DATE DUE

ENCYCLOPEDIA OF ROCK

This 1988 edition published by
Schirmer Books
A Division of Macmillan, Inc
866 Third Avenue, New York,
N.Y. 10022

Editor: Lorrie Mack
Art Editor: Simon Webb
Designer: Valerie Wright

Printing number
1 2 3 4 5 6 7 8 9 10

ISBN 0-02-919562-4

Filmset by
Wyvern Typesetting Ltd

Printed and bound in Spain by
Graficromo SA

PHIL HARDY

DAVE LAING

ENCYCLOPEDIA OF ROCK

SCHIRMER BOOKS
A Division of Macmillan, Inc
New York,

ADDITIONAL MATERIAL

STEPHEN BARNARD

DON PERRETTA

INTRODUCTION

This is a considerably expanded edition of the highly acclaimed *Encyclopedia of Rock*, which was first published in 1976 by Panther Books. Edited by Phil Hardy and Dave Laing, the *Encyclopedia* was widely regarded as the most comprehensive work of its kind, drawing as it did on the knowledge and opinions of well over forty of the best writers on rock music from both Britain and the US. In revising the text and providing a large number of additional entries, the editorial team responsible for this second edition has sought to build on the strengths of the first to create a volume of possibly unparalleled breadth, and one that provides a balanced, authoritative overview of well over thirty years of rock.

The entries are wide ranging, summarising not only the careers of the most influential and important artists in rock, but also those of the backroom figures – the entrepreneurs, record producers, session musicians and songwriters whose role in the evolution of rock was at least as vital as the acts whose talents they helped nurture. As for the artists themselves, the two main criteria for inclusion are, first of all, chart success in either the US or UK or both (though chart artists with no obvious rock connections are not featured); and secondly, historical influence and artistic significance. The *Encyclopedia* also gives due weight to the work of musicians from areas which border on rock and which have exerted considerable influence on it; to the record companies that helped mould the music's creative and commercial course; and to the role of the media within rock – there are individual entries on film, television, radio and video. The length of each entry has been determined by the editors' estimate of the importance of the subject to rock music as a whole.

Alongside entries on specific artists and institutions, there are entries on such rock or rock-related genres as a cappella, Cajun music, disco, doo-wop, folk-rock, gospel, hip hop, traditional jazz (listed under 'Jazz, Traditional'), jazz-rock, lovers rock, new wave, power pop, pub rock, punk rock, rap, reggae, rockabilly, skiffle, surf music, swamp-pop and western swing. Also covered separately are African music, Band Aid, British R&B, cover versions, festivals, girl groups, instrumentals, metal-bashing, new romantics, the Rock Against Racism movement, screen stars, and sound systems.

Because the aim of the *Encyclopedia* is to provide information and informed comment for the general reader, no discographies as such have been included, though in most cases reference is made to an artist's most significant recordings and the record company of origin. In any case, a definitive discography of all the artists in the *Encyclopedia* would fill a book at least as big as this. For the purposes of the book, a 'hit' is defined as a record that reached the UK Top 40, *Billboard* magazine's US Hot Hundred or either of the US country or R&B (rhythm and blues) charts; all chart placings mentioned in the text have been verified by reference to *The Guinness Book of Hit Singles* (Guinness Books, 1985), in the case of the British charts, and Joel Whitburn's *Record Research* in the case of the US charts.

Regarding use of the *Encyclopedia*, some explanatory notes may be helpful. First of all, the entries are given in alphabetical order in the style of a telephone directory, with those artists whose surnames begin with 'Mc' appearing under 'Mac'. In the case of Little Richard, the relevant entry will be found under the letter 'L', while Guitar Slim will be found under 'G'. Groups are listed according to the first letter of the first main word: Jefferson Airplane, for example, is entered under 'J'. Where a name appears in bold type, a separate entry exists which can be used for cross-reference. These cross-references apply to solo artists, groups, composers, producers and managers, and are generally not given for entries concerning record labels, recording studios or places. Titles of compositions, singles and individual album tracks appear within quotation marks, while album titles appear in italic type. Standard rock terminology is used throughout, including the abbreviation of rhythm and blues to R&B, country and western to C&W, artists and repertoire to A&R, adult-oriented rock to AOR, middle-of-the-road to MOR, and disc jockey to DJ.

The compilers of this updated edition echo Phil Hardy and Dave Laing's acknowledgement, in the original *Encyclopedia*, of the debt owned to a number of publications and individuals, namely *Bigtown Review, Billboard, Bim Bam Boom, Blues and Soul, Blues Research, Blues Unlimited, Blues World, Boppin' News, Cashbox*, Barrett Hansen, *Jazz & Blues, Let it Rock, Living Blues, Melody Maker, New Musical Express, Penniman News, Record Mirror, Rock File, R&B Monthly, R&B Magazine, Rollin' Rock, Rolling Stone, Shout, Soul Bag*, Joel Whitburn and *Who Put the Bomp*. Mention should also be made of the Orbis partwork, *The History of Rock*, which proved an unfailingly reliable aid in the gathering of information and comment, and in verifying career detail.

Finally, while every effort has been made to ensure the consistent accuracy of the text, it would be naïve not to acknowledge that it may contain some errors. The success of a volume such as this depends on input from a great many individuals and sources, and the publishers would welcome any comments or suggestions from readers regarding omissions or errors they find in the text, so that it may be amended in time for any future edition.

This book is a revision and updating of Phil Hardy and Dave Laing's *The Encyclopedia of Rock*, which was originally published in three volumes by Panther Books in 1976. The revision is by Stephen Barnard and the new entries are written by Don Perretta.

Contributors to the First Edition

Clive Anderson	Rob Finnis	Ian Hoare	John Pidgeon
Stephen Barnard	Mike Flood Page	Mick Houghton	Clive Richardson
John Broven	Pete Fowler	Jonh Ingham	Tony Russell
Ron Brown	Dave Gelly	Norman Jopling	Peter Simons
Peter Carr	Jerry Gilbert	Dave Laing	Graham Taylor
John Collis	Mick Gold	David McGillivray	John Tobler
Tony Cummings	Michael Gray	Phil McNeill	Ray Topping
Robin Denselow	Phil Hardy	Bill Millar	Dave Walters
David Downing	Martin Hawkins	Jonathan Morrish	Cliff White
Dr. Rock	Gary Herman	John Morthland	Richard Williams
Adam Finnis			

Consultant Editors to the First Edition

Charlie Gillett	Greil Marcus	Bill Millar	Greg Shaw

Contributors to the Second Edition

Geoff Brown	John Gill	Don Scully	Johnny Waller
Simon Garfield	Chris May		

A&M RECORDS The company was formed in the summer of 1962 by band leader **Herb Alpert** and West Coast promotion man Jerry Moss – thus A&M. Their first single release was 'Lonely Bull' by Herb Alpert and the Tijuana Brass. It was a world-wide hit, immediately establishing the Los Angeles-based company, which was then housed in a converted garage. By 1966 Herb and the Tijuana Brass had five albums in the Top 20 and had signed Sergio Mendes and Brasil '66, another big-selling easy listening group, produced by Alpert. Other successes that year included 'The More I See You' by **Chris Montez** and 'Guantanamera' by the Sandpipers. Of the 25 albums released by A&M, 16 went gold.

By 1968 A&M had acquired wholly owned subsidiaries in London and Toronto, signed their first rock-oriented band, the **Flying Burrito Brothers**, and opened their own studios on the West Coast. Not long after, in 1969, **Joe Cocker** signed to the label and **Phil Spector** also returned as a producer in conjunction with his own Phil Spector Productions.

By 1970 Lou Adler had brought his Ode label to A&M for distribution, which resulted in solo success for **Carole King** and Cheech and Chong. **Leon Russell**'s Shelter Records also signed a distribution deal with A&M, releasing several solo albums plus albums by **Freddie King**. The **Carpenters** were also contracted to the label, becoming A&M's biggest-selling act. Other major signings included **Humble Pie**, **Joan Baez**, **Rick Wakeman**, **Stealers Wheel**, and **Supertramp**, together with distribution of **George Harrison**'s Dark Horse label. **Styx**, Quincy Jones, the **Police**, **Joe Jackson**, and **Squeeze** were among the important acts who kept A&M's fortunes riding high into the Eighties. *See also* **Herb Alpert**.

A CAPPELLA Derived from the Italian word *cappella* (chapel) and originally applied to 16th-century church music, a cappella is the term used to describe almost any kind of unaccompanied singing, though it most often refers specifically to vocal groups.

The absence of instrumentation was normal in the pre-war gospel field, but some early secular black groups, the Four Vagabonds and the Virginia Four, for example, also sang without backing. A cappella enjoyed a brief boom between 1964 and 1966 on the East Coast, partly in reaction to the **Beatles** (who were anathema to most doo-wop fans) and partly through the discovery of ten-year-old a cappella practice tapes by the **Nutmegs**. The tapes, which included 'Let Me Tell You' and 'Down in Mexico', were issued on the Times Square label by Slim Rose. They sold a mere 2000 copies but inspired all the kids who had been singing the old songs down in the subway (because of the echo) to try their hand at recording. Rose, Eddie Gries (Relic) and Stan Krause (Catamount) were besieged by street corner quartets.

Mediaeval, Old Timer, Siamese and Harlequin were among the dozens of a cappella labels. Some recorded up to 30 groups, most of whom were white, i.e. Spanish, Italian, and Puerto Rican (young blacks had moved on to soul). They were often absurdly polished with high, pure, strong voices that avoided the graceless vibrato so common in imitative R&B.

A cappella discography is riddled with oldies: songs originally cut by the **Skyliners**, Harptones, **Orioles**, and **Moonglows** were revived with an honesty and affection unparalleled in rock. The form was carried on almost single-handedly during the Seventies by the Persuasions, but the Zircons, Dennis Ostrum and the Citadels, and the Velvet Angels – just three of the best groups from the golden years – deserve to be remembered.

ABBA Although Abba first emerged as a recording entity in 1971, all four members had known each other and worked together for some years. Each was a superstar of sorts in their native Sweden: Anni-Frid Lyngstad (born 15 November 1945) had been a dance band singer since the age of 15; Benny Andersson (16 December 1946) and Bjorn Ulvaeus (25 April 1945) had sung together as a folk-style duo and had been members of the Hep Stars and the Hootenanny Singers respectively; and Agnetha Fältskog (5 April 1950) had found considerable chart success in Scandinavia since making a chart-topping debut with 'I Was So in Love' in 1967. Agnetha and Bjorn's marriage, followed later by that of Benny and Anni-Frid, made their combination as a working group almost inevitable, and the song 'Ring Ring' – written for the Swedish heats of the Eurovision Song Contest – put the name of Abba into the European charts for the first time during 1973.

A year later, Abba won the Contest proper with 'Waterloo', written by Andersson and Ulvaeus together with their producer, Stig Anderson. A Number 1 in the UK, the record was a power-house production in the style of **Roy Wood** and the British glam-rock bands, but it failed to establish the group as an important chart act. The real breakthrough came in late 1975 with the ballad 'S.O.S.', which began a run of 18 consecutive UK Top 10 hits, eight of which were chart-toppers. Their blend of easy-listening harmonies, disco rhythms and cosy glamour won them a devoted cross-generation following, and even those who dismissed them as purveyors of inconsequential MOR pop had to admire their imaginative approach to pop production and the sheer consistency of their hit-making touch. By 1980, their world sales of albums and singles totalled 150 million, matching those achieved by the **Beatles**, and their popularity extended to both the US and the USSR, where they were one of very few Western pop groups to be endorsed officially by the authorities. Disintegrating relations within the group and the subsequent divorces of both couples led to an expected break-up in 1982, after which Lyngstad and Faltskog each recorded solo albums and Andersson and Ulvaeus collaborated with Tim Rice on the musical *Chess*, which opened in London during 1986.

ABC Under the guidance of singer Martin Fry, Sheffield band ABC combined grandiose, melodramatic pop music with a chic B-movie image to great effect in the early Eighties. Formed early in 1981 by Fry with Steve Singleton (sax), Mark White (guitar), Mark Lickley (bass) and David Palmer (drums), they quickly found success with their first single, 'Tears Are Not Enough', which made the UK Top 20 in October.

The next year, 1982, proved to be ABC's most successful, with a string of UK Top 5 singles and a widely-acclaimed album. These were made possible when the interest generated by the first single enabled them to hire producer **Trevor Horn**, who became an important factor in their progress by giving them a bright, crystal-clear sound that complemented Fry's elaborate ideas. The collaboration gave them the hits 'Poison Arrow', 'The Look of Love' and 'All of My Heart' (the first two were also hits in the US), and the

The Sheffield band ABC rode the 'new romantic' wave to success in the early Eighties, but their pretentious image dated fast

album *Lexicon of Love*, a debut LP that was hailed as a pop masterpiece and became a UK Number 1.

Fry's obsession with image, although it was a superb marketing tool, made ABC easy targets for the critics, yet for the most part the quality of the music fended off the jibes. But they soon became the victims of this image since it dated quickly, and their fortunes took a downward turn in 1983 when Fry made a disastrous concept video – *Mantrap* – that was deeply embarrassing for all those involved. In the wake of this, *Beauty Stab* (1983) was heaped with derision and the singles taken from it fared badly. ABC waited until 1985 to release their third LP, *How To Be a Zillionaire*, which, while not as poor as their previous effort, was received just as badly by critics and public alike, suggesting that ABC were unlikely to rediscover the glorious pop with which they had made their mark in 1982.

ABC RECORDS Formed in Hollywood in 1955 as a subsidiary of Paramount Pictures, ABC was one of the first major record companies to embrace rock'n'roll. Under company president Sam Clark, the label built its success on the efforts of music director Don Costa and freelance A&R man **Buck Ram**, and its first important chart acts included teen idols **Paul Anka** and **George Hamilton IV**, girl group the

Poni-Tails and New Orleans R&B singer **Lloyd Price**. **Dick Clark** – host of *American Bandstand*, networked by Paramount's television arm of ABC-TV – acted as label consultant and introduced to the company such briefly popular names as the Royal Teens and **Danny and the Juniors**.

ABC's interest in black music developed with the signing of the **Tams** and the **Impressions** in the early Sixties, and the success of **Ray Charles** in particular compensated for the loss of Paul Anka (and the rights to his material) in 1962. After distributing the releases of **Lou Adler**'s California-based independent, Dunhill, ABC bought up the company in 1966 and maintained its chart prominence with **Barry McGuire**, the **Mamas and Papas**, **Steppenwolf**, and others. One of its biggest-selling albums of the decade was the soundtrack to the film *Easy Rider* (1969). The Seventies brought major hit singles and/or albums from **Three Dog Night**, **Steely Dan**, **Jim Croce**, **Rufus**, and **B.B. King**, while inroads were made into the country music market with the signing of Freddy Fender and the Amazing Rhythm Aces. In 1978, ABC-Dunhill (as the company had been known since 1966) was absorbed into the giant MCA corporation.

ABNER, EWART Abner's career in the record industry began in 1950 on the staff of Chance Records in Chicago,

writing songs and producing acts like the **Flamingos** and the **Moonglows**. The company never achieved national prominence and folded in 1954, by which time Abner had helped to form Vee Jay Records, where he teamed up with Calvin Carter to write and produce many hits for acts including the Dells and **Dee Clark**. Abner's forte, however, lay in promotion and marketing. The Falcon subsidiary was formed in 1957 and later renamed 'Abner' to avoid confusion with an existing label. This subsidiary was active up to 1960, by which time Abner had become president of Vee Jay. During the early Sixties, the company was well represented in the charts with such acts as **Gene Chandler** and the **Four Seasons**, but in 1963 Abner was deposed as president and quit. He was reinstated as general manager in 1965, but despite chart success the company was financially unsound and folded in 1966. Abner then joined Motown as a producer, moving to the West Coast with them and eventually becoming president of the corporation in 1973. *See also* **Vee Jay Records**.

AC/DC's Bon Scott, a softly-spoken, genial man, despite his macho image

AC/DC Australian heavy metal band AC/DC became one of the leading groups of the genre in the Eighties, amassing multi-platinum and gold sales worldwide. Led by Angus Young, a fiery lead guitarist with a schoolboy stage persona (he was only 14 when the band was formed), they produced raucous, smutty songs and sweaty live shows that won them a huge international following.

Formed in Sydney, Australia in 1973 by the Scottish-born Young brothers, Angus and Malcolm (rhythm guitar), the original AC/DC line-up also included the gravelly-voiced Bon Scott, drummer Phil Rudd and bassist Mark Evans. By 1975 they had released two albums and their domestic following was growing rapidly. In 1976 the international label Atlantic released *High Voltage* (a compilation of the first two Australian albums) worldwide and, remarkably, the band conquered the UK on their first visit, at the height of punk. In 1978 AC/DC produced their classic document, the live album *If You Want Blood You've Got It*.

Continuous tours across the world and a string of LP's culminating in *Highway to Hell* (1979) paid off. This album, the first that was not produced by elder brother George Young (himself a hit-maker in the early Sixties with the **Easybeats**) and his partner Harry Vanda, was tailored by Robert John 'Mutt' Lange to US radio, and sold 3½ million copies. The group's success seemed assured, but then, in February 1980, vocalist Bon Scott died tragically, having choked on his own vomit after one of his drinking bouts. Brian Johnson, formerly of a band called Geordie who had a couple of UK hits in the Seventies, joined as replacement.

The fact that Johnson's vocal style was very similar to Scott's allowed AC/DC to continue where they had left off, and another album, *Back in Black* (1980), sold over 10 million worldwide. Successful LP releases continued but at much greater intervals with *For Those About to Rock (We Salute You)* (1981), *Flick of the Switch* (1983) and *Fly on the Wall* (1985), but they never again reached their early level of excellence or success.

ACE, JOHNNY Born on 9 June 1929, in Memphis, Tennessee, as John Marshall Alexander Jnr, R&B singer Johnny Ace began his career as a pianist with Adolph Duncan's Band. Ace joined the Beale Streeters – whose other members included **B.B. King**, **Bobby Bland**, and **Rosco Gordon** in the late Forties – following naval service during the war. His solo debut, the plaintive 'My Song' (Duke), topped the R&B charts in 1952, and subsequent discs – generally sensitive baritone performances of love ballads accompanied by understated small combo support – enjoyed great success. Stylistic parallels include **Jesse Belvin**, **Charles Brown** and **Nat 'King' Cole**, though Ace occasionally recorded jump items in the style of **Roy Brown** or **Amos**

Milburn. He toured constantly, and was voted 'Most Programmed R&B Artist of 1954' in Cashbox's DJ poll. His life came to an early, tragic end when he shot himself playing Russian roulette backstage at the City Auditorium in Houston on Christmas Eve, 1954. A measure of immortality was assured by his posthumous hit, 'Pledging My Love', which reached Number 17 in the US Hot 100 during 1955.

ACE RECORDS Despite operating within the small-time atmosphere of the Southern country town of Jackson, Mississippi, Ace Records became a major independent label in the late Fifties thanks to its active involvement in the fermenting New Orleans R&B scene and the use of such sessionmen as **Lee Allen** (tenor) and Red Tyler (baritone). Founded in 1955 by Johnny Vincent, Ace had an early regional R&B hit with Earl King's 'Those Lonely, Lonely Nights'. **Huey 'Piano' Smith** took Ace into the Hot 100 charts in 1957 with 'Rockin' Pneumonia and the Boogie Woogie Flu', followed quickly by 'Don't You Just Know It'. This inspired a succession of hits from **Joe Tex**, **James Booker**, Bobby Marchan and Eddie Bo. Vincent then had even bigger success with white rock'n'rollers **Jimmy Clanton** ('Just a Dream') and **Frankie Ford** ('Sea Cruise'), and straining for further commercial success, turned Ace into a dire MOR pop label. In 1962, Ace merged with Vee Jay, had another massive hit with Jimmy Clanton's 'Venus in Blue Jeans' and then fell apart at the seams – a long way from its New Orleans roots.

ACKLES, DAVID A cult figure in the early Seventies, singer-songwriter David Ackles was born into a show-business family in Rock Island, Illinois, on 20 February 1937. He started his career in vaudeville at the age of four and became the child-star of a series of successful B-films featuring a dog called Rusty. He studied literature at college while writing ballet and choral music; later he gained experience in musical comedy, theatre and film.

Elektra signed him as a songwriter after hearing 'Blue Ribbons' (which resurfaced on his first album); eventually they were persuaded to allow him to record. In the course of three Elektra albums he achieved huge critical acclaim but little commercial success. His brooding, elegant and eclectic style – seen at its best on the album *American Gothic* (1972, produced by **Elton John**'s songwriting partner **Bernie Taupin**) – is an acquired taste; super-

ficially it can seem simply depressing. Ackles is a writer and performer of remarkable power, perhaps doomed to remain underrated. Elektra dropped him in 1972; one Columbia album followed, but he has not recorded since.

ACKLIN, BARBARA R&B singer and songwriter Barbara Acklin was born in Chicago on 28 February 1943, and first sang in a gospel choir. In 1964, her mellow voice was heard on background sessions for the St Lawrence label and on a handful of unsuccessful solo recordings, which were issued under the pseudonym of Barbara Allen. Signed by Brunswick in 1967, she scored a US Top 40 hit with 'Love Makes a Woman' a year later and recorded a series of duets with **Gene Chandler**, one of which – 'From the Teacher to the Preacher' – became a small national hit. Her other recordings included 'Just Ain't Love' and 'Am I the Same Girl' – the original local version of Young-Holt Unlimited's million-selling 'Soulful Strut' – both in 1969. She also developed her songwriting career in partnership with Eugene Record, producer of her own discs and those by the **Chi-Lites**. She moved to Capitol in the Seventies and subsequently renewed her association with Chandler, who produced her recordings for Chi-Sound Records in Chicago.

ACUFF, ROY One of country music's true pioneer figures, Roy Acuff was born on 15 September 1903 at Maynardsville, Tennessee. His period of greatest musical influence was during the middle and late Thirties and early Forties when he led a band called the Smokey Mountain Boys, whose sound was echoed by many contemporaries. Featuring a thick-textured fabric of fiddle and steel guitar, it was heard regularly on the *Grand Ole Opry* radio show and elsewhere in Acuff's native Tennessee. The coupling of 'Wabash Cannonball' and 'Freight Train Blues' – the latter the original for **Bob Dylan**'s version – was a hit, but was eclipsed by the fundamentalist 'Great Speckled Bird', and Acuff continued to evoke Southern rurality through railroads and religion. His status encouraged him to run for State governorship – unsuccessfully – and in 1947 to found, with Fred Rose, the Acuff-Rose music-publishing concern, now a substantial power in country music. Still performing in the Eighties, Acuff remains one of the few Nashville personalities of consequence who adheres to an uncompromisingly old-time approach.

ADAMS, BRYAN Singer/songwriter Bryan Adams (born in Vancouver, Canada, on 5 November 1959) achieved his first successes at the age of eighteen, when his compositions were recorded by a host of North American rock acts including Loverboy and **Kiss**. Adams established himself as a popular performer in his own right with a tough-edged guitar sound that produced a variation on the traditional North American hard rock form.

Adams teamed up with drummer Jim Vallance in 1977 to form a songwriting duo and in 1979, after having material performed by various name acts, Adams was signed to A&M Records who released his first solo LP *Bryan Adams* in 1980. *You Want It – You Got It* and *Cuts Like a Knife* followed in '81 and '83 respectively, and it was the third album that conquered the charts, giving Adams his first US platinum LP and hit single, 'Straight From the Heart'.

Reckless (1984), Adams' fourth album, returned similar sales figures and gave him another personal first, a US Number 1 single with 'Heaven'. It also continued to sell into 1985 and proved to be the album that finally cracked the UK market, going gold within a month and yielding a string of hit singles ('Run to You' being the biggest). The same year also saw him on a major tour with **Tina Turner** (with whom he recorded 'It's Only Love') and writing (with Vallance) 'Tears Are Not Enough' for Northern Lights, the Canadian rock establishment's contribution to the **Band Aid** appeal.

ADAMS, JOHNNY The most important quality soul singer to emerge from New Orleans, Johnny Adams scored locally with his early records for Ric, 'Come On' (1960) and 'A Losing Battle' (1962). These initial releases had a more blatantly pop approach than the mainstream New Orleans R&B sounds of the time, but his strong, soulful voice was well able to compete with full orchestras and heavenly choirs. After recording for Watch in 1963, he fell out of favour, but was rescued from oblivion in 1969 when he had three successive and classy Hot 100 hits for SSS International with 'Release Me', 'Reconsider Me', and 'I Can't Be All Bad'.

ADE, KING SUNNY Since the early Eighties, Nigeria's King Sunny Ade has enjoyed two parallel careers: in his own country, Ade, Ebenezer Obey and Dele Abiodun form the ruling juju music triumvirate, while in

King Sunny Ade had been a star in his native Nigeria for almost a decade before his breakthrough in Britain in early 1983

Europe and North America he is responsible for taking juju (a style that added electric instruments to the traditional multiple drum sound) beyond a small cult following and onto the edge of the mainstream album market. Ade's British (and subsequent European and North American) breakthrough can be said to have come with a triumphant 3½-hour concert that he and his band, the 23-piece African Beats, gave in January 1983 at London's Lyceum Ballroom, where critics hailed him as one of the emergent dance-music stars of the year.

Ade's career began in 1965, when he became lead guitarist with Moses Oolaiya's highly regarded band. The following year he left to form his own Green Spots outfit (the name was a cheeky challenge to the grand old man of juju, I. K. Dairo, whose Blue Spots had ruled the roost since the early Fifties). Ade's first release, 'Challenge Cup', a partisan song about a local football championship, became a national hit in 1967.

Ade first played Britain in 1975, about the same year that he reached star status in Nigeria, where, between 1975 and 1984, he released over forty albums. By the early Eighties, the average sale of each was in excess of 200,000 copies (an achievement only barely minimized by the fact that a substantial proportion of these sales were of bootlegged pressings, bootlegging being economically crippling to the legitimate recording industry in Nigeria and other African countries).

ADLER, LOU One of the key figures in the development of California pop, Lou Adler was active as early as 1959, when he managed **Jan and Dean** and worked with **Herb Alpert** on his first records. Together they collaborated on early **Sam Cooke** hits including 'Only Sixteen', under the pseudonym of Barbara Campbell. He subsequently became involved with Screen Gems and their Colpix and Dimension labels. At Colpix he met Shelly Fabares, whom he later married, while at Dimension he worked with **Carole King** and the rest of **Don Kirshner**'s impressive Brill Building stable, and also discovered a number of young artists including **Steve Barri**, **P.F. Sloan**, and Carol Connors.

In 1964 he started Dunhill Productions and Trousdale Music, employing the talents of Steve Barri and P.F. Sloan, who wrote, produced and recorded hundreds of songs in styles ranging from surf music to protest rock, a style that found its home on the Dunhill label, launched in 1965. After two years of hits by the **Mamas and Papas**, P.F. Sloan, the **Grass Roots**, **Barry McGuire**, the Brass King and Richard Harris, and hit productions for non-Dunhill artists including **Johnny Rivers** and Jan and Dean, Adler became one of the organizers of the Monterey Pop Festival, which brought the whole California music explosion into focus in June, 1967.

After he sold Dunhill Records to ABC in 1966, Adler formed Ode Records, whose first hit was 'San Francisco (Be

Sure to Wear Some Flowers in Your Hair)' by **Scott McKenzie** in 1967. Other early Ode acts included **Spirit** ('I Got a Line on You', 1969) and the City, featuring Carole King. King, who'd been in a commercial slump since 1963, made one of the most successful comebacks in the history of rock on Ode in 1971 where, under Adler's direction, she led the singer-songwriter trend. Other successes on Ode include Cheech and Chong, and the symphonic version of *Tommy*.

In later years, Adler became involved in films (*Phantom of the Paradise*), theatre (he produced the L.A. production of the *Rocky Horror Show*), and club management, in addition to producing Carole King's records and running Ode Records. A peripheral figure in Eighties rock – his last record production work of note was for Carole King's *Speeding Time*, released on Atlantic in 1983 – he will always be seen as the archetypal West Coast rock hustler, a shrewd entrepreneur, and one of the all-time great rock talent-spotters.

ADVERTS Self-proclaimed 'One Chord Wonders' (the title of their first single on Stiff), the Adverts came onto the scene at the very beginning of the British punk explosion in 1976, and were among the first bands to top the bill regularly at the Roxy, London's punk mecca.

Fronted by Tim 'T.V.' Smith (vocals) the group comprised Laurie Driver (drums), Howard Pickup (guitar) and Gaye Advert (bass-vocals); not only did the band include this first female punk star, it was also one of the first to score a UK hit single, with 'Gary Gilmore's Eyes' which reached Number 18 in August 1977. The LP *Crossing the Red Sea* made the UK Top 40 in 1978 as did the single 'No Time To Be 21'. They made one more album, *The Cast of Thousands* (1979) on RCA, but by this time punk had already wound itself down and the LP went almost unnoticed. Shortly afterwards the Adverts' manager Michael Dempsey died tragically when he accidentally electrocuted himself and the band fell apart.

AEROSMITH A no-nonsense, no-frills heavy metal band from the Boston area, Aerosmith came together in 1970 around the nucleus of bassist Tom Hamilton (born 31 December 1951 in Colorado Springs), lead guitarist Joe Perry (10 September 1950 in Boston) and singer Steven Tyler (26 March 1948 in New York). Drummer Joey

Kramer (21 June 1950 in New York) and guitarist Brad Whitford (23 February 1962 in Massachusetts) completed the line-up a year later, and the band's high-voltage, high-decibel live set and their strong local following persuaded Columbia Records boss Clive Davis to award them a contract during 1972. After two modest-selling albums and several years of constant touring, the band made a major national breakthrough with *Toys in the Attic* (1975). The album stayed in the US chart for the best part of two years, ultimately selling over four million copies, and represented the perfect distillation of the Aerosmith sound – a muscular but surprisingly agile rhythm section, with the twin guitars howling and snapping around Tyler's vocal lines. *Rocks* (1976) repeated the formula, while an uncharacteristically long break from touring during 1977 enabled them to complete their fifth and in some ways most ambitious album, *Draw the Line*.

By 1978, Aerosmith had established themselves as one of America's premier arena bands, and they even emerged unscathed from Robert Stigwood's disastrous film version of *Sgt Pepper's Lonely Hearts Club Band*, in which they performed 'Come Together'. The track gave them their

sixth US Top 40 single. 1979 brought the first change in personnel when Perry left to form the Joe Perry Project and was replaced by Jim Crespo, former guitarist with Flame. In 1981, Whitford departed to form the Whitford-St Holmes Band; his replacement was Rick Dufay.

AFRICAN MUSIC Any consideration of African music needs to be prefaced by the observation that Africa is not one vast and monolithic place, but a continent embracing many hundreds of different cultures and traditions, so that both traditional and modern African music display a stylistic diversity on a level with that to be heard in the musics of the Americas.

A second basic observation that should be made is that all modern African music (which can perhaps most usefully be defined as that combining indigenous folk music with Western/electric strains) owes huge debts to the traditional styles of the peoples and the regions it came from. Thus **Manu Dibango's** futuristic abele and makossa style is rhythmically and melodically rooted in Cameroonian abele and makossa folk music, **Hugh Masekela's** jazz-influenced output is rooted in the mbaqanga music of South Africa, and

Large bands, like Sunny Ade's 23-piece African Beats, have spearheaded the African assault on the Western music scene in the Eighties

the same applies with every other modern African star known in the West today.

Perhaps the greatest single conceptual difference between traditional and modern music the world over lies in traditional music's narrow dividing line between performer and audience. While modern Western music is essentially a spectator form, with a rigid distinction between (paying) audience and (paid) performer, traditional music recognizes a much smaller distinction. Feedback from the audience, often in the form of choral responses to lead vocal cues from the band, is a distinguishing characteristic of many traditional African styles and one that continues to shape modern forms that have developed out of those styles.

The blurring of the line between audience and performer is also reflected in the way in which professional musicians are paid in Africa today. In traditional rural culture, performers are frequently unpaid (in the case of, say, the village band leading local ritual or community events), while paid performers will generally receive their money direct from individual members of the audience rather than from a middleman promoter. While such Western financial structures as recording royalties and set performance fees are now increasingly common in Africa, a major modern-music star like Nigeria's **Sunny Ade** will still receive the bulk of his performance fee in cash from members of the audience (who press the notes onto his sweaty brow, from where they are collected by a band member specifically responsible for the task).

Of course, traditional music shapes not only the conceptual and financial structure of modern African music, but also the music itself. At the root of practically every modern style lies a group of traditional folk rhythms, from which the style frequently draws its name. As already noted, Manu Dibango's makossa style – whose rhythms are often, mistakenly, assumed to be borrowed from Western disco/dance music – is based on a centuries-old makossa rhythm. The fact that this rhythm corresponded to the prevailing Western disco beat at the time of the release of Dibango's 'Soul Makossa' was simply a commercially fortuitous coincidence.

Instrumentation, too, in modern African music is frequently based on traditional folk band line-ups, with large batteries of drummers and percussionists in many of the most futuristic modern bands. And just as

Teen idols A-ha. Norway's first international pop success

the contribution of drummers and percussionists is often of paramount importance in a traditional band, so they have retained their central role in much modern music, with guitars and keyboards assuming a secondary importance. Even such highly Western-related bands as those led by Sunny Ade and **Fela Kuti** place a crucial importance on traditional drums and percussion.

These distinctions having been made, African music should be enjoyed precisely as modern Western music is enjoyed. Indeed, the growing popularity of Afro-American-rooted dance music in the West suggests a continuing breakthrough of African musicians and styles. Whether African music will ever achieve the level of Western breakthrough its propagandists hope for is, however, open to doubt. It is unlikely, for instance, that African music sung in African languages – as most modern African music continues to be – will ever find an enthusiastic audience beyond the specialist, album-oriented market.

AFRIKA BAMBAATAA With a name taken from a Zulu chief living at the turn of the century, DJ rapper and guiding force of the hip hop movement Afrika Bambaataa was, along with **Grandmaster Flash** and Cool DJ Herc, one of the pioneer practitioners of **rap**. A strong force in the development of hip hop right from 1975, after the first wave of popularity had died down (in

the wake of Grandmaster Flash's 'The Message'), Bambaataa with his group Soul Sonic Force resuscitated the whole scene, more or less single-handedly, in 1982 by releasing the single 'Planet Rock', a masterpiece of mixing that fused **Kraftwerk**'s 'Trans Europe Express' with a sequence of popular hip hop records. It took off all over the world and catalysed a whole new interest in rap and hip hop, which ceased to be mere novelties and became important musical forces. Bambaataa continued to release powerful records with 'Looking for the Perfect Beat' and 'Renegades of Funk' (a UK Number 30 in 1984) inspiring a whole new generation of rap artists.

A-HA Stepping in to take over the mantles of **Duran Duran** and **Wham!** as the leading pop pin-ups in the teen market, A-ha arrived in the latter part of 1985 to become Norway's first international pop act.

Guitarist Pål Waaktaar (born 6 September 1961) and keyboard player Magne (Mags) Furuholmen (1 November 1962) had been playing together from the age of ten in their native town of Manglerud, a suburb of Oslo, forming a number of different bands. After one abortive trip to London seeking an international recording contract, they returned to Norway £2000 poorer but then met up with singer Morten Harket (14 September 1959). As a trio they returned to London in 1984 and eventually managed to convince Warner Brothers of their commercial viability.

In spite of their obvious marketability in terms of their boyish good looks, their first single had to be released three times, re-recorded and they then had to have two videos shot for it before the lightweight pop of 'Take On Me' became the international hit they desperately wanted. It finally reached the UK Number 2 spot in October 1985, shortly after scoring a US Number 1. Three further hit singles and a hit album, *Hunting High and Low*, followed into 1986, whereupon they embarked on a world tour and released their second LP, *Scoundrel Days*.

AIR SUPPLY Although originally from Australia, Air Supply became one of the biggest soft-rock bands in the USA during the Eighties. Based around the songwriting partnership of Russell Hitchcock and Graham Russell, Air Supply came into being in 1976 and quickly achieved success in their native country. In the following year they acted as support band for **Rod Stewart**'s 60-date US tour, which exposed them to a massive new audience receptive to their brand of rock. Besides Hitchcock (vocals) and Russell (guitar/vocals), the touring band comprised Frank Esler-Smith and Ken Rarick (keyboards), Wally Stocker (guitar), Donald Cromwell (bass) and Ralph Cooper (drums). Little happened in terms of chart success until their record company, Arista, released the single 'Lost in Love' into the US market in 1980. An immediate hit, it reached Number 3 and over the next few years the group was regularly in the Top 5, three of their singles going gold including 'The One That You Love', which also topped the chart. Their biggest single in the UK was 'All Out of Love', which reached Number 11 in September 1980. In the US album charts *Lost in Love* (1980), *The One That You Love* (1981) and *Now and Forever* (1982) all gained gold, then platinum, status.

Ska pioneer Laurel Aitken

AITKEN, LAUREL A pioneer of Jamaican ska, Laurel Aitken was born in Cuba in 1928 and moved to Jamaica in 1956. His 'Little Sheila' (1960) was the first Jamaican-produced record ever to be issued in Britain, soon after which Aitken settled in Britain and began recording for a variety of labels, among which were (briefly) EMI and the independents Direct, Blue Beat, Ska Beat, and Pama. Although he was never a chart name in the UK, releases such as 'Bugaboo', 'The Lion of Judah', and 'You Was Up' sold well among both Britain's immigrant West Indian population and the mods and skinheads of the mid- to late Sixties. He

recorded in a variety of styles, from plaintive ballads like 'You Left Me Standing' to songs with political content ('Landlords and Tenants'), and tracks detailing sexual chicanery ('Fire in My Wire', 'Pussy Price'). A major influence on the growth of an indigenous British reggae scene, the Two-Tone (ska revival) movement of 1979–81 brought his name to the fore once again and prompted his signing with I-Spy, a division of Arista. His 1980 release, 'Rudi Got Married', finally gave him a British chart entry.

ALABAMA Formed in 1969, country-rock band Alabama had to wait until the early Eighties before becoming one of America's widest selling acts in that genre, achieving a string of hit singles and gold and platinum LPs. Originally a trio comprising the three cousins Jeff Cook (guitar/fiddle/vocals), Randy Owen (guitar/vocals) and Teddy Gentry (bass/vocals), under the name of Young Country they performed semi-professionally in their home town of Fort Payne, Alabama.

Under the new name Alabama (and with a drummer, Rich Scott) they moved to South Carolina in 1973 and started to play some of their own compositions in local clubs; after a few self-financed records they clinched a deal with GRT in 1977. This signing proved unproductive and with new drummer Mark Herndon, they moved to MDJ and scored their first country hit with 'I Wanna Come Over' in 1980, quickly followed by 'My Home's in Alabama'. Their first Number 1 US country single, 'Tennessee River', was with RCA the same year.

ALADDIN RECORDS Formed in Los Angeles in 1945 by brothers Eddie and Leo Mesner, the Aladdin label was swept along in the emergent post-war record boom and by the mid-Fifties was one of the premier R&B companies. With Maxwell Davis as staff producer, there was a series of early R&B hits from artists such as **Charles Brown** (the classic 'Drifting Blues'), **Amos Milburn**, Peppermint Harris, **Lightnin' Hopkins** and the Five Keys. The company hit the national Hot 100 charts with the million-selling 'Let the Good Times Roll' by **Shirley and Lee** in 1956, and in early 1958 Thurston Harris' 'Little Bitty Pretty One' reached the US Top 10. These discs apart, Aladdin never really came to grips with rock'n'roll and was a spent force by 1960. In 1962, the entire catalogue was purchased by Imperial and selected reissues have since been made.

ALARM Inspired by the political ferocity of the **Clash** and the emotional fire of **U2**, the Alarm were four young idealists from Rhyl in Wales who determined to follow their heroes to the top of the charts and into stadium super-stardom.

Mike Peters (vocals/guitar), Dave Sharp (guitar), Eddie MacDonald (bass) and Nigel Twist (drums) were originally a derivative pop outfit called Nineteen, but once they had recorded their first punk-influenced song, 'Alarm, Alarm', they changed their direction and their name and set about winning audiences by intensive touring in 1981/2.

Their anthemic, declamatory style (occasionally with an acoustic backing) contained echoes of both **Bob Dylan** and **Bruce Springsteen**, and brought them well-deserved UK hit singles with '68 Guns' (1983), 'Where Were You Hiding When the Storm Broke?' (1984) and 'Spirit of 76' (1985), before showing signs of maturity on their second album, *Strength* in 1985.

ALEXANDER, ARTHUR Born in Sheffield, Alabama, in 1942, Arthur Alexander was the first hit artist to emerge from **Rick Hall**'s Muscle Shoals studio with a beautifully understated interpretation of the self-penned 'You Better Move On' (1962) – a seminal performance, reflected by many later Southern soul hits.

Recorded before Hall had formed his own Fame label, it was released by Dot who proceeded to market Alexander as a pop singer. Despite less sensitive productions, he was equally impressive on the **Barry Mann** and Cynthia Weil song 'Where Have You Been?' and his own 'Anna' (1962) and 'Go Home Girl' (1963), and although he was indifferently received at home, all four records were much admired and covered by British acts (the latter two by the **Beatles** and the **Rolling Stones** respectively). Subsequent records for Dot, Sound Stage 7 (1965–9), Monument (1968), and a fine album on Warner Bros, nearly all excellent examples of Southern country soul, were ignored until he returned to the Hot 100 with his own 'Everyday I Have to Cry a Little' in 1975.

ALEXANDER, J.W. One of the most important backroom men in the Los Angeles black music scene of the late Fifties and early Sixties, J.W. Alexander was born in Tulsa, Oklahoma, in 1917. His first involvement was with gospel music, including spells singing with, managing and recording such noted gospel groups as the Pilgrim Travellers and the **Soul Stirrers**. In 1961, with ex-Soul Stirrer **Sam Cooke** (whom Alexander had actively encouraged to forsake the gospel scene for the white pop market), he set up the Sar and Derby labels as showcases for new gospel talents like **Johnnie Taylor**, **Mel Carter**, the **Valentinos**, and **Billy Preston**. On Cooke's death in 1964, Alexander devoted most of his energies to grooming Lou Rawls as an international soul star. He also recorded some fine blues sides for his own label, Truth.

ALLEN, LEE Born in Pittsburgh, Kansas, on 2 July 1926, Lee Allen performed searing tenor sax solos on countless classic New Orleans R&B sessions of the Fifties. He started playing in the clubs of New Orleans in the late Forties with Paul Gayten's band, and in between recording sessions he also played with the bands of **Fats Domino** and **Dave Bartholomew**. After helping make hit records for many other artists, he finally had his own hit in 1958 with the R&B instrumental, 'Walking with Mr Lee'. In the early Sixties he moved to the West Coast.

ALLISON, MOSE Jazz singer/pianist/trumpeter Mose Allison was born in Tippo, Mississippi, on 11 November 1927. His early influences included the blues of **John Lee Hooker**, **Sonny Boy Williamson**, and **Charles Brown** and the jazz of Duke Ellington and Charlie Parker. The result was a richly individual style first heard on record in 1957 with the critically acclaimed album *Back Country Suite* (Prestige) and other accomplished compositions.

Allison's greatest impact on rock has been through his dry, idiosyncratic singing on 'Parchman Farm', 'Seventh Son' and 'I Love the Life I Live' which has exerted a lasting influence on British singers, notably **Georgie Fame**. Allison's later recordings were for Columbia, Atlantic and Elektra.

ALLMAN BROTHERS BAND

Spearheading a salutary return to blues and country roots in rock music in the early Seventies, the Allman Brothers Band stood out from the many basic boogie bands of the era because of the skill and sensibility of twin lead guitarists Duane Allman and Richard Betts.

The group was formed by Duane Allman (born on 20 November 1946). Raised in Nashville and then Daytona Beach, Florida, he recorded first in Los Angeles in 1968 with Hour Glass, a

Hour Glass, the vehicle for Duane and Gregg Allman's first albums

group that included his brother Gregg (born 8 December 1947) on keyboards. A first album on Liberty led to further sessions at **Rick Hall**'s studio in Muscle Shoals. When these tapes were rejected by Liberty, Duane returned at Hall's request to play on sessions by **Wilson Pickett**, **Percy Sledge**, **Aretha Franklin**, **Boz Scaggs**, and others. Many examples of his solos for other artists crop up on the album *Duane Allman: An Anthology* (Capricorn, 1972).

An abortive solo album was cut at the insistence of Atlantic's Jerry Wexler, following which Duane signed to Phil Walden's Capricorn Records of Macon, Georgia, and set about forming a band. From Jacksonville, Florida, came bass-player Berry Oakley (born 4 April 1948) and guitarist Richard Betts (born 12 December 1943, who was formerly with **Tommy Roe**'s Romans). Gregg Allman returned from California and drummers Jai Johanny Johanson (born 8 July 1944) and Butch Trucks completed the line-up.

They began to tour extensively in the South, forming the kind of relationship with the region that the **Grateful Dead** had with the West Coast. Their first album (*The Allman Brothers Band*, 1969) found them, like the **Rolling Stones** and the **Paul Butterfield Blues Band** before them, reworking rock's blues inheritance, but with far greater fluidity and assurance. Central to the Allmans' sound on this and *Idlewild South* (1970) was the combination of Duane Allman's slide guitar and Betts' more delicate electric patterns. The latter, which included the original version of 'Midnight Rider' with vocals

Duane Allman, one of the outstanding guitarists of his generation

from Gregg, broke nationally, earning the group a gold album.

Duane continued to play some sessions, notably those for **Eric Clapton**'s *Layla* album. Their duets on the title track and others were among Allman's finest work, though the emotional power of his live playing with the Allman Brothers Band was preserved on *Live at the Fillmore East* (1971). These were virtually Duane Allman's last recordings before he died in a motorcycle accident on 29 October 1971 in Atlanta.

Wisely, no attempt was made to replace Duane, who had been, in many respects, the most complete guitarist of his generation. The remainder of the band went on to complete *Eat a Peach* (1972), another Top 10 album. Without Duane, the group gravitated towards a more melodic, country-influenced sound exemplified on 'Ramblin' Man' and Betts' instrumental 'Jessica' from the next album, *Brothers and Sisters* (1973). On 11 November 1972, Berry Oakley was killed in similar circumstances to Duane, and the band gained two new members: Chuck Leavill (keyboards) and Lamar Williams (bass).

The success of 'Ramblin' Man' and 'Jessica' established the Allman Brothers Band as a singles group, and by now their success had fostered interest in a whole host of Southern rock bands. Next, both Gregg Allman and

Betts cut solo albums, with Gregg also forming a band to tour in 1974, later releasing a live double album. By the mid-Seventies, the band itself no longer seemed the central force it had been during Duane's lifetime, something the selection of tracks for their double greatest-hits album (*The Road Goes on Forever*, Capricorn, 1975) emphasized.

In 1976, Gregg's evidence against the Allmans' road manager Scooter Herring helped convict the latter on narcotics charges, and his action created a schism within the group's ranks. Refusing to work with Gregg again, Betts formed a new band called Great Southern, while Gregg himself forged a recording partnership with **Cher** – they married in 1975 – and put together the Gregg Allman Band, whose *Playin' Up a Storm* was released in 1977. The Allman Brothers Band was reunited a year later, with Great Southern guitarist Dan Toler and bass-player David 'Rook' Goldflies also joining. The albums *Enlightened Rogues*, *Reach for the Sky* (Arista, 1980), and *Brothers of the Road* (1981) followed.

Gregg Allman held the Allman Brothers Band together after brother Duane's death in 1971, but also branched out to make his own albums solo and with the Gregg Allman band

ALMOND, MARC See **Soft Cell**

ALPERT, HERB The founder (with partner Jerry Moss) of A&M Records, and a best-selling instrumentalist in his own right, Herb Alpert was born in Los Angeles on 31 March 1937, and took up the trumpet at the age of eight. After US Army service he began songwriting in partnership with **Lou Adler**: their songs for Keen Records included the **Sam Cooke** hit, 'Wonderful World'. They became producers for Dore Records, handling the early hits by **Jan and Dean** and together with Lou Rawls set up the Shardee label, but after friction over Alpert's own recording and acting ambitions they separated. Acting took him no further than being an extra for *The Ten Commandments*, and initially recording too was fruitless.

Trumpeter Herb Alpert led his Tijuana Brass to the top of the charts

He found a new partner, Jerry Moss, a promoter and co-producer of the sole Dore Alpert single, issued through RCA, and they set up Carnival Records, later A&M. Their third venture was the Mexican-sounding 'The Lonely Bull' by the Tijuana Brass, on A&M. It launched Herb Alpert simultaneously as a recording star and a MOR label executive. He became a household name with a run of gold albums, sellout concerts and television specials.

In 1968, an uncharacteristic vocal track – a version of **Burt Bacharach**'s 'This Guy's in Love with You' – took him to Number 1 on both sides of the Atlantic. A year later, facing declining popularity, he took a five-year sabbatical, concentrating on the production side of A&M and grooming the **Carpenters**. In 1979, with the disco market in mind, he recorded the instrumental 'Rise' and returned to the transatlantic charts for the first time since 1968. The track reached Number 1 in the US. *See also* **A&M Records**

ALTERED IMAGES Formed in Glasgow in 1979, Altered Images were one of a number of bright Scottish guitar pop bands that found success in the early Eighties. Three school friends, Johnny McElhone (guitar), Tony McDaid (bass) and Michael 'Tich' Anderson (drums) formed the band; they were then joined by Jim McIven (guitar/keyboards) and soon after by pretty, pouting singer/actress Clare Grogan.

The group established a live following in Glasgow, and gained a support slot with **Siouxsie and the Banshees** that brought them to the attention of DJ **John Peel**. Soon after, they signed to Epic and in September 1981 released their first album *Happy Birthday*; the title track, a sparkling pop record, reached Number 2 on UK singles chart. In May 1982 they released the moderately successful follow-up LP *Pinky Blue*, produced by **Martin Rushent**. Soon after, McIven and Anderson left the band, to be replaced by Stephen Lironi on guitar and a succession of session drummers. With Lironi they recorded their last album, *Bite* (1983), which yielded the sophisticated dance pop hit 'Don't Talk to Me About Love'. The band split at the end of the year, Grogan leaving to pursue her acting career.

AMBOY DUKES Comprising **Ted Nugent**, guitar; Steve Farmer, rhythm guitar; Dave Palmer, drums; Bill White, bass (replaced by Greg Arama); Rick Lober, piano, organ (replaced by Andy Solomon), and John Drake, vocals (replaced by Rusty Day, ex-Detroit Wheels), the Amboy Dukes hailed from Detroit. They broke through nationally in the US with the Top 20 hit 'Journey to the Centre of the Mind' in 1968 on Mainstream.

Personnel changes didn't deter their rank bad taste: Steve Farmer really knew how to write a pretentious lyric, and brash, abrasive Ted Nugent, the first to put himself in a class with **Jimi Hendrix** or **Jeff Beck**, was a dab hand at adapting to other influences. He pulled out all the stops in their wild stage shows, and did so again with the new Amboy Dukes, which resurfaced in 1974 with *Call of the Wild* (DiscReet). The man who learnt his licks from Keith Richard and Jim McCarthy of the Godz could still turn in the grossest ever version of 'Maybellene'. The closest they came to a good album was *Migration*, their last in 1969. Ted Nugent, however, has since gone on to heavy metal megastardom as a solo act. *See also* **Ted Nugent**

AMERICA

AMERICA Formed in 1969 by the sons of UK-stationed servicemen, America – Dewey Bunnell (born 19 January 1952), Dan Peek (born in 1950) and Gerry Beckley (born 12 September 1952) – made their chart debut in the US two years later with the million-selling 'A Horse with No Name'. Their sound was a softer version of the acoustic guitar/harmony style pioneered by **Crosby**, **Stills and Nash**, while vocally they bore more than a passing resemblance to **Neil Young**.

Concentrating mostly on melodic material tailored to the requirements of the American FM radio networks, America were leaders in the field of Seventies AOR and enjoyed consistently high album sales for much of the decade. All their album releases between 1974 and 1977, beginning with *Holiday* and culminating in *Live*, were produced by **George Martin**. Dan Peek left the trio in 1977 to become a born-again Christian, but Bunnell and Beckley carried on somewhat less successfully as a twosome. After a six-year absence from the US singles chart, America had a major hit in 1982 with 'You Can Do Magic', written by Russ Ballard, who also produced *Your Move* (1983).

Leaders in the field of adult oriented rock in the Seventies, America were successful in concert as well as on record: Beckley (left), Peek (centre) and Bunnell

Andy Fairweather Low contributed his highly original vocal sound to Amen Corner's late Sixties hits

AMEN CORNER A leading R&B band from the Cardiff area, Amen Corner – who comprised Andy Fairweather Low, vocals; Neil Jones, guitar; Blue Weaver, organ; Clive Taylor, bass; Dennis Bryn, drums; Allen Jones, baritone sax; Mike Smith, tenor – had their first British Top 20 record in 1967 at the end of the mod wave with the powerful 'Gin House' (Deram). Their material became progressively more commercial, never fulfilling early promise. After providing Immediate with a Number 1 in 1969 with 'Half As Nice', they were caught up in the label's collapse. As Fairweather they dropped the brass section and had a Top 5 hit, 'Natural Sinner', in 1970, but soon became disillusioned and disbanded. Blue Weaver went to the **Strawbs**, Dennis Bryn to the **Bee Gees**, and Andy Fairweather Low rested his thin voice through several years' isolation in Wales before re-emerging with *Spider Jiving* (A&M) in 1974.

AMON DUUL II

AMON DUUL II Formed in Munich in 1968, Amon Duul II had a line-up that comprised Renate Knaup-Kroetenschwanz (vocals), John Weinzier (guitar), Chris Karrer (guitar, violin, sax), Falk Rogner (keyboards), Lothard Meid (bass) and Danny Fischelscher (drums). The band's origins lay in a politico-musical commune that underwent a factional split – the revolutionary but short-lived Amon Duul I represented the rival faction – and they became the first German group to make a sustained impact in the European and US markets. Their music originally owed much to the **Pink Floyd**'s early space-inspired work, but Syd Barrett's sense of awe in the face of the universe was transformed by Amon Duul II into a harsher vision of fearful mysteries waiting just beyond the boundaries of normal experience. Their solid rock base was complemented by electronic effects and avant-garde jazz improvisation, heard best on *Yeti* (1970) and *Dance of the Lemmings* (1971), both issued by Liberty. During the Seventies the band made 20 albums in commercially unspectacular spells with Atlantic, Sonopresse, and the German record labels BASF, Brain, Metronome, and Straud.

ANDERS AND PONCIA

ANDERS AND PONCIA Peter Anders (Andreoli) and Vinnie Poncia first worked together as members of the Videls, whose 'Mr Lonely' was a minor US hit in 1960. Contracted to the music publishing company Hill and Range, they became regular suppliers of songs to producer **Phil Spector** and provided hits for the **Ronettes**, the **Crystals**, and **Darlene Love**, as well as penning **Cher**'s unsuccessful **Beatles** cash-in of 1964, 'I Love You, Ringo'. Breaking with Spector that year, they formed their own production company and wrote, produced and sang (as the Tradewinds) 'New York's a Lonely Town', which became a US Top 40 hit on **Leiber and Stoller**'s Red Bird label. They later joined Kama Sutra and continued to record as the Tradewinds ('Mind Excursion') and as the Innocence, whose 'There's Got to Be a Word!' was a small hit in 1967. After recording *The Anders and Poncia Album* for Warner Brothers in 1969, the team split and Poncia worked as producer on albums by **Fanny**, Melissa Manchester, Ellen Foley, and Lynda Carter (of *Wonderwoman* fame). In the mid-Seventies, they resumed their partnership and shared joint production credits on albums by **Kiss**, Mary Travers, **Ringo Starr** (on his 1978 release, *Bad Boy*), and others.

ANDERSEN, ERIC

ANDERSEN, ERIC A folk singer who perpetually seemed to be on the brink of a popular breakthrough, Eric Andersen was born in Pittsburgh, Pennsylvania, on 14 February 1943, and was brought to New York by **Tom Paxton** after serving his folk club apprenticeship in and around Cambridge, Massachusetts. One of several singer-songwriters of the early to mid-Sixties to be heralded as 'the new Dylan', Andersen impressed many with his poetic lyrics, his handsome, ethereal presence and his gift for haunting melodies. Among his strongest works were the romantic 'Violets of Dawn', the passionate 'Come to My Bedside', the socially conscious 'Thirsty Boots' and the anti-Dylan 'The Hustler'.

After recording for Vanguard and Warner Bros, he moved to Columbia, developing strong background arrangements that never detracted from his supple, involved singing. Beatles manager **Brian Epstein** had planned a major management push for Andersen only months before his death. In 1974 he was signed by Clive Davis to the Arista label, but that long-awaited breakthrough never came.

ANDERSON, LAURIE

ANDERSON, LAURIE New York performance artist Anderson (born 1947, in Chicago) reached the British Top 5 in 1981 with the 8-minute single, 'O Superman'. Her first pieces were heard on the *Airwaves* compilation and on the collaboration with poets John Giorno and William Burroughs, 'You're the Guy I Want To Share My Money With'. Her strong dislike for the self-consciously serious nature of the art scene made her wit and sense of song a natural to cross over into rock, especially the ever-expanding 7-hour multi-media stage piece United States. The first part of United States, *Big Science*, was recorded and released as an album by WEA in 1982, followed two years later by a full, five-album set of the entire work to date. In the intervening period she released the lighter, more song-oriented *Mr Heartbreak*, and 1986 saw her third studio album, *Home of the Brave*. Her use of bizarre technology and her preoccupations with conspiracies, nuclear war and urban alienation can be misleading – Anderson is in fact a droll stand-up comic; part, as she says herself in United States, of 'the great sweep of American humour'.

Laurie Anderson bridged the gap between the avant-garde New York art scene and rock music with her multi-talented hi-tech performances

ANDREWS, CHRIS

His squeaky voice and tubby appearance made him an unlikely mid-Sixties pop star, but Chris Andrews won brief fame in 1965 with the self-composed 'Yesterday Man' and 'To Whom It Concerns', both Decca releases. Born in Romford, Essex, in 1938, he was a night-club musician in Hamburg before finding regular work on the *Oh Boy!* TV show and leading a modestly successful pre-**Beatles** era group, Chris Ravel and the Ravers. He turned to songwriting in the early Sixties, his first hit being 'The First Time' for **Adam Faith** in 1963, and he also wrote and produced most of **Sandie Shaw**'s early singles. Their jerky, upbeat rhythm became one of the most familiar British sounds of the mid-Sixties. He continued recording throughout the Sixties but with no further chart success.

ANDREWS, LEE AND THE HEARTS

The four-man Hearts – Roy Calhoun, Butch Curry, Jimmy McAlister and John Young – first recorded with Lee Andrews for Eddie Heller's Rainbow label in 1954 and Irwin Ballen's Gotham in 1955. Inspired by the **Orioles**, this Philadelphia group had 1957 US hits with 'Long Lonely Nights' (Number 45) and 'Teardrops' (Top 20), which Chess purchased from Jocko Henderson's Main-Line label. The following year, 'Try the Impossible' – which United Artists bought from Casino – reached the Top 40. Later members included Wendell Calhoun, Ted Weems and Gerald Thompson, but the group split up when doo-wop became unfashionable. With and without the Hearts, Lee Andrews also recorded for Gowen, Lost Nite, Parkway, Jordan, Swan, RCA and Crimson. In the Seventies he led new groups, First Born and Congress Alley.

ANGELIC UPSTARTS

Fiercely political, determined to stand up for the rights of an oppressed working class – and to rage against the iniquities imposed upon it – four-piece band Angelic Upstarts (from Sunderland in north-east England) combined a strong sense of melody (especially in their flair for chorus hook-lines) with some of the angriest lyrics to be encountered in British post-punk music. The Upstarts came into being following the **Clash**'s famous 'White Riot' tour of 1977; inspired by the London band, the group's members Mensi (vocals), Mond (guitar), Decca (drums) and Steve (bass) formed their own tough, politicized punk outfit. A drug problem saw the replacement of Steve by Ronnie Wooden and in 1978, with this line-up, they self-financed the recording and release of their debut single, 'The Murder of Liddle Towers', a raw, angry protest song about the death of a local man while in police custody.

Signed to Warners (via a false start with Polygram), they released a number of minor UK chart hits, including 'I'm an Upstart', 'Teenage Warning' and 'Never 'Ad Nothing', as well as two albums, *Out of Control* (1979) and *We've Gotta Get Out of This Place* (1980). Unhappy with Warners, the Upstarts left the label for EMI in 1980 and in July that year released the single 'Last Night Another Soldier', followed by an album, *2,000,000 Voices*. At the tail end of 1983 a compilation of their best work was released, *Angel Dust (The Collected Highs 1978–1983)*.

ANIMALS

Arguably the greatest stylists among the bands that led the British R&B boom and certainly the most significant force to emerge outside London's suburbs, the Animals came together in Newcastle during 1963 as the Alan Price Combo. The original line-up – **Alan Price** (organ, vocals, born on 19 April 1942), Hilton Valentine (guitar, 21 May 1943), Bryan 'Chas' Chandler (bass, 18 December 1941), and John Steel (drums, 4 February 1941) – were the main Saturday night attraction at the city's shabby, crowded Downbeat club and later at the smarter

The Animals on and off stage: key members of the group were Alan Price (right, second from left) and Eric Burdon (right, centre)

Club A Go-Go, by which time they had gained a charismatic lead singer in **Eric Burdon** (11 May 1941). In early 1964, the group moved to London and changed its name en route to the Animals.

Almost immediately the group inspired a following on the London club circuit as ardent as that they had left in Newcastle. The core of their sound was the counterpoint of Burdon's authentically 'black' voice and Price's engine-room organ playing, coupled with an on-stage aggression that prompted one American bluesman to admit, 'Man, them Geordies are really mean – I gotta fight to keep the limelight when they're playing.' With record companies looking for R&B groups in the wake of the **Rolling Stones**' Top 10 success, the Animals signed with EMI's Columbia label, where their discs were produced by a then relatively unknown independent record producer, **Mickie Most**. For their first single, Most ignored the R&B

classics that went down so well on stage and opted instead for an unfamiliar blues standard that had recently appeared on **Bob Dylan**'s first album as 'Baby Let Me Follow Me Down': with key changes to the lyric, the song became 'Baby Let Me Take You Home' and reached Number 21 in the UK. The follow-up, 'House of the Rising Sun', came from the same source, but Price's compellingly powerful arrangement transformed it into a rock classic. As well as topping the transatlantic charts and establishing the group worldwide, it was reputedly this success that prompted Dylan to work with a rock band himself. Although they were seen as part of the R&B boom in Britain, they came to be regarded in the US – because of the Dylan connection – as part of the folk-rock movement.

After recording their own 'I'm Crying', which hinted at their later inability to make the transition from interpretations to originals, they returned in 1965 to American material with **Nina Simone**'s 'Don't Let Me Be Misunderstood', **Sam Cooke**'s 'Bring It on Home to Me' and, interestingly, with 'We've Gotta Get out of This Place' by Brill Building writers Mann and Weil. After two albums, *The Animals* (1964) and *Animal Tracks* (1965), Alan Price left in May 1965. He was replaced by Dave Rowberry (born 27 December 1943) from the Mike Cotton Sound, who imitated his style completely, and in February 1966, the **Nashville Teens**' Barry Jenkins took over from John Steel.

The reshaped Animals moved to Decca for 'Inside Looking Out', 'Don't Bring Me Down' and the album *Animalisms*, but, in September, Burdon unexpectedly broke up the group. He re-emerged at the end of the year as the leader of Eric Burdon and the Animals – John Weider (guitar, violin), Vic Briggs (guitar), Danny McCulloch (bass), Barry Jenkins (drums) – which had a further string of psychedelically inspired hits in America where the group was based. These included Burdon's twin hymns to hippiedom in 1967, 'San Franciscan Nights' and 'Monterey', followed by 'Sky Pilot' the year after.

In 1969 Burdon finally laid the Animals to rest to follow an erratic solo career. The original line-up reformed briefly in 1976 and subsequently recorded *Before We Were So Rudely Interrupted*, and in 1983 they again came together for various concert dates and new recordings. *See also* **Eric Burdon**; **Alan Price**

ANKA, PAUL One of the more talented and durable teen idols of the late Fifties, Paul Anka was born on 30 July 1941, in Ottawa, Canada, and entered show business as an impersonator at the age of 12. In 1956, under the supervision of Ernie Freeman, he cut his first (unsuccessful) record, 'I Confess', for Modern Records. The following year, while staying in New York with the Rover Boys, who were contracted to ABC, he took their advice and contacted Don Costa who signed him to ABC and produced 'Diana'. That song, the story of his love for a 20-year-old girl – 'I'm so young and you're so old' – reached Number 1 in the US and went on to sell nine million copies worldwide. It was followed by a string of hits, including 'Lonely Boy', 'Put Your Head on My Shoulder' (both in 1959), and 'Puppy Love' (1960) – this last supposedly reflecting his admiration for **Annette** (**Funicello**).

Anka was no manufactured idol. Through a mixture of luck and good judgment in the Fifties and early Sixties, he made the middle ground – between the aggression of **Elvis Presley** and the repression of 'good guy' **Pat Boone** – his own. Anka's market was the girls between 12 and 14 who had few stars they could relate to before the arrival of the **Beatles**, **Monkees**, and **Osmonds**. Anka, with his calculatingly honest songs of teenage *angst*, could

make 12-year-old girls cry in their beds – and it would be his songs that the Osmonds would later revive.

A prolific songwriter, as well as his own hits he wrote 'It Doesn't Matter Anymore' for **Buddy Holly** before moving on to the mainstream with the English lyrics of 'My Way' for Sinatra and 'She's a Lady' for **Tom Jones**, among others. Anka was also a shrewd businessman – on leaving ABC for RCA in 1962, he bought back all his ABC masters. By then he had sold 30 million records throughout the world and could not have been particularly worried by his declining chart success. Moreover, his songwriting and various business concerns were going well. In the Sixties, Anka spent most of his time working behind the scenes – for example, he gave singer/songwriters **Steve Goodman** and **John Prine** their starts in the record industry. However, in 1970, he began to feel the urge to perform again. He quit RCA for Buddah and then United Artists, for whom in 1974 he wrote and recorded – at **Rick Hall**'s Muscle Shoals studio – the sickly, but very successful, 'You're Having My Baby'. The wheel had come full circle. Later albums included *Headlines* (1979) and *Walk a Fine Line* (1983), recorded with the help of Michael McDonald, Kenny Loggins and Karlo de Vito of **Meat Loaf**.

ANNETTE *See* **Funicello, Annette**

Paul Anka graduated from pop to cabaret (below left) in the Sixties, when he also wrote the hugely successful 'My Way' (performed by Paul, below right)

ANT, ADAM Born Stuart Goddard in London on 3 December 1954, Adam Ant adopted his new name on the formation of his group, Adam and the Ants in 1977. As leader of an out and out punk outfit, he found only limited success, but with a new look and a change of direction, Adam Ant suddenly became the biggest teenage pop sensation since the early Seventies.

Dressed in S-M and bondage garb, Adam and his Ants were strictly second division punks; derided by the music press and ignored by the punters, their survival was due solely to the music business' enthusiasm for signing punk bands in the late Seventies. By 1979 Adam's future looked bleak until in October he met the great punk entrepreneur **Malcolm McLaren**, who for a fee of £1000 agreed to re-shape the Ants' music and inject some fresh ideas.

While McLaren stole the Ants from Adam (to form the nucleus of **Bow Wow Wow**), he introduced him to the primitive rhythms of the African Burundi tribe. Inspired, Adam assembled a new group: guitarist and musical co-organiser Marco Pirroni, drummers Terry Lee Miall and Merrick (Chris Hughes) and bass player Kevin Mooney (although he was later replaced by Gary Tibbs). A cleverly-conceived fantasy image was constructed around Adam's swashbuckling togs and the Red Indian warrior war paint on his undeniably striking face. Combined with the new euphoric jungle sound, it impressed CBS enough for them to offer the re-styled group a contract. In July 1980, a new single, 'Kings of the Wild Frontier', was released. The record's rapturous whooping and pounding – a curious hybrid of a Zulu battle party and the Glitter band – was a triumphant departure from previous Ant efforts, and scraped into the UK Top 50.

Marco and Adam repeated the formula on the follow-up, 'Dog Eat Dog', and this time the tribal drums and warrior imagery – helped by an appearance on BBC TV's *Top of the Pops* – captured the public imagination. In October, 'Dog Eat Dog' reached Number 4; another single, 'Ant Music', made Number 2 the next month, and by February Antmania was rampant in the adolescent market. Adam and the Ants had five singles in the Top 40. Their new LP, *Kings of the Wild Frontier*, stood at Number 1 in the UK LP chart, and a previous album *Dirk Wears White Sox* reached Number 16.

1981 belonged to Adam Ant; a series of cleverly-crafted pop singles was promoted by visually stunning videos –

With his Red Indian war paint and swashbuckling image, Adam Ant led the resurgence of colourful escapism in the post-punk era

directed by Mike Mansfield and devised by Adam himself – in which the singer adopted various enticing looks and fully exploited his teen appeal. 1981 releases 'Stand and Deliver' and 'Prince Charming' both made the top of the UK charts while 'Ant Rap' reached Number 3. By the end of the year, Adam Ant had become the biggest pop phenomenon since the **Bay City Rollers**. Poster magazines and

Ant highwayman kits for tiny tots abounded while the Ant features were plastered across the covers of colour magazines and other glossies.

By 1982, Adam believed he had taken the tribal sound as far as he could and he decided on a change. In the spring, he dispensed with the services of the Ants – although Pirroni was retained as musical partner – and produced his first solo single in May. A rather meaningless attempt to emulate the rock'n'roll idiom, 'Goody Two Shoes' gave Adam his third Number 1, but the panache of old seemed lacking. The autumn's album, *Friend or Foe*, and the single of the same name, were lacklustre efforts, sadly short on drive or ideas. A further single, 'Desperate But Not Serious' failed to make the Top 30 and Adam's bubble appeared to have burst.

But then, in the autumn of 1983, he came bouncing back with a new album, *Strip*, and single, 'Puss'n'Boots'. The accent was back firmly on a dominant drum sound (courtesy of producer **Phil Collins**) and the whole thing was a conglomeration of sinister, howling rhythms and party tunes. The single climbed to Number 4 in the UK and the LP sold healthily.

Adam failed to capitalize on the success of 'Puss'n'Boots' and little of interest followed. An album, *Vive Le Rock!*, arrived in spring 1985 but neither it nor the title track, released as a single, made any real impression on the charts. There had been nothing particularly new about Adam and the Ants, but the inspired mixture of borrowed elements had arrived in the right place at the right time. Adam could justly claim that he had spearheaded a renaissance in colourful escapist pop music, a lead that new teen idols such as **Duran Duran**, **Spandau Ballet**, **Culture Club**, and **Wham!** were quick to follow.

ARGENT Formed in 1969 by ex-**Zombies** keyboard player Rod Argent (born 14 June 1945), Argent matched progressive rock leanings to a pop sensibility in a manner that predated the mid-Seventies efforts of bands like **Queen** and **Supertramp**. Making up the band were Russ Ballard (born 31 October 1947) on guitar and vocals; Jim Rodford (born 7 July 1945) on bass; and Robert Henrit (born 2 May 1946) on drums. Both Ballard and Henrit were ex-members of the Roulettes and Unit 4 + 2. The group's organ-based sound was well showcased on their albums *Argent* (CBS, 1970 – including the track 'Liar', later a hit in the US for **Three Dog Night**), *Ring of Hands* (1971), and *All Together Now* (1972), which featured the transatlantic Top 10 hit, 'Hold Your Head Up'. On *In Deep* (1973) and *Nexus* (1974), Rod Argent's mellotron and synthesizer playing began to dominate. 'God Gave Rock'n'Roll to You' reached the UK Top 20 in 1973. Following a live double album, *Encore* (1974), Ballard left for a solo career, and was replaced by John Grimaldi (guitar) and John Verity (vocals, guitar), but the

Rod Argent, Zombies keyboard player and later leader of his own band

Joan Armatrading blended many styles in her music, turning increasingly to electric rock in the Eighties

revised line-up broke up after two albums in 1975, *Circus* (Epic) and *Counterpoints*. Rodford, Henrit and Verity formed a band called Phoenix, which Rodford left to join the **Kinks** in 1978. Ballard has produced albums by **Roger Daltrey**, **Leo Sayer**, and **America**.

ARMATRADING, JOAN Born on 9 December 1950 on St Kitts, West Indies, black singer/songwriter Joan Armatrading moved to Birmingham, England at the age of eight. By her early twenties, urged on by friends, she was performing around the Birmingham area, and was soon being lauded as a performer of great potential, many (largely inappropriate) comparisons being drawn with **Joni Mitchell**.

On Cube Records she recorded *Whatever's For Us* (1973) with lyricist Pam Nestor and then, writing exclusively on her own, Armatrading signed to A&M. *Back to the Night* was released in 1975, but she maintained a low profile until 1976 and a third LP *Joan Armatrading*, which came out in a

blaze of publicity, received excellent reviews (praising her mellow voice in particular), and contained her only UK Top 10 single, 'Love and Affection'. Her combination of confident musicianship and personal diffidence endeared her to the public, and she became a special favourite of feminist audiences at a time when there were few female performers of Armatrading's authority operating in British rock.

Up to 1985 she recorded another eight albums, from *Show Some Emotion* (1977) to *Secret Secrets*, turning in consistently well-received collections of songs, and illustrating her remarkable ability to blend tastefully folk, gospel, jazz-funk, soul, reggae and, increasingly in the Eighties, rock. This individual formula slowly and unspectacularly built Armatrading a strong adult following; she never took the charts or the media by storm, but nor did she find it difficult to sell out major concert halls. Probably Armatrading's most popular period covered the albums *Me, Myself, I* and *Walk Under Ladders* in 1980/81, which received substantial airplay and had long runs in the UK album chart Top 10. *The Key* (1983) included 'Drop the Pilot', a Number 11 UK hit.

Joan Armatrading remains among the few solo performers to have retained a measure of consistency and integrity in her quest for commercial success.

ARNOLD, P.P.

Los Angeles-born Pat (P.P.) Arnold began her career in the early Sixties as a session-singer and first came to the UK in 1966 as a member of the Ikettes, **Ike and Tina Turner**'s backing group. She signed with **Andrew Loog Oldham**'s newly formed Immediate label and made her UK chart debut in 1967 with an impassioned version of a **Cat Stevens** composition, 'The First Cut is the Deepest'. Of her subsequent releases, only 'Angel of the Morning' reached the Top 30, although her debut album *Kafunta* was produced by Mick Jagger and Steve Marriott.

She appeared in the rock musicals *Catch My Soul* and *Jesus Christ Superstar* but was best known during the Seventies for her session work on albums by **Dr John**, **Nils Lofgren**, **Graham Nash**, **Freddie King**, **Humble Pie**, and others. Her original backing band, the **Nice**, formed in 1967 to accompany her on tour, quickly became one of the leading bands of the new progressive era under the leadership of Keith Emerson.

ASHFORD AND SIMPSON

Nicholas Ashford and Valerie Simpson are black singers/songwriters *extraordinaire*. Nick (born 4 May 1943) moved from Detroit to New York, meeting Valerie (born 26 August 1948) at Harlem's White Rock Church where she sang in the choir and had formed a gospel group, the Followers. Valerie and Nick became a singing duo (recording with Glover) and songwriting team (penning 'Let's Go Get Stoned', eventually a hit for **Ray Charles** in 1966, and others for Maxine Brown and **Chuck Jackson**). Signed to Motown Records as staff writers, the duo began a fruitful period of working with such as **Marvin Gaye** ('You're All I Need to Get By') and **Diana Ross** ('Ain't No Mountain High Enough'), and moved into production before Valerie was eventually launched by Motown as a solo recording artist. Despite two brilliant albums, the critical acclaim wasn't matched in sales. Nick and Valerie left Motown in 1973, to sign with Warner Bros Records, where two albums, *Gimme Something Real* and *I Wanna Be Selfish*, displayed their subtle, warm, sensitive music.

They married in 1974 and continued to record together, literally striking gold with the albums *Send It* (1977), *Is It Still Good to Ya* (1978) and *Stay Free* (1979). They undertook production work for **Chaka Khan**, **Diana Ross**, **Gladys Knight** and others, and partwrote the score for the film musical, *The Wiz*. 'Solid' was a major US and UK hit for the duo in 1985.

ASIA

British supergroup Asia, comprising Steve Howe (guitar) from **Yes**, John Wetton (bass/vocals) from various groups including **King Crimson** and **Roxy Music**, Carl Palmer (drums) from **ELP** and Geoffrey Downes from **Buggles**, was formed in 1981, uniting, in the tradition of rock supergroups, a group of well-known and experienced musicians.

Signing to Geffen and working with mainstream rock producer Mike Stone, Asia took five months to record their debut LP *Asia*, which was released in April 1982 and sold well worldwide, going triple platinum in America and quintuple platinum in Canada, and scoring numerous gold awards elsewhere.

A second LP, *Alpha*, followed in August '83 and was also a big seller, settling Asia into that stable of big-time transatlantic rock groups who could safely release formula album after formula album, with heavy sales more or less guaranteed.

ASSOCIATES

Originating from Dundee, Scotland in 1977 the Associates comprised the duo of Billy Mackenzie (vocals) and Alan Rankine, although they used a number of other musicians for selected projects, including former **Cure** bassist Michael Dempsey and drummer John Murphy. Their debut album, *The Affectionate Punch* combined intense, Bowie-influenced soul vocals with abrasive, 'experimental' sounds and was released on Fiction Records to extravagant critical praise in 1980. After a spell on Situation 2 Records the Associates signed to WEA and enjoyed a series of hit singles: 'Party Tears Two' (Number 9), 'Club Country' (13), and '18 Carat Love Affair'/'Love Hangover' (21). Their 1982 album, *Sulk*, made the UK Top 10 but unfortunately the Associates could not live up to the intense commercial expectations their success had brought them, and they split early in 1982.

Mackenzie's distinctive and highly mannered vocal delivery had brought him to the attention of Ian Craig Marsh and Martyn Ware of BEF (British Electric Foundation), who featured him on their showcase album *Songs of Quality and Distinction* (1982). Mackenzie worked on other solo projects before reforming the Associates in 1984 and releasing a new album, *Perhaps*, featuring Mackenzie and a new working partner, guitarist Stephen Reid.

ASSOCIATION

A vocal harmony group, the Association straddled the worlds of conventional pop and the new California consciousness of the late Sixties. The group included Russ Giguere (vocals, guitar), Ted Bluechel (drums), Brian Cole (bass, vocals), Terry Kirkman (keyboards), Larry Ramos (replaced by Gary Alexander, lead guitar, vocals) and Jim Yester (guitar, vocals). 'Along Comes Mary' and 'Cherish' – their first two records – were both Top 10 US hits on Valiant in 1966, despite accusations that 'Mary' was a 'drug song'. The Association followed with another ambiguous ditty, 'Pandora's Golden Heebie Jeebies', but after they joined Warner Bros in 1967, their material became straightforwardly romantic. 'Windy' and Never My Love' reached Number 1 and Number 2 respectively, while 'Everything That Touches You' and 'Time for Livin'' were smaller hits. By 1972, when they recorded for Columbia, their popularity had waned. In 1981, the group re-formed for cabaret appearances, minus Brian Cole, who had died in 1972 of a drug overdose.

ASWAD Formed in the Ladbroke Grove-Harlesden area of West London in 1975, Aswad (derived from the Arabic word for 'black') were among the pioneers of home-grown UK reggae. Based around a nucleus of Brinsley Forde (guitar and vocals), Angus Gaye (drums) and George Oban (bass), Aswad were quickly signed by Island Records. Their first release was the rock-steady 'Back to Africa', soon followed by the album *Aswad*. Although they were a Rastafarian band, Aswad had a musical approach that was free of the negative fundamentalism often associated with this creed; they absorbed the influence of black street life in Britain to achieve their own radical reggae synthesis. Their concerns were reflected in their music: the social injustice suffered by blacks in Britain ('Babylon') and police harassment in particular.

George Oban left the group at the end of 1979 to pursue his interests in jazz/rock, while Gaye and Forde, with the addition of new bass player Tony 'Gad' Robinson, moved towards a tougher Jamaican roots reggae. The album *Hulet* was followed by the classic single 'Warrior Charge', a track used in the film *Babylon*, which featured Brinsley Forde in the leading role.

Towards the end of 1980 Aswad left Island for CBS where they consolidated their progress with *New Chapter* and *Not Satisfied*, but after two years their hopes of breaking into the American market had not been realised and they returned to Island. Aswad's first live album *Live and Direct*, was released at the end of November 1983; recorded at the Notting Hill Carnival the previous August it ably demonstrated their power when playing on the concert stage. The following year they were in Jamaica working on new songs that included 'Chasing for the Breeze' and '54–56 That's My Number' – a reworking of the **Toots and the Maytals'** classic.

ASYLUM RECORDS David Geffen (born in New York on 21 February 1943) started Asylum Records in 1971 with $400,000 and an artist roster that included **Jackson Browne**, Jo Jo Gunne, David Blue, and Judee Sill. A year later he sold out to Warner Communications for $5 million, although he remained company president. In July 1973 he took over the running of Elektra Records (also part of Warner Communications) and merged it with Asylum. In so doing he dropped 25 of the former's recording artists. By this time he had signed the **Eagles** and

Linda Ronstadt to Asylum, and he followed that by spiriting **Bob Dylan** (briefly) away from Columbia and **Joni Mitchell** from Reprise. In the first year of Geffen's tenure, Elektra-Asylum sales were in excess of $18 million. In 1975, Geffen moved into films, and Joe Smith replaced him as president, but Geffen launched his own eponymous label under the Warner Communications umbrella with a roster including Joni Mitchell – whose song 'Free Man in Paris' on her *Court and Spark* album was dedicated to him – and **John Lennon**. *See also* **Elektra Records**.

ATKINS, CHET A leading force in the popularization of country music from the late Fifties onwards, Chet Atkins was born in Luttrell, Tennessee, on 20 June 1924, as Chester Burton Atkins. He took an early interest in country music and before he left school joined Bill Carlisle and his Dixieland Swingers on WNOX radio in Knoxville, Tennessee. Eventually he moved to Nashville and by the time the town became a really important recording centre in the Fifties, he had established himself as one of its leading musicians.

By 1960, Atkins, a guitarist in the Merle Travis tradition, already had a long association with RCA both as performer and producer, and was moving out of the straight country music field. He ran a small jazz-oriented nightclub group of drums, bass, guitarists Grady Martin and Hank Garland, and pianist **Floyd Cramer**. They threw out the conventional instrumentation, piano and the guitars taking the lines that had formerly belonged to the fiddle and steel guitar. The resulting rhythm had a light, rocking feel, and when Atkins took it back into the studio it became known as the 'Nashville Sound'.

As an A&R director with RCA, among his responsibilities was the career of the newly-arrived **Elvis Presley** whose records he supervised. He was also responsible for much of the **Everly Brothers'** early work, but is best known for the resuscitation of the ailing body of country music. Hank Locklin, **Bobby Bare**, **Skeeter Davis**, **Jim Reeves**, **Don Gibson**, and **John D. Loudermilk** all gained important successes with Atkins. He and Floyd Cramer played on

Established as a leading Nashville musician in the Fifties, Chet Atkins later pioneered the small-group 'Nashville Sound'

most of the records themselves and it was his fluent guitar and Cramer's tinkling right-hand piano that characterized many records of this period. At one time he was the most powerful man in Nashville. He stayed with RCA and has encouraged new singers such as Charley Pride, **Waylon Jennings**, Dottie West, Connie Smith and **Jerry Reed** (another graduate Nashville sideman).

But like most of Nashville's defences against musical impurity, Atkins' fabled 'Sound' lived on to become a barrier to progress. The original small group sound was soon lost in a mush of strings and crooning singers that ossified into a musical orthodoxy that Nashville applied to all who recorded there. It is no coincidence that RCA was the last of the major recording companies to give cover credits to sidemen: under RCA's guidance, they were all starting to sound the same. Some singers, notably Waylon Jennings, moved out of the Atkins orbit to experiment on their own, but others, like Charley Pride, remained, their later records standing as tedious (though profitable) testimony to Nashville's inherent musical conservatism. Atkins was elected to the Country Music Hall of Fame in 1973 and has continued to produce and record ever since, though generally in an easy-listening vein. *See also* **Nashville**

ATLANTIC RECORDS

One of the most consistently creative and commercially successful independent companies of the rock'n'roll era and beyond, Atlantic Records was formed in 1947 by Herb Abramson and Ahmet Ertegun with the help of a $10,000 loan from the latter's dentist.

At a time when the US music market was dominated by majors like Columbia, RCA, and Decca, with franchises in the key stores, distribution was an early problem: national distributors didn't think that the music Atlantic was recording for the customers of the side-street stores – a rough, danceable combo blues – would be successful. However, Ertegun quickly discovered the importance of setting up national distribution and was aided by Sticks McGhee's big 1949 hit, 'Drinkin' Wine Spo-De-O-Dee', and in the next few years a consistent string of hits followed by **Ruth Brown**, the **Clovers**, and **Joe Turner**.

In 1953 Abramson left and his place was taken by Jerry Wexler. Often, however, at this stage, the majors were being successful with songs – 'Such a Night', 'Tweedle Dee', 'Sh-Boom' and of course 'Shake, Rattle and Roll' – that

Atlantic had originally recorded. They used identical arrangements, very often the same musicians, but with white singers. In Britain, the situation was considerably worse, as the Atlantic originals were never even released, and it wasn't until 1955 that Decca started to issue Atlantic's material on its London label.

However, the company's growth wasn't to be checked and several factors in the second half of the Fifties ensured its expansion. With the advent of rock'n'roll came the breakdown of all previous distinctions between R&B and pop, between the majors and the 'indies'. In short, the whole industry was radically altered. While rock'n'roll had been a new name for R&B to disguise the fact that the singers were black, it wasn't – as R&B had once been – solely confined to black singers. Moreover, in **Jesse Stone**, a man intimately acquainted with Southern rhythm and blues records, Atlantic had someone whose arrangements and compositions ('Money Honey' and 'Shake, Rattle and Roll') recreated the bass patterns, rhythms and all-round level of energy for other arrangers to copy, gratefully. Atlantic had discovered how to record rock'n'roll successfully.

The arrival in 1956 of the ingenious producing-arranging-writing team of **Jerry Leiber and Mike Stoller** and the signing of **Bobby Darin** helped reduce the number of cover versions that had kept Atlantic's records out of the charts. In the following four years – an era renowned for its one-hit wonders – the company (plus the subsidiary Atco) had 84 hits in the Hot 100, of which 56 were contributed by five performers – the **Coasters** (15), **LaVern Baker** (11) and the **Drifters**, **Clyde McPhatter** and Bobby Darin (10).

The pop field was not Atlantic's only concern. In 1956, Ahmet's brother, Nesuhi, moved in and expanded the company by setting up the LP department and enlarging the roster of jazz artists – Charlie Mingus, John Coltrane and Ornette Coleman were among those who recorded for the company over the next few years, with the Modern Jazz Quartet easily their most successful jazz artists.

Before the arrival of the **Beatles** and the industry's next radical change, the company went from strength to strength. The Drifters, Bobby Darin, **Solomon Burke**, **Nino Tempo and April Stevens** all had hits at a time when much cornier songs prevailed – an augury of the soul explosion to come. But, above all, the company

showed a foresight, integrity and genuine interest in music (like releasing British-produced records in America – most successfully with **Acker Bilk**'s 'Stranger on the Shore' – and the signing of a distribution deal with Satellite, later to become Stax) that exemplified their philosophy of providing good material for good singers. It was their broader perspective and refusal to be categorized as a specialist label that ensured their survival.

With the coming of the Beatles and the British invasion *circa* 1964, Atlantic retained its R&B bias and was instrumental in the development and popularization of soul music, not only through its association with Stax but through its nurturing of a staggering range of black vocal talent – notably **Wilson Pickett** and **Aretha Franklin**, both of whom were northern-based artists who found their ideal recording environment courtesy of veteran Atlantic producer Jerry Wexler, in the studios of Memphis and Muscle Shoals respectively. In the pop market, meanwhile, Atlantic enjoyed considerable success with blue-eyed soul boys the **Rascals**, and **Sonny and Cher**, whose records were released on Atco. One of the consequences of the opening of a Los Angeles office was the signing, in 1966, of the **Buffalo Springfield**, one of the various offshoots of which – supergroup **Crosby, Stills, Nash and Young** – became one of Atlantic's most commercial signings, marking the label's entry into the rock field in a major way. The contracting of **Led Zeppelin** in late 1968 consolidated Atlantic's position while also setting new business precedents: Zeppelin won total control over everything from record production to merchandise marketing, and received the largest advance ever given to a new act.

Atlantic was incorporated into the Warner Brothers-Seven Arts group in 1967 and was sold with the group to Kinney Communications in 1969, though its A&R policies and its commitments to R&B, soul, jazz and the new rock were generally unaffected. Atlantic subsequently became one part of the WEA (Warner Brothers/Elektra/Atlantic) triumvirate, and during the late Seventies and Eighties its roster was even more catholic, including such diverse acts as **Chic**, **Foreigner**, Leif Garrett, **Mink DeVille**, **AC/DC**, and – for American release – **Abba** and **Phil Collins**. The Atlantic story from 1947 to the mid-Seventies is told in Charlie Gillett's model study of a record company, *Making Tracks* (W. H. Allen).

ATOMIC ROOSTER

ATOMIC ROOSTER Formed in 1969, Atomic Rooster was a hard rock outfit that enjoyed a sizeable British college following during the early Seventies. The band's founders were organist Vincent Crane and drummer Carl Palmer, former members of the Crazy World of **Arthur Brown**; completing the original line-up, which debuted with the album *Atomic Rooster* on the B&C label in 1970, was bassist Nick Graham. Palmer and Graham left soon after that album's release, to be replaced by John Cann and Paul Hammond (who left in 1972 to form Hard Stuff), and **Chris Farlowe**, John Mandella, Steve Bolton and Bill Smith also figured in the line-up at various points during Rooster's life. The band recorded eight albums in the Seventies (for B&C, Elektra, Pegasus, Dawn and Mooncrest) and enjoyed two UK hits during 1971, with 'Tomorrow Night' (a Number 11) and 'The Devil's Answer' (Number 4). In 1982, Crane recruited Cann and Hammond back into the group and secured a contract with Towerbell: *Headline News* followed in 1983.

AUDIENCE One of several London-based bands to build up a loyal following on the thriving UK college circuit of the late Sixties, Audience – Howard Werth (guitar, vocals), Tony Connor (drums), Trevor Williams (bass), and Keith Gemmell (sax) – won critical acclaim with their first two Charisma albums, *Friend's Friend's Friend* (1970) and *House on the Hill* (1971). The band toured the US with the **Faces** in the early Seventies and attracted a large underground following as a result, but friction between Gemmell and the rest of the band precipitated a split in 1972. Top US session men Bobby Keyes and Jim Price played on that year's final Audience album, *Lunch*, but only their producer Gus Dudgeon – who also guested as a percussionist on *House on the Hill* – and Howard Werth succeeded in furthering their own careers after the break-up.

AUGER, BRIAN Born in London on 18 July 1939, Brian Auger first made his name on the music scene when he formed a jazz group in the early Sixties; Auger played piano, and the other members included **John McLaughlin** on guitar and Rick Laird on bass. Although Auger had a promising career in prospect – he won the 'New Star' section in a *Melody Maker* readers' jazz poll in the early Sixties – he abandoned it in 1964 to take up the Hammond

organ and play R&B. With Rick Brown (bass) and Mickey Waller (drums), he formed the Brian Auger Trinity, which quickly evolved into Steampacket after the addition of guitarist Vic Briggs and vocalists **Julie Driscoll**, **Long John Baldry**, and **Rod Stewart**. The band lasted only a year, but Auger revived the Trinity concept and brought in bassist Dave Ambrose, guitarist Gary Boyle and drummer Clive Thacker to back himself and Driscoll in a new working line-up. Their one hit, 'This Wheel's on Fire' (1968), was a mesmeric version of a lesser-known **Bob Dylan** song, but its success persuaded Driscoll to strike out on a solo career and the band soon folded. In late 1970, Auger formed Oblivion Express with Robbie McIntosh, later one of the founders of the **Average White Band**, but the band's jazz-rock leanings meant little commercially. In 1983 he recorded a reunion album with Driscoll (known as Julie Tippett since her marriage to jazz composer Keith Tippett). He is now resident in San Francisco. *See also* **Julie Driscoll**

Brian Auger and Julie Driscoll performed together in the Brian Auger Trinity

AVALON, FRANKIE Like his label-mate **Fabian**, Philadelphia-born Avalon (born Francis Avallone on 18 September 1939) epitomized the stereotyped American teen idols who peopled American pop in the late Fifties. He began his career as a trumpet-playing child prodigy, appearing on the Paul Whiteman *Teen Club* television show in Philadelphia and recording instrumentals for RCA's Vik and 'X' subsidiaries. As he outgrew his novelty appeal, he opened a youth club called Frankie Avalon's 'Teen and Twenty Club' (under the sponsorship of two local businessmen, Bob Marcucci and Peter de Angelis), where Avalon, Fabian and **Bobby Rydell** would hang out in their pre-fame days.

In 1957, he joined a local group called Rocco and the Saints, then began recording solo for Marcucci and de Angelis' newly formed Chancellor label. After two flops, Avalon finally broke into the national chart with 'De De Dinah' (1958), a pubescent idiot chant that sold a million. Other hits followed – 'Gingerbread', 'Venus' (a 1959 US Number 1), 'Bobby Sox to

Frankie Avalon, wholesome teen idol of the Fifties

Stockings', 'Just Ask Your Heart', and 'Why' among them – before he moved into films and cabaret. During the early Sixties, his bronzed, clean-cut Italian-American features figured in a series of beach party movies in which he usually co-starred with the pneumatic **Annette Funicello**, and he also appeared in *The Alamo*, *Voyage to the Bottom of the Sea* and *The Carpetbag-*

In the Sixties, Avalon appeared in a number of films to sustain his popularity

gers. In 1976, he made a minor chart comeback with a disco remake of 'Venus'. Two years later, in 1978, he appeared in the film version of *Grease*, and in 1980 his brief pop career formed the basis of the film *The Idolmaker*.

AVERAGE WHITE BAND

Six experienced Scottish musicians, who had first met and played together in and around the Dundee and Glasgow areas in the mid-Sixties, got together in 1972 and formed the Average White Band. The members were: Alan Gorrie, bass, lead vocals (born 19 July 1946); Hamish Stuart, guitar, lead vocals (8 October 1949); Onnie McIntyre, lead guitar (25 September 1945); Robbie McIntosh, drums (1950); Roger Ball, alto and baritone saxes, keyboards (4 June 1944); and Malcolm Duncan, tenor and soprano saxes (24 August 1945). Their first real break came playing support to **Eric Clapton** at his comeback Rainbow performance in January 1973. The AWB consolidated this success with an impressive debut album, *Show Your Hand* (MCA), a few months later.

Their music is a derivation of modern black soul, their near-perfect re-creations as close as any British band has come to emulating the real thing. They bring to mind certain British R&B groups of the mid-Sixties in their striving for authenticity. With their second album *Average White Band* (Atlantic) they broke into the American market in a big way, and

spent most of 1974 and 1975 living and touring there. On 23 September 1974 Robbie McIntosh died after an accidental overdose of heroin. The group was stunned. They had always been close friends as well as a well-integrated musical unit. But within a couple of weeks they were back on tour with pick-up drummers, before adding Steve Ferrone. A third, less exceptional but more successful album *Cut the Cake* (1975) followed, introduced to America by a Top 20 single, 'Pick Up the Pieces'. Thereafter, the AWB continued to record an album per year without ever reaching the commercial heights. They joined with **Ben E. King** for the 1977 album, *Benny and Us*.

AXTON, HOYT

The son of Mae Axton, composer of 'Heartbreak Hotel', singer-songwriter Hoyt Axton was born on 25 March 1938, in Duncan, Oklahoma. He cut his first album, *The Balladeer*, for the Horizon label in 1962, and had his first major songwriting success a year later, when the **Kingston Trio** took 'Greenback Dollar' to Number 21 in the US chart.

Two of Axton's songs dealing with drug abuse – 'The Pusher' and 'Snowblind Friend' – were recorded by **Steppenwolf**, the former appearing on the best-selling *Easy Rider* soundtrack album. Later pop single hits came with 'Joy to the World' (**Three Dog Night**) and 'No No Song' (**Ringo Starr**), while 'Never Been to Spain' is perhaps his most-recorded song.

Axton's compositions span the divide between folk, country and rock, with the result that over 30 artists have recorded his material, ranging from Tiny Tim to **Joan Baez**. He has released a total of 19 albums, for CBS, Capitol, A&M, MCA, and other labels. Since 1979, he has recorded for his own company, Jeremiah.

AYERS, KEVIN

A founder member of **Soft Machine** and self-confessed professional eccentric, Kevin Ayers was born in Herne Bay, Kent, on 16 August 1945. He began his solo career with the Harvest album *Joy of a Toy* (1969). It contained the themes that have remained central to his work, presented with subversive wit and frequently disturbing effect: dreams, relationships with the audience, and personal relationships.

In 1970 he formed The Whole World (including Lol Coxhill, David Bedford and **Mike Oldfield**), the first of a series of freewheeling agglomerations such as Banana Follies (1973) and the Soporifics (1974) which have contained many

of the key figures of the British *avant-garde*, among them Steve Hillage, Archie Leggett, **Robert Wyatt**, and Ollie Halsall. An erratic performer, he has also guested with Gong and Henry Cow, while continuing to represent the spirit of 1967 in songs like 'Stranger in Blue Suede Shoes' from *Whatever-shebringswesing* (1971), though often despairing of its viability as in 'Shouting in a Bucket Blues' from *Bananamour* (1973). In 1974 he moved to Island and recorded *The Confessions of Dr Dream*, containing a remake of his classic 'It Begins with a Blessing . . .', and teamed up with the disparate talents of **John Cale**, Eno and **Nico** for a concert at London's Rainbow Theatre which yielded a live album, *June 1, 1974*. A cult figure with a strong European following, he continues to record and tour occasionally, though he is now semi-resident in Majorca.

AZTEC CAMERA

Scottish band Aztec Camera emerged in the early Eighties during a period when Scotland produced a sizeable crop of fine young bands. The group has gone through numerous personnel changes, but singer, songwriter and guitarist Roddy Frame and bassist Campbell Owens have remained constant.

Aztec Camera's first releases came in 1980 (when Frame, a superb guitarist, was only seventeen) on Postcard, Alan Horne's independent Scottish label, and the gentle acoustic arrangements of 'Just Like Gold' and 'Mattress of Wire' won many admirers. They signed to Rough Trade in 1982 and released the album *High Land Hard Rain*, which also spawned their biggest UK hit, 'Oblivious' (Number 18 in '83) when it was re-released on their new label, WEA. The first album for WEA, *The Knife* did not appear until 1984 and achieved only moderate success.

Scottish band Aztec Camera showed a gift for subtle arrangements

B

B-52s Formed in late 1976 in Athens, Georgia, the B-52s came together as a celebration of all that was kitsch in American life. Comprising Fred Schneider (vocals), Kate Pierson (keyboards and vocals), Cindy Wilson (vocals), Ricky Wilson (guitar) and Keith Strickland (drums), they put their shared exaggerated dress sense and unorthodox musical taste to positive advantage by forming the band, which took its name from Sixties slang for the lofty, beehive hairstyle favoured by the girls (itself derived from the huge American B-52 bomber). Early 1978 saw the release of their debut single, 'Rock Lobster'/'52 Girls' (which made the UK Top 20 when it was re-issued eight years later), and that summer they headed for Max's Kansas City and CBGBs in New York to put a toe in the water of popular taste. They were swiftly signed to Warner Bros in the US, and Island for the rest of the world.

Their sound consisted of a brisk top-heavy drum beat and deep synthesized bass, over which were spread the unlikely chords of a four-string electric guitar. A collection of bongoes, wireless receivers and toy percussion filled in the cracks, all of which gave a free rein to the unsettling vocal delivery of Fred Schneider. In June 1979 the group's first album *The B-52s* was released. A European tour, during which they developed a cult following, ensued but it was in Australia that they made most impact: a reworking of 'Rock Lobster' made the Top 10 in 1979, while a 1980 tour sold out.

The second album, *Wild Planet*, was released in 1980 and was disappointing, despite making the Top 20 in the UK. David Byrne of **Talking Heads** produced a mini-album, *Mesopotamia*, which reached Number 18 in the UK chart. The B-52s never regarded their music as anything more than an enjoyable hobby, and by the release of the 1983 album, *Whammy!*, the magic had gone from the music. Ricky Wilson died prematurely of cancer on 13 October 1985, aged 32, effectively bringing the group to an end.

BACHARACH, BURT Although rarely credited for his innovation in the fields of pop composition and arrangement, Burt Bacharach was one of the most interesting and quietly influential

The B-52s combined an unorthodox music sound and an outrageous sense of humour to produce one of the most unlikely styles of the late Seventies, but they never took their meteoric rise to fame seriously

figures of the early Sixties. Born in Kansas City, Missouri, on 12 May 1929, he studied music at McGill University in Montreal and, upon graduating, chose the classic route of becoming a piano accompanist to balladeers like Vic Damone and Steve Lawrence. He worked as Marlene Dietrich's musical director between 1956 and 1958, by which time he had become a songwriter in partnership with Hal David. They were successful with neat songs like 'The Story of My Life' (Marty Robbins, 1957) and 'Magic Moments' (Perry Como, 1958). Bacharach also worked briefly with Bob Hilliard, with whom he composed two memorable songs for the **Drifters**, 'Mexican

Divorce' and 'Please Stay' (both 1961).

It was, however, with David that Bacharach formed his most famous and productive partnership. David's sharp, witty, literate images (he had worked on Broadway) provided the perfect foil for Bacharach's increasingly sophisticated melodies. Both men were steeped in a tradition that went back way beyond pop music to the classic show songs of Cole Porter, Irving Berlin, and George Gershwin, yet both had enough appreciation of the finer points of pop consciousness to be able to roll off dozens of hit songs in the early Sixties. **Dionne Warwick** – discovered by Bacharach singing backgrounds on a Drifters session – was their *protégée*, their mouthpiece, and success came immediately through her with songs like her first US hit 'Don't Make Me Over' (Number 21 in 1962), 'Anyone Who Had a Heart', 'Walk On By' (both Top 10 in 1963), 'You'll Never Get to Heaven', 'Reach Out for Me', 'Here I Am', and many others on Scepter. Instantly apparent was the iconoclasm of Bacharach's melodic sense: few other singers could have coped with the daringly wide intervals, odd phrase-lengths, and uneven rhythms with which he confronted Warwick. Given his head as producer and arranger, he emphasized the more eccentric aspects of the songs, employing unusual instrumental groupings and almost melodramatic orchestral punctuation. By the standards of contemporary pop he kept to no rules, and his exemplary knowledge and taste allowed him to get away with it. During this period Bacharach and David also composed for other performers, and among their greatest artistic successes were **Gene Pitney**'s smash '24 Hours from Tulsa' (with its famous two-trumpet phrase) and Jimmy Radcliffe's lesser known but equally attractive 'Long After Tonight Is All Over'.

Inevitably, as the rest of the world plagiarized their methods, the couple's success ratio declined, but in 1970 one of their earliest songs, 'One Less Bell to Answer', was renovated and became a Number 2 hit for the **Fifth Dimension**, thanks to its typical combination of sumptuous melody and imaginative lyric idea. Towards the end of the Sixties they wrote a Broadway musical called *Promises, Promises* – but it was not as successful as their previous efforts and ultimately the partnership was dissolved. Their last major hit collaboration was 'Raindrops Keep Fallin' on My Head' for B.J. Thomas in 1969, from their Oscar-winning score for *Butch Cassidy and the Sundance Kid*. Since 1963 Bacharach had been recording (for MCA and A&M) in his own right, largely due to the popularity of TV specials and series built around him, and his own albums contain interestingly developed versions of songs like 'Walk On By', 'Close to You', 'The Look of Love', 'Any Day Now', 'I Say a Little Prayer', and 'This Guy's in Love with You'. Without David, however, his creative energies appeared to dwindle, and his songs were conspicuously absent from the world charts during the first half of the Seventies. A return to commercial form came in 1981 with the chart-topping 'Arthur's Theme', from the film *Arthur*, which Bacharach wrote with the song's performer,

Bachman-Turner Overdrive, the pop end of the heavy-rock spectrum

Christopher Cross, and Carol Bayer Sager. A year later, Bacharach and Sager were married. *See also* **Dionne Warwick**

BACHMAN-TURNER OVER-DRIVE
Randy Bachman, founder member and lead guitarist of Canadian band the **Guess Who**, formed Bachman-Turner Overdrive in 1972. After quitting the Guess Who in 1970, while his composition 'American Woman' was still riding high in the transatlantic charts, Bachman teamed up with brother Robbie Bachman (drums), C. F. (Fred) Turner on bass, and the original Guess Who singer Chad Allan to form Brave Belt. They made two albums for Warner Bros, dabbling in the country end of rock, the second with Tim Bachman replacing Allan. Both were indifferently received and it was only after some persuasion that Mercury signed the group with a third album already in the can which was released under the

name of Bachman–Turner Overdrive. Very soon they had notched up monster hits: 'Takin' Care of Business' (1973), 'You Ain't Seen Nothing Yet' (1974), and 'Let It Ride' (1975) – all compelling examples of the pop end of the heavy-rock spectrum – and had seen *BTO* and *BTO II* (both, 1973) go gold.

Tim Bachman departed and the group brought in guitarist and sex symbol – the rest of them were somewhat overweight – Blair Thornton. Things went from better to better still with two more platinum albums, *Not Fragile* (1974) and *Four Wheel Drive* (1975), but they began to be superseded by a new crop of British and American heavy metal outfits who played even louder, wilder doses of primal energy. Randy Bachman left in 1978 and was replaced by Jim Clench, but after two more albums – *Street Action* and *Rock-'n'Roll Nights* (both 1978) – the group broke up.

BAD COMPANY

BAD COMPANY Formed in late 1973, Bad Company comprised four musicians from established British groups: Paul Rodgers (vocals) and Simon Kirke (drums) came from Free; Mick Ralphs (guitar) was a founder-member of **Mott the Hoople**; and Boz Burrell (bass) came from **King Crimson**, where he had been taught by **Robert Fripp**. They embarked on their first US tour in 1974, initially as a support group, and proved so successful that they later headed the bill. Following on from this acclaim, their first album, *Bad Company* (Island 1974) topped the US charts and the single taken from it, 'Can't Get Enough' went to Number 5 (UK Number 15). The album also went to the top of the UK chart, and they were established as a first-rate heavy rock group. They were unable, however, to sustain this level of achievement. They had four more US Top 20 hits, only one of which – 'Feel Like Making Love' – also reached the UK Top 20. Each of their five remaining albums sold steadily, and *Burnin' Sky* sold more than a million copies. The group broke up in summer 1982, Paul Rodgers joining **Jimmy Page** in the Firm. Early in 1987 the group reformed with Brian Howe (ex-**Ted Nugent**) as vocalist.

BAD MANNERS Formed in 1979, North London manic ska/R&B band Bad Manners enjoyed a brief period of chart success during the ska revival of the early Eighties. Led by the corpulent singer Fatty 'Buster' Bloodvessel (real name Doug Trendle), the nine-piece band built up a reputation for wacky, goodtime live shows and for foot-tapping, singalong tunes that were mindless but huge fun. Bad Manners scored nine UK Top 40 hits from 1980–82, the best-known being 'Special Brew' (Number 3 in 1980) and 'Can Can' (Number 3 in 1981). After 1983 their popularity declined as ska went completely out of vogue and, because they were without the musical skills of contemporaries **Madness**, who managed to transcend the limitations of the form, Bad Manners disappeared from the charts. The band's name continued to be seen on the London pub and club circuit well into the Eighties, but there was no sign of their regaining their earlier successes.

BADFINGER One of the few signings by the **Beatles**' Apple label to achieve major chart success, Badfinger were briefly taken to the public bosom in the early Seventies as a surrogate fab four. Tom Evans (bass, born in 1947)

and Joey Molland (guitar, keyboards, born in 1948) were both Liverpudlians, while Pete Ham (vocals, guitar, born in 1947) and Mike Gibbins (drums, born in 1949) both hailed from Swansea. As the Iveys, the group had played the Cavern during the Merseybeat heyday. Boasting good looks, solid musicianship and a pleasant line in McCartney-like melodies, they joined Apple in 1969 and reached Number 4 in the UK a year later with the McCartney-composed 'Come and Get It', which was featured on the soundtrack of the Peter Sellers–**Ringo Starr** film *The Magic Christian*. 'No Matter What', written by Ham, was the successful follow-up.

More singles success followed, together with guest appearances on albums by Apple artists (including the now solo Beatles) and a supporting spot in **George Harrison**'s concert for Bangla Desh in 1971. A Ham/Evans composition, 'Without You', also provided **Harry Nilsson** with a transatlantic Number 1 in 1972. The group left Apple in 1973 to join Warner Brothers, but the association was an unhappy one and Molland departed within a year to form Natural Gas with ex-**Humble Pie** drummer Jerry Shirley. In April 1975, Ham committed suicide and the band disintegrated. In 1977, Evans and Molland re-formed Badfinger with new members Tony Kaye and Peter Clarke (ex-**Stealers Wheel**), and a deal was signed with Elektra. After only moderate sales of their album *Say No More* (1981), however, Badfinger disbanded once more. In almost a carbon copy of Pete Ham's death, Tom Evans was found hanged at his Surrey home in November 1983, the victim of severe depression over allegedly unpaid royalties.

Endowed with a superb natural singing voice, Joan Baez put her talents at the service of her political beliefs with a passionate intensity

BAEZ, JOAN Whatever her theme, her voice always rings with strength and clarity. Whether singing folk or contemporary material in her purling soprano, or enunciating her views on pacifism and brotherhood (and sisterhood), Joan Baez projects an identifiable, persuasive and compelling sound. Her fusion of music and social conscience was an Old Left folk-movement convention, which she carried along into the New Left of the Sixties.

She made a striking debut at the first Newport Folk Festival, in 1959, and has been a star ever since, but a star obdurately indifferent to showbiz image or style. She was born in New York City on 9 January 1941, daughter of an English-Scots mother, a drama teacher, and a Mexican-American physicist. Both her grandfathers had been ministers. Her Latin descent gave her a command of Spanish as well as early experience with discrimination in California. To keep up with her father's shifting assignments, the family moved to Boston after high school. Joan fell in with the Harvard Square folk scene in her first tentative attempts to sing and play guitar. She attended Boston University for only one month, then pursued a career in music, folklore and humanist politics that was entirely self-taught. Baez's first few albums featured traditional material. Then she fell under the sway of **Bob Dylan** and the topical song movement. By the end of the decade, she was writing her own songs.

The Baez voice is generally regarded as a marvel of untrained purity, always controlled, often rolling with reined passion, light in texture, quite unforgettable once heard. Her singing has a stunning projection, clear-as-glass intonation, a focus that many a highly schooled conservatory singer would envy. Her acoustic guitar-playing is consistently secure, supple and refined. Whatever her stylistic excursions, even into country music, she is a master of idiom. Among her best early recordings were 'Silver Dagger', 'All My Trials', 'Donna Donna', 'Engine 143', 'What Have They Done to the Rain?', 'Mary Hamilton', 'There But for Fortune', and 'Bachianas Brasilieras No. 5'. *The First Ten Years* double album recapitulates her first decade with Vanguard Records. After 17 albums on that label, she switched to A&M. Among her most unusual work have been an unreleased experiment into folk-rock, co-produced by the late **Richard Fariña**, her brother-in-law; *Any Day Now*, a double album of Dylan material in which she began recording

Ginger Baker, regarded by many as the world's best rock drummer

in Nashville; *Where Are You Now, My Son?*, including tapes from North Vietnam, and *Gracias a La Vida*, a Spanish collection.

Joan's influence has been in political activism, music and in her lifestyle, as well. Her diffidence towards stardom and towards false shibboleths was widely imitated. Her career was never just in music, but on the battlefronts of social reform. In 1962, her three Southern concert tours maintained a strict non-discrimination policy. She began, in 1964, a running battle with American tax authorities by withholding that proportion earmarked for arms and war. In 1965, as an outgrowth of her interest in pacifism, she founded the Institute for the Study of Nonviolence near her home in Carmel, California. In 1967, after participating in a draft-resistance action, she, her mother, and sister Mimi spent 10 days in jail. Later that year, Joan was jailed again briefly for a similar violation. Her autobiographical book, *Daybreak*, appeared in 1968, the year she was married to David Harris, a peace activist who served a long prison term. Their son, Gabriel Earl Harris, was born in December 1969. The couple were divorced later. In the Seventies, Baez became active with Amnesty International, ultimately joining the American chapter's board. Late in 1972, on a visit to Hanoi, she survived the 11-day American bombing of the North Vietnamese capital. The experience underscored her long opposition to war. 1975 saw her returning to the rock mainstream with *Diamonds and the Rust* (A&M). Recorded in Los Angeles rather than Nashville, it was her most commercially successful record for some time.

Also during 1975, she joined Dylan on his quirky Rolling Thunder tour,

and three years later she appeared in his feature film, *Renaldo and Clara*. Her political activities still occupy much of her time, and in the Eighties she has been particularly associated with human rights campaigns in Central and South America. *See also* **Folk Revival (1960s)**

BAKER, GINGER Born in Lewisham, South London on 19 August 1939, Peter 'Ginger' Baker was a racing cyclist and trumpeter as a teenager; he went on to gain early experience as a drummer with the increasingly popular traditional jazz bands of the late Fifties, including **Acker Bilk** and Terry Lightfoot. Following a residency at Ronnie Scott's Jazz Club in London, he joined Blues Incorporated in 1962, replacing Charlie Watts. In February, 1963, he broke away with **Graham Bond** and **Jack Bruce** and stayed with the Graham Bond Organisation until 1966, when he formed **Cream** with Bruce and **Eric Clapton**. He and Clapton stuck together after Cream broke up late in 1968 and teamed up with **Stevie Winwood** and Rick Grech in the short-lived **Blind Faith**.

Widely acclaimed as the world's best rock drummer, Baker developed a passionate interest in African music, which provided the impetus for his ten-piece Airforce in 1970 and prompted his move to Akeja, Nigeria, where he built a recording studio and made a TV documentary about Nigerian music. He visited Europe with **Fela Kuti** and Salt, and returned to England in 1974 where he formed the Baker-Gurvitz Army with Adrian Gurvitz, ex-leader of Gun. The band lasted until the late Seventies, after which Baker moved to Italy to record and perform, reportedly for tax reasons. *See also* **Cream; Blind Faith**

BAKER, LAVERN Atlantic's premier female vocal star of the Fifties, LaVern Baker was born in Chicago on 11 November 1929. She first sang in Detroit clubs where, as Little Miss Sharecropper, she is said to have had an enduring influence on **Johnnie Ray**, before recording unsuccessfully for Columbia and – with Todd Rhodes' orchestra – for King in 1952. The following year, she was snapped up by Atlantic, where she remained until 1965. Many of her earliest recordings –'Tweedle Dee', 'Bop-Ting-a-Ling' (both written by Winfield Scott) and 'Play It Fair' for example – were deliberately pop-slanted with bland, stereotyped, vocal choruses, and hardly stand up today. None the less, her records were ruthlessly covered at the time by white 'name' artists. So much so that she gained useful publicity by writing to her Detroit congressman about the practice.

Her warm, broken-note voice had a sexy, playful quality, and by 1956, she was given the material she deserved. 'Jim Dandy', 'Jim Dandy Got Married' and 'Voodoo Voodoo' established her as one of the finest female rock'n'rollers of all time, while her ballad hits, 'I Cried a Tear' (1958) – her only big hit in the 'pop' charts – and 'I Waited Too Long' (1959) demonstrated the relaxed, gospel feel that earned her a place in the ranks of the first pioneers of soul. 'Tiny Tim', 'Shake a Hand', 'Bumble Bee' (a rockabilly song, replete with twangy guitar), 'You're the Boss' (a duet with the **Ravens**' bassman, Jimmy Ricks), 'Saved' (a rumbustious neogospel **Leiber and Stoller** composition) and 'See See Rider' kept her (just) in the charts until 1963. Her subsequent records for Brunswick were less successful.

BAKER, MICKEY 'GUITAR'
See **Mickey and Sylvia**

BALDRY, LONG JOHN A folk and jazz singer in the Fifties, Long John Baldry (born on 12 January 1941 in London) left Blues Incorporated a few months after its formation in 1962 to tour Germany with a jazz band and joined Cyril Davies' breakaway R&B All-Stars on his return. On Davies' death in January 1964 he renamed the band the Hoochie Coochie Men and led it for more than a year with **Rod Stewart** as second singer, then took Stewart to join Steampacket.

After a subsequent stint with Bluesology, he was tempted into pop in 1967 for the only hits of his career – the British chart topper 'Let the Heartaches

LaVern Baker was the leading female vocalist of the Fifties, projecting her warm, playful presence in a string of rock numbers and ballads

Begin' (Pye, written and produced by Tony Macaulay) and 'Mexico' (1968). In the Seventies he attempted a return to blues, but despite label changes and the production assistance of former colleagues, Rod Stewart and **Elton John** (Bluesology's Reg Dwight), he met with little success.

BALLARD, HANK Best remembered as the creator of 'The Twist', Hank Ballard was born in Detroit, Michigan, on 18 November 1936. In 1953 he joined the Royals – Lawson Smith, Norman Thrasher (later replaced by Charles Sutton), Billy Davis (replaced by Arthur Porter) and Henry

Hank Ballard (second from the left) and the Midnighters in high-steppin' form: their 'Annie' discs all reached the R&B Top 10

Booth (replaced on his death by Sonny Woods) – as lead singer. The following year, the group's name was changed to the Midnighters to avoid clashing with the Five Royales – like them, a King Records act – since both groups were becoming successful. In 1954, the Midnighters scored with their now-famous 'Annie' discs – 'Work with Me, Annie', 'Annie Had a Baby' and 'Annie's Aunt Fanny' (Federal). All reached the R&B Top 10, but were considered too risqué for pop exposure. The group recorded steadily over the next four years without spectacular success, then in 1958 they switched from the Federal subsidiary to the main King label – Ballard getting headline billing for the first time – and immediately made the national charts with 'Teardrops on Your Letter'. Its B-side was the original issue of 'The Twist'. 1960 saw the group in the Top 10 with 'Let's Go, Let's Go, Let's Go' and 'Finger Popping Time', a characteristically gritty jump performance featuring the mandatory rasping tenor sax solo. The success of **Chubby Checker**'s version of 'The Twist' led King to re-promote the original, which sold a million.

The next two years brought chart success with mainly dance-aimed songs, but sales were diminishing. Following a period in 'soul limbo', Hank resurfaced in 1968 under the wing of **James Brown**, touring with his Revue and recording a series of stereotyped funky dance songs. In 1970, he switched briefly and unsuccessfully to Lelan Rogers' Silver Fox label, but soon returned to the Brown fold. Still in search of renewed fame, he signed with Stang Records in 1974.

BANANARAMA The apotheosis of the 'girls just wanna have fun' school of rock music, all-girl vocal trio Bananarama met in London in 1979, drawn together by their mutual love of soul music, dancing and night clubs, and by 1981 they had decided to form a band.

In the same year, Keren Woodward, Siobhan Fahey and Sarah Dallin released their first single, 'Aie A Mwana', an infectious tribal dance number that secured them a deal with London Records and a brief (but successful) liaison with the **Fun Boy Three**, who used the girls as back-up on 'It Ain't What You Do' and then returned the compliment on Bananarama's first hit, 'Really Saying Something' in 1982.

Their natural exuberance and down to earth appeal made them media darlings for a while, but the girls were given little chance to progress and explore their own talents after the commercial failure of their self-penned single, 'Cheers Then'. London placed them under the guiding hands of production team Jolley and Swain who forced them into more cover versions, the hits 'Na Na Hey Hey Kiss Him Goodbye' and 'Venus'. Over two moderately impressive albums their high point was the atmospheric song 'Robert De Niro's Waiting' (a UK Number 3 in 1984), but after this they seemed to lose direction and never again captured that initial burst of irrepressible fun.

BAND AID/LIVE AID In late November 1984, the cream of Britain's pop talent were brought together by Bob Geldof in Sarm West Studios in London to record a single, 'Do They Know It's Christmas?'. Geldof (of the **Boomtown Rats**) and Midge Ure (of **Ultravox**), prompted by a harrowing TV News report on the Ethiopian famine, had written the song and recruited the big names from the pop world (including the likes of **U2**, **Duran Duran**, **Wham!**, and **Culture Club**) to donate their time and voices for charity. Geldof and Ure also managed to persuade the businesses involved at every stage of production – manufacture, distribution, sales and so on – to waive all costs. Only the Conservative government of the time could not be urged to lift the tax element. Out of every £1.35 charged in the shops, 96.03p would go to famine relief.

In a welter of publicity, public response to the single was overwhelming. The record went straight to the UK Number 1 slot, stayed there for five weeks and became the biggest selling British single of all time, with sales of over £7 million. Yet Band Aid (the collective name for the group and the charity) was only the first step. As Geldof realised, even the sum of £8 million raised by the record would only scratch the surface of the famine problem so he and Ure were personally committed to overseeing maximum efficiency in the purchase and distribution of the aid. Even more importantly, the example set by their release was followed by 'We Are the World', an American all-star famine relief record that notched up similarly huge sales.

As well as inspiring a spate of other benefit recordings, the achievements of Band Aid led Geldof, through the sheer persistence and bull-headedness for which he came to be notorious, to realize a grandiose project called Live Aid. Justifiably hailed as the greatest rock spectacle ever, this consisted of two mammoth concerts, one in Philadelphia and one in London, staged on Saturday 13 July 1985. Six-figure crowds filled the stadiums and a TV audience of one and a half billion watched the event as it was beamed live around the world, living up to its 'global jukebox' tag. The star-studded line-up consisted of the biggest names from all over the pop world – particularly memorable performances were turned in by **Queen**, **Madonna** and **U2** – and made compulsive viewing. The sixteen hour transmission, including music from the Soviet Union, reaped £50 million from telethon donations and television sales.

With hints of a possible repetition of Live Aid, plus the re-appearance of 'Do They Know It's Christmas?' in the UK charts late in '85, Geldof and Ure continued to be closely involved with the relief operations. On a wider level, the existence of Band Aid highlighted the possible interplay of popular music and social/political issues, and has been followed by several campaigns and movements such as Farm Aid and Sports Aid. In June 1986, Geldof was created a Knight of the British Empire (KBE) and also in that year he was nominated for the Nobel Peace prize, but lost out to American author and human rights campaigner Elie Wiesel.

BAND, THE A pivotal group in American rock at the turn of the Seventies, The Band comprised Levon Helm, drums (born 1935); James Robbie Robertson, guitar (5 July 1943); Garth Hudson, organ (2 August 1937); Richard Manuel, piano (3 April 1943); and Rick Danko, bass (29 December 1942). They came together in the late Fifties as the Hawks, the backing group of the Toronto-based rock'n'roller, **Ronnie Hawkins**. All were Canadian, except for Helm who came originally from Arkansas. With Hawkins, they toured Canada and recorded R&B standards like 'Who Do You Love?' and **Muddy Waters**' '19 Years Old', which featured Robertson's tough but understated guitar playing and Helm's vocals.

Leaving Hawkins, they played small venues across Canada and the United States, billed as the Canadian Squires or Levon and the Hawks, cutting a few singles including Robertson's 'The Stones I Throw'. In New York, they played with white blues singer **John Paul Hammond**, and through him met **Bob Dylan**, who saw them as the ideal group to accompany his intended move into electric music. The first recording that Dylan and The Band made together was the single 'Can You Please Crawl Out Your Window' (1965) and some members played on selected *Blonde on Blonde* tracks. But certainly the most powerful music made by Dylan and The Band at this time were the rock concerts of Dylan's 1965–6 tour. Their sound has been preserved on 'Just Like Tom Thumb's Blues' (issued on the flip side of 'I Want You') and on a widely circulated bootleg recording of Dylan's Albert Hall, London concert which demonstrates that The Band had made Dylan's sound more anarchic and turbulent than his studio recordings. On this tour Mickey Jones played drums instead of Helm, and the rhythm section propelled Dylan's voice along like a battering ram while Robertson played searing guitar lines on top, leading Dylan to praise him as 'a mathematical guitar genius'. After Dylan's motorbike crash in July 1966, The Band settled in Woodstock, to make music with him while he recuperated. These sessions resulted in a collection of songs, originally widely circulated in bootleg recordings known as *The Basement Tapes* and finally officially released by Columbia in 1975. These songs possessed a more subdued, mellow, funky feeling, and were indicative of the effect that Dylan and The Band were having on each other.

The Band, particularly Robertson, assimilated some of Dylan's gift for metaphor and imagery, while Dylan developed a less violent, more rural musical vocabulary. The results of this interaction were first heard on Dylan's *John Wesley Harding* album, and subsequently on the first recording released under the name of The Band, *Music from Big Pink* (Capitol, 1968). The album was remarkable for the 'white soul' sound of the singing, primitive but powerfully honest, the 'natural' sound of the instruments, undistorted by electronic tampering, the ease with which lead vocals were tossed around the group on 'We Can Talk', and the subtlety with which the shifting rhythms wove 'The Weight' together. *Big Pink* was a powerful stylistic achievement, synthesizing influences from country, soul, fairground music, Baptist hymns, Bob Dylan, and rock'n'roll, and succeeding through a gift for understatement and subtlety that came as a distinct contrast to the aggressive virtuosity of the 'progressive' rock scene. However, on their second album, *The Band*, Robertson created a set of songs that, verbally, displayed the same range as The Band's musical resources, e.g. 'The Night They

Drove Old Dixie Down', 'King Harvest' and 'Up on Cripple Creek'. Despite its timeless feel, the album evoked a strong response in the America of late 1969. A sense of growing disillusion surrounded youth and rock culture, and *The Band* was welcomed as the work of adults, displaying a broader grasp of American experiences than the transient obsessions of one age group or one moment in history – an achievement that wasn't compromised by any ponderous, self-conscious artistry, or loss of rock'n'roll vitality.

Having emerged from Dylan's shadow, they undertook some lengthy tours that led to the title song of their third album, *Stage Fright*, which dealt with the perils of performing. Equally powerful was the album's closing song, 'The Rumor', in which The Band brought their history of the American identity up to date to embrace the paranoid and vindictive quality of life in the Seventies under Nixon and Agnew. As a whole, though, *Stage Fright* lacked the stylistic coherence of *The Band*, a result of emerging from their protective bubble of historical perspectives to look at the present. This

process continued on *Cahoots* (1971) where they seemed to be expressing despair at the values of contemporary society and began to sound ponderous in their role of custodians of traditional values. At the same time, their rock energy began to be neutralized by their 'maturity'.

They produced no new material in the three years following *Cahoots*, suggesting that their misgivings about life in the Seventies have, to some extent, stifled their creativity. They produced a good live album, *Rock of Ages*, and also a 'golden oldies' album, *Moondog Matinee*, their liveliest recordings since *The Band*. The album displayed the strength of their affection for the roots of rock, and renewed conviction as musicians and singers. They also worked again as Bob Dylan's back-up band: on his *Planet Waves* album, a pleasant piece of work but scarcely a triumph for Dylan or The Band, and also on Dylan's 1974 tour, recorded and released as *Before the Flood*. When backing Dylan, The Band displayed noticeably more musical daring and attack (particularly Hudson's organ and Robertson's guitar) than when

James Robert Robertson, guitarist of The Band (left), is joined on stage by Bob Dylan in the group's farewell performance, Thanksgiving Day, 1976

playing their own songs, which sounded like rather wooden versions of acknowledged masterpieces.

The disappointing *Northern Lights –Southern Cross* (1975) gave signs that inspiration was fading, and they took the bold step of splitting up at the height of their career. They gave their farewell concert on Thanksgiving Day 1976, at San Francisco's Winterland Ballroom, before 5000 fans; the event – which included guest appearances by **Neil Young**, **Joni Mitchell**, **Van Morrison**, Ronnie Hawkins and Dylan himself – was captured on film by director Martin Scorsese and released as *The Last Waltz*. The Band's final album, *Islands*, was issued in 1977; Robertson went into production and film work, while Helm and Danko put out promising solo albums in 1977 and 1978. On 4 March 1986, Richard Manuel hanged himself in Florida.

BARBER, CHRIS A benefactor of the skiffle, trad jazz and R&B scenes of the late Fifties and early Sixties, Chris Barber was born on 17 April 1930, in Welwyn Garden City, Hertfordshire. He formed his first band in 1949 with himself on trombone and Dickie Hawdon and Ben Cohen on twin cornets (in the manner of King Oliver's band during the period it featured Louis Armstrong). In 1953, he and clarinettist Monty Sunshine organized a band for Ken Colyer to join on his return from New Orleans. Colyer, whose approach to New Orleans jazz was fundamentalist, dismissed the rhythm section in May 1954, whereupon Barber and Sunshine resigned. The new Barber band included Pat Halcox on trumpet and **Lonnie Donegan** on guitar and banjo, with Ron Bowden (later to join Kenny Ball) on drums. It often appeared at Humphrey Lyttelton's club at 100 Oxford Street, London. The band's repertoire included a few 'skiffle' numbers played by Barber (string bass), Donegan (guitar) and Beryl Bryden (washboard).

Donegan left the Barber band in April 1956, following the success of 'Rock Island Line', but by this time Barber had added female vocalist Ottilie Patterson to the band. It became more jazz-oriented but Barber never lost his interest in the blues to which skiffle paid homage. Throughout the early Sixties, Barber's interest in blues developed: he brought American bluesmen to Britain to tour with his band – many for the first time – and became involved in what was to become Britain's annual Folk and Blues Festival. It was through these activities, far more than through

The Barber band backs singer Big Bill Broonzy, with Lonnie Donegan on banjo. Chris Barber was a major influence on the jazz and blues scenes in the Fifties and Sixties, not so much through his own music as through his encouragement of other performers and the introduction of black artists like Broonzy from the United States to British audiences

his own music, that Barber positively influenced and supported the emergent British R&B movement. The band had one UK Top 10 hit in 1959 with 'Petite Fleur', but Donegan's 'Rock Island Line' hit was, in fact, a recording made by the Barber skiffle group. *See also* **Jazz, Traditional**; **British R&B**; **Lonnie Donegan**; **Skiffle**

BARCLAY JAMES HARVEST
In spite of their perseverance and the fashionably opulent presentation of their work, Barclay James Harvest have remained a cult band since their formation in Manchester in 1967.

The group – Woolley Wolstenholme (keyboards, vocals, born 15 April 1947), Melvin Pritchard (drums, born 20 January 1948), Les Holroyd (bass, born 12 March 1948) and John Lees (guitar, born 13 January 1948) were one of the first bands to use mellotron. On selected gigs they also presented their own orchestra.

Despite being launched on the new Harvest label, which was reputedly named after them, and winning large critical acclaim with their second album *Once Again* (1971), the band's classically oriented music never really found favour with large audiences. In 1973 front-liners Woolley Wolstenholme and John Lees embarked on solo projects, but in 1975 the group's new album *Time Honoured Ghosts* (Polydor), which was produced by Elliot Mazer, saw them returning to their **Moody Blues**-like blend of soft-rock and classical orchestration. *Octoberon* (1976) and *Gone to Earth* (1977) continued the formula, and by the end of the decade the group was a major act on the European mainland and particularly in West Germany. Their Eighties albums included *Turn of the Tide* (1981), *A Concert for the People* (Berlin, 1982), *Ring of Changes* (1983), and *Victims of Circumstance* (1984).

BARE, BOBBY A label error ensured that it was Bobby Bare's partner, Bill Parsons, who got the credit for Bare's 1958 hit recording of 'The All-American Boy' – a Number 2 in the US. Boyhood friends, Parsons and Bare (born in Ironton, Ohio, on 7 April 1935) made demo tapes for Cherokee, whose owner Orville Lunsford leased them to the Fraternity label. Bare was drafted into the Army two days later and let Parsons take the credit for his narration of the record, which parodied a rock-'n'roller's (some said Elvis's) meteoric rise to fame. Bare had previously recorded for Capitol, and when his Army service was over, he cut further records for Valiant, Fraternity, RCA and Mercury, where he broke down the barriers between country and pop with many huge hits, such as 'Detroit City', '500 Miles Away From Home' and 'Shame on Me'. In the Seventies he made some headway as a 'progressive' country singer.

BARNUM, H.B. Singer H.B. Barnum claimed to have arranged the **Leiber and Stoller**-produced Robins' classic, 'Riot in Cell Block No. 9' in 1954 as well as the group's many records on Whippet. A utility voice with the group, Barnum went solo and recorded for Fidelity, Eldo – where he made the pop charts with the instrumental 'Lost Love' in 1961 – Imperial and RCA before developing into a jack-of-all-trades. He led a 30-piece band behind rock'n'roll shows at San Francisco's Cow Palace, owned many small labels (Little Star, Prelude, MunRab) and scored for commercials. By the late Sixties, he was a rich man via arrangements for artists on RCA, Sue, Imperial (**Irma Thomas**) and Capitol (Lou Rawls). He later emerged into the pop limelight with arrangements for Motown stars and the **Osmonds**.

BARRETT, RICHARD A very important backroom figure in girl group pop of the early Sixties and, ten years later, the 'Philly Sound' developed in the recording studios of Philadelphia, Richard Barrett received his first big break in 1956 when Morris Levy of Roulette Records bought his song 'Creation of Love' for $100. It was in his native Philadelphia that his performing career began, as leader of the Angels and the Valentines, vocal groups who recorded for the independent labels Gee and Rama respectively. While the Valentines were appearing at the Apollo in New York, **Frankie Lymon** and the Teenagers pestered Barrett into auditioning them, after which **George Goldner** signed them to Gee and produced their first, million-selling hit 'Why Do Fools Fall in Love?' in 1956. A further discovery was the **Chantels**, featuring the distinctive voice of Arlene Smith, who scored nationally in 1958 with 'Maybe'. He quit the Valentines to concentrate on production, artist management and songwriting, though he still pursued a limited solo recording career with spells at MGM, Atlantic, 20th Century-Fox and other labels. His song 'Some Other Guy' became a particular favourite with Merseybeat groups very early in the Sixties, and a version by the **Big Three** ultimately became a minor UK hit. Working as right-hand man to George Goldner, then boss of numerous small New York labels, Barrett signed such acts as the **Isley Brothers**, **Little Anthony and the Imperials** and the **Flamingos**, and in 1964 joined Swan Records in Philadelphia. He then devoted much of his time to developing the career of the **Three Degrees**, who recorded several very minor hits in 1965–6 but emerged in the early Seventies as a surrogate **Supremes**, their sophisticated soul styling very much a part of Philadelphia's renaissance as a recording centre.

BARRI, STEVE Together with **Lou Adler** and **P.F. Sloan**, Steve Barri virtually launched folk-rock/protest music in California in the mid-Sixties. A writer, producer, record executive and occasional performer, Barri started his career in 1959 with solo singles on the tiny Rona label and compositions for the Nortones, Carol Connors and others. With Connors, he formed the Storytellers, whose recordings for Dimension brought him into contact with Lou Adler; Adler hired Barri and Sloan to work as a songwriting team for his Dunhill Trousdale publishing/production concern. Barri and Sloan were together responsible for hundreds of songs – among them hits for **Johnny Rivers** (such as 'Secret Agent Man in 1966), the **Grass Roots**, and **Jan and Dean** – and for a string of surfing discs released under the name of the Fantastic Baggys.

In 1968, the Barri/Sloan partnership ended with Sloan moving to New York and Barri to an executive position within ABC-Dunhill. In the early Seventies, he drew praise for his production work on albums by R&B pioneer **Bobby Bland**. His later production credits included albums for **Cher**, **John Sebastian**, **Dion**, Mel Brooks and the **Temptations**. See also **Lou Adler**; **Folk-rock**; **P.F. Sloan**

BARRY, JEFF Born in Brooklyn, New York, on 3 April 1938, Jeff Barry entered the music business as a singer but became best-known as the writer and producer of numerous New York-recorded hits of the Sixties. As a solo artist, he cut ten singles between 1959 and 1962, the year in which he met and married a young songwriter named Ellie Greenwich. He had also written a few hits for others, notably 'Tell Laura I Love Her' (**Ray Peterson**, RCA), 'Chip Chip' (**Gene McDaniels**, Liberty), and with Greenwich he developed one of the hottest writing teams in New York, turning out hits for **Lesley Gore**, Ray Peterson, the **Exciters**, the **Shirelles**, the **Chiffons**, and others.

In early 1963, he and Ellie began recording for Jubilee as the Raindrops, scoring two hits with 'What a Guy' and 'The Kind of Boy You Can't Forget'. At the same time, they were involved heavily with **Phil Spector**, knocking out hits including 'Da Doo Ron Ron', 'Then He Kissed Me' (for the **Crystals**), 'Be My Baby', 'Baby I Love You', 'Chapel of Love' (for the **Ronettes**), 'Wait Till My Bobby Gets Home' (for **Darlene Love**), 'Not Too Young to Get Married' (for Bob B. Soxx), and 'River Deep, Mountain High' (for **Ike and Tina Turner**), as well as lesser hits for all these artists. In 1964, they were also working for **Leiber and Stoller**'s newly formed Red Bird label, where they wrote, arranged and/or produced most of the label's output by the Jelly Beans, **Dixie Cups**, and the **Shangri-Las**. It was there they discovered **Neil Diamond**, taking him to Bang Records in 1966, where they produced five albums and 12 singles with him, also writing most of his hits. His production work in the Seventies included albums by **Sha Na Na**, **Tommy James**, King Harvest and John Travolta.

BARRY, JOHN Having learned his basic arranging skills from a Stan Kenton correspondence course, John Barry wielded a prodigious influence over British rock in the late Fifties. Born John Barry Prendergast in York in 1933, he was an arranger for big bands before forming his instrumental group, the John Barry Seven, in 1957. This unit was a staple ingredient of pop shows and package tours for the next five years, during which time Barry was also active in other fields, the most significant of which was the launching of **Adam Faith**'s career. Having introduced him to TV – *Drumbeat* – and films – *Beat Girl* – Barry went on to score all his early records. The pizzicato string arrangements (inspired perhaps by middle-period **Buddy Holly**) later became the basis of the 'new sound' of 1960. Among Barry's other contributions to this movement were the theme tunes to TV's *Juke Box Jury* and radio's *Easy Beat*. In 1962, Barry left his group to concentrate on writing film and TV scores. Best known for his work on the James Bond series of films, he has composed a number of jangly TV themes. In 1971, he returned to the charts after a long absence with his music for *The Persuaders*. His film work includes Oscar-winning scores for *Midnight Cowboy* (1969) and *Out of Africa* (1986).

BARRY, LEN The king of blue-eyed soul for six months during 1966, Len Barry was born in Philadelphia on 12 June 1942. He sang on the Bosstones' wild rocker 'Mope-Itty Mope' on Boss in 1958, and moved on to chart success with the **Dovells** in 1961–3, performing on their series of hit dance records, initiated by 'Bristol Stomp'.

As a solo artist, he had his greatest moments in 1965 and 1966, with '1–2–3' and 'Like a Baby' (Decca) respectively, both of which have since become disco classics. Barry's high tenor singing kept him in business into the Seventies, with records on American Decca and RCA, but when the hits stopped coming he was forced to tone down his **James Brown**-inspired stage act and adapt his style for the cabaret circuit.

BARTHOLOMEW, DAVE The architect behind **Fats Domino**'s superstardom in the Fifties, Dave Bartholomew was born in Edgard, Louisiana on 24 December 1920. The son of Louis Bartholomew, a noted tuba player, he was soon immersed in the New Orleans music scene. The young Bartholomew started to make a name for himself playing trumpet with Fats Pichon's band on the S.S. *President* riverboat as it chugged up the Mississippi to St Paul and back. A spell in the Army halted his rising star temporarily, but on demob in 1946 he formed his first band in New Orleans, playing the lavish balls, fraternity dances and school hops that abounded in the Crescent City. It became the city's major orchestra, playing everything from R&B and jazz to popular standards, and he kept it that way by exerting strict discipline over the top musicians he was attracting.

Bartholomew recorded initially for De Luxe in 1949 and 'Country Boy' sold close on 100,000 copies. Then he met Lew Chudd, of Imperial Records, who was looking for an R&B producer. Bar-

tholomew had all the right qualifications and was hired. He hit the jackpot first time out with '3 × 7 = 21' by Jewel King and, more notably, with 'The Fat Man' by Fats Domino. He worked for Imperial on a freelance basis, and notched up hits for Specialty with **Lloyd Price**'s 'Lawdy Miss Clawdy' and Aladdin with **Shirley and Lee**'s 'I'm Gone'. However, he was put on a long-term Imperial contract in 1952 when Chudd could see the possibility of Fats Domino becoming a big money-spinner. Besides producing those monumental hits for Domino over the years, Bartholomew was successful with **Smiley Lewis**' 'I Hear You Knocking', Bobby Mitchell's 'Try Rock-'n'Roll', the Spiders' 'You're the One' and **Earl King**'s 'Trick Bag'; he also recorded a host of other classic New Orleans artists – **Guitar Slim**, Tommy Ridgley, Sugar Boy Crawford, **Huey 'Piano' Smith**, **Frankie Ford**, and **Bobby Charles**. He backed these men with members of his band and recorded prolifically in his own right, although his records were too idiosyncratic to sell. But as a producer, Bartholomew had fallen upon a hit formula based on a wholly commercial outlook, with a penchant for simple, almost singalong, melodies dressed up with riffing saxes and exuberant second-line rhythms.

In 1963, Chudd sold Imperial to Liberty, and Bartholomew turned down other offers that would have meant leaving New Orleans. He was content just to put a band together for occasional gigs in the city, living off the huge royalties he had amassed as co-writer of most of Domino's hits. *See also* **Fats Domino**; **Imperial Records**

Bartholomew (standing) with Fats Domino

BASS, FONTELLA R&B singer Fontella Bass was born on 3 July 1940 in St Louis, Missouri, and first played organ and piano in the Oliver Sain Band, with whom she made her first records (on **Ike Turner**'s Prann label and on Bobbin) in 1963. She also recorded for another of Turner's labels, Sonja, before he moved to the West Coast, but her first hit came with a duet with Bobby McClure on Checker Records, 'Don't Mess Up a Good Thing', which reached the R&B Top 5 in 1965.

Bass followed this success with 'Rescue Me', which featured a Motownesque production by Billy Davis. It topped the R&B charts and reached Number 4 in the pop listings. Smaller hits from this period included 'Recovery' and 'I Surrender'. In 1969, she recorded (with her husband, jazz trumpeter Lester Bowie) in Paris for the Art Ensemble of Chicago. On her return to the US the following year she appeared in the R&B charts with records for the Jewel/Paula label, produced by Oliver Sain.

BASS, RALPH A white, New York-born record producer, Ralph Bass gave great service to the R&B cause. He worked as a violinist in New York society bands before moving into jazz production (working with Dizzy Gillespie, Charlie Parker, Erroll Garner and others) and subsequently hustling his way into the burgeoning Los Angeles 'race' market. His first R&B hit, 'Open the Door Richard' for Jack McVea (on Black and White, 1947), led to a spell with Savoy Records. There, as West Coast A&R man for the label, he produced hits for **Johnny Otis**, Little Esther, and the Robins.

Touring the South with the Johnny Otis revue was a revelation to Bass; thereafter, he left the sophistication of jazz for a lifelong association with some of the earthiest R&B on record. In the Fifties he masterminded the King subsidiary, Federal, where his productions for the **Dominoes**, **Hank Ballard** and the Midnighters, the Five Royales, and, later, **James Brown** and the Famous Flames, monopolized the R&B charts. 'Sixty Minute Man', 'Work with Me, Annie', 'Please, Please, Please' – all these and many, many more black anthems owed their success to Bass's love for and belief in a rough, raw and gospel-tinged brand of R&B. In 1960, he teamed up with Chess, recording **Etta James**, Moms Mabley, **Ramsey Lewis** and the many Chicago blues greats as well as pioneering pop-gospel with the Violinaires.

BATT, MIKE One of Britain's top independent producers and an occasional performer and composer in his own right, Mike Batt (born 6 February 1950) rose from staff songwriter with a London music publishing house to become A&R manager of Liberty Records' UK office. Among his early productions were albums for the **Groundhogs** and Hapshash and the Coloured Coat, although his independent work also included the creation of a series of budget-priced orchestral albums of **Beatles** and **Rolling Stones** material and numerous advertising jingles. In 1973, he wrote and recorded the theme song to the children's TV series *The Wombles* and scored a surprise UK hit, which he followed with a string of big-selling singles on a variety of Womble themes. Among them were such pastiches as 'Wombles Beach Party' (surf), 'Wombling White Tie and Tails' (Fred Astaire), a Womble minuet, Womble rock'n'roll, and 'Superwomble'. Under the guise of the Wombles, Batt was, amazingly, the most successful chart act of 1974.

He continued to demonstrate his worth as a rock producer by handling the production work on albums by **Steeleye Span**, Linda Lewis, pub rockers the Kursaal Flyers and others. Batt has also proved adept at writing hit material for artists like **Art Garfunkel** (the 1979 chart-topper 'Bright Eyes', featured in the film *Watership Down*) and **David Essex** ('A Winter's Tale' in 1982, co-written with Tim Rice). In addition, he has recorded a number of albums under his own name.

BATTISTE, HAROLD His first step to becoming a respected recording producer came when Harold Battiste was put in charge of Specialty's New Orleans branch office in 1957. At first his efforts to get the operation off the ground took second place to the label's success with **Little Richard** and **Larry Williams**, and so his discoveries like **Irma Thomas**, **Ernie K-Doe**, and **Chris Kenner** had to wait a little longer for their Gold Discs, although **Jerry Byrne** had a local hit with 'Lights Out', a rock'n'roll classic. In 1960 Battiste joined the staff of Ric Records and arranged **Joe Jones**' US Top 10 hit, 'You Talk Too Much'.

Alarmed at the way New Orleans musicians were being exploited, Battiste masterminded the AFO (All For One') label as a black cooperative and had an enormous hit with Barbara George's 'I Know'. But his ambitious plan of making AFO a black Atlantic

ended in discord and he headed for the West Coast, where he arranged for **Sam Cooke** and others, notably **Sonny and Cher**'s 'I Got You Babe'. He evolved the **Dr John** character with Mac Rebennack in 1967, but Rebennack grabbed all the accolades for putting the Voodoo Rock and good old-fashioned New Orleans funk sound into the grooves, leaving Battiste (who also recorded for Uptown) on the outside looking in – a man of good ideas reduced to a comfortable but obscure career in TV jingles.

BAUHAUS Emerging from the nihilism of punk, Bauhaus combined glam-rock with the theatrical minimalism of black and white horror movies.

Formed in Northampton in 1979, Bauhaus were Daniel Ash (guitar), Kevin Haskins (drums), David Jay (bass, Haskins' elder brother) and charismatic singer Peter Murphy who dominated the band's live shows with a pretentious but enthralling blend of high camp, low sexual ballet and vocal histrionics. They first came to prominence with their single 'Bela Lugosi's Dead', a hypnotic maudlin homage that immediately set them apart from their 100mph thrash peers.

Throughout the course of three patchy albums (the best was 1984's *Mask*) Bauhaus were most revered for their occasionally electrifying singles on the Beggars Banquet label – 'Kick in the Eye', 'Terror Couple Kill Colonel' and 'The Passions of Lovers' – before they burnt out with their commercial

swansong, a cover version of Bowie's 'Ziggy Stardust' in 1982. Murphy then had a musical fling with ex-**Japan** bassist Mick Karn as a duo called Dali's Car while the other three members of Bauhaus later re-formed as Love and Rockets.

BAY CITY ROLLERS The teenybopper sensation of 1974–6, Edinburgh group the Bay City Rollers made a brief chart entrance in 1971 with the **Jonathan King**-produced 'Keep On Dancin'' but found a surer pop footing under the wing of producer/songwriters Bill Martin and Phil Coulter and, a little later, **Sweet** producer Phil Wainman. The group's members were: Derek Longmuir (drums, born 19 March 1955), Alan Longmuir (bass, born 20 June 1953), Eric Faulkner (guitar, 21 October 1955), Stuart 'Woody' Wood (guitar, 25 February 1957) and Leslie McKeown (vocals, 12 November 1955). Their sound was a watered-down imitation of early-period **Four Seasons** – their first Number 1, 'Bye Bye Baby' (1975), was an old Seasons number – and their image drew on football terrace culture, all tartan scarves, tank-tops and Oxford bags. The Rollers had 11 UK Top 20 hits and fared respectably in the US, where 'Saturday Night' (1975) reached Number 1. By 1977, however, the party was over, and the group's career met a messy conclusion in management scandals, legal wrangles and newspaper revelations over alleged sexual misbehaviour backstage.

The Bay City Rollers, tartan teenybopper tearaways of the mid-Seventies

BEACH BOYS Formed in 1961, still going in the Eighties, the Beach Boys were America's only real challenge to the **Beatles** and certainly the most prominent white American group of the pre-psychedelic era. The group's formation took place in the middle-class Los Angeles suburb of Hawthorne, and was centred around the teenage Wilson Brothers – Brian (born 20 June 1942); Dennis (4 December 1944); and Carl (21 December 1946) – their cousin Mike Love (15 March 1941); and friend Alan Jardine (3 September 1942). When the Wilson parents took a holiday in Mexico in September 1961 it was a perfect opportunity for the kids to rent instruments and start a group in their living room.

It was Dennis's addiction to the California sport of surfing that gave the group their initial identity. He suggested that the group sing about the pastime, and a song (written by Brian and Mike) called 'Surfin'' was the immediate result. Their father, Murray Wilson, himself a songwriter, took the boys along to his music publisher and the song was recorded in somewhat improvised conditions with Carl on guitar, Alan on acoustic bass, and Brian providing percussive support on a garbage can. The publisher procured a release for the record on the local X label and then the slightly larger Candix label, and against all the odds it stuck around the lower limits of the American Hot 100 for six weeks – based mainly on sales to Californian surfer boys and girls, no doubt. They also began to appear in public, initially as the Pendletones (after a make of heavy plaid shirt that surfers wore and that became their early uniform), briefly as Carl and the Passions, and ultimately as the Beach Boys, a name suggested by Candix's promotion man. Their concert debut under this name was in the **Ritchie Valens** Memorial Concert in Long Beach Municipal Auditorium on 31 December 1961.

Jardine left around this time to pursue his dentistry studies, and was replaced by neighbour David Marks who played rhythm guitar, enabling Brian to switch to bass guitar. Dennis played drums, while Mike Love shared the lead vocals with Brian.

When Candix, a small label, folded early in 1962, Murray Wilson took the boys along to Capitol Records and played producer Nik Venet acetates of 'Surfin' Safari' and '409' – the latter a hymn in praise of the singer's car. Venet grasped the possibilities, signed the group, and 'Surfin' Safari' became a national Top 20 hit. 'Ten Little Indians', the follow-up, was a comparative flop, but the next one, 'Surfin' USA', reached Number 3 in the early summer of 1963. In addition, it laid bare the influences behind the growing talent of Brian Wilson, who was coming to the forefront as the group's real creative force. For 'Surfin' USA' Brian had borrowed the tune and treatment from **Chuck Berry**'s 'Sweet Little Sixteen', adding new words and a lead vocal surrounded by the beginnings of a cool, liquid harmony style strongly reminiscent of the Four Freshmen (and, by implication, the American glee-club tradition).

The next single, 'Surfer Girl', a wistful, yearning ballad, emphasized the harmonies even more heavily and added a gimmick adapted from East Coast vocal group records – Brian's cool, cruising falsetto, which became a major trademark. 'Surfin' USA' and 'Surfer Girl' marked the complementary modes that Brian and the group explored for the next three years. The up-tempo style led to 'Fun Fun Fun', 'I Get Around' (a Number 1), 'When I Grow Up (To Be a Man)', 'Dance Dance Dance', and 'Help Me Rhonda' (another Number 1) – all Top 10 hits in 1964 and 1965 – while the possibilities of the ballad form were explored with ever more trance-like effect in such classics as 'In My Room', 'The Lonely Sea', 'Girls on the Beach', 'Don't Worry Baby', 'The Warmth of the Sun', 'She Knows Me Too Well', 'Kiss Me Baby', and 'Please Let Me Wonder' from the same period. By this time, Jardine had returned to the fold, displacing Marks.

On a wider front, the group's own influence had become widespread. Their early surfing records sparked off a complete genre, opening the way for many other performers like **Jan and Dean** ('Surf City'), Bruce (Johnston) and Terry (Melcher) with 'Summer Means Fun', Ronnie and the Daytonas ('Beach Boy'), **Jack Nitzsche** ('The Lonely Surfer'), Dick Dale and the Del-Tones ('Surf Beat'), and hundreds of aspiring Californian garage bands. When surfing's vogue dropped off, the Beach Boys put out an album of car songs called *Little Deuce Coupe*, featuring '409' alongside other beauties like 'Our Car Club', 'Cherry Cherry Coupe', 'No-Go Showboat', and 'Custom Machine'. Sure enough, others responded: **Jan and Dean** with 'Dead Man's Curve' and 'Drag City', Bruce and Terry with 'Custom Machine' and 'Hot Rod USA', Ronnie and the Daytonas with 'GTO', the Rip-Chords with 'Hey Little Cobra' and 'Three Window Coupe'.

Through all this, Brian Wilson was absorbing and reflecting the emerging lifestyle of teenage California, which – luckily for him – kids everywhere wanted to emulate. Although many of his early lyrics lack grace and wit in print, sung by the group they are perfect expressions of teen *angst* in all its forms. Among his external collaborators were Roger Christian, a local deejay who helped out with the car songs, and **Garry Usher**.

When the Beatles first blitzed America, at the beginning of 1964, the

The Beach Boys survived the stylistic changes of the Sixties, with a few changes of personnel as well

Beach Boys were little affected. In an apparently unassailable position, Brian strengthened the musical content of their records by adding elements of another influence: the production techniques of **Phil Spector**. From Spector, Brian borrowed the wall-of-sound technique, particularly the batteries of percussion instruments, which can be heard among the growing complexities of peak-era Beach Boys records like 'California Girls', 'The Little Girl I Once Knew', and 'Wendy', all perfect blends of teen consciousness and musical innovation. Brian reached his personal summit with the album *Pet Sounds* in 1966 and the single 'Good Vibrations', a Number 1 for the group later that year. Employing unusual instrumental grouping and apparently endless vocal overdubs with complete mastery and a tireless attention to detail, he was producing music that set the pop world on its ear.

A combination of circumstances, however, proved cumulatively tragic: *Pet Sounds* was badly upstaged by the Beatles' *Sgt Pepper*, which followed it within a matter of months. Brian abandoned (amidst a mass of neuroses) his next project, an album called *Smile* which was to have dwarfed even *Pet Sounds*; and then the West Coast 'psychedelic revolution' occurred. Whereas the Beatles remained in the vanguard of the new rock, the Beach Boys lagged fatally behind, the victims equally of Brian's personal uncertainties and of the innate conservatism of several other members of the group, who felt that they should never have left the simplicities of surf music. Within months they were old hat, and the tattered remnants of *Smile*, issued in skeletal form as *Smiley Smile*, did their reputation no good.

In the face of change, though, they stuck together. Bothered by partial deafness in one ear (which still renders him unable to hear stereo sound), Brian quit touring and was replaced in the road band first, briefly, by **Glen Campbell**, and then by Bruce Johnston, who stayed to contribute a number of songs to their repertoire. But while other groups were exploring the possibilities of two- and three-hour sets, the Beach Boys continued to parade their 45-minute 'medley of hits' in front of concert audiences. Yet on record, and particularly in Europe, they maintained some semblance of hit status: 'Wild Honey', 'Darlin'', 'Do It Again', 'I Can Hear Music', and 'Break Away' were all fine – and successful – records, and albums like *Friends*, *20/20*, and *Sunflower* contained superb songs and

matchless production, despite Brian's ever-diminishing participation.

They were also enmeshed in lawsuits with their former managers and with Capitol – the latter dispute boiling up after they'd formed their own label, Brother Records, in 1967, distributed first through Capitol and (from 1970) through Warner–Reprise Records. Brother, one of the early artist-run labels, was one of the many pioneering efforts for which they have received little credit.

In 1971, though, their affairs took a turn for the better when their management was taken over by a former journalist, Jack Rieley, who understood their position and their importance. As well as writing intelligent lyrics for songs by Brian and Carl, Rieley also unearthed the incomplete tapes of a song called 'Surf's Up', which was to have been the centrepiece on *Smile* back in 1967. He persuaded them to finish it off, made it the title-track of their new album, and went about refurbishing the group's image by abandoning stage uniforms and allowing them to play two-hour sets including both the hits and more obscure material. To a degree, Rieley's strategy worked –and the track 'Surf's Up', with controversial, typically elliptical words by **Van Dyke Parks** and fragile melodies by Brian, may well prove to be their masterpiece. Shortly after the release of this album, Bruce Johnston left to pursue a career with his own group.

In an attempt mainly to shake Brian out of his torpor, Rieley took the group in its entirety to Holland in 1972, built them a complete recording studio there, and came up with an album called *Holland*. Critically well-received, it was not a major hit, and when Rieley left them shortly afterwards the group resorted to releasing an accurate if unspectacular double album culled from live concerts. In person at this time they were highly impressive, thanks to a new rhythm section including two South Africans – Blondie Chaplin (guitar) and Ricky Fataar (drums) – but it seemed that they had lost the ability to make hit singles. Chaplin and Fataar left during 1974, **Jim Guercio** (of **Blood, Sweat and Tears** and **Chicago** fame) took over their management, and the group reverted almost to its original 1961 configuration, with Guercio playing bass on stage in Brian's place. Though Dennis and Carl were by now composers of considerable strength, and despite having regained a place in the affections of the rock audience, business problems and their collective uncertainty as to

the band's role kept their future insecure for much of the Seventies. In 1976, however, Brian returned to the band in a performing capacity for a new album, *15 Big Ones*, which proved to be their last for the Brother label. Recording for Caribou from 1977 onwards, they had minor success with *L.A. (Light Album)* (1979) and a revival of the **Del-Vikings'** hit, *Come Go With Me*, in 1981. Dennis Wilson died in a swimming accident on 28 December 1983, and once again there were doubts raised about the group's continuation. But in 1985 they were still together, looking good and still sounding fresh during their spot on the Live Aid con-

cert. One of American pop music's greatest institutions, their importance is twofold: no group in pop history has shown a more consistent creative development over a long period, and none has been more influential in the field of vocal harmonies. *See also* **Surf Music**

BEAT A Birmingham based band formed in 1978–9, the Beat played a mixture of ska, reggae and rock. Closely associated with Jerry Dammers' 2-Tone label, they produced brightly pulsating dance music that set them apart from labelmates the **Specials** and the **Selecter**. By the time they had disbanded in 1983, having put over much social and political comment, they had achieved five Top 20 hits in the UK chart.

The group had its start when Midlands guitarists Dave Wakeling and Andy Cox met on the Isle of Wight in 1978 and teamed up with local bassist David Steele. They then returned to Birmingham and recruited Everett Morton, an experienced West Indian drummer. Early in 1979 they began playing gigs in Birmingham pubs and were joined by extrovert black punk

The Beach Boys as Seventies megastars in concert

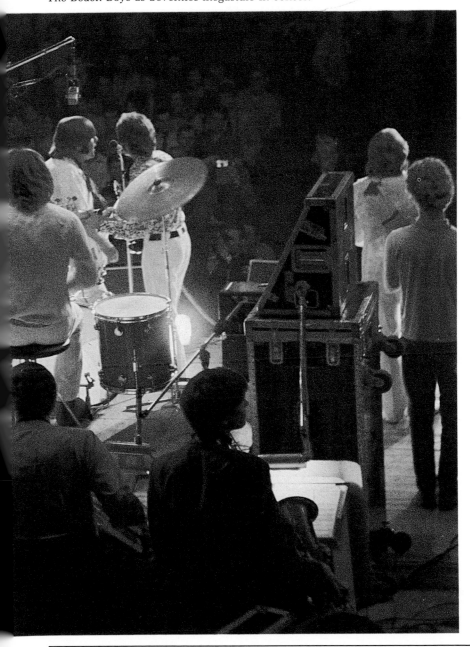

toaster/rapper Ranking Roger, who fronted the group with Wakeling. They also took on Saxa, a middle-aged West Indian saxophonist who had once sided for ska doyen **Prince Buster.**

After supporting the Selecter at various gigs, they recorded their first single – on the 2-Tone label – at the end of 1979. This record, the Motown classic 'Tears of a Clown' went to Number 6 and stayed in the UK chart for 11 weeks. Following this initial success, the band set up their own label, Go-Feet, distributed by Arista, and quickly followed up with the hit singles 'Hands Off . . . She's Mine' and 'Mirror in the Bathroom'.

They released their first album *I Just Can't Stop It* in April 1980, with an anti-nuclear track off the album, 'Stand Down Margaret' also being released as a single and the proceeds donated to CND. Shortly after, the band appeared in the Joe Massot film *Dance Craze*. In December their single 'Too Nice to Talk To' reached Number 7. By the time their second album *Wha'ppen* was released in May 1981, the Beat had found their characteristic sound – the interplay of Wakeling and Cox on guitars overlaid by Morton's strong reggae rhythms and the echoing saxophone improvisations of Saxa.

Some of the old urgency, however, had gone. Saxa retired in April and was replaced by Wesley Magoogan, a seasoned sessionman. In October 1982 the new line-up released the band's third and last album *Special Beat Service*. Innocent of political comment and packed with strongly hooked pop songs, it nevertheless failed to emulate its two predecessors' UK chart performance. In spite of the Beat's considerable recording success, their absences on extensive tours of Europe and the US lost them status with the UK audiences and after five singles in a row failed to make the Top 30, Arista dropped them. In April 1983 the Go-Feet label released 'Can't Get Used to Losing You' a quirky Andy Williams cover, surprisingly scoring the Beat's last and biggest hit. Three months later they disbanded with Roger and Wakeling forming General Public, releasing the albums *All the Rage* (1984) and *hand to MOUTH* (1986) which were far-better received in the US than in the UK. Cox and Steele joined forces with young black singer Roland Gift to form Fine Young Cannibals who stormed into the UK charts with superb soul/jazz first single 'Johnny Come Home' in 1985 and followed it up with an impressive eponymous debut album and a string of hits.

BEATLES The paramount import-ance of the Beatles makes it impossible to provide a neat summary of their career and its significance. The Beatles became more than **John Lennon**, **Paul McCartney**, **George Harrison**, **Ringo Starr**, music-makers; they became the worldwide representatives of the great explosion in British popular music in the Sixties, and the symbols of a new way of regarding the possibilities of pop. They were a *phenomenon*, and if it was their music that gave the Beatles cultural force, their history is not just a musical one.

The Beatles were part of the gener-ation, teenaged in the Fifties, of English working-class kids who grew up after the war, in conditions of comparative affluence and with, after the 1945 Edu-cation Act, at least a chance of second-ary education and more. They also experienced the full impact of Ameri-can rock'n'roll and its artistic and material possibilities. John Lennon (born 9 October 1940) formed his rock-'n'roll group, the Quarrymen, in 1955 while he was still at school; by 1958,

when he was at art school, the group included Paul McCartney (18 June 1942) and George Harrison (25 Febru-ary 1943), who had previously had his own group, the Rebels. But the Quarrymen weren't just another English rock'n'roll group, they were a Liverpool rock'n'roll group, with the advantages of growing up in a cosmo-politan port. Most importantly, Ameri-can R&B records officially unavailable in Britain were brought to the city by local seamen. In addition Liverpool, because of its size and diversity, con-tained any number of clubs where gutsy, sexy music was in demand, and it was therefore possible to make a liv-ing from providing it.

In 1959 the Silver Beatles were formed – John, Paul and George, Stuart Sutcliffe on guitar, Pete Best on drums – and they soon widened their pro-fessional horizons by making frequent appearances in the West German city of Hamburg – another port, another club scene, and another centre of American music.

It is impossible to overestimate the

importance of these early *professional* years for the Beatles' subsequent music. The group learnt its basic tech-nical and crowd-pleasing skills in very specific circumstances: the music had to be loud and hard, there was no space for subtlety; the clubs were small, the equipment poor, the resulting sound was dependent on the combined beat of drums, bass and rhythm guitar. Although the Beatles occasionally backed a lead singer, Tony Sheridan, as a group they didn't have a leader but rather built their vocals around harmonies and back-up voices – tech-niques learnt from R&B and particu-larly from the gospel-based soul sound of early Motown records. By 1961 the Beatles were making a distinctive local music – and making it better than anyone else. They had survived their apprenticeship and they possessed, in John and Paul, two of the finest singers on the scene.

The group had also become suffi-ciently popular – they were the win-ners of *Mersey Beat*'s first poll – to come to the attention of **Brian Epstein**, the manager of the record department (North End Music Stores) in his family's Liverpool furniture store, who became their manager. He groomed them (cleaning up their stage act, tak-ing them out of leather and into suits), he got them a record contract (with EMI's Parlophone label), and he masterminded their successful assault on the charts, on the concert halls, and on the nation's consciousness. But if Epstein's achievement was to make the Beatles the most successful act in the British music business, his signifi-cance was that he was not himself a part of that business. The key to the Beatles' career between 1961 and 1964 was that they became successful without having to tread the traditional pop path. The crucial factor was John and Paul's songwriting ability – they wrote all the group's hit singles of this era – which was important for two reasons: it ended the domination of American rock records, and it com-pletely broke the hold of the music publishing industry, with its hustling songwriting hacks, over British pop.

The group that Brian Epstein signed comprised George Harrison on guitar, Paul McCartney on bass, John Lennon on rhythm, and Pete Best on drums (Stuart Sutcliffe had left the group in Hamburg and subsequently died of a brain tumour). Shortly after this Pete Best was replaced by Ringo Starr (born Richard Starkey, 7 July 1940) from Rory Storme and the Hurricanes. If it took Epstein months to get the EMI contract,

The recording session that produced 'Love Me Do' in September 1962, supervised by studio producer George Martin (extreme left)

John Lennon, always the most rebellious of the group

George Harrison, lead guitarist but never leader of the band

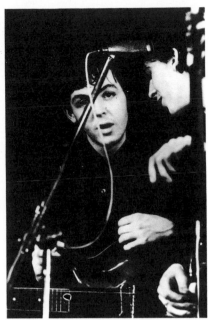

Paul McCartney's lyricism was a foil to Lennon's toughness and drive

success was then rapid. 'Love Me Do' made the Top 20 in December 1962; 'Please Please Me', 'From Me to You', and 'She Loves You' all made Number 1 and established the Beatles in the summer of 1963 as teen idols. Record sales became accompanied by all the trappings of hysteria – sell-out, police-ringed concerts, obsessive press coverage, desperate record companies searching for 'new Beatles'.

But even then the group were more than just the latest flames. They didn't disappear into their own hype; they remained interesting, individual, articulate characters; as people, personalities, they were real in a way that **Cliff Richard** and the **Shadows** had never been. Their qualities were not those of showbiz – they came across as cynical, arrogant, restless. Beatle trappings – Beatle haircuts, Beatle jackets and Beatle boots – came to represent an attitude as well as the usual fan fervour. The Beatles brought pop appeal to a mass audience that had previously been uneasy in its relationship to pop. When Beatle music came out of the Cavern it was not heard just by other working-class kids, it also became the music of middle-class young people. This audience had had a similar generational experience to the Beatles themselves, and the Beatles were the first English pop group that didn't insult their intelligence. The contrast between the covers of the Beatles' first and second albums is symbolic: *Please, Please Me* had the boys grinning in

their cheap suits, chirpy, very working-class; *With the Beatles* had four artistically posed heads, grainy, serious, black polo-necked, the Beatle cuts, soft and floppy – they looked like *students*.

If it was extraordinary that the Beatles' personalities could survive the success of their music, it was even more extraordinary that the music itself continued to carry weight. The group brought to the charts a fresh style of melody, of harmony, of rhythm, that was exhilarating and compulsive. The rough Hamburg edges were smoothed, but the verve remained, the songs became more polished but retained their originality. By the end of 1963, in little over a year, the Beatles had achieved everything possible for a pop group in Britain. The next and ultimate step was the conquest of America (Europe and the Commonwealth had already fallen) and this was achieved in stunning fashion in February 1964. Thanks partly to careful planning by Brian Epstein (including a top billing on the *Ed Sullivan Show*), partly to £20,000 worth of hype from Capitol Records, but mostly to the vacuum in American teenage pop, when the Beatles arrived in New York they took over the charts. Beatlemania flooded the States, bringing in its wake success for every group with an English accent, transforming attitudes to pop there as successfully as in Britain.

In retrospect, the real achievement of the Beatles in 1964 was not to arouse for the first time (and for ever) Ameri-

ca's interest in British pop, but to retain a musical creativity throughout the traumas and trappings of super-stardom. From then on their career ran along two separate, if parallel, lines – business success on the one hand, musical progress on the other. As a business, the Beatles made hit record after hit record, signed a new deal with EMI, formed a publishing company, Northern Songs; there were sell-out world tours (which finally stopped in 1966) complete with a growing entourage of hangers-on and ceaseless media attention. Everywhere the Beatles went so did the merchandisers, offering everything from Beatle wigs and Beatle knickers to Beatle tea-cloths. They made so much money that early in 1965, they were honoured as an export industry, being awarded MBEs.

Even in their attainment of riches the Beatles were original. Their films, *A Hard Day's Night* and *Help!* were not quick exploitations, but were inventively and artily directed by Dick Lester, and his tricks – plus the Beatles' own wit – won the films critical as well as box-office success. The key Beatle image occurred in *Help!* – the boys enter their row of terraced houses to reveal, behind the façade, a huge communal, luxury pad. The Beatles, in their starry world, were cut off now from their roots. Their music was no longer, as in Hamburg days, a direct response to their performing situation, it was made *despite* the pressures. Their workplace was the studio, their musical history became a history of albums. And the significance of that history is that their music progressed – as they absorbed new influences, as they used their newly acquired wealth and resources, as their artistic ambitions grew. No one had expected the original rock'n'rollers to progress and few of them did, but the Beatles' music developed inexorably – despite the day-to-day pop pressures and the limitations of their musical origins. In transforming the attitudes of their audiences towards pop, the Beatles had transformed their own. By 1965, they were sustaining and being sustained by a new world of musicians – eclectic, ambitious, self-conscious. Pop was no longer a suitable word as the Beatles and **Bob Dylan** became mutual influences on each other, as folk and rock'n'roll and blues and teenage ballads were swirled together in a new cultural frenzy; the Beatles were the first rock stars.

The staging posts of their progress were *Rubber Soul*, which came out in December 1965, and *Revolver* (August 1966). The albums still had their pretty tunes (if more elaborately orchestrated) but there were no more straight rockers, no more simple songs. Instead, the melodies became complex (as Paul McCartney moved from his instant standard, 'Yesterday', to the deliberate calculation of 'Eleanor Rigby'); the lyrics became 'interesting' (as Lennon absorbed Dylan and the group's philosophical pretensions showed); above all there was an outburst of new sounds – George's sitar, banks of strings, French horns, all producer **George Martin**'s technical tricks. By 1967, it seemed that nothing was impossible for the Beatles as artists or for their audience as listeners, and in June they put out *Sgt Pepper's Lonely Hearts Club Band* – elaborately conceived, elaborately packaged, an amazingly consistent pop package of all the elements of 1967 youth culture – drugs, electronics, mysticism and hope – and all with the familiar Beatle harmonies, tunes and charm.

The Beatles had become hippies. They grew their hair long, admitted to smoking dope, took up with the Maharishi; they believed in love, planned the *Magical Mystery Tour* for television, and put together Apple, the company that was going to use their profits creatively, joyously, for the people. Summer 1967 was the end of the beginning and the beginning of the end. Brian Epstein died, the *Magical Mystery Tour* flopped, Apple became a wheeling, dealing paradise. The

John Lennon and Paul McCartney: the most successful songwriting partnership of their day

Beatles began to be rent by the contradictions – between their role as the people's hippies and their lives as rich superstars; between their pop appeal and their increasing distance from 'ordinary' concerns; above all, between their individual musical and material ambitions. The break-up was slow and disguised, but between 1967 and 1969 the Beatles ceased to be the Beatles and became John Lennon, Paul McCartney, George Harrison and Ringo Starr. They continued to make records together and while the double *White Album* (November 1968) may be the finest showcase of the group's talent – as songwriters, singers, arrangers, performers and artists – it is also a showcase of *individual* talents. There are John songs and Paul songs and George songs, and they were now produced that way.

When the group finally split it hardly made any musical difference – the solo work had begun before then and the Beatles continued to be each other's sessionmen afterwards. But the split was symbolic – not just in its bitterness, in its business ramifications, but simply in the loss of a name. An era was over, in which the musical possibilities of rock'n'roll, of pop, had been first realized and explored, an era in which music had seemed to carry cultural, social, political, *revolutionary* force. The Beatles had symbolized optimism, their disintegration symbolized optimism fading. In the end the Beatles left us with not just a collection of fine songs (recorded by countless other artists as well as by themselves), but also with the reminder of a spoiled dream;

they left us with the most nostalgic music in the history of rock. *See also*: individual entries; plus **Brian Epstein**; **George Martin**; **Rock Films**

BEAU BRUMMELS Formed in San Francisco in 1964, the Beau Brummels – Ron Elliott (guitar), Sal Valentino (vocals), Ron Meagher (bass) and John Petersen (drums) – were an early American 'answer' to the **Beatles** and the British beat group invasion that followed. Signed to DJ **Tom Donahue**'s Autumn label, the group charted with 'Just a Little' and 'Laugh Laugh' in 1965, both tracks produced by Sylvester Stewart of **Sly and the Family Stone** fame. Their sound was very influenced by that of the **Searchers**, matching 12-string guitar work to soft harmonies, plaintive harmonica and minor-key melodies, and they laid the ground for the folk-rock of the **Byrds**, the **Seeds** and other California-based groups. The band moved to Warner Brothers in late 1966 and lost Petersen to **Harpers Bizarre**, but in *Triangle* they produced one of the most intriguing yet neglected psychedelic albums of 1967. They broke up a year later, Elliott switching to full-time songwriting and occasional session work for the **Everly Brothers**, **Randy Newman** and others, and Valentino to a spell with multi-member travelling rock band Stoneground. Elliott recorded a charming solo album, *Candlestickmaker*, for Warners in 1970 and formed a new group, Pan. The Brummels re-formed four years later for a reunion album but lack of public interest prompted a second disbanding.

BE-BOP DELUXE The band that put leader and guitarist Bill Nelson on the musical map, Be-Bop Deluxe had a brief spell in the mid-Seventies as a band tipped for the rock big time, but they failed to turn their considerable potential into large-scale success.

Yorkshireman Nelson, an accomplished and innovative instrumentalist, first put Be-Bop Deluxe together in 1972. Based around Nelson's talents as a singer and composer, the band went through several changes of line-up, but the best known and most successful consisted of Nelson, Charlie Tumahai (bass), Simon Fox (drums) and Andrew Clarke (keyboards). Playing in a thoughtful, complex guitar-based rock/pop style, they gained considerable critical acclaim but managed only one UK Top 30 single, 'Ships in the Night' in 1976, and out of six albums, only one, *Live! In the Air Age* (1977) made the Top 10. Nelson disbanded the group in 1979.

He immediately formed a new band, Bill Nelson's Red Noise, which recorded just one album, *Sound on Sound* (1979), a fine collection of pop songs that saw him move more towards electronic sounds. This venture, too, was short-lived and Nelson has since continued as a solo artist and producer, recording a string of albums on Cocteau, his own label, and staying outside the mainstream workings of the industry. His work has varied from the complex but highly marketable (the excellent 1980 single 'Do You Dream in Colour?' inexplicably missed the UK Top 40 but the album *Quit Dreaming and Get on the Beam* (1981) reached Number 7) to the increasingly experimental. Some of Nelson's later work borders on the pretentious and impenetrable, but he remains a gifted, enterprising musician not content to limit himself to a merely commercial formula. In 1986, he signed to CBS, on which he released the album *Getting the Holy Ghost Across* and a six-track mini-LP *Living for the Spangled Portrait*.

BECK, JEFF When **Eric Clapton** left the **Yardbirds** in March 1965, the Tridents' lead guitarist, Jeff Beck (born in Surrey on 24 June 1944), was recommended by **Jimmy Page** to replace him. He remained with the group until December 1966 and contributed much to the 'new' sound of the Yardbirds on records like 'Shapes of Things' and 'Over Under Sideways Down' (Columbia, 1966), experimenting with electronic sounds and exploring Eastern as well as Western influences. He formed

his own Jeff Beck Group with **Rod Stewart** (vocals), Ron Wood (bass) and Ray Cook (drums), Cook being replaced by Mickey Waller following a disastrous debut on a **Roy Orbison/Small Faces** package tour in March 1967, from which the group was immediately removed. During the next two and a half years the group – subsequently joined by Nicky Hopkins (keyboards) – released two albums, *Truth* (Columbia, 1968), and *Beck-Ola* (1969), and earned a strong reputation in America. Beck's plans to re-form the group with Stewart and **Vanilla Fudge**'s Tim Bogart (bass) and Carmine Appice (drums) fell through, and a car smash forced him to retire for some 18 months. A second Jeff Beck Group appeared in 1971 with *Rough and Ready* (Epic) and new personnel: Bob Tench (vocals), Max Middleton (piano), Clive Chaman (bass),

and Cozy Powell (drums). The break-up of Bogart and Appice's band, Cactus, led to the formation of Beck, Bogart and Appice in 1972. An album and a tour later, Beck was again solo, returning in 1975 with his best playing for several years on *Blow by Blow*, produced by **George Martin**. He toured with the **Mahavishnu Orchestra** during 1976 and collaborated with keyboards player **Jan Hammer** on *Wired* (1976), *Live* (1977), and *There and Back* (1980). His completely uncharacteristic 1967 solo hit single, 'Hi-Ho Silver Lining' (produced by **Mickie Most**), was a chart re-entry in both 1972 and 1982, since when he has made sporadic appearances – notably with a host of Sixties guitar heroes at multiple sclerosis benefits organized by **Ronnie Lane** in London and New York during 1983. *See also* **Yardbirds**

Jeff Beck established himself as a guitar hero with his revolutionary use of controlled feedback and scintillating individual playing style

BEE GEES Consummate masters of the art of adapting to changing musical fashion, the Bee Gees have a history that dates back to 1955, when the three Gibb brothers – Barry (born 1 September 1947), Robin, and Maurice (both born 22 December 1949) – first began performing publicly as children in Manchester. In 1958, they emigrated with their parents to Brisbane, Australia, where they built up a local following via television appearances, and signed (in 1962) to the Festival label. By 1967 – when they returned to the UK as the Bee Gees – they had released two albums and a dozen singles.

Back in England, they were signed to a management deal by Robert Stigwood, an ex-**Brian Epstein** employee, who in turn placed them with Polydor. Vince Melouney (guitar) and Colin Peterson (drums) joined them at this time. Their first UK hit, the eerie 'New York Mining Disaster 1941', reached Number 14 in mid-1967. The style of both this debut hit and subsequent releases – 'Massachusetts' and 'I've Gotta Get a Message to You' (both UK Number 1s) in particular – was heavily Beatles-influenced. They also dabbled in hard-rock guitar sounds on 'World' (1968) and even soul styling ('To Love Somebody', later covered by **Nina Simone**).

In 1969, Robin Gibb left the group to go solo – he had one major hit in that year with 'Saved by the Bell' – but he was comparatively unsuccessful, and by 1972 the group was together again and getting American Top 20 hits like 'My World' and the country-flavoured 'Run to Me'. In 1975, after a period of little success, they returned to the top of the US charts with two smash hits, 'Jive Talkin'' and 'Nights on Broadway', from the **Arif Mardin**-produced *Main Course* (RSO), an album that saw them producing their nasal harmonies in front of funkier rhythms than ever before. The album set the tone for much of their later work, which included recording with Miami rhythm sections on 'You Should Be Dancing' (another US Number 1) and the staggeringly successful soundtrack album for the Robert Stigwood-produced film *Saturday Night Fever* (1977), sales of which topped 30 million. The album was a clinically perfect interpretation of the soul-influenced disco sound then sweeping the US, and it confirmed yet again the Gibb brothers' extraordinary capacity for homing in on current trends and refashioning them subtly as their own. And 1977 and 1978 were certainly their years: 'How Deep Is

Your Love', 'Stayin' Alive', and 'Night Fever' (all from the album) each topped the US chart, as did their three next singles – 'Too Much Heaven', 'Tragedy', and 'Love You Inside Out'. They also wrote the theme song for another Stigwood-financed box office smash-hit, *Grease*, in 1978.

Their next project, a movie treatment of the **Beatles**' *Sgt Pepper's Lonely Hearts Club Band*, was a critical and commercial disaster, and began a comparatively dry spell in the group's career. They broke with Stigwood in 1980, releasing their final album for his RSO label, *Living Eyes*, a year later. They have recorded intermittently since, but their most interesting work has been as providers of hits for other artists – Barry's writing and production work for **Dionne Warwick**, Barbra Streisand, and **Diana Ross** has been particularly notable.

The essence of Bee Gees music is the self-pitying ballad, lushly orchestrated around Robin's ingratiating tremolo and his brothers' distinctive nasal harmonies. In this style the Gibbs are facile songwriters (their songs are widely used by cabaret artists), but doubts remain about their place in rock history. Their achievement was initially to take some aspects of the Sixties English group style – the harsh harmonies, the 'impure' lead voice, the risky melodies – and apply them to traditional pop; they were never a rock group. As the Beatles and other groups moved out of the world of pure pop, the Bee Gees were left filling a significant gap, and their continuing ability to strike the right musical chord at any given time is likely to ensure their future in pop for many years to come.

BELAFONTE, HARRY The leader of the calypso music boom that began in the US during the mid-Fifties, Harry Belafonte (born in Harlem, New York, in 1927) spent eight years in the US, then five in Jamaica before returning to New York. He had an uneven career before establishing himself as the 'King of Calypso': it included a spell in the US Navy, attempting to become an actor, and succeeding in becoming a messenger. He then sang with a jazz group, quit to start a restaurant in Greenwich Village, and there became a convert to the folk scene. An engagement at the Village Vanguard, and a contract with Victor Records, followed. His album *Calypso* – which included his hit composition, 'Banana Boat Song' – was released in 1956. Three years later it had sold a million copies. Belafonte's smooth singing style

appealed to both folk and easy listening audiences, and by popularizing West Indian styles he was to lead the way for the folk and rock world's later fascination with the Caribbean. He also appeared in films (*Carmen Jones*, *Island in the Sun*, *Buck and the Preacher*) and in 1985 was one of the prime movers behind USA for Africa, the famine relief project that grew out of **Band Aid**.

Calypso crooner Harry Belafonte sold more than a million copies of his 1956 release 'Banana Boat Song', earning the title 'King of Calypso'

BELL, FREDDIE AND THE BELL BOYS One of the earliest rock'n'roll combos, Freddie Bell and the Bell Boys closely modelled themselves on **Bill Haley and the Comets**. Comprising Jack Kane (sax), Frank Brent (bass), Jerry Mayo (trumpet), Russ Contic (piano), Chick Keeney (drums), and Bell (vocals), they appeared with Haley in the first rock movie, *Rock Around the Clock* (1955). The first American rock'n'roll act to visit Britain, they toured with **Tommy Steele** in 1956. They had a British hit with the tepid 'Giddy Up a Ding Dong', which reached Number 4 on Mercury's British licensee of the time, Pye Records. They also originated the arrangement of **Elvis Presley**'s 'Hound Dog'.

BELL, MAGGIE Born in Glasgow on 12 January 1945, Maggie Bell had a singing style heavily influenced by soul and blues. Her first professional experience came with the Power, a local group led by Alex Harvey's brother Leslie. Signed in 1969 by **Led Zeppelin** manager Peter Grant, their name was changed to Stone the Crows. Two albums for Polydor – *Stone the Crows* and *Ode to John Law* – followed, with Colin Allen (drums), Jim Dewar (bass) and John McGinniss (keyboards).

In 1971, Ronnie Leahy and Steve Thompson replaced McGinniss and Dewar. Bell was being acclaimed as the most powerful female singer in Britain, inspiring inevitable comparisons with **Janis Joplin**. *Teenage Licks*, in the same year, was the most assured album to date, but in between sessions for *'Ontinuous Performance* (1972), Harvey was killed in an on-stage accident at Swansea.

Maggie Bell determined to carry on, bringing in Jimmy McCullough after an abortive attempt to lure **Peter Green** back into live performance. Stone the Crows split in 1973, after which Bell released two solo albums – *Queen of the Night* (1973) and *Suicide Sal* (1975), the former produced by Jerry Wexler. Her only UK solo hit came in 1978 with the theme song from the television series *Hazell*. Her voice could also be heard over the credits of two further crime series, *Widows* and *Taggart*, in the early Eighties. In 1981, a duet with B.A. Robertson, 'Hold Me', took her to Number 11 in the British chart.

BELL RECORDS Originally the record outlet of Columbia Pictures, Bell was formed in the mid-Fifties and developed its rock and R&B catalogue through its subsidiaries Mala and Amy. Among the Bell artists to fare well in the US charts in the early to mid-Sixties were **James and Bobby Purify**, **Del Shannon**, **Lee Dorsey**, and the **Box Tops**. Later in the decade, the label brought its various subsidiaries under the one umbrella company and established a policy of releasing cheaply purchased master tapes from small labels rather than signing or developing its own talent. Most of Bell's early Seventies hits were therefore products of deals with foreign labels or with independents. This policy changed with the success of the Partridge Family and **David Cassidy**, and with the domination of the UK singles market by acts signed by Bell's British division, e.g. **Gary Glitter**, Barry Blue, and the rejuvenated **Drifters**. In 1974, ex-Columbia head Clive Davis took charge of the company's transformation into Arista, and under him the label became more rock and easy listening-oriented with such signings as **Patti Smith**, Barry Manilow, Whitney Houston, the **Kinks**, and **Billy Ocean**.

Thom Bell, one of the highly talented arrangers who created the distinctive Philadelphia sound with his orchestral scores

BELL, THOM Soul music has seen few more intriguing developments than the infusion of 'classical' orchestrations into the hovering soft vocal styles that were the direct successor of the Fifties doo-wop groups. Thom Bell, more than any other single producer/arranger, recognized the full potential of this synthesis during the late Sixties and Seventies and thus broadened the whole spectrum of the black music experience. Born in Philadelphia, Bell came from a middle-class background and grew up studying classical piano and playing 'serious music' with his brother and sister.

In 1959 he teamed up with a school-friend, Kenny Gamble (later of **Gamble and Huff**), and recorded a vocal duet for Jerry Ross's Heritage label. It flopped, but a seed had been sown. Bell then joined Kenny Gamble's Romeos, playing little clubs and doing some recording (for Jimmy Bishop's Arctic

Records). They were to become the nucleus of Philly's famed MFSB (Mother, Father, Sister, Brother) session band. While doing session work at Cameo Records the young Bell was introduced to the vocal group the **Delfonics** by Stan Watson. Bell's productions and arrangements for the group (discs on Moon Shot and Cameo) were unsuccessful, but when Cameo went bust, Watson formed a label of his own – Philly Groove. Suddenly Bell's Delfonics productions for Philly Groove proved immensely successful. Smashes like 'La La Means I Love You' and 'Break Your Promise' (1968) poured forth. In 1969 Bell teamed up with the flourishing production team of Gamble and Huff, and his arrangements for acts like **Jerry Butler** brought more success. Teaming up with a French lyricist, Linda Creed, Bell began to write a series of beautiful new songs for his next major venture, the **Stylistics**, for whom Avco commissioned him to arrange and produce in 1971. 'Stop Look and Listen', 'You Are Everything' (1971),'Betcha by Golly, Wow', 'Stone in Love with You' (1972): the string of quivering falsetto-led hits continued. At the same time, Bell did some of Gamble and Huff's arrangements (including stunning work for the **O'Jays**) and produced such Columbia acts as Ronnie Dyson and **Johnny Mathis**. Another run of hit productions occurred with the **(Detroit) Spinners**, and he also worked with **Dionne Warwick**, **Elton John**, and **Deniece Williams** later in the decade.

BELL, WILLIAM Born in Memphis in 1939, William Bell was one of the earliest recruits to the Stax label, and the maker of some of its biggest US R&B hits during the mid- to late Sixties. Starting his career as a member of the Del-Rios, Bell went solo in 1961 and made a major impression with 'You Don't Miss Your Water' (1962) and 'I'll Show You' (1963). His best run of chart success came between 1966 and 1968, when Memphis soul was at its peak, with the ballads 'Everybody Loves a Winner' and 'Tribute to a King' (dedicated to the memory of **Otis Redding**). Also in 1968, he scored a Top 10 UK hit with 'Private Number', a duet with Stax stablemate Judy Clay that he co-wrote with **Booker T.** Jones. His other compositions included 'Born Under a Bad Sign', an R&B hit for **Albert King**. Further duets with Clay, Mavis Staples (of the **Staple Singers**) and **Carla Thomas**, an attempt at soul-reggae, and some pretentious-sounding albums did little for his career in the early Seventies. In

1973 he signed with Mercury, and recorded two albums in New Orleans with producer **Allen Toussaint** and the single 'Tryin' to Love Two' (1977), which brought him his first success in the mainstream US pop chart.

BELLE STARS All-girl seven-piece band the Belle Stars had a short burst of moderate success in the UK during the early Eighties with a string of basic, good-time rock/pop dance numbers.

The Belle Stars were born out of all-girl 2-Tone group the Bodysnatchers who had a UK Top 30 hit with 'Let's Do the Rock Steady' in 1980. A second single, 'Easy Life', failed and the band split; Sarah-Jane Owen (guitar), Stella Barker (guitar), Miranda Joyce (sax) and Judy Parsons (drums) formed the nucleus of the Belle Stars, while vocalist Rhoda Dakar emerged later with the Special A.K.A.

Jennie McKeown (vocals), Lesley Shone (bass) and Clare Hirst (sax) were recruited and the Belle Stars started gigging furiously in the UK and in Europe. They signed to Stiff in April 1981 and released a couple of singles, but had to wait until June '82 and their cover of the **Dixie Cups**' 'Iko Iko' for their first UK chart record. They scored their biggest hit in 1983 with 'Sign of the Times' reaching Number 3, but apart from the album *Flat Out* (1983) their popularity waned to the extent that their last chart single, '80's Romance' reached a miserable Number 71.

BELVIN, JESSE Born in Texarkana, Arkansas, on 15 December 1933, Jesse Belvin was a singer, composer and pianist whose influence cannot simply be measured by the success of 'Goodnight My Love' (an R&B hit on Modern in 1956) or 'Funny' and 'Guess Who', his **Nat 'King' Cole**-type pop hits for RCA in 1959. The extent of his prolific activities among the tangled world of West Coast independent labels may never be fully catalogued. After graduating from **Big Jay McNeely**'s band, Belvin became a father-figure to many younger singers and the leader of a Los Angeles group fraternity who sang and practised together. In 1953, he cut an R&B hit, 'Dream Girl' (Specialty) as one half of Jesse and Marvin. The following year, he wrote 'Earth Angel', and legend insists that he wrote many more songs that now have someone else's name on the credits. Until his death in a car crash in 1960 (aged 27) Belvin made numerous solo discs for Specialty. He recorded for Hollywood, Modern,

Kent, Knight, Candlelight, Cash, Class, and Jamie. He also doo-wopped his way through a dozen groups including the Cliques (Top 50 with 'Girl of My Dreams' in 1956), the Sharptones (Aladdin), Three Dots and a Dash (Imperial), and the Sheiks, whose original 'So Fine' (Federal) was revived by the Fiestas in 1959.

BENATAR, PAT American hard-rock singer Pat Benatar was born Patricia Andrzejewski in New York in 1953 and grew up on nearby Long Island, from where she began serious operatic vocal training at Juilliard when she was seventeen. Dissatisfied with the strict regime at the school, she left, and at eighteen married Dennis Benatar (her high-school sweetheart) with whom she moved to Virginia, where he was stationed as a G.I. There she worked in a bank and then as a singing waitress, but by 1975 the couple had returned to New York.

Finding little success on the cabaret circuit, she toughened up her sound and with a new rock direction and a more glamorous image, she was signed to Chrysalis in 1978. The next year, Benatar released *In the Heat of the Night* which went platinum on the strength of the US Top 30 hit single, 'Heartbreaker'. Soon after this she and Dennis Benatar were divorced. Benatar has since been a regular presence in the US charts, but her superior, tuneful brand of US guitar rock did not conquer the UK charts until 1985 with the singles 'Love is a Battlefield' and 'We Belong' reaching the Top 20. By the time the LP, *Seven the Hard Way*, was released at the end of 1985, Benatar had sold 25 million albums.

BENNETT, CLIFF From the **Beatles** onwards, everybody professed to respect Cliff Bennett in the British rock scene of the mid-Sixties, though people rarely bought his records. Bennett was born in Slough, Berkshire, England on 4 June 1940, and formed his group, the Rebel Rousers, in 1961. The group included Dave Wendells (lead guitar), Maurice Groves and Sid Phillips (saxes), Frank Allen (bass, replaced by Bobby Thompson), and Mike Burt (drums). His music was soul-based, and the band's repertoire included songs by **Bobby Bland**, the **Drifters**, **Ray Charles**, and **Bobby Parker**.

Bennett and the Rebel Rousers had two Top 10 hits in the UK, with efficient remakes of the Drifters' 'One Way Love' (1964) and the Beatles' 'Got to Get You into My Life' (1966, produced by

Paul McCartney). Allen left the band in 1965 to become Tony Jackson's replacement in the **Searchers**, and the Rebel Rousers limped on until 1969, when Bennett broke up the group and joined would-be progressive rock band Toe Fat as vocalist. Toe Fat found little favour with anyone and disbanded within two years, following which Bennett formed Cliff Bennett's Rebellion and, in 1975, Shanghai. By the early Eighties he was working for an advertising company – his was the voice on a long-running series of TV commercials for Carling Black Label.

BENSON, GEORGE

Born in Pittsburgh, Pennsylvania on 22 March 1943, jazz guitarist/vocalist George Benson began singing at an early age and at four he won a local singing contest. He was given a guitar at the age of eight and, heavily influenced by virtuoso jazz guitarist Wes Montgomery, he was playing the local clubs by the time he was 15. During the Sixties Benson travelled the jazz circuit, releasing a number of records (on Columbia, Verve and A&M), gaining him experience if not much commercial success. In 1971 Benson settled in with producer Creed Taylor at CTI and during the next five years he fulfilled his considerable promise as a guitarist, recording six albums – notably *White Rabbit* (1972) and *Bad Benson* (1974) – and building a strong following in jazz circles. A 1975 single, 'Supership', made the Top 30 in the UK, but Benson remained largely unknown to a mass audience.

This state of affairs changed dramatically the following year when Benson

George Benson's jazz roots infuse his fine guitar work and soulful vocals

left CTI to join Warner Brothers. There, he was teamed with ace producer Tommy LiPuma and they recorded the album *Breezin'* (1976). Although five of the six tracks were instrumentals, LiPuma gave Benson the freedom to show off his unique vocal style on a smoochy half-jazz, half-soul version of **Leon Russell**'s 'This Masquerade'. Released as a single, it reached Number 10 in the Billboard Hot 100, while *Breezin'* went platinum and later became the biggest selling jazz album of all time. Having found the magic hit formula, Benson, again with producer LiPuma, recorded *In Flight* (1977), a million-selling follow-up aimed at a pop audience and comprised of four vocal and only two instrumental tracks.

The success of *In Flight* brought Benson superstar status, with world tours, guest appearances on recordings by artists ranging from **Herbie Hancock** to **Minnie Riperton**, a string of Grammy awards and lilting duets with **Aretha Franklin**, **Chaka Khan** and Patti Austin. Benson's recordings had now moved into the pop/soul field – to the almost total exclusion of jazz – a transition that was confirmed in the 1980 album *Give Me the Night*. Produced by Quincy Jones, this late-night, disco-inspired album provided two smash hit singles in the title track (a US Number 4) and 'Love × Love' (a UK Number 10).

His style well-set – in an artistic rut that was nevertheless a commercial goldmine – Benson released a steady flow of albums in the Eighties that in turn ensured him a regular place in the singles charts on both sides of the Atlantic. Benson's 1984 album *20/20* was notable in that it contained contributions from a wide range of songwriters who included Cecil and Linda Womack, Neil Larson, Michael Masser, Steve Lukather, James Newton Howard, the Sembello Brothers and Gerry Goffin.

Benson's popularity with the record-buying public is undoubted and his success in crossing over from mainstream jazz to mainstream pop showed the way for a new wave of jazz musicians, like Grover Washington Jr, Mezzoforte and Central Line.

BENTON, BROOK

Born on 19 September 1931 in Camden, South Carolina, Brook Benton was a warm-voiced balladeer who came into his own during the lull between rock'n'roll and the return of heavy rhythms in the mid-Sixties. After singing with the Bill Landford and Golden Gate gospel quartets he recorded for Epic and Vik

(scoring a minor hit, 'A Million Miles from Nowhere', in 1958), but survived by making demo recordings for writer/publisher Clyde Otis. Through Otis' successful association with Mercury Records (he'd given them several winners, including 'The Diamonds' and 'The Stroll') Benton was signed to the company, and together Belford Hendricks, Otis, and Benton himself wrote his first three hits in 1959 – 'It's Just a Matter of Time', 'Endlessly', and 'Thank You Pretty Baby'. For nearly four years he couldn't go wrong, recording a succession of smoky vocals supported by swirling strings and a chorus arranged and conducted by Hendricks. His hits included 'So Many Ways' (1959), 'Kiddio', and 'Fools Rush In' (1960); perhaps his finest sides, two million-selling duets with **Dinah Washington**, 'Baby (You've Got What It Takes)' and 'Rockin' Good Way' (1960); two folk songs, 'Boll Weevil Song' and 'Frankie and Johnny' (1961); and many more until 'I Got What I Wanted' and 'My True Confession' (produced by **Shelby Singleton**, arranged by **Bill Justis**), his last big hits for Mercury in 1963. Sojourns with RCA (1965–7) and Reprise (1967–8) failed to revive his career, but he successfully adapted to the soul market on the Atlantic subsidiary Cotillion, scoring several hits including a particularly fine version of 'Rainy Night in Georgia' (1970). Subsequent releases on MGM, Brut, and Stax were not so impressive.

BERNS, BERT

Sixties R&B producer and writer Bert Berns (also known as Bert Russell and Russell Byrd) was a master at matching gospel voices with slow and climactic ballads of extraordinary passion. Born in 1929, he worked first as a record salesman, music copyist and session pianist. In 1960 he began writing songs with Phil Medley. While Austin Taylor's 'Push Push' on Laurie was probably their first hit song, the most famous was 'Twist and Shout'. Originally written for the Topnotes on Atlantic, it became a Top 10 hit when revived by the **Isley Brothers**, on Wand, in 1962.

During the early Sixties, Berns compositions appeared on records from a number of small New York labels including Cameo (**Don Covay**), United Artists (the Electras, **Marv Johnson**, the **Exciters**, **Garnet Mimms**), Scepter (the Rocky Fellers), Diamond (Johnny Thunder), MGM (**Conway Twitty**) and his own label Keetch (Linda Laurie). At Atlantic/Atco, Berns took over from **Leiber and Stoller** in the dual role of songwriter-producer.

His publishing company, Webb IV, was formed to provide material for **Barbara Lewis**, **Ben E. King**, the **Drifters**, **Tony Orlando**, Tami Lynn, the Bluebelles and, most notably, **Solomon Burke**. 'Cry to Me', 'Down in the Valley', 'If You Need Me', 'Goodbye Baby' and 'Everybody Needs Somebody to Love' were among Burke's best recordings and Berns helped to write and/or produce them all. Berns also collaborated frequently with other top writers, producers and arrangers, producing a soul classic on almost every occasion. They included the **Vibrations**' 'My Girl Sloopy' (written with **Wes Farrell**), Betty Harris' 'Cry to Me' and 'His Kiss' on Jubilee (produced with Mike Stoller) and the Drifters' hit 'Under the Boardwalk' (arranged with Mike Leander). His compositions with **Jerry Ragavoy** established Garnet Mimms as Solomon Burke's only real rival. 'One Girl', 'Look Away', 'It Was Easier to Hurt Her' and 'I'll Take Good Care of You' were among Mimms' deep soul masterpieces. In a more commercial vein, 'Little Lonely One' and 'A Little Bit of Soap' (a US Top 20 hit in 1961) by the Jarmels were equally seminal Berns productions.

With assistance from Atlantic, Berns set up his Bang label in 1965. It was a sustained attempt to enter the white pop field and the Bang roster of artists included **Neil Diamond**, the Strangeloves and **Van Morrison**. Morrison's group, **Them**, had already recorded Berns' 'Here Comes the Night' and Berns brought him to the US following the group's break-up. He also signed ethnic Spanish performers, and his interest in Latin music was reflected in the catchy 'La Bamba' rhythm that permeated some of his greatest hits – the **McCoys**' 'Hang On Sloopy', the Isleys' 'Twist and Shout', and Tami Lynn's 'I'm Gonna Run Away From You' (a belated UK hit in 1971). Bang's R&B subsidiary, Shout, featured a host of good soul performers including **Roy C.**, George Freeman, Bobby Harris, Erma Franklin ('A Piece of My Heart') and Freddie Scott ('Are You Lonely For Me, Baby', 'Cry to Me', and 'Am I Grooving You'). Berns also recognized the struggle for black identity with 'Up in the Streets of Harlem', written for the Drifters in 1966.

Apart from running Shout, Berns continued to write for Atlantic artists and for those with other companies – such as **Lorraine Ellison** on Loma, Garnet Mimms on Veep – until his death in December 1967. Deprived of one of its major writers and producers, the golden era of deep soul died with him.

BERRY, CHUCK The significance of Chuck Berry lies partly in his own stylistic innovations and the vivid articulation of a spirit of rock'n'roll rebellion in his lyrics. And, partly, it lies in the fact that his career uniquely encapsulates the links between the rock-'n'rollers of the Fifties and latter-day rock bands; between blues and pop, between black and white musical cultures. His origins are, in many ways, representative of the black artists primarily responsible for hammering out the musical identity of rock. Born Charles Edward Berry in St Louis, Missouri, on 18 October 1931, he began singing in a church choir at the age of six. He learned the rudiments of guitar while still at high school, and made his debut performance at the school glee club review, playing the Chicago blues standard, 'Confessin' the Blues' – which, he has recalled, was avidly welcomed for what was seen at the time as an almost risqué earthiness.

Berry's next move was equally part of a wider pattern: the journey to Chicago itself, following in the steps of the many Southern country blues artists who had subsequently abandoned their intimate, solo approach in favour of the heavily amplified and raucous bar blues style associated with the northern city. One such was **Muddy Waters**. Berry – an ardent admirer – played with the Waters band in early 1955, and the blues star recommended that he get in touch with Leonard Chess, whose Chess and Checker labels provided the major outlet for black artists in the area. Berry got the audition he wanted and was signed up immediately. His first recording, 'Maybellene', was released in May 1955. It sold a million in a matter of weeks and reached Number 5 in the national singles charts. 'Maybellene' sprang from a blues environment, but the song – written by Berry himself – owed almost as much to C&W influences. This was clearly indicated by the oddly foreign hillbilly title, of which Berry once remarked, 'The only Maybellene I ever knew was the name of a cow.' Moreover, the performance itself, with its heavily accentuated backbeat, bore a notable resemblance to the rockabilly style being developed by Sun's white country-rooted artists in Memphis – though the harshness, the heaviness and the whining guitar were pure Chicago. The major popularizer of rock-'n'roll, DJ **Alan Freed**, was credited as co-writer, and it seems likely that the sound that eventually emerged was inspired in part by a desire to match the commercial success being enjoyed by the new Southern hybrid music. Berry's own remark that 'The dollar dictates what music is written' tends to confirm that impression. This is not to say that the C&W tradition was completely alien to him: he has frequently said that he had listened to a great deal of country music on the radio.

Berry became securely established as a performer with mass appeal only when the blues element in his work had undergone considerable modifications. His fourth single, 'Roll Over Beethoven', reached the Top 30 in 1956 and pointed the way forward. Over the next two years, he produced his most important music in a string of commercially successful singles. 'School Day' and 'Rock and Roll Music' both achieved Top 10 successes in 1957. The following year saw his biggest seller, 'Sweet Little Sixteen', reach Number 2, while 'Johnny B. Goode' went to Number 8 and 'Carol' also entered the Top 20. There were no other major hits in the Fifties, but several of his minor successes exemplified his mature style at its best and most influential. In 1957, there was 'Oh Baby Doll', which failed to get beyond the bottom half of the Hot 100. In 1958, 'Beautiful Delilah', 'Sweet Little Rock and Roller', 'Jo Jo Gunne', and 'Run Rudolph Run' all entered the lower reaches of the charts. The story was the same the following year with 'Anthony Boy', 'Almost Grown', 'Little Queenie', and 'Back in the USA', and in 1960 with 'Too Pooped to Pop' and 'Let It Rock'. Berry was a prolific writer, and several of the songs for which he is best remembered were not even released as A-sides at the time – such as 'Memphis, Tennessee' and 'Reelin' and Rockin''.

Berry's style in this period had a number of distinctive features. The bold 'rocking' beat of 'Maybellene' was filled out with 'rolling' rhythms, achieved mainly by swiftly alternating between a handful of chords, particularly the 'blue' sixths and sevenths. His records were also instantly recognizable by the wailing, chiming guitar sound and the fast, cutting, high-pitched solos he used as introductions. The overall impression of speed was strengthened by the machine-gun rhythms of the lyrics; and his vocal style lacked the coarseness generally associated with city blues and rock-'n'roll. He articulated the words extremely clearly, a characteristic that probably derived partly from another of his idols, **Louis Jordan**. By singing in a manner not totally given over to wildness and emotionalism, he allowed room for humour to enter the picture.

And because virtually every word could be understood, the lyrics themselves came to have a more essential function than they did with most other rock'n'rollers.

In his lyrics, Berry defined a new audience. He crystallized the meaning of white teenage rock'n'roll in terms of a lifestyle in which the search for physical excitement – especially in the form of dancing, driving and sex – was paramount. If rock'n'roll was implicitly anti-romantic and anti-puritan, Berry made it explicitly so. His songs were celebrations of the pleasures available to the dedicated American consumer, typified by 'Back in the USA', with its richly detailed references to sizzling hamburgers, drive-ins, skyscrapers and the long freeway. But they were also songs of rebellion. The kids might want to have fun, but there were forces that stood in their way – work and school, parents and the law, old age.

Berry became one of the leading rock'n'roll stars, with four film appearances to his credit to prove it: *Rock, Rock, Rock* and *Mr Rock and Roll* in 1957, *Go Johnny Go* in 1959, and his performance at the Newport Jazz Festival in *Jazz on a Summer's Day*. Then, late in 1959, his career was sharply interrupted. He was charged with transporting a minor over a State line for immoral purposes. Accounts of the incident vary, but it appears that he brought an Indian girl from Texas to work as an assistant at his night club in St Louis. The police suspected she was working as a prostitute. At some point, Berry gave her the sack, and she then confessed to the police that she was only 14. Local court records say that he was convicted after a series of trials and started a two-year prison sentence in February 1962. Berry has denied this, claiming he was acquitted and that he had, in any case, been led to believe that the girl was over 20.

Berry's disappearance coincided with a period when rock'n'roll had lost a great deal of its original energy and momentum. When he returned in 1964, the British renaissance was in full spate and he was its major hero. Chuck Berry songs were a key part of the repertoire of almost every British group. The **Beatles** recorded 'Roll Over Beethoven' and 'Rock and Roll Music', and his influence was clearly apparent in such Lennon-McCartney compositions as 'I Saw Her Standing There' and 'Little Child'. The **Rolling Stones'** first single was Berry's 'Come On'; their debut album included 'Carol', together with his arrangement of 'Route 66'. They

later recorded 'Bye Bye Johnny', 'Round and Round', and other Berry songs, such as 'Little Queenie' and 'Johnny B. Goode', were highlights of their stage act. Berry's enormous impact in Britain can be partly attributed to the fact that his lack of major hits in that country – only 'Sweet Little Sixteen' had reached the Top 20 – made him acceptable to the many new rock musicians and fans who saw 'commercialism' as the main enemy of worthwhile music. He appealed to both the R&B 'purists' and to those who made a cult of relatively obscure Fifties rock'n'roll. At the same time, he had been a chart star in America, so the possibility of good music achieving mass success could never be totally ruled out by his admirers.

Chuck Berry earns the name Crazy Legs

His influence was also evident in the work of many American performers in the Sixties. The **Beach Boys** took the melody and guitar figures of 'Sweet Little Sixteen' and merely adapted the lyrics to a Californian surfing context for their first hit, 'Surfin' USA'. When **Bob Dylan** adopted a rock style in 1965 with 'Subterranean Homesick Blues', he based the tune, the metric pattern and even the mood of the lyrics on Berry's 'Too Much Monkey Business'.

Berry resumed his own recording career in 1964 with 'Nadine' and 'No Particular Place to Go'. The lyric of 'Nadine' was a re-wording of the car-

chase motif of 'Maybellene', but the performance was far more relaxed. The record was a Top 30 hit in America and also sold well in Britain, where the upsurge of interest in his music had put the re-issued 'Memphis Tennessee'/ 'Let It Rock' in the Top 10 the previous year. 'No Particular Place to Go' – a song based on 'School Day' but with new lyrics about 'cruising' – was a Top 20 entry on both sides of the Atlantic.

In 1966 Berry left Chess and signed a $50,000 contract with Mercury. He made five albums for the label over the next three years, devoting much of his studio time to drab remakes of Fifties songs. But his reputation as a live performer reached its zenith during these years. His cherry-red Gibson and the crouched gliding shuffle that he called the 'duck walk' and that had earned him the nickname 'Crazy Legs', had become trademarks of his act. In Britain, his tours were remarkable for the way they drew together Fifties rock-'n'roll fans and the new generation of Beatles and Stones followers.

He returned to Chess in 1969 and by 1971 had recorded two new albums, *Back Home* and *San Francisco Dues*. The music was more consistently and overtly blues-based than ever before, a mature re-exploration of his roots. It seemed that the pop charts had seen the last of him. However, a tour of Britain early in 1972 reversed all expectations. He was received more ecstatically than ever, and a live recording made at the Lanchester Arts Festival in Coventry gave him not only half of the next album, *London Sessions*, but also the biggest hit of his career, 'My Ding-a-Ling'. He had previously recorded much the same song as 'Mr Tambourine' for Mercury, and it had a history stretching back through various R&B artists to 1950 at least. But the new version, publicized and promoted with maximum efficiency, gave him his first Number 1 in both America and Britain. The mild sexual innuendo of the record apparently broadened his appeal, attracting a younger audience.

Berry has recorded prolifically since, though his sales have been unspectacular. He made a memorable appearance in the Alan Freed biopic *American Hot Wax* (1976) and has continued to tour regularly, although the legend of his meanness – as regards both the duration of his stage shows and the sums he demands – has by no means dissipated with time. In 1979, he completed a 100-day jail term for tax evasion. He now spends much of his time at his fabulously equipped amusement park home in Wentzville, Missouri.

BERRY, DAVE An ardent admirer of **Chuck Berry**, Dave Berry was born David Grundy in Woodhouse, Sheffield, England in 1941. He changed his surname to that of his idol and formed the Cruisers, an R&B group, in 1961. Their first two records for Decca ('Memphis, Tennessee' in 1963 and 'My Baby Left Me' the following year) were pure British R&B.

Subsequently Berry was tempted into more commercial pop with Top 5 songs like 'The Crying Game' (1964) and 'Mama' (1966) before moving into the Northern club circuit in the late Sixties. Berry always found it difficult to sing in tune, but compensated for this by evolving an enjoyably eccentric stage act revived by **Alvin Stardust** in the Seventies. Since the Sixties, he has kept working and he remains a popular artist in Europe.

BERRY, RICHARD An influential singer and composer of the late Fifties and Sixties, Richard Berry was born in New Orleans in 1935. He moved to California in the Forties and began writing songs with **Jesse Belvin**, subsequently becoming one of the first 'session' singers, a position he retained until the early Sixties. His first single with the Flairs in 1953, 'She Wants to Rock' (on Flair) was produced by **Leiber and Stoller**, who brought Berry into the Robins to guest on 'Riot in Cell Block No. 9', a dramatic vignette that he narrated perfectly. He cut solo sides for Modern and RPM until 1956, when he formed the Pharaohs and made the original version of 'Louie, Louie' (on Flip) which sold a million by the **Kingsmen** in 1963. Berry made some 30 singles in all – on Paxley, Hasil, K&G, Smash, AMC, Bold Soul and others. But he enjoyed greater success on other people's records, duetting with **Etta James** on 'Roll With Me Henry' (Modern) and sobbing behind Donald Woods on 'Death of an Angel' (Flip). In the Seventies, he led a soul band in West Los Angeles and has played piano behind Chuck Higgins for Rollin' Rock.

BIG BOPPER The Big Bopper – real name J. P. Richardson – won rock'n'roll immortality through one major hit ('Chantilly Lace') and his death in the same plane crash that killed **Buddy Holly** and **Ritchie Valens**. He was born in Sabine Pass, Texas, on 29 October 1932, and worked part-time as a disc jockey and compere while still at high school in Beaumont, Texas. In the early Fifties, he was voted top disc jockey on KTRM radio station in Beaumont, and adopted the name 'Big Bopper' to

The arrow points to Big Bopper J. P. Richardson, the Texas DJ who managed only one major hit in his short singing career

match his ebullient personality. His career was interrupted by two years of Army service as a radio instructor, but on discharge he returned to work as the station's programme director and found more time for songwriting. Richardson sent some demos to Pappy Daily, a veteran Houston distributor, who signed him to a recording contract, and in 1957–8 he recorded two hillbilly singles under his real name for Mercury. In 1958, Richardson recorded a novelty song titled 'The Purple People Eater Meets the Witchdoctor' under his Big Bopper alias, but it was the flip, 'Chantilly Lace' that registered internationally, reaching the Top 10 in America and the Top 20 in England. He followed this in December 1958 with 'The Big Bopper's Wedding' (a Top 30 record in America) before he died on 3 February 1959. Richardson's small legacy of recordings suggests that he was a talented songwriter – he wrote **Johnny Preston**'s 'Running Bear', for example – rather than an artist of any durability.

BIG BROTHER AND THE HOLDING COMPANY Formed in San Francisco in 1966, Big Brother and the Holding Company comprised Sam Andrew, guitar; James Gurly, guitar; Pete Albin, bass; Dave Getz, drums; and **Janis Joplin**, vocals. A top group from the Bay area, they produced only one album that did them justice. *Big Brother and the Holding Company* (Mainstream, 1967), was ironically a demo tape that the group fought against being released. But it showed a rough-

ness behind the obvious excitement of Joplin's voice that Columbia, when they signed the group in 1968, was unwilling to risk on record again. By 1969, Big Brother and Janis were separate entities. *Be a Brother* (1970), on which the original members were augmented by Nick Gravenites and David Schallok, saw the group developing a smoother, if less exciting, sound. They disbanded in 1972, after one further album, *How Hard It Is*. See also **Janis Joplin**

BIG COUNTRY The creation of guitarist Stuart Adamson, Big Country, along with **U2** and **Simple Minds** led the return of guitar-based rock music into the British charts after the synthesizer domination of the early Eighties. Their tough, rousing sound and their anthemic songs, coupled with Adamson's honest and straightforward approach to the music industry, made them a popular act all over the world.

After Adamson had left the **Skids** in 1981, he played with guitarist Bruce Watson, a friend from Dunfermline, in a short-lived band, and at the end of that year the duo went down to London to record a demo for Phonogram. To support them on it, they called in a session team, Rhythm for Hire (consisting of bassist Tony Butler and drummer Mark Brzezicki), and the resulting tape was so good that they were recruited full-time, and Big Country was born.

Signed to Phonogram, they released their debut single 'Harvest Home' in

Big Country staged a rock revival with their tough guitar-based sound, which was a success worldwide in 1983/4

mid-'82, and although it didn't chart, it received a lot of attention and showcased their strident, escalating guitar work and their ability to compose a catchy hookline. They developed a reputation for exhilarating live shows and quickly built up a strong grass roots following.

1983 proved to be the year that Big Country broke through, with three hit singles and a hit album. With producer Steve Lillywhite, who played an important part in defining the band's huge sound, they recorded another LP, *The Crossing*, which received excellent reviews and went gold, reaching Number 3 in the UK. Successive tours were a huge success and Big Country established themselves in the first division of British bands.

They started 1984 with a superb single, 'Wonderland', which featured Brzezicki's phenomenal powerhouse drumming and the close guitar harmonies of Adamson and Watson. It was their biggest hit to date, but one they failed to follow up, taking most of the rest of the year to tour and to write and record a second album, *Steeltown*, released in November '84. A disappointment after the power and freshness of its predecessor, it failed to emulate its success. A couple of singles from it were released, only one of which, 'East of Eden', made the Top 20.

There then followed a long period of rest and recuperation for Big Country, whose heavy touring schedules had taken their toll. The silence was finally broken in the spring of 1986 with their third album, *The Seer*.

BIG MAYBELLE A big-voiced blues shouter of the Fifties, Big Maybelle was born Mabel Smith in 1926, in Jackson, Tennessee. She recorded with Christine Chatman's Orchestra in 1944 until her solo debut in 1947 on King Records. In 1952 she was with Okeh as 'Big Maybelle', and 1953 brought three R&B Top 10 hits including 'Gabbin' Blues'. She moved to Savoy in 1956 and 'Candy' became another R&B hit, but the late Fifties saw a steady output of ballads and jump-blues fail to make further commercial impact. The Sixties brought moves to Brunswick, Scepter, Rojac, Port and Chess, while a return to Rojac in 1966 brought success with 'Don't Pass Me By' and '96 Tears' (both R&B hits, the latter also giving Maybelle her only national 'pop' hit). Apart from one disc on Brunswick in 1968, she remained with Rojac until her death in 1972.

BIG STAR Formed out of the remnants of the **Box Tops** and other stalwarts of the local Memphis pop scene in 1972, Big Star was the most successful product of Ardent Studios, which in three years produced several excellent records by other groups such as Cargoe and the Hot Dogs on the Ardent label. All these groups, and the producers and musicians who made up the Ardent crew, shared a deep interest in British pop, banding together to form a minority in the predominantly black-oriented Memphis recording scene.

The first Big Star album, *Number 1 Record* (1972), featuring Alex Chilton's **Byrds**-like vocals and the distinctive tunes of co-leader Chris Bell, with Andy Hummel (bass) and Jody Stephens (drums), was a critical success, and Big Star became one of the city's most popular live attractions. They suffered a setback following Bell's departure (a result of personality conflict) but came back with an interesting second album, *Radio City*. Sales on both were poor, however, and three impressive singles ('When My Baby's Beside Me', 'Don't Lie to Me', and 'September Girls') failed to take off, which along with other factors led to the group's disbanding when the Ardent label folded in 1975. Bell was killed in a car crash in 1978, while Chilton began a solo career with the European album releases, *Bach's Bottom* and *Like Flies on Sherbert* (1980), and achieved a notable cult following among the rock cognoscenti.

BIG THREE One-time members of top Merseybeat group Cass and the Casanovas, Brian Griffiths (guitar), Johnny Gustafson (bass) and Johnny Hutchinson (drums) combined as the Big Three in 1962 but proved to be one of **Brian Epstein**'s least successful signings. Although they were arguably the most accomplished beat musicians in Liverpool, various personnel changes, an unsympathetic record company (Decca) and an inability to transfer the excitement of their live performances to disc (with the exception of their EP, *Live at the Cavern*) halted their progress, with only 'Some Other Guy' and 'By the Way' (both 1963) making a minor Top 40 impact. After two members of Faron's Flamingos, Bill Russley and Paddy Chambers, replaced Gustafson and Griffiths in late 1963, Epstein dropped the group because – as he tersely put it in his autobiography, *A Cellarful of Noise* – 'I don't approve of groups breaking . . . there was a lack of discipline and this cannot be tolerated because it is bad for business, awful for reputation and extremely bad for morale'. Gustafson and Griffiths joined fellow Liverpudlians the Seniors, soon after which Gustafson replaced Bob Garner in established Liverpool band the **Merseybeats**. He later played in Quatermass, Hard Stuff and **Roxy Music** and, in 1973, was briefly reunited with Griffiths for a Polydor album, *Resurrection*.

BIG YOUTH Though it was U Roy who, in the early Seventies, was largely responsible for the emergence of toasting as a major recorded-reggae style (it had previously been the preserve of live sound system DJs), Jamaican DJ Big

Youth (real name Michael Buchanan) was another important pioneer (along with King Stitt and Dennis AlCapone). His first major hit single was 1972's 'Ace 90 Skank', which was quickly followed by others in 'Screaming Target', 'The Killer', 'Cool Breeze' and 'Rocking'. By the end of 1974, Big Youth was widely known as The Human Gleaner (*The Gleaner* being Jamaica's leading daily popular newspaper), for it was from his records that many young Jamaicans learnt what was going on in society around them. 1975 was Big Youth's last really massive year – along with **Burning Spear**'s seminal 'Marcus Garvey', his 'House of Dreadlocks' was one of *the* singles of the year. The late Seventies saw Big Youth eclipsed by successive waves of younger DJs; he is now comparatively inactive.

BILK, ACKER Jazz clarinettist Bernard 'Acker' Bilk became a highly popular recording act with British middle-of-the-road audiences during the early years of the Sixties. Born in Pensford, Somerset, on 28 January 1929, Bilk played the clarinet in a semi-professional band in Bristol before joining Ken Colyer in 1954 – replacing Monty Sunshine. In 1958 he formed the Paramount Jazz Band – the most representative line-up of which was Colin Smith (trumpet), John Mortimer (trombone), Ron McKay (drums), Roy James (banjo), and Stan Greig (piano) – and had a British Top 10 hit with 'Summer Set' in 1960. The band's success owed more to their bowler hat and striped waistcoat image than to their dedication to traditional jazz. Largely on the strength of this image and other ideas devised by Bilk's inventive publicist, Peter Leslie (he dreamed up 'The Bilk Marketing Board' as a jokey piece of self-description), the band had eight Top 20 hits, including Bilk's self-composed solo outing 'Stranger on the Shore' – a piece of pure pop that reached Number 1 in the American as well as the British chart in 1962. It was this success more than anything else that helped the band move into the lucrative cabaret and TV variety show circuit just as the trad boom was collapsing. *See also* **Jazz, Traditional**

BISHOP, ELVIN Born in Tulsa, Oklahoma, on 21 October 1942, Elvin Bishop played guitar in the **Paul Butterfield** Blues Band until 1968 when he left to form his own group. Although **Mike Bloomfield** played lead guitar on the first three Butterfield records, Bishop had preceded him in the band, and took over for two later albums,

including *In My Own Dream*. The Elvin Bishop Group was formed in San Francisco, and included Art Stavro (bass), Steve Miller (organ) and drummer John Chambers, formerly of Loading Zone. Three albums were cut for CBS/Epic between 1968 and 1972, the band undergoing various personnel changes and moving through various blues, gospel and soul styles. In 1974, with a new band including Phil Aaberg (keyboards), Bishop signed with Capricorn Records to produce some pleasant albums very much in the **Allman Brothers Band**'s 'southern funk' mould, notably *Juke Joint Jump* in 1975. In 1976, he reached Number 3 in the US with the single 'Fooled Around and Fell in Love'.

BLACK, BILL One of the Sun label's noted team of session players, Bill Black linked the pre-rock'n'roll sounds of country with the Sixties rock and soul sounds of the South. Born in Memphis on 17 September 1926, he became a string bass player with Sun and teamed up with **Elvis Presley** for five years, playing on all his early hits and appearing in a number of Presley films, including *Loving You*. The insistent bass sound of Sun-vintage Presley was carried over into the Bill Black Combo, formed in 1959, by which time he was playing electric bass. His combo originated a genre of Memphis instrumentals with hits like 'Smokie' (1959), 'White Silver Sands', 'Josephine' and 'Don't Be Cruel' (all 1960). Aided by innovative saxophonist Ace Cannon, the Combo backed Jumpin' Gene Simmons on his 1964 US hit 'Haunted House', but it took groups like the **Mar-Keys** and **Booker T and the MGs** (also Memphis-based) to develop Black's sound further into soul music. Black died on 21 October 1965, but the Combo continued performing into the Seventies.

BLACK, CILLA Born Priscilla White on 27 May 1943, Cilla Black used to check in the coats at Liverpool's Cavern and occasionally sang a song with one of the local groups. **Brian Epstein** saw her as perfect material for mainstream pop stardom and masterminded her rise to the top of MOR show business in Britain. Her name was changed to Cilla Black, and after an unsuccessful debut with Lennon/McCartney's 'Love of the Loved' (Parlophone, 1963), she resorted to the old tradition of covering American hits – **Dionne Warwick**'s 'Anyone Who Had a Heart' and a fairly feeble version of 'You've Lost That Lovin' Feeling' among them – and a girl-next-door

Cilla Black's home-spun working-girl image had lasting appeal

image was skilfully promoted. In Britain she had over a dozen Top 20 hits which led by the Seventies to top cabaret appearances and a regular BBC series. In the Eighties, she hosted two prime-time ITV shows, *Blind Date* and *Surprise, Surprise*.

BLACK OAK ARKANSAS A boogie-cum-heavy metal band from America's southern states, Black Oak Arkansas originally comprised Jim Dandy Mangrum (vocals, born 30 March 1948, in Black Oak, Arkansas), Stanley Knight (guitar, born in Little Rock, Arkansas, on 12 February 1949), 'Little' Jimmy Henderson (lead guitar, born in Jackson, Mississippi, on 20 May 1954), Pat Daugherty (bass, born in Jonesboro, Arkansas, on 11 November 1947), Tommy Aldridge (drums, born in Nashville, Tennessee, on 15 August 1950) and Rickie Lee Reynolds (guitar, born in Manilla, Arkansas, on 28 October 1948).

Formed in 1964, they first hit the road under the name of Knowbody Else and recorded an album for Stax in 1969. The change of name followed their move to Los Angeles that year, after which they signed with Atlantic and released a clutch of crude Southern boogie albums (including *Keep the Faith* in 1971 and *Raunch'n'Roll Live* in 1973) before the Richard Podolor-produced *High on the Hog* (1974) gave them their first gold album. Their stage act, heavily featuring Dandy's machismo histrionics, endeared them to teenage audiences during the mid-Seventies, but they were somewhat eclipsed by the new wave of stadium bands who emerged later in the decade. The band's personnel changed all the time, and by 1977, Jim Dandy was the only remaining member from the original line-up.

BLACK SABBATH Consummate masters of singleminded apocalyptic heavy metal rock, Black Sabbath originally comprised Geezer Butler, bass (born 17 July 1949), Tony Iommi, guitar (19 February 1948), Bill Ward, drums (5 May 1948), and **Ozzy Osbourne**, vocals (3 December 1948). All from Aston, Birmingham, they changed their name from Earth in 1969 to launch upon an astonished world an act remarkable for its use of sheer volume, extreme musical simplicity and overtones of black magic.

Touring Europe for a year, Sabbath returned to Britain in 1970 with a first album, *Black Sabbath*. Their second album, *Paranoid*, included the single 'Paranoid' – an instant hit. Black Sabbath set the format for the albums that followed one a year until 1974. Musically it consisted of sub-**Cream** power chords and riffs delivered with sledgehammer relentlessness; lyrically it combined the themes of atomic war, death, doom and destruction with drugs and teenage revolt. The group's appeal, particularly in America, was based upon a one-to-one identification with a young audience. This overcame a barrage of negative criticism and virtually no radio air-play to gain the band gold albums – notably *Masters of Reality* (1971) and *Sabbath Bloody Sabbath* (WWA, 1973) – and sell out audiences for their almost non-stop world tours. In mid-1974, the year their management company World Wide Artists collapsed, they went into semi-retirement. In 1975 Black Sabbath returned with a sixth album, *Sabotage* (NEMS), and toured America and Britain.

Sabotage (1975) adhered to the basic heavy rock formula, but the sessions for *Technical Ecstasy* (1976) saw Iommi experimenting with overdubbing and even a horn section. Osbourne left in 1977 but rejoined a year later, ousting his replacement Dave Walker (formerly with Savoy Brown). One more album followed, *Never Say Die* (1979), before Osbourne again departed to launch his solo project, Blizzard of Oz.

While Ozzy's career took off with two albums – *Blizzard of Oz* (1980) and *Diary of a Madman* (1982) – Sabbath recruited ex-**Rainbow** singer Ronnie James Dio in his stead. (Bill Ward retired for health reasons and was replaced by Vinnie Appice, younger brother of former **Vanilla Fudge** drummer Carmine Appice.) However, tension developed between Dio and the other Sabbath members, with Iommi alleging that Dio had tampered with the mixes of *Live Evil* (1982) to make the vocals more prominent. Late in 1982, Dio and Appice left to form their own band, called Dio.

BLACK SLATE Formed in the early Seventies, London-based reggae band Black Slate had matured by the mid-Seventies into leading lights of the first wave of genuinely 'British' reggae talent – like their contemporaries **Matumbi**, confident enough in their own abilities to cast off the previously widespread approach of simply copying what was coming out of the Kingston studios. Two singles from that period remain substantial listening today, 'Sticks Man' and 'Piano Twist', though – apart from one UK Top 10 single, the catchy 'Amigo' in 1980 – Slate never lived up to the promise they seemed to be showing in 1975/6.

BLACK UHURU One of the fresher breaths of air to emerge from reggae when they came together in 1980 (at a time dominated by overly repetitive

Tony Iommi of Black Sabbath looking very cool as the band hammer out their archetypal heavy metal sounds behind Osbourne's frenzied vocals

and derivative toasters), Jamaica's Black Uhuru were a glorious return to the great harmony trio tradition of Jamaican popular music – their style having all the vocal richness of the rock-steady era, with lyrics suitably updated to embrace militant Rastafarianism. Working with producers Sly Dunbar and Robbie Shakespeare, Uhuru released a succession of unusually powerful records between 1980 and 1982 – of which the 1981 album *Red* is arguably the finest. They were also unusual for their time in including a woman, the American Puma Jones, in their line-up (alongside Michael Rose and Duckie Simpson). A handful of solo artists aside, women were then in little active evidence within reggae – while lyrics dealing with sexual politics from a woman's point of view were even rarer. Uhuru's 1983 tracks 'Puff She Puff' and 'Sistren' were trailblazers in this area.

BLACKWELL, 'BUMPS' The studio mastermind behind **Little Richard**'s string of Fifties hits, Robert A. 'Bumps' Blackwell was born on 23 May 1918, and had the distinction of heading an early Fifties R&B band that included both **Ray Charles** and Quincy Jones in its line-up. He became studio assistant to Art Rupe at Specialty Records in Los Angeles in 1955 and was despatched to New Orleans to arrange and produce Little Richard's first sessions for the label, from which 'Good Golly Miss Molly' and 'Rip It Up' – co-written by Blackwell with Richard – both resulted. In 1956, he recorded **Sam Cooke**'s first solo tracks, and he later took Cooke to Keen Records when Rupe sold him the master-tapes plus Cooke's contract in lieu of royalties. He became A&R manager of Mercury Records in the early Sixties and worked as Little Richard's personal manager. He died on 9 March 1985, in California.

BLACKWELL, OTIS The composer of 'Fever' (for **Little Willie John**), 'Handy Man' (for **Jimmy Jones**), 'All Shook Up' (for **Elvis Presley**), 'Great Balls of Fire' (for **Jerry Lee Lewis**), and many other classic songs of the rock-'n'roll era, Otis Blackwell was born in Brooklyn, New York, in 1931. A blues fan in his teens, he began his career singing in local amateur shows and neighbourhood bars and made his recording debut in 1953 with 'Daddy Rolling Stone' for the Jay-Dee label, a song later revived by the **Who**. He turned to full-time songwriting around 1956 and established his reputation with a string of hit songs for Elvis Presley – 'Don't Be Cruel', 'One Broken Heart for Sale' and 'Return to Sender' among them. Presley's versions reputedly drew very heavily on Blackwell's own demo recordings of the songs.

Blackwell found his songwriting services less in demand during the Sixties and returned to recording, this time for the Gale, Atlantic, Date and MGM labels. In 1976 he started to receive overdue recognition, with **Stevie Wonder** acknowledging him publicly by passing on his own Best Male Vocalist award to Blackwell at a music industry gathering. In 1977 he recorded an album, *These Are My Songs*, and began work on the score for a biographical film of Presley's life: his recording of the theme song, 'The No. 1 King of Rock'n'Roll', on his own Fever label, was one of the better Presley tributes to appear following the singer's death.

Songwriter Otis Blackwell provided the greats of rock'n'roll with some of their biggest hits – his compositions have sold 30 million records

BLAINE, HAL A legendary West Coast session drummer of long standing, Hal Blaine was born in 1932. He began playing at nine in his home town of Hartford, Connecticut, and then played in groups first in the Army and afterwards on the road with various acts. During the early Fifties he spent three years at the Roy Knapp School of Percussion in Chicago. Then, in 1957, he joined a Texan rockabilly group, the Raiders, and moved to Hollywood. There they backed pop star Tommy Sands on stage and record until Sands was conscripted in 1960. Blaine then toured with Patti Page and in 1961 met producer **H.B. Barnum**, who persuaded him to stay in Los Angeles and work sessions.

Soon after, he played on the **Crystals'** 'He's a Rebel' session and became a regular member of **Phil Spector**'s West Coast session crew. It was Spector who encouraged Blaine to unleash his full potential on hits like 'Be My Baby' and 'Da Doo Ron Ron'. From then on, everyone hired Blaine and since the early Sixties he has played drums on countless hit singles and albums.

BLANCMANGE Along with **Soft Cell** and **Depeche Mode**, Blancmange emerged from the early Eighties British electro-pop scene and went on to establish themselves as an international pop act who coincidentally still used synthesizers.

First coming together in 1980, Neil Arthur (vocals/guitar) and Stephen Luscombe (keyboards) released an experimental EP called 'Irene and Mavis', before being invited to contribute a track to the now-notorious *Some Bizarre* compilation LP. Their instrumental single, 'Sad Day', prompted London Records to sign them.

Blending the aloof precision of the synthesizer sound with Arthur's soulful vocals, Blancmange released their debut album *Happy Families* (1982) and scored UK Top 10 hits with two singles from it, 'Living on the Ceiling' and 'Blind Vision'. After a quiet spell the band returned in 1984 with a second album *Mange Tout*, on which Luscombe explored his fascination with Eastern music and provided them with a surprise hit with a cover of **Abba**'s 'The Day Before You Came'.

Blancmange released a third album, *Believe You Me* in 1985, scoring a couple of minor single hits from it before splitting up in June 1986. Both planned to write film soundtracks; Luscombe also indulged his interest in Eastern culture, while Arthur intended to pursue a solo career.

BLAND, BILLY R&B singer Billy Bland was born in Wilmington, North Carolina, on 5 April 1932. An ex-ballroom dancer, Bland recorded for Old Town in 1955, making two excellent blues, 'Chicken in the Basket' and 'Chicken Hop' (with **Sonny Terry** on harp). He hit the Top 10 with an atypically bouncy pop song, 'Let the Little Girl Dance' in 1960. Old Town, with which he remained until the mid-Sixties, issued a large number of extremely varied Billy Bland singles, including three smaller chart entries – 'Born to Be Loved', 'Harmony' and 'My Heart's on Fire'. His excellent version of **Bobby Bland**'s 'Little Boy Blue' should be in any representative collection of deep soul.

BLAND, BOBBY 'BLUE' One of the leading figures in modern blues, Bobby Bland was born Robert Calvin Bland in Rosemark, Tennessee, on 17 January 1930. He was raised in Memphis, and by the late Forties had joined the Beale Streeters, a loose assemblage of young talent that included **B.B. King**, **Rosco Gordon**, **Johnny Ace**, and **Junior Parker**. Bland's singing style came straight from the Southwest – deft, swinging, articulate, with a unique dusty blues feeling. In 1954 he made a guest appearance at a Houston talent show, which gained the attention of Don Robey, president of Duke Records. Robey quickly signed him to a recording contract and April 1955 saw the release of 'It's My Life Baby', his first R&B chart success. This was followed by 'I Smell Trouble', 'Little Boy Blue' and 'Farther Up the Road', which reached the national Hot 100 in 1957 and stayed there for a remarkable 21 weeks. Once established Bland took to the road, touring the well-worn circuit of one-night stands, concerts, dances and theatres such as Harlem's Apollo and the Regal in Chicago. With him went a band so strongly identified with Bland that it has earned its own legend. Led by tenorist Bill Harvey and trumpeter-arranger Joe Scott – whose importance as Bland's longtime musical director cannot be overstated – it was driving and bluesy, loose and loping, with a jump and bite reminiscent of the exciting big bebop bands of the Forties. There was also the stunning lead guitar of Wayne Bennett, who is present on most of Bland's hits. The songs Bland performed were mostly written by Scott and others, under the alias 'Deadric Malone'. The material and arrangements were impeccable, thus ensuring a consistent stream of R&B chart successes.

Bland's early Sixties hits included 'Cry, Cry, Cry', 'I Pity the Fool', 'Call On Me', 'Ain't Nothing You Can Do', and 'Two Steps from the Blues'. As the Sixties progressed, Bland began to experiment with modern soul styles, his songs occasionally sounding almost Motown in their presentation. Producer Andre Williams took over from Joe Scott, although Bland still maintained a regular output of persuasive, bluesy records between his more pop-oriented hits. In 1972, the vast ABC/Dunhill record complex gobbled up Duke and belatedly turned the white rock market onto Bland. Dunhill teamed up with producer **Steve Barri** who was then working with the **Four Tops**. His *California Album* was into a rock framework, but one that had not eroded Bland's gospel roots. There were songs by 'Deadric Malone' but they nestled alongside compositions by Gerry Goffin and **Leon Russell**. The album sold very well and paved the way for the subsequent *Dreamer* set, again produced by Barri. Later albums included two collaborations with B.B. King (*Together for the First Time*, 1974; *Together Again . . . Live*, 1976), *Reflections in Blue* (1977), *Sweet Vibrations* (MCA, 1980), *Try Me, I'm Real* (1981), and *Here We Go Again* (1982).

BLIND FAITH Blind Faith existed for most of 1969 when **Eric Clapton** and **Ginger Baker**, on the rebound from **Cream**, teamed up with **Stevie Winwood** from **Traffic** and **Family**'s bassist, Rick Grech. They recorded one album, *Blind Faith* (Polydor, 1969), played a series of US dates and a free summer concert in London, and then broke up – victims of the extraordinary demands made of such 'supergroups' in the late Sixties by businessmen, press and public alike. Blind Faith simply could not live up to the expectations raised by their formation, and the experience caused Clapton, for one, radically to reassess his musical outlook; among the first fruits of this reappraisal was his re-emergence a year later as leader of **Derek and the Dominos**. *See also* **Cream**; **Eric Clapton**; **Ginger Baker**; **Steve Winwood**

BLONDIE At their height the most successful band to come out of the US new wave, Blondie staged a fully-fledged assault on the airwaves with a joyous modern blend of pop that embraced a wide variety of musical styles and gave them five UK and four US Number 1 hits. With such an effective focal point as a blonde 'sex kitten', the eminently photogenic singer

Deborah Harry, their glamorous, colourful image and fun outlook won them a loyal international following.

Blondie grew out of tacky New York garage band the Stilettoes, in which Debbie Harry was one of the three girl singers and her boyfriend Chris Stein played guitar. Harry and Stein poached the Stilettoes' rhythm section, consisting of bassist Fred Smith and drummer Billy O'Connor, to form Blondie in 1974. They played around the New York club circuit and in 1976, having signed to the small label Private Stock, they recorded their first album *Blondie*. The LP was a good-humoured, B–movie-inspired collection of raw pop tunes and served as an early indicator of what Blondie could do. By this point both Smith and O'Connor had left (Smith to join **Television**), to be replaced by Gary Valentine and Clem Burke respectively.

Blondie began to tour across America but their impact remained strictly local, with the notoriously conservative US radio stations reluctant to air anything labelled 'punk' or 'new wave'. In autumn 1977 they toured the UK with Television and in September they scored their first hit single with 'In the Flesh', reaching Number 2 in Australia. Chrysalis decided to invest in the band on the strength of that one hit, a gamble that paid off very quickly when 'Denis' (a female inversion of the 1963 Randy and the Rainbows US hit) reached Number 2 in the UK early in 1978. Shortly after this they released the LP *Plastic Letters*, a rockier, more adventurous album than its predecessor, which reached Number 10 in the UK and stayed in the charts for over a year.

Having recruited a new bass player, Englishman Nigel Harrison, they went into the studio with renowned hit producer Mike Chapman and recorded the album that was to break the band worldwide, *Parallel Lines*. Released in September 1978, this LP spent 100 weeks on the UK chart alone, and was the perfect manifesto for Blondie's pop talent, containing five huge hit singles, most notably 'Heart of Glass'. This disco-flavoured song was the first to bridge the fields of disco and new wave, and as such became a milestone in the development of popular music. It gave them their first UK Number 1 and – disco music being officially acceptable on American radio – finally broke them in the US, reaching the top slot there.

By 1979, Blondie were a hugely successful group all over the world, hounded by the popular press, and when *Eat to the Beat* came out late that year, it had no difficulty emulating the success of the previous album, even though it did not match up in quality. The first ever LP to be released simultaneously as a video, it too was loaded with hit songs including 'Atomic', 'Dreaming' and 'Union City Blue', the number originally intended for the low-budget black comedy *Union City*, Harry's first film role and Stein's first soundtrack.

The next single, 'Call Me', was released in 1980 and marked the final step in Blondie's quest for world domination. Taken from the soundtrack to the film *American Gigolo*, it was produced by **Giorgio Moroder** and sold enormously all over the world, giving them another transatlantic Number 1. Chapman was back at the mixing desk later the same year for *Autoamerican*, an album that expanded their use of dance and Caribbean rhythms, as amply shown by the muted reggae of 'The Tide is High' and the jokey white rapping on 'Rapture'. It was poorly received, however, inspite of its being released after the band's 1980 tour, which saw them on cracking form. From then on, Blondie's future became more and more unsure, with Harry's increasing commitments to films and TV fuelling rumours of an imminent split.

In 1981, Stein and Harry teamed up with Nile Rodgers and Bernard Edwards of **Chic** to record Harry's first solo LP *Koo Koo*, a release that seemed likely to signal the end of the band. A mechanical and cold effort, it sold only moderately and provided a solitary minor hit, 'Backfired'.

In the event, there was to be one more Blondie record, the dreary 1982 release *The Hunter*, which took Harry and Stein's obsession with rapping to ridiculous lengths. The band began to go their separate ways; 'Island of Lost Souls' (1982) proved to be the group's last UK Top 20 hit single, and reached only Number 37 in the US. Nevertheless, Blondie had done more than prove themselves America's biggest musical export of the late Seventies. Their look and sound had been widely imitated and, for a while, Debbie Harry was the most photographed woman in rock. The activities of Stein and Harry virtually came to a standstill after the demise of the band; Stein's pet venture, his own label Animal Records, was curtailed due to a serious illness – pemphigus, a chronic skin disease. Harry spent considerable time nursing Stein, and by late 1986 his health was restored sufficiently for him to work on the soundtrack of a film entitled *Tales from the Dark Side*. In the same year, Harry revitalized her career with *Rockbird* which spawned the UK Top 10 single 'French Kissing in the USA'.

Exploiting vocalist Debbie Harry's image as a punk sex-kitten, Blondie became the United States' biggest musical export of the late Seventies

BLOOD, SWEAT AND TEARS

The brainchild of **Al Kooper**, Blood, Sweat and Tears was formed after the demise of his **Blues Project** in 1968. One of the first rock bands with a full horn section, it was founded on the premise that rock is art, or at least arty eclecticism. On their debut album, *Child Is Father to the Man* (Columbia), the eclecticism worked more often than not. The original line-up was Kooper (keyboards, vocals), Steve Katz (guitar), Jim Fielder (bass), Bobby Colomby (drums), Randy Brecker, Jerry Weiss (trumpets), Dick Halligan (trombone) and Fred Lipsius (alto sax). But Kooper left almost immediately, and leadership of the band fell to Katz (also ex-Blues Project) and new singer David Clayton-Thomas, a big-voiced Canadian. And where the first album had mixed rock, folk, blues, jazz and classical music into something resembling coherence, the second presented a taste of rock here, a smattering of jazz there, a classical interlude elsewhere. 'You Made Me So Happy' was a huge hit in 1969, and there was no turning back.

Commercial success grew by leaps and bounds, as did charges of pretentiousness. By 1970, most of the group's original audience was gone, replaced by the sort of man who picks his mood music by scanning the *Playboy* Jazz and Pop Poll. They duplicated their records almost note-for-note in concert. There followed Las Vegas engagements, State Department tours behind the Iron Curtain, and albums full of songs by Lennon/McCartney, Jagger/Richard, Satie, **Little Walter**, Prokofiev, and **James Taylor** – none of which bore any resemblance to the original in the BS&T version, although they certainly sounded a lot like each other. Personnel changes increased until 1976, when they were dropped by Columbia. Colomby left and Clayton-Thomas remained as leader and resident creative force, though the critical reception for *Brand New Day* (ABC, 1977) was mixed. *Nuclear Blues* (1980) did little to improve the band's fortunes. *See also* **Blues Project**; **Al Kooper**

BLOODSTONE

The four original members of this band – Charles McCormick, Henry Williams, Charles Love, and Williss Draffen – all grew up together in Kansas City. They worked as the Sinceres, before moving to Los Angeles where they recorded for Pzazz Records. Returning to Kansas and learning instruments, they moved into **Sly and the Family Stone**-influenced black rock with a new name, Bloodstone. Coming to Britain in 1972, unknown and unrecorded, they appeared on a soul package and created a storm. Subsequently signed to English Decca, their first album was a disaster, but their second, brilliantly produced at Chipping Norton by **Mike Vernon**, brought forth a classic sweet soul ballad, 'Natural High', a double million-seller in America in 1973. Their follow-up albums, *Unreal* and *Riddle of the Sphinx*, were also successful in the soul market. They released five more albums before the end of the decade – the last, *Don't Stop*, marked their brief association with Motown in 1979 – and in 1981 McCormick left, to be replaced by Los-Angeles-born Ron Wilson and Ronald Bell.

BLOOMFIELD, MIKE

Son of a wealthy Chicago restaurant supplies manufacturer, Mike Bloomfield was born on 28 July 1944, and spent the early Sixties on the South Side, learning blues guitar from the black masters. It was there that he met **Bob Dylan**.

When Dylan went electric in 1965, he brought along Bloomfield, already familiar with the studios by virtue of his sideman role on blues albums. His fast, piercing guitar helped define the Dylan rock style. By then, he had also taken up with the **Paul Butterfield Blues Band**. Butterfield was another white veteran of the South Side, and his integrated band brought blues to the colleges and rock ballrooms, spawning a wave of white blues bands.

Bloomfield's technique was impeccable (he was often unjustly criticized for just that), and he was by now recognized as *the* guitarist. So much so that when Butterfield played New York, Bloomfield often stood with his back to the audience to prevent the guitarists in the front row from watching his hands and stealing his licks. The epochal *East–West*, which fused blues and Eastern modes, further enhanced his reputation.

In 1967, he moved to northern California and formed the **Electric Flag**, with whom he played his last consistently good guitar. The complaint that he was all technique started looking more accurate as he freelanced – joining **Al Kooper** on the first *Super Session* (which, again, spawned many imitators); joining other white musicians and the **Muddy Waters** Band on a Chicago reunion, *Fathers and Sons*; dabbling in production; and releasing a solo album that was mostly uninspired country music. He hated to tour, and thus played only the Bay Area club circuit, with a makeshift band of other white blues veterans.

As the Seventies progressed he

Singer David Clayton-Thomas leads the powerful brass of Blood, Sweat and Tears. The band's artistic pretentions eventually provoked hostility

became less and less visible except for a 1973 'Supersession' with **John Paul Hammond** and **Dr John** (*Triumvirate*, Columbia), a 1974 Electric Flag reunion and a gig scoring porn movies for the Mitchell Brothers Film Group. In 1975, he played in KGB with Barry Goldberg, Carmine Appice, Rick Grech and Roy Kennedy, but left after one album. He recorded a number of solo albums during the late Seventies but died on 15 February 1981, of an accidental drug overdose.

Mike Bloomfield, pioneer of electric blues guitar, high on technique

BLUE CHEER San Francisco bands of the late Sixties progressed at a tangent to the influence of British power rock bands like **Cream** and the **Jeff Beck** Group, but many of their second and third generation outfits were completely overawed by the Britons. Accordingly, when Blue Cheer – Paul Whaley, drums (from Sacramento's Oxford Circle); Dick Peterson, bass, lead vocals; and Randy Holden, lead guitar – erupted on the scene with shatteringly loud performances and an excessively overburdened version of 'Summertime Blues' (Philips), a hit in the summer of 1968, there seemed little to distinguish them from British trios apart from extra volume. By their second album, *Outside Inside*, Holden had been replaced by Leigh Stevens. It is their most interesting album, noteworthy for Paul Whaley's excellent heavy rock drum technique. Like the **Grateful Dead**, they abounded in mystique and local legend but failed to project their aura of excitement on to any of their four albums. Too inward-looking, they nevertheless possessed a musical identity that in a later group, **Grand Funk Railroad**, proved to be a vehicle for enormous success.

BLUE ÖYSTER CULT Originally the Soft White Underbelly, Blue Öyster Cult were formed in 1970 in New York under the auspices of Sandy Pearlman, a critic for the rock magazine *Craw-*

daddy. They went out on the road, joined and left Elektra, and eventually were signed by Columbia. The group – Donald (Buck Dharma) Roeser, lead guitar, vocals; Eric Bloom, guitar, synthesizer; Albert Bouchard, drums, vocals; Joe Bouchard, bass, vocals; and Allen Lanier, rhythm guitar, keyboards – quickly gained a deserved reputation as *the* intelligent heavy-metal band, partly through their relationship with Pearlman and critic and occasional lyricist Richard Meltzer, partly through their use of extravagant symbolism in their stage act and on their album covers. Their lyrics have always been undecipherable, apart from title lines like 'OD'd on Life Itself' and 'Hot Rails to Hell'; the music, at its best on *Blue Öyster Cult* (1972) and *Tyranny and Mutation* (1973), is quintessential heavy-metal – layers of vicious guitar riffs over a thudding rhythm section, growled and screeched vocals.

Once called 'a portable Altamont', they themselves attribute their music to the 'primal paranoia' in the air. Certainly, with the odd exception like the lyrical 'Last Days of May' on their first album, their music has little of the light or sense of joy possessed by their predecessors, **Cream** and **Jimi Hendrix**. It is usually fast, always powerful and clear, like a well-tuned motorcycle. They have been a major box office draw since 1976, when their album *Agents of Fortune* (containing contributions from **Patti Smith**) precipitated a long-awaited chart breakthrough. In 1980, they shared top billing with **Black Sabbath** on the cross-America Black and Blue tour.

BLUEBEAT The Bluebeat label, run by Melodisc, existed from 1960 until 1967. Originally set up to provide West Indian immigrants living in London with home-grown boogie, 'blues' and gospel music from independent Jamaican producers Coxsone Dodd, Duke Reid, Smiths, Beverley, etc., it later found a market amongst white British youth who linked cult R&B with the raw Jamaican sound, itself derivative of New Orleans jump music. Discs featuring the offbeat piano rhythms and honking saxes of the new, uptempo 'ska' dance included Theo Beckford's 'Bringing in the Sheep' and **Prince Buster**'s 'Tongue Will Tell'.

In the resulting confusion, the music became known as 'bluebeat' (after the label) by the British buyers while the West Indians themselves referred to it simply as 'the blues'. It was not, however, quite as simple as that. The very earliest recordings in the Bluebeat

catalogue feature a very dissonant variety of styles, including Fifties teen doo-wop from the Jiving Juniors on 'My Heart's Desire'; ska-gospel from **Laurel Aitken** with 'Judgment Day'; mainstream low-church gospel from Basil Gabbidon's Mellow Larks on 'Time to Pray (Alleluia)'; and simple pop-flavoured love songs such as Derrick Morgan and the Ebonies' 'Don't Cry'. The legendary Folks Bros' 'Oh Carolina' had Rastafarian overtones. Furthermore, many of the discs that were popular during the bluebeat craze of 1963–4 were not on the Bluebeat label: **Millie**'s 'My Boy Lollipop' (Fontana); Derrick and Patsy's 'Gypsy Woman' (Island); Prince Buster's 'The Lion Roars' (Dice); Rezo Reco's 'King of Kings' (Columbia).

The label continued to flourish long after 'bluebeat' had died its death. The older artists, Kentrick Patrick, Monty Morris, Cosmo, gave way to the Skatalites, the Charmers, and the Maytals. The perennial **Owen Gray**, Prince Buster, Derrick Morgan and Laurel Aitken remained popular too. By 1967, however, Buster was the only one left. Apparently, Melodisc were unpopular in the record shops, and newer labels like Island, R&B, Doctor Bird, and Pama were more forward-looking and popular with the record buyers. Bluebeat issued all the most important Prince Buster rock-steady sides including 'Judge Dread', 'Ghost Dance' and 'Judge Dread Dance the Pardon', before shutting shop to emerge with the Fab label, distributing all Prince Buster product, and later the Prince Buster label itself.

BLUEBELLS The brainchild of Robert Hodgens, who got the idea for the group when interest was expressed in one of the fictitious bands he featured in his own fanzine, the Bluebells joined the ranks of the smart Scottish pop bands who brightened up the British music scene in the Eighties. Hodgens (vocals, guitar) began by writing songs and, after several unsuccessful attempts to recruit suitable musicians, he put together a line-up of Russell Irvine (guitar), Ken McLusky (harmonica, vocals), David McLusky (drums), and Laurence Donegan (bass) in Glasgow in 1981. The band eventually signed a deal with London in 1983 after recording an impressive demo with **Elvis Costello** at the controls. There followed a string of bright pop singles and in 1984 they scored a big UK hit with 'Young at Heart' (Number 8), as well as releasing their debut album *Sisters*.

BLUES PROJECT The Blues Project was the title of a blues collection released during 1965 by Elektra: it featured a number of Greenwich Village folk and blues musicians, and one of them, Danny Kalb, adopted the same name for New York's first native electric blues band. The original line-up comprised: Tommy Flanders, vocals; Steve Katz, guitar, vocals; Danny Kalb, lead guitar; **Al Kooper**, organ, vocals; Andy Kulberg, bass, flute; and Ray Blumenfeld, drums. Katz had been in the Even Dozen Jug Band, Flanders in Boston's Trolls, Kulberg was studying music and Blumenfeld just hanging around. Al Kooper joined, to improve his nascent and highly praised organ-playing first heard on Dylan's *Blonde on Blonde*. The high-energy Project tore the New York scene apart, especially at Bleeker Street's Café A Go Go, venue for their first (live) album in 1966 on Verve. Genuinely exciting, it represents Flanders' only recorded work with the original band. Kooper and Katz filled the vocal role on *Projections* (1966) and *Live at the Town Hall* (1967).

Friction with Kalb led Kooper to leave, then Kalb fell ill and disappeared and finally Katz was enticed into Kooper's newly founded **Blood, Sweat and Tears**. Kulberg and Blumenfeld added Richard Greene, violin, Don Kretmar, bass and sax, and John Gregory, guitar and vocals. They cut *Planned Obsolescence* as Blues Project though they were already metamorphosing into Sea Train. In 1971 Kalb, Blumenfeld and Kretmar came back with *Lazarus* and *Blues Project*, the latter plus Tommy Flanders and ex-Fish David Cohen. That version fell apart in April 1972, and the final chapter was the reunion of the originals, minus Flanders, that led to *Reunion in Central Park* (MCA) in 1973. *See also* **Al Kooper**

BLUNSTONE, COLIN Lead singer with the **Zombies** until their break-up in 1967, Colin Blunstone (born 24 June 1945) subsequently embarked on a solo career, achieving his first hit in 1969 with a re-recording of his former group's best-known record, 'She's Not There'. The track was credited, however, to Blunstone's pseudonym of Neil MacArthur. In 1971, he re-emerged under his own name with the album *One Year* (Epic), with breathy interpretations of songs by **Tim Hardin** and others; a year later came the hit single 'Say You Don't Mind', which had originally been recorded by its writer, **Denny Laine**.

The formation of a permanent backing group – Pete Wingfield (piano), Derek Griffiths (guitar), Terry Poole (bass), Jim Toomey (drums) – caused a divergence between his recorded work, which tended towards lush arrangements to highlight his airy, floating vocals, and his live performances fronting a band that wanted to rock more than he did. He broke up the band, after the release of *Journey* in 1974, to work alone. His later albums included *Planes* (1976) and *Never Even Thought* (1978). In 1981, he sang on Dave Stewart's UK hit revival of **Jimmy Ruffin**'s 'What Becomes of the Broken-Hearted', which reached Number 15 in the UK on Stiff Records.

BOB AND EARL Despite their 30 years of activity in the R&B field, Bobby Relf and Earl Nelson are still best known for 'Harlem Shuffle', a shrill discothèque hit that reached the US Top 50 on the Marc label in 1963 and the UK Top 10 on re-issue in 1969. The original 'Bob' was Bobby Byrd, alias **Bobby Day** of 'Rockin' Robin' fame. He met Nelson when the latter joined Byrd's group, the Hollywood Flames, in 1957. They recorded as Bob and Earl for Class between 1957 and 1959, after which Byrd departed and Relf joined Nelson to record prolifically for Chene, Tempo ('Don't Ever Leave Me' was a small hit on the label in 1962), Loma, and Mirwood. Relf also recorded solo for Flair, Cash, Dot, and (as Bobby Garrett) Mirwood, while Nelson cut solo sides for Class, Ebb, Mira (as Earl Cosby), Keyman, Mirwood (as Jackie Lee, under which name he had a US Top 20 hit with 'The Duck' in 1965), and (as Jay T.) for Warner Brothers in 1973. Relf also wrote 'Walking in the Rain', a 1974 hit for Love Unlimited, who were protégés of Bob and Earl's long-time arranger, **Barry White**. 'Harlem Shuffle' was successfully revived by the **Rolling Stones** in 1986.

As vocalist of the Zombies, Colin Blunstone displayed an anguished voice that was totally distinctive. His solo career featured several hit singles

BOLAN, MARC See **T. Rex**

BOND, GRAHAM Organist and sax player Graham Bond (born c.1937) was voted one of UK jazz's 'brightest hopes' in the early Sixties, when he was still spending his days working in a sales office and his evenings playing with the Don Rendell Quintet. He left the group in November 1962 to replace **Cyril Davies** in Blues Incorporated but stayed only a few months, finally quitting to form the Graham Bond Trio with **Jack Bruce** and **Ginger Baker**. Guitarist **John McLaughlin** joined a little later but was replaced within six months by Dick Heckstall-Smith, after which the band became known as the Graham Bond Organisation. Critical success followed, despite the departures of Baker and Bruce, but the Organisation's brand of jazzy, aggressive blues never found commercial favour and Bond moved to the US after its final break-up in 1965. On his return 18 months later he became involved in a long series of abortive groups, including Ginger Baker's Airforce and the band Holy Magic, formed with his wife, ex-Airforce singer Diane Stewart. A brief partnership with **Cream**'s lyricist **Pete Brown** followed, resulting in the album *Two Heads Are Better Than One* (1972). He died on 8 May 1974, after falling under an Underground train at Goodge Street Station in London.

BONDS, GARY 'U.S.' An important US hit-maker of the early Sixties and a key influence on **Bruce Springsteen**, Gary 'U.S.' Bonds was born Gary Anderson in Jacksonville, Florida, on 6 June 1939. He moved to Norfolk, Virginia, as a child and sang in church choirs. In 1952, he formed his own high school group, the Turks, and then went solo. In 1960, he met local record shop owner **Frank Guida** and recorded 'New Orleans' for Guida's Legrand label, reaching the Top 20 in both Britain and America early in 1961. His follow-up, 'Not Me', flopped completely, but his third record 'Quarter to Three' went to Number 1 in America and reached the UK Top 10. Bonds then had a series of consecutive American hits including 'School Is Out', 'School Is In', and 'Twist, Twist Señora', all featuring distinctive riffs and a muzzy, boisterous semi-live effect created by crude phasing and tape-echo techniques. In an era of tinny, thin-sounding records, Bonds' records proved revolutionary, and had a great influence on Britain's burgeoning R&B beat group scene. However, Bonds' sound palled through repetition, and he turned to songwriting with

Swamp Dogg, recording and performing only occasionally. By 1981, however, Bonds was back – with the well-publicized backing of long-time fan Bruce Springsteen, who frequently closed his shows with a version of 'Quarter to Three'. Bonds' comeback album, *Dedication*, was produced by Steve Van Zandt of Springsteen's E. Street Band, while the hit single 'This Little Girl Is Mine' (a Number 8 in the US during 1981) was a Springsteen composition. *On the Line* (1982) was another Springsteen/Van Zandt production.

BONEY M One of the most successful acts in the Eurodisco field, Boney M was the brainchild of German producer Frank Farian. Created specifically to perform Farian's music, they were put together in 1977 in Munich when one of his songs, spuriously credited to Boney M, required an act to sing it on television.

The record, 'Baby, Do You Wanna Bump?', a studio creation made entirely by session men, became a big hit in West Germany. Four black singers, Liz Mitchell, Marcia Barrett, Bobby Farrell and Maizie Williams

Gary Bonds astonished everyone by a re-emergence to stardom in 1981 almost two decades after his earliest recording successes

were recruited, but the first record they actually sang on the single was 'Daddy Cool'. It became the first of nine consecutive UK Top 10 hits, including, in 1978, two massive Number 1s, 'Rivers of Babylon'/'Brown Girl in the Ring' (in the charts for 40 weeks) and 'Mary's Boy Child'. They also had three UK Number 1 albums in a row, *Night Flight to Venus* (1978) being especially popular all over Europe, before the bubble burst with their last Top 40 single, 'I'm Born Again', in 1980.

BONZO DOG DOO DAH BAND

The Bonzos' first publicity photographs in 1966 implied that they were merely a Sixties version of the **Temperance Seven**, but interpretations of Twenties kitsch formed only part of their act. Formed by art students from several London colleges, the band began playing in pubs in 1965, and many of the members were still studying when the Bonzos moved on to clubs and cabaret in 1966.

The same year, the success of the New Vaudeville Band, another group of Twenties revivalists, encouraged the Bonzos to widen their musical range, and the result can be heard on their first, and most inventive, LP, *Gorilla* (Liberty, 1967), which includes characteristic Bonzo humour ('The Intro and the Outro'), Thirties novelty ('Mickey's Son and Daughter'), and rock ('The Equestrian Statue'). The band personnel was now stabilized and the final line-up consisted of Vivian Stanshall (vocals, trumpet); Neil Innes (vocals, piano), who produced most of the band's comic and satirical song material; Roger Ruskin Spear, who generally supervised the props, dummies and robots; Rodney Slater (sax); 'Legs' Larry Smith (drums); Vernon Dudley Bohay-Nowell (guitar, banjo); and Sam Spoons (Martin Stafford) (percussion). Following their 1968 British Top Five single, 'I'm the Urban Spaceman', the Bonzos became widely known through TV and concert appearances. Innes' influence made them increasingly psychedelic and rock-oriented, but Stanshall also retained his repertoire of pre-war curiosities, so that the Bonzos' act finally developed into a (literally) explosive display of school concert-like eclecticism.

The strain of having to devise new routines for their every appearance proved too great in 1970, and, after several albums, *The Doughnut in Granny's Greenhouse* (1968), *Tadpoles* (1969) and the legendary *Keynsham* (1969), the Bonzos went their separate

ways. Stanshall formed several new groups but eventually went solo and became a radio and TV personality (he was the narrator on **Mike Oldfield**'s *Tubular Bells*); Innes developed his composing talents, created the Beatles spoof *The Rutles* for television, and was a fixture in children's television programmes (*Puddle Lane*, *The Wide Awake Club*) in the mid-Eighties; Spear toured with his 'Kinetic Wardrobe', a one-man show; Slater left the business; and the others joined Bob Kerr's Whoopee Band, a cruder version of the Bonzos as they were in 1966.

BOOGIE WOOGIE

The style known as 'boogie woogie' remains essentially a piano idiom, in which blues are played with a prominent eight-to-the-bar left hand bass supporting right-hand improvisations. The style probably took shape as a club and dance-hall music, and was developed at house parties and similar gatherings during the Twenties and Thirties. The earliest record of the style was Pine Top Smith's 1928 performance 'Pine Top's Boogie Woogie', but examples were soon added by players like Meade Lux Lewis (especially his famous 'Honky Tonk Train Blues'), Albert Ammons, Pete Johnson (often in accompaniments to the blues-shouter **Joe Turner**) and many other blues pianists, such as the obscure but seminal Lee Green, Cripple Clarence Lofton, Montana Taylor and Romeo Nelson, all working around Chicago.

Ammons, Lewis and Johnson were among the most creative of these musicians, and it was appropriate that in the boogie-woogie craze of the Forties the three men should form a group and make a number of deft and exciting solo, duet and trio recordings. Another player to attain a reputation at that time was the Chicago-born Jimmy Yancey, an altogether individual player with a spare and restrained style far removed from the hard-driving attack favoured by most of his peers. After World War II a more brittle and showy kind of boogie woogie found wide favour, as played by musicians like Freddie Slack, and this was distantly echoed in the technically crude but well-received records of **Merrill Moore** and other performers on the fringe of rockabilly. Following the hit recording of 'Guitar Boogie' by country guitarist Arthur Smith, and the guitar duet stylings of hillbilly artists like the Delmore Brothers, there was a great fashion for boogie-woogie guitar, and Jimmy Yancey's bass figures appeared in the Delmores' 'Blues Stay Away From Me' and many contempor-

ary recordings, mostly based on Avery Parrish's piano solo 'After Hours'.

With the death of the creators and chief transmitters of boogie woogie, the idiom as a purely pianistic form passed to younger musicians who attempted, with varying success, to re-enact the documented originals. Both in America and Europe, there has been lively patronage of boogie-woogie piano playing; meanwhile the general lessons of the form have been incorporated into rock music in many ways, and are implicit in the manner, if rarely explicit in the repertoire, of innumerable bands.

BOOKER, JAMES

Rock'n'roll pianist/organist James Booker, who once declared, 'Between the penitentiary, the crazyhouse and the music business, I never had a chance!', was born in New Orleans on 17 December 1939, to a family with a long musical heritage, and was known as a child genius on piano. After recording for Imperial and Ace while still in his teens, he had a Number 43 national hit record in 1960 as Little Booker, with the frolicking R&B organ instrumental, 'Gonzo', on Peacock. He was much in demand for recording sessions in New Orleans in the early Sixties but then sank from sight. It was another ten years before he began to do justice to his undoubted talents by playing with such rock luminaries as **Dr John** and the **Doobie Brothers**.

BOOKER T. AND THE MGs

For ten years, Booker T. and the MGs were the nucleus of the Stax Records houseband, and the cornerstone of the company, its sound, and its success. Their line-up comprised Booker T. Jones (born 11 December 1944, in Memphis), a multi-instrumentalist, primarily on keyboards; **Steve Cropper** (21 October 1941), guitar; Al Jackson (17 November 1945), drums; and Donald 'Duck' Dunn (24 November 1941), bass, who replaced original bassist Louis Steinberg. 'MG' stood for 'Memphis Group'.

Originally the rhythm section of the **Mar-Keys**, the four men were recorded at an impromptu session minus horns, resulting in 'Green Onions', a bluesy organ riff slashed through by Cropper's razor-sharp tones, riding on a simple but persuasive bass and drum line. Issued on the new subsidiary Volt, it was transferred to the parent Stax label and distributed by Atlantic to a million sales in August 1962. Tighter than the average small R&B combo, their economic and expressive interplay of ideas was effective on moody, small-hours blues or hard-driving dance tunes, displayed in over a dozen albums and 20 more singles, including 'Bootleg' (1965), 'Hip Hug-Her', 'Groovin'' (1967), 'Soul Limbo' (1968), and 'Time Is Tight' (1969) from their soundtrack to the film *Uptight*. Even more impressive was their contribution to virtually every hit created in the Stax studio in the Sixties. They backed not only the company's own stars, but also provided other Atlantic artists with the most consistently successful answer to the Motown Sound.

In 1971, tired of the pressures in a company that had long outgrown its intimate beginnings, Booker T. escaped to a new career with his wife, Priscilla Coolidge (sister of Rita), on the West Coast; Dunn stayed on in Memphis; Cropper became a roving writer/producer and sessionman. Jackson

remained a leading session drummer until his death in a shooting incident in 1975. Jones, Cropper and Dunn reunited for recording sessions in 1976 and 1978, with Willie Hall (ex-Bar-Kays) joining in Jackson's place. *See also* **Stax Records**

BOOMTOWN RATS Emerging out of Dublin at the same time as the **Sex Pistols** were making their presence felt on the UK punk scene, the Boomtown Rats were among the first of the new wave bands to break into the mainstream. They went on to become one of the best selling acts to have come out of Eire, with a string of increasingly eloquent and sophisticated singles that won over a wide following and considerable critical acclaim.

Formed in 1975 as Bound for Glory, the group consisted of Garry Roberts (guitar/lead vocals), Johnny Fingers

(keyboards), Gerry Cott (guitar), Pete Briquette (bass), Simon Crowe (drums) and Bob Geldof, ex-bulldozer driver, English teacher and journalist, who alternated between the posts of manager and lead vocalist. By 1977, after intensive gigging around Ireland, a successful trip to Holland and a re-organization that involved Geldof fronting the band full-time and writing many of their lyrics, they had progressed from their R&B roots and, re-named the Boomtown Rats, moved to London after signing a deal with Ensign. The first album, *The Boomtown Rats*, was released in August and the single taken from it, 'Looking After No. 1' reached Number 11 the same month, establishing them as a top-flight punk/new wave act and the first to crack the UK charts.

A couple of minor hits followed, but it was their second, and their best, album, *A Tonic for the Troops* released in June '78, that made the big breakthrough. It reached Number 8, stayed on the UK LP chart for 44 weeks, and contained the single 'Rat Trap', which gave them their first Number 1. The Boomtown Rats, and especially the articulate, media-conscious Geldof, were much sought after.

While on a promotional visit to the US in 1979, Geldof heard the story of Brenda Spencer, a 16-year-old Californian who took potshots at the people in her school yard on a Monday morning, killing two of them. Her stated rationale behind this act provided him with the story for their next – and best-known – single, 'I Don't Like Mondays', which reached Number 1 in both the UK and Australia, but was virtually banned from US airplay on the grounds that it could be prejudicial to the girl's defence. It was also the standout track on an otherwise drab album, *The Fine Art of Surfacing*, which was released later the same year.

The year 1980 found the Boomtown Rats maintaining a high level of popularity; the singles 'Someone Looking at You' and 'Banana Republic' both made the UK Top 5 and the band completed an exhausting world tour. But with the arrival of 1981, and the LP *Mondo Bongo*, the group's fortunes started to go into decline. The album received poor reviews and it was also the last to feature guitarist Cott, who left the band soon after its release. The Rats continued as a five-piece, and another album, *V Deep*, appeared the next year but performed very badly in the chart, reaching only Number 64. Their last Top 30 single was 'House on Fire' in March 1982. Had it not been for Geldof's constant presence in the

Memphis-based Stax label artists Booker T. and the MGs, one of the few racially integrated bands of the Sixties: (left to right) Donald 'Duck' Dunn, Booker T. Jones, Steve Cropper and Al Jackson Jr

Bob Geldof with Rats Pete Briquette and Gerry Cott

All-American Pat Boone performing in The Main Attraction

media due to his well-publicized relationship with TV personality Paula Yates and his founding of **Band Aid**, the Boomtown Rats would have been all but forgotten.

Geldof's commitments to Band Aid were often cited as the cause of the Boomtown Rats' fall from grace, but in fact the decline had set in long before. The group continued to tour into '86, but it was indicative of their standing with audiences that the most rapturous applause always came when the band performed 'Do They Know It's Christmas', the song Geldof had written with Midge Ure for Band Aid.

In June 1986, Geldof was created a Knight of the British Empire (KBE) and also in that year, he was nominated for the Nobel Peace prize, but lost out to American author and human rights campaigner Elie Wiesel.

In October of the same year he released his first solo single, 'This Is the World Calling' and an album *Deep in the Heart of Nowhere*.

BOONE, PAT Born Charles Eugene Pat Boone on 1 June 1934, in Jacksonville, Florida, Pat Boone was, next to **Elvis Presley**, the most successful singer of the early rock'n'roll era, with dozens of hit singles stretching from 1955 to the early Sixties. He was popular simply because he was the total opposite of Presley in every respect. Where Elvis was sensual, menacing and intense, Boone was the decent, All-American Boy (with a neat

and pretty wife and four kids) who refused to kiss the leading ladies in his films. His records represented the successful domestication of the predominantly black sound of rock-'n'roll, his polite tenor transforming it into an acceptable sound for the children of Middle America.

Boone moved to Nashville as a child, where his early years found him singing C&W for Republic Records – he married C&W star Red Foley's daughter Shirley – and studying for his degree in English and Speech. In 1955 he was signed to Dot Records by the astute Randy Wood, who turned Boone into the king of the cover versions. In 1955–6 he recorded somewhat embarrassed versions of 'Ain't That a Shame', 'Tutti Frutti' and 'Long Tall Sally'. All were big hits.

At this point, Boone was a fully-fledged teenage idol as well as a Columbia University student and a permanent member of the Arthur Godfrey Show. On record he graduated to insipid romantic ballads, while screen roles in *Bernadine* and *April Love* made him the Number 3 box office attraction of 1957.

Pat Boone's hits of 1957 to 1962 – records like 'Love Letters in the Sand', 'April Love' (1957), 'If Dreams Came True', and 'Sugar Moon' (1958) – had only tenuous connections with rock. They represented the essence of the Pat Boone sound, a lush crooning style in the Bing Crosby tradition. The only exceptions were his two solitary Top

10 records after 1958, the powerfully arranged death ditty, 'Moody River' (1961) and the mock-Mexican 'Speedy Gonzales' (1962).

Part of the Boone legacy is his book, *'Twixt Twelve and Twenty*, a manual for good, wholesome teenage living. The contents are entirely in character – get your hair cut, don't go to parties without a chaperone, don't rebel against authority because they know best. For many teenagers caught between the raucous rebellion of authentic rock'n'roll and parental hostility, the Boone compromise came as a welcome relief. Few, however, shared his fundamentalist Christianity, which has grown stronger over the years. His occasional performances are now mostly in a religious context, usually with members of his large, all-singing family. His daughter Debby reached Number 1 in the US in 1977 with 'You Light Up My Life'.

BOSTON Mainstream American rock band Boston appeared in a blaze of glory in 1976 with the fastest selling debut album in rock history. The brainchild of Tom Scholz (guitar/keyboards), a senior product designer for Polaroid who recorded tapes in his spare time, the band adopted a successful formula aptly described by him as 'power guitars, harmony vocals and double-guitar leads'.

Scholz played his tapes to Epic Records, who signed him, with a group of local musicians, Brad Delp (guitar/vocals), Barry Goudreau (guitar), Fran Sheehan (bass) and Sib Hashian (drums) making up the band. The resulting album, *Boston*, was essentially a reworking of Scholz's tapes done on 24-track. It sold $6\frac{1}{2}$ million copies and Boston became immediate members of the stadium band super-league.

Their second album, *Don't Look Back*, appeared two years later, but showed no departure from the formula of the first album, and sold a relatively disappointing $3\frac{1}{2}$ million copies. A waning interest in the band sent them into a prolonged period of inactivity; their third album, *Third Stage* didn't appear until 1986.

BOVELL, DENNIS In his own right as a solo artist and producer, and as leader of **Matumbi**, Dennis Bovell is undoubtedly the single greatest reggae talent Britain has so far produced. Starting out in the early 1970s as key musician and songwriter with Matumbi, Bovell had by mid-decade become the most in demand and successful British reggae producer – in the same week in 1976 that Janet Kay's Bovell-produced single 'Silly Games' first topped the British reggae charts (also a UK Number 2 pop hit), no less than 16 out of the remaining 19 entries in the Top 20 were Bovell productions! As Matumbi gradually split up during the late 1970s, Bovell effortlessly made the transition to solo artist and, later, leader of the Dub Band (in reality, a line-up who reproduced onstage what Bovell the multi-instrumentalist was recording in his own South London Studio 80).

Bovell's greatest solo outing to date is the 1981 double album *Brain Damage*, which he wrote, played and produced entirely on his own. It took reggae deep into previously uncharted waters – to the considerable outrage of the purist audience, who were particularly incensed by Bovell's reworking of the Matumbi classic 'After Tonight'. Bovell declared that he had done this because 'too many reggae listeners are too set in their ways, their brains have ossified'. At the same time, Bovell's production work for **Linton Kwesi Johnson** demonstrates a sure touch for in-the-tradition reggae when called for. A major talent, he is perhaps *too* talented for his own commercial good.

BOW WOW WOW Created in 1980 out of the ashes of the original Ants (**Adam Ant**'s backing group) by ex-**Sex Pistols** svengali **Malcolm McLaren**, Bow Wow Wow were designed with qualities that were part of the blueprint for all future pop groups: teenage sex appeal, Burundi drum rhythms, spaghetti Western guitar lines and a sense of adolescent abandon.

Bow Wow Wow fronted by Annabella Lwin and packaged by McLaren

Ex-Ants Matthew Ashman (guitar), Lee Gorman (bass) and Dave Barbarossa (drums) were now fronted by the then 14-year-old Burmese beauty Annabella Lwin, who – the legend goes – had been discovered in a North London launderette by McLaren. His manipulative management secured a huge deal with EMI and a hit single, 'C30, C60, C90, Go', followed by the innovative tape-only release 'Your Cassette Pet' which encouraged under-age sex and home taping and was promoted with the slogan 'sun, sea and piracy'.

Signed now to RCA, they released a debut album *See Jungle! See Jungle!* (1981) that was an exhilarating mix of influences as Bow Wow Wow exploited Annabella's youthful infectiousness; from it, they scored another single hit with 'Go Wild in the Country'. The rough edges were smoothed off by producer Kenny Laguna on the 1982 bubblegum hit 'I Want Candy', and by the time their Mike Chapman-produced third album *When the Going Gets Tough, the Tough Get Going* (1983) was released, they had passed into blandness. Shortly afterwards, Annabella quit and later re-appeared as a solo artist.

BOWIE, DAVID The single most influential performer in British rock since the early Seventies, David Bowie (who was born David Jones in Brixton, London, on 8 January 1947) started his musical career playing tenor saxophone for a school group at the age of 15. A year later he was in a progressive blues group, the Lower Third, until, 'frustrated by amps', he went solo with an acoustic guitar and recorded a series of confessional love songs sung in an **Anthony Newley** style for Decca; these were re-released in 1973 as *Images 1966–67*.

The music didn't set the world on fire, and Bowie dropped out of the music business for almost two years, pursuing his involvement with Buddhism almost to the point of a head-shave, and writing and performing for Lindsay Kemp's mime company. In 1969 he went out again with a guitar and started an arts lab in Beckenham to 'try and promote the ideals and creative processes of the underground'. At the same time he recorded the mysterious 'Space Oddity' for Mercury, which surprisingly became an international hit. As a result, he went on tour as a support act, but he did not enjoy the experience, and went back to his one-man show in Beckenham.

So by the turn of the decade there was little sign of the superstar to come.

Bowie was initially criticised as 'just an image', but he has proved his enduring talents not only for music, but drama and mime as well

The ingredients of his music, though, were slowly gathering, and the ideological themes of the *Space Oddity* album would be followed, in a logical enough way, right through to the Orwellian cataclysm of *Diamond Dogs* in 1974. The ideals of the underground provided the social framework, the commitment to change. Buddhism supplied the paradoxes and vicious circles that made a mockery of those hopes. His interest in mime suggested the theatrical context in which the themes would be presented.

The music to complement the vision was also coming together. His second, and last, album for Mercury, *The Man Who Sold the World* (1970), featured **Mick Ronson** and Mick Woodmansey on guitar and drums; they would later form his backing group with Trevor Bolder. *The Man Who Sold the World* was a far cry from the acoustic *Space Oddity*, featuring dark and heavy music, Ronson's vicious guitar riffs and a spacey moog, Bowie's voice at its coldest and most metallic. The music suited the subjects: outsiders drifting on the edge of sanity, through a netherworld of sexual doubts and death-wishes.

The album started a cult following for Bowie, particularly in America, where he toured as a latter-day Garbo, complete with long dresses and flowing hair. But a cult following was not what he wanted, and the next album saw the pendulum wrenched violently to the other extreme. *Hunky Dory* (1971), the first RCA album, saw his voice at its warmest and his tunes at their most melodic. It was still a tortured vision but it didn't *sound* it. And it started the bandwagon rolling in earnest. By early 1972 Bowie was the coming star. He had the image and the album ready to make the most of it. Not that *The Rise and Fall of Ziggy Stardust and the Spiders from Mars* (1972) was anything other than an artistic advance on the earlier albums. The diverse personae struggling for precedence in his previous work were all subsumed in the doomed figure of Ziggy, Bowie's solution to the paradox of a life both unchangeable and unacceptable, the rock'n'roll star who stood outside the problem and so could solve it. Musically it claimed the middle ground between *The Man Who Sold the World* and *Hunky Dory*, between acid-rock and pop, heavy and accessible. Imagewise it turned Bowie into Ziggy, the bisexual astronaut from another world, both harbinger of doom and prophet of extravagance.

Ziggy Stardust was to be the first of four monolithic concept albums, over all of which hovered this spectre of doom. *Aladdin Sane* (1973) was Bowie's most realized album, showcasing all his talents and few of his faults. The lyrics were clear and insightful, rather than spectacularly obscure, and Bowie's musical eclecticism served as a springboard rather than as an end in itself. Above all, Mick Ronson was finally let off the leash, which enabled him to conjure out of his guitar the necessary blind power to set beside Bowie's driving vocals.

Aladdin Sane viewed the disintegration of world society from the vantage point of an American tour; *Pin-Ups* demonstrated the process by dressing up the hopes of mid-Sixties British music in 1975 guise. Thus, for example, the **Kinks'** 'Where Have All the Good Times Gone' was given a resonance beyond mere nostalgia. *Diamond Dogs* (1974) was the culmination of this phase; a musical re-working of Orwell's *1984*, that sorely missed the departed Ronson's guitar. Despite its limitations it presented Bowie's vision at its most acute, tying together the themes of the previous years. Ziggy's spaceman-rock hero-saviour mutates into the doomed figure of George Orwell's Winston Smith.

The bisexual astronaut tours of 1972–3 became the Bowie Armageddon extravaganza of 1974, with the star in powder-blue Oxford bags singing of

Bowie's frequent changes of musical style and stage performance reflect an insatiable taste for experiment; this is the 1978 version of the man

the end of it all beneath vast theatrical props of the urban desert. After that, however, came an abrupt change of course with *Young Americans* (1975), on which he emulated the Philadelphia soul sound at the city's Sigma Sound Studios. 'Fame', co-written with **John Lennon** and featuring his guest vocals, was lifted from the album to become Bowie's first US Number 1. By 1975, too, he had turned his attention to acting, starring in Nicolas Roeg's *The Man Who Fell to Earth*.

1976 brought another Bowie excursion into what he himself called 'plastic soul' with *Station to Station*, a transitional album that wrapped up the past four years and opened the doors to the next three. His persona this time was the Thin White Duke, and the music was cold, metallic and densely produced – a hint at the electronic music that would follow. In London in 1976 he met Brian Eno, late of **Roxy Music**, and the two worked together in Berlin on a cycle of experimental albums. *Low* and *'Heroes'* (both 1977) found Bowie deliberately distancing himself from the pop mainstream, and the final Eno collaboration, *Lodger* (1979), was a patchy set notable for his extended use of the random 'cut up' or collage technique of writing pioneered by novelist William Burroughs. As if sensing his recording career had reached a hiatus, Bowie returned to acting and turned in a very well-received performance on the Broadway stage as *The Elephant Man*.

Scary Monsters (1980) was Bowie's next album, a venture into modernist electro-pop with bubbling synthesizers and distorted electric guitar courtesy of ex-**King Crimson** leader **Robert Fripp**. It was his biggest seller for some years and contained his first UK Number 1 since 1975, 'Ashes to Ashes', the lyrics of which updated the story of Major Tom told in 'Space Oddity'. A three-year silence followed, broken only by an extended-play release of music from *Baal*, a Brecht play in which Bowie appeared on British television, and a single recorded with **Queen**, 'Under Pressure' (1981), which was another UK chart-topper. In 1982, he starred in the films *The Hunger* and *Merry Christmas Mr Lawrence*, and switched record companies, moving from RCA to EMI for *Let's Dance* (1983), produced by Bowie in collaboration with Nile Rodgers of **Chic**. Bowie called it 'the most positive, emotional, uplifting album I've made in a long time', and its title track reached Number 1 in both the US and UK charts. *Tonight* followed in 1984, providing the hit single 'Blue

Jean' (Number 6 in the UK, Number 8 in the US), and in 1985 he formed two new temporary partnerships for recording purposes – with the Pat Metheny Group for 'This is Not America' (taken from the soundtrack of *The Falcon and the Snowman*), and with Mick Jagger for 'Dancing in the Street'. Released in aid of Live Aid and premiered during the July 1985 internationally networked concert, the duet reached Number 1 on both sides of the Atlantic and in many countries across the world.

Clichés about Bowie's chameleon-like character abound, but as a general rule he has spent his career anticipating trends rather than following them. It is precisely his ability to change and experiment that has enabled him to survive in the rock world, while maintaining a level of critical and commercial success almost unequalled within post-**Beatles** popular music.

BOX TOPS Along with the **Gentrys**, the Box Tops – Alex Chilton, lead guitar; Billy Cunningham, bass; Gary Talley, guitar; Danny Smythe, drums; and John Evans, organ – were among the few white acts to achieve success from the soul-oriented studios of Memphis during the late Sixties. Formed in 1967, they recorded at American Recording Studios with Chips Moman, **Dan Penn** and **Spooner Oldham**, who wrote their third hit ('Cry Like a Baby', a Number 2 in the US in 1968) and produced all their major hits, including their first, 'The Letter', a strong and intensely catchy record that went to Number 1 in the US in the late summer of 1967, and has since been successfully covered by many others including **Joe Cocker**.

Although they had many subsequent US Top 40 hits ('Neon Rainbow', 'Choo Choo Train', 'I Met Her in a Church', 'Sweet Cream Ladies, Forward March', and 'Soul Deep'), only 'Cry Like a Baby'

The Box Tops at the height of their popularity in 1968: a perfectly packaged group that had a string of hits in the US charts

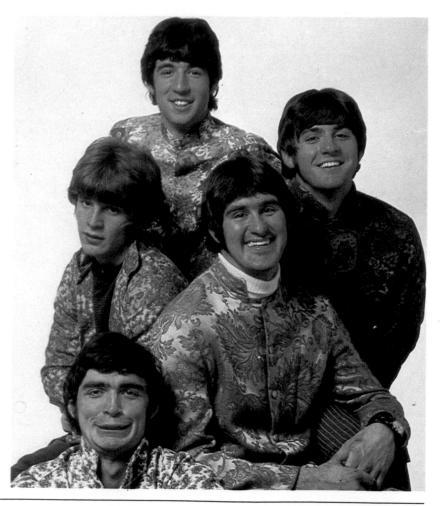

approached the sales of 'The Letter', and the Box Tops never managed to sustain their popularity. After they disbanded in early 1970, lead singer Alex Chilton (whose winsome voice had made the Box Tops' records so appealing) joined up with his songwriting partner Chris Bell and other pop-minded Mempheans at the newly formed Ardent Productions to form **Big Star**, a group that released two highly acclaimed albums: *Number 1 Record* (1972) and *Radio City* (1974). The group disbanded in 1975 and Bell was killed in a car crash three years later, just as Chilton's solo career was beginning to take off. Chilton's subsequent albums include *One Day in New York* and the UK-made *Like Flies on Sherbert* (1980). *See also* **Big Star**

Billy Bragg: an improbable success in the hi-tech Eighties music scene

BRAGG, BILLY Born in Barking, Essex on 20 December 1957, radical left-wing singer/songwriter Billy Bragg is one of the most unlikely success stories of the Eighties. Touring constantly across Europe and the US as a one man show – aided solely by electric guitar and amplifier – he produced protest lyrics and tuneful stripped-down lone minstrel performances that were completely at odds with the studio- and technology-dominated mid-Eighties music scene.

Bragg's musical career started in 1977 with Riff Raff, a punk/R&B band operating in and around Peterborough in Northamptonshire. The band split in 1981 and Bragg spent a very brief stint in the army – he bought himself out for £175 after only 90 days. In 1982 he reappeared as a solo artist and set about gigging non-stop all over Britain, where through sheer hard work he built up a sizeable cult following with his thrilling live performances. His first LP, *Life's a Riot With Spy vs Spy*, originally recorded on two track as a demo, was released on independent label Go!

Discs after all the major labels turned Bragg down. In the shops in November 1983, it sold over 135,000 copies. A year later, his second LP *Brewing Up With Billy Bragg* was released to great acclaim, peaking at Number 16 in the UK chart. January 1985 saw **Kirsty MacColl**'s version of Bragg's best known song, 'A New England', rise to Number 7 in the UK singles chart and pave the way for his own 'Between the Wars' EP to appear in April.

By in the latter half of '85, he had generated a great deal of interest in the US, and released his second single, 'Days Like These', and he continues to play the innumerable benefit gigs in aid of many and varied causes for which he has become famous. Bragg released a third LP, *Talking with the Tax Man about Poetry*, in 1986.

BRANIGAN, LAURA American mainstream rock songstress Laura Branigan (born 2 July 1955) scored a handful of transatlantic solo hits between 1982–84. Considered too poppy by hard rock enthusiasts, Branigan took the single 'Gloria' to the US Number 2 spot in 1982 (Number 6 in the UK) but really surprised audiences with the subtle and far superior 'Self Control' in 1984. She also released two albums in that period with the awe-inspiring titles *Laura Branigan* (1982) and *Laura Branigan 2* (1983).

BREAD A Los Angeles soft-rock harmony group who racked up six gold albums in a career lasting less than four years, Bread was formed in 1969 by three session musicians – David Gates from Tulsa, Oklahoma, James Griffin from Memphis, Tennessee, and Robb Royer. Gates had previously produced an album by Pleasure Faire, a group that included Royer and for which Griffin had written songs. All were multi-instrumentalists and prolific songwriters in that professional manner which at its best can marry the emotional power of rock with the smoothness of mainstream balladry. After an unsuccessful but critically acclaimed first album for Elektra, the hits started coming: 'Make It With You' (1970); 'If' (later recycled by TV cop Telly Savalas), 'Baby I'm-a Want You' (1971); and 'The Guitar Man' (1972). These and other songs mostly featured David Gates' high, pure and countryish tenor.

Although Jim Gordon played drums on the first album, Mike Botts from Sacramento, California, joined as permanent percussionist. Between the third and fourth albums (*Manna*, 1971, and *Baby I'm-a Want You*, 1972), Royer

left to be replaced by veteran session keyboards man Larry Knechtel. Following one more album (*Guitar Man*, 1972), the group dissolved following disagreements between Griffin and Gates, both of whom became solo artists. Bread re-formed in late 1976 for an album, *Lost Without Your Love*, but disbanded within the year. Gates' solo hits have included 'Never Let Her Go' (1975) and 'The Goodbye Girl' (1978, from the film of the same name).

BREAKDANCING/BREAKING An integral part of the hip hop/electro funk scene that emerged out of New York via deejays/rappers like **Afrika Bambaataa** and **Grandmaster Flash** at the end of the Seventies, break dancing, or breaking, is the name applied to a specific form of supra-athletic dancing (including head and back spins) practised by hip hop fans. It takes its name from 'breaks' – the drum and percussion passages on records played by hip hop deejays (deejays would often play only the break part of the records). Some observers of break dancing have suggested that the designation follows from the fact that careless practitioners are likely to break some of their bones; appropriate, but wrong.

BREWER AND SHIPLEY A close-harmony duo best known for their 1971 song 'One Toke Over the Line', which was eventually banned from the airwaves because of its drug connotations, Mike Brewer (born in Oklahoma in 1944) and Tom Shipley (born in Ohio in 1942) teamed up as songwriters under contract to A&M in 1965. They cut an uneventful album for the label before moving to Kama Sutra to work with San Francisco producer Nick Gravenites. *Weeds* (1970) and *Tarkio* (1971) were fine examples of Bay Area soft rock, with backing by Nicky Hopkins, Jerry Garcia, Mark Naftalin and Red Rhodes.

Based in rural Missouri, Brewer and Shipley cut two more albums for Kama Sutra – *Shake Off the Demon* (1971) and *Rural Space* (1972) – before moving to Capitol in 1974. After two albums, they switched to Mercury for *Not Far From Free* (1978).

BRINSLEY SCHWARZ The band called Brinsley Schwarz was comprised of **Nick Lowe**, bass; Bob Andrews, keyboards; Billy Rankin, drums; Ian Gomm, guitar; and Brinsley himself, guitar and sax. The nucleus of the group came from Kippington Lodge, an unsuccessful harmony group that was signed to EMI's Parlophone label in the mid-Sixties by Mark Wirtz. In 1970, on the verge of collapse, they signed a management contract as Brinsley Schwarz with Famepushers, who signed them to British Liberty/UA with the biggest piece of hype in rock's recent history: they flew the British press to witness the group's debut at New York's Fillmore East. The hype failed – though, ironically, the album that accompanied it, *Brinsley Schwarz* (Liberty, 1970), which was an uneasy mixture of 'heavy' blues and **Crosby, Stills and Nash**-type harmonies, turned out to be their biggest seller.

However, after a promising second album, the aptly titled *Despite It All* (1970), they came back with two magnificent albums, *Silver Pistol* (UA, 1971) and *Nervous on the Road* (1972). The change stemmed from the band's assimilation of influences seemingly as diverse as **The Band** and New Orleans R&B, Nick Lowe's development as a songwriter and singer, the addition of Ian Gomm on guitar, which thickened their sound, and the group's renewed pleasure in playing tightly together during their pioneering discovery of the pub circuit then opening up in London. But, though those and subsequent albums – *Please Don't Ever Change* (1973) and *The New Favourites of . . .* (1974) – were critically well received, they didn't sell.

In 1975, tired of the endless touring, either as the support act to less talented groups, or as the 'stars' of the pub circuit, the Brinsleys broke up. All the members pursued independent projects, with Nick Lowe enjoying the most notable subsequent success. *See also* **Nick Lowe**

BRISTOL, JOHNNY When singer

Johnny Bristol's **Barry White**-influenced 'Hang On in There Baby' (MGM) soared up the UK and US charts in 1974, it was the culmination of a 14-year career. Bristol's first release in 1961 was as part of the duo Johnny and Jackey, who recorded for Tri-Phi; Jackey was Jackey Beavers. The song was the original version of 'Someday We'll Be Together', which in 1969 became an American chart-topper for the **Supremes**. After the duo's demise, Bristol worked at Motown, writing and producing for the **(Detroit) Spinners**. With **Harvey Fuqua**, he was responsible for a string of hits including **Marvin Gaye** and **Tammi Terrell**'s 'Ain't No Mountain High Enough' (1967) and **Stevie Wonder**'s 'Yester-Me, Yester-You, Yesterday' (1969). Bristol's greatest success, however, was undoubtedly with **Junior Walker**

and the All Stars, who scored a massive chain of hits. In 1973, Bristol left Motown and joined US Columbia as a house producer, working with **O.C. Smith**, **Boz Scaggs**, **Jerry Butler**, **Buddy Miles** and others. Because Columbia would not sign him as a solo artist, he negotiated an outside deal with MGM, for whom he recorded his 1974 hit and a well-received album of the same name. He subsequently recorded for Polydor (*Bristol Creme*, 1976) and Hansa (*Free to Be Me*, 1981), besides producing albums for **Johnny Mathis**, **Tom Jones**, Tavares and various other acts.

BRITISH R&B The British R&B

boom of the Sixties that produced the **Rolling Stones**, the **Animals** and a whole wealth of new rock talent in London and the regions had its roots in the Fifties jazz scene and the efforts of **Chris Barber**, **Alexis Korner** and **Cyril Davies** in particular. A key event was the 1955 transformation, by Korner and Davies, of the Skiffle Centre (at the Roundhouse pub in London's Wardour Street) into the London Blues and Barrelhouse Club. The club's Thursday night sessions drew local enthusiasts and, later, visiting American bluesmen like **Muddy Waters**, **Otis Spann**, and **Big Bill Broonzy**.

Chris Barber had meanwhile been experimenting with blues within the framework of his traditional jazz band since 1953, when a blues trio featuring himself (bass), Beryl Bryden (washboard) and **Lonnie Donegan** (vocals, guitar) previewed the skiffle craze. Through the late Fifties, when his popularity was at a peak, he brought a series of blues artists to Britain to tour with his band – Bill Broonzy, Sister Rosetta Tharpe, **Sonny Terry and Brownie McGhee**, and, most significantly in 1958, Muddy Waters, whose use of amplification which so offended the 'purists' inspired Davies and Korner to wire up their own instruments.

After an American tour the following year, when he saw Muddy Waters play in Chicago, Barber invited Davies (harmonica) and Korner (guitar) to back his singer (and wife) Ottilie Patterson for brief R&B sets during his band's performances. So successful was this innovation that Davies and Korner left to form their own electric R&B band, Blues Incorporated. However, Barber stuck to jazz, seeing his music threatened by the debased 'trad' fad at the start of the Sixties, and didn't return to R&B until he replaced acoustic bass and banjo with bass and

lead guitars in 1964 when, ironically, he was condemned as a bandwagoner.

Initially shunned by the clannish jazz club circuit, Davies and Korner opened their own club in a basement beneath the ABC teashop, near Ealing Broadway Underground station, on 17 March 1962. Blues Incorporated was the houseband, but the club was a spawning ground for R&B groups like the Stones and **Manfred Mann**, whose future members would jam regularly. At the beginning of May, Blues Inc. were offered a residency for a Thursday 'Rhythm and Blues Night' at the Marquee Club, 165 Oxford Street, W1, where two months later the Rolling Stones made their first public appearance. During that summer another West End jazz club, the Flamingo in Wardour Street, was developing its own brand of R&B with the Blue Flames, whose leader, **Georgie Fame**, quickly absorbed the musical tastes of the predominantly black audience.

As the music's following grew, jazz clubs turned to R&B as a substitute for the increasingly lifeless trad, and new clubs opened around London's suburbs. By 1963 a distinct club circuit had evolved and a wave of bands had emerged to fill them.

Under the broad banner of R&B there were four basic and distinct forms: the long-hair-and-maracas rock style of the Stones and later groups like the **Yardbirds**, the **Pretty Things** and the Downliners Sect; the 'black' Flamingo sound, pioneered by Fame and adopted by **George 'Zoot' Money**'s Big Roll Band, **Chris Farlowe** and the Thunderbirds, Ronnie Jones and the Nightimers, and other resident groups; and following Davies' split with Korner in November 1962, the uncompromising revival of 1958 Muddy Waters by Davies' R&B All-Stars – which had parallels in **John Mayall**'s self-styled blues crusade – and the subsequently jazzier, horn-driven riffing of Korner's Blues Inc. and **Graham Bond**'s spin-off Organisation.

So engrossed was the music industry with the Northern groups boom (and the feeble Home Counties competition from the **Dave Clark Five** and **Brian Poole** and the Tremeloes) that London's R&B movement flourished almost unnoticed by record companies and the pop press. Moreover, the music being played in the R&B clubs was generally considered too rough-hewn for conventional taste. What changed this notion was the Top 10 success of the Stones' second single, 'I Wanna Be Your Man', in the first week of January

1964. Previously, only a handful of R&B records had been released – their status plainly indicated by the budget price tag on Blues Incorporated's *R&B from the Marquee*. But as 1964 progressed, the releases multiplied.

Hit singles, of course, forced groups out of the clubs into ballrooms across the country, and they were frequently obliged to dilute their style. The groups that replaced them in the clubs had invariably learned their repertoire at second hand from their predecessors,

and this double effect of success brought about the grass roots breakdown of British R&B. The other factor was the source of the music itself. Faced in 1962 with an apparently inexhaustible reservoir of black music dating back over many years, few musicians had contemplated the possibility of it drying up and the need to provide their own material. Yet even before the boom started, influential figures like **Chuck Berry**, **Bo Diddley**, **John Lee Hooker**, **Jimmy Reed** and Muddy

Waters had passed their creative peak, and by 1965 the music of black America had moved on to a level of sophistication that precluded, on the whole, re-creation by British groups.

The Stones showed the way when, after several early derivative R&B-based attempts, Mick Jagger and Keith Richard developed a distinctive songwriting style of their own. Not every band had the inclination or the ability to adapt; some broke up, others hung on unchanged for a while. But for those who made the change, R&B had been an invaluable apprenticeship.

A young Jagger sits in as vocalist with Blues Incorporated (from left, Korner, Bruce and Davies) in the early days of the British R&B boom

BRONSKI BEAT One of the few openly homosexual bands, Bronski Beat became a major transatlantic success in the mid-Eighties with a bouncy, danceable blend of electro-pop and radical gay politics.

Formed in South London in 1983 by two Glaswegians, Steve Bronski and Jimmy Somerville, and an East Londoner, Larry Steinbachek, Bronski Beat began by playing in London's pubs and clubs. Before long Somerville's distinctive, high-pitched voice backed by the rhythmic electronic work-outs of the other two started to get attention, and the music press gave them plenty of positive coverage. Signed to London, they released their debut single 'Smalltown Boy', a remarkable record that frankly discussed the problems of young gays, and became a surprise UK Number 3. More singles, 'Why?', 'It Ain't Necessarily So' and 'I Feel Love' (a cover of the **Donna Summer** song sung with Marc Almond of **Soft Cell**) followed it into the UK charts and an album, *The Age of Consent* (1984) also sold well.

But their whirlwind success and Somerville's radical politics did not mix. The rift that began with his conviction on a charge of gross indecency, causing the cancellation of a visit to the US just as the trio were beginning to break there, grew to a crisis in early '85, when Somerville left. He formed a duo, the **Communards**, with a friend, pianist Richard Coles, and continued a successful recording career with their first release, 'You Are My World'. In 1986, they had a huge Number 1 hit with their cover of 'Don't Leave Me This Way'.

Bronski Beat also continued with a new vocalist, Jon Foster, and scored hits almost straight away with 'Hit That Perfect Beat' and 'C'mon C'mon', notably devoid of the political content of some of their earlier work.

BROOKS, ELKIE A noted British rock singer who made the leap to international stardom in 1977 with a little help from old hands **Leiber and Stoller**, Elkie Brooks was born in Manchester on 25 February 1945. She began singing at 15 as 'Manchester's answer to **Brenda Lee**', later joining Eric Delaney's dance band and working with Humphrey Lyttelton as a jazz singer. After a spell as a session and back-up singer, she joined up with guitarist Pete Gage (born 31 August 1947), formerly the arranger with Geno Washington's Ram Jam Band, in DaDa, an experimental progressive 12-piece jazz/rock band that cut one album for Atlantic in 1971.

Elkie Brooks enjoys a jet-setting lifestyle, plied with champagne by Record Mirror's *ace reporter of the Sixties, Norman Jopling*

DaDa was the prototype for Vinegar Joe, which emerged in the following year to critical acclaim. A hard-driving soul-inflected band, it was again led by Gage and the vocals were shared by Elkie Brooks and **Robert Palmer** (born 19 January 1949). Brooks' energetic **Tina Turner**-style stage presence caused a stir, but the group's records – *Vinegar Joe* (Island, 1972), *Rock 'n' Roll Gypsies* (1972), and *Six Star General* (1973) – didn't make the charts. They disbanded in 1974, with Palmer and Brooks both set on solo careers. She moved temporarily to the US, joined Southern rock band Wet Willie as a backing singer and toured with them for just over a year.

Her first solo album, recorded in Britain, was *Rich Man's Woman* (A&M, 1975), which included a number of self-written tracks. The album caused a few ripples of interest without accomplishing much commercially, but for *Two Days Away* (1977) she worked with producers Leiber and Stoller and found a much surer commercial touch. Two singles taken from it, 'Pearl's a Singer' and 'Sunshine After the Rain' became Top 10 UK hits. 'Lilac Wine', 'Don't Cry Out Loud' (both 1978) and 'Fool If You Think It's Over' (1982) provided further Top 20 placings, though success in the US proved more elusive. She has a strong MOR following, and albums like *Live and Learn* (1982) and the film-song set *Screen Gems* (1984) seem a far cry from her blues-singing days, but she chooses her material well – her versions of the **Moody Blues**' 'Nights in White Satin' and **Neil Young**'s 'Only Love Can Break Your Heart', both minor UK hits, are especially notable.

BROONZY, BIG BILL Born in Scott, Mississippi, in 1893, Big Bill Broonzy was of the first generation of recorded bluesmen, but stylistically he made every transition possible in his lifetime. The last ten years before his death in 1958 were spent chiefly in introducing the blues from concert and club platforms to Americans and Europeans, who were encouraged by fashion and Broonzy's patrons to believe that he represented uniquely the rural workman/blues-singer. His many records of that period, mostly European-made, accorded with this image – which had little to do with the forceful Chicago band blues that had been Broonzy's chosen and mastered idiom throughout the Thirties and Forties. From early on a supremely accomplished guitarist, he was also an astute composer and clear, expressive singer, besides being a reliable accompanist. His personality lent much distinction even to his last phase, but his stature as a creative blues musician was established by the earlier work.

BROTHERS JOHNSON George (guitar, vocals) and Louis (bass, vocals) Johnson were child prodigies in music, working the Los Angeles club scene while still in school and cutting classes to tour in **Billy Preston**'s band or take up the offer of lucrative session work. In 1975 they became part of Quincy Jones' prestigious set-up writing for and performing on the *Mellow Madness* LP, after which Jones produced their debut album, *Look Out For No 1*, for A&M. Louis' terrifically nimble yet heavily authoritative bass playing and George's flowing, slightly jazzy guitar lines behind the duo's light, pleasant voices formed a melodically attractive sheen to the tight, modern R&B rhythms. The next three albums – *Right On Time*, *Blam!!* and *Light Up the Night* – all contained solid and varied hits from the lush ballad 'Strawberry Letter 23' to the compulsive dance-cut 'Stomp!' But in the Eighties the brothers lost their way, as evinced by a series of disappointing albums. Louis went on to record as part of a pop-gospel trio, Passage, while George, signed to Qwest, acted as 'creative consultant' on yet another attempted come-back by **Sly Stone**, this time for A&M in 1986.

BROUGHTON, EDGAR/ EDGAR BROUGHTON BAND

Emerging out of the London underground club scene of the late Sixties, the Edgar Broughton Band – formed in 1969 – comprised Robert Edgar Broughton (born 24 October 1947, in Warwick; guitar and vocals), his brother Steve (born 20 May 1950; drums), Art Grant (born 14 May 1950; bass), and Victor Unitt (born 5 July 1946; guitar). Playing regularly at benefits up and down the country, the group rose to prominence as much for their anarchic politics and espousal of 'free music' as for their playing. Broughton's anthem-like 'Out Demons Out' was a crowd-please heard at virtually every free festival. Signed to Harvest in 1969, they recorded several uneven albums, including *Sing Brothers Sing* (1970), *Edgar Broughton Band* (1971) and *Oora* (1973) before a series of management problems temporarily halted their recording and performing career. Edgar and Steve re-emerged later in the decade with a new line-up under a new name – the Broughtons – but still treading the same musical paths.

BROWN, ARTHUR

Although he was a pioneer of pyrotechnic rock stagecraft and a considerable influence on the likes of **Peter Gabriel**, **David Bowie**, and **Alice Cooper**, Arthur Brown achieved little in commercial terms beyond his one 1968 UK Number 1, 'Fire'. He was born in Whitby, Yorkshire, England on 24 June 1942, and sang in a number of small-time mid-Sixties R&B bands while studying philosophy at Reading University. He teamed up with keyboards player Vincent Crane in 1967 and, performing under the name of The Crazy World of Arthur Brown, they built up a major cult following in the fledgling underground clubs of flower-power London. Their act really built up from appearances at the UFO club once they fell in with the **Who**'s managers, Kit Lambert and Christ Stamp, who knew well the power of media outrage.

The Crazy World of Arthur Brown were just right for the times. Clearly influenced by **Screamin' Jay Hawkins**, Brown came on stage grotesquely made up, wearing Sun God robes flowing freely as he gyrated around the stage singing, screaming and howling. The group, later adding drummer Carl Palmer, played frenzied and tight music as a perfect foil for Brown's antics, which culminated in his blazing crown during 'Fire'. This was their *tour de force*, which gave the group a trans-atlantic smash hit, led to a lawsuit with Peter Ker and Michael Finesilver who were later co-credited with its authorship, and also led to the break-up of the band. Earlier the group had cut a mostly exciting and timely album, *The Crazy World of Arthur Brown*, but Brown's outrageousness soon became *passé*, and, once Crane and Palmer left to form **Atomic Rooster**, his back-up musicians failed to come up to standard. In 1971 he re-emerged as the force behind an interesting rock theatre band, Kingdom Come. Following its demise he travelled widely, playing to Israeli troops with just a guitar, and in 1975, after six months at a meditation school, returned with a new album and tour plans. He also secured a small part in Ken Russell's *Tommy*. He then began working with German synthesizer specialist Klaus Schulze, but settled in the US during 1980 to work on such projects as *Requiem*, a concept album about the effects of a nuclear holocaust.

Arthur Brown's performance of 'Fire' ended with his crown in flames

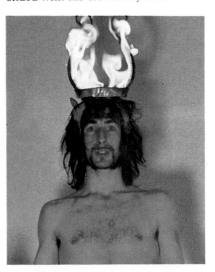

BROWN, BUSTER Born in Criss, Georgia, on 11 August 1914, Buster Brown sang and played harmonica locally before recording for Bobby Robinson in New York City in 1959. In a powerful and intensely rhythmic style reminiscent of **Sonny Terry**, Brown reached the Top .40 with the much-imitated 'Fannie Mae', on Fire, in 1960. Smaller hits included 'Is You Is Or Is You Ain't My Baby' and 'Sugar Babe' (covered in Britain by Jimmy Powell) in 1962. Brown also recorded for Serock, Gwenn, Checker, Nocturn and Astroscope. He died on 31 January 1976.

BROWN, CHARLES Singer/pianist Charles Brown was born in Texas City, Texas, in 1920, and joined guitarist Johnny Moore's Three Blazers during the early Forties. Records under Moore's name for Exclusive, including 'Drifting Blues' (an historic session on which **Johnny Otis** played drums) and 'Merry Christmas, Baby', monopolized the R&B charts from 1946 to 1948. Los Angeles blues enjoyed national popularity at that time, and Brown was the leader of the field. His records with Moore were followed by seven Top 10 R&B hits under his own name. His was a cool, late night, almost cocktail blues style. Sophisticated, relaxed, and reflective, it had an indelible influence on many of the West Coast performers. In addition, most of Brown's hits for Aladdin – 'Get Yourself Another Fool', 'Trouble Blues', 'My Baby's Gone', 'Black Night', and the **Leiber and Stoller** composition 'Hard Times' – have become blues standards. His popularity waned somewhat in 1953, but he came bouncing back with a pop hit in 1961, 'Please Come Home for Christmas', on King. He has also recorded for Ace, Mainstream and Jewel. His mentor, Johnny Moore, died in 1968 at the age of 62.

BROWN, CLARENCE 'GATE MOUTH' Probably the outstanding Texas blues guitarist during the early Fifties, Clarence 'Gatemouth' Brown became one of Duke/Peacock's biggest-selling artists. Born on 18 April 1924 in Orange, Texas, he cut his first sides in 1947 for the Los Angeles-based Aladdin label, accompanied by the **Maxwell Davis** orchestra. He moved to Houston in late 1949 and was discovered by Don Robey, who signed him to Peacock. Among his hits are the intense 'Dirty Work at the Crossroads' and 'Ain't That Dandy', with backing by the Bill Harvey band. His guitar solos are near-legendary in blues circles, and have given inspiration to countless young musicians. In addition to his singing and guitar playing, Gatemouth is accomplished on the harmonica and fiddle. Since the Seventies, he has made a regular living at various blues festivals. His Eighties recordings include *Alright Again!* (Rounder 1982) *San Antonio Ballbuster* (1982), *One More Mile* (1983) and *Atomic Energy* (1984).

BROWN, DENNIS Reggae singer Dennis Brown (born February 1956 in Kingston, Jamaica) came to be periodically hailed in the years immediately following **Bob Marley**'s death as the successor to the great man's international mantle. However, Brown had by that time in fact long since given his best shot. By 1981, the year of Marley's death, he was making blandly inoffensive crossover records that in the main committed the cardinal sin (in crossover terms) of failing to cross over.

In his time, however, Brown released

Dennis Brown rose from child prodigy to international superstar

some genuinely spellbinding material. A child star, he was discovered in 1967 by legendary producer Clement Dodd, who gave him his first hit single two years later with 'No Man Is An Island', also the title track of his successful 1972 LP. The bulk of his later work, however, has been produced by Joe Gibbs – including his two *chefs d'œuvre*, the 1977 albums *Visions* and *Wolf and Leopard*.

BROWN, JAMES The greatest or the most boring; overblown or underestimated; sincere or just plain shrewd? The only unanimous opinion about James Brown is that he is unique, and the only indisputable fact is that for nigh on 15 years he had been the most consistently successful black entertainer bar none. Mixing gospel and blues roots with the energy of his own aggressive personality, he created some of the most fervent records of the late Fifties and a dynamic road show that, by 1962, had made him America's leading R&B star – 'Soul Brother No. 1'. Sidestepping the traditional fate of top black talent (limited rewards or compromise to mainstream, white-controlled showbiz) Brown then extended his music into an expression of defiant independence that was spiritually closer to the great jazz revolutionaries than to other 'soul' singers, but used compulsive dance rhythms to attract mass audiences, and brought about the polarization of jazz and soul in the form of Seventies 'street-funk'.

As one of the first entertainers to assume complete control of his own career, Brown paved the way for many other such independent ventures, and using his popularity as a platform for active participation in social reform, he became a major figure in the fight for black equality. Now, disentangled from the main body of politics, he remains a champion of the underprivileged and is still a top-selling name in an era when the changes he helped to pioneer have given birth to many equally committed performers. However, the startling paradoxes in his personality and music have so far robbed him of much of the critical acclaim usually heaped upon artists of similar stature. For never before had such an uncompromising talent made such a determined bid for commercial success, or indeed, been so successful.

Born near Augusta, Georgia, on 3 May 1928, Brown was first noticed in Macon leading the Famous Flames, the vocal group that he used as a foil on the gospel-style interaction of his early hits, and then disbanded in favour of

complex rhythm accompaniment. Signed by **Ralph Bass** to Federal, a division of King Records of Cincinnati, they recorded 'Please, Please, Please' in February 1956. A strong regional hit, this raw wailing dirge was reworked in several less successful guises before a beautifully adapted gospel song, 'Try Me', put Brown in the national charts in November 1958. On the strength of this success he was signed by Universal Attractions booking agency where he came to the attention of the owner, Ben Bart, who chaperoned Brown's emergence as a major star and taught him how to take care of business. Given much wider exposure, and his first regular band, Brown expressed his restless imagination by redefining R&B in a succession of fiery hits that were even more persuasive on stage.

Using the fast numbers ('Good, Good Lovin', 'I'll Go Crazy', 'Think', 'Night Train') as the basis of intricate dance routines; extending the slow songs ('Bewildered', 'I Don't Mind', 'Baby

Soul Brother No. 1 James Brown gives tortured, extravagant performances . . .

You're Right', 'Lost Someone') into hysterical sermons; and crowning the whole package with precision timing and a wardrobe that made his rivals look positively drab, Brown criss-crossed America, breaking box-office records in every major black venue with the wildest show ever assembled. In October 1962, the show was captured on *Live at the Apollo*, resulting in a million-selling album – then unprecedented for an R&B album – that introduced an unsuspecting white market to 'The Hardest Working Man in Show Business'. Almost immediately he scored his first pop Top 20 entry with an emotional interpretation of the schmaltz ballad, 'Prisoner of Love', but before getting trapped in the middle of the same road as **Ray Charles**, Brown and Bart risked a manoeuvre that enabled him to reach an even larger audience without diluting his music. Forming their own production company, Fair Deal, they sent new recordings to Smash, part of the nationwide Mercury Corporation. The third release, 'Out of Sight' (1964), used a tighter band and a strong bass line to bind the co-ordination of his previous records into a solid dance rhythm that hit with an international *and* bi-racial audience. At the same time, he shrugged off conventional patterns of song construction. Returning to King, and aided by his band director, Nat Jones, he recorded progressively less formal hits ('Papa's Got a Brand New Bag', 'I Got You', 'Ain't That a Groove', 'Money Won't Change You', 'Bring It Up'), checked only by 'It's a Man's, Man's, Man's World', a wailing ballad with orchestra and chorus, and a kids-stay-in-school special, 'Don't Be a Dropout'.

In 1967, Alfred Ellis succeeded Jones in shaping Brown's ideas. Their first collaboration, 'Cold Sweat', was completely divorced from any other form of popular music and introduced some of the most unique black records of the era, including 'There Was a Time' (a live extension of an earlier hit 'Let Yourself Go'), 'I Got the Feeling', 'Licking Stick', 'Give It Up or Turnit a Loose', 'I Don't Want Nobody to Give Me Nothing', and the last three big hits with his famous Sixties band, 'Mother Popcorn', 'Let a Man Come In', 'It's a New Day'. During this period he was caught in the crossfire of racial conflict. Harangued for apparently supporting both factions with 'America Is My Home' and 'Say It Loud, I'm Black and I'm Proud' (actually two shades of the same emotion), he toned down his political involvement, but reaffirmed black roots in a series of superb Afro-rhythmic hits featuring younger musicians (including five who went on to join Funkadelic): 'Sex Machine', 'Get Up, Get Into It, and Get Involved', 'Superbad' (1970), 'Soul Power', 'Hot Pants' (1971); and two tracks that were issued after his switch to Polydor, 'Talking Loud and Saying Nothing', and 'I'm a Greedy Man'.

Recording for Polydor since 1971 with yet another band, Fred Wesley

. . . dressed up in a bright and colourful choice of wardrobe

and the JBs (including Maceo Parker, St Clair Pinckney, and others who accompanied him in the Sixties), he survived the changes stimulated by successors like **Sly Stone** and continued to produce exciting hits – 'Make It Funky' (1971), 'Get on the Good Foot' (1972),'Doing It to Death' (1973), 'The Payback', 'Papa Don't Take No Mess' (1974). But with younger bands (**Kool and the Gang**, the **Ohio Players**) surpassing the JBs, and the increasing use of pre-recorded backing tracks destroying much of his spontaneous creativity, Brown began to seek new worlds to conquer. After scoring two successful movie soundtracks (*Black Caesar* and *Slaughter's Big Rip-Off*) in 1973, he crossed the arc lights for a starring role

in *Come to the Table* in 1974. However, his fortunes by this time were ill-starred: his son Teddy was killed in a car accident, his second marriage failed, and there were stories of a payola scandal involving him. Mid-Seventies disco revived his career somewhat and his cameo appearance as a gospel preacher in *The Blues Brothers* (1980) was widely praised. He has recorded and performed tirelessly since, and in 1986 he scored his first US and UK hit for some years with 'Living in America', from the soundtrack of *Rocky IV*. It is likely he will reach even wider audiences with the extraordinary personality that has dominated nearly 100 R&B and pop hit records and a legendary rags-to-riches career.

BROWN, JOE One of British rock-'n'roll's most talented instrumentalists and a consistent hit-maker during the pre-Merseybeat years of the early Sixties, Joe Brown was born Joseph Roger Brown in Swarsby, Lincolnshire, on 13 May 1941, and moved to Plaistow, East London, at the age of two. He was a founder member of a skiffle group, the Spacemen, in 1956, and was used regularly as a backing musician on package tours by pop entrepreneur **Larry Parnes**. Spotted by television producer **Jack Good** at an audition in Southend in 1959, he was hired as a backing guitarist on *Boy Meets Girl*, Good's follow-up show to *Oh Boy!*

With his blond crew-cut and easy stage presence, he seemed a natural for a solo spot and he began doing instrumentals, but soon graduated to singing *and* playing and a name billing. Brown released a number of records on Pye between 1959 and 1962, starting with 'People Gotta Talk' and 'Darktown Strutters Ball' (on which the Spacemen became the Bruvvers). It wasn't until 'Picture of You' was released in the summer of 1962 that he had his first hit, to be followed by 'It Only Took a Minute' at the end of the year and 'That's What Love Will Do' in 1963. He quickly moved on to films which consolidated his image as lovable Cockney 'sparrer' – in particular one of the better British pop films, *What a Crazy World* (1963). During the latter part of the Sixties, he turned more and more to acting and made an unspectacular comeback with the countryish Brown's Home Brew in the early Seventies. He had his own TV series in the early Eighties. He still tours regularly, mixing country and rock material with his old hits.

BROWN, NAPPY R&B singer Napoleon 'Nappy' Brown had a Southern background and a church choir education, but it was after he moved to Newark, New Jersey, that he became the Savoy label's star attraction with over 25 singles between 1954 and 1961. Several of his giant R&B hits – 'Don't Be Angry', 'Pitter Patter' (both 1955), 'Little By Little' (1957), 'It Don't Hurt No More' (1958), and 'Cried Like a Baby' (1959) – also reached the pop charts. His slower ballads were exceptionally soulful, and included 'The Right Time', 'I'm Getting Lonesome', and 'It's Really You' – on which Brown wailed, screamed and barked like a dog. After a long spell in prison, he returned to recording in 1969 – with Elephant – and later cut gospel sides for Jewel with the Bell Jubilee Singers.

BROWN, PETE Poet, songwriter and bandleader Pete Brown was an important catalyst in the British rock scene of the Sixties. Born on 25 December 1940, in London, Brown (with Michael Horovitz) initiated the jazz and poetry movement which involved several musicians who were to be active in the British R&B scene, notably **Jack Bruce** and **Graham Bond**. In the mid-Sixties, Brown founded a series of experimental rock groups – Battered Ornaments, Piblokto, etc. – whose members included Kokomo's Jim Mullen and guitarist Chris Spedding. He also wrote extensively with Bruce for **Cream**, composing such songs as 'Sunshine of Your Love' ('It'll pay my rent for the rest of my life,' he once said) and 'Politician'. His records include three Piblokto albums on Harvest and *The Not Forgotten Association* (1973), a jazz-and-poetry album on Deram. *Party in the Rain* (1982) was a collaboration with Ian Lynn.

BROWN, ROY Born in New Orleans on 10 September 1925, Roy Brown is best remembered for his pioneering vocal style. In 1948 he recorded 'Good Rockin' Tonight' for De Luxe, and turned the national spotlight on New Orleans. The song was also successfully covered by **Wynonie Harris** (on King) and later by **Elvis Presley** (on Sun). Brown quickly made a name for himself singing in local clubs and concert halls. In 1950 he had topped the R&B charts with 'Hard Luck Blues', and thereafter every Roy Brown record turned 'gold' – 'Boogie at Midnight', 'Love Don't Love Nobody', 'Long About Sundown', and 'Big Town'. In 1952 he moved to King, but suffering a decline in popularity, he signed with Imperial in 1956. Teamed with **Dave Bartholomew**'s band, Brown hit the charts again with a cover of **Buddy Knox**'s 'Party Doll', then – in 1957 – with 'Let the Four Winds Blow'. But by this time the rock'n'roll craze was at its peak, and Brown's success couldn't last. Apart from a few sporadic releases, he was virtually forgotten until 1970 when **Johnny Otis** brought him back for a guest appearance at the Monterey festival. Many artists were inspired by Brown's gospel-tinged vocals and his influence has been acknowledged by such names as **B.B. King**, **Bobby Bland**, **Little Richard**, **Jackie Wilson**, and **James Brown**. He died of a heart attack on 25 May 1981, in Los Angeles.

BROWN, RUTH Easily the most prolific female R&B singer of the Fifties, Ruth Brown was born on 30 January 1928, in Portsmouth, Virginia. Called 'Miss Rhythm', itself an indication of her singing style, her output of some 87 sides released by Atlantic between 1949 and 1962 established her as the label's top-selling artist of the decade, even surpassing the recorded totals of **Ray Charles**, **LaVern Baker**, **Clyde McPhatter** and the **Drifters**. Her first R&B Number 1 seller was 'Teardrops from My Eyes', released in 1950. Other chart-topping hits included 'Mama, He Treats Your Daughter Mean', '5–10–15 Hours', 'Oh What a Dream', and 'Lucky Lips' (also a US Top 40 hit). In 1956, she was voted by deejays in a *Cash Box* poll the 'most programmed female vocalist in the R&B field'. Ruth was also a vitally important part of the pop music scene, and made numerous appearances at **Alan Freed**'s rock'n'roll extravaganzas. She came out of 'retirement' in the early Seventies to tour clubs and record new material for the Cobblestone label.

BROWNE, JACKSON One of the most enduringly creative talents to emerge out of the singer-songwriter movement at the start of the Seventies, Jackson Browne was born in Heidelberg, West Germany, on 9 October 1948. He moved with his parents to Los Angeles in the early Fifties. In 1967, he travelled to New York where he performed on the club circuit for a year, establishing a reputation as a songwriter. Returning to LA, he waited three years before releasing an album, although his songs had already been recorded by **Tom Rush** ('These Days'), **Nico** (also 'These Days'), and the **Nitty Gritty Dirt Band** ('Jamaica Say You Will'). His first two Asylum albums, *Saturate Before Using* and *For Everyman* (1974), saw the burgeoning of a formidable talent, increasingly imaginative music alongside a vision ever more acute. His themes – the ambiguity of love as salvation and as prison, the struggle in the cities and the peace of the countryside, the hopes of a better world and the fears of apocalypse – have been handled with both insight and a poetic economy, forged into a world-view as integrated for the times as any since **Bob Dylan**. His music was much improved by the skills of David Lindley on lead guitar and violin, who Browne used to good effect on the third (and most successful) album, *Late for the Sky* (1974), a loose concept album that convincingly fused the personal and social aspects of life in the US in the mid-Seventies. The **Jackson Five** ('Doctor My Eyes') and the **Eagles** ('Take It

Jackson Browne, a talented singer-songwriter of the post-Dylan era

Easy') were among the artists who found chart success with Browne songs.

The Pretender (1976) was a bleak album, recorded following the suicide of his first wife Phyllis, while *Runnin' on Empty* (1978) was a live set that included a revival of **Maurice Williams and the Zodiacs**' 'Stay', which reached Number 20 in the US. *Hold Out* followed in 1980 and *Lawyers in Love* in 1983, since when he has toured regularly and has produced albums for Warren Zevon. He lent his name to the anti-nuclear cause in the Eighties and appeared at numerous 'No Nukes' concerts. *Lives in the Balance* was a 1986 release.

BROWNS Vocal trio the Browns – comprising two sisters and a brother – hailed from Pine Bluff, Arkansas. Jim Ed was born on 1 March 1934, Maxine on 27 April 1932, and Bonnie on 7 June 1936. Appearances on the *Louisiana Hayride* led to an RCA recording con-

tract and a lachrymose version of Edith Piaf's French hit, 'Les Trois Cloches'. 'The Three Bells' topped the charts for four weeks in 1959. Later records included a version of the **Harry Belafonte** hit, 'Scarlet Ribbons'. During the Sixties, Jim Ed Brown established himself as a country singer, still with RCA.

BRUCE, JACK Born in Glasgow on 14 May 1943, Jack Bruce began his career playing acoustic bass in Jim McHarg's Scotsville Jazzband and the city's dancehalls before coming to London where he joined Blues Incorporated in 1962. He quit **Alexis Korner**'s band with altoist-organist **Graham Bond** and drummer **Ginger Baker** in February 1963, and played with the Graham Bond Organisation until late 1965 when he left for a short stint with **John Mayall**'s Bluesbreakers, followed by six months with **Manfred Mann**, before the formation of **Cream**. His dazzling improvised duets

with **Eric Clapton** raised bass guitar playing to a new level of artistry, and he developed considerably both as a singer and – in partnership with **Pete Brown** – as a songwriter.

After the break-up of Cream, Bruce pursued a solo career using various combinations of 'friends' who included **Larry Coryell**, Art Themen, Mike Mandel, Mitch Mitchell, **John McLaughlin**, Tony Williams, Chris Spedding, John Marshall, Graham Bond, Dick Heckstall-Smith and Jon Hiseman, to record a series of albums – *Songs for a Tailor* (Polydor, 1970), *Things We Like* (1971), *Harmony Row* (1971) – and for occasional live performances, where he successfully ignored demands for Cream oldies. He took part in Carla Bley's jazz suite *Escalator over the Hill*, but dropped his sights when he joined ex-**Mountain** members Leslie West and Corky Laing in the sub-Cream group West, Bruce and Laing in 1972, which lasted until the following year.

After the release of *Out of the Storm* (RSO, 1974), he formed a short-lived new band with ex-**Rolling Stone** Mick Taylor, Ronnie Leahy, Carla Bley (keyboards), and Bruce Gary (drums). *How's Tricks* followed in 1977 and *I've Always Wanted to Do This* in 1980, the same year he went on the road with former **Humble Pie** guitarist Clem Clempson and ex-**Bruce Springsteen** pianist David Sancious. In the early Eighties, he collaborated with **Robin Trower** on *BLT* (1981) and *Truce* (1982). *See also* **Cream**

Jack Bruce, bass guitar maestro

BRYANT, FELICE AND BOUDLEAUX A songwriter team responsible for a string of hits for the **Everly Brothers** and others in the late Fifties, Felice and Boudleaux Bryant began writing professionally around the time of their marriage in 1948. Boudleaux was born in Shellman, Georgia, in 1920, and came from a part-Indian background; Felice was born in Milwaukee, Wisconsin, in 1925. Their first hit composition was 'Country Boy', originally recorded by hillbilly artist Jimmy Dickens but also covered by numerous others. In the early Fifties, Mitch Miller, the head of A&R at American Columbia, made a habit of covering C&W hits for the national pop market; among the Bryants' songs covered were 'Have a Good Time' (Tony Bennett), 'Hey Joe' (first recorded by country singer Carl Smith but covered by **Frankie Laine** who made it an international hit), and 'Willie Can' recorded in Britain by Alma Cogan. The Bryants moved to Nashville in 1950 and were among the few people working there solely as songwriters; the other writers were usually also recording artists. In 1957, Archie Bleyer of the New York Cadence label introduced his new signings, the Everly Brothers, to the Bryants, who wrote 'Bye Bye Love' for the duo. 'Bye Bye Love' sold a million, and as a result the Bryants were commissioned to provide further material, writing either one or both sides of the duo's next five singles, including 'Wake Up Little Susie', 'Problems', 'Bird Dog', 'All I Have to Do Is Dream', and 'Poor Jenny' – all million-sellers. In 1958, they wrote 'Raining in My Heart' for **Buddy Holly**, which became a posthumous hit for him in 1959 as the B-side of 'It Doesn't Matter Anymore'. In 1960 the Bryants wrote Bob Luman's million-seller 'Let's Think About Living', but then their success in the pop market began to dwindle as the New York publishing houses took a firm hold on pop music.

BUBBLEGUM This was a musical style that became a major commercial trend in American pop during 1968 and 1969. What started out as a rigidly defined formula (heavy, repetitive bass beat, simple nursery-rhyme lyrics, and affectedly nasal vocals) gradually became the object of intense ridicule from the 'progressive' faction, and the term 'bubblegum' was applied to almost anything that could be labelled 'commercial'.

Credit for its invention generally goes to Jerry Kasenetz and Jeff Katz,

Nashville songwriting team Felice and Boudleaux Bryant – their songs included 'Wake Up Little Susie' and 'Raining in My Heart'

whose Super-K Productions began with seminal bubblegum records by the Rare Breed and the Music Explosion on Attack Records, then moved to Super-K (their own label), which found its spiritual home under the wing of Buddah Records, headed by Neil Bogart, formerly of Cameo Records. The earliest bubblegum records – 'Try It' and 'Beg, Borrow and Steal' by the Ohio Express, 'Capt. Groovy and His Bubblegum Army' by Capt. Groovy, 'Shake' by the Shadows of Knight, and 'Go Away' by the 1910 Fruitgum Co., sounded more like garage band punk than what most would call bubblegum. But soon the formula emerged: the musical structure defined above, and a calculated distillation of sub-teen subject matter, expressing love in metaphors of candy, gumdrops, and children's games.

In late 1967, Katz and Kasenetz moved their operation to Buddah, and were joined there by other young

The 1910 Fruitgum Company – bubblegum poppers

studio pioneers including Joey Levine, Artie Resnick, and Richie Cordell (from Kama Sutra Productions). At the same time, Andy Kim and **Jeff Barry** were leaving Red Bird Records to join **Don Kirshner** in creating the Archies, a faceless cartoon act designed to surpass even the **Monkees** in TV and record drawing power. The Archies' 'Sugar Sugar' subsequently became the biggest grossing record of 1969, thanks largely to the presence of Ron Dante from Ohio on vocals. Curiously, a large number of other bubblegum artists were also Ohio-based: the Ohio Express, of course, but also the Music Explosion, the Lemon Pipers, Dick Whittington, and the Royal Guardsmen. Although there were many interesting records by all these acts, and some very unusual recordings (ranging from Spector-imitations to hot-rod tunes) by other more ephemeral bubblegum aggregations, the genre is best remembered for the hits of the Ohio Express ('Yummy Yummy Yummy', 'Chewy Chewy'), the 1910 Fruitgum Co. ('Simon Says', '1, 2, 3, Red Light', 'Indian Giver'), the Lemon Pipers ('Green Tambourine', 'Jelly Jungle'), Crazy Elephant ('Gimme Gimme Good Lovin'', another Super-K production), and the Archies ('Sugar Sugar', 'Jingle Jangle').

The bubblegum era effectively ended around 1970, though its legacy could be felt well into the next decade in the records of various cartoon groups created for American television (Josie and the Pussycats, for example) and in the choice of material accorded the likes of Little Jimmy Osmond and **Dawn**. The best that can be said is that bubblegum pop did provide a fertile training ground for some important producers and writers.

BUCHANAN, ROY Born in Ozark, Arkansas, on 23 September 1939, Roy Buchanan was propelled into the ranks of guitar superheroes through a Polydor contract in 1971. Poor support bands failed to blunt an incomparable technique perfected over two decades of picking with some of the finest rock-'n'roll combos around. Influenced by black (Blind Boy Fuller, **Johnny 'Guitar' Watson**) and white (**Scotty Moore**, Roy Nicholls) musicians alike, he played in local groups until joining **Dale Hawkins** in 1958. The breaks on Hawkins' 'My Babe' and the folksy accompaniment to 'Grandma's House' (Checker) were years ahead of their time. He also recorded with Gerry Hawkins, Bob Luman, the Hawks, **Freddy Cannon** and Bobby Gregg and cut solo

sides for Swan and Bomarc before retiring to Washington DC in 1962.

Ten years later he was promoted as the new guitar saviour, a role for which his introspective personality was particularly ill-suited. Versatility was a keynote of all nine of his Polydor albums, with slow and steamy versions of 'Sweet Dreams' and 'After Hours' being among the finer cuts. Despite all the critical acclaim, however, he remained essentially a cult artist and never translated all the positive reviews into big record sales.

BUCKLEY, TIM Born in Washington DC on 14 February 1947, Tim Buckley was a leading figure on the fringes of mainstream rock after 1966. He began in various southern Californian country bands before moving on to the Los Angeles folk circuit. There he found a manager, Herb Cohen, and a record company, **Jac Holzman**'s Elektra.

Holzman and **Paul Rothchild** produced Buckley's first album which, like

the three that followed, was firmly folk-rooted but musically sophisticated. His most famous song of this period, 'Morning Glory' from the *Hello and Goodbye* album (1967, produced by Jerry Yester), was written with poet Larry Beckett, a partnership that continued sporadically. It was, however, the richness and variety of Buckley's singing which did most to establish his reputation. And the next phase of his career found him moving towards John Coltrane-style jazz on *Lorca* and *Starsailor* (1970), his first record for Straight, the label set up by Cohen and **Frank Zappa**. This free-form scat singing provoked mixed reactions, however, and *Greetings from L.A.* (1972) found Buckley returning to a more accessible urban R&B style, singing of sex rather than romance. *Sefronia* (1973, on another Cohen-Zappa label, DiscReet) was a synthesis of that hard-edged style with the earlier more lyrical singing. He died on 29 June 1975, in Los Angeles.

Tim Buckley's unique vocal style earnt him many admirers

BUCKS FIZZ Like **Abba** and second only to them, Bucks Fizz achieved their early successes as a direct result of winning the Eurovision Song Contest. While on record the foursome were merely the medium for the inoffensive, ultra-commercial pop ideas of Svengali-like producer Andy Hill, their exuberant and highly professional live work revealed talented performers.

Four experienced but largely unknown singers Mike Nolan, Cheryl Baker, Bobby Gee and Jay Aston were brought together especially for Eurovision in 1981 by co-managers Nichola Martin (who was married to Hill) and Jill Shirley, but after that success it was Hill, with his phenomenal studio prowess and ear for a strong hook-line, who masterminded their career from then on. Bucks Fizz records ranged from the totally crass (especially the Eurovision winner 'Making Your Mind Up') to the irritatingly catchy, but with the two UK Number 1s 'The Land of Make Believe' and 'My Camera Never Lies' (both 1982), they released two of the best pure white pop songs since **Blondie** were at their height.

In 1985, Aston left the group in a well-publicized internal dispute, to be replaced by Shelley Preston, selected from the hundreds of young girls who turned up for the auditions. Bucks Fizz's mass popularity in the charts has waned, but their good-humoured, broad appeal has guaranteed large attendances at their concerts.

BUDDAH RECORDS Buddah was formed in September 1967, by Neil Bogart, formerly of Cameo-Parkway Records. Through arrangements with Kama Sutra Productions, Super-K Productions, **Anders and Poncia**, and other independent songwriting and production outfits, Buddah soon became one of the most prolific singles-oriented independents.

The label's initial success was with what became known as 'bubblegum' music. Early hits by the Lemon Pipers ('Green Tambourine'), the 1910 Fruitgum Co. ('Simon Says', '1, 2, 3, Red Light' and others) and the Ohio Express ('Yummy Yummy Yummy' and others) established Buddah as the home of bubblegum – a sound created almost entirely by a handful of producers – that was a huge commercial success during 1968–70 and disappeared almost completely thereafter.

But although few of Buddah's non-bubblegum releases were hits in those years, they had built a solid roster of pop and R&B. The Brooklyn Bridge (featuring Johnny Maestro of the **Crests**) had numerous hits from 1968 on, starting with 'The Worst That Could Happen'. **Lou Christie** made the Top 10 in 1969 with 'I'm Gonna Make You Mine', and other established artists including **Teddy Randazzo**, **Johnny Tillotson**, and **Chubby Checker** joined the label. In the early Seventies, having taken over Kama Sutra Records and affiliated with other labels including the **Isley Brothers**' T-Neck, Buddah's roster widened to include **Melanie**, **Brewer and Shipley**, the **Stairsteps**, the **Edwin Hawkins Singers**, Biff Rose, **Freddy Cannon**, **Paul Anka**, **Len Barry**, and a number of R&B acts – particularly **Gladys Knight and the Pips**, who were Buddah's most popular artists of the Seventies. After Bogart's departure in 1974 to launch Casablanca Records, Buddah's mainstays were Knight, Les Variations, Isis, Barbara Mason, and (on Kama Sutra) **Stories**, **Charlie Daniels**, and **Sha Na Na**.

BUFFALO SPRINGFIELD A seminal mid-Sixties West Coast group, Buffalo Springfield incorporated the talents of two future members of **Crosby, Stills, Nash and Young – Steve Stills** (born in Dallas, Texas, on 30 January 1945) and **Neil Young** (born in Toronto, Canada, on 12 November 1945). Stills and Richie Furay (born in Dayton, Ohio, on 9 May 1944) were New York folksingers of meagre repute. Up in Toronto, Neil Young was doing better with a similar act, but getting restless for the big time. Drummer Dewey Martin (born in Chesterville, Ontario, on 30 September 1942) was with the **Dillards**, and bassist Bruce Palmer (born in Liverpool, Canada, in 1947) was a friend of Neil's. They came together in Los Angeles in 1966, by chance more than anything else, and took their name from a steamroller. People who were there often insist that Buffalo Springfield was the best of the mid-Sixties LA groups.

They were certainly one of the most exciting live groups, thrilling Whiskey A Go-Go audiences nightly with a show that featured two lead guitars (Stills and Young), three lead singers (Stills, Young and Furay), a rhythm section that had obviously been listening to the recent Stax singles, and an onstage kineticism that reintroduced showmanship to the Sunset Strip. That was live. On record, it was a different story. Their debut LP on Atlantic, *Buffalo Springfield* (1967), sounded sludgy, and it took them some time to learn their way around a studio. The exception was their first, and only, US Top 10 single, the Stills-penned 'For What It's Worth' (1967), a most effective topical song about the Sunset Strip hippie riots that quickly became an anthem.

Hits or no hits, no one disputed their originality. They didn't play the folk-rock of their contemporaries, though folk was a major influence, and their country pop leanings were several years ahead of everyone else. Stills could move from hard rock ('Rock-'n'Roll Woman') to Latin-influences ('Uno Mundo'). Young was also a master of hard rock ('Mr Soul'), but experimented with sound collages ('Broken Arrow'), showed a soft touch on ballads ('I Am a Child') and wrote lyrics that conveyed an intense, poetic sense of terror (as on 'Mr Soul'). Furay and Jim Messina (who replaced Palmer on bass) showed the strongest country

Niel Young: (left) and Steve Stills developed an intense rivalry that could be creative, but led to the breakup of Buffalo Springfield in 1968

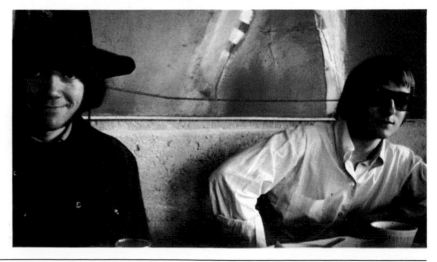

predilections ('Kind Woman'). When all these talents merged cohesively, as often occurred live and as captured on *Buffalo Springfield Again* (1968), they added up to something many felt was the American answer to the **Beatles**.

But none of the Springfield's next four singles rose even to the top half of the charts. They suffered from poor management, and were never able to mount a single national tour. Stills and Young were often at each other's throats, to the extent that Young didn't even appear for their crucial Monterey Pop Festival engagement. *Last Time Around* (1969), their final album, was almost like the Beatles' *White Album*, with group dynamics being discarded and each member doing his own songs his own way. After that, each member bar Martin went on to a Seventies supergroup, none of which showed half the range of the Springfield – Stills and Young to CSN&Y, Messina and Furay to **Poco**. Additionally, Stills and Young enjoyed major success as solo acts. *See also* **Crosby, Stills, Nash and Young**; **Steve Stills**; **Neil Young**

BUGGLES Geoff Downes and **Trevor Horn** first met in 1977 while they were both session musicians in London, and two years later, as Buggles, they had one of the first electropop Number 1s with 'Video Killed the Radio Star'. A surprise hit, it gave Island their first ever chart-topper, yet although both had been musicians for a long time, it soon became clear that they were not cut out for pop superstardom. Three subsequent singles and an LP *The Age of Plastic* (1980) failed to register the same volume of sales, and in 1980 the duo moved on to a short-lived liaison with **Yes**. Eventually Downes went on to find success with **Asia**, while Horn became a widely-respected and influential producer.

BURDON, ERIC Following the break-up of the **Animals** in 1966, lead singer Eric Burdon (born 11 May 1941, at Walker-on-Tyne, England) retained the group's name for a new backing band and pursued an increasingly erratic course across the counter-culture of the late Sixties. Under the influence of LSD, flower power and meditation, the hard-drinking white soul singer became the philosopher of a new lifestyle. With the first version of his new Animals, Burdon had hits on MGM with 'Good Times', 'San Franciscan Nights', and 'Monterey'. But a new line-up including **Zoot Money** on organ and Andy Summers (later of the **Police**) on guitar was less

Eric Burdon, a wild and frenzied performer with a raucous blues voice

successful, and in 1968 Burdon quit. He returned two years later with black R&B group **War**, cutting two albums with them and a single, 'Spill the Wine' (a US Number 3 in 1973), which suggested he was returning to his old form. But War broke away to make a series of hits on their own, while Burdon made an album with bluesman **Jimmy Witherspoon** called *Guilty!* (United Artists, 1971). In the Seventies he seemed to be forever on the verge of making a comeback, but his albums –

Ring of Fire (Capitol, 1974), *Sun Secrets* (1975), *Stop* (1975), and *Survivor* (1978) – had unspectacular sales. He recorded a reunion album with members of the original Animals in 1977 – *Before We Were So Rudely Interrupted* (United Artists) – and appeared in a number of European-made films. 1983 saw a further reunion. Burdon's own account of his career in rock, *I Used To Be An Animal But I'm Alright Now*, was published by Faber and Faber in 1986.

BURKE, SOLOMON

King Heavy, The King of Rock'n'Soul – Solomon Burke was for many years the big man and big voice of black music. Born in Philadelphia in 1936, by the age of nine he was starring as the soloist in church, which led to local broadcasts on his own radio show *Solomon's Temple*, and stage appearances as 'The Wonder Boy Preacher'. His early recordings for the New York Apollo label (1955–8) were nearly all quasi-religious ballads or sentimental love songs, presumably aimed at the same audience that enjoyed **Roy Hamilton**, but after a few sides on Singular (1959, subsequently re-issued on Atlantic), including one untypical rocker, 'Be-Bop Grandma', he was signed by Atlantic where he became the first, and according to some the greatest, of the company's formidable and impressive armoury of soul talent.

From his earliest sessions with the company (1960–62) he gave new meaning to a catholic selection of material, including country-weeper 'Just out of Reach (of My Two Empty Arms)', the traditional 'Down in the Valley', and three Fifties R&B favourites, 'I Almost Lost My Mind', 'You Can Make It If You Try', and 'Send Me Some Lovin''. But finest of all were two new songs, 'I'm Hanging Up My Heart for You' (a John Berry/**Don Covay** composition) and his most famous hit, 'Cry to Me', written and produced by **Bert Berns**. Berns, the man behind many of New York's best contributions to soul, produced with Jerry Wexler all of Burke's greatest recordings, following the early hits with a smoother but equally convincing cover-version of **Wilson Pickett**'s 'If You Need Me' (1963). This was including the first of several preaching scorchers, including 'Can't Nobody Love You', 'You're Good for Me', 'Goodbye Baby (Baby Goodbye)', all arranged by Garry Sherman, climaxing with 'The Price' (1964), which even after so many other intense performances, was a stunning end to what can only be described as a very fruitful relationship.

It may have been coincidence, but with Berns no longer in the studio Burke was never again so impressive on record, although he immediately scored his biggest hit with the catchy 'Got to Get You off My Mind' (1965), arranged by Gene Page. The same year, 'Tonight's the Night' – coupled with an uncomfortable version of **Bob Dylan**'s 'Maggie's Farm' – were his last best-sellers. For three more years he continued to turn out performances that compared favourably with contemporary soul records but seemed lifeless,

compared to his earlier work. After minor hits with 'Take Me (Just As I Am)', recorded in Memphis in 1967, and 'I Wish I Knew' (1968), he left Atlantic.

Recording in the South again, he cut some fine sides for Bell (including 'Proud Mary' and 'That Lucky Old Sun' – 1969) and then spent an erratic three years with MGM, where several good issues (particularly 'Love's Street and Fool's Road' – 1972) were sandwiched between some of the worst recordings of his career. In 1974, after a partially successful tribute album to Dr Martin Luther King, *I Have a Dream*, he changed tack completely, jumping straight into the Seventies by reuniting with Gene Page on two singles heavily influenced by hitmaker **Barry White**: 'Midnight and You' (Dunhill), and 'You and Your Baby Blues' (Chess). In 1975 he released *Music to Make Love by* (Chess).

In 1979, Burke cut the album *Sidewalks, Fences and Walls* (Infinity) but recorded only intermittently thereafter. During the early Eighties, he released some gospel material through the Savoy label, and appeared with fellow members of the formidable 'Soul Clan' – **Joe Tex**, Don Covay and Wilson Pickett.

Burke in the studio with Atlantic's top A&R man and producer Jerry Wexler

'The King of Rock'n'Soul' Solomon Burke displays his outstanding talents in a Sixties TV performance, preaching the gospel of soul

BURNETTE, DORSEY The brother of **Johnny Burnette**, Dorsey Burnette began his career playing string bass in Johnny's Rock'n'Roll Trio alongside guitarist Paul Burlison. The Trio recorded for Coral between 1956 and 1958. Before that, Dorsey – who was born in Memphis on 28 December 1932 – had been a boxer and an employee at Crown Electric with **Elvis Presley**. As a solo act from 1958 onwards, Dorsey's rich, deep voice was heard on rockers like 'Bertha Lou' for Cee Jam, but major success came in 1960 with the ballads 'Tall Oak Tree' and 'Big Rock Candy Mountain', recorded in Hollywood for Era. Later a successful C&W singer, Burnette also wrote many hit songs for **Rick Nelson**, **Jerry Lee Lewis** and numerous country artists. He died of a heart attack on 19 August 1979, in California.

BURNETTE, JOHNNY Rock-'n'roll singer Johnny Burnette had a career filled with incident. Born on 25 March 1934, in Memphis, Tennessee, he attended the same school as **Elvis Presley**; in 1953, he worked at the Memphis electrical firm, Crown Electric, where Presley drove a truck. He then tried boxing, following in his elder brother Dorsey's footsteps. But after a period as a lightweight, he decided to roam the South, working as a deckhand on a Mississippi river barge. He then made his way to California but was unable to find a job and hitched the 2000 miles back to Memphis in late 1955. After singing for a month in St Louis, Burnette persuaded his brother (who played bass) and a family friend, Paul Burlison (a guitarist), to form a rockabilly trio as Elvis had done with **Scotty Moore** and **Bill Black**. Sam Phillips at the local Sun label rejected them as being too Presleyish, but the trio drove to New York where they won Arthur Godfrey's Amateur Hour show three times in succession. Singing with Decca-Coral, the Johnny Burnette Trio recorded their first single, 'Tear It Up', on 7 May 1956. In 1956–7 they appeared on the Steve Allen TV show, toured with **Gene Vincent**, mimed in the film *Rock, Rock, Rock*, and made three more singles for Coral. None was a hit, and in the summer of 1957 Johnny and Dorsey headed for California where they wrote songs for Imperial's **Rick Nelson** and **Roy Brown**. They also recorded 'Bertha Lou' for a small local label, but their vocals were erased when Coral objected to the duo's breach of contract.

In the autumn of 1958, Johnny joined Liberty's newly formed Freedom subsidiary, recording three singles in 1958–9. He was transferred to Liberty in 1960, and under the supervision of whizz-kid producer **Snuff Garrett**, recorded five consecutive American hits including 'Dreamin'', 'Little Boy Sad', and 'You're Sixteen'. He enjoyed two years as a teen idol but by 1963, following moves to Capitol and Chancellor, his fortunes had waned. He recorded for Sahara in 1964 before forming his own Magic Lamp label. He died on 14 August 1964, in a boating accident while fishing.

BURNING SPEAR Since the mid-Sixties, the name Burning Spear has variously been the tag for a solo vocalist, a vocal duo and a vocal trio – the common (and dominating) denominator of all three incarnations being vocalist/composer Winston Rodney. (The name Burning Spear itself was taken by Rodney from the Kenyan leader Jomo Kenyatta, who was known to his people as 'the Burning Spear').

Like so many other major reggae talents of his generation, Rodney/Burning Spear arrived on the recording scene via producer Clement Dodd, who first recorded Rodney under his own name in 1969 (on the single 'Swell Headed'). Since then Rodney has always recorded as Burning Spear. Already a major roots artist by the early Seventies – with the singles 'Foggy Road' and 'Ethiopians Live It Out' and the albums *Burning Spear* and *Rocking Time* (all produced by Clement Dodd, and all roots classics) – Spear's international breakthrough came in 1975 with the Jack Ruby-produced (and UK-released via Island) album *Marcus Garvey* and single of the same name. Though Spear never achieved the international acceptance of Bob Marley, he was an equally important figure within reggae during the Seventies, a consummate vocal stylist and superb message-oriented songwriter. Still active, Spear's greatest records have probably all been made, but he remains a compelling figure in live performance.

BURTON, JAMES Like **Roy Buchanan** and Al Casey, James Burton was one of the group of influential rockabilly guitarists who survived through to the present with session work and played a major part in the West Coast country-rock scene of the Sixties and Seventies. He first appeared as a guitarist in Shreveport, Louisiana (where he was born on 21 August 1939), and recorded with **Dale Hawkins**, whose 'Suzie Q' on Checker was a rock'n'roll hit in 1957. The heavy, deliberate, and

– for its time – very inventive guitar work enabled Burton to gain work in California, where he joined the band of the young **Rick Nelson**. Burton's 'Sun-style' electric lead picking was an important factor in the success of Nelson's discs, and the solos on 'Waitin' in School', 'Believe What You Say', and 'My Bucket's Got a Hole in It' were definitive statements of the **Carl Perkins**, **Scotty Moore** guitar school. Burton remained with Nelson into the Sixties and has guested on guitar with successive waves of post-**Byrds** country-rockers, including the new-style **Everly Brothers**, **Mike Nesmith**, **Delaney and Bonnie**, and **Gram Parsons**. He cut a solo album for A & M and, in 1969, backed Dale Hawkins on a comeback album and joined the newly rejuvenated **Elvis Presley**'s entourage of backing musicians.

BUSH, KATE Undoubtedly one of the finest and most distinctive artists ever to come out of British rock music, Kate Bush possesses unique gifts as a singer-songwriter, dancer, arranger and producer that have always made her difficult to categorize.

Born on 30 July 1958 in Welling, Kent, she grew up in a musical family environment, first studying the violin and then moving on to the piano. By the time she was 14 she had begun to compose her own material, and three years later, **Pink Floyd**'s Dave Gilmour (who met Bush through mutual friends) arranged and financed a demo tape at

Off-stage Kate Bush presents herself as quiet and demure

Kate Bush on stage: dramatic use is always made of her striking appearance and her dance training in videos and live performances

London's Air studios. EMI Records were sufficiently impressed to sign her up; they took the unusual step of advancing her £3500 to go away and work on her songs. Kate's first album, *The Kick Inside*, was released in 1978 to wide critical acclaim, and it spawned the extraordinary single 'Wuthering Heights', which introduced Bush's characteristic high-pitched vocal technique to the UK charts, reaching Number 1.

The sharp contrast between Bush's demure off-stage personality and her intense, almost demonic performing style annoyed critics and frequently led to negative coverage in the UK music press. Yet when her second album *Lionheart* was released at the end of 1978, it went to Number 6 in the UK chart, and in the same year she won top newcomer, female singer and songwriter awards from the British Phonographic Institute. Six months later she undertook her first British tour, a gruelling singing and dancing extravaganza that was a sell-out everywhere.

Her next UK album, which she co-produced, was *Never For Ever*. It took almost a year to put together and appeared in 1980, accompanied by a Keith MacMillan video. Her imaginative use of promotional videos, in which she put her striking looks and dance training to good use, came to be one of her trademarks. The albums made the Number 1 spot and remained a best-seller for almost six months. *The Dreaming*, released two years later, was Kate Bush at her least accessible and although it went to Number 3 in the charts, sales quickly slumped and a single, 'There Goes a Tenner', did not make the chart at all – her first such failure.

Her next album did not appear until September 1985. *Hounds of Love* was the product of her own studio (supervising the construction of which had occupied some of the three year gap between releases), and amid much publicity and positive reviews, returned her to the top of the album charts. A single from the album, the haunting 'Running Up That Hill', reached Number 4 in the UK singles chart and re-established her as a top-flight recording artist.

BUTLER, JERRY One of Chicago soul music's favourite sons, Jerry Butler was brought up in the city but was born in Sunflower, Mississippi, on 8 December 1939. A Chicago resident from the age of three, his early activities in various church choirs and gospel groups helped pave the way for his current status as one of America's top black vocal stylists of the past 15 years.

He met **Curtis Mayfield** in the Traveling Souls Spiritualist Church Choir and, together with three ex-Roosters from Tennessee, formed Jerry Butler and the **Impressions**. They wrote 'For Your Precious Love' which became a Top 10 tune of 1958, and later that year Butler quit to go solo and cut a string of Vee Jay smashes which often crossed over to white markets: 'He Will Break Your Heart', 'Need to Belong' (both written with Mayfield), 'Moon River' (by Henry Mancini and Johnny Mercer who publicly thanked Jerry for his help in making it Song of the Year 1961), and 'Make it Easy on Yourself' (by **Burt Bacharach** and Hal David). His cool on-stage delivery earned him the tag of 'The Iceman' – though the soubriquet also stemmed from Butler's one-time ambition to be a chef and ice sculptor. He diversified his activities considerably after he received his own award for the 'Let It Be Me' duet with **Betty Everett** in 1964.

He entered the field of producing and publishing and wrote songs for Count Basie, **Jackie Wilson** and **Otis Redding** (I've Been Loving You Too Long). When Vee Jay folded (after grossing $20 million during their last year of operations) he joined Mercury, went pop for 'Mr Dream Merchant' and then teamed up with the unknown **Gamble and Huff**. The classic results included the gold 'Only the Strong Survive' and two smash albums *The Iceman Cometh* and *Ice on Ice*. Gamble and Huff quit Mercury in 1970 and Jerry floundered with his ill-fated labels Fountain and Memphis. However, he made a personal comeback when he got together with Brenda Lee Eager to make the gold record 'Ain't Understanding Mellow' (1972).

In 1975, Butler joined Motown and recorded four albums and a number of singles. None of them were top 40 hits, and by the end of the decade, he had left Motown and was back recording with Gamble and Huff. Since the early Seventies, he has run the Butler Music Workshop on Chicago's South Side, cultivating new writers, producers and performers. *See also* **Impressions**

BUTTERFIELD, PAUL Born in Chicago on 17 December 1942, Paul Butterfield became America's leading white blues harmonica virtuoso. He acquired his technique while playing the black clubs on Chicago's South Side. Influenced by the harp styles of **Little Walter**, **Junior Wells** and James Cotton, he formed his first blues outfit in 1963, bringing in two ex-members of **Howlin' Wolf**'s band – Jerome Arnold (bass) and Sam Lay (drums), plus guitarist Smokey Smothers. **Elvin Bishop** later replaced Smothers, and in 1965 was joined by a session guitarist from Columbia records – **Mike Bloomfield**. Their first recordings were released that same year on the Elektra sampler *What's Shakin'*. Widely acclaimed as the most vital of the new American R&B groups, a debut album quickly followed.

Butterfield was always at his best when accompanied by Bloomfield. They provided superb back-up on **Chuck Berry**'s vintage 'It Wasn't Me' (1965) and they peaked on *East–West* (1966), which was highlighted by the 13-minute title track – a futuristic instrumental built on an Indian raga scale. Triumphant, the band came to Britain, but proved too way-out for London's blue-eyed soul scene. However, Butterfield did manage to cut an EP with **John Mayall**'s Bluesbreakers, featuring **Peter Green**'s guitar.

In 1967, Bloomfield quit the band to work with **Bob Dylan** and subsequently the **Electric Flag**. Butterfield released *The Resurrection of Pigboy Crabshaw* (1967), adding a horn section for the first time. *In My Own Dream* followed, in pretty much the same style, but his 1969 recording, *Keep on Moving*, produced by **Jerry Ragavoy**, introduced a completely new line-up, and veered musically towards the soul/jazz market. Even so, he returned to his roots briefly that year to cut a double album for Chess called *Fathers and Sons*. It reunited Butterfield with Bloomfield, but was really a showcase for the legendary **Muddy Waters**. In 1971 Butterfield met with **Todd Rundgren**, who produced *The Paul Butterfield Band – Live* double album in Los Angeles. A few months later Butterfield cut his final album for Elektra – *Sometimes I Just Feel Like Smilin'*, this time featuring guitarist Ralph Wash, who was later to join **Van Morrison**'s band.

The Paul Butterfield Blues Band finally disbanded in the autumn of 1972, after completing eight best-selling albums (plus the anthology, *Golden Butter*). Butterfield moved to Woodstock, where he met Ronnie Bar-

Paul Butterfield, the supremely gifted blues harp player, jams with Maria Muldaur in an open-air concert of the early Seventies

ron, **Bobby Charles**, Geoff Muldaur and Amos Garrett, and recruited them into a new band called Better Days. The debut album, released on Bearsville in 1973, was distinguished only by fairly sophisticated interpretations of folk/blues standards plus a couple of contemporary songs. A second album, *It All Comes Back*, was a little more outgoing, but still failed to capture the excitement of the early albums. Butterfield died in May 1987.

BUZZCOCKS In the late Seventies, Manchester's Buzzcocks led the Northern branch of the punk rock explosion, but it was with their tuneful, vulnerable love songs that they found most success.

Formed initially in January 1976 by their permanent leader Pete Shelley (born McNeish, 17 April 1955) and

The Buzzcocks were one of the first out-of-London punk-era bands

Howard Devoto (later of **Magazine**) with John Maher on drums and Steve Diggle on bass, they began by gigging locally. They gained publicity from a support slot with the **Sex Pistols** in July and were consequently offered more and better gigs until December when producer Martin Hannett gave them studio time. They raised £500 to put the resulting punk classic *Spiral Scratch* EP out on their own New Hormones label, and it sold 16,000 copies.

Devoto left in 1977; Shelley took over lead vocals, Diggle lead guitar and bassist Garth was brought in. They signed to United Artists in September and over the next three years recorded some of the best punk pop songs of that era, including the singles, 'Ever Fallen in Love (With Someone You Shouldn't Have)', their most successful, reaching Number 12 in the UK in 1978, and 'Harmony in My Head'. Their three albums *Another Music in a Different Kitchen* (1978), *Love Bites* (1978) and *A Different Kind of Tension* (1979) were considered staple listening for the discerning punk/new wave follower long after the band's demise in 1980 when, disappointed at their lack of international success, they split. Shelley embarked on a solo career, producing a string of poorly received electro-pop songs, and Diggle formed the punky guitar rockers Flag of Convenience. However, neither recaptured the success and the quality that had been achieved with the Buzzcocks.

BYRDS Hailed as the American **Beatles** and the originators of folk-rock, the Byrds dominated the American music scene for a brief period in 1965. They were never again to be as celebrated, yet with virtually each record between 'Mr Tambourine Man' (1965) and the *Sweetheart of the Rodeo* (1968) album, moving from folk-rock through acid-rock and space-rock to country-rock, they outlined vast areas that other bands would later begin to explore. Moreover, the Byrds weren't merely musical pioneers. Their work also saw the creation of one of rock's most assured styles through which seemingly disparate musical elements were transformed into a unique Byrds sound.

In the early Sixties, while rock'n'roll was dying, across America in the coffee houses and colleges the folk boom in which most of the Byrds began their musical careers was getting underway. Jim, later **Roger**, **McGuinn** – born 14 July 1942, in Chicago – the only Byrd with a musical education, started backing the Limeliters, joined the Chad

The Byrds were one of the most innovative and original of all the rock-folk bands of the Sixties. After the group's major songwriter Gene Clark left to pursue a solo career in 1966, the line-up was as above: Jim McGuinn (seated centre), Chris Hillman (standing left), Dave Crosby (standing right) and drummer Michael Clarke. The band reassembled in varying combinations in the Seventies (opposite)

Mitchell Trio and in 1962 started session work and supporting **Bobby Darin** who had introduced a folk spot into his night-club act. Similarly, **Gene Clark** – born 17 November 1941, in Tipton, Missouri – had done a stint with the New Christy Minstrels, and **Dave Crosby** – born 14 August 1941, in Los Angeles – had been a Les Baxter Balladeer for a while. **Chris Hillman** – born 4 December 1942, in Los Angeles – began playing folk music in coffee bars, like McGuinn, before temporarily leaving it for bluegrass, first with the Scottsville Squirrel Breakers and then with his own group, the Hillmen, a joint folk and bluegrass outfit.

By 1964, the Byrds as individuals were old troupers of a folk scene that was rapidly changing. **Peter, Paul and Mary** had opened the door to the charts with their prettied-up versions of **Bob**

Dylan, and folk was quickly leaving the coffee bars for the concert halls: like rock'n'roll before it, folk was being swallowed up by the record industry. But if folk was happening, the event of 1964 for America was the Beatles, who opened up the floodgates of the British invasion and brought excitement back to rock. Suddenly the charts seemed important again, it seemed possible to play rock without having to be perpetually compromised, and McGuinn and a lot of other ex-folkies began starting rock groups. In the summer of 1964, McGuinn, Clark and Crosby began rehearsing as the Jet Set in Los Angeles. They quickly turned to Jim Dickson, who was trying to sell an album he'd produced for the Hillmen. When it became apparent the Jet Set wouldn't make it as a trio, Dickson persuaded Hillman to join and trade in his mandolin for a Japanese bass guitar. With the addition of Michael Clarke – born 3 June 1944, in New York – a conga-playing acquaintance of Crosby's, on drums, the group was complete. Dickson had the run of World Pacific studios so they decided to rehearse there and make a tape of their songs. Later McGuinn would describe their early music as a synthesis of Dylan and the Beatles, but when those tapes were released eventually as *Preflyte* (Together Records) – which includes a trial version of 'Mr Tambourine Man' – it was the Beatles' influence that stood out. On the basis of that tape, Dickson secured the group a one-record-and-option deal with Elektra, for whom, as the Beefeaters, they put out the very Beatlish 'Please Let Me Love You' in the autumn of 1964. The record failed and the band, now officially the Byrds, switched to Columbia and began looking once again for a song to record.

Earlier that year the **Animals** recorded 'Baby Let Me Follow You Down' and 'House of the Rising Sun' (an American Number 1), both rocked-up pieces of Dylan material, if not Dylan compositions. So Dickson suggested they remake 'Mr Tambourine Man'. They did – with the aid of sessionmen **Hal Blaine**, **Leon Russell** and Larry Knetchel; of the group, only McGuinn played on the single. After six months it soared to the top of the American and British charts where it was seen as signalling the arrival of folk-rock and as stemming the tide of the British Invasion.

But the Byrds' chart success was short-lived: their second record, 'All I Really Want to Do', was beaten to the top by a **Sonny and Cher** cover version and though their third, 'Turn! Turn! Turn!', was a US Number 1 in the autumn of 1965, from then on their singles struggled in the charts. Their last American Top 20 single was 'Eight Miles High' which made Number 14 in September 1966 before it was discovered to be a 'drug song' and promptly received no more airplay.

In the two years between 'Mr Tambourine Man' and 'Eight Miles High', the Byrds changed a lot. Columbia allowed the group to play on the album *Mr Tambourine Man* (1965), which was the expected mixture of Dylan, traditional folk songs and their own compositions. But if the material was straight folk-rock, the Byrds' treatment of it showed them to be more interested in three-part harmony, sound textures and circular rhythmic patterns as, song by song, the group stylized their

material. By the next album, *Turn! Turn! Turn!* (1966), the group had folk-rock down pat and from material like Gene Clark's 'Set You Free This Time' and Dylan's 'Lay Down Your Weary Tune' they created diamonds of formal perfection that lacked only a sense of excitement: the Byrds seemed weary before their time. *Fifth Dimension* (1966), the third album, saw the Byrds

tire of folk-rock and begin experimenting with electronics. Gene Clark, the group's major songwriter, left to pursue a solo career after *Turn! Turn! Turn!*

On the group's singles McGuinn was the Byrds; it was his voice and distinctive 12-string guitar that were the trademarks, but on albums he was merely one of the group. This was amply demonstrated on *Younger Than*

Yesterday (1967), which brought the electronic experimentation of *Fifth Dimension* to absolute perfection. McGuinn provided probably his strangest piece of 'space-rock', 'CTA 102', but the album belonged to Crosby ('Everybody's Been Burned' and 'Renaissance Fair') and Hillman ('Have You Seen Her Face' and 'Thoughts and Words'). Also featured was McGuinn and Hillman's world-weary 'So You Want to Be a Rock'n'Roll Star'. But if the group had never sounded tighter on record, outside the studio the incessant touring – the price of chart failure – led to bad feeling, with Crosby in particular forever threatening to leave. The crisis came to a head during the recording of *Notorious Byrd Brothers* (1968). Crosby refused to sing Gerry Goffin and **Carole King** 'pop' songs – 'Goin' Back' and 'Wasn't Born to Follow' – demanded more political songs and then finally quit for a cash payment leaving the group with a half-completed album. The Byrds finished it as a trio and, once again, it was superb; even more importantly, it was well reviewed and sold well. Classified as a singles group, the Byrds were neglected by the new audience that sprang into being after 1967 and *Younger Than Yesterday*, the album that might have rescued them, was completely overshadowed by *Sgt Pepper's Lonely Hearts Club Band*. The reception of *Notorious* in 1968 confirmed that the Byrds had a definite (and developing) following, and while the larger 1967 audience still eluded them, another *Notorious* might have given the group the San Franciscan seal of approval.

Instead, the Byrds added **Gram Parsons**, from the International Submarine Band, replaced Mike Clarke with Kevin Kelley, and headed for Nashville where they played the Grand Ole Opry and recorded *Sweetheart of the Rodeo*, virtually creating country-rock and alienating their putative audiences at the same time. Later, *Sweetheart* would be seen as an enormously influential album, but in 1968 no one in either Nashville or Los Angeles was willing to accept a rock group singing songs by the Louvin brothers *and* **William Bell** *and* Dylan *and* **Merle Haggard**. *Sweetheart* not only lost the Byrds the 'progressive' audience, it also more or less destroyed the group. The next time they came to record, McGuinn would be the only Byrd left.

First Parsons quit rather than do a tour of South Africa, and then on the group's return, when McGuinn wanted out of the country trip, Hillman, whose idea it had been, left to form the **Flying Burrito Brothers** with Parsons. The new Byrds' debut album, *Dr Byrds and Mr Hyde*, with Gene Parsons – born 9 April 1944 – on drums, Clarence White – born 6 June 1944, in Maine – on guitar and John York on bass, was uncharacteristically muddy. Moreover, to McGuinn's chagrin, he seemed unable to get away from country-influenced musicians and henceforth there would always be a country flavour to the Byrds' music. At this low point, luck entered the picture in the form of the phenomenally successful *Easy Rider* film which used some of their songs on its soundtrack. Almost respectable, and with a better album, *The Ballad of Easy Rider* (1970), the Byrds seemed to be on the way up again.

In 1970 Skip Battin – born 2 February 1934, in Gallipolis, Ohio – half of **Skip and Flip**, an early Sixties imitation Everly Brothers, replaced John York and after some hard touring the group finally won themselves a reputation as a live band. Indeed they were so sure of themselves that half of the double album, *Untitled* (1971), consisted of live recordings. And as if that wasn't enough, the other half saw McGuinn back on form as a writer. He'd been commissioned to write a rock musical version of Ibsen's *Peer Gynt* (renamed *Gene Tryp*) with Jacques Levy, and though that fell through, out of it came a batch of songs some of which, like 'Chestnut Mare' and 'Just a Season', fitted perfectly into the classic Byrds' mould of weary resignation. None the less, *Untitled* was just marking time, and finally, in 1972, after two more desultory albums, *Byrdmaniax* and *Farther Along*, McGuinn folded the band in order to re-form the original Byrds and see if the group could take off again in an atmosphere of revived oldies. The resulting album, *Byrds* (Asylum, 1973) was an artistic disaster, demonstrating that the individual Byrds had developed away from each other and completely lost any sense of balance. Whereas previously they had played as a group, *Byrds* saw them acting as each other's sessionmen, which they were to continue to do in their various individual projects in the Seventies.

For a while it looked as though McGuinn, who of all the group had most assiduously cultivated Dylan, might find further success through his association with him, but after the Rolling Thunder Review in 1975 he, too, turned back to gigging with his fellow former Byrds. The last such album, *McGuinn and Hillman* (1981), saw both Hillman and McGuinn in

McGuinn and Hillman made a final album together in 1981

decidedly low key, going through the paces of soft, empty LA country-rock to little purpose.

If the Byrds lacked the ability to stay the course that, say, the **Rolling Stones** have displayed, they were in their time one of the most influential and assured of groups. They were memorable both for the doors they opened in their experimental and innovative albums and for achievements like 'Eight Miles High'. Well after the event, McGuinn – speaking of 'Mr Tambourine Man' – said: 'I tried to make my voice sound like a cross between Dylan and **John Lennon**'s.'

Precisely; the Byrds' success was that they yoked together the pop of the Beatles with the visions of Dylan. It was a staggering achievement, and one that seemed to burn out the group and its members before their time. *See also* **Gram Parsons**; **Gene Clark**; **Roger McGuinn**; **David Crosby**; **Chris Hillman**.

BYRNE, DAVID See **Talking Heads**

BYRNE, JERRY A contemporary of the young New Orleans rock'n'rollers, **Bobby Charles**, **Frankie Ford** and Mac Rebenack (**Dr John**), Byrne's claim to fame rests on just one record, 'Lights Out'. Recorded for Specialty in 1958 by producer **Harold Battiste** when Byrne was a 17-year-old (white) high school student, the record sold only in the South. It is, however, now recognized as a rock'n'roll classic, with its ferocious rhythm and **Art Neville**'s pounding piano solo. Because it sold in only moderate quantities, Byrne continued to play hops and dances around New Orleans, showing a strong **Ray Charles** influence. Then, in the words of Rebennack: 'Jerry got into some trouble and had to go off-the-set for a while.'

C., ROY Born Roy Charles Hammond in New York City in 1943, Roy C. changed his name to avoid confusion with **Roy Hamilton** and **Ray Charles**, and sang lead with the Genies (Claude Johnson, Buddy Fason, Bill Gaines, Fred Jones) on Shad, Hollywood, Warwick and Forum. When the group split up, Roy went solo, scoring an R&B hit with 'Shotgun Wedding' which went to Number 14 in the US in 1965 and reached the British Top 10 the following year.

Other discs on Black Hawk and Shout (produced by **Bert Berns**) made little impact, and in 1969 he formed his own record company, Alaga. He issued a long series of consistently good soul singles, dealing blatantly with sexual problems and pleasures. 'Divorce Court', 'I Found a Man in My Bed', 'Gotta Get Enough of Your Sweet Love Stuff' and others were later repackaged in album form as *Sex and Soul* by Mercury to whom he signed in 1973. Roy C. also wrote and produced the Mark IV's million-selling 'Honey I Still Love You', for Mercury in 1972. He remains one of the least acclaimed masters of contemporary soul music.

CABARET VOLTAIRE Named after the experimental performances by Paris-based artist/writer Tristan Tzara in the Twenties, the 'Cabs' as they quickly became known, had been working together in Sheffield as the central duo of Richard H. Kirk and Stephen 'Mal' Mallinder since the early Seventies. They perfected a rock version of the experimental electronic and tape music of John Cage and Karlheinz Stockhausen, anchoring dense, disjointed noise to a hard new wave beat. With singles such as 'Mix-Up' and albums like *Red Mecca* (1981), all on Rough Trade, they became the godfathers of the so-called 'Sheffield Scene', and famed around the world's punk grapevine as the leading new wave experimentalists.

Signed, briefly, to Virgin in the mid-Eighties for two albums, they produced a leaner mixture of dance-beat, roaring electronics and radio/television recordings that even won them modest chart success. Unable to turn them into 'stars', Virgin let them go in 1986. They continued to work happily in their Sheffield studios, touring regularly.

CADENCE RECORDS Formed in New York in 1953 by Archie Bleyer, Cadence is best remembered for the seven Nashville-based million-sellers by the **Everly Brothers**, including 'Bye Bye Love' in 1957 and 'Wake Up Little Susie' in 1958. Bleyer himself hit with the novelty 'The Naughty Lady of Shady Lane' in 1954, and **Johnny Tillotson** reached Number 2 in the US in 1960 with 'Poetry in Motion'. Heavier rock sounds like **Link Wray**'s original 'Rumble' appeared, too, while Cadence also fielded several ballad singers headlined by Andy Williams and his 1957 transatlantic Number 1, 'Butterfly'. Williams and the Everly Brothers left in 1960, and, partly as a result, Cadence ceased operations a year later; Bleyer sold the masters to Williams.

CADETS Fifties R&B quintet the Cadets – Aaron Collins, Willie Davis, Ted Taylor, Dub Jones and Lloyd McCraw – were a group with a double identity. As the Cadets they covered rock'n'roll songs for Modern, and as the Jacks cut ballads and jump tunes for RPM. They covered a host of hits (e.g. 'Heartbreak Hotel', 'Church Bells May Ring') but failed to improve on the originals until their version of the Jayhawks' comic 'Stranded in the Jungle', with its exotic, nocturnal sounds and Jones' sour narration, reached the US Top 20 in 1956.

On the Jacks' 1955 R&B hit, 'Why Don't You Write Me' (originally recorded by the Feathers) the lead was taken by Davis who, together with Collins, joined the Flairs. Jones moved on to the **Coasters** and Taylor became a much-admired soul singer. Aaron Collins' sisters, Betty and Rosie, formed the Teen Queens of 'Eddie My Love' fame.

CADILLACS New York R&B quintet the Cadillacs – Earl Carroll (born 1937), Bobby Phillips (1935), Lavern Drake (1938), Gus Willingham (1937) and John Clark (1937) – made their first appearance in 1954, when they started their recording career with Josie. Their slow ballads are favoured by present-day devotees, but the group themselves preferred a faster, harder style consistent with the most choreographed of all rock'n'roll stage acts. 'Speedoo' (Number 30 in 1955), a perfect crystallization of the up-tempo East Coast group sound, was a private joke – 'Some folks call me Speedoo but my real name is Mr Earl' – while 'Peekaboo' (Top 30 in 1958) was inspired by the **Coasters**. Carroll's voice was light, happy and tuneful. He was one of the best group singers, inspiring many other street-corner groups, black and white. While their manager, Esther Navarro, often took the credit, much of the Cadillacs' material was written by Carroll and other members: his replacement as lead singer, Bobby Spencer, wrote 'My Boy Lollipop' for singer Barbie Gaye – the original of **Millie** Small's 1964 British hit. After Carroll teamed up with the Coasters in 1961, the Cadillacs carried on recording for Smash, Capitol, Mercury and Polydor.

CAJUN MUSIC The sweaty swamplands of southwest Louisiana are the home of Cajun, one of the last bastions of indigenous American folk music. It has flourished in splendid isolation from the American way of life, its roots dating back to 1604 when the first settlers from France arrived in the Canadian province of Arcadia. Following the war between Britain and France, the Arcadians (now 'Cajuns') were forced to leave Canada, and, sailing down the eastern seaboard, finally settled in the hostile and virtually unpopulated lands of Louisiana. The music, like all folk forms, has undergone much change in the past 60 years. For example, the accordion was the prominent instrument in the Twenties but, by the Thirties, with the hillbilly influence strong, the fiddle took over. By the Seventies, both instruments were featured equally, and there was a noticeable influx during that decade of black music traditions (when played by black musicians the form is known as 'Zydeco'). But this did not allow its basic functions to alter: Cajun is primarily a dance music consisting of waltzes and two-steps.

Joe Falcon was Cajun's pre-war recording star, along with Joe Werner and the Hackberry Ramblers. Harry Choates' 'Jole Blonde' (the Cajun 'national anthem') and Nathan Abshire's 'Pine Grove Blues' were massive hits in the Forties, while the big names of the Fifties were Iry Le Jeune, Aldus Roger, and Lawrence Walker.

Cajun's biggest-ever commercial success came in 1961 when Cleveland Crochet's classic 'Sugar Bee' with Jay Stutes (on Goldband) broke into the lower reaches of the Hot 100. Supplying the loyal local record market since about 1970 have been George Khoury (Lyric), Lee Lavergne (Lanor), Jay Miller (Kajun), Carol Rachou (La Louisianne), Eddie Shuler (Goldband), and – biggest of all – Floyd Soileau (Jin and Swallow). *See also* **Clifton Chenier**.

CALE, J.J. Born in Tulsa, Oklahoma, in 1939, J.J. Cale began playing rock-'n'roll with a local group, J.J. Cale and the Valentines, in the mid-Fifties, before following **Leon Russell** to Los Angeles. There he recorded a psychedelic album and began writing. Back in Tulsa, Carl Radle sent a tape of Cale's to Russell, who signed him to his Shelter label. His first album, *Naturally* (1972), included two American Top 40 hits, 'Crazy Mama' and the much-recorded 'After Midnight'. Featuring the playing of Tim Drummond (drums), Carl Radle (bass), Norbert Putnam (bass), David Briggs (keyboards), Weldon Myrick (steel guitar), and Mac Gayden (slide guitar) amongst others, the album was notable for the relaxed yet insistent rhythms around Cale's guitar, his soft growling of the words of his songs and Audi Ashworth's sympathetic production. He has recorded further albums in the same mould for Shelter: *Really* (1972), which produced another Hot 100 hit, 'Lies', and *Okie* (1974). He subsequently recorded *Troubadour* (1976), *Number 5* (1979), *Shades* (1981) and *Grasshopper* (1984).

CALE, JOHN Born in Garnant, South Wales, in 1942, John Cale studied viola and keyboards at Goldsmiths College, London, before moving to the US on a music scholarship and working with avant-garde composer La Monte Young. He then formed the **Velvet Underground** with **Lou Reed** but left the group after the release of their second album, thereafter working as a producer with Iggy and the Stooges (*see* **Iggy Pop**) and **Nico**. While employed as a staff producer, initially with US Columbia and then with Warner Bros, he began to record albums of his own songs. *Paris 1919* (Warner Bros, 1973) attracted critical acclaim for its combination of musical elegance with literate, surrealistic lyrics. In 1974 he moved back to Britain, signed with Island Records and recorded *Fear*, a more abrasive album featuring a metallic, urban sound and images of paranoia. He has recorded regularly since, his releases including *Slow Dazzle* and *Helen of Troy* (both 1975), *Guts* (1977), *Sabotage* (1980), and his 1981 debut for A&M, *Honi Soit*. Recording for the Ze label since 1982, he released *Music for a New Society* during that year and followed it with *Caribbean Sunset* (1983) and *John Cale Comes Alive* (1984). An unpredictable stage performer and a highly eclectic and idiosyncratic recording artist, Cale has complemented his solo activities

with production work for **Patti Smith**, the Modern Lovers, **Squeeze**, and Dave Kubinec, and soundtrack work on the films *Caged Heat* and *Heat*.

CAMEO US funk band Cameo is led by singer, writer and producer Larry Blackmon, a New York City-bred drummer who has guided Cameo's fortunes since the mid-Seventies. Signed to Chocolate City/Casablanca in 1975 and founded in a hard funk style on their first LPs (*Cardiac Arrest* and *Ugly Ego*), the band's personnel grew at one time to eleven, building a strong reputation through incessant touring and extravagant stage shows, and often rivalling Parliament (see **George Clinton**) and **Earth, Wind and Fire** in their showmanship. In the Eighties, their music started to sound flabby and Blackmon decided to strip Cameo down to a basic four-piece. As a result, 1982's *Alligator Woman* and the subsequent *She's Strange* put the band back to the top of the R&B charts and, in the case of the latter album, the pop charts. In 1985 Blackmon pared the band down even further, to a trio, with Nathan Leftenant and Tomi Jenkins, had an even bigger pop hit, 'Single Life', and became somewhat tetchy with anyone who dared describe the band's music as 'funk' or 'black'. In 1986, both the album *Word Up* and the

single of the same name cemented Cameo's pop chart success on both sides of the Atlantic.

CAMEO-PARKWAY RECORDS Formed in 1956 by two Philadelphian songwriters, Kal Mann and Bernie Lowe, Cameo-Parkway Records achieved an unparalleled run of success in the early Sixties with a series of dance records based on the phenomenally successful 'Twist'. While working in New York's Tin Pan Alley, Mann and Lowe wrote 'Butterfly', and rather than sell the song to a name artist, they decided to launch their own 'Cameo' label and had a local singer, **Charlie Gracie**, record the song. Both Gracie's version and a cover rendition by Andy Williams became hits, as did Gracie's follow-up, 'Fabulous', in 1957.

Cameo were able to take advantage of Philadelphia's burgeoning record scene, which centred around **Dick Clark**'s *American Bandstand*, a TV rock show which attracted a huge national audience and became, in effect, the industry's sole criterion for assessing a record's potential. Cameo struck up a good working relationship with Dick Clark (who chose all the acts and records) and the label geared its entire output towards the show. In 1957, Cameo scored with 'Silhouette'

John Cale's eerie viola sound made an edgy contribution to Velvet Underground's first two albums, before he moved on to wider fields

by the Rays (leased from the XYZ label) and John Zacherle's ghoulish 'Dinner with Drac' as well as smaller hits by the Applejacks, Timmie Rogers and Bernie Lowe's Orchestra.

In 1959, they signed **Bobby Rydell**, a 17-year-old Philadelphian who quickly blossomed into America's foremost teenage idol with a colossal run of hits, including 'Volare', 'Kissin' Time', 'Wild One' and 'Forget Him'. Also in 1959, the label signed one Ernest Evans, who had plucked chickens in a shop patronized by Kal Mann, and renamed him **Chubby Checker**. After one flop, one moderate hit ('The Class' on which Checker mimicked **Elvis**, the **Coasters**, **Fats Domino** and the Chipmunks), then two more flops, Checker recorded 'The Twist', an undistinguished dance-disc that became a US Number 1 in August 1960. He followed that with several more dance hits before recording 'Let's Twist Again' which re-focused attention on 'The Twist' and sparked off the biggest dance craze in years. His original 'Twist' disc was re-released and reached Number 1 in America for the second time in November 1961. Cameo demonstrated an unmatched flair for exploitation by cashing in shamelessly with more dance discs, including Checker's 'Limbo Rock', 'Slow Twistin'', 'The Fly', the **Orlons'** 'Wah-Watusi' and 'South Street', and Dee-Dee Sharp's 'Mashed Potato Time' – all big American hits.

By 1963, however, the formula had grown stale and Mann and Lowe sold their label to retire as extremely rich young men. Their timing, as always, was exemplary – by 1964, Cameo's hits had dried up and although Bunny Sigler and **Question Mark and the Mysterians** had huge hits in 1965–6, the label folded in 1968.

CAMPBELL, GLEN
Although best known as a middle-of-the-road vocalist with country leanings, Glen Campbell – born in Oklahoma on 22 April 1938 – played guitar on recording sessions in Nashville and Los Angeles before beginning his singing career. Producer Nik Venet recorded some vocal and instrumental sides with him in 1961, and 'Turn Around Look at Me' was a minor hit on Crest, but soon after, Campbell returned to session work, playing behind the **Monkees**, **Mamas and Papas** and others, as well as accompanying the **Beach Boys** on tour for a short time. He resumed his own recording career with Capitol in the mid-Sixties, covering **Buffy Sainte-Marie**'s 'Universal Soldier', then hav-

ing a worldwide hit with 'Gentle on My Mind', composed by 'New Nashville' songwriter **John Hartford**. Since then, Campbell has had many hits in his pop/country crooning style, often with above-average ballads. In particular, he brought the work of **Jimmy Webb** to the fore with 'Wichita Lineman', 'Galveston' and others. In the Seventies, Campbell remained one of the better middle-of-the-road artists, introducing the songs of Kenny O'Dell, Kinky Friedman, **Allen Toussaint**, and **Merle Haggard** to audiences beyond the country and rock fraternities, although the frequent blandness of his singing – as on, say, his 1975 worldwide smash hit, 'Rhinestone Cowboy' – often contrasted with the original power of his chosen material.

CAN
Formed in the summer of 1968, Can were classically and jazz-trained musicians – students of German avant-garde composer Karlheinz Stockhausen – who believed that rock was the idiom of greatest potential at that time. They started by making film soundtracks in their rented castle outside Cologne, and after a struggle secured a record contract with United Artists. Their albums, from *Monster Movie* (1970) to *Soon Over Baballuma* (1975), have done justice both to rock

and to the musical education of Can's members. They have been the most consistently experimental of the well-known German groups, producing albums as varied as the stark *Ege Bamyasi* (1972) and the smooth-textured *Future Days* (1974). At that point the line-up included Irmin Schmidt, piano (born 29 May 1937); Holger Czukay, bass guitar (24 March 1938); Michael Karoli, guitar (29 April 1948); Jackie Liebesit, drums (26 May 1938), and Damo Suzuki, vocals (16 January 1950). They moved to Virgin in 1975 and two years later added Rosko Gee and Reebop Kwaku Baah (both ex-**Traffic**), who made their debut on *Saw Delight*. Can's members became involved in solo projects towards the end of the Seventies, notably Czukay, whose *Movies* (EMI, 1979) was well received.

CANNED HEAT
Blues band Canned Heat won international fame when their atmospheric version of the Memphis Jug Band's 'On the Road Again' reached Number 8 in Britain and Number 16 in America in 1968. The group was formed in 1965 by blues collector Bob ('The Bear') Hite (vocals, born on 26 February 1945), Henry Vestine (guitar, 25 December 1944) and Al ('Blind Owl') Wilson (slide guitar,

The driving force behind Canned Heat was a profound love of the traditional blues. Vocalist Bob Hite, known as 'the Bear', and Al 'Blind Owl' Wilson shared a passion for collecting old blues recordings

harmonica, vocals, 4 August 1943). All were students of country blues and their first Liberty album – *Canned Heat* (1967) was an expert reworking of rural songs in an electric blues style, with Larry Taylor (bass, 26 June 1942) and Frank Cook (drums), replaced in 1968 by Fito De La Parra (8 February 1946).

Both 'On the Road Again' and 'Going up the Country' (another Top 20 hit, in 1969) featured Wilson's high-pitched singing, and established the band in the forefront of white blues exponents. Numerous Liberty albums followed including one with veteran bluesman **John Lee Hooker** (*Hooker 'n' Heat*, 1971). Their biggest European hit was a reworking of **Wilbert Harrison**'s 'Let's Work Together' (a Number 2 in Britain) in 1970. Wilson's death on 3 September 1970 precipitated several personnel changes, with Taylor leaving to join **John Mayall**, a route later followed by **Harvey Mandel** who had replaced Wilson. By the mid-Seventies, only Vestine and the 260lb Hite remained of the original line-up, having been joined by Hite's brother Richard (guitar, bass, vocals, born in 1950), James Shane (guitar, bass, vocals) and Ed Beyer (keyboards). Hite died on 5 April 1981, in California.

CANNON, FREDDY A teen star of the late Fifties, Freddy Cannon was born Freddy Picariello in Lynn, Massachusetts, on 4 December 1940. Cannon had Boston disc jockey Jack McDermott to thank for putting him in touch with **Bob Crewe** and Frank Slay of Swan Records; it was with them that Cannon enjoyed an unbroken string of 18 hits beginning with 'Tallahassie Lassie' (written by his mother, Crewe and Slay) in 1959. 'Way Down Yonder in New Orleans' (1959) and 'Palisades Park' (1962) also made the Top 10.

Crewe, Slay and the studio musicians sat around for hours trying to make the records simpler, but the combination of brassy horns and Cannon's sore throat vocals – he must have taken singing lessons from **Fabian** – has not stood the test of time. 'Buzz Buzz a Diddle It', with a powerful **Bo Diddley**-style guitar intro from Kenny Paulson (who added the glitter to 'Tallahassie Lassie') rates as his finest hour. He also had Top 20 hits with 'Abigail Beecher' and 'Action' on Warner Brothers in 1965–6. Cannon subsequently recorded for Sire, We Make Rock'n'Roll Records, and Metromedia, but met with little success.

CAPALDI, JIM An original member of **Traffic**, Jim Capaldi was born in Evesham, Worcestershire, on 2 August 1944. He first found professional fame with Birmingham-based band Deep Feeling before joining Traffic as drummer. He immediately achieved an uncanny relationship with **Steve Winwood**, the spirit of whose music was perfectly matched by Capaldi's lyrics. His solo songwriting efforts were heard on the first album, *Mr Fantasy* ('Dealer', for example), but it was not until 1972 that he released a solo album, the excellent *Oh How We Danced* (Island), recorded in Muscle Shoals and featuring the studio's resident musicians together with various members of Traffic including Steve Winwood and **Dave Mason**. Several Traffic tours later he released the ecologically oriented *Whale Meat Again* (1974) and had a Top 20 UK hit with 'It's All Up To You'. In 1975 he had further hits with a revival of 'Love Hurts' and the album *Short Cut – Draw Blood*. Subsequent Capaldi albums included *The Contender* (1978), *The Sweet Smell of . . . Success* (Carrere, 1980), *Fierce Heat* (WEA, 1983) and *One Man Mission* (1984).

CAPITOL RECORDS In the spring of 1942 Capitol was founded by record shop owner Glenn Wallichs (of 'Wallich's Music City'), film producer Buddy DeSylva and songwriter Johnny Mercer on the basis that Wallichs would handle the business aspects and Mercer the musical scores, while DeSylva looked after the finances. The war years were not auspicious for the formation of a new record company, but with DeSylva investing more money in the concern, Capitol survived to sign a young black jazz pianist-vocalist named **Nat 'King' Cole** in 1943. By 1950, Cole had stepped into the front ranks of record personalities with hits such as 'Nature Boy', 'Mona Lisa' and 'Too Young', and accounted for a quarter of the label's turnover. During the early Fifties, Capitol consolidated its position with such pre-rock acts as **Les Paul and Mary Ford**, Frank Sinatra, and the orchestras of Les Baxter and Nelson Riddle.

In 1948, the label also activated a successful country music division by signing the popular Tex Ritter, and staff producer Ken Nelson quickly developed an outstanding country roster, including **Tennessee Ernie Ford**, Jean Sheppard, Faron Young, Hank Thompson and Merle Travis, who all registered hits in that market. In 1954, Capitol announced a $20 million

Freddy Cannon pounded out a series of lightweight hits in the late Fifties and early Sixties, re-emerging in the Seventies rock revival

turnover and the following year, EMI in Britain bought Capitol for £8½ million.

Ken Nelson also masterminded Capitol's entry into rock'n'roll by signing **Gene Vincent**, whose 'Be-Bop-A-Lula' sold a million in 1956. Other Capitol rock acts at this time included **Esquerita**, Tommy Sands, **Merrill Moore** and **Johnny Otis**, but the label's success in this field was extremely limited due to its condescending attitude towards the idiom – a reaction after the fabulous success of the post-war years. Then, in 1961, a young staff producer named Nik Venet signed the popular Lettermen vocal group and in 1962 he contracted the **Beach Boys**, who quickly went on to become the foremost US act of the mid-Sixties. The acquisition in 1964 of the **Beatles**, **Peter and Gordon**, and other UK acts consolidated Capitol's position in the rock field and precipitated a boom period. In the country market, **Buck Owens**, **Merle Haggard**, and Sonny James all became major acts.

During the late Sixties, Capitol was slow in catering for hard rock audiences but made amends by signing **Joe South**, **Steve Miller** and **Grand Funk Railroad** – the latter accounting for ten million record sales in three years (1971–3). The company also had **The Band**, the **Raspberries**, **Anne Murray**, and **Glen Campbell**, together with US rights to releases by **Paul McCartney** and Wings. In the early Eighties, Capitol could claim one of the biggest acts of the so-called 'second British invasion' in **Duran Duran**, and arguably *the* comeback artist of the decade – **Tina Turner**.

CAPTAIN BEEFHEART AND HIS MAGIC BAND

Don Van Vliet, the Captain (born in Glendale, California, on 15 January 1941), was a little too bizarre for even the most steadfast crazies in the music biz. He first appeared with his band in 1966 with two singles – 'Diddy Wah Diddy' and 'Frying Pan' – of bone-crunching blues-rock. His cult started growing with the release of *Safe as Milk* (Kama Sutra) which featured **Ry Cooder**, Jimmy Semens, John Drumbo French and Herb Besman.

The Captain had an amazingly deep, gruff voice with an unprecedented range, and most felt he could have been the greatest white blues singer ever. But his own inclinations took him further and further from the mainstream. With his third album (*Trout Mask Replica*, Straight, 1969), he achieved his finest, and most avant-garde, work. The album featured a new Magic Band –

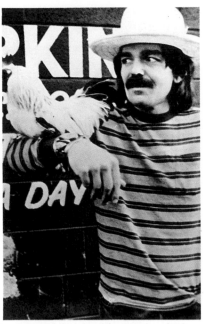

The controlled insanity of Captain Beefheart, tearful or bird-brained: a little too crazy for even the extremists in the music world

Semens, guitar; Zoot Horn Rollo, guitar; the Mascara Snake, bass clarinet; and Rockette Morton, bass. It was rooted in Delta blues, but sounded nothing like the blues. There was a blues feeling to it, but the horn players were blowing lines more reminiscent of the new wave jazz of Ornette Coleman and John Coltrane. Tempos jumped about crazily, melodies disappeared faster than they could be absorbed. The Captain's lyrics were an outrageously wacky series of word plays, puns and surrealist images which carried very serious thoughts. Beefheart considered his music great art, but saw no reason why he shouldn't reap the rewards of a pop musician. He felt that managers and record company executives tried to compromise his work; consequently most of his records came out on different labels. Live performances were irregular.

After *Trout Mask Replica*, he started moving slowly back towards the pop mainstream on his own initiative. By 1974, he had come up with *Unconditionally Guaranteed* (Mercury in America, Virgin in Britain), a baroque and bluesy album that was quite accessible. However, success still eluded him. Worse, perhaps the best incarnation of the Magic Band (including guitarists Zoot Horn Rollo and Rockette Morton) left him to form a group, Mallard. He had taught most of them to play from scratch, and their looks and musicianship were integral to his music. In 1975 the Captain rejoined his oldest musical comrade, **Frank Zappa**, as vocalist with the Mothers of Invention. Three years later he was back with Warner Bros for the album *Shiny Beast* and enjoying a cult following among the new wave cognoscenti. *Doc at the Radar Station* (1980) and *Ice Cream for Crow* (1982) were both released by Virgin after a legal battle over the rights to Beefheart recordings. *Blue Jeans and Moonbeans* followed in 1984.

CAPTAIN SENSIBLE

Initially making his first outings as a solo artist while still a member of the **Damned**, Captain Sensible (real name Ray Burns, born 24 April 1960) was so christened on the return ferry journey from a festival in France, during which the extreme idiocy of his behaviour inspired the ironic nickname. He had a surprise UK Number 1 single in 1982 with his catchy oddball version of 'Happy Talk' from Rogers and Hammerstein's *South Pacific*. This was quickly followed up by another single, 'Wot', which, although only a minor success in the UK, was a huge worldwide dancefloor hit, and the album *Women and Captains First*.

Sensible continued to work with the Damned until 1984, when the release of *The Power of Love*, prompted his departure. This gave him his second UK Top 10 hit with 'Glad It's All Over', but he failed to follow this up, and subsequent releases showed no likelihood of making an impact on the charts. *See also* **Damned**.

Underground band Caravan, here preparing for a TV appearance on 'Colour Me Pop', developed a wistful, gently avant-garde style

CARAVAN One of the longest-lasting of British underground bands, Caravan was formed in 1967 by members of Canterbury group the Wilde Flowers, whose line-up had included **Kevin Ayers** and **Robert Wyatt**, founder members of **Soft Machine**. Caravan's original personnel comprised Pye Hastings (guitar, vocals), David Sinclair (keyboards), Richard Sinclair (bass, vocals), and Richard Coughlan (drums); they made one album for MGM and two for Decca's Deram label between 1968 and 1970, all featuring wistful, eccentric songs and gentle *avant-garde* playing. David Sinclair left to join Robert Wyatt in Matching Mole and subsequently joined Hatfield and the North, who in turn recruited his cousin Richard in 1972. Various replacements were tried (including pianist Steve Miller from Delivery) but it was only when David Sinclair rejoined Caravan – now including Geoff Richardson (viola) and John Perry (bass) – that the band's music began to reach out to new audiences. They toured the US in 1974 and made a minor impact with their seventh album, *Cunning Stunts* (Deram), but David Sinclair left for a second time during the following year.

They continued recording until the end of the decade – *Blind Dog at St Dunstans* (Arista, 1976), *Better by Far* (1977) – and released their swan-song, *The Album*, in 1980.

CARMEL Born in Scunthorpe, England on 24 November 1958, Carmel McCourt came to the fore as one of the prime exponents of the moody, jazz-influenced pop that blossomed during the so-called British jazz revival of the mid-Eighties. Brought up as a Catholic, Carmel sang in church as a child, but her singing career proper began while at art college in Manchester. After performing occasionally with the group Bee Vamp she eventually joined up with bassist Jim Paris in 1981 and they set up on their own as Carmel, finding a drummer in Gerry Darby.

The group released a single, 'Storm', to great acclaim in 1982, followed by a mini LP on Red Flame, generating enough interest for major label London Records to snap them up. Two UK Top 30 singles followed, 'Bad Day' in 1983 and 'More More More' in 1984, plus a debut album *The Drum is Everything*. The group disappeared from the public eye for a while but resurfaced in 1986 with a new album, *Sally*.

CARNES, KIM American mainstream singer/songwriter Kim Carnes (born in 1948 in Los Angeles) spent most of the Seventies recording unsuccessful albums consisting mainly of ballads before releasing the best-selling US single of 1981, the rock-oriented 'Bette Davis Eyes'.

Some of Carnes' songs had been covered by the likes of Frank Sinatra and Barbra Streisand, but her big break came when **Kenny Rogers** (who had also recorded some of her songs) duetted with her on 'Don't Fall in Love With a Dreamer' (a US Number 4 in 1980). By this stage she had already been concentrating on more rock-inclined material and she went on to have a US Number 10 in her own right with 'More Love' in 1980. In 1981 she released the album *Mistaken Identity* which included 'Bette Davis Eyes' (also a UK Number 10). She further explored the rock sound, bordering on hard rock on the album *Voyeur* (1982). The calmer *Café Racers* was released in 1984.

CARPENTERS One of America's most commercially successful easy-listening acts of the Seventies, the Carpenters were a brother and sister duo – Richard (born 15 October 1946, keyboards and vocals) and Karen (born 2 March 1950, vocals and drums) – from New Haven, Connecticut. Moving to California in the late Sixties, they sang together in a six-member group called Spectrum, whose emphasis on soft harmonies and orchestrations heralded their later work as a twosome. **Herb Alpert** heard a tape of the group and signed the Carpenters to his A&M label in 1970. There they enjoyed a stream of hit singles and albums, including the worldwide sellers 'Goodbye to Love' (1972) and 'Top of the World' (1973), both written by Richard with his songwriting partner John Bettis. Their hits also included songs by Lennon/McCartney ('Ticket to Ride', 1970), Bonnie Bramlett (of **Delaney and Bonnie**) and **Leon Russell** ('Superstar', 1971), Brian Holland (of **Holland, Dozier and Holland**) ('Please Mr Postman', 1974), and **Hank Williams** ('Jambalaya', 1974). The latter two songs plus the Carpenter–Bettis original 'Yesterday Once More' both came from a concept album, *Now and Then* (1973), that immaculately reflected the fad for musical nostalgia at that time. The duo cut down drastically on recording during the late Seventies and early Eighties, with 'Touch Me When We're Dancing' providing their only US Top 40 hit during the latter decade. Karen died suddenly on 4 February

1983, from heart failure brought on by anorexia nervosa. 'Make Believe It's Your First Time' became a posthumous hit in the UK during the same year.

CARR, JAMES A Southern soul wailer born in Memphis on 13 June 1942, James Carr started off sounding like **Otis Redding**, developed a similarity to **Percy Sledge**, and was considered by many to be better than either of them. After signing with the **Soul Stirrers** gospel group, he signed to Goldwax Records of Memphis and recorded a succession of intense performances ('You Got My Mind Messed Up', 'Love Attack', 'Pouring Water on a Drowning Man' in 1966; 'Dark End of the Street', 'A Man Needs a Woman' in 1967) and a few up-tempo sides (including 'That's What I Want to Know', 1966, and 'Freedom Train', 1968) that have since become disco favourites. He was last heard on Atlantic in 1971.

CARS Boston's the Cars burst onto the scene in 1978 as America's fastest selling new wave act, their first two albums registering sales of more than six million copies each. Their success, although not on so large a scale, continued into the Eighties as they became the favourites of North American AOR audiences.

Ric Ocasek (guitar/vocals) and Ben Orr (bass/vocals) had been working together for years in Cleveland before they moved to Boston in 1972. Playing with various musicians and picking up permanent band members on the way, they had, by 1976, settled on a line-up of Elliot Easton (guitar), David Robinson (drums) and Greg Hawkes (keyboards) and called themselves the Cars. Record company interest picked up as they gained a good reputation around Boston, and in 1977 they signed to Elektra. The next year they recorded their debut album, *The Cars*, in London, and it was in the UK that they had their first hit, a Number 3 with the raunchy guitar pop single 'My Best Friend's Girl', followed into the Top 20 by 'Just What I Needed'. The Cars only repeated their UK success six years later with 'Drive', but in America and the rest of the world, subsequent albums have sold in large quantities. In 1983, Ocasek released a poorly received solo album, *Beatitude*.

'Drive' re-entered the charts in 1985 as a result of its use during the Live Aid concert (*see* **Band Aid**) over a harrowing film of a starving African child attempting to stand.

CARTER AND LEWIS Born in Small Heath, Birmingham, in 1942, songwriters John Carter (real name John Shakespeare) and Ken Lewis (Kenneth Hawker) formed the group Carter, Lewis and the Southerners (which included **Jimmy Page**) in the Sixties. Between 1962 and 1963 they were hardly off the air and had a minor hit with 'Your Momma's out of Town'.

In 1964 Carter and Lewis joined forces with songwriter Perry Ford (real name Bryan Pugh; born 1940 in Lincoln) to provide vocal backings – for example on the **Who**'s 'I Can't Explain' in 1965. The trio then decided to put out their own recordings under the name of the Ivy League and, in 1965, had a couple of British Top 10 hits in a close-harmony style influenced by both the **Beach Boys** and the **Four Seasons**, 'Funny How Love Can Be' and 'Tossing and Turning', both on Piccadilly. Carter then left the group and was replaced with yet another songwriter, Tony Burrows. In 1967 the Ivy League was augmented by one, became the Flowerpot Men and had a solitary hit with a Carter–Lewis song, 'Let's Go to San Francisco'. In 1968, after the failure of the over-produced 'A Walk in the Sky', they changed their name to Friends in an abortive attempt to halt their decline. Meanwhile Carter and Lewis returned to session singing and entered the lucrative world of commercials. John Carter later reappeared in the British and US charts as the lead singer on the First Class's 'Beach Baby'; another member of the 'group' was Tony Burrows.

CARTER, CLARENCE Blind since childhood, Clarence Carter first recorded with Calvin Scott (or Thomas) as Calvin and Clarence and the C and C Boys, for Fairlane, Duke and Atco. When Scott was injured in a car crash, Carter went solo for **Rick Hall**'s Muscle Shoals-based Fame label, entering the charts with 'Tell Daddy' and 'Thread the Needle' in 1967.

In 1968 he signed with Atlantic and recorded a succession of solid soul hits which reached both R&B and pop charts. They included 'Looking for a Fox', 'Slip Away' (national Top 10 in 1968), 'Too Weak to Fight', 'Snatchin' it Back', 'Patches' (taken from a Chairmen of the Board album, it reached Number 2 in Britain in 1970), 'It's All In Your Mind', and 'The Court Room'. He left Atlantic for ABC, but reappeared during 1981 on the Venture label, with *Let's Burn*. Carter also nurtured the career of soul singer Candi Staton, whom he later married.

CARTER FAMILY The most influential singing group in rural American music, the Carter Family was composed of A.P. Carter (1891–1960), his wife Sara (born 1898) and her cousin Maybelle (born 1909), all from southern Virginia. The trio performed locally during the Twenties but achieved fame throughout the South after their first recordings (Victor, 1927). In contrast with contemporary fiddle bands and solo singers, they defined the style of the family harmony group, employing two- and three-part vocal arrangements of traditional ballads, lyric songs and hymns. Their instrumental accompaniments – two guitars, or guitar and autoharp – lent prominence to Maybelle Carter's innovative fashion of melody-line guitar-playing.

Recording regularly throughout the Thirties, the family touched upon most idioms of Southern song and devised some of their own. A.P. Carter was an astute collector of songs, obtaining material from both white and black informants and channelling it into a stream of commercial records, which in turn became a legacy for later artists. Songs associated with the Carters are current today among many bluegrass and C&W artists. 'Wildwood Flower' has become a test-piece for country guitarists, while 'Keep on the Sunny Side', 'Worried Man Blues', 'Will the Circle Be Unbroken' and a score more have permanent places in the idiom.

The original trio disbanded in 1943, and the numerous Carter children provided the basis for two distinct groups. One of these still performs, headed by Maybelle and including her daughter June, wife of **Johnny Cash**. The recordings of the original family, made between 1927 and 1941, have been extensively reissued.

CARTER, MEL Born in Cincinnati on 22 April 1943, Mel Carter worked with Paul Gayten's band before moving to gospel where he sang with the Robert Anderson Singers and his own group, the Carvetts. In 1960 he moved to California where **Sam Cooke** signed him to Derby, the label on which he brushed the Top 50 with the romantic soul ballad, 'When a Boy Falls in Love' in 1963. More substantial hits followed on Imperial. With the singles 'Hold Me, Thrill Me, Kiss Me' (which reached the Top 10 in 1965), 'All of a Sudden My Heart Sings', 'Band of Gold' and 'You You You' (all Top 50 hits) Carter strayed more towards an MOR, singalong style that led to a durable chart career.

Johnny Cash, rueful folk champion of society's all-time losers

CASH, JOHNNY The first country singer since **Jim Reeves** to achieve international stardom, Johnny Cash's reputation is built upon his instantly recognizable (if limited) voice, his ability to write communicative songs, and a 'natural' presence on stage and on film. Additionally, the range of his interests and friendships – prisoners, Indians, railroads, Christianity, **Bob Dylan** – has won him a following among both liberals and Middle Americans.

Born John R. Cash in Kingsland, Arkansas, on 26 February 1932, he spent his early life farming, selling vacuum cleaners, serving in the Air Force, and writing poetry. In 1954, he formed a country band in Memphis. In 1955, his first record, 'Cry! Cry! Cry!', made the country Top 10 on the Sun label. Soon Cash was to develop a unique echoing, sparse, melancholy sound that led to hits such as 'Folsom Prison Blues' and 'I Walk the Line'. In 1958 he gained a producer in **Jack Clement** who took him into the Top 20 of the Hot 100, with 'Ballad of a Teenage Queen' and 'Guess Things Happen That Way', a manager in Bob Neal who got him into movies, and a new record company in Columbia. Columbia recorded Cash in much the same way as Sun, making the most of his distinctive voice, and hits have been forthcoming ever since, including 'Don't Take Your Guns to Town' (1959), 'Ring of Fire' (1963), 'Folsom Prison Blues' (1968), 'A Boy Named Sue' (1969), 'What Is Truth' (1970), and 'Sunday Morning Coming Down' (1971). He has also had 40 or so country hits.

Cash's audience broadened considerably in 1968 when he recorded an album 'live' in Folsom Prison and gained a national TV series and an international reputation. At this time he recorded 'Girl from the North Country', with Bob Dylan, and began to encourage young singer/songwriters such as **Kris Kristofferson** and Glen Sutton. He had already issued several concept/conscience albums, like the *Ballads of the True West*, *Bitter Tears*, and *Ride This Train*, and was in demand for TV documentaries.

During the Seventies he continued to expand his activities, visiting, writing and singing about Jerusalem and Vietnam, and recording a 'family' album – he is married to singer June Carter of the famous country music **Carter Family**. As an actor he starred with Kirk Douglas in *A Gunfight*, having starred in Hollywood 'B' features a decade earlier, and he just failed to outwit Columbo on television.

Johnny Cash has become a larger-than-life figure, whose importance goes beyond country music, or even rock. For country music, he became an international ambassador and undoubtedly he greatly helped to popularize the sound without projecting a stereotyped image. For rock, his early hits opened the way for an injection of country sounds by others, and his recording with Dylan influenced the thoughts of many country artists and promoters about the viability of country-rock. *See also* **Sun Records**

CASSIDY, DAVID Born in Englewood, New Jersey, on 12 April 1950, David Cassidy was for a short time the leading team idol of the early Seventies. His father was the Hollywood actor Jack Cassidy, his stepmother the actress/singer Shirley Jones, and his pop career began when he was booked to co-star with her in a TV series, *The Partridge Family*, in 1970. Previously he had been a small-time actor, playing the odd TV role and appearing in minor roles in Broadway shows. The *Partridge Family* – produced by Screen Gems–Columbia, who had been responsible for *The Monkees* TV series four years earlier – featured Cassidy as the lead singer of a mythical pop family, and soon he, Jones and a group of session musicians were making hits under the show's title. 'I Think I Love You' went to the top of the US charts in 1970. Cassidy's solo career was, for a brief period, phenomenal. By 1972 he was the hottest property in pop, and his international tours were sellouts despite the bland simplicity of songs like 'How Can I Be Sure' (1972) and the UK chart-topping 'Daydreamer' (1973). His complaints that he wanted to be taken seriously as a singer (with the 1975 concept album *I Write the Songs*)

David Cassidy's success depended on a baby face and breathy vocals

coincided with many of his fans deserting him in favour of a younger idol, Donny, of the **Osmonds**, but enough people accepted the new image to put two singles from the album in the British Top 20. During 1976 he left Bell, for whom he had recorded both solo and as a member of the Partridge Family, for RCA. His popularity dwindled, however, and he took only the occasional TV role before attempting a modestly successful comeback in 1985 with 'Last Kiss', a Top 20 hit in the UK.

CASTOR, JIMMY Born on 22 June 1943 in New York, Jimmy Castor sang on street-corners with the likes of **Frankie Lymon** and the Teenagers. The latter recorded 'I Promise to Remember', which Castor had composed and previously cut on Wing with his own group, the Juniors, consisting of Orton Graves, Johnny Williams, and Al Casey Jr, son of the famous jazz guitarist. Castor also sang with the Teenchords, recorded as a solo artist for Winley, Clown, Jet-Set, and Decca, and played saxophone on Dave 'Baby' Cortez's 'Rinky Dink'. In 1966 he had a Top 40 hit on Smash with a Latin calypso, 'Hey, Leroy, Your Mama's Calling You'. After other records on Compass and Capitol, he reached the top with a ferocious discotheque classic, 'Troglodyte' (RCA). Subsequent discs for Atlantic, including the aptly titled 1974 album *The Everything Man* and

the 1975 hit 'King Kong', demonstrated Castor's exceptional versatility. By 1982, he was recording for the Salsoul label and enjoying success in the soul and disco market with 'E-Man Boogie 82', basically an update of his earlier hits.

CBS RECORDS See **Columbia Records**

CHAD AND JEREMY The aura of the British public school surrounded ex-Central School of Speech and Drama students, Chad (born 10 December 1943) and Jeremy (born 22 March 1944). They were polite and well-spoken and, accordingly, highly popular for a time in America. Their early material was a mixture of folk and pop which evolved into post-**Byrds** folk-rock and thence to post-*Sgt Pepper* ideas expressed in the 'Progress Suite', a five-movement piece on *Of Cabbages and Kings* (Columbia, 1967), scored and arranged by Chad Stuart, who always took the weight of the musical duties, leaving Jeremy Clyde to concentrate on the lyrics. Both played guitars, Chad adding a variety of keyboard and stringed instruments, and both sang. Their considerable success in America in the wake of the **Beatles** – they had three Top 20 records, 'A Summer Song', 'Willow Weep for Me' (World Artists, 1964) and 'Before and After' (Columbia, 1965) – was never reflected in their native Britain where 'Yesterday's Gone' (1964) was their only Top 40 hit. They went their separate ways in 1969, Chad trying his hand at writing musicals and Jeremy Clyde taking up acting. His best known performance was in *Conduct Unbecoming* in London's West End, which also marked the stage debut of ex-**Manfred Mann** singer **Paul Jones**. They were briefly reunited during 1985 when both took roles in the West End production of the musical show, *Pump Boys and Dinettes*.

CHAIRMEN OF THE BOARD One of the most intriguing groups in the black music mainstream of the early Seventies, the Chairmen of the Board were formed in 1969 by ex-Motown production team **Holland, Dozier and Holland** as one of the initial acts for their Invictus label, it consisted of General Norman Johnson (the wheezing-voiced ex-lead singer of the Showmen), Eddie Curtis, Harrison Kennedy, and Danny Woods. With every singer on occasion singing lead and also possessing an ability to play a variety of instruments, the group none

the less worked mainly as a showcase for the extraordinary vocal and songwriting talents of General Johnson on hits like 'Give Me Just a Little More Time' (a million-seller in 1970) and the US Top 20 'Pay the Piper' (1970). By 1972 the group had become a trio through Curtis leaving, and each group member also cut solo albums. With Johnson spending a good deal of his time writing and producing (with Greg Perry) for others, Chairmen of the Board's successes became more infrequent, partly because of the gradual winding down of Invictus. The group was officially disbanded in 1976, after Johnson and Woods had completed a tour of the UK without the other members. Johnson became a solo artist with Arista.

CHAMBERS BROTHERS An early, influential band in the soul-funk mode, the Chambers Brothers were Lester (born 13 April 1940), George (26 September 1931), Joe (22 August 1942) and Willie (2 March 1938), all from Lee County, Mississippi. They moved to Los Angeles in the Fifties, and, by 1961, were becoming known as a gospel quartet in the southern California area. Their subsequent records on Vault included magnificently rough versions of soul songs like 'Your Old Ready' and 'People Get Ready', each heavily featuring mouth-harp, that were acclaimed by fans of downhome blues. Augmented by drummer Brian Keenan, who had once played with **Manfred Mann**, the Brothers joined Columbia and made their chart debut with 'The Time Has Come Today', the title track from their first album, in 1967. It reached Number 11 in the US, and the follow-up, 'I Can't Turn You Loose', was also a Top 40 hit in 1968. The band's stoned black hippie image was taken up by the underground press and white audiences. 'Shout', an ecstatic Vault re-issue, was another 1968 hit, while 'Funky' reached the R&B Top 40 in 1971. The Brothers broke up in 1972 but re-formed two years later to record two albums for Avco, *Unbonded* (1974) and *Right Move* (1975).

CHAMPS A largely instrumental rock'n'roll combo based in California, the Champs were Chuck 'Tequila' Rio (tenor sax), Dave Burgess and Dale Norris (guitars), Dean Beard (piano), Van Norman (bass) and Gene Alden (drums). They were West Coast sessionmen who made eight hits on Joe Johnson's Challenge label between 1958 and 1962. The first, 'Tequila', reached Number 1 and stayed in the charts for 19 weeks. The other brash and gutty hits included 'El Rancho Rock', 'Chariot Rock', 'Too Much Tequila' and 'Limbo Rock'. Rio and Alden left to be replaced by Jimmy Seals and Dash Crofts (later to become **Seals and Crofts**), while Burgess and Beard made solo rock'n'roll records of considerable distinction.

CHANDLER, GENE

Sporting a top hat, cloak, and cane, Gene Chandler shot to fame in 1962 with the ludicrous but irresistible dook, dook, dook, 'Duke of Earl' (Vee Jay). Seemingly doomed by such an outrageous gimmick, Chandler – born 6 July 1937 in Chicago – was rescued by **Curtis Mayfield** who gave him further hits with some of his best songs, including 'Rainbow' (1962), 'Man's Temptation' (1963), both on Vee Jay; and 'Think Nothing About It', 'Just Be True (1964), 'Nothing Can Stop Me' (1965) on Constellation. Chicago remained his base and, he continued to record successfully for the city's major black music outlets, notably Checker, with 'I Fooled You This Time' (1967); Brunswick, 'Girl Don't Care' (1967), 'From Teacher to the Preacher' with **Barbara Acklin** (1968); and Mercury, 'Groovy Situation' (1970), 'Ten and Two' with **Jerry Butler** (1971). He recorded for Mayfield's Curtom label in the early Seventies and for his own label, Mr Chand Records, while A&M had him under contract as a producer between 1974 and 1977. The disco-inspired 'Get Down' gave Chandler a small US hit in 1979, but since then he has worked mainly behind the scenes, principally as a vice-president of the Chi-Sound label.

CHANNEL, BRUCE

Best remembered for 'Hey Baby', a US Number 1 in 1962, Bruce Channel was born in Jacksonville, Texas, on 28 November 1940, and was a regular on the *Louisiana Hayride* TV show at the age of 17. He made a series of unsuccessful country-rock records (for King and others) before cutting 'Hey Baby'. Originally, only 200 copies were pressed by the producer, Major Bill Smith, for release on the LeCam label, but demand soared, and Smash bought the master. It was a seminal white blues disc, heavily played on R&B stations before television appearances revealed that Channel wasn't black. His unvarnished vocal and Delbert McClinton's harmonica accompaniment impressed the **Beatles**, with whom Channel shared the bill at a Liverpool concert in 1962. 'Love Me Do' was said to have owed a lot to Channel's sound. An astute per-

former, he came back with hits every now and then, including a Dixieland rocker, 'Going Back to Louisiana' (LeCam, 1964), 'Mr Bus Driver' and 'Keep On' (Mala, 1968).

CHANTELS

The premier girl group of the mid-Fifties, the Chantels – Rene Minus (born 1943), Lois Harris (1940), Sonia Goring (1940), Jackie Landry (1940) and lead singer Arlene Smith (1941) – scored with a handful of choral hits – 'He's Gone', 'Maybe', 'Every Night' and 'I Love You So' – on **George Goldner**'s End label. Produced by **Richard Barrett**, they were innovatory records, doomy and inspirational, with lashings of echo over which Arlene, then 15, sang with exceptional power and clarity. The group returned to the charts in 1961–3 with 'Look in My Eyes' and 'Well I Told You' (an answer to **Ray Charles**' 'Hit the Road Jack') on Carlton and 'Eternally' on Ludix. While Barrett switched his attentions to the **Three Degrees**, the Chantels recorded for Verve and RCA without success. Arlene, who doubled as a housewife in the Bronx, also made some sides for Spectorious and Big Top.

CHAPIN, HARRY

The title of Harry Chapin's third album for Elektra, *Short Stories*, was an accurate term to apply to his songs as a whole – each an acute, telling commentary on events or persons, often told in the first person. He was born in New York City on 7 December 1942, the son of a jazz drummer. Before embarking on a recording career in 1972, he flew aeroplanes, became expert at pool, received an Academy Award nomination for directing a silent film about boxing, and wrote songs for the celebrated shark film *Blue Water, White Death* (1971). He was also temporarily part of the Brothers and Sisters, whose other members included Lucy and **Carly Simon** and his brother Tom.

His debut album was *Heads and Tales* (1972), which included the minor US hit 'Taxi', but he established himself as a leading singer-songwriter with *Short Stories*. The single taken from it – 'W.O.L.D.', a look at life from the point of view of an ageing AM disc jockey – reached Number 36 in the US and Number 34 in the UK. His 1974 album, *Verities and Balderdash*, included the chart-topping US hit, 'Cat's in the Cradle'.

All his subsequent albums sold well – *Portrait Gallery* (1975), *On the Road to Kingdom Come* (1976), *Dance Band on the Titanic* (1977), *Living Room Suite* (1978), *Legends of the Lost and*

Found (1979) – and he became heavily involved with a number of charities and causes. He was killed on 16 July 1981, in a car accident on the Long Island Expressway.

CHARLES, BOBBY

Singer/writer/producer Bobby Charles was born in Louisiana in 1938 as Robert Charles Guidry. He grew up with an ear to the local black radio stations and also to the music of the French-speaking Arcadian peoples of Louisiana, absorbing a synthesis of raw, earthy R&B and accordion-dominated Cajun music. From these influences he composed such rock'n'roll classics as **Fats Domino**'s 'Walking to New Orleans', **Bill Haley**'s 'See You Later Alligator' and **Clarence 'Frogman' Henry**'s 'But I Do', sometimes under the name of Robert Guidry. His own solo career began around 1955 in Chicago with the Chess record company, working in both a recording and A&R capacity. Then, after a brief three-year period, he was back down South with New Orleans-based Imperial Records, and in 1967 was signed to Paula, a subsidiary of Stan Lewis's independent Jewel Records of Shreveport, Louisiana.

In 1972, Bobby made his album debut on Bearsville with *Bobby Charles*. An excellent collection of new songs like 'Small Town Talk', 'Tennessee Blues' and 'Street People', the album was critically acclaimed, most notably for the superb, relaxed back-up support from **The Band** plus Amos Garrett and **Dr John**. Since then he has been inactive, save for brief appearances on both Better Days albums featuring **Paul Butterfield**, and an appearance on The Band's farewell concert in 1976.

CHARLES, RAY

On 23 September 1930, Ray Charles Robinson was born in Albany, Georgia. Blind at six – he suffered from glaucoma – he studied music at a school for the blind in Florida until he was orphaned in 1947. After a lean couple of years gigging around Florida, he moved to Seattle, Washington, and formed the Maxim Trio, blatantly based on the then commercial piano/guitar/bass sound of the **Nat 'King' Cole** group: Charles sang, played piano, sometimes organ, plus alto saxophone and clarinet. They cut a number of Nat Cole-type ballads and **Charles Brown**-influenced blues for Swingtime, displaying enough potential for Atlantic to buy up Charles' contract in 1952. It was around this time too that R. C. Robinson became 'Ray Charles' to avoid confusion with Sugar

Ray Robinson, a boxer who became an entertainer.

Charles had freelanced with **Lowell Fulsom**, **Guitar Slim**, and **Ruth Brown** in between regular club and TV engagements with the trio, and the welding of this varied experience to the influence of his Baptist church upbringing resulted in a gospel-tinged 'soul' sound. He took the typical gospel rhythms, call-and-response patterns and 16-bar chord progressions, and sang secular lyrics over them with the yelled asides, exhortations and catches in the voice of a Southern service in full swing. 'Talkin' 'Bout Jesus' became 'Talkin' 'Bout You', and even 'My Bonnie Lies over the Ocean' and Stephen Foster's 'The Old Folks at Home' (as 'Swanee River Rock') were given the treatment, with a four-girl vocal group (the Raylettes, later 'Raelets') on responses, the melody lines recast and the 'new' songs credited to Charles.

Signed to Atlantic and making regular visits to the American charts with 'I Got a Woman', 'A Fool for You', 'Lonely Avenue', 'Hallelujah I Love Her So', etc., he also recorded several instrumental jazz albums with groups from his own band and with Milt Jackson, vibraharpist with the Modern Jazz Quartet. They featured Ray's piano style – the funkiest of blues filled out with modern jazz harmonies – and his Charlie Parker-derived alto. In 1959, only months after cutting his most basic hit – 'What'd I Say', complete with fundamental 12-bar riff and call-and-response with the Raelets – Charles recorded some sides with strings and voices, arranged by Ralph Burns. Later that year, he accepted a contract offer from ABC-Paramount, and Burns was hired to arrange the first single, 'Georgia on My Mind'; thanks to ABC's superior promotion and distribution machine, it topped the charts on both sides of the Atlantic.

At first, there were still plenty of soul/gospel rockers like 'Hit the Road, Jack' and 'Sticks and Stones', and even the *Modern Sounds in Country and Western Music* LPs were split between string and big-band backings (Volume Two had 'You Are My Sunshine', a superb holy leg-pull right out of the 'My Bonnie' bag); soon, though, sentimental ballads accounted for nearly all the singles. Selling-out wasn't involved, since Charles had always been eclectic in his choice of material, and what's more was able to produce something worthwhile in each of the idioms he tackled: some of the items with strings ('Come Rain Or Come Shine', 'Georgia', 'Take These Chains

from My Heart') were among the finest recordings he made. It was more a question of balance, as the entire output gradually veered towards a smooth and inoffensive repertoire. Concerts became dominated by old favourites, most of them sounding very tired, but Charles' charisma, his inability to stop swinging, and the odd snatch of his still spine-tingling piano ensured that there was always something to be had from a live performance. Albums like *A Message from the People*, featuring good songs delivered with conviction, were few and far between. Only one jazz LP came out during the Sixties, a big-band album with Ray on organ throughout, *Genius + Soul = Jazz*.

In 1962, Charles started his own record label, Tangerine, which was distributed until 1973 by ABC. In 1977, Charles placed his label, now renamed Crossover, with Atlantic in a marketing and distribution deal; five years later, Charles himself signed with Columbia and debuted for the company with *Wish You Were Here Tonight* (1983), an album recorded in Nashville that saw Charles return to the country styling of his early Sixties work.

Whether or not Ray Charles' future work will return to the level of his greatest records, he is already acknowledged as one of the most important influences on the course of post-war black music. His profane mingling of secular and sacred styles proved to be the blueprint for the many varieties of

soul music that dominated the R&B and often the pop charts throughout the Sixties. And when young white singers turned towards black music for inspiration in that decade, it was Ray Charles who was most influential, just as **Chuck Berry**'s guitar style could be heard in the playing of hordes of white guitarists. Among those who have openly copied the master are David Clayton-Thomas, **Righteous Brother** Bill Medley, **Joe Cocker**, **Long John Baldry** and **Steve Winwood**. And the wheel came full circle when Nat 'King' Cole reached the charts in 1962 with a country and western song, 'Dear Lonely Hearts', phrased unmistakably in the manner of the man who had once paid him the same compliment.

CHEAP TRICK Hugely popular around the world in the late Seventies, America's Cheap Trick worked its way up to platinum status with a highly commercial blend of pop and hard rock. Formed in 1974 in Rockford, Illinois, by oddball guitarist (and rare guitar collector) Rick Neilsen and bassist Tom Petersson (with whom he had played in various groups) the band later recruited vocalist Robin Zander and drummer Bun E. Carlos (real name Brad Carlson). Their first few years were spent touring incessantly, opening for big name acts like **Kiss**, **Boston** and various others.

Signed to Epic, they released their first few albums, which sold only

Charismatic Ray Charles brought the sound of gospel out of the churches into the commercial world in an inspired mix with soul

moderately in the US but went gold in Japan, where they recorded an LP *Live at Budokan* (1978). This went platinum in the States, helped by the US Top 10 success of the single 'I Want You to Want Me'. Big sellers *Dream Police* (1979) and *All Shook Up* (1980) followed and Cheap Trick were established as one of the top live draws in the world.

The band's fortunes then went into a sharp decline, but they eventually recorded a new LP, *One on One* (1982), with new bassist Jon Brant. When the album failed to emulate their earlier successes, Cheap Trick dropped from the world stage, but in 1986 there was sign of a comeback when low-key touring and recording activities resumed.

CHECKER, CHUBBY Born on 3 October 1941 in Philadelphia, Ernest Evans was working in a chicken market when his boss, impressed by his singing, contacted Kal Mann, a staff-writer with the local Parkway label, who signed him to a long-term contract in 1959. Ernest Evans then became Chubby Checker and his first disc 'The Class' was quite successful, but a later disc changed the course of pop history. 'The Twist' had been the flipside of a **Hank Ballard** and the Midnighters hit in 1959: it seems that **Dick Clark** called in Checker as a replacement when Ballard didn't show for rehearsals of his *American Bandstand* TV show and he recorded the song to accompany his appearance. Clark's wife created his stage-name, remarking that he resembled a young **Fats Domino** – hence Chubby Checker! 'The Twist' was a Number 1 hit (twice) and Checker went on to capitalize by recording nebulous dance songs – 'Pony Time', 'Let's Twist Again', 'The Fly', etc. – over the next six years, most achieving chart status but few creating any musical landmarks, being largely nasal tenor chants accompanied by somewhat tuneless vocal choruses and stereotyped rhythm/saxophone bandtracks. It was obviously what the public wanted, however, since he had no less than 31 chart entries up to Parkway's demise in 1968, regularly featuring on TV and movies demonstrating his dances. He made a brief comeback on Buddah in 1969, and a disastrous foray into 'reggae' and 'Progressive' sounds on Chalmac in 1971, but then settled into a comfortable niche on rock'n'roll revival shows, featuring in the movie *Let the Good Times Roll*. Recording for MCA from 1979, he had a number of small, mainly disco, hits in the US.

Chubby Checker (right) teaches square, but enthusiastic, Lionel Blair to twist

CHENIER, CLIFTON Born on a farm near Opelousas, Louisiana, on 25 June 1925, Clifton Chenier is the foremost exponent of 'Zydeco', the little-known equivalent of Cajun music found among the French-speaking blacks of the Louisiana and Texas Gulf Coast. His blues accordion playing and funky English/French patois vocals have long enjoyed considerable local appeal. Since the mid-Fifties he has recorded for numerous labels, including Elko, Part, Specialty, Checker and Zynn. Prolific sessions for the Arhoolie label with his older brother Cleveland (on washboard) were met with universal acclaim by blues enthusiasts throughout the Sixties. *See also* **Cajun Music**

CHER Born Cherilyn Sarkasian LaPier on 20 May 1946 in El Centro, California, Cher came to prominence in 1965 with a series of hit recordings with her husband Sonny Bono, whom she had met while singing back-up vocals on **Phil Spector**'s sessions. She soon launched her solo career with **Bob Dylan**'s 'All I Really Want to Do' (Imperial), and a succession of hits followed: 'Where Do You Go' (1965), 'Bang Bang' (1966), and 'You'd Better Sit Down Kids' (1967), all dramatically produced and arranged by Bono and **Harold Battiste**. A label switch to Kapp in 1971 resulted in even greater success. 'Gypsies, Tramps and Thieves' (1971), proved to be the biggest seller in the label's history, and the album of the same name turned gold, as did the *Half*

Breed album. Her last MCA/Kapp hit was 'Dark Lady' in 1974, after which she and Sonny split up. Cher signed with Warner Bros to cut *Stars*, produced by **Jimmy Webb** and featuring her rich-voiced interpretations of songs by **Neil Young**, **Eric Clapton**, and **Jimmy Cliff**. She also cut a disastrous single for Warner-Spector, 'A Woman's Story'.

Unlike Sonny, who disappeared from view once the duo split, Cher became a top draw in rock and fashion circles and featured regularly in the gossip columns thanks to her relationships with Gregg Allman of the **Allman Brothers Band**, Gene Simmons of **Kiss** and Les Dudek of Black Rose, with whom she recorded. She guested on the 1981 **Meat Loaf** single 'Dead Ringer for Love' but made most impact in the Eighties as an actress, appearing in *Come Back to the Five and Dime, Jimmy Dean* on stage and on film, and opposite Meryl Streep in *Silkwood*. *See also* **Sonny and Cher**

CHESS RECORDS Perhaps the supreme blues and R&B label, Chess Records has been responsible for dozens of classic recordings and some of the biggest hits in the field of popular black music. It has also, by sheer virtue of its artistic roster, influenced and shaped – either directly or indirectly – the entire white rock movement from the early Sixties on.

The company was formed by Leonard and Phil Chess, Jewish immigrants from Poland who settled in Chicago in 1928. They worked their way into the liquor business and by the Forties owned a string of bars on Chicago's South Side. From there they purchased a night-club, the Macomba, which featured names like Billy Eckstine and Gene Ammons. The popularity of these artists with the black clientele was quickly appreciated by Leonard Chess, as was the lack of local recording facilities for the newer names who appeared at the club. Satisfied that a demand existed, the Chess brothers started Aristocrat records in 1947, and hit lucky when blues pianist Sunnyland Slim hustled a recording date, bringing with him a Mississippi-born singer/guitarist named **Muddy Waters** who was recorded as an afterthought. One of Muddy's songs, 'I Can't Be Satisfied', was released and became an immediate hit as thousands of disillusioned black migrants identified with his lyrical invitation to return 'back down South, 'cos I just can't be satisfied and I just can't keep from cryin''. He followed it with 'You're Gonna Miss Me' and 'Screamin' and Cryin'', and within three years Leonard Chess had become a major producer in black music and Muddy the biggest name in blues.

In June 1950 the Chess label was launched and Aristocrat slipped into history. The first Chess single was by tenorist Gene Ammons and led to releases by **Howlin' Wolf**, **Elmore James**, **Rosco Gordon**, and **Willie Dixon**, who subsequently acted as musical adviser, arranger, producer and session bassist for the Chess brothers. Three years later, the Checker subsidiary label introduced **Little Walter**, **Lowell Fulsom**, **Little Milton**, and the **Flamingos**. While Phil stayed in Chicago taking care of business, Leonard made innumerable trips down South, selling records from the back of his car as well as making contacts. From Sam Phillips he bought the rights to Jackie Brenston's 1951 recording of 'Rocket 88' (with Ike Turner on piano), which is often cited as the first rock-'n'roll record. Leonard Chess appreciated the importance of the DJ as an advertising asset, and was one of the first associates of **Alan Freed**, who greatly helped spread Chess sales and ultimately caused the label to expand its horizons. Perhaps the greatest years for Chess were 1954–5, when records by Muddy, Wolf, Walter, **John Lee Hooker**, **Sonny Boy Williamson**, Eddie Boyd, **Willie Mabon**, Jimmy Rogers and the **Moonglows** continually dominated the R&B Top 10. Soon after, **Chuck Berry** and **Bo Diddley** came to Chess, pushing the name into the national charts with a constant stream of hits. As the Fifties progressed, Chess and its subsidiaries, Checker and Argo, looked more towards the rock'n'roll and soul market, signing up such acts as the **Dells**, **Jimmy McCracklin**, **Dale Hawkins**, **Clarence 'Frogman' Henry**, **Etta James**, Johnny and Joe, the **Monotones**, **Ramsey Lewis**, and **Bobby Charles**. By the late Fifties Chess had dropped all their blues acts with the exception of Muddy, Wolf, Sonny Boy, Walter, **Otis Rush** and **Buddy Guy**, going into the Sixties with **Sugar Pie De Santo**'s 'Soulful Dress', Koko Taylor's 'Wang Dang Doodle', and **Fontella Bass**' 'Rescue Me'. By the end of the Sixties, the company's main hit-makers were the Dells, on Cadet. On 16 October 1969 Leonard Chess died and the Chess organization was bought out by GRT, America's second largest tape corporation. Phil left to run a radio station, and Marshall Chess, Leonard's son, went to work for the **Rolling Stones**. The head office subsequently moved back to New York supervising Chess and its subsidiary Janus, Checker, Cadet, GRT, Westbound, and Concept. Chuck Berry's surprise 1972 hit with 'My Ding a Ling' revitalized the company temporarily, with hits by **Solomon Burke** and albums by the Baker-Gurvitz Army following in the mid-Seventies. GRT then sold all the labels to All Platinum in New Jersey, who released all the artists from their contracts and began re-packaging the archive material.

CHIC Bassist Bernard Edwards and guitarist Nile Rodgers, the leaders of Chic – probably the most successful dance band of the Seventies – were part of the road band used by soul band New York City ('I'm Doing Fine') at the beginning of the Seventies disco boom. By the end of the boom and the end of the decade Edwards and Rodgers had produced arguably the best dance music of the era and were set to go on to become respected producers and writers in a very much wider field. Recruiting drummer Tony Thompson and a brace of women singers (the longest-serving were Alfa Anderson and Luci Martin), Edwards and Rodgers evolved a sophisticated, melodic, clean sound with the guitarist's instantly recognizable rhythmic chording giving the Chic records especial distinction. 'Dance Dance Dance' (1978) started off the group's run of marvellously conceived dance hits – 'Everybody Dance' and 'Le Freak' followed in quick succession while 'I Want Your Love', slower and more spacious, revealed the band's broader canvas. These successes were complemented in the same year by the release of the magnificent album *C'est Chic*. Their 1979 album, *Risqué*, further illustrated the Rodgers/Edwards ability to move away from the strict regimen of dance-floor music. By now, word about their prowess as producers was out and henceforward their work with Chic would be adversely affected by the increasing demands on them as writers and producers for others. The first project was with Norma Jean Wright, a fine single, 'Saturday', followed by a disappointing album, but **Sister Sledge**'s *We Are Family* album (1979) and the major hit from it, 'He's the Greatest Dancer', firmly established them. Prestigious offers poured in. The success of **Diana Ross**' 1980 LP *Diana* was almost entirely due to their writing and production (though Ross controversially remixed portions of the set), **David Bowie** used Rodgers as guitarist and co-producer on his 1982 album *Let's Dance* and he also co-produced Mick Jagger's 1985 solo LP debut *She's the Boss*. Chic's own LPs – *Real People* (1980), *Take It Off* (1981), *Tongue in Chic* (1982) and *Believer* (1983) were increasingly less satisfactory, since the material Edwards and Rodgers were preparing for them was not of the highest order in terms of melody. But the outside production work never diminished – Sheila B Devotion records, **Blondie** lead singer Debbie Harry's solo album, *Koo Koo* (1981), possibly the worst Chic production, among others. Edwards released his own, disappointing solo album, *Glad To Be Here*, in 1983 while in the same year Rodgers' set *Adventures in the Land of the Good Groove* was only slightly better. His *B-Movie Matinee* two years later was an improvement. Meanwhile drummer Tony Thompson had teamed up with **Robert Palmer** and a couple of **Duran Duran** members to become, briefly, Power Station. Rodgers, though, remained the most prolific Chic member producing 'Wild Boys' and 'The Reflex' EP for Duran, arranged **Hall and Oates**' 'Adult Education' and played with many top rock acts ranging from **Jeff Beck** to **Peter Gabriel**, **Madonna** to **Brian Ferry**, his unmistakeable guitar sound often imitated but never perfectly duplicated. The greatest monument to Chic, however, remains the *Risqué* and *C'est Chic* LPs.

CHICAGO The most successful and most criticized jazz-rock group of the early and mid-Seventies, Chicago adapted their approach so effectively during the latter half of the decade that they became one of the leading bands in the nebulously termed field of AOR. The group was originally known as the Chicago Transit Authority and comprised, on its formation in 1968, Robert Lamm (keyboards, vocals, born 13 October 1944), Terry Kath (guitar, vocals, 31 January 1946), Jim Pankow (trombone, 20 August 1947), Walter Parazaider (saxes, clarinet, 14 March 1945), Lee Loughnane (trumpet, flugelhorn, 21 October 1946), Peter Cetera (bass, vocals, 13 September 1944) and Dan Seraphine (drums, 28 August 1948).

Their first album for Columbia, *Chicago Transit Authority* (1969), followed hard on the heels of the pioneering brass-rock arrangements of **Blood, Sweat and Tears**. Produced by the group's mentor, **Jim Guercio**, it bobbed in and out of the album charts for the next six years, becoming one of the biggest-selling records ever. Pankow's horn arrangements were strong and melodic, if not exactly innovative by contemporary jazz standards. Combined with Lamm's lukewarm, quasi-political lyrics, they mirrored the mood of the end of the decade. The succeeding albums – all vast sellers – were simply numbered *Chicago I–XVI* and appeared regularly on an annual basis, with the exception of the fourth, a live album named *At Carnegie Hall* (1971), and the Phil Ramone-produced *Hot Streets* (1978).

Hot Streets was their first since parting company with Guercio in 1977 and confirmed the band's switch away from the brass domination of their early albums towards a sleek AOR-styled sound featuring the vocals of Kath and Cetera. Their late 1976 single, 'If You Leave Me Now', had been a giant worldwide hit – a Number 1 on both sides of the Atlantic – and it was in this mode that they continued to record, charting again with 'Baby, What a Big Surprise' (1977), 'Alive Again' (1978), 'No Tell Lover' (1979), and another US chart-topper, 'Hard to Say I'm Sorry' (1982). There were various personnel changes during these years, notably the recruitment of Donnie Dacus in place of Terry Kath, who died in 1978 after accidentally shooting himself, and the band also switched record labels during 1982 – from Columbia to the Warner Bros subsidiary Full Moon. They were joined for the Tom Dowd-produced *Chicago XVI* (1983) by guitarist Bill Champlin, and 'Hard Habit to Break' (from *Chicago XVII*) gave them another major transatlantic hit during late 1984. In the meantime, Peter Cetera began a parallel solo career, reaching both the UK and US charts with 'The Glory of Love' in 1986.

CHICAGO BLUES

CHICAGO BLUES A phenomenon of the late Forties and early Fifties, blossoming from an amalgam of Southern regional blues styles, the sound of Chicago blues was characterized by heavily amplified guitars, piano, bass, drums and usually harmonica and remains best exemplified by the band of the late **Muddy Waters**, considered the finest ever to emerge from that city.

The style reached its creative peak in 1954–5, when Chicago blues records dominated the national R&B Top 10. A handful of key names can be cited as having made a real and innovative contribution to the pure strain of Chicago blues. **Sonny Boy Williamson** No. 1 (John Lee) was the first bluesman to score a major impact on the Chicago scene of the Forties. His records for RCA Victor paved the way for the group

Chicago: from the left, Pete Cetera, Danny Seraphine, Robert Lamm, Lee Loughnane, Terry Kath, Walter Parazaider and Jim Pankow

ensemble sound of later years. The most commercially successful artist to perform in the style was undoubtedly **Little Walter**, often regarded as simply Muddy Waters' harp player. He did, in fact, sell more records than any other Chicago blues artist, Waters included. Walter was a total innovator and his revolutionary harmonica sound – deeply rooted in jazz – remains unsurpassed. His Top 10 R&B hits like 'Juke' and 'Last Night' – cut for Chess in the early Fifties – mark the pinnacle of Chicago blues. Another Waters' sideman, guitarist Jimmy Rogers, must share credit for his contribution to the music. His solo records, usually with the Waters band in attendance, are again brilliant examples of the undiluted Chicago blues sound. Nor can **Jimmy Reed**'s stature in the 'Windy City' be overlooked. From 1955 to 1961 he was continually in the charts with a succession of hit singles for Vee Jay including 'Honest I Do' and 'Bright Lights, Big City'. In the Seventies the Chicago blues style survived in the work of **Junior Wells**, Carey Bell and a host of lesser known bluesmen active in the clubs and bars of South Side Chicago. The influence of Chicago blues on rock musicians since the Fifties – whether direct or indirect – has been enormous. For instance, the **Rolling Stones** based their early sound and line-up on that of the Muddy Waters band.

CHICKEN SHACK Part of **Mike Vernon**'s Blue Horizon stable which dominated the British blues renaissance of the late Sixties, Chicken Shack was formed in Birmingham in 1965 by guitarist Stan Webb, bassist Andy

Silvester and drummer Dave Bidwell. By the time the band came to London in 1968, Christine Perfect had joined as lead singer, and her reading of **Etta James**' blues classic 'I'd Rather Go Blind' gave the band its only major hit single a year later. Soon after her departure that same year – to team up with husband John McVie in **Fleetwood Mac** – Bidwell and Sylvester left to join Savoy Brown. Webb carried on with new personnel but disbanded Chicken Shack in 1973, shortly after which he himself joined Savoy Brown. In 1975, Webb formed the short-lived Broken Glass with Tony Ashton, Miller Anderson and Robbie Blunt. Later the same year he revived Chicken Shack, which went through several changes of personnel until early 1982. The final line-up was Webb, guitarist Paul Butler, bassist Andy Pyle and drummer Ric Lee.

CHIFFONS A successful black female vocal group of the early Sixties, the Chiffons were contemporaries of other early-Sixties pop-oriented acts like the **Crystals** (produced by **Phil Spector**) and the Cookies (produced by Gerry Goffin and **Carole King**). The Chiffons were produced by Bright Tunes Productions Inc. of Brooklyn, who were essentially Margo/Margo/Medress/Siegel of **Tokens** fame. The group comprised Judy Craig (born 1946), Barbara Lee (16 May 1947), Patricia Bennet (7 April 1947) and Sylvia Peterson (30 September 1946), plus resident guitarist Butch Mann (from **Ruby and the Romantics**, later with the **Drifters**). Their first record was 'Tonight's the Night' on Big Deal in 1960, then came a string of hits on

Laurie, including, 'He's So Fine' (their only Number 1, in 1963, written by their manager, Ronald Mack, and later acknowledged to have been the source of **George Harrison**'s 'My Sweet Lord'), 'One Fine Day', 'Sweet Talking Guy' (a Top 10 in Britain when reissued in 1972), 'A Love So Fine' and 'I Have a Boyfriend'. They also recorded as the Four Pennies, under which name they reached the Hot 100.

CHI-LITES Dominated by Eugene Record, the extraordinary singer/songwriter/producer and creator of one of the most sensuously romantic soul sounds, the Chi-Lites hailed from Chicago. Formed in 1960, they comprised Marshall Thompson, Robert Lester, Creadel Jones and Eugene Record. Originally using names like the Chanteurs and the Hi-Lites, they changed to the Chi-Lites in 1967 and recorded locally for James Shelton Jr before gaining their first national hit in 1969 with 'Give It Away', on Brunswick. It was the start of a phenomenal hit run including the shuddering slab of black rock '(For God's Sake) Give More Power to the People' (1971), the unashamedly sentimental 'Have You Seen Her?' (Top 5 in 1971 and a reissued hit in Britain in 1975), 'Oh Girl', an American Number 1 in 1972, the soaringly produced 'Coldest Days of My Life' (1972) and the charmingly lilting 'Homely Girl' (1973). Eugene and his fellow Chi-Lites brought a unique blend of rich, billowing sophistication to the black music mainstream that was threatened by the mid-Seventies disco boom yet managed to outlast it. In the Eighties, the Chi-Lites remained a working unit, despite Record's solo excursions on WEA and a paucity of hits since the 1973 Top 30 hit, 'Stoned Out of My Mind'.

CHINA CRISIS Developing out of the musical friendship of two Merseyside schoolboys, China Crisis emerged as one of the more successful, if lightweight, keyboard-influenced groups of the early Eighties. Garry Daly (keyboards) and Eddie Lundon (guitar) formed the core of China Crisis, later to be joined by Gary Johnson (bass) and Kevin Wilkinson (drums) on a full-time basis. The Liverpool-based Inevitable label released their impressive first single, 'African and White', which caught the ear of Virgin Records, who snapped them up. The group's debut album *Difficult Shapes and Passive Rhythms* was released on Virgin in 1982 and from this came the hit single 'Christian'

which reached Number 12 in the UK, while the follow-up album, *Working with Fire and Steel*, provided a Top 10 hit in the shape of 'Wishful Thinking'. To admirers, China Crisis are seen as masters of the delicate but tuneful pop song, although their detractors would argue that their pastel tones were bland to the point of nothingness. The third album, the Walter Becker-produced *Flaunt the Imperfection*, was released in April 1985 and reached the UK Top 30, spawning a handful of hit singles including 'King in a Catholic Style' and 'Black Man Ray'.

CHORDETTES Bridging the gap between Fifties pop and the rock'n'roll era, the Chordettes consisted originally of four girls from Sheboygan, Wisconsin – Dorothy Schwarz, Jinny Osborne, Janet Ertel, and Carol Bushman. Before they came to notice via the Arthur Godfrey show, Dorothy and Jinny were replaced by Lynn Evans and Margie Needham. Following the Godfrey appearance, they were signed to Cadence by Archie Bleyer, and their first record, 'Mr Sandman', was at Number 1 for seven weeks in 1954. They appeared frequently in the charts until the early Sixties with records like 'Eddie My Love', 'Lay Down Your Arms' (unusually, an American cover version of a UK hit, in this case by Anne Shelton), 'Lollipop' (a British hit for the Mudlarks in 1958), 'A Girl's Work Is Never Done', 'Born to Be with You' and 'Never on Sunday'.

CHORDS *Billboard* wrote of the Chords in April 1954: 'Playful bounce and tasty restrained styling will appeal to customers in both R&B and pop markets', and the group certainly made a trailblazing contribution to rock-'n'roll with 'Sh-Boom'. Covered by the Crewcuts, parodied by Stan Freberg – 'stuff some old rags in your mouth and take it again from the top' – and revived by **Sha Na Na**, the song is universally famous. But the Chords, who became the Chordcats, could never repeat its success despite further records for the Atlantic subsidiary, Cat. Claude and Earl Feaster (or Feister), Jimmy Keyes, Floyd McRae, James Edwards, and Bobby Spencer were among the personnel.

CHRISTIE, LOU Born Lugee Salo on 19 February 1943, in Glen Willard, Pennsylvania, Lou Christie had two spasms of success each out of time with the music scene around him. In 1963 he scored two US Top 20 hits with 'The Gypsy Cried' and 'Two Faces Have I'

(both on Roulette), reviving the dying embers of an era of high-image falsetto rockers in the **Jimmy Jones/Del Shannon** fashion – this in the year before the **Beatles** began unsettling the old pop order. He returned in 1966 with the US Number 1, 'Lightnin' Strikes' (also a UK hit), a fine rock ballad with a Motown-style beat and a throwback baritone-to-falsetto vocal which this time was set against the punk stance of the song's lyric, a conscience-ridden lad lusting after his girl. His album of that year *Lightnin' Strikes* (MGM) was another paean to the Fifties, with its 'sweet side' of current covers and more interesting 'rockin' side' (all Lou Christie/Twyla Herbert originals). Lou Christie's career was strangely schizoid in this way. The Top 20 follow-up, 'Rhapsody in the Rain', was actually banned in Britain for its too graphic sexual rhythms and 'makin' love in a storm' lyrics, despite its dated musical/vocal dressing. Three years later Lou came up with a further hit, 'I'm Gonna Make You Mine' (Buddah), surprisingly trite after his earlier classics.

In later years, Christie married an English beauty queen, changed his name, became a long distance lorry driver in Montana, and, subsequently, an offshore oil driller in Louisiana.

CIMARONS Formed in 1967, the Cimarons (the name is based on that of the Jamaican Maroon people, who successfully rebelled against British colonial power), along with **Matumbi** and **Black Slate**, were among the first wave of British reggae bands to throw off slavish adherence to Jamaican studio innovations and forge a style both 'British' and original. Between 1968 and 1972, they were virtually the only established homegrown reggae band in existence, and in that time they backed almost every Jamaican singer to tour or record in the UK. Widely tipped for a big breakthrough in the mid-Seventies, the Cimarons were in fact the least successful of the three bands – in record terms, anyway – though they were a consistently powerful live outfit. By 1974, however, they had become a name to contend with by successfully exporting reggae to Jamaica. They released the album *On the Rocks* and scored a huge hit single with their version of **Bob Marley**'s 'Talking Blues', which was a Jamaican Number 1 for seven weeks. However, this success was not repeated elsewhere – a combination of inconsistent songwriting and unfortunate recording contracts meant that the Cimarons never achieved the expected breakthrough.

CLANTON, JIMMY Singer Jimmy Clanton – born in Baton Rouge, Louisiana, on 2 September 1940 – was discovered by New Orleans studio engineer Cosimo Matassa and signed by Ace Records in 1958. His second record, 'Just a Dream', a wistful R&B ballad, shot up the charts to Number 4 and won Clanton a gold disc. Ace quickly saw the potential of making the good-looking high-school kid into an all-American teen-idol and so encouraged a commercial-pop approach. This scheme paid hefty dividends for a while with a series of hit records, culminating in another million-seller, 'Venus in Blue Jeans' in 1962. After this it was all downhill; his time as teen-fodder was up.

CLAPTON, ERIC The outstanding British rock guitarist of his generation, Eric Clapton was born in Ripley, Surrey, on 30 March 1945, and joined his first group, the Roosters, at the invitation of Tom McGuinness early in 1963. When the group folded that August he and McGuinness went to Casey Jones' backing group, the Engineers, but Clapton quit within two months to replace Tony Topham as lead guitarist with the **Yardbirds**, who had recently taken over the **Rolling Stones**' residency at Richmond's Crawdaddy club. It was with the Yardbirds that Clapton first encountered adulation as a guitar hero, but his development as a player was limited by the Yardbirds' ambitions, and their decision to record the pop-oriented 'For

Eric Clapton, the peerless master of rock guitar performance

Your Love' (Columbia UK) prompted him to leave in March 1965.

John Mayall at once asked him to join his Bluesbreakers, but Clapton stayed only for a short time before departing with a makeshift group, the Glands, on an abortive world tour that wound up in Greece, from where some weeks later Clapton travelled home to rejoin Mayall. During this second period with the Bluesbreakers between November 1965 and July 1966 (when he formed **Cream** with **Jack Bruce** and **Ginger Baker**) Clapton's status amongst the growing army of British blues fans grew to the point of deification. The guitar hero, meanwhile, demonstrated his outstanding talent on *Bluesbreakers* (Decca, 1966).

The format and musical ambitions of Cream inspired Clapton to progress far beyond the role of blues copyist into areas of improvisation previously ignored in rock. After the trio split up at the end of 1968, he teamed up with **Stevie Winwood**, Ginger Baker and Rick Grech in **Blind Faith**, a 'supergroup' that was unable to live up to the public's expectations or survive commercial pressures.

In search of anonymity and a release from the intense demands of both fans and businessmen, Clapton joined **Delaney and Bonnie** Bramlett's backing group and recorded a solo album, *Eric Clapton* (Polydor, 1970), with them, produced by Delaney. He eventually took three of the Bramletts' 'friends' – Bobby Whitlock (keyboards), Carl Radle (bass), Jim Gordon (drums) – to form **Derek and the Dominos** in May 1970, adding Duane Allman on the recording sessions for the magnificent *Layla* (Polydor, 1970).

After a live album, Derek and the Dominos broke up in May 1971. Apart from his performance at **George Harrison**'s Bangla Desh concert three months later, an unannounced appearance with **Leon Russell** that December, and his own concert in January 1973 with Pete Townshend, Ron Wood, Stevie Winwood, Rick Grech, **Jim Capaldi**, Jim Karstein, and Reebop (recorded as *Eric Clapton's Rainbow Concert*, RSO, 1973), he virtually retired, amidst increasing speculation about his health and future. He emerged in 1974 with a new group – George Terry (guitar), Dick Sims (keyboards), Carl Radle (bass), Jamie Oldaker (drums), **Yvonne Elliman** (vocals) – and a newfound serenity in his music. His evident distaste for the role of guitar idol having forced his development as both singer and songwriter, his next release – *461 Ocean*

Boulevard (RSO, 1974) – contained his most balanced work yet, and featured what was to be his biggest single hit of the Seventies, a version of **Bob Marley**'s 'I Shot the Sheriff'. A Number 1 in the US and a Number 9 in the UK, it set the scene for an impressive run of solo albums, beginning with *There's One in Every Crowd* (1975). *No Reason to Cry* appeared in 1976 and the platinum *Slowhand* a year later, the latter containing 'Lay Down Sally', a Number 3 hit in the US.

Another album – *Backless* (1978) – followed, before Clapton formed a new band featuring vocalist/pianist Gary Brooker from **Procol Harum**, keyboardist Chris Stainton (ex-**Joe Cocker** accompanist), bassist Dave Markee, drummer Henry Spinetti, and guitarist **Albert Lee**. They cut a double live album, *Just One Night* (1980), and the studio set *Another Ticket* in 1981. He signed with Warner Bros in 1982 and debuted with *Money and Cigarettes* (1983).

Early in 1984, Clapton brought together a new band comprising Chris Stainton, Tim Renwick (guitar), 'Duck' Dunn (bass, ex-**Booker T.**), Jamie Oldaker (drums), and vocalists Marcy Levy and Shaun Murphy. *Behind the Sun* appeared in 1985 and *August* a year later, the latter produced by **Phil Collins** and **Tom Dowd** and featuring guest appearances by **Tina Turner** and Stephen Bishop. Clinically clean and technically perfect in every way, his mid-Eighties studio work – which has also included guest spots on albums by artists as varied as **Lionel Richie** and Bob Geldof (*see* **Boomtown Rats**) – was that of an elder rock statesman in tune with the times but no longer a major influence upon them. He remains, nevertheless, one of the Sixties' great survivors.

CLARK, DAVE/DAVE CLARK FIVE The first British group to provide a popular alternative to Merseybeat, the Dave Clark Five's trade mark was a harsh combination of shouts and thumps that was for a time referred to as the 'Tottenham Sound'. Formed in that North London suburb in 1960, the group (who, in spite of their music, had a decidedly clean-limbed image) were Clark on drums (born 14 December 1942), Lenny Davidson on guitar and bass (30 May 1944), Rick Huxley on guitar (5 August 1942), Denis Payton on sax (1 August 1943) and singer/keyboard-player Mike Smith (12 December 1943). Four chartbusters followed their first big hit, 'Glad All Over' on Columbia (Epic in America), in 1964, but their

British popularity declined as their US success increased. In 1968 Clark, who had always fancied himself as an actor, ploughed some of the group's fortunes into TV film production. One programme, starring Clark, was screened, but a projected series did not materialize.

The group's last major UK hits were 'Good Old Rock'n'Roll' (1969), a medley of rock'n'roll songs, and a version of the **Youngbloods'** US hit, 'Everybody Get Together' (1970). Mike Smith left to move into record production and a recording collaboration with ex-**Manfred Mann** singer **Mike d'Abo**, but the Five continued with various personnel changes until the mid-Seventies. Clark, an astute businessman who hired the group members as employees rather than pay them on a percentage basis, then put most of his energies into his various business interests, which included buying the rights to ITV's *Ready Steady Go!* and issuing compilation editions of the shows in video form. In 1986, he produced and co-wrote the West End musical *Time*, starring **Cliff Richard** and Sir Laurence Olivier.

CLARK, DEE

Born in Blythville, Arkansas, on 11 July 1938 as Delecta Clark, Dee Clark moved to Chicago, where he sang in gospel groups prior to recording with the Hambone Kids for Okeh in 1952. He subsequently joined the Kool Gents, who recorded for Vee Jay. Recognizing Clark's ability to imitate either **Little Richard** or **Clyde McPhatter**, the company signed him as a solo artist. A string of discs on Falcon, Abner and the parent label, Vee Jay, followed, including hits with 'Nobody But You', 'Just Keep It Up', 'Hey Little Girl' (all Top 30 in 1958–9), 'How About That', 'Your Friends' and 'Raindrops' (Number 2 in 1961). Skilfully produced and memorably tuneful, they were among the best black pop records of their era. Clark also recorded for Constellation, Columbia, Wand and Liberty, and helped to write 'You Can't Sit Down' (a hit for the Phil Upchurch Combo in 1961) while on tour with Upchurch.

CLARK, DICK

A key figure in the process by which rock'n'roll was rendered wholesome and presentable to a mass audience during the late Fifties, Dick Clark was born in Mount Vernon, New York, on 30 November 1929, and graduated from radio announcer to host of Philadelphia's top TV show *Bandstand* in 1956. Clark's perceptive choice of music (solid rock and pop) and programme format (stomping Philly High School regulars) interested the giant ABC network. In 1957, it was dubbed *American Bandstand* and went national, and the daily 90-minute show began to draw up to a million fan letters weekly. Clark single-handedly established **Frankie Avalon**, **Fabian**, and **Connie Francis** among others, and began other ventures including the weekly *Dick Clark Show*, a syndicated newspaper column, working as a tour emcee, and the ill-fated *World of Talent*. When the payola crisis hit rock in early 1960, he was called 'the single most influential person' in the popular music industry, and was made to divest himself of some business interests after the Congressional probe. Despite that, ABC kept on the show and the sponsors continued their support. Clark made more movies throughout the Sixties on everything from high-school dropouts to acid casualties, moved to Hollywood for *Where the Action Is*, and swung into the Seventies with *In Concert* and, briefly, *Soul Unlimited*. His later TV projects included the TV movies *Elvis* and *Birth of the Beatles*.

CLARK, GENE

A member of the New Christy Minstrels in the early Sixties, Gene Clark – born 17 November 1941 – founded the **Byrds** with Jim, later **Roger**, **McGuinn** and **David Crosby** in 1964. His plaintive voice and distinctive love songs were prominent features of the Byrds' first two albums, but he left the band in 1966, ostensibly because of his fear of flying, but perhaps also as a result of his diminishing control over the group's direction. He then made an album with the Gosdin Brothers and two with Doug Dillard, the first of which – *The Fantastic Expedition of Dillard and Clark* (A&M, 1969) – was a beautifully constructed example of the country-rock fusion that would dominate West Coast rock in the early Seventies. He then made several solo albums of simple folk/country rock, featuring sparse instrumentation behind a succession of outstanding songs. *Gene Clark/White Light* (A&M, 1971) and *Roadmaster* (1973) were followed by *No Other* (Asylum, 1974), and all contained characteristic Clark lyrics that used simple words in complex ways to explore Sixties themes in a Seventies context. Three years passed before Clark's next solo release, *Two Sides to Every Story* (RSO, 1977), after which he partnered McGuinn and another former Byrd, **Chris Hillman**, on *McGuinn, Clark and Hillman* (Capitol, 1979) and *City* (1980). The Takoma label released Clark's *Firebyrd* in 1984, among its tracks a new version of 'Mr Tambourine Man'.

CLASH

Standing alongside the **Sex Pistols** as the founding fathers of the British punk movement, the Clash were formed in London in the summer of 1976 by Mick Jones (guitar, born in 1956) and Paul Simonon (bass, 1956). After meeting Joe Strummer (real name John Mellor, born in 1953) in an employment exchange, the duo went to watch him front the R&B pub band, the 101ers, and he was recruited as vocalist. Terry Chimes (drums) and guitarist Keith Levine (later to surface with **Public Image Ltd**) completed the first line-up and they set about rehearsing in a North London warehouse, where Simonon coined the band's name.

The Clash played their first live dates in the autumn, and these were quickly followed by the departure of both Levine and Chimes. Chimes was eventually replaced by Nicky 'Topper' Headon (born in 1956), and the band settled into a four-piece. After playing with the Sex Pistols on their 'Anarchy in the UK' tour, they signed to CBS Records in January 1977.

Their debut album, *The Clash* (recorded over three weekends), was released in April 1977, entered the UK chart at Number 12 and was instantly recognized as a classic. A potent mixture of raw energy and devastatingly simple anthemic hooklines, it perfectly summed up the spirit of punk and established the Clash as the most important and influential British band of the late Seventies. 'White Riot', their debut single taken off the album, is still regarded as the theme song of the punk movement.

Major British and European tours followed and received extensive press coverage, especially over their numerous confrontations with the police and the authorities. These culminated in a notorious incident where a surveillance helicopter spotted members of the band on a roof carrying air rifles, taking potshots at pigeons; they were subsequently arrested by armed police.

Further single releases followed quickly, including 'Complete Control' produced by Jamaican **Lee 'Scratch' Perry** (the Clash had already been experimenting with reggae on their gritty version of Junior Murvin's 'Police and Thieves' on the first album), and 'White Man in Hammersmith Palais', recorded with American producer Sandy Pearlman. The partnership was continued to produce their second album, *Give 'Em Enough Rope*, in the autumn of 1978. This album gave them their first real UK single hit, 'Tommy Gun', which peaked at Number 19 in December. At the same time the Clash were taking their well publicized 'Sort It Out' tour around England and in the process lost the services of their manager, Bernie Rhodes.

They toured America for the first time in February 1979 (encouraged by the success of the first album which had sold an unprecedented 100,000 copies on import) and were enthusiastically received by press and punters alike. The group returned to England to work on the film *Rude Boy*, which they later dismissed as boring and directionless. In August they entered the studio again to record their third LP, the double set *London Calling*. Released in December, it was another significant step in the evolution of the band, retaining their power but indulging in a wider range of styles. The title track reached Number 12, giving them their biggest hit single, and the album became their biggest seller to date, earning several gold disc awards.

In 1980 the Clash toured America again, supported by the likes of **Sam and Dave**, **Bo Diddley**, and **Joe Ely** who was persuaded to join them on the British leg of the tour. June the same year saw them entering studios in New York to start work on the triple LP *Sandinista!* which was released in December to a mixed reception, registering the worst sales of any Clash album.

Then followed a traumatic period for the group. At a time when he felt disappointed with *Sandinista!*, Strummer accidentally bumped into Bernie Rhodes in London, and by March 1981 Rhodes was reinstalled as manager. The band went to New York to play for seven nights at Bonds International Casino, and they finally managed to complete the problem-dogged residency by playing seventeen shows in fifteen days. Later the same year, Simonon was charged for possession of cocaine in the UK. *Combat Rock*, their fifth LP, was to be cut in New York at the end of the year, but they interrupted recording to tour the Far East, and eventually finished the recording in London in the spring of 1982. Just as the band were set to tour to promote the release of the album, Strummer disappeared. The album was released in May in his absence, and two weeks later Strummer was located in Paris. On his return, disgruntled by the publicity caused by Strummer's little break,

Headon left the band to be replaced temporarily by original drummer Chimes, rejoining them for their biggest US tour.

Combat Rock proved to be a major success and produced the Clash's biggest international single hit 'Rock the Casbah', a surprise Number 8 hit in the US. American interest in the Clash swelled at this time, the LP selling well over a million copies and their name reaching a prominent position in several magazine polls, most notably *Rolling Stone's*. At the same time they also supported the **Who** on their farewell tour and proved a very difficult act to follow.

May 1983 brought the recruitment of a new permanent drummer, Pete Howard, but even this appointment did not end the internal chaos. In September, Strummer and Simonon announced that they had told Mick Jones to leave the band because he had 'drifted apart from the original idea of the Clash'. Jones later went on to form his own band, Big Audio Dynamite, while he was replaced in the Clash by two guitarists, Vince White and Nick Shepherd, in January 1984.

There then followed a long period of silence, finally broken by the release of *Cut the Crap* in autumn 1985, which signalled a return to the raw Clash sound but made no real impression on the charts. Amazingly, the band again split, just before going on the road to promote the album, with no indication of what the future was likely to hold.

CLASSICS IV Best-known for their debut hit, 'Spooky', a Number 3 in the US early in 1968, Classics IV hailed from Jacksonville, Florida, but subsequently moved to Atlanta. They comprised Dennis Yost, vocals; James Cobb, guitar; Wally Eaton, rhythm guitar; Kim Venable, drums; and Joe Wilson, bass. 'Spooky' (Imperial) was their first release and established them as a group specializing in soft, sincere ballads and smoothly commercial arrangements. As a session group they backed **Tommy Roe**, Billy Joe Royal and the **Tams**. While they kept coming up with strong material (most of it written by Cobb and Buddie Buie, who also arranged and produced the records), Classics IV with a much-changed line-up continued having hits. 'Stormy', 'Traces' and 'Everyday With You Girl' were all US Top 20 entries during 1968–9. But despite large sales and an attempt in 1969 to promote lead singer Dennis Yost as a star along the lines of **Bobby Goldsboro** or Gary Puckett, he and the group had never created

enough of an identity to pull it off. Leaving Imperial/Liberty (which had just merged with United Artists), the group resurfaced on MGM-South (a label over which their mentor, Bill Lowery, had more direct control) in 1972 with 'What Am I Crying For?', which got to Number 39. Buie and Cobb then joined the Atlanta Rhythm Section, whose albums included *Dog Days* (Polydor, 1975).

CLEFTONES Comprising Charlie James (born 1940), Berman Patterson (1938), Warren Corbin (1939), William McClain (1938) and lead singer Herbie Cox (1939), the Cleftones were students from Jamaica High, New York, when they first recorded for Gee in 1956. Hits followed with Patterson's 'You Baby You' and Cox's 'Little Girl of Mine'. Returning from the limbo to which most black groups were consigned by the rise of rock'n'roll, the Cleftones re-entered the charts in 1961–2, with 'Heart and Soul' (Top 20), 'I Love You for Sentimental Reasons', and 'Lover Come Back to Me'. Under the guidance of Henry Glover, and with new members including Pat Span and Gene Pearson, these revitalized standards were an ideal showcase for Cox's soulful rasp. The group also recorded for Rama, Roulette and Ware.

CLEMENT, JACK Born Jack Henderson Clement in Memphis in 1932, Jack Clement was for many years one of the most colourful characters on the Nashville scene. His career began in Washington, in 1950, in a bluegrass duo called Buzz and Jack, at which time Clement began to master the guitar, mandolin, bass, steel guitar and drums, enabling him to become a sessionman and eventually a record producer in Memphis during the rockabilly boom of the Fifties. He has recorded country material for Sheraton, Sun and RCA, and has a distinguished, if unsuccessful, country vocal style. His 'Ten Years' was a minor success for Sun in 1958.

As a writer and producer, he has contributed much to country-influenced rock. He was responsible for commercializing the **Johnny Cash** sound with his own songs 'Ballad of a Teenage Queen' and 'Guess Things Happen That Way', and for Dickey Lee's Hallway recordings. His production work began in 1955 with Fernwood in Memphis and continued with Sun and his own label, Summer, until in 1960 he moved to the Hallway label in Beaumont. In 1966, he launched the first commercially successful black country artist, Charley Pride, with 'Just Between You and Me' on RCA, and produced seven years of sustained top country hits. He has also a considerable reputation as an unpredictable joker and has written many comedy songs, such as the Johnny Cash hits 'Everyone Loves a Nut' and 'The One on the Right Is on the Left'. By the mid-Seventies he was a freelance producer in Nashville, controlling sessions varying from those by the traditional Doc and Merle Watson to the modern Area Code 615.

CLIFF, JIMMY Born in St Catherine, Jamaica, in August 1944 as James Chambers, Jimmy Cliff was reggae music's first true superstar. He began his career in the early Sixties, recording for a number of producers, notably Leslie Kong ('Hurricane Hattie', 'Miss Jamaica'). On a government-sponsored tour of America with Byron Lee and the Dragonaires, he met Chris Blackwell of Island Records. Settling in Britain, having signed with Blackwell, Cliff developed a strong club following, but had little success disc-wise until 1968 when he won the Brazilian Song Festival, with a self-penned song, 'Waterfall'. A year later he scored worldwide with the catchy reggae song 'Wonderful World, Beautiful People' and had European success with its follow-up 'Vietnam'.

In the interim, two albums, *Hard Road to Travel* (1967) and *Jimmy Cliff* (1969), had demonstrated the artist's considerable talent, particularly on painful, emotive songs like 'Sitting in Limbo' and 'Many Rivers to Cross'. Another hit, in 1970, with **Cat Stevens**' plaintive 'Wild World', spotlighted his versatility, but lost him much of his ethnic following.

Ironically, it was as an actor, in the lead role in *The Harder They Come* (the soundtrack of which was released by Island in 1972), that Jimmy Cliff gained his greatest success and earned the 'superstar' tag. Musically, he tended increasingly to pop, with the Muscle Shoals-recorded *Another Cycle*, the uneven EMI sets *Unlimited* (1973), *House of Exile* (1974), and *Brave Warrior* (1975), and with hit songs for the Pioneers ('Let Your Yeah Be Yeah') and **Desmond Dekker** ('You Can Get It If You Really Want').

In 1975, Cliff joined WEA, who insisted that his Jamaican-recorded tapes be brought to the US to have backing tracks added by American session musicians: *Brave Warrior* and *Follow My Mind* (1976) were the first fruits of this policy. He spent much time in Africa during this period, giving concerts and recording them on film, and he finally tired of WEA with the release of *Give Thanx* (1978), and formed his own label, Sunflower Records, based in Jamaica. He also created a subsidiary, Oneness, to be devoted entirely to the recordings of young Jamaican artists.

1981 saw the release of *Give the People What They Want*, a self-produced set, but within a year he had again switched labels, moving this time to CBS. *Special* (1982) was followed by the film *Bongo Man*, which was in essence Cliff's own personal celebration of African culture.

CLIMAX BLUES BAND Comprising Colin Cooper, Peter Haycock, Arthur Wood, Derek Holt, Richard Jones, and George Newsome (Jones dropped out after their first album, and Newsome was replaced by John Cuffley in 1973), the Climax Blues Band were originally called the Climax Chicago Blues Band. They began in the Stafford area in 1968 as part of the British blues revival, playing in a fairly traditional post-war blues style, but recording mostly original songs for Harvest. A 1972 tour introduced them to American audiences. A live album recorded in New York (*FM Live*, 1974), became a top seller and made them FM radio favourites. Their albums since then, notably *Rich Man* (1972) and *Sense of Direction* (1974), produced by Richard Gottehrer, have refined the group's tightness, economy and fullness of sound. *Gold Plated* (1976) included the Number 3 US hit 'Couldn't Get It Right', while *Flying the Flag* (1980) featured the Number 12 hit 'I Love You'. The line-up has changed considerably over the years: indeed by 1983, Haycock and Cooper were the only remaining members of the band's original personnel.

Jamaican reggae superstar Jimmy Cliff has devoted much of his long career to uniting black people worldwide through his music

CLINE, PATSY

Arguably the finest female country singer of the late Fifties and early Sixties, Patsy Cline was born in Winchester, Virginia, as Virginia Hensley, and made her performing debut in a 1957 edition of the Arthur Godfrey Talent Scouts Television Show. Signed by Decca, she made an immediate impression on the national pop chart with 'Walkin' After Midnight', written by Ben Hecht, who described her as the one person who could 'cry on both sides of the microphone'. It was this unique quality in her voice that allowed her to dominate the modern 'weepie' genre with songs like 'She's Got You', 'Faded on Your Mind', 'Faded Love' and 'I Fall to Pieces'. By the time she recorded this last song she was the undisputed top female country singer in America. That was in 1963, the year she died, with Hawkshaw Hawkins and Cowboy Copas, in a plane crash. In 1973 she was elected to the Country Music Hall of Fame, and in 1985 her life story was dramatized in the film *Sweet Dreams*.

CLINTON, GEORGE

One of the three semi-legendary pioneers of the tough, rhythmic style of soul/R&B known as 'funk', singer/bandleader George Clinton (born 22 July 1940) was as important a figure in that style of music through the Seventies as **James Brown** and **Sly Stone** had been in the Sixties and early Seventies.

A giant in black music, for some 13 years Clinton led the Parliaments, a vocal quintet that had one US hit single, '(I Wanna) Testify' (1967). In 1969, increasingly influenced by the blooming drug scene, he changed the name of the band to Funkadelic, far more suitable for the psychedelic era. Funkadelic signed to Westbound and released albums (*Funkadelic* (1970), *Free Your Mind and Your Ass Will Follow* (1970) and *America Eats Its Young* (1972)) that were more instrumentally slanted, using long but never boring guitar solos, and lyrically bizarre. His kernel of musicians – guitarists Ed Hazel and Gary Shider, bassist William 'Bootsy' Collins, keyboard-player Bernie Worral – would stay with him, off and on, for the decade – some longer.

When *Standing on the Verge of Getting It On* (1974) came out, however, Clinton had found a way to give the anarchic yet purposeful Funkadelic a soul band alter ego. He simply signed the same group to another label, Casablanca, as Parliament (dropping the 's') and altered their emphasis, making them more pop-oriented and leaning more towards vocals. They had more immediate commercial appeal and developed into a band full of invented characters around which an extraordinary stage show was built. *Up for the Downstroke* (1974) expressed Clinton's rhythmic secret (in his words, 'everything is one the one', i.e. the first beat of every 4/4 bar is heavily emphasized, then an unusual style).

After the similarly styled *Chocolate City* (1975), Clinton's vision finally paid off in an extravagant way. *Mothership Connection* (1975) placed funk in a comic sci-fi setting as he and his crew, on seven songs, described encounters between extra-terrestrials and Harlemites. The same year, *The Clones of Dr Funkenstein* introduced, as well as a series of varied, compelling funk grooves, a second set of strip-cartoon characters, who were defined even further on *Funkentelechy vs the Placebo Syndrome* (1977), as Dr Funkenstein used his protégé, Starchild, to rid the world of the misanthropic Sir Nose D'Voidoffunk.

This all made excellent visual and aural material for the Parliafunkadelicment Thang (as the collective of musicians came to be known) tours when the whole entourage would go on the road and present both aspects of Clinton's musical persona in a startling show that included an inflatable, gaudy limousine – a veritable pimpmobile – and a flying saucer. By now, too, Clinton had expanded his musical web to include many other acts for whom he wrote and produced – for example, Parlet and the Brides of Funkenstein – while many of his band, Bootsy Collins most notably, had begun to record solo albums.

Having made Parliament a vastly successful enterprise, Clinton set about doing the same for Funkadelic. He signed them to Warner Bros and, after the aforementioned 'P-Funk' tours, they had an international hit single with 'One Nation Under a Groove', an essential funk anthem. Despite slightly less successful Parliament (*Motor Booty Affair* (1978) and *Gloryhallastoopid* (*Pin the Tail on the Funky*) (1979)) and Funkadelic (*Uncle Jam Wants You* (1979), *Electric Speaking of War Babies* (1981)) albums, a difficult time starting his own Uncle Jam label and a decision to split up all his bands, Clinton remained prolific in the Eighties, finding time to produce and act as mentor for others (from Sweat Band to the late Philippe Wynne, once lead singer for the **(Detroit) Spinners**) before signing to Capitol as a solo artist.

Uniquely funky and quirky, his first three solo albums – *Computer Games* (1982), *You Shouldn't-Nuf Bit Fish* (1983) and *Some of My Best Jokes Are Friends* (1985) – displayed his grasp both of funk and of left-field thought. His P-Funk All Stars project was successful, white acts started owning up to their admiration of him when **Thomas Dolby** cut 'Cube' with him, and in 1986 he confirmed continuing funk lunacy with the single, 'Do Fries Go With That Shake', the album *R&B Skeletons* (*in the Closet*) and the soundtrack to George Lucas's film, *Howard the Duck*.

CLOVERS

Fifties R&B group the Clovers began as a trio – Harold Lucas, Thomas Woods and Billy Shelton – in 1946 at school in Washington. John Bailey was soon added, and in the late Forties Matthew McQuator replaced Woods. Harold Winley then replaced Shelton and, in 1949, guitarist Bill Harris joined the throng. In 1950 they were introduced to Lou Krefetz, who became their manager and had them record for Rainbow; the disc didn't sell and Krefetz placed them with Atlantic, where their first two discs, Ahmet Ertegun's 'Don't You Know I Love You' and 'Fool Fool Fool', were Number 1 R&B hits during 1951. Both raw beat ballads, they sold 250,000 and 500,000 respectively – massive quantities in their limited market. In 1952, Bailey was drafted and replaced by Billy Mitchell, who was retained when Bailey returned after Army service, making a sextet.

Enjoying a string of 17 R&B hits up to 1956, they varied their style between harmonic ballads ('Blue Velvet') and novelty jump items ('Nip Sip'). Their magic ran out by 1957 when they left Atlantic for Poplar, making a couple of undistinguished singles and an LP subsequently issued by United Artists, whom they joined in 1958. The next year saw their biggest hit, 'Love Potion No. 9' (which reached Number 23 nationally), in their novelty 'jump' style. But after brief outings on Port and Atlantic, the sextet split in 1961, different factions subsequently recording for Winley, Porwin, Brunswick, Tiger, and Josie. A Clovers group led by Lucas was still playing revival shows as late as the mid-Seventies. Harris became a respected jazz guitarist.

COASTERS

Created in 1955 from the nucleus of a Los Angeles-based group, the Robins, the Coasters were the agents through which **Leiber and Stoller** marketed some of the most entertaining songs of the Fifties. Founder member Bobby Nunn had led

The late Fifties Coasters line-up (from left) Billy Guy, Will 'Dub' Jones, Carl Gardner and Cornel Gunter, here with Adolph Jacobs

the Robins through numerous West Coast labels, recorded with **Johnny Otis** on Savoy, and had a hit with Little Esther Phillips, 'Double Crossing Blues' (1950), before teaming with Leiber and Stoller on RCA in 1953. When the writing and producing duo formed their own label, Spark, a year later, they scored several local hits with the Robins, notably 'Riot in Cell Block No. 9' (featuring **Richard Berry**), 'Framed' (Nunn), 'The Hatchet Man' (Nunn), and 'Smokey Joe's Café' (Carl Gardner). Eight cuts from this period were later included on the first Coasters' album and have subsequently been regarded as Coasters' recordings.

Attracted by the success of 'Smokey Joe's Café', Atlantic signed them to their subsidiary label, Atco, retaining Leiber and Stoller as the creative force behind the group. Gardner and Nunn, with newcomers Billy Guy and Leon Hughes (also from California), were renamed the Coasters, and achieved widespread popularity with their first releases 'Down in Mexico' and 'One Kiss Leads to Another' (1956), which were followed more emphatically by 'Searchin''/'Young Blood' (1957) – a Top 10 pop hit.

After three less successful outings, Nunn and Hughes were replaced by Will 'Dub' Jones and Cornel Gunter who, with Guy and Gardner, formed the quartet that recorded all the other famous Coasters' hits: 'Yakety Yak' (1958) – their only Number 1 – 'Charlie Brown', 'Along Came Jones', 'Poison Ivy' (1959), and 'Little Egypt' (1961). The arrangement of these records used the differing character of each singer's voice to full effect around a catchy guitar figure (often Mickey Baker) or a fruity sax break (**King Curtis**). The production, particularly on the Robins' and early Coasters' releases, was far superior to any contemporary group efforts; and the lyrics, humorous cameos each neatly deriding an aspect of teenage and/or black ghetto life, were more adventurous than most other popular songs. In short, they were a unique series of statements influencing many other groups (the **Cadillacs**, the Olympics, the Hollywood Argyles) and yet never bettered. Hilarious stage routines worked out for each song ensured that they were as entertaining in person as on record. Apart from the hits, other sides – 'My Baby Comes to Me' (1957), 'The Shadow Knows' (1958), 'I'm a Hog for You' (1959), and 'Shopping for Clothes' (1960) – were equally fine examples of the partnership.

In 1961 Earl 'Speedoo' Carroll from the Cadillacs replaced Gunter, and the group continued on Atco until 1966, without Leiber and Stoller. Despite a couple of good releases – 'T'ain't Nothin' to Me' (recorded live at The Apollo in 1963) and 'Let's Go Get Stoned' (1965) – the Coasters' audiences dwindled. On Date in the late Sixties (reissued on King in the Seventies) Leiber and Stoller made an attempt to revive the Coasters' flagging career. Although the best of these recordings, 'Down Home Girl' and 'D. W. Washburn', were just as good as the Fifties hits, they were completely ignored by a new generation of record buyers.

COCHRAN, EDDIE Rock'n'roll guitarist and singer Eddie Cochran was born in Oklahoma City on 3 October 1938, the youngest of five children. Soon after his birth, the family moved north to Albert Lea, Minnesota, where they remained until he was 11. In 1949, they moved again to California, land of post-war opportunity, and settled in the Bell Gardens area. Here Eddie took up the guitar in earnest, and in 1953 he met Connie 'Guybo' Smith who later became his bassist.

In 1954, Cochran began his professional career as back-up guitarist behind an obscure hillbilly singer, Hank Cochran. Though unrelated, Hank did resemble Eddie and before long they hit the road as the Cochran Brothers, one of many hillbilly duos playing local fairs and dances in the south-west. In 1955, they recorded two straight hillbilly singles for the small Ekko label in Hollywood ('Guilty Conscience' and 'Mr Fiddle') but switched to rock'n'roll late in 1955 after seeing **Elvis Presley** (then still on Sun) in a Dallas stage show. Augmented by a heavy-handed drummer and an excitable pianist, the Cochrans cut 'Tired and Sleepy' and 'Fool's Paradise', progressing from acoustic hillbilly to frantic country-based rock, the spirit of which had now caught Eddie's fancy.

In 1956, Hank and Eddie split up and

Eddie Cochran, probably the most widely talented rock star of the Fifties

Eddie teamed up with Jerry Capehart, a songwriter who secured a deal with American Music, a Hollywood music publishing company, and Eddie recorded 'Skinny Jim' for their small Crest label. Using 'Skinny Jim' as a demo, Capehart, by now Cochran's manager and confidant, secured Eddie a contract with Liberty who in turn found him a part in the forthcoming movie, *The Girl Can't Help It*. Although Cochran sang '20 Flight Rock' in the film, his first Liberty release was 'Sittin' in the Balcony', a smoochie 'rockaballad' which reached Number 18 in America in May 1957. Despite this flying start, however, Cochran had problems finding a follow-up, and had to wait until September 1958, for his next big hit – 'Summertime Blues', a million-seller rock'n'roll classic.

Although contracted to Liberty, Cochran spent a great deal of time in the studio surrounded by musician friends and singers under the auspices of American Music. The results were often released on obscure American Music subsidiaries such as Silver Capehart, Crest, and Zephyr credited to the Kelly Four (Cochran's backing group), Jewel and Eddie, and others.

After 'Summertime Blues' came 'C'mon Everybody', 'Weekend', 'Somethin' Else' and 'Cherished Memories' – all much bigger hits in Britain where, like **Gene Vincent**, he was more popular than in America. Cochran appeared in two other films, *Untamed Youth* (1957) and *Go Johnny Go* (1959). Finally, in 1960, he was booked to tour England with his close friend, Gene Vincent. He was ecstatically received both on stage and TV (*Boy Meets Girl*) and made his final appearance at the Bristol Hippodrome on 16 April 1960. The following day, the car in which he was travelling to London Airport skidded and crashed into a lamp standard. Cochran was killed and passengers Gene Vincent and Sharon Sheeley (Cochran's fiancée) were badly injured. Ironically, his British chart hit at the time was 'Three Steps to Heaven'.

When Cochran died at 21, he was only beginning to realize ambitions which went far beyond the scope of most of his contemporaries, in terms of studio activity. He was not merely a singer and a talented guitarist and songwriter, he was also an arranger and an A&R man. Moreover, considering him only as a singer-songwriter, if some of his records seem a little too slick now, the wit of his running commentary on teenage life, seen from within, puts him only a couple of notches below **Chuck Berry**.

COCKER, JOE Originally a gas fitter and pub singer from Sheffield, England, where he was born on 20 May 1944, Joe (born John Robert) Cocker made his recording debut in 1963 as a member of Vance Arnold and the Avengers, with a version of the **Beatles'** 'I'll Cry Instead'. He dropped out of performing soon after but returned in 1966 with the Grease Band, who were signed by **Denny Cordell** to the Regal Zonophone label, of which he was head. 'Marjorine' was a small UK hit in 1967 and drew national attention to Cocker's raw, anguished, powerful blues voice. The follow-up – a soulful reading of the Beatles' 'With a Little Help from My Friends' – was a British Number 1 in 1968 and a success throughout the world, leading to a first album of the same name which featured **Jimmy Page**, **Albert Lee**, **Stevie Winwood**, and Henry McCullough, among others.

The Grease Band, comprising Bruce Rowland, Chris Stainton, Alan Spenner, and McCullough in addition to Cocker, toured America and played Woodstock in 1969. There Cocker met **Leon Russell**, whose song 'Delta Lady' was to be Cocker's third British hit, and (together with session musicians and the Grease Band) he recorded the album *Joe Cocker!* under Russell's supervision. Russell put together Mad Dogs and Englishmen for an American tour in 1970 when the Grease Band quit; the tribe of over 20 musicians and

singers, included the pirated **Delaney and Bonnie** Band, was a runaway success. A live double album (which went gold) and film resulted and Russell emerged a superstar. But Cocker, who reportedly made only $800 from the tour, retired to England after recording one more song, 'High Time We Went', a minor American hit.

In 1972, he made a disastrous comeback bid with a tour, opening in the States and closing in Australia, where repeated arrests led to his deportation. That year he released a further album, *Something to Say*, which showed a marked limitation and deterioration in his vocal powers. In 1974, he returned once more with a better album, *I Can Stand a Little Rain*, which none the less ranked below his former greatness. He began to tour again in the summer of 1974, opening with a concert in Los Angeles that ran into many difficulties. However, he persisted with live work and by March 1975, had a US Top 10 hit with a track from the album, 'You Are So Beautiful'. His other Seventies albums included *Jamaica Say You Will* (1975) and *Luxury You Can Afford* (1978), but it was 1982 before Cocker again made a significant international impact, with the album *Sheffield Steel* (Island) and a US chart-topping duet with Jennifer Warnes, 'Up Where We Belong' (from the film *An Officer and a Gentleman*). He joined Capitol in 1984 and debuted later that year with *Civilised Man*.

Joe Cocker was instantly recognisable by his raw, powerful blues voice and the strange jerking movements he made on stage. His band usually included a brass section

Leonard Cohen, singer and writer

COHEN, LEONARD

An established novelist and poet long before he became known within the rock music world, Leonard Cohen was born on 21 September 1934, in Montreal, Canada. He studied English literature at McGill and Columbia Universities and made his literary debut in 1966 with his novel, *Beautiful Losers*, which contained an attractive mixture of eroticism, spiritual longings, slapstick and existential despair. He repeated this mixture on his first two albums, *The Songs of Leonard Cohen* (Columbia, 1967) and *Songs from a Room* (1969) which were enormously successful. Cohen's droning voice, his minimal backing, his attitude of humorous desperation towards existence and sexual relationships, made him a major figure in the 'bedsitter' singer/songwriter league. His songs, particularly 'Suzanne' and 'Sisters of Mercy', became acknowledged classics, and Cohen achieved commercial success by turning his concerts into experiences of communal catharsis (as documented on 'Please Don't Pass Me By' on *Live Songs*, 1973). The subsequent *New Skin for the Old Ceremony* (1974) displayed an undiminished gift for subtle imagery and striking political/sexual metaphors. After living on a Greek island for a spell, he returned to touring and recording in 1976: *Death of a Ladies Man* (1977) was produced by **Phil Spector** and included vocal contributions by **Bob Dylan**. Unhappy with the results, Cohen shifted gear on *Recent Songs* (1979) and returned to the acoustic settings of earlier albums.

COLE, LLOYD AND THE COMMOTIONS

Formed in Glasgow in 1983, Lloyd Cole and the Commotions almost immediately became a favoured critics' band, playing a fresh, delicate brand of post-new wave guitar pop/rock.

Lloyd Cole (guitar/vocals) and Blair Cowan (keyboards) knew each other from university and got together with Neil Clark (guitar) before completing the line-up with Lawrence Donegan (bass) and Stephen Irvine (drums) in 1984. Polydor signed them almost immediately and the debut single 'Perfect Skin' was released the same year to loud critical applause, eventually breaching the UK Top 30 in June.

Their debut LP *Rattlesnakes* was released in November, again to good reviews, and Lloyd Cole and the Commotions came to be regarded as an 'important' band, the most likely one to imbue the charts with a touch of quality. *Easy Pieces* (1985) confirmed that the first album was no fluke, spawning the minor hit single 'Brand New Friend', but the big hit that would give them the major international band status that many predicted for the Commotions continued to elude them.

COLE, NAT 'KING'

A pioneer of the sophisticated West Coast nightclub style of singing and playing that was later followed by **Charles Brown**, **Floyd Dixon**, **Ivory Joe Hunter** and a host of others, Nat 'King' Cole remains the only black performer in this style to attain lasting acceptance by a mass white audience.

Born 17 March 1917, in Montgomery, Alabama, he first attracted attention as an Earl Hines-influenced pianist in his brother's band in Chicago. By 1939, he had formed his own trio with Oscar Moore on guitar and Wesley Prince on bass and was playing regularly in Hollywood night spots. *Downbeat* jazz magazine voted the Nat Cole Trio the Top Small Combo from 1944 to 1947, while Moore topped the guitarists section from 1945 to 1948. During the mid-Forties, Cole started to make a series of recordings for the then newly formed Capitol label which ultimately brought him fame as a highly polished, commercial singer. In 1948, he scored his first Gold disc for 'Nature Boy', then a year later he received a second for 'Mona Lisa' and a third in 1951 for 'Too Young'. All three songs were successfully covered in later years by **Bobby Darin**, **Conway Twitty**, and Donny Osmond.

By 1953, Cole was a huge name, knocking Billy Eckstine from the Top Male Vocalist slot in the annual *Downbeat* poll. In 1957, he cut perhaps his best-remembered hit, 'When I Fall in Love' and was given his own national TV series, but abandoned the project that same year, complaining that the attitude of advertising agencies had resulted in his failure to find a regular sponsor (a year earlier Cole had been physically attacked by a gang of Southern racialists while performing to a predominantly white audience of 3000 in Birmingham, Alabama).

In August 1962 Cole again broke into the US national charts with the million-seller 'Ramblin' Rose'. 'Those Lazy, Hazy Days of Summer' brought him his last US Top 10 hit in mid-1963. Although performed in a pedestrian singalong style, they proved Cole's staying power over two decades. He died of cancer on 14 February 1966.

COLE, NATALIE

The daughter of **Nat 'King' Cole**, Natalie Cole (born 6 February 1950) in Los Angeles) became a prominent US soul and TV star in the late Seventies, scoring a string of gold and platinum albums as well as several Grammys, and was at one point hailed as the new **Aretha Franklin**.

She attended the University of Massachusetts and began singing in the local Amherst clubs. Cole signed to Capitol in 1975 and released her first album, *Inseparable*, sent on its best-selling way by the single, 'This Will Be' (a US Number 6). Her successful releases continued with an album a year and several hit singles including 'I've Got Love On My Mind' (Number 5 in 1977) and 'Our Love' (Number 10 in 1978). However, after 1980 and the LP *Don't Look Back*, her popularity waned, and her recording activities came to a virtual halt. 1983 found her re-emerging with *Unforgettable*, a tribute album to her father recorded with **Johnny Mathis**.

COLLINS, ALBERT

Born in Leona, Texas, in 1930, Albert Collins' blues vocal and guitar style was formed in the clubs of the Houston ghetto where his career began. He has not always done himself justice on record, considering the brilliance of his live performances. The important singles – 'The Freeze' on Kangaroo in 1958 and 'Defrost' on Great Scott in 1962 (but also issued on Hallway and Smash) – sold well in the South without reaching the national charts. Under the guidance of producer Bill Hall, Collins' subsequent singles and albums for TCF-Hall, Tracie, 20th Century-Fox, Blue Thumb, Imperial and Tumbleweed achieved considerable fame among white blues enthusiasts.

His Eighties releases included *Frozen Alive* (Sonet, 1981) and *Live in Japan* (1984).

COLLINS, JUDY Along with **Joan Baez** and **Joni Mitchell**, Judy Collins is one of the three great female singers who emerged through the American folk scene in the Sixties. Born in Seattle on 1 May 1939 and originally trained as a classical pianist, she began singing in the folk clubs of Denver and Central City, Colorado, before moving east to Greenwich Village, New York. Her first album *A Maid of Constant Sorrow* (Elektra, 1961) demonstrated her exquisite, crystal-clear voice on traditional material.

As the folk scene developed, Collins managed to keep at least one jump ahead. She moved from folk to contemporary songs by up-and-coming writers. So, in 1963, she recorded **Bob Dylan** tracks, and in 1966 she was the first to record **Leonard Cohen**'s 'Suzanne'. On *Wildflowers*, in 1967, she took another step forward by including some of her own songs for the first time. By now her style had broadened to include ballads and *chanson*, and she was rightly recognized as a superb interpreter of writers as varied as Jacques Brel, Brecht/Weill, Joni Mitchell and **Randy Newman**. This album qualified for a gold record, as did *Who Knows Where the Time Goes* (1968), which included **Stephen Stills** among the backing musicians. Collins later had hit singles with 'Both Sides Now' and 'Amazing Grace', and in all her recordings retained her magnificent, clear voice.

She has been active in politics, including help in registering black voters in Mississippi in 1964. In 1974 she seemed to be drifting away from music when *Antonia: Portrait of a Woman*, a film she helped make about her classical teacher, Antonia Brico, was nominated for an Academy Award. But in 1975 she returned to the charts with a bang following the success of Stephen Sondheim's 'Send in the Clowns', which came from the Broadway show *A Little Night Music*. In 1980, she left Elektra for Columbia.

COLLINS, PHIL Since his promotion from drummer to frontman for **Genesis**, Phil Collins has been one of the most versatile and consistently acclaimed figures in mainstream rock, and one of the few to find outstanding success as a group member, solo artist, sessioneer and producer.

Born on 31 January 1951, Collins was educated at drama school and his earliest success was as the Artful Dodger in a London production of *Oliver*. He had also been drumming since the age of twelve, and, in 1970, he

Phil Collins has one of the most distinctive voices in Eighties rock

left the world of acting to join Genesis. He really only came into the public eye, however, when **Peter Gabriel** left the group and Collins took over the vocals. Under his influence, they developed in a more accessible direction and attained a new level of worldwide popularity. Yet, even in the face of this resounding success, Collins' achievements outside Genesis were even greater.

Collins had already played with the renowned, moderately successful jazz-oriented group Brand X during his time with Genesis. Only a part-time endeavour, it produced a couple of albums of which *Moroccan Roll* (1977) was the bigger seller. But in 1981 he set out as a solo artist proper and, with the aid of top session players, recorded his debut LP, *Face Value*, which proved phenomenally successful, staying in the UK charts for over a year and spawning the international hit 'In the Air Tonight'. It was sophisticated, mainstream adult rock, and won him scant praise from the critics, but it was very easy on the ears and solidified Phil Collins' reputation as a singer in the minds of many people. The album established him among the elite of best-selling rock artists.

Another LP, *Hello, I Must be Going*, was released in 1982, and while it failed to emulate the success of its predecessor, it produced a UK Number 1 hit single, 'You Can't Hurry Love', which widened his appeal with pop audiences. His solo success spurred Collins on to produce albums by other artists, among them **Adam Ant**, **Eric Clapton**, and **John Martyn**, as a result of which he started to get commissions for film scores, most notably the 1984 film *Against All Odds*, whose soundtrack album reached the top of the charts around the world.

Early in 1985, after drumming and singing on the **Band Aid** single 'Do They Know It's Christmas?', Collins released his third solo album *No Jacket Required*, and while it did not depart from his already successful formula, it consolidated his success and soared straight to the UK Number 1 spot, supported by a lengthy world tour. He was the only performer to appear in both UK and US Live Aid concerts in the summer of the same year, and early in 1986 he won the British Phonographic Institute Award for male artist of the year.

While Phil Collins' solo work could never be described as pushing back the barriers of popular music ('ordinary' is a word often used by reviewers), his unflappable, workaholic approach to so many fields will ensure his longevity and continuing large-scale success in the rock world.

COLOSSEUM An attempt to develop the fruitful interplay between jazz, blues and rock characteristic of Sixties London R&B bands like those of **Graham Bond** and **John Mayall** gave rise to Colosseum. Drummer Jon Hiseman (born in Blackheath, London, on 21 June 1944) had worked with both groups, as had horn player Dick Heckstall-Smith (born in Ludlow, Shropshire on 26 September 1934).

They were the nucleus of the group which was formed in 1968. Other members were Dave Greenslade (keyboards, vibes), Jim Roche (guitar), and Tony Reeves (bass). Roche was later replaced by first James Litherland, then Dave Clempson. Mark Clark replaced Reeves. Colosseum's records were dominated by Hiseman's penchant for extended pieces, on *Those Who Are About to Die Salute You* (Fontana, 1969) and notably *Valentyne Suite* (Vertigo, 1969). In 1970 singer **Chris Farlowe** joined the group for the last studio album, *Daughter of Time*.

A year later, the band broke up, leaving a live album released on Bronze. Hiseman formed Tempest with guitarist Ollie Halsall in 1972, while both Heckstall-Smith (briefly) and Greenslade formed their own bands; the latter (called Greenslade) featured an unusual double keyboards line-up with Dave Lawson and made three albums on Warner Bros. In 1975, Hiseman formed Colosseum II with Gary Moore (guitar), Don Airey (keyboards), Neil Murray (bass), and Mike Starrs (vocals). They recorded three albums – *Strange New Flesh* (Warner Bros), *Electric Savage* and *Wardance* (both MCA) before disbanding in 1978.

COLUMBIA RECORDS (CBS)

Formed in 1887 in the US as the Columbia Phonograph Company, Columbia Records is better known in the UK as CBS (Columbia Broadcasting System). In 1890, the company introduced the first pre-recorded cylinders and the record industry was born. Yet while the company has always been at the fore in technical advances in recording and merchandising – including the introduction of the long-playing record in 1947 and the first major company subscription club in 1955 (the Columbia Record Club) – the Fifties saw Columbia, under the direction of Mitch Miller, who replaced Mannie Sachs as head of Columbia's A&R department in 1950, attempt to bury its head in the sand as far as rock'n'roll was concerned.

One reason for this was its undeniable success in the early Fifties, when **Frankie Laine**, Rosemary Clooney, **Guy Mitchell**, Doris Day, **Johnnie Ray**, and Jo Stafford marched up the singles charts, almost in rotation, with few other artists even getting a look-in, while Mitch Miller and his gang persuaded America to 'Sing Along with Mitch' on numerous very successful albums. Indeed, Columbia's only failure in these years was the loss of Frank Sinatra to Capitol in 1950. (Sinatra had objected to the regimentation of Columbia's A&R department.)

Where other companies were looking for R&B songs for their artists to cover, Miller, with writers pounding on his door all the time, could afford to give 'Singing the Blues' to Guy Mitchell for the pop market and to **Marty Robbins** for the country market, and get both to Number 1 in their respective charts in 1956. He did the same thing again with 'Knee Deep in the Blues', only a little less successfully, during the following year. Moreover, while the country singers signed to other labels were, by 1957, becoming interested in rock'n'roll, those on Columbia's roster were kept on the straight and narrow by Miller, whose notion of country was of a country- (or folk-) inflected pop song. None the less, Miller bid for **Elvis Presley** in 1955 when the latter was ready to leave Sun for a bigger company, and a couple of Columbia's country singers, notably **Ronnie Self** and Sid King and the Five Strings, were allowed to record some of the best rockabilly cuts of the Fifties.

Similarly, where most other labels' black artists were heavily R&B-influenced, Columbia's **Johnny Mathis** was a remarkably successful singer of sweet, smooth ballads. The only part of Columbia's empire to come to terms with rock before the mid-Sixties was the autonomous subsidiary Okeh, which had the Treniers, **Chuck Willis**, and Titus Turner among others. Johnnie Ray, whose 'Cry' sold a million in 1951, was originally issued on Okeh and sold remarkably well in the R&B market. Later, in 1956, Okeh produced arguably the most bizarre piece of rock-'n'roll ever recorded in **Screamin' Jay Hawkins'** 'I Put a Spell on You'.

Columbia entered the Sixties with a healthy stable of MOR stars (Mitch Miller, Doris Day, Andy Williams, etc.) and a string of enormously successful Broadway cast albums (*South Pacific*, *My Fair Lady*). Yet by 1966, with only the **Byrds**, **Bob Dylan**, **Simon and Garfunkel**, and **Paul Revere and the Raiders** – their best-selling rock act – and with post-**Beatles** rock transformed into the major concern of the record industry, things looked decidedly bleak, though the country music division was healthy and soul hits came sporadically on Okeh and Dare. While in the rock field Dylan gave them prestige, he did not sell in vast quantities, and Simon and Garfunkel would not become real moneyspinners until 1968. By then, the whole problem had been solved by a mixture of good luck and good judgment when Clive Davis, the company's new president, went to the Monterey Pop Festival, saw rock's future and waved the corporate cheque book. A few years of frenzied signings later, **Janis Joplin**, **Sly Stone**, **Johnny Winter**, and **Blood, Sweat and Tears** had been added to the roster, and the cash expectations of groups looking for a record contract had drastically risen. This was topped off by an advertising campaign that invited people to 'Join the Revolution' – and this at a time when in Britain, the newly independent CBS's only sizable hits were with pop groups like the **Tremeloes**. That said, the result of Columbia's burst of activity was that by 1969, the company again was well balanced and extremely profitable, with soul the only area left to be explored.

The signing of a distribution deal with **Gamble and Huff's** Philadelphia International label – the home of early to mid-Seventies hits by the likes of the **Three Degrees**, **Harold Melvin and the Blue Notes**, and **Billy Paul** – went some way towards filling this gap, as did Columbia's nurturing of **Earth, Wind and Fire**. Meanwhile, Columbia's subsidiary, Epic Records, grew in strength with a range of black talent including the **Isley Brothers**, **Johnny Nash**, and – after their 1976 break with Motown – the **Jacksons** and **Michael Jackson** as a solo artist. The departure of Clive Davis in 1973 – he was sacked over claims that he had misused company funds – had no immediate impact on Columbia's profitability, and indeed many of the mainstays of the label during the Seventies and early Eighties were his signings, among them **Billy Joel**, **Kris Kristofferson**, **Neil Diamond**, and the hugely successful **Bruce Springsteen**.

Britain was never a particularly significant source of talent for Columbia until the Eighties, when CBS (UK) found a succession of post-new wave artists – **Bonnie Tyler**, **Paul Young**, **Alison Moyet**, and **Wham!** among them – who were suitable for global marketing. All these examples were acts who had originally been signed to other companies, and generally speaking the label's success in actually discovering *new* talent was less impressive.

COMMANDER CODY AND HIS LOST PLANET AIRMEN

A Seventies band who specialized in an inventive and innovative blend of Western Swing, rockabilly, country music and R&B, Commander Cody and his Lost Planet Airmen was the brain-child of keyboards player George Frayne. While studying at Michigan University in Ann Arbor, he formed a variety of bands (including the Amblers, the Fantastic Surfing Beavers and Lorenzo Lightfoot) with John Tichy (guitar), before amalgamating with the R&B band of Billy C. Farlow to form the Airmen in 1967.

The line-up of the much-changing group eventually settled down to Frayne (Commander Cody), Tichy, Farlow, Lance Dickerson (drums), Andy Stein (fiddle, sax), Bill Kirchen (lead guitar), Buffalo Bruce Barlow (bass) and the West Virginia Creeper (steel guitar) when the band moved to Berkeley in 1969, where they soon acquired the reputation of being the best bar band in town. Signed to ABC-Paramount in 1971, they recorded their most successful and influential album *Lost in the Ozone*, which included the infamous 'Seeds and Stems' and saw the band mixing rockabilly and traditional country music. The Commander's novelty song – there was one on every album – a version of Johnny Bond's 'Hot Rod Lincoln', gave them a Top 10 hit in 1972. Subsequent albums for ABC, including *Hot Licks, Cold Steel and Truckers' Favourites* (1972), and *Country Casanova* (1973), which included their only other major US hit, another Cody novelty song, 'Smoke! Smoke! Smoke! (That Cigarette)', revealed a fondness for trucking songs and Western Swing, but were not as powerful as the first. In 1974 they switched to Warner Bros, releasing two better-produced but unexciting albums in 1975.

The group disbanded in 1976 after a tour of Europe, but Frayne continued to record under the name of Commander Cody. Their experience with Warner Bros was the subject of a book by Geoffrey Stokes, published in 1978, called *Starmaking Machinery*.

COMMODORES

A sextet formed at Tuskegee Institute, Alabama, in the late Sixties as the Jays, the Commodores emerged on Motown in the mid-Seventies as that label's trump card in the self-contained band stakes. At the time, disco was at its zenith and the band, which wrote its own material, tapped this market with a series of prime, hard-hitting funk tunes such as 'Machine Gun' (also the title of their 1974 debut album), '(Do) the Bump', 'Slippery When Wet' and 'I Feel Sanctified', the last-named also giving some indication of their gospel roots. But massive, world-wide success came later in the form of ballads penned by their keyboard-player, tenor saxophonist and singer **Lionel Richie**; the group's other members were Milan Williams (keyboards, trombone, guitar), William King (trumpet), Walter Orange (drums), Ronald LaPread (bass, trumpet) and Thomas McClary (guitar). Their hits, 'Just To Be Close to You', 'Sweet Love', 'Zoom', 'Easy' and 'Three Times a Lady' all had a distinctive style – warm melody romantically realized by Richie's pleasantly convincing voice – that was highly distinctive, and contrasted vividly with their tougher funk pieces.

As these ballads increasingly became the artistic and commercial strong-point of the band, it seemed increasingly evident that Richie would quit to pursue a solo career, and in 1981 he did just that. He continued to work with James Anthony Carmichael, the producer who had shepherded the Commodores through the Seventies' successes, and stayed with Motown for the albums *Lionel Richie* (1982) and the massive-selling *Can't Slow Down* (1983), which illustrated the degree to which his ballad ('Hello') and funk ('All Night Long') styles were still in harmony with public taste. After a long spell resting, Richie returned in 1985 with a song written for the film *White Nights*, 'Say You, Say Me', which won an Oscar in 1986. Richie won a Grammy that year too for 'We Are the World', the American all-star recording effort in aid of African famine relief. Meanwhile, the remaining members of the Commodores were found to be

Lionel Richie quit the Commodores for a successful solo career

somewhat lacking in broad appeal without their former ballad writer, and their live shows – previously tight, varied and largely excellent – now became laboured, with no one able to render Richie's ballads as well as he did. McClary left and in 1984 released an eponymous album on Motown; it sold poorly, and deservedly so. A British singer, J. D. Nicholas, was then recruited; he had previously been with Heatwave, who had supported the Commodores, and the Commodores' manager subsequently offered him the chance to join the group.

In 1985, now working with producer Dennis Lambert, the quintet recorded 'Nightshift', a touching tribute to **Jackie Wilson** and **Marvin Gaye**, two great soul singers who had recently died, and it gave the group its biggest hit since the departure of Richie.

In 1986 Ronald LaPraed left, and the group left Motown for Phonogram.

COMMUNARDS

Formed as a duo by Jimmy Somerville and Richard Coles in 1985 after Somerville had left **Bronski Beat**, the Communards debuted early in 1986 with the single 'You Are My World', which marked something of a departure from the rigid synthesizer rhythms of Somerville's previous band. His soaring falsetto was still in evidence, but it was now accompanied by a much mellower sound orchestrated by pianist Coles.

Because of Somerville's previous successes, many observers were surprised by the failure of the first single and the low chart placing of subsequent releases. However, matters were put right by the astonishing success of their rousing version of 'Don't Leave Me This Way', which was a Number 1 in the UK for over a month in the latter half of 1986 and featured the deep, sonorous voice of Sarah-Jane Morris, a part-time member of the band. The same year they released the debut album *The Communards* which performed well in the UK on the strength of their huge Number 1 hit.

CONLEY, ARTHUR

An **Otis Redding** protégé born on 1 April 1946 in Atlanta, Georgia, Arthur Conley had unsuccessful releases on Stax, Volt, and the star's Jotis label before 'Sweet Soul Music' (Atco) became a Top 5 hit in 1967. Originally written and recorded by **Sam Cooke** as 'Yeah Man', Redding and Conley's adaptation included the names of top soul stars and used a classic Memphis arrangement to create an anthem for the music that was ultimately ridiculed as a cliché-ridden parody. Conley never really recovered. After half-a-dozen smaller hits, including 'Funky Street' and 'People Sure Act Funny' (1968) he joined Capricorn Records in 1971. He has not had a hit since.

CONTOURS Comprising Hubert Johnson, Billy Gordon, Sylvester Potts, Joe Billingslea and Billy Hoggs, the Contours were introduced to Motown's Berry Gordy by Johnson's cousin, **Jackie Wilson**, in 1961. The following year the frenetic 'Do You Love Me?' topped the R&B charts and reached Number 3 in the US national charts. It was covered in Britain by **Brian Poole and the Tremeloes** and the **Dave Clark Five**. Other distinctively hoarse dance releases entered the middle reaches of the Hot 100, including 'Shake Sherrie', 'Don't Let Her Be Your Baby' (1963), 'Can You Do It', 'Can You Jerk Like Me' (1964), 'First I Look at the Purse' (1965), and 'Just a Little Misunderstanding' (1966). A ballad, 'It's So Hard Being a Loser' (1967), completed their chart run. Later members of the Contours included Joe Stubbs (brother of the **Four Tops**' Levi) and Dennis Edwards (subsequently with the **Temptations**).

COODER, RY A former session musician who attracted critical acclaim and a cult following during the Seventies for his expertise on slide guitar and his exploration of half-forgotten American folk styles, Ry Cooder was born Ryland Peter Cooder in Los Angeles on 15 March 1947. He received his first guitar at the age of four and developed his distinctive 'bottleneck' guitar style under the tutelage of blues legends like the Reverend Gary Davis. He formed a duo with **Jackie DeShannon** in the early Sixties and joined guitarist **Taj Mahal** in a group called the Rising Sons, who recorded a single, 'Candy Man', and an unreleased album. At the same time, he began taking on extensive session work and appeared on records by a host of major West Coast pop names, among them **Paul Revere and the Raiders** and **Harpers Bizarre**. A friendship with arranger/producer **Jack Nitzsche** led to slightly more prestigious recording gigs, including the *Safe as Milk* album by **Captain Beefheart and his Magic Band**, and albums by **Randy Newman**, **Phil Ochs** and the **Rolling Stones**: his contributions to the Stones' *Let it Bleed* (1969) and *Sticky Fingers* (1971) added to Cooder's growing reputation.

In 1970, Cooder landed a solo recording deal with Reprise and cut *Ry Cooder*, which was followed by *Into*

Ry Cooder, steeped in US folk

the *Purple Valley* (1972), *Boomer's Story* (1973), *Paradise and Lunch* (1974), and *Chicken Skin Music* (1976). Common to each was a wide range of repertoire from all manner of sources – blues, R&B, Cajun, Tex-Mex, rock-'n'roll, the folk songs of **Woody Guthrie** and **Leadbelly** – and a fine array of accompanying musicians. Most of all, the albums marked Cooder as an archivist, unearthing often obscure material and wrapping it in appropriate yet very contemporary arrangements. Sometimes this misfired – as on his first studio album for Warner Bros, *Jazz* (1978), which featured jazz greats like Earl Hines on songs by Bix Beiderbecke, Joseph Spence and Jelly Roll Morton. However, his acute understanding of America's musical heritage was such that, by the late Seventies, he was much in demand among US filmmakers for soundtrack work on projects like Walter Hill's 1980 Western, *The Long Riders*, the same director's *Southern Comfort* (1981), and Tony Richardson's *The Border* (1981).

Cooder's digitally recorded *Bop Till You Drop* (1979) finally brought Cooder some commercial success, and *Borderline* (1980) marked the beginning of his association with singer-songwriter John Hiatt. *The Slide Area* followed in 1982, and a compilation set, *Why Don't You Try Me Tonight?* in 1986.

COOKE, SAM Born one of a family of eight in Chicago on 22 January 1931, Sam Cooke first sang publicly in his local Baptist church, at the age of nine, when he got together with two sisters

Sam Cooke, cool crooner of pop-soul

and a brother under the name of the Singing Children. In his early teens he moved to another young Baptist group, the Highway QCs. They were coached for a while by R.B. Robinson, the baritone with a leading gospel quartet, the **Soul Stirrers**. When the Stirrers' lead tenor, Robert (R. H.) Harris, retired in 1950, Cooke was invited to take over, and he sang with the group until 1956.

The Soul Stirrers had already been responsible for major innovations in their field. Apart from being one of the first itinerant quartets to deal solely in hymns and modern gospel songs – rather than jubilees and spirituals – the group also singled out and emphasized the lead vocal to a far greater extent than their predecessors. They introduced a 'second lead' to fill in the tenor harmonic line and with this freedom Harris was able to develop a highly individual style of syncopated improvisation, prominently featuring his falsetto. Cooke's mature vocal style built on the groundwork done by Harris.

Once he had found his feet with the Soul Stirrers, Cooke also confirmed the uniquely contemporary and exciting atmosphere the group had brought to gospel. He became the idol of thousands of young girl fans, projecting the sexuality that had always been central to gospel, but bringing to it a cool, urban sophistication. The Soul Stirrers did their first session for Specialty early in 1950, and many of Cooke's recordings with them – such as 'Touch the Hem of His Garment' and 'Were You There' – show his pop-soul style fully developed.

In 1956 **'Bumps' Blackwell** encouraged Cooke to record some pop songs. A number of ballads were released, of which 'Lovable', 'That's All I Need to Know' and 'I'll Come Running Back to You' were the most notable, the last-named a million-seller on its belated release in 1957. Initially, he recorded under the name Dale Cook to avoid offending the gospel world. (He was christened Sam Cook, and the 'e' was added to his surname during his period at Specialty.) When Blackwell added a white female vocal chorus to sweeten Cooke's recording of 'You Send Me', Art Rupe (Specialty's owner) offered to sell them the tape and release both of them from their contracts in return for forgoing their past royalties. Blackwell took the tapes to Bob Keene on whose Keen label 'You Send Me'/'Summertime' was a national chart topper and eventually sold some two-and-a-half million copies. Other major hits on Keen were 'Only Sixteen' and 'Wonderful World' in 1959.

On these early pop records, the smooth, open delivery and lyrical purity of Cooke's gospel style remained virtually intact. His singing was a little more restrained and wistful, fitting the teenage-fantasy-sentimentality of the lyrics. But the controlled passion and the adlibbed mannerisms of 'You Send Me' – such as the wailing 'whoa-uh-oh-ah-oh' with which he extended many of the lines, giving weight to an insubstantial lyric and tune – were direct transpositions from his church style. It was a style without a clear precedent in mass popular music, and one that contrasted sharply with the dominant hot, raucous mood of rock'n'roll.

The switch to pop caused a final rift with the Soul Stirrers and they replaced him with future Stax performer **Johnnie Taylor**, who had also been in the Highway QCs. Cooke didn't lose touch entirely with his church music roots, however. In association with J. W. Alexander – late of the Pilgrim Travellers gospel group – he spent much of 1958–9 forming his own company, Sar Records, one of the first black-owned labels. Sar put out a series of strongly gospel-flavoured R&B hits in 1960–2, including the Sims Twins' 'Soothe Me', Johnnie Taylor's 'Rome (Wasn't Built in a Day)' and 'Lookin' For a Love' by the **Valentinos** – a group featuring **Bobby Womack**, who was not only heavily influenced artistically by his mentor but was later to marry Cooke's widow.

Meanwhile, Cooke had signed as a performer with RCA-Victor. By retaining his basic vocal style, Cooke was able to transcend the generally inflated and unsympathetic orchestral backings created by producers **Hugo and Luigi**, and many of his RCA performances were as influential and artistically convincing as they were commercially successful. The major hits included 'Chain Gang' (Number 2) and 'Sad Mood' in 1960, 'Cupid' in 1961, and in 1962, 'Twisting the Night Away', 'Having a Party' and 'Bring It on Home to Me', which featured ex-Pilgrim Traveller, Lou Rawls, as second vocalist. 1963 produced 'Little Red Rooster', with **Ray Charles** on piano and **Billy Preston** on organ; and in the following year came 'Ain't That Good News', 'Tennessee Waltz', 'That's Where It's At' and 'Shake'. The flipside of 'Shake' was one of Cooke's greatest compositions, 'A Change Is Gonna Come', with its seemingly prophetic expression of the imminent upsurge in black political and social consciousness. But by the time the record reached the Top 10 early in 1965, Cooke was dead. He was shot at a Los Angeles motel on 10 December 1964. The court returned a verdict of justifiable homicide.

Sam Cooke's influence was enormous. He stands at the head of the entire sweet soul ballad tradition, and performers such as **Otis Redding**, **Al Green**, **Smokey Robinson**, **Johnny Nash**, and **Marvin Gaye** have openly borne witness to their debt to him. Part of his importance lay in the fact that, like Ray Charles, he demonstrated that an R&B artist could retain a vital relationship with the black audience while surviving in the teenage pop market and in a Las Vegas night-club context as a performer of standards. He was also a significant force in British rock, with **Rod Stewart** modelling his style on Cooke's and a number of groups scoring important hits with songs he made famous – including the **Animals** ('Bring It on Home to Me') and even **Herman's Hermits** ('Wonderful World'). The latter song provided Cooke with a posthumous UK hit when reissued in 1986 following its use in a Levi's Jeans commercial.

COOKIE AND HIS CUPCAKES
A tremendously popular Louisiana group in the late Fifties and early Sixties, Cookie and his Cupcakes toured constantly throughout the South, distilling their distinctive brand of swamp-pop. Led by Huey Thierry and Shelton Dunaway, they recorded prolifically for the tiny Khoury label of Lake Charles, and reached Number 47 in the US chart in 1959 with the archetypal Louisiana ballad, 'Mathilda', which was leased to Judd; they also brushed the charts in 1962 with 'Got You on My Mind' on Chess. Like so many similar acts, they never really survived the onslaught of the British groups on America in the mid-Sixties.

COOLIDGE, RITA
A singer who occupies the middle ground between country music and mainstream American rock, Rita Coolidge was born in Nashville, Tennessee, on 1 May 1944. Schooled in country and gospel music with her sister Priscilla (who married and recorded with **Booker T.** for A&M), she came to prominence as a backing singer on the **Joe Cocker** Mad Dogs and Englishmen tour in 1970, having previously worked with **Delaney and Bonnie**.

Signed to A&M as a solo artist the following year, she went on to make a series of albums alone and with **Kris Kristofferson**, whom she married in 1973. The most outstanding were *The Lady's Not for Sale* (1972) and *Fall into Spring* (1974), both produced by David Anderle, although the biggest sales were achieved by *Anytime ... Anywhere* in 1977, which produced three hit singles in 'Higher and Higher' (Number 22 in the US), 'We're All Alone' (Number 7, a **Boz Scaggs** composition), and 'The Way You Do the Things You Do' (Number 20). She appeared in the films *Convoy* and *A Star is Born* alongside Kristofferson, from whom she was divorced in 1979.

The Eighties found her working with producer **Andrew Gold** on *Heartbreak Radio* (1981) – its cuts including revivals of **Dusty Springfield**'s 'Wishin' and Hopin'' and **Marvin Gaye**'s 'One More Heartache' – and with Anderle again on *Never Let You Go*, which included the hit single 'All Time High' (from the James Bond film, *Octopussy*) and versions of **Culture Club**'s 'Do You Really Want to Hurt me' and **Yazoo**'s 'Only You'. *Inside the Fire* (1984) was a **Tom Dowd** production.

COOPER, ALICE
'Alice Cooper' is the adopted stage persona of Vincent Furnier (born in Detroit on Christmas Day 1945), who carved his niche in Seventies rock with a blend of heavy metal music and shock-horror theatrics. Furnier spent most of his early life in Phoenix and formed his first band, the Earwigs, in 1965. A year and several personnel changes later, he renamed the band the Spiders and based its musical direction on that of the **Rolling Stones** and the **Who**, stressing outrage and a general anti-social stance. In late 1966, he changed the

Alice Cooper, Seventies antihero of shock rock, dealt in images of sex, violence and depravity

group's name once more to the Nazz (not to be confused with **Todd Rundgren**'s contemporaneous group of the same name) and began making use of props and ultra-violet light effects in live performances.

Yet another name change occurred towards the end of the decade: legend had it that the band members made contact through a Ouija-board with a spirit named Alice Cooper and that, when asked who Alice Cooper was, the insistent reply was 'Alice Cooper is Vincent Furnier'. Trading on the ambiguity and outrage implicit in the name, the group made their first appearance under their new appellation at a Lenny Bruce Memorial Party and drove the audience from the club, leaving only Shep Gordon and **Frank Zappa**. Fascinated by the spectacle, Gordon agreed to manage the group and Zappa signed them to his record label, Straight. Two albums resulted, but Zappa granted Alice a contractual release in 1970, and they signed with Warner Brothers, at the same time working out the right balance of vio-

lence and depravity for their stage show, which included simulated chicken- and baby-killing. 'Eighteen' gave the band its first US hit in 1971, following which Alice teamed with producer Bob Ezrin to devise the first of three thematic albums in *Killer*. The accompanying stage act found Alice fondling snakes, throwing money at the crowd, dismembering a baby doll, and being hanged for his sins. This ritualistic violence atoned for by death became a mainstay of the Cooper show.

By mid-1972, Alice Cooper was a world act on the strength of hits like 'School's Out' and 'Elected', but Alice himself began to tone down his image with appearances on TV game shows and on the pro-am golfing circuit. The group's three-month *Billion Dollar Babies* tour in 1973 left him disgusted at the violent behaviour of his audience, and, as part of an attempt to rehabilitate himself within the rock world, he reconstituted his band in 1974 and brought in new members Dick Wagner and Steve Hunter from **Lou Reed**'s band. Three of his original sidemen, Michael Bruce, Dennis Dunaway, and Neal Smith, left in 1977 to form their own band – called Billion Dollar Babies to capitalize on the Cooper association – and during the following year, Alice underwent extensive treatment for alcoholism, an experience explored on his low-key album *From the Inside* (for which he wrote some of the songs with **Bernie Taupin**). No longer much a chart force by the end of the decade, he nevertheless had the satisfaction of seeing such new and fashionably outlandish acts as Wayne County, **Kiss** and the **Damned** ape his particular brand of kitsch-style horror. Musically, too, the gothic hard rock of bands like **Meat Loaf** echoed the Alice Cooper of old. His Eighties albums include *Da Da* (1982) and *Zipper Catches Skin* (1983).

COOPER CLARKE, JOHN

Manchester-born John Cooper Clarke was the original Seventies punk poet – his ranting, quick-fire delivery and his humorous treatment of topical sociopolitical issues inspiring a new generation of young poets.

Though he had little to do with the music of punk, he shared its look and attitude. Remarkably, he regularly headlined bills that included prominent bands, and he commanded a strong following. Cooper Clarke has made a string of recordings, usually of his poetry set to urgent mood music, firstly in 1977 with an independent EP and later, when he was signed to a

major label, Epic. His debut album, *Disguise in Love* appeared in 1978 and he has followed this up with several more recordings, including the first orange triangular single, 'Gimmix!'. None of his LPs have sold particularly well, and his major achievements remain his influence on the new Ranter Poets (like Jools, Seething Wells and Attila the Stockbroker) and his live performances, as captured in the 1982 film, *Ten Years in an Open Neck Shirt*.

CORDELL, DENNY A leading Six-

ties rock entrepreneur-cum-producer, Denny Cordell was born Dennis Cordell-Laverack in Brazil in 1942, the son of an English father and a Brazilian mother. After attending public school in England, he worked for **Brian Epstein**'s Seltaeb company, set up in 1964 to merchandise **Beatles** goods. He stumbled into record production by discovering the original Bessie Banks version of 'Go Now' in 1965 and passing it to the **Moody Blues**, who were contracted to Seltaeb at that time. Although Cordell was heavily involved in the production of the Moody Blues' hit treatment of the song, the production credit on the label went to the more experienced Alex Murray. None of the group's subsequent Cordell-produced follow-ups made much chart impact, however.

Between 1965 and 1966, Cordell – a non-musician – also produced discs by the Mark Leeman Five, Jackie Edwards and a number of obscure names before beginning a highly successful association with the **Move** – like the Moody Blues, another Birmingham-based band. The Move's first hit was 'Night of Fear' in 1966, the same year that saw Cordell produce the chart-topping 'Getaway' for Georgie Fame and the two UK Top 20 follow-ups, 'Sunny' and 'Sitting in the Park'. 1967 brought the commercial high-point of his production career, with the worldwide success of **Procol Harum**'s 'A Whiter Shade of Pale', shortly after which Cordell joined EMI as head of the newly revived Regal Zonophone subsidiary. Cordell-produced hits released by the label included the Move's 'Flowers in the Rain', Procol Harum's 'Homburg' (both 1967), and **Joe Cocker**'s 'With a Little Help from My Friends' (1968). The Cocker link brought Cordell into contact with **Leon Russell**, with whom he produced Cocker's best-selling *Mad Dogs and Englishmen* album for A&M in 1970. From 1971 onwards, Cordell became Russell's full-time partner, administering the Russell-established Shelter Records from its base in

Russell's home town of Tulsa, Oklahoma. His production work has since included two **Tom Petty and the Heartbreakers** albums, *Tom Petty and the Heartbreakers* (1976) and *You're Gonna Get It* (1978).

COREA, CHICK Born in Massachusetts on 12 June 1941, Chick Corea was one of the leading forces in jazz-rock during the Seventies. A session musician during the Sixties, when he worked as pianist and resident composer with Stan Getz on albums such as *Sweet Rain* (Verve, 1967), he joined **Miles Davis** in 1969 and played on such important Davis albums as *Bitches Brew* and *In a Silent Way*. He co-led a rather forbidding free-improvisation group, Circle, before settling on the small-band format of Return to Forever, which took its name from Corea's solo album of 1972. Featuring the great Stanley Clarke on bass, Return to Forever tended towards the Latin side of jazz-rock; other members at various times included Airto Moreira (percussion), Lenny White (drums) and Bill Connors (guitar). In 1976, after Clarke and guitarist Al DiMeola left the group, Corea expanded Return to Forever into a 13-member combination, but a year later he dropped the name and returned to solo work and guest sessions with other jazz notables. He also played extensively with **Herbie Hancock** and with vibraharpist Gary Burton.

CORNELIUS BROTHERS AND SISTER ROSE This group produced one of the most insidiously memorable American hits of 1971 with the churning 'Treat Her Like a Lady'. Creatively, if not commercially, it was the zenith for the Miami-based group. Born in Fort Lauderdale, Florida, brothers Eddie and Carter and sister Rose Cornelius began singing in a family gospel quintet, the Split Tones, before 'crossing over' and signing with a tiny Miami independent, Platinum Records. Producer Bob Archibald recorded Eddie Cornelius' droning, pulsating 'Lady'. It became a local hit and the master and the group's contract were snapped up by United Artists. Just after the record had gone gold the group were in a car crash and 11 months elapsed before a follow-up was released – 'Too Late to Turn Back Now', another Top 5 record in 1972. The group went on to score with 'Don't Ever Be Lonely' (1972), 'Big Time Lover' (1973) and several more, but their overproduced, limp pop soul featuring Eddie's flat, rather unmusical voice had

palled by 1974 and they had no further hits.

CORYELL, LARRY A jazz guitarist who made his first impact with the Gary Burton Quartet in 1967–8, Larry Coryell (born in Galveston, Texas, on 2 April 1943) is an immaculate player with a seemingly inexhaustible supply of ideas and techniques. He led his first band in 1969, the line-up including **Jack Bruce** and Mitch Mitchell from the **Jimi Hendrix** Experience. On *Spaces* (Vanguard, 1970) he was partnered by Billy Cobham, **Chick Corea**, **John McLaughlin**, and Miroslav Vitous. His Seventies bands included Eleventh House, whose one album was *Introducing the Eleventh House with Larry Coryell* (1974), and he also recorded a series of albums with Philip Catherine, former guitarist with **Focus**.

COSTELLO, ELVIS Born Declan MacManus in London on 25 August 1954, Elvis Costello is the foremost British rock talent to have emerged from the punk/new wave explosion. From his first appearance on the scene in 1977, he has grown to be a singer/songwriter of great stature, and while Costello has never quite made it into the record sales super-league, he commands enormous respect from both peers and critics.

When his parents divorced (his father Ross sang with the Joe Loss Band), Declan took his mother's surname and moved with her to Liverpool. After playing in various garage bands there, he returned to London and performed both as the front-man for pub-rockers Flip City and, under the name of D.P. Costello, as a solo singer in folk clubs. By 1976 he had accumulated a collection of his own material, and after a series of rejections from major companies' A&R men, he arrived at the then newly-formed Stiff Records. In early 1977, Jake Riviera signed Costello, re-named him Elvis and put him into the studio with house producer **Nick Lowe**. There followed three stand-out singles, 'Less Than Zero', 'Alison' and 'Red Shoes' and his debut album *My Aim is True*, which served notice that a major new talent had emerged.

One problem with the album was the lukewarm performance of the backing band but this was quickly remedied by the formation in June '77 of the Attractions: Steve Nieve on keyboards, Pete Thomas on drums and Bruce Thomas on bass. Their arrival immediately expanded Costello's live sound and the trio – especially the imaginative Nieve

– became an important factor in Costello's material. They played together for the first time in July at a packed-out Dingwalls in London, and subsequent gigs in the capital were increasingly difficult to get in to as Costello became a hot property. They joined the national Stiff tour, which also featured **Ian Dury**, **Dave Edmunds** and Nick Low. A fourth single, 'Watching the Detectives', was released at the same time and made the charts, reaching Number 15. At the end of the year, Riviera took Costello away from Stiff and onto the emerging Radar label.

This Year's Model appeared in March '78 to ecstatic reviews, and it remains Costello's finest LP. A collection of powerful songs including the hit '(I Don't Want To Go To) Chelsea', it expressed a wave of derision and contempt as Costello proved himself a potent lyricist as well as a master tunesmith. It proved a difficult album to follow, and although *Armed Forces* (1979) provided Costello's biggest hit 'Oliver's Army' (a UK Number 2), it was – apart from a couple of songs – glib by comparison.

Costello's popularity in the US had been increasing with his regular visits, but it suffered a major setback in the spring of '79 when in a drunken altercation at the Holiday Inn, Columbus, Ohio, he is alleged to have described **Ray Charles** as 'an ignorant blind nigger'. He was immediately branded a racist, his gigs were picketed by anti-racist groups, and he didn't tour the US again for eighteen months.

Back in the UK, he produced the **Specials**' debut album and in the autumn began working on a new album of his own. Since Radar was being wound down by Warner Brothers, Riviera formed his own label, F-Beat, and early in 1980, another LP, *Get Happy!!*, was released. With an ironic title that expressed the degree to which recent events had affected him, it packed twenty short pop songs into forty-seven minutes, and included a foot-tapping cover of **Sam and Dave**'s 'I Can't Stand Up For Falling Down' which gave him another Top 5 hit. Nonetheless it was still a gloomy time for him and after a perfunctory promotional tour, Costello temporarily parted company with the Attractions.

The rest of 1980 saw only the release of a compilation LP of Costello obscurities, *10 Bloody Marys and 10 How's Your Fathers* (*Taking Liberties* in the US) until the very end of the year, when a rejuvenated Costello released an excellent, brooding single, 'Clubland', but this was not a commercial success.

The greatest songwriter of the new wave, Elvis Costello

Another LP, *Trust*, followed early in '81 and performed as badly as the single had in the charts, yet it showed again Costello's passion, depth and versatility as a songwriter. Soon after *Trust*, he went to Nashville to cultivate his love for country music; an album of country rock standards, *Almost Blue*, was the result. Reviewers praised its freshness and emotion and this LP fared much better than the previous one in the charts. 'Good Year for the Roses' was a surprise Top 10 hit single at the end of the year.

The year 1982 arrived with Costello playing an extravagant New Year's show at the Royal Albert Hall where he – together again with the Attractions – was augmented by the Royal Philharmonic Orchestra. There was a gap until July and the release of *Imperial Bedroom*, but the over-elaborate recording techniques he had used backfired and the album was very flat, the over-production detracting from the songs. The LP reached Number 6 in the UK but stayed there for only a short while, and a succession of singles failed to impress. Commercially, Costello was at a low ebb, but he still managed to produce one of his finest works during that time, the single 'Shipbuilding', which he co-wrote with Clive Langer for **Robert Wyatt**.

Another single, 'Pills and Soap', a comment on the state of the nation that he recorded under the name The Imposter, revived his career in June 1983. A fervent political address, it was, as a marketing ploy, deleted by the record company on election day and therefore generated enough interest to reach Number 16. An album, *Punch the Clock*, came out in July to mixed reviews. Much under-rated, it contained 'Pills and Soap', his own recording of 'Shipbuilding', a couple of excellent singles in 'Everyday I Write the Book' and 'Let Them All Talk', and the punchy brass power of a group of horn sessionmen, called TKO Horns.

Yet another album, *Goodbye Cruel World*, was released in June 1984 to a general chorus of approval and saw Costello allay all the critics' fears. Much mellower than his previous work, it saw him continue to deal with the depressing subjects of loneliness and despair and produced two classic singles in 'The Only Flame in Town' and 'I Wanna Be Loved'. The latter reached Number 25 and was backed with 'Turning the Town Red', his theme tune to the TV show *Scully*, in which he also played the protagonist's simpleton brother.

During 1985, Costello took his solo show to Australia, New Zealand and Japan, accompanied by guitarist/producer T-Bone Burnett. Together they formed the Coward Brothers and released a single, 'The People's Limousine'. That summer Costello took part in Live Aid (*see* **Band Aid**), performing a rousing version of the **Beatles**' 'All You Need is Love'. He also took on another acting role in the film *No Surrender*, and then went off to Los Angeles to record, predominantly with a host of American sessioneers, although the Attractions performed on the album too.

The resulting album, *King of America*, emerged early in 1986 and marked a change of direction, displaying a heavy traditional country and R&B influence, but it was charged with Costello's fierce wordplay and his special, intense vitality. The album was credited to the 'Costello Show featuring the Attractions and the Confederates' (the US sessioneers), and on the production credits he billed himself as Declan Patrick Aloysius MacManus, suggesting a new, irreverent and less belligerent Costello. This good-humoured man and his new album were greeted with a flood of approval, provoking intensive press coverage and bringing universal proclamations of Costello's status as one of the greatest songwriters ever.

COUGAR MELLENCAMP, JOHN

American mainstream rock singer/songwriter John Cougar Mellencamp (born John Mellencamp in Indiana, 7 October 1951) was spotted as a potential chart-topper in 1975 when Tony DeFries, **David Bowie**'s ex-manager, signed him to his management company. It wasn't until 1982, however, that he finally scored a US Number 1 with 'Jack & Diane' and had a triple platinum album, *American Fool*.

Mellencamp had played in various bands since adolescence but took his first career step in '75 by moving to New York. DeFries re-christened him John Cougar, and negotiated a lucrative deal for him, as a result of which Mellencamp recorded his first LP, *Chestnut Street Incident*. Consisting solely of cover tunes, the album flopped and he was dropped by MCA. Mellencamp, having signed to Riva, then came to England to record *A Biography* (1978) and to play some dates, but despite considerable exposure, he still failed to chart. Through successive LPs (and the eventual re-inclusion of his real surname), John Cougar Mellencamp's mainstream rock appeal grew in the US; his 1980 release *Nothing Matters and What If It Did* sold half a million copies. He then made his breakthrough with 'Jack & Diane' (which also made Number 25 in the UK). Subsequent albums, *Uh Huh* (1983) and *Scarecrow* (1985), also sold well and confirmed his status as a major US rock star.

COUNTRY JOE AND THE FISH

Berkeley, California, saw Country Joe and the Fish begin life as a jug band in 1965. Joe McDonald (born 1 January 1942 in El Monte, California) wrote their lyrics, drawing his material from the current political talking points of Berkeley, and also from the social life and drug experimentation there. The songs were powered by the Fish's acid-rock sound, particularly Barry Melton's fluid guitar work. Their first album (produced by Sam Charters on Vanguard), aptly titled *Electric Music for the Mind and Body* (1967), successfully integrated love songs ('Grace'), political skits ('Superbird'), social satire ('Not So Sweet Martha Lorraine') and drug songs ('Flying High'). McDonald's sharp lyrics were influenced by the political songs of **Woody Guthrie** and **Bob Dylan** and the Fish were more disciplined and melodic than other psychedelic West Coast groups.

Their second album in 1967 had a less optimistic feel, and featured McDonald's insanely catchy, suicidal, Vietnam marching song, 'I-Feel-Like-I'm-Fixin'-To-Die Rag', as the title track. The Fish were still impressive as a musical combo, and their Indian instrumental, 'Eastern Jam', displayed Melton's guitar work at its most high-powered. However, Country Joe and the Fish, never the most stable of groups, subsequently went through personnel changes and recurrent break-ups. McDonald, the central figure, alternated between dominating the group and despairing of them. Their recordings only occasionally recaptured the power of their first two albums – the Vietnam song, 'An Untitled Protest' on *Together* (1968), the drugs and death warning on 'Crystal Blues', and the optimistic rebirth described in 'Here I Go Again'. In 1970, they split up for the final time, accurately reflecting the fragmentation of the youth/drugs/protest society that spawned them. Joe McDonald has since recorded solo for Vanguard and Fantasy, while 1977 brought the Fish together again briefly for the album *Reunion. See also* **Joe McDonald**

COUNTS Snappy purveyors of blues-rock, the Counts were led by Bobby Comstock (born 28 December 1943, at Ithaca, New York). The other members were Gus Eframson (guitar), Chuck Ciaschi (bass) and Dale Sherwood (drums). They reached the US charts with 'Tennessee Waltz' (on Blaze in 1959), 'Jambalaya' (Atlantic in 1960) and 'Let's Stomp' (Lawn in 1963). Comstock's greatest solo record was an edgy, cavernous revival of **Bo Diddley**'s 'I'm a Man' (a Feldman-Goldstein-Gottehrer production). It was not a hit, but rock'n'roll revival shows kept him and the band busy right into the Seventies, when they were the backing band for acts appearing in the movie *Let the Good Times Roll*.

COVAY, DON Soul singer and songwriter Don Covay – born in Orangeburg, South Carolina, in March 1938 – was the son of a Baptist preacher, and received his musical grounding in a family gospel quartet, the Cherry-Keys, formed when the Covays moved to Washington. He entered the secular field at high school in his mid-teens, joining the Rainbows after they had had a hit locally with 'Mary Lee' (on Red Robin) in 1955.

Covay's solo career began when **Little Richard** played Washington in 1957 – he hustled a job as warm-up vocalist on the show, and Richard was sufficiently impressed to record him (as 'Pretty Boy'). Atlantic issued his single 'Bip Bop Bip' in 1957. Don soon reverted to his own name, label-hopping to Sue, Columbia, Epic, RCA and Big Top before scoring a regional hit in 1961 with 'Pony Time' (Arnold). 'Popeye Waddle' – another stereotyped Philadelphia dance disc – was a 1962 hit on Cameo, but singles on Parkway and Landa were ignored. In 1964 Covay

and his Goodtimers group signed to Rosemart and immediately reached the Top 50 with the atmospheric, bluesy 'Mercy Mercy'. Rosemart was distributed by Atlantic, who then took over his contract, but despite recording in various styles, his only other hit in the Sixties was 'See Saw' (1965).

An unsuccessful attempt to regain hit status in a blues idiom came in 1970, and the following year Covay signed with Janus, moving to Mercury in 1972 as A&R director/performer, soon attaining chart status with 'I Was Checkin' Out, She Was Checkin' In', a searing soul ballad, followed by the highly acclaimed *Superdude I* album and a further hit single, the dynamic gospel-soul 'It's Better to Have and Don't Need'. A prolific and most successful songwriter, Covay was a Grammy nominee in 1968 when his 'Chain of Fools', sung by **Aretha Franklin**, was a Number 2 American hit.

COVER VERSIONS A cover version is, strictly speaking, either a version issued to compete with the original, or a carbon copy issued to capitalize on the original, often in another market. Rock'n'roll, largely music spawned in the urban black ghettos of the late Forties, finally reached middle America through the agency of **Bill Haley** and **Elvis Presley**. The former wrote much of his material but nevertheless achieved national fame with 'Shake, Rattle and Roll', a number recorded earlier in 1954 by Joe Turner on Atlantic, which Haley severely edited in order to remove the explicitly sexual references in the original. Presley cut hundreds of black R&B tunes, but in his own inimitable style and invariably after a gap of some years. Often accused of covering **Arthur Crudup**, it must be emphasized that Presley's epoch-making 'That's All Right' on Sun in 1954 came nearly seven years after the bluesman's original. One might just as well deny **Ray Charles** access to a country standard like **Hank Williams**' 'Your Cheatin' Heart'.

The real offenders were those whites with no feeling for R&B, but a good ear for commercial possibilities. Those undercutting black performers included **Pat Boone**, the Crewcuts, the **Diamonds**, the Fontane Sisters, the Four Lads, Georgia Gibbs, the McGuire Sisters, Kay Starr, and Gale Storm. The righteous Pat Boone rushed out lucrative covers for Dot of **Fats Domino**'s 'Ain't That a Shame' and **Little Richard**'s 'Long Tall Sally' in 1955 and 1956. The Crewcuts (Mercury) fastened

onto the **Penguins**' 'Earth Angel' (Dootone) in 1955 but fortunately the latter still went gold. In 1954, the Crewcuts had notched a million with 'Sh-Boom' which nevertheless still sold well for its originators, the **Chords**, on Cat. Georgia Gibbs built her career by recording, and subsequently diluting, R&B originals. Like Haley, she readily changed the lyrics of the songs she copied in order to avoid sexual references. 'Roll With Me Henry', a hit in the R&B market for **Etta James** under the title of 'Wallflower' on Modern, became 'Dance With Me Henry' when performed by a white woman for a white audience. Etta James' version sold 400,000 – Georgia Gibbs sold a million.

Not all cover versions cross racial boundaries, however. In cut-throat competition, Elvis Presley covered **Carl Perkins**' 'Blue Suede Shoes' and raced him up the charts. The same process happens with black singers – Little Richard recorded Eddie Bocage's 'I'm Wise' as 'Slippin' and Slidin'' in 1956. Similarly, sometimes covers cross national boundaries. Indeed, in the Fifties and early Sixties, British rock-'n'roll – with a few notable exceptions – consisted almost entirely of covers of American hits, white and black. The careers of **Marty Wilde**, **Tommy Steele**, **Billy Fury**, and Craig Douglas, and many others were liberally dotted with (usually inferior) versions of American hits – a practice that was greatly aided in the early Fifties by the fact that a significant amount of American R&B and rock'n'roll was not issued in Britain. Even Mersey Beat and the British R&B movement depended heavily on unoriginal material, though with a radical change of emphasis: songs were revived by the British groups, rather than merely covered by them.

In the fiercely chaotic world of reggae, covers (often uncredited) are a frequent occurrence. Thus Jamaican reggae fans preferred their own Lorna Bennett with 'Breakfast in Bed' in 1973, rather than the black American, Baby Washington, whose number it was. Generally, however, it was the reggae song that was covered. In 1974, **Eric Clapton** scored internationally with 'I Shot the Sheriff'. Very few Anglo-American rock devotees realized – or cared – that the song was written and recorded earlier that year by reggae star **Bob Marley**.

While the 'progressive' music of the Sixties saw few cover versions, the charts in almost any week of the early Seventies looked strangely familiar to those of the Fifties, with a few bizarre changes thrown in for good measure. Thus, in 1975, soul star **Betty Wright** enjoyed success with 'Shoorah, Shoorah' in both America and Britain at the expense of **Frankie Miller** who had failed to register with it at the end of 1974. But, then, he cut it for **Allen Toussaint** in New Orleans long after **Chris Kenner**'s original version.

A contrast of the British and American charts of 1974 showed a similar situation. In Britain, Paper Lace and **Leo Sayer** were racing up the charts with 'Billy Don't Be a Hero' and 'The Show Must Go On' respectively, while in America cover versions of their songs, by Bo Donaldson and the Heywoods and **Three Dog Night** were doing precisely the same thing. Since the mid-Seventies, cover versions have become less and less frequent as artists and bands record their own material almost as a matter of course: the trend, if it can be called that, has been for groups to mine pop music's heritage and revive classic hits of the past, sometimes (as in the case of Doctor and the Medics' 1986 revival of **Norman Greenbaum**'s 'Spirit in the Sky') by means of note-for-note re-creations.

CRAMER, FLOYD One of the outstanding and most commercially successful pianists in post-war country music, Floyd Cramer was born in Shreveport, Louisiana, on 27 November 1933 and came to public attention playing piano as a sideman on the *Louisiana Hayride* radio show in the early Fifties. **Chet Atkins** brought him to Nashville in 1955 and he quickly became one of the top session players there and an RCA Victor stalwart, backing artists as diverse as **Jim Reeves** and **Elvis Presley**.

If Atkins masterminded the 'Nashville Sound', it was Cramer's 'slipnote' style of playing that characterized it. This technique he describes as a whole-tone slur, and he likens it to the distinctive guitar style of Maybelle Carter (of the **Carter Family**). It's a right-hand device used at the treble end of the keyboard with the intended note hit precisely on the beat as the last of a triplet. Every other piano player in town quickly mastered the trick, and, as the 'Nashville Sound' flagged into stereotype through the Sixties, it became a mechanical feature of almost every successful country record. Cramer continues to work in Nashville as a session player and as a recording artist in his own right with some 20, mostly mediocre, albums to his credit. But his single, 'Last Date', which sold a million copies in 1960, is the definitive statement of the 'Nashville Sound', and it still sounds as fresh and imaginative as the day it was made. *See also* **Nashville**

CRASS Fiercely independent punk anarchists Crass first achieved wide renown in 1984, when a joke tape they had produced, purporting to be a politically controversial conversation between Margaret Thatcher and Ronald Reagan, fell into the hands of a newspaper who took it for real and started a minor press scandal.

Apart from this incident, the ten (and often more) members of Crass, formed in 1978 and loosely guided by Steve Ignorant and Penny Rimbaud, stayed stubbornly out of the 'pop' arena, living in a commune outside London in a manner that was almost reminiscent of the hippie era. This style was offset by their angry, eloquent and eclectic music, heard on such albums as *Yes Sir, I Will* (1983), which was an attack on Falklands policy. They had a strongly loyal following among alternative punks and their left-wing politics, barely staying this side of treason, were the most radical that Britain had ever seen in pop, or was ever likely to.

CRAWFORD, RANDY Although she was born in the South – in Macon, Georgia, in 1952 – Crawford was raised in the industrial north of the USA – in Cincinnati, Ohio. She sang in church, listened to the young **Aretha Franklin** and to jazz stylists such as **Dinah Washington** and Billie Holiday. At 16 she began singing with a jazz trio whose leader encouraged her to study music. In New York she worked briefly with another young rising jazz musician, guitarist **George Benson**, before she moved to Los Angeles where she was eventually booked on the first concerts promoted by the World Jazz Association, sharing a bill that included Quincy Jones, Benson, Stan Getz and Bob James. On the strength of her performance, Warner Bros offered Crawford a contract, but her initial recordings found her searching for a style; *Everything Must Change* (1976) was jazz flavoured, *Miss Randy Crawford* (1977) had a harder R&B edge, while *Raw Silk* (1979) was a collection of finely drawn ballads, which won plaudits, critical awards but, like its two predecessors, sold poorly. But then the Crusaders used her as vocalist on the single 'Street Life' and produced her *Now We May Begin* album and the combination was an immediate commercial success, giving her a big, world-wide hit with her beautifully wistful reading of 'One Day I'll Fly Away'. Three Tommy LiPuma-produced LPs followed – *Secret Combination* (1981), *Windsong* (1982) and *Nightline* (1983) – each less artistically satisfying than the previous set but which showcased her beautiful voice – a blend of soul sauce, gospel fervour and jazz phrasing. Crawford then spent the next couple of years looking for a new, compatible producer. Early in 1987, her single 'Almaz', produced by Reggie Lucas, got to Number 4 in the UK charts.

The Crusaders provide the backing for Randy Crawford's vocals – a combination that proved a great commercial success in 1980

CREAM Recognized in retrospect as the original 'supergroup', Cream was a trio formed in the summer of 1966 when **Eric Clapton** left **John Mayall**'s Bluesbreakers with a reputation as Britain's finest blues guitarist. He teamed up with two former members of the **Graham Bond** Organisation, **Ginger Baker** (drums), and **Jack Bruce** (bass), who, after being bullied out of the Organisation by Baker, had spent the previous six months languishing in pop with **Manfred Mann** – he played on 'Pretty Flamingo' – and getting his kicks staging harmonica battles with **Paul Jones**. Cream's pedigree in British blues was immaculate, their individual technique superb, and, having all had to fight for prominence in egocentric line-ups, they possessed a rare equilibrium.

In contrast to the heavy, blues-oriented performances of their early live work, the group's first single, 'Wrapping Paper' (Reaction, October 1966), was emphatically low-key, and flopped. But 'I Feel Free' and the more stylistically characteristic album *Fresh Cream*, released in December that year, both made the charts. On stage their forte became extended improvisation, and following *Disraeli Gears* (1967) – like the first album a studio production – their albums juxtaposed long, live work-outs of mainly blues material with shorter studio songs, usually by Jack Bruce and **Pete Brown**, such as 'White Room' and 'Politician' on *Wheels of Fire*.

Since the group had been spending much of their time in America, where their impact on audiences generally ignorant of the first wave of British blues had been greater than at home, the 'Live at the Fillmore' set on the double *Wheels of Fire* (Polydor, 1968) was a revelation to the many British fans who had never seen them on stage. Although the energy of 'Spoonful' and Baker's drum feature, 'Toad', became dissipated over a quarter of an hour, the reworking of **Robert Johnson**'s 'Crossroads' was a startling demonstration of Cream's considerable qualities – its stunning solo by Clapton urged on by Bruce's challenging bass patterns and Baker's restless drumming.

Apparently at a peak of creativity and universal popularity, but privately dissident, they announced their intention to split, which they did at the end of 1968. *Goodbye* (Polydor, 1969), included, besides some of their best live work, their third and final hit single, 'Badge', written by Clapton and **George Harrison**. At their best, masters of blues interpretation and rock musi-

Ginger Baker, Jack Bruce and Eric Clapton performed together as Cream for less than three years, but it was time enough to build a legend

cianship, at their worst, purveyors of empty virtuosity, Cream's influence was twofold – they encouraged the worst excesses of extreme self-indulgence as well as inspiring individual expression. As if to emphasize the fact that the group had broken up before exploring their full potential, their recordings were subsequently repackaged in seemingly endless permutations. *See also* individual entries

CREEDENCE CLEARWATER REVIVAL Masters of an updated rockabilly sound that also drew on the influence of Memphis soul, Creedence Clearwater Revival were one of America's leading late Sixties bands yet a group curiously out of step with rock at that time. Although they hailed from San Francisco, all they had in common with contemporaries like **Country Joe and the Fish** and the **Grateful Dead** was

geography: eschewing psychedelic exploration, hippie sloganeering, and a 'progressive' orientation, Creedence looked back to Fifties rock'n'roll, country and R&B, and wrote songs evoking images of riverboats, Louisiana swamps and bayou dances.

The band consisted of two guitar-playing brothers, John Fogerty (born in Berkeley, California, on 28 May 1947) and Tom Fogerty (9 November 1941), bassist Stu Cook (Oakland, 25 April 1945) and drummer Doug 'Cosmo' Clifford (24 April 1945). They first played together while at junior high school in El Cerrito in 1959, and under the name Tommy Fogerty and the Blue Velvets were regular performers at San Francisco Bay area school hops. During the British beat invasion, they called themselves the Blue Velvets and recorded for the local Orchestra label before signing with Fantasy Records as the Golliwogs, a name chosen by the

Creedence Clearwater Revival on stage in Paris, delivering one of the swamp-rock classics that won them phenomenal success worldwide

with the new direction and left soon after *Pendulum* was released; *Mardi Gras* (1972) found John Fogerty allowing his fellow band members more space, but the composing abilities of Cook and Clifford were limited, and the result was an album of uncharacteristic unevenness. Although a million-seller, it precipitated the break-up of the band.

Clifford recorded a solo album, *Doug 'Cosmo' Clifford* (1973), before teaming up with Stu Cook in the Don Harrison Band in 1976. Tom Fogerty also recorded solo and later in the Seventies launched a band of his own, Ruby. John Fogerty, meanwhile, pursued a solo career as the Blue Ridge Rangers, recording C&W and gospel standards – for example, 'Jambalaya', 'Hearts of Stone' and 'Workin' on a Building' – on which he played all the instruments and sang all the vocal parts. 'Jambalaya' was a US Top 20 single for him in 1972. The album, *The Blue Ridge Rangers* (Fantasy, 1972), found Fogerty demonstrating his mastery of studio technique and his ability to inject new life into old material. Three years later, after a lengthy dispute with his record company, he re-emerged with another hit single, 'Rockin' All Over the World', and the fine *John Fogerty*, a collection of mostly original songs performed in the Creedence manner. He recorded *Hoodoo* in the late Seventies, but Asylum, his new record label, reportedly rejected it. Signing with Warner Bros in the early Eighties, he scored a US Top 10 hit with the brilliantly simple 'Rock and Roll Girls', from the album *Centerfield* (1986).

CRESTS A racially mixed but otherwise archetypal late Fifties East Coast vocal group, the Crests were led by Johnny Maestro (born John Mastrangelo in New York on 7 May 1939). His light and youthful voice took them into the charts ten times between 1957 and 1960. Early records for Joyce were followed by a Number 2 on Coed with 'Sixteen Candles', a slow ballad of great charm. Equally melodic hits included 'The Angels Listened In', 'Step by Step' and 'Trouble in Paradise'. Among the original members of the Crests were Harold Torres, Tommy Gough and Jay Carter, but later personnel changes were intricate, with Eddie Wright, Chuck Foote and Leonard Alexander singing on later records. Maestro's later solo career included one Top 20 hit ('Model Girl' in 1961). In 1968 he became lead singer for the Brooklyn Bridge, who had one massive US hit with 'Worst That Could Happen' on Buddah a year later.

label's bosses. On Christmas Eve 1967, the band changed their name to Creedence Clearwater Revival and, under the auspices of Fantasy's new owner, Saul Zaentz, the group began developing their distinctive brand of southern-influenced rock. Their eponymous debut album, released in 1968, mixed R&B standards like **Screamin' Jay Hawkins**' 'I Put a Spell on You' and **Dale Hawkins**' 'Suzie Q' with John Fogerty originals. 'Suzie Q', the single taken from the album, reached Number 11 in the US in September 1968. *Bayou Country* (1969) featured all Fogerty compositions with the exception of a version of **Little Richard**'s 'Good Golly Miss Molly', and produced a Number 2 hit single in 'Proud Mary', which was also their debut hit in the UK (reaching Number 8). From *Green River* (1969) came 'Bad Moon Rising', another US Number 2 but a Number 1 in the UK, and the

album's title track (US Number 2); from yet another 1969 album, *Willy and the Poor Boys*, 'Down on the Corner' was released as a single and reached Number 3 in the US.

Arguably their finest album, however, was *Cosmo's Factory* (1970), which included an 11-minute version of 'I Heard It Through the Grapevine' and the singles 'Travellin' Band' and 'Lookin' Out My Back Door'. It was the perfect distillation of the Creedence sound, though by this time the band were being criticized for supposed one-dimensionalism. *Pendulum* (1970) was Fogerty's response, and saw the band attempt to extend their basic formula to encompass more experimental arrangements and instrumentation. The original Creedence trademarks – the chugging rhythm and biting lead guitar – were now swamped by heavy-handed organ, saxophones and vibes. Tom Fogerty, for one, was not happy

CREWE, BOB A greatly respected record producer of long standing, Bob Crewe was born in Bellville, New Jersey, in 1931. A male model, an interior decorator and a singer at various times in his career, he met Frank Slay Jr, a Texan who needed a demo singer for his songs, in 1953; later that year Crewe made his first record (co-written by Slay) for BBS, a small Philadelphia label. Between 1954 and 1956, Crewe recorded unsuccessfully for Jubilee and Spotlight. Then in 1956, again with Slay, Crewe began independently producing records of their songs by Charlie and Ray (for Herald) and the Rays (for Chess), and in 1957 they activated their own label, XYZ. They were at this time among the few independent producers in the US, along with **Leiber and Stoller** and **Lee Hazlewood**.

In 1957, their composition 'Silhouettes' by the Rays – originally issued on XYZ but leased to Cameo – sold a million, and Slay and Crewe quickly notched up other hits, including 'La Dee Dah' by Billy and Lillie, and 'Tallahassie Lassie' by **Freddy Cannon** (both for Swan). After co-producing several more Cannon hits, including 'Way Down Yonder in New Orleans' (1959), they parted company. Slay became a producer for Swan while Crewe attempted unsuccessfully to break into films as an actor. He recorded his first hit, 'The Whiffenpoof Song', for Warwick in 1961.

Returning to production in 1962, Crewe began supervising recordings for the **Four Seasons**, initially for the Gone label ('Bermuda') and then for Vee Jay, where they scored immediately with the US chart-topping and million-selling 'Sherry' (1962). Between 1962 and 1968, Crewe produced an unbroken run of hits for the group, most of which he co-wrote with group member Bob Gaudio. During the mid-Sixties, Crewe formed New Voice Records and had big sellers with 'Walkin' My Cat Named Dog' by Norman Tanega and 'Jenny Take a Ride' by **Mitch Ryder and the Detroit Wheels**, which sold a million. Crewe also had a Top 20 US hit of his own in 1966 with the catchy instrumental, 'Music to Watch Girls By'.

In 1969, he formed the Crewe label and enjoyed a million-selling success with pop singer Oliver's 'Good Morning Starshine'. However, a quieter period followed in the Seventies, though Crewe made a solid comeback in 1974 after his label folded with his productions for Disco Tex and the Sex-O-Lettes and former Four Season singer Frankie Valli.

CRICKETS Originally **Buddy Holly**'s group, the Crickets separated from him in 1958 but continued recording, mostly in Los Angeles. They remained with Coral until 1961, releasing several unsuccessful singles, and then switched to Liberty. Throughout numerous personnel changes, the backbone of the group remained drummer Jerry Allison and singer/guitarist Sonny Curtis.

In 1962, they toured Britain with **Bobby Vee** and cut an album with him containing several authentic-sounding versions of rock'n'roll standards. Although neglected by American record buyers, the group had two British hits at this time – 'Please Don't Ever Change' (a Gerry Goffin and **Carole King** song) and Curtis' 'My Little Girl'. The arrival of the **Beatles** left the Crickets, like so many others, stranded, and they officially disbanded in March 1965. Curtis and Allison concentrated on songwriting and session work in Los Angeles. They played on **Eric Clapton**'s 1970 solo album, and it was possibly the interest caused by this that led to the revival of the Crickets soon after. The new band, which included two Englishmen, Rick Grech (bass) and **Albert Lee** (guitar), made three albums on Mercury (two in Britain). The production of the albums was by **Bob Montgomery**, Buddy Holly's partner in his first-ever recordings.

In 1977 and 1979, Curtis and onetime Crickets Joe Mauldin and Jerry Allison re-formed the group for Buddy Holly Week, organized by **Paul McCartney** each year since 1977 and held in London. *See also* **Buddy Holly**

The three Crickets in 1957

CRITTERS The initial claim to fame of the Critters was in recording 'Younger Girl', a **John Sebastian** song from the first **Lovin' Spoonful** album. This, and the Top 20 follow-up, 'Mr Dieingly Sad', were both substantial US hits in 1966. The group – Chris Darway, autoharp; Kenny Corka, bass; Jeff Pelosi, drums; Bob Spinella, organ; and guitarist Jim Ryan, who also arranged some of their material – recorded for Kapp. Their first album, *Younger Girl*, was a delightful summery disc in 1966. They made a second for Kapp, *Touch 'n' Go*, and a final album, *The Critters*, for Project Three, the label set up by the production company responsible for their earlier albums.

CROCE, JIM Jim Croce's introspective love songs found wide public favour in the US during the early Seventies. A singer, guitarist and songwriter, he was born in Philadelphia on 10 January 1943, and served his apprenticeship in the customary way – playing the folk clubs and coffeehouses of downtown Manhattan and touting his songs around the record companies. Capitol signed him in 1969 but lost interest after the commercial failure of his album *Approaching Day*, which was produced by his wife Ingrid. Two years later, Croce signed with ABC at the instigation of producers Terry Cashman and Tommy West. The resulting album, *You Don't Mess Around with Jim*, was the source of two 1972 singles in the title track (a Number 8 US hit) and 'Operator', and his chart success continued with the chart-topping 'Bad Bad Leroy Brown', 'I Got a Name' and 'Time in a Bottle' (all 1973). A homely and engaging live performer, Croce's developing career was cut tragically short on 20 September 1973, when the plane he had chartered for touring purposes crashed shortly after take-off from an airfield in Louisiana. His death inspired enormous sales of his singles and albums. One of his posthumous hits, 'I'll Have to Say I Love You in a Song' (1974), became an easy-listening standard.

CROPPER, STEVE Having played permanent under-secretary to the Sixties' changing guitar heroes, Steve Cropper has shunned the glare of solo superstardom to make his mark in his Memphis studio, TMI. Working on most of Stax's biggest hits as arranger/co-writer, he cut into the heavy Memphis beat with clean, incisive licks that made him the most distinctive accompanist of the era.

Born in Willow Spring, Missouri, on 21 October 1941, by the age of 16 he was in Memphis, where he formed a high-school band, the **Mar-Keys**, and had his first composition, 'Flea Circus', recorded by local hitmaker **Bill Justis**. 'Last Night' (1961) and other releases by the Mar-Keys on the embryo Satellite/Stax labels led to further instrumentals by various permutations of house musicians (the Triumphs, the Van-Dells, **Booker T. and the MGs**), each featuring Cropper. It was for his work with the latter quartet that he became widely known, but like the rest of the group his contribution to the growth of Stax was most fully realized supporting the company's vocal stars. For several years he was heard on most tracks cut at the McLemore Avenue studios, as well as collaborating on many of their most famous recordings, with **Eddie Floyd** ('Knock On Wood', 'Raise Your Hand'); **Don Covay** ('See Saw', 'Sookie Sookie'); **Wilson Pickett** ('In the Midnight Hour', 'Don't Fight It', '634-5789' – written with Floyd – 'Ninety-Nine-and-a-Half Won't Do'); and **Otis Redding** ('Mr Pitiful', 'Fa-Fa-Fa-Fa-Fa', 'The Dock of the Bay').

When the company expanded and the old corps dispersed, Cropper stayed in Memphis as a freelance jack-of-all-trades and producing for his own TMI label. In 1969 he recorded a pleasant solo album, *With a Little Help from My Friends* (Volt), the help in question coming from **Buddy Miles**, **Leon Russell**, the Memphis Horns, and others. In the mid-Seventies, Cropper returned to session work – he played on **Rod Stewart**'s *Atlantic Crossing* – and in 1978 became involved with the Blues Brothers' travelling show. *See also* **Booker T. and the MGs**

CROSBY, DAVID Born on 14 August 1941 into a Los Angeles movie family, David Crosby served his musical apprenticeship as a folk singer on the West Coast club and coffee-house circuit before founding the Jet Set, which evolved into the **Byrds**. His rhythm guitar, harmony singing and songwriting abilities were a mainstay of the group through their first four albums. In 1967, he was sacked after losing a struggle for the group's leadership. The large cash settlement bought him a yacht, but by 1968 he had formed a new partnership with **Steve Stills** and **Graham Nash** in **Crosby, Stills and Nash**. During that group's part-time existence (and that of **Crosby, Stills, Nash and Young**), he sang harmony on sessions for many friends, notably the **Jefferson Starship** and **Jackson Browne**, and recorded a solo album, *If I Could Only Remember My Name* (1971), which featured the softer side of Crosby's dialectic trip between the politics of anger and the oceanic lifestyle. It was followed by a weaker joint album, *Crosby and Nash* (Atlantic, 1972), and a 1973 reunion album with the Byrds. The association with Nash continued on *Wind on the Water* (1975), *Whistling down the Wire* (1976), and *Live* (1977), and he also took part in a CSN reunion in the same year. Crosby recorded a second solo set in 1980 but Capitol refused to release it: some of the songs appeared on yet another CSN reunion album, *Daylight Again*, in 1982. The following year, he toured Europe as part of CSN to promote *Allies*, but was convicted in 1985 on drugs and weapons charges and committed to the Texas State Penitentiary.

David Crosby (left) with Stephen Stills (centre) and Graham Nash

CROSBY, STILLS AND NASH/ CROSBY, STILLS, NASH AND YOUNG

'One night round at Joni's place' (**Joni Mitchell**) in late 1968, refugees from the **Byrds** (Crosby), **Buffalo Springfield** (Stills) and the **Hollies** (Nash) decided to form a new group. They made one album as a trio, *Crosby, Stills and Nash* (Atlantic, 1969), with Dallas Taylor helping out on drums, which featured Stills' desperate love songs, Nash's gentler celebrations of 'peace and love' consciousness, and Crosby's mixture of romanticism and angry politics – all smoothed into a soft electric/acoustic music topped off by dazzling virtuoso harmony singing. To go out on the road, and to add a darker ingredient, they added a second Springfield refugee in mid-1969, Neil Young. They played their second gig at Woodstock in August, and made one studio album, *Déjà Vu*, early in 1970. The sound was tougher, more electric than CSN's, counterpointing Nash's soft admonitions to 'teach your children' with Young's wails of pain, Crosby's politics with Stills' intense self-preoccupation. The overall effect was an album – and a group – that offered a multi-faceted view of American youth in the year of the Kent State shootings. The level of musicianship displayed on the album was reflected in their stage shows through late 1969 and 1970. The concerts contained an acoustic half in which the four of them sang solo and together, and an electric half of rock-'n'roll in which the hired rhythm section and Crosby's rhythm guitar laid down the base for Stills and Young to engage in ferocious electric guitar duelling.

What separated CSN&Y from the rank and file was their conquest of both the Los Angeles and the San Francisco approaches to rock. In the studio, they were as perfectionist as the Byrds had been; on stage, they were every bit as real, as separate personalities singing for each other as much as for the audience, in the manner of **Jefferson Airplane**. They sparked an infectious joy in the making of music. Some of it was captured on the live *Four-Way Street* album (1971), particularly in devastating performances of Crosby's 'Long Time Gone' requiem for Robert Kennedy and Young's 'Southern Man'.

At the end of 1970 they went their separate ways, partly to pursue directions that couldn't be pursued in the always loose structure of the group, partly because of more personal differences. Crosby and Nash would continue to extol nature and love, Stills to explore his desperation in countrified rock, Young to mirror the doubts and anguish of a dissolving dream. In 1974 they reunited for an American tour, after attempts in previous years had failed, but they parted again soon after. Thereafter, Young's stock continued to rise, even if the praise he received from reviewers was not always reflected by the albums he sold. His reunion album with Stills was half completed when Crosby and Nash were invited to dub the necessary vocals and transform it into a CSN&Y revival; then Stills had second thoughts and *Long May You Run* was finally issued without the additional harmonies, and credited to Stills and Young. Understandably furious, Crosby and Nash insisted that they would never work with their erstwhile partners again, though they did combine with Stills for *CSN* in 1977 and *Daylight Again* in 1982. Young meanwhile kept his distance, choosing not to appear with the trio in the Philadelphia Live Aid concert (he performed with his own band), and Crosby's imprisonment for drugs offences during 1985 cast some doubt on CSN's long-term future as a recording and performing entity. *See also* individual entries

CROSS, CHRISTOPHER

Singer/songwriter and multi-Grammy award winner Christopher Cross scored instant success with his soft pop/rock when his debut album, *Christopher Cross* (1980) went platinum on the back of a US Number 2 single, 'Ride Like the Wind'.

Born Christopher Geppert (1951, Texas), he fronted various local Texan bands through the Seventies until he signed a solo deal with Warner Brothers in 1978. His debut album appeared two years later, and in 1981 he took the Grammy Awards by storm, winning five of them including Best Record, Best Album and Best Song. The same year he scored a US Number 1 with his theme for the film *Arthur*, a song that also won an Oscar.

In 1983 he released *Another Page* and scored another US Top 10 single with 'Think of Laura', but after that Cross maintained a low profile.

CROWS

One of the first black vocal groups to move outside the R&B market into the pop field, the Crows' record, 'Gee', is often credited with marking the start of the rock'n'roll era. From Harlem, Sonny Norton (lead), Bill Davis (baritone and occasional lead), Harold Major and Mark Jackson (tenors), and Gerald Hamilton (bass) recorded for **George Goldner**'s Rama label. Probably it was Goldner who instructed the group to sweeten their delivery in order to increase their exposure on white radio stations. The ploy certainly worked: in April 1954, 'Gee' (a Bill Davis composition) made the Top 20. Although the group's other records for Rama and Tico failed to please, 'Gee' – still one of America's favourite oldies – became the name of yet another of Goldner's labels. The flip of 'Gee', 'I Love You So' was subsequently successfully revived by the **Chantels** and made the Top 50 in 1958. By then, however, the Crows had disbanded, and Hamilton and Norton have since died.

CRUDUP, ARTHUR

Born in Forest, Mississippi, in 1905, Arthur 'Big Boy' Crudup enjoyed wide success in the Forties, recording a series of blues that reached not only their primary market but a substantial number of those whites who were to become both the musicians and the audience of rockabilly. 'Rock Me Mama', 'That's All Right' and 'My Baby Left Me' (all on Victor, 1942–50) were taken up by singers from **Elvis Presley** on down – an acknowledgment less of Crudup's sparse instrumental sound than of his piercing vocal attack and his musically suggestive reworkings of traditional blues themes. Rediscovered in the late Sixties, he cut some more albums in a virtually unaltered style and appeared before many American and European audiences. He died in 1973.

CRUSADERS

Originally known as the Jazz Crusaders, Wilton Felder (tenor, alto saxes), Joe Sample (piano), Wayne Henderson (trombone) and Stix Hooper (drums) began playing together in 1953 in their native Dallas, Texas – first as the Swingsters – when their ages ranged from 13 to 15. By the time they'd completed their education at the Texas Southern University and signed to Pacific Jazz Records in 1961, their style of jazz – funky in a typically Texan vein driven by Hooper's firm drumming – was considerably more energetic and powerful than that performed by many of their contemporaries. This simple, direct and vigorous approach did not, however, prove consistently appealing to jazz enthusiasts and so they dropped the 'Jazz' from their name and in 1972 unveiled *Crusaders 1* on Blue Thumb and *Hollywood* on Mowest. The former album's first track, 'Put It Where You Want It', a punchy, piano-based instrumental written by Sample, set the tone for their music for the next decade and a half – 'Way Back Home', 'Hard Times', 'Stomp & Buck Dance', 'Chain Reaction', 'Keep That Same Old Feeling' were further examples of the group's musical ability and powerful delivery. Their line-up, lacking a bassist, was regularly augmented and in the mid-Seventies they most often used Pops Popwell (bass) and Larry Carlton (guitar) to good effect.

In 1976, Henderson became the first original member to quit the line-up, preferring to concentrate on his role as a producer with his At Home company. Others chose to pursue solo careers in tandem with membership of the group. Joe Sample recorded *Rainbow Seeker*, the first of his handful of solo albums, in 1978; Wilton Felder followed suit later in the year with *We All Have a Star*; as did Hooper in 1979 with *The World Within*. Between times, their recording as a group received an enormous boost when they used **Randy Crawford** as vocalist on 'Street Life', a big hit in 1979 (there was also an album of the same name). The success prompted them to use singers on at least one track on subsequent albums – **Bill Withers** on *Rhapsody and Blues* (1980), **Joe Cocker** on *Standing Tall* (1981) and **Bobby Womack** on Felder's *Inherit the Wind* (1979) and *Secrets* (1985). Commercially the decision was fully justified. At the beginning of the Eighties the group recorded one studio album, *Standing Tall*, and then concentrated on solo projects, the only Crusaders LP being *Royal Jam*, a live set with **B.B. King** and the Royal Philharmonic Orchestra. Soon after Hooper decided to leave the group, being replaced on drums by Ndugu Chancler, who made his debut on record on the *Ghettoblaster* album in 1984. Felder and Sample continued to release solo LPs.

CRYSTALS A girl group whose chart success owed everything to the production ingenuity of **Phil Spector**, the Crystals comprised Brooklyn schoolgirls Dee Dee Kennibrew, Dolores Brooks, Mary Thomas, Barbara Alston and Pat Wright. Their debut Top 20 hit for Spector's Philles label was 'There's No Other Like My Baby' in 1961, followed some months later by 'Uptown', but their third release – 'He Hit Me (And It Felt Like a Kiss)' – was withdrawn following objections to its title. The next Crystals release, the **Gene Pitney** composition 'He's a Rebel', topped the US chart in November 1962, and ushered in Spector's classic 'wall of sound' era. Ironically, however, the disc featured not the real

Crystals but a Los Angeles session group headed by **Darlene Love**, who also sang on the successful follow-up, 'He's Sure the Boy I Love' (1963). By this time, Mary Thomas had left the group, and it was as a quartet that the Crystals enjoyed their two biggest sellers of all, 'Da Doo Ron Ron' and 'Then He Kissed Me' (both 1963). Spector's growing commitment to Crystals stablemates the **Ronettes** and declining public interest in the girl group sound sent the Crystals' chart fortunes plummeting during 1964, with both 'Little Boy' and 'All Grown Up' failing to reach the US Top 40. They bought out their contract with Philles and subsequently joined United Artists, for whom they recorded two unsuccessful Motown-styled singles. In the Seventies and early Eighties, the Crystals were still performing, albeit with a much-changed line-up.

CULTURE CLUB Like **Spandau Ballet** a product of the underground London club scene, Culture Club were another British pop group of the Eighties who found huge international success with a careful blend of soulful pop and colourful image. Formed in 1981 when one of the best-known faces on that club circuit, Boy George O'Dowd (vocals) and his musical partner Mikey Craig (bass), met Jon Moss (drums) and then went on to recruit Roy Hay (guitar). The group quickly built up a *risqué* image based

Boy George O'Dowd, Culture Club vocalist and gender-bender

around Boy George's outrageous dress and his androgynous appearance.

Boy George (born 14 June 1961), from the suburbs of South-East London, had been flitting around the edges of the music scene for a while and gained notoriety for his weird clothes and his presence at all the trendiest parties. He even had a stint as guest vocalist with **Bow Wow Wow**, but the poor reviews after a debut appearance at London's Rainbow Theatre curtailed that liaison. Moss had a more extensive grounding in the business, drumming in various bands (including a brief stint with the **Clash**), and dabbling as a studio engineer and promoter. Hay was a hairdresser from Southend, and Craig had been a reggae session musician.

As they played more gigs, media attention grew and they signed a deal with Virgin Records. They released a couple of singles that were largely ignored, but then the big break came in November 1982 with, 'Do You Really Want to Hurt Me', which made Culture Club, and especially Boy George, a household name. A smooth, classy blend of pop and reggae, it was Number 1 in the UK for three weeks and reached the top in eighteen other countries.

The national press became obsessed with Boy George after his debut appearance on BBC TV's *Top of the Pops*, where his largely female attire threw the conservative tastes of the nation. George became the object of ridicule, but the constant press coverage gave the band unprecedented publicity and British youth went out and bought their undeniably well-crafted white pop-soul in their droves.

From that point until mid-1984, Culture Club were probably Britain's biggest pop group, successive albums *Kissing to Be Clever* (1982) and *Colour by Numbers* (1983) selling exceptionally well all over the world. At this time, too, they acquired the backing vocals of Helen Terry, which gave them a fuller, more escalating sound. In the UK seven singles in a row made the Top 5, including their classic hit 'Karma Chameleon', which stayed in the charts for five months and finally established Culture Club worldwide. Their accessible music charmed Britain's housewives to such an extent that the initially negative publicity was forgotten and Boy George became the darling of the press. Culture Club had even managed to conquer the notoriously conservative Americans, scoring a Number 1 with 'Karma Chameleon'.

By this point, however, the backlash had begun to set in and the banal 'War Song', despite reaching Number 2, gave fuel to the increasing numbers of Culture Club detractors. The follow-up single 'The Medal Song', reached only Number 32, which by their standards was a major disaster resulting in the album *Waking Up with the House on Fire* (1984) failing to sustain the large sales of the previous two.

Culture Club took extended leave for most of 1985, releasing no new material, and went into the studio at the tail end of the year to record a new album, *From Luxury to Heartache*, which was released in April '86. A predictable collection of pop/soul, it immediately spawned the Top 10 hit 'Move Away'.

Later in 1986 the band was rocked by a drugs scandal when it was revealed in banner headlines that Boy George was a heroin addict. Although he escaped imprisonment and attended a drug dependency clinic, his troubles were not over. He was served a short time later with a multi-million pound lawsuit by the family of American musician Mike Rudetski, who had died from a drugs overdose in O'Dowd's house while the singer was staying elsewhere. O'Dowd bounced back early in 1987 with the solo UK hit single, 'Everything I Own', which cast some doubts as to the future of the band.

CURB, MIKE Born in Savannah, Georgia, on 24 December 1944, Mike Curb was once touted as the 'Boy Wonder' of the record business. At the age of 25, he was appointed president of MGM Records in 1968. Prior to that, he had been extremely active for over five years as a Los Angeles producer and songwriter. His talent was for finding musicians on the street, turning

The Cure, an influential post-punk band of the Eighties

them into studio groups overnight, and leasing masters to a variety of labels. All this was done under the banner of Sidewalk Productions, who provided many recordings for the Tower label, and also released quite a few on Curb's own Sidewalk label. Notable among these were early tracks by the Mugwumps, the **Electric Flag**, the Stone Poneys, and Davie Allan and the Arrows.

More than anything else, however, Curb was known for assembling soundtrack albums (using mostly the same groups who recorded for Sidewalk) for American International Pictures, a leading maker of so-called 'youth exploitation' movies. Curb's soundtracks included *Riot on Sunset Strip*, *Psych-Out*, *Teenage Rebellion*, *Mondo Hollywood*, *Freakout U.S.A.*, and *The Wild Angels*. Through AI, he became involved with Transcontinental Entertainment Corp, for whom he acquired and ran a number of small labels, all of which were discontinued when he joined MGM. He lasted three or four years at MGM, but failed to bring the ailing label the 'youth image' they had hoped for.

In the Seventies, Curb set up his own label with distribution through Warner Bros. Called Warner/Curb, the company had some success with Shaun Cassidy, younger brother of **David Cassidy**, and Debby Boone, daughter of **Pat Boone**. Both artists had Number 1 US hits during 1977, with 'Da Doo Ron Ron' and 'You Light Up My Life' respectively.

CURE One of the foremost British post-punk bands, the Cure emerged in 1979 with the stark 'Killing an Arab'/'10.15 on a Saturday Night', a single that instantly won them huge critical acclaim. While not achieving more than moderate commercial success, under the leadership of singer/songwriter/guitarist Robert Smith (who also had two spells playing with **Siouxsie and the Banshees**), the band crafted skilful atmospherics that proved a strong influence on post-punk bands in the Eighties.

First formed under the name Easycure in Crawley, Sussex, in 1976, the trio of Smith, Laurence Tolhurst (drums) and Michael Dempsey (bass) had abbreviated the name long before the release of the first single. The good reviews this inspired encouraged them to tour the UK early in the year and to release in May the first album, *Three Imaginary Boys* (1979). Their first showing in the UK charts wasn't until 1980 with 'A Forest', a moody, sombre

single that characterized the Cure's recorded output through the albums *Seventeen Seconds* (1980), *Faith* (1981) and *Pornography* (1982).

Going through several line-ups, but always based around a core of Smith and Tolhurst (who had moved on to keyboards), the Cure began to produce work that was somewhat brighter in tone with the lighthearted mewling pop hit single, 'The Love Cats', in 1983. Subsequent albums *The Top* (1984) and *The Head on the Door* (1985), and the 1985 Top 20 single 'In Between Days', confirmed the apparent change of mood as the Cure grafted a new pop sensibility onto their carefully constructed songs.

CYMBAL, JOHNNY In the Fifties, one of the commonest tricks employed to capture the listener's immediate attention was to bring the bass singer into far greater prominence than usual and make a feature of his 'bom, bom' vocal phrases. In 1963, Johnny Cymbal, from Cleveland, Ohio, wrote and performed his tribute to these little-known heroes of rock'n'roll, 'Mr Bass Man', which reached Number 16 in the US on Kapp. The bass part, the core of the record, was taken by Ronald Bright – an ex-member of the Valentines and **Cadillacs** and later of the **Coasters** – who had previously put the bomp in **Barry Mann**'s 'Who Put the Bomp?' in 1961. After a couple of less successful follow-ups, 'Teenage Heaven' and 'Dum Dum De Dum', Cymbal left Kapp. In 1968, under the name Derek, he had a Top 10 hit with 'Cinnamon' and then a smaller hit with 'Back Door Man' the following year. He later worked as a record producer.

CYRKLE Beginning life as the Rondells, the Cyrkle was a Pennsylvania singing group spotted and subsequently renamed by the **Beatles'** manager, **Brian Epstein**, who then exposed them nationally in America through a supporting slot on the Beatles' 1966 tour there. Group members, Tom Dawes (born 25 July 1944), Don Danneman (9 May 1944) and Marty Fried (1944) – later joined by Michael Losekamp (1947) – had a light, friendly sound, not unlike **Gary Lewis and the Playboys**. Their first release, the **Paul Simon** composition, 'Red Rubber Ball' (Columbia) was an American Number 2 in 1966. Produced – and frequently joined – by John Simon, they had a second Top 20 record with 'Turn-Down Day' and several good, but decreasingly successful, follow-ups. They disbanded in 1969.

D'ABO, MIKE Best known as the singer who replaced **Paul Jones** in **Manfred Mann** in 1966, Mike d'Abo (born in Surrey in 1944) began his rock career in the Band of Angels, an R&B band formed by boys from Harrow School. As Manfred Mann's vocalist, d'Abo sang on numerous hits, beginning with 'Just Like a Woman' (1966) and including 'Semi-Detached Suburban Mr James' (1966), 'Ha Ha Said the Clown' (1967), and 'Mighty Quinn' (1968), at the same time developing a second career as a songwriter. His hit compositions during the late Sixties included 'Build Me Up Buttercup' for the **Foundations**, 'Handbags and Gladrags' for **Chris Farlowe**, and he wrote the score for a musical version of *Gulliver's Travels* in which he also appeared. In 1969, he sang the part of Herod in the original album recording of Tim Rice and Andrew Lloyd Webber's highly successful *Jesus Christ Superstar*.

After leaving Manfred Mann later that year, he cut three solo albums and in 1976 teamed up with Mike Smith (ex-**Dave Clark Five**) to record *Smith and D'Abo*. Since then, he has composed extensively for films and TV commercials.

DAF (DEUTSCHE AMERIKANISCHE FREUND-SCHAFT)
Named, with bitter irony, after Berlin street posters promoting 'German-American friendship', DAF were formed in Düsseldorf in 1979, effectively dating the start of the second wave of homegrown German music.

Their first album, *Produkt* (1979), on the German label Warning, owed much to earlier German innovators and showed little of the taut, muscular style they were to develop with further British album releases such as *Die Kleinen und die Bosen*, *Geld und Liebe* and *Für Immer*. A duo of drummer Robert Gorl and singer Gabi Delgado-Lopez, backed live and on record by prerecorded electronics, they mixed a bare, minimal electronic disco beat with disturbing political and sexual imagery. They split up in 1984 to pursue solo careers, but reunited in late 1985 to record the (unsuccessful) single, 'Brother'.

DALE AND GRACE Two young Louisiana kids – Dale Houston and Grace Broussard – achieved the ultimate in high-school dreams when their starry-eyed version of **Don and Dewey**'s R&B hit, 'I'm Leaving It All Up To You', shot up the charts all the way to Number 1 in the US in 1963 (the song was a British hit again in 1974 for Marie and Donny of the **Osmonds**). Recorded by Sam Montel for his Montel label out of Baton Rouge, the duo (both born in 1944) had a lot of the soulful feel of Louisiana swamp-pop music and enjoyed a big follow-up hit with 'Stop and Think It Over', which reached Number 8 in 1964. Dale Houston also recorded prolifically in his own right and had a Southern hit with 'I'm the One' in 1961.

DALTREY, ROGER Lead singer with the **Who** from its formation to its break-up in 1983, Roger Daltrey (born in Hammersmith, London, on 1 March 1944) developed a convincingly unmannered voice and a powerful and distinctive stage presence during his years with the group. He began a parallel solo career in 1973 with the album *Daltrey* (Track), which featured songs by **Leo Sayer** and Dave Courtney, and was produced by Courtney and **Adam Faith** in his home studio at Burwash, Sussex. It included his 1973 UK hit single, 'Giving It All Away'. He took the title role in Ken Russell's film version of the Who's *Tommy* in 1974, and in the following year played the composer Franz Liszt in Russell's *Lisztomania*. His later album releases included *Ride a Rock Horse* (1975) and *One of the Boys* (1977), but his main extra-curricular activities prior to the Who's dissolution involved film work, notably his roles in *Sextet*, *The Legacy*, and a project he helped initiate, *McVicar* (1980), based on Great Train Robber John McVicar's autobiography.

DAMNED With 'New Rose' in November 1976, the Damned just beat the **Sex Pistols** as the first punk band to have a nationally distributed single, and went on to become the first punks to appear on the cover of a music paper (*Sounds*). Even though they were clearly punk pioneers, the Damned have never commanded the same respect as their most illustrious contemporaries, like the Sex Pistols or the **Clash**, because of their shameless 'take the money and run' attitude to the music industry. Yet they, of all of them, managed to continue into the Eighties as one of Britain's most colourful and exuberant rock acts.

The Damned evolved from a smaller band with an ever-changing line-up, London SS, formed in 1975 by bassist Tony James and guitarist Mick Jones. James left to form Chelsea and later **Generation X** and **Sigue Sigue Sputnik**, and Jones left for the Clash, leaving Brian James on guitar and drummer Rat Scabies (real name Chris Miller). They invited Ray Burns, a friend of Scabies', to join the group on bass, and then found singer Dave Vanian (real name Letts) propping up the bar at the Nashville, then the heart of London's pub-rock scene.

As a result of their success at a festival in France (after which, on the ferry crossing, Burns behaved in such an idiotic fashion that he was rechristened **Captain Sensible**), they were signed to a new independent label, Stiff. Their first single, 'New Rose' became a high energy punk classic, and they built up a sizeable following, especially through their whirlwind live sets, usually compressed into a 25-minute onslaught which left them, and their audience, exhausted.

After becoming the first British punk band to play in the US, they released the first punk LP *Damned Damned Damned* in February 1977, and it remains a perfect document of the joys of early punk. Their next album, *Music For Pleasure*, released later the same year, was a seriously watered down effort produced under the pressure of sustaining chart success. Disgusted with the album, Rat Scabies left, to be replaced by Jon Moss (later of **Culture Club**). Even though he was an adequate drummer, it was clear that Scabies had been an integral part of the live act and their audiences declined. Jake Riviera, the man who had signed them, left Stiff; the band found themselves without a recording deal, and they decided to disband in April 1978.

Their various individual projects failed, but there remained a demand for the Damned, and Sensible (switching to guitar), Vanian and Scabies joined Lemmy of **Motörhead** for a one-off gig as Les Punks to raise some money at the end of 1978. It was such a success that, having added a full-time bassist, Henry Badowski, they continued to gig as the Doomed. Badowski was replaced early in 1979 by Algy Ward, and they reverted to the name under which they had been most successful – the Damned. Signing to Chiswick records, they had two hits with 'Love Song' and 'Smash It Up'.

After the recording of the album *Machine Gun Etiquette* Ward was replaced by Paul Gray from **Eddie and** the Hot Rods, and it became clear that the Damned were moving towards the more melodic brand of loud guitar-music that was first in evidence on 'Love Song'; this was borne out by *The Black Album* in 1980. Even though they continued to be marketed as a hardcore punk band, the Damned had mellowed and their recordings lost their appeal for the lovers of thrash. Symptomatic of this movement away from punk was Captain Sensible's jokey solo LP *Women and Captains First* and the surprise Number 1 placing in June 1982 of his version of Rogers and Hammerstein's 'Happy Talk' from *South Pacific*. This and the follow-up single 'Wot' unexpectedly turned the Captain into a top disco act in Europe.

Despite this success, and the heavy live schedule they continued to undertake, their single sales were poor, and they found themselves without a recording contract in 1983. Nevertheless, they released an album, *Live in Newcastle* on their own label, Damned, but the line-up was depleted by the departure in August 1984 of Captain Sensible, who wanted to concentrate on his solo work.

A new line-up of Scabies and Vanian, plus Roman Jugg (guitar) and Bryn Gunn (bass) signed a deal with MCA and by early 1985 they had found their way back into the charts with a string of eccentric but catchy singles and an album, *Phantasmagoria*.

Throughout their lengthy, erratic career the Damned have remained resolutely British, proudly sustaining their oddball reputation, but always managing to appeal to a substantial audience. They remain one of the most exciting bands on the live circuit.

DANIELS, CHARLIE
Born in 1937 in Wilmington, North Carolina, Charlie Daniels graduated from highly respected session player to fully-fledged platinum selling international country artist, playing an eclectic blend of country, blues, bluegrass and Tex-Mex.

Turning professional in 1958, he spent ten years learning his craft as a guitarist/fiddler in the Jaguars and then in 1967 moved to Nashville as a session player where he added bass and banjo-playing to his repertoire. He played on innumerable country sessions and on albums by **Leonard Cohen**, **Pete Seeger** and **Bob Dylan**, among others.

He formed the Charlie Daniels Band in 1971 after recording the LP *Charlie Daniels* on Capitol the previous year, and extensive gigging soon built him up a loyal following in the south and

west of the US. The success of the LPs *Honey in the Rock* (1970) and *Nightrider* (1975) was such that Epic lured him away for a reported sum of $3 million in 1975. *Saddle Tramp* (1976) proved to Epic that Daniels had been a shrewd investment.

Daniels showed himself to be something of a workaholic, following tours with albums and more tours (including a set at President Carter's inaugural ball), and releasing the milestone LPs *High and Lonesome* (1977) and *Million Mile Reflections* (1979). The latter elevated Daniels to platinum status and yielded the international hit single 'The Devil Went Down to Georgia' (a US Number 3), which earned Daniels a Grammy Award for Best Country Vocal performance.

DANNY AND THE JUNIORS
Formed as a street corner group in Philadelphia late in 1957, Danny and the Juniors comprised Danny Rapp, lead singer (born 1941); Dave White, first tenor (1940), later replaced by Bill Carlucci; Frank Maffe, second tenor (1940); and Joe Terranova, baritone (1941). They were taken by singer friend, Johnny Madara, to his vocal coach, Artie Singer, who had just formed a small label, Singular. White, Madara and Singer co-wrote 'Do the Bop' for the group but on **Dick Clark**'s recommendation, they changed the lyrics and title to 'At the Hop' before recording it. The record sold 7000 copies locally on Singular before ABC-Paramount bought the master and turned it into a US chart-topper and an international million-seller. They followed that up with Dave White's similar-sounding 'Rock and Roll Is Here to Stay', which reached Number 19 in 1958, before commencing upon a string of boring dance records on Swan and Guyden – 'Twistin' USA', 'Doin' the Continental Walk', etc. – each of which gained progressively lower chart places. They disbanded in 1963. Danny Rapp died on 5 April 1983.

DARIN, BOBBY
Born Waldo Robert Cassotto on 14 May 1936, in Philadelphia, Bobby Darin blew with the wind. It is possible to listen to the records he made throughout his career and sense the directions the music was taking. Not that you will discover anything about Bobby Darin, because in a musical sense he had no independent existence – he was, instead, a series of identities, a collection of counterfeits.

After an unsuccessful year at Decca, covering **Lonnie Donegan**'s 'Rock Island Line' and recording atrocities

such as 'Blue-Eyed Mermaid', Darin moved to Atco in 1956. There he began his proper career as a young rocker, blasting out of the Atlantic stable with 'Splish Splash', 'Queen of the Hop' and 'Plain Jane' – the songs shot up the US charts through sheer force and energy. Not that the records were bad – as a writer and performer Darin was always a superb craftsman and these early records stand the test of time more than adequately. Darin was never satisfied, however, and he turned his hand to writing an all-time rock classic using the perennial C/Am/F/G7 chord changes. Of all the hundreds of hit songs that have used this sequence, his adaptation of it for 'Dream Lover' (1960) must rank alongside 'All I Have to Do Is Dream' as one of the very best.

A Fifties rocker outlives his time: the later Bobby Darin

It was after 'Dream Lover' that Darin first switched roles, and he emerged overnight – with his US Number 1 record 'Mack the Knife' – as a finger-clicking hipster, a Sinatra in embryo. This particular phase, however, lasted not much more than a year, for in the meantime he had discovered **Ray Charles** and responded to his love for his music by writing a song better suited to Charles than anything else he was recording. 'You're the Reason I'm Living' was a smash hit for Darin in

1962 on Capitol, the label he had moved to as a replacement for Sinatra.

He had rung the changes many times – even starting what looked like becoming a respectable film acting career with an Oscar-winning performance in *Captain Newman MD* – but the British Beat Invasion in the mid-Sixties left him stranded. Darin was only able to pick up the pieces of his career in the late Sixties after the new breed of singer-songwriters had emerged in the wake of **Bob Dylan**. However, Darin himself could not write that sort of material and his only real success – which coincided with his return to Atlantic in 1966 – was a version of **Tim Hardin**'s 'If I Were a Carpenter'. He died of a heart attack on 20 December 1973.

DARREN, JAMES Early Sixties teen idol James Darren – born James Ercolani on 3 October 1936, in Philadelphia – won a contract with Columbia Pictures. One of the Philadelphia school of good-looking Italian boys (**Fabian**, **Frankie Avalon**, etc.), his first record on Colpix was the title song from the movie *Gidget*. 'Goodbye Cruel World' was his first hit, reaching Number 3 in America and Number 15 in Britain, where it was released on Pye. Its success was due mainly to a gimmicky fairground organ sound, though the following year (1962), Darren growled his way through two more Top 20 records, 'Her Royal Majesty' and 'Conscience'. In 1967, he resurfaced on Warner Bros with the minor hit, 'All', and starred in the science-fiction TV series, *The Time Tunnel*.

DARTS British doo-wop revivalists the Darts made their reputation in the late Seventies as one of the most entertaining and accomplished live acts on the circuit, and successfully converted their on-stage vitality into a string of hit singles.

Rita Ray (vocals), Griff Fender (vocals), Horatio Hornblower (sax) and Den Hegarty (vocals) had all been members of Rocky Sharpe and the Replays from Brighton in Sussex, before moving up to London in 1976, recruiting Thump Thompson (bass), Hammy Howell (piano), George Curry (guitar) and John Dummer (drums) to form the original Darts. They were signed to Magnet Records and their first single, 'Daddy Cool – The Girl Can't Help It', an instant UK Top 10 hit in November 1977, was followed by three consecutive Number 2s ('Come Back My Love', 'Boy From New York City' and 'It's Raining') by which time Hegarty had

been replaced by New Yorker Kenny Andrews (bass vocals).

In November 1982 they starred in a stage musical, *Yakety Yak*. Conceived for the fringe theatre, it was a showcase for songs by **Leiber and Stoller** and opened at the Half Moon in London's East End. In January 1983 it transferred to the Astoria in the West End where it ran for six months; this made the Darts the first established group to star in a West End musical. The line-up, dating from early 1982, was Rita Ray, Griff Fender, Horatio Hornblower, Thump Thompson, Kenny Andrews, Pikey Butler (vocals), Jimmy Compton (keyboards), Nosmo King (drums) and Duncan Bashted (guitar), and the show went on to make a successful UK tour.

After three albums and twelve UK chart singles, contractual wrangles ended Darts' association with Magnet, and by 1985 they had released several singles on their own Choice Cuts label (financed by the success of *Yakety Yak*) but none had made any impact on the charts, and as the band members became more and more involved in projects outside the band, the Darts' career was effectively put on hold.

DAVIES, CYRIL Born in Denham, Buckinghamshire, in 1932, Cyril Davies was a panel-beater by day and played banjo in jazz and skiffle outfits before opening the London Blues and Barrelhouse Club with **Alexis Korner** in 1955. After switching to harmonica, he worked with Korner backing Ottilie Patterson, and in 1961 the two formed Blues Incorporated. His hatred of saxophones led him to quit in November 1962, to lead his own **Muddy Waters**-style band. He converted **Screamin' Lord Sutch**'s Savages, who included Nicky Hopkins on piano, into his R&B All-Stars, adding a black vocal trio, the Velvettes, and **Long John Baldry** for 'Country Line Special'/'Chicago Calling' (Pye), his best-remembered single in 1963. Davies collapsed and died of leukaemia on 7 January 1964.

DAVIS, BILLIE White soul singer Billie Davis, who barely survived an accident-prone career, was born Carol Hedges in Woking, Surrey, in 1945. She was groomed for stardom by Robert Stigwood, teamed with Mike Sarne for 'Will I What?', and then allowed to go solo for 'Tell Him' (Decca), which became a Top 10 hit in 1963. Immediately afterwards, she met ailing ex-**Shadows** bass guitarist Jet Harris and began a long, over-publicized relationship. Throughout the Sixties she persevered for further hits, graduating

from pop to soul and reaching maturity in 1967 with her version of 'Angel of the Morning'. Her talents have long been acclaimed in Europe but her full potential was never realized.

DAVIS, MAC Country-pop singer-songwriter Mac Davis was born in Lubbock, Texas, in 1941 and moved to Atlanta, Georgia, in his teens. In the late Fifties he began writing songs and formed his own rock'n'roll group. He quit performing in 1961 to become the regional manager for Vee Jay Records until 1965, when he moved over to Liberty and then transferred to Hollywood as head of Liberty's Metric Music, a position that allowed him to present his own songs to a wider range of singers much more easily – e.g. 'You're Good to Me' (Lou Rawls), 'Within My Memory' (**Glen Campbell**) and 'A Little Less Conversation' (**Elvis Presley**). In 1969 Presley gave Davis his first Top 10 songs with his versions of 'In the Ghetto' and 'Don't Cry Daddy'. Other hits Davis has written include: 'Daddy's Little Man', 'Friend, Lover, Woman, Wife' (**O.C. Smith**, 1969), 'Watching Scotty Grow' and 'Something's Burning' (Top 20 hits for **Bobby Goldsboro** and **Kenny Rodgers** respectively in 1970). In 1970 he signed with Columbia and scored a Number 1 US hit in 1972 with 'Baby Don't Get Hooked on Me'. That began a string of successful singles and albums (*I Believe in Music*, 1972 and *Mac Davis*, 1973), each a commercial mixture of sentimentality, melodrama and sensuality. In 1974 he hosted his own TV show. 'It's Hard to be Humble' (Casablanca) reached the Top 30 in 1980.

DAVIS, MAXWELL An important figure in black music for nearly 20 years as a saxophone player, A&R man and arranger, Maxwell Davis was born in Independence, Kansas, on 14 January 1916. He moved to Los Angeles in 1937 and played tenor with the bands of Fletcher Henderson and Happy Johnson. From 1948 to 1954 he was effectively A&R chief for Aladdin, and later for Federal and Modern. Davis wrote for, directed and played on innumerable R&B sessions, including many by **Percy Mayfield**, **Amos Milburn**, **B.B. King** and **Etta James**. His extremely adaptable sax playing was also heard on jazz and rock'n'roll records for Capitol, notably those of Ray Anthony and Ella Mae Morse. He was perhaps the most influential behind-the-scenes presence of West Coast R&B. Davis died in 1967. His last R&B hit was **Lowell Fulsom**'s 'Tramp', which he arranged.

DAVIS, MILES The founding father of jazz-rock fusion, Miles Davis was born in Alton, Illinois, on 25 May 1926, and made his recording debut on 25 November 1945. The junior member of altoist Charlie Parker's band, Miles displayed in his choice of apprentice-master (as in so many other things) instinctive good judgment. Over the next 30 years or so he brought about a number of decisive and radical changes in jazz, both technical and stylistic. In 1949 he introduced a completely new orchestral conception to the music and brought belated recognition to arranger Gil Evans as one of the most original composers in jazz. In the mid-Fifties there was the classic quintet with tenor-saxist John Coltrane; towards the end of the decade came his bold introduction of modal improvisation, and the Sixties saw his first moves into the world of rock music. It was only the latest of a series of examples of his genius for grasping a musical problem and proposing its solution in a single imaginative leap.

His album *Miles in the Sky* (Columbia, 1967) gave the first indication of his interest in rock forms, and the numbers on it, particularly 'Big Stuff', contained the seeds of all his later explorations of the idiom. The fragmentary, attenuated theme and sidelong approach to the beat provided a perfect sketch for the records which followed. On these he dropped the quintet format in favour of larger, irregular line-ups, and began to abandon tight chorus-structure in favour of free-flowing meditation on a single harmonic and rhythmic mood. Typical of this period was *Live Evil* (1972), with its brilliant use of the bass clarinet, which wandered from front-line to rhythm section in a most haunting and disturbing way. As the form became looser, the results became less and less predictable. Live appearances varied wildly in quality, while the albums, particularly *In Concert* and *At the Fillmore* (1971), were rather forbidding slabs of go-for-broke improvisation.

This loosening of form threatened to pass the point of balance and topple into incoherence; after his extension of electronics to include his own trumpet sound, the notes themselves became almost meaningless and all significance became invested in rhythmic tension and tonal distortion. This was not entirely satisfactory, especially since Miles had been, for over a quarter of a century, a 'notes' man *par excellence*. It was certainly true, however, that the interface between jazz and rock in its early Seventies form existed through the influence of Davis. Ex-Davis players like **Herbie Hancock**, Joe Zawinul, Billy Cobham, **Chick Corea**, and Keith Jarrett were (and remain) not only leading figures: they can be considered as a stylistically identifiable 'school', the characteristics of their style and procedure deriving from their experience with his bands during the period 1968–72.

1972 was in some ways a watershed year for Davis. A car crash put him out of action for some time and he became increasingly reclusive, while his albums between then and 1975 – *On the Corner* (1973), *Get Up With It* (1974), and *Agharta* (1975) – elaborated on the course he had begun taking with the seminal *Bitches Brew* in 1970, featuring fewer solos and heavier use of electronics. *Agharta* was his last all-new album for five years, and rumours persisted that he would return at the end of the decade – as he had done previously in the Forties, Fifties and Sixties – with a brand new direction to astound his fans. In 1981, he re-emerged with *The Man with the Horn* and resumed touring, this time with a six-piece band featuring Marcus Miller (bass), Bill Evans (soprano sax), Mike Stern (guitar), Al Foster (drums), and Mino Cinelu (percussion). A live album, *We Want Miles*, was recorded in both Boston and Tokyo and released in 1983. Although the album marked no radical change in Davis' music, it served to show that the master's playing had lost none of its grace or economy.

DAVIS, SKEETER Country singer Skeeter Davis – real name Mary Frances Penick – had a major crossover hit with 'The End of the World' in 1963. Born in Dry Ridge, Kentucky, on 30 December 1931, she formed the Davis Sisters with schoolmate Betty Jack Davis in 1953. Later that year, after a Number 1 country success with a version of 'I Forgot More Than You'll Ever Know', Betty Jack died on the road returning from a show. Skeeter gave up performing until **Chet Atkins** persuaded her back five years later. In 1959, she hit the country chart with 'Set Him Free' and then she made her best couple of singles – 'Last Date', a vocal version of **Floyd Cramer**'s hit and 'I'm Falling Too', a response to Hank Locklin's 'Please Help Me I'm Falling'. Skeeter Davis has never enjoyed an easy relationship with the Nashville establishment. 'The End of the World' – a million-seller and a Number 2 in the pop chart – was dismissed as a rock tune, and in 1974 she was barred from the stage of the *Grand Ole Opry* after using it for an attack on the Nashville police department for their harassment of the religious sect with which she was associated.

Innovative trumpeter Miles Davis blazed the trail to the new jazz-rock

DAVIS, SPENCER/SPENCER DAVIS GROUP Originally known as the Rhythm and Blues Quartet, the Spencer Davis Group were a pioneer Birmingham, England, R&B group comprising brothers **Stevie Winwood**, guitar, keyboard and vocals (born 12 May 1948) and Muff Winwood, bass (15 June 1945), Pete York, drums (15 August 1942), all from trad jazz backgrounds, and Spencer Davis, guitar (17 July 1942), a folk-blues performer. The keynote of the group was Stevie Winwood's amazingly mature and strong blues voice, perfect for their material, which was culled from black American sources, e.g. **Sonny Boy Williamson** and **Bo Diddley**.

Discovered in Birmingham by Chris Blackwell in 1964, they recorded unsuccessfully for Fontana throughout 1964 and 1965 until two songs by Jamaican singer, Jackie Edwards, propelled them into the charts. The first, 'Keep On Running', made Number 1 in December 1965 and was distinctive among British R&B for Winwood's voice and Muff's prominent, compulsive bass. Similar hits followed in 1966 with 'Somebody Help Me' (the second song composed by Edwards), 'When I Come Home' and 'Gimme Some Loving' – their first American Top 10 record. The group toured R&B clubs and played all-nighters throughout Britain, culminating in their last hit, in February 1967, 'I'm a Man', a Stevie Winwood composition.

In early 1967, both Winwoods left, Stevie to found **Traffic**, Muff to work for Chris Blackwell's Island Artists, and since then Davis, who was largely a figurehead, has kept various groups together under the same name without ever achieving another chart success. *See also* **Traffic; Steve Winwood**

DAVIS, TYRONE Chicago-based singer Tyrone Davis is best-known for the extraordinarily hypnotic 'Can I Change My Mind' (Dakar, 1968). Born in Greenville, Mississippi, in 1938, Davis worked as 'Tyrone the Wonder Boy' and employed a rasping, gasping vocal style on recordings for Tangerine (including an early version of 'Can I Change My Mind') and 20th Century-Fox, with little success. Signing with Carl Davis' Dakar Records, Tyrone cut his immortal 'Change' (though as a flip side) which months later hit the US Top 10, in December 1968. Subsequent hits have included the lilting 'Turn Back the Hands of Time' in 1970, 'You Keep Me Holding On' in 1971, and the 'concept-production' 'I Had It All the Time' in 1973. Although limited in the

kind of mid-tempo material he invariably chooses, Davis' mixture of smooth crooning and raw-edged emoting, vaguely similar to that of **Bobby Bland**, is one of the most riveting black music voices.

DAWN Dawn was the brainchild of **Tony Orlando** (born in New York on 3 April 1944), who in the early Sixties had been a successful singer in the **Ben E. King** mould. He moved from performing into the management side of the music business, rising to general manager of Columbia Records' April Blackwood publishing division by 1970. During that year he was approached by Hank Medress, a former member of the **Tokens** and a producer for Bell Records, with a song he wanted Orlando to record. The result was 'Candida', an almost clinically perfect pop disc recorded with two back-up singers – Thelma Hopkins (born in Louisville, Kentucky, on 28 October 1948) and Joyce Vincent (born in Detroit on 14 December 1946) – who had sung on various Motown sessions. 'Candida' (which was credited to Dawn) mirrored the then emerging MOR strand in US pop and reached the Top 20 on both sides of the Atlantic. The follow-up, 'Knock Three Times', was a transatlantic Number 1 in 1971, the year that Orlando left publishing to concentrate on recording and performing full-time. 'What Are You Doing Sunday' was another 1971 hit, while the million-selling 'Tie a Yellow Ribbon Round the Old Oak Tree' (1973, another transatlantic chart-topper) was the first on which Orlando shared label billing with Dawn, the legend reading 'Dawn featuring Tony Orlando'. 'Say, Has Anybody Seen My Sweet Gypsy Rose' (1973) and 'Who's in the Strawberry Patch with Sally' (1974) brought further hits and the group began touring the American cabaret circuit. In 1976, Orlando ended his association with the group and embarked on a solo career. *See also* **Tony Orlando**

DAY, BOBBY R&B singer Bobby Day enjoyed considerable success in the pop market during the late Fifties. He was born Robert Byrd in Fort Worth, Texas, in 1934, and moved to Los Angeles as a child, where he appeared in the Barrelhouse Club run by **Johnny Otis**. In 1957, he wrote and recorded 'Little Bitty Pretty One', but a cover version by Thurston Harris outsold his own. Among 11 other singles for the Class label, 'Rockin' Robin' was the most successful, reaching Number 2 in the US in 1958. Lesser hits included

'Over and Over', 'Bluebird, Buzzard and Oriole' and 'Gotta New Girl'.

Day's distinctive baritone also appeared on discs for Rendezvous, RCA and Sureshot, and as lead vocal for the Day Birds (on Jama). He also sang with the Hollywood Flames, whose novelty rock'n'roll records (notably 'Buzz Buzz Buzz', which reached the Top 20 in 1957) were more successful than their many beautiful ballads. Bobby Day's songs were revived by various artists in the Sixties and Seventies, the most successful being the **Dave Clark Five** and the **Jackson Five**.

DE SANTO, SUGAR PIE A diminutive but fiery R&B singer whose exciting stage presence was rarely captured on record, Sugar Pie De Santo was discovered by **Johnny Otis** in the mid-Fifties. She recorded for Federal and Aladdin before scoring regional hits on the Check and Veltone labels, and she toured with the **James Brown** Revue in 1960. Four years later she achieved national success with 'Slip-In Mules' (an answer record to **Tommy Tucker**'s 'Hi Heel Sneakers') and 'Soulful Dress' on Checker – the only records to do her justice. Later releases on Cadet, Brunswick, and Soul Clock were poor, though her early Seventies recordings for Jasman were better.

DEAD KENNEDYS San Francisco punks the Dead Kennedys caused a great deal of upset with their highly politicized garage thrash. Formed in 1978 with a line-up of Jello Biafra (vocals), East Bay Ray (guitar), Klaus Fluoride (bass) and Bruce Slesinger (drums), they released their debut single the following year, 'California Uber Alles', a scathing attack on US imperialism and power-hunger. This record clearly displayed the band's preoccupation with politics, a stance that they consistently held and which allegedly earned them death threats. Later, Biafra stood for mayor of San Francisco, coming fourth out of ten.

In 1980, the band released their debut album, *Fresh Fruit for Rotting Vegetables*, two sides of manic hardcore thrash, and in 1981 they outraged the world with the single 'Too Drunk to Fuck'. Airplay bans were slapped on the single everywhere, but it predictably reached the UK Top 40.

Recording activities subsided as they set about running their own label, Alternative Tentacles, but they remained one of the leading punk bands until early 1987 when the band split up. Jello Biafra went on to form a new band, the Kage.

DEAD OR ALIVE Led by androgynous singer Pete Burns, Liverpool's Dead or Alive developed from a cult punk band into a camp white funk outfit, scoring an international hit with 'You Spin Me Round' in 1985.

Always a background for the imposing stage presence of the flamboyantly dressed Burns, Dead or Alive's line-up was not stable until 1982 with Mike Percy (bass), Tim Lever (keyboards/sax) and Steve Coy (percussion) making up the unit. After a couple of well-received independent singles, they signed to Epic in 1982 but had to wait until 1984 for their first UK Top 30 hit, a cover of **KC and the Sunshine Band**'s 'That's the Way (I Like It)' from their first album *Sophisticated Boom Boom* (1984). *Youthquake* followed in 1985 and spawned 'You Spin Me Round', a UK Number 1.

DEAN, JIMMY Born in Plainview, Texas, on 10 August 1928, Jimmy Dean came to international fame through his semi-recitation 'Big Bad John' (1961), which established him as a pop-country entertainer. He began his country music career in 1951 with radio station WLS in Washington, singing with his group the Texas Wildcats, and became known in country circles for the hit 'Bumming Around' in 1953. After 'Big Bad John' came hits for RCA and Columbia, among them 'PT 109', 'The Cajun Queen' and 'Little Black Book', and a TV series for ABC in the US that repeated the success of his syndicated Fifties CBS-TV show, *The Jimmy Dean Show*. He has successfully straddled the pop-country fence ever since.

DEATH DISCS Discs taking death as their theme were a common feature of the charts in the late Fifties and early Sixties, but in a sense they only carried an old tradition into a new medium. Death, in the form of the murder ballads that were hawked through the streets of London in the 18th century, has some claim to be seen as the cornerstone upon which Tin Pan Alley was built.

By the early 20th century, when Tin Pan Alley had established itself as the source of popular songs, death was no longer considered a fit subject for song material. Thus in the Twenties, Thirties and Forties, death only appeared in the 'folk musics of the day', notably the blues and country music – the first million-selling country record was Vernon Dalhart's 'Wreck of the Old '97' in 1924. In the blues, death was treated as a fact of life, and hence

generally appeared in either a comical guise ('Stack O'Lee'), or at the most treated bitterly ('Frankie and Johnnie'); but never tragically as it was in country music (and popular music when it made its rare appearances), for example 'Wreck on the Highway', 'Put My Little Shoes away', 'The Death of Little Kathy Fiscus', etc.

Hence it was not surprising that what was probably the first death record of the rock'n'roll era, the **Kingston Trio**'s 'Tom Dooley' in 1958, was a dilution of an old folk song. Not surprisingly, it (and the discs that followed) was attacked by assorted clergymen and parent-teacher groups as being corrupt and depraved. Later that year, there was David McEnery's 'New Star Tonight' (dealing with the death of Presley's mother), and in 1959 came Ruby Wright's 'Three Stars' (later recorded by **Eddie Cochran**) about the deaths of **Buddy Holly**, **Ritchie Valens**, and the **Big Bopper**. While this number is fondly remembered to this day, songs of this kind – which include Mike Berry's 'Tribute to Buddy Holly' (Britain, 1961), tributes to **Johnny Ace** (e.g. the **Ravens**' 'Salute to Johnny Ace' and the Five Wings' 'Johnny's Still Singing', both in 1955) and later records such as the **Righteous Brothers**' 'Rock and Roll Heaven' in 1974 – belong more to the commemorative tradition than the rock'n'roll death song proper.

The classic death songs of the Fifties and early Sixties were simply translations of the minor traumas of teenage life through the application of excessive doses of romanticism into *the* trauma. Examples included: 'Endless Sleep' (**Jody Reynolds**, 1958); 'Teen Angel' (Mark Dinning, 1959); 'Tell Laura I Love Her' (**Ray Peterson**, 1959), which brought the reply 'Tell Tommy I Miss Him' from Marilyn Michaels; 'Running Bear' (**Johnny Preston**, 1960); 'Ebony Eyes' (the **Everly Brothers**, 1961); 'Leah' (**Roy Orbison**, 1962), 'Give Us Your Blessing' (Ray Peterson, 1963); 'Leader of the Pack' (the **Shangri-Las**, 1964); 'Dead Man's Curve' (**Jan and Dean**, 1964), and 'Last Kiss' (Frank J. Wilson and the Cavaliers, 1964). The period saw other death discs: 'The Three Bells' (the **Browns**, 1959), **Marty Robbins**' gunfighter ballads ('El Paso' and 'Big Iron' in 1959 and 1960, respectively), **Jimmy Dean**'s 'Big Bad John' (1961) and 'Steel Man' (1961), and even Abner Jay's 'The Thresher', about the missing submarine, in 1963 – but their origins lay outside the world of rock'n'roll.

The emergence of the **Beatles** saw a decline in the genre. A few death

records were made, such as 'I Can Never Go Home Anymore' by the Shangri-Las in 1966, Jimmy Cross' 'I Want My Baby Back' in 1965, **Bobby Goldsboro**'s million-selling 'Honey' in 1968, and the Goodee's 'Condition Red' in 1968, but in the changed world of rock that followed the arrival of the Beatles, the **Rolling Stones** and **Bob Dylan**, death was no longer the comfortable subject it had been earlier. The death of **Jimi Hendrix** and the threatening prescience of the real world in rock closed the door to the innocent world in which Ebony Eyes and Laura lived – and died.

DECCA RECORDS (UK) The Decca Record Company was started in Britain in 1929 and rapidly moved to the forefront of the home record industry, sharing the traditional honours as leading company in the British market with EMI. An American subsidiary was formed in 1934, which has since become part of the Music Corporation of America. Under the chairmanship of Edward Lewis, Decca made some remarkable advances in electronics, particularly in the radar field, but also introduced high-fidelity recording techniques in 1944 (*ffrr* – full frequency range recording), and the LP record into Britain in 1950. At the end of the Forties, the newly formed American Capitol entered into a licensing arrangement with British Decca, which lasted until 1954. Decca's most important deals, however, were with RCA and Atlantic – both made in 1957. RCA titles came out under their own name and included **Elvis Presley**'s records from 'Teddy Bear' onwards in the summer of 1957. The Atlantic titles came out under the Decca London, and then London American, label.

The London label covered releases from many American companies, including titles by **Fats Domino**, **Duane Eddy**, **Chuck Berry**, **Roy Orbison**, **Bobby Vee**, the **Crystals**, the **Ronettes**, the **Ventures**, Slim Whitman, **Larry Williams**, **Del Shannon**, **Ricky Nelson**, **Little Richard**, **Jerry Lee Lewis**, the **Everly Brothers**, and **Pat Boone**. Not surprisingly, with such an impressive roster, the London-American label was considered *the* label by both R&B and rock'n'roll British collectors until well into the Sixties when the American record companies it represented began to set up their own British organizations.

Earlier, in 1956, Decca had picked up **Tommy Steele** and seemed set to tie up the British rock'n'roll market since they already had **Bill Haley** and **Buddy**

Holly and the Crickets. However, with the exception of Billy Fury, their later British signings were not very successful, though the strength of the American artists they released continued to give them a large share of the market. Possibly because their success was founded on America, the company felt secure enough for A&R man Mike Smith to reject the Beatles in 1962. A year later, aware by now of the way the tide was flowing, they did something to correct that mistake by signing the Rolling Stones.

The Stones apart, few of Decca's pop and rock names stayed with the label very long – Lulu, the Animals, the Small Faces, and Alan Price all moved to other labels after initial success there – and one of its most astute signings, the Zombies, built a bigger following in the US than at home. Decca set up its own 'progressive' subsidiary, Deram, in 1967, and fared very well with Amen Corner, Cat Stevens, the Move, and Procol Harum, but its most important rock act of the late Sixties was the Moody Blues, who recorded initially for Deram but then set up their own label, Threshold, with distribution through Decca.

Decca's position within the UK record industry was sustained for a while by the success of its strong MOR roster – the perennially popular Mantovani and his Orchestra, Gilbert O'Sullivan, and singers Tom Jones and Engelbert Humperdinck – but its decline was marked during the Seventies, and in 1979 Decca's recording operations were taken over by Polygram.

DECCA RECORDS (US) Decca was a British company whose American subsidiary was launched in New York in 1934 by Jack Kapp. It quickly built up a mainstream popular reputation with artists such as Bing Crosby and, later, Sammy Davis Jr. Much attention was paid to jazz and, later, R&B – the Ink Spots, the Mills Brothers, Ella Fitzgerald, and Louis Jordan all being highly successful.

The first major to set up an office in Nashville, Decca picked up several of the best C&W artists, including Webb Pierce, Ernest Tubb and Red Foley. This enterprising attitude led to the surprising acquisition of Bill Haley and his Comets from the Philadelphia label, Essex, in 1954. The wisdom of this move was soon demonstrated when Haley became the sensation of the nation with the release of 'Rock around the Clock', produced by Milt Gabler, who had previously supervised Louis

Jordan's recordings. The following year, country-boogie pianist Roy Hall was signed, and several fine rock'n'roll singles resulted. Decca also recorded rock'n'roll with Johnny Carroll, Webb Pierce, Jackie Lee Cochran, Eddie Fontaine, whose 'Cool It Baby' was a regional hit, and Brenda Lee. Only Lee was commercially successful, and Decca transferred the rest of its rock activities to its subsidiary label, Coral. With Bob Thiele in charge of A&R, it had been formed in 1949 (originally as Decca's R&B label) and was reactivated late in 1956.

Both labels featured products from Norman Petty's studios in Clovis – Coral with Buddy Holly and Peanuts Wilson, and Brunswick with the Crickets. Memphis rockabilly was represented by the Johnny Burnette Trio and Billy Lee Riley, but the most successful artist, with Haley and Holly, was Jackie Wilson, whose R&B rockers, like the Dick Jacobs-arranged 'Reet Petite', were followed by a string of more soulful R&B hits.

During the course of the Sixties, the American Decca organization was merged into the new MCA set-up, but by then its concentration on rock had more or less ceased.

DEE, DAVE DOZY, BEAKY, MICK AND TICH This group's cumbersome name derived from the nicknames of its members: David Harman (born 1943), Trevor Davies, John Dymond, Michael Wilson, and Ian Amey, all born in 1944. When they arrived in London from Salisbury, Wiltshire, to record 'No Time' in 1965, they sported a comic image, but this was dropped when success arrived at the end of the year with 'Hold Tight' on Fontana and, by 1967, they were leaders of fashion. Their hits (driving disco fodder written by their managers Ken Howard and Alan Blaikley) numbered almost a dozen, and made them the most prolific chart-toppers of the period. In 1969 Dave Dee left to become an actor, failed, and returned in 1973 as A&R chief of Atlantic Records' London office. He also worked briefly for Capital Radio in London. The remaining members, renaming themselves DBM&T, had a modest UK Top 40 hit in 1970 with the cod protest song 'Mr President'.

DEE, JOEY, AND THE STARLITERS This group gyrated to the top of the American charts and into the British Top 20 in 1961 with 'Peppermint Twist' on Roulette (EMI's Columbia label in Britain). Written by

Dee and producer Henry Glover, the song was an undistinguished paean of praise to the Peppermint Lounge, a small fashionable New York night-club that had attracted the city's many socialites.

Dee was born in Passaic, New Jersey on 11 June 1940. With the Starliters – Carlton Latimor (organ), Willie Davis (drums), Larry Vernieri and David Brigati (singers/dancers) – he appeared in a couple of Twist-flicks and managed to stay on the charts until 1963 with other dance records for Roulette. His weak, rather anonymous voice could hardly do justice to such frenetic neo-gospel tunes as 'Hey Let's Twist' (Number 20), 'Shout' (Number 6) and 'Hot Pastrami with Mashed Potatoes' (Number 36), but he excelled on the attractive Johnny Nash ballad 'What Kind of Love Is This?' (Number 18), and his two black musicians were a joy to watch on stage. The Starliters proved to be a breeding-ground of talent. Three members of the Young Rascals – later the Rascals – (Felix Cavaliere, Gene Cornish, and Brigati's brother Eddie) were in the 1963 line-up, and Jimi Hendrix is said to have played briefly with the group in 1966.

DEE, KIKI Born Pauline Matthews in Bradford, Yorkshire, in 1947, Kiki Dee spent most of the Sixties decorating the outskirts of pop. Despite being a familiar figure on TV pop shows and on package tours, she had no chart success of any kind until 1973, when she returned to the UK after an abortive spell with Tamla Motown as the label's first white UK singer.

During that year she was signed by her old friend Elton John to his newly formed Rocket label. Her first release, a version of Veronique Sansom's tale of lost virginity, 'Amoureuse', reached Number 13 in the UK, and further hits followed with 'I Got the Music in Me' (1974), 'How Glad I Am' (1975), and 'First Thing in the Morning' (1977). Her duet with John, 'Don't Go Breaking My Heart' (written by John and partner Bernie Taupin under the pseudonym of Ann Orson and Carte Blanche), topped the UK chart for six weeks in mid-1976. She also toured extensively with the Kiki Dee Band – Bias Boshell, Phil Curtis, Jo Partridge and Roger Pope – and was the supporting act on Steely Dan's 1974 UK tour.

After a four-year absence from the Top 40, Kiki Dee re-emerged in 1981 with 'Star' (for her new label, Ariola). In 1984, she made her West End acting debut in the musical show Pump Boys and Dinettes.

DEEP PURPLE Formed in 1968, Deep Purple were one of the most popular of the British rock groups of the early Seventies. Originally playing a blend of rock and pop with a pseudo-classical touch, they achieved their biggest success when they moved on to loud, guitar-dominated heavy metal.

The first line-up of Ritchie Blackmore (guitar), Rod Evans (vocals), Nick Simper (bass) (ex-**Johnny Kidd** and the Pirates), Jon Lord (keyboards) and Ian Paice (drums), made three albums and found early success in the US, scoring a Top 5 single with their version of 'Hush' in 1968. Ian Gillan and Roger Glover were brought in to replace Evans and Simper in 1970 as the group sought to venture into heavier material, and it was with this line-up that the group enjoyed their biggest successes.

Their sound became increasingly reliant on Blackmore's pounding guitar riffs, and after they had broken through in the UK with a Number 2 single, 'Black Knight', in 1970, Deep Purple Mark II recorded a series of increasingly successful LPs, starting with *In Rock*. Their biggest seller was *Machine Head* (1972) which was a UK Number 1, sold four million copies in the US and spawned another US Top 5 single, 'Smoke on the Water', probably their best-known song.

After recording their double live LP *Made in Japan* (1972), Gillan and Glover left in 1973 to be replaced by David Coverdale (later of **Whitesnake**) and Glenn Hughes respectively. Gillan went to form his own band, **Gillan**, and Glover turned to production. Deep Purple Mark III continued the success with *Who Do We Think We Are* (1973) and four more albums until 1975, when Ritchie Blackmore left to form **Rainbow**. He was replaced by Tommy Bolin, previously of the **James Gang**, and the group recorded just one more LP, *Come Taste the Band* (1975) before disbanding in the summer of 1976.

After years of continual rumour, the Deep Purple Mark II line-up finally reformed in 1984, spurred on by the renewed public interest in heavy metal, and recorded *Perfect Strangers*. The album sold well worldwide and the band toured through 1985, grossing millions of dollars and headlining the Knebworth Fayre in the summer.

DEF LEPPARD One of the leading bands of the so-called new wave of British heavy metal, Sheffield's Def Leppard found great success in America with their good-humoured, accomplished hard rock.

Formed in 1977 by Joe Elliott (vocals), Pete Willis (guitar), Rick Savage (bass), Steve Clark (guitar) and Rick Allen (drums), they recorded an EP, 'Getcha Rocks Off', on their own Bludgeon Riffola label. Signed to Polygram, they released their first album, *On Through the Night* in 1980; this made the UK Top 20 and was well received in the US, where the band set about touring on various support slots. The American crowds warmed to them and their following increased with the second album, *High 'n' Dry* (1981), but it was *Pyromania* (1983) (on which Phil Collen had replaced Willis), an ambitious blend of electronics and heavy metal, that put the band into the US platinum bracket, selling over 2 million copies.

In 1984 drummer Rick Allen lost an arm in a car crash, which effectively put the group's career on hold as they contemplated their next move.

Jamaican Desmond Dekker took reggae into the international charts

DEKKER, DESMOND Born in Jamaica in 1943, Desmond Dekker was a protégé of producer Leslie Kong who came to prominence in 1967 when '007' (Pyramid), a disc glorifying the rude boy era, climbed into the British singles charts. It was a light, infectious rock-steady number with a catching melody, and he continued in similar vein with more than 20 consecutive chart-toppers in Jamaica, including 'Hey Grandma' and 'Music Like Dirt', before 'Israelites' gave him a second British hit, climbing to Number 1 in April 1969 and to Number 10 in the US on Uni. Sung in a mixture of English and Creole patois, it was immensely popular, and paved the way for further reggae chart entries, 'Return of Django' and 'The Liquidator'. A follow-up, 'It Mek', was almost as successful, and the following year he had his fourth British hit with 'You Can Get It If You Really Want' before fading from the limelight because of poor material. Re-released in 1975, 'Israelites' was a hit again. In 1980, he signed with Stiff Records for the well-received *Black and Dekker* album and a year later was teamed with producer **Robert Palmer** (ex-Vinegar Joe) for *Compass Points*.

DELANEY AND BONNIE This couple acted as a focus for many of the best musicians of the early Seventies with their successful American and European tours. Delaney Bramlett was born in Pontotoc County, Mississippi, on 1 July 1939, and joined the famous Shindogs, the house band for **Jack Good**'s *Shindig* television show.

There he met and married Bonnie Lynn (born in Acton, Illinois, on 8 November 1944). Their first album was made for Stax in 1968, with **Don Nix** producing, and the next year they put together Delaney and Bonnie and Friends to tour with **Blind Faith**. The resulting album, *Accept No Substitute* (Elektra, 1969) involved such then unknown players as Carl Radle (bass), Jim Keltner (drums), Bobby Whitlock (guitar), Jim Price (trumpet), Bobby Keys (sax) and singer **Rita Coolidge**. So infectious was the band's brand of white soul that **Eric Clapton** joined them for the subsequent tour, which produced *On Tour with Eric Clapton* (Atco, 1970).

Then the entire band deserted the Bramletts for the **Leon Russell/Joe Cocker** extravaganza, Mad Dogs and Englishmen. After the couple divorced in 1972, each released a solo album through Columbia, and in 1975 Bonnie signed with Capricorn, for whom she recorded two albums. Delaney returned to recording with *Class Reunion* (Prodigal) in 1977.

DELFONICS Ace soul harmonizers the Delfonics first came together as the Four Guys in Philadelphia in 1964, the line-up comprising William Hart (born 17 January 1945, in Washington), his brother Wilbert (19 October 1947, in Philadelphia), Randy Cain (2 May 1945, in Philadelphia) and Ritchie Daniels.

Cain left to study in 1965, returning in 1967 when Ritchie was conscripted, and the trio became the Delfonics at manager Stan Watson's instigation. Discs on Fling and Moon Shot flopped, so Watson formed his own Philly Groove label for the group, and the debut 'La La Means I Love You' was a Top 5 hit in 1968. Subsequent releases (including 'Break Your Promise', 'Ready Or Not Here I Come', 1968, and 'Didn't I (Blow Your Mind This Time)') were also substantial hits, though in 1971 Cain quit the group to be replaced by Major Harris, from Richmond, Virginia, who in late 1973 in turn was replaced by Chicagoan Bruce Peterson. The wistful, melodic sweet-soul trio subsequently signed to **Curtis Mayfield**'s Curtom Records but enjoyed no further large-scale chart success.

DELLS Black vocal quintet the Dells have a very long history behind them, having first come together in 1953. During that year, Marvin Junior (first tenor), Verne Allison (tenor), Mickey McGill (baritone), Lucius McGill (tenor), Johnny Funches (lead), and Chuck Barksdale (bass) formed a vocal group at high school in Harvey, Illinois, and recorded without success, for Checker, as the El Rays. Lucius quit in 1954 and the group signed with Vee Jay as the Dells, recording prolifically through the next six years. Funches left in 1958 after a serious car crash – replaced by ex-**Flamingo** Johnny Carter – and in 1962, the group returned to Chess where '(Bossa Nova) Bird' (Argo) became their first (minor) national hit. 1964 saw them back on Vee Jay, whose demise in 1966 led to their return to Chess, where they have since remained, enjoying more than 20 R&B hits of varying proportions, plus the US Top 10 entries 'Stay in My Corner' (1968) and a re-recording of their 1956 R&B hit, 'Oh What a Night' (1969). The medley 'Love Is Blue/I Can Sing a Rainbow' (1969) was the group's only British Top 20 hit.

DEL-VIKINGS A mixed black and white vocal group from a Pittsburgh USAF base, the Del-Vikings (originally spelt Dell-Vikings) comprised Clarence Quick, Corinthian Jackson, Dave Lerchey, Norman Wright, and Gus Backus. They first recorded for Luniverse in 1956. The following year, with new member Kripps Johnson, they had two memorable Top 10 hits with 'Come Go with Me' and 'Whispering Bells', which were leased to Dot by the small Fee-Bee label. Members of the Dell-Vikings tended to form splinter groups whose personnel changed rapidly. They changed the spelling and moved on to Mercury (where 'Cool Shake' made the Top 50), ABC-Paramount, United Artists, Alpine, and Gateway. Backus became a cabaret artist in Germany while Chuck Jackson, another important member, became a successful soul balladeer in the Sixties.

DENNY, SANDY After she left **Fairport Convention** at the end of 1969, Sandy Denny pursued an erratic career as a singer and songwriter. She had emerged on the British folk scene a few years earlier, and after a series of performances at the Troubadour and Les Cousins in London, she joined the **Strawbs** briefly in 1968, recording one album with them.

As a lead singer with Fairport Convention, Denny (born 6 January 1947) was instrumental in introducing traditional folk songs into the group's repertoire, as well as her own material, notably 'Who Knows Where the Time Goes', later recorded by **Judy Collins** and other singers. Leaving Fairport, she formed Fotheringay with her future husband Trevor Lucas and American guitarist Jerry Donaghue. The band was short-lived, and Denny went on to record three solo albums of her own songs for Island: *The North Star Grassman and the Raven* (1971), *Sandy* (1972), and *Like an Old Fashioned Waltz* (1974).

In 1974, she rejoined Fairport Convention, which now included Lucas and Donaghue. After an uncertain beginning, she re-established herself as a fully integrated member of the band with her work on *Rising for the Moon* (1975), though she and Lucas departed once more during February 1976. A solo album, *Rendezvous*, followed in 1977, but it was to be her last recording: she died on 21 April 1978, from head injuries received in a fall at her home. *See also* **Fairport Convention**

DENVER, JOHN An immensely successful singer-songwriter whose music draws equally on folk, country, and pop influences, John Denver was born John Henry Deutschendorf in Roswell, New Mexico, on 31 December 1943. Raised in the South, he moved to Los Angeles after leaving college in 1964, and played the city folk clubs before joining the Chad Mitchell Trio during the following year. The Trio recorded for Mercury and lasted until 1969, when Denver signed a solo deal with RCA and recorded *Rhymes and Reasons*, which contained his own version of 'Leaving on a Jet Plane', a Denver song that **Peter, Paul and Mary** took to Number 1 in the US chart later that year. Denver's early songs were mainly second-generation folk protest, centring on the evils of social injustice and war, while some of his best compositions were on ecological themes. 'Take Me Home, Country Roads' and 'Rocky Mountain High', for example, combined an evocation of natural wonder with lyrics that stressed the fragility of such feelings in the contemporary world. The sense of space in his songs was conveyed by powerful acoustic guitars behind his nasal, but clear singing voice. Both were US Top 10 hits, in 1971 and 1973 respectively.

Denver was one of America's biggest-selling artists by 1974, when both 'Sunshine on My Shoulders' and 'Annie's Song' topped the US chart (the latter also reached Number 1 in the UK). He moved into TV work, hosting his own series on BBC-TV and even appearing with Frank Sinatra on a TV special and album, and he made his film debut in *Oh God!* in 1977. He seemed committed to a career as an easy-listening entertainer, yet continued to record albums of some considerable charm and inventiveness – *Autograph*, for example, in 1980 – and to put his weight behind political causes. He started his own label, Windsong Records, in 1976, whose first hit single was 'Afternoon Delight' by the Starland Vocal Band (also 1976).

DEPECHE MODE Initially dismissed as either fatuous New Romantics or unmelodic synth-pop merchants, Depeche Mode have finally become recognized as accomplished tunesmiths whose simplistic singalong ditties often conceal a surprising degree of perception and humour.

Formed in 1980 in Basildon, Essex, the group were originally a conventional bass-guitar-drums trio called Composition of Sound, which featured Vince Clarke, Martin Gore and Andy Fletcher, but they soon teamed up with vocalist Dave Gahan and made the timely switch to synthesizers.

Through their involvement with Stevo and the Some Bizarre compilation album, they signed to Daniel Miller's independent Mute label, where they have remained ever since. Their debut single, 'Dreaming of Me' (February 1981) reached Number 57 in the UK and was quickly followed by 'New Life' and 'Just Can't Get Enough', insistent, catchy tunes penned by Clarke that pushed into the Top 20.

When Clarke quit in 1981 to form **Yazoo**, critics predicted the demise of Depeche Mode, but Martin Gore stepped in to take on the songwriting, and with new member Alan Wilder, the band continued to have hit singles through 1982 with 'See You' and 'Leave in Silence'. However, neither of their two albums (*Speak and Spell* (1981) and *Broken Frame* (1982)) amounted to more than a couple of good singles padded out with synth fillers.

Construction Time Again (1983) changed all that. Fashioned by Gore to blend immaculately smooth melodies with harsh industrial sound effects and lyrics concerning capitalism, socialism and socializing, the album proved that Depeche Mode could successfully mix politics and pop. 'Everything Counts' and 'People Are People' were huge hit singles that gave the band the confidence to experiment even more, and the result was 1984's *Some Great Reward* LP, which featured the hit 'Blasphemous Rumours', a sardonic ballad with a gently mocking tone.

In 1985 there were yet more hits with 'Shake the Disease' and 'It's Called a Heart', both of which were included on the compilation album, *The Singles 81–85.*

DEREK AND THE DOMINOS

Originally formed by **Eric Clapton** to play a charity concert in London in June 1970, Derek and the Dominos comprised members of **Delaney and Bonnie**'s band – Bobby Whitlock (organ), Carl Radle (bass), Jim Gordon (drums), and ex-**Traffic** guitarist **Dave Mason**. The group's name reflected the post-**Cream** Clapton's desire for anonymity. He kept the group together – minus Mason – for a low-key British tour later that year which was interrupted for recording sessions in Miami that produced the brilliant double album, *Layla* (Polydor, 1970), featuring Duane Allman on slide guitar. It was a song-cycle incorporating originals by Clapton and Whitlock as well as classics like Chuck Willis' 'It's Too Late'. *Layla* showed Clapton to be not just a guitarist, but a writer and singer of range and power. It was said later to have been inspired by his relationship with Patti Harrison.

After recording a live album, not released until 1973, the group broke up in May 1971, reportedly after disagreements during the sessions for a projected second album. 'Layla' (the single) reached Number 7 in the UK during 1972 but went three places better when re-issued ten years later.

DERRINGER, RICK

Derringer (real name Zehringer, born in 1949) was a member of the **McCoys**, whose 'Hang On Sloopy' (Bang, 1965) was a Number 1 US hit. With his brother Randy, he was later brought in by manager Steve Paul to form the nucleus of **Johnny Winter**'s backing band. Rick Derringer also produced the next four albums by Winter.

During Johnny Winter's long lay-off to undergo treatment for narcotics addiction, Derringer became lead guitarist for the **Edgar Winter** Group. His best-known number, 'Rock and Roll Hoochie Koo', appeared on albums by both Winter brothers, as well as his own first solo record, *All American Boy* (Epic, 1974), a technically proficient set of heavy metal rock.

In 1976, he formed the group Derringer with guitarist Danny Johnson, Vinnie Appice (drums), and Kenny Aaronson (bass). They recorded four albums between 1976 and 1979, by which time Derringer decided to re-enter the East Coast club scene from which he had originally emerged, playing solo sets or guesting with other bands. *See also* **McCoys**

DESHANNON, JACKIE

Born in Hazel, Kentucky, on 21 August 1944, Jackie DeShannon was responsible for an impressive number of Sixties hit tunes. She began her career as a writer for the **Kalin Twins** and **Brenda Lee** ('Dum Dum') amongst others before recording in 1960 with a group called the Nomads.

Signed to Liberty as a solo artist, she released many singles and albums. Working with arranger **Jack Nitzsche** and other songwriters, including Sharon Sheeley and **Randy Newman** (she co-authored some of his first songs), DeShannon's songs were covered extensively, particularly by English groups like the **Searchers** who had a transatlantic hit with 'When You Walk in the Room'. Her own biggest hits were 'What the World Needs Now Is Love' (Imperial, 1965), and 'Put a Little Love in Your Heart' (Imperial, 1969), both Top 10 records. In 1972, she moved to Atlantic Records, where she released two fine solo albums, before moving on to Columbia for the powerful but commercially unsuccessful *New Arrangement* (1975). Her albums since have included *You're the Only Dancer* (Amherst, 1978) and *Songs* (Capitol, 1979). In 1981, she co-wrote (with Donna Weiss) the **Kim Carnes** hit, 'Bette Davis Eyes'.

(DETROIT) SPINNERS

Formed in 1955, the (Detroit) Spinners were a five-man team (Pervis Jackson, Bobbie Smith, Henry Farnborough, Billy Henderson, George W. Dixon, later replaced by G. C. Cameron) from Detroit signed by ex-**Moonglows** leader, **Harvey Fuqua**, to his Tri Phi label. They scored with their first release, 'That's What Girls Are Made for' in 1961. Absorbed by the expanding Tamla Corporation, the Spinners next appeared on Motown: 'I'll Always Love You', 'Truly Yours' (1965–6) – and its subsidiary VIP – 'Message From a Black Man', 'It's a Shame' (1970); but transferred to Atlantic in 1972. Teamed with **Thom Bell**, and sporting a new line-up including Phillipe Wynne and Crathman Spencer, a succession of classy soul ballads ('I'll Be Around', 'Could It Be I'm Falling in Love', 'I'm Coming Home', and 'Then Came You' with **Dionne Warwick**) established them as one of the top black groups of the Seventies. In Britain the group have been known as both the Motown Spinners (on Tamla) and the Detroit Spinners (on Atlantic) to avoid confusion with the British folk group, the Spinners. Wynne left in the mid-Seventies. Their last major hits were the 1980 releases, 'Working My Way Back to You' (Number 1 in the UK and Number 2 in the US) and a medley, 'Cupid/I've Loved You for a Long Time'.

DEVIANTS

Originally known as the Social Deviants, this 1967-founded group were a community band led by Mick Farren, then working at *International Times* and the first London 'underground' club, UFO. They came together for a series of 'total assault' gigs in the early underground clubs and for free concerts. After drummer Russ Hunter joined, the band moved on to a more semi-pro basis but the other musicians were less committed and the Social Deviants broke up. Farren and Hunter put together a new band, the Deviants, producing, pressing and distributing their first album themselves. *Ptoof* was on the Underground Impressarios label and was just sold through *It* and *Oz*, notching up 8000 in sales before Decca subsequently re-released it. A more stable line-up completed by bass player Duncan Sanderson and guitarist Paul Rudolph recorded a second album, *Disposable*. The group originally was heavily – if anarchically – political but changed later to a policy of simply trying to create a good-time atmosphere on stage. They were never a very accomplished musical outfit, the family ideal outweighing their development as musicians. In 1968, during a vast American tour, they called it a day, with Hunter, Sanderson and Rudolph joining Twink (late of the **Pretty Things**), whom they had backed on a solo album, to form the Pink Fairies. The Fairies had a similar spirit but greater musical ambition, although that ambition was to remain unfulfilled.

DEVO

Formed in Akron, Ohio, in 1975, eccentric five-piece Devo first came to the attention of British audiences on the crest of America's first wave of new music following the punk explosion of 1976. They stand out as originals, having cornered the market for jerky, irreverent, mechanistic punk/pop, played with a contrived amateurism that either charms or appals, depending on the listener's tolerances.

Consisting of two sets of brothers, Jerry (bass, vocals) and Bob (vocals, keyboards, guitar) Casale, Mark (vocals, keyboards, guitar) and Bob (lead guitar, vocals) Mothersbaugh, plus Alan Myers on drums, Devo, like most new American artists of that period, got their first break in Britain. They had already released two singles – 'Jocko Homo' and 'Satisfaction', later to be regarded as classics of the period – on their own Booji Boy label and were included in an Akron compilation put together by Stiff in 1977. Stiff also released the two singles in the UK. After intense competition from all the majors, Virgin finally signed them on a long-term deal.

The first album Q: *Are We Not Men? A: We Are Devo!* (1978), produced by Brian Eno, was a clear statement about Devo – wacky visuals, manic songs, bizarre lyrics expounding their obscure doctrine of 'de-evolution' – and captured the band's live feel, which British audiences revelled in when Devo played their first headline tour later that year. This was followed in 1979 by another LP, *Duty Now for the Future*, which indicated a broader musical base, was more widely accessible, and led to 1980's *Freedom of Choice*, Devo's first real dance album. The Americans finally warmed to the band and the electro-dance single 'Whip It' (on WEA in the States) reached Number 15 in the US chart.

The band continued to tour and release albums (*New Traditionalists*, a lampoon on the British New Romantics (1981), *Oh No! It's Devo* (1982) and *Shout!* (1984)) but their earlier popularity had gone. The latter two LPs were not well received in the UK, and represented no leaps in style like their predecessors. In addition, Devo's efforts to be taken seriously in other media, particularly cinema, detracted from their music.

Devo brought a unique style and freshness of approach to rock music in the Seventies and Eighties, but widespread commercial success was sacrificed to the over-cultivation of their crazed image and their refusal to conform with music business convention. Yet it was precisely these attitudes that made Devo what they were.

DEXYS MIDNIGHT RUNNERS One of the more erratic bands to come out of the British post-punk period, Dexys Midnight Runners, led by the enigmatic Kevin Rowland, went through short-lived bouts of widespread popularity over the tortuous course of their career. With Rowland firmly at the controls, the group's oft-changing musical direction has always been subject to his whim, but despite sometimes lengthy gaps between releases, Dexys Midnight Runners scored some of the UK's biggest selling singles of the Eighties and retained a loyal following.

Formed in the Midlands in 1978 as an eight-piece by Rowland and guitarist Al Archer after their previous band, the Killjoys, had split, Dexys Midnight Runners first came to the public eye on a 1979 2-Tone tour. Brought in halfway through to replace the errant **Madness**, they impressed audiences with their tight, Sixties soul-influenced dance music that made a marked contrast to the ska of the other two bands on the bill, the **Selecter** and the **Specials**. Even at that early stage, it was clear that Rowland was in charge, and he insisted that the music be all-consuming, right down to determining the kind of clothes the band should wear to reinforce their sound most effectively. This authoritarian approach was to cause several changes of line-up.

Rejecting their association with 2-Tone, Dexys turned to ex-**Clash** manager Bernie Rhodes' Oddball Records, on which they released their debut single 'Dance Stance', a fine record that just made the Top 40 in January 1980. Shortly afterwards they signed to EMI, and in March their second single 'Geno' hit the UK Number 1 spot, remaining in the charts for over three months. Their growing number of new fans clamoured to hear 'Geno' at their concerts, but Dexys (i.e. Rowland) insisted that the rest of their show be taken equally seriously, gaining the band a cantankerous reputation. Rowland never got on with the press and has gone through long periods of refusing to talk to them, but when the LP *Searching for the Young Soul Rebel* was released in July, it received ecstatic reviews and made Number 6 in the UK.

At the end of 1980, after returning from some successful dates in the US, four of the band left following a disagreement over 'Keep It Part II', the fourth single. The single flopped; the departed members formed the Bureau and in March 1981 released the magnificent 'Only for Sheep', which did no

better. After the commercial failure of another single and an album, they split. Mick Talbot, who had been a member of both Dexys and the Bureau, later joined Paul Weller in the **Style Council**.

Meanwhile, Rowland, Archer and Big Jim Paterson (the trombonist who had been with the band from the start), recruited more members, after which Archer struck out on his own and was replaced by guitarist Billy Adams. The group's comeback single was the exuberant 'Plan B', which only made Number 58 but showed that Dexys were still a musical force. At this point, their long-running feud with EMI was settled and the band left to sign with Phonogram. Their first release with this company, 'Show Me', returned the band to the UK Top 20 in July '81.

After that success, they released a disastrous single, 'Liars A-E', but a year later, after a quiet period, they reappeared with a radically altered sound and image. On the next single, 'The Celtic Soul Brothers', the Emerald Express, a string trio led by Helen O'Hara were featured and the powerful horns that characterized their sound had all but gone to be replaced by a rhythmic Irish folk lilt and a new, scruffy gipsy image. Although it only reached Number 45, it signalled the way for their biggest international hit, the stomping rock/folk dance number 'Come On Eileen', which was a huge summer Number 1 and stayed in the UK charts for over four months.

Kevin Rowland, Runners' leader

Too Rye Ay, a tough blend of Irish folk, soul and R&B, was released in August and made Number 2, and there followed a string of Top 20 singles into 1983. Dexys fulfilled a heavy touring schedule, and then took a long rest.

They did not re-emerge until two years later, this time with yet another change of image, a clean-cut, suburban white-collar look. Now, with the Dexys unit consisting of Rowland, Adams and O'Hara plus sessioneers, an LP, *Don't Stand Me Down*, came out in autumn 1985, accompanied by announcements that there would be no singles. This stance was dropped with the slow commercial progress of the album, however, and 'This Is What She's Like' was released, but it failed too, and after a moderately successful tour, Dexys Midnight Runners again disappeared from the limelight.

Despite the often hostile music press reaction, usually engendered by Rowland's uncompromising approach and his bizarre obsession with image, his charismatic stage presence and songwriting talents are undoubted, and his ability to surround himself with excellent musicians has meant that Dexys Midnight Runners remains a strong voice in British rock.

DIAMOND, NEIL

An immensely popular singer and songwriter for nearly two decades, Neil Diamond was, like **Carole King**, another talent to emerge from the song factories of New York's Brill Building during the early

Ambition and introspection marked Neil Diamond's Seventies career

Sixties. He was born on 24 January 1941, in Brooklyn, New York, and attended New York University medical school before dropping out to work for a number of music publishers, including **Don Kirshner**'s Aldon Music. His potential as a performer was first realized by **Jeff Barry** and **Ellie Greenwich**, who took him to **Bert Berns**' newly established Bang label in 1965.

His first single for the label, 'Solitary Man', was a minor hit, but he followed with a series of five Top 20 records, beginning with 'Cherry Cherry' in 1966. Diamond's compositions were also recorded by the **Monkees** ('I'm a Believer'), **Elvis Presley** and **Deep Purple** ('Kentucky Woman'), and **Lulu** ('The Boat That I Row').

Up to this point, Diamond's songs were well-crafted Brill Building commercial pop. In 1968, artistic ambitions took him to Uni where 'Brooklyn Roads', his first single, was a self-consciously autobiographical piece. Over the next few years, his work included calculated pop ('Cracklin' Rosie'), experimental sequences ('African Trilogy', described as a folk-ballet, on *Tap Root Manuscript*, 1970) and a handful of classic songs, notably 'I Am . . . I Said' and 'Stones' (both 1971).

As his success grew, his artistic horizons (critics called them pretensions) kept pace. In 1973, he signed to Columbia for a vast advance, releasing his songs for the soundtrack of *Jonathan Livingston Seagull* as his first album for them. It justified critical scepticism about his judgment, though *Serenade* (1974) did something to redress the balance.

His next album, *Beautiful Noise* (1976), was a nostalgic tribute to his Brill Building beginnings, and was produced by Robbie Robertson of **The Band**, on whose farewell concert he guested the same year. His 1978 duet with Barbra Streisand, 'You Don't Bring Me Flowers', was a US Number 1, and endorsed his increasing appeal to MOR audiences; his film debut in *The Jazz Singer*, 1980, consolidated that appeal.

DIAMONDS

Prominent at a time when adult castigation of rock'n'roll was rife, the Diamonds were among the prime perpetrators of diluted, 'acceptable' cover-versions of R&B hits. In the five years from 1956 to 1961 Canadians Dave Somerville and Mike Douglas, and Californians John Felton and Evan Fisher achieved some 16 hits, ten of which were 'covers' of R&B discs which (as exemplified by the biggest hit, the Gladiolas' 'Little Darlin'') employed semi-parodic arrangements

of the originals. Significantly, the demise of 'doo-wop' style black groups at the turn of the Sixties also saw the end of the Diamonds' run of success.

DIBANGO, MANU

While hardly geriatric – he was born in 1934 – Cameroonian saxophonist/keyboardist Manu Dibango is nevertheless one of the oldest African musicians on the contemporary recording and gigging scenes and at the same time one of the most adventurous and forward-looking. In stark contrast to the attitude towards old people in the West, where advancing age brings diminished respect and inspires impatience, in Africa, the older a person becomes, the greater the esteem in which he or she is held.

His first taste of Western success came in 1973 when the American chart breakthrough of his 'Soul Makossa' single triggered off hit status for the record almost throughout the world. Always catholic and unpredictable, in 1984 he embraced the emergent hip hop music of New York to cut what was for many people the most exciting African single of the year, the Martin Meissonnier-producer 'Abele Dance'. The following year he teamed up with producer Bill Laswell to continue the experiment on his own and other Laswell-produced albums (notably the all-star *Deadline*).

He has subsequently lived in New York, Cameroon and (for the most part since the mid-Seventies) Paris, and his own brand of music has become increasingly global in outlook. An avid believer in experiment, Dibango is incensed by Western critics who frown on change in African music: 'Africa is not a museum,' he points out, 'and we have as much right to progress and electronics as anybody else'.

DICK AND DEEDEE

Dick (St John) and Deedee (Sperling) were one of many teenage couples to enjoy brief chart success in the US. Dick (born in 1944) had originally recorded for Liberty, but with no success. He then called on schoolfriend Deedee (born 1945) – they both came from Santa Monica, California – to record his song called 'The Mountain's High', which climbed to Number 2 in the Hot 100. A remarkable record, its tremulous harmonies sounded as if they had been recorded in a garage. The duo alternated between touring and studying at school during the record's success in 1961. Their follow-up releases ('Tell Me', 'Young and in Love') never sold as well, but they had a brief comeback in 1964 with 'Thou Shalt Not Steal'.

DIDDLEY, BO Born Ellas McDaniel on 30 December 1928, in McComb, Mississippi, Bo Diddley switched from violin to playing guitar in Chicago's Maxwell Street market, a spawning ground for many leading blues figures. In July 1955, he successfully auditioned for Checker, a subsidiary of Chess Records. That same year he wrote and recorded his famous self-dedication, 'Bo Diddley' – a nickname he acquired as a boxer in his youth. The song was a major hit, and stands as one of the greatest R&B records ever made, while his 'jungle-rhythm' blues-based music in general remains a key factor in the origin and development of rock.

From then on he continued to score regular hits, his vocal and writing style often revealing a debt to R&B singer **Louis Jordan**, whose recordings during the Forties – generally containing witty lyrics – were popular with both black and white audiences. Diddley recorded all his songs in the Chess studios in Chicago, usually accompanied by Jerome Green (maracas), Otis Spann (piano), Billy Boy Arnold (harmonica), and Frank Kirkland (drums), while his half-sister, known as 'The Duchess', was sometimes featured on rhythm guitar. (Incidentally, Diddley and stablemate **Chuck Berry** sometimes sat in on each other's sessions – Bo plays rhythm guitar on Berry's 'Memphis Tennessee' and 'Sweet Little Rock and Roller'.) Diddley's unique sound – raw vocals and a heavily amplified guitar underscored by a pounding 'jungle beat' – has been copied and used by a variety of artists. **Buddy Holly** covered 'Bo Diddley', while **Johnny Otis** emulated the Diddley sound on 'Willie and the Hand Jive'. It was even rumoured that **Elvis Presley** copied Diddley's stage antics wholesale when he first came to New York in 1956. But it was the British R&B boom of the early Sixties that really brought Bo Diddley's name into prominence.

The **Rolling Stones**' original stage act featured such Diddley numbers as 'Mona', 'Diddley Daddy', 'Pretty Thing', 'Hey Bo Diddley', 'Road Runner', 'Bring It to Jerome', 'Cops and Robbers', 'Nursery Rhyme', and – not surprisingly – 'Bo Diddley'. Other British groups who revived Diddley compositions include the **Who**, **Yardbirds**, **Manfred Mann**, Downliners Sect, **Johnny Kidd** and the Pirates, and the Zephyrs, who reached Number 27 in the British charts with 'I Can Tell'. One band, the **Pretty Things**, was even named after a Diddley song. Running through the Bo Diddley catalogue, 'Who Do You Love' stands out as the song that has received more cover versions than any other. The list is headed by the **Doors**, **Tom Rush**, **Ronnie Hawkins**, **Quicksilver Messenger Service**, **Juicy Lucy**, and **Bob Seger**. Diddley's influence is just as prevalent today; his songs were featured regularly by British pub rock bands like Chilli Willi and the Red Hot Peppers, **Dr Feelgood**, and the Michigan Flyers. Diddley has returned to prominence in recent years by touring America and Europe with various rock revival shows. He can be seen to good effect in the D. A. Pennebaker film *Keep On Rockin'*.

Big Bo Diddley, far ahead of his time as a guitar player

DILLARDS Originally comprising Doug (born 6 March 1937) and Rodney Dillard (18 May 1942), Dean Webb (28 March 1937) and Mitch Jayne (7 May 1930), the Dillards were richly imbued with the inbred and isolated traditions of the Ozark Mountains in the Southern states of America. Their music was high-powered bluegrass with a strong emphasis on comedy, notably on their second album *Live Almost* in 1964. Doug played banjo, Rodney guitar – both sharing work on fiddle and dobro – Dean Webb played mandolin and Mitch Jayne, once a local DJ, played bass and handled all the introductions and routines. Later they added a young but accomplished fiddle player, Byron Berline, for occasional gigs and sessions, most notably their more old-timey album *Pickin' and Fiddlin'* (1965).

The group arrived in LA in 1963 and were signed by the (then) essentially folk-blues label Elektra. A shared management brought them into early contact with the **Byrds**. The new electric sound turned Doug Dillard's head and he left, unhappy about the group's direction. By 1968 he had teamed up with ex-Byrd **Gene Clark** to form the short-lived but highly influential Dillard and Clark.

The Dillards, with Herb Pederson replacing Doug, trod initially well and tastefully between country and rock on two albums, *Wheatstraw Suite* (1968) and *Copperfields* (1969). Pederson left a year later and was replaced by Billy Ray Latham. It was at this point that the group strayed further from its original path, featuring electric instruments with greater regularity on albums like *Roots and Branches* (Liberty, 1972) and *Tribute to the American Duck* (1973).

DION AND THE BELMONTS

With the possible exception of the **Four Seasons**, Dion and the Belmonts were the finest and most influential white vocal group to emerge on the US East Coast during the post-rock'n'roll era. The group's leader was Dion DiMucci, who was born on 18 July 1939, in the Bronx, New York, the son of a singer and an actress, and who started singing at the age of five. He made his first professional appearance on Paul Whiteman's *Teen Club* TV show in Philadelphia in 1954. By 1957 he had formed his own street-corner group, Dion and the Timberlanes, and recorded one unsuccessful single, 'The Chosen Few' for the Mohawk label in New York. In 1958, he formed a new group featuring Fred Milano (second tenor), Angelo D'Aleo (first tenor) and Carlo Mastrangelo (baritone) and named them the Belmonts after the main Bronx thoroughfare where they lived.

They signed with the newly formed Laurie label and made one unsuccessful single before recording 'I Wonder Why', an inane but engaging vocal workout which reached Number 22 in America. The group followed up with two more American hits, 'No-one Knows' and 'Don't Pity Me', before securing a worldwide hit with the now classic 'Teenager in Love'. That same year, D'Aleo was conscripted and the group continued as a trio, notching up more hits with 'Where Or When' (Number 3 in America) and 'When You Wish upon a Star'. They were, by this time, the most popular young white vocal group in America.

Late in 1960, Dion was persuaded by his management to break with the Belmonts and pursue a solo career. The Belmonts joined another label, Sabina, and achieved moderate American success in 1961–3 with 'Tell Me Why' (Number 18) and 'Come On Little Angel' (Number 25) but it was Dion who went on to major stardom. Initially he scored with 'Lonely Teenager' in November 1960, a fairly typical 'rock-aballad' which reached the Top 20 in America. But his next two releases flopped and it seemed as if his solo career had lost its impetus. Then he stormed back late in 1961 with a newly adopted style that could be described as early punk-rock. 'Runaround Sue' reached Number 1, as did the sequel, 'The Wanderer' and from then on Dion appeared to be commercially infallible. His next four records – 'Lovers Who Wander', 'Sandy', 'Little Diane' and 'Love Came to Me' – all reached the American Top 10.

Late in 1962, Dion moved to Columbia (CBS in the UK), but did not let the label's then middle-of-the-road orientation affect his music. Rather than adapt a cabaret image like so many of his contemporaries, he grew funkier. Four more hits followed – 'Ruby Baby' (Number 2), 'Donna the Prima Donna', 'Drip Drop' and 'This Little Girl' – before his sudden fall from popularity early in 1964. This has been attributed to American Beatlemania, which obviously had some bearing. But, in fact, he suffered from a serious narcotics problem (despite his ostensibly boy-next-door image) and spent most of 1964–5 in seclusion. During this time he released a series of R&B numbers – 'Johnny B. Goode', 'Chicago Blues', 'Hoochie Koochie Man', and 'Spoonful' – long before they became fashionable in American pop circles. They met with little success despite their excellence.

In 1967, Dion re-emerged to re-unite with the Belmonts and released two excellent singles ('Mr Movin' Man' and 'Berimbau') and an album on ABC, but with little success; in 1969, however, he achieved a meteoric comeback (ironically on his old label, Laurie) with 'Abraham, Martin and John' which reached Number 2 in America and heralded the new 'folkie' and introspective Dion. This new Dion was not that new in fact. As early as 1963, he had recorded simple folk songs on the B-sides of his Columbia hits and, it is said, wished to pursue a career similar to fellow Columbia act, **Bob Dylan**, but was dissuaded by his management. He signed with Warner Brothers in 1970, and then recorded a series of albums as a singer-songwriter, at one time recording under **Phil Spector**, who has long considered him one of rock's greatest talents. *Streetheart* (1976) was Dion's last solo album.

DIRE STRAITS Formed in 1976 in Deptford, South-East London, Dire Straits emerged at the height of punk but had little in common with that movement, eventually acquiring mainstream rock supergroup status. Successive albums have sold in huge quantities worldwide, owing much of their success to the characteristic, Dylan-influenced vocal delivery and virtuoso guitar-picking of leader Mark Knopfler.

Knopfler was in his late twenties and had been through two other careers (journalist and teacher) before embarking on a career in music. Over this time he had absorbed a great many musical influences (most notably **Bob Dylan** and **J.J. Cale**) and his skills as a songwriter and guitarist had matured fully, two factors that contributed greatly to Dire Straits' early acceptance in serious music circles.

After joining forces with his flatsharers, brother David (guitar) and John Illsley (bass), Knopfler added drummer Pick Withers to the line-up and they started to gig on the London pub circuit. Eventually they made a demo for £120 which included 'Sultans of Swing', their all-time classic, and this was picked up on by Radio London DJ Charlie Gillett. As a result, the record companies swarmed round to sign the group; in 1978 they signed to Phonogram who released 'Sultans of Swing' plus an album *Dire Straits*, which, although the critics admired it for its slick professionalism, the fans in the UK largely ignored. The album was more suited to American rock tastes, however, and it was therefore more acceptable for radio airplay than most of what was coming out of Britain at the time. Suddenly they had a US hit single and album on their hands.

This success was repeated elsewhere including back in the UK, where the single peaked at Number 9 and the album reached Number 5; after this Dire Straits quickly became an enormously successful international act. The LP *Communiqué*, released in 1979, differed little from its predecessor and also sold well worldwide. After its release, David Knopfler left the group to go solo. In 1980, another LP, *Making Movies*, featured Roy Bittan from **Bruce Springsteen**'s E Street Band who gave the album a fresher sound. For the 1980 tour, the band were joined by guitarist Hal Lindes and keyboard player Alan Clark.

Meanwhile, Mark Knopfler's reputation as a guitarist continued to grow and he left the group temporarily to do some work with Bob Dylan and **Steely Dan**. There was therefore a lengthy gap before the release of the fourth LP *Love*

Sultans of Swing Dire Straits in 1983: from the left, Mark Knopfler, John Illsley, Hal Lindes, Terry Williams and Alan Clark

Over Gold in 1982, which was produced by Knopfler and sold even better than the previous albums. Knopfler was now one of the most respected men in rock and found himself in great demand, writing film scores (*Local Hero*, *Cal* and *Comfort and Joy*) and producing Bob Dylan's *Infidel* and **Aztec Camera**'s *Knife*. In 1984 the live set album *Alchemy* was released, but the fans had to wait until 1985 for the next studio album, *Brothers in Arms*. Needless to say, it was a best-seller worldwide. That summer Dire Straits took part in Live Aid (*see* **Band Aid**) to cap yet another very successful year.

In commercial terms Dire Straits, and especially Mark Knopfler, had proved themselves among the most successful acts since the Seventies, selling in the region of twenty million albums worldwide. Yet, the excellent 'Sultans of Swing' apart, Dire Straits' releases have often been criticized for their blandness, and the suspicion remains that Knopfler is more of a highly-skilled artisan than a genuinely original talent.

DISCO An abbreviation of *discothèque* (French for dance club) the word 'disco' initially described specifically black dance music, although in the Seventies it came to be used for any cool, trendy dance music. The term soon became *passé*, however, and although the dance market did not disappear, new phrases to describe the music were invented by those who sold it.

Providing accompaniment to dance had always been one of two major functions of black music as far back as the blues and jazz of the Twenties and even further – the other was expressing emotion. White rock'n'roll was lifted directly from black dance music, and one of the great appeals of Tamla Motown in the Sixties was its easy danceability. By the early Seventies however, dancing had become extremely unfashionable and the vogue was for incredibly pompous white rock bands performing interminable, pretentious 'pieces'. But still, in small enclaves in the north of England like the Blackpool Mecca and the Wigan Casino, fanatics danced to obscure Fifties and Sixties R&B records which came to be termed 'Northern Soul'.

Meanwhile in the south of England, in Europe and in the gay community, a return to the 'physicality' or danceability inherent in black-influenced pop music became evident. In the United States, a new white generation embraced new black sounds produced not by the major recording companies but by smaller independents away

from New York and Los Angeles. The TK group in Miami, Philadelphia International, and All Platinum in New Jersey were just a few that blossomed in the Seventies. Dance records like **James Brown**'s 'Get on the Good Foot' and the **(Detroit) Spinners**' 'I'll Be Around' were hits in 1972, and the next year the cool insouciant rhythm behind Timmy Thomas' 'Why Can't We Live Together', the drive of **Stevie Wonder**'s 'Superstition' and 'Higher Ground', and the glide of **Eddie Kendricks**' 'Keep On Truckin'' made them equally popular. The record industry, however, always slow to react to grass-roots movements, never quite grasped the significance – until the appearance of the word 'rock' in song titles alerted them to the fact that it was the suitability of the tracks for dancing that was largely responsible for their success. **George McCrae**'s 'Rock Your Baby' and the Hues Corporation's 'Rock the Boat' signalled a new, lighter type of dance record with a less aggressive rhythm, a more hummable melody and therefore a broader appeal. McCrae's stable-mates **K.C. and the Sunshine Band** eventually milked the Miami style most proficiently, while Philadelphian acts like the Tramps and People's Choice, and the New Jersey-based group the Moments were all successful 'disco' acts, although they had recorded for several years in blissful ignorance of the word. The style flourished for much of the period 1974-8, and a surprising number of tracks still sounded fresh long after the industry-dubbed boom was said to be over – Tavares and the Real Thing, for example, had hits in 1986 with re-mixed Seventies disco tracks.

At this time, the success of a disco record depended heavily on support from club DJs (though this support was not enough on its own – if the customers wouldn't dance to a given track, he couldn't make them), and this led to the development of the cult of the DJ. The club factor, too, was responsible for the tyranny of the 'bpm' (beats per minute), which were voguishly quoted on the record's label. Since disco relied so much more on a strong beat than on expressive singing, this was also a period when hit-making came into the province of producers, like the Europeans Frank Farian, **Giorgio Moroder**, Pete Bellotte, and Mario Malavasi. For a while quality soul/R&B singers suffered, but they were soon able to adapt – **Marvin Gaye**'s 'Got To Give It Up' and **Diana Ross**' 'Love Hangover' were among the best songs of the period, while others,

like **Johnnie Taylor**'s 'Disco Lady' were less happy compromises.

In disco music, the gay scene was reflected most overtly by Sylvester (1978's 'You Make Me Feel (Mighty Real)' was his best) and **Village People** ('Y.M.C.A.', 'In the Navy', 'Go West'), while the mainstream pop scene best captured the genre in the soundtrack to the John Travolta movie *Saturday Night Fever*, which made the **Bee Gees** household names again. If any image of the Seventies disco boom persists, it is likely to be the Travolta one.

DIXIE CUPS Comprising Barbara Ann Hawkins (born 1943), Rosa Lee Hawkins (1944), and Joan Marie Johnson (1945), the Dixie Cups were a black vocal trio discovered at a New Orleans talent contest by bandleader **Joe Jones**. They were still attending Southern University when 'Chapel of Love' – a song originally written for the **Ronettes** by **Phil Spector** and others – reached the top of the charts on Red Bird in 1964. Four other hits followed: 'People Say', 'You Should Have Seen the Way He Looked at Me', 'Little Bell' and the semi-traditional New Orleans chant 'Iko Iko'. When Red Bird folded in 1966, the group recorded for ABC/Paramount without success.

DIXIE HUMMINGBIRDS A gospel group known to rock audiences through their association with **Paul Simon** in the early Seventies, the Dixie Hummingbirds were founded by James L. Davis in Greenville, South Carolina, in 1928. They gained national prominence in the black gospel field during the Forties, their harmonies built around the rollicking deep bass of William Bobo and the versatile lead of Ira Tucker, and their innovative, frenzied showmanship established the stage precedent for the **James Browns** of soul music. With the 1952 addition of alternate lead James Walker and guitarist Howard Carroll, they began a 20-year string of gospel/R&B hits for the Peacock label. In 1973, they were heavily featured as backing vocalists on Paul Simon's album, *There Goes Rhymin' Simon*: one of its songs, 'Loves Me Like a Rock', was released as a single under the credit of Paul Simon with the Dixie Hummingbirds and reached Number 2 in the US. In 1979, the Hummingbirds made further inroads into the rock market with the album *We Love You Like a Rock*, its tracks including their own version of the Simon song and of **Stevie Wonder**'s 'Jesus Children of America', with Wonder on keyboards. *See also* **Gospel Music**

DIXON, FLOYD A West Coast R&B singer and pianist who recorded extensively in the late Forties and early Fifties, Floyd Dixon was a protégé of the influential **Charles Brown**. He first recorded in 1947 for the Supreme label of Los Angeles, switching to the Biharis' Modern label in 1949 where he scored with 'Dallas Blues'. His lazy, dragged-out vocals and tinkling piano followed the tradition set by **Nat 'King' Cole** and Charles Brown. Around 1950, Dixon signed to Aladdin, teaming up with Johnny Moore's Three Blazers, which initially featured Brown on lead vocals. Sixteen sides were cut before Dixon went solo, this time working with arranger **Maxwell Davis**. After hitting the charts with 'Tired, Broke and Busted' and 'Call Operator 210', his popularity began to slacken off. In 1953, he signed to Specialty, then in 1958 to Chess and several smaller labels – but without too much success. Dixon just couldn't adjust to the influx of rock'n'roll and the changing public taste in R&B.

DIXON, WILLIE Born in Vicksburg, Mississippi, on 1 July 1915, Willie Dixon made a contribution to postwar urban blues which stands as a major and energizing force that subsequently laid the basic foundations for the popular music of today. In his combined roles as composer-producer-studio bassist-A&R man for Chess records in the Fifties and Sixties, he was responsible for hit recordings by **Muddy Waters**, **Chuck Berry**, **Bo Diddley**, **Howlin' Wolf**, **Little Walter**, **Sonny Boy Williamson**, **Buddy Guy**, **Otis Rush**, and others. His compositions include 'Hoochie Coochie Man', 'My Babe', 'Spoonful', 'You Shook Me', 'Whole Lotta Love', 'I Just Want to Make Love to You', 'Little Red Rooster' and 'Seventh Son'. Dixon's songs have been recorded by such artists as the **Rolling Stones**, **Led Zeppelin**, **Ten Years After**, **Jeff Beck**, Savoy Brown, the **Animals**, and the **Spencer Davis Group**.

DOGGETT, BILL Born in Philadelphia on 6 February 1916, Bill Doggett became a pianist in Jimmy Gorham's Band in 1935, and the band's leader in 1938. He soon relinquished the position to Lucky Millinder, though remaining with the band until 1949 when he succeeded Bill Davis in **Louis Jordan**'s Tympani Five. In 1952 he began fronting his own combo, recording prolifically for the King label over some nine years, the peak of his career coming in 1956 with 'Honky Tonk', a jogging instrumental featuring Clifford Scott's sax and Billy Butler's deft guitar. A succession of smaller hits followed before Doggett moved to Warner in 1961. He subsequently recorded for Columbia, Sue, ABC, and Roulette.

DOLBY, THOMAS Born on 14 October 1958, Thomas Dolby was an original, indeed eccentric, figure amid the flood of electronic pop acts inspired by the **Human League** in the late Seventies. He had been experimenting with electronics since the early part of the decade, inspired by Brian Eno (of **Roxy Music**) and **Kraftwerk**, and had worked as live sound mixer and occasional keyboard player for the likes of **Lene Lovich** and Bruce Wooley's Camera Club. A number of unsuccessful indie singles preceded his 1981 hit, 'Europa and the Pirate Twins', which was featured on his debut album, *The Golden Age of Wireless*, released in 1982. The album actually produced three more singles that year and the next: 'Airwaves', 'Radio Silence', and 'Windpower', the last reaching Number 31 in the UK. 1983's 'She Blinded Me With Science' only reached Number 69 in the UK but the American mix reached Number 5 in the US. American success effectively made his name around the world, and also led to a number of producing roles, most notably with **George Clinton**, with whom he also composed and played, and Prefab Sprout's *Steve McQueen*. In 1984 he produced his second album, *The Flat Earth*. American involvements took Dolby away from Britain, at one point resulting in a collaboration with **Stevie Wonder** and **Herbie Hancock**. In June 1985, Dolby unveiled Dolby's Cube, a studio band whose debut single, 'Get Out of My Cube', boasted Clinton, Lovich and members of Parliament and **Earth, Wind and Fire**. At the time of writing (spring 1987), Dolby was working on an album from his star-studded studio band.

DOLLAR Thanks to a combination of pouting good looks, the dazzling production skills of **Trevor Horn** and a sharp collection of soft electro-pop dance tunes, blonde girl/boy duo Dollar became the apotheosis of early Eighties pop packaging.

David Van Day and Therese Bazaar took such disposable pop classics as 'Love's Gotta Hold On Me', 'Hand Held in Black and White' and 'Give Me Back My Heart' into the UK Top 20 during 1979–82, and although they were the recipients of a great deal of derision at the time, they earned a modicum of retrospective critical respect. This was entirely due to the involvement of Horn who later went on to the glories of **Frankie Goes to Hollywood** and the ZTT label. These later successes were no doubt a factor in the re-formation of Dollar in 1986 after Van Day and Bazaar had had unsuccessful solo stints.

DOMINO, FATS Born Antoine Domino in New Orleans, on 26 February 1928, Fats Domino has been playing piano publicly since he was ten. His first engagement was at the Hideaway Club where bassist Billy Diamond's band dubbed him 'Fats'. Lew Chudd, president of Hollywood Imperial, seeking New Orleans talent, signed him up in 1948.

Domino worked a rich cultural heritage. For over two hundred years New Orleans has proved a unique meeting point for Spanish, French, West African, Creole, Protestant American, and Caribbean influences. 'Hey La Bas', from Domino's first session, unconsciously assimilates African and Catholic elements. The majority of slaves brought into New Orleans came from Dahomey (now Benin) and were practitioners of 'vodun' or 'voodoo'. Legba, the omniscient god of crossroads, luck and fertility, became identified with St Peter, the keeper of the keys. African ritual was preserved because Catholic Orleans preferred to defuse by absorption rather than engage in a theological war of attrition. Papa Legba underwent a transition to Limba, Laba, and finally to 'Hey La Bas'.

Another example is the instrumental 'Second Line Jump' made in 1952. Repetitious to a fault, it nevertheless storms along defying anyone to stay seated. But title and repetitions imply more. Jazz may have been nurtured in the clubs and brothels of Storyville, but it was not born there. It began in a thousand places. Just one of them was the 'second line' in a funeral parade, characterized by lively 2/4 music and ecstatic dancing.

A final example of the fusions in New Orleans music is the custom of 'lining out'. The call-and-response pattern, obvious in gospel and soul, and imitated instrumentally in blues and jazz, represents a wedding of African chant and British psalmody where lines from the preacher were repeated by an illiterate congregation.

Nor did Domino spring from some personal artistic limbo. Piano-playing contemporaries working New Orleans included Salvador Doucette, **Amos Milburn**, **Little Richard**, Roy Byrd

(**Professor Longhair**), Leon T. Gross (Archibald), Joseph Pleasant (Smilin' Joe), S. Q. Reeder (**Esquerita**) and Eddie Bocage (Eddie Bo). The prime influence, though, was an outsider, boogie pianist Albert Ammons who died the year of Fats' recording debut. Ammons' trilling right hand, played off against the rolling anchor of the left, fits Fats perfectly.

Fats Domino sold a million with his first release, 'The Fat Man', the second number he cut on 10 December 1949. An ebullient eight-bar blues, it has a relatively long piano introduction before he broke into that familiar 'wah wah' vocal approximation of a harp. On the flip was the first song from that first session, 'Detroit City Blues', a powerful side opening with the inimitable Domino right hand, then the horns and Domino shouting the blues in sudden excitement. With Frank Fields' remorseless bass and the endless sax riffs, the die was cast.

Domino worked closely with trumpeter and bandleader, **Dave Bartholomew**, writing and arranging with great success for the first six years. Bartholomew found Domino's approach difficult – allegedly the Fat Man couldn't or wouldn't keep time – but the hits kept coming. There was always something to hold attention. 'Little Bee' (Imperial 5065) is a most attractive performance with a stinging, buzzing little guitar figure from Ernest McLean, substantial piano, and memorable lyrics –

'She's 42 in the hip, 31 in the bust
She's got big fine legs
And she knows how to strut her stuff!'

Fats proved deceptively varied. 'Hideaway Blues' (Imperial 5077), yet another from the debut session, employs a similar opening gambit to 'Detroit City Blues' and there is the repetition of sound and structure usual in his work. That it does not become monotonous is a tribute to the charm of this music, and there are often moments of leavening humour – the sly reference to 'catch a body coming through the rye', for example. Recorded in December 1951 but not released until March the following year was Fats' second gold disc, the bland 'Goin' Home' (Imperial 5180) and there were several releases before Fats came up with a *bona fide* classic in 'Mardi Gras in New Orleans'. Cut in October 1952, it is virtually a cover of the Professor Longhair song replete with what Jelly Roll Morton would have termed the 'Latin tinge'. It's a great number, atypical for Fats, employing rhumbalero rhythms and faultlessly

executed. Coupled with 'Going to the River', it sold a million in 1953. This latter song exhibits a new assertiveness with just a suggestion of ossification, twelve-bar slickness, that points to the greater simplifications of the rock-'n'roll era.

From 1955 to 1960 Fats was at his commercial peak, although some would argue a decline in artistry. Despite riotous acclaim coast-to-coast, there were decided lapses in the quality of recorded output – for example, the appalling 'I'm in the Mood for Love' which only sold because it was slapped on the reverse of 'I'm Walkin'', a considerable rocker. That was in February 1957. But the first real smash came with 'Ain't That A Shame' in April 1955. Cornelius Coleman drums up a storm, while Walter Nelson's guitar chops along underneath. From then on the hits came thick and fast – the melancholy 'Blueberry Hill', recorded in Los Angeles and released in September 1956; 'Blue Monday' cut in New Orleans a year earlier but held over; 'Whole Lotta Lovin'' in 1958; 'I'm Ready' in 1959; and a slow slide into straight pop culminating in the string-laden 'Walking to New Orleans' in 1960.

Much of his success rested on a relaxed command of a characteristic New Orleans sound, slightly lugubrious, rolling with effortless charm. It also depended on the long service and high calibre of sessionmen like Jimmie Davis, Frank Fields (bass), Ernest McLean, Roy Montrell, Walter Nelson, Harrison Verrett (guitar), Wendell Duconge (alto), Buddy Hagans, Herb Hardesty (tenor), Cornelius Coleman and Earl Palmer (drums). And, on some rock'n'roll sides such as 'The Big Beat' in 1957, Fats was replaced at piano by **Allen Toussaint**, **James Booker**, or Edward Frank. Fats also played on Imperial sessions for **Smiley Lewis**, **Lloyd Price**, and **Joe Turner**. His songs have been recorded by **The Band**, **Chuck Berry**, **Pat Boone**, **Johnny Burnette**, **Bobby Charles**, **Ronnie Hawkins**, **Buddy Holly**, **Jerry Lee Lewis**, **Rick Nelson**, **Elvis Presley**, **Little Richard**, Warren Storm, and **Larry Williams**. His influence in the growth of Jamaican ska and reggae is undeniable.

He went to ABC in Nashville in 1963 and, although he never recovered his former glory, much of the material was agreeable, especially 'There Goes My Heart Again' and 'Sally Was a Good Old Girl'. His last, modest success came with a version of the **Beatles**' 'Lady Madonna', released in 1968 on Reprise.

DOMINOES Recruited by New York composer, pianist and singing coach, Billy Ward, from among his best students in 1950 the Dominoes' line-up was **Clyde McPhatter**, James Van Loan (tenors), Joe Lamount (baritone), and Bill Brown (bass). Brown sang lead on 'Sixty Minute Man', the best-selling R&B disc of 1951, while McPhatter wailed 'Have Mercy Baby', an R&B Number 1 the following year. Producer **Ralph Bass** rang the changes from jump blues to highly emotive churchy ballads, all on Federal. With a succession of lead singers, including **Jackie Wilson** and Gene Mumford, the Dominoes also recorded for King, Jubilee, Decca, Liberty ('Stardust' and 'Deep Purple' were two of the group's symphonic black pop hits in 1957), and Melbourne. *See also* **Clyde McPhatter**; **Jackie Wilson**

DON AND DEWEY Although they never enjoyed chart success themselves, Don and Dewey's songs proved to be big sellers when revived by the Olympics ('Big Boy Pete'), the Premiers ('Farmer John'), **Dale and Grace**, and Donny and Marie of the **Osmonds** ('I'm Leaving It Up to You'). Don 'Sugarcane' Harris and Dewey Terry had formed a duo in their native Los Angeles in 1955 after singing with the Squires. Records for Spot and Shade led to a contract with Specialty, where records like 'Jungle Hop', 'Koko Joe', and 'Justine' adhered to the fast and frantic rock-'n'roll formula common to many of Art Rupe's post-**Little Richard** signings. After further discs for Rush and Highland, each concentrated on his own career. Terry recorded for Tumbleweed, while Harris played blues violin with **Johnny Otis**, **Frank Zappa**, and **John Mayall**.

DONAHUE, TOM A pioneer of rock on FM radio in the US during the late Sixties, Tom 'Big Daddy' Donahue was born on 21 May 1928, in South Bend, Indiana. His professional radio career began with a DJ stint at station WTIP in Charleston, Virginia, after which he joined WBIG in Philadelphia. He settled in San Francisco during 1961 and presented Top 40-oriented shows on station KYA. In 1964, with fellow DJ Bob Mitchell, he promoted the Cow Palace shows and the **Beatles**' and **Rolling Stones**' appearances there. In the same year as they set up Autumn records, using the KYA studios to record in, they had a national hit with their second release, Bobby Freeman's 'C'mon and Swim'. Sylvester 'Sly' Stewart joined the company as arranger and producer and even recorded some songs himself. Donahue himself recorded such bands as the **Beau Brummels**, the Charlatans, the Great Society, even the **Grateful Dead**, and helped negotiate **Jefferson Airplane**'s recording contract with RCA. However, for various reasons – mostly financial – Autumn records never took off, and folded in 1966.

Donahue's involvement with the San Francisco music scene was total. In the summer of 1965 he opened a North Beach club, Mothers, with the help of Mitchell, where they put on outside bands like the **Byrds** and the **Lovin' Spoonful**. Mitchell died in 1966, but Donahue continued in his various roles as DJ and producer. In 1968, after the demise of Autumn records, he left KYA and set up the revolutionary KMPX-FM station and later KSAN-FM. Among the various groups that he managed were Stoneground, the Fast Bucks, and Bad Rice. If not as well remembered as his contemporary **Bill Graham**, Donahue – who died on 28 April 1975 – epitomized the early San Francisco approach to music. *See also* **Radio (US)**

DONEGAN, LONNIE The chief popularizer of skiffle music during the Fifties, Lonnie Donegan was born Anthony Donegan on 29 April 1931, in Glasgow. He was immersed in American folk music as a youth and at 17 bought his first guitar. A year later, he made his first appearance with a jazz band before being called up for National Service in 1949. He played drums with the Wolverines Jazz Band in the Army and, on discharge, played banjo with Ken Colyer's band where he was first exposed to the 'skiffle' style. In 1951, Donegan formed his own group and after appearing on the same bill as his idol, Lonnie Johnson, at the Royal Festival Hall, he changed his name to 'Lonnie'. By 1953, he had joined **Chris Barber**'s band on banjo, and in 1954 he recorded 'Rock Island Line' in a skiffle style as part of Barber's *New Orleans Joys* album.

Released as a single in 1956, 'Rock Island Line' unexpectedly reached the charts and caused a sensation with its then wild and undisciplined sound. It went on to become one of the first British records to reach the American Top 20. Within months, the sales of guitars shot up as hundreds of skiffle groups were formed throughout the UK. Leaving Barber's band to go solo in 1956, Donegan scored again with 'Lost John' (Number 2 in Britain) and from then on registered an incredible 24 consecutive hits (a figure topped only by

Cliff Richard) including 'Cumberland Gap', 'Dixie Darling', 'Putting on the Style', 'Battle of New Orleans', 'My Old Man's a Dustman' and 'Pick a Bale of Cotton'.

Branching out into comedy and variety in the early Sixties, Donegan developed an act that stood him in good stead for the rest of his career, though it did detract from what 'authenticity' he had. His run of hits terminated abruptly in 1963 with Beatlemania, but he still performed in cabaret and at country music festivals. He it was who struck the first immortal chords for Britain's rock empire in the Fifties – an achievement acknowledged by his 1978 album of re-recordings of his old hits (*Puttin' on the Style*, United Artists), on which appeared many of the musicians he influenced. They included **Adam Faith**, **Leo Sayer**, **Ringo Starr**, **Elton John**, Ron Wood, Brian May, Mick Ralphs, and **Rory Gallagher**. *See also* **Skiffle**

DONNER, RAL Born in Chicago on 10 February 1943, Ralph Stuart Donner first recorded in 1958 for Scottie. Moving to New York, he signed with Gone, and reached the Top 20 with 'The Girl of My Best Friend' (a song from **Elvis Presley**'s *Elvis Is Back* album) in 1961. As Presley became more of a Neapolitan balladeer than a rock'n'roller, Donner continued to sing in the manner to which early Elvis fans had been accustomed. His heavily stylized, hot-potato-in-the-mouth vocals smouldered through a string of blistering soul ballads. They included 'You Don't Know What You've Got' (Number 4), 'Please Don't Go', 'She's Everything' (another Top 20 hit), and 'What a Sad Way to Love Someone'. Donner recorded also for Tau (1960), Reprise (the fine 'I Got Burned' in 1963), Fontana (1965), Red Bird (1966), Rising Sons (where he was produced by **Billy Swan** in 1968), Mid Eagle, M. J. (1971), Chicago Fire, and Sunlight (1972).

DONOVAN Born Donovan Leitch on 10 May 1946, in Glasgow, Donovan started as one of the hundreds of early **Bob Dylan** imitators who flourished in the British folk clubs in the mid-Sixties. Appearances on the TV show *Ready, Steady, Go* – with a guitar sticker proclaiming 'This Machine Kills', omitting the vital word 'Fascists' from the slogan originally coined by **Woody Guthrie** – led to a contract with Pye, and his first hit, 'Catch the Wind' (1965). His style was so similar to Dylan's that the British folk scene was unsure how to react.

Donovan then switched from Dylan to flower power, which by 1966 was blossoming across the Atlantic. With their soft-rock backing, and rhythmic, trance-like tunes, his songs 'Sunshine Superman' (1966) and 'Mellow Yellow' (1967) brilliantly captured the mood of the new movement, and both became million-sellers. The resulting album, *Sunshine Superman* (1967), which included 'Young Girl Blues' and 'Hampstead Incident' amongst others, and was produced by **Mickie Most**, saw Donovan at his observational best, and was a deserved classic. Donovan moved on – or off – to publicly renounce drugs, take up with Eastern mysticism and then leave Mickie Most in the search for a musical identity. Along the way he has recorded an album of children's songs (*HMS Donovan*, 1971), scored four feature films, and interrupted his cosmic philosophizing for a study of spacemen's toilet arrangements ('The Intergalactive Laxative', on *Cosmic Wheels*, 1973). In 1974, he wrote a theatrical stage show called *7-Tease*, that dealt with the fate of hippie mind-searching and drugs. The accompanying album, produced by Norbert Putnam in Nashville, showed he was still developing – this time as a mainstream rock balladeer. 1977 found him touring again for the first time in years, and he also renewed his partnership with Mickie Most for an album, *Donovan*, on Most's RAK label. In 1981, he appeared at the Cambridge Folk Festival and seemed set for a recording and performing comeback, though little has appeared on record since.

Donovan began his career in the mid-Sixties as a Dylan imitation

DOOBIE BROTHERS Starting life as an archetypal West Coast boogie band, the Doobie Brothers developed into a sharp, sophisticated yet bland AOR outfit during their 12-year career. The group was formed in 1970 when John Hartman (drums) moved from West Virginia to San Jose, California, intending to re-form **Moby Grape** with Skip Spence. He was introduced by Spence to Tom Johnston (guitar) and with Dave Shogren (bass) they formed a band called Pud. In the course of playing the San Francisco Bay Area they met Pat Simmons (guitar) and one night over a 'doobie' (California slang for a joint) changed their name to the Doobie Brothers.

They were signed to Warner Bros by A&R man Ted . Templeman on the strength of a demo tape; Templeman (former leader of **Harpers Bizarre**) then made his production debut with the band. Their first success came in mid-1972 with the Top 20 US hit, 'Listen to the Music', by which time they had added second drummer Michael Hossack and replaced Shogren with Tiran Porter. From this time they had a string of hits based on the infectious rhythm and phrasing of 'Music'. In 1973 Hossack left to join Bonaroo; he was replaced by Keith Knudsen. The following year they were joined by guitarist Jeff 'Skunk' Baxter, late of **Steely Dan**.

Stampede (1975) was their second album with the new line-up, and it included a revival of the **Holland, Dozier and Holland** classic, 'Take Me in Your Arms (Rock Me)'. However, the Doobies' sound was by now becoming stereotyped and drawing critical flak; this died down when Tom Johnston was replaced by Michael McDonald (another ex-member of Steely Dan), and McDonald and Baxter were responsible for much of the material on the group's sixth album, *Takin' It to the Streets* (1976). *Livin' on the Fault Line* (1977) consolidated their AOR appeal, while *Minute by Minute* (1978) was heavily disco-influenced, and included the Grammy-winning single 'What a Fool Believes', composed by Michael McDonald with **Kenny Loggins**.

Baxter left in 1979 and Hartman shortly after, and for *One Step Closer* (1980) the band recruited John McFee from Clover, drummer Chet McCracken and saxophonist/keyboard player Cornelius Bumpuson. It turned out to be the band's last studio album, and they bade farewell with a double live set, *Farewell Tour*, which was released in 1983. Of the band's various one-time members, Michael McDonald has made the most impact, both as a solo artist and in partnership with **Patti LaBelle** – their single, 'On My Own', was a big transatlantic hit in 1986.

DOOLEYS Led by singer/songwriter Jim, the Dooleys were a family group from Manchester who had a handful of UK hits during 1977–80 with their ultra-commercial mainstream dance pop.

Paying their dues on the Northern club cabaret circuit, the Dooleys signed to GTO in 1977 and had their first hit with 'Think I'm Gonna Fall in Love You', a UK Number 13. Further hit singles followed, the best seller being 'Wanted', a Number 3 in 1979, as well as a heavily TV-promoted Top 10 album *The Best of the Dooleys* (1980), before the hit-making formula dried up on them. They continued to trade on past glories on the international cabaret circuit well into the Eighties.

DOORS A Los Angeles band whose influence has spanned the years since their 1965 formation, the Doors came together when would-be poet Jim Morrison (born in Melbourne, Florida, on 8 December 1943) met keyboard player Ray Manzarek (Chicago, 12 February 1935) in the film-making department of UCLA. They subsequently teamed up with ex-jugband guitarist Bobby Krieger (Los Angeles, 8 January 1946) and drummer John Densmore (Los Angeles, 1 December 1945). They took their name from William Blake (via Aldous Huxley) – 'If the doors of perception were cleansed/All things would appear infinite' – and Morrison's lyrics and performances concentrated on acting out images and obsessions from his own poetry.

After performing as a support band around LA, the Doors succeeded in being fired from their most important booking, at the Whiskey A Go-Go, for performing 'The End', a semi-spoken, semi-improvised musical melodrama filled with apocalyptic imagery and Freudian references: 'Father, I want to kill you/Mother, I want to . . . (piercing shrieks) . . .!' Their show was rather too dramatically convincing for current tastes. However, **Jac Holzman** of Elektra Records had seen them in action, and rewarded their daring with a lucrative contract. Their debut album, *The Doors* (1967), featured a lengthy rendition of 'The End', and 'Light My Fire', an extended, rhythmically tough but melodic invitation to erotic ecstasy. An edited version of this became a Number 1 single in the US. Other successes on the album were 'Break On Through (to the Other Side)' which succinctly expressed the Doors' philosophy, and 'Soul Kitchen', a catchy account of mind/body alienation.

The Doors album worked because the instrumental energy packed enough power to sustain Morrison's dramatics – he projected an image halfway between street punk and depraved poet. The second album, *Strange Days* (1967), smoothed the rough edges off their music and contained their most carefully crafted work. Themes of alienation pervaded the album from the bizarre cover photo, via the haunting ballad, 'People Are Strange', to the lengthy concluding statement 'When the Music's Over' which tied the apocalyptic mood of 'The End' to more specific concerns – the Vietnam war, ecological awareness, and the almost magical significance of rock music. The rich imagery of Morrison's songs, Manzarek's classical/rock keyboards, Krieger's versatile guitar, and Densmore's drumming combined to create the musical energy to sustain their pretensions. Live, the Doors' music was a full-scale attempt at electronic, musical ritual, centring around Morrison's skin-tight leather theatricals.

1968 saw another Number 1 single, 'Hello I Love You', and the album *Waiting for the Sun* which carried the Doors further into political poses, and caused them problems. To 'underground' fans their politics appeared shallow. To promoters and police, their performance of songs announcing 'They've got the guns but we got the numbers!' coupled with Morrison's incitements to sexual frenzy, spelled trouble. It culminated in Morrison's arrest for allegedly exposing himself on stage in Miami, in March 1969. The mood of liberation and psychic exploration which gave the Doors their context for performing had crumbled, and the Doors' musical ritual began to look absurd and over-inflated. Morrison reduced the number of live performances they gave, and his final recordings, *Morrison Hotel* (1970) and *L.A. Woman* (1971), returned to the earthy roots of R&B. The music was tight and beautifully performed, possibly the Doors' best, but seemed somewhat perfunctory. Finally, Morrison left for Paris to concentrate again on poetry, and there he died – suddenly and mysteriously – on 3 July 1971. Without him, the Doors recorded two further albums, demonstrating their musical excellence, but lacking a clarity of focus without Morrison. They disbanded in 1973.

Manzarek recorded two solo albums, formed a band called Nite City, and in

1983 combined with avant-garde composer Philip Glass on a rock version of *Carmina Burana*, the Carl Orff cantata. Densmore and Krieger formed the Butts Band, which broke up after two years.

The Doors were the group who most successfully carried 'underground' music beyond an audience of freaks and students to a mass teen market – they had six Top 20 singles. At his peak, Morrison successfully combined **Elvis Presley**'s physical magnetism with highbrow, intellectual restlessness, claiming Céline and Camus as his major influences. Morrison's charisma, and the Door's chart success, earned them a huge audience, while their music explored the mysteries, totems and taboos of contemporary America.

DOO-WOP

This was the term applied to the singing style of American R&B vocal groups of the Fifties, originating from the fact that the harmony support to lead vocals was often derived from simple phrases like 'doo wop'. Such groups, generally four or five strong, usually consisted of a tenor or baritone lead singer supported by a second tenor, baritone, and bass voices and were thus, basically, musically self-supporting. In fact, many recorded initially with minimal instrumental accompaniment, partly to avoid detracting from intricate vocal harmonies and partly for economy.

The style is also known as 'street-corner music', since some groups actually rehearsed on the street corners of their neighbourhood, singing 'a cappella' (without instruments; literally 'as in chapel'), though often preferring the acoustic qualities of subways or hallways. Doo-wop music had its roots in the late Thirties when the **Ink Spots** climbed to world fame featuring Bill Kenny's high tenor lead and Hoppy Jones' bass voice. The 'jubilee' (multi-voice harmony lead) and 'quartet' (solo lead with harmony support) styles of gospel groups were the inspiration behind the immediate post-war 'race' market success of earliest doo-wop performers the **Orioles** (Natural Records), led by the cool and clear tenor of Sonny Til, and the **Ravens** (National) featuring Jimmy Ricks' bass lead. Coincidentally, these names were precursors of a vast number of 'bird' groups to record during the Fifties – Larks, **Crows**, **Penguins, Flamingos**, etc. The Orioles were also the first group to gain 'mass-market' acceptance when 'Crying in the Chapel' became a national pop hit in 1953. The song's pop success was due to the relative sophistication of the Orioles' delivery which, in contrast to

that of earthier R&B hits, did not immediately give away their colour.

The following year, 1954, was perhaps the turning-point for acceptance of doo-wop (and R&B in general), with the Crows' 'Gee', the **Chords**' 'Sh-Boom' and the Penguins' 'Earth Angel' selling in huge quantities 'across the board', paving the way for the subsequent success and popularity of the **Platters, Coasters, Drifters, Moonglows,** etc. during the rock'n'roll heyday of the mid- and late Fifties. This, in turn, inspired the literally hundreds of similar groups in doo-wop hotbeds like New York and Philadelphia in the east, and Los Angeles in the west, many of which had national hits.

The essence of doo-wop was simplicity, and passing years saw arrangers become more ambitious until vocal harmonies became engulfed in string and brass sections of studio orchestras. The last vestiges of the style are evident *circa* 1962, leading into the era of soul vocal groups where the **Four Tops, Isley Brothers**, etc. perpetuated the lead/harmony format over the sophistication of complex orchestral arrangements.

DOO-WOP, WHITE

The interpretation by white vocal groups of the black harmony sound became a craze in the US during the late Fifties and reached epidemic proportions between 1961 and 1963. The first white doo-woppers were straight copycat outfits like the Crewcuts and the **Diamonds**, but they gave way to white groups whose love of black harmony brought an honest authenticity to their performances. Most of these pioneers – Slades, Aquatones, Mellokings, Capris, **Dion and the Belmonts, Skyliners** – came from the cities of the north-east where European immigration was greatest and where the vocal tradition ran deepest. The first exponents (not in fact 'white' by American WASP standards) sprang from the lower status minority groups – Italians, Puerto Ricans, Poles and Spaniards, etc. Ignoring the candid language of black R&B, their original songs expressed love in Puritan terms.

This immature strain led to a series of hugely popular lullabies by the Mystics ('Hushabye') and the Elegants ('Little Star'). Others revived Tin Pan Alley standards – the Chimes ('Once in a While'), the Dimensions ('Over the Rainbow'), Vito and the Salutations ('Unchained Melody') – as well as dusty R&B hits. The Earls ('Remember Then') and Nino and the Ebbtides ('Juke Box Saturday Night') and the Devotions ('Rip Van Winkle') contributed to

this fierce blast of *déjà vu*. Apart from using bass and falsetto voices in weird and diverting ways, many of the lead singers – Jimmy Beaumont (Skyliners), Lenny Cocco (Chimes), Dion (Belmonts) and Larry Chance (Earls) – were among the finest of their generation. Rangy, piquant, mobile, they had a purity of tone that often escaped the black singers they idolized.

Despite the increasing segregation of R&B radio playlists, most white doo-woppers made the R&B charts because R&B radio stations couldn't tell what colour they really were. That's probably the best tribute that can be paid.

DORSEY, LEE

Born in New Orleans on 24 December 1924, Lee Dorsey enjoyed worldwide success in the mid-Sixties with a series of jaunty dance records on Amy. Beginning with 'Ride Your Pony' in 1965, Dorsey reached Number 44 in the US with 'Get Out of My Life, Woman', Number 8 with 'Working in the Coalmine', and Number 23 with 'Holy Cow'. The last two were Top 10 hits in Britain on Stateside. Formerly a boxer and US Marine, Dorsey first came to national prominence in 1961 when the infectious 'Ya Ya' was a Number 7 hit for Bobby Robinson's Fury label, with 'Do-Re-Mi' as the carefully calculated follow-up. The company collapsed and Dorsey moved to Amy to work with the Marshall Sehorn–**Allen Toussaint** team, with the latter producing his hit recordings. Later singles were unsuccessful and in 1970 Dorsey signed with Polydor to make a concept album called *Yes We Can*, again produced by Toussaint. He remained active within the New Orleans music scene during the Seventies but recorded little, his major release being the 1978 album, *Night People*, on ABC, which consisted entirely of Toussaint compositions. He died of emphysema on 2 December 1986. *See also* **Allen Toussaint**

DOT RECORDS

Formed in 1950 by Randy Wood in Gallatin, Tennessee (near Nashville), Dot Records blossomed within five years into a major concern with acts such as **Pat Boone**, Billy Vaughn and the Hilltoppers, plus one-hit-wonders like Robin Luke, the Shields and the **Del-Vikings**.

Leaving the US Air Force in 1945, Wood opened a neighbourhood appliance shop and started stocking a few records as a customer service. The record sideline quickly took over, and by 1950 'Randy's Record Store' boasted the largest mail-order catalogue in the South. Having bought a small local radio station to advertise his business, Wood began producing records after hours in the station's studio, releasing them on his newly formed Dot label. He had hits with honky-tonk pianist Johnny Maddox and various R&B and hillbilly acts, including the Griffin Brothers, Margie Day, and Mac Wiseman.

In 1952, 'Trying' by a white vocal quartet, the Hilltoppers, reached the national Top 10 and in 1955 Dot signed Pat Boone who rapidly became a Fifties superstar, initially through covering R&B hits for the white masses ('Tutti Frutti', 'Long Tall Sally', 'Ain't That a Shame') and later by adopting a mawkish crooning style on million-sellers like 'It's Too Soon to Know' and 'Love Letters in the Sand'.

Moving from Gallatin to Hollywood in 1956, Dot became one of the first independent labels to license masters from smaller companies, and, although many of these records fell by the wayside, a significant number became hits, including such classics as 'The Fool' by **Sanford Clark**, 'You Cheated' by the Shields, and Robin Luke's 'Susie Darlin''.

By 1963, Pat Boone's fortunes had waned considerably, but Dot scored with three huge instrumental hits, 'Wipeout' (the Surfaris), 'Pipeline' (the Chantays), and 'Boss' by the Rumblers, which, again, had all been leased from small labels. In 1965, Wood sold Dot to Gulf and Western, the film combine responsible for Paramount, and started Ranwood Records.

DOVELLS The Dovells had a series of eight raucous dance craze hits on Cameo-Parkway between 1961 and 1964. Beginning with 'Bristol Stomp' (Number 2), and moving on through 'Bristol Twistin' Annie', 'Hully Gully Baby', a vocal version of 'You Can't Sit Down' (Number 3) and 'Betty in Bermudas', they petered out with the arrival of the British groups. A white quintet from Philadelphia, their lead singer, **Len Barry** (born 6 December 1942), went on to success as a solo artist, unlike the other members – Arnie Satin (baritone, 11 May 1943), Jerry Summers (first tenor, 29 December 1942), Mike Dennis (3 June 1943), and Danny Brooks (bass, 1 April 1942). On their albums, the Dovells frequently sang in the style of the black doo-wop groups they idolized, but, as Barry said later, 'Sometimes we were great, sometimes we stank.' Barry's subsequent solo hits included '1–2–3' (1965, a million seller), 'Like a Baby' and 'Somewhere' (both 1966). *See also* **Len Barry**

DOWD, TOM A pioneer in the development of post-war recording techniques, Tom Dowd started his career as an engineer for Atlantic Records in 1948. The clarity of the many hit records he worked on for **Joe Turner**, **Ray Charles** and others was much envied by rival companies. Among independent record companies, Atlantic led the way in the use of stereo and eight-track recorders, on which Dowd worked with **Leiber and Stoller** for hits by the **Coasters** and the **Drifters**. He was equally influential at the Stax studios where he engineered sessions by several of the major Memphis soul artists in the Sixties. Eventually he became a fully fledged producer, working with many singers and groups, among them the **Rascals**, **Aretha Franklin**, **Eric Clapton**, **Rod Stewart**, the **Allman Brothers Band**, **Black Oak Arkansas**, **Cher**, **Chicago**, **Wishbone Ash**, **Lynyrd Skynyrd**, and **Meat Loaf**.

DOWNING, BIG AL A talented R&B vocalist and writer, Big Al Downing has recorded since 1956 in the rock-'n'-roll, R&B, soul, and even C&W idioms. Downing recorded first for East West, Whiterock, Challenge, Columbia, and Carlton. Rockers like 'Down on the Farm' incorporated the best of rockabilly guitar styles and usually had a solid New Orleans sound. 'Just around the Corner' and 'Georgia Slop' were especially fine. Soul duets with Little Esther for Lenox were followed by 'Cornbread Row' and 'Soul Medley', recorded in 1968–9 for Silver Fox in Nashville. He had some disco hits for Janus during the Seventies.

DR FEELGOOD (GROUP) One of the few British pub-rock bands of the mid-Seventies to achieve a measure of sales success, Dr Feelgood began life on Canvey Island in the Thames Estuary under the leadership of guitarist Wilko Johnson (real name John Wilkinson). The group took its name from the pseudonym of blues pianist Willie Perryman (see next entry). Johnson had played in local bands the Roamers and the Heap before studying English literature at Newcastle University; on his return to Canvey he was approached by Lee Brilleaux (vocals, harmonica) and John B. Sparks (bass) – schoolmates who shared an interest in R&B – to form Dr Feelgood. With John Martin completing the line-up on drums, the band played its first dates in the Southend area in 1972 and broke into the embryonic London pub circuit two years later. Their first album, *Down*

by the Jetty (United Artists), was released that year; *Malpractice* followed a year later. *Stupidity*, recorded live in Southend and Sheffield, reached Number 1 in the UK album chart during 1976. In March 1977, Johnson walked out during recordings for their fourth album and was replaced by John Mayo; between then and 1981, the Feelgoods produced seven albums of varying quality, and a track from *Private Practice* (1978), 'Milk and Alcohol', became a UK Top Ten hit. *Let It Roll* (1979) was produced by long-time British blues devotee **Mike Vernon**, *A Case of the Shakes* (1980) by **Nick Lowe**. In 1981, Mayo left and a year later Sparks and Martin departed. Still in existence in the mid-Eighties but with a much changed line-up, the Feelgoods continue to keep the spirit of Seventies pub-rock alive. The band's importance lay in helping to pave the way for the punk revolution of 1976–8: bands such as the **Clash**, Vibrators, Chelsea and **Boomtown Rats** owed much to the Feelgoods' boozy raucousness and complete disregard for current musical trends.

DR FEELGOOD (SOLO) This was the pseudonym adopted in 1962 by Atlanta bluesman, Willie Perryman, who had recorded prolifically as Piano Red for RCA/Groove between 1950 and 1958. In that period his best-selling R&B records – 'Rockin' with Red', 'Red's Boogie', 'Wrong Yo Yo' and others – were characterized by gruff, good-humoured singing and a rumbustious piano style. 'Yo Yo' had previously been recorded in 1930 by his brother Rufus Perryman (alias Speckled Red). Piano Red also recorded for Jax, Checker, and Arhoolie. Emerging as Dr Feelgood and the Interns, Willie Perryman made the pop charts with two exuberant rockers, 'Dr Feelgood' and another version of 'Right String but the Wrong Yo Yo', on Okeh. The flip of the first, 'Mr Moonlight', sung by Roy Lee Johnson, was later recorded by the **Beatles** on their *Beatles for Sale* album.

DR HOOK AND THE MEDICINE SHOW A country-oriented rock outfit imbued with a fine sense of the absurd, Dr Hook and the Medicine Show originally comprised Ray Sawyer (vocals, guitar, born 1 February 1937 in Alabama), Dennis Locorriere (vocals, guitar, born 13 June 1949 in New Jersey), William Francis (keyboards, born 16 January 1942 in California), Richard Elswit (guitar, born 6 July 1945 in New York), George Cummings (guitar, steel guitar, born 28 July 1938), Jance Garfat (bass, born 3 March 1944 in California), and John David (drums, born 8 August 1942 in New Jersey), replaced by John Wolters. Originally known as the Chocolate Papers, the group was formed in the late Sixties in New Jersey. Manager Ron Haffkine put them in touch with *Playboy* cartoonist, songwriter and singer Shel Silverstein, who was writing the score for the film *Who Is Harry Kellerman and Why Is He Saying Those Terrible Things about Me?* and asked them to perform it. As a result the group secured a contract with Columbia in 1971.

In 1972 they had their first British and US Top 10 hit with Silverstein's plaintive 'Sylvia's Mother'. 'The Cover of "Rolling Stone"' followed 'Sylvia' into the US Top 10 but was banned in Britain by the BBC for advertising. They recorded three albums for Columbia, *Dr Hook and the Medicine Show*, *Sloppy Seconds* (1972), and *Belly Up* (1973), before leaving the company for Capitol. They were best known at this time as the performers of Silverstein's comic songs – though Silverstein recorded a collection of them himself, *Freakin' at the Freakers' Ball* (Columbia, 1972), and also wrote in a more serious vein for artists like **Johnny Cash** and **Bobby Bare**. *Bankrupt* (1975), however, saw the group expanding their range through versions of songs like 'Only Sixteen'; it also marked the beginning of their move into an AOR vein, developing their countrified rock music with mainstream audiences in mind. The first fruits of this policy were the hit singles 'A Little Bit More' (1976) and 'When You're in Love with a Beautiful Woman' (1979), which went to Number 2 and Number 1 respectively in the UK chart. By the beginning of the Eighties, Dr Hook were more popular abroad than in the US.

Sawyer quit the group in 1983, leaving Locorriere as Dr Hook's focal point. Under his leadership, the group continued as a recording and touring entity until 1985, when the band split up after a final farewell tour of the UK.

DR JOHN (THE NIGHT TRIPPER) A survivor of the darker sides of the music business, and a vehement champion of New Orleans music and musicians, Dr John was born Malcolm (Mac) Rebennack in that city in 1941, and first recorded in 1958 as session guitarist for R&B labels Ace, Ebb, Ric, Ron, and Specialty, while writing and arranging for several artists on these labels – notably **Jerry Byrne** ('Lights

Out', 'Carry On'). He also toured behind local rock stars like Byrne and **Frankie Ford**, and recorded one single himself – a fiery instrumental called 'Storm Warning' (Rex). After he was shot in the hand in 1961 he played bass in a dixieland band before learning organ and resuming session work for **Harold Battiste**'s AFO organization. Transferring to Los Angeles, he continued working with Battiste and other producer/arrangers (René Hall, **J. W. Alexander**, **H. B. Barnum**, Gene Page) until his disenchantment with West Coast ideas forced him to form his own bands – Drits and Dravy (with Ronnie Barron), the Zu Zu Band (with Jessie Hill), Morgus and the Three Ghouls – and take part in sessions with the New Orleans Musicians Association in Los Angeles. In 1968 he emerged as voodoo man, Dr John Creaux The Night Tripper, with the startling *Gris-Gris* (Atlantic), a collection of hypnotic chants and mystic symbolism, including the eerie 'I Walk on Gilded Splinters', that was far more impressive than bemused critics would allow. Following releases in the same general style were less well conceived, although *Babylon* (1969) had some memorable cuts (particularly 'Twilight Zone'), and some of *Remedies* (1970) anticipated his return to basic New Orleans R&B – as celebrated on his fifth album *Gumbo* (1972). A masterly tribute to the Crescent City's contribution to popular music, it established Dr John as a creditable artist without frills or gimmicks, and paved the way for his excellent *In the Right Place* (1973) and *Desitively Bonnaroo* (1974) albums – both produced by fellow New Orleans veteran, **Allen Toussaint**.

Rebennack parted company with Atlantic in 1975 and subsequently recorded for DJM (*Cut Me While I'm Hot*, 1975), United Artists (*Hollywood Be Thy Name*, 1976), and Horizon (*City Lights*, 1978; *Tango Palace*, 1979). He performed rarely in the Eighties but could still be seen at the annual New Orleans Jazz Heritage Festival, beguiling the faithful with his hallucinatory music, spells, incense, and his ever-bizarre costume.

DRAKE, NICK A British singer-songwriter in whose lyrics many saw a tragic presentiment, Nick Drake (born in Burma on 18 June 1948) first became known in progressive music circles towards the end of the Sixties, when he was signed by **Fairport Convention** manager Joe Boyd to his management company Witchseason. Drake's first album, *Five Leaves Left* (Island, 1969),

received little exposure or promotion at his own apparent insistence, and part of his mystique was that he never spoke on stage, rarely acknowledged the audience's presence and refused all requests for press interviews. His small but fanatical following grew with the release of *Bryter Later* in 1970, but by that time he had stopped giving live appearances altogether. He became a virtual recluse after delivering the master tape of *Pink Moon* to Island's offices in 1972, and nothing further was heard from him until his death from an overdose of anti-depressants on 25 November 1974, in Birmingham. He left behind four songs from an unfinished album he had begun with producer John Wood, which eventually appeared on a boxed-set compilation *Fruit Tree* in 1979. The success of this release prompted new interest in Drake's work, and his influence could be strongly heard in the heavily introspective, angst-ridden songs of New Order, the Dream Academy, Prefab Sprout and other Eighties UK bands.

DREAD, MIKEY Jamaican reggae DJ, toaster and producer Mikey Dread (real name Michael Campbell) first made his name in the late Seventies as a radio DJ with the Jamaican Broadcasting Corporation. His *Dread at the Controls* reggae programme (1978–9) became so popular in ghetto areas that the authorities, frightened at the power Dread was generating, closed it down. As well as mixing some of the tracks on British punk band the **Clash**'s *Sandinista* album (and so winning some useful international recognition), he supported the band on a UK tour in 1980. The radio DJ then became a toasting DJ and reggae producer in his own right, forming his own Dread At The Controls label and releasing tough roots music from artists like Earl Sixteen, the Ovations and Gilly Buchanan. As a producer, Dread came up with two of the early Eighties' most covered instrumental tracks ('rhythms') in 'Jumping Master' and 'Warrior Stylee'.

DRIFTERS Not just one group but a corporate identity for several different groups permutated over two decades from more than 40 individuals, the Drifters date back to 1953. The group was formed that year around lead singer **Clyde McPhatter** and signed to Atlantic. The first six Drifters' records ('Money Honey', 'Such a Night', 'Honey Love', 'Someday', 'White Christmas', 'Whatcha Gonna Do') were all Top 10 R&B hits. Their strength lay

in an exciting blend of gospel phrasing and 'bird-group' harmony, a technique already successful for the Five Royales and originally introduced to the Drifters by McPhatter from his previous group, the **Dominoes**. His influence was so strong that when he left the Drifters for a solo career, their popularity immediately waned.

Without McPhatter's distinctive lead, they were unable to find an identity strong enough to satisfy the young rock'n'roll audiences beginning to dictate the market. Using five lead singers (David Baughn, Johnny Moore, Bill Pinkney, Gerhart Thrasher, Bobby Hendricks) in three years, they tried a variety of styles from **Platters**-type ballads to stomping rockers, until the group was disbanded in 1958. Their most popular recordings from this period, 'Ruby Baby' (led by Moore) and 'Drip Drop' (featuring Hendricks) were **Leiber and Stoller** songs, the writer-producers who sparked off a seven-year run of hits with a new set of Drifters in 1959. This line-up (**Ben E. King**, Charlie Thomas, Doc Green, Elsbeary Hobbs) had been recording unsuccessfully in New York as the Crowns. Signed by manager George Treadwell to replace the sacked personnel, and teamed with Leiber and Stoller at Atlantic, their first recording as the Drifters, 'There Goes My Baby', was a smash hit in both the R&B and pop charts. The startling, almost experimental, arrangements of the song, involving strings, tympani, and Latin rhythms, made the Drifters a top name

The Drifters at the very start of a long career, way back in 1953

again, this time with a multi-racial audience. Their following releases ('Dance with Me', 'This Magic Moment', 'Lonely Winds') were equally popular, climaxing with their most famous hit, 'Save the Last Dance for Me', in October 1960.

By the time the record reached Number 1, King had left the group to be replaced by Rudy Lewis from the Clara Ward Singers. For the next three years, Lewis was the only distinctive voice to be heard on Drifters' recordings. The production techniques first tried in 1959 had been perfected into a glossy formula, blending the rest of the group with a female quartet (Dee Dee and **Dionne Warwick**, Cissy Houston and **Doris Troy**) and submerging them all in fancy orchestration. Arrangers **Phil Spector**, **Burt Bacharach**, **Bert Berns**, and Garry Sherman each in turn added their ideas to the mixture. The songs were provided by Gerry Goffin and **Carole King**, **Barry Mann** and Cynthia Weil, Bacharach and Hal David. The results made the Drifters the most consistently successful pop-orientated black act until Motown took over the market in the mid-Sixties. Of the dozen hits at this time, 'Sweets for My Sweet' and 'When My Little Girl Is Smiling' are the best examples of their pure pop style, while 'Please Stay' and 'Let the Music Play' give a truer indication of Lewis' vocal talent. But it was 'Up on the Roof' and 'On Broadway' that were their best sellers, two good songs that took a deeper look at city life than previous pop records had cared to. This theme was repeated, less successfully, in 'Rat Race' and then, after Lewis' death in 1964, diluted to an endless romantic fantasy.

After six years' absence, Johnny Moore had rejoined the group in 1963, just in time to record their last major hit before leading them slowly to near oblivion. The Drifters' string of hits had been achieved in the few years when the tastes of black and white audiences were more closely aligned than at any other period. As British groups began invading the pop market, black record buyers turned to the rawer soul singers and Motown captured the remaining middle ground. The Drifters and their contemporaries (like the **Shirelles** and Phil Spector's groups) were gradually squeezed out of the charts. 'Under the Boardwalk' (led by Moore) coupled with 'I Don't Want to Go On Without You' (Charlie Thomas) was a superb double-sided hit in August 1964, and for three more years they survived, scoring progressively lower entries with following instalments of the same

story – 'I've Got Sand in My Shoes', 'Saturday Night at the Movies', 'At the Club', 'Come On Over to My Place', 'I'll Take You Where the Music's Playing'. By 1968, however, they were a spent force, left with inferior material by the record company and relegated to performing in supper-clubs and lounges.

Shortly after the expiration of their Atlantic contract in 1972, British Atlantic started to hit with re-issues of their old records. Taking advantage of the renewed interest, the Drifters signed to Bell Records and were teamed with British pop veterans Roger Cook, Roger Greenaway and Tony Macaulay who gave them Top 10 UK hits with 'Like Sister and Brother' in 1973, and two new episodes of their Sixties saga, 'Kissin' in the Back Row of the Movies', 'Down on the Beach Tonight', in 1974.

At the same time, back in America another set of Drifters re-formed around Charlie Thomas and they, too, attempted to re-create the old magic with 'A Midsummer Night in Harlem', on Musicor. In 1985, the group was still around, performing the old, familiar hits in cabaret and on rock'n'roll revival shows.

From a raw R&B group to an MOR pop act the Drifters, in one form or another, have survived all the changes of post-war entertainment. With such a flexible arrangement, the name will probably still be around in another 30 years. *See also* **Ben E. King**; **Clyde McPhatter**

DRISCOLL, JULIE Born on 8 June 1947, in London, Julie Driscoll was working as secretary to producer **Giorgio Gomelsky** and running the **Yardbirds**' fan club when Gomelsky suggested she should join **Long John Baldry** and **Rod Stewart** in Steampacket. When first Stewart and then Baldry left a year later and Steampacket folded, she stayed with fellow member **Brian Auger** as vocalist in his band, the Brian Auger Trinity. Signing with Gomelsky's Marmalade record label, the Trinity had an international hit single in 1968 with a version of **Bob Dylan**'s 'This Wheel's on Fire', though Driscoll quit the band on the subsequent US tour. A period of semi-retirement followed, though she did emerge occasionally to sing with Centipede, the multi-member experimental jazz-rock band formed by her husband, Keith Tippett. She recorded a solo album, *Julie Driscoll*, in 1971 with Tippett on keyboards, and was briefly associated with his band Ovary Lodge during the mid-Seventies.

DUKE, GEORGE Long before he became known as a commercially attuned producer of hits (for **Jeffrey Osborne**, **Deniece Williams**, Stephanie Mills, A Taste of Honey, among many), keyboard player George Duke had run up an extraordinarily long list of collaborations and solo hits that left one in no doubt of his manifold talents. While being classically trained at San Francisco's Conservatory of Music, he was moonlighting in the evenings as a pianist in local jazz clubs. In the early Seventies his work as a backing musician was as prodigious as it was varied – **Frank Zappa**'s Mothers of Invention, Cannonball Adderley, Jean-Luc Ponty – and by the late Seventies he had become a successful bandleader/producer in his own right with his LPs (*From Me To You*, *Reach For It*, *Don't Let Go*) and singles. His music was a blend of **George Clinton**esque funk, and light Latin flavourings (he'd worked with Flora Purim and Milton Nascimento) allied to a precise ear for what made current hit sounds work. Not all of his collaborations were successful. A co-operative band with drummer Billy Cobham was somewhat pretentious but proved a minor misjudgment as Duke returned to making solo albums in whatever style happened to be contemporary and turned his attention to producing many hits for many artists. His finger firmly on the pulse, he even had some success moving out of the purely black market as a producer for Melissa Manchester, **Kenny Loggins** and other white mainstream acts.

DUKE/PEACOCK RECORDS

A key R&B record label of the post-war years, Don Robey's Houston-based company was responsible for the emergence of **Bobby Bland**, **Junior Parker**, **Johnny Ace**, **Rosco Gordon** and a host of other R&B and gospel acts.

The company was formed by Robey, who in the mid-Forties owned a large night-club in Houston called the Bronze Peacock which attracted a black clientele. Most of the popular black performers were booked into the club and it was **T-Bone Walker** who, in 1947, suggested that Robey catch the performance of San Antonio singer-guitarist **Clarence 'Gatemouth' Brown**. The industrious Robey was so impressed with Brown that he became his manager and, after several unsuccessful deals with local recording companies, decided to start a record concern of his own. So, in 1949, Robey issued 'Mary Is Fine' by Gatemouth Brown on the Peacock label. It was an instant local hit, and from then on Robey never looked back.

On 2 August 1952, he took over the Duke label, which was owned by Memphis DJ James Mattis. At the same time, Johnny Ace was making his debut on the label, and was soon to become a very big name with hits like 'Angel', 'The Clock', and 'Pledging My Love'. The following year, 1953, saw Duke/Peacock's most significant contribution to rock'n'roll. It was **Leiber and Stoller**'s 'Hound Dog', recorded by **Willie Mae Thornton** backed by the **Johnny Otis** band. Willie Mae's powerhouse vocal and a piercing, high-register guitar solo anticipated **Elvis Presley**'s multi-million-selling version of the same song three years later.

In 1954, Robey negotiated a deal with Sam Phillips to bring Little Junior Parker to Duke. The harmonica-playing blues singer had already scored a few hits on Sun, but was to establish himself with the help of Robey's guiding hand. A year later Duke made its biggest-ever signing in Bobby Bland, a huge name on today's contemporary blues scene. Robey discovered him in a local talent show and subsequently nurtured his career right through into the Seventies. Bland's string of R&B hits is near-endless and includes national chart entries. Other artists signed by Robey during the Fifties included **Jimmy McCracklin**, Earl Forrest, Larry Davis, Fention Robinson and Norman Fox, and the Rob Roys (who had a chart hit in 1957 with 'Tell Me Why').

A healthy amount of gospel material has also been issued on Peacock over the years. The artist roster is substantial and includes the **Dixie Hummingbirds**, Spirit of Memphis Quartet, Mighty Clouds of Joy, Sensational Nightingales, and Inez Andrews and the Andrewettes (on the subsidiary Songbird label). In all, there are over 120 gospel albums in the catalogue.

The continued success of Duke/Peacock and its prestigious position with R&B record buyers can be attributed in part to Robey's total supervision of the recording sessions, his insistence on using only top arrangers, producers and accompanying musicians such as Johnny Otis, trumpeter Joe Scott, tenorist Bill Harvey, guitarists Wayne Bennett and Pat Hare, pianist **James Booker** and drummer Sonny Freeman. Harvey's band – usually with arrangements and production by Scott – can be heard on most of the hits by Bland, Parker and Brown, while James Booker played on the Davis and Robinson sessions. The ubiquitous Johnny Otis band provided back-up for Johnny Ace and several other acts.

Duke/Peacock's standing as a major independent label ended abruptly in 1972 when it was purchased by the vast ABC/Dunhill record group. Since then Bobby Bland has become an important figure in the rock world, no doubt helped along by Dunhill's vastly superior coast-to-coast distribution outlets. Don Robey died in 1975.

DUNCAN, JOHNNY

Best known in Britain for his association with the mid-Fifties skiffle boom, singer/guitarist Johnny Duncan was born in 1931 in Oliver Springs, Tennessee. He was a member of a gospel quartet until the age of 16 when he took up the guitar and went on to join Bill Monroe's Blue Grass Boys. He joined the Army and in 1953 was stationed in Britain where he married a British girl later that year. Returning to Britain after his discharge, he replaced **Lonnie Donegan** as the skiffle singer in **Chris Barber**'s Jazz Band. In 1956, he left to form his own Blue Grass Boys – Denny Wright, electric guitar; Johnny Bell, bass, and Lennie Hastings, drums. In 1957, the group had a Number 2 hit on the British charts with 'Last Train to San Fernando', the success of which had a lot to do with Duncan's 'authentic' American whine. Further records were only moderate hits, and in the early Sixties he returned to America and joined Columbia, with whom he had a string of minor country hits from 1967 onwards.

DUPREE, CHAMPION JACK

A boxer during the Depression (hence the 'Champion' tag), Dupree was born in New Orleans on 4 July 1910. The supreme barrelhouse pianist, he recorded for Okeh from 1940, cutting many superb blues in an exuberant rough-house style. Moving to New York in 1944, he recorded for numerous labels including Joe Davis, Apollo, Continental, and King, on which he reached the R&B Top 10 in 1955 with 'Walking the Blues'. A later Atlantic session which produced the album *Blues from the Gutter* was critically acclaimed. A British resident in the Seventies (he lived in Halifax, Yorkshire), his later records were aimed at the white blues collector, but earlier sides (especially 'Junker Blues') had a seminal influence on **Fats Domino**.

DURAN DURAN

British five-piece Duran Duran proved to be the apotheosis of early Eighties pop, their style, danceability and glossy videos conquering an idol-hungry teen-market worldwide and making them very wealthy young men in the process.

Duran Duran – Nick Rhodes took the name from a character in the 1968 film *Barbarella* – came together in the city of Birmingham in 1977, when Rhodes and John Taylor first hit on the idea of a group that crossed the energy of punk with the danceability of disco. The band went through a series of short-lived line-ups that had Taylor on lead guitar and Rhodes on keyboards, and at one point featured Stephen 'Tin Tin' Duffy (who went on to a successful solo career) on vocals. With the establishment of a firm unit however, consisting of Rhodes, John Taylor (now on bass), drummer Roger Taylor (recruited from local band Crucified Toad) and guitarist Andy Taylor, who had answered an ad in *Melody Maker*, Duran Duran's fusion of rock and disco began to take shape. The last member to join (in the summer of 1980) was singer Simon Le Bon, a drop-out from the local University Drama course, whom they met at the Rum Runner, a Birmingham club that had for some time been the centre of the Midlands' New Romantic scene.

Donning the foppish clothes of the movement and playing a slick, if superficial, brand of dance-pop, the band were tailor-made for the style-obsessed New Romantics. Gigs at the Edinburgh Festival, London's Marquee and the Lyceum were followed by a support slot with **Hazel O'Connor** in late 1980. As they had no record company to help them financially, manager Michael Berrow, co-owner of the Rum Runner, sold his house to finance these appearances, during the course of which they were spotted and signed by EMI.

Early in 1981 they released their debut single, 'Planet Earth'. By February it had peaked at Number 12 in the UK chart (it made Number 1 in Australia) and by March Duran Duran

were headlining a national tour. The serious music press did not take to the band, accusing them of being frivolous and trivial, but the newer, image-oriented magazines like *Smash Hits* and *The Face* welcomed the opportunity to fill their pages with glossy photos of the boys. The same year their first album *Duran Duran* sold well, reaching Number 3 in the UK, and spawned two other hit singles, including 'Girls on Film'.

It was 'Girls on Film', with its mildly pornographic promo video, that brought the band most attention and gave them their first Top 5 hit. Their audience was rapidly expanding, but even at this stage the group's potential teen appeal was inexplicably underestimated. It was Duran Duran's use of video that would prove to be their most effective promotional tool, and they paid as much attention to video production as they did to their appearance. They indulged their every flight of fancy, and in so doing provided an escapist, travel-brochure world that delighted their fans.

The group managed to ditch the New Romantic tag in 1982, thereby reaching a wider audience; that year brought a string of successes. Their second album, *Rio*, made Number 2 in the UK and produced four hit singles, most importantly the slow moody number 'Save a Prayer', which reached Number 2 in the UK and is by far the best song (most critics would say the only good song) in their repertoire. To promote the album, they made a string of videos in exotic locations with Australian director Russell Mulcahy and then embarked on an eight month world tour.

All this hectic activity soon began to pay off – they had already won the hearts of British teenagers, sweeping the board in several polls; their videos were proving popular on America's

rock-music cable TV channel, MTV, and 'Hungry Like the Wolf' became their first US hit, reaching Number 3 in the charts. In March 1983 they finally made the top of the British charts with 'Is There Something I Should Know'. The group spent most of the rest of the year either in tax exile or recording their third album, *Seven and the Ragged Tiger*; released at the end of the year it went into the charts at Number 1.

The year 1984 saw them consolidating their success worldwide, achieving transatlantic Numbers 1 and 2, with 'The Reflex' (re-mixed by Nile Rodgers of **Chic**) and 'Wild Boys' respectively, both peaking in the UK and US in the same week, but their repetition of a successful formula won them no new friends. They also released the live album *Arena* in December, but it did not perform as well as the previous releases, failing to make the Top 5. If anything, they only just lost out on the popularity stakes to **Wham!** but their diehard fans made sure they maintained their lead at the top of the *Smash Hits* readers' poll.

Group activities in 1985 were limited to just one single, the James Bond film theme tune 'A View to a Kill' (which reached Number 2 in the UK), but various band members took time off to pursue interests outside Duran Duran. First, John and Andy Taylor joined with **Robert Palmer** and a host of prominent American session musicians to form a dull rock outfit called Power Station and released an album of the same name, scoring the Top 20 single 'Some Like It Hot' and making an appearance at Live Aid (*see* **Band Aid**). Later, the rest of the band got in on the act, formed a new band called Arcadia (who sounded not entirely unlike Duran Duran) and released the album *So Red the Rose* and a Top 10 single with 'Election Day'.

Duran Duran's future was in no way compromised by these extra-mural indulgences and in 1986 they came back together for the rehearsal and recording of a fourth studio album, destined to sustain their success. Musically, Duran Duran are no more than accomplished studio stylists, skilful welders of a host of disparate elements – hard rock, electro, white soul and, latterly, scratch and hip hop – into an eminently commercial sound. Far more important was their marketing success, whereby they capitalized on their obvious visual attractions through the media (video and the glossy pop magazines), a technique that became increasingly important in the music industry in the Eighties.

Simon Le Bon leads Duran Duran in this 1985 line-up

DURY, IAN Combining an art-school background, a love of rock'n'roll and a vaudeville presentation, Ian Dury used the spontaneity of the late Seventies punk explosion to become one of Britain's most exciting, funniest and best-loved rock performers.

Born on 12 May 1942 in Billericay, Essex, and crippled by polio since childhood, he studied at the Royal College of Art in London, then became a teacher in the Kent town of Canterbury before forming Kilburn and the High Roads, a group that build up a cult following and had a profound effect on several other fledgling bands like the **Sex Pistols** and **Madness**, before splitting up in 1976, when they were still virtually unknown.

Dury then spent a year writing new lyrics and teamed up with guitarist Chas Jankel to collaborate on the material that became his first solo album, *New Boots and Panties* (1977), on the aggressive indie label Stiff. The album became an immediate favourite and a subsequent single, 'Sex and Drugs and Rock and Roll', despite failing to reach the charts, achieved the status of cult anthem. This song was also adopted as the theme tune for 1977's Be Stiff tour where Dury unveiled his new backing group, the Blockheads, featuring Jankel on guitar and keyboards along with Davey Payne

(sax), Norman Watt-Roy (bass) and Charley Charles (drums).

'What a Waste' (1978) became Dury's first hit single and the next year, 'Hit Me With Your Rhythm Stick' (UK Number 1) and 'Reasons to be Cheerful' (Number 3) plus a second LP *Do It Yourself*, established him as a favourite, albeit eccentric, British character.

This success was maintained by 1980's *Laughter* album and the irresistible hit 'I Wanna Be Straight', both of which featured guitarist Wilko Johnson, Jankel having left to pursue a solo career.

It was at this time that Dury left Stiff for Polydor in search of international success. Tragically, his first single on the new label, 'Spasticus Autisticus' (recorded to coincide with the Year of the Disabled) was regarded by many radio stations as offensive to the handicapped, despite Dury's own disablement. The blow severely affected Dury's career and his subsequent albums *Lord Upminster* (1983) and *4000 Weeks Holiday* (1984) failed to receive the attention the music deserved.

Dury remained one of the most respected artists in the music business even though his recording career was put on hold when he appeared in the 1986 BBC TV drama series *King of the Ghetto*.

Ian Dury; respected and much-loved rock performer

DYLAN, BOB The most influential singer-songwriter of the rock era, Bob Dylan was born Robert Allan Zimmerman in Duluth, Minnesota, on 24 May 1941. At high school in nearby Hibbing, he played briefly in a rock'n'roll band, and then attended the University of Minnesota at Minneapolis for a year. Here Robert Zimmerman became Bob Dylan the folk singer, who set out to make his name in the mecca of the folk scene, New York's Greenwich Village. He was determined to become a 'famous folk singer' and consequently he trimmed his sails and ignored many of the other musical influences of his teenage years.

On the first few albums he cut after veteran producer **John Hammond** signed him to Columbia in 1961, there was little evidence of his love for **Hank Williams** or **Chuck Berry** – though occasionally he let slip an **Everly Brothers** riff. Instead, Dylan's music was very much in the mainstream of the folk revival. And it was good, sometimes brilliantly so. He quickly became known as the most talented of the young writers (like **Phil Ochs** and **Tom Paxton**) whose songs became anthems for the white students involved in the civil rights and anti-war movements. There were protest songs like 'Blowin' in the Wind' and 'A Hard Rain's Gonna Fall', love songs like the traditional 'Corrina' and the traditionally based 'Girl from the North Country', and funny songs like the various renditions of 'I Shall Be Free'. The tunes were relatively simple (often lifted from traditional folk material), and his technical ability (both singing and playing the guitar and harmonica) was, in the field of folk music, primitive. But the impact was unusually hard-hitting – Dylan was creating a mood, and the scenarios he was painting needed no sophistication. The voice, the guitar playing and the sometimes vicious harp sounds, helped set the tone in which his stories could unfold and hit home. There was nothing more moving in the world of the Cuban missile crisis and CND than to listen to Dylan singing 'Masters of War' and 'Hard Rain'.

It was in this period (1961–4) that Dylan became the hero of the folk set and the radicals, but in the wider world of pop music his songs were known only in the versions of others, notably those of **Peter, Paul and Mary**. All that changed for two reasons. First, his typecasting as a radical guru began to irritate him, and the irritation showed in his songs, notably on the fourth album, *Another Side of Bob Dylan*

(1964). The seminal track, 'My Back Pages', found Dylan railing against 'the lies that life is black and white' and commenting on his earlier firm commitment that 'I was so much older then, I'm younger than that now'. Second, and more important, was the revolution in British pop around 1963 and 1964. Dylan reportedly 'jumped out of his car seat' when he first heard the **Animals** singing his version of the traditional 'House of the Rising Sun' because of the sheer brashness of the adaptation. It opened his eyes to a new musical world, and made him realize that it was possible to express his love for Chuck Berry and **Woody Guthrie** at the same time. His next album was called *Bringing It All Back Home*, a subtle reference to his admiration for the way in which the British artists had revived his own interest in American rock'n'roll. One side of the album was devoted to rock songs, with a **Rolling Stones** riff on every other one of them. 'I have given up the struggle for perfection', he acidly noted on the sleeve, and his music leapt along joyously and uninhibitedly, romping through 'Subterranean Homesick Blues', a direct descendant of Chuck Berry's 'Too Much Monkey Business'.

Dylan's switch in direction caused a few missed heartbeats among his erstwhile followers, but at least the album had another side to it, which included 'Mr Tambourine Man' and the almost political 'It's All Right, Ma'. But the concerts he gave during 1965–6, beginning with his performance with the **Paul Butterfield** Blues Band at the Newport Folk Festival, divided his audience dramatically, and Dylan became a rock idol virtually by default, the success of 'Like a Rolling Stone' – it reached Number 2 in 1965 – more than compensating for the lost purist folk audience. The albums of this period – *Highway 61 Revisited* and the double *Blonde on Blonde* – represent the pinnacle of Bob Dylan's recording career. The musicians he worked with – **Al Kooper**, Robbie Robertson and Nashville sidemen like **Charlie McCoy** and Kenny Buttrey – were perfect choices to carry through the fusion of the various styles Dylan had absorbed over the years. Musically, the songs were still constructed simply, using well-worn chord sequences, but they were often longer and more flowing. With Kooper's lush organ sound the effect of, for instance, 'Queen Jane Approximately' and 'Like a Rolling Stone', was magisterial. And Dylan's lyrics were still centrally important, though now linear coherence had collapsed before the rush of rich, myriad images. Their landscape was now an interior one, with the power and special logic of dreams. Sometimes ('Tombstone Blues', 'Desolation Row') they were peopled with historical figures in strange conjunctions, elsewhere they were intensely lyrical with archetypal images from blues or country music transformed in Dylan's intense inner visions of the urban nightmare ('Visions of Johanna' and the 12-minute 'Sad Eyed Lady of the Lowlands'). And Dylan's zany, deadpan humour was still evident on 'Rainy Day Women' and 'Leopard Skin Pill Box Hat'.

Dylan's own lifestyle was accurately reflected in the kaleidoscopic chaos of the songs he was writing, and he seemed to be driving himself onwards at a terrifying pace (*Highway 61* and *Blonde on Blonde* – three albums in all – were released in the space of a few months). 'He'll be a legend,' said **Pete Seeger**, 'if he doesn't blow up first', and the sense of impending implosion was especially strong in the cathartic performances of his 1966 tour with the Hawks (later to become **The Band**).

In August 1966 Dylan's career was abruptly interrupted by a motorcycle smash, and he vanished from public view for two years. His presence, though, was everywhere, from the posters in every head shop to constant press rumours of his imminent return, and bootleg recordings of concerts, like the famous 1965 Albert Hall show in London, were widely distributed. Paradoxically, his silence caused his mystique to grow, and Dylanologists of varying degrees of credulity and sanity flourished. For a period during 1967 Dylan lived in Woodstock with The Band – his 1965–6 touring group – and his musical development continued in this secluded atmosphere. The recordings made at this time (which soon became available in bootleg form) were tortured probings into Dylan's post-King of Rock and Roll mind. Some songs were hilariously funny drunken ravings ('Please Mrs Henry', 'Million Dollar Bash'), but the overall mood, set by the more sombre of the numbers, was penitent and full of an ominous sense of foreboding. On 'Tears of Rage' and 'Too Much of Nothing' he seemed to feel overwhelmingly guilty for his past and sorry for those he had – admittedly unwittingly – led. On 'I Shall Be Released' and 'Wheel's on Fire', he seemed aware, vaguely and subconsciously, of an imminent explosion that might or might not be a kind of liberation. The songs prove an unnerving experience to listen to, but on the simple emotional level they are the most personal and moving of all of Dylan's songs. There is none of the

The prophet of his generation: far-sighted Dylan tells it as it is

detachment that characterizes most of his previously issued work, none of the confidence and none of the arrogance – he sings them plaintively and rawly, occasionally aided by Richard Manuel's harmony lines. *The Basement Tapes*, the title given to the bootleg album that contains all of his tracks recorded with The Band in 1967, is the most atmospheric and the most direct Dylan album. And if *Sgt Pepper* and *Blonde on Blonde* are the finest celebrations of the optimism of the new Sixties counter-culture, *The Basement Tapes* is the crucial expression of the other side of that optimism. In that respect it must rank as the forerunner of a whole series of major Seventies records that have all eschewed Utopian statements in favour of explorations of the prevailing nightmare. Finally, in 1975, the tapes were officially released on Columbia, eight years after they were made.

Dylan presented a new stance to the public at large with the release of *John Wesley Harding* in 1968. In marked contrast to the prevailing trend toward complexity (musical and lyrical), the songs were direct and simple, and continued to explore themes of guilt and self-doubt. But the last two tracks, 'Down along the Cove' and 'I'll Be Your Baby Tonight', pointed towards the mellower tone of the two country albums that followed, *Nashville Skyline* (1969) and *Self Portrait* (1970). These albums brought Dylan his first real critical attacks since the move into rock in 1965. He was accused of a retreat into the banality and sentimentality of country music, while *Self Portrait*, a double album of other people's songs, was said to be mere self-indulgence. In fact, this was yet another instance of the emergence of an early musical influence on Dylan: his friendship with **Johnny Cash**, who duetted with him on 'Girl from the North Country' on *Nashville Skyline*, dated from the early Sixties. The albums marked the beginning of an important rapprochement between rock and country music, as many artists, from the **Byrds** to **Joan Baez**, followed him in recording in Nashville. They were, however, the last of Dylan's albums to have that pioneering effect. In the Seventies, he played a minor role in the development of rock, and some of his records were diffuse and uneven. On *New Morning* (1970) and *Planet Waves* (1973) he often sounded contrived and even hackneyed, often presenting the persona of a conventional family man far removed from the acute and acerbic love songs of earlier

years. *Pat Garrett and Billy the Kid* (1973) was a soundtrack album containing one classic song ('Knocking on Heaven's Door'). *Blood on the Tracks* (1975), in contrast to the preceding albums of the Seventies, saw Dylan in a more questioning mood, with songs like the embittered 'Idiot Wind', the cryptic 'Lily, Rosemary, and the Jack of Hearts', and the deceptively gentle 'A Simple Twist of Fate'. A similar feeling was evident on 'Hurricane' (1975), the story of Reuben Carter's wrongful imprisonment.

Dylan was still receiving the kind of attention he had attracted in the previous decade. His fragmentary, surrealistic novel, *Tarantula*, was published in 1971, he played a cameo role in Sam Peckinpah's *Pat Garrett* movie, and his few public appearances (the Concert for Bangla Desh, and the Woody Guthrie memorial event) foreshadowed the enormous response to his 1974 American tour with The Band. Over six million applications were made for tickets, and the resulting live album, *Before the Flood*, found both Dylan and The Band returning to their greatest songs of earlier years in a powerful way. That record and *Planet Waves* appeared on Asylum (Island in Britain), the label to which Dylan had moved when his Columbia contract ran out. The relationship with Columbia had been stormy, particularly after the two-year lay-off and the emergence of the brash Clive Davis as chief executive. He seemed to personify the image of the corporate music business, while David Geffen of Asylum Records had

Dylan as the anguished poet and sardonic rebel of the mid-Sixties

apparently grown with his artists. Columbia then released the appalling *Dylan* (1974), a cynical collection of out-takes, of interest only to the (many) Dylan fanatics. In the event, the relatively low sales of *Planet Waves* led in 1974 to a re-signing with Columbia for a further five-year period.

The mid-Seventies found Dylan presenting himself as a musician among his peers on the Rolling Thunder tour (with Joan Baez and others). He was, however, bedevilled by rumour and the intense scrutiny of Dylanologists like the indefatigable A. J. Weberman, who was always ready with accusations of pro-Israeli sympathies or 'revelations' about Dylan's private life. Not that his relationship with wife Sara was free from problems: it was worsening, and the pain and desperation of impending separation informed *Blood on the Tracks* (1974) and *Desire* (1975), the latter containing a number of songs co-written with Jacques Levy. Dylan and Sara formally separated in February 1977, and Dylan immersed himself in another Rolling Thunder tour, out of which emerged the four-hour film *Renaldo and Clara*, which intercut concert footage with semi-autobiographical scenes acted out between Dylan, Sara, and Joan Baez. 1978, the year of the film's release, also saw the appearance of *Street Legal*, on which Dylan could be heard clearly moving towards the religious conversion that was soon to claim him, both in its imagery and in the gospel-like responses of the backing vocalists. In 1979, Dylan proclaimed himself a born-again Christian, and spiritual themes were at the core of his next four albums – *Slow Train Coming* (1979), *Saved* (1980), *Shot of Love* (1981), and *Infidels* (1983). *Empire Burlesque* appeared in 1985, *Knocked Out Loaded* a year later – the latter featuring collaborations with playwright Sam Shepard, Carole Bayer Sager and **Tom Petty**.

In 1986, Dylan was back on tour, this time with Tom Petty and the Heartbreakers as his backing band, and still packing concert halls and stadiums. His legacy, however, remains fundamentally Sixties-bound: without Dylan, there is no doubt that rock in that decade would have taken a different route. There would have been no *Sgt Pepper*, no *Beggar's Banquet*, no *Music from Big Pink*. That was the level of his impact. He did much to mould the sensibility of a whole generation in industrialized countries, and his music is crucial to any understanding or analysis of the Sixties.

The Eagles, epitome of the Californian rock'n'roll dream

EAGLES Their immaculate combination of neat harmonies and countrified rock music made the Eagles the premier Los Angeles rock band for much of the Seventies. The group came together in 1971, all four members having had playing experience in other bands: Randy Meisner (bass, born 8 March 1946 in Nebraska) had played with **Rick Nelson**, **Poco**, and **Linda Ronstadt**; Glenn Frey (guitar, 6 November 1948) had been a member of several bands in his native Detroit and had also accompanied Ronstadt, as had Don Henley (drums, 22 July 1947 in Texas) who had drummed in a Texas group called Shiloh; Bernie Leadon (guitar, 19 July 1947) was a former member of the **Flying Burrito Brothers**.

Their first album, *Eagles* (Elektra, 1972), included the Glenn Frey/**Jackson Browne** composition, 'Take It Easy', which became a US Top 20 hit. *Desperado*, a concept album on the gunslinger theme, followed in 1973 and included two further hits in the title song and 'Tequila Sunrise'. For *On the Border* (1974), the band added Florida-born Don Felder on guitar and brought in Bill Szymczyk as producer in place of Glyn Johns, who had worked on the previous two; an accomplished album, it again explored the central theme of their earlier releases – the rock star as mythical hero, outlaw and loner. *One of These Nights* (1975) established them as a major name in the UK, where they began a run of six Top 40 hits with the title track. Leadon left soon after its completion to form the Bernie Leadon–Michael Georgiades Band and was replaced by **Joe Walsh**, former guitarist with the **James Gang**. He made his Eagles debut on *Hotel California*, their biggest-selling album (11 million copies worldwide) and an extended comment on the West Coast superstar lifestyle in which the group had become entangled.

In 1977, Meisner departed for a solo career and was replaced by another former Poco bassist, Tim Schmit, and a further two years elapsed before the band next released an album – *The Long Run*, which turned out to be their last. It provided them with their fifth US Number 1 in 'Heartache Tonight' and, like its two predecessors, went platinum, but the group announced their break-up in late 1979. Walsh, Frey and Henley all recorded solo, with the latter two enjoying particular success in the early Eighties – Frey with albums on Asylum and MCA and the 1985 hit 'The Heat is On' (from the film *Beverly Hills Cop*); Henley with the album *Building the Perfect Beast* (1985), which included the US Top 10 hits, 'The Boys of Summer' and 'All She Wants to Do Is Dance'. *See also* **Joe Walsh**

EARTH, WIND AND FIRE More than any other black band, Earth, Wind and Fire fulfilled the promise offered by a jazz-funk fusion. Formed by singer/drummer Maurice White in Chicago in the mid-Sixties (and recording for Capitol as the Salty Peppers) the band were eventually picked up by Warners in 1971 after **Sly and the Family Stone** had made it obvious that 'progressive black music' was a commercial proposition. Their first single, 'Love Is Life', was a minor hit but their two Warners albums failed despite massive promotional campaigns. The bulk of the band split and Maurice and brother Verdine formed a new group with Philip Bailey, Jessica Cleaves, Roland Battista, Larry Dunn, Ronald Wayne Laws and Ralph Johnson. Pulling free from jazz elements into wickedly electric rhythms, the group's reputation began to build with the Columbia 1972 album *Last Days of Time* which was followed with hit discs like 'Open Our Eyes', 'Head to the Sky' and 'That's the Way of the World'.

Subsequent albums – notably *Head to the Sky*, *Open Our Eyes* (both 1974) and *That's the Way of the World* (1975) – revealed White's fascination with mystic ideas, and a maddening feature of Earth, Wind and Fire music for the rest of the Seventies was their persistent matching of superb, densely layered productions and intoxicating rhythms with lyrics of unbridled pretentiousness and whimsy. *That's the Way of the World* did, nevertheless, mark the beginning of mass acceptance for the band, which was confirmed by the success of *Gratitude* (1975), *Spirit* (1976) and *All'n'All* (1977), the last-named being notable for White's obsession with Egyptology, pyramid power and other arcane matters. They enjoyed success in the singles market, too, with 'Shining Star' (1975), 'Sing a Song' (1975), 'Got to Get You Into My Life' (1978, from the film *Sgt Pepper's Lonely Hearts Club Band*), 'September' (1978) and 'After the Love Has Gone' (1979) all reaching the US Top 10.

Their stage shows from the mid-Seventies onwards were an extraordinary mixture of music, illusion, sci-fi pyrotechnics and choreography, although by the start of the Eighties they were beginning to look and sound dated compared to newer funk outfits like **Shalamar**. *Raise* (1981) and *Powerlight* (1983) were the customary big sellers, though the early part of the decade was particularly notable for the outside recording projects of the various EW&F members. Maurice White, having produced such artists as **Ramsey Lewis**, **Deniece Williams** and the Emotions, turned his attention to Jennifer Holliday; Verdine began producing Britain's **Level 42** with the assistance of Larry Dunn, whose own ventures included work with Stanley Turrentine; and singer Philip Bailey struck out on his own with *Continuation* in 1983 and had a Number 1 in the UK in 1985 with 'Easy Lover', on which he duetted with **Phil Collins**.

EASTON, SHEENA

Born on 27 April 1959 near Glasgow, Scotland, singer Sheena Easton was given her big break when, in 1979, she was selected for BBC TV's *The Big Time*, a series that gave unknowns an opportunity to work at the top level of their chosen field. Her first single, 'Modern Girl' just failed to make the UK Top 50, but when the programme showing Easton's auditions with EMI was screened in July 1980, the second single 'Nine to Five' ('Morning Train' in the US) stormed up the charts to Number 3. Interest in 'Modern Girl' was reawakened and it made Number 8.

Easton's US success came the following summer when 'Morning Train' was Number 1 for two weeks, with 'Modern Girl' in the Top 10 at the same time. From that point on, Easton found US audiences more receptive to her easy-listening pop style and she went on to become a US TV personality. In 1981 she was given the accolade of singing the theme song to the Bond film *For Your Eyes Only*, and the next year was awarded a Grammy for best new artist.

EASTWOOD, CLINT AND GENERAL SAINT

Originators of the tandem style of British reggae DJing that subsequently produced Laurel & Hardy *et al* – and through its crossover success paved the way for such solo DJs as **Smiley Culture** and Tippa Irie in 1985/6 – Clint Eastwood and General Saint started working together in 1980, achieving their first specialist UK chart success with the single 'Tribute to General Echo' (a DJ friend of Eastwood's who'd been gunned down in Kingston). Subsequent outings were avowedly more crossover in direction, but contained sufficient humour to retain the duo's roots following at a time when their appeal broadened to include the mainstream pop audience.

Eastwood, the more experienced DJ of the two, was already a name artist by the time he arrived in Britain in 1979, having recorded in Kingston for producers Joe Gibbs and Bunny Lee, and by 1978 had acquired a reputation on a par with Trinity and Dillinger. He met up with Saint by chance in London and the tandem DJing developed as the two friends found they shared the same gift for mimicry and verbal gymnastics.

EASYBEATS

The top national group in Australia by mid-1966, with four chart-toppers to their credit, the Easybeats came to the UK with a lineup comprising George Young (born 6 November 1947), Gordon Fleet (16 August 1945), Dick Diamonde (28

The Easybeats, stars from Down Under, dressed up and going places

December 1947), Harry Vanda (22 March 1947) and Little Stevie Wright (20 December 1948). All were the sons of European expatriates.

Recording for United Artists in London, with **Shel Talmy** producing, they made their British chart debut with 'Friday on My Mind', written by guitarists Vanda and Young. The disc reached Number 6 in the UK, Number 16 in the US, and Number 1 in Australia. Failure to match the success of that single – still one of the best-ever expressions of teenage frustration with the nine-to-five routine – caused them to change their style in an attempt to accommodate new audiences. Their album *Vigilu* (United Artists, 1967) was, accordingly, a curious mixture of easy-listening songs like 'Can't Take My Eyes Off You', soul-inflected material like 'Hit the Road Jack', and pseudo-psychedelic excursions such as 'We All Live Happily Together'. Two tracks taken from that album, however, did become minor hits in Britain – the Dylanesque 'The Music Goes Round My Head' and the booming, almost symphonic 'Hello, How Are You?' (both 1968). A further release, 'St Louis' (issued on Rare Earth) was a Hot 100 hit in the US in 1969.

The band broke up at the tail end of 1970 and Vanda and Young stuck together to record under a variety of names, including Paintbox, Band of Hope, Marcus Hook, and Flash and the Pan. 'Natural Man' (Regal Zonophone, 1972) was a particularly fine but unsuccessful single by the Marcus Hook Band. Later in the Seventies they branched into production work and nurtured the career of Australian heavy-metal band **AC/DC**, whose lineup included George Young's younger brothers, Malcolm and Angus.

ECHO AND THE BUNNYMEN

Widely regarded as the pre-eminent post-punk guitar band, Liverpool's Echo and the Bunnymen passed from cult status to chart success with the release of their debut album *Crocodiles* (1980). While they never achieved the worldwide sales of kindred bands **U2** and **Simple Minds**, in the UK they retained a strong following and were in no way overshadowed by them.

Led by the brash, fresh-faced Ian McCullough (who had been in the Crucial Three, a band that gave rise to **Wah!** and the **Teardrop Explodes**), Echo and the Bunnymen played their first gigs late in 1978. Comprising McCullough, Les Pattinson (bass), Will Sargeant (guitar) and a drum machine called Echo, they released the single 'Pictures on My Wall' in 1979. Drummer Pete De Freitas joined later that year and in 1980 they recorded the single, 'Rescue', and the first LP – releases that established the band as an innovative and exciting rock outfit.

Their critical reputation grew with the release of *Heaven Up Here* (1981), and while they were attracting sizeable live audiences, real commercial success came only in 1983 with *Porcupine* and the single, 'The Cutter', which both made the UK Top 10. Another album, *Ocean Rain*, was released in 1984, again to rave reviews, and there then followed a lengthy gap, with the only new material released up to the end of 1985 being the single 'Bring On the Dancing Horses'.

EDDIE AND THE HOT RODS

When punk exploded in 1975, Eddie and the Hot Rods' brand of energetic rhythm and blues was aggressive enough to satisfy hard core punk fans but also melodic enough to score several hit singles.

First formed in and around Southend in 1975, the Rods (as they came to be known) featured Barrie Masters (vocals), Dave Higgs (guitar), Simon Gray (bass) and Paul Nicol (drums). After building up a solid local following, they began to make an impression on the London pub scene and soon secured a deal with Island Records. Their first release, recorded at London's Marquee club, was a live EP that featured four stage favourites (including **Bob Seger**'s 'Get Out of Denver' and the **Rolling Stones'** 'Satisfaction') and reached Number 43 in the UK singles chart.

A debut album, *Teenage Depression* (1976), with its virtues of speed and exhilaration, capitalized on the punk excitement of the time and the title track became their second minor hit. At this time, they augmented their line-up with second guitarist Graeme Douglas and recorded a second album, *Life on the Line*, based on a concept by manager/producer/lyricist Ed Hollis. A single taken from the album, the anthemic 'Do Anything You Wanna Do' became their biggest hit, a Number 9 in 1977. This was followed by 'Quit This Town', which peaked at Number 36.

The band were never able to repeat their early success, but even though their chart days were over, they still were regulars on the London pop circuit well into the mid-Eighties.

EDDY, DUANE A star guitarist of the 1958–63 period, when he had a run of fifteen US Top 40 hits, Duane Eddy was born on 28 April 1938, in Corning, New York, and moved with his family to Phoenix, Arizona, in 1951. At five, Eddy took up the guitar and after leaving Coolidge High School at 16, he played at local dances before meeting guitarist Al Casey in 1955. He sat in with Casey's combo and began studying under jazz guitarist Jim Wybele. In 1957, **Lee Hazlewood**, a Phoenix DJ, and his partner, Lester Sill, signed Eddy, leased the recording to the Jamie label and made 'Movin'n'Groovin'' featuring Eddy and his 'twangy' guitar as one of the Rebels, a sax/guitar group comprising Al Casey, Larry Knechtel and Steve Douglas. Eddy and Hazlewood had stumbled across the 'twangy' sound by playing the melody on the bottom instead of the top strings and feeding it through a combination of echoes. This sound was epitomized on Eddy's next record 'Rebel Rouser' (co-written with Hazlewood) which sold a million in the summer of 1958.

Eddy followed up with more hits including 'Ramrod', 'Cannonball' and 'Peter Gunn' and by 1960 was one of the highest paid pop instrumentalists, although much of his success can be attributed to Hazlewood's superb production. He was especially popular in Britain where he had nine consecutive Top 10 hits and was voted Number 1 Pop Personality by the *New Musical Express* in 1960.

In 1961, Eddy and Hazlewood parted company and Eddy began producing himself, with disappointing results – 'The Avenger', a self-produced final single for Jamie flopped totally late that year. In 1962, he joined RCA and made a modest comeback with 'Deep in the Heart of Texas' and 'The Ballad of Palladin' before re-uniting with Hazlewood and recording 'Dance with the

Guitar Man', which featured vocals by a girl session group specially christened the Rebellettes. 'Guitar Man', co-written with Hazlewood, reached the Top 10 in both Britain and America but apart from the follow-up, 'Boss Guitar', early in 1963, Eddy never had another hit despite many more releases on RCA. He signed with Colpix in 1967 and recorded the atrocious *Duane Does Dylan* and *Duane A Go Go* albums with no success.

Eddy still visits Britain periodically where he maintains a strong following in rock'n'roll circles. After working as a producer for MCA in Hollywood, he was temporarily rescued from oblivion as a recording artist in 1975 by the British chart success of 'Play Me Like You Play Your Guitar', written and produced by Tony Macaulay. After more years spent in relative obscurity, he emerged yet again in 1986 with a UK hit remake of 'Peter Gunn', made with the help of **Trevor Horn**'s Art of Noise.

The Duane Eddy who rocked the US charts with his 'twangy' guitar (above) in the late Fifties and early Sixties, is still recognisable in his more recent style (below)

EDMUNDS, DAVE Spanning more than twenty years, Dave Edmunds' career as a singer, guitarist and producer began in his native Cardiff during the early Sixties. Edmunds (born 15 April 1944) played guitar in various local bands before forming a group with bassist John Williams and drummer Bob Jones called Love Sculpture, whose repertoire consisted of early rock standards and lightning-speed guitar adaptations of classical themes – one of which, 'Sabre Dance', was a Top 10 hit single on Parlophone in 1968. It was the group's only hit, however, and subsequently they disbanded. Edmunds signed with Gordon Mills' management agency, then retired to Wales with Kingsley Ward in order to build his own recording studio, Rockfield.

Rockfield soon became one of the most active studios in Britain, with a distinctive 'sound' that couldn't be matched elsewhere. He spent months experimenting, until he could produce exact replicas of his favourite records, from early Sun rockabillies to the most elaborate **Phil Spector** masterpieces. The first product of his considerable applied talents was 'I Hear You Knockin'', an electrifying tribute to his Fifties idols that was a worldwide smash on MAM towards the end of 1970, reaching Number 1 in Britain and Number 8 in America.

Among his productions have been records by the **Flamin' Groovies**, Deke Leonard, **Brinsley Schwarz**, Ducks Deluxe, **Shakin' Stevens** and the Sunsets and **Del Shannon**. In 1972 and 1973, Edmunds released two singles on the Rockfield label glorifying the Phil Spector sound, 'Baby I Love You' and 'Born to be With You', which were Top 10 hits in Britain. In 1974 he appeared in the **David Essex** film *Stardust*, incidentally creating all the music supposedly done by the Beatles-like group in the film. In 1975 he released a long-awaited second album *Subtle as a Flying Mallet*, which included songs and accompaniment by **Nick Lowe**, with whom Edmunds toured as a member of Rockpile in 1977. He returned to the UK chart that year with 'I Knew the Bride' and in 1979 reached Number 4 with **Elvis Costello**'s 'Girls Talk', from the album *Repeat When Necessary*.

In the Eighties, he produced albums by new wave rockabilly band the **Stray Cats** and became involved in numerous other recording projects, including solo albums (*D.E. 7th, Information*) and guest appearances on albums by Shakin' Stevens amongst others.

EDWARDS, TOMMY

EDWARDS, TOMMY Originally a composer – he wrote 'That Chick's Too Young to Fry' for **Louis Jordan** – Tommy Edwards made his name as a singer in 1958 with a US and UK chart-topping version of 'It's All in the Game'. Edwards was born in Richmond, Virginia, on 17 February 1922, and first recorded the song (the melody of which was composed by former US Vice-President Charles Dawes) in 1951, but the 1958 version featured a heavier backing. It has since been recorded as a 'beat ballad' by many singers; a version by **Cliff Richard** reached Number 2 in the UK in 1963. Edwards had five other Top 40 hits in the US, all for MGM. He died on 22 October 1969.

EEK A MOUSE

EEK A MOUSE A graduate DJ of the Virgo, Gemini, Papa Roots, Black Ark and Jah Roots sound systems in Jamaica, Eek A Mouse (Ripton Joseph Hylton, born 19 November 1957; Jamaica) began recording in 1974, though it was not until 1980 that he achieved major breakthrough (in Jamaica as in Britain) with the single 'Wa Do Dem'. A scat singer rather than a talking DJ – but a major talent however you label him – Eek A Mouse had the misfortune to emerge at more or less the same time as Yellowman, an infinitely less original performer but one whose 'slackness' lyrics (i.e. sexually explicit in Jamaican patois) made him the bigger commercial success. Eek A Mouse had three excellent albums released in Britain by Greensleeves in 1982/3 – *Wa Do Dem*, *Skidip* and *The Mouse and the Man* – all of which combined peerless singjaying (toasting along to well-known pop) with substantial lyric matter but which failed to achieve the success they deserved.

ELBERT, DONNIE

ELBERT, DONNIE With a distinctive – and influential – use of falsetto that took 'What Can I Do' into the lower reaches of the Hot 100 on DeLuxe in 1957, Donnie Elbert has recorded for many labels. They include Vee Jay, Red Top, Jalynne, Cub, Parkway, Checker, Gateway (songs like 'A Little Piece of Leather' were popular in London clubs), Atco and, in Britain, New Wave and CBS. Elbert reached the US Top 20 with 'I Can't Get Over Losing You', on Rare Bullet, in 1970. A disco revival of the **Supremes**' 'Where Did Our Love Go?' (recorded in London in 1969 but turned down by various record companies) was a Top 10 hit on All Platinum in 1971. He moved to Avco during the following year and scored an international hit with a revival of the **Four Tops**' 'I Can't Help Myself'.

ELECTRIC FLAG

ELECTRIC FLAG When first conceived, the Electric Flag was to be an 'American music band' comprising **Mike Bloomfield**, the great white hope of the blues guitar; Nick (the Greek) Gravenites, the gifted Chicago singer-composer; **Buddy Miles**, the gigantic black soul drummer; and a full horn section. Their Stax-styled soul and South Side Chicago blues, seasoned with a dash of psychedelia and electronics, was brash and flashy, thunder and lightning. Their debut before an uncritical audience at the Monterey Pop Festival in 1967 was widely acclaimed, as were subsequent live appearances. Inexplicably, their first LP (*A Long Time Comin'* on Columbia) earned only mild praise from critics, but it certainly justified the Flag's tremendous reputation. A victim of hard drugs and clashing egos, the band disintegrated almost as quickly as it had burst on to the scene; a second album by a Miles-led Flag was a pale shadow of the first. Miles launched the Buddy Miles Express and joined **Jimi Hendrix**'s Band of Gypsies, while Gravenites joined **Big Brother and the Holding Company**. Bloomfield, Miles, Gravenites and some-time member **Barry Goldberg** reunited in 1974 for *The Band Kept Playing* (Atlantic), but no further albums were made. *See also* **Mike Bloomfield**; **Buddy Miles**.

ELECTRIC LIGHT ORCHESTRA (ELO)

ELECTRIC LIGHT ORCHESTRA (ELO) Originally conceived by Carl Wayne and **Roy Wood** as a classically oriented offshoot of the **Move**, ELO (initially Roy Wood, **Jeff Lynne**, and Bev Bevan) made one critically acclaimed album in 1972, then split apart. Wood and ex-Move bassist Rick Price formed Wizzard, and Lynne and Bevan were joined by Richard Tandy (keyboards), Mike De Albuquerque (bass), Mike Edwards, Colin Walker (cellos) and Wilf Gibson (violin), the last three from the London Symphony Orchestra (Walker and Gibson were replaced in 1974 by Hugh McDowell and Mike Kaminski). This group scored almost immediately with 'Roll Over Beethoven', a single cleverly combining themes from Chuck Berry and Beethoven. In subsequent albums, ELO have refined and developed their concept of using classical instruments and motifs in a rock format, with occasional hit singles ('Showdown', 'Can't Get It Out of My Head') and a heavy American touring schedule. *Eldorado*, a rock symphony, became their first gold album in 1975. By this time, the band had changed labels from Harvest to Warner Bros. 1976 saw them move to their own label, Jet, and enjoy their biggest US success yet with *Olé ELO* and *A New World Record*. By 1978, ELO were the top-selling British band

Rock guitars remained a fundamental part of the ELO sound, despite the band's use of violin, cello and orchestra

in America and their stage presentations were becoming ever more elaborate, involving the use of laser technology and the construction of an actual-size 'spaceship' for their US tour that year. In 1980, Lynne lent his commercial touch to the film *Xanadu*: although it was a box-office flop, the title song (recorded by ELO with **Olivia Newton-John**) reached Number 1 in the UK. ELO have since recorded and toured with customary professionalism and a continuingly brilliant sense of showmanship and musical pastiche, though they remain deeply unfashionable with rock critics. *See also* **Jeff Lynne; Move; Roy Wood**

ELECTRIC PRUNES Comprising Jim Lowe, Ken Williams, Mark Tulin, Preston Ritter, and 'Weasel', the Electric Prunes recorded in Los Angeles from 1965 to 1969. Their Number 11 hit, 'I Had Too Much to Dream (Last Night)' (Reprise, 1966), was a minor punk-rock classic, chiefly because of Dave Hassinger's production gimmickry. He took advantage of the latest technological advances in fuzz and reverb to create a sound that was 'freaky' without being too blatantly underground. They had one follow-up hit, 'Get Me to the World on Time' but kept recording for several years, producing two of the first 'concept' albums, *Mass in F Minor* and *Release of an Oath* (Reprise), both written and arranged by David Axelrod. By their fifth and final album, *Just Good Old Rock and Roll* (Reprise, 1968) none of the original members remained in the group.

ELEKTRA RECORDS One of the most respected labels for musical tastes and policy throughout the Sixties, the Elektra Record Company was founded in October 1950 by **Jac Holzman** with an initial budget of $600. The company grew from Holzman's twin fascinations with engineering and music, and was originally run from his dormitory at St John's College in New York State.

For the first five years of its existence, Elektra released around thirty obscure albums catering to minority tastes. But, in 1955, a turning point occurred when Josh White, a folk blues singer, and Theodore Bikel, a purveyor of multilingual folk songs who later featured in **Frank Zappa**'s film, *200 Motels*, were signed to the label and gave the company some commercial appeal. At this time, budgetary restrictions confined Elektra to recording folk singers, since recording costs for such artists were very limited, and among other early

artists on the label were Oscar Brand, Ed McCurdy and Bob Gibson. The earliest Elektra artist who remains significant in the Eighties is **Judy Collins**, who was signed to the label in the early Sixties. Other familiar folk singers of the time who started their careers on Elektra include **Tom Paxton** and **Phil Ochs**, who were quick to follow the lead established by **Bob Dylan**. Holzman's desire to extend the breadth of Elektra's catalogue led to a number of 'project' albums, and among the artists who contributed tracks to such a collection as *The Blues Project* were Dave Van Ronk, Geoff Muldaur, Eric Von Schmidt and Koerner, Ray and Glover, the last named of which produced the first white blues-type albums for Elektra. The pianist on Von Schmidt's tracks was Bob Dylan, working under the alias of Bob Landy. Others in the 'project' series included such latter-day artists as Peter Rowan. Richard Greene, David Blue and **Richard Fariña**, while an intended 'Electric Guitar Project', which was finally released as *What's Shakin'*, featured **Paul Butterfield**, **Mike Bloomfield**, the **Lovin' Spoonful**, **Eric Clapton**, **Stevie Winwood**, **Tom Rush** and **Al Kooper**.

Paul Butterfield was the first fully electric artist to sign to the label, and after the success enjoyed by the Butterfield band, a near-miss at signing the Lovin' Spoonful, and a couple of early tracks with the **Byrds**, Holzman entered the field of rock. Signings included **Love**, the **Doors**, **Tim Buckley**, Tom Rush, Clear Light, Earth Opera, the **Dillards**, **Lonnie Mack**, **Fred Neil**, the **Incredible String Band**, the Stooges, the **MC5**, **Nico**, **David Ackles**, and Rhinoceros, who are all either famous in their own right, or whose members subsequently formed part of such bands as **Crosby, Stills and Nash**, the Mothers of Invention and Sea Train. Later signings, such as the **New Seekers**, together with a flock of English material purchased for America, tended to subvert the label's image 'quality', but the contracting of artists like **Carly Simon**, Mickey Newbury, **Harry Chapin** and **Bread** went some way towards restoring that image.

In August 1973, Jac Holzman was appointed senior vice-president of Warner Communications Inc., and relinquished his post as president of the record company that he had single-handedly built during its 23-year history. He handed over his duties to David Geffen, who merged Elektra with his own company, Asylum Records, under the corporate banner of Warner Communications. Subsequent signings

like **Tom Waits**, the **Cars** and **Television** maintained Elektra's reputation for cultivating slightly left-field artists, while the early Eighties were marked by diversification into Latin music (Ruben Blades), reggae (Steel Pulse), black music (**Teddy Pendergrass**), heavy metal (Dokken, Motley Crue) and what the industry chose to call 'new music' – 10,000 Maniacs, the Unforgiven, Joe Lynn Turner and, from the UK, **Simply Red**. Since the departure of David Geffen to form his own eponymous label in 1975, Elektra has been headed by Bob Krasnow.

ELGINS One of the lesser lauded outfits of Berry Gordy's Motown stable, the Elgins made a minor impact on the US R&B charts in 1966 with 'Put Yourself in My Place', 'Darling Baby' and 'Heaven Must Have Sent You'. The group's leader was singer Johnny Dawson, who had previously headed the Emeralds and the Downbeats, though much of the charm of their records lay in the lead vocals of Saundra Edwards. Ironically, Edwards had left the group by the time 'Heaven Must Have Sent You' reached Number 3 in the UK on re-release in 1971. Her replacement was Yvonne Allen of the Donays, the makers of the original version of 'Devil in Her Heart', which the **Beatles** recorded on their *With the Beatles* album in 1963. The other three original members were Norman McClean, Cleotha Miller and Robert Fleming.

ELLIMAN, YVONNE Hawaiian-born singer Yvonne Elliman first came to fame in a memorable performance as Mary Magdalene on the original album of *Jesus Christ Superstar* in the early Seventies. She also played the role in the American stage version.

After taking the song 'I Don't Know How to Love Him' from this show into the US Top 30 in 1971, Elliman had only minimal chart success (two US Top 20 singles) in the following seven years. In 1974 she sang on the sessions for **Eric Clapton**'s album *461 Ocean Boulevard* and subsequently joined his group. In 1978 she had a huge US Number 1 (UK Number 4) with 'If I Can't Have You', taken from the film soundtrack of *Saturday Night Fever*.

ELLIOTT, CASS Born on 19 September 1943, in Alexandria, Virginia, Cass began her career in New York singing with the Big Three, via whom she met Denny Doherty and then John and Michelle Phillips. The four sang together as the **Mamas and Papas** between 1966 and 1968, and for a short period in 1971. Following the first break-up of the group she employed her strong and distinctive voice on more pop-oriented music and cut a number of solo albums, notably *Dream a Little Dream* (Dunhill, 1968) and *Make Your Own Kind of Music* (1969). In 1970 she worked briefly with ex-**Traffic** member **Dave Mason**, returning to the rock music she had abandoned, but following the failure of the Mamas and the Papas' comeback she went back once more to the TV/cabaret scene. She died of heart failure in a London hotel on 29 July 1974. *See also* **Mamas and Papas**

ELLIOTT, RAMBLIN' JACK A

colourful archetype of the American folk-song rambler 'citybilly', Jack Elliott was born in Brooklyn on 1 August 1931. He so thoroughly absorbed rural speech, manners and performing styles that he typified the American Everyman from Everywhere. As a teenager, he became **Woody Guthrie**'s friend, disciple, travelling companion and interpreter. Guthrie once said of him: 'Jack Elliott sounds more like me than I do.' While mostly identified with the Guthrie songbag, wit and lifestyle, Elliott also mastered the idioms of **Jimmie Rodgers** and **Hank Williams**. An important influence on **Dylan**, perhaps his most successful recording, apart from the Guthrie material, was **Jesse Fuller**'s 'San Francisco Bay Blues'. Working in England and France in the late Fifties, Elliott introduced American folk and C&W music to a vast European following in the late Fifties. His audiences on both sides of the Atlantic also rollicked in his Will Rogers-style folksy anecdotage and corn-fed humour. A major interpreter of warmth, charm and undeniable musical identification with the silent greats.

ELLIS, SHIRLEY Born in New

York in 1941, Shirley Ellis is best remembered for three US Top 20 hits – 'The Nitty Gritty', 'The Name Game', and 'The Clapping Song' – all of which were soul-flavoured nursery rhyme novelty numbers written for her by her husband and manager Lincoln Chase. His previous hit compositions included such rock'n'roll standards as 'Such a Night' for the **Drifters** and 'Jim Dandy' for **LaVern Baker**, while he had also recorded as a singer for Decca, Liberty, Splash, Dawn, Columbia, RCA Victor, and Swan. Although Shirley had some smaller hits on Congress and Columbia, she retired from performing towards the end of the Sixties.

ELLISON, LORRAINE Philadel-

phia-born soul singer Lorraine Ellison had her first R&B hit in the US in 1965 with 'I Dig You Baby' (Sharp). A contract with Warner Brothers led to the recording of a classic track in soul music, her extraordinarily emotive reading of 'Stay With Me Baby' which, although only a minor US chart hit, became an instant favourite with soul buffs and critics in the US and UK. Nothing else on her three albums for Warners had anything like the neurotic depth of emotion on this track, which was produced in New York by **Jerry Ragavoy**. She recorded no further hits, but her compositions with Sam Bell of the Enchanters were covered by numerous Philadelphia-based soul singers in the mid-Sixties to early Seventies.

ELO *See* **Electric Light Orchestra**

ELP Leading lights of the classically

tinged rock that came to the fore in the early Seventies, Keith Emerson (keyboards), Greg Lake (bass/guitar/vocals) and Carl Palmer (drums) formed the enormously successful Emerson, Lake and Palmer in 1970.

Emerson, then leader of the **Nice**, had a chance meeting with Lake, of **King Crimson** and, aware that their respective careers were flagging, they teamed up with Palmer. The trio immediately gelled into a tight unit, displaying a high degree of musical proficiency and showmanship. ELP made their debut at the Isle of Wight Festival in 1970 with a rock version of Mussorgsky's *Pictures at an Exhibition* which became their third album and established them as principals players in their field.

Though slow to take off in the UK, each of their first five albums went gold in the US (*Trilogy* (1972) and their eponymous debut album went platinum). In 1973 ELP started their own label, Manticore, which also released material by acts like Italian art-rockers PFM. Joining the ranks of the supergroups, ELP did a huge world tour in 1973–4 that required 36 tons of equipment and was showcased on their triple album set, *Welcome Back My Friends to the Show That Never Ends*.

By 1975, having notched up enormous sales all over the world, ELP took a two-year break during which each member pursued solo work. Lake had a surprise Christmas hit with the uncharacteristically mellow 'I Believe in Father Christmas' in 1975. They resumed group activity in 1977, but after three comparatively unsuccessful albums (the last of which was *Love Beach* in late 1978) demonstrated their

waning popularity, they split up.

In 1985, ELP was re-formed by Emerson and Lake after unremarkable solo careers, but since Palmer had become a member of the Eighties supergroup **Asia**, the third place was filled (conveniently, since no change was needed to the band name's last initial) by drummer Cozy Powell. He had a long track record with a series of heavy rock bands including **Rainbow** and had scored a solo UK Top 5 single, 'Dance with the Devil' in 1973. In 1986, they released *Emerson, Lake and Powell*, which was supported by a US tour.

ELY, JOE Born in Amarillo, Texas in

1947 and raised in nearby Lubbock, Joe Ely produced a style of music that places him firmly within the musical tradition of west Texas, along with **Buddy Holly**, **Roy Orbison** and **Waylon Jennings**. Having moved to Austin, Texas, Ely was signed to MCA and in 1977 they released his debut album, *Joe Ely*, a mix of fresh Texan lyrical sophistication and rockabilly vitality. During the late Seventies, Ely and his band were packing honky-tonks, juke joints, showcase clubs and concert halls from coast-to-coast. In 1980 Ely crossed the Atlantic to play in Britain with the **Clash**, forging one of the oddest Anglo-American musical alliances ever. Ely had toured with the Clash in the US and helped bring the pioneering punk group to Texas, and they persuaded him to tour with them in the UK. Ely's album, *Live Shots*, was recorded in England while he was touring with the Clash and it revealed a new, hard-driving, urban sound. *Musta Notta Gotta Lotta* was released late in 1981, and it ably demonstrated Ely's ability to transcend the Texan country-rock stereotypes to produce the strongest rock of his career. Despite acclaim from the critics, the album did not break Ely into the popular market as he had hoped, and his problems were compounded by the death of his drummer and the departure of his disaffected guitarist, the widely respected Jesse Taylor. Moving away from the rigours of constant touring, Ely spent more time assembling and working in his home studio and, employing synthesizers and the latest computer-aided studio techniques, he recorded *Hi-Res* (1984), the title (an abbreviation of high resolution) being an allusion to the highly technical nature of the work. The album was an abject failure and effectively put Ely's solo career on hold. He continues as a session player, widely active in various bands on the Texas scene.

EMERSON, LAKE AND PALMER See ELP.

EMI RECORDS EMI Limited, the
registered name of the group of companies built up around the original Electrical and Musical Industries, was formed in 1931 by a merger of the Gramophone Company and the Columbia Graphophone Company. The Gramophone Company had earlier swallowed the Marconiphone Company which, in turn, had swallowed His Master's Voice. The companies' main activities covered the production and development of radio receivers and record players, but as with all early companies producing gramophones, EMI quickly realized that the best way to increase demand for playing and receiving equipment was to make and sell recorded music for playing and receiving. EMI rapidly became the market leader in the field and since the Fifties has maintained a constant 20 per cent proportion of the world market in records.

During the Fifties, EMI marketed three British labels – His Master's Voice, Columbia and Parlophone, as well as distributing a number of other independent and semi-independent British labels and being involved in licensing and distribution deals with American labels such as MGM and Mercury. In 1954, the British company bought a controlling investment in the American Capitol label. This followed on the termination of a licensing deal with American Columbia (CBS). CBS subsequently went with the new Philips British subsidiary. In 1957 RCA moved from EMI to Decca, taking **Elvis Presley** and Perry Como with it.

A catalogue deal with Roulette Records, of New York, led to EMI's issuing **Frankie Lymon**'s 'Why Do Fools Fall in Love?' in Britain and a deal between EMI and ABC Records, of New York, gave EMI a string of phenomenal **Paul Anka** hits, starting with 'Diana' in 1957. By this time, EMI's own three labels were being run by a triumvirate of enormously successful label managers: Norman Newell at HMV, Norrie Paramor at Columbia, and **George Martin** at Parlophone. The group had found a new chairman in 1954 in Joseph Lockwood and towards the end of the Fifties it became clear that EMI, having achieved a very strong position in its native British market, would try for a big push into the US.

While the British market was no longer wholly dominated by US performers, it did not necessarily follow that the US market was prepared to be dominated by UK performers. EMI's attempt to break into the US, notably with **Cliff Richard** in 1960, were marked failures until Capitol took up its option to release the **Beatles**' fifth single, 'I Want to Hold Your Hand', in early 1964. George Martin's signing of the Beatles to Parlophone had been on his own initiative and marked the end of the days when Columbia had been EMI's major label with a string of American stars and thinly disguised British derivatives.

With Capitol behind the Beatles in the US from 1964 onwards, the way was open for EMI to expand its markets and to diversify its own interests. It was the Beatles who provided the company with a secure foundation to the Sixties: in Britain its music profits rose by 80% in 1964, though in the US – despite the success there of the British groups, the **Beach Boys** and its country music division – a series of bad management decisions at Capitol restricted the company's growth. Only after the appointment of Baskhar Menon from EMI India as president did the company, with the aid of groups like **Grand Funk Railroad**, return to the black.

In the wake of the emergence of underground rock around 1967, EMI set up its own 'progressive' label, Harvest, but even with the success of groups such as **Pink Floyd** the company's major assets remained the Beatles and the fact that it distributed and manufactured half of the records sold in Britain. Accordingly, EMI's fortunes also fluctuated with the rise and fall of the market and changes in its licensee rights. This latter point became especially important in the late Sixties and early Seventies when American companies were more concerned than ever to integrate their international operations and open their own British offices, to sign new acts as much as to oversee the selling of their own product. For example, MCA moved in and ABC and Elektra/Asylum out of EMI House in 1974–5.

However, by the mid-Seventies, under the direction of Gerry Oord from Bovina Records in Holland (who kept all the individual Beatles bar George Harrison), EMI established a corporate EMI label on which **Queen** were phenomenally successful; it also kept the rights to important American companies such as Motown and Fantasy and signed a successful production deal with **Mickie Most** (RAK Records). In so doing, EMI reaffirmed its place as the British market leader and its position as the world's largest record company. Nevertheless, EMI's problems were far from over: with the recession in the record industry at the end of the Seventies, EMI found itself overextended, and a merger with the electronics firm Thorn took place in 1980. The company's financial position was turned around, but at the expense of cutbacks in EMI's music division. During the Eighties, Thorn-EMI diversified into video production and cable TV while maintaining its visibility in (if not its domination of) the world marketplace with acts such as **Duran Duran**, **David Bowie** (who switched from RCA to EMI early in the decade), **George Thorogood**, **Kim Carnes**, **Sigue Sigue Sputnik**, and the ever-dependable Queen and Cliff Richard.

EPSTEIN, BRIAN One of the most
successful yet ultimately tragic managers in rock history, Brian Epstein was born on 19 September 1934, the son of a Liverpool department store owner. After a year's National Service in the Army, he was discharged as emotionally unfit and spent an abortive year at the Royal Academy of Dramatic Art in London. In 1957, he returned to Liverpool to take charge of the record department of the family store, North End Music Stores (NEMS), which he turned into the city's most respected record retail outlet. He took pride in following up customers' enquiries, which included a request for 'My Bonnie' by the **Beatles** on 28 October 1961 – a date recorded faithfully in his 1964 autobiography, A Cellarful of Noise. In search of the disc, he discovered that the group were playing at the nearby Cavern Club where he watched them several times. Despite warnings about their unreliability from Alan Williams, the group's ex-manager, Epstein signed the Beatles to a management contract – attracted by what he called their 'very considerable personal magnetism', which reawakened his own creative yearnings.

By the middle of 1962, Epstein had secured a recording deal for the Beatles with EMI's Parlophone label, with **George Martin** as producer. As the group's fortunes rose meteorically during 1963, he signed other Liverpool acts to his company, NEMS Enterprises – among them **Gerry and the Pacemakers**, **Billy J. Kramer and the Dakotas**, the **Big Three**, **Cilla Black** and Tommy Quickly, all of whom enjoyed some measure of chart success during the brief Merseybeat boom. His commitment to the Beatles remained total, however: he cajoled them into stage suits and a clean-cut mop-top image, and masterminded their hysteria-spawning tours, in the planning and execution of which his attention to detail and protectiveness were most called for. But by August 1966, the four Beatles themselves were tired of the showbusiness aura that Epstein had done so much to create around them. When they ceased touring, he effectively became redundant.

Epstein continued to take a personal interest in the careers of his other signings, notably Cilla Black, but his attempts to groom non-Liverpool acts for pop stardom – pop-folk group the Silkie, southern R&B boys **Cliff Bennett** and the Rebel Rousers, instrumentalists Sounds Incorporated – were conspicuously unsuccessful. He was hit hard by the growing distance between his original protégés (especially Lennon) and himself, and he died on 27 August 1967, from an overdose of sleeping pills, just as the Beatles were beginning a meditation weekend with the Maharishi Mahesh Yogi in Wales. The coroner's verdict was 'accidental death'.

EQUALS The reputation of the Equals – a pop band with reggae and soul leanings – rests almost entirely on the success of 'Baby Come Back' (President), which was a European million-seller and a Number 1 in the UK in 1968. The group had originally recorded the song in late 1966 as a B-side. Although they had only two more Top 20 hits over the next three years, the original personnel – the twins, Dervin and Lincoln Gordon, vocals and guitar respectively (born 29 June 1948); **Eddy Grant**, lead guitar (5 March 1948); Pat Lloyd, guitar (17 March 1948); and John Hall, drums (25 October 1947) – stayed together until Grant left to pursue a highly successful solo career in 1971. His replacement, Jimmy Haynes, was in turn replaced by Dave Martin in mid-1973. Neil McBain took over from Hall early in 1975. The group left President after a legal battle in 1973 and subsequently recorded for Grant's label, Ice Records, before splitting up in 1977. They re-formed, minus Grant, in 1981 for a tour of Germany, where they had always been popular. *See also* **Eddy Grant**

ESQUERITA One of a number of singers who tried to out-scream and shout **Little Richard** in the late Fifties, Esquerita released a series of records on Capitol in 1958 including 'Oh Baby' and 'Rockin' the Joint', but made no impact whatsoever. He went home to New Orleans and enjoyed some local

success under the name of Eskew (derived from his real initials, S. Q.) Reeder with an organ instrumental of the **Jim Lowe** hit, 'Green Door', on Minit in 1962. He also recorded for Okeh and Instant, and although something of a legend among rock'n'roll collectors, his reputation in New Orleans was slight. He died in early 1987.

ESSEX, DAVID After an undistinguished career as a pop singer dating back to the mid-Sixties, David Essex (born in London on 23 July 1947) achieved his first success in the London stage version of *Godspell*. The part of Jim McLain in the film *That'll Be the Day* (1973) proved to be prophetic, as Essex himself went on to become a rock star with a string of hit singles on CBS ingeniously produced by Jeff Wayne with the artist himself as a composer. Among them were 'Rock On' (1973, a big American hit), 'Lamplight' (1973), 'Gonna Make You a Star' (1974), 'Stardust' (1975), 'Hold Me Close' (1975) and 'If I Could' (1975). His singing ranged from a staccato, heavily echoing style on the earliest discs to a more coy English-accented voice developed out of the **Anthony Newley/David Bowie** manner. He maintained his success well into the Eighties with further starring roles in films (*Silver Dream Racer, Stardust*) and on the London West End Stage – playing Che Guevara in *Evita* and Fletcher Christian in his own production of *Mutiny!*, a musical savaged by the critics but one of the biggest box office hits of 1985.

David Essex came to stardom via the role of Jesus in the musical Godspell

EURYTHMICS/TOURISTS

Dave Stewart (born 9 September 1952) and Annie Lennox (born Christmas Day 1954), the core of the Eurythmics, are among the few rock artists who can claim to have had success with two different groups. First of all they enjoyed moderate domestic fame with the rock pop of the Tourists, but as the Eurythmics they combined Stewart's grasp of modern music technology and Lennox's expansive voice to procure an international stage for their soulful brand of electronic pop.

Lennox and Stewart – she from a classical music background, he with a track record of many bands ranging from folk to blues – met in London in 1976. They became lovers and musical partners and formed the Tourists with another songwriter, Peet Coombes, bassist Eddie Chin and drummer Jim Toomey. In 1979 they signed a deal with Logo Records, and over the following eighteen months scored four UK Top 40 singles, including a cover of **Dusty Springfield**'s 'I Only Want to Be with You', which reached Number 4. The band released three albums, the last of which, *Luminous Basement* (1980), came after they had joined RCA. Manufactured for pop success and doomed by their own restrictions, the Tourists split up that winter in Bangkok in the middle of a Far East tour.

Eurythmics were born when, toward the end of 1980, Lennox and Stewart went to work in Cologne, at the studios of the eminent German musician Connie Plank. Plank heard the songs they had developed for that session at a New Year's Eve party and took an immediate interest in them. Taken up by RCA, they released their debut album, *In the Garden*, in 1981 and this featured **Blondie** drummer Clem Burke, Robert Görl from **DAF** and Holger Czukay of **Can**. Between mid-1981 and early 1983, the Eurythmics released a string of unsuccessful singles after which Stewart and Lennox, needing some breathing space, ceased to be lovers. This change in their personal relationship seemed to revitalize their musical partnership and in January 1983, the LP and single *Sweet Dreams (Are Made of This)* were released. The single reached Number 2 and demonstrated beyond doubt that young record buyers were finally ready for the Eurythmics' epic pop.

Once they had regular access to TV airtime, their imaginative use of video undoubtedly helped them to enchant a massive new audience, and they scored another three UK Top 10 singles in '83, including the re-released 'Love Is a

Stranger', which had been ignored on its previous issue in September '82. The video factor also helped in the US where, with the arrival of MTV, 'Sweet Dreams' made it to Number 1.

Another album, *Touch*, was released in the autumn of 1983, and although it was not so well received by the critics, it marked a progression to a generally warmer but varied sound, from the furious dance tempo of 'Right By Your Side' to the strangely moody single 'Here Comes the Rain Again'.

The year 1983 had been successful (over six million records sold worldwide), and 1984 saw the Eurythmics undertaking a world tour to consolidate their success. Following this, amid much controversy, they were commissioned to write a new film score for the film *1984* after the first one was rejected, the producers having resorted to the increasingly common ploy of using a 'name' commercial pop soundtrack to sell the film. The music was released as an LP, even though much of what they had written was not used on the film after protests from the original composer. A single taken from the album, 'Sex Crime (Nineteen Eighty Four)', gave them yet another hit, reaching Number 4.

The LP *Be Yourself Tonight* was released in 1985, confirming their status as one of the most popular and invigorating pop bands of the Eighties, and this year also saw Eurythmics score their first UK Number 1 single with 'There Must Be an Angel'. The same year, Lennox tangled voices on a collaboration with an even more powerful singer, **Aretha Franklin**, for the single 'Sisters Are Doing It for Themselves'. Dave Stewart also found time to produce albums for the likes of ex-Undertones' singer **Feargal Sharkey** and young American country rockers Lone Justice. They released the album *Revenge* in 1986.

EVERETT, BETTY R&B vocalist Betty Everett, born in Mississippi in November 1939, recorded unsuccessfully for Chicago labels Cobra, Onederful, and C.J. before scoring national hits on Vee Jay with catchy pop songs – 'You're No Good' (1963), 'It's in His Kiss (The Shoop Shoop Song)', 'Getting Mighty Crowded' (1964), and a romantic duet with **Jerry Butler**, 'Let It Be Me'. After the company's collapse and an inauspicious year with ABC-Paramount, she surfaced with 'There'll Come a Time' (1968) and others on UNI, and has remained a consistent name in the soul charts, recording for Fantasy since 1970.

EVERLY BROTHERS Although the roots of rock'n'roll are usually traced to black R&B, in retrospect the total picture of rock in the Fifties can be seen to owe as much to white country music. The 'landmark' artists – **Haley**, **Presley** and **Holly** – added black influences to their country heritage; the Everly Brothers, however, were simply the most successful hillbilly act ever.

Both born in Brownie, Kentucky, Don (1 February 1937) and Phil (19 January 1939) came from a country-music family; their parents, Ike and Margaret, were hillbilly performers with their own Kentucky radio show. As soon as Don and Phil could stand in front of a microphone it became a family act. In 1956 Ike persuaded **Chet Atkins** in Nashville to take an interest in them, and they cut their first single, 'Keep A-Lovin' Me', for Columbia in the same year. They switched to Archie Bleyer's Cadence label in 1957 and the hits started coming. By this time, the family had moved to Tennessee, and the brothers met songwriter **Boudleaux Bryant**. Bryant, writing either alone or with his wife Felice, was to provide many of their hits, which were recorded in Nashville. The Bryant songs were archetypal teenage love ballads whose frequently lachrymose tone perfectly suited the keening, plaintive harmonies of the Everlys.

The first hit (May 1957) was 'Bye Bye Love', followed the same year by 'Wake Up Little Susie'. The brothers' association with Cadence continued until 1960, producing sixteen Hot 100 entries – of which nine made the Top 10 – including 'Bird Dog', 'Problems' and 'When Will I Be Loved?'. The records were melodramatic and forceful, with the Brothers' harmonies soaring above impressive rock arrangements. The act then signed with the new Warner Brothers label, and had an immediate Number 1 in both America and Britain with 'Cathy's Clown'. The big hits continued until 1962, including 'So Sad', 'Walk Right Back', 'Ebony Eyes' and 'Crying in the Rain'.

Like all established American acts, the Everly Brothers felt the impact of the British Invasion, but continued to have the occasional success until 'Bowling Green' (1967). Their biggest mid-Sixties British hit was 'Price of Love' (1965). The relationship between the two brothers began to deteriorate, however, and from being indistinguishable halves of a harmony act, they became two distinct personalities: Phil lighter and pop-oriented, Don darker and brooding.

They continued to record, and in 1968 produced a classic album aptly titled *Roots*: country songs interleaved with tape excerpts from the old Everly radio show. A friendship with **John Sebastian** resulted in the 1972 album *Stories We Could Tell*, backed by a host of superstars, and later the same year they returned to their old mentor Chet Atkins for *Pass the Chicken and Listen*, on RCA. The brothers broke up in mid-1973 in acrimonious circumstances and concentrated on solo careers, but by 1984 the rifts appeared to have been healed sufficiently for Don and Phil to give a reunion concert at London's Royal Albert Hall. They still sounded as fresh and engaging as ever.

Phil and Don Everly – perfect vocal harmony, but personal discord

EVERYTHING BUT THE GIRL

Ben Watt and Tracey Thorne came together in the early Eighties as Everything But the Girl, among the first in Britain to play a lightly jazz/swing-influenced pop that became increasingly fashionable in the Eighties.

Watt and Thorne, both established solo performers and recording artists in their own right with Cherry Red Records, met at Hull University in 1980 and then proceeded to record and perform as a duo while still studying for their degrees. Their first single was a cover of Cole Porter's 'Night and Day' which instantly won acclaim. Switching labels to Blanco Y Negro, the duo had their first chart success four years later with the UK Top 30 single 'Each and Everyone', a success that pushed the highly jazz-influenced album (featuring Simon Booth of **Working Week**) *Eden* (1984) up the charts too.

Successive single releases failed to make the charts and sales of the second album *Love Not Money* (1985) suffered due to a lack of radio airplay. A similar fate awaited their next album in 1986, *Baby the Stars Shine Bright*.

EXCELLO RECORDS The

Excello label was formed in Nashville, Tennessee, in 1952 by record man Ernie Young as an outlet for blues and R&B recordings so that the parent label, Nashboro, could concentrate exclusively on the gospel market. The first releases were poor in quality and did not sell until Arthur Gunter clicked in 1954 with 'Baby Let's Play House' (later recorded by **Elvis Presley**). This inspired Young to expand his blues activities and in 1955 he set up a long-term deal with Jay Miller of Crowley, Louisiana, that led to hit R&B recordings with **Slim Harpo** ('I'm a King Bee', 'Rainin'' in My Heart', 'Baby Scratch My Back') and a consistent output of Southern downhome blues by Lightnin' Slim, Lonesome Sundown, Lazy Lester and many more. Ernie Young had national hits with the original versions of 'Little Darlin'' by the Gladiolas in 1957 and 'Oh Julie' by the Crescendos on the Nasco affiliate in 1958.

For over a decade Excello was a prime source of authentic R&B, but when Ernie Young retired in 1966 the new management adopted a far more commercial approach, specializing particularly in soul music.

EXCITERS Although their chart

success was minimal, the Exciters recorded the original versions of several classic early Sixties pop songs. Members Brenda Reid, Carol Johnston,

Lillian Walker and Herb Rooney all hailed from Jamaica, New York, and their records – produced by **Leiber and Stoller**, written by such composers as **Burt Bacharach**, **Van McCoy** and **Bert Berns**, and arranged by Teacho Wilshire – employed the ethereal strings, marimba and tom-tom baion beat of **Drifters** discs. Their releases included 'Tell Him' (1962, their only US Top 10 hit) and 'I Want You To Be My Baby', both of which were successfully covered in the UK by **Billie Davis**, and 'Doo Wah Diddy Diddy', which was covered in Britain by **Manfred Mann**. The Exciters had spells with Roulette, Bang and RCA during the late Sixties and found belated popularity in the UK at the height of the Seventies 'northern soul' boom, when a number of their early releases achieved cult status.

FABIAN Philadelphia teen idol

Fabian – real name Fabiano Forte Bonaparte – was born on 6 February 1943, and shared the same background, manager and record label as **Frankie Avalon**. It was said that he was 'discovered' walking down the street by a talent scout impressed by his Italianate profile. If Stan Freberg's character, Clyde Ankle, was a satire on any one figure, it was Fabian. His record company (Chancellor) released five singles in 1959 in the hope that he might catch on as another **Elvis Presley**. These included 'I'm a Man', 'Turn Me Loose', 'Tiger', 'Come On and Get Me' and 'Hound Dog Man'. All figured in the Hot 100 although, in Britain, where his appearances on TV shows like *American Bandstand* were not seen, his contrived image never caught on in the same way. His films included *Hound Dog Man* (1959), *North to Alaska* (1960) and *Fireball 500* (1966).

FACENDA, TOMMY 'BUBBA'

Born on 10 November 1939 in Portsmouth, Virginia, Facenda was a classmate of **Gene Vincent** and in 1957 he joined Vincent's group, the Blue Caps, as a background singer and dancer. Leaving Vincent in 1958, he pursued a modest solo career, recording one single for Nasco in Nashville, before meeting Portsmouth record shop owner **Frank Guida**, for whom he cut 'High School USA', a novelty rock'n'roll song that was mastered in 28 different versions – one for each distributor – each

listing the important high schools in the distributor's area. Leased to Atlantic, the song reached Number 28 on the Hot 100 late in 1959, but Facenda only managed one follow-up before being drafted into the Army. On his discharge in 1962, he joined the Portsmouth Fire Brigade.

FACES The Faces were a coalition of

three leaderless **Small Faces** – **Ronnie Lane**, bass (born in London on 1 April 1946), Ian McLagan, keyboards (12 May 1946), and Kenny Jones, drums (8 September 1948) – and two refugees from the **Jeff Beck** Group, **Rod Stewart** (10 January 1945) and guitarist Ron Wood (1 June 1947), whom Beck had temporarily converted to bass. The group worked hard on the road for two years after their formation in 1969 before establishing themselves in Britain by reason of their ebullient live performances and Stewart's solo hit, 'Maggie May' (Mercury, 1971). They were, however, accepted sooner in America, where Stewart enjoyed a lingering reputation from his days with Beck. The band's boozy, easy-going approach tended to work less well in the recording studio, and the group's albums, consistently overshadowed by Stewart's solo efforts, moved from the patchily successful *First Step* (Warner Bros, 1970), *Long Player* (1971), and *A Nod's As Good As a Wink to a Blind Horse* (1972), to the disappointing *Ooh La La* (1973) and, apart from a live album in 1974, apparent stagnation. Lane left in mid-1973 to be replaced by Tetsu Yamauchi, and Wood and Jones made their own solo albums. By 1976, Stewart's rising superstar status caused friction within the band and his own commitment to its continuance was called into question. Wood left to join the **Rolling Stones** and Jones, after a short spell with a re-formed Small Faces, became Keith Moon's replacement in the **Who**. The Faces officially disbanded in 1977, though they reunited for a one-off concert in May 1986. *See also* **Small Faces**; **Rod Stewart**; **Ronnie Lane**

FACTORY RECORDS The most

innovative and abiding new wave label in terms of sound and marketing, Factory was the Bauhaus of punk. It was launched in Manchester, January 1978, by TV presenter Tony Wilson, host of the short-lived but adventurous rock show, *So It Goes*. Initially formed to house Wilson's signing **Joy Division**, it soon began signing other bands from Manchester and the North-West: **Orchestral Manoeuvres in the Dark**, the Durutti Column, A Certain Ratio and others.

With Joy Division as a lucrative, and controversial, flagship, Factory introduced, and still maintains, an eccentric operating style. Rather like an art book publisher, it retains a distance from the marketing processes of the industry, requires bands to produce, manage and publicize themselves, and prides its resistance to 'hyping' practices. Some bands complain about this; others relish the freedom and note that Factory pays better royalties than elsewhere.

The success of Joy Division – notably the fluke Number 1 success of their 1980 album *Closer* – allowed Factory to expand. It had already opened The Factory nightclub in a Manchester suburb, but closed this to open the larger, more sophisticated Hacienda, in central Manchester. As well as the Hacienda's three bars and hair salon, Factory also launched Ikon Video, producing videos of and by its own bands, as well as independent productions such as the full-length experimental movie *Feverhouse* (1985). In 1984 Wilson also announced plans for Factory clothing, and Factory 'loft' housing in Manchester, but these have yet to be realized.

Controversy has always surrounded Factory. Joy Division took their name from a forced-prostitution area of the Nazi death camp, Treblinka; New Order, the name the band adopted after the suicide of leader/singer Ian Curtis, while suggesting the Nazi 'Final Solution' in fact comes from the manifesto of the Khmer Rouge regime in Cambodia. Both names are said to be the idea of New Order manager Rob Gretton, like Wilson a university-educated left-wing radical. While the label thrives, no other signing has had the success of Joy Division/New Order. Wilson retains a full-time TV career, allowing the label to run its own eccentric way.

FAIRPORT CONVENTION

Fairport Convention are best known as the first exponents of British folk-rock, though during the various line-ups (at least nine in their first ten years alone) the band veered through American West Coast music to the highly original songs of **Richard Thompson** (born 3 April 1949) and **Sandy Denny** (6 January 1947). The original Fairport band was formed in 1967, played Dylanish, Byrdish, Butterfieldish material in London's 'underground' clubs, and gloried in being the scruffiest outfit in town. The founding line-up was Richard Thompson, Simon Nicol

(guitars), Ashley Hutchings (bass), Martin Lamble (drums) and Judy Dyble – later augmented with **Ian Matthews** as additional singer.

Only with the arrival of Sandy Denny from the folk-club scene after Dyble's departure did a British traditional element creep in: 'Nottamun Town' and 'She Moves Through the Fair' on their second album, *What We Did on Our Holidays* (Island, 1969), were the first-ever British folk-rock tracks. Denny's exquisite voice and the discreet muted backing ensured they were a success. Two albums later, with *Liege and Lief*, the band concentrated on what they called a 'folk-rock project'. By now the line-up had changed again: Lamble had been killed when the band's van crashed, and Dave Mattacks (born 1948) had taken over on drums; Matthews had left, and one of the folk scene's finest instrumentalists, fiddler Dave Swarbrick (born 5 April 1941) had joined. *Liege and Lief* (1969) was a milestone, for the Fairports now used all-out amplification, with long instrumental workouts, on lengthy narrative ballads. The music was loud, electric and exciting, yet the narratives and the strong folk melodies still came across. Inevitably for the Fairports, more splits followed. Sandy left for a solo career, and Ashley left to found Steeleye Span, Dave Pegg (born 2 November 1947) taking his place on bass. The band was still excellent, thanks largely to Richard Thompson's guitar work, and the musical approach began to veer away from folk to include more of his songs. After *Full House* (1970), Thompson left and the band began to lose its musical direction. A folk-rock 'concept album', *John Babbacombe Lee* (1971) was a partial success but lacked musical guts. The decline continued with Simon Nicol's departure, and reached rock-bottom with *Rosie*. From 1973 onwards, after yet more changes in personnel, the band began to regain the old excitement. When Sandy Denny rejoined in 1974 it was clear that the Fairports could again be a major force in British rock. By now they had progressed to a very varied musical format, with Sandy's fine, moody ballads interspersed with Swarbrick's fiddle jigs, traditional songs, and new material from the rest of the band, as exemplified on the fine *Rising for the Moon* (1975).

That album's release, however, preceded news of the departure of Sandy Denny, her husband Trevor Lucas (born 25 December 1943) – who had joined in 1971 – and Dave Mattacks,

which seemed to spell the end of the band. The others carried on as Fairport, with an enlarged line-up that included Bruce Rowland (from **Joe Cocker**'s Grease Band) and Dan Ar Bras, but their album *Gottle o' Geer* (1976) was a disappointment. Simon Nicol subsequently rejoined and the band – now Fairport Convention once more – signed with Vertigo. Three albums followed (*The Bonny Bunch of Roses*, 1977; *Tippler's Tales*, 1978; and *Farewell Farewell*, 1979) before what was announced as a final disbandment in the summer of 1979.

Almost inevitably, given the Fairports' history of splits and re-formations, there was still more to come: a reunion concert was held at the village of Cropredy, Oxfordshire, in 1980, that turned out to be the first of an annual event. 1984 found them back in the studios again for *AT2* and *Moat on the Ledge*, both released on the small Woodworm label.

Although he was low on singing technique, Adam Faith scored high marks for style and looks

FAITH, ADAM Born Terry Nelhams in Acton, London, on 23 June 1940, Adam Faith was second only to **Cliff Richard** as Britain's teenage idol in the early Sixties. His first ambition was to be a film editor and after school he worked as a messenger boy at Rank Screen Services. But caught up in the skiffle craze, he became vocalist with the Worried Men, a group formed by workmates at Rank, until after a year, **Jack Good** – the scholarly father figure of English rock'n'roll – suggested that

Nelhams go solo as Adam Faith.

He left his job, appeared on *Six-Five Special* twice, went on the road four times and cut two flops for HMV in 1958. Losing heart, he returned to Rank where he worked as an assistant cutter. Early in 1959, after a year's absence from showbiz, **John Barry** recommended Faith for a residency on a forthcoming TV rock series, *Drumbeat*, and after a successful audition, Faith stayed with the show for its 22-week run. He also recorded another flop, 'Runk Bunk' for Top Rank and appeared in the teen-movie *Beat Girl*.

On *Drumbeat*, he met songwriter Johnny Worth, a member of the Raindrops, who offered Faith his composition 'What Do You Want?' Recorded at EMI in late 1959 with John Barry providing novel pizzicato string backing over which Faith hiccuped the lyrics, 'What Do You Want?' became the biggest British hit of 1960, finally establishing the singer. He followed up with a series of huge hits, including 'Poor Me' (another Number 1), 'Someone Else's Baby', 'Lonely Pup' and 'Who Am I?', all in the same little-boy-lost style. Though not technically a singer, Faith's contrived enunciation and emasculated vocal style aroused a protective feeling among the era's girl fans, and visually he was quite chic for the period, eschewing greasy forelocks for a French college boy haircut. Abandoning his recording career in 1965, he went into repertory and for two years he toured the provinces in obscurity. In 1971, he was widely acclaimed for his portrayal of the loser villain 'Budgie' in the TV series of the same name and many thought he stole the limelight from co-star **David Essex** in the film *Stardust*. He masterminded **Leo Sayer**'s rise to fame in 1973 and remained his manager for the rest of the Seventies, while 1974 found Faith attempting (with only limited success) to re-launch his own career as a singer with the album *I Survive*. Since then, he has divided his time between his business interests, his passion for tennis (playing and watching) and acting roles like that in the 1986 West End production, *Down an Alley Full of Cats*.

FAITHFULL, MARIANNE

Born in Ormskirk, Lancashire, in 1947, Marianne Faithfull was an ex-convent schoolgirl discovered by **Rolling Stones** manager **Andrew Loog Oldham** at a party. He asked her to record a Jagger/Richard composition, 'As Tears Go By'. Her plaintive, cultured folky tones made a refreshing change in 1964 and the record (plus three follow-ups) made the charts. She then absented herself to have a baby. In 1967 her notorious affair with Mick Jagger tarnished her pure image, but initially furthered her new career as an actress. She appeared in a play by Chekhov and several films, but after her break with Jagger, her personal life was disrupted by drug problems. Between a series of appearances on the London stage she returned to recording in 1976 with *Dreamin' My Dream* and then signed with Island to make *Broken English*, a bitter set of songs utterly different in tone and content from her releases of a dozen years earlier. The album sold well, especially in the US, and she has since recorded two further albums for Island, *Dangerous Acquaintances* (1981) and *A Child's Adventure* (1983).

FALCONS

'You're So Fine' (Unart) by the Falcons reached the US Top 20 in 1959 and was one of the first obviously soulful records. Originally recorded for a Detroit label, Flick, it featured pungent guitar work and a heartbreakingly sad lead vocal from Joe Stubbs, the brother of Levi Stubbs of the **Four Tops**. The rest of the group — Mack Rice, Lance Finnie, **Eddie Floyd** and Willie Schofield — harmonized in deliciously dusty fashion. With a new lead singer (**Wilson Pickett**), the group returned to the charts on Lupine in 1962 with 'I Found a Love'. It was their last hit, but the Falcons' recording career had stretched from Mercury in 1956 (when Floyd sang lead), through Savoy, Falcon, Chess, United Artists, Atlantic, Big Wheel and others in the Sixties. Stubbs joined the **Contours**, while Floyd, Rice and Pickett became solo soul singers of varying distinction. *See also* **Eddie Floyd**; **Wilson Pickett**

FAME, GEORGIE

One of British R&B's most original and dynamic performers, Georgie Fame began his career backing the likes of **Eddie Cochran** on multi-date, nationwide package tours. Born Clive Powell in Leigh, Lancashire, on 26 June 1943, he was given his stage name by British rock'n'roll impresario **Larry Parnes**, who hired him as a member of the Blue Flames — the backing group assigned to **Billy Fury** — on a 1960 tour. Fame stayed with the Parnes organization for a year or so before switching to his first love, American R&B, and making his first, semi-legendary appearances at London's Flamingo Club on Sunday afternoon sessions early in 1962. The Blue Flames — Colin Green (guitar), Tex Makins (bass) and Red Reece (drums) — became his permanent backing band.

Augmented by a tenor saxophone (first Al Watson, then Mick Eve), the Blue Flames were given a residency at the Club's Saturday all-nighter session. **John McLaughlin** replaced Green that summer and, in November, Fame radically altered the group's sound when he bought a Hammond organ and Leslie speakers. However, the biggest change in the Blue Flames' music was prompted by the club's predominantly black audience — a mixture of American GIs on weekend leave and West Indians — who introduced Fame to his major influence, **Mose Allison**, and the beginnings of soul and ska. Green returned in place of McLaughlin and the line-up was expanded to include John Marshall (baritone sax), Eddie Thornton (trumpet), Cliff Barton (bass) and Speedy Acquaye (congas), although personnel changed frequently. Apart from two instrumental singles for R&B, the small independent label, Fame's first release was a live album, *Rhythm and Blues at the Flamingo* (Columbia (UK), 1964), and he recorded a second before 'Yeh Yeh' made Number 1 in January 1965. Subsequent hits launched him on a solo career and allowed him to achieve his ambition to sing with big bands. He broke up the Blue Flames in September 1966 (drummer Mitch Mitchell joined **Jimi Hendrix**), recorded *Sound Venture* (Columbia, 1966) with the Harry South Band, won jazz polls, and the following year appeared at the Albert Hall with Count Basie. His biggest hit, 'The Ballad of Bonnie and Clyde', marked the nadir of his artistic career at the end of 1967. He later partnered **Alan Price**, mainly for television and cabaret work, but the sum of their talents proved less fruitful than the parts. In 1974, he reformed a large and unwieldy Blue Flames and recorded *Georgie Fame* (Island).

The late Seventies found Fame developing his jazz career further, and he became particularly associated with the music of songwriter Hoagy Carmichael, in tribute to whom he recorded the album *Hoagland* (1981) after working with him in California. In late 1983, in collaboration with Sylvia Vrethammar, he recorded *In Goodman's Land* (Sonet), a homage to jazz clarinetist Benny Goodman. In 1984, he re-cut several of his old hits plus a number of rock'n'roll standards for *My Favourite Songs* (Polygram) with fellow British R&B veterans Andy Fairweather Low and **Zoot Money**. Two years later he guested as vocalist on the Mondo Cane single, 'New York Afternoon'.

Georgie Fame made his name performing a blend of R&B, jazz and rock at the Flamingo Club, but his career drifted off into light entertainment

FAMILY In the late Sixties and early Seventies, Leicester band Family were one of the most talked-about British bands, yet they never quite broke into the top league. Originally they set out as Jim King and the Farinas but changed their name and soon made two fine albums, *Music in a Doll's House* (Reprise, 1968) and *Family Entertainment* (1969). The frenetic approach of their cadaverous lead singer Roger Chapman (born 8 April 1944) set a new trend in vocal styles although the band's performances were often erratic and their personnel was never constant for long, only Chapman, Charlie Whitney (24 June 1944) and Rob Townsend (7 July 1947) remaining throughout the band's career.

Rick Grech (born 1 November 1946), an original member, left to join **Blind Faith** and Jim King returned to Leicester. With Poli Palmer (born 25 May 1943) and John Weider (21 April 1947), Family recorded two further albums before John Wetton replaced John Weider. *Fearless* (1971) and *Bandstand* (1972) did something to restore the band's flagging credibility but with the departure of Wetton and Palmer, Family could scarcely accommodate further personnel changes. With Tony Ashton and Jim Cregan they recorded *It's Only a Movie* (1973) for the short-lived Raft label, but later that year Chapman and Whitney decided to wind up Family. The band went out in

a blaze of glory with a memorable farewell tour and Chapman and Whitney formed Streetwalkers, who subsequently enjoyed limited success.

FANNY All-female rock group Fanny first came together in California in 1970. The group's founders were singer and guitarist June Millington (born in Manila, Philippines, in 1949) and her sister Jean (bass, born in Manila in 1950), who played in a high-school outfit called the Sveltes before touring the Californian club circuit as Wild Honey during the late Sixties. With Nicole Barclay joining on keyboards and Alice de Buhr on drums, the group signed with Warner Brothers in 1969 and changed their name to Fanny at the suggestion of **George Harrison**. Their first three albums, *Fanny* (1970), *Charity Ball* (1971) and *Fanny Hill* (1972) were all Richard Perry productions, the last-named recorded at Apple studios in London. *Mother's Pride*, produced by **Todd Rundgren**, followed in 1973. A year later, Jean Millington and De Buhr left, to be replaced by Brie Brandt-Howard (drums) and Patti Quatro (**Suzi Quatro**'s sister, bass). Their next album, *Rock and Roll Survivors*, (Casablanca, 1975), was a poorly received rock opera. In 1975, the group broke up. Nicky Barclay went on to form Good News, who debuted on Ariola with *Diamond in a Junk Yard* (1976).

FARIÑA, RICHARD AND MIMI The Fariñas were a singer-songwriter couple who irradiated the mid-Sixties with distinctive, gentle folk-rock songs of love and social commentary. Born in 1937, Richard married Mimi (born 1945) in 1963 in Paris. Richard was emerging as a promising novelist (*Been Down So Long It Looks Like Up To Me*) and songwriter when he was killed in a motorcycle accident near Carmel, California, on 30 April 1966, on his wife's 21st birthday. Mimi has since been an actress, solo singer and songwriter. She is the sister of **Joan Baez**.

Fariña, of Irish-Cuban descent, played dulcimer; his wife played guitar and both sang in warm harmony. They attracted national attention at the 1965 Newport Folk Festival, playing in the rain to a mesmerized audience. While very much derivative of Dylan and Joan Baez, the duo established a new quality of swinging folk-rock that was 'pure' enough to appeal to traditionalists. Their approach towards topical material was fresh and without clichés. Three albums were issued by Vanguard, *Celebration for a Grey Day*, *Reflections in a Crystal Wind* (1965) and *Memories* (1968). Better known songs include 'Pack Up All Your Sorrows', 'Hard-Lovin' Loser', and 'House Un-American Blues Activities Dream'.

FARLOWE, CHRIS Born John Deighton in London on 13 October 1940, Chris Farlowe began his singing career as the teenage leader of the John Henry Skiffle Group which won the All-England Skiffle Championship in 1957. As Chris Farlowe he fronted the Thunderbirds, whose personnel included **Albert Lee** (guitar) and Dave Greenslade (organ), singing rock'n'roll and – by 1962 – a brand of R&B that landed them a residency at London's Flamingo Club.

Prior to the patronage of the **Rolling Stones'** Mick Jagger and Keith Richard, which brought him a Number 1 UK hit in the summer of 1966 with 'Out of Time' (Immediate), he had no chart success though he recorded two cult singles, the mods' anthem, 'Buzz with the Fuzz' (Columbia, 1965) and a version of 'Stormy Monday Blues' (Sue, 1965) as Little Joe Cook which fooled some British blues enthusiasts into thinking he was black. The hit changed his style, pulled him out of the clubs where his following was strongest, and led to the break-up of the Thunderbirds. He reorganized the group as a trio with Lee, Pete Shelley (drums) and Carl Palmer (also drums) in 1967 and kept them together for a year. Later, he rejoined Greenslade in **Colosseum**, and three months after the band's split in November 1971, joined **Atomic Rooster**. He temporarily quit rock in 1973 to pursue his business interest in Nazi memorabilia. He has never been able to find a satisfactory showcase for his powerful, bluesy voice and informal style outside of the Thunderbirds and the London R&B club circuit of the mid-Sixties. Accordingly, when he returned to performing in 1975 it was as part of a band (which included Albert Lee), and his first album was a live recording, *The Chris Farlowe Band, Live* (Polydor).

FARRELL, WES Born in New York in 1940, Wes Farrell had a successful executive career in pop music spanning two decades, starting in the late Fifties with his songwriting partnerships with Luther Dixon and **Bert Berns**. As one of the managers of the Roosevelt Music publishing company, he signed the young **Neil Diamond**, and co-wrote various hits for the **Shirelles**, **Jay and the Americans**, **Solomon Burke**, the **Vibrations**, and others. 'My Girl Sloopy', written for the Vibrations in 1964, was re-recorded a year later by the **McCoys** as 'Hang On Sloopy', in which form it became a US Number 1. By 1967, Farrell had become one of the major figures in the burgeoning 'bubblegum' business, responsible for the chart success of the Cowsills, Beacon Street Union, Every Mother's Son and other teen-oriented pop bands. Producing discs for each of these acts, Farrell's policy was to lease the tracks to major labels, especially MGM. In 1970, Farrell played a key part in the creation of *The Partridge Family* television series and the promotion of its star, David Cassidy, as a teen idol. Farrell produced many of his hits, some of which were revivals of Farrell-published songs from the Sixties. His Chelsea and Roxbury labels (formed in 1972) had a number of disco hits in the Seventies.

FASHION Despite an abundance of ambitious ideas (both musically and image-wise), Fashion failed to convert their early post-punk electro-dance incarnation into the successful pop group they always felt destined to be.

Formed in Birmingham in 1978, the original trio of Luke (vocals/guitar), Dik (drums) and Mulligan (bass/synth) predated **Sigue Sigue Sputnik** by eight years with their fascination for narcissism, technology and rock heritage. Two singles on their own label ('Steady Eddie Steady' and 'Citinite') preceded

their innovative debut album *Product Perfect*, released on Miles Copeland's Faulty Products label in 1980.

The sudden and mysterious departure of Luke saw the band take a new direction: Martin Recci (bass) and Dee Harris (vocals/guitar) were drafted in as Fashion purported to adopt the New Romantic style and were rewarded with a contract by Arista. An album, *Fabrique* (1982), contained the germs of several ideas that were never developed and Harris left soon after. He was replaced by ex-**Teardrop Explodes** man Troy Tate (vocals/guitar), Alan Darby (guitar) joined the group and Fashion released a third album *Twilight of Idols* (1983) with CBS, before disintegrating the next year.

FEARON, PHIL *See* **Galaxy**

FEATHERS, CHARLIE A vocalist and guitarist from backwoods Mississippi, Charlie Feathers was born on 12 June 1932, in Hollow Springs, Mississippi. He never had a hit record, but his importance to rock was his contribution to the mélange of country music and R&B known as 'rockabilly'. Many recordings, mostly made in Memphis (for the Flip, Sun, Meteor, King, Hi (unissued), Kay, Walmay, Memphis, Holiday Inn, Pinewood, Barrelhouse, and Rollin' Rock labels) and his backings for other artists all testify to his unique rhythmical influence on the sound that spawned **Elvis Presley**. His band retained their original rockabilly style well into the Seventies.

FELICIANO, JOSÉ Blind since his birth on 10 September 1945, in Puerto Rico, José Feliciano grew up in New York's Harlem. Always fascinated by music, at 18 he dropped out for a life in Greenwich Village coffee houses like the Café Id. His residency there led to an RCA contract, a single 'Everybody Do the Click' and album *The Voice and Guitar of José Feliciano* in 1964. He showed a diversity of style – rock-'n'roll, R&B and native Latin influences. Spanish language recordings propelled him to spectacular success in Central and South America and later in America and Europe with 'Light My Fire', 'California Dreamin'' and the *Feliciano* album in 1968. In time, however, the originality and freshness of his arrangements and interpretations began to lose their impact through constant repetition of a tried formula. In the Seventies, he appeared on **Joni Mitchell**'s *Court and Spark* album (1973), sang the theme song to the television series *Chico and the Man*, wrote

'Destiny' for Canadian easy-listening entertainer **Anne Murray**, and contributed to the soundtrack score of the film *MacKenna's Gold*. His albums included *Compartments* (1973), recorded with ex-Stax guitarist **Steve Cropper**, but much of his recording work by the end of the decade showed an unwillingness to diverge from the middle of the road. In 1980, he surprised many by joining the now California-based Motown label; his first album for Motown, *José Feliciano*, was produced by Berry Gordy himself.

FERRY, BRYAN The founder, lead singer and creative force behind **Roxy Music**, Bryan Ferry was born in Washington, County Durham, on 26 September 1945. An ex-Newcastle Art College student, Ferry began a solo career – initially to parallel his activities with the group – in late 1973 with the album *These Foolish Things* (Island), and followed it a year later with *Another Time, Another Place*. Unusually, it was the group that recorded his own compositions, while his solo efforts carried his interpretations of songs from a wide range of popular music sources – from **Bob Dylan** ('A Hard Rain's Gonna Fall') to the **Platters** ('Smoke Gets in Your Eyes') to mid-Sixties soul (a revival of **Dobie Gray**'s 'The In Crowd'). Both albums featured his own polished arrangements and drily exaggerated enunciation to create that particular mood of romantic nostalgia that is clearly redolent of its own falsity. Ferry stared out of the record covers in tuxedo and bow-tie, his expression half-

The inimitable Bryan Ferry in his mellower style of the Eighties

way between amusement and a malicious irony. The pattern changed somewhat after Roxy Music broke up in 1975 and his own career assumed a new importance, though *Let's Stick Together* (1976) contained more reworkings of old pop favourites ('The Price of Love' and 'Shame, Shame, Shame' included). *In Your Mind* (1977) featured Ferry originals, and *The Bride Stripped Bare* (1978) was a mixture of new songs and old, among them 'Hold On, I'm Coming' and 'That's How Strong Love Is'. Since that album's release, he has been writing and recording with a reconstituted Roxy Music.

FESTIVALS The outdoor festival was an integral part of the jazz and folk music calendar long before the first such rock event at Monterey, California, in 1967. The annual events at Newport, Rhode Island, were the most prestigious concert dates that jazz musicians and folk singers could play during the Fifties and early Sixties, although it was not unknown for rock performers – notably **Chuck Berry** at the 1959 Newport Jazz Festival and **Bob Dylan** at its 1964 folk equivalent – to run the gauntlet of abuse from the purists and appear there. Similarly, small-scale jazz festivals in the UK became a platform for the new R&B and beat groups of the mid-Sixties.

The Monterey event was organized by Los Angeles music mogul **Lou Adler** in conjunction with John Phillips of the **Mamas and Papas**, although its steering committee also included the likes of **Paul Simon** and **Paul McCartney**. Its purpose was to present the 'new music' of the flower-power era in an appropriate setting. Its immediate inspiration came from the open-air concerts in San Francisco, notably the famous Human Be-In of January 1967. Featuring **Jimi Hendrix**, the **Who**, **Janis Joplin**, **Jefferson Airplane**, **Otis Redding**, **Ravi Shankar** and others, Monterey set the pattern for what was to follow, not least in the respect that the film rights were pre-sold. Many of the then lesser-known acts who appeared there also benefited from the attentions of US record companies eager to own a slice of the potentially highly profitable post-San Francisco scene.

During the next three years about 30 festivals were held in America, attended by an estimated 2½ million people. Woodstock's 450,000 attendance was not exceeded until 1973, when 600,000 turned up at Watkins Glen, Indiana, to hear the **Allman Brothers**, **The Band** and the **Grateful Dead**. But that was only a one-day event, unlike the major festivals of the Sixties when most of the audience would camp out for up to a week.

A hippie mystique developed around the rock festivals, and anthems were written about them by **Joni Mitchell** and **Eric Burdon**. They were, it was said, the prototype communities of a new society, evidence that 'we' were going to spread the gospel of peace and love all over the nation. It was true that many festival-goers had to practise self-help over food, shelter and sanitary facilities since, in most cases, the provision made by the organizers was hopelessly inadequate. Yet the audiences were also at the mercy of the elements, and baking sun or torrential rain could make a festival site look somewhat like a refugee camp.

There were also large sums of money involved. Festivals were a promoter's dream, since they could accommodate ten times the audience of the largest hall. And even if only a minority of those attending actually paid to get in (as was often the case), there was always the future income from film and record rights. The promoters of Woodstock, for instance, sold $1.4 million worth of tickets, and paid the artists a total of $150,000, according to an investigation by *Variety* magazine. Even though the cost of preparing the site was massive, the profit margin was undoubtedly enormous.

The festival boom died down with the arrival of the Seventies. Promoters were increasingly harried by authorities worried about civil disorder and radicals who felt festivals should be free and tried to make them so – like those at the Isle of Wight Festival in 1970 (starring Dylan and The Band) who occupied a hill overlooking the stage. Also, the philosophy which had fuelled the major events had suffered a fatal blow at the Altamont Raceway in 1969, when a young black was knifed by Hell's Angels in front of the stage on which the **Rolling Stones** were performing. However, festivals spawned a new PA technology which led to regular concerts by superstars in outdoor (usually sports) arenas to audiences far bigger than any auditorium could hold, thereby permanently removing successful artists from relatively 'intimate' concert halls. Such one-day 'festivals' became the norm during the Seventies and Eighties, though the original festival ethic was kept alive by heavy metal fans in the UK at events like that held annually at Reading – large, noisy, anarchic affairs lasting up to three days.

The Live Aid concerts (*see* **Band Aid**), held at London's Wembley Stadium and Philadelphia's John F. Kennedy arena on 13 July 1985, were heartwarming and timely reminders of just how well organized (and how altruistic) all-star outdoor events could be: as a result of worldwide television coverage, a total of £54 million was raised for famine relief in Africa.

FIFTH DIMENSION Practitioners of an exuberant and highly commercial brand of pop-laced soul music, the Fifth Dimension were spawned in Los Angeles where Florence LaRue Gordon and Marilyn McCoo were born in 1943 and 1944 respectively. The three male members – Billy Davis Jr, Lamont McLemor (born 1939) and Ron Townson (born 1933) came from Louisiana. First known as the Versatiles, then the HiFis, they were touring as part of the **Ray Charles** Revue when they met manager Mark Gordon, who signed them to **Johnny Rivers'** Soul City Records. They adopted their now familiar name in 1967. Their novel, soul-flavoured harmony work, combined with the then unknown **Jim Webb**'s songs and Bones Howe's arrangements and production, captured public imagination with 'Up, Up and Away' and polished albums like *Magic Garden* and *Stoned Soul Picnic*. After 'Aquarius' in 1970, they became increasingly soulless, sophisticated and slick, but they stayed together until 1975, when McCoo and Davis left to work as a duo – their 'You Don't Have to be a Star' was a 1976 US Number 1. The remaining members again joined forces with Jim Webb for the album *Earthbound* (1975). McCoo and Davis broke up their partnership in 1980.

FIREBALLS The instrumental record vogue of the late Fifties and early Sixties produced major hit-makers in the Fireballs, all of whom – with the exception of Illinois-born pianist Jimmy Gilmer – came from Raton, New Mexico. Gilmer formed the group in 1959, and it comprised Gilmer, guitarist George Tomsco, bass-player Stan Lark, and drummer Eric Budd. They were managed by **Norman Petty**, who used the Fireballs to overdub various **Buddy Holly** demo tracks in the early Sixties. As the Fireballs, the band had four US hits in the years 1959–61, starting with 'Torquay'; they reappeared in 1968–9 with three more successes. The 1961 hit, 'Quite a Party', also scored in Britain. As Jimmy Gilmer and the Fireballs they had a US Number 1 in 1963 with 'Sugar Shack', following this with two minor hits.

FIVE SATINS

FIVE SATINS Best remembered for the haunting 'In the Still of the Night', the Five Satins were formed by lead singer Fred Parris in 1956. He had previously formed the Scarlets in 1953 and recorded with them for Red Robin. 'In the Still of the Night', written by Parris and cut in the basement of a New Haven church, was first released on Standard but bought from the label by Ember, the label on which it reached Number 24 in the US in 1956. They say the song hangs in the air over New York City; certainly it's one of the most beautiful R&B ballads ever recorded. Parris, Al Denby, Jim Freeman and Ed Martin were responsible for the weird but thrilling harmony, while Jessie Murphy played piano. Other hits included 'To the Aisle' – on which Bill Baker sang lead – and 'I'll Be Seeing You', which the group revived a cappella in the film *Let the Good Times Roll*. The group also recorded for First, Club, Chancellor, Warner Bros, Roulette and Mama Sadie.

FLACK, ROBERTA

FLACK, ROBERTA Black ballad singer Roberta Flack, born in Asheville, North Carolina, on 2 February 1937, was exposed to musical expertise from her earliest days – her mother was a classical pianist, while her father played jazz. She graduated with a BA in music from Howard University, Washington, and, after teaching music for a year, began to accompany opera singers. Finally in 1967 she took a job playing and singing jazz at a Washington club. Roberta was spotted by eminent jazz pianist Les McCann, upon whose recommendation she was signed to Atlantic by producer Joel Dorn. Having enjoyed some chart success in duet with **Donny Hathaway**, Roberta topped the American charts in 1972 with the haunting 'First Time Ever I Saw Your Face' – also a British Top 20 hit – taken from her first album, *First Take*. She followed that with another huge international hit in 1973, Charles Fox and Norman Gimbel's 'Killing Me Softly With His Song'. Supposedly inspired by seeing Don McLean, 'Killing Me' made it clear that Flack was rapidly becoming a jazz-tinged MOR singer and leaving 'soul' far behind.

Between 1974 and 1977, Flack spent much of her time working on educational projects for disadvantaged youth. She returned to recording with the album *Blue Lights in the Basement* (1977) and renewed her partnership with Hathaway for *Roberta Flack Featuring Donny Hathaway*, although he died before the release date. In 1980, she began a new partnership with Peabo Bryson – a live album, *Live and More*, was issued in 1981. *See also* **Donny Hathaway**

FLAMIN' GROOVIES

FLAMIN' GROOVIES Formed in San Francisco in 1966, the Flamin' Groovies were originally known as the Chosen Few, then the Lost and Found. Cyril Jordan, George Alexander, Roy Loney, Tim Lynch, and Danny Mihm were the first line-up as the Flamin' Groovies, with Lynch replaced by James Farrell and Loney by Chris Wilson in 1971, and Mihm replaced by David Wright in 1973. Never an accepted part of the San Francisco scene, the Groovies were rock'n'roll purists with a traditional approach, doing Fifties rock, Beatle music and folk-rock in a no-nonsense, anti-progressive style that built them a solid cult following but held back the attention more fashionable groups received.

A self-issued album in 1968 was followed by an album on Epic (*Supersnazz*) the next year. A contract with Kama Sutra resulted in two albums, *Flamingo* (1970) and *Teenage Head* (1971). With the latter, the Flamin' Groovies were hailed as the new Rolling Stones, and it seemed that mass idolatry was just around the corner, but then a two-year stay in England under the auspices of United Artists resulted in only two singles (produced by **Dave Edmunds**) and a series of misunderstandings that found the group back in San Francisco in 1973. Their cult following was by now immense, and their recordings collectors' items. Enormously popular in Europe, they toured France and were treated as heroes. Back home, the group exercised more caution in dealing with the record industry, releasing only one single (the Edmunds-produced 'You Tore Me Down'), on the independent Bomp Records label, an offshoot of *Who Put the Bomp?*, a leading fanzine, resulting in a contract with Sire Records in 1975. *Shake Some Action* (1976) was produced by Dave Edmunds. In the late Seventies, the Groovies found new fame in Europe among punk and new wave audiences following their tour with the **Ramones**.

FLAMINGOS

FLAMINGOS An R&B quintet from Chicago, the Flamingos were formed in 1952 by Zeke and Jake Carey, Solly McElroy and Paul Wilson. Their unusually broad range of influences – from gospel to the Four Freshmen, a close harmony group – left them well equipped to survive the radical changes to overtake black group singing during their twenty-year history. The Fats Washington ballad 'I'll Be Home' (covered by **Pat Boone**) made the R&B Top 10 in 1956, and they subsequently made the pop charts with a string of equally romantic tunes on End. They included 'Lover Never Say Goodbye', 'I Only Have Eyes for You' (Number 11 in 1959), 'Love Walked In', 'I Was Such a Fool', 'Nobody Loves Me Like You' (Number 30 in 1960) and 'Time Was'. Later hits in the soul vein included 'Boogaloo Party' (on Philips in 1966), 'Dealin'', (Julma in 1969) and 'Buffalo Soldier' (Polydor in 1970). Johnny Pearson, Terry Johnson, Nate Nelson (who joined the **Platters**), Tommy Hunt (a Sixties soul star), Doug McClure and Larry Clinton were among later personnel, while Johnny Carter joined the **Dells**. The Flamingos also recorded for Parrot, Decca and, in 1972, Ronze.

FLASH CADILLAC AND THE CONTINENTAL KIDS

FLASH CADILLAC AND THE CONTINENTAL KIDS 1969 was a year in which many groups did well with parodies of Fifties rock, with **Sha Na Na** the model for dozens more such as Big Wheelie and the Hubcaps and Vince Vance and the Valiants who became fixtures on all the regional club circuits over the following few years. Flash Cadillac and the Continental Kids – Sam McFadin, Warren Knight, Linn Phillips, Kris Angelo, George Robinson and Ricco Masino – formed in Colorado in 1969, were arguably the only such group to bring any originality to the genre, while also being closest to the true spirit of Fifties rock'n'roll. They moved to California in 1970 and made a strong impression with the press and audiences, then went on to appear in the film *American Graffiti* and from there to a recording contract. Their first album for Epic consisted of fairly well-known classics, but the second (*There's No Face Like Chrome*, 1974) presented a surprising synthesis of Fifties, Sixties and Seventies pop styles, not unlike groups such as Ducks Deluxe in the UK. A version of Barry Blue's 'Dancin' on a Saturday Night' flirted with the charts, while 'Good Times, Rock and Roll', their first on the Private Stock label, was a smallish hit in early 1975. 'Did You Boogie (with Your Baby)?' – recorded in 1976 with DJ Wolfman Jack – does, however, remain their only US Top 40 hit.

FLEETWOOD MAC

FLEETWOOD MAC The story of Fleetwood Mac is really that of two distinct groups – the hard-edged UK-based blues band of the late Sixties and the phenomenally salesworthy Californian AOR band of the mid-Seventies and beyond. Originally known as **Peter Green**'s Fleetwood Mac, the group played its first engagement on 12 August 1967 as part of that year's National Jazz and Blues Festival. As a result of their appearance, they were signed to a recording contract with Blue Horizon records. Fleetwood Mac then consisted of Peter Green, vocals/guitar (born 29 October 1946); Jeremy Spencer, vocals/slide guitar (4 July 1948); John McVie, bass (26 November 1945); and Mick Fleetwood, drums (24 June 1947). *Fleetwood Mac* (Blue Horizon, 1968) reached Number 1 and stayed in the album charts for almost thirteen months. This was followed by 'Black Magic Woman' and the bluesy 'I Need Your Love So Bad', both of which were minor British hits.

Later in 1968, Peter Green's friend, guitarist Danny Kirwan (born 13 May 1950), was recruited into the Fleetwood Mac line-up. A month later the band cut their million-selling single, 'Albatross' – a British Top 5 hit again when it was re-released in 1973. In August 1969, Fleetwood Mac signed with Reprise, continuing their hit formula with 'Oh Well' and 'The Green Manalishi' in addition to two top-selling albums, *Mr Wonderful* and *Then Play On*. After 'The Green Manalishi', Peter Green quit the band, and his place was taken by John McVie's wife, Christine Perfect (born 12 July 1943), formerly of **Chicken Shack**. The band was now very much aware that they had to find a new direction without their former leader, and recorded several new songs for the hit album *Kiln House* (1970), their passport to the States. In February 1971, while in America, Jeremy Spencer disappeared and was later found to have joined a Los Angeles religious cult, the Children Of God. Ironically, as California took Jeremy away, it also provided a replacement in guitarist Bob Welch. The group's next album, *Future Games* (1971), ushered in a new era. They had left behind the 12-bars that initially made their name, but the blues in its root form remained a major influence. In mid-1972, following Danny Kirwan's departure, guitarist Bob Weston joined the band, creating a more complex overall sound. The subsequent *Penguin* and *Mystery to Me* (1973) involved further musical exploration. In 1973, the group decided to settle permanently in America – but without Weston.

A year later they released *Heroes Are Hard to Find*, their first album made wholly in America, but by early 1975 had once again changed the line-up. Lead guitarist Bob Welch left the group to concentrate on production work, and was replaced by San Franciscans Lindsey Buckingham (vocals, guitar, born 3 October 1947), and girl vocalist, Stevie Nicks (born 26 May 1948), who previously worked as a duo. The addition of Buckingham and Nicks made the group a much more formidable commercial force. Their asexual tenor/alto vocal ranges augmented an already developed sound, and they brought with them their own backlog of songs and fresh ideas. Buckingham was to emerge as the new 'leader' of Fleetwood Mac, writing the catchiest of the band's more disposable pop songs – 'Go Your Own Way', 'Monday Morning', 'Never Going Back Again' – and playing all guitar parts on their records, mixing acoustic and electric stylings. Nicks was the group's most eccentric member with her penchant for antique knitted shawls and Isadora Duncan-like stage moves. *Fleetwood Mac* (Reprise, 1975) included 'Say You Love Me', 'Warm Ways' and 'Rhiannon', and gained platinum status within months. Their success, however, precipitated the collapse of the relationships of the two couples within the band: Buckingham and Nicks drifted apart during the summer of 1976, and Christine McVie celebrated her divorce from husband John by getting herself sterilized – a fashionable Californian trend in the Seventies. She then embarked on a two-year affair with Dennis Wilson of the **Beach Boys** while further complications arose when Currie Grant, the band's long-serving lighting engineer, revealed his involve-ments with both Christine and Stevie in the pages of *Rolling Stone*. Their 1977 album *Rumours* chronicled the group's various romantic upheavals and set the scene for an untold number of subsequent 'involvements' that verged on both the bizarre and the outrageous. As John McVie said at the time, 'it was like an extract from a diary of our lives'.

Rumours eventually sold 25 million copies worldwide and contained a clutch of hit singles – 'Go Your Own Way', 'Dreams' (a US Number 1), 'Don't Stop' and 'You Make Loving Fun'. Their next album, *Tusk* (1979), was the most expensive rock album ever recorded at that time, totalling ten months of prime studio time at a total of over one million dollars. It sold four million copies – a relative failure by the standards of *Rumours* – and featured a large proportion of Buckingham's left-field experiments in song structure and mixing. A double album, *Fleetwood Mac Live*, followed in December 1980 but it was 1982 before the group again combined to record a studio album, *Mirage*, which received mixed reviews but again demonstrated their collective commercial strength. Amid constant speculation about a Fleetwood Mac break-up, Nicks, Buckingham and Fleetwood became heavily involved in solo projects as the Eighties wore on. Notable solo releases included Nicks' *Bella Donna* (1981) and *The Wild Heart* (1983), Buckingham's *Law and Order* (1981, from which the US Number 9 hit single 'Trouble' was taken) and Fleetwood's *I'm Not Me* (1983). Christine McVie also made her solo debut for Warners with *Christine McVie* (1984).

John McVie and Lindsey Buckingham let rip as Fleetwood Mac notch up another successful concert in their phenomenally lucrative career

FLEETWOODS A vocal trio formed in 1958 at Olympia High School, Olympia, Washington, the Fleetwoods were Gary Troxel (born 28 November 1939), Barbara Ellis (20 February 1940) and Gretchen Christopher (29 February 1940). They originally called themselves Two Girls and a Guy before changing their name to the Fleetwoods. Their first record, the self-penned 'Come Softly to Me', was a Number 1 in the US in 1959 on Liberty/Dolton, as was their second and best De Wayne Blackwell composition, 'Mr Blue'. However, their gentle harmony sound soon fell out of favour and their last Top 10 hit was a revival of Thomas Wayne's 1959 hit 'Tragedy' in 1961.

FLOYD, EDDIE Although best known for his recordings for Stax in the late Sixties, Eddie Floyd (born in Montgomery, Alabama, on 25 June 1935) began his singing career as a member of the Detroit-based **Falcons**, whose impassioned gospel style anticipated the coming of soul music. Floyd was the group's featured soloist on their records for Mercury, but he left to go solo in 1962 and recorded for the Lupine, Atlantic and Safice labels – the last-named his own company, run jointly with Al Bell and Chester Simmons – before moving to Stax in 1966. While he never achieved the status of such Stax contemporaries as **Otis Redding** or **Isaac Hayes**, he co-wrote (with **Steve Cropper**) and recorded at least one soul classic in 'Knock on Wood' (1966) and reached the US Top 40 on two further occasions, with 'I've Never Found a Girl' and a revival of **Sam Cooke**'s 'Bring it On Home to Me' (both 1968). He left Stax in the mid-Seventies for the Malaco label and switched to a more disco-based style, but with little success.

FLOYD, KING An underrated singer from New Orleans, King Floyd was born on 13 February 1945. He had local hits on Uptown (1964–6) and Pulsar (1967) produced by **Harold Battiste**, before breaking nationally with the Top 10 hit 'Groove Me' (Chimneyville, 1970). Recorded at Malaco studio in Jackson, Mississippi, and produced by another Crescent City veteran, Wardell Quezergue, it was prematurely acclaimed as the start of a 'Malaco Sound'. Apart from Jean Knight's 'Mr Big Stuff' (1971) the studio had no more notable successes, but Floyd continued to score minor hits, including the Top 30 'Baby Let Me Kiss You' (1971), 'Think About It' (1973), and 'Don't Cry No More' (1974).

FLYING BURRITO BROTHERS The Burritos were formed in Los Angeles in 1968 by musicians interested in an integration of rock and country music. The original line-up was **Gram Parsons** (guitar, born 5 November 1946), **Chris Hillman** (guitar, born 4 December 1942), 'Sneeky' Pete Kleinow (pedal steel, born c. 1935), Joe Corneal (drums), and Chris Ethridge (bass) – the first four of whom had played on the **Byrds**' ground-breaking album *Sweetheart of the Rodeo* (1968). The band never made more than one album with the same line-up. Temporary band members included Bernie Leadon (guitar), Rick Roberts (guitar), Al Perkins (pedal steel), Byron Berline (fiddle), Martin Scougat (triangle).

The original concept was more than a simple fusion of country and rock music. It was also a 'cosmic' American fusion, a bringing together of Sixties lifestyle and consciousness with the full width of the American musical heritage, from uptempo jigs to 'the saddest love songs ever heard', from biblical righteousness to country breezes. A song like 'Sin City', from their first and finest album *The Gilded Palace of Sin* (A&M, 1969), managed to sound as beautiful as an updated **Everly Brothers**, retaining the bits of the traditional country theme of uprootedness in the context of the vanished Sixties dream. This vision, though, was largely Gram Parsons', and found its fullest expression in his sadly truncated solo career – he died on 19 September 1973. After his departure from the Burritos in 1970, the group pursued a new aim, in which the early bite was sacrificed for a simpler music that still proved too subtle for commercial success. Their albums after *Burrito Deluxe* (1970) – *The Flying Burrito Bros* (1971) and *Last of the Red Hot Burritos* (1972) – while boasting some fine music, suffered in comparison with the half-realized vision of the early years. The 1974 double album *Close Up the Honky Tonks*, a compilation of the first two albums plus unreleased material, was a fitting epitaph for the group. However, the appeal of the name was so strong that in 1975 Kleinow and Ethridge got together another band of Burritos (including Joel Scott Hill, ex-Byrd Gene Parsons and cajun fiddler Gib Guilbeau) and secured a Columbia record contract. Ethridge left in 1976 and was replaced by Skip Battin of **Skip and Flip** fame. The final album bearing the Flying Burritos Brothers' name was *Airborn* in 1976. *See also* **Gram Parsons**

FLYING LIZARDS The brain-child of musician, composer and producer David Cunningham, Flying Lizards scored a novelty hit single in 1980 with a ramshackle version of 'Money', allegedly recorded for less than £5. No such success attended later singles, or the three albums, *Flying Lizards* (1980), *Fourth Wall* (1981) or *Top Ten* (1984), the last-named being a series of pop classics 'deconstructed' by Cunningham and friends. Although a line-up ventured briefly into London's Riverside Studios for a live performance in 1984, Flying Lizards are essentially a studio group. Masterminded by Cunningham, and abetted, on a part-time basis, by such friends as multi-instrumentalist Steve Beresford, singer Patti Palladin (ex-Snatch) and 'systems music' composer Michael Nyman, the group brought Cunningham's experience in the classical avant-garde to bear on his liking for pop, dub reggae and electronics. Cunningham continues to work in pop and the avant-garde.

FLYING PICKETS Six-piece group the Flying Pickets stored the first ever UK a cappella Number 1 with their version of **Yazoo**'s 'Only You', which occupied the top slot for five weeks over Christmas 1983.

Rick Lloyd, Brian Hibbard, David Brett, Gareth Williams, Ken Gregson and Red Stripe all met in 1980 while performing in the political musical *One Big Blow* for the radical 7:84 Theatre Company (the name represented the statistic that 7% of the population own 84% of the wealth). The show toured Europe for two years and by the end of its run, they had polished their vocal harmony abilities to the point where they began touring on the UK small club and cabaret circuit as the Flying Pickets. With the novelty value of the a cappella style and an adventurous choice of material, the group soon became a live favourite across the country. They signed a recording deal with Virgin offshoot 10 Records in November 1983 and by Christmas that year they had taken 'Only You' to Number 1.

'When You're Young and In Love' made Number 7 in April 1984, but later that year their version of **Eurythmics**' 'Who's That Girl?' reached a miserable Number 71 and indicated a decline in their fortunes as recording artists, although they retained their popularity as a live band. Their album *Lost Boys* (1984) contains ingenious versions of 'I Heard it Through the Grapevine', 'Masters of War' and 'Tears of a Clown'.

FOCUS A Dutch group who came together in 1969 as the back-up musicians to the Amsterdam version of the musical *Hair*, Focus originally comprised four formidable musicians – Thijs Van Leer (organ, flute, vocals, born 31 March 1948), Jan Akkerman (guitar, born 24 December 1946), Burt Ruiter (bass, 26 November 1946), and Pierre Van der Linden (drums, 19 February 1946). With the exception of the self-taught Ruiter, the group has behind it an extensive array of formal musical education. From 1969 onwards they produced a number of albums, notably *Moving Waves* (Blue Horizon, 1971), *Focus 3* (Polydor, 1972) and *Focus at the Rainbow* (1973), featuring their unique style of music, combining elements of rock (**Cream**, **Traffic**), modern jazz (Davis, Coltrane, Parker) and classical music from Bach through to Bartok, all moulded into a driving instrumental sound topped off by Thijs Van Leer's extraordinary scat-singing and Akkerman's imaginative guitar solos. 'Sylvia' and 'Hocus Pocus' were British Top 20 hits for the group in 1973. Van Leer and Akkerman also cut solo albums, for CBS and Harvest respectively. Akkerman left in 1976 and Philip Catherine joined; further personnel changes saw Steve Smith replace Van der Linden on drums and Eef Albers join on guitar. Their last album was *Focus Con Proby* (1978), a bizarre matching of talents with **P.J. Proby**.

FOGELBERG, DAN A singer-songwriter from Peoria, Illinois, Dan Fogelberg (born on 13 August 1951) made his recording debut for Columbia in 1972 with the Nashville-recorded album *Home Free*. A former art student, he had earlier worked as a session musician on guitar and keyboards, at one time backing **Van Morrison** on tour. While *Home Free* attracted some critical attention, it was *Souvenirs* in 1974 that made the Fogelberg name widely known, including as it did the US hit single 'Part of the Plan' (it reached Number 31). *Captured Angel* followed a year later and *Netherlands* in 1977, by which time he had moved to Boulder, Colorado; *Twin Sons of Different Mothers* (1978), recorded with flautist Tom Weisberg, went platinum, though his biggest selling record proved to be *Phoenix* in 1979. He sang on the *Urban Cowboy* soundtrack in 1980 and continued recording, though his live performances were few. Fogelberg's Eighties albums included *The Innocent Age* (1981) and *Windows and Walls* (1984).

FOLK REVIVAL (1960s) The unparalleled revival of interest in folk music that began about 1958 in America involved considerably more than a change in music tastes. It was also a political and social movement, a search for an alternative culture, and the start of a 'back-to-the-country' movement that has still not run its course. 1958 marked the start of the revival, for in that year the **Kingston Trio** had a chart hit with the unlikeliest sort of song, 'Tom Dooley', a traditional murder ballad. But it caught the popular imagination and set out the twin directions the revival would take – on one hand, traditional music and performers were discovered and lionized; on the other, an upsurge of city and college-based performers worked in folk style or neo-folk style. The folk revival brought into the popular mainstream of American music a different beat; music of earnest simplicity; meaningful lyrics; old story-songs and modern protest/topical commentaries.

An earlier major folk revival had happened during World War II, in the spirit of the New Deal and anti-Fascist populist movement. Two giants of that period, **Leadbelly**, the black Texas powerhouse, and **Woody Guthrie**, the white Oklahoma Dust Bowl bard, left a legacy that the post-1958 revival developed. The strongest link between the two revivals was **Pete Seeger**, who, with the Almanac Singers, the **Weavers**, and then on his own, is regarded as the 'father' of the folk revival. Several other older performers set the stage for the new revival, among them **Harry Belafonte**, Burl Ives and Josh White: sophisticated interpreters with roots out in the country. The success of the Kingstons sparked other group efforts. Among them were the Limeliters, Brothers Four, Chad Mitchell Trio, Tarriers, Rooftop Singers, and the Highwaymen. Shaped in the image of both the Kingstons and the Weavers were **Peter, Paul and Mary**, the dominant folk group of the 1960s.

Other new interpreters emerged: Odetta with her rich voice; **Judy Collins** and **Joan Baez**; Bob Gibson, Eric Weissberg and Billy Faier explored instrumental virtuosity; Dave Van Ronk, Eric Von Schmidt and **John Paul Hammond**, showed that white city boys could empathize with the blues. **Jack Elliott** kept Woody's style vibrant. Soon, it wasn't enough to do the songs of the country stylists, but the recordings and the rural performers themselves were rediscovered. City audiences marvelled at the blues of **Robert Johnson**, **John Lee Hooker**, **Muddy Waters**, **Lightnin' Hopkins**, **Sonny Terry and Brownie McGhee**, the Rev. Gary Davis and black songsters like Mississippi John Hurt and Mance Lipscomb. The white rural ballad tradition came alive again, too, unearthing great ballad-singers like Roscoe Holcomb, Frank Proffit, Horton Barker, Mother Maybelle Carter, and Sarah Ogan Gunning. The Citybilly trio, the New Lost City Ramblers, revived old string-band sounds, while a succession of able urban bands, like the Bluegrass Boys and the Charles River Valley Boys pointed in the direction of that virtuoso bluegrass style pioneered by Bill Monroe and such famous alumni as **Earl Scruggs** and Lester Flatt.

The settings for the great revival were many, but coffee-houses and campuses seemed especially suitable for folk song. Regional and college folk festivals abounded, while the annual Newport Folk Festivals became national extravaganzas, the meeting of the hip new with the dedicated old. Some folk festivals had a quasi-religious feel, invested with high purpose, brotherhood and ethical content, through and beyond the music. Recordings proliferated, on specialist labels like Folkways, Vanguard, Prestige, Elektra, but soon every major label also had its folk roster. When the music business got into the revival, there was a dilution of material, but a broadening of the audience. The TV show, *Hootenanny*, embattled and unbalanced, turned the revival for two years into a craze. Around 1964, the heat cooled as rock and the **Beatles** arrived, and **Dylan** and the **Byrds** explored folk-rock. But the revival had discovered great music and traditions, and the rediscovery continued in myriad ways and with many voices.

FOLK-ROCK (U.K.) Despite occasional experiments with traditional jazz bands and dabblings in the skiffle boom, the leaders of the folk-revival, such as Ewan MacColl and A. L. Lloyd, kept their distance from the pop world. The result was that, by the mid-Sixties, hundreds of folk clubs thrived in Britain, forming a parallel musical culture to the dance-halls and clubs of the beat group scene.

In many clubs a cheerful eclecticism prevailed. British traditional songs existed side by side with ragtime guitarists, jug bands and **Woody Guthrie** imitators. The most important development, though, was the emergence of the contemporary songwriter, often modelling himself on **Bob Dylan** or **Tom Paxton**. The first to break through into rock music proper was **Donovan** whose naïve protest songs appeared in the charts in 1965. But, like others who came after, **Ralph McTell, Roy Harper, Incredible String Band**, he had little to do with folk songs as such. It was simply that the clubs, with their intense audiences and tolerant atmosphere, offered the only place for the new songwriters to perform.

As a musical genre 'folk rock' can be defined as the mingling of traditional or traditionally influenced material with rock instrumentation. Among its earliest exponents were the Irish group Sweeney's Men and **Fairport Convention**, who added British folk songs to their repertoire of West Coast music when ex-folk singer **Sandy Denny** joined in 1968. Their 1969 album, *Liege and Lief*, was Britain's first full-scale folk-rock work.

Steeleye Span, formed in the same year, took a different musical stance. Their philosophy was that the only way to make traditional songs relevant to present-day audiences lay in placing them in a rock context. A more purist attitude was taken by former Fairport and Steeleye bassist Ashley Hutchings whose Albion Country Band and Etchingham Steam Band, plus his productions for his wife Shirley Collins (notably the album *No Roses*, 1971) stuck more closely to traditional melodies and rhythms.

More eclectic were Fairport Convention and **Pentangle**, based around the 'folk-baroque' guitar playing of **Bert Jansch** and John Renbourn, while another former club guitarist, **John Martyn**, had by the mid-Seventies developed a style using electronics and owing much to Indian and East European folk music as well as jazz. A different strategy was taken by Mr Fox, formed by Bob and Carole Pegg in 1971, which performed electric songs written in a traditional vein.

By the early Seventies, much of the energy of folk-rock came from Irish, Scottish and Breton bands, notably Horslips, Alan Stivell, Planxty and the JSD Band, while **Lindisfarne** and its successor Jack The Lad, from Newcastle, mixed local folk songs with original material. All had many valid musical ideas, but without exception were eventually defeated by their position in a no man's land between the introverted folk world and the increasingly conservative rock scene, where promoters and recording executives were suspicious of new ideas. Eventually the sheer cost of keeping an electric group on the road took its toll.

The folk-rock exemplified by Steeleye Span and Fairport Convention died sometime in the late Seventies, but the notion of a merging of the energies of folk music and rock still retained its potency. In 1982, **Dexys Midnight Runners** boldly experimented in fusing folk with white soul and scored a Number 1 hit with 'Come On, Eileen', while a succession of singers and bands have come up with the odd folk-influenced single whose novelty has caught the public's imagination.

FONTANA, WAYNE Best remembered for his mid-Sixties hits with the **Mindbenders**, Wayne Fontana was born Glyn Ellis in Manchester in 1947 and began his pop career playing in a school skiffle group called the Velfins. With the Mindbenders (also from Manchester) as his backing group, his first record was a cover version of **Bo Diddley**'s 'Road Runner', which was released on Philips' Fontana label in June 1963. A year later, the group scored its first major chart success with a cover of **Major Lance**'s 'Um Um Um Um Um Um', which reached Number 5 in the UK. The subsequent 'Game of Love' (1965) brought the group worldwide acclaim, peaking at Number 1 in the US, Canada and Australia, and Number 2 in Britain. Later singles failed to click, however, and Fontana and the Mindbenders split in February 1966; ironically, it was his former accompanists who triumphed – with 'A Groovy Kind of Love', a Number 2 in the UK in 1966 – while Fontana's solo chart fortunes slumped somewhat. He reached Number 16 with 'Come on Home' and Number 11 with 'Pamela, Pamela' during 1966, but no further Top 20 hits were forthcoming. During the Seventies he toured the US appearing in rock'n'roll revival shows. *See also* **Mindbenders**

FORBERT, STEVE A native of Meridian, Mississippi, where he was born in 1955, Steve Forbert emerged in the late Seventies as a quirkily original singer-songwriter in the **Loudon Wainwright/John Prine** mould. He played in rock bands at high school and later graduated to the New York folk club scene. He made his debut for the small Nemperor label in 1978, with the album *Alive on Arrival*, which featured perhaps his best-known song, 'Thinkin''. *Jackrabbit Slim* (1979) contained the hit single 'Romeo's Tune', a Number 11 in the US during 1980. Later albums included *Little Stevie Orbit* (1980) and *Steve Forbert* (1982), each featuring his band the Flying Squirrels in support.

FORD, FRANKIE Born in 1941 in Gretna, Louisiana, Frankie Ford rose to fame when his second record, 'Sea Cruise', was a Top 20 hit in 1959 on the Ace label. It is now recognized as a New Orleans rock'n'roll classic, but the hit was obtained at the expense of **Huey 'Piano' Smith**, whose original vocal tracks were wiped off in favour of Ford's – the same thing happened with the follow-up 'Alimony'. In 1960 Ford had a small hit with a cover version of **Joe Jones**'s 'You Talk Too Much' on Imperial but a spell in the Army in 1962 effectively ended his career as a recording star. He has recorded on and off without much success since then, and now plays standards with great poise for the throng of tourists in his own nightclub in New Orleans' French quarter.

FORD, TENNESSEE ERNIE One of the Capitol label's roster of country singers during the Fifties, Tennessee Ernie Ford was born Ernest Jennings Ford in Bristol, Tennessee, on 13 February 1919, and worked as a DJ before beginning his professional singing career on local radio in Pasadena. Signing with Capitol in 1948, he scored major national hits with 'Mule Train', 'Smokey Mountain Boogie' and 'Anticipation Blues' (all 1949), but scandalized the country purists by recording 'I'll Never Be Free' and 'Nobody's Business' with mainstream pop singer Kay Starr in 1950. His first million-seller, the self-composed 'Shotgun Boogie', came during the same year.

He struck gold again in 1955, this time with a semi-rock record, 'Sixteen Tons'. One of the fastest selling records in history, 'Sixteen Tons' allowed Ford to make his final break with the country music establishment. CBS gave him his own television show and he slipped quickly into the mainstream of American showbusiness. When he retired, still successful, in the early Sixties, he had accumulated some 20 albums of songs, the most popular of which were his religious collections.

FOREIGNER Almost the first group that comes to mind when the term 'AOR' is used, Foreigner employed their mastery of a widely accessible and undemanding rock form to sell albums in vast quantities across the world. Formed in New York City in 1976 by two Englishmen, veteran guitarist Mick Jones (ex-**Spooky Tooth**) and ex-**King Crimson** multi-instrumentalist Ian McDonald, they quickly recruited Lou Gramm (vocals), Ed

Gagliardi (bass), Al Greenwood (keyboards) and Dennis Elliott (drums).

Foreigner was released in 1977 and achieved quadruple platinum sales, setting a pattern for its successors. The group became a huge live attraction, scoring US Top 10 singles, and successive album releases all achieved multiple platinum sales, with *Double Vision* (1978) selling over seven million copies. Naturally the critics were none too impressed, but the next LP, 4 (1981), converted many hard rock reviewers who had considered the band too lightweight. By this stage Foreigner had been reduced to a four-piece, with McDonald and Greenwood gone, while a new bassist, Rick Wills, was added.

The next album, *Agent Provocateur* did not appear until 1985, and, if anything, it out-performed its predecessors by providing Foreigner with the massive transatlantic Number 1 single, 'I Want to Know What Love Is'. By this stage Foreigner had sold well over 20 million albums, with no sign of slowing down.

FORTUNES A Birmingham group formed in 1964, the Fortunes were UK Decca's first provincial signings along with the **Rockin' Berries**. Both had a strong commercial strain and not surprisingly outlived most of the other, highly derivative, Birmingham beat groups by becoming typical Northern cabaret mainstays after the flow of hits was over.

The Fortunes – Glen Dale, vocals, guitar; Barry Pritchard, vocals, guitar; David Carr, keyboards; Rod Allen, bass guitar; Andy Brown, drums – were a strong harmony group far removed from the cut-and-thrust R&B scene. Their early reputation rested on their recording of 'Caroline', the theme song for the pirate radio station and thus heard daily. In 1965, they had three British and American chart hits, 'You've Got Your Troubles', 'Here It Comes Again' and 'This Golden Ring' – all pleasant, totally inoffensive examples of British pop, though they earned more money by recording 'It's The Real Thing' for Coca Cola. After a stream of personnel changes they re-emerged as a chart force in 1972 with two British Top 20 records, 'Freedom Come Freedom Go' and 'Storm in a Teacup'. It might still have been 1965 for all their style had changed.

FOSTER, FRED Already established in the Nashville music scene when he founded Monument Records in 1958 in Andersonville, Tennessee,

Fred Foster immediately achieved success in the national chart with a country artist, Billy Grammer, whose 'Gotta Travel On' reached Number 4 that year. Grammer followed that hit with a version of Pee Wee King's song, 'Bonaparte's Retreat'. Foster had further hits with country artists Dick Flood and Jack Eubanks, and with the black vocal group the Velvets, until he found a star to cement his label's success – **Roy Orbison**, whose internationally famous lachrymose ballad style was developed with Foster at Monument in early Sixties hits like 'Uptown' (the first in 1960), 'Only the Lonely', 'In Dreams', 'Running Scared' and 'Oh Pretty Woman'. Boots Randolph also tasted success in 1963 with the instrumental 'Yakety Sax', and **Billy Swan** – later a recording star himself – joined Foster as a producer. In 1969, Monument launched **Tony Joe White** and ushered in an era of laid-back country soul with 'Polk Salad Annie', and a year later **Kris Kristofferson** made his debut on the label. One of Kristofferson's most recorded early songs, 'One Day at a Time', was co-written with Foster.

FOUNDATIONS A million-selling single, 'Baby Now That I've Found You' (Pye), written and produced by Tony Macaulay, launched the Foundations in October 1967. The group – Clem Curtis, vocals (born 28 November 1940); Tony Gomez, organ (13 December 1948); Eric Allandale, trombone (4 March 1936); Pat Burke, saxophone (9 October 1937); Mike Elliott, saxophone (6 August 1929); Alan Warner, guitar (21 April 1947); Peter Macbeth, bass (2 February 1943) and Tim Harris, drums (14 January 1948) – had a string of hits over the next 18 months, including a second million-seller with the Macaulay-d'Abo composition, 'Build Me Up Buttercup', in 1968. That year Elliott left and Curtis was replaced by Joey Young. Following an unsuccessful period, the group broke up late in 1970. A different line-up later appeared under the same name.

FOUR PREPS An early influence of the **Beach Boys**, white vocal group the Four Preps consisted of Bruce Belland and Marvin Inabett (lead tenors), Ed Cobb (bass) and Glenn Larson (baritone). Their arranger-producer Lincoln Mayorga stayed offstage. They first sang together in the Hollywood High School Choir and made their debut with **Ricky Nelson**, at Hamilton High School, Los Angeles. Clean cut, but with a sense of humour, they had a

gold record with '26 Miles' in 1958 and 'Big Man', with its distinctive piano, played by Mayorga, was a Top 5 hit on both sides of the Atlantic. Their live act included jump numbers, ballads, novelty songs and even vocal impressions.

FOUR SEASONS With Frankie Valli's piercing falsetto as their trademark, the Four Seasons were the most successful and influential of all the East Coast vocal groups. The original quartet was Valli (born Francis Castelluccio in Newark, New Jersey, on 3 May 1937), Nick Massi (Newark, 1935), Tommy DeVito (Bellville, New Jersey, 1936) and his brother Nick. Originally known as the Variatones, they signed to RCA as the Four Lovers in 1956 and scored a small hit with 'You're the Apple of My Eye'. In 1960, Valli met **Bob Crewe** of Swan Records, who signed the group as session-singers and players. He also began to write songs for them with new member Bob Gaudio (born in the Bronx, New York, on 17 November 1942), who had replaced Nick DeVito. Success came in 1962 with two chart-topping million-sellers, 'Sherry' and 'Big Girls Don't Cry', on Vee Jay. For the next four years the Seasons had an unbroken series of hits, including a further Number 1 in 'Rag Doll' (American Philips). Making use of all the effects of uptown R&B production techniques under the guidance of Crewe, their style was based on that of Fifties groups like the **Diamonds** and **Maurice Williams and the Zodiacs**: the Seasons provided essentially a white interpretation of a black sound. They also recorded a version of **Dylan**'s 'Don't Think Twice' under the pseudonym of the Wonder Who in 1964 just to prove that their records were not selling on the strength of the name alone. The record reached the charts at the same time as 'Let's Hang On' and Valli's solo release, 'You're Gonna Hurt Yourself', were in the US Top 10.

Refusing to change their style when the **Beatles** threatened their status, they maintained a healthy following throughout the latter half of the Sixties, although they failed to match the success of their earlier recordings. In 1968, they attempted to go progressive with an album called *Genuine Imitation Life Gazette* but its relative failure led indirectly to Bob Crewe breaking off his association with the group and to Gaudio taking over the role of producer. Litigation with Philips left the group with no recording outlet for a couple of years until, moving to the

Evergreen chart-toppers the Four Seasons on stage in the Seventies: falsetto lead singer Frankie Valli kept the group's identity intact

further hits on Motown in 1972, the group moved to Dunkhill and enjoyed a Top 10 hit with 'Keeper of the Castle'. Under the wing of a new writer/production team, Dennis Lambert and Brian Potter, they continued to prosper, although the years 1973 to 1981 were marked by a complete absence from the US Top 40. That period ended, however, with their signing by Casablanca and their return to the US and UK charts with 'When She Was My Girl'.

Motown's Four Tops in their mid-Sixties heyday, grouped around Beatles manager Brian Epstein

West Coast, they helped launch Motown's subsidiary label, Mo-West. Valli developed a concurrent solo career by concentrating particularly on the MOR market, hitting the US and UK charts with 'My Eyes Adored You' and 'Swearin' to God' (1975); he scored a US chart-topper in 1978 with the title song from the film *Grease*. The group signed with Warner Brothers and made a major comeback in 1975–6 with a run of hit singles that included 'Who Loves You' and 'December 63 (Oh What A Night)', a US Number 1, but broke up in 1977. In 1980 Valli and Gaudio reformed the Four Seasons with Don Ciccone, Jerry Corbetta and Gerry Polci.

FOUR TOPS One of the great Motown vocal groups of the label's most productive era, the Four Tops originally came together as the Four Aims in Detroit in 1953. The members, then as now, were Levi Stubbs, Renaldo Benson, Lawrence Payton and Abdul Fakir. In 1956 they signed with Chess as the Four Tops, recording one unsuccessful single, 'Kiss Me Baby'.

The late Fifties were spent playing endless club and cabaret dates in a variety of musical styles, and they spent some time touring with Billy Eckstine's roadshow before **John Hammond** signed them to Columbia in

1962. Singles on Columbia and Riverside didn't sell, but attracted the attention of Berry Gordy, whose Motown organization was growing rapidly. He signed them in 1964, initially assigning them to his short-lived Workshop jazz label, but actually releasing their first disc, 'Baby I Need Your Loving', on Motown. This atmospheric, storming beat ballad was a Top 20 smash, and began a sequence of 28 chart entries over eight years (a reissued Columbia track even sneaked a small hit), largely comprising mid-tempo ballads with a heavy beat, and often written by the prolific trio of **Holland, Dozier and Holland.** Their first chart-topper was the 1965 million-seller 'I Can't Help Myself', while in 1966 'Reach Out, I'll Be There' was a transatlantic Number 1. This track in particular shows how far and how fast Holland, Dozier and Holland, the Four Tops and Motown had developed in just two years. The instrumentation – flutes, oboes and Arab drums – was unusual, pointing to future developments in soul. Similarly, Stubbs' dramatic and imaginative lead vocal galvanized the lyric. Moreover, the song was the first of a sequence of equally dramatic hits, including 'Standing in the Shadows of Love', 'Bernadette' and 'Seven Rooms of Gloom' (1966–7). However, despite

FOWLEY, KIM American singer/producer/composer Kim Fowley was born in Los Angeles on 27 July 1942, and became involved in music in high school, working with schoolmates **Gary Paxton** and Skip Battin, producing groups he assembled from kids picked at random on the street. Some of the groups he wrote and produced for were the Jayhawks ('Stranded in the Jungle'), the Paradons ('Diamonds and Pearls'), B. Bumble and the Stingers ('Nut Rocker'), the Innocents ('Honest I Do'), **Skip and Flip** ('Cherry Pie'), and the Hollywood Argyles ('Alley Oop'). In the early Sixties he was involved with the **Rivingtons** ('Papa Oom Mow Mow'), and **Paul Revere and the Raiders**. In addition, there were dozens of records either written, produced or sung by Fowley released on countless local labels – and many on his own Living Legend label.

He spent 1965 in England, working with a number of acts who later achieved fame, among them the **Rockin' Berries**, **P.J. Proby**, the **Soft Machine**, **Cat Stevens**, **Dave Mason** and **Jim Capaldi**. Back in America, he joined the Mothers of Invention for their first album, then returned to solo work. Currently he confines his activities to songwriting (in the mid-Seventies his songs were recorded by the **Byrds**, **New Riders of the Purple Sage**, Leo Kottke, **ELP**, **Sir Douglas Quintet**, Masters of the Airwaves, **Blue Cheer**,

REO Speedwagon, Helen Reddy and others), publishing and talent spotting. None the less, precisely what Fowley did for the various people whose careers he has been 'involved' in has always been unclear; indeed often his 'involvement' has been disputed. That said, musically, Fowley had an undeniable talent for novelty songs and uncomplicated teenage anthems. His fourteen albums – among them *Outrageous* (Imperial, 1968) and *International Heroes* (Capitol, 1973) – are noted for their satiric qualities, while the hundreds of singles he has been involved in have inspired a cult following.

FOXX, INEZ AND CHARLIE

A sister/brother team from Greensboro, North Carolina, Inez and Charlie first hit with the million-seller 'Mockingbird' (1963) – a bouncy adaptation of a children's song. Other gimmicky records on the Symbol label ('Hi Diddle Diddle', 'Hurt By Love') gave little hint of Inez's fine, emotive voice. Writer/producer Charlie (born on 23 October 1939) also contributed background chants and the energetic parts of their stage routine. Later releases on Musicor/Dynamo were better, particularly 'I Stand Accused – Guilty' (1967), although their biggest hit, 'Count the Days', was somewhat similar to their earlier work. Since 1969, Inez – born 9 September 1942 – has performed solo, recording in Memphis for the Stax and Volt labels.

FRAMPTON, PETER

A mercurial rock talent whose album *Frampton Comes Alive* (A&M, 1976) sold nearly 15 million copies worldwide, Peter Frampton was born on 22 April 1950, in Beckenham, Kent, and began his pop career with the Herd at the age of sixteen. Named 'the face of '68' by several British music papers seeking the star of tomorrow, Frampton was quickly disenchanted with teeny-bopper music and formed Humble Pie with the similarly disenchanted Steve Marriott. After two years, he left to pursue his own music – a gentler, more romantic style of rock than that of Humble Pie. His main strength was his lead guitar playing, and it is this which dominated his solo albums, lifting an average songwriting ability into music that at times comes close to Eric Clapton's definitive rendition of the romantic guitar on *Layla*. His lyrics centred on romance, displaying – particularly on the second album *Frampton's Camel* (A&M, 1973) – a powerful knack for marrying telling hook lines to imaginative guitar-playing. This album found him playing alongside Rick Wills (bass), Mickey Gallagher (keyboards), Frank Camillo (guitar) and John Siomos (drums), a line-up which remained with him on concert and recording dates until 1974, when he settled semi-permanently in the US. Within two years he was being touted by American critics as the guitar hero of the Seventies, and the success of *Frampton Comes Alive* and the live singles taken from it – 'Show Me the Way' and 'Baby I Love Your Way' – seemed to confirm his status. *I'm in You* (1977) came close to repeating the earlier album's sales but after that Frampton's career appeared to nosedive. In retrospect, his appearance in the disastrous Robert Stigwood film *Sgt Pepper's Lonely Hearts Club Band* and the injuries he suffered in a car crash in the Bahamas in 1978 had a negative effect on his long-term progress. He has recorded and toured regularly since, but without the same spectacular level of acclaim. By 1984, he was back in Britain.

FRANCIS, CONNIE

Born Constance Franconero on 12 December 1938, Connie Francis sold vast quantities of records after rock'n'roll and before the Beatles. She graduated from the *Arthur Godfrey Talent Show* at 11, but not from New York University where she abandoned her studies in favour of a musical career.

She sang on Marvin Rainwater's MGM hit 'Majesty of Love' in 1957, but her own records were at first unsuccessful. Then, a revival of the standard, 'Who's Sorry Now?', became a hit in 1958. For the following five years Connie Francis was never out of the charts, having 25 American hits in that time. The songs were well split between bouncy novelty sub-rock numbers ('Lipstick on Your Collar', 'Stupid Cupid') and throbbing ballads ('Everybody's Somebody's Fool', 'Don't Break the Heart That Loves You'). Many of the latter were dusty old hits from the pre-war era. 'Who's Sorry Now?' was composed in 1923, and 'Among My Souvenirs' and 'Together' in 1928. They were generally more successful than the up-tempo songs.

The arrival of the Beatles brought her career as a singles artist to a close. Resourcefully, she turned to an MOR audience, for whom she purveyed albums of Jewish, Italian, Country, and Latin American songs in her powerful but unfocused singing style. She was nevertheless the most important female singer of the post rock'n'roll era, and remained so until the late Sixties.

Connie Francis has left little trace on rock history, yet she may be the biggest-selling female singer ever

FRANKIE GOES TO HOLLY-WOOD

At that period of rock in the early Eighties when, for many popular bands, style far outweighed content, Frankie Goes To Hollywood rode a phenomenal tide of success to become one of the biggest selling bands ever. Carefully crafted and marketed, they were possibly the ultimate pop style package.

Formed in their home town of Liverpool, Frankie made their first appearances in 1982 when singer Holly (né Billy) Johnson (who had already worked with cult new wave band Big in Japan) joined forces with Brian Nash (guitar), Mark O'Toole (bass) and Peter Gill (drums). (Fellow frontman Paul Rutherford didn't join until 1983.) Early performances were augmented by the Leatherettes, two female dancers/singers. After an appearance on TV show *The Tube*, **Trevor Horn** offered them a deal with his new label, ZTT, who released their first single, 'Relax', produced by Horn, in October 1983. Progress up the charts was slow at first but the band, fronted by two outspoken homosexuals dressed in leather and bondage gear and armed with a single full of sexual innuendo, soon came to the notice of the national press and inspired a growing controversy in the papers. The single had reached Number 6 when Radio One DJ Mike Read, after studying the none-too subtle lyrics, vowed never to play it again. Within two weeks, it rose to Number 1, and even though it was banned from BBC TV's *Top of the Pops*, it stayed at the top for five weeks. The ban – a lavish publicity campaign orchestrated by ex-journalist Paul Morley – and the ensuing controversy turned Frankie into instant media stars.

'Relax' was a sophisticated, elegant slice of pop – its lively sound the result of Horn's incredible prowess in the studio. It was a sleek blending of different musical styles – heavy funk, European electro, mainstream disco and art-rock sound effects – into an eminently danceable, commercial package, one that was repeated with the follow-up single, 'Two Tribes' (Number 1 for nine weeks) and later toned down for the smoochy Number 1, 'The Power of Love'. In October 1984, ZTT released the LP *Welcome to the Pleasure Dome*, a brilliant piece of packaging but one that was rather thin on content, comprising a few powerful tunes padded out by (admittedly highly accomplished) studio effects. Even though it did well by most group's standards, reaching Number 1, it could not, after the initial huge advance

Frankie Goes to Hollywood: their first three singles all made Number 1

orders, sustain the massive sales performance of their earlier singles.

After this, Frankie remained suspiciously quiet for some time, but no matter how well they continued to perform (they had another Top 5 single, 'Rage Hard' in mid-1986), they could never outdo their astonishing early success. The statistics are awesome – they reached sales of over five million worldwide with 'Relax' and their debut album, *Two Tribes*, sold a record 807,000 copies on 12″, and much more. They released their second LP, *Liverpool*, late in 1986 but it performed poorly by comparison. Whilst on tour in Europe early in 1987, a rift developed between Johnson and the rest of the band. The antipathy grew to such a pitch that after a series of snubs on Johnson's part, the band could no longer continue as a unit and they split in March the same year.

FRANKLIN, ARETHA

Like **Ray Charles** before her, Aretha Franklin exorcized her own personal demons through the ecstasy of gospel emotion initially on recordings that gained her much respect but limited success, before eventually seducing an international, multiracial audience. Ironically it was Atlantic, the company that lost Charles just before his breakthrough, who guided Aretha to stardom. But in the years between their handling of the two performers, times had changed. Whereas Charles was not accepted by a mass audience until he'd disguised his black roots with a liberal coating of whitewash, it was precisely by reject-

ing ambiguous compromise that Aretha emerged as a major name.

Unlike Charles, who had adopted gospel phrasing to give his blues new expression, Aretha was a true daughter of the church. Born in Memphis on 25 March 1942, one of six children of the Reverend C.L. Franklin, she was raised in Detroit surrounded by the ballyhoo of her father's success. A wealthy and, by all accounts, devastating Baptist preacher, he held sway over a large and devoted congregation, commanded pop star fees on his crusading personal appearances, and recorded a whole library of religious albums for Battle (Detroit) and Chess (Chicago). The Franklin home was open house for the top black personalities of the day. In particular, the two reigning gospel queens, **Mahalia Jackson** and Clara Ward, were close friends who helped to mould the young Aretha. By the age of nine, she was singing in her father's choir; at twelve, she was the star soloist; and then, in 1956, the fourteen-year-old protégée began cutting solo recordings for Chicago labels JVB and Checker. After four years of recording straight gospel, heavily influenced by Clara Ward, Aretha was encouraged by **Sam Cooke** to follow his switch to commercial success. In 1960, she left her father and settled temporarily in New York where she was signed to Columbia records by **John Hammond**.

In six years Columbia tried many settings for Aretha's emotive vocal style, but with every change of direction they were always one step out of tune with the times. Following her initial bluesy sides, she attacked show-biz standards; a collection of **Dinah Washington**'s hits; other artists' pop chart entries; after-hours jazz ballads; and a few originals that were arranged in a Columbian approximation of soul music. Although she scraped the charts half a dozen times (notably 'Rock-A-Bye Your Baby with a Dixie Melody', 1961, 'Don't Cry Baby', 1962, 'Runnin' Out of Fools', 1964) and survived the endless round of nightclubs, it was an abysmal waste of talent, akin to RCA's persistent attempts to make another Sammy Davis Jr out of Sam Cooke.

In November 1966, she found a more sympathetic home at Atlantic records. Supervised by the company's veteran producer Jerry Wexler, she was recorded at the Muscle Shoals studio in Alabama, just simply wailing her heart out over a beautifully economic backing. The stunning result, 'I Never Loved a Man (The Way I Love You)', went straight to the top of the soul charts, hit the Top 10, and sold a million. There followed a string of equally convincing performances ('Respect', 'Baby I Love You', 'Natural Woman', 'Chain of Fools', 'Since You Been Gone', 'Think'), each as enthusiastically received as the first. By the end of 1968 Wexler had twice been acclaimed 'Producer of the Year' and Aretha was being showered with gold records and effusive rhetoric.

The next two years were not so golden. Disturbed by the pressures of success and suffering the pangs of a broken marriage to manager Ted White, Aretha seemed confused. Many of her recordings lacked the intensity of the previous hits and her stage shows were similarly disappointing. Not only was her ponderous road band unable to match the excellent studio musicians, but audiences were less than delighted by her alarming tendency to break into a hearty rendition of 'There's No Business Like Show Business'. By the autumn of 1970 she had remarried, scrapped the large band in favour of a tighter combo led by **King Curtis**, and had begun to pull out of the trough. A successful appearance at New York's Philharmonic Hall in December of that year which had critics proclaiming 'Aretha returns to life', and her superb interpretation of **Ben E. King**'s 'Don't Play That Song', seemed to prove it. The following spring a confident self-portrait, 'A Brand New Me', preceded a triumphant concert at Fillmore West in San Francisco (recorded, and released on album). The Queen of Soul was back on top, after which she seemed set to establish herself as the leading black female entertainer – not quite as relevant to younger audiences as the new heroines like **Millie Jackson**, and perhaps a little too fond of reworking other people's hit songs, but still a unique and influential vocalist who could pack the concert halls of Europe while whupping all those funky bands in the soul charts. (Indeed, she has achieved more Number 1 soul hits than everyone except **James Brown**.)

In the spring of 1972, before the congregation of the Temple Missionary Baptist Church in Watts, Los Angeles, Aretha joined with gospel star James Cleveland and the Southern California Community Choir to record the benefit concert that was later released as *Amazing Grace* (1973). Clearly moved by his daughter's performance, the Reverend C.L. Franklin had no doubts about the true strength of her talent. 'If you want to know the truth, Aretha has never left the church. If you have the ability to feel, and if you have the ability to hear, you know that Aretha is still a gospel singer.'

Aretha's career since then has been uneven, but with occasional moments of pure triumph. She recorded with a succession of producers – Quincy Jones for *Hey Now Hey (The Other Side of the Sky)* (1973), **Curtis Mayfield** for *Sparkle* (1976), Lamont Dozier for *Sweet Passion*, and **Van McCoy** for *La Diva* (1979) – without quite touching the heights she had reached while under Wexler's tutelage, and in 1980 she left Atlantic to join Arista Records. During that year she appeared in *The Blues Brothers* (delivering an unforgettable version of her old hit, 'Think') and debuted for the label with *Aretha*, which like her second Arista release, *Love All the Hurt Away* (1981), was produced by **Arif Mardin**. *Jump to It* (1982) and *Get it Right* (1983) found her once again on something like top form, the title song from the former album giving her a US Top 40 hit for the first time since 1976. Her best year saleswise, however, was 1985, which found her enjoying renewed success in the US and the UK with the album *Who's Zoomin' Who* and the single 'Sisters Are Doin' It for Themselves', a duet with Annie Lennox of **Eurythmics** released on RCA. In early 1987, her duet with George Michael, 'I Knew You Were Waiting', was a UK Number 1.

'Lady Soul' herself, Aretha Franklin, preaching the hot gospel

FRAZIER, DALLAS A noted country and pop composer, Oklahoma-born (in 1939) Dallas Frazier recorded intermittently in his own right during the Fifties and Sixties. Moving to Bakersfield, California, in his teens, he won a Ferlin Husky-sponsored talent contest and cut a number of children's novelty songs for the Capitol label. His predilection for comic book characters showed in his first major hit composition, 'Alley Oop', which became a US Number 1 in a version by the Hollywood Argyles. Frazier himself was present on the session, alongside singer **Gary Paxton** and drummer **Sandy Nelson**. He made several discs for small Californian labels before rejoining Capitol, but it took other artists to turn his songs into hits – among them the **Coasters** ('Ridin' Hood'), **Charlie Rich** ('Mohair Sam'), **O.C. Smith** ('Son of Hickory Holler's Tramp'), Engelbert Humperdinck and **Elvis Presley**, who both recorded 'There Goes My Everything'. His own records were of greater interest: 'California Cottonfields' (later recorded by **Merle Haggard**) told the story of his father's move from the midwest to 'the Promised Land'.

FRED, JOHN, AND HIS PLAYBOY BAND Born in Baton Rouge, Louisiana, on 8 May 1941, John Fred had a minor hit in 1959 with 'Shirley' and for years led one of the most popular Louisiana-based touring bands, the seven-man Playboys. The group's big break came in late 1967 with the worldwide success of 'Judy in Disguise (With Glasses)', a spoof on the **Beatles**' 'Lucy in the Sky With Diamonds'. It reached Number 1 in the US but proved to be the Playboy Band's only Top 40 entry. In 1982, 'Shirley' was recorded by British rock'n'roll revivalist **Shakin' Stevens** and taken to Number 6 in the UK chart.

FREDDIE AND THE DREAMERS Early participants in the British beat boom of 1963–5, Freddie and the Dreamers were from Manchester and comprised Freddie Garrity (born 14 November 1940); Pete Birrell, bass (9 May 1941); Roy Crewsdon, guitar (29 May 1941); Bernie Dwyer, drums (11 September 1940) and Derek Quinn, lead guitar (24 May 1942). They performed happy-go-lucky songs while posturing and leaping about. Pint-sized Freddie had been a milkman before the group passed a BBC audition in 1963. They appealed to a much younger audience than their contemporaries and, after seven hits on UK Columbia – including 'I'm Telling You Now' (an

They didn't look like teen idols, but they were: ex-milkman Freddie Garrity (left) and Dreamers Pete Birrell (centre) and Roy Crewsdon

American Number 1) and 'You Were Made for Me' – became more involved in children's entertainment. They broke up at the end of the Sixties but Freddie and Pete Birrell stayed together to star in the long-running children's TV series *Little Big Time*. The group reformed for beat revival concerts in the Seventies and early Eighties.

FREE One of the many blues-based bands to form in the shadow of **Cream** and the blues renaissance of 1968, Free were given their name and some early encouragement by **Alexis Korner**. Their line-up comprised Paul Rodgers, vocals (born on 12 December 1949); Paul Kossoff, guitar (14 September 1950); Andy Fraser, bass (7 August 1952); and Simon Kirke, drums (28 July 1949). From the start they mixed original compositions with blues standards, and their bare-wired style quickly earned them a strong reputation with club audiences, although neither of their first two albums – *Tons of Sobs* (Island, 1968) and *Free* (Island, 1969) – nor the singles taken from the latter made any impact on the charts. Then 'All Right Now', released in May 1970, became one of the year's major singles. Let down by the failure of the follow-up, the excellent 'Stealer', and perhaps too young to handle their sudden stardom, the group split up early the following year.

Rodgers and Fraser, Free's songwriters, formed the bands Toby and Peace respectively, while Kossoff and Kirke teamed up with Tetsu Yamauchi (bass) and John 'Rabbit' Bundrick (keyboards). The original line-up re-formed in 1972 for the patchy *Free At Last* and a hit single, 'Little Bit of Love', but live work was frequently disrupted by Kossoff's drug problems. Fraser left to form Sharks with Chris Spedding, and Tetsu and Rabbit rejoined; Kossoff's increasing unreliability led to the bulk of *Heartbreaker* (1973) being recorded without him, and he quit altogether at the end of 1972. Wendell Richardson was used on an American tour early the following year, but after Tetsu's departure for the **Faces** that summer, Free folded, Rodgers and Kirke subsequently forming **Bad Company** with Mick Ralphs (guitar) and Boz Burrell (bass), while Kossoff and Fraser put together their own groups. Kossoff died in New York on 19 March 1976.

FREED, ALAN As one of the first white disc jockeys to espouse the rock-'n'roll cause and the first to give the music a national platform, Alan Freed deserved the description of the Pied Piper of rock'n'roll. Of Welsh-Lithuanian descent, he was born on 15 December 1922 in Johnstown, Philadelphia, and at high school organized a jazz band, the Sultans of Swing. He started work in radio in 1942, successively holding jobs as a programme director and sportscaster with WKST, WKBN and WAKR in Ohio and Philadelphia. He moved to WJW in Cleveland in 1951. Encouraged by a local record store owner, Leo Mintz, Freed began to play R&B records on a show which he called Moondog's Rock'n'roll Party. He adopted the new name for the music that he played to avoid the racial stigma he thought inherent in existing names like 'rhythm & blues' and 'race music'. Rock'n'roll would probably have gained large-scale acceptance without Freed, but he was the catalyst. Throughout his radio show he would thump out the beat on a telephone book and his enthusiasm, as charismatic as the records he played, built up vast listening figures. His first stage-show, in March 1952, was cancelled when 30,000 kids tried to get into the 10,000 capacity Cleveland Arena. Freed was surprised to find that a substantial minority of the disappointed audience was white.

In September 1954, Freed moved to New York, where he hosted Rock-'n'Roll Party over WINS. The following January, he assembled a package show at St Nicholas Arena with a host of groups, virtually all black. By now the audiences were 70 per cent white. He had become a household name by 1957, the year in which he appeared in three films (*Rock Around the Clock*; *Rock, Rock, Rock* and *Don't Knock the Rock*). He also shared composing credits on many rock'n'roll hits – by **Chuck Berry**, the **Moonglows** and others – and very often songwriters were only too pleased to give him a cut in return for continued airplay. Freed, of course, did accept payola but he could not be bribed to play a record he didn't like. He thought black music was honest and refused to play the myriad inspired white cover versions of R&B originals. Those who did, he accused of racialism. His outspoken defence of black music incurred the wrath of the music business establishment. Although charges of anarchy and incitement to riot after a Boston concert were dismissed in 1958, Freed was made a scapegoat for his part in the payola scandals that racked radio and the US record industry during 1959. In 1962 he pleaded guilty to accepting bribes and received a suspended prison sentence and a fine. Attempts to revive his career were unsuccessful and he died in a Palm Springs hospital on 20 January 1965. 'He had suffered the most', proclaimed an article in *Cashbox*, 'and was perhaps singled out for alleged wrongs that had become a business way of life for many others.' Today, most people – not least the performers he helped – recognize his major contribution to the advancement of black music. See *also* **Radio (US)**

FRIPP, ROBERT Guitarist Fripp (born May 1946, in Wimborne, Dorset) was one of the founders and leaders of noted British art-rock group **King Crimson**. With Van Der Graaf Generator, King Crimson concentrated on the darker, heavier side of the rock classicism spearheaded by **Yes** and **ELP**. Unlike most of his contemporaries, Fripp discovered a new lease of creative life in the early 1970s, as part of the growing rock avant-garde. Working with Brian Eno (ex-**Roxy Music**), he recorded the albums *No Pussyfootin'* and *Evening Star* (1975), on the latter essaying what he called 'Frippertronic' guitar. Arising from his and Eno's interest in 'minimal' electronic music, 'Frippertronics' involved feeding the guitar through a series of tape loops, resulting in a circular, treated guitar sound that would continue long after the notes or chords had actually been struck. He went on to develop this technique on the 'drive to 1985' albums *Exposure* and *Under Heavy Manners*.

King Crimson had dissolved in the late 1970s after numerous personnel changes and an uninspired foray into complicated jazz-rock figures. In 1980, Fripp formed the League of Gentlemen, featuring ex-**XTC** keyboard player Barry Andrews (who would go on to found Shriekback with **Gang of Four** bassist Dave Allen). The League of Gentlemen toured widely, recording one, same-name, album for EG, which mixed Fripp's tortuous style with Andrews' organ-heavy bop. Fripp disbanded the group shortly afterwards, disappointed at its lack of technical ability.

In 1982 he re-formed King Crimson with a totally new line-up of American bassist Tony Levin, guitarist Adrian Belew and drummer Bill Bruford. After two albums, *Respect* and *Heartbeat* (after the biopic of writer Jack Kerouac), this line-up also foundered. Fripp remains one of rock's most innovative forces, however, he and Eno being two of the very few figures to survive transition to the new wave.

Eccentric guitar virtuoso Robert Fripp was the main inspiration behind King Crimson, one of the most acclaimed progressive rock bands

FUGS Created by the diversification of the Beat poets into rock, the Fugs became the first of a line of New York bands who made outrage their stock-in-trade. Founded by poets Ed Sanders, Tuli Kupferberg and Ken Weaver, the group was signed by the avant-garde jazz label, ESP, in 1965. Their three albums for the company show a progression from musically crude political chants like 'Kill for Peace' and versions of William Blake poems, to drugs and sex songs like 'New Amphetamine Shriek' and 'Coca Cola Douche'. The Fugs were signed by Reprise in the hippie atmosphere of 1967 and went on tour, augmented by genuine musicians including bassist Charlie Larkey and guitarist **Stefan Grossman**. Their three albums for Reprise brought them a cult following which survived the group's demise at the end of the Sixties, after which Sanders recorded two solo albums and wrote a best-selling account of the trial of Charles Manson (for the murder of actress Sharon Tate). Both maintained their underground connections through to the Eighties, when Kupferberg became Director of Revolting Theater in New York.

FULLER, BOBBY / BOBBY FULLER FOUR A quartet from El Paso, the Bobby Fuller Four played Texas rock'n'roll. They welded their own rough-hewn vocal harmonies to the loose, loping West Texas rhythms and scored twice in 1966 with Sonny Curtis' 'I Fought the Law' and with **Buddy Holly**'s 'Love's Made a Fool of You' on Mustang. But success was short-lived. Within months, Bobby died in a freak car accident. His brother, Randy, stuck around to make a couple of singles, but soon joined fellow-members DeWayne Quirico and Jim Reese back in Texas and obscurity.

FULLER, JESSE Country-bluesman Jesse Fuller was born in Jonesboro, Georgia, on 12 March 1896. His metier was the one-man-band: he played 12-string guitar, harmonica, kazoo, hi-hat and fotdella (an instrument of his own devising, a sort of pedal-operated string bass). To this he adapted a repertoire of blues, good-time songs and spirituals, which made him, especially in the early days of blues appreciation, popular as a club and folk-festival act. 'San Francisco Bay Blues' was much copied in the early Sixties, but after its vogue little attention was paid to its creator, and he stayed out of the public eye until his death in 1976. His several albums for Good Time Jazz are representative.

FULSOM, LOWELL Born in Tulsa, Oklahoma, in 1921, Lowell Fulsom was a singer-guitarist who became one of the chief exponents of West Coast dance-hall blues. Early work with Texas Alexander led to many discs on a prolific number of labels, beginning with those owned by Bob Geddins and Jack Lauderdale in Oakland, California, in 1946. His R&B hits included 'Come Back Baby' for Downbeat in 1949 and 'Every Day I Have the Blues', 'Blue Shadows' (a Number 1) and 'Lonely Christmas' for Swingtime in 1950–1. 'Reconsider Baby', now a blues standard, heralded Fulsom's move to Checker in 1954. He finally made the US charts on Kent with 'Black Night', 'Tramp' (a Number 52 in 1967) and 'Make a Little Love'. His guitar improvisations were submerged among the brass arrangements of **Maxwell Davis**, but few bluesmen made the pop charts with such minimal stylistic change.

FUN BOY THREE Early Eighties pop trio Fun Boy Three were formed from the debris of the **Specials**, who split in mid-1981. Over the next two years, Terry Hall (vocals), Lynval Golding (guitar) and Neville Staples (vocals) scored a string of hits in the UK with their sparse, rhythmic style.

Moving away entirely from the 2-Tone sound, they had a hit with their first single, the haunting 'The Lunatics (Have Taken Over the Asylum)', late in 1981. The second single was a collaboration with **Bananarama**, a cover of a Thirties jazz standard, 'It Ain't What You Do (It's the Way That You Do It)', which proved to be their biggest hit, reaching Number 4 early in 1982. They scored another five hit singles and two UK Top 20 albums, *Fun Boy Three* (1982) and *Waiting* (1983), which was produced by David Byrne of **Talking Heads**. Byrne drew the best out of the trio to record an album of subtle, stripped down intensity – the critics raved.

1983 saw them begin to crack the US market, but after their only tour there, Hall abruptly disbanded the group. He went on to form the Colourfield, who recorded an album, *Virgins and Philistines* (1985), while Golding and Staples formed Sunday Best, with an assortment of other musicians. Neither venture recaptured the success of their previous groups.

FUNICELLO, ANNETTE Regularly appearing in Hollywood beach party movies (usually opposite **Frankie Avalon**) during the early Sixties, actress/singer Annette Funicello was born in Utica, New York, on 22 October 1942. Moving to the West Coast, she joined Walt Disney's Mousketeers in October 1955 and three years later was launched as a singer at the male teenage market by the Disney organization. Her first record, 'Tall Paul' (on the Disney label, Vista) reached Number 7, and was followed by a series of forgettable hits. The biggest were 'First Name Initial' (Number 20 in 1959), 'O Dio Mio' (Number 10 in 1960) and 'Pineapple Princess' (Number 11 in the same year). All were recorded with her backing group, the Afterbeats, and were credited simply to 'Annette'.

FUQUA, HARVEY One-time member of the **Moonglows** and later an important figure within the Motown Corporation, Harvey Fuqua was born in Louisville, Kentucky, on 27 July 1929. He began his musical career when he moved to Cleveland in 1951 and helped form the Moonglows, who recorded prolifically and successfully for Chance and Chess until 1959, their best-known hits being 'Ten Commandments of Love', featuring Harvey's bass lead vocal, and 'Sincerely'. When they split in 1959, Fuqua recruited the Marquees (including **Marvin Gaye**) to record with Chess – as the Moonglows – for a while before becoming A&R director at Chess in 1960, taking Gaye with him to the subsidiary Anna label. At this time he recorded some successful duets with **Etta James**, issued on Chess, then married Anna label owner, Gwen Cordy. Breaking with Chess, Fuqua formed the Harvey and Tri-Phi labels, subsequently incorporating into the Motown organization, with whom he worked as writer/producer until 1969. He then began his own production company, channelled through RCA, and achieved success with the Nitelighters, New Birth, and revived Moonglows.

FURY, BILLY Born Ronald Wycherly on 17 April 1941 in Liverpool, Billy Fury was perhaps the most talented of the adolescent Britons who aped American rock'n'roll in the late Fifties. He was discovered in the classic manner – late in 1958, while working on the Mersey tugboats, he had written a couple of songs, and when one of the marathon rock shows promoted by impresario **Larry Parnes** came to Birkenhead, he talked his way into **Marty Wilde**'s dressing-room in the hope of interesting the star in his songs. The end result was that Parnes gave Ronald a new name and a spot on the rest of the tour.

Fury's first hit, 'Maybe Tomorrow', followed in April 1959. After a few misses he returned to the charts in 1960 with two of his own numbers, 'Colette' and 'That's Love', and produced one of the classic rock'n'roll albums in *The Sound of Fury*. It was almost authentic rockabilly throughout, and yet Fury had written all of the songs and the lead guitarist was Cockney **Joe Brown**.

Fury then turned to the common pattern, of covering American hits and big ballads, 'Halfway to Paradise', 'Jealousy' and 'I'll Never Find Another You', and when his chart reign ended in 1966 he had been in the British Top 20 nineteen times. By this time, he had made the switch to Northern clubs and cabaret for a living.

Ill-health dogged Fury's career, and his dream was always to leave showbusiness and found a bird sanctuary. But *The Sound of Fury* and his almost unprecedented chart run put him among the British pop greats. In what was almost a reprise of his classic style, Fury played the role of the rock'n'roll singer Stormy Tempest (sic) in the acclaimed movie, *That'll Be The Day*, in 1973. During the last ten years of his life he recorded little but could still be seen at rock'n'roll concerts and on television specials, gamely singing the old hits. He died on 28 January 1983.

G

GABLER, MILT During the late Thirties, Milt Gabler formed the pioneering independent Commodore label for which he supervised Billie Holiday's earliest sessions as well as Jimmy Yancey, Meade Lux Lewis, James P. Johnson, Jelly Roll Morton and many others. Joining Decca in 1941, Gabler was responsible for supervising the firm's 'race', jazz and hillbilly (C&W) sessions and throughout the decade he presided over a vast number of recordings by Burl Ives, Ella Fitzgerald, the **Ink Spots**, the **Weavers**, Red Foley and **Louis Jordan**, who became the biggest black recording star of the Forties with Gabler-supervised hits like 'Caldonia', 'Choo Choo Ch' Boogie' and 'Saturday Night Fish Fry'. In 1954, Gabler signed **Bill Haley** to Decca and produced such classics as 'Rock Around the Clock' and 'See You Later Alligator'. During the Sixties, Gabler gradually assumed the role of executive producer. He was one of the record industry's unsung greats.

GABRIEL, PETER After coming to fame as the flamboyant frontman of supergroup **Genesis**, Peter Gabriel left for a solo career. An enigmatic performer, he has straddled the experimental and rock/pop fields, and found sporadic success in the charts across the world.

Born on 13 February 1950, Gabriel attended Charterhouse School with the other original members of Genesis, and when they turned professional in 1968, he stayed with the band for seven years, as many albums, and endless tours during which time he was particularly well-known for his live performances, each one a theatrical spectacle of masks and weird costumes. He left the band in 1975, not to reappear on the rock scene until 1977 with his first solo album, *Peter Gabriel*, also the title of several subsequent albums ('like issues of a magazine'). A thoughtful collection of tough pop songs, it was an instant critical and public success and gave him his first solo hit single, 'Solsbury Hill'.

A second *Peter Gabriel* album, produced by Robert Fripp, also performed well reaching UK Number 10 in 1978, but his biggest success came with the release of his third album in 1980. Produced by Steve Lillywhite, it gave Gabriel his first Number 1 and produced the worldwide hit single, 'Games Without Frontiers'. It also saw Gabriel merging African rhythms with studio technology to produce the powerful song 'Biko'. In Gabriel's fourth album he went further with his fusion of complex rhythms and the latest music technology, resulting in yet another worldwide hit 'Shock the Monkey' (1982).

Peter Gabriel, heavily into make-up

Throughout this period Gabriel continued to perform live; he also financed the first WOMAD (World of Music, Arts And Dance) festival in 1982, which brought Third World music to Britain. To cover the loss made on the festival, Genesis were re-formed for a one-off concert. In 1983 Gabriel released the live double *Peter Gabriel Plays Live*, and his soundtrack album for the Alan Parker film *Birdy* came out in 1985. In 1986, he released his fifth studio LP – *So* – not given his name. This contained a huge hit single, 'Sledgehammer' and the album made UK Number 1.

GALAXY Galaxy is the brainchild of singer/songwriter/producer Phil Fearon, one of the most consistent hitmakers in British black dance music ever since the late Seventies. Fearon's first big hit came in 1979 as a member of Kandidate with the single 'I Don't Wanna Lose You'. After leaving Kandidate he scored a minor club hit with 'Pay Up', a song recorded with his brother Lenny, and that experience encouraged Fearon to set up his own London studio, FJR.

One of his projects to come out of FJR was the band he named Galaxy; midway through 1982 Fearon approached Ensign with a demo tape of Galaxy tunes and signed a deal. In 1983, by this time assisted by twin vocalists Julie Gore and Dee Galdes, Galaxy released the catchy 'Dancing Tight', which made the UK Top 5, followed by a string of hit singles and a gold album, *Phil Fearon and Galaxy* (1984). In 1985 Galaxy released their second album, *This Kind of Love*.

GALLAGHER AND LYLE A popular mid-Seventies singing and songwriting duo, (Benny) Gallagher and (Graham) Lyle began their professional careers with an Apple Music songwriting contract in 1968. One of their songs, 'International', was recorded by **Mary Hopkin**. When Apple went into decline, they left to join **McGuinness Flint**, writing two Top 10 hits for the band: 'When I'm Dead and Gone' (1970) and 'Malt and Barley Blues' (1971). Gallagher and Lyle eventually signed to A&M as a duo, with Glyn Johns as producer, and also had a brief spell with **Ronnie Lane**'s Slim Chance in 1974. Their songs were melodic and thoughtful, with a concern for the history and contemporary situation of their native Scotland, notably *Seeds* (1973). *The Last Cowboy* (1974) and *Breakaway* (1976) saw them further develop their incisive harmony singing. They had two UK Top 10 hits during 1976, 'I Want to Stay With You' and 'Heart on My Sleeve'. Their last album together was *Showdown* (1978), since when Graham Lyle has written songs with a number of collaborators. **Tina Turner**'s 1985 hit, 'What's Love Got to Do With It?', was written by Lyle with Turner's producer, Terry Britten.

GALLAGHER, RORY A guitar hero of the early and mid-Seventies, Rory Gallagher was born in Ballyshannon, Co. Donegal, Irish Republic, on 2 March 1949. He played guitar with the Impact showband before forming his first trio to play in Hamburg in 1965. The following year he teamed up with Norman Damery and Eric Kittringham to form Taste. By this time Gallagher was moving away from **Chuck Berry**-influenced rock'n'roll towards his modern blues style. In 1968 John Wilson (born 3 December 1947) and Richard McCracken (26 June 1948) joined on drums and bass and Taste signed with Polydor.

Four albums including *On The Boards* (1970) were produced by Tony Colton between 1968 and 1970, when Taste disbanded and Gallagher continued with Wilgar Campbell (drums) and Gerry McAvoy (bass), the others forming Stud. On *Rory Gallagher* (1971) and *Deuce* (1971), he introduced some of his own compositions while retaining his committed blues approach. He remains perhaps the only white guitarist to have maintained the Sixties commitment to blues without seeming either narrow-minded or rigidly purist, and subsequent albums like *Calling Card* (1976), *Photo Finish* (1978) and *Jinx* (1982) have for the most part maintained the standard.

GAMBLE, KENNY AND HUFF, LEON One of the most celebrated partnerships in soul music history, Kenny Gamble and Leon Huff are producer/writers who in the Seventies became the uncrowned kings of the 'Philly Sound'. Their Philadelphia International label was one of the most powerful and creative forces in Seventies soul music, boasting virtually every topline name in the genre – **Harold Melvin and the Blue Notes**, the **O'Jays**, the **Three Degrees** *et al.* When they met up in 1964, Huff had already established a reputation as a top New York R&B session pianist, working out of **Leiber and Stoller**'s offices on numerous sides. He moved back to his home town of Philadelphia, and had a hit with Patti and the Emblems in 1964 ('Mixed Up Shook Up Girl'). Kenny Gamble had been singing and song-

Leon Huff (left) and Kenny Gamble, uncrowned kings of 'Philly Sound'

writing since leaving school. Huff played on Candy and the Kisses' 'The 81', one of Gamble's songs, and a partnership was born, Huff replacing **Thom Bell** in Kenny Gamble's Romeos.

In 1966, the duo formed Excel Records, and recorded the **Intruders**, scoring a local hit. The company's name was changed to Gamble. Both soul and Hot 100 hits emerged from the new company by the Intruders, all written and produced by Gamble and Huff. Although 1968 was a rough year for Philadelphia – with Cameo being forced to fold – Gamble Records continued to have hits and the duo began to work as outside producers for Atlantic (breaking Archie Bell and the Drells) and Mercury (**Jerry Butler**). In 1970, a hook-up with Leonard Chess was arranged, resulting in the launch of Neptune Records. Despite a brilliant roster of acts – the O'Jays, the **Vibrations**, the Three Degrees, Bunny Sigler, **Billy Paul**, etc. and encouraging sales, Neptune folded when Leonard Chess died and his Chess Records were swallowed by the GRT conglomerate. Still getting hits with the Intruders and independent productions (notably for **Wilson Pickett**) they regrouped and in 1971 secured a Columbia Records tie-up and formed Philadelphia International Records (PIR). For a year things moved slowly, but once the Ebonys and then Harold Melvin and the Blue Notes broke through to the national charts, Columbia began to pay real attention to Philadelphia International. Million-selling smashes for the O'Jays and Billy Paul brought waves of interest in the 'Philly Sound'. Certainly Gamble and Huff's immaculate fusion of sophisticated orchestrations (supplied by the brilliant MFSB session band and recorded at Philly's Sigma Sound studio) and rich, vibrant soul vocalists brought immense success – and payola

investigations – and more evidence that the diverse threads of black music had become inseparably interwoven into the pop music mainstream.

Later in the Seventies, Gamble and Huff produced hits by the **Jacksons**, ex-Blue Notes singer **Teddy Pendergrass**, and Jerry Butler, but the beginning of the next decade found the fortunes of Philadelphia International waning dramatically. In 1982, Gamble and Huff tried a further venture with the launch of Peace International, a label devoted to gospel music with a roster including the legendary Five Blind Boys of Mississippi. However, during the following year PIR's distribution deal with Columbia was terminated and the label was forced to fold.

GANG OF FOUR Yorkshire contemporaries of the **Human League** and **ABC**, Gang of Four formed in Leeds in 1977 and immediately made startling headway with their brand of tough 'radical dance music', which blended punk aggression, provocative lyrics and funk rhythms.

Their debut release – the 'Damaged Goods' EP on the independent Fast label – created such a stir that they signed a major deal with EMI and followed this up with the intriguing 'At Home He's a Tourist' single and *Entertainment* (1979) album. The early (seminal) line-up of Jon King (vocals), Andy Gill (guitar), Dave Allen (bass) and Hugo Burnham (drums), was regarded as standard bearer for a new breed of intelligent Eighties groups, but they sadly promised more than they delivered, as shown by their patchy second album, *Solid Gold* (1981).

Their best work can be found on a retrospective live album, *At the Palace* (recorded in May '84, just before they split), which features Sara Lee on bass and Steve Goulding on drums.

Jon King, vocalist of Leeds radical dance band Gang of Four

GARRETT, TOMMY 'SNUFF'

Born in Dallas, Texas, in 1939, Tommy Garrett was one of the leading record producers of the early Sixties and, later, an MOR celebrity in his own right. His career began at 15 years of age, when he undertook promotion for a distribution company in Dallas. From promotion he expanded into record sales and, at 17, left Dallas to become a DJ at KDUB in Lubbock, Texas, where he met **Buddy Holly** and the **Crickets**. He then moved to Wichita Falls, Texas, where he ran his own TV show and a teenage nightclub, 'Snuff's Record Hop'.

In 1958 he went to Hollywood where he took a job as local promotion man with Liberty before returning into record production. He was asked to produce the hitherto unsuccessful **Johnny Burnette** for Liberty, and after only two records under Garrett, Burnette achieved his first hit with 'Dreamin'', a 1960 million-seller. In 1959, Garrett signed **Bobby Vee**, a 17-year-old from Minnesota, and had him cover **Adam Faith**'s 'What Do You Want?' for the American market. This flopped, but Vee's sequel, 'Devil Or Angel' reached Number 6 in America and under Garrett's masterful supervision, Vee went on to become a major American teen idol with such hits as 'Rubber Ball', 'Take Good Care of My Baby' and 'Run to Him'. Meanwhile, Burnette registered with two more hits, 'Little Boy Sad' and 'You're Sixteen' and Garrett even managed to launch a failed jazz singer named **Gene McDaniels** with a series of hits including 'A Hundred Pounds of Clay' and 'Tower of Strength'. In the period between 1961 and 1963, Garrett was probably the most successful A&R man in America. At 22, he was made head of A&R at Liberty and hired a contemporary prodigy, named **Phil Spector**, to work for Liberty in New York.

Although Garrett's productions were generally aimed at America's white middle-class and epitomized the artless sterility of pop in the early Sixties, he was, nevertheless, solely responsible for Liberty's inroads into the mainstream rock market. He also launched a series of best-selling MOR albums in the *50 Guitars of Tommy Garrett*. During 1965–6, Garrett produced no less than ten successive American Top 10 hits by Jerry Lewis' son, **Gary Lewis and the Playboys**, most of which were arranged by **Leon Russell**.

He left Liberty in 1966 to form his own Viva label, but had no hits at all. He retired in 1969 but produced a run of come-back hits for Cher in 1973.

Art Garfunkel: he divided his energies between music and acting after the break-up of his partnership with Paul Simon

GARFUNKEL, ART

Art Garfunkel has divided his time between music and film-acting since the break-up of his partnership with **Paul Simon** in 1970. The albums *Angel Clare* (Columbia, 1974) and *Breakaway* (1975, co-produced by Richard Perry) continued the lush arrangements characteristic of the later **Simon and Garfunkel**, while the vocals retained the high, breathy tone of 'Bridge Over Troubled Waters'. The songs were selected from the work of various writers of the previous twenty years, and in 1975 Garfunkel enjoyed international hits with his mawkish version of 'I Only Have Eyes For You', a Fifties doo-wop hit for the **Flamingos**, and **Gallagher and Lyle**'s 'Breakaway'.

Simon and Garfunkel reunited briefly for 'My Little Town', which appeared on the second solo album, but the impression remained for some time that Garfunkel's commitment to a musical career was far less than his former partner's. Nevertheless, both 'I Only Have Eyes For You' (1975) and 'Bright Eyes' (1979, from the film *Watership Down*) were Number 1 hits in the UK, and his revival of Sam Cooke's 'Wonderful World' (recorded with Simon and **James Taylor**) was a Top 20 US hit in 1978. His film appearances have been uniformly excellent, including *Catch 22* (1969), *Carnal Knowledge* (1971) and *Bad Timing* (1981). *See also* **Simon and Garfunkel**; **Paul Simon**

GAYE, MARVIN One of Motown's greatest stars and an inspiration to literally scores of soul singers, Marvin Gaye was born in Washington, DC, on 2 April 1939, and received his musical grounding singing in the choir and playing organ at the Washington church where his father was minister. His career in the popular field began when he won the school talent show: the show was judged by **Harvey Fuqua** and Marvin won singing his song 'Ten Commandments of Love'.

At his father's instigation he enlisted in the USAF on graduation, but was soon demobbed on psychological grounds. He immediately renewed his friendship with Fuqua, singing in the **Moonglows** in the twilight of their career, including their 1959 Chess release 'Mama Loocie'. In 1960 Gaye and Fuqua moved from Chicago to Detroit, where Fuqua formed his Harvey and Tri-Phi labels, beginning an association with the Gordy family. Berry Gordy had recently formed the fledgeling Motown Corporation which soon engulfed the Fuqua labels, while Berry's sisters, Gwen and Anna, were soon married to Harvey and Marvin respectively. Berry heard Marvin sing at an informal party in Detroit, and subsequently signed him to the Tamla label in 1961.

Marvin's first three releases meant little, but the fourth, 'Stubborn Kind of Fellow', a crisp, mid-tempo beat ballad with gospel chanting by the Vandellas in the background was a Top 50 hit late in 1962, starting a run of some 28 Top 50 hits over the next ten years, ten discs reaching the Top 10, peaking with the chart-topping 'I Heard It Through the Grapevine' in 1968. Much of Marvin's material was in the beat ballad idiom, ideally suiting his soft tenor voice. There were some notable exceptions – the rasping 'Hitch Hike' dance song (his second hit, in 1963); the storming 12-bar blues format gospel rocker 'Can I Get a Witness' (later in 1963); a similar, if less frantic 'You're a Wonderful One' (1964) and the powerful Bo Diddley-beat 'Baby Don't You Do It' (1964). In 1964, Marvin was teamed with **Mary Wells** for a duet album, both sides of the spin-off single making the Top 20, but the success was short-lived since Mary Wells quit Motown for 20th Century soon after. A partnership with **Kim Weston** followed, yielding a 1967 Top 20 hit 'It Takes Two', but then Kim Weston left for MGM.

The beautiful **Tammi Terrell** was Marvin's third distaff partner, beginning in 1967, and this time the combination was more permanent, scoring

Marvin Gaye basks in the limelight at the Albert Hall in 1976, although by then his personal life was already well on the downward track

ten Hot 100 entries – four of them Top 10 – over three years. But this pairing was tragically terminated in 1970 when Tammi died after undergoing several operations on a brain tumour. Tammi's death had a profound effect on Gaye: his mid-1970 hit was aptly entitled 'The End of Our Road', following which he quit touring and spent many months reshaping his recording career, resurfacing in 1971 with the deeply introspective 'What's Going On', 'Mercy Mercy Me (The Ecology)', and 'Inner City Blues' in a subdued, philosophical vein, vastly different from his Sixties teen-ballad hits. During 1972 he wrote the soundtrack for 20th Century-Fox movie *Trouble Man*, and the title single brought him another Top 10 hit, while in May 1972 he returned to stage appearances following which a musically excellent and critically acclaimed 'live' album was issued. Gaye's success with such diverse projects as the *What's Going On*

song cycle and the three-million seller, 'Let's Get It On', demonstrates his importance within contemporary black music, while his independent attitude towards recording forced Motown to allow other artists, including **Stevie Wonder**, more freedom in the studio and to treat albums as more than 'two hits and 10 fillers'.

Gaye's personal life took a downturn in the mid-Seventies, and a judge's instruction that Gaye should relinquish all profit from his forthcoming album in lieu of unpaid alimony due to his ex-wife Anna inspired the sardonically-titled *Here My Dear* (1978). He recorded one more album for Motown – *In Our Lifetime* (1981) – before parting company with the Corporation and joining Columbia in 1982. His first album for the label, *Midnight Love* (1982), contained the transatlantic hit single, 'Sexual Healing'. He was shot dead by his father on the morning of 1 April 1984.

GAYLE, CRYSTAL Born Brenda Gail Webb in 1951 in Paintsville, Kentucky, Crystal Gayle shrugged off the millstone of being **Loretta Lynn**'s younger sister to have a successful career as a country singer in her own right.

Going on the road with her sister and **Conway Twitty** straight after graduating from high school, Crystal Gayle soon secured a recording contract and had an instant country hit single with 'I Cried (the Blue Right Out of My Eyes)', a song written by her sister, in 1970. However, Gayle had a lean period in the charts for the next few years, until 1977, when 'Don't It Make My Brown Eyes Blue', a revamped version of her first single, became a big transatlantic hit (US Number 2, UK Number 5).

Although through sheer hard work Gayle had maintained moderate sales in the country charts, she achieved crossover success with the LP *Crystal* (1976). Her wide appeal reached its peak with the next album, *We Must Believe in Magic* (1977) which went platinum in the US. 'Talking in Your Sleep' (from the album *When I Dream*) became another big hit in 1978, her second single to break the UK charts, but after this Gayle's popularity tailed off as her subsequent releases maintained a lower profile in the charts. She aroused a great deal of interest when she duetted with **Tom Waits** on several tracks for his film soundtrack album, *One From the Heart* (1982).

GAYNOR, GLORIA Born in Newark, New Jersey, on 7 September 1949, Gloria Gaynor was America's 'Queen of Disco' in the early to mid-Seventies. After an unsuccessful **Johnny Nash**-produced single on Jocida in 1965, she sang with a touring band, the Soul Satisfyers, for two years. In 1973, she began working with manager Jay Ellis (who found her at a Manhattan night club), Tony Bongiovi, whizz-kid recording engineer, and Meco Monardo, musical consultant. With the canny crew producing her, Gaynor became just part of an immaculately conceived disco sound, tailor-made for dancing the night away. The hits (for MGM) began with 'Never Can Say Goodbye' (1974), and 'Reach Out I'll Be There' (1975), but it was a depressingly faceless, robot-like soul that Gloria and Bongiovi/Monardo/Ellis conceived for the disco audiences. Her star faded a little during the latter half of the Seventies, when the Eurodisco productions of **Giorgio Moroder** for **Donna Summer** rendered the Gaynor-Monardo mix unfashionable, but she made a triumphant return to the US national and soul charts with 'I Will Survive' (Polydor) in 1979. A rousing assertion of female independence, it topped US and UK Top 40s, though her follow-up singles and albums were far less successful. Her biggest hit since has been 'I Am What I Am' (1983), a disco treatment of a song from the Broadway show *La Cage Aux Folles*.

GEILS, J./J. GEILS BAND Formed in Boston in 1967, the J. Geils Band spent well over a decade as a solid rock/R&B recording band with a faithful live following on the East Coast of America but limited commercial success. Their years of perseverance paid off however, since their twelfth album *Freeze Frame* (1981), gave them an international stage.

The band was named after guitarist Jerome Geils but the focal point was always singer/lyricist Peter Wolf. Geils, Danny Klein (bass) and Magic Dick (Dick Salwitz, harmonica) were playing around Boston together as an acoustic trio but by the time Wolf (ex-DJ and painter) joined, they had switched to electric instruments, with Bladd recruited as drummer. Seth Justman (keyboards) joined in 1968.

Gigging solidly through the Seventies, they managed to instil enough of a contemporary feel to their basic rock to keep them ticking over respectably, scoring a few minor US hit singles ('Must Of Got Lost' reached Number 12 in 1974), and two gold albums with *Bloodshot* (1973) and *Sanctuary* (1978). The breakthrough LP, the radio-oriented pop/rock style *Freeze Frame*, followed a huge world tour, and yielded two international hit singles, the title track and 'Centrefold', which made Number 1 both sides of the Atlantic in 1981, staying at the US top spot for six weeks.

The live LP *Showtime!* (1982) sought to consolidate this success but failed to match up to its predecessor, receiving poor reviews. Wolf left the band shortly after a split that mortified the band's diehard fans, but the group bounced back with a new LP, *You're Getting Even While I'm Getting Old*, in 1984.

GELDOF, BOB See **Boomtown Rats; Band Aid**

GENE AND EUNICE Mid-Fifties R&B duo Gene Forrest and Eunice Levy were based in California, where Forrest recorded with his orchestra for RPM and Aladdin before joining Eunice for vocal duets. Their first hit was 'Ko Ko Mo' in 1955 on Combo Records, recorded by Aladdin, which, when covered by Perry Como, sold a million. Further Aladdin discs failed to register, and their biggest 'pop' hit came in 1959 when 'Poco-Loco' reached the America Top 50 on Case Records. After another disc, on Lilly, no more was heard of the duo, whose style was mellower than **Shirley and Lee** but harsher than **Mickey and Sylvia**.

GENERATION X Formed in 1976 in London by **Billy Idol** and Tony James, Generation X were a punk band who promised much but failed to deliver, getting caught up in their glossy image and the distractions of the rock'n'roll lifestyle.

The first bona fide line-up of Idol (vocals), James (bass), Mark Laff (drums) and Bob 'Derwood' Andrews (guitar) caused a tremendous amount of interest, with major record companies falling over each other to get to the band, confident that Idol's blonde pouting good looks was a foolproof marketing tool. Chrysalis eventually won the race to sign the band in 1977, but in the end they only produced one single of any lasting worth, 'Ready Steady Go' (1978), which nevertheless failed to reach the UK Top 40, and one Top 20 single, 'King Rocker' (1979).

Generation X released three albums, the last of which, *Kiss Me Deadly* (1981) took an exceptionally long time to record and featured a whole host of guitarists including Steve Jones of the **Sex Pistols** and Danny Kustow of the **Tom Robinson** Band, but it had a great many production problems and the debacle eventually broke the group. When the widely-tipped single 'Dancing with Myself' failed miserably, Generation X split up. Idol went on to a successful solo career and James formed **Sigue Sigue Sputnik**.

Billy Idol fronts Generation X at the Marquee in the heyday of punk

GENESIS One of the more enduring products of late Sixties progressive rock, UK-style, Genesis was formed in 1966 by a group of songwriting enthusiasts at a public school near London. The original members were Tony Banks (keyboards, born 27 March 1950), Michael Rutherford (bass, 2 October 1950) and **Peter Gabriel** (vocals, 13 May 1950). Signed to Decca by Jonathan King, they made an uninspiring album (*From Genesis to Revelation*, 1969) with John Mayhew on drums and guitarist Anthony Philips.

The arrival of **Phil Collins** (drums, born 31 January 1951) and Steve Hackett (guitar, 12 February 1950) for *Trespass* (Charisma, 1970) strengthened the band, while Gabriel was beginning to explore the theatrical dimensions of their act. Genesis gained a wider following with *Nursery Cryme* (1971) and *Foxtrot* (1972), where the music matched the melodrama of live performances. *Selling England by the Pound* (1973) consolidated their popularity, and by the time *The Lamb Lies Down on Broadway* was released in 1974, the band had stepped into the major league of post-progressive rock era groups, appealing to both the student market and younger fans, who came to Genesis via their 1974 hit single, 'I Know What I Like (In Your Wardrobe)'.

Peter Gabriel left late in 1974 for a slow-starting but eventually very suc-cessful solo career, and for a time the group's future was in doubt. Phil Collins took over as vocalist after a lengthy series of auditions failed to turn up anyone else, and Bill Bruford was enlisted to share drumming honours with him. The theatrical approach that Gabriel had favoured was dropped and the band developed a tighter, less expansive sound that was well featured on *A Trick of the Tail* (1976). *Wind and Wuthering* (1976) and *... And Then There Were Three* (1977) fared particularly well in the US, and their chart career picked up with a string of hit singles from 1977 onwards, among them the Top 10-placed 'Follow You, Follow Me' (1978), 'Turn it on Again' (1980) and 'Abacab' (1981).

Steve Hackett left in 1977, but the group's line-up has since been stable. The album *Abacab* (1981) saw the band augmented by a horn section (courtesy of **Earth, Wind and Fire**), which had also appeared on Phil Collins' debut album, *Face Value*, that same year. Collins' influence on the band's direction became particularly noticeable at this time, though his own career took off spectacularly with both his two-million selling debut album, *Face Value*, and the subsequent *Hello, I Must Be Going!* (1983): by 1986, he was one of the UK's most consistent hit-makers and biggest musical exports. Suggestions that his success might undermine the future of Genesis were persistently dismissed.

Genesis in the early Seventies: singer Peter Gabriel (in make-up mask), and from left to right, Tony Banks, Phil Collins, Steve Hackett and Michael Rutherford. Gabriel left in 1974 and Hackett followed in 1977

GENTLE GIANT The Glasgow-born brothers, Ray (born 8 December 1949) and Derek (2 February 1947) and Phil Shulman (27 August 1937) were founder members of Simon Dupree and the Big Sound, who had a British Top 10 hit with 'Kites' in 1967. In 1969, frustrated with the cabaret nature of the group, they planned Gentle Giant. They teamed up with Kerry Minnear (2 April 1948), newly graduated from the Royal Academy of Music; a multi-instrumentalist, lead guitarist Gary Green (20 November 1950); and John Weathers, an experienced Welsh musician who had once been with the Eyes Of Blue and the Grease Band, on drums. The brothers themselves played a wide range of instruments: Ray, bass, guitar, violin, drums and piano; Derek, lead vocals, bass, alto; Phil, tenor sax and trumpet.

Gentle Giant slipped into a multi-instrumental experimental niche. Their fourth release, *Octopus* (Vertigo), was a surprise hit in America in 1973. Phil Shulman left in 1973, after which Giant released the rushed-sounding *In a Glasshouse* (WWA), the freer, more spontaneous *Power and the Glory* (1974), and *Free Hand* (1975) – all offering plenty of light and shade from delicate acoustic playing to climactic heavy riff building often featuring well-arranged vocal interweaving.

A Giant Step (1975), *Interview* (1976) and *Playing the Fool* (1977) followed before the group changed pace for *The Missing Piece* (1977), an album that featured more conventional rock treatments and shorter songs. Their 1980 release, *Civilian*, was produced by Lee Abrams.

GENTRY, BOBBIE The singer and writer of one of the most enigmatic songs in pop history, 'Ode to Billie Joe', Bobbie Gentry was born in Chickasaw County, Mississippi, on 27 July 1945. She studied at the Los Angeles Conservatory of Music before working as a secretary and, briefly, as a night-club dancer in Las Vegas. Recording 'Ode to Billie Joe' for Capitol in 1967, she scored a Number 1 US hit and a Top 20 hit in the UK, but follow-up songs such as 'Okalona River Bottom Band', 'Mississippi Delta' and 'Chickasaw County Child' – all individualized statements of Deep South living – failed to make the same impression. In Britain, she had a Number 1 with a version of **Burt Bacharach**'s 'I'll Never Fall in Love Again' during 1969 and also starred in her own BBC-TV series; a year later she reached Number 3 in the UK chart with 'All I Have to Do is Dream', a duet with

Glen Campbell, but she never became the major international star that the BBC and Capitol envisaged. She married Jim Stafford, singer of the 1974 UK and US hit 'Spiders and Snakes', in 1978.

GENTRYS Memphis, Tennessee's answer to the British-inspired beat scene of 1965, the Gentrys recorded for the local Youngstown label after several months of playing local clubs, talent competitions, teen fairs and even Ted Mack's Amateur Hour. The group comprised Larry Raspberry (guitar, vocals), Jimmy Johnson (trumpet, organ), Larry Wall (drums), Pat Neal (bass), Bruce Bowles (vocals), and Jimmy Hart (vocals). Their second single, 'Keep on Dancing' – revived by the **Bay City Rollers** in 1971 – was picked up by MGM and was a US Top 10 hit in September 1965. It was a period classic, one of those songs dedicated to and designed for dancing, mentioning all the top dances of the day and filled out with a solid beat and punk organ sound reminiscent of some of the tougher Texas groups of the time. Like most groups of this era who were favoured with one phenomenal hit, they were never able to follow it up, although they made a fairly strong comeback in 1970 with 'Why Should I Cry' and 'Cinnamon Girl' on the newly reactivated Sun label. In 1973, Larry Raspberry launched his own group, the Highsteppers, who recorded for Stax. The rest of the Gentrys recorded briefly for Capitol.

GERRY AND THE PACE-MAKERS Consisting of Gerry Marsden (vocals, guitar, born 24 September 1942), Les Maguire (piano, 27 December 1941), Les Chadwick (bass, 11 May 1943) and Freddie Marsden (drums, 23 November 1940), Gerry and the Pacemakers were the second group to be signed by **Brian Epstein**, in 1962. Like those by the **Beatles**, their records were produced by **George Martin**. Their first album, *How Do You Like It?* (Columbia, 1963) showed they were well-schooled in rock'n'roll and R&B standards, but as a singles group they emphasized Gerry Marsden's cheeky-chappie image. Each of their first three records went to Number 1 in Britain (an unprecedented chart feat), and the first two (Mitch Murray's 'How Do You Do It?' and 'I Like It') also reached the American Top 20. The third was the *Carousel* ballad, 'You'll Never Walk Alone', which was quickly adopted by Liverpool soccer fans and later by fans of every other

team in England. The hits continued into 1965 and included the theme song from a movie, *Ferry 'Cross the Mersey*, in which the group starred. Soon after, the Pacemakers split up, with Gerry going on to a career as a television and cabaret entertainer. He starred in the West End show *Charlie Girl* in 1969, taking over from **Joe Brown**. In 1985, he earned himself another place in chart history by becoming the first artist ever to take the same song back to Number 1: 'You'll Never Walk Alone', credited to the crowd but featuring Marsden prominently, was a record conceived by him to raise money for victims of the stadium fire at Bradford City's football ground.

GIBSON BROTHERS Born and raised in Martinique, but resident in Paris since their mid-teens, the Gibson Brothers – Chris, Patrick and Alex Gibson – came and went in the summer of 1979 in a brief, concentrated flurry of catchy dance tunes. The songs – 'Cuba', 'Ooh! What a Life', 'Que Sera Mi Vida (If You Should Go)' and 'Better Do It Salsa' – were co-written by the trio's producer Danial Vangarde, and were without exception loud and very merry sounds. But a year can be a long time in pop music and by 1980, a style that had been infectious and jolly began to sound merely banal, a feeling exacerbated by the Gibson's drift away from more exotic rhythms (salsa) and a tendency to attempt to conform to standard American R&B formulae.

GIBSON, DON Born in Shelby, North Carolina, on 3 April 1928, Don Gibson has been writing and singing country music for most of his life, but somehow he's never fulfilled his early promise. He began as a straight honky-tonk singer, but when **Elvis Presley** threw down his challenge to the country traditionalists Gibson adapted his style.

In the late Fifties and early Sixties, **Chet Atkins** had gathered around him a group of musicians and performers at RCA Victor in Nashville, one of whom was Gibson. Atkins was doing his best to stem the flood of rock'n'roll and in Gibson he had, potentially, his greatest ally. The idea was to create a semi-rocking sound around essentially country singers, but for Gibson it was a technique that simply didn't go far enough and the result was the emasculation of a genuinely soulful voice. He had a string of hits – 'Oh Lonesome Me', 'Blue Blue Day', 'Heartache Number One', 'Legend in My Time' – but it was often left to others to reveal the true worth of his writing. **Neil Young** may have failed to better him on 'Oh Lonesome Me' – a Top 10 pop hit for Gibson in 1958 – but his own version of 'I Can't Stop Loving You' pales beside the **Ray Charles** version. His last really important record was probably his best yet ironically not one of his own compositions – the archetypal country/rock single, Harlon Howard's 'Sea of Heartbreak', a pop hit in 1961. He still works in Nashville.

Gerry and the Pacemakers make a live television appearance

GILLAN Formed by ex-**Deep Purple** vocalist Ian Gillan in 1979, Gillan came into being at a time when British heavy metal was undergoing a renaissance. During the three years of their existence, fronted by an exceptional hard rock vocalist, they became one of the leading heavy metal bands in the world, consistently finding chart placings with their releases.

After leaving Deep Purple in 1973, Gillan took a couple of years leave before his next LP (credited to the Ian Gillan Band), *Child in Time* in 1976. After releasing another three albums, all only moderate sellers, he folded that band and set up a new one – Gillan. The band went through several changes of line-up, but the best known and longest-standing was Bernie Tormé (guitar), Colin Towns (keyboards), John McCoy (bass) and Mick Underwood (drums).

The first Gillan album was *Mr Universe* (1979), an immediate success due to the £3 price, considerably lower than usual, and four other albums followed, the most successful of which was *Future Shock*, a UK Number 2 in 1981. Gillan also scored two UK Top 20 singles, 'Trouble' and 'New Orleans' in 1980 and 1981 respectively. At the end of 1982 Ian Gillan announced his retirement from music under doctors orders to rest his ailing vocal chords, and the group disbanded.

Late in 1983, Ian Gillan made a surprise announcement that he would return to singing, not to re-form Deep Purple as everyone had suspected, but to join **Black Sabbath**. But this liaison was short-lived, however, and didn't last out 1984, by which time he had rejoined Deep Purple.

GILLEY, MICKEY Until the mid-Seventies, Mickey Gilley was a vocalist and pianist who lived both stylistically and commercially in the shadow of cousin **Jerry Lee Lewis**. Born in Mississippi, but living in Houston since 1957 when Lewis became a star, Gilley recorded rock'n'roll during that year for Minor Records. A series of rock and country classics on small Southern labels followed and country hits with 'Is It Wrong' (1960), 'Lonely Wine' (1964), 'Now I Can Live Again' (1968) and 'Room Full of Roses' (1974) were achieved. He opened his own nightclub in Houston in 1971. His best year was 1977, when he won four Academy of Country Music awards – as Entertainer and Top Male Vocalist of the Year, for Best Single ('Bring It on Home') and Best Album ('*Gilley's Smoking*).

GIRL GROUPS (1960s) Girl vocal groups were an almost purely American phenomenon of the early Sixties, although the Teen Queens, Hearts and **Chordettes** had made an impact during the previous decade. The trend started when the **Shirelles** had a big hit in 1960 with 'Will You Love Me Tomorrow?', which led to a string of American hits. Male groups were already a part of American pop, but a consistently successful girl group was something quite new.

As audiences then tended to buy the sounds first, then look to see who was singing afterwards, images hardly counted and producers looked upon girl groups as pliable studio puppets who were even more naive than their male counterparts. By the same token, however, most of the female vocal groups were only modestly talented and were therefore only too happy to be manipulated by some whizz-kid producer if it resulted in their earning $800 a night, touring on the strength of a hit.

By 1963, most of the teenage idols of the late Fifties and early Sixties had declined in popularity and American record producers were making an increasing number of studio-contrived girl-group discs. As a consequence, many quaintly named one-hit wonders reached the American charts including the Murmaids, the **Jaynetts**, the Girl-friends, the Angels, the Dixiebelles, the Cookies, the Sherrys and **Reparata and the Delrons** – the list is endless. The majority of these records were made either by professional session-singers

Innocent smiles from one among many girl groups – the Chiffons

or by semi-pros who were coaxed into the studio with a few dollars' advance. By using session-singers, a producer was able to avoid clashes of temperament with self-opinionated artists and at the same time ensure greater profits for himself, since they were only paid a standard fee.

Girl-group records became so fashionable in the States that early in 1964, **Leiber and Stoller** and the late **George Goldner** formed the legendary Red Bird label as a vehicle for instant girl-group hits. Red Bird's first release, 'Chapel of Love' by the **Dixie Cups**, topped the charts and thereafter the firm's small but shrewd writer-producer workshop gave Red Bird a hit with virtually every other release by anonymous entities like the Jelly Beans, the **Shangri-Las** and the Butterys, etc.

The same year, 1964, saw the emergence of a new generation of fans who, like their older brothers and sisters a decade earlier, wanted real heroes and real personalities rather than the plethora of faceless girl groups and one-hit wonders that the industry was churning out. Thus the advent of the 'British Invasion' signalled the demise of the girl-group sound. *See also* **Red Bird**

GIRLSCHOOL All-girl British heavy metal foursome Girlschool had trouble being taken seriously when they first emerged out of South London in 1979, but when it became clear that they could in fact play their instruments and thump out the power chords with the best of them, they became valued as more than a novelty act.

Originally formed at school under the name of Painted Lady by Kim McAuliffe (guitar/vocals) and Di 'Enid' Williams (bass/vocals), they changed their name when Kelly Johnson (guitar/vocals) and Denise Dufort (drums) joined. They quickly built up a following as a result of their appearances at local gigs, and then had a major hit with **Motörhead** (masquerading under the name Headgirl), 'The St Valentine's Day Massacre' EP, which reached Number 5 in 1981. They went on to record a series of moderately successful albums on Bronze, culminating with *Play Dirty* in 1984, before dropping from the public eye.

GISCOMBE, JUNIOR Norman Junior Giscombe was born in South London on 6 June 1957. Because of his tendency to pick pockets to obtain money, he was thrown out of school. An enthusiastic reggae fan, he formed a vocal group, recorded an indie single and moved to New York, but later returned to Britain when he was signed by Phonogram, who combined his talents with those of Linx's co-producer, arranger and keyboard player Bob Carter. Giscombe had previously sung background for Linx, and he and Carter wrote several songs together including 'Mama Used To Say' and 'Too Late', both of which appeared on Giscombe's 1982 debut LP *Ji*. By the time of its release, Junior was a hit artist on both sides of the Atlantic. 'Mama', which he'd originally written for a previous band of his called Atlantis, was remixed and released in the US after gaining only minor success in Britain, and its smart, bright British black sound pushed aside some of the tired-sounding elder American pop-soul. Junior became only the second British artist (after **David Bowie**) to appear on the famed US TV show *Soul Train*. His second album, *Inside Lookin' Out*, appeared in 1983 but didn't quite recapture the vivacity and sharpness of *Ji*. In 1986, Junior appeared on the Red Wedge tour with Paul Weller, **Billy Bragg** and other socially aware UK acts, and released another LP, *Acquired Taste*.

GLITTER, GARY

Born Paul Gadd in Banbury, Oxfordshire, on 8 May 1940, Gary Glitter pursued a singing career as Paul Raven which survived through the Sixties on stamina rather than success. He appeared on the original *Jesus Christ Superstar* album, before changing his record company – to Bell Records – in 1971, and his name. In 1972, the B-side of his first single in his new identity 'Rock And Roll Part 2' became an enormous and unexpected US and UK hit after 'sleeping' on the lower reaches of the chart for several months. The consistent success of the string of singles that followed over the next years ('Do You Wanna Touch Me?', 'I'm the Leader of the Gang' (1973), 'Always Yours' (1974), etc. prompted him to develop his persona into an extravagant parody. He wrote all his songs with his producer Mike Leander and by 1974 had become part of pop's showbiz *élite* and launched his backing group, the Glitter Band, on their own career.

The hits continued into 1975, but by then glam-rock was passé and the parody had worn thin. He appeared in *The Rocky Horror Show* in New Zealand and carried on playing the college circuit where he had always had a loyal if slightly surprising following, until the early Eighties brought him fresh recognition via **Adam Ant**'s updated version of the Glitter Stomp and comic theatricals. In 1984, Gary was back in the UK chart with 'Dance Me Up' and 'Another Rock and Roll Christmas', both on Arista.

GLOVER, HENRY

An important backroom figure in Fifties R&B, Henry Glover was born in Manhattan, New York. After leaving college in 1943, Glover did graduate work at Wayne University, almost attaining an MA in music before joining Buddy Johnson's band on trumpet in 1944. He then played with Willie Bryant and Tiny Bradshaw before joining Lucky Millinder's band, with whom he was working when King Records boss Syd Nathan appointed him as A&R director – having first ascertained that he could write and arrange music.

Glover's duties included recording Bullmoose Jackson, Lonnie Johnson and numerous R&B acts, together with **Moon Mullican**, Cowboy Copas and many of the company's C&W artists. He also helped Nathan design an echo-chamber, and worked on many other business projects with him. Glover became a prolific songwriter, often collaborating with Lois Mann, and was shrewd enough to get full copyright protection on his material including the now standard 'Drown in My Own Tears' and the Midnighters' infamous 'Annie Had a Baby'. He recorded acts such as **John Lee Hooker**, **Roy Brown**, **Little Willie John** and **Wynonie Harris** before moving to Roulette on its inception in 1956. Here he began a further fruitful songwriting partnership with his co-director Morris Levy, also handling production/arranging duties, and was responsible for a vast amount of material by Dave Cortez, Essex, **Joey Dee** (he co-wrote the million-selling 'Peppermint Twist'), **Sam and Dave**, etc. before returning to King in 1963 and attaining the vice-presidency before the Leiber/Stoller/Neely combine bought the company, now Tennessee Recording and Publishing Co. *See also* **King Records**

GODLEY AND CREME

Kevin Godley (born 7 October 1945 in Manchester) and Lol Creme (17 September 1947, Manchester) worked together as musicians, composers, producers, authors and video directors to become the most talented all-rounders in the music world.

After they left **10cc** in 1976, Godley & Creme released their ridiculously overblown triple LP *Consequences* (1977) to mixed reviews, but the album demonstrated that after the clean-cut pop of their previous band, they were trying something altogether more ambitious. *L* (1978) was a more down-to-earth affair and was released to rave reviews, followed by the coolly-received *Freeze Frame* (1979), neither of which sold in great numbers. However, the single taken from the latter, 'An Englishman in New York', allowed them to direct their first video and was such a success that they went on to make award-winning videos for **Duran Duran**, **Frankie Goes to Hollywood**, **Police** and many others.

Their work on videos increasingly prevented them from recording, but in 1981 the album *Ism Ism* gave them their first real chart success since leaving 10cc, with the two UK Top 10 singles 'Under Your Thumb' and 'Wedding Bells'. *Birds of Prey* (1983) passed by largely unnoticed, and expanding extra-curricular activities meant that it was followed by only two items of original material in three years, the singles 'Golden Boy' (1984) and the superb 'Cry' (1985). The latter release showcased the extent of their talents, a brilliant marriage of sound and image, promoted by a devastatingly simple video which consisted of a constantly mutating, sad face mouthing the lyrics.

GOFFIN, GERRY *See* **Carole King**

GO-GO'S

Formed in Los Angeles in 1978, West Coast all-girl band the Go-Go's overcame tortuous bad luck to become one of the most successful female acts of all time, notching up a US Number 1 with their debut album.

Jane Wiedlin (guitar) and Belinda Carlisle (vocals) met at a party and decided to form a band, completing the Go-Go's with Charlotte Caffey (guitar), Margot Olavarria (bass) and Gina Schock (drums). In England they opened for **Madness** before they released their first single, 'We Got the Beat' on Stiff in 1980. Returning to the US, (with a new bassist Kathy Valentine) they released the LP *Beauty and the Beat* (1981), which topped the US charts, and there followed *Vacation* (1982) and *Talk Show* (1984), establishing them as a major band and a top live draw.

However, their progress was dogged by problems, ranging from an uncooperative record company and a disappearing manager to bouts of ill-health – Caffey was temporarily paralysed in the left hand and Schock underwent heart surgery – to the point where the stress was overpowering, causing them to split in 1985.

GOLD, ANDREW Musician, singer/ songwriter and arranger, Andrew Gold (born 2 August 1951 in Burbank, California) played in **Linda Ronstadt**'s band before finding success as a solo mainstream rock/pop artist.

Coming from a musical family (his father Ernest was a film soundtrack composer, his mother Marni Nixon overdubbed Natalie Wood's singing voice in *West Side Story* and many others), Gold became a proficient musician (he is a multi-instrumentalist) and in 1969 formed Bryndle. A short-lived folk-pop band that included Karla Bonoff and Wendy Waldman (who later became prominent singer/songwriters in their own right), they never released a record and Gold went on to become a respected sessioneer around Los Angeles.

In the early Seventies, he joined Linda Ronstadt and played on several of her albums while at the same time embarking on a solo career, starting with the LP *Andrew Gold* in 1975. Gold cut another three albums before 1980, and in that time scored three UK Top 20 singles (most notably 'Never Let Her Slip Away', Number 5 in 1978) and one US Top 10 hit, 'Lonely Boy' in 1977.

After 1980, Gold abandoned his solo career for several years but continued to work as a musician, and several of his songs were covered by **Cliff Richard**, **Leo Sayer**, **Art Garfunkel** and many others. In 1986 Gold partnered ex-**10cc** man **Graham Gouldman** to form pop duo Wax, and they released the single 'Ball and Chain', which met with little chart success.

GOLDBERG, BARRY Blues pianist and songwriter Barry Goldberg's career began in the late Fifties in Chicago, when he sat in with bluesmen like **Otis Rush**, **Muddy Waters** and **Buddy Guy** and becoming well established in the South Side clubs. In 1965, he played with **Bob Dylan** on the controversial electric set at the Newport Folk Festival. He had been enticed there by **Michael Bloomfield**, with whom he had played occasionally in the **Butterfield Blues Band**. On his return to Chicago he set up the Goldberg-Miller Blues Band (also known as the Third World War Blues Band) with **Steve Miller**, recording an album, *Blowing My Mind*, in 1966, though Steve Miller had already left for San Francisco by the time of its release. A much respected player, Goldberg has never made a really worthwhile album despite surrounding himself with fine and willing musicians like **Duane Allman**, **Harvey Mandel** (who had replaced Miller in the Blues Band) and Mike Bloomfield on albums like *Two Jews' Blues* and *Blasts From My Past* (Buddah, 1968 and 1969 respectively). Bloomfield enticed him to California when he set up the **Electric Flag** in 1968. Eventually he made the switch from being purely a keyboard player to a self-contained singer, musician and writer, and in 1973 he produced his most pleasing album, *Barry Goldberg*, at Muscle Shoals and worked on Gerry Goffin's solo album, *It Ain't Exactly Entertainment* (Adelphi). A live album, *Barry Goldberg and Friends*, was released in 1976.

GOLDNER, GEORGE Manhattan-born George Goldner began his career as a mambo teacher with a string of dance halls in New York in the latter years of the Forties. Tico, the first label he worked for, specialized in Latin-American music and had a roster which included Tito Puente and Machito. Increasing black interest in the mambo craze led Goldner to form Rama, his first R&B label, and following the success of the **Orioles**' 'Crying in the Chapel' in 1953, he realized that a great many black vocal groups could also 'go pop' if they were produced with the white audience in mind. Accordingly, with Joe Kilsky and, later, **Richard Barrett**, Goldner began to pull in groups off the street corners of New York: the Five Budds, the Valentines, the **Crows**, the Pretenders, the Heartbeats, the Wrens, the Rainbows – groups galore were whisked into rented studios. Their records were inevitably stereotyped, with a jaunty teenage lead tenor, a heavy drumbeat, Jimmy Wright's obligatory tenor saxophone solo and breaks in the simple arrangement where the bass singer could offer his glamorous contribution. Many of Goldner's acts made the Hot 100 on the strength of New York sales alone. Others, particularly **Frankie Lymon** and the Teenagers, became internationally successful manifestations of New York's street-corner sound. The Teenagers – with three Top 20 hits to their credit and well over three million records sold outside America – were a black/Puerto Rican group. Goldner never worried about creed or colour. Provided a group or vocalist could sing falsetto ballads or hot, impromptu scats, he would give that act a chance on one of his numerous labels. Consider this list, most of whom had major hit records: on Gee – the **Cleftones**, the Heartbeats, the Regents; on Gone – the Channels, Jo Ann Campbell, **Ral Donner**; on End – the **Chantels**, Lewis Lymon and the Teenchords, the **Flamingos**, **Little Anthony and the Imperials**; on Mark-X – the **Isley Brothers**, Dickie Goodman; and on Goldisc – the **Temptations**, the Royaltones. Juanita and Cindy were among Goldner's less successful labels. After heavy gambling, Goldner's interests were acquired by Roulette, for whom he continued to supervise many recording sessions.

In 1964, he joined **Leiber and Stoller** as president of the hugely successful Red Bird label, and when that was dissolved he gambled another fortune away. In December 1969, he formed his last label, Firebird, with a view to producing hard rock with a Fifties feel. However, the dream turned sour when he signed such acts as the Crewcuts who had only their hairstyles going for them in the first place. Goldner died on 15 April 1970, aged 52. Next to the Atlantic label, he was the most important force in New York rock'n'roll. He was the original Fifties bubblegum king, without a mind for traditional blues. Nor was he entirely punctilious over royalty payments, but he cut a lot of wonderful records and did more for integration than the Supreme Court.

GOLDSBORO, BOBBY At the peak of his popularity in the late Sixties, Bobby Goldsboro – born in Marianna, Florida, on 18 January 1941 – was responsible for many much-recorded pop and country songs. He began his career as a guitarist, working in a variety of local rock studios and touring for two years as a member of **Roy Orbison**'s backing band, and signed with Laurie Records in 1962. His first release for them, 'Molly', reached Number 70 in the Hot 100 during 1963. Later that year he joined United Artists, where he was produced by **Bob Montgomery**: 'See the Funny Little Clown' reached Number 9 in the US. It was a further four years, however, before he had a hit of similar size – the million-selling 'Honey', unusually not one of his own compositions but a song by Bobby 'Little Green Apples' Russell, which topped the US chart and gave him his first hit in the UK (a Number 2). He had his own TV series in the US between 1972 and 1975 and had a second UK hit in 1973 with perhaps his best record, a sultry tale of first love inspired by the film *Summer of '42*, 'Summer (The First Time)'. 'Hello Summertime', adapted from a Coca Cola jingle, reached the UK Top 20 in 1974 and a reissue of 'Honey' repeated the track's original UK chart placing during the following year.

Since then, he has worked mainly in a country-pop vein, scoring the occasional hit in the country chart.

GOMELSKY, GIORGIO One of a handful of promoters who saw the early potential of British R&B, Giorgio Gomelsky started Sunday night sessions at the Station Hotel, Richmond (the first location of his Crawdaddy club), and gave the **Rolling Stones** a residency in February 1963. His reluctance to bind the group to a written managerial contract allowed **Andrew Loog Oldham** to sign them up, and he was more careful with the group who took over the Stones' residency, the **Yardbirds**. He went on to manage other Crawdaddy club bands, including the **Brian Auger** Trinity and the T-Bones, and brought Steampacket together (its personnel including **Rod Stewart** and **Julie Driscoll** in 1965). He subsequently formed his own record company, Marmalade, with backing from Polydor Records, but despite the international success of Julie Driscoll and the Brian Auger Trinity with 'This Wheel's On Fire' in 1968, the label was short-lived and he left England for France to establish an 'alternative' circuit for groups like **Gong** and Magma (whom he also managed). A series of albums cut from tapes in his possession appeared on the French BYG label under the collective title of *Rock Generation* and featured material by groups with whom he had been involved in London (though not the Stones). He set up Utopia Records in 1975, for whom he recorded blues guitarist **Albert King** and others.

GONG After **Hawkwind**, Gong (formed in Paris in 1970) were the definitive hippy/space rock band. Brought together by wandering Australian guitarist, bohemian and poet Daevid Allen (who co-founded **Soft Machine**), they recorded their first album, *Camembert Electrique*, for the French label Byg in 1971. Together with Gilli Smith (vocals), Christian Tritsch (bass), Pip Pyle (drums) and Didier Malherbe (sax and flute), Allen was based in the French countryside, and Gong became one of the most popular avant-garde bands working in France. Allen broke up the group in 1972, however, in order to concentrate on writing, but a recording contract from Virgin later encouraged him to re-form the band, and although the personnel changed often, it became established around Allen, guitarist Steve Hillage and synthesizer player Tim Blake.

British success came in 1973 when Virgin released the LP *The Flying Teapot*, the first of Gong's *Radio Gnome Invisible* trilogy. This was a drug-induced fantasy about 'pot-head pixies' who journey through inner space in bright green teapots fitted with helicopter rotors. *Angel's Egg* (1973) and *You* (1974) completed the trilogy, seeing the group moving toward more sophisticated, jazz-rock riffing. It also saw the departure of the three main figures, Hillage to a successful solo career, Blake to obscurity on a French electronic label and Allen, it would appear, into thin air. Gong successfully completed its transition into jazz-rock, under the leadership of classically-trained percussionist Pierre Moerlen, on albums such as *Shamal* (1976). By 1980, Gong and its individual members had fallen silent.

GOOD, JACK The history of British pop music cannot be written without mention of Jack Good who, almost single-handedly, brought it to the British television screen in 1957. Born in Palmers Green, London, in 1931, and educated at Balliol College, Oxford, Good joined the BBC in 1956 as a trainee. The following year, intrigued by rock'n'roll and the media's fear of it, he devised the legendary *Six-Five Special* and apparently hoodwinked the Corporation into letting him produce it by pretending that it was to be a young people's magazine programme. In 1958 Good was wooed across to the commercial network, who gave him *carte blanche* to produce his own show. The result was *Oh Boy!*, arguably British television's shrewdest exploitation of rock music. He then produced, in descending order of popularity, *Boy Meets Girl* (1959) and *Wham!* (1960), but during this time introduced a wealth of new talent to the screen and became a celebrity in his own right as the 'intellectual' of rock.

He saw himself as star-maker through television and, with mixed results, attempted to create images for performers like **Cliff Richard** and **Adam Faith**. He also brought a degree of critical intelligence to the British pop press through an incisive weekly column in *Disc*. In 1962, after two years in the doldrums, Good went to America 'for a year'. He stayed for eight during which time he produced *Around The Beatles*, *Shindig* and spectaculars for the **Monkees** and Andy Williams. He returned to Britain in 1970 to play Othello in his stage musical *Catch My Soul* and, in 1973, wrote and produced an abortive screen version. *Oh Boy!*

Gene Vincent (left) and Joe Brown on Jack Good's Boy Meets Girl *show*

returned to the screen in the early Eighties, with Good again producing, but it had the air of a parody – a self-consciously comic re-creation of British pop in the pre-Beatle years. **Shakin' Stevens** was one of its resident stars.

GOODHAND-TAIT, PHILIP Singer-songwriter Philip Goodhand-Tait was born in Hull on 3 January 1945, and became involved in the London R&B scene around 1965 as a member of the Stormsville Shakers. A popular London club band, they backed American musicians including **Larry Williams** and **Johnny 'Guitar' Watson**. With the advent of the underground, they became Circus, and sported beads, droopy moustaches and kaftans.

Leaving Circus shortly before they recorded for Transatlantic, Tait signed with Dick James Music as a songwriter. He embarked on a solo career, cutting four pleasant and workmanlike albums for DJM between 1970 and 1973. Their lack of success was partially attributable to comparisons drawn between Goodhand-Tait and **Elton John**. His backing group – Andy Latimer (guitar), Andy Ward (bass) and Doug Ferguson (drums) – left in 1972 to form Camel with Peter Bardens. Camel's *Snow Goose* (Deram, 1975) made them one of the most successful newer British bands of the year and marked the start of a long recording career. Goodhand-Tait moved from DJM after five albums to join Chrysalis, for whom he recorded *Oceans Away* (1976) and *Teaching an Old Dog* (1977).

GOODMAN, STEVE A cheerfully unpretentious, country-oriented singer-songwriter from Chicago, Steve Goodman – born 25 July 1948 – is best remembered for creating one of the finest and most recorded train songs of the modern era in 'City of New Orleans', though the 1972 hit version of the song was by **Arlo Guthrie**. Goodman's background was in folk music, but his career took off around 1971 thanks to the joint backing of **Paul Anka** and **Kris Kristofferson**, both of whom also took an active interest in the career of Goodman's friend and long-time playing partner **John Prine**. Goodman's two albums for Buddah were well received but sold poorly, and it was as a live performer that he made most impact: his appearances at the Lincoln and Cambridge Folk Festivals in the UK during 1972 were still talked about years later. Despite signing for Elektra in 1974, Goodman's recording career never quite took off and he spent the last decade of his life in relative obscurity, the royalties from 'City of New Orleans' his chief source of income. After a long battle against leukemia, he died in Seattle, Washington, on 20 September 1984.

GOONS The Goons first emerged in a BBC radio comedy show which began in 1951 under the name *Crazy People*. The original Goons were Terence (Spike) Milligan, Peter Sellers, Harry Secombe and Michael Bentine. The show added a certain satirical attitude to an already existing tradition of surreal radio comedy. The Goon shows proper of the mid-Fifties incorporated musical interludes by Max Geldray (harmonica) and Ray Ellington's band. Two records released in 1956, 'I'm Walking Backwards for Christmas' and 'Bloodnock's Rock and Roll', reached the British Top 10 and predated later lunacy by the **Bonzo Dog Doo Dah Band**. Sellers and Secombe have both had individual record successes – Sellers with such **George Martin**-produced novelties as 'Goodness Gracious Me' (1960, with Sophia Loren) and Secombe in a straight vocal vein. In 1973, general nostalgia for things British and old met the new teenybopper market head-on to give the Goons a re-issue British Top 10 hit with their 1956 recording of the unique 'Ying Tong Song'.

GORDON, ROSCO Memphis-based R&B singer and pianist Rosco Gordon helped launch the careers of several top R&B acts besides cutting a string of hit records. During the Forties,

Gordon was a popular entertainer in and around Memphis. In 1948 he helped form the Beale Streeters, which included **B.B. King** on guitar, **Johnny Ace** on piano and Earl Forrest on drums. By 1952 the Beale Streeters were signed to Duke and issuing sides under their various names. Gordon later introduced **Bobby Bland** into the act, offering him encouragement and advice throughout the early years. By this time, Gordon was already recording for Sam Phillips, who leased his first record, 'Booted', to Chess in Chicago. **Ike Turner** was in charge of the Phillips sessions, and produced many more fine sides for Gordon including the excellent 'No More Doggin''. Gordon sang with near-fury through most of his hits, and was usually supported by a chunky backing band with a growling tenor sax. He eventually switched to Vee Jay and cut his most famous R&B hit, 'Just a Little Bit', which was to be re-recorded by countless British R&B outfits during the early Sixties, even becoming a minor hit in 1964 for the Liverpool group the Undertakers.

GORE, LESLEY Born on 2 May 1946, in Tenafly, New Jersey, Lesley Gore was one of the few singers to emerge in the 1962–5 girl group era who survived into the late Sixties, mainly on the strength of her material, style and the large following generated by the string of seven straight Top 10 records that started her career. Her first hit was the US Number 1, 'It's My Party' (Mercury, 1963), followed by an answer to that, 'Judy's Turn to Cry' and then 'She's a Fool' and 'You Don't Own Me', which she also sang in a stunning performance in *The T.A.M.I. Show*. These records shared certain key elements: strong productions, impassioned, crying vocals, and the themes of teenage love triangles. 'That's The Way Boys Are' and 'Maybe I Know' followed in the same vein, but later hits such as 'Look of Love', 'Sunshine, Lollipops And Rainbows' and 'California Nights' found her moving towards more of a mainstream pop sound. After ten years with Mercury and a spell with Bob Crewe Records, she signed with Motown's subsidiary Mowest in 1972 and then A&M in 1975, for whom she recorded *Love Me by Name*, produced by Quincy Jones. She worked on the soundtrack score of *Fame* in 1980, writing lyrics to her brother Michael's music: their song 'Out Here on My Own' was a US Number 19 hit for one of the film's stars, Irene Cara, during that year.

GOSPEL MUSIC Stripped of their cultural heritage through slavery, the early Afro-Americans found the Church the only institution able to explain and mollify their new position. The simple life-after-death theology, delivered through parable preaching and inspirational singing, enabled the Black Churches to flourish through the 19th century. They 'Africanized' the early Anglican hymns in aural transmission, transmuting and reassembling them into the Negro Spirituals – the call and unison response of 'Swing Low, Sweet Chariot', the long sustained melody of 'Noboy Knows the Trouble' and the syncopated clap-rhythmic 'Shout All Over God's Heaven'.

The early 20th-century upsurge of fundamentalist churches in the dehumanizing industrial ghettos brought ecstatic, testifying shouts, holy dancing and musical instruments into church music. Reflecting this, the pre-Depression recording boom waxed a wide range of styles of religious material, from Rev. J. M. Gates' short sermons and answering congregation, to the piano-playing evangelist singer, Arizona Dranes, to the religious blues of guitarist Blind Willie Johnson and the ruggedly harmonized versions of the spirituals by 'jubilee' (multi-voice harmony lead) quartets like the Golden Gate and the Norfolk Quartets.

In the Thirties, traditional spirituals were supplanted by new gospel material. Earlier, Rev. Charles A. Tindley had published 'Stand By Me' and 'Understand It Better By and By' and Lucie Campbell produced 'Something Within Me' and 'In the Upper Room', but Thomas A. Dorsey (*aka* Georgia Tom) is regarded as the Father of Gospel Music. In 1932, he co-founded the National Convention of Gospel Singers which promoted the spread of material like his own 'Precious Lord' and 'Peace in the Valley'. With performers like Sallie Martin, Roberta Martin and **Mahalia Jackson** pushing them, the sentimental, optimistic blue-note ridden gospel numbers swept the nation, finding white acceptance through artists like Red Foley and the Stamps-Baxter Quartet. Though Mahalia was the 'Gospel Queen', others were important. Willie Mae Ford Smith, an instructress at Dorsey's Conventions, taught many younger singers, like Brother Joe May, the improvising slurs, note bending and rephrasing techniques of gospel, while Sister Rosetta Tharpe took the gospelly blues 'This Train' into the race charts.

The golden age for gospel began in

1945. New independent recording labels like Apollo, King and Specialty prospered issuing gospel material; radio stations featured early morning and Sunday gospel shows; and the gospel highway of one-night theatre stands, church benefits, and anniversary programmes was thick with travelling groups. Run by matriarch Gertrude, the Famous Ward Singers – who used daughter Clara's arrangements, Marion Williams' solos and Rev. W. Herbert Brewster's material like 'Move On Up a Little Higher' – and their rivals, Albertina Walker's Caravans – who nurtured current solo stars including Shirley Caesar, Inez Andrews, Dorothy Norwood, and, more briefly, James Cleveland and Bessie Griffin – featured strong emotional lead singers in front of imaginative background harmonies, usually accompanied by simple piano or organ lines. Clara Ward exerted a considerable stylistic influence on the young **Aretha Franklin**, whose first recordings were made in her father's (Rev. C. L. Franklin) New Bethel Church.

Others, like the Consolers with ethereal guitar and organ-backed versions of 'heart-warming spiritual hymns' like 'Waiting for My Child' and the early **Staple Singers**, of the hillbilly harmony 'Will the Circle Be Unbroken?', appealed more to Southern audiences.

Male a cappella 'quartets' were also developing. Using gospel material and a second tenor to complete the four-part harmony behind the high, clear tenor voice of Rebert Harris, the **Soul Stirrers** gave gospel and – through **Sam Cooke** – soul music, one of its lasting styles. Likewise, the contrast of Claude

Gospel group the Staple Singers: Pop Staples and his daughters

Jeter's falsetto and the harsh shouter leads of the **Swan Silvertones** presaged the **Temptations**, while the devil-demolishing ecstatic screams of the Five Blind Boys' Archie Brownlee were picked up by the young **James Brown**, whose stage movements could be a parody of the frenzied movement of Ira Tucker of the **Dixie Hummingbirds**.

The end of a cappella came with the addition of guitarists, like Howard Carroll of the Dixie Hummingbirds, and in the Sixties popular groups like the Mighty Clouds Of Joy and the Violinaires used falsetto harmony behind the preaching lead voices of Joe Ligon and Robert Blair respectively. Now the

instrumentation of gospel groups can be as full as soul groups, enabling the Rance Allen Group to rework secular hits, alongside the smooth jubilee hymns of the Harmonizing Four or the cool sophisticated homophonic Voices-Supreme.

James Cleveland's 'Love of God' with the Voices Of Tabernacle and 'Peace Be Still' with the Angelic Choir in the Sixties ushered in the era of choirs and soloists, with his Gospel Music Convention promoting large interdenominational choirs, and the surprising pop success (in 1969) of the **Edwin Hawkins Singers'** 'Oh Happy Day'.

Sister Rosetta Tharpe, an influence on the young Elvis Presley

GOULDMAN, GRAHAM One of the most talented British pop song-writers of the mid-Sixties, Graham Gouldman (born 10 May 1946) played guitar in the Manchester group the Mockingbirds. His first successful composition was 'Listen People', which fellow Mancunians **Herman's Hermits** took into the US Top 10 during 1966, and his 'No Milk Today' provided the group with a further hit a year later. In between came the **Hollies**' recordings of Gouldman's 'Bus Stop' and 'Stop Stop Stop' (1966), both of which demonstrated his keen eye for unusual settings for conventional pop lyrics. He wrote three major chart hits for the **Yardbirds** – 'For Your Love', 'Heart Full of Soul' and 'Evil Hearted You' – before moving to New York in late 1967 to work in the Kassenetz-Katz bubblegum music organization. Returning to Britain in 1969, he began working on an album for **Giorgio Gomelsky**'s Marmalade label with Lol Creme and Kevin Godley, an association which was to provide the basis for **10cc**. After the demise of 10cc in the early Eighties, Gouldman concentrated most of his energies in the field of record production. In 1986 he formed the pop duo, Wax, with **Andrew Gold**. *See also* **Bubblegum**; **10cc**

GRACIE, CHARLIE Born Charles Anthony Graci in Philadelphia on 14 May 1936, of Sicilian ancestry, Charlie Gracie had a US Number 1 in 1957 with 'Butterfly' (Cameo) but had first recorded in a rockabilly vein for Cadillac and 20th Century in 1953–6 with limited success. An enormously commercial piece of rock'n'roll, 'Butterfly' was written by Bernie Lowe and Kal Mann but was credited to Tony Mammarella, the producer of television's *American Bandstand*, under the pseudonym of Anthony September. Other bit sellers – 'Fabulous' (1957), 'I Love You So Much it Hurts' and, in the UK, 'Wanderin' Eyes' – led to a part in the film *Disc Jockey Jamboree*, and Gracie was one of the few rock'n'rollers to be praised by *The Times* of London: 'the test of a rock'n'roll expert is presumably whether he can convert his staider audience to the delights of this intoxicating rhythm, and your critic must confess to conversion', ran the review. Much was made of the fact that Gracie was a proficient guitarist, though guitar solos rarely featured on his discs. He subsequently recorded for Coral, Roulette, Felsted, President, Diamond and, in 1968, Sock'n'Soul. Gracie toured England in 1979 and again in 1981.

Charlie Gracie was a massively successful rock'n'roller in the Fifties, and the Eighties rock revival brought him back to British stages

GRAHAM, BILL Born in Berlin in 1931, Bill Graham, who oscillated from business manager of the San Francisco Mime Troupe to promoter of **Bob Dylan**'s 1974 American tour, was one of the few people to outlast the San Francisco boom of 1967–9. Starting with a couple of benefits for the Mime Troupe in 1965–6, Graham slowly moved into full-time promotion. 1966 saw him looking after the Fillmore Auditorium (an important venue) and temporarily managing the **Jefferson Airplane**; 1968 looking after the Fillmores West and East (the latter was in New York) plus a record label (Fillmore, of course) that soon folded. By now he had a virtual monopoly of promotions in the Bay Area and was beginning national promotions. Always outspoken, Graham was often accused by the San Francisco 'head community' of being nothing more than a dollars and cents man. However, his continued involvement in live music and his reputation of being a tough, but fair, businessman demonstrates that his interest in music is more than merely mercenary. He played a crucial role in the staging of the US Live Aid concert on 13 July 1985.

GRAHAM, DAVEY Born in 1940 of Scottish-Guyanese parents, Davey Graham became the largely unrecognized father of the British 'folk baroque'

guitar style. As an itinerant musician in Europe and North Africa, he absorbed jazz, folk, Arab and Indian influences, and blended them all in his playing. His experiments with **Alexis Korner** on *3/4 A.D.* (1961) and then with folk singer Shirley Collins on *Folk Roots, New Routes* (Decca, 1965) were largely ignored because they were so far ahead of their time – but they pointed to a whole variety of eclectic styles that were to come. Illness in the late Sixties affected his career, but by the mid-Seventies he had recovered and was back playing on the folk circuit. He recorded two albums in the late Seventies for Kicking Mule – *Complete Guitarist* (1978) and *Dance for Two People* (1979).

GRAND FUNK RAILROAD Originally the brainchild of pop Svengali Terry Knight, Grand Funk Railroad were formed from the remnants of Terry Knight and the Pack and other Flint, Michigan bands. The group – Mark Farner (guitar, vocals, born 29 September 1948), Mel Schacher (bass, born 3 April 1951), Don Brewer (drums, born 3 September 1948) – asked Knight for help after an initial failure managing themselves. He signed them to Capitol Records and engineered an unpaid appearance at the 1969 Atlanta Pop Festival where they stole the show. They quickly

Blunt, loud and powerful, Grand Funk Railroad in concert

became a growing attraction, but the press and radio showed universal revulsion for their unrelenting, ear-splitting, rhythmic attack. Knight turned this to the band's advantage, making them a generational emblem for their largely teenage audience. By December 1970, with albums like *Grand Funk* and *Closer to Home*, Grand Funk were the hottest group in America, without benefit of reviews, features, or much radio play. In late 1971, the band severed relations with Knight in a flurry of million-dollar suits and countersuits. The band added Craig Frost on keyboards and in 1973, the suits settled, **Todd Rundgren** produced *We're an American Band*, the title song becoming their first Top 20 hit. Over the next year, with singles like 'Locomotion', they consolidated their now broader-based popularity and began establishing their reputation outside of America. In 1976, they announced their decision to split up after the release of *Born to Die*, but one more album appeared – *Good Singin', Good Playin'* – which was produced by **Frank Zappa**. Following the break-up, Mark Farner released two solo albums, *Mark Farner* (1977) and *No Frills* (1978) on Atlantic, before reuniting

with Brewer in 1981 and new bassist Dennis Bellinger as a reborn Grand Funk. *Grand Funk Lives* (Full Moon) sold well, but the band broke up once more in 1983. Brewer then joined **Bob Seger**'s Silver Bullet Band.

GRANDMASTER FLASH
Although Kurtis Blow (real name Kurt Walker) had the first genuine rap hit (in 1979, with 'Christmas Rappin'') and the Sugarhill Gang scored an outstanding success the same year with 'Rapper's Delight', there is no doubt that Grandmaster Flash and the Furious Five were the most colourful, inventive, streetwise, cool and convincingly polemical of all the rap acts, with their irresistible blend of declamatory 'lyrics', break dancing and scratch mixing. Formed in New York City in 1977, the Flash entourage comprised Flash himself (real name Joseph Saddler), Melle Mel, Raheim, Cowboy, **Kid Creole**, Mr Ness and E-Z Mike. In 1982 their hit single 'The Message' (US Number 36, UK Number 3) with its politically upfront protestations built on the hard street-life experience they knew from the Bronx, the area in which they had been brought up, was a powerfully atmospheric antidote to much of the flaccid black pop of the early Eighties. Yet their style had limitations; it could be as dully repetitive as disco without even the saving grace of a melody, and therefore became tedious if the 'lyric' was ever less than exact in the aim of its observation or anger. Moreover the rap boom led to a rash of less interesting rappers/scratchers who soon saturated the market with poor, boring work. In addition, the novelty appeal of the style made its staying power (and particularly that of Grandmaster Flash and the Furious Five) appear to be tenuous as a commercial pop enterprise. Nevertheless, because the mechanics of rap require a comparatively low level of both personal skill and financial investment, the style in which GF and the FF excel will always have an appeal in one form or another.

GRANT, EDDY
Born in Guyana on 5 March 1948, singer/songwriter Eddy Grant had his first hits in the late Sixties with the **Equals**, but it was as a solo artist in the Eighties that his exuberant pop/reggae style found most success.

In the Fifties, Grant's family moved to North London where he grew up and developed an obsession for music and soccer. He bought his first guitar while still at school, and there he formed a

band that eventually became the Equals. Grant penned several hits for the group, most notably 'Baby Come Back' which was a huge UK Number 1 in 1968. The Equals had their last hit in 1970 with 'Black Skin Blue Eyed Boys', after which Grant developed a more business oriented outlook, built his own recording studio and bought the publishing rights to all his own songs.

During the Seventies he produced bands like the Pioneers and Ninety Degrees, and in that time he widened his knowledge and experience of the business aspects of the music industry, to the point where he was able to establish his own label, Ice, in 1977. His first solo release on the label was the album *Message Man* (1977), but it wasn't until 1979 and the single 'Living on the Frontline' that he scored his first solo UK hit. That single established the laid-back reggae-based dance pop style that characterized his subsequent work.

Grant's increasing solo success in the UK, especially the Number 1 single 'I Don't Wanna Dance' and the gold album *Killer on the Rampage* (both 1982), plus a US Number 2 'Electric Avenue' had enabled him to build his own studios – Blue Wave – in Barbados, that not only became the centre of his own operations, but also attracted numerous recording artists with its luxuriously equipped facilities and exotic location.

In 1986, Eddy Grant released his eighth solo album, *Born Tuff*, a title that underlined his resilience and determination to take on the large music corporations and find success on his own terms.

GRASS ROOTS
One of the most enduring hit singles groups of the Sixties, Grass Roots' first records came out in 1966, at the height of folk-rock, and were in fact written and performed by **P.F. Sloan** and **Steve Barri** for the first year. 'Where Were You When I Needed You' (a US Number 28) was their biggest hit during this period. By 1967, a real group had been assembled – Warren Entner, vocals, guitar; Rob Grill, vocals, bass; Ricky Coonce, drums and Creed Bratton, guitar – and 'Let's Live for Today', a cover of an Italian hit by the Rokes, was a Top 10 hit. From there, the Grass Roots were launched on a series of hits that included 'Things I Should Have Said', 'Midnight Confessions', 'Bella Linda', 'I'd Wait a Million Years', 'Heaven Knows', 'Temptation Eyes', 'Sooner or Later', 'Two Divided By Love', continuing to 1972.

GRATEFUL DEAD One of the handful of important and influential bands to emerge out of the San Francisco rock scene of 1966–8, the Grateful Dead played a very active part in its evolution. The band had its origins in Mother McCree's Uptown Jug Champions, late in 1963. The Jug Champions were: Jerry Garcia, guitar, banjo, vocals (born 1 August 1942); Pigpen (Ron McKernan), harmonica, piano, vocals (8 September 1945); John 'Marmaduke' Dawson, guitar, vocals (later of the New Riders); Bob Matthews, guitar, vocals (later a member of the family as recordings and equipment man); and Bob Weir, jug and kazoo (16 October 1947), then a guitar novice taking lessons from Jorma Kaukonen. Work was scarce for the Jug Champions until Dana Morgan, owner of a music store where Garcia had worked, provided the equipment for them to become an electric band, the Warlocks. Dawson and Matthews had left to be replaced by Bill Sommers (actually Kreutzmann – born 7 April 1946) and Morgan himself, on bass. He was quickly replaced by Phil Lesh (15 March 1940) then a musician of classical leanings, who took a two-week crash course in bass playing to complete the now familiar Dead line-up.

The Warlocks played their first date in July 1965 and dealt in pretty straight rock'n'roll until they collectively started taking LSD. The sets immediately became more diffuse, the numbers being stretched out and the volume increased. This led to the Dead's involvement with the Pranksters, typified by the Acid Tests and culminating in the Ken Kesey-organized Trips Festival. By now the Warlocks had become the Grateful Dead, the name itself the outcome of an evening of stoned lexicology, and were already the nodal point of a family of musicians – they acquired a second drummer, Mickey Hart, in the summer of 1967, and keyboard player Tom Constanten, a friend of Lesh's, was intermittently with the group – associated sound and light show operatives, road crew, wives, friends and children. The family included designer Rick Griffin, lyricist Robert Hunter and engineer Owsley. Owsley's role was threefold; he was a chemist of highly potent LSD, an electronics wizard who supervised the building of their impeccable sound system and, for a while, their financial benefactor.

The family grew after they moved to 710 Ashbury, San Francisco, and with it grew the myth surrounding them and the 'Frisco scene. This phenomenon

Live performances were the cornerstone of Grateful Dead's work, providing the occasion for lengthy experiments in free improvisation

was about to explode in a blaze of publicity with the Dead at its centre in their communal house, playing for free in the park and with Garcia (Captain Trips) – despite his denials – as a kind of guru figure. Finally, the Dead signed with Warner Bros. Their first three albums – *The Grateful Dead* (March 1967), *Anthem To The Sun* (August 1968) and *Aoxomoxoa* (June 1969) – were charged with the group's presence and multi-directional consciousness, but never had the commercial possibilities of the **Jefferson Airplane**'s early albums. They ended up over 100,000 dollars in debt to Warners, as well as owing them an album. The essence of the Dead had always been their phenomenal live show, and finally on the double album *Live/Dead* (1970) they allowed people outside 'Frisco a glimpse of the band's real power. They were also by now touring more widely than ever, including a first European visit.

Success came with the realization of their studio capabilities on two stylish country-rock albums, *Workingman's Dead* and *American Beauty* in 1971, on which they showed, for the first time, a previously undeveloped vocal strength. Garcia, Weir and Lesh sounded like a rough and ragged, less

sterile **Crosby, Stills and Nash**. Similarly, lyricist Robert Hunter made the transition from the complex word patterns of 'Dark Star' to the simplicity of 'Uncle John's Band'. The tighter Dead had achieved a synthesis of Haight Street freeness and country-rock precision and discipline. It was amply illustrated on their next album, another live double set, *Grateful Dead*, winning them their first gold album. This was followed by a dangerous period of over-exposure. Jerry Garcia, in particular, played countless sessions. Three members of the group made albums in 1972 – Jerry Garcia (*Garcia*), Bob Weir (*Ace*), and the soon-to-leave Mickey Hart (*Rolling Thunder*) and the Dead themselves celebrated their two-month European tour with a triple live album, *Europe '72*. Though beyond their control, the Dead additionally fell foul of a mixed spate of bootlegs and some weak early live recordings dredged up from 1966 on MGM.

The group, however, rode it all out. The death of Pigpen in March 1973 was obviously a deeply felt setback but he had been ill for over a year with a serious liver disease, and a keyboard player, Keith Godchaux, had already been added to the group. He gave a fresh impetus to the band at a time when they were flagging, and his wife Donna sang with them from time to time. The Dead were also taking care of business: they set up their own record company, Grateful Dead Records, on which their latest studio albums, *Wake of the Flood* and *From the Mars Hotel* appeared, and Round Records on which they released the less commercial albums of the Dead family. They also developed complementary fields. By 1975, their 150-member family was running the Fly By Night travel company, Out of Town Tours, a booking agency, Ice Nine Publishing Company, a recording studio, and more besides.

The Dead underwent minimal personnel changes during the late Seventies, when they signed with Arista: Godchaux left, together with Donna, in 1979, and was replaced by Brent Mydland. Godchaux died a year later in a car crash. Their Arista albums included *Terrapin Station* (1976), *Shakedown Street* (1978), *Go to Heaven* (1980) and *Reckoning* (1981).

Perhaps the secret of the Dead's prolonged life is that all the individual members are free to involve themselves in a variety of projects – exemplified in Jerry Garcia's many ventures, notably the spin-off band, the **New Riders of the Purple Sage**, now a completely separate unit. This, combined with the astute business sense of their current manager, John McIntire, has given them a great stability. The remarkable history of the Grateful Dead, from jug band to social institution – 'what a long, strange trip it's been' – is a testament to the power of the hopes and ideals that were pinned to rock's mast in the heady days of 1966–7. None the less, however naive and aimless their endless jamming may appear on occasion, it's the Dead's music, far more than the organization of their business affairs, that has shown them consistently struggling to develop those ideas. Certainly, no other group, outside of those heavily influenced by jazz, has introduced as much *structured* free-form music into rock. Never as reflective as **Country Joe** (and the Fish) or as anarchic as Jefferson Airplane, the Dead are none the less *the* representative San Franciscan band.

GRAY, DOBIE Country-soul singer Dobie Gray was born in Brookshire, Texas, in 1943 and first appeared on the Hot 100 Charts in 1963 with 'Look at Me' (Cor Dak), recorded after he had travelled to Los Angeles in search of a recording contract. He had his first big hit with the insistent dance record, 'The In Crowd' (Charger) in 1965, which he co-wrote. A follow-up, 'See You at the Go Go', reached the lower part of the Hot 100 later that year but it was eight years before Gray had another major hit with the Mentor Williams composition/production, 'Drift Away' (MCA, 1973), an anthem to the power of rock to soothe as well as excite. In between, Gray cut demo discs (which is how he met Paul Williams and through him his brother Mentor), worked with the group Pollution, acted in Rip Torn's New York production of *The Beard* and appeared in *Hair*. Under Mentor Williams' direction Gray recorded three albums for MCA, *Drift Away, Loving Arms* (1973) and *Hey Dixie* (1974) – all fine examples of progressive Southern music – before moving to Capricorn where, with Troy Seals producing, he released *New Ray of Sunshine* (1975). *Midnight Diamond* (Infinity) appeared in 1978.

GRAY, OWEN Born in Jamaica, Owen Gray was a classic reggae singer, barely changing his style through the years, but always abreast of the trends. Popular from the very outset of his career with discs like 'Sinners Weep' and 'No Good Woman', he continued to cut material of the highest quality. 'Millie Girl', 'Darling Patricia' and 'Tree in the Meadow' were extremely popular ska discs, while his faultless 'Girl What You Doing to Me' was among the best of the early reggae sounds, skirting the British charts in 1969. In the Seventies, Island Records promoted him on commercial reggae cuts including a version of **John Lennon**'s 'Jealous Guy'.

GREEN, AL A vocal stylist who dramatically switched from commercial soul to the gospel music field at the end of the Seventies, Al Green is one of black music's true giants. He was born in Forrest City, Arkansas, on 13 April 1946, and was raised in Grand Rapids, Michigan, where he sang with the Creations before his first recording 'Back Up Train' (Hot Line) gave him a Top 50 hit in 1967. This beautiful soul ballad was followed unsuccessfully by similar releases, and he had slipped back into obscurity by 1969 when he was signed by **Willie Mitchell**, producer and vice-president of Hi Records, Memphis. After trying deep soul ('One Woman'), adapted pop ('I Wanna Hold Your Hand'), and a bit of thump-and-strut ('Right Now, Right Now'), they finally cracked the charts with a bluesy interpretation of the **Temptations**' 'I Can't Get Next to You' (1970). A similar treatment of 'Drivin' Wheel' was not so well received, but Green's own song 'Tired of Being Alone' (1971) gave him a hit – and the formula – that made him one of the major black stars of the Seventies. Green employed all the vocal gymnastics of a typical gospel-influenced soul singer, yet stayed so restrained that often he was barely audible; Mitchell's band set up insidious rhythms without ever driving the songs to any sort of dramatic conclusion. The

The young Al Green with a long and varied career ahead of him

effect of tightly reined emotions was heard in a dozen US hits (including 'Let's Stay Together', a Number 1 in 1971; 'I'm Still in Love with You', 'You Ought To Be with Me', 1972; 'Livin' for You', 1973; 'Sha-La-La', 1974) but after four years the Green style was in need of rejuvenation.

The turning point came in 1974, when a one-time girlfriend attacked him with boiling grits and then killed herself; Green was hospitalized for some time and during the enforced lay-off underwent the beginnings of a spiritual rebirth. Returning to the studio in 1977, he recorded *Belle* and seemed back to his old form, though this time he was undertaking his own production and much of the writing. *Truth 'n' Time* (1978) skilfully pleased both ballad and disco lovers, but the real shock came in 1980 with *The Lord Will Make a Way* – an excursion into the gospel world that Hi seemed to disassociate themselves from completely. The album nevertheless won Green a Grammy Award for Best Vocal Performance.

Since 1980, Green – now billed as the Rev. Al Green – has devoted more of his time to his church, choosing to win over the American public from the pulpit instead of from the stage.

GREEN, PETER The founder and original lead guitarist of **Fleetwood Mac**, Peter Green was born in Bethnal Green, London, on 29 October 1946. On leaving school, Green played with various semi-pro bands before joining **Rod Stewart**, Peter Bardens and Beryl Marsden in the 1966 club band, Steampacket. His big break came later that same year when he replaced **Eric Clapton** in **John Mayall**'s Blues-breakers. Influenced by both **B.B.** and **Freddie King**, Green's reputation as a guitarist soon grew and he was heavily featured on Mayall's 1967 album *A Hard Road*. After a year with the Blues-breakers, he left to form Peter Green's Fleetwood Mac. Green was responsible for writing most of their biggest hits including the multi-million seller instrumental 'Albatross', 'Oh Well', 'The Green Manalishi', 'Man of the World' and 'Black Magic Woman', which was covered in later years by **Santana**. Green left Fleetwood Mac in May 1970, following a traumatic illness, and devoted himself to religious matters. Little was heard of him until January 1977, when he was committed to a mental hospital after a shooting incident over a Fleetwood Mac royalty cheque. *See also* **Fleetwood Mac**

GREENBAUM, NORMAN Universally remembered for just the one international hit, 'Spirit in the Sky' in 1970, Norman Greenbaum was born on 20 November 1942, in Malden, Massachusetts, and became an occasional folk singer while at Boston University. He moved to LA where he put together Dr West's Medicine Show And Junk Band (inspired by Boston's **Jim Kweskin Jug Band**). The group – Bonnie Wallach, vocals, guitar; Jack Carrington, washtub, bass, guitar, banjo; and Evan Engber, percussion – plus Greenbaum, anachronistic though they were in 1966, had a surprise Top 50 hit with 'The Eggplant That Ate Chicago' (Go Go), but hardly found their style flourishing in the changing climate of the mid-Sixties. Ironically, after the single hit, they toured widely to odd reactions among audiences, who saw in their appearance (painted faces and light shows) all the nastier manifestations of California psychedelia.

In 1967 the group split up. A fortuitous meeting with Eric Jacobsen in 1968 resulted in Greenbaum recording his first solo album, *Spirit in the Sky* (Reprise). The title track, with its compelling fuzz-tone riff, gave Greenbaum a million-seller worldwide. Greenbaum again failed to follow this up and consolidate his success,

releasing the weaker 'Canned Ham' and patchy second album *Back Home* (1970). He has been in semi-retirement since, mixing music (he released a third solo album for Warners, *Petaluma*, in 1972) and goat breeding in Petaluma, California.

'Spirit in the Sky' was revived in 1986 by UK nouveau-psychedelic band Doctor and the Medics, who took their note-for-note re-creation of Greenbaum's arrangement to Number 1.

GREENWICH, ELLIE Best remembered in pop and rock circles for her songwriting partnership with **Jeff Barry**, Ellie Greenwich – born on Long Island, New York, in 1940 – began her career as a singer, recording unsuccessfully for RCA in the late Fifties as Ellie Gay. In 1960, she majored in English at college and worked as a teacher for a short spell before breaking into the songwriting field by co-writing (with Tony Powers) 'This Is It' for **Jay and the Americans** and 'He's Got the Power' for the **Exciters**. In 1963, she began co-writing with her husband Jeff Barry, and, working in close alliance with producer **Phil Spector**, they notched up a series of hits by the **Ronettes**, the **Crystals** and Bob B. Soxx. Drifting away from Spector in 1964, Greenwich and Barry were responsible for 80 per cent of the Red Bird label's early output, including such hits as 'Chapel of Love' and 'Goodnight Baby', and, during 1965–7, they performed a similar role (despite their divorce) for **Bert Berns**' Bang label, where they produced **Neil Diamond**. In the late Sixties, she retired temporarily before trying a comeback as a singer-songwriter with an album on Verve in 1973 called *Let It Be Written, Let It Be Sung*, consisting mostly of her most familiar songs.

GREENWICH VILLAGE Manhattan's Latin Quarter, a few square miles of turf below New York's 14th Street, has long been a magnet for provincials seeking personal freedom and the artistic life. In the middle Sixties, the section turned middle-class and the bohemians went West in droves, while their successors, the hippies, populated the adjacent East Village.

Jazz clubs and ethnic music abounded and, later, rock became firmly rooted in the East Village. Folk music was always in its natural environment in and around 'The Village'. Annual folk song and dance festivals near the fountain below Washington Arch date back to the Thirties. Since then, outdoor Sunday hootenannies have brought together

singers, pickers and fiddlers the way London's Speaker's Corner attracts opinion-hawkers. Village radical politics and lifestyles drew folkniks of every description – **Woody Guthrie**, **Pete Seeger** and The Almanac Singers lived there in World War II on West Tenth Street; Josh White and Billie Holliday started at Café Society Downtown at Shiridan Square; while **Harry Belafonte** began at the Village Vanguard. The Village Gate carried on that tradition as a major centre for folk and jazz.

In the heat of the folk revival, after 1960, small clubs mushroomed with folk singers. Gerde's Folk City, the Gaslight, the Bitter End, the Café Wha? and the Thirdside offered a continuing stream of talent. Coffee-houses were especially important locations for mobile singer-guitarists. Nearly every established folk singer, from **Tom Paxton** to **Phil Ochs** to **Peter, Paul and Mary** to **Dylan** got their major impetus and developed an audience in The Village. Although young talent was often exploited by club and coffee-house managements, the venues were unequalled as an incubator for successful performers. The gloss and the charm have since worn thin, but Greenwich Village still stands as a national campus for students and practitioners of the alternative culture. *See also* **New York – local scenes**

GROSSMAN, STEFAN Country blues guitarist Stefan Grossman – born in New York on 16 April 1945 – first made his mark in 1965–6 as part of those amorphous New York City dinosaurs, the Even Dozen Jug Band and the **Fugs**. He was an avid student of the blues, worshipping the old East Coast ragtime pickers and in particular the Rev. Gary Davis. He spent many hours learning first hand from Davis and by the time the country blues revival took place in Britain around 1968, Grossman had crossed the Atlantic to show the way.

His popularity in Europe grew and he settled down to live in Rome, recording a number of instructional albums for Transatlantic. Hotly tipped to join forces with **Paul Simon** after the split with **Art Garfunkel**, all that happened in the end was that the duo cut a single track on Simon's first solo album. He continues to compile tablature books and albums on all styles of blues guitar playing and in 1972–3 launched his own Kicking Mule label in an effort to focus attention on the large school of unknown folk/blues instrumentalists throughout Europe and North America.

GROUNDHOGS Named after a **John Lee Hooker** song, the Groundhogs were in the forefront of the purist British R&B groups during the early Sixties. They comprised Tony McPhee (guitar, vocals, born 22 March 1944), Pete Cruikshank (bass, born 2 July 1945), Ken Pustelnik (drums) and Steve Rye (harmonica).

After three standard blues albums for United Artists, Rye quit and the remaining trio joined the ranks of the progressive bands. With *Thank Christ for the Bomb* (1970) and *Split* (1971), McPhee took to electronics and social comment. He went on to record a guitar/synthesizer solo album as well as two further Groundhogs records (*Who Will Save The World?*, 1972 and *Hogwash*, 1973) before finally winding up the trio at the end of 1974. In 1976, McPhee re-formed the group with new sidemen.

GRYPHON Although Amazing Blondel had tried before, Gryphon were the first band to achieve popularity by adapting medieval tunes and instruments (such as the crumhorn and glockenspiel) for a rock context. The group, formed in 1971 as Spell Thorn, comes from London and the Home Counties and comprises Brian Gulland (born 1951), Richard Harvey (1953), Graeme Taylor (1954) and David Oberle (1953). Malcolm Bennett was a later addition. It was not until 1973 that their arrangements of minstrel airs, Beatle music and 'Chattanooga Choo Choo' caught on, and since then the band has played a much wider field (lecture tours, incidental music for Peter Hall's *Tempest*, etc.) than most rock musicians. In time, they eschewed all connection with medieval music, becoming a skilful if less original mainstream rock band for the albums *Raindance* (1975) and *Treason* (1977).

GUERCIO, JIM An important musician-cum-backroom figure in American rock from the mid-Sixties onwards, Jim Guercio began his career in Chicago, where he played guitar in bars while a student of classical composition at the city's university. On a mid-West tour as a member of a backing group with a **Dick Clark** Caravan Show, he met J. Holvay who handed him a song called 'Kind of a Drag' which Guercio recorded with a local Chicago outfit, the Buckinghams, in 1966. Two years later, Guercio had become one of four guitarists with the Mothers Of Invention in Los Angeles, then at their most outrageous. At the same time he was planning a brass rock group. **Al Kooper** pipped him to the post with **Blood, Sweat And Tears**, but Guercio had the satisfaction of producing their second, most successful album, *Blood, Sweat And Tears* (Columbia, 1969) after Kooper had left. It was Guercio's own group Chicago Transit Authority (later shortened to **Chicago**) that coveted the brass rock niche thereafter. Their debut album *CTA* (Columbia) released in April 1969 was an enormous critical and commercial success. Critical acclaim became scarcer, however, as Guercio sustained Chicago's impressive work rate – three two-record sets in under two years, all packaged with posters, lyric sheets and colour photographs, culminating in a dubious four-record set recorded live at Carnegie Hall in 1971. A torrent of critics screamed overkill but Guercio, still in his twenties, ploughed on relentlessly.

Chicago became part of James William Guercio Enterprises along with his Caribou studios in Colorado, where **Elton John**, among others, has recorded. He had less dramatic success and even failures like the Chicago group, Illinois Speed Press, and his period as manager of Firesign Theatre. The film *Electra Glide In Blue* (1972), produced, directed and scored by Guercio, marked a new diversification in his interests. In 1975 he took temporary control of the **Beach Boys**' affairs and appeared with them on live dates. Chicago broke with him in 1977, since when Guercio has been extensively involved in further film work.

GUESS WHO Canada's leading rock band in the first half of the Seventies, the Guess Who comprised Burton Cummings (lead vocals, keyboards), Randy Bachman (guitar, vocals), Jim Kale (bass) and Gary Peterson (drums). Bachman was replaced in summer 1970 by Greg Leskiw and Kurt Winter (guitars); Leskiw and Kale by Don McDougall (guitar) and Bill Wallace (bass, vocals) in 1972. Winter and McDougal were replaced by Dominic Troiano (guitar and vocals) in 1974.

The Winnipeg group Chad Allen and the Expressions became the Guess Who in 1965 after Allen left and scored a minor hit, 'Shakin' All Over'. Their run of million-sellers began in 1969 with 'These Eyes', 'Laughing' and 'No Time' mostly written by Bachman (who left while his composition 'American Woman' was Number 1) to re-join Chad Allen in Brave Belt which later evolved into **Bachman-Turner Overdrive**. Jack Richardson has produced all their eleven albums of which the foremost are *The Best Of The Guess Who, Volumes I And II*. The arrival of ex-Hawk and **James Gang** member Troiano shifted the balance of the band slightly, but only three further albums resulted – *Flavours* (1974), *Power in the Music* and *Born in Canada* (both 1975) – before the group broke up in 1976. Kale, Peterson, McDougall and Winter re-formed the Guess Who in 1977, but the line-up has since changed on several occasions.

GUIDA, FRANK A record-shop owner who branched out temporarily into record production in the early Sixties, Frank Guida achieved ten consecutive hits (including three million-sellers) in three years with a sound so radical that the records created attention by that virtue alone.

Born in New York of Italian heritage, Guida moved to Portsmouth, Virginia, in the early Fifties and opened 'Frankie's Birdland' which soon became Virginia's leading R&B record shop. Looking to expand, Guida formed Legrand records and recorded former **Gene Vincent** Blue Cap, **Tommy Facenda**, singing 'High School USA', a novelty record which reached the Top 30 in the US in 1959. In 1960, he began recording **Gary 'U.S.' Bonds** in the back of his record shop where the poor acoustics and barely adequate equipment, combined with primitive phasing and tape-echo techniques, resulted in a synthetic 'live' effect with Bonds yelling above a muzzy, distorted background of voices and thumping rhythms. Although Guida had problems convincing his own distributor that his records were not recorded in a toilet, Bonds' hits, 'New Orleans', 'Quarter to Three', 'Twist Twist Señora' and 'School Is Out', had a great influence on English beat groups and, it is said, on **Phil Spector**'s techniques.

When Bonds' sound began to pall, Guida formed a subsidiary, SPQR, on which 'Twistin' Mathilda' by Jimmy Soul made the Top 30 early in 1962. A year later, Soul scored again with the infectious 'If You Wanna Be Happy', an American Number 1 and million-seller. Beatlemania effectively ended Guida's run of hits, after which he ran several record shops and released occasional records on Peanut County. Years later Bonds dismissed suggestions that Guida was one of pop's great unsung architects: 'It's been said that a lot of minds were set to make that sound, but I could never see it myself. We'd just go in there and make a lot of noise'. See *also* **Gary 'U.S.' Bonds**

GUITAR SLIM Born in Greenwood, Mississippi, on 10 December 1926, Eddie 'Guitar Slim' Jones was responsible for the biggest blues record of 1954, the passionate, soul-flecked 'The Things That I Used To Do'. A genuine blues standard, it was cut in New Orleans for Specialty, with **Ray Charles** on piano. Jones had previously recorded for Imperial and Bullet during 1951–2, but moved to Atco before his death in New York on February 7, 1959. He was held in awe by fellow New Orleans musicians who envied his spectacular stage act.

GUTHRIE, ARLO Guthrie worked hard to overcome the twin handicaps of living in his father Woody's shadow and the 'arch-hippie' tag which followed his appearance in Arthur Penn's movie, *Alice's Restaurant*. Albums like *Hobo's Lullabye* (Reprise, 1972) and *Last of the Brooklyn Cowboys* (1973) established his personal synthesis of folk and country traditions with contemporary themes.

Born in New York on 10 July 1947, his earliest success came in 1967, the year of Woody's death. The epic ballad 'Alice's Restaurant' spawned an album and the film, and was followed by five more Reprise albums before the live double with Pete Seeger in 1975. In 1973 he had a Top 20 hit with **Steve Goodman**'s 'City of New Orleans', a song that summed up Guthrie's own clear-eyed stance towards the American past, while 'Presidential Rag', dealing with Watergate, was a vigorous piece of social comment in the best family manner.

Arlo became a Catholic in 1977 and toured and recorded with his backing band, Shenandoah. In the Eighties he became actively involved in the ecology and anti-nuclear movements. *See also* **Woody Guthrie**

GUTHRIE, WOODY Probably the most influential single figure in American folk music, Woody Guthrie was born in Okemah, Oklahoma, on 12 July 1912, and left a legacy of a thousand songs, several books, hundreds of articles, folk poems and essays, and a lifestyle that still impels young hopefuls to pack bedrolls, guitars and don boots to discover the real and gritty world at the end of the dusty highway.

Woody was really too short to be a giant, too lean and delicate-faced to be a hero, terribly ungrammatical to be a poet, with too flat and nasal a little voice to be considered a great singer. Yet Woodrow Wilson Guthrie was all those: a giant of humanism, a hero of

the American little man, a major folk poet and a singer and composer of some of the country's greatest songs: for instance, 'Pastures of Plenty', 'Deportees', 'Hard Traveling', 'Dust Bowl Refugees', 'This Land Is Your Land' and 'So Long, It's Been Good to Know You'. Guthrie has been called 'America's best contemporary ballad composer', 'the best folk ballad composer whose identity has ever been known', a 'rusty-voiced Homer' and 'an influence on America as great as Walt Whitman'.

As with Whitman, Thomas Wolfe, Carl Sandburg, and, later, Jack Kerouac, the Guthrie vision of America was a heady one, intoxicated with the breadth and richness, the variety and promise of the American soil and character. He would pile up his images upon each other like a drunken mason building a dream house. His early years were recounted in his 1943 autobiography, *Bound for Glory*, most notable for its portrait of rural hardship in the great Depression. Fragmentarily, Guthrie's story incorporated childhood in a boom town; life on the road into Texas; the agonies of the Dust Bowl refugees; the lure and heartbreak of California; daily radio shows for a dollar a day on Los Angeles' WKVD; friendships with Will Geer, the actor, and Cisco Houston, folk singer; trips to migrant labour camps; the trek East and contact with the Left-oriented folk movement; Library of Congress recordings for **Alan Lomax** (released commercially later by Elektra); the singing with Hally Wood and Burl Ives and The Almanac Singers, who included Sis Cunningham and Gordon Friesen, who later edited *Broadside* magazine; restless trips back and forth across the continent with **Pete Seeger**; recording *Dust Bowl Ballads* for Victor, and the beginning of extensive recordings for Stinson and Folkways; deep involvement with the trade-union movement; writing columns for *The People's World*; the marriages and divorces and the children; the death in a fire of his daughter, Kathy Ann; the birth of his son, **Arlo**. And through it all, the writing, adapting, rewriting and arranging of songs out of the **Carter Family** songbook, out of country standards, out of hymns and union song traditions, the re-awakening in a contemporary vein of an old tradition.

In the late Forties, Woody fell prey to the degenerative nerve illness that had killed his mother, Huntington's chorea. Gradually, his pen and voice were stilled. Then began the endless years in Eastern hospitals, where his limbs shook convulsively and uselessly,

Woody Guthrie, an itinerant singer of the Depression years, was the US folk movement's romantic hero

where he could barely talk or show recognition. On 3 October 1967, with no possible hope for any other end to nearly two decades of suffering, he died. Through the efforts of Harold Leventhal, his longtime agent, and **Bob Dylan**, his best-known disciple, memorial concerts were held on both coasts, involving most of the leading figures of American folk music. It was a testimony to the key importance of Guthrie to the folk movement.

GUY, BUDDY Born in Lettsworth, Louisiana, on 30 July 1936, Buddy Guy was one of the younger generation of 'Chicago' bluesmen. George 'Buddy' Guy learned his blues from records by **Lightnin' Hopkins**, **John Lee Hooker**, etc., on the radio, experimenting on a homemade guitar before his father bought him a real instrument. He played in Big Poppa Tilley's group and toured Louisiana, backing Excello label artists like **Slim Harpo**; he recorded for Ace in Baton Rouge before migrating to Chicago in 1957 and played the Chicago clubs for some while before signing to Artistic Records in 1958, where he met **Willie Dixon**. Artistic folded in 1959 and Dixon took Guy to Chess Records, where his first session yielded the renowned 'First Time I Met the Blues', performed in Guy's characteristic style – high-pitched, near-hysterical vocal and a biting, penetrating guitar accompaniment. Guy had an R&B chart hit with 'Stone Crazy' in 1962, worked steadily as a name act and sessioneer for Chess until 1968, and subsequently recorded for Blue Thumb, Vanguard and Atco.

H

HAGEN, NINA East German singer/actress Nina Hagen first came to the public eye in 1976 when, already a popular performer in her native country, she acquired a permanent exit visa and arrived in London at the height of the punk scene. It was an encounter that fuelled her interest in punk, and she became known for her soaring operatic voice and extreme spiky-haired appearance.

Once the novelty wore off, British interest in her waned (she sang in German and the critics hated her) but Hagen's shrieking, aggressive brand of punk won a strong following on the continent, the albums *Nina Hagen Band* (1979) and *Unbehangen* (1980) selling well across Europe and Japan. In 1980 Hagen moved to the United States and settled there, recording several albums (including *Fearless* in 1984 with **Giorgio Moroder**), but never acquiring more than a cult following, although her popularity in non-anglophone countries, especially Japan, remained as strong as ever. In 1985 Hagen released *Nina in Ekstasy*, promoted with an extensive worldwide tour, including a successful appearance at the Rock in Rio Festival in Brazil.

HAGGARD, MERLE Probably still best known outside the country market for 'Okie From Muskogee', a song seemingly defending small-town American virtues, which topped the country charts for several weeks in 1969 and also made the lower reaches of the Hot 100. Haggard's most successful record was 'If We Make It Through December', a Top 40 pop hit in 1974 describing urban unemployment.

Haggard is a country superstar, the best-known product of the strong Californian country scene centred on the town of Bakersfield. Nearby Hollywood and Los Angeles have always been foremost recording centres and country music has long been established in California since half the population came from the rural South anyway. Haggard's family came from Oklahoma, and Merle was born in Bakersfield on 6 April 1937.

During the early Sixties the most renowned singers in the area were Billy Mize, Wynn Stewart and **Buck Owens**, until 1963 when Fuzzy Owens

began to record Merle Haggard, a rough, tough product of the oilfields, and lately out of San Quentin prison, on his Tally label. By 1965 Haggard had scored three country hits including the Top 10 hit '(All My Friends Are Gonna Be) Strangers'. A move to Capitol brought a Number 1 country hit in 'I Am a Lonesome Fugitive', and in 1968 'Mama Tried', which embodied an idealized Haggard life story but idealized in an unusual manner – for Haggard is the bad boy who's going to go straight, but not deny his past experiences. By now, Haggard had not only married Buck Owens' ex-wife, Bonnie, but also was challenging Buck Owens' reputation as the Nashville-West superstar. Songs like 'Working Man Blues', 'Daddy Frank' and 'Okie From Muskogee' had a sense of purpose and a simple brilliance wrapped in an interestingly formulated instrumental sound, featuring session guitarist **James Burton** or his own back-up man, Roy Nichols. Haggard also recorded tribute albums to country stars **Jimmie Rodgers** and Bob Wills, and a double album of gospel songs.

He and Bonnie Owens divorced in 1977, and he then married Leona Williams. He has taken acting roles on television (*The Waltons, Centennial, The Adventures of Huckleberry Finn*) and in films (*Killers Three, Bronco Billy*) and has continued to record extensively. *Poncho and Lefty* (1982) was an album of duets with **Willie Nelson**.

HAIRCUT 100 Becoming a success virtually overnight, Haircut 100 had a glorious six months in 1981/2 when they stormed the UK Top 10 with four consecutive snappy dancefloor pop singles. They inspired countless scenes of teenage adoration before the pressures of fame caused a split.

Haircut 100 was formed on a Sunday afternoon in 1980 by three South London schoolfriends, Nick Heyward (vocals/guitar, born 20 May 1961), Les Nemes (bass) and Graham Jones (guitar), in a spirit of lighthearted whimsy that characterized their music. The band was rounded off by Phil Smith (sax), Blair Cunningham (drums) and Mark Fox (percussion), all of whom had previous experience as sessioneers.

Fronted by the photogenic Heyward, the band were very quickly signed up by Arista early in 1981 after only a handful of gigs, and the debut single, 'Favourite Shirts (Boy Meets Girl)', reached Number 4 in October. Three other singles, the best of which, 'Love

Plus One', made the Top 3, established Haircut 100 as a teen favourite as well as winning approval from the critics.

Pelican West (1982) reached Number 2 in the UK LP chart before internal dissent caused Nick Heyward, the songwriter and main inspiration of the band, to leave at the end of 1982, during the recording of the second LP (which never appeared). The band retained the name, Mark Fox took over vocals, and they moved unsuccessfully to Polydor, while Heyward almost immediately returned to the charts with the mellow 'Whistle Down the Wind'. Two further Top 20 singles followed and the album *North of a Miracle* (1983) made the Top 10. But Heyward's career also slumped as a procession of mediocre singles fared poorly in the charts through 1985, and at the end of the year it looked as though only a major shot in the arm would revive his flagging fortunes.

HALEY, BILL Born William John Clifton Haley at Highland Park, a Detroit suburb, on 6 July 1925, Bill Haley spent a decade in obscurity before finding fame in the mid-Fifties as the first idol of the rock'n'roll era.

When Haley was four, his parents – both musical – moved to Booth-Winn, Pennsylvania, where they bought and ran a farm. As a teenager, Haley attempted to launch himself as a hillbilly act in local fairs and amusement parks. He played guitar for two years with Cousin Lee's band in Booth-Winn during the early Forties, made his first solo record, 'Candy Kisses' at 18 in 1945, and spent the next four years on the road with various obscure cowboy bands. While Haley had been on the road, a small radio station, WPWA, had been built in Chester, Pennsylvania, adjacent to Booth-Winn. In 1949, Haley returned home, worked as a deejay at WPWA and formed his own band – the Four Aces Of Western Swing – who broadcast regularly from the station. During the late Forties, he cut several more hillbilly records for small labels (including one for Atlantic) before signing, in 1950, with Essex, Dave Miller's small Philadelphia label.

In 1951, Haley covered Jackie Brenston's R&B hit 'Rocket 88' in an aggressive rockabilly style. Released on an Essex subsidiary, Holiday, it sold a meagre 10,000 copies but Haley's next record, 'Rock the Joint', another cover of an R&B song, sold about 75,000 on Essex. Between these formative rock efforts, however, Haley recorded a variety of unsuccessful hillbilly songs in 1952. Finally in 1952, Bill Haley's Saddlemen – as the group was then known – dropped its hillbilly image and became Bill Haley and the Comets. Then in 1953, the group – John Grande, Billy Williamson, Rudy Pompelli, Al Reed, Francis Beecher and Don Raymond – cut the pacy 'Crazy Man Crazy', a Haley original which reached the national charts. This record crystallized the driving dance-band style for which Haley would become famous.

Despite Haley's successes, however, Dave Miller tended to neglect him in favour of more popular orchestral recordings by another Essex artist, Monte Kelly, and in 1954 Haley's manager, Dave Myers, took him to New York and accepted an attractive offer from Decca. At his first Decca session on 12 April 1954, Haley recorded 'Rock

Around the Clock' as a favour to Myers who had co-written and published it some eighteen months earlier when Sunny Dae had recorded it. The Milt Gabler-produced record sold moderately well but Haley's follow-up, 'Shake, Rattle and Roll' (a dilution of Joe Turner's original) reached the Top 10 in both Britain and America and eventually sold a million. This prompted Decca to re-release 'Clock', which also sold a million and was included in the opening sequences of *The Blackboard Jungle*, a 1955 film about juvenile delinquents. Partly through the film's influence and partly because public tastes were rapidly changing, 'Rock Around the Clock' became an instant youth anthem and Haley's Comets – at

best a driving little hillbilly dance band – became unlikely cult figures for the new rock generation.

Between 1955 and mid-1956, Haley was the biggest rock attraction in the world and he notched up twelve hits including 'Burn That Candle', 'See You Later Alligator', 'R-O-C-K', 'Hot Dog Buddy Buddy' and 'Rudy's Rock'. It must be said, however, that in chart terms Haley was infinitely more popular in Britain, where he had no opposition, than in his home country where only five of his records reached the Top 20. Up to March 1957, every record released by Brunswick in Britain reached the Top 20 and in February 1957, Haley arrived in Britain to a tumultuous welcome. He rode from Southampton to London in state on the Bill Haley Special, a train laid on for him by the *Daily Mirror* and, at Waterloo, he was met by three thousand cheering fans, many of whom had waited all day. Someone called the event 'The Second Battle of Waterloo'.

Despite the triumph, Haley's British tour also proved to be his undoing, for audiences saw him as he really was – chubby, married and rather sedate, not the sort of figurehead on which the new generation based their fantasies. He had starred in two Hollywood exploitation films, *Rock Around the Clock* and *Don't Knock the Rock* and they did well at the box-office but by 1958 it was over for him. He had an American comeback hit that year with 'Skinnie Minnie', but passed into the nostalgia category as an entertainer. Although it is generally assumed that the rise of **Elvis Presley** and Haley's own reluctance to digress from his basic dance-hall style contributed to his demise, time has shown that Haley simply knew his limitations and stuck to them. He died on 9 February 1981, at Harlingen, Texas.

HALL AND OATES Formed in Philadelphia in 1969, Hall and Oates are the most successful American duo in the history of the charts, their rock/R&B scoring them five US Number 1 singles since they first charted in 1976. Since then they have become the darlings of American rock radio.

Daryl Hall (born 11 October 1949 in Pottstown, Pennsylvania) and John Oates (born 7 April 1949, New York City) first came together in 1967 when both were singing with doo-wop groups in and around Philadelphia. Hall's group, the Temptones, were competing against Oates' group, the Masters, in a battle of the bands competition; legend has it they shared a lift

Chubby ex-hillbilly Bill Haley became the idol of the rock generation

while escaping from a gang fight. They began composing together, then joined a band, Gulliver, which recorded one album for Elektra before quitting.

As a duo, they signed to Atlantic in 1972 and released three albums with them. These produced little of interest, save the second album *Abandoned Luncheonette* (1973) and the song 'She's Gone', which was a Number 1 R&B hit for Tavares (and later a Number 7 for themselves). *War Babies* (1974), album number three, produced by **Todd Rundgren**, was a rock concept LP that sold well in New York but nowhere else. At the end of 1974 they were dropped by the label.

They immediately signed to RCA and cut *Daryl Hall/John Oates* in 1975, which gave them their first US hit single, 'Sara Smile'. The album, *Bigger Than Both of Us*, was released in '76 and contained their first US Number 1 song, 'Rich Girl'. In its wake, the two previous albums went gold and *Bigger* became their first platinum LP. But between 1977 and 1980 they had a lean period, three albums yielding only minor hits until *Voices* (1980) produced no less than four US Top 30 singles including the Number 1, 'Kiss on My List'. The album went platinum.

Having rediscovered a successful pop/rock formula, Hall and Oates continued to be very popular in the US, but it wasn't until 1982 and H_2O that they made their mark in the UK, scoring Top 10 hits with 'I Can't Go For That (No Can Do)' and 'Maneater'. Subsequently, *Rock 'n' Soul Part 1* (1983), *Big Bam Boom* (1984) and *Live at the Apollo* (1985) have all done moderately well in the UK, but Hall and Oates' biggest successes remained in their own country.

HALL, RICK A leading independent producer/arranger/engineer, Rick Hall was responsible for a solid string of hits from Muscle Shoals, Alabama. Born 31 January 1932 in Mississippi, Hall progressed from session musician at Hi studios in Memphis to a songwriting partnership with **Billy Sherrill**. In 1961 he opened his own Fame studios near Muscle Shoals, and cut his first hit, **Arthur Alexander**'s 'You Better Move On'. By 1964 Hall had formed his own label, Fame – distributed by Vee Jay – and scored an immediate chart success with Jimmy Hughes' 'Steal Away'. That same year Buddy Killen used the studios to produce **Joe Tex**'s million-selling 'Hold What You've Got'.

When Vee Jay went bankrupt in 1965, Hall switched outlets to Atlantic and recruited a regular unit of studio musicians – Jimmy Johnson (guitar), Norbert Putnam, Albert Lowe and David Hood (bass), Roger Hawkins and Jerry Corrigan (drums), **Spooner Oldham** and David Briggs (keyboards), Chips Moman, Eddie Hinton and Duane Allman (guitars). Later session men included Barry Beckett and Tommy Cogbill. The studio quickly gathered attention with hits like **Percy Sledge**'s 'When a Man Loves a Woman', **Wilson Pickett**'s '634–5789' and **Aretha Franklin**'s 'I Never Loved a Man (The Way I Loved You)'. Other Fame hits include Wilson Pickett's 'Hey Jude' and **Clarence Carter**'s 'Patches'. The studios were also used by such artists as **Boz Scaggs**, **Ronnie Hawkins**, **Bobbie Gentry** and **Cher**.

In 1967, Moman and Cogbill left Hall to launch their own AGP studios in Memphis, eventually recording **Elvis Presley**, the **Box Tops** and **King Curtis**. A year later, Hall withdrew his Fame label from Atlantic following a disagreement over advances and signed a new deal with Capitol, although still continuing to produce his protégé, Clarence Carter. Dissatisfied with the new set-up, Johnson, Beckett, Hood and Hawkins quit in 1968 to open their own studio, Muscle Shoals Sound, picking up the Atlantic projects. Hall wound up Fame Records in 1974, but continued to work out of his studio with artists like the **Osmonds**, **Paul Anka**, **Mac Davis**, Candi Staton, and **Otis Rush**. *See also* **Muscle Shoals**

HALL, TOM T. Born in Olive Hill, Kentucky, on 25 May 1936, Tom T. Hall worked in factories, stores, the US Army and as a DJ until he set his sights on becoming a songwriter in the Nashville of the Sixties. 'I Washed My Face in the Morning Dew', and two redneck war songs, 'Hello Vietnam' (a country Number 1 in 1964) and 'What Are We Fighting For', endeared him to the Southern country establishment. Then he wrote 'Harper Valley P.T.A.' an international hit for **Jeannie C. Riley** in 1968 and his success was assured.

By now a singer as well, he started writing songs directly from his own experiences – his nickname is 'The Storyteller' – and, hostile to the MOR direction country music was taking, was a forerunner of the 'new' Nashville rebel singer/songwriter fraternity with **Willie Nelson**.

'The Year That Clayton Delaney Died' ushered in an era of country hits for Hall on Mercury. 'Ballad of Forty Dollars', 'Ravishing Ruby', 'America the Ugly' and 'Trip to Hyden' were in the best traditions of the understated realism country music is capable of.

HALLYDAY, JOHNNY Although once rumoured to be American, Johnny Hallyday was for many years France's leading exponent of rock'n'roll.

Hallyday was born Jean-Philippe Smet in Paris on 15 June 1943. He covered all the leading US and UK hits, a practice generally referred to as *yéyé* in France, even visiting British studios and Memphis to get the sound right for the French market. His multilingual version of 'Let's Twist Again' ('Viens Danser le Twist') was a million-seller for him in 1961. A spectacular performer at his peak in the pre-**Beatles** Sixties when he frequently caused riots, Hallyday was the first to credit the role of his manager, his elder stepbrother, Lee, and the excellence of his backing group, the Golden Stars. A typical album, *Johnny Hallyday Sings America's Rockin' Hits* (1962), reveals him to be much better than British exponents of the cover-version syndrome. He never actually had a hit in Britain or America, not for want of trying or through any real deficiency on his part. In France, paralleling **Cliff Richard**, he has always remained sufficiently in touch with trends to survive gracefully over 25 years of rock.

HAMILTON IV, GEORGE A country singer far more popular overseas than in his native US, George Hamilton IV was born in Salem, North Carolina, on 19 July 1937. He became a teen idol at the age of 19 with the success of 'A Rose and a Baby Ruth' on ABC Records and continued recording in the same mode – 'Only One Love', 'High School Romance', 'Why Don't They Understand' – with declining success. However, he had always had a leaning towards country music and in 1961 he joined RCA Victor and the cast of WSM's *Grand Ole Opry* in Nashville. Never very successful with 'country' songs, he found a role for himself as Nashville's country/folk singer, recording songs by writers as different as **John Hartford**, **John D. Loudermilk** and even **Leonard Cohen**. He had a Top 20 hit with 'Abilene' in 1963, but when his career sagged in the late Sixties, he came to Britain; he allowed himself to be appointed 'Mr Country Music' by the BBC for whom he fronted a series of television shows featuring local talent and the least adventurous of Nashville's performers. Since the early Seventies he has been semi-resident in the UK and a familiar figure at European country music festivals.

HAMILTON, ROY Fifties R&B star Roy Hamilton was born on 16 April 1929, in Leesbury, Georgia, and sang with the Searchlight Gospel Singers in New Jersey in 1948. Local disc jockey Bill Cook became his manager and secured him a contract with Epic, for whom Hamilton topped the R&B chart with 'You'll Never Walk Alone' in 1954. His fame was instantaneous, audiences regularly storming the stage when he appeared. Other Top 10 records – 'If I Loved You', 'Ebbtide', 'Hurt' and 'Unchained Melody' (the best-selling R&B disc of 1955) – were among the vehicles for his powerful, near-operatic baritone. He strongly influenced the **Righteous Brothers,** who cut two of his hits. Hamilton also excelled on secularized gospel songs, enjoying hits with 'Don't Let Go' (Number 13 in 1958) and the vibrant 'You Can Have Her' (Number 12 in 1961). But chart success eluded him on later records for MGM, RCA, and AGP. He died from a heart attack in 1969.

HAMMER, JAN Synthesizer wizard Jan Hammer (born in Prague, Czechoslovakia, on 17 April 1945) first made his name in the jazz field as keyboards player with Sarah Vaughan and Elvin Jones, before joining the fledgling **Mahavishnu Orchestra** in 1971. He stayed with the Mahavishnus for three albums – *Inner Mounting Flame* (1971), *Birds of Fire* (1973) and *Love Devotion Surrender* (1973).

In 1974 he made his recording debut under his own name with *Like Children* (Atlantic), a collaborative effort with Mahavishnu violinist Jerry Goodman. His band, the Jan Hammer Group, toured and recorded with **Jeff Beck** in 1976–7 (resulting in the CBS album, *Live with Jeff Beck*, in 1977), and his other collaborations included *Time is Free* (Vanguard, 1978) with David Earle Johnson and *Untold Passions* (CBS, 1982) with Neil Schon of **Journey.** His session credits have been many, and he runs his own studio, Red Gate. In 1985, his theme for television's popular series, *Miami Vice*, reached Number 5 in the UK on its release by MCA.

HAMMOND, ALBERT A successful pop songwriter before he turned to recording, Albert Hammond was born in London in 1944 but was brought up in Gibraltar. He became a highly successful Spanish language artist before he was 21. He moved to England, where his initial success was in writing songs for artists like Leapy Lee ('Little Arrows') and the Pipkins ('Gimme Dat Ding') in collaboration

Cockney Rebel in 1974: from the left, Paul Avron-Jeffreys, Jean-Paul Crocker, Steve Harley, Milton Reame-James and Stuart Elliott

with Mike Hazlewood. In the early Seventies, Hammond moved to Los Angeles, and registered strongly in 1972 with 'It Never Rains in Southern California' – which was actually written in Fulham, West London. After three successful Columbia solo albums in America, Hammond gained an additional songwriting partner – Hal David, who previously worked with **Burt Bacharach**. Hammond's biggest hit song of the Seventies was 'The Air That I Breathe', the original version of which he included on his *It Never Rains in Southern California* album in 1973. It was the **Hollies**, however, who took it into the UK and US charts during 1974.

HAMMOND, JOHN Born into a wealthy middle-class family on 10 December 1910, in New York City, John Hammond became known in the Thirties for using his money, position, pen and energies in the cause of mainstream jazz. Educated at Yale University and a classical music student at the Juilliard School of Music, his career spanned American popular music from **Bessie Smith** to **Bob Dylan.**

As a writer, he was involved with *Melody Maker* and *The Gramophone* in Britain, *Down Beat* in America, contributed pieces on race relations to several publications, and was for a time vice-president of the National Association for the Advancement of Colored Peoples. As an impresario, he presented black bands at his own theatre and organized integrated recording sessions and tours at a time when they were unheard of. In various executive

positions with a number of labels, he offered recording opportunities to Count Basie, Teddy Wilson, Billie Holiday, Lester Young, Charlie Christian and several boogie pianists including Meade Lux Lewis. In 1938 and 1939, Hammond presented the 'From Spirituals to Swing' concerts at Carnegie Hall, featuring varied line-ups including Young, Christian, Benny Goodman, **Big Bill Broonzy** and **Sonny Terry**. **Robert Johnson** was booked for the first concert, but was killed a few weeks before the date; years later, Hammond was involved in the preparation of the classic Columbia LP *Robert Johnson, King of the Delta Blues Singers*, and in the early Sixties produced the comeback album by Son House, whose Thirties records had influenced Johnson.

Although Hammond has been associated with some of the greatest names in jazz, none were well known when he first heard them, and he continued to back his own personal taste through the Sixties, persuading Columbia to sign **Aretha Franklin** and **Pete Seeger**, and negotiating a particularly lucrative deal for Bob Dylan who was known in the company as 'Hammond's Folly' before his records began to sell. He produced Dylan's first Columbia album in 1962 and signed **Bruce Springsteen** to the label in 1973.

HAMMOND, JOHN PAUL The son of the renowned writer, talent scout and blues champion **John Hammond**, John Paul was born in New York City on 13 November 1943, and became one of America's outstanding white blues singers of the Sixties. He inherited his father's enthusiasm for the country blues of **Robert Johnson** and others and, after cutting a folk/ blues album for Vanguard, he formed an electric band in 1964, recording an album for **Leiber and Stoller**'s Red Bird label which featured Robbie Robertson, then of the Hawks, on guitar. The record was not released until 1968 when Atlantic bought the tapes. Since then, Hammond has continued singing and playing guitar and harmonica, while cutting occasional albums, including *Triumvirate*, with **Dr John** and **Mike Bloomfield** in 1973. He could also be heard on the soundtrack of the film *Little Big Man* in 1970.

HANCOCK, HERBIE

Born in Chicago on 12 April 1940, Herbie Hancock first became widely known as a pianist through his work with the classic **Miles Davis** Quintet of the mid-Sixties, although his career had got off to a flying start some years earlier with the hit composition, 'Watermelon Man'. After participating in Miles' early excursions into rock, Hancock left to lead his own band. His music at this time was a beautifully poised amalgam of the jazz and rock idioms, with highly controlled dynamics and exquisite ensemble voicing. As a composer he admitted he owed a debt to Gil Evans which was evident in his grasp of instrumental colour and the fine precision with which he controlled the band's sound.

Hancock composed soundtrack music for the films *Blow Up* (directed by Michaelangelo Antonioni, 1967) and *Death Wish* (Michael Winner, 1974), while the best of his post-Miles albums of the Seventies were *Speak Like a Child* (Blue Note, 1970), *Mwandishi* (Warner Brothers, 1971), *Head Hunters* (Columbia, 1974) and *Thrust* (Columbia, 1974).

While the bias in these albums was towards a jazz-flavoured brand of electric funk, his work with V.S.O.P. (which stood for Very Special Onetime Performance) demonstrated his interest in acoustic jazz: the line-up he brought together included Wayne Shorter from **Weather Report**, Ron Carter, Tony Williams and Freddie Hubbard. The album *V.S.O.P.* was released in 1977. He recorded and toured with **Chick Corea** in 1979 and had considerable success in the electro-funk/disco field with the singles 'I Thought It Was You' (1978), 'You Bet Your Love' (1979) and 'Rockit' – all of them Top 20 hits in the UK. Hancock's career continued strongly into the Eighties.

HARDCASTLE, PAUL

Producer/ keyboard player Paul Hardcastle fused his mastery of studio technology and his abilities as an arranger with the talents of a string of vocalists to great effect in the mid-Eighties.

Born on 10 December 1957, he acquired his first synthesizer while working in a hi-fi store in 1980, and scored a handful of club dancefloor hits as keyboard player with the bands Direct Drive and First Light. By 1984 he had formed his own Total Control label, and a couple of his singles found their way to the US where they became dance hits. Administration of the label became a problem, and he signed a deal with Chrysalis.

In 1985, inspired by a TV documentary on the Vietnam War, Hardcastle constructed the scratch-inspired single '19', using the narration from the programme on the single. It was a massive hit, a UK Number 1 for four weeks and sold over 3½ million copies worldwide. 'Just for Money' and 'Don't Waste My Time' (featuring the vocals of Carol Kenyon) were lesser hits and *Paul Hardcastle*, his debut LP featuring most of his previously released material, was released in November 1985, achieving moderate success.

HARDIN, TIM

The career of singer-songwriter Tim Hardin (born in Eugene, Oregon, on 23 December 1941) began soon after his discharge from the US Marines in 1961, when he became part of the folk movement in Boston's many folk clubs.

By the time he released his first Verve album, in 1966, his style was maturely formed, owing more to jazz and blues than folk. He used his emotionally charged voice as a musical instrument and his first two albums – *Tim Hardin 1* and *2* – contained a clutch of subsequent standards, 'Reason to Believe', 'Misty Roses', 'If I Were a Carpenter' and 'The Lady Came From Baltimore' among them. His fame spread when **Bobby Darin** had a Top 10 hit with 'Carpenter' in 1966 (ironically, Hardin had only one Hot 100 entry himself, and that was with Darin's 'Simple Song of Freedom' in 1969).

The third Hardin album consisted of forgotten tapes recorded when he was 22, showing the strong blues influence in his early work. Following a live concert album, Hardin left Verve for Columbia for whom his first album was the ambitious *Suite for Susan Moore and Damion* (1969), a thematic album dedicated to his wife and child and incorporating poetry. *Bird on a Wire*, consisting of other writers' songs, fol-

lowed in 1971 and the unsatisfactory *Painted Head* in 1973. His British contract with GM produced *Nine* (1974), in which year Verve repackaged his first two albums. Hardin's career was bedevilled by ill-health and 'bad advice', and he never quite matched the quality and originality of his first two albums in later recordings. He died in Los Angeles on 29 December 1980, reportedly of a heroin overdose.

HARLEY, STEVE AND COCKNEY REBEL

Based around Steve Harley's macabre, theatrical stage persona, Cockney Rebel emerged from the tail-end of the Seventies glam-rock era to achieve huge (if fleeting) success with their hybrid brand of insidious art-school anthems.

Formed in 1973 by ex-journalist Harley (real name Steven Nice, born 29 February 1951), the original Cockney Rebel leaned heavily on the influences of **Roxy Music**, **David Bowie** and the film *A Clockwork Orange*, and featured Jean-Paul Crocker (guitar/violin), Milton Reame-James (keyboards), Paul Jeffreys (bass) and Stuart Elliott (drums).

Two albums – *The Human Menagerie* (1973) and *The Psychomodo* (1974) – established a cult following for the group, which helped them to achieve two hit singles in 'Judy Teen' (UK Number 5 in 1974) and 'Mr Soft' (Number 8). By now Harley's compulsive artistic ego was dominating the group to such an extent that internal dissatisfaction caused him to leave the band. Jim Cregan (guitar), George Ford (bass) and Duncan Mackay (keyboards) joined him in time for a major appearance at the Reading Festival in September 1974, where they were billed for the first time as Steve Harley and Cockney Rebel.

The year 1975 witnessed Harley's peak – both artistically and commercially – when the sublime single, 'Make Me Smile (Come Up and See Me)', reached Number 1 in the UK, followed by the *Best Years of Our Lives* album and 'Mr Raffles' single.

After this, Harley seemed to lose his sense of purpose and direction, and despite minor successes – his cover of the **Beatles**' 'Here Comes the Sun' (a UK Top 10 single) and two patchy solo albums *Timeless Flight* and *Love's a Prima Donna* (all 1976) – he remained an ex-star for almost ten years.

Then suddenly, in 1986, Harley became involved with Andrew Lloyd-Webber and *Phantom of the Opera*, teaming up with Sarah Brightman to have a UK hit with the title track.

HARPER, ROY One of UK rock music's great individualists, Roy Harper was born in Manchester on 12 June 1941, and joined the RAF at 15. His career included spells in mental hospital and prison before his highly personal songs made him a cult figure on the London folk scene in 1965. The next year he made his first album (*The Sophisticated Beggar*) for Strike.

Other albums for CBS and Liberty followed, before Harper signed a long-term contract with Harvest in 1970. The resulting albums were a faithful reflection of Harper's erratic live performances, in which he would often harangue audiences for long periods of time. *Flat, Baroque and Berserk* (1970) featured two songs that were to become classics in Harper's repertoire – 'I Hate the White Man' and 'McGoohan's Blues' – while *Stormcock* (1971) comprised just four songs and offered some superlative string arrangements by David Bedford. *Made* appeared in 1972 and *Lifemark* – one side of which featured Harper's apocalyptic 'The Lord's Prayer' – in 1973, and one further album followed (*Valentine*, 1974) before he formed his first band, Trigger, with Bill Bruford from **Yes** and guitarist **Chris Spedding**. Their album, *HQ* (1975) was especially notable for the elegiac 'When an Old Cricketer Leaves the Crease'.

In 1976, Harper quit Britain for the US but returned for *Bullinamingvase*, which featured Paul and Linda McCartney on backing vocals. Thereafter, he seemed to lose his creative momentum: *Commercial Break* (1977) was initially rejected by EMI, and neither the subsequent *The Unknown Soldier* (1980) nor *Work of Heart* (1982) were up to the standards set by *Stormcock*, which in retrospect seems his finest work.

HARPERS BIZARRE Starting out in the San Francisco Bay area around 1963, Harpers Bizarre – **Ted Templeman**, Dick Scoppetone, Dick Yount and Eddie James – originally called themselves the Tikis and played surf music in imitation of the **Beach Boys**. They recorded briefly for **Tom Donahue**'s Autumn label in San Francisco alongside major chart act the **Beau Brummels**, whose drummer John Petersen joined the Bizarre in late 1966. In 1967, both the Brummels and the Bizarre signed with Warner Brothers and were placed with house producer **Lenny Waronker**, who put an impressive array of young songwriting and arranging talent – **Randy Newman**, **Van Dyke Parks** and **Leon Russell** included – to

Folk rocker Harper has never achieved the degree of commercial success his talents deserve, held back by his turbulent personality

work on their respective albums. The Bizarre scored early with a bubbling version of **Paul Simon**'s '59th Street Bridge Song (Feelin' Groovy)', a Number 13 US hit in 1967, and had further minor hits with imaginative revivals of pre-rock'n'roll era songs like Cole Porter's 'Anything Goes' and Glenn Miller's 'Chattanooga Choo Choo'. The group's intricate five-part harmonies won them a sophisticated easy-listening following but little favour among the hip rock clientele, and they disbanded in 1970 after four albums. Petersen rejoined the Beau Brummels in 1975 and Templeman became a staff producer at Warner Brothers, his credits including albums by the **Doobie Brothers**, **Van Morrison**, **Captain Beefheart** and **Van Halen**.

HARPO, SLIM Born James Moore on 11 January 1924, in Lobdell, Louisiana, Slim Harpo made his initial public appearances as 'Harmonica Slim' before meeting Excello Records

boss, Jay D. Miller, in 1957, who signed and recorded him. His first disc, 'I'm a King Bee'/'I've Got Love If You Want It', meant little commercially, but both sides were later revived by British R&B groups. Slim's first taste of success came in 1961 when 'Raining in My Heart' was a substantial pop and R&B hit in America. Little different to his preceding material, it was a relatively simple song with drawled vocal backed by harmonica and a small rhythm section. Further discs in the same vein sold only locally until 'Baby Scratch My Back' soared into the Top 20 in 1966. However, in succeeding years Slim produced just two small R&B hits, and he died of a heart attack in February 1970.

HARRIS, EMMYLOU One of the most enduringly creative exponents of country-rock fusion, Emmylou Harris was born on 2 April 1949, in Birmingham, Alabama, but grew up in

Washington DC and attended Greensboro's University of North Carolina. She sang folk and country music from an early age, graduating to New York's Greenwich Village in the late Sixties and recording for the small Jubilee label. A little later she met **Gram Parsons**, founder of the **Flying Burrito Brothers**, and recorded and toured with him in the months prior to his death in 1973. Her song 'Boulder to Birmingham', included on her first Reprise album *Pieces of the Sky* (1975), was dedicated to his memory. With an impressive array of instrumental talent behind her – including **James Burton** (guitar), **Albert Lee** (guitar), Glen D. Hardin (piano) and Hank De Vito (pedal steel) – Emmylou began making a major impression in country music circles in 1975, when her single 'If I Could Only Win Your Love' topped the country chart, and in rock circles around 1976–7, with the release of *Elite Hotel* and *Luxury Liner*. She married Brian Ahern, her producer, in 1977 and in 1979 won a Grammy award for Best LP by a Country Singer with *Blue Kentucky Girl*. She guested on albums by numerous other rock and country luminaries, among them **Dolly Parton**, **Linda Ronstadt**, **Neil Young** and **Little Feat**, and consolidated her reputation into the Eighties as one of the most graceful vocalists in contemporary music with such albums as *Cimarron* (1981), *Last Date* (1982) and *White Shoes* (1983).

HARRIS, JET, AND MEEHAN, TONY

Jet Harris (born 6 July 1939) and Tony Meehan (2 March 1942) were possibly the first example of a trend that by the end of the Sixties was to become widespread. First bassist Harris and then drummer Meehan left the **Shadows** to develop their musical talents rather than remain in the rut of touring. Harris charted with 'The Man with the Golden Arm' (the theme from the film) in 1962 and combined with Meehan for a string of successful Decca singles in 1963, all in the Shadows mould – 'Diamonds' (a UK Number 1), 'Scarlett O'Hara' and 'Applejack'.

They existed more as a friendly business relationship rather than a permanent recording and performing partnership. Meehan had a small solo hit, 'Song of Mexico', in 1964 and continued working for Decca as a record producer; Harris had an unhappy solo career, bedevilled by revelations about his private life and a serious road accident in 1963 which wrecked his nerves.

HARRIS, WYNONIE Born in Omaha, Nebraska, in 1915, Wynonie Harris started his life in music as a drummer, then became a dancer and finally, about 1940, a blues singer. He first became known as a vocalist with Lucky Millinder's band with which he recorded in 1944. By 1945, he was recording solo in Hollywood with bands led by **Johnny Otis**, Jack McVea, Oscar Pettiford and Illinois Jacquet. His real success started in 1947 when he joined King and made a series of records which had pop as well as jazz/R&B appeal, including 'Good Morning Judge', 'Lovin' Machine', 'All She Wants To Do Is Rock' and his fondly remembered 1955 British hit, 'Bloodshot Eyes'. By the late Fifties, however, Harris had faded from the scene and did not record again. He was a rousing, humorous, slick performer who shouted his lyrics with an infectious spirit. He died, aged 54, in Los Angeles in 1969.

George Harrison: songwriter, singer, guitarist and film producer, living well in the material world

HARRISON, GEORGE As a Beatle, George Harrison grew from guitarist and harmony singer into a writer and singer in his own right, eventually becoming a third creative force alongside **John Lennon** and **Paul McCartney**. It was primarily his interest in Eastern religion, and the subsequent (temporary) involvement of Lennon, that pushed the Beatles, and helped to push popular music in general, into a cultural stance heavily indebted to Eastern modes of thought. His songs on Beatle albums from *Revolver* onwards were usually explorations of common romantic themes through Hinduistic perspective, centring on the possibilities of egoless love.

This philosophy illuminated the first four solo albums he made after the Beatles' demise. The first, *All Things Must Pass* (Apple, 1970) – made after two experimental albums, *Wonderwall* (1968) and *Electronic Sounds* (1969) – in particular represented a further development of the music bequeathed by the Sixties, and ranked as one of the classic albums of the Seventies.

Much of the credit for this must go to the production of Harrison and **Phil Spector**, which, with an infinite attention to detail in the creation of a massive, multi-layered sound, managed to make the most of Harrison's strengths and minimize his weaknesses. The thinness of his singing voice became a strength set against the imagination of the music; the guitars of himself, **Eric Clapton**, and **Dave Mason** rang clearly regardless of the complexity of instrumentation. All combined to give the songs an emotional strength both compelling and uplifting, seen most notably on 'My Sweet Lord', the international hit that launched the album. On this and his second album, *Living in the Material World* (1973), Harrison continued the role that much rock performed in the Sixties, that of proselytization. He is still a believer: in the wrongs of the present and the vision of another way. Similarly the Seventies' obsession with relationships was treated as thoughtfully in Harrison's songs as any others.

His belief in rock music's duty to a wider world received its most obvious expression in the Concert For Bangla Desh, organized in 1972 to make money for the relieving of the plight of that country. George got **Ringo Starr** and **Eric Clapton**, among others, to play with him, and even coaxed **Bob Dylan** on stage to sing a few of the old protest songs. *Rolling Stone* called the concert 'a brief and incandescent revival of all that was best about the Sixties'.

Harrison subsequently kept out of the public eye, except for the overpublicized separation from his wife. The third album, *Dark Horse*, received less than critical acclaim, as did his tour of the States in 1974. He seemed to have lost the power of the previous two solo albums, although *Extra Texture (Read All About It)* (Capitol, 1975) saw a return to form. In 1974, he launched his own label, Dark Horse, with Splinter, a singer-songwriter duo whose 'Costafine Town' was a Top 20 hit in the UK during that year. An album also called *Dark Horse* (1974) was Harrison's own debut for the label, which was followed by two further Seventies albums, the disappointing $33\frac{1}{3}$ (1976) and *George Harrison* (1979). *Somewhere in England* (1981) was chiefly of interest for its inclusion of 'All Those Years Ago', a jaunty tribute to the recently murdered John Lennon, which provided Harrison with his biggest UK hit single (a Number 10) since 'Give Me Love' in 1973. *Gone Troppo* followed in 1982.

His non-musical activities include extensive financial and creative involvement in the film company HandMade Films, whose productions have included *The Life of Brian*; *The Long Good Friday*, *Time Bandits*, *The Missionary* and **Madonna**'s *Shanghai Surprise*.

HARRISON, WILBERT

A truly original but often underrated R&B talent, Wilbert Harrison was born on 6 January 1929 in North Carolina. He first recorded on Rockin ('This Woman of Mine') and De Luxe in Miami during the early Fifties, and followed with records on Savoy. In 1959, 'Kansas City' – a hypnotic revival of the **Leiber and Stoller** blues, for Fury – reached Number 1 in the US, but Harrison moved from one small uncaring label to another: Seahorn, Neptune, Doc, Port, Vest. Unable to afford sidemen, he turned eventually to a one-man band format and scored with 'Let's Work Together', a US Top 40 hit on Sue in 1969 that was successfully covered that year by **Canned Heat**. An album of the same name received critical acclaim in 1970. Harrison's work has a breadth and inventiveness at which his sporadic hits can only hint; unaffected by his limited success, he remains undeniably authentic but never tedious. Seventies discs for Buddah, Hotline and Brunswick continued to couple his idiosyncratic diction with the exuberance of vintage R&B.

HARTFORD, JOHN

Born on 30 December 1947, singer-songwriter John Hartford served his musical apprenticeship first as a fiddle player at square dances, then playing rock guitar in East St Louis and West Memphis honky tonks. This background of extremes left its mark and is evident on some of Hartford's far-ranging, erratic work. He arrived in Nashville in 1965, quickly forged a reputation as a session picker (guitar, banjo and fiddle) and earned a certain notoriety as the local hippie. This changed when **Glen Campbell** recorded his 'Gentle on My Mind', a minor country hit for Hartford in 1967. Campbell's recording was a spectacular hit, setting him on the road to superstardom and country music in the direction of the sweet and lush countrypolitan sound which Hartford himself despised.

Hartford moved from Nashville to Los Angeles, the natural home of countrypolitan, where he cut his sixth solo album, *John Hartford* (RCA, 1969). A supporter and advocate of country rock in its beginnings, Hartford played fiddle and banjo on the **Byrds'** classic pioneering country rock album, *Sweetheart of the Rodeo*. *Aereo-Plain* (Warner Bros 1971) – which included his own 'They're Tearing Down the Grand Ole Opry' – similarly demonstrated his ongoing commitment to traditional country styles. Later albums included *Mark Twang* (Flying Fish, 1976), for which he won a Grammy award; a collaboration with Rodney and Doug Dillard of the **Dillards**, *Dillard, Hartford and Dillard* (1977); and *Slumberin' on the Cumberland* (1979).

HATHAWAY, DONNY

A star of the Seventies soul field who became particularly known for his best-selling duets with **Roberta Flack**, Donny Hathaway was born in Chicago on 1 October 1945. He grew up in St Louis, getting his musical grounding in the gospel field – his grandmother was a noted performer of sacred music. He gained a scholarship to Howard University, Washington, where he studied piano and music teaching before majoring in musical theory. While in Washington he played and sang in church before joining a 'cocktail' jazz trio, then met **Curtis Mayfield** who invited him to Chicago as a producer for his Curtom label for which he also recorded with June Conquest as June and Donny. Pressure of work forced him to quit Curtom, and Donny signed with Chess as staff musician/producer, though also dabbling freelance with Uni, Kapp and Stax before establishing his own independent production company. He met up with **King Curtis**, who introduced him to Atlantic Records, where he signed as performer, writer and producer, and enjoyed chart success both on his own – e.g. 'The Ghetto' (1970) and 'I Love You More Than You'll Ever Know' (1972) – and with Flack – most successfully with 'Where Is The Love?', a Top 5 record in America in 1972. The most accomplished Flack-Hathaway collaboration was the 1979 release, *Roberta Flack Featuring Donny Hathaway*, but his association with Flack tended to overshadow his solo work and also his production and writing for other artists, including **Aretha Franklin** and **Jerry Butler**. He died on 13 January 1979, after a fall from a New York hotel room.

HAVENS, RICHIE

Born in New York on 21 January 1941, Richie Havens became an underground star in the late Sixties through his idiosyncratic guitar playing and singing. Havens had been a part of the Greenwich Village folk scene as early as 1962, one of the few black singers in a mainly white idiom, although his early gospel singing experience contributed to his later style. Rather like **José Feliciano**, Havens' particular talent was to transform well-known songs by other artists into an instantly recognizable, personal sound, based on the insistent acoustic rhythms of his E-chord open-tuned guitar and a gruff, but soft, singing voice. By the early Seventies he had cut a dozen albums, the most outstanding being *Richard P. Havens 1983* (Verve, 1969), which included sensitive renderings of 'Strawberry Fields Forever', 'She's Leaving Home' and 'I Pity the Poor Immigrant'. The high point of his career was his Woodstock appearance in 1969. His only US Top 20 record was 'Here Comes the Sun' in 1971, a version of the **George Harrison** song. He recorded for A&M, Polydor and Elektra during the Seventies and appeared in the film *Catch My Soul* in 1974.

HAWKINS, DALE Born on 22 August 1938 in Goldmine, Louisiana, as Delmar Allen Hawkins, Dale Hawkins was among the first group of rockabilly singers to reach the pop charts, with 'Susie Q' (Checker), which entered the Top 30 in 1957. The fusion of a raunchy black beat (he had heard a similar blues by **Howlin' Wolf**), white country picking and the unorthodox use of a cowbell resulted in a fine snappy style. Other Checker singles were less popular, but no less authentic. 'My Babe', 'Class Cutter', 'Liza Jane' and 'La Do Da Da' were studded with bursts of frantic energy, with innovatory guitar work from Kenny Paulsen, **Roy Buchanan**, **Scotty Moore** or **James Burton**. In 1961, Hawkins left Checker to record for Tilt, Zonk, Atlantic, Roulette and ABC-Paramount. In the late Sixties, he produced hits for **Bruce Channel** and the **Five Americans**.

HAWKINS, EDWIN/EDWIN HAWKINS SINGERS
The man behind one of 1969's unlikeliest hits, 'Oh Happy Day', Edwin Hawkins was born in Oakland, California, in August 1943. While studying at the University of California, Berkeley, in 1967, he became choir director at a Berkeley church where he formed the North California State Youth Choir with leading soloists from other choirs in the San Francisco area. They recorded an album to sell in aid of choir funds and went on to represent North California at a youth convention in Cleveland, Ohio, selling their album there. In 1969, an Oakland disc jockey began playing 'Oh Happy Day' from the album, featuring soloist Dorothy Coombs Morrison (who was born in Longview, Texas, in 1945), and Pavilion Records signed the choir as the Edwin Hawkins Singers. The song became a surprise US and UK Top 10 hit that year, although they failed to repeat its success. Dorothy Morrison went on to enjoy a limited career in the secular field.

HAWKINS, RONNIE With a not wholly unjustified reputation as the last of the original rock'n'rollers, Ronnie Hawkins is now a successful club owner and TV star in Canada. More important, perhaps, his band, the Hawks, once included Levon Helm and Robbie Robertson and formed the basis of **The Band**. Hawkins was born on 10 January 1935 in Huntsville, Arkansas, and formed his first C&W band of Hawks in 1952 at the University of Arkansas. By early 1957, he was in Memphis auditioning as a rockabilly singer for Sun. Unsuccessful on this occasion, he developed an intense rock'n'roll style and was a capable rock singer with a strong voice who favoured a semi-screaming style at times. In 1957 he moved to Toronto and Quality Records, recording 'Bo Diddley', whose beat Hawkins often utilized. In 1959 he joined Roulette and enjoyed hits with 'Forty Days', 'Mary Lou' and others which were mostly powerful rockers in a soft rock era. In 1963, his classic version of **Bo Diddley**'s 'Who Do You Love?' employed almost psychedelic lead guitar work from Robertson. He recorded on his own Hawk label in the mid-Sixties before appearing on Atlantic with a tight Muscle Shoals back-up in 1969 and joining Monument in 1972. He was one of the stars of The Band's farewell concert in 1976, which was recorded for posterity in the film *The Last Waltz*. 1981 found him playing a small acting role opposite **Kris Kristofferson** in the film *Heaven's Gate*. *See also* **The Band**

HAWKINS, SCREAMIN' JAY With gaudy costumes, an outlandish stage act and a series of bizarre recordings, Screamin' Jay Hawkins achieved brief success but lasting notoriety as rock'n'roll's weirdest offspring. Born in Cleveland, Ohio, on 18 July 1929, he first worked as a pianist/singer with Tiny Grimes, Lynn Hope, and other name R&B bands before launching a solo career in 1953. Records on Timely, Mercury, Wing and Grand displayed his talent for wryly humorous lyrics, but it was 'I Put a Spell On You' (Okeh) in 1956 that became his most famous performance, completing his reputation as a voodoo man. Trapped by the image, he spent the rest of his career label-hopping from obscure (Enrica, Providence, Queen Bee) to major (Decca, Philips, RCA) companies, trying to re-create that success. Equally powerful records, 'I Hear Voices' (1962), 'Poor Folks' (1965), 'Feast of the Mau Mau' (1967), and several hit cover-versions of 'Spell' failed to attract modern audiences to his brand of macabre theatre, the influence of which could be seen most clearly on **Arthur Brown** of Crazy World fame.

Screamin' Jay Hawkins warns of the evils of death-dealing tobacco

HAWKWIND Originally called Group X, Hawkwind emerged in 1970 from London's Ladbroke Grove, the nearest thing in Britain to a hippie ghetto. X became Hawkwind Zoo, then plain Hawkwind when their manager Doug Smith signed them to United Artists. Formed by Dave Brock (guitar, vocals) the original line-up included Huw Lloyd Langton (guitar), Terry Ollis (drums), Nick (later Nik) Turner (saxophone), Dave Anderson (bass) and Dikmik (electronics).

The band became known as regulars on the free festival circuit and the first album (*Hawkwind*, 1970) was unimpressive. But the following year, poet and writer Bob Calvert joined the ensemble and inspired Hawkwind's 'space-rock' persona on *In Search of Space* (1971), and their surprise hit single 'Silver Machine' (1972).

Various personnel changes occurred as Hawkwind consolidated a large, youthful following on both sides of the Atlantic. Langton, Ollis and Anderson left, with Lemmy Kilminster (bass), Simon King (drums) and Del Detmar (electronics) joining. The statuesque Stacia eventually became a permanent fixture as a dancer, while in 1974 Dikmik and Calvert departed, the latter to follow a solo career. The next year Lemmy was fired: he then formed **Motörhead**, a hard rock band whose lack of prowess was reminiscent of the early Hawkwind.

Further tours and albums (e.g. *Hall of the Mountain Grill*, 1974) saw Hawkwind continuing in their time-warp, their anachronistic image and pulp sci-fi material appealing to teenage audiences unfamiliar with flower-power and all its trappings. *Warriors on the Edge of Time* featured the voice of science-fiction writer Michael Moorcock and *Astounding Sounds, Amazing Music* (1976) – their first after leaving United Artists for Charisma – was their last before a major reshaping of personnel that left the band's line-up reading: Brock, Calvert (who had returned on a temporary basis), King, Adrian Shaw (bass) and Simon House (keyboards). The album (*Quark, Strangeness and Charm*, 1977) followed before Brock disbanded Hawkwind and formed a new outfit, Hawklords, with Calvert. *25 Years On* (1978) was released before friction forced Calvert out for good.

A new Hawkwind emerged in September 1979, consisting of Brock, King, Harvey Bainbridge (bass), Huw Lloyd Langton (guitar)and Tim Blake (keyboards). In many ways a hippie hangover, the band has maintained a sizeable following into the Eighties with releases like *Choose Your Masques* (1982) and *Independents Day* (1984). They have at least to some extent adjusted to the modern world in their lyrics and presentation.

Nik Turner of Hawkwind, keeping the hippy tradition alive

HAYES, ISAAC One of the key backroom figures behind the Memphis Sound associated with Stax Records during the mid-Sixties, Isaac Hayes was born on 6 August 1938 in Covington, Tennessee, and learned to play piano and saxophone in his teens. He sang in local clubs and cut his first discs in 1962 for tiny labels. They were mainly **Brook Benton** imitations. A long-standing friendship with David Porter led him to join Stax Records as a writer/producer. The Hayes/Porter working partnership led to gold records for **Sam and Dave** ('Hold On I'm Coming' and 'Soul Man') and proved to be one of the key factors in the emergence of the Memphis Sound.

When the Gulf and Western Corporation bought Stax in 1968, the label was asked for 30 albums, so Hayes cut an album himself – *Hot Buttered Soul*. Unlike its predecessor (the jazz-styled *Presenting Isaac Hayes*), it was complex, sophisticated, sensuous and highly controlled, a watershed between the old, raunchy Stax sounds, and the later 'sophistisoul' releases. *Hot Buttered Soul* was an immediate success and subsequent albums featuring extended raps, huge orchestrations and pungent rhythm tracks quickly made Hayes into a superstar, culminating in *Black Moses*. When asked to write the score for the film *Shaft*, Hayes created a double set that some consider his masterpiece, and established his name internationally.

However, despite his *Wattstax* movie appearance, subsequent albums on Stax (including two tepid film scores) failed to sell like Hayes' earlier discs (or those of a new sophistisoul star, **Barry White**). Hayes finally left Stax in 1974 after a publicized royalties wrangle. Early in 1975 he signed with ABC Records and the success of his *Chocolate Chip* album indicated that the bald-headed, chain-vested prophet of Middle American soul could rediscover his immense audience.

Later albums failed to repeat that success, however, and his most notable contributions to the music scene of the late Seventies and Eighties were his various writing, arranging and production assignments for Linda Clifford, **Dionne Warwick** and Donald Byrd.

HAZLEWOOD, LEE An important backroom figure in late Fifties and Sixties pop, Lee Hazlewood was born on 9 July 1929, and attended Southern Methodist University before the Army took him to Korea. On his discharge in 1953, he became one of the most popular deejays in Phoenix, Arizona, where he broadcast C&W music locally. In 1955, he branched out into songwriting and began dabbling in record production after experimenting in his radio studio. His production of 'The Fool', by **Sanford Clark**, sold 800,000 copies on Dot Records in 1956 and Dot subsequently signed him as a record producer for a year, but he failed to make another hit.

In 1957, he teamed up with entrepreneur Lester Sill and they formed the Jamie label in Philadelphia with a distributor and **Dick Clark** of *Bandstand* fame. Through *Bandstand*, they launched **Duane Eddy** with the 'twangy' guitar sound which made him a star. In three and a half years, Hazlewood sold 20 million Duane Eddy records that despite their crass commerciality were the earliest 'sound' productions in rock.

In 1961, Hazlewood and Sill formed the Gregmark label which scored with Phil Spector-produced records by the Paris Sisters (Sill and Hazlewood had earlier run two less successful labels called Trey and East-West). They parted company in 1962 and Hazlewood formed an unsuccessful label, Eden. In 1964, he left the business but the following year, Jimmy Bowen at Reprise asked him to produce the bubblegum trio of Dino, Desi and Billy for whom he produced four consecutive hits. He also began recording Nancy Sinatra at Reprise and established her as a potential chart-force with 'These Boots Are Made for Walkin'' and recorded countrified duets, like 'Jackson', with her. In the late Sixties, he ran his own LHI label in Hollywood but lack of success ended the project. Always something of a bohemian, Hazlewood – in semi-retirement since the early Seventies – commutes between homes in Sweden, Paris and Los Angeles.

HEAD, ROY Born in Three Rivers, Texas, on 1 September 1941, singer Roy Head formed his group, the Traits, in 1958. His first records were for TNT and Renner under the direction of **Huey Meaux**. Subsequent discs, mainly R&B revivals, were leased to Scepter/Wand. In 1964, Head signed with Backbeat, the label on which 'Treat Her Right' reached Number 2 in the US. The funky rhythm and tightly knit brass arrangement gave Head the reputation of a blue-eyed soul brother, but the singing and guitar-work on later records, like 'Apple of My Eye', 'My Babe', 'Wigglin' and Gigglin'' and 'You're Almost Tuff', showed him to be a latent rockabilly performer of considerable accomplishment, as was his lesser-known brother, Don. But despite a dynamic, rubber-legged stage act and equally fine singles on Mercury, Dunhill and other labels, Head was unable to do more than grace the lower reaches of the country charts during the Seventies.

HEAVEN 17 One of the groups instrumental in bringing about the synthesizer UK chart domination of the early Eighties, Heaven 17 stunned critics with their debut single, '(We Don't Need This) Fascist Groove Thang' in March 1981. The song premiered their tough, politicized dance-electro, and while subsequent releases failed to match the quality of the first, they retained a strong following.

Founders Ian Marsh and Martyn Ware, having left pioneer electronic band the **Human League** in 1980, teamed up with old friend Glenn Gregory on vocals. As Heaven 17 they made a policy decision to stick to studio work (as well as experimenting with their pet project, the British Electronic Foundation) and concentrate

on producing technically excellent records and videos.

The first four singles were minor hits but the albums, *Penthouse and Pavement* (1981) and *The Luxury Gap* (1982) sold well and were showered with praise by reviewers. However, when the singles 'Temptation' and 'Come Live with Me' became their first UK Top 5 hits in 1983, Heaven 17 had lost the hard-edge that had won them such strong critical approval. The release of an LP, *How Men Are*, at the end of 1984 did little to answer the growing accusations of insubstantiality.

HEBB, BOBBY Best remembered for his worldwide hit, 'Sunny', in 1966, Bobby Hebb was born in Nashville on 26 July 1941. He played the Grand Ole Opry at the age of 12 at the invitation of **Roy Acuff** and moved to Chicago in the early Fifties where he sat in with **Bo Diddley** on spoons. In 1961, he recorded for Battle with Sylvia Shemwell (later of the Sweet Inspirations) as Bobby and Sylvia. Many other records followed on FM, Rich, Smash and Boom. Hebb achieved his first major success in 1966, when 'Sunny' on Philips reached Number 2 in the US and Number 12 in Britain. His brother, Hal (a member of the Marigolds, an Excello recording group) had died on the day following President Kennedy's assassination, and both events were said to have inspired the song's melancholic lyric. His later Philips records, 'A Satisfied Mind', 'Love Me' and especially 'Love Love Love', made him a firm favourite on the British Northern soul scene by 1973, when he was recording for a new label, GRT. He has recorded little since.

HELL, RICHARD AND THE VOIDOIDS Born Richard Myers on 2 October 1949 in Lexington, Kentucky, Richard Hell (bass/vocals) was an original member of **Television** before forming, in 1976, the stark, uncompromising Voidoids who became major protagonists in the New York punk scene.

Reputedly the man on whom **Malcolm McLaren** based the torn-clothes image of punk, Hell formed the Voidoids with Marc Bell (drums), Robert Quine (guitar) and Ivan Julian (guitar) to perform his own songs. Like so many US punk acts, they first gained recognition in the UK where they recorded the 'Blank Generation' EP on Stiff in 1976. The title song, plus 'Loves Comes in Spurts' off the debut LP *Blank Generation* (1977), became two

of the most enduring punk anthems and overshadow the rest of Hell's work.

In 1979 the Voidoids recorded a single, 'The Kid with the Replaceable Head', with **Nick Lowe**; Hell didn't surface again until 1982 and the album *Destiny Street*. Despite his importance in the development of punk, he remained a cult figure basking in relative obscurity, a situation that was compounded by his increasingly rare appearances.

HENDRIX, JIMI Born James Marshall Hendrix on 27 November 1942 in Seattle, Washington, Jimi Hendrix rose from a poor black background to become at once the fêted genius of the electric guitar and a victim of the destructive forces of the recording industry in the late Sixties. Hendrix taught himself to play guitar while still at school and listened avidly to the recorded work of Southern-born bluesmen from **Robert Johnson** to **B.B. King**. In 1961, he enlisted in the US Paratroopers, played in military clubs and met bass-player Billy Cox, whose musicianship and friendship Hendrix called on years later when under great pressure at the height of his career.

Returning to civilian life, Hendrix worked on various tours of the South, backing up his idol B.B. King, **Sam Cooke** and many others after a brief spell in a band, the Flames. He then worked for **Little Richard** and **Ike and Tina Turner** before moving to New York City. After trying to support himself playing behind the **Isley Brothers**, King Curtis and others on the limited black club circuit, he met entrepreneur Ed Chalpin, who signed him to a management and recording deal and made him lead guitarist in **Curtis Knight**'s band. Hendrix's already extraordinary gifts as a guitarist were recognized by Chas Chandler, originally the **Animals**' bassist, who brought Hendrix to England at the end of 1966.

In London, the Jimi Hendrix Experience was formed – a three-piece band of astonishing power – with Hendrix on lead guitar and vocals, Noel Redding (bass) and Mitch Mitchell (drums). Hendrix was an overnight sensation. He caught the attention of the élite of British pop society (**Eric Clapton** and **Pete Townshend** reportedly went to every club gig Hendrix had in London that winter). By the summer of 1967, he had completed a successful tour of Britain, Germany and Scandinavia, and had record success with 'Hey Joe' and 'Purple Haze' and the album *Are You Experienced?* (on Track). On **Paul McCartney**'s insistence, he was lined up for the Monterey Festival where his performance made him a star. Getting 'thrown off' a follow-up tour of America headed by the **Monkees** perfected the Hendrix image of a wild black anti-hero. A black freak was good music-press copy and Hendrix had developed a highly charged, controversial stage-act that included a pretence at sexual assault upon his amplifiers and sometimes setting his guitar on fire. Yet it was noticeable that his audience was almost entirely white. While it was one of Hendrix's achievements that he became the first black star to win a mass white audience, he was to find himself, by 1969, under heavy political pressure to forge a solidarity with black Americans. It was a pressure he didn't understand in political terms and which caused him much strain and difficulty.

In commercial terms, 1968 was his most successful year – gold albums (*Axis Bold As Love*, 1967, and *Electric Ladyland*), massive earnings from concerts, undisputed superstar status – and in terms of his development as a musician. He was, by the end of the year, considered light-years ahead of all other 'progressive rock' guitarists, with a unique style of keening, soaring, imaginative leaps rooted in a strong melodic sense and an earthy blues feel. **Miles Davis** even considered that Hendrix would become a great jazz player, so wide, it seemed, was the scope and experimental urge in his playing. But as his success increased, so did personal and professional problems. In January, 1968, he spent a night in jail after a violent row with Noel Redding, a sign of their rapidly deteriorating relationship. A month later, on his second and headlining American tour, Hendrix renounced all the showbiz gimmickry of his stage act and played his complex music straight. The reception was hostile, and Hendrix's attempt to ride out this response was not helped by having to fulfil a schedule of 54 dates in 47 days while living out a chaotic round of encounters with groupies and drugs. He lost a lot of weight and became convinced that his management were mishandling his earnings.

Despite the sustained magic of his name among the public, 1969 was an even more corrosive year. Chas Chandler was eased out of Hendrix's management; the Jimi Hendrix Experience broke up; a Toronto drugs bust hung over the star throughout the year; his money was poured, at times it seemed hopelessly, into his dream-studios, Electric Ladyland in New York; his personal life was even more anarchic;

and he came under enormous political pressure to aim at black audiences and form an all-black band. His live appearances were fewer, though in July 1969 he played at Newport, using Mitch Mitchell but bringing in his old friend, Billy Cox, on bass. A month later he played the Woodstock Festival – the last high of his career. His all-black Band Of Gypsies finally came together in December, but Hendrix was bewildered and highly dissatisfied with the band's debut. At the follow-up gig at Madison Square Garden, in January 1970, Hendrix walked out on 19,000 people in the middle of the second number. It was the end of the Band Of Gypsies.

Hendrix went back to using Mitch Mitchell and Billy Cox (the Band Of Gypsies had been Hendrix, Cox and **Buddy Miles**); he filmed in Hawaii; he played more concerts; he recorded at the now open Electric Ladyland studios; and, in August, he left America – for the last time – to play at the Isle of Wight Festival. His performance received a poor critical reception, though in retrospect it was at times controlled, moving and full to strain-

ing-point with ideas and power. The European tour that followed was cut short, and Hendrix returned to England alone in mid-September. On 18 September 1970, he died, suffocating on his own vomit.

Many consider that Hendrix's death came at a time when his creativity was already waning. In the best sense a simple person who didn't realize, until too late, that rock stars need to protect themselves against the ravages of their profession, he had no idea how to erect such protective barriers. It is hard to claim that his creativity was declining in the light of his 1970 work, and it is unfortunate that one measure of how profoundly important his music was in its impact has led to the barrel-scraping for material since issued to cash in – only Alan Douglas' *Crash Landing* compilation (Polydor, 1975) is worthy of Hendrix's name. Musically, his influence has proved a dangerous one for his many followers. The virtuoso technique and the fluent imagination to which it was harnessed have resulted too often in more emulation rather than inspiration. That, in itself, is an indication of his power and stature.

Hendrix's experimental, imaginative guitar style transformed the use of the instrument, leading him into areas of sound previously undreamed of

HENRY, CLARENCE 'FROG-MAN' Born in Algiers, New Orleans, on 19 March 1937, and after dabbling in music at high school, Clarence 'Frogman' Henry became an overnight star in 1957 when his novelty rock'n'roll number, 'Ain't Got No Home' (where he imitated frog noises), was a Number 30 hit on Argo. For a while it looked as if he was a one-hit wonder, but he came back again in 1961 with **Bobby Charles'** composition 'But I Do', a compulsive slice of New Orleans R&B produced by Paul Gayten and **Allen Toussaint** which reached Number 4 in the US chart. He consolidated this success with a series of minor hits in the early Sixties, and was one of the few artists still putting down 'oldies but goodies' R&B in the clubs of New Orleans until his death in the Crescent City in 1984.

HENRY COW The Leaders in British avant-garde rock in the early Seventies, Henry Cow produced some of the most complex, eclectic and uncompromising records ever made. Their wildly diverse music covered rock, classical, jazz, free improvisation and many other forms; this eclecticism, along with their left wing political consciousness and firmly anti-commercial stance, ensured that they never acquired more than a tiny fanatical following.

Formed in Cambridge in 1968 by Fred Frith (guitar/violin/piano) and Chris Cutler (drums) and joined by Tim Hodgkinson (keyboards/reeds), John Greaves (bass) and Geoff Leigh (sax), their ideological stance kept them in virtual obscurity until they played the Glastonbury Festival in 1971, and then in 1973 recorded their critically acclaimed first album, *Legend*. After a second album, *Unrest* (1974), Henry Cow joined forces with bizarre cabaret outfit Slapp Happy (Dagmar Krause, Anthony Moore and Peter Blegvad) and in 1975 collaborated on both *Desperate Straits* and *In Praise of Learning*. Moore and Blegvad left in 1976 for various offbeat musical ventures, but Krause remained with Henry Cow.

After the mid-Seventies, the activities of Henry Cow as a group virtually ceased but several members, notably Frith and Krause, remained highly active on the avant-garde rock scene.

HERD Discovered and groomed by successful UK pop entrepreneurs **Ken Howard** and **Alan Blaikley**, the Herd emerged in late 1967 with an image that was the embodiment of post-flower-power chic. Their first two hits, 'From the Underworld' (1967) and 'Paradise Lost' (1968), were both Howard/Blaikley compositions rich in self-conscious musical and verbal allusions to the new underground culture. By mid-1968, they were one of Britain's leading young pop bands, and lead vocalist/guitarist **Peter Frampton** had been voted the 'Face of '68' by readers of *Rave* magazine. Disillusioned by the band's failure to achieve artistic respectability, Frampton left in 1969 to form **Humble Pie** with Steve Marriott of the **Small Faces**. In the mid-Seventies, he became a big-selling Clapton-style guitar hero with a massive US following. The Herd struggled on without him but disbanded in 1970. Keyboard player Andy Bown joined **Andy Fairweather-Low** in Fairweather and bassist/singer Gary Taylor took the surprising step of joining BBC Radio One as a disc jockey. *See also* **Peter Frampton**

HERMAN'S HERMITS Originally known as the Heartbeats, Herman's Hermits were far from being the leading Manchester group when **Mickie Most** singled them out to record. At that time, Manchester boasted a considerable number of better musical units, with greater local followings, but it was the potential image of Peter Noone (born 5 November 1947), the group's boyish singer, that was the deciding factor for Most. The rest of the group – Derek Leckenby, guitar (14 May 1946); Keith Hopwood, guitar (26 October 1946); Karl Green, bass (31 July 1946); and Barry Whitwarn, drums (21 July 1946) – were almost superfluous. They didn't even play on most of the group's hits.

Herman's Hermits' first British single, 'I'm Into Something Good' in August 1964, took them to Number 1. More importantly, it established them, if gently, in America. Subsequent British releases over the next three years gave them ten Top 20 hits, but their easy rocking style had only intermittent appeal and few of their successes were sizeable.

In America, however, their timing was perfect: by 1965 many of the other early British beat groups were already spent forces and Herman's arrival with the classic 'little boy' and 'British' persona allowed him to clean up. The group was also solidly 'good time' when much of the other current British product was aggressively R&B-flavoured and accordingly jogged its way straight into America's hearts with eleven Top 10 hits, including two Number 1s, 'Mrs Brown' and 'I'm Henry VIII I Am'. Despite a flagging following in America and Britain, the group stayed together until 1970 when Herman went solo under his real name – though he did team up with the group again for Richard Nader's 'English Invasion Revival' in 1973. The Hermits stayed in America while Peter Noone carried on with his solo career, still associated with Mickie Most, and recording for his Rak label.

Noone formed and recorded with a rock'n'roll revival outfit called the Tremblers in the early Eighties and appeared as the Pirate King in the London production of the rocked-up *The Pirates of Penzance*.

HEYWARD, NICK See **Haircut 100**

HICKS, DAN AND HIS HOT LICKS From Santa Rosa, New Mexico, Dan Hicks was a member of one of the first important San Francisco groups, the Charlatans, with George Hunter (vocals) – who was later to become a renowned poster artist – Mike Vilhelm (guitar), Mike Ferguson (piano), and Sam Linde (drums). Hicks left the group in 1968 to form Dan Hicks and his Hot Licks, the line-up of which originally comprised John Girton (guitar), Sid Page (violin, mandolin), Maryann Price (vocals, cornet), Jaime Leopold (bass), and Naomi Eisenberg (vocals, violin). They recorded a series of interesting albums for Blue Thumb, *Where's the Money* (1970), *Strikin' It Rich* (1972), and *Last Train to Hicksville* (1973), all gentle mixtures of folk, blues, Forties jazz and Western Swing. However, the band was beset by personnel problems and in 1973, at a time when *Hicksville* was climbing up the American album charts, Hicks folded the group.

He released a solo album, *It Happened One Bite*, on Warner Bros in 1978.

HILL, JESSIE Jessie Hill was shot from the ghettos of New Orleans into the national spotlight when 'Ooh Poo Pah Doo' was a Number 28 hit on the Minit label in April 1960. With the use of call-and-response devices much loved by **Ray Charles**, the record had a raw wildness and latent power which time has not dissipated. Despite the presence of producer **Allen Toussaint**, Hill was unable to repeat this commercial success in a fine series of releases on Minit and in 1963 he left New Orleans for the West Coast. There he teamed up with several exiled musicians from New Orleans including **Dr John**, and cut several singles and an album for Blue Thumb in 1970.

HILLMAN, CHRIS One of the best bluegrass mandolin players on the US West Coast during the Sixties, Chris Hillman fronted his own group, the Hillmen, before joining the nascent **Byrds** as bassist in 1964. He played a fairly passive role in the band's first three years as members Jim (later **Roger) McGuinn**, **David Crosby** and **Gene Clark** sparred for the leadership, but following the departures of the latter pair his songwriting and jazz-influenced bass playing became a major feature of the Byrds' music on *Younger Than Yesterday* and *The Notorious Byrd Brothers*. He brought **Gram Parsons** into the group and, with him, led the Byrds into electrified country. In 1968, Hillman and Parsons left the Byrds to form the **Flying Burrito Brothers** and further define the new genre of country-rock.

Hillman – a native Californian, born in Los Angeles on 4 December 1942 – subsequently played with **Stephen Stills** in Manassas and then formed the Souther-Hillman-Furay Band with J. D. Souther and ex-**Buffalo Springfield** guitarist Richie Furay. This new band, though adept in its command of solid Los Angeles country-rock, was a publicist's dream turned sour, its commercial potential eclipsed by the more successful **Eagles**. The band split up after two albums and Hillman went on to record the solo efforts, *Slippin' Away* (1976) and *Clear Sailin'* (1977), both for Asylum.

HIP HOP Although it has come to be used as a term for describing the New York City street music of the Eighties – in particular, rap – hip hop in fact has a much wider meaning as a collective term for all the various elements of the New York street culture of the time, of which rap was one of many.

Besides rap, the other vital ingredients of the hip hop lifestyle are: 'scratch mixing', rhythmic audio distortions DJs make when moving a record back and forth on the turntable with their hands; 'quick mixing', when a DJ moves from one record to another without any audible delay; break dancing, and body popping (both dance forms of extraordinary athleticism and originality); Adidas training shoes and tracksuits (although trade marks tend to go through waves of popularity); and the bright, intricate and highly stylized graffiti that customized many street corners and subway trains. As the popularity of rap and electro music increased in Britain in the second half of the Eighties, so did the number of adherents to hip hop styles.

HODGES, EDDIE Born on 5 March 1947, in Hattiesburg, Mississippi, Eddie Hodges first came to public attention as a contestant on the television game show *Name That Tune*. As a result of these appearances, he was offered a part in the Broadway musical *The Music Man* at the age of twelve, and later starred as Frank Sinatra's son in *A Hole in the Head*, in which he duetted with Sinatra on the Oscar-winning song, 'High Hopes'. In 1961, Hodges was signed to Cadence and his 'I'm Gonna Knock on Your Door' and 'Girls, Girls, Girls Are Made to Love' both made the Top 20 in 1961 and 1962 respectively. His freckle-faced, wholesome charm and kiddie tenor delighted sub-teen listeners and infuriated others. He also cut the original version of the Brook Brothers' British hit, 'Ain't Gonna Wash for a Week' and returned to the charts for the last time with a revival of **Gary 'U.S.' Bonds'** 'New Orleans' on Aurora in 1965.

HOLLAND, DOZIER AND HOLLAND During the mid-Sixties, a period known to some as the 'golden age of Motown', a vast percentage of the product emanating from the Detroit studios bore the composer and production credit legend 'Holland-Dozier-Holland'.

Lamont Dozier was born in Detroit on 16 June 1941 and raised in a musical environment; both parents sang and he joined his church choir at an early age. He made his recording debut at 15, with the Romeos, on the local Fox label in 1956, but the group soon split and Lamont went to New York, where he married and took a regular job. 1958 saw him back in Detroit, however, where he met Motown founder Berry Gordy through a childhood friend, Ty Hunter, who was signed to Anna Records. He started a solo recording career as Lamont Anthony on Anna and Melody, meeting little success, but as the Motown Corporation began to grow, so did Lamont's songwriting prowess, and in 1961 he met up with Brian Holland, then producing for the company with Robert Bateman – they'd produced the **Marvelettes'** 'Please Mr Postman'. Bateman left Motown, suggesting that Dozier team with Brian. Thus Holland and Dozier became a regular writing and production team, at which time Brian's brother, Eddie, was a hit artist with the company.

Eddie Holland, born in Detroit on 30 October 1939, dropped out of college to work for Berry Gordy's music publishing company, where he would sing demos of Gordy's songs, and later col-laborated as a writer himself. Impressed with Eddie's voice, Gordy signed him as an artist, with initial discs leased to United Artists. Soon afterwards Motown was formed, and Eddie's first release was 'Jamie', a heavily orchestrated beat ballad with a vocal style identical to that of **Jackie Wilson** (for whom he had sung demos). It was a Top 30 hit in 1962. Three of his next eight discs were small hits, by which time Eddie had teamed up with his brother and Lamont Dozier to write and produce. Brian (born in Detroit on 15 February 1941) was introduced to Berry Gordy by Eddie, and Gordy coached him as a writer and producer up to the time of the trio's collaboration.

From 1962, almost everything the trio touched turned to gold as they wrote and produced a long succession of hits for the **Supremes**, **Temptations**, **Four Tops**, **Marvin Gaye**, **Martha and the Vandellas** and the **Isley Brothers** as well as less renowned groups and performers within the Motown Corporation. However, passing years created some friction between them and Gordy, and in 1968 they quit Motown to form their own company with twin labels Invictus and Hot Wax.

In May 1969, the trio were legally restrained from operating pending a lawsuit in which Motown alleged breach of contract, but the matter was settled out of court, and Invictus/Hot Wax rapidly accrued success as **Chairmen of the Board**, **Freda Payne** and **Honey Cone** soared into the Top 10, the last-named gaining the company's first chart-topper with 'Want Ads' in 1971. Brian and Lamont returned to active recording themselves, scoring pop and R&B hits as a duo in 1972/73, but Lamont quit the Hollands in 1973 to sign as a solo act with ABC Records on the recommendation of his longtime friends, the **Four Tops**, and proceeded to record some fine albums with related hit singles. He later recorded for Warner Brothers and Columbia and undertook a number of independent production projects, among them the supervision of **Aretha Franklin**'s 1977 album *Sweet Passion*. *See also* **Motown**

HOLLIES An amalgamation of two other Manchester groups, the Deltas and the Dolphins, the Hollies were formed in 1962 and comprised Allan Clarke, vocals (born 15 April 1942); **Graham Nash**, guitar (2 February 1942); Don Rathbone, drums; Eric Haydock, bass; and Tony Hicks, lead guitar (16 December 1943). Their first two singles, 'Ain't That Just Like Me' (Parlophone) and 'Searchin'', were two old **Coasters'** numbers and while the second made the Top 20 in 1963, it was 'Stay' (the **Maurice Williams and the Zodiacs** number) which started their string of chart entries that, amongst British groups, only the **Beatles** could rival.

Without being as accomplished as musicians or songwriters as the Beatles, and lacking a strong image, the Hollies' success was based on their knack of choosing commercial songs and their unmistakable way of singing them; Clarke's voice and Nash's tight harmonies were inimitable. After successes with 'Just One Look', 'Here I Go Again', 'We're Through' (1964), 'Yes I Will', 'I'm Alive' (their first British Number 1), 'Look Through Any Window' (1965), they had their first relative failure with a cover of **George Harrison**'s 'If I Needed Someone', which only just scraped into the British Top 20. After 'I Can't Let Go' (a Number 2 in early 1966) Eric Haydock left the group to be replaced by ex-Dolphins' bassist Bernie Calvert (16 September 1944) and in the meantime **Jack Bruce** played bass on the 'After the Fox' session. This period, prior to the departure of Graham Nash, saw the group at their peak. They were masters of the singles medium and their lyrics – they were writing their own songs by now – without ever being as outrageously gimmicky as **Dave Dee** and company, for example, were carefully constructed vignettes describing people and situations that had a real charm and humour of their own – 'Bus Stop' (the song that finally established them in America, on Imperial), 'Stop, Stop, Stop' (1966), 'On a Carousel', 'Carrie Anne', 'King Midas in Reverse' (1967) and 'Jennifer Eccles' (1968).

The Hollies' success, however, lay almost exclusively in the singles market. Although their first album, *Stay with the Hollies* (Parlophone, 1964), sold well, their subsequent album releases never matched their singles sales. It was possibly their lack of image and uniformity of style that resulted in their missing the psychedelic flower-power boom of 1967. Furthermore, Tony Hicks was phased out of the group at a time when guitar heroes were just becoming fashionable. None the less, the albums of that year, *Evolution* and *Butterfly*, still contain superb examples of the much-overlooked songwriting team of Clarke, Hicks and Nash.

At this stage, the group lost something of its direction and finally Graham Nash, having already expressed his dissatisfaction with 'Jennifer Eccles' ('I want to make records that say something'), decided to quit for California and eventual superstardom with **Crosby, Stills, Nash and Young**. Ex-**Swinging Blue Jean**, Terry Sylvester (born 8 January, 1945), replaced Nash but something of the balance of the Hollies was destroyed. They still chose their singles well – often with better results in America than Britain, e.g. 'Long Cool Woman' – but they could never decide on albums whether they were still a pop group or a rock band.

In 1971, Clarke, too, left them to pursue a more fashionable career as a solo artist. He made three albums that failed to establish him and then rejoined the group, replacing temporary recruit Michael Rickfors, in 1973. A giant hit, 'The Air That I Breathe', followed a year later, since when the group has stayed together, playing cabaret venues and scoring the occasional hit.

HOLLOWAY, BRENDA Born on
21 June 1946 in Atascadero, California, Brenda Holloway studied classical violin before signing as a singer to Motown for whom she recorded the classic slow soul ballad 'Every Little Bit Hurts', which featured the piano of Lincoln Mayorga and, more importantly, was the company's first West Coast-produced hit: it reached Number 13 in the US in 1964. Lesser hits included 'When I'm Gone' and her own composition, 'You've Made Me So Very Happy', later a much bigger success for **Blood, Sweat and Tears**. She retired in the late Sixties, returning only for occasional sessions with **Joe Cocker** and records with the San Remo Strings.

HOLLY, BUDDY One of the pivotal
figures in the development of rock music, Buddy Holly was born on 7 September 1936 in Lubbock, Texas, and christened Charles Hardin Holley. Lubbock's geographical position meant that Holly would have heard hillbilly, Mexican and black music on the radio during his formative years; this cosmopolitan musical background was to prove vital to the versatility he later displayed in his own work.

As a youngster he took up the violin, but soon changed to guitar. He showed an early interest in country and western, and while still at school had his own show on KDAV, the local radio station. He was partnered by **Bob Montgomery**, and in 1954 they made some hillbilly demo records which were posthumously issued as *Holly in the Hills*. Together with bass-player Larry Welborn, Buddy and Bob would

Holly's untimely death in 1959 created a legend, consigning him to an eternal youth while other Fifties rockers lived on to age and decline

sometimes fill the 'local talent' spot when travelling package shows visited the area. As a result of this exposure, and with help from KDAV disc-jockey Dave Stone, Nashville agent Eddie Crandall and publisher Jim Denny, Buddy Holly was signed to Decca in 1956 to cut some singles in Nashville. Two were released without success, and before his contract with Decca was up Holly was beginning to look elsewhere, guessing that the option would not be renewed.

Although Decca handled Holly rather insensitively (i.e. no more nor less off-handedly than any other bright young hopeful) these early sessions did produce at least two Holly classics, 'Midnight Shift' and 'Rock Around with Ollie Vee', and Holly worked with musicians like Sonny Curtis and Jerry Allison who were later to be involved in the **Crickets**. The tapes were eventually issued as *That'll Be The Day*. Allison and Holly had been schoolfriends, and had often played together as a drum/guitar duo. The limitations of this line-up helped forge their style; the smooth switch from rhythm to lead in Buddy's guitar-playing, the versatility of Jerry's drumming. In 1955, when the two started playing together professionally, it was still unusual to find drums in a country line-up.

Soon after his last Decca session, Holly started working at **Norman Petty**'s studio in Clovis, New Mexico. Petty, who was also a middle-of-the-road band leader, was a pioneer of the small, independent recording studio; he was also unusual in that he charged per song rather than per hour, which put less pressure on musicians. Holly, Allison and Welborn, together with a vocal quartet that included Cricket-to-be Niki Sullivan, recorded 'That'll Be the Day' and 'I'm Looking for Someone to Love' in February 1957. Petty first submitted the songs to Roulette in New York, since they had already had hits originating from his studio with **Buddy Knox** and Jimmy Bowen. They weren't interested, but Holly and the Crickets were soon signed by Coral. The record reached Number 3 in America and Number 1 in Britain, and was followed with almost equal success by 'Oh Boy'/ 'Not Fade Away'. By this time, Joe Mauldin had become the Crickets' bass-player, with Niki Sullivan on rhythm guitar.

Before long Petty, who had quickly assumed a managerial position, began to record Holly solo as well as with the Crickets, though the musicians were often the same. Holly's first hit under his own name was 'Peggy Sue', late in

1957, followed in Britain by 'Listen To Me' and in both countries by 'Rave On' and the **Bobby Darin** number 'Early in the Morning' (by mid-1958, Holly had begun to record in New York without the Crickets, as well as in Clovis).

After a British tour with the Crickets in that year, Holly married Maria Elena Santiago and moved to New York. The rest of the Crickets didn't want to make the move and so split from Holly. This was probably inevitable. Petty was trying to broaden Holly's career and one of the first results was to record him with the Dick Jacobs Orchestra (notably 'It Doesn't Matter Anymore'). Holly's backing group on live dates at this time included Tommy Allsup, whom he had brought into the Crickets earlier to play lead guitar (it is a mistake to assume that Holly fulfilled this role on all his records). Other notable musicians with whom he worked at this time were saxophonist King Curtis, and **Waylon Jennings**, whose first solo record, 'Jole Blon', was produced by Buddy Holly.

Early in 1959, Holly's career was at a crossroads. In spite of the significant early impact both with the Crickets and as a solo performer, and in spite of his own single-minded attitude towards success and the attempts he was making to create the basis for a long career, there was little in strict commercial terms to suggest (except with hindsight) that he was any different from many other rock performers of the time. It is, of course, inconceivable that, had he lived, he would not have risen further from the pack and still be accorded the respect that his prolific few years have so justly earned for him. He died on 3 February 1959, together with **Ritchie Valens** and the **Big Bopper** when their plane crashed soon after taking off from Mason City airport in Iowa, *en route* between package-tour concerts in Clear Lake, Iowa, and Fargo, North Dakota. His current record, 'Heartbeat', was barely making an impact on the Hot 100.

The first posthumous release, 'It Doesn't Matter Anymore'/'Raining in My Heart', was a huge hit in both America and Britain. And in Britain a series of processed tapes put out by Norman Petty kept Holly's name in the charts until the mid-Sixties, while an album of his best-known tracks was still in the Top 10 of the budget-price charts ten years later.

Buddy Holly said 'We owe it all to Elvis'. Countless stars of the Sixties owe a similar debt to Holly. He was one of the two great singer/songwriter/ musicians of the pop Fifties (the other being **Chuck Berry**). He was a pioneer

of the subsequently-standard two-guitars/bass/drums line-up, and of double-tracking. Almost anything that a pop song can say was said in the late Fifties by Buddy Holly, who was only twenty-two years old when he died. *See also* the **Crickets**

HOLMAN, EDDIE Soul balladeer Eddie Holman's major moment of chart fame came in 1969, with the US Number 2 success of 'Hey There Lonely Girl' (originally a hit in 1963 for **Ruby and the Romantics**). Born in Norfolk, Virginia, in 1946 he had formal vocal training at the Victoria School of Music and Art in New York. His recording career began in 1965, with the soul hit 'This Can't Be True', and further releases like 'I Love You', 'It's All in the Game', 'I'm Not Gonna Give Up' and 'Since I Don't Have You' consolidated his reputation within black music circles. After the impact of 'Hey There Lonely Girl' – which repeated its US success in the UK some five years later, Holman identified himself solidly with Philadelphia's 'Philly Sound' and recorded for the city's GSF label. By 1977, he was trying his luck in the disco field and completing an album, *A Night to Remember*, for the Salsoul label.

HOLT, JOHN Kingston-born John Holt emerged as one of Jamaica's top music stars in the late Sixties, after a period as lead vocalist with the heavily soul-influenced Paragons. Between 1964 and 1966, the Paragons recorded numerous local hits including 'Wear You to the Ball' and 'Love at Last' for Coxsone Dodd's Studio One label, but their switch to producer Duke Reid coincided with a move into the new rock-steady field that in turn resulted in a run of sixteen Jamaican Number 1 hits. Holt left the group in 1968 and made an immediate impact with a series of smooth, sentimental rock-steady ballads, including 'Let's Build Our Dreams' (produced by Duke Reid), 'Love I Can Feel' (produced by Coxsone Dodd) and 'Close to Me' (a **Prince Buster** production). By the mid-Seventies, Holt had begun to make some real impact internationally: his gentle reggae version of **Kris Kristofferson**'s 'Help Me Make It Through the Night' brought him his first UK hit in late 1974. His albums and singles continued to sell well to Jamaican and British reggae record-buyers right into the Eighties. Notable John Holt albums include *One Thousand Volts of Holt* (1974), *Pledging My Love* (1975) and *Up Park Camp* (1975).

HOLZMAN, JAC Jac Holzman founded **Elektra Records** in 1950 and remained its chief executive until 1973. Trained as an engineer, Holzman at first ran virtually a one-man operation, recording folk singers like Jean Ritchie and Theodore Bikel, who had been blacklisted in the early Fifties. The company grew with the folk revival and Holzman recorded **Judy Collins**, **Tom Paxton** and the **Paul Butterfield Blues Band** among many others. Elektra's sister label, Nonesuch, also developed its catalogue of classical and ethnic recordings. During the Sixties, Holzman gradually shifted his attention from East Coast folk to West Coast rock, signing Los Angeles groups **Love** and the **Doors**. In the Seventies, **Carly Simon** and **Bread** were successful Elektra signings, though by this time the exclusive mystique which had attached to the label in earlier years had all but disappeared. In 1970, the company was taken over by the Kinney Corporation and three years later grouped together with Asylum Records as a division of the massive Warner Communications Inc. The new operation was headed by Asylum's David Geffen, while Holzman became senior vice-president of the parent company, in charge of developing quadrophonic sound systems. *See also* **Elektra Records**

HONEY CONE An all-female soul trio of the early Seventies, Honey Cone comprised Carolyn Willis (born in Los Angeles in 1946), Edna Wright (born in Los Angeles in 1944), and Shellie Clark (born in Brooklyn, New York, in 1943). All had previously worked as session-singers or had sung in various line-ups before being put together as a backing group for an Andy Williams television show in 1969: Willis had toured with **Bob B. Soxx and the Blue Jeans**; Wright had sung on sessions for the **Righteous Brothers** and had been a member of **Ray Charles**' Raelettes; while Clark had backed **Ike and Tina Turner** as one of the Ikettes. As Honey Cone, the trio signed in 1970 to the Hot Wax label just formed by the ex-Motown team of **Holland, Dozier and Holland** and charted a year later with the powerful 'Wants Ads' (a US Number 1), 'Stick-Up' and 'One Monkey Don't Stop No Show'. 'The Day I Found Myself' followed in 1972. Three albums and a handful of minor singles successes later, the group disbanded and the individual members returned to session work. In 1976, Carolyn Willis featured prominently on **Seals and Crofts**' US Top 10 hit, 'Get Closer'.

HOOKER, JOHN LEE A leading figure in the mid-Sixties blues boom, John Lee Hooker was born on 22 August 1917, in Clarksdale, Mississippi. He moved to Memphis in his teens and started playing guitar with bluesmen like Robert Nighthawk. In 1943 he moved to Detroit, where five years later he signed to the Modern label. His first session produced the million-selling single 'Boogie Chillen', featuring just Hooker's vocals and throbbing electric guitar. It was an excellent introduction to his hypnotic, Afro-American rhythms which have since become his trademark. He followed up with 'Driftin'' and 'Hobo Blues' – two more unaccompanied numbers. Although contracted to Modern, he recorded under such pseudonyms as Texas Slim and Johnny Williams for Chess, King, DeLuxe and Chance.

In 1955, Hooker officially switched labels to the Chicago-based Vee Jay company, where he made some of his best sides. They included 'Maudie', 'Crawlin' King Snake', 'Tupelo', 'Birmingham Blues' and 'I'm in the Mood', which had been a huge R&B hit for him when he first recorded it for Modern in 1951. As the Sixties progressed, Hooker's sound became even more urbanized, often featuring a horn section and girl singers. This period produced his biggest hits – 'Boom Boom' and 'Dimples', which was even a minor success in the British pop charts in 1964. Many rock bands have covered Hooker songs including the **Animals** ('I'm Mad Again') and the **J. Geils Band** ('Serve You Right to Suffer').

HOPKIN, MARY While watching TV's *Opportunity Knocks*, Twiggy took a liking to an angelic-looking Welsh folk singer named Mary Hopkin, and recommended her talents to **Paul McCartney**. He signed her to Apple, and produced her first record, 'Those Were the Days', which reached Number 1 in the UK and Number 2 in the US in 1968. Apple promoted their star (born in Pontardawe, Glamorgan, on 3 May 1950) as a paragon of chapel-bred virtue, and she was consequently maligned in the press. This did not prevent her from achieving further hits over the next year; but the crunch came when she was sent out on the road and revealed her lack of stage presence. Nevertheless, she sang Britain's entry in 1970's Eurovision Song Contest ('Knock Knock Who's There?', a Number 2 hit in the UK) and seemed to be heading for MOR stardom, until she decided to retire from performing on

her marriage to producer Tony Visconti. Apart from occasional session work and the odd television appearance, she has since stayed out of the pop limelight.

HOPKINS, LIGHTNIN' Lightnin' Hopkins remains many people's idea of what a blues-singer should be: an endlessly inventive folk-poet, whose imagination is touched by almost everything but whose singing and playing express nothing but the blues. And this, despite some 30 years of performing and recording, and all the pressures that might have made him something else, he unswervingly was throughout his lifetime. But he was not, outside his own community, very obviously influential on either American or British rock; his blues, sung by others, are not self-sustaining, as are many of those by Chicago blues artists.

His early recordings, in the Forties and Fifties, were characterized by thunderous amplification, but his first ventures into a different market, with acoustic guitar, compensated in subtlety for what they lost in force (e.g. the Folkways and some Bluesville albums). Later sessions placed him with accompanying groups, rarely successfully, though his album for Jewel was an exception. Through all these records he balanced slow blues with vivid boogies, occasionally leaving his guitar to essay an idiosyncratic piano style.

Born in Centerville, Texas, in 1912, he spent most of his life in Houston, and his refusal to extract himself from that milieu is the chief reason for his undiminished authenticity as an observer, through the blues, of black life. He died in 1986.

HORN, TREVOR Undoubtedly the most influential record producer of the 1980s, Trevor Horn did more than anyone to define the bright, smooth and synthetic sound that characterized Eighties pop. He combined the insight and instinct of a musician with complete mastery of studio technology to instil his work with a special clinical vibrancy that none could equal.

Horn first made his name as half of electro-popsters **Buggles** in 1979, and then went on to have a short-term liaison with art-rockers **Yes**. He enjoyed limited success as a musician, but it was as a producer that he discovered his greatest talents and acquired the producer/mentor status that had not been seen since the Sixties and the likes of **Phil Spector**.

Turning his hand to winsome pop

duo **Dollar**, he fashioned for them an irresistible dance sound that scored a succession of hits from 1979–82. With **ABC** he produced the classic Eighties pop album, *Lexicon of Love* (1982), embellishing their pedestrian pop-funk with dramatic, crashing drum treatments and flurries of epic strings. Horn also worked with that other famous music mentor, **Malcolm McLaren**, on his *Duck Rock* (1983) album.

Horn's greatest achievements came with the formation of ZTT, a label he formed with ex-journalist Paul Morley, and his production work for **Frankie Goes to Hollywood** in 1984. Horn took an unremarkable punk/funk band from Liverpool and, with a stroke of genius, turned them into one of the hardest sounding white funk outfits around. The towering strength of the bass and drum sounds on the songs 'Relax' and 'Two Tribes' made them huge international hits and milestones in the history of dance music.

Unfortunately, on occasion, Horn's expertise in the studio has been used to excess, as when he devised several extended (and completely gratuitous) remixes of the Frankie singles, which did wonders for sales but little for his reputation. With the completely over-the-top special effects gimmickry on Frankie's *Welcome to the Pleasure Dome* LP, his interventions even bordered on the annoying. Nevertheless, Horn remains one of the most sought-after producers in the world.

HORTON, JOHNNY Killed in a Texas automobile crash in November 1960, Johnny Horton was at the height of his popularity, following a string of pop hits with country-based story and saga songs like 'Springtime in Alaska', 'North to Alaska', 'Battle of New Orleans' and 'Sink the Bismarck'. Despite the wide appeal of these songs' lyrical content, he retained many elements of conventional acoustic country instrumentation and was, in retrospect, a significant artist in breaking down the rigid categorization between country and popular singers.

Born in Tyler, Texas, on 30 April 1927, Horton started his career under the title of the 'Singing Fisherman' on KLTV, Tyler, and graduated in 1948 to a starring spot on Shreveport's KWKH country shows with **Hank Williams** and **Jim Reeves**. He recorded first with Mercury and Dot before successfully transferring to Columbia, gaining rockabilly-influenced country hits on 'Honky Tonk Man' and 'Honky Tonk Hardwood Floor', prior to his success in the pop charts.

Hot Chocolate on Top of the Pops

HOT CHOCOLATE The origins of Hot Chocolate, one of Britain's most successful soul/dance bands, lay in the songwriting team of Tony Wilson and Errol Brown. The duo began their career in 1969 supplying songs for the **Beatles**' short-lived Apple label. They composed **Mary Hopkin**'s 1970 Top 20 hit 'Think About Christmas', and 'Bet Yer Life I Do' for **Herman's Hermits**. The collapse of Apple saw them move over to **Mickie Most**'s RAK Records where they became recording artists in their own right, under the name of Hot Chocolate. With Most as producer they came up with 'Love Is Life', a Top 10 hit in August 1970. This marked the start of a fruitful relationship with RAK which generated twelve Top 10 hits. A full group was assembled in order that live dates could be undertaken: Patrick Olive (congas), Larry Ferguson (keyboards), Harvey Hinsley (guitar) and Tony Connor (drums) joined Wilson on bass with Brown vocalizing.

In November 1975 Wilson left the group, leaving Brown as the sole driving force within the band. Wilson's departure proved less of a problem than expected; Olive replaced him on bass and the hits continued, with 'You Sexy Thing' reaching Number 2 at the end of 1975. By this time Hot Chocolate was beginning to break into the American market and both 'You Sexy Thing' and 'Every 1's A Winner' (1978) were certified as million sellers. In the UK they finally topped the chart in the summer of 1977 with 'So You Win Again'. In early 1987, 'You Sexy Thing' was re-released and shot to Number 10 in the charts. However, this success coincided with Brown's decision to leave the band and pursue a solo career.

HOUSEMARTINS Side-by-side with the **Smiths**, the Housemartins took their rousing, melodic brand of pop into the 'hit' category and gave the beleaguered independent labels the rare opportunity to break the majors' dominant grip on the UK charts, as well as finding great success throughout Europe.

Though not all the members originally came from Hull, the Housemartins started to come together in that city when singer Paul Heaton (born 9 May 1962) met guitarist Stan Cullimore (6 April 1962) early in 1984 when they discovered that they lived seven doors away from each other. Drummer Hugh Whitaker (18 May 1961) joined shortly after as did original bass-player Ted Key. They impressed greatly as a live act with their lively grasp of melody and the rare attribute of having four members who could all sing, and allied to their great sense of fun, the Housemartins were a much-sought-after band. They eventually signed to Go! Discs, the same small independent label as **Billy Bragg**, in late '84.

Though they received rave notices, it wasn't until their third single, 'Happy Hour', that the band broke into the pop charts. It reached the UK Number 3 spot in June 1986 (by which time new bassist Norman Cook, born 31 July 1963, had joined) and was followed by 'Think for a Minute' (UK Top 20) and a Number 1 with their a cappella version of the **Isley Brothers**' 'Caravan of Love'. The album, *London 0 Hull 4* went platinum, establishing the band as a leading UK act. The band went into 1987 looking to conquer the US market.

HOWARD, KEN AND BLAIKLEY, ALAN

After **Mickie Most**, Ken Howard and Alan Blaikley were the most successful British pop operators of the mid-Sixties. They came into the business from an intellectual background (university and the BBC) but their first success was with the Honeycombs, a straightforward pop group whom they discovered in a pub in London's Balls Pond Road and took to Number 1 in 1964 with 'Have I The Right?' (on Pye). In America it reached Number 5 on Interphon. The Honeycombs split after a couple of follow-ups and Howard and Blaikley turned their attention to **Dave Dee, Dozy, Beaky, Mick and Tich**, for whom they wrote ten successive Top 20 hits, (on Fontana) between 1966 and 1968.

The secret of DDDBMT's success was not the songs as such (clever variations on a basic beat, lots of innuendo – 'Bend It' was the best) but the image Howard and Blaikley created for them: flash, young, sexy, noisy. DDDBMT were the pop expression of mod teenage culture: calculated rebellion, safe but never family entertainment. By 1968 this teenage generation had grown up and Howard and Blaikley had to change tack: they gave DDDBMT more sophisticated songs (notably 'Legend of Xanadu', their only Number 1) and responded to the hippy atmosphere of 1967 with the **Herd**'s 'From the Underworld' (Fontana), an elaborate arrangement of hippy clichés. They continued with both groups but by the Seventies their time had passed and their attempts to get into rock (Flaming Youth's concept album, *Arc*, and **Matthew's Southern Comfort**'s first album) enjoyed a critical but not a popular success.

Howard and Blaikley wrote seventeen Top 20 singles in their time but their importance was more commercial than musical: they were among the first British businessmen to take teenage pop seriously. Moving out of pop in the mid-Seventies, they collaborated with Melvyn Bragg on an unsuccessful West End musical, *Mardi Gras*, and became involved with television work: Howard composed the theme to ITV's *The Flame Trees of Thika* and, in 1985, wrote and produced *John Lennon*, a BBC-TV dramatization of Lennon's life.

HOWLIN' WOLF

One of the best-known names in post-war blues, Howlin' Wolf was born in Aberdeen, Mississippi, on 10 June 1910, as Chester Arthur Burnett. He learnt guitar (and his guttural 'howlin'' vocal style) from country bluesman Charley Patton and harmonica from **Sonny Boy Williamson** (Rice Miller). In 1948, Wolf was spotted performing in a Memphis club by Ike Turner, who subsequently signed him to the Modern label. Rival sessions with other companies followed, and he was recorded by Sam Phillips for Sun and eventually by the Chess brothers.

Wolf's 270lb frame and aggressive demeanour became well-known in the blues clubs of Chicago, his often suggestive stage-act blending perfectly with his choice of songs – usually reflecting either infidelity or sexual prowess. All his major hits were cut between 1954 and 1964 at the Chess studios in Chicago and, more often than not, featured the excellent Hubert Sumlin on lead guitar. Wolf's work has made a significant impact on the rock world, prompting dozens of cover versions of his hits, including 'Smokestack Lightning' (**Yardbirds**, **Manfred Mann**), 'Spoonful' (**Cream**, **Ten Years After**), 'Little Red Rooster' (**Rolling Stones**), 'I Ain't Superstitious' (**Rod Stewart/Jeff Beck**, Savoy Brown), 'Back Door Man' (**Doors**), 'Killin' Floor' (**Electric Flag**) and 'How Many More Years?' (**Little Feat**).

In 1972, Wolf came to London to record an album at the request of the Rolling Stones. On the session were such rock luminaries as **Eric Clapton**, **Ringo Starr**, **Stevie Winwood**, plus several of the Stones themselves. He died on 10 January 1976.

H. P. LOVECRAFT

Formed in Chicago in 1966, H. P. Lovecraft comprised George Edwards, guitar; Dave Michaels, keyboards; Tony Cavallari, lead guitar; Mike Tegza, drums and Gerry McGeorge, ex-**Shadows of Knight**, bass, who was later replaced by Jeffrey Boylan. All shared vocals. They made their earliest recording in February 1967 – a version of the **Troggs**' 'Anyway That You Want Me' (on the album *Early Chicago*) which featured only Edwards and Michaels plus three of Chicago's Roving Kind. *H. P. Lovecraft* later that year established them on the West Coast. The highpoint of the album was 'The White Ship', from an early story written by their namesake, lingering and haunting, beautifully sung and sympathetically arranged. *H. P. Lovecraft II*, which followed their move to Los Angeles, was their acid album, hypnotic and powerful, the psychedelics usually superfluous. There were no further recordings, though Tegza later formed Lovecraft and produced the lame *Valleys of the Moon*.

HUDSON FORD

Richard Hudson and John Ford, both born in London in 1948, played in Elmer Gantry's Velvet Opera before joining the **Strawbs** in 1969. They were between them responsible for much of the band's more commercial material, including their biggest hit 'Part of the Union' in 1973, but musical differences led them to quit after the Strawbs' second American tour in 1973. Their first single together, 'Pick Up the Pieces', was tailor-made chart material, but subsequent releases failed to emulate its UK Top 10 success. They recorded three albums before breaking with their label, A&M, in 1975, but re-emerged four years later as the Monks, a pseudo punk rock band. A single, 'Nice Legs, Shame About the Face', became a minor novelty hit.

HUDSON, KEITH

Born in Trenchtown, Jamaica, on 18 March 1949, Keith Hudson was an important figure in the development of reggae in the late Sixties. His production work for artists like **John Holt**, **Delroy Wilson** and **Ken Boothe** was mainstream in orientation, but he established his reputation as an experimental, 'rebel' producer with his early Seventies productions for **U Roy**, **Big Youth** and **Dennis Al Capone**. From 1973 onwards, Hudson began recording in his own right and achieved healthy sales with two widely acclaimed 'message' albums, *Torch of Freedom* and *Flesh Off My Bones*, and a dub set, *Pick a Dub*. He died of cancer on 14 November 1984, in New York.

HUGO AND LUIGI

Hugo and Luigi first gained public acclaim as recording artists when 'Young Abe Lincoln' was a small pop hit on Mercury in 1955. New York Italians, Hugo Peretti and Luigi Creatore moved into exclusive circles in 1957, buying Roulette Records from **George Goldner**, handling producing and writing duties (they wrote under the pseudonym Mark Markwell) and scoring hits including **Jimmy Rodgers**' 1957 million-seller 'Falling in Love Again'. In 1959 they left Roulette to Morris Levy and Henry Glover, moving to RCA where they hit as artists ('La Plume de Ma Tante') and also produced material for such as the **Isley Brothers** (1959 million-seller 'Shout') and **Sam Cooke**. The duo remained with RCA for some years, producing much of Cooke's material, and came to the fore again in 1973 as vice-presidents of Avco Records, where they took over writing and producing for the **Stylistics**. Peretti died in 1986.

HUMAN LEAGUE A hugely successful electro-pop chart band worldwide, the Human League originally came together at the experimental stages of electronic music. Ian Marsh and Martyn Ware, two Sheffield computer operators turned synth players, formed the group with vocalist Philip Oakey, a plastic surgery hospital porter, in June 1977. They all shared a complete lack of musical expertise, as did the final recruit, visual director Adrian Wright, who completed the first line-up and provided the on-stage imagery.

The band developed as innovators both in live performance, with Wright's back-drops complementing the musical ideas, and on record with the landmark singles 'Being Boiled/Circus of Death' and the 12-inch 'The Dignity of Labour' (both on the independent Edinburgh label Fast Product). As a result, the music papers latched on to them and by April 1979 they had been signed to Virgin Records, who released two albums *Reproduction* (1979) and *Travelogue* (1980), and several singles. Although these served to establish the Human League as one of the pioneering British modern electronic bands, and accumulated considerable critical approval, they had only limited commercial success.

At the end of 1980, only a week before they were due to embark on a European tour, Ware and Marsh left to form **Heaven 17**, leaving Wright and Oakey to take care of Human League. Ian Burden (an old friend) was dragged in and two 17-year-old girls, Joanne Catherall and Susanne Sulley, neither of whom had sung professionally before, were recruited from the dance floor of a Sheffield nightclub. Jo Callis (from Scottish punk band the Rezillos) later joined to make the band into a six-piece.

This new line-up gelled straight away, scoring four UK hit singles in 1981, including the worldwide smash single 'Don't You Want Me', and releasing the album *Dare* to score a Number 1 single and album in the US and sell in large quantities all over the world. They toured Europe, USA and Japan to consolidate their success and then took a long rest.

Since 1982, releases from the Human League have been few and far between, with only one new album, *Hysteria* in 1984 (*Love and Dancing* was an instrumental version of *Dare*) and a handful of singles, all selling well and keeping the group very much in the pop mainstream. In 1986, they produced a further album called, *Crash*, which spawned the successful UK hit single, 'Human'.

HUMBLE PIE Formed in 1969 in the then fashionable 'supergroup' manner, Humble Pie comprised **Peter Frampton**, guitar, vocals (born on 22 April 1950 in Beckenham, Kent) from the **Herd**; Steve Marriott, guitar, vocals (born on 30 January 1947 in London) from the **Small Faces**; Greg Ridley, bass, vocals (23 October 1947) from **Spooky Tooth**, and Jerry Shirley, drums (4 February 1952). Humble Pie wavered between the straightforward rock style of their first single, 'Natural Born Bugie' (Immediate, 1969), and the lightweight tastes of Frampton until, during a period of extensive American work, Marriott rediscovered his former confidence and began to dominate the group, as *Live at the Fillmore* (A&M, 1971) demonstrated. Frampton quit and was replaced by guitarist Dave 'Clem' Clempson (born 5 September 1949) from **Colosseum** as the music grew steadily heavier, apart from a brief flirtation into soul with the addition of a vocal trio, the Blackberries (Clydie King, Venetta Fields, and Billie Barnum). The band, always at its best on stage, where Marriott's audience control and showmanship remained superb, broke up in 1974. Marriott formed Steve Marriott's All Stars out of its ashes in 1975, while Shirley formed Natural Gas in Los Angeles and Clempson joined Greenslade and then Strange Brew, which featured Ridley and Cozy Powell, drums (ex-**Jeff Beck**), in its line-up. After a short spell in a reunited Small Faces in 1977, Marriott re-formed Humble Pie with Shirley and another Jeff Beck acolyte, singer Bobby Tench. They toured the US in the early Eighties but broke up after two albums, *On to Victory* (Atlantic, 1980) and *Go for the Throat* (1981). *See also* **Peter Frampton**

HUNTER, IVORY JOE Blues singer Ivory Joe Hunter, born at Kirbyville, Texas, in 1914, was first recorded by **Alan Lomax** for the Library of Congress in 1933. Moving to Los Angeles, he recorded for a number of small labels, having R&B hits with 'Blues at Sunrise' (on his own label, Ivory) and 'Pretty Mama Blues' (Pacific). In 1947, a King contract

Human League were originally a highly experimental multi-media group, but they achieved commercial success as a more orthodox pop outfit

resulted in further hits: 'Guess Who', 'Landlord Blues' and 'I Quit My Pretty Mama'. Moving to MGM, Hunter's successes included 'I Almost Lost My Mind' (Number 1, in the R&B chart in 1950) and 'I Need You So'.

Having joined Atlantic, Hunter broke into the rock'n'roll market in 1956 with a Top 20 hit, 'Since I Met You Baby'. His own subsequent discs for Dot, Capitol and Veep sold poorly, but **Nat Cole**, the **Five Keys**, **Pat Boone** and **Elvis Presley** all did well with his songs. Hunter subsequently based himself in Nashville where, as a member of the *Grand Ole Opry*, he had hopes of a fresh career in country music, the field with which his soulful blues ballads and understated barrelhouse piano had close affiliations. He died of cancer in a Memphis hospital on 8 November 1974.

HYLAND, BRIAN Born on 12 November 1944, in Queens, New York, Brian Hyland was only 15 when his recording of the Paul Vance and Lee Pockriss song, 'Itsy Bitsy Teeny Weeny Yellow Polka Dot Bikini' on Leader went to the top of the Hot 100. A gimmick record reminiscent of Paul Evans' 'Seven Little Girls', it was followed by 'Lop-Sided, Overloaded and It Wiggled When I Rode It'. 'Let Me Belong to You' was more successful a year later and in 1962 he had two straight Top 10 entries on ABC, 'Ginny Come Lately' and 'Sealed with a Kiss' – a Top 10 hit again in Britain when reissued in 1975 – both controlled exercises in teen *angst*. This was the high point of Hyland's career, though he has continued recording with ABC, Philips, Dot – on which he had a Top 20 hit with the **Snuff Garrett**-produced and **Leon Russell**-arranged 'The Joker Went Wild' in 1966 – and Uni, with whom he had his last hit, 'Gypsy Woman' in 1970.

I

IAN, JANIS Born Janis Eddy Fink in New York City on 7 May 1951, Janis Ian effectively had two careers – as a young and angry Greenwich Village-based folk singer in the mid-Sixties, and as a mature, intense singer/songwriter in the mid-Seventies. She was brought up in New Jersey and attended the Manhattan High School of Music and Art. *Broadside* magazine published her first song, 'Hair of Spun Gold' in 1964, and she produced shock waves when

she first performed at a *Broadside Hoot* at the Village Gate. At only 15, she signed to MGM and recorded 'Society's Child', a bitter personal protest at the hypocrisy of the older generation in the face of an inter-racial relationship. An eponymous album full of angry 'generation gap' songs followed in 1967 – and for a writer of her age they showed astonishing maturity. After a couple of years performing, she quit and moved to Philadelphia and then California to write songs for others.

She re-emerged in 1974 with *Stars* (Columbia), which contained her version of the song 'Jesse', a minor hit for **Roberta Flack** during the previous year. *Between The Lines* (1975) was a platinum album and included the Number 3 hit in the US, 'At Seventeen', for which she won a Grammy award for Best Female Vocal. She has recorded consistently since, though with less spectacular success.

IDOL, BILLY Born William Broad in Middlesex on 30 November 1955, Billy Idol first found fame as the lead singer with punks **Generation X**, but it was as a solo singer that he had his

Singer Billy Idol emerged from punk as a stateside superstar

biggest success, building up a teen following in the US that rivalled **Duran Duran**'s.

When Generation X finally split up in 1981, Idol headed for New York and didn't re-emerge until 1982, with a new batch of songs and a thirst for success. With guitarist Steve Stevens, he recorded a mini-LP *Don't Stop*. It got played in the clubs, but not on US radio, although the response was sufficient to inspire the album, *Billy Idol* (1982), which gave Idol his first US hit single, 'Hot in the City', which reached Number 23.

Further hit singles followed, and then a second album, *Rebel Yell* in 1983, and aided by extensive exposure on MTV, his glamorous punk image and a danceable fusion of rock and pop won over a new, younger audience. By 1985 the LP had sold nearly two million copies in the US and Idol, the superstar, was playing to packed stadiums from coast-to-coast. For a while the UK was indifferent to Idol-fever with a solitary Top 20 hit, 'Eyes Without a Face', in 1984, but a year later 'White Wedding' crashed into the UK Top 10, two years after it had been a hit in America.

IFIELD, FRANK Britain's most popular balladeer of the early Sixties, Frank Ifield was born in Coventry, Warwickshire, on 30 November 1936 but spent his childhood and teens in Australia. Returning to the UK in 1959, he was signed by EMI's Columbia label and recorded by Norrie Paramor, whose arrangements and productions played up Ifield's Slim Whitman-like yodel. Most of Ifield's hits were little more than MOR fare, enlivened by country-styled harmonica breaks that were mimicked by the **Beatles** on their early singles (notably 'Please Please Me' and 'From Me to You'), but his output included some interesting reworkings of standards like 'I Remember You', 'The Wayward Wind' and the **Hank Williams** favourite, 'Lovesick Blues'. He was the first-ever UK artist to enjoy a run of three consecutive British Number Ones (beginning with 'I Remember You' in 1962), but his chart career went into decline around 1964 and caused Ifield to concentrate almost exclusively on overseas markets like mainland Europe and Australia itself, where his popularity held firm for some years. In the Seventies, Ifield returned to performing the country music that had in fact always been his first love, making a number of appearances both at British country festivals and on television.

IMAGINATION Formed in 1981, black trio Imagination became the most popular British dance group of the early Eighties with a string of bass-heavy club favourites including several UK hits. Bedecked in deliberately over-the-top glam outfits, singer Lee John's clean falsetto trilled to great effect over the dense rhythms of Ashley Ingram (drums) and Errol Kennedy (bass).

Imagination came together after several chance encounters around the UK gig circuit, finally recording a demo that included 'Body Talk', the song that clinched them a contract and became their first UK hit, making Number 4 in May 1981. Their flamboyant image and good humour served them well on TV appearances and they quickly became media favourites, especially in the glossy teen pop magazines. They followed the first hit with seven UK Top 40 singles (including 'Just an Illusion', a Number 2 in 1982) and became big sellers across Europe and the Far East.

By mid-1983, however, the impetus slowed and several releases failed to reach the Top 40, with only one single making any impression – 'Thank You My Love', a long runner in the lower reaches of the charts at the end of 1984. Imagination released their sixth album, *Trilogy* in 1986.

IMPALAS Truly an overnight phenomenon, the Impalas were propelled from a Brooklyn street corner to Number 2 on the US charts with 'Sorry, I Ran All the Way Home' on Cub in 1959. This bright, brash novelty, written by Gino Giosasi of Gino and Gina (who had their own hits on Mercury) qualifies as an early example of bubblegum. But black lead singer, Joe Frazier, sang with a punch that rivalled his famed namesake, while the rest of the group – white kids Richard Wagner, Lenny Renda and Tony Calouchi – harmonized with verve. After a smaller hit, 'Oh, What a Fool', they moved to 20th Century-Fox and Checker without success.

IMPERIAL RECORDS Imperial Records was formed in 1947 in Los Angeles by Lew Chudd, a university graduate who dabbled in electronics. He guided Imperial to spectacular success in the Fifties through his vision, drive and energy, and thanks to him the label became recognized as one of the top independent recording companies. 'Imperial Records promoted records well and was a very, very fine company,' producer **Dave Bartholomew** has said. 'Lew Chudd was on fire, by this I mean he was a terrific worker. He could sell more records in the world than anybody else if he wanted to.'

Chudd had started out recording the West Coast jump blues bands of Charlie Davis, Poison Gardner and King Porter, but by this time these sounds were rapidly being ousted by the new rhythm and blues craze, and the early releases did not sell. His luck changed when he met up with New Orleans bandleader Dave Bartholomew in Houston in 1949 and talked Bartholomew into producing for him. Although De Luxe Records had been cleaning up in New Orleans the city was wide open for recording talent and the Chudd/Bartholomew team hit the jackpot first time when they signed and recorded the young **Fats Domino**; his initial release 'The Fat Man' shot into the R&B charts and over the next four years sold enough copies to qualify for a gold record. Domino stayed with Imperial for 14 years and his constant flow of hit platters was primarily responsible for its overall success.

Imperial enjoyed other early New Orleans R&B hits with Jewel King, Archibald and Tommy Ridgley. Lew Chudd also flirted in the hard blues, gospel and country and western markets (turning up another international star in Slim Whitman). However, when Fats Domino started to string his hits together in 1952, Chudd decided to concentrate on the more lucrative R&B field and signed Dave Bartholomew to an exclusive producing contract. Besides Domino, **Smiley Lewis**, Bobby Mitchell and the Topper and the Spiders were selling well in the mid-Fifties.

Then along came rock'n'roll and those million-selling Fats Domino records, 'Ain't That a Shame', 'I'm in Love Again', 'Blueberry Hill', 'Blue Monday' and 'I'm Walkin'': the Fat Man was doing more business than anyone except **Elvis Presley**. Bartholomew was also churning out further New Orleans hits by **Roy Brown** and **Chris Kenner**, and on the West Coast, Ernie Freeman had a Top 20 hit with 'Raunchy'. By now there was no stopping Imperial and Chudd made another masterstroke when he snapped up young teen-idol **Rick Nelson** from Verve in 1957, giving him a double-headed line-up as every Domino and Nelson release careered up the Hot 100 charts in the late Fifties.

By the early Sixties, **Sandy Nelson** was another big-selling star and the bulging coffers were swelled further by the acquisition of the hit-making Minit label of New Orleans. However, rock-'n'roll and R&B were starting to run out of steam, and seeing gloomy prospects ahead Chudd felt it was time to cash in his chips. The sale of Imperial to Liberty in 1963 marked the end of the golden era of independent labels.

IMPRESSIONS Formed in Chicago in 1957, the Impressions were originally an anonymous drone behind **Jerry Butler**'s beautiful recording debut, 'For Your Precious Love' (Falcon, 1958). Three years later, it was another founder-member, **Curtis Mayfield**, who came to dominate the group with his distinctive songs, soft expressive voice, mellow, fluid guitar, and unique ideas in production. He made the Impressions the most readily identifiable group of the Sixties and eventually emerged as one of black music's superstars.

After Butler's departure, Mayfield led the revamped group (Richard and Arthur Brooks, Sam Gooden, and Fred Cash) and supplied most of the songs for the rest of their unsuccessful recordings on Abner. When the label was absorbed by the parent company, Vee Jay, the Impressions were dropped. While Gooden and Richard Brooks took the lead on singles for Bandera (Chicago) and Swirl (New York), Mayfield created his first hits, writing and accompanying several of Butler's early Vee Jay releases, before doing the same thing for the Impressions with their first ABC-Paramount release, 'Gypsy Woman' (1961), cut in New York. Five more singles were less successful, perhaps because Mayfield was busy giving his most interesting songs to **Gene Chandler** and his most commercial to **Major Lance**. Then, back in Chicago as a trio, Mayfield, Cash and Gooden recorded their biggest hit, 'It's All Right' (1963). Arranged by Johnny Pate, its gentle, infectious rhythm and lilting harmonies supported two more years of solid hits – bouncy love songs ('Talking About My Baby', 'You Must Believe Me', 'Woman's Got Soul') – the wistful ('I'm So Proud') – and the first stirrings of deeper thought ('Keep On Pushing', 'Amen', 'People Get Ready', 'Meeting Over Yonder').

With the group at their peak, and many other performers recording his songs, Mayfield made two premature attempts to launch his own record companies, Windy C (1966) and Mayfield (1967). While these ventures quietly collapsed, the Impressions' records started to sound like out-takes from Motown sessions. 'You Been Cheatin'' (1965), 'Since I Lost the One I Love', 'Can't Satisfy' (1966), and 'You Always Hurt Me' (1967) were all hits that owed

Impressions of the Seventies: from left to right, Fred Cash, Sam Gooden (both founder members) and new boy Reggie Torian

more to the sound of Detroit than Chicago, and it seemed that Mayfield had lost his touch. In their last year with ABC, they recovered with two prophetic titles ('We're a Winner' and 'We're Rolling On') which they promptly confirmed by transferring to Mayfield's third, successful, company – Curtom. From their first release, subtle changes in his guitar playing and the overall production showed that he acknowledged the new wave of young black musicians and the use of modern technology. With heavier songs like 'This Is My Country' (1968), 'Choice of Colours', 'Mighty Mighty Spade and Whitey' (1969), 'Check Out Your Mind' (1970) he began attracting audiences who wouldn't have listened to his earlier work, and left the group for a solo career in 1970.

Replacing Mayfield with Leroy Hutson, the Impressions survived as a trio for two more years without a memorable hit. When Hutson also left to go solo, Cash and Gooden brought in Reggie Torian and Ralph Johnson, recorded the successful 'Three the Hard Way' film soundtrack, and by 1974 were back at the top with 'Finally Got Myself Together', written and produced by veteran Ed Townsend. They had their only UK hit in 1975 with 'First Impressions'. In 1976, they left Curtom for Vee Jay and subsequently joined 20th Century where they made the albums *Come to My Party* and *Fan the Fire. See also* **Jerry Butler**; **Curtis Mayfield**

INCREDIBLE STRING BAND

The Incredible String Band began as a three-man jug band in 1965, playing in Glasgow at Clive's Incredible Folk Club. Only after Clive Palmer left did the other two, Robin Williamson (born 24 November 1943) and Mike Heron (12 December 1942), blossom out to invent a new, global folk form. Both were extremely versatile musicians: using instruments and influences from anywhere they could, and actually being able to play the gimbris, mandolins, whistles, or other assorted instruments they got hold of, they were popular in both the folk clubs and the emergent 'Underground'. The freshness and unspecific idealism in their early work summed up the best in the new, vague hippie culture, notably on *The 5,000 Spirits or the Layers of the Onion* (Elektra, 1967). The follow-up album, *The Hangman's Beautiful Daughter*, reached Number 7 in the UK album charts and in the autumn of 1968 they released a highly successful double album, *Wee Tam and the Big Huge.*

As they became more successful they moved to the rock circuit and expanded the band. For many years it included two girls, Rose and Licorice, and then a dancer turned musician, Malcolm Le Maistre. During the Seventies the String Band moved to Island where they gradually lost their magic, and moved to a conventional rock line-up. The band eventually broke up in 1974 after recording their final album,

Hard Rope and Silken Twine.

Heron went on to form his own band, Mike Heron's Reputation and Williamson moved to the US West Coast later in the decade where he formed Robin Williamson's Merry Band.

INGRAM, LUTHER The creator of one of soul music's finest-ever single performances, the million-selling 'If Loving You Is Wrong (I Don't Want to Be Right)', Luther Ingram was born in Jackson, Tennessee, and served his singing apprenticeship in local Baptist Church choirs. His early **Leiber and Stoller**-produced recordings for Smash in New York included the original version of Jamo Thomas' R&B hit 'I Spy for the FBI', but chart success came towards the end of the Sixties following his signing by the Stax-associated label, KoKo. 'If Loving You Is Wrong' reached Number 3 in the US during 1972 and proved the high point of his career, coinciding as it did with his appearance in the film *Wattstax* alongside numerous, more widely-known soul music luminaries. His hits also included the beautiful 'Ain't That Loving You (For More Reasons Than One)' (1970).

INK SPOTS The most influential black vocal group ever, the Ink Spots originally comprised Jerry Daniels (lead tenor), Charles Fuqua (second tenor), Deek Watson (baritone) and Orville 'Hoppy' Jones (bass), who first recorded together for Victor in New York during 1935. In 1939, with Bill Kenny (Daniels' replacement) on 'If I Didn't Care', they dropped jazz'n'jive vocals to concentrate on the ballads of Tin Pan Alley sung in a fairly conventional manner, which found favour among a large white audience.

The Ink Spots established a pattern followed by black groups ever since. The second tenor, baritone and bass harmonize an accompaniment to the lead – in this case Kenny's ice-smooth choirboy voice. The spoken verses by Jones provide a novelty effect. His was the archetypal 'talking' bass, copied extensively by the **Drifters**, **Coasters** *et al.* **Elvis Presley** hoped to sound like all the Ink Spots on 'Are You Lonesome Tonight?', while Deek Watson's classic composition, 'I Love You for Sentimental Reasons' has been recorded by numerous R&B acts, particularly groups. The rise of the Ink Spots from street-corner concerts (as The Percolating Puppies) to global tours and Hollywood films is related by Deek Watson in Lee Stephenson's book *The Story of the Ink Spots.*

INSTRUMENTALS

INSTRUMENTALS Instrumentals in pop have always been of two kinds: dance tunes and melodic or mood pieces, often using strings and often movie themes. With the arrival of rock'n'roll, dance band records of the old kind almost disappeared completely from the charts, but mood music was still much in demand and was going strong throughout the Fifties and into the Sixties.

The bands of Percy Faith, Billy Vaughn, Don Costa, Frank Chacksfield, Perez Prado, Bert Kaempfert, Henry Mancini and Lawrence Welk all had hits with film themes like 'The Sundowners' or novelty pieces like 'Calcutta', a Number 1 for Welk in the US in 1960. Alongside them were Ferrante and Teicher, playing their piano duets of middlebrow classical music for Middle America. But from 1957 onwards, rock'n'roll set the pace for pop instrumentals. Spearheaded by **Bill Doggett**'s 'Honky Tonk', a whole range of boogie-based instrumentalists and groups entered the best-selling lists. The most consistent were Doggett, the two Bills from Memphis (**Black** and **Justis**), the novelty sounds of **Johnny and the Hurricanes**, the pounding drums of **Sandy Nelson**, the twangy guitar of **Duane Eddy** and the restrained melodic sound of the **Ventures**, who represented a dilution of the raw original sounds of rock just as surely as **Frankie Avalon** or **Johnny Tillotson**. In the meantime, Britain was producing its own breed of top-selling instrumentalists, notably the **Shadows**, their former members **Jet Harris and Tony Meehan**, the **Tornados** and a string of lesser lights. Among these were **Bert Weedon**, and the Spotnicks, who were actually a Swedish group based in the UK.

Many less successful, but often more exciting, rock'n'roll instrumentalists also made the charts between 1957 and 1962. The veteran New Orleans pianist Paul Gayten had minor hits in the US with 'Nervous Boogie' (1957) and 'The Hunch' (1959), and his compatriot Lee Allen scored with 'Walking with Mr Lee' in 1958 on Ember. In that year, too, the jazz drummer Cozy Cole took 'Topsy, Part 2' to Number 3 in the US on the Love label. Then there were two raucous saxophone and guitar records, 'Weekend' by the Kingsmen (alias **Bill Haley**'s Comets) on East-West, and 'Poor Boy' by the Royaltones on Jubilee. The important newcomer in 1959 was Dave 'Baby' Cortez, whose record 'The Happy Organ' on Clock went to Number 1. From Detroit, his real name was David Cortez Clowney,

and he was born in 1939. He had to wait until 1962 for another big hit, the classic 'Rinky Dink' on Chess. Santo and Johnny (the Farina brothers from New York) created a strange Hawaiian-guitar sound on 'Sleep Walk' and 'Tear Drop', for Canadian-American. But the hard rockers of the year came from Preston Epps ('Bongo Rock' on Original Sound), the Wailers from Seattle ('Tall Cool One' and 'Mau Mau' on Golden Crest), and the Rock-A-Teens, with 'Woo Hoo' on Roulette. The group comprised Vic Mizell, Bill Cook, Bill Smith, Paul Evans, Boo Walker and Eddie Robinson. The record was pure New York garage band rock'n'roll. The following year, 1960, saw the arrival of Nashville-originated instrumental hits from **Chet Atkins** and **Floyd Cramer**, whose 'Last Date' on RCA reached Number 2 in the US. The Fendermen made a substantial impact with their version of the **Jimmie Rodgers** classic 'Muleskinner Blues' on Soma. And the Joiner, Arkansas, High School Band reached Number 53 with 'National City'.

Jazz instrumentals from Cannonball Adderley and the Dave Brubeck Quartet ('Take Five' and 'Unsquare Dance') were a feature of the charts in 1961, and surf music swept in with Dick Dale's 'Let's Go Trippin'' (Deltone), while 'Stick Shift' by the Duals got to Number 25. The Ramrods did the 1949 Vaughn Monroe hit 'Ghost Riders in the Sky' with a girl drummer and lots of bass strings and cattle calls. And Ferrante and Teicher were finally matched by Kokomo's 'Asia Minor', which was topped only in the Roll-Over-Beethoven stakes by B. Bumble and the Stingers' 'Nut Rocker' (based on Tchaikovsky's Nutcracker Suite) in 1962. Guitarist **Lonnie Mack** had an unexpected hit in 1963 with **Chuck Berry**'s 'Memphis', which got to Number 5 in the US, and the Chantays did well with a crisp, resonant guitar sound on 'Pipeline' (US Number 4; UK Number 16).

Instrumentalists figured in the transatlantic charts far less frequently after the emergence of the **Beatles** and the British beat boom, although **Billy J. Kramer**'s group the Dakotas did reach the UK chart with the Shadows-like 'The Cruel Sea' in mid-1963. Since then, instrumental hits have generally been confined to either those hardy perennials, film themes, or straight novelty numbers like Lieutenant Pigeon's UK chart-topper 'Mouldy Old Dough' (1972), Hot Butter's 'Popcorn' (1972) and the Tweets' 'The Birdie Song' (1981).

INTRUDERS An important act in the development and commercial expansion of the 'Philly Sound' boom in the early Seventies, the Intruders comprised Sam 'Little Sonny' Brown, Eugene Daughtry, Phil Terry, and Robert Edwards. All were native Philadelphians who first came together in classic doo-wop fashion around 1961, as a group of street-corner harmonizers. In 1964, they teamed up with a young pianist/producer, Leon Huff, who was then about to launch his own Excel record label in partnership with **Kenny Gamble**. Chart success followed in the shape of big-selling R&B discs like '(We'll Be) United' and 'Cowboys to Girls', which also reached Number 6 in the national pop chart during 1968. In the Seventies, the group continued to benefit from their association with the Gamble/Huff production team, although it was in the UK that their brand of sophisto-soul made the most impact: 'I'll Always Love My Mama' and 'Win, Place or Show (She's a Winner)' each achieved higher placings in Britain than in the US during 1974.

IRON BUTTERFLY Prototype heavy metal band Iron Butterfly began life in Los Angeles in 1967, soon settling to a line-up of Doug Ingle (born 9 September 1945) organ, vocals; Ron Bushy (23 September 1941) drums; Lee Dorman (15 September 1942) bass; and Eric Braunn (10 August 1950) guitar. Danny Weiss also flirted with the band for a while before joining Rhinoceros and can be heard on their first album, *Heavy*. The album, released in 1968, established the group as unsubtle and instrumentally obvious, with a too solid rhythm section and an overweight sound only lightened by Ingle's ponderous organ work. Despite an inauspicious start, a strong following launched their second album, *In A Gadda Da Vidda*, to massive sales. To this day it remains Atlantic's largest grossing rock album – and maybe their largest gross selling album. Braunn was replaced in 1971 by two guitarists – Mike Pinera (born 29 September 1948) and Larry Rheinhardt (7 July 1948) – but their contribution failed to raise *Metamorphosis* to a higher critical standpoint.

The group came to a grinding halt in 1971 but resurfaced three years later under the dual leadership of Eric Braunn and Ron Bushy, assisted by Phil Kramer (bass) and Howard Reitzes (keyboards). Together they produced two expendable albums, *Sun and Steel* and *Scorching Beauty*.

Iron Maiden's original vocalist Paul Di'anno, who left the group in mid-1981, shrieks out a raucous song, backed by steamhammer-rock guitars

IRON MAIDEN One of the leading bands of the British Eighties' heavy metal revival, Iron Maiden found favour with the fans for their uncomplicated guitar riffs, super-distorted power chords and shrieking vocals.

Formed in East London in 1976 by bassist Steve Harris, the line-up did not settle down until 1978 when he was joined by Dave Murray (guitar), Paul Di'anno (vocals) and Doug Sampson (drums) in the studio to record a four-track demo that was eventually released on their own Rock Hard Records. The demo aroused plenty of interest, and after supporting **Motörhead** at the Marquee club and performing a headline date of their own, they were hailed by the music papers as one of the leaders of a 'new wave' of British

heavy metal groups, alongside **Def Leppard** and **Saxon**. Iron Maiden were signed by EMI in 1979. Sampson was replaced on drums by Clive Burr, a second guitarist Dennis Stratton joined, and the result was the screaming heavy metal of *Iron Maiden* (1980). It reached Number 4 in the UK following a tour second on the bill to **Judas Priest**.

In 1981 Di'anno left to be replaced by Bruce Dickinson, late of Samson, who sang in a more traditional heavy metal singing style. Their steamhammer approach to music, a dense sound of awesome mindlessness, has remained unchanged since then, and after scoring a UK Number 1 album with *The Number of the Beast* in 1982, they started to break into the American

market. Successive albums adorned with violent imagery have sold well both sides of the Atlantic; they remain a popular live attraction and are the only heavy metal band to score regular UK Top 20 singles. The macho posture of *Live After Death* (1985), a live double album, serves as the ultimate Iron Maiden statement.

IRWIN, BIG DEE Five years before his 1963 British Top 10 duet with Little Eva, 'Swinging on a Star', Big Dee Irwin made the American Top 30 as the lead singer with the Pastels – Richard Tavers, Anthony Thomas, and B. J. Willingham – whose lovely ballad, 'Been So Long' was purchased from Mascot by the Chess subsidiary Argo in 1957. As a soul singer, Irwin (born on 4 August 1939 in New York) recorded prolifically – with discs on Hull, Bliss, 20th Century, Fairmont, Rotate, Redd-Coach, Imperial, etc. – but he is best known as a writer (under his real name, Defosca Ervin) and, since the late Sixties, as a producer for Ripple.

ISAACS, GREGORY The possessor of the most sweetly aching tenor voice in reggae, Jamaican singer Gregory Isaacs (born 16 June 1950) – the 'Cool Ruler' – is the music's most consummate singer of love songs, but by no means a **'lovers' rock'** vocalist. His regular forays into message material, together with the deeper roots essence which drenches even his most sentimental performances, mark him out as something far more substantial.

Isaacs' international breakthrough came in 1980 with the albums *Lonely Lover* and *More Gregory*, and followed ten years of prolific recording at roots level. He began recording in 1970 as a member of a vocal group called the Concords, before switching to a solo career (and producer Rupie Edwards) in 1973. He subsequently recorded for producers **Prince Buster** and Phil Pratt before, frustrated at both the deals and the general lack of success he was achieving, setting up his own African Museum label with fellow singer Errol Dunkley in 1974. Releases for African Museum, plus one-offs for outside producers like Niney and Prince Tony, followed before Isaacs made his first big score with the self-produced *Extra Classic* album in 1977. His first major single success came a year later, with the **Dennis Brown**-produced 'Mr Know It All'. The late 1970s saw him cement his Jamaican and British specialist market success with the albums *Mr Isaacs, Cool Ruler* and *Soon Forward*, before the mainstream acceptance which followed *Lonely Lover* and *More Gregory*. He carried on into the Eighties as a successful artist and his *Night Nurse* LP (1982) became one of the biggest-selling reggae albums ever. Conflicts with the law in Jamaica in the mid-Eighties have kept Isaacs in relatively low profile, but his audience is as loyal as ever and his day far from over.

ISLAND RECORDS Formed by Chris Blackwell in 1962 to distribute Jamaican record labels (including his own) in Britain, Island slowly expanded its repertoire, first licensing the New York Sue R&B label and then plunging headlong into 'progressive' rock when it signed **Traffic** in 1967. Formed following the break-up of the **Spencer Davis Group** which Blackwell had managed but placed with Philips because Island was too specialist a label for the group, Traffic provided Island with its first hit single, 'Paper Sun', and album, *Mr Fantasy*, in 1967, and created the image of a progressive label that Island was to henceforth carefully nurture. The signing of groups like **Fairport Convention** and **Free** confirmed this image and by 1970, when WEA offered Blackwell six million dollars for the company, Island was the most successful independent record company in Britain.

Since the mid-Sixties, Island had assigned its Jamaican product to Trojan Records and in 1972 it sold its interest in Trojan to B&C Records, only retaining progressive reggae acts such as **Bob Marley and the Wailers** and **Toots and the Maytals**, a move anticipated by the financing of *The Harder They Come*, the film that more than anything else paved reggae's way to becoming a part of the rock mainstream rather than purely a specialist music.

By the mid-Seventies, Island had maintained its position in the progressive rock market-place with the successful signing of acts like **Cat Stevens**, the Chieftains, **Roxy Music** and **Bad Company**, as well as signing a licensing deal with Fania (a Caribbean label) which gave it the cream of 'salsa' music, and making tentative steps into the pop field with the signing of **Sparks**. At the same time, it made distribution deals with smaller companies like Rocket, Chrysalis and Virgin, set up its own pressing plant, and formed an American company which by 1976 had signed **Joe South** and given Island its first US Top 20 hit, **War**'s 'Low Rider'.

During the late Seventies, Island built on its success with Marley by setting up its own reggae subsidiary called Front Line as a specific UK outlet for the records of **Big Youth**, **Burning Spear** and other Jamaican artists, and the company also became a leading promoter of Nigerian juju artists – notably **King Sunny Ade**. In the Eighties, Island's most spectacular sales came via **Frankie Goes to Hollywood**, who were assigned their own ZTT subsidiary. A merger with Stiff Records was effected in January 1984.

ISLEY BROTHERS The Isley Brothers – Rudolph (born on 1 April 1939), Ronald (21 May 1941) and O'Kelly (25 December 1937) – survived twenty years of musical changes, scoring definitive hits in each era along the way, to emerge as one of the most innovative black groups of the Seventies. Raised in Cincinnati, Ohio, the brothers moved to New York in 1957 where they recorded mediocre doo-wop/rock'n'roll sides for Teenage, and

George Goldner's Cindy, Mark X, and Gone labels before signing with RCA. Produced by **Hugo and Luigi**, their driving gospel style enlivened a weak selection of pop material, but was best displayed by 'Shout' (1959), an exciting adaptation of the climax to their wild stage act which has since become a rock classic. They next worked with writer/producers **Leiber and Stoller** (Atlantic, 1961–2) and **Bert Berns** (Wand, 1962–3; UA, 1963–4), who tried unsuccessfully to fit their raw sound into a commercial package, although it was Berns who gave them 'Twist and Shout' (1962), a one-take, end-of-session dance riff that became their first Top 20 pop hit, later immortalized by the Beatles. Forming their own production company, T-Neck, in 1964–5 they cut several memorable sides (including the rousing 'Testify' and dramatic ballad 'The Last Girl') featuring their young guitarist,

The Isley Brothers are one of the very few groups to have released hit records in four consecutive decades, from the rock'n'roll era to disco

Jimi Hendrix, before joining Tamla.

After hitting with some typically slick corporation products (the Top 20 'This Old Heart of Mine' and 'I Guess I'll Always Love You', for example, in 1966) the trio were relegated to second-rate material and quit to revive T-Neck in 1969. From their first release, the million-selling 'It's Your Thing', they projected a new heavy image and soon began using two younger brothers (Ernie, on guitar, and Marvin, on bass) and Chris Jasper (keyboards) to create 'progressive' hits that anticipated modern trends in black music and brought them to the attention of wider audiences. By the early Seventies they were interpreting songs by **Steve Stills** (the Top 20 hit 'Love the One You're With', 1971) and **Dylan** ('Lay Lady Lay', 1971) and including Hendrix's traumatic 'Machine Gun' in their act. In 1973, they crystallized all their influences and ideas in the highly acclaimed 3 + 3 album, which included the million-selling 'That Lady'. Subsequent releases in a similar style (*Live It Up*, *The Heat Is On*) kept them to the forefront of black music, and they adapted easily to the disco boom with albums such as *Showdown* and *Winner Takes All* (both 1978) and singles like 1979's 'It's a Disco Night (Rock Don't Stop)', which was a Top 20 hit in the UK. They began the Eighties on yet another strong note – with *Grand Slam* and *Inside You* (both 1981), the latter of which found the Isleys using orchestrations for the first time. *The Real Deal* followed in 1982 and the sultry (and appropriately titled) *Between the Sheets* in 1983. O'Kelly Isley died of a heart attack on 31 March 1986.

IT'S A BEAUTIFUL DAY A
second-generation San Franciscan group comprising David LaFlamme, electric violin (born 5 April 1941); Bill Gregory, guitar; Val Fuentes, drums (25 November 1947); Tom Fowler, bass; and Pattie Santos, vocals (16 November 1949), It's a Beautiful Day had their first album, *It's a Beautiful Day* (Columbia) released in the summer of 1969. It featured a blend of rather ordinary rock and the impassioned violin-playing of their leader, the classically trained LaFlamme, heard at its best on the group's one memorable number, 'White Bird'. With each subsequent album, *Marrying Maiden*, *Choice Quality Stuff* and *Live at Carnegie Hall*, the group shed members and changed styles until, by 1973, they were unrecognizable as the group who originally performed 'White Bird'. They disbanded in 1974 after six albums.

JACKSON, CHUCK R&B singer Chuck Jackson was born on 22 July 1937 in Winston Salem, North Carolina, moved to Pittsburgh to join the **Del-Vikings** shortly after the group's 'Whispering Bells' hit in 1957. His lead singing can be heard on early Seventies records on Bim Bam Boom. He made solo discs for Clock and Beltone before producer Luther Dixon signed him to Wand. The resulting rich-voiced soul ballads were constantly in the middle reaches of the charts between 1961 and 1964. Among them were 'I Don't Want to Cry', 'I Woke Up Crying', 'Any Day Now' (a fine **Burt Bacharach** song), 'I Keep Forgetting' (a **Leiber/Stoller** composition), 'Tell Him I'm Not Home', 'Beg Me' and 'Since I Don't Have You'. In 1965, Jackson's partnership with Maxine Brown produced a series of hits, including 'Something You Got'. Two years later, he joined Motown where 'Are You Lonely For Me Baby' was a small R&B hit. Subsequent records for Dakar and ABC-Paramount were less successful although he returned to the charts with the **Steve Barri** production, 'I Only Get This Feeling', in 1973.

Always a distinctive singer, Jackson became firmly established during the Seventies in the cabaret soul market.

JACKSON FIVE/JACKSONS
In the early Seventies, the Jackson Five appeared to be popular music's ultimate anomaly. Promoted and packaged as teenybop whimsy at the same time as the **Osmonds** and the Partridge Family (see **David Cassidy**), their music differed considerably: the Jacksons were black and their music still retained links with the continually evolving soul music mainstream.

Born and raised in Gary, Indiana, Michael (born 29 August 1958), Jermaine (11 December 1954), Jackie (4 May 1951), Marlon (12 March 1957) and Tito Jackson (15 October 1953) were the sons of Joe Robinson, a musician/singer and one-time member of the **Falcons**. The Jackson Five began playing local hops around Indiana, eventually recording two obscure discs (for Steeltown Records). When 'discovered' by superstar **Diana Ross**, as future publicity had it, they were immediately whisked away by the Motown Record Corporation and given one of the most extensive groomings ever. Staff writers, producers and musicians (including a couple of the **Crusaders**) worked for weeks on some of the most pungently rhythmic tracks the Detroit company had ever laid down and when 'I Want You Back' was

The Jackson Five fused pulsating music with tightly-rehearsed dance routines: from the left, Tito, Marlon, Jackie, Michael and Jermaine

released in 1969 its success was immediate. More gold discs quickly followed: 'ABC', 'The Love You Save' and 'I'll Be There', all American chart-toppers in 1970. Lead singer Michael was sometimes asked to use his high quavering soprano on maudlin ballads rather than the highly charged dance numbers with which the group excelled, but considering the size and relative immaturity of their mass audience the Jacksons' discs were often staggeringly good. A slump did occur, however, when Michael began to record solo albums (*Got to Be There* and *Ben*) and when the group were asked to parody their original effervescent style (as on 'Little Bitty Pretty One' in 1972). Motown, still ringing the changes, launched Jermaine Jackson as a fairly successful solo act and as late as 1974 the group had a million-seller with 'Dancing Machine'.

But the group's failure to develop as songwriters, to move sufficiently in new musical directions (though the riveting electro-funk of 'Dancing Machine' was an intriguing possibility) and especially to shake off their decidedly *passé* image, caused a decline from the stupendous successes of old, though the change from Motown to Epic Records (with Jermaine electing to stay put) saw the group recover their commercial strength. With a $20 million law suit from Motown hanging over them – eventually settled in 1980 – the three remaining brothers relaunched themselves as the Jacksons and had a string of major US hits, including 'Enjoy Yourself' (1979), 'Shake Your Body' (1979) and 'Lovely One' (1980). Michael and Jermaine continued their solo careers, the former with spectacular success in the early Eighties, but friction between the various brothers has fuelled persistent speculation of a split in the Jacksons' ranks. *See also* **Michael Jackson**; **Jermaine Jackson**

JACKSON, JERMAINE Born 11
December 1954 and condemned to live for ever in the shadow of his younger brother Michael, Jermaine Jackson nevertheless emerged from the **Jackson Five** as a solo artist of occasional touching charm. He'd already recorded solo albums (*Jermaine*, *Come into My Life*) by the time the brothers decided to quit Motown. Alas, he'd already married Hazel Gordy, daughter of the Corporation's boss, Berry, and felt it right that he should stay behind at his father-in-law's somewhat beleaguered firm. He was 21. After three interesting though never thoroughly convincing albums

(*My Name Is Jermaine*, *Feel the Fire*, *Frontiers*), and despite a willingness to experiment within the pop-soul format, Jermaine teamed up in 1979 with **Stevie Wonder** who co-produced 'Let's Get Serious' and 'You're Supposed to Keep Your Love for Me', two of Jermaine's best tracks as a solo performer. Alone, he was more successful at recapturing the sunny warmth of the latter (as in 'You Like Me Don't You', 'Tell Me I'm Not Dreamin'', 'Sweetest Sweetest') than the funky power of the former. In 1983, Jermaine finally quit Motown and signed for Arista debuting with 1984's *Dynamite*, on which album he was reunited with his brothers on the silly 'Escape from the Planet of the Ant Men'. He also went on the road with his brothers as part of the 'Victory' tour which promoted a very poor Jacksons LP. His 1986 single release, 'I Think It's Love', was a further collaboration with Stevie Wonder and the album, *Precious Moments*, again exuded the warmth and genuine 'niceness' which seems to be the basis of Jermaine Jackson's character and, thus, his music.

JACKSON, JOE Born 11 August
1955 in Burton-on-Trent, Staffordshire, and raised in Portsmouth, Joe Jackson has remained one of the more innovative mainstream British singer/songwriters of the post-punk period. Suffering initially from comparisons with **Elvis Costello**, Jackson has surprised critics frequently by drawing on a variety of musical sources and experimenting with various styles.

After attending the Royal College of Music, he became a full-time musician, putting in a short stint as a musical director on the cabaret circuit before coming to London and forming the Joe Jackson Band with Graham Maby (bass), Gary Sanford (guitar) and Dave Houghton (drums). In 1978, signed to A&M, they recorded *Look Sharp*, a no-frills, finely-honed collection of pop songs including the classic 'Is She Really Going Out with Him', which had to appear on the US singles chart in 1979 before finally being re-released and making the charts in the UK. This pattern was to continue throughout his career; a loyal following supported him in the UK, but the real commercial impact took place across the Atlantic. *I'm the Man*, a richer and more complex album, was released late 1979, went gold in the UK, and charted high all over the world, while 'Different for Girls', a single taken from the LP, proved to be his biggest UK hit, making the Top 5. Touring extensively to promote

the album, the band developed into one of the tightest and most exciting on the circuit at that time.

The reggae influenced LP, *Beat Crazy* came out in November 1980, but it received poor reviews and sold badly, and, two months later, a disillusioned Jackson broke up the band. He quickly recovered his enthusiasm however, and a long-time interest in all forms of jazz led him to put together a goodtime swing outfit called Jumpin' Jive. Originally intended as a short-term fun venture, the group unexpectedly recorded an album, *Jumpin' Jive*, a collection of swing standards that did surprisingly well despite a panning from the purists, and introduced swing to a new young audience. After successfully touring the US and the UK, they disbanded and Jackson went to live in New York.

His fifth album, *Night and Day*, clearly influenced by the salsa, latin and jazz scenes in New York, was released in June '82 and proved to be his most successful release, yielding a sizeable worldwide hit in the single 'Steppin' Out'.

In March 1984 came the release of the even more jazz-influenced *Body and Soul*, which was notable for the extraordinary care taken in its recording; the clarity and authenticity of the real acoustic sounds on it remain a testament to modern production technology. The material on the album was disappointing, however, even though it included two US Top 20 hit singles.

Maintaining a low-profile for two years, Jackson took the unusual step of recording, in early 1986, an album of completely new material on a live stage, direct and untreated, on to a two-track tape recorder. The resulting album, *Big World*, was Jackson's seventh and it marked a return to a more traditional rock sound.

Although to a great extent deprived of the critical acclaim he deserved, especially as a lyricist, Jackson has always managed to stay ahead of the market and consistently given memorable live performances. He remains one of the few artists who refuses to stick with a successful formula.

JACKSON, MAHALIA Although
raised in New Orleans (where she was born on 26 October 1911), Mahalia Jackson's talent really blossomed in Chicago where she recorded a stream of gospel hits for Apollo between 1946 and 1953. With tastefully simple piano accompaniment from Mildred Falls, and material like 'Move on up a Little Higher' by Rev. Brewster, 'Prayer

Changes Things' by Robert Anderson and 'Dig a Little Deeper' by Kenneth Morris, her powerful natural contralto couldn't be faulted. Moving to Columbia she continued recording while becoming a public figure known for her work for the civil rights movement and her reassuring 'We Shall Overcome'. She died in 1972.

JACKSON, MICHAEL Originally the lead singer of the **Jackson Five**, later known as the Jacksons, Michael (born 29 August 1958) emerged in the late 1970s as the period's greatest pop idol in the world. When the Jackson Five's contract with Motown ended in 1976 they went to Epic, who also took on a commitment to record Michael's solo albums. Although *Got to Be There*, *Ben* and *Forever Michael* had sold reasonably well for him on Motown, there was clearly a need to wean him from the teeny-bop, cute style (if not audience) if he was to have longevity. It came in the most extraordinary fashion through two albums – *Off the Wall* (1979) and *Thriller* (1982) – both of which were blueprints for mass appeal pop-soul recordings and, indeed, led a stampede of white acts in search of black producers, musicians, sounds. And not for the first time. The success of *Off the Wall* was due to the splendid production of Quincy Jones and the ineffably catchy songs written by Rod Temperton, a former member of the Brit-funk band Heatwave ('Rock with You' and the title track particularly). The album also revealed Jackson as a fine writer in his own right – 'Don't Stop Til You Get Enough', 'Working Day and Night' and, with Louis Johnson, 'Get on the Floor' – all tapped the new generation's desire to get back on the dance-floor and, coincidentally, were well-timed for the exercise-to-music aerobics boom. However well *Wall* sold, nothing could have prepared the observer for the preposterous sales achieved by *Thriller*. This LP was perfectly timed to tap a third sales device that was to become crucial in the Eighties – video. Michael, ever a stunning dancer, was made for the medium and once he'd broken down the never-stated but tacitly understood racist policy of the American rock video station MTV (by including a hard rock guitar solo on one track and cutting another as a duet with former Beatle **Paul McCartney**) the world became his cash register. Towards the end of '83 the album had sold 24 million copies, and carried on selling. A million alone had been sold in both Los Angeles and Britain. Epic

Michael Jackson in leather for the 1983 video of 'Billie Jean'

had lifted no fewer than five of its nine cuts as Top 10 hit singles in most countries; it had gone platinum in 14 countries; it was selling 200,000 a week in the USA alone, and it was still selling. An industry – books, a video *The Making of Thriller*, itself a video based on the LP's title-track, magazines – and an extraordinary barrage of gossip stories grew atop this edifice. The gossip was fuelled by Michael's shyness and unwillingness to be interviewed. Questions about his romances (Tatum O'Neal), looks (a nose job) and home (loves animals, collects mannequin dolls, dances all day Sunday, fasts too) and private life (who's his latest girlfriend? is he gay? the filing of paternity suits) were generally met with a wall of silence, increasing pulp journalists' determination to portray him as 'loony'. He was, however, a very hard business negotiator. The group he shared with his brothers was eclipsed totally.

He produced and/or wrote for other artists (e.g. **Diana Ross**, 'Muscles'), narrated the movie soundtrack album to E.T., but was slow to follow up his own movie debut as The Scarecrow in *The Wiz*, the Diana Ross musical vehicle, a black version of *The Wizard of Oz*. The film wasn't a success; Jackson's role was. A new project was slow to emerge, though in 1985 he was filming for Walt Disney when he injured a hand, a less alarming accident than the singed scalp he suffered earlier while making an ad for Pepsi. Whatever his future as a film star, Jackson's skill as a pop-soul singer, writer and producer makes him an intriguing performer. Many acts benefitted by his absence from the market during 1985, by which time *Thriller* had just about stopped selling.

JACKSON, MILLIE Arguably the greatest of the many impressive black girl singers to have emerged since the Seventies, Jackson's raw emotive style has inhibited mass acceptance, but within 18 months of her first hit, 'Ask Me What You Want' (1972), she was voted Top R&B Vocalist with **Aretha Franklin**. Born in Thompson, Georgia in 1944, she moved to New York in the Sixties where she played local clubs and recorded unsuccessfully for MGM before signing to Spring in 1971. From her first release – the devastating portrayal of ghetto life, 'Child of God' – she hardly cut a bad track and proved equally at ease on uptempo dance tunes ('Ask Me What You Want', 'My Man a Sweet Man' – 1972), sensuous love songs ('It Hurts So Good' from the film *Cleopatra Jones* – 1973), or down-on-the-knees wailers ('If Loving You Is Wrong' – 1975). This last track was drawn from her beautiful concept album *Caught Up* which also provided the hit single 'I'm Through Trying to Prove My Love to You' and was one of the most highly acclaimed black music albums of 1975.

Feelin' Bitchy (1977), *Get It Out Cha System* (1978), and *A Moment's Pleasure* (1979) all consolidated her reputation, while the titles hinted at the raunchiness of her performances – many of her releases were not played on American radio because of the uncompromising language used. In 1979, she recorded an album of duets, *Royal Rappins*, with **Isaac Hayes**, and in 1985 she had a major transatlantic hit with **Elton John**'s 'Act of War'.

JACKSON, WANDA Wanda Jackson was one of the very few girl singers in the Fifties to achieve an energy and wildness comparable to the rock'n'roll styles of her male contemporaries, and this despite a solid background in country music. Born Wanda Goodman in Maud, Oklahoma, 20 October 1937, she worked on radio KLPR in Oklahoma City from 1952, and in 1953 began recording for Decca. She joined Hank Thompson's successful Western Swing band and in 1956 joined Capitol, who saw her as a female **Gene Vincent**. The raw power and strangled vocalizing on singles like 'Mean Mean Man' were followed by an album *Rockin' With Wanda* and a national pop hit in 1958 with 'Let's Have a Party'. The spirited backings included Vincent's Blue Caps, guitarist Roy Clark and pianist **Merrill Moore**, but by 1961 she had returned to country when the ballad 'Right or Wrong' began a continuing series of hits.

JAM One of the foremost bands of the punk explosion and eventual leaders of the mod revival, the Jam was formed in Woking, Surrey, out of the schoolboy partnership of Paul Weller (vocals/guitar) and Rick Buckler (drums), who met during school breaks to jam with other school musicians (thus inspiring the band's name). Steve Brookes (guitar) and Bruce Foxton (bass) joined later, and as a fourpiece the band played local youth and social club gigs. By mid-1976, when they had graduated to the London circuit, Brookes departed, leaving the Jam as a trio.

Although their sound and image were inspired by the mod era, they found themselves involved in the early stages of punk, playing the same clubs as the **Sex Pistols**, the **Clash** and other leading lights of the time. Their smart haircuts, mod suits and rickenbacker guitars initially provoked hostile reactions from punk audiences, but their tuneful mod sensibility, coupled with the naked aggression of punk, generated a loyal following.

In February 1977 they signed to Polydor and their debut single, 'In the City', was released. It reached Number 40 and started a long run of outstanding hit singles, including three that entered the UK charts at Number 1 ('Going Underground', 'A Town Called Malice' and 'Beat Surrender'). Three further albums, *In the City* (1977), *This Is the Modern World* (1977) and *All Mod Cons* (1978, generally rated as their best) were released and by 1979 the Jam were competing with **Police** as the most popular band in Britain.

That year also saw a revival of interest in mod culture, for which they could claim much of the responsibility and which, ironically, increased their popularity no end. The film *Quadrophenia* ensured further interest and encouraged a handful of mod bands to appear briefly, but the Jam were the sole outfit to outlive the fad.

Their phenomenal success continued on through the albums *Setting Sons* (1979) and *Sound Affects* (1980), each of which displayed an increased sophistication and continued to yield hit singles. Their popularity was confined to the UK however until the release of their sixth album *The Gift* in 1982, and the single 'A Town Called Malice/Precious' which made inroads into the US and Australian markets. This breakthrough was not followed up, however, as the Jam announced in October of that year that they were disbanding, professing disillusionment with the music industry. They undertook a farewell British tour in

December, and released their final album, *Dig the New Breed*, a live anthology chronicling their evolution from London's 100 Club in 1977 to the Glasgow Apollo in 1982.

Each member of the band went on to pursue separate musical projects, but it was Weller who was to sustain a high profile in the charts with his new band, the **Style Council**.

By the time the Jam split in December 1982, they had not only enjoyed five years as the most consistently successful and critically acclaimed group to have emerged from the punk era, but, with the likes of 'Strange Town', 'Down in the Tube Station at Midnight' and 'Absolute Beginners' they had also recorded some of the very best pop songs of the time.

JAMES, DICK Best known in pop circles for his association, as publisher of their songs, with the **Beatles** and **Elton John**, Dick James began his career in music in 1936 under the name of Lee Sheridan, singing with various dance bands in his native North London. In the Forties, as Dick James, he sang with the bands of Geraldo and Cyril Stapleton before becoming a member of the Stargazers, an immensely popular vocal group on BBC radio who topped the UK chart with 'Broken Wings' in

1953. Two years later, as a solo artist, he recorded a hit version of the theme song of the television series *Robin Hood* for Parlophone, with **George Martin** producing.

James quit performing in the late Fifties and joined Sydney Bron's publishing company as a plugger. He set up his own publishing company in 1960, which was given a spectacular boost in October 1962, when George Martin put him in contact with **Brian Epstein** to publish songs for the Beatles and future NEMS artists. James then set up Page One Records, with Larry Page, in November 1965, scoring immediately with the **Troggs**' 'Wild Thing'. Four years later, when James and Page parted company, he set up his own DJM label. His luck and judgment continued – in James' studios cutting demos was Reg Dwight, whom James teamed with **Bernie Taupin** to launch another English rock phenomenon, Elton John.

James was the centre of some controversy in 1978, when – against the wishes of the Beatles – he decided to sell Northern Songs, the publishing company he had established for Beatle material, to ATV Music. A dispute between James and Elton John (who broke with DJM in the mid-Seventies) over ownership of copyrights resulted in litigation in late 1985, with the court

The Jam in action: Bruce Foxton (left), Rick Buckler (on drums) and Paul Weller (right). They gave a Sixties sound to punk aggression

ruling largely in Elton's favour. James died within weeks of the case's conclusion, in February 1986.

JAMES, ELMORE As an important blues figure of the Fifties and Sixties, Elmore James was born on 18 January 1918, at Richland, Mississippi. He started out playing at Saturday night dances, occasionally working with **Sonny Boy Williamson** (Rice Miller) and blues legend **Robert Johnson**. His first record was a cover of Johnson's 'Dust My Blues', recorded in Jackson in 1951 for the Trumpet label. The single made the R&B Top 10, which inspired James to adapt the theme for several of his later songs. His best known sides were cut for the Chess, Chief and Fire labels between 1957 and 1962. This period produced such contemporary-sounding blues classics as 'It Hurts Me Too', 'The Sun Is Shining', 'Rollin' and Tumblin'' and 'Shake Your Money Maker'. His regular band on these sessions included his cousin Homesick James (rhythm guitar), Little Johnny Jones (piano) and J. T. Brown (tenor sax). All the songs were characterized by James' intense, tortured vocal delivery and fierce, heavily amplified slide-guitar playing. His records influenced countless British blues groups during the mid-Sixties, in particular **Fleetwood Mac** and **John Mayall**'s Bluesbreakers. But recognition came too late for Elmore, who died of a heart attack on 23 May 1963.

JAMES, ETTA Born in Los Angeles in 1938, Etta James had a career which fell into four distinct phases – phase one followed her discovery by **Johnny Otis** while playing San Francisco clubs in the early Fifties. Otis took her under his wing and placed her with the local Modern label, where she had two R&B Top 20 hits in 1955, 'Roll With Me Henry', an answer-disc to the Midnighters' sexually euphemistic 'Work With Me Annie', and 'Good Rockin' Daddy'. Following these, she spent some four or five years touring with various rock'n'roll shows and recording profusely, but not too successfully, for Modern.

Late 1959 saw her on a show with the **Moonglows** (Chess Records) in Chicago; she and the group were broke, so **Harvey Fuqua** (Moonglows' bass singer) recommended Leonard Chess to sign her in return for payment of hotel bills. Chess bought her contract from Modern – thus began phase two. 'All I Could Do Was Cry' was an immediate R&B hit, followed by 18 more over the next four years (including 'At Last', 'Pushover', and 'Stop the Wedding'), largely searing blues ballads, though 'Pushover', her biggest hit of the time, was a relatively simple teenage beat ballad.

Following a brief lull, phase three began in 1967 with a session at **Rick Hall**'s Muscle Shoals, Alabama studio, from which 'Tell Mama' reached the American Top 30 and four subsequent discs were progressively smaller hits. Phase four began in 1973 when, after a rehabilitation course following a drug problem, Etta began recording for Chess again, producing a series of critically-acclaimed LPs and making a welcome return to the R&B charts. Later in the Seventies she appeared with the **Rolling Stones** on a US tour and performed at the Montreux Jazz Festival.

JAMES GANG One of the more imaginative and dynamic American hard-rock bands of the late Sixties, the James Gang was formed in Cleveland, Ohio during 1967 by Jim Fox (drums), Glen Schwartz (guitar) and Tom Kriss (bass). Both Schwartz and Kriss left the group within the next two years, the former to join Pacific Gas and Electric, and the Gang's critical reputation was thereafter built on the outstanding playing of replacements **Joe Walsh** (guitar) and Dale Peters (bass). Between the release of *Yer Album* (1969) and *Live in Concert* (1971), the band produced its best work – thinking man's hard-rock, intelligently and sensitively performed – but Walsh's departure in 1971 created a gap that neither guitarist Dominic Troiano nor singer Roy Kenner could fill. Troiano left after one album, *Straight Shooter* (1972), and joined the **Guess Who**, and his replacement Marty Bolin appeared on just two albums before joining **Deep Purple**. In 1974, the James Gang officially disbanded, though Fox reconstituted the band a year later with guitarists Bubba Keith and Richard Shack. Two further albums resulted, *Newborn* (1975) and *Jesse Come Home* (1976), but the Gang broke up for a second time in late 1976. *See also* **Joe Walsh**

JAMES, RICK In 1978, a new artist released his first album on Motown, and soon after, the mixture of tight funk grooves and streetwise lyrics was termed 'punk funk'. The album, *Come Get It!* and its successor, *Bustin' Out Of L Seven*, propelled the writer/producer/singer/guitarist Rick James to stardom at such a rate that by 1979 he was lying in a hospital bed with a severe case of hepatitis and a stern warning from his doctors to slow down or die. He slowed down, lived better and carried on refining the punk funk style which had been best illustrated, on the first album, by 'You and I' and 'Mary Jane', an ambiguous paean to marijuana or his girlfriend. After two further LPs, *Fire It Up* and *Garden of Love*, James released 1981's *Street Songs*, comfortably his best album to date, mixing sensual ballads ('Fire and Desire', 'Make Love to Me'), openly sexual invitations ('Super Freak', 'Give It to Me Baby') and commentaries on social conditions in black America ('Ghetto Life', 'Me Policeman').

Born in Buffalo, New York, on 1 February 1952, as James Johnson, Rick James had a somewhat eventful period as a teenager playing in local bands before joining the US Navy (at 15), deserting (since pardoned: he was under-age when called up), and fleeing to Canada where he played in the Mynah Birds with **Neil Young**. He spent a year-and-a-half learning and going hungry in London, went back to the States and later joined Motown as a staff writer and producer for a few years before returning to Canada and forming a band named White Cane. His next band, Main Line, recorded an album which James played to Motown and, renamed Rick James and the Stone City Band, the set became *Come Get It!* Since *Street Songs* James has released a couple of none-too enthralling LPs, but has put much effort into producing others – the Stone City Band, the Mary Jane Girls and Val Young among others – which was probably just as well for ill health again dogged him in 1982 when he collapsed during a concert in Dallas, Texas, and later fled Britain in rather murky circumstances during a promotional tour.

The funk'n'roll of Rick James added rock licks to urban soul

JAMES, TOMMY AND THE SHONDELLS

Initially known simply as the Shondells, this Michigan group first came together in 1964 and released a cover version of the Raindrops' 'Hanky Panky' on the small Snap label in Michigan. Two years later, it was heard by a DJ in Pittsburgh and, released nationally by Roulette, the record climbed to Number 1 in the US. Tommy James – born 29 April 1947 – and his new Shondells (the original group had long since split) – Mike Vale, bass (17 July 1949); Ronnie Rosman, piano (28 February 1945); Peter Lucia, drums (2 February 1947); Eddie Gray, guitar (27 February 1948) and others – followed that with another Top 30 record in the same vein, 'Say I Am', but eventually they changed their style to become a less raunchy, more candy-coated bubble-rock group. Their many hits during 1967–9 (mostly written by James and Bob King) included 'I Think We're Alone Now', 'Mirage' and 'Gettin' Together' (1967); 'Mony Mony' (a Number 3 in the US and Number 1 in the UK) 'Do Something to Me' and 'Crimson and Clover' (1968); 'Sweet Cherry Wine', 'Crystal Blue Persuasion' and 'Ball of Fire' (1969). After the group disbanded in 1970 James returned to the US Top 40 as a solo act with 'Draggin' the Line' and 'I'm Comin' Home' (both 1971), but had no further success until 1980 when his 'Three Times in Love' reached Number 19. The rest of the Shondells recorded briefly as Hog Heaven in the early Seventies.

JAN AND DEAN

Kingpins of the California surf music and hot rod crazes of the early Sixties, Jan Berry (born in Los Angeles on 3 April 1941) and Dean Torrence (born in the same city on 10 March 1940) were entrenched in an era when pop was fun and by no means culture. Had their career not been abruptly terminated, it's difficult to imagine that their success would have continued much beyond 1966. Both attended Emerson Junior High School in LA and discovered their singing capabilities in the shower room after football practice. The season over, it was into the garage with two tape recorders and a few friends, among them Bruce Johnston, the future Beach Boy, to record 'Jenny Lee' as Jan and Arnie – Arnie Ginsberg – a song about a local burlesque stripper. A few months later in 1958, it was a Top 10 hit (on Arwin). Further hits followed under the name of Jan and Dean, notably 'Baby Talk', a Number 10 in 1959 (on Dore), produced and arranged by Herb

Alpert and Lou Adler, while they were still at college, Berry studying to be a doctor and Torrence studying design.

For 'Heart and Soul', a Top 30 hit in 1961, they moved to Challenge, and then signed with Liberty in 1962 and started singing about one of their favourite pastimes – surfing. The group had been gigging with the Beach Boys, and when Brian Wilson played them a demo of 'Surf City', which they recorded and took to Number 1 in 1963, it opened up a vintage period for Jan and Dean who, alongside the Beach Boys, fought off the British Invasion with a string of hot rod, surfin' and high-school epics like 'Drag City', 'Little Old Lady From Pasadena' and 'Dead Man's Curve', all Top 10 hits during 1963–4 on Liberty. They hosted The TAMI Show, disastrously took on folk-rock with a 1965 album, Folk'n'Roll, and often sang on Beach Boys sessions; Jan actually sang lead on the Beach Boys' Party hit 'Barbara Ann'. Brian Wilson had a hand in most of their classic hits between 1963 and 1965.

Then while filming Easy Come – Easy Go early in 1966, Jan crashed his car into a parked truck and all but sliced off the top of his head. It took years for him to recover fully but, though he cut some sides for A&M in the early Seventies, no permanent return to Jan and Dean was ever likely. Dean has been involved with the Legendary Masked Surfers and California Music but more importantly now runs a flourishing studio in Hollywood, Kittyhawk, designing posters and album sleeves. Their contribution to the less complicated Sixties pop is best remembered through their hits on either their Legendary Masters or Gotta Take That One Last Ride albums released in 1974.

JANSCH, BERT

Born in Glasgow on 3 November 1943, Bert Jansch worked as a gardener in Edinburgh before moving to London to become one of the most successful guitarists on the folk scene. Originally influenced by bluesmen like Big Bill Broonzy and Lightnin' Hopkins, he followed Davy Graham as a leading exponent of the 'folk baroque' style. Jansch applied this guitar technique to his own songs, of which 'Needle of Death' (on Bert Jansch, Transatlantic, 1965) was the best known. He then concentrated on using this technique on traditional songs (as on the 1966 Transatlantic album Jack Orion). On all his solo recordings the voice is weak but effectively propped up by the intricate accompaniment.

In 1966, Jansch recorded an excellent album of jazz-tinged instrumentals with his friend, John Renbourn, entitled Bert and John, and the following year he and Renbourn formed a band, Pentangle, along with Danny Thompson, Jacqui McShee and Terry Cox. Pentangle was an amplified acoustic band, and mixed folk with jazz, blues and contemporary songs. It was a success, internationally, but the muted, sophisticated approach often sounded monotonous. In 1974, after Pentangle had broken up, Jansch recorded an album for Charisma, L.A. Turnaround, backed by American country musicians and produced by Mike Nesmith – a fusion that brought new life to his excellent guitar technique. More recently, he has recorded Santa Barbara Honeymoon and A Rare Conundrum (1977) which inclines to his earlier folk style, and he continues to collaborate with John Renbourn. See also Pentangle

JAPAN

Despite their basic glam rock/funk origins, Japan's later work proved to be some of the most subtle and innovative synthesizer-based rock to emerge out of the early Eighties.

Japan came together at school in Catford, South London during the early Seventies, with the Batt brothers David (guitar/vocals) and Steve (drums) (who renamed themselves Sylvian and Jansen respectively), Mick Karn (bass) and Richard Barbieri (keyboards). In 1977 (with the addition of guitarist Rob Dean), Japan's made-up, glam image was completely at odds with the 'summer of punk'. At this point they were still a guitar-heavy band, and their label (Ariola/Hansa) tried to promote them as a hard rock outfit. But Japan were clearly not in that market as was shown by the poor audience reaction they inspired on a support slot with the Blue Öyster Cult. They made three albums for Ariola, but it wasn't until the third, the highly underrated Quiet Life (1978), that Japan essayed the complex electronic arrangements for which they came to be known.

Because Sylvian's voice was vaguely similar to Bryan Ferry's, and also due to the band's glam past, they were unjustly tagged as Roxy Music copyists. Poor reviews sabotaged album sales and Japan signed to another label, Virgin. After a year they emerged with Gentlemen Take Polaroids (1980), and with synthesizers in vogue at the time, it elicited a far more positive critical response. Dean left soon after, to later re-emerge with Gary Numan. Sales picked up, and in 1981 Japan released

David Sylvian, front man of inscrutable androgynous Japan, predictably had more solo success than the others after the band's break-up

their classic album, *Tin Drum*. A beautifully textured collection with a clear oriental influence, it featured the haunting 'Ghosts' and the powerful 'Visions of China', probably their finest work.

Having earned the respect of their peers, various members of Japan began to do more and more outside the band, particularly Sylvian who had already worked with Riuichi Sakamoto of the **Yellow Magic Orchestra**. This drew them increasingly further apart and in 1983, they released their last album, the live LP *Oil on Canvas*. Of all Japan's members, Sylvian scored the greatest success after the demise of the band, starting his solo recording career with the album, *Brilliant Trees* (1984) which gave him three UK hit singles, most notably 'Red Guitar'.

JAY AND THE AMERICANS In
1962, the year of the twist and hootenanny epidemics, Jay and the Americans climbed their way to the American Top 5 with 'She Cried' (United Artists). Jay Black (born 2 November 1947) provided the plaintive lead voice while Kenny Vance (9 December 1943), Sandy Deane (30 January 1960), Marty Saunders (28 February 1941) – also their lead guitarist – and Howie Kane (6 June 1942) added the neatly dovetailed chorus and harmonies. Sincere and emotional and anachronistic; simple arrangements in the age of **Phil Spector**; clean-cut, All-American image in the era of the British Invasion – despite or because of it all they had a steady flow of hits – 18 between 1962 and 1970, mostly produced by **Wes Farrell**, notably 'Come a

Little Closer' and 'Cara Mia' (both Top 5) with Jay Black also enjoying some favour on solo ventures. They seemed oblivious to all that was changing around them, though this very fact was possibly the key to their surprising longevity. Black and Vance both recorded solo albums for Atlantic in 1975.

JAYNETTS Mary Sue Wells, Ethel Davis, Ada Ray and Yvonne Bushnell were the members of the Jaynetts. From New York's Bronx, they first appeared on Zell Sanders' J&S label in 1956. However, it was not until 1963 that they came to the fore with the driving, hypnotic 'Sally Go 'Round the Roses', a Top 5 record on Sanders' Tuff subsidiary. Sanders' daughter, Johnnie Louise Richardson – who was also half of hitmakers Johnnie and Joe of 'Over the Mountain' fame – recorded but did not perform with the group, which, after a minor hit as the Hearts ('Dear Abby'), disbanded in 1968.

JAZZ-ROCK During World War II, jazz began to separate itself from black entertainment music in general, though throughout the immediate postwar period it would have been impossible to draw a confident line between current jazz style and, say, the idioms of R&B or jump blues. Records by **Wynonie Harris**, Sonny Thompson or Tiny Bradshaw contain passages, particularly tenor-sax solos, that could easily have been played at a Jazz At The Philharmonic concert, while the jazz playing of Illinois Jacquet or Charlie Ventura would fit perfectly into any R&B band. A common basis in the blues

rendered this a perfectly natural state of affairs, and in the work of Gene Ammons, Stanley Turrentine and many organ-led combos this jazz/R&B fusion continued almost unaltered through to the Seventies.

The arrival of rock'n'roll brought a mass white audience for the first time to black popular music, which coincided with a movement in jazz towards greater complexity and a view of the musician as artist rather than entertainer. Jazz, in consequence, vanished from popular music almost overnight. In the middle Sixties, this process went into reverse. Jazz had, by now, assumed a more explicit and extrovert manner, while rock music was entering an experimental phase. In both the US and Britain, a generation of musicians appeared to take advantage of this situation and refused to make a sharp distinction between the two idioms. Gary Burton's quartet, for instance, played in a style almost exactly midway between jazz and rock and their example encouraged a host of others, as did that of **Miles Davis** during the early Seventies. In Britain, several groups came into being composed of young players with a jazz background who moved, as if by instinct, into the rock world. Among them were **Soft Machine**, Nucleus and **Colosseum**, whose members had served their apprenticeship with bands as diverse as the New Jazz Orchestra, John Mayall's groups and the **Graham Bond** Organisation.

It is impossible to overemphasize the effect of this cross-fertilization on the development of rock. Improvisation, the stock-in-trade of jazz, was brought to a music which hitherto had concentrated on finished, definitive performance. **Cream**, perhaps the most influential progressive rock band, was two-thirds composed of players whose musical imagination had developed in a jazz context, and their emphasis on long, exploratory solos derived directly from the jazz tradition.

Of much less importance has been the practice, often described as 'jazz-rock', of simply adding brass and reed sections to rock bands. The pioneers in this field, **Blood, Sweat and Tears**, produced some interesting music on their first two albums but soon degenerated into mannerism and displays of mere virtuosity, as did **Chicago** and other groups who followed.

The relationship between jazz and rock is a complex one and no two groups work in exactly the same way, but there are those who believe that jazz-rock reached its peak in the early to mid-Seventies, notably with the **Mahavishnu Orchestra**'s *The Inner Mounting Flame* (1971), and the various bands put together by ex-Miles Davis sidemen like Stanley Clarke, **Chick Corea**, Joe Zawinul (founder of **Weather Report** with Wayne Shorter) and **Herbie Hancock**. According to this argument, the ability of the jazz-rock groups to add anything creative to rock seemed to die around the mid-Seventies, gradually becoming the sound of filler music on television shows or in advertisements where a certain hip but not too young image was required. Jazz-rock built up its own establishment, its own set of musicians who tended to play in each other's bands and who considered themselves jazz musicians; these people saw themselves using rock styles merely as an aid to mass communication or mass money-making, depending on which way you looked at it. By the early Eighties, jazz-rock was no longer part of rock; the nearest it got was in its close links with the technically expert but emotionally dead hand of disco-funk, or when its musicians were used as session men. In the light of these kinds of arguments, perhaps the only generalization that can be made is that the jazz tradition has at the very least reasserted itself as a vigorous current in popular music.

JAZZ, TRADITIONAL

Britain had its first real taste of traditional (or 'trad') jazz during World War II when many British musicians first heard recorded New Orleans jazz – courtesy of some thousands of American servicemen. Probably the first and most influential British traditional jazz band was George Webb's Dixielanders, formed around 1944 by George Webb. The band broadcast in 1945 with a line-up borrowed from King Oliver's Creole Jazz Band – piano, two cornets, clarinet, trombone, banjo, tuba and drums. By 1947, Humphrey Lyttelton had joined the band and they had reverted to the traditional Hot Seven line-up using only Lyttelton's cornet. The Dixielanders broke up in 1948, leaving Lyttelton fronting a band composed mainly of ex-Dixielanders. In 1951 he and clarinetist Wally Fawkes reorganized the band using a rhythm section of piano, guitar and banjo, bass and drums, and in 1953 they added the alto saxophone of Bruce Turner. To the disgust of the most purist fans, the sacrosanct tradition of New Orleans marching bands was giving way.

In 1951, the National Federation of Jazz Organisations put on a traditional jazz concert at the Festival Hall in London, graced by the presence of the then Princess Elizabeth, future Queen of England. By this time the number of working 'trad' bands had enormously proliferated. Among the best-remembered pioneers are **Chris Barber** (whose band included **Lonnie Donegan** and Monty Sunshine), Ken Colyer (whose important influence fell on musicians such as Barber, **Acker Bilk**, **Alexis Korner** and Micky Ashman), Mike Daniels (who used Cy Laurie, Charlie Galbraith and Micky Ashman in his Delta Jazzmen), Mick Mulligan (whose vocalist was blues shouter George Melly), and Alex Welsh.

Trad quickly became associated with radical politics and the bohemian image of the music attracted a sizeable following in the record-buying public. In some ways the world of trad jazz (clubs, beatniks and beer rather than coffee) became a symbol of rebellion in Britain. However, as the music grew in popularity it lost most of its purist connotations and the biggest hit records associated with trad – Acker Bilk's 'Stranger on the Shore' (1961) and Chris Barber's 'Petite Fleur' (1959) emphasized that trad had been merged with Tin Pan Alley. Nevertheless, the skiffle movement flourished within trad itself, and the Chris Barber and Ken Colyer skiffle groups had earlier provided the motor for a new resurgence in British pop – leading directly to the success of Lonnie Donegan, an increasing interest in the blues and small-group music, indirectly to the success of a host of British pop stars (culminating with the Beatles) who all started in skiffle groups, and to the development of the British R&B of the Sixties.

JEFFERSON AIRPLANE/JEFFERSON STARSHIP

The Airplane became synonymous with the 'San Francisco Sound' in 1967 when both 'Somebody to Love' and 'White Rabbit' were Top 10 US hits on RCA. Although the critical consensus is that the Airplane reached their peak in 1970, they remain, with the **Grateful Dead**, the most long-lasting and prolific of the groups to emerge from Haight-Ashbury in the late Sixties. Formed on the initiative of singer Marty Balin, who had recorded solo sides for Challenge in the early Sixties, the group was born out of a bunch of ex-folk musicians, who began playing folk-rock at the Matrix in the summer of 1965. One of the earliest San Francisco bands to establish themselves at the centre of the growing local culture, they were the first to secure a recording contract. The advance paid by RCA was said to be $25,000, and by the time the first album (*Jefferson Airplane Takes Off*) was recorded the following winter, the group was fully electric.

Although it was, in parts, derivative of the **Beatles** and the **Lovin' Spoonful**, the record showed how innovative the Jefferson Airplane were to be. From the beginning they saw their music as a means of breaking down established traditions and mores: hence the unabashed way they celebrated the drug culture, as early as 1965. Following the release of *Takes Off*, singer Signe Anderson left to be replaced by Grace Slick from the Great Society, another San Francisco group. Drummer Skip Spence also departed, to form **Moby Grape**. The remaining personnel remained together for the next four years. They were Jorma Kaukonen, lead guitar (born 23 December 1940), Jack Casady, bass (13 April 1944), Paul Kantner, guitar and vocals (12 March 1942), Marty Balin, vocals (30 January 1943), Grace Slick, vocals (30 October 1939) and Spencer Dryden, drums (7 April 1943). They were a co-operative, multi-media band, with posters, album-sleeves, dance promotion and Glenn McKay's Headlights light show all integral parts of their activity. The late Sixties also saw them at a creative zenith as a recording group with *Surrealistic Pillow* (1967), *After Bathing at Baxters* and *Crown of Creation* (1968), the live *Bless Its Pointed Little Head* and the politically oriented *Volunteers* (1969). Grace Slick was an important addition to the band; she strengthened its visual and musical identity (through her harmonies with Balin), and she was the composer of the Airplane's two hit singles, 'White Rabbit' and 'Somebody to Love'. Equally important was the group's electronic experimentation, in the extended instrumental passages of songs like '3/5 of a Mile in 10 Seconds' and 'The Ballad of You, Me and Pooneil'. The pressures on the Airplane during these four years were immense and the cracks started to appear in 1970 when Casady and Kaukonen, who wanted to get back to playing blues again, formed Hot Tuna. Similarly Balin, whose contributions on each successive album were becoming less and less, left the band he had nurtured, a disillusioned figure, and although involved at the outset of Hot Tuna, left them, too, to form his own band, Grootna. Not even the arrival of violinist Papa John Creach prior to Balin's departure could cement the Hot Tuna/Balin/Slick/Kantner factions of the band together. It wasn't until 1971 –

Grace Slick of Jefferson Airplane

after Slick's car crash and baby, the formation of their own record label, Grunt, the second Hot Tuna album and the bombastic *Blows Against The Empire* of the retitled Jefferson Starship – that *Bark* appeared to prove that the Airplane were still in existence.

Although members of the band contributed to splinter Grunt productions like *Sunfighter*, *Papa John Creach*, *Burghers* and *Black Kangaroo*, it was another year before the insipid *Long John Silver* appeared. Technically the last Airplane album, it showed that the totality of the band was no longer the primary interest of its members. Ex-**Quicksilver Messenger Service** bassist, David Freiburg, joined for the 1972 American tour and afterwards produced the impressive *Baron Von Tollbooth and the Chrome Nun* (1973) with Slick and Kantner followed by Slick's first 'solo' venture, *Manhole*.

The next 'group' venture, with Craig Chaquico on lead guitar and Pete Sears on bass and keyboards, was the Starship's *Dragonfly* (1974), an even more marked return to form that was indeed worthy of the Jefferson prefix. With Balin returning to the band (he sang one track on *Dragonfly*), the vocal depth of the band was strengthened and the content of songs became more diverse; it was when Balin's love songs were phased out in the Sixties, that iconoclasm had become the order of the day. Significantly, it was with his 'Miracles' from *Red Octopus* that the band returned to the singles (and album) charts in 1975.

Spitfire (1976), like *Red Octopus*, was a platinum album, but Slick and Balin let after one further album – the 1978 release, *Earth*. Mickey Thomas, previously the singer with the **Elvin Bishop** band, joined in 1979 and Aynsley Dunbar shortly after, both of them debuting with *Freedom at Point Zero*. By 1981 and the release of *Modern Times*, Grace Slick was back as

a permanent member. *Winds of Change* followed in 1983 and *Nuclear Furniture* in 1984, while two years later the band – now billed as Starship – finally achieved a major UK hit with 'We Built This City'.

The Airplane/Starship were and still are a very important band. Pioneers in many fields, they created sensuous music of the highest order, and if at times over-emphatic lyrically and self-indulgent, they were powerful spokesmen for a generation intensely critical of prevailing American values.

JENNINGS, WAYLON Waylon Jennings had a bit part in a 1966 movie, *Nashville Rebel*, and has since done much to earn that title. Born on 15 June 1937 in Littlefield, Texas, he played bass with **Buddy Holly** in 1959 and 'Jole Blon', his first record on Brunswick was produced by Holly. He moved to a folk-country style, recording for Trend, J.D.'s (leased to Vocalion), Ramco and A&M. In 1965, Jennings became involved in mainstream country when **Chet Atkins** signed him to RCA. He had hits with 'Green River', 'Only Daddy That'll Walk the Line' and 'MacArthur Park', but soon found the existing country scene musically restricting.

By the early Seventies, Jennings had dispensed with house producers and began to make his own, fine, country-rock albums like *Lonesome, 'Ornrey And Mean*. He toured with the **Grateful Dead** and was recognized as a member of the loose 'Nashville underground' circle which included **Willie Nelson**, Tompall Glaser and Billy Joe Shaver. Shaver contributed several songs to the 1973 album, *Honky Tonk Heroes*, which featured Jennings' road band rather than the conventional Nashville session men, and Jennings collaborated with Nelson, Glaser and his wife, Jessi Colter, on the 1976 release *Wanted: The Outlaws* – the first country album to go platinum.

Jennings had a number of crossover hits during the later Seventies, including 'Luckenbach, Texas' (1977) and a 1976 duet with Willie Nelson, 'Good Hearted Woman', and by the early Eighties was firmly regarded even by the Nashville establishment as one of the great contemporary country talents.

JETHRO TULL Formed in 1968, Jethro Tull comprised Ian Anderson (flute, vocals, born in Edinburgh on 10 August 1947), Clive Bunker (drums, born 12 December 1946), Mick Abrahams (guitar, born 7 April 1943) and Glen Cornick (bass guitar, born 24

April 1947). Anderson spent the early Sixties in various bands in and around Blackpool, but formed Tull in London. He taught himself flute about six months before, his early playing owing much to Roland Kirk.

Naming themselves after the inventor of the seed drill, they were an immediate success in the clubs but their first single on Island Records, 'Song for Jeffrey', was not a hit. Changing to Chrysalis Records, they continued to enjoy singles success in Britain, though none made a dent in America, where the albums took off instead. Anderson's penchant for a tatty overcoat and manic stage presence – playing the flute while dancing on one leg becoming an early trademark – gave him instant appeal to both critics and public. By early 1969, however, changes were happening. Mick Abrahams left to form Blodwyn Pig, being replaced by Martin Barre (born 17 November 1946); Clive Bunker left to form Jude, and was replaced by Barriemore Barlow (born 10 September 1949); Glen Cornick left to form Wild Turkey and was replaced by Jeffrey Hammond-Hammond (born 30 July 1946). In 1971 John Evans (born 28 March 1948) joined on keyboards.

Anderson attempted his first concept album in 1971 with *Aqualung*, questioning organized religion and lamenting social injustice. These themes were further developed in *Thick as a Brick* (1972), which introduced stage props, low humour and film. As Tull continued moving further from the concept of a rock band playing music, their audiences grew by quantum leaps, though critics were turning the other way. In 1973 *A Passion Play* was greeted with universal critical scorn and sell-out tours; Anderson took the criticism to heart and announced the end of the band, apparently counting on a huge fan response which never materialized. In 1974 the group returned to performing their peculiar brand of rock, theatre and puerile comedy and in 1975 recorded the awful *Minstrel in the Gallery*.

A compilation album, *M.U.* (short for Musicians Union) appeared in 1976, as did *Too Old to Rock'n'Roll: Too Young to Die*, a concept album originally conceived as a stage musical for **Adam Faith**. A further three studio albums were released before the close of the decade, by which time Jethro Tull had become a distinctly unfashionable band. *The Broadsword and the Beast* (1982) and *Under Wraps* (1984) did little to help, though the group have maintained a loyal following.

JETT, JOAN, AND THE BLACKHEARTS Perennial girl rocker Joan Jett's solo career provided her with the success that evaded her while she was leader of the West Coast teenage all-girl hard rock outfit the Runaways. Her stripped-down, primitive Seventies guitar rock proved very successful, especially in the United States.

Born in Philadelphia on 22 September 1960, Jett moved with her family to Southern California when she was 14. She was a fan of the British glam-rock acts such as **Sweet** and **Gary Glitter**, but most of all **Suzi Quatro** who became an important role model for her. When she was 15, Jett joined the Runaways after meeting producer/manager **Kim Fowley** at a party. The band had a hard time at the hands of the critics, who brought into question the girls' ability to play their instruments. They split at the end of 1978, and after a protracted illness, Jett teamed up with Kenny Laguna (producer of **Jonathan Richman**) and Ritchie Cordell (legendary bubblegum producer and songwriter) to record the album *Joan Jett* in 1980. At first released only in Europe, it had a positive US press reaction, and was therefore released in the States with a new title, *Bad Reputation*, but it still failed to sell.

Jett recruited a band (which she called the Blackhearts) and recorded a second album, *I Love Rock'n'Roll* (1981). The heavy rock-pop of the title track, a cover of an Arrows B-side, became a US Number 1 single in 1982 (it reached Number 4 in the UK) and the album went platinum. Another single, 'Crimson and Clover' was also a US Top 10 hit the same year, but subsequent releases failed to equal this success.

JIVE FIVE Eugene Pitt and the Jive Five (Billy Prophet, Richard Harris, Norma Johnson and Jerome Hanna) reached Number 3 in the US with the Joe Rene-arranged 'My True Story' on the King-distributed Beltone label in 1961. Pitt, who wrote the song, made listeners weep with his impassioned cry of teenage *angst*. After less successful discs for Beltone and Sketch, they staged a comeback on United Artists with the Top 40 hit 'I'm a Happy Man' in 1965 and the wonderful 'Bench in the Park', which sold poorly. In the Seventies, they changed their name to the Jyve Fyve and with fresh personnel (including Casey Spencer, Webster Harris and Johnny Watson) they had some small soul hits on Avco Embassy. Eugene Pitt had previously sung with the Genies whose 'Who's That Knockin'' was a hit on Shad in 1959.

JOEL, BILLY Billy Joel's path to becoming America's most salesworthy singer/songwriter of the late Seventies and Eighties was by no means smooth. He was born in Hicksville, Long Island, on 6 May 1949, and boxed professionally in his teens before forming a rock band, the Hassles, who recorded two albums for United Artists. When the band split up he formed a duo, Attila, with fellow Hassle Jonathan Small, but the partnership lasted for only one album. He then signed a songwriting deal with Artie Ripp's Family Productions and made his solo debut the following year with *Cold Spring Harbor* (Family/Philips, 1972), a somewhat sombre collection of songs in the then-fashionable introspective mode. Legal and managerial problems led to Joel's absence from recording for nearly two years, during which time he moved to California and earned a living playing the piano bars under the name of Bill Martin – an experience which provided the basis for the Top 40 hit single 'Piano Man' (1974) and the album of the same name, his first for Columbia.

Street Life Serenade and *Turnstiles* followed in 1975 and 1976, neither of them spectacular sellers, but it was *The Stranger* (1977) that finally put Joel into the major league of performers. Produced by Phil Ramone, it included five US hit singles – 'Just the Way You Are', 'Movin' Out (Anthony's Song)', 'Only the Good Die Young', 'She's Always a Woman' and 'My Life' – and also established Joel internationally. Stung by criticism of his MOR leanings (*The Stranger* was the most played album of 1977–8 on America's AOR stations), he demonstrated his rock credentials on the album *Glass Houses* (1980), and topped the US chart during that year with a single taken from it, 'It's Still Rock and Roll to Me'. *Songs in the Attic* (1981) was a live album highlighting some of his early to mid-Seventies compositions, while *The Nylon Curtain* (1982) was a piece of extended social commentary that included one of his best songs, 'Allentown', about small-town unemployment.

His next album, *An Innocent Man* (1983), was far lighter in tone but more original in conception – a tour through America's urban pop heritage, featuring immaculate re-creations of the sounds and styles of **Little Anthony and the Imperials** ('The Longest Time'), the **Four Seasons** ('Uptown Girl') and others. The latter track was a UK Number 1 in 1983, and another

Singer, songwriter and pianist Billy Joel, a huge success with the public, but not the critics

single from the album – 'Tell Her About It' – matched that achievement in the US. At his best writing punchy, forthright, streetwise love songs, Billy Joel is an engagingly unfussy performer with some claim to be regarded alongside the likes of **Bruce Springsteen** and **Bob Seger**. Only the very scale of his success has prevented him being taken more seriously by the critics.

JOHN, ELTON One of the most successful rock entertainers of the Seventies, Elton John was born Reginald Kenneth Dwight on 25 March 1947 in Pinner, Middlesex. He began his career as a weekend pub pianist at the Northwood Hills Hotel for £1 a night in 1964 and spent four years as organist with the soul group, Bluesology, which backed visiting American acts such as **Major Lance**, **Patti LaBelle** and the Bluebelles, **Billy Stewart**, and the **Ink Spots**. He wrote and sang the

Elton John: 'The clothes I wear have always been to conceal the fact that I'm horribly shy'

group's first Fontana single 'Come Back Baby' in 1965. Bluesology became **Long John Baldry**'s backing band in 1967, the year of Baldry's British Number 1 hit with the ballad 'Let the Heartaches Begin' but Dwight, who had changed his name to Elton John – taken from Elton Dean, the group's saxophonist, and John Baldry – grew eager to leave. He failed a Liberty Records audition but was put in touch with **Bernie Taupin**, a lyricist from Lincolnshire, whom he finally met after six months of putting music to his lyrics. Helped by Caleb Quaye (former guitarist with Bluesology), they got a three-year writing contract with DJM for £10 a week each and John left Bluesology.

Taupin and John tried unsuccessfully to write Top 40 material and John performed on Marble Arch and Music For Pleasure budget albums covering current hits, while he released one single, 'I've Been Loving You', in 1968 and recorded an unreleased album of flower power material. Encouraged by DJM song-plugger Steve Brown, they wrote 'Skyline Pigeon', 'Lady Samantha' and finally the first album *Empty Sky* (DJM), released to warm reviews in the summer of 1969. Producer Gus Dudgeon and arranger Paul Buckmaster transformed the sound of the second album, *Elton John* (1970), which, containing 'Your Song' and 'Border Song', revealed John as a romantic and sensitive performer. However, it gained little British success. A band comprising two former Spencer Davis sidemen,

drummer Nigel Olsson (born 5 February 1949) and bassist Dee Murray (born 3 April 1946) caused a stir when premièred at the Rock Proms backing John's exuberant showmanship.

In 1970, the trio opened above **David Ackles** at the Troubadour Club in Los Angeles to an ecstatic reception, swiftly echoed in New York and Philadelphia with the effect that *Elton John* on MCA swept into the *Billboard* album charts at Number 17, a feat repeated later in the year by the third album *Tumbleweed Connection* (1970), steeped in Taupin's obsession with the American Old West. In Britain the American reaction was reflected by the chart entry of the second and third albums in spring 1971.

Meanwhile a film soundtrack *Friends* on Paramount, a live tape of a New York Radio show *17-11-70*, and the grandiose *Madman Across the Water* were released in quick succession in 1971. *Madman* introduced guitarist Davey Johnstone from Magna Carta, and its doomy melodramatic arrangements were almost Buckmaster's last fling. A critical backlash greeted the flood of product in Britain but in America it made Elton John the first artist since the **Beatles** to have four albums simultaneously in the Top 20.

His music, a synthesis of current styles that betrays his fan-like mentality but fails to project a distinct musical persona, arrived at a time when the distinction between pop and rock was beginning to blur. His easygoing command of a multiplicity of styles, his flair for outrageous showmanship, and his appeal to romantic sensibilities enabled him to become highly successful on stage and record. Lyricist Taupin developed from his earlier poetic pretensions to a more direct, jaunty vein on the next album, *Honky Château*, recorded in France and released in 1972. With *Don't Shoot Me, I'm Only the Piano Player* (1973) it re-established John's critical and popular appeal on both sides of the Atlantic, which grew even greater in 1973, the year he set up Rocket Records and released the double album *Goodbye Yellow Brick Road* arranged by Del Newman, which showed a broadening musical range and Taupin's increased interest in film mythology. Despite the mediocre *Caribou*, 1974 saw his popularity increase until his monthly royalties cheque surpassed the Beatles' earnings at their peak. In 1975, the autobiographical *Captain Fantastic and the Brown Dirt Cowboy*, dealing with his and Taupin's early career, shipped platinum for American sales

in excess of one million units, the first album ever to do so, and he augmented and reformed his band. It was followed later in the year by *Rock of the Westies*.

1976 put Elton at the top of both the US and UK charts with 'Don't Go Breaking My Heart', recorded with Rocket stablemate **Kiki Dee** and written with Taupin under the pseudonyms of Anne Orson and Carte Blanche. A year later, he announced what turned out to be a temporary retirement from performing and became heavily involved in the day-to-day running of Watford Football Club, of which he remains Chairman. He broke with Taupin to form a brief partnership with lyricist Gary Osborne – they collaborated on Elton's albums *A Single Man* (1978) and *Victim of Love* (1979) – and he hired **Thom Bell** as producer for The Thom Bell Sessions, which featured the hit single 'Mama Can't Buy You Love' (1979).

Reunited with Taupin in 1980, Elton signed an American recording deal with Geffen and made a strong return to the UK charts after some years of indifferent chart placings with the singles 'Blue Eyes', 'I Guess That's Why They Call It the Blues' and 'I'm Still Standing'. Not only his musical success but his surprise marriage in 1983 and the remarkable achievements of Watford F.C. under his astute command became major talking points between 1983 and 1986.

At the beginning of January 1987, after having suffered recurring and increasing problems with his throat, John underwent exploratory surgery in Sydney, Australia, during which nodules were removed from his vocal cords. Although these were found not to be cancerous, doctors advised that he give up singing for at least a year.

Behind the intimidating statistics, Elton John remains an elusive artist, lacking a defined musical character. Rather his success reflects his ability to synthesize the prevailing styles and postures in an amiable – and sometimes moving – manner.

JOHN, LITTLE WILLIE An important influence on **James Brown** and many other soul performers, Little Willie John was born in Camden, Arkansas, on 15 November 1937. His first forays into the studio are obscure, but by the age of 16 he had toured with the Paul Williams Orchestra and had recorded for Prize, Savoy and Rama. In 1955 he joined King Records, where his fourteen R&B best-sellers revealed an assurance and presence that few teenage singers possessed. His biggest hits (all Top 30) included 'Fever', 'Talk to Me' and 'Sleep', all of which were produced by **Henry Glover**. Sunny and the Sunglows, **Elvis Presley**, Peggy Lee, **Johnny Preston**, **Fleetwood Mac** ('Need Your Love So Bad') and many others revived his hits, faithfully copying the arrangements of his vocal inflections. His sister Mable recorded for Stax and was a member of **Ray Charles**' backing group, the Raelettes. Few black performers from the Fifties had the authority or long-term potential of Willie John, who died while incarcerated in Washington State Prison on 26 May 1968.

JOHNNY AND THE HURRICANES
Originally from the Toledo, Ohio area, Johnny and the Hurricanes – Johnny Paris (tenor sax), Paul Tesluk (organ), Dave Yorko (guitar), Lionel 'Butch' Mattice (bass) and Don Staczek (drums) – first got together at high school and they played local hops and dances behind a vocalist at Toledo's Pearson Park. As instrumentalists, they were signed to a management contract early in 1959 by Irving Micahnik and Harry Balk, two Detroit entrepreneurs who placed them with Morty Craft's newly-formed Warwick label.

Their first record, a frantic, exciting dance-disc titled 'Crossfire', reached Number 23 in the US in July 1959, but did not feature the prominent organ-sound for which they became famous. Their follow-up 'Red River Rock' (an adaptation of the traditional 'Red River Valley') reached Number 5 in the US and Number 2 in the UK, establishing the group internationally. By this time, Bill 'Little Bo' Savitch from the Royaltones had replaced Staczek on drums – not that fans knew it in an era when group members were anonymous faces in photographs. Two more hits, 'Reveille Rock' (1959) and 'Beatnik Fly' (1960), followed on Warwick before the group switched to Big Top in New York where they continued their run with 'Rocking Goose' (which reached Number 3 in the UK but only Number 60 in America), 'Down Yonder' and 'Ja-Da' (1961) before flopping with 'Old Smokie' and 'Minnesota Fats' in 1962.

The original 1959 line-up had disbanded by 1961, and during 1962–3 the touring line-up underwent constant personnel changes with only leader Johnny Paris remaining static. While the group toured, sessionmen made the records, a precedent which had been established as early as 'Beatnik Fly' in 1959.

Johnny and the Hurricanes were the archetypal Fifties instrumental group, even if they were merely a trademark for a highly marketable sound. In all probability, the group's management profited most from the group's existence since Micahnik and Balk took writer credits (as Tom King and Ira Mack respectively) for most of their early records.

JOHNSON, LINTON KWESI
Black poet Linton Kwesi Johnson, born in Jamaica in 1952, came to the fore in the late Seventies at a time when there was renewed interest in reggae and punk poets, led by **John Cooper Clarke** (with whom Johnson often co-headlined), were becoming increasingly popular. Concerts, consisting of a varied bill of music and verse, found a new wide audience as the 'poetry recital' acquired a contemporary relevance.

Johnson moved to Brixton, London, in 1963 and after leaving school and working as a tailor, he took a part-time sociology degree course at the University of London. During this time he became involved in black politics, the black power movement and the works of black political thinkers. In 1971 he

Linton Kwesi Johnson, reggae poet of British black protest

began writing himself and later published two anthologies, *Voices of the Living and the Dead* (1974) and *Dread Beat and Blood* (1975). His politicized verse pulsed with the strong rhythms of the Afro-Caribbean tradition, and being a Jamaican, he imbued his poems with a strong reggae beat.

In 1977, Johnson made his first recording, a four-track EP for Virgin Records that featured poems recited over reggae rhythms and constituted the start of a prolonged recording career that married poetry and music. In 1978, *Dread Beat and Blood*, his debut album, was released to wide acclaim. He then signed to Island and released *Forces of Victory* (1979), which saw him become more ambitious and experimental as regards the musical content of his recordings, a process that continued through subsequent releases like *Bass Culture* (1980) and *LKJ in Dub* (1982).

JOHNSON, MARV
Born on 15 October 1938, in Detroit, singer Marv Johnson began his career as a member of the Serenaders. Going solo in 1959, he scored nine consecutive R&B hits before 1961 which collectively represented the first rumblings of the new Detroit soul sound. Produced for United Artists by Berry Gordy Jr, they were both crisper and more frothy than most black pop of the day: in retrospect, the sound was distinctly Motown-like. Girls sang thin, reedy 'bop shoo bops' while a bass singer hummed the kind of 'bottom' at which James Jamieson would later excel. Instantly hummable, 'Come to Me', 'You Got What It Takes', 'I Love the Way You Love' and 'Move Two Mountains' (all Top 30) hinted at the seductive aura of later Motown classics. Johnson eventually followed his mentor to Tamla-Motown-Gordy, where he scored with 'I Miss You Baby' (1966) and 'I'll Pick a Rose for My Rose' in 1968.

JOHNSON, ROBERT
Often cited as the greatest, most expressive and harrowingly poetic blues singer ever to record, Robert Johnson remains to this day a figure firmly shrouded in mystery. The only hard fact is that he cut some 29 songs during 1936–7. They are all gripping, magnificent performances that stand unrivalled in blues history. These recordings – Johnson's songs and the manner in which they were performed – represent the ultimate flowering of the Mississippi blues style. He died in 1938 at the age of

26, probably as the result of poisoning by a jealous girlfriend. Many rock bands have recorded Johnson's compositions including the **Rolling Stones** ('Love in Vain'), **Cream** ('Crossroads' and 'From Four Till Late') and **John Mayall**'s Bluesbreakers ('Dust My Blues' and 'Rambling on My Mind').

JOHNSTON, BOB A staff producer for Columbia's country music division throughout the Sixties, Bob Johnston worked on albums by **Bob Dylan**, **Simon and Garfunkel**, **Johnny Cash** and **Leonard Cohen**. He was the 'Bob' addressed by Dylan when he calls out 'Is it rolling, Bob?' on the *Nashville Skyline* album. A Texan, Johnston's first success came with production work for MOR singer Patti Page. He went on to produce six Bob Dylan albums, from *Highway 61 Revisited* (1965) to *Self Portrait* (1970), and the Simon and Garfunkel hit single, 'Homeward Bound' (1966). In the late Sixties, he succeeded Don Law as head of Columbia's Nashville operation, but was ostracized by the country music establishment (because of associations with rock) and replaced by **Billy Sherrill**. As an independent producer in the Seventies, he worked with several artists on the UK Charisma label, including **Lindisfarne** – both *Fog on the Tyne* (1971) and *Dingly Dell* (1972) were Johnston productions – and Bell and Arc. He also produced albums for **Jimmy Cliff**, **Doug Kershaw**, Alvin Lee, **New Riders of the Purple Sage**, and **Loudon Wainwright III**, among many others.

JONES, GEORGE Influenced by **Roy Acuff** and **Hank Williams**, George Jones came out of Saratoga, East Texas, in 1954, at a time when rockabilly upstarts were threatening to make country music extinct. But even though he cut a couple of rockabilly sides under the name of Thumper Jones, he was – as his first country hit, 'Why Baby Why', for the Starday label in 1955, showed – a purist at heart. Despite a long string of superb records, Jones did not receive his due until 1962 and 1963, when disc jockeys voted him Number 1 male country singer. His honky-tonk music was matched by a lifestyle debilitated by drinking, and he did not maintain his position as 'king of country music'. Nevertheless, such mid-Sixties recordings as 'The Race Is On' (covered for the pop market in 1965 by singer Jack Jones, who was no relation) were as 'traditional' as any in a field leaning increasingly towards MOR music. In 1967 he went on tour

with **Tammy Wynette** and they married soon after. He shared her label (Epic) and her producer (**Billy Sherrill**), whose ornate, pop-oriented arrangements did much to blunt the classic Jones style. By the time their dream marriage dissolved in 1974, Jones had recorded some 100 albums (for Starday, Mercury, Musicor, United Artists and Epic), embracing virtually every form of country music, and if anything his stature grew within country circles as the Seventies progressed. In 1980, he won a Grammy award for Best Male Country Vocal Performance, for his single 'He Stopped Loving Her Today', and also won his first Country Music Association award for the album on which it appeared – *I Am What I Am*.

JONES, GRACE Jamaican-born (19 May 1952) model-turned-singer-and-actress Grace Jones became the darling of the nightclub set in the late Seventies. Symbolic of the power of image in rock, Jones' outrageous dress and androgynous image challenged normal notions of race, gender and

decorum and won a sizeable following for her largely pedestrian rock disco.

Arriving in Paris from New York in the mid-Seventies, Jones proceeded to become one of the best known high-fashion cover girls in the world. In 1977 she began to record as a singer in France and later signed to Island Records in the UK. Her popularity grew in the New York gay disco scene and her exotic performances captivated exclusive, jet set audiences. Jones' limited vocal abilities did not detract from her bizarre appeal and her early, formularized releases became disco hits without denting the main charts.

Large scale success eluded Jones until the release of the album *Warm Leatherette* in 1980. It abandoned the disco clichés of her previous work and moved into sparser, solid reggae/funk that the critics began to warm to, and the single 'Private Life', a cover of the **Pretenders** song, became her first UK Top 20 hit. Jones' next album, *Nightclubbing* (1981) was voted album of the year by the *New Musical Express*, and the following album, *Living My Life* (1982) was also well received, but con-

Grace Jones, model, singer and actress, in one of her more restrained outfits: she proved that a glamour image could carry a subversive message in sexual politics

sidering her critical acclaim, Jones' albums sold only moderately well and her singles consistently failed to reach the Top 40 on both sides of the Atlantic. The situation was redressed when after a long period of recording inactivity, the re-released single 'Pull Up to the Bumper' made the UK Top 20 at the end of 1985.

JONES, HOWARD Waiting until his late twenties before taking up a full-time career in music, singer/songwriter Howard Jones produced catchy, unpretentious synth-based pop that made the UK Top 5 at the first attempt; his debut album *Human's Lib* (1984) entered the UK charts at Number 1 and instantly went gold.

Born on 23 February 1955, Jones studied classical piano at Northern School of Music in Manchester but returned to his High Wycombe base in the late Seventies disillusioned with the classical establishment. While working in a plastics factory, Jones began writing songs. He acquired electronic keyboards and kept on plugging away until in March 1983 he recorded a session for Radio One; in May he played support on a **China Crisis** tour and in June he signed a recording contract with WEA.

The debut single 'New Song' was an immediate hit in September '83, and was followed by a string of hit singles and the highly successful LPs *The 12″ Album* and *Dream into Action*, which both made the UK LP Top 20 in 1985, amid growing critical acclaim. Jones continued his consistent UK chart success into 1986 with the single 'No One Is To Blame' at the start of the year.

JONES, JIMMY R&B singer Jimmy Jones scored two major UK and US hits in 1960, 'Handy Man' and 'Good Timin'', for MGM. He was born on 2 June 1937 in Birmingham, Alabama, and moved to New York in his teens, when he recorded with a number of groups including the Sparks Of Rhythm (Apollo), the Pretenders (Rama Central, Holiday, Whirlin' Disc) and the Savoys (Savoy). Despite later solo discs on Savoy, Arrow and Epic, he was poverty-stricken when **Otis Blackwell** took him to MGM where he recorded for the company's R&B subsidiary, Cub. 'Handy Man' and 'Good Timin'' relied chiefly on Jones' falsetto breaks for their appeal. Despite an acrobatic stage act and lesser hits with 'That's When I Cried' and 'I Told You So', Jones was typecast as a novelty singer – and the novelty soon wore off. He later recorded both for Vee Jay and

for Roulette before he finally faded out altogether.

JONES, JOE Born in New Orleans on 12 August 1926, Joe Jones was an opportunist, if not a great artist, and he had a special talent for acquiring some of the best New Orleans musicians in his band for recording and live dates. He struck gold in 1960 with 'You Talk Too Much', a novelty R&B number which climbed to Number 3 in the US charts on Roulette. After a minor hit with 'California Sun' and a fine album, he left New Orleans for New York to concentrate on artist management and for a time had success with two New Orleans acts, **Alvin Robinson** and the **Dixie Cups** (who had a Number 1 hit with 'Chapel of Love' in 1964). He later expanded his business interests to include his own label (Joe Jones) and recording studios.

JONES, PAUL Originally known as **Manfred Mann**'s pixie-faced 'one-in-the-middle', Paul Jones was a regular visitor to the Ealing Club throughout 1962, where as P.P. ('permanently pissed') Pond he would perform impromptu duets with Brian Jones behind huge sunglasses. A moderate singer, Jones – born on 24 February 1942 – left Manfred Mann in 1966 to pursue a solo career. He recorded two British Top 10 singles on his own – 'High Time' (1966) and 'I've Been a Bad Bad Boy' (1962) – but had stronger ambitions as an actor. He appeared in dramatic roles on stage, television, and in films, starring in Peter Watkins' *Privilege* (1967). In the late Seventies, he returned to performing as a member of R&B revivalists the Blues Band, and by 1986 he had begun a new career on radio as presenter of BBC Radio 2's *Rhythm and Blues* programme.

JONES, RICKIE LEE Singer/songwriter Rickie Lee Jones (born 8 November 1954, Chicago) had an instant platinum success with her eponymous debut album, a sophisticated and individual blend of folk, jazz and rock.

Jones grew up in Arizona, moving at the age of 19 to Los Angeles, where she began performing in small clubs, delivering a set of beat-poet style monologues set to a minimal rhythmic backing. In 1977 she met **Tom Waits** and it was during her friendship with Waits that Jones wrote many of the jazz-tinged songs about down-and-out people that appeared on her first LP.

In 1978 a set of her demos aroused the interest of Warner Brothers, and as her reputation began to grow, Lowell

George of **Little Feat** used a song of hers, 'Easy Money', on his solo album. Her own LP, *Rickie Lee Jones*, appeared in 1979 and the first single from it, 'Chuck E's in Love', undoubtedly Jones' best-known song and an international hit (US Number 4), pushed the album to US platinum sales.

As Jones' songs moved into more complex and less accessible structures, subsequent releases failed to produce a big hit single and album sales diminished, but *Pirate* (1981) still went gold. 1983 saw a 10-inch EP of ballad covers, *Girl at Her Volcano*, and on the LP *Magazine* (1984) she assumed the role of producer for the first time.

JONES, TOM Born in Treforest, Glamorgan, Wales, on 7 June 1940 as Thomas J. Woodward, Tom Jones first changed his name to Tommy Scott as a bar-room rock'n'roller in the late Fifties, singing for beer and change, brawling enough to bust his nose several times, and working by day as a labourer to support the wife and child he'd had since sixteen. Turned down in 1963 by **Joe Meek**, he was 'discovered' in a Pontypridd club a year later by ex-novelty singer and harmonica player, Gordon Mills, who was there to watch Mandy Rice Davies' act.

Then a songwriter, Mills took him to London as a demo-singer, changed his name to Jones, and let him record a song he'd demoed, 'It's Not Unusual' (Decca), which reached Number 1 in Britain in March 1965. Over the next two years Jones had more flops than hits, but then found his true audience on TV and in cabaret and never looked back. The mawkish 'Green, Green Grass of Home' stayed seven weeks at Number 1 over Christmas 1966, and Tom went on to win female hearts in America as a substitute Presley.

JOPLIN, JANIS One of rock music's most outstanding vocal talents, Janis Joplin (born in Port Arthur, Texas, on 19 January 1943) had a tragically short but ultimately deeply influential career. She spent the first seventeen years of her life in the South, acquiring a love of the blues through listening to the recordings of **Leadbelly** and **Bessie Smith**. Then she joined the national odyssey to San Francisco, on her first visit singing alone in folk clubs and bars, on her second joining **Big Brother and the Holding Company** as lead singer. The band played a raucous amalgam of rock and blues behind Janis' dramatic vocals. Little subtlety was in evidence; above all the music expressed enthusiasm, in the making of

Tomboy superstar Janis Joplin at the height of her brief career

music and in the community it was made for. The *Cheap Thrills* album (Columbia, 1968), for all its musical shoddiness, saw Janis at a peak. In particular the classic 'Ball and Chain' and 'Piece of My Heart' displayed her power as singer and symbol. They were desperate cries for love and security, transforming themselves in the emotional energy of the performance into triumphs of a will to continue.

In late 1968 Janis left the band, convinced that they had exhausted their collective potential. But with the undoubtedly more competent musicians with whom she thenceforth worked, Squeeze and later Full Tilt Boogie, the old enthusiasm was never quite recaptured, although her singing perhaps showed a finer control. Both *Kosmic Blues* (1969) and the posthumously released *Pearl* (1971) are fine records but somehow lack the bite of *Cheap Thrills*' joyous intensity. Janis

was now a superstar, confronting greater expectations with less human support. In addition, she faced the contradiction of the tomboy superstar, defying the feminine stereotypes, but also the traditional female blues persona of the eternal loser. A combination of these pressures eventually overwhelmed her. She died of a heroin overdose on 4 October 1970, in Hollywood. *See also* **Big Brother and the Holding Company**

JORDAN, LOUIS Born in Brinkley, Arkansas, in 1908, Jordan served a big-band apprenticeship and in 1938 formed his own combo, the Tympany Five, which he fronted as singer and alto saxophonist. For more than a decade this group produced blues, novelty blues and just novelties, making important versions of 'Caldonia' and 'Let the Good Times Roll' and sustaining the insouciance of 'Saturday

Night Fish Fry'. Titles like 'School Days' and 'Blue Light Boogie' hint at an influence upon **Chuck Berry** and Berry has been quick to admit his debt. Many blues and R&B artists who grew up to Jordan's music have remembered it fondly, and its effect upon early white rock'n'roll was not insignificant. The album *Let the Good Times Roll* (Decca) is a just sample of this exuberant music. Louis Jordan died in 1975.

JOURNEY One of the biggest-selling acts in rock, Journey produced a mainstream FM style that has ranked them among America's all-time favourite bands. They have achieved phenomenal record sales and filled stadiums all over their home country, but these figures have not been echoed worldwide, least of all in the UK where they have made only a very minor impression on the charts.

Formed in 1973 at the instigation of manager Walter James 'Herbie' Herbert II, the original line-up consisted of Greg Rolie (keyboards), Neal Schon (guitar), Ross Valory (bass) and Aynsley Dunbar (drums). During 1974–8, they toured steadily to promote their first three LPs, which all sold moderately. In 1978 they recorded a fourth, *Infinity*, with producer Roy Thomas Baker, which brought a change in their fortunes. It marked the recruitment of a proper vocalist in Steve Perry and the departure of Dunbar, to be replaced by Steve Smith. The LP yielded their first three chart singles and went on to earn double platinum status.

Journey broadened their appeal and started to sell records in ever greater quantities, making the US Top 20 for the first time with 'Lovin', Touchin', Squeezin'' in 1979, and notching up huge sales for three more new LPs. In 1981, after they released the double live set *Captured*, Greg Rolie retired from the gruelling tour schedules to live a more quiet life, and was replaced by Jonathan Cain, previously the leader of the Babys. Cain's arrival gave Journey a far poppier sound, and with him the band recorded in late '81 the mega-selling album *Escape* (the first album to inspire a video game) which achieved quintuple platinum sales in the US and spawned a bagful of hit singles into 1982.

Journey have always been the object of enormous critical derision, accused of being retrogressive, over-commercial and completely unadventurous by the likes of *Rolling Stone*, but despite this their records have sold exceptionally well and no doubt will continue to do so in the future.

JOY DIVISION/NEW ORDER

The most influential post-punk band to emerge in the late Seventies, Joy Division influenced many groups – **U2**, the **Cure**, **Echo and the Bunnymen** and more – who carried some of their introspective (some would say miserable) atmosphere into the Eighties, while New Order, the band that rose from its ashes, developed their music into a lighter electronic pop.

Coming together in Manchester with a line-up of Ian Curtis (vocals), Bernard Sumner (aka Dickin, aka Albrecht, guitar), Peter Hook (bass) and Stephen Morris (drums), the group started life under the name Warsaw in 1977. By 1978 they had changed their name to Joy Division (named after a Nazi prostitution camp) and released the EP 'An Ideal For Living' on the independent Enigma label. They then signed to the newly-formed Factory Records, and in June the next year released the single 'Transmission' and the first Joy Division LP, *Unknown Pleasures*. An album of rawness and power, produced by Martin Hannett who had produced the **Buzzcocks**' single 'Spiral Scratch', it caught the spirit of the economic depression and, virtually overnight, Joy Division became the darlings of the music press.

Although the group acquired enormous underground cult status and the album sold well on the independent charts, radio airplay was almost nil, since most stations found their material too gloomy. The only exception was Radio One DJ **John Peel**, who championed the band from the very beginning. Records were not, however, the main reason for Joy Division's success; their live dates were a spectacle of harrowing intensity as Curtis captivated audiences with his arhythmic twitches and anguished voice.

After a successful tour of Europe in January 1980, the band went into the studio to record a second album. Then, on May 18, on the point of leaving to tour the US, Curtis (a manic depressive who had attempted suicide twice previously), hung himself in a fit of depression brought on by the break-up of his marriage and his apparently progressive epilepsy. Their classic single 'Love Will Tear Us Apart' reached Number 13 in June, and the second album, *Closer*, was released in July. Compared to its predecessor, the tone of the record was hushed; it was a dark foray into the depths of emotion, and many considered it a masterpiece. A final compilation of unreleased tracks and a live concert, the LP *Still*, brought the works of Joy Division to a close.

After Curtis' death, the remaining three decided to continue under a new name, New Order, which brought accusations of fascist overtones, but the band maintained that all it signified was a new start. In fact, it was inspired by the manifesto of the Khmer Rouge regime in Cambodia. After a tour of America, they recruited an old friend, Gillian Gilbert, to join them on keyboards, and went on to essay a more electronic sound with the single 'Ceremony'/'In a Lonely Place' in March '81, followed by 'Procession'/'Everything's Gone Green' in September, and the album *Movement* in November. The reviewers gave it a lukewarm reception, but it sold well nevertheless. It was not until April 1982 however that the group fully developed the dance rhythms that were their real strength with the single 'Temptation', a song that gave them their biggest hit to date, reaching Number 29. Observers of their tours noted the change from a sombre attitude to bouncier, more dance-oriented songs.

By 1983 the dance element had become even more pervasive and in April they scored their massive club hit, 'Blue Monday', which stayed on the chart for a total of 38 weeks, and sold over a million worldwide. In May they released the sombre *Power, Corruption and Lies*, which received favourable reviews, and as a result they opened up a little, giving their first press interviews in years. Yet, while still maintaining a sizeable cult status, they chose to keep the low profile that has since characterized their progress. Their third album *Low-life*, a more light-hearted work, did not appear until 1985 and it was again well-received. Early in 1986 the swinging single 'Shellshock' returned New Order to the UK Top 30.

JOY OF COOKING

A rock group with folk leanings from Berkeley, California, Joy of Cooking started out in 1967 as an outlet for the talents of Toni Brown and Terri Garthwaite, then both at the University of California. It was an unusual group with two girls at the helm – Toni Brown, vocals, keyboards, guitar (born 16 November 1938); Terri Garthwaite, vocals, guitar (11 July 1938); Fritz Kasten, drums, alto sax; Jeff Neighbor, bass (19 March 1942); Ron Wilson, congas, bongos, harp (5 February 1933). Toni Brown contributed most of the songs. Their first two albums, *Joy of Cooking* (Capitol, 1970) and *Closer to the Ground* (1971), established their distinctive rhythmic approach building on closely woven patterns between drums, bass, conga, Terri's rhythm guitar and Toni's lyrical piano work. *Closer to the Ground* saw Toni Brown's country leanings coming out in her singing and in the slight shift in the group's direction. But more importantly, behind their rhythmic playing lay an adult orientation in lyrics, dealing with the period following youth and finding your feet/facing the world subject-matters. A third album, *Castles* (1972), was disappointing but Toni and Terri took time out to cut an album together in Nashville, the impressive *Cross Country* (1973). Toni left the group following the release of the album to record a solo album, *Good for You Too* (MCA), 1974, while Terri remained another year before recording her own solo album for Arista (1975). The group, who added another guitarist, Glan Frendel, and piano-player Steve Roseman, remained without a recording contract for some time but returned with *The Joy*, for Capitol, in 1977. Critically well received, it sold poorly and the group disbanded.

JUDAS PRIEST

Emerging from the UK's heavy metal capital Birmingham in 1972, Judas Priest at first conquered the UK and then plugged away to become eventually one of the most revered and hardest rock outfits in the world, joining the ranks of the big stadium bands.

Originally put together by guitarist KK Downing and bassist Ian Hill in 1969, Judas Priest didn't have anything like a stable line-up until 1972 when the duo were bolstered by Rob Halford (vocals) and Glenn Tipton (guitar). This foursome remained the nucleus of the band as they went through a procession of drummers right through their career. They released two albums on Gull, *Rocka Rolla* (1974) and *Sad Wings of Destiny* (1976), the latter still regarded as a classic by heavy metal aficionados. Neither album sold well, and the band made a move to the major label clout of CBS to further their fortunes in 1977.

All the while, led by the leather-clad Halford, the band were building up a reputation as an exceptionally heavy live band, and each successive album release saw them increase in stature. Like many heavy metal outfits, Judas Priest found the Japanese very receptive to their music, and in 1979 while on tour there, they recorded the live set *Unleashed in the East*, which remains a perfect record of their stagecraft. The album sold well and put the band into rock's first division.

Their seventh album *British Steel* (1980) broke the band in America, and subsequent releases like *Screaming Vengeance* (1982) and *Defenders of the Faith* (1984) have sold in vast quantities across the world.

JUICY LUCY A British-based blues band, Juicy Lucy was formed on the American model in 1969 by steel-guitarist Glenn Campbell. He had previously been with the Misunderstood, whose 'I Can Take You to the Sun' was a cult single among the London underground. Other members were Chris Mercer (sax, keyboards) – a **John Mayall** alumnus – Mick Moody (guitar), James Leverton (bass), Rod Coombes (drums) and Paul Williams (vocals), previously with **Zoot Money**.

Their first single, the **Bo Diddley** song 'Who Do You Love' (Vertigo, 1970) was a Top 20 hit, but later records were less successful. Juicy Lucy made four albums (two for Vertigo, one each for Bronze and Polydor) before splitting up in 1972. Campbell returned to his native America, Mercer played sessions and formed Gonzalez, while Williams sang briefly with Jon Hiseman's Tempest.

JUSTIS, BILL 'Raunchy', dominated by Bill Justis' alto-sax playing, was a huge hit single for Phillips International in 1957 and one of the first in a series of rock instrumentals which paved the way for the success of the **Champs**, the **Ventures** and **Duane Eddy**. Justis, born in Birmingham, Alabama, on 14 October 1927, was a professional jazz musician and arranger who came to rock'n'roll production with Sun in Memphis in 1957. Besides his own recordings, he arranged hits for **Johnny Cash**, **Jerry Lee Lewis** and **Charlie Rich** and was active in mellowing the raw sounds of Sun rock'n'roll for a national pop audience. In 1959, he formed his own short-lived label, Play Me, and then joined Groove-RCA as an artist and producer, again working with Charlie Rich. He moved to Monument and Sound Stage 7 in Nashville, producing big hits for the Dixiebelles.

KAJAGOOGOO The ultimate teenypop package, Kajagoogoo produced frivolous pop that resulted in an instant Number 1 with their debut single, 'Too Shy' in January 1983. A carefully manufactured blend of image and sound designed to appeal to a young female audience, it clearly demonstrated the power of good marketing.

Foursome Nick Beggs (bass), Jez Strode (drums), Steve Askew (guitar) and Stuart Neale (keyboards) from Leighton Buzzard in Bedfordshire were brought together with singer Limahl (Chris Hamill) in 1982 via a classified ad. Their pretty boy looks and the bland commerciality of their material made Kajagoogoo a natural for the charts, and, supported by the major resources of EMI, 'Too Shy' was an obvious hit. 'Ooh To Be Ah' followed it into the UK Top 10, and an album, *White Feathers* (1983), was a Top 5 UK LP.

The honeymoon was shortlived, however, and Limahl was sacked from the band in August under circumstances never clearly explained. Nick Beggs took over on vocals and 'The Big Apple', a tougher, more dance-oriented single, became, in September, their first hit without Limahl, who went into a solo singing career, also scoring a hit first time out with 'Only for Love'. The next year he followed it up with 'Never Ending Story', after which his chart entries dried up. 1984 was a lean year too for Kajagoogoo, who changed their name to just Kaja. Although Limahl continued to record as a solo artist, Kajagoogoo split up in 1986.

KALEIDOSCOPE A reminder of the danger of over-eclecticism in rock, Kaleidoscope's first two remarkable albums *Sidetrips* (Epic, 1967) and *A Beacon From Mars* (1968) ranged through old-timey music, English ballads, Cajun fiddle music, Eastern modal music, R&B and brilliantly sustained feedback work by guitarist David Lindley who also played fiddle, harp guitar and banjo. The rest of the crowd were Solomon Feldthouse, guitar, caz, oud and other stringed instruments; Chris Darrow, bass, mandolin; John Vidican, drums, and Fenrus Epp, keyboards, fiddle and harmonica.

On the four albums that the group made in their heyday, Epp masqueraded under a different name (Max Buda, Templeton Parceley or Connie Crill) while for their final albums more changes brought in Paul Lagos, drums, and Stuart Brotman, bass. Under that line-up they cut *Incredible* (1969), the brilliant but obscure single 'Just a Taste', and the weakish *Bernice*, the last before they split up in 1970. Their live perform-

ances deserved the legendary tag, showcasing their eclectic tendencies in spectacular fashion. Flamenco dancers would accompany Feldthouse's Spanish guitar piece and a belly-dancer their Eastern jam, 'Taxim'. Kaleidoscope went unnoticed while less deserving Los Angeles bands monopolized the critical acclaim until it was too late. Chris Darrow later followed a solo career (with three albums) while Dave Lindley is best known for his work with **Jackson Browne**. The 1975 album *When Scopes Collide* (Pacific Arts) was the product of a brief reunion.

KALIN TWINS A genuine pair of twins, Harold and Herbie Kalin (born on 16 February 1939) were discovered by Clint Ballard Jr – composer of the **Betty Everett/Linda Ronstadt** hit, 'You're No Good' – who signed them to American Decca in 1958. The Paul Evans and Jack Reardon song, 'When' took them to the Top 5 in America and the Number 1 spot in Britain for five weeks – on the strength of which they were among the first rock'n'rollers to visit Britain. Though their next record, 'Forget Me Not', also made the US Top 20, they soon faded from sight. In retrospect, what was appealing about 'When' was the arrangement, not so much the high-pitched harmonizing of the twins.

KANE, EDEN A popular British singer in the **Billy Fury** mould, Eden Kane achieved a string of UK hits between 1961 and 1964. Born Richard Sarstedt in Delhi, India, on 29 March 1942, he supposedly took his stage name from the Orson Welles film *Citizen Kane*. He appeared in the film *Drinks All Round* in 1960 before turning to singing and was the subject of careful grooming by his managers, Michael Barclay and Philip Waddilove. His first record, 'Hot Chocolate Crazy' was used to advertise a proprietary brand of drinking chocolate on Radio Luxembourg. His Decca releases 'Well I Ask You', 'Get Lost' (1961), 'Forget Me Not' and 'I Don't Know Why' (1962) all made the Top 10 in Britain and were promoted as being in the hully-gully vein – a combination of heavy beat and growl. A change in label, after 'House to Let' and 'Sounds Funny to Me' had failed, brought him back to the charts with 'Boys Cry'. In 1973, he re-emerged with his brothers, Robin and **Peter Sarstedt** as the Sarstedt Brothers, but the partnership lasted for only one album, *Worlds Apart Together*.

KANE GANG Blending the powerful soul influences of **Wilson Pickett** and **Hall and Oates** with a hard-edged lyrical style inflamed by living in the depressed northeast of England, the Kane Gang emerged in the early Eighties as a pop band with a great future ahead of them.

Formed in Newcastle in 1982, the group – Martin Brammer (vocals), Paul Woods (vocals) and Dave Brewis (instruments) – were originally called the Kings of Cotton, but changed their name in time for their debut release, the 12″ single 'Brother Brother' on the local Kitchenware label.

An appearance on the television show *The Tube* created a stir and the band signed a licensing deal (through Kitchenware) with London Records, scoring a UK Top 20 hit with 'Closest Thing to Heaven' before subsequently releasing their debut album, *The Bad and Lowdown World of the Kane Gang* in February 1985.

K.C. AND THE SUNSHINE BAND

Formed in Florida in 1973, K.C. and the Sunshine Band were the prime exponents of a good-time, tropical funk disco/dance music known as the Miami Sound, scoring five US Number 1s and a Number 2.

Based around the songwriting partnership of Harry Wayne Casey (vocals/keyboards) and Rick Finch (bass) at the TK Studios in Hialeh, just outside Miami, they recorded as K.C. and the Sunshine Junkanoo Band. Under that name they recorded one single, 'Blow Your Whistle' (a Number 27 on the US R&B charts), in 1973, before dropping the 'Junkanoo' for their subsequent work.

A couple of early single successes made it possible to release the debut LP *Do It Good* (1974) which became a hit in Europe, giving them a UK Number 7 single with 'Queen of Clubs'. Casey and Finch's first major success came the same year when they wrote, arranged and produced for **George McCrae** the international Number 1 'Rock Your Baby', which went on to sell over 10 million copies.

In 1975 'Get Down Tonight' was a US Number 1 for the band and commenced a three-year domination of the charts and dancefloors in America ('That's the Way [I Like It]', '[Shake, Shake, Shake,] Shake Your Booty' and 'I'm Your Boogie Man' all topping the US charts) as disco-fever swept the country. There was a brief lull in the hits through 1978 but in 1979 'Please Don't Go' suggested they had rediscovered the hit-making formula.

However, after 1979, their US chart appearances tailed off, and despite a UK Number 1 in 1983 with 'Give It Up', K.C. and the Sunshine Band were never able to regain their former chart popularity.

K-DOE, ERNIE Best remembered for his 1961 US chart-topper, 'Mother-in-law', Ernie K-Doe was born the son of a Baptist minister in New Orleans in 1937. His real name was Ernest Kador, but as Ernie K-Doe he became a member of that group of young black New Orleans R&B artists who turned so much national attention towards the funky Crescent City sounds in the early Sixties. After the success of 'Mother-in-law', a compulsive R&B novelty record, he had further small hits on Minit but he couldn't repeat his initial success. An extrovert showman, he can still be found in the New Orleans clubs, singing modern soul songs to local audiences.

KENDRICKS, EDDIE Born in Birmingham, Alabama, on 17 December 1939, Eddie Kendricks was an original member of the **Temptations** who left the group to go solo in 1971. He scored only minor hits in 1971–2 but had a US Number 1 and UK Top 20 hit with 'Keep on Truckin'' (Tamla) in 1973, on which his normally tender tenor was a little rougher than usual. 'Boogie Down', a Number 2 US hit, followed in 1974, and his numerous subsequent R&B hits included 'Shoeshine Boy', 'Happy' (both 1975) and 'He's a Friend', the last-mentioned from an album of the same name which was produced by Norman Harris and exhibited a clear Philadelphia sound influence. He left Motown for Clive Davis' Arista label in 1978 but recorded only one album, *Vintage '78*, before signing with Atlantic in 1980. His releases for them included *Love Keys* (1981), recorded in a musically sympathetic setting – Muscle Shoals, Alabama – that at last brought out the best in Kendricks' considerable vocal talent.

KENNEDY, JERRY Previously a Nashville session guitarist and independent producer, Jerry Kennedy took over the plum position of Nashville A&R man and production head for Mercury Records from **Shelby Singleton** in 1967. He had earlier worked for Singleton at his Bayou Record Shop in Shreveport, Louisiana, during the Fifties, and recorded rockabilly sides for Decca as well as a solo album for Smash Records in 1965.

Doubling as a guitarist on sessions he supervised, Kennedy developed a personal approach to production that paid dividends in a string of hits for his top artists – **Jerry Lee Lewis**, Faron Young and **Tom T. Hall** among them – and also for newcomers such as Johnny Rodriguez.

KENNER, CHRIS New Orleans R&B singer Chris Kenner was born on 25 December 1929, in Kenner, Louisiana, a suburb town of the city. He began his career as a spiritual singer with the New Orleans Harmonizing Four, and it was a marriage of gospel and New Orleans R&B which gave his records such a distinctive flavour. He hit the big time in 1961 with the novelty-dance tune, 'I Like It Like That', a Number 2 record on the Instant label which was voted 'Best Rock-'n'Roll Record of 1961'. He followed this with a local hit, 'Something You Got' and in 1963 'Land of 1,000 Dances' crept into the charts at Number 77. This latter song has been covered countless times by artists like **Wilson Pickett**, **Fats Domino** and **Tom Jones**. Kenner also recorded without much success as a comeback for Baton, Imperial ('Sick and Tired'), Prigan and Uptown amongst others.

KERSHAW, DOUG Multi-instrumentalist Doug Kershaw, born in Tel Ridge, Louisiana, on 24 January 1936, was easily the best-known exponent of Cajun music during the Sixties. His background was classic Cajun: born into a French-speaking community, he only learned English at the age of eight and became a master of around thirty different musical instruments by his mid-teens. He formed a duo, Rusty and Doug, with his 16-year old brother and moved to Nashville in 1955 to record for Hickory Records. Five years later, their autobiographical 'Louisiana Man', written by Doug, became a major country hit and was subsequently covered by numerous country singers and groups. Although the duo broke up in 1961, Kershaw used his regional success as a springboard into the growing folk market. In 1968, following his appearance on television's *Johnny Cash Show* alongside **Bob Dylan**, he found acceptance within rock circles and began a ten-year association with Warner Brothers as one of their 'prestige' acts. He moved back into the country field towards the end of the Seventies and contributed suitably 'authentic' Cajun music to several films, among them *Days of Heaven* (1978).

KERSHAW, NIK Singer/songwriter Nik Kershaw (born 1 March 1958 in Bristol) came to the fore in the mid-Eighties at a time when solo artists consistently found placings in the UK charts. Kershaw's abilities as a sharp tunesmith and arranger and his array of sophisticated but accessible pop songs won him many admirers.

Kershaw's first musical outings were at school in Ipswich in Suffolk (he started playing guitar at the age of fourteen), and he eventually joined local jazz-funk outfit Fusion who gigged extensively around Suffolk and Essex. Fusion broke up in 1982, and after writing a batch of songs at home, Kershaw did the rounds of the record companies. He eventually won a deal with MCA, who put him into the studio in 1983; a debut single 'I Won't Let the Sun Go Down' made the UK Top 50, paving the way for 'Wouldn't It Be Good' to reach Number 4 in 1984. Kershaw had another two Top 5 singles that year and released two albums, *Human Racing* and *The Riddle*, the latter reaching the UK Top 5. The year 1985 was spent touring the world, and included an appearance on Live Aid (*see also* **Band Aid**).

KHAN, CHAKA Though she first made her name fronting soul band **Rufus**, Chaka Khan came into her own as a solo singer. Born in the Chicago suburb of Great Lakes on 23 March 1953, Yvette Marie Stevens dropped her given name for the more exotic Chaka Khan (apparently meaning fire, war and red) when she began her professional singing career in Chicago in 1968. Chaka teamed up with the Midwest group Rufus as lead singer, to begin her apprenticeship playing in the clubs. Success came with the album *Rags to Riches*, from which was released the million-selling 'Tell Me Something Good'. Other Top 10 hits followed in the shape of 'Once You Get Started' and 'Sweet Thing'.

A dazzling live performer with a superb voice, at once both lyrical and passionate, Chaka was the natural focus of the band, and it was almost inevitable that she would eventually go solo. In 1977, Chaka made the break from Rufus, and in the following year Warner Brothers released her disco classic, 'I'm Every Woman', written by **Ashford and Simpson**. Over the next few years she was involved in a number of projects, including that of jazz-rock guitarist Lenny White, in which she contributed the vocals to a series of Fifties jazz classics.

In the Eighties, Chaka's collabora-

tions with producer **Arif Mardin** began to bear fruit, when the success of *What Cha' Gonna Do For Me* was followed by *Chaka Khan* and *I Feel For You*. The last album provided the single of the same name which – with rap introduction from Grandmaster Melle Mel and harmonica solo by **Stevie Wonder** – was a smash hit on both sides of the Atlantic towards the end of 1984. The follow up, 'This Is My Night', was released in 1985, making Number 14 in the UK chart. *See also* **Rufus**

Chaka Khan, gifted with a passionate voice and thrilling stage presence

KID CREOLE AND THE COCONUTS Kid Creole was the enigmatic creation of August Darnell (né Browder), a zoot-suited cool cat and undisputed leader of the band who – with their irresistible, eminently danceable blend of soul, Latin jazz, big-band swing and rock – were the darlings of the UK nightclub set in the early Eighties.

Born in Montreal but raised in the Bronx, a suburb of New York City, Darnell had a Master's degree in English Literature and spent the early part of his career teaching English. His first band of any substance was Dr Buzzard's Original Savannah Band, a dance outfit with an eclectic style similar to that of the Coconuts. Formed in 1974 with his brother Stony Browder, this early outfit also included Andy Hernandez, a manic vibes player who was later to become Kid Creole's sidekick. For the Savannah Band, Darnell wrote lyrics that ironically set the New York urban working class in a glamorous backdrop, and this approach gave them one major US hit single, 'Cherchez La Femme', Number 27 in 1976, but their fortunes declined and they split up after being dropped by their record company, RCA.

Scantily clad Coconuts give their all as creole kid August Darnell delivers his cool ironical lyrics

In 1980, Darnell became the house producer for Ze Records and at the same time set about forming Kid Creole and the Coconuts with Hernandez (under his stage name Coati Mundi). The Kid Creole character gave the band a mythological front man, a hybrid representative of all America's rich immigrant cultures; he was supported by the Coconuts, a seductive trio of singer/dancers in colourful costumes led by Darnell's wife Adriana Kaegi, plus red-hot horn and rhythm sections. After a few exuberant live performances and the release of their debut album *Off the Coast of Me* (1980), they began to generate a good public response. This encouraged the second album, *Fresh Fruit in Foreign Places* in 1981 and the British press hailed Darnell as a 'modern soul genius'. 'Me No Pop I' was a minor hit (credited to Kid Creole and the Coconuts present Coati Mundi), but the group were unable to capitalize on the UK interest since lack of funds precluded a tour, and so they remained a small cult band.

They finally toured the UK in May 1982 to promote the third album *Tropical Gangsters* (*Wise Guy* in the US), and two weeks later the single 'I'm a Wonderful Thing Baby' started to move up the charts. The live show was a phenomenal success, the band made a TV special and for the rest of the year UK discos were full of people dancing to the soundtrack of a succession of Kid Creole and the Coconuts' hits ('Annie, I'm Not Your Daddy' was the biggest, reaching Number 2 in October).

After such a stunning year their performance since has been disappointing and they have never managed to crack the US market. In 1983 Darnell produced albums for the Coconuts (*Don't Take My Coconuts*) and Coati Mundi (*Coati Mundi – The Former 12 Year Old Genius*) and the fourth Kid Creole and the Coconuts album *Doppelganger*, which was the soundtrack to a planned stage-show, but they all performed miserably and *Doppelganger* received a critical panning. The live shows continued to be large-scale extravaganzas with intricate sets and routines, yet while they sold out regularly, record sales remained poor. *In Praise of Older Women . . . And Other Crimes*, the fifth album, did not appear until 1985, after a change of label to Sire, and while it marked something of a return to form, the swinging single 'Endicott' failed to chart, and Darnell was left finding it difficult to recapture the peak of popularity that had been achieved three years previously.

KIDD, JOHNNY Born Frederick Heath in London on 23 December 1939, Johnny Kidd has become something of a legend. At the end of the Fifties he and his band, the Pirates, featuring guitarist Mick Green, developed a form of R&B which stood in direct contrast to the careful cover jobs and polite rock of so many British artists, and predated the R&B revival by two or three years.

This reputation exceeds Kidd's actual chart successes – four British Top 20 entries and no impression whatsoever in America. But his first hit, 'Shakin' All Over' (released on HMV and co-written by Kidd and his manager, Gus Robinson) is now a rock standard; he followed it in the same year, 1960, with 'Restless' and in 1963 scored with 'I'll Never Get Over You' and 'Hungry for Love'. 'Please Don't Touch' is another Kidd classic; his stage style, complete with gimmick eye-patch, is indicated by these titles.

Tragically, Kidd couldn't climb back to the top when R&B arrived in force, in spite of his 1963 success. His later recordings were heavily Beatle-influenced, and by the time of his death in a Lancashire car crash on 7 October 1966, the Pirates had been reduced to low-priced support gigs. They later became a favourite pub-rock band and recorded for Warner Brothers and Cube during the late Seventies.

KILLING JOKE Formed in London in 1979, cult band Killing Joke was the brainchild of founders Jaz Coleman (vocals and keyboards) and Paul Ferguson (drums), who were brought together by a shared interest in the occult. They then went on to recruit guitarist Geordie and bassist 'Youth' (Martin Glover). Rehearsals in a small studio in Cheltenham were followed by a series of live dates that included support slots for the likes of the **Ruts** and **Joy Division**. As a result, the group signed with EG Records who had a distribution deal with Polydor.

Developing a raw, uncompromising style – an amalgam of punk, heavy metal and black magic – Killing Joke undertook the gruelling life of a touring band, which while it gave them a devoted cult following, did not translate into commercial success; their first two albums *Killing Joke* and *What's This For!* did not make any impression on the charts.

The group's future was suddenly placed in jeopardy in early 1982 when Coleman and Geordie disappeared, eventually to resurface in Iceland playing with a local band. The errant pair returned to the fold, however, to be joined by Paul Raven who replaced Youth on bass. (Youth went on to form Brilliant, a stylish pop-soul trio who surfaced in 1985.)

Hard work and renewed enthusiasm slowly began to pay off and their third album, *Revelations*, reached Number 12 on the UK chart in 1982. The release of 'Love Like Blood' in January 1985 marked the beginning of success in the UK singles market (it reached Number 16), heralding a new commercial future for Killing Joke.

KING Surfacing in 1983 as the brainchild of singer Paul King and manager Perry Haines, King, from Coventry in the English midlands, ranked among the biggest-selling and most-photographed mainstream pop groups of the mid-Eighties.

After the break-up of his previous band, the Reluctant Stereotypes, Paul King met Haines and together they gathered a unit of local lads, Tony Wall (bass), Jim 'Jackal' Lantsbury (guitar) and Mick Roberts (keyboards) who were joined on a semi-permanent basis by ex-Members drummer Adrian Lilywhite. They debuted as support to **Wah!** and signed to CBS Records.

Touring incessantly around Britain, they built up a sizeable live following and received positive music press coverage, but three singles and an album *Steps in Time* sold poorly until, at the end of '84, they played support to **Culture Club**, bringing them to a new, younger audience. As a result, one of their original singles, 'Love and Pride' was re-released early in 1985 and reached the UK Number 2 slot, while the album made the Top 10. The new teenage fans dragged King into the pin-up market, ensuring wide media coverage and confirming them as one of the big new pop acts. King continued to do well in the charts throughout Europe, scoring a string of hit singles and a second hit album *Bitter Sweet*, which was released at the tail-end of 1985. After a protracted period of inactivity, the band split late in 1986, with Paul King starting a solo career.

KING, ALBERT A top blues guitarist and a major influence on Sixties and Seventies rock, Albert King was born in Indianola, Mississippi, on 25 April 1923. Inspired by the guitar-playing of **T-Bone Walker**, King travelled to Chicago where he ended up playing drums behind **Jimmy Reed** and on a few early sessions for Vee Jay Records, including those by the **Spaniels**. He did sing and play guitar on 'Bad Luck Blues', a one-off single for Parrot Records which he cut in 1953. He did not record again until 1959, when he signed with the St Louis label, Bobbin Records; these sides were later leased to King Records. In 1965, he recorded for the Coun-Tree label in East St Louis, and a year later he signed with Stax. This marked the turning point in his career as, together with the label's solid house band, he recorded some of the most dynamic blues sides of the Sixties, among them 'Laundromat Blues', 'Crosscut Saw' and 'Personal Manager' on the album *Born Under a Bad Sign*.

An extremely imposing figure, King stands six feet four inches and weighs about 250lb. He plays a left-handed Gibson Flying Arrow guitar in a distinctly recognizable style which more than complements his raw and husky vocals. His guitar breaks build to a climax, incorporating clusters of fast, single-note runs – usually on a minor scale – with hard, biting notes that almost scream. This technique influenced dozens of rock guitarists; his songs were covered by **Free** ('The Hunter'), **Paul Butterfield** ('Born Under a Bad Sign'), **John Mayall** ('Oh Pretty Woman') and the **Electric Flag** ('You Threw Your Love on Me Too Strong').

Since leaving Stax in 1974, King has recorded for **Giorgio Gomelsky**'s Utopia label – the 1975 album, *Truck Load of Lovin'* – and for the Tomato label, but the most representative selection of his work remains the 1982 Atlantic anthology, *Albert King Masterworks*.

KING, B.B. Perhaps the best-known and most influential bluesman of them all, B.B. King was born Riley B. King on 16 September 1925, in Indianola, Mississippi. After World War II, he travelled to Memphis, where he renewed a friendship with his cousin, the legendary blues singer/guitarist, Bukka White. Encouraged by White and influenced by the guitar-playing of **T-Bone Walker**, Django Reinhardt and Charlie Christian, King began working sessions on local radio shows and eventually landed a job as DJ on station WDIA. He became known as the Beale Street Blues Boy, which he later abbreviated to just B.B. In between radio shows he kept playing, often sitting in with whichever jazz and blues artists were in town.

In 1950, he signed with Modern Records, cutting his first million-seller, 'Three O'Clock Blues', which stayed at Number 1 in the R&B charts for eighteen weeks. The song featured King on vocals and guitar, **Ike Turner** (piano), **Willie Mitchell** (trumpet) and Hank Crawford (alto). It was the first of a string of hits for Modern/RPM, as King recorded literally hundreds of sides for the label over a ten-year period. They included 'Everyday I Have the Blues', a million-seller in 1955, 'Sweet Little Angel' (1956) and 'Sweet Sixteen' (1960). All were polished city blues, mostly featuring horns and occasionally strings.

Initially, B.B. played guitar to accompany himself, but by the time he cut his first records, he was playing single-string runs in a group context. Gradually he began to develop different ways of punctuating phrases. He sometimes played a barrage of notes to introduce a whole section of extended improvisation, and to this would add a vibrato sound while 'bending' notes. The idea did not originate with him, since a number of jazz guitarists had done the same thing before – but the frequent use of bent notes has since become a B.B. King trademark. He also possesses a potent vocal style, most distinctive, again, in the way he tends to punctuate phrases with his clear falsetto wail and gospel-blues voice.

In 1961 King signed with ABC, which led to R&B hits like 'Don't Answer the Door' and his second million-seller in 1969, 'The Thrill Is Gone', the latter revealing a more contemporary approach to his material. During the early Seventies, King teamed up with **Leon Russell** and **Carole King** for *Indianola Mississippi Seeds*; with **Joe Walsh** and **Taj Mahal** for *LA Midnight*, and worked with **Ringo Starr**, Pete Wingfield, Steve Marriott and others on *B.B. King In London*. He also recorded with **Bobby Bland** – *Together for the First Time . . . Live* (1974) – and with the **Crusaders** in 1982, besides issuing a steady flow of solo albums, among them *Kingsize* (1977), *Midnight Believer* (1978), *Take it Home* (1979), and the Grammy award-winning *There Must Be a Better World Somewhere* (1981). But his best album remains *Live at the Regal*, recorded in Chicago during the early Sixties.

KING, BEN E. One of the finest balladeers in post-rock'n'roll black music, Ben E. King was born Benjamin Earl Nelson in Henderson, North Carolina in 1938. He first sang professionally with a New York group, the Crowns. When they were signed to Atlantic Records as the **Drifters** in 1959 he was brought to the attention of a mass audience as lead singer, notably on their biggest hit 'Save the Last Dance for Me' in 1960. Three months later, he had his first solo success, 'Spanish Harlem' (Atco), followed by 'Stand By Me', considered a black music classic. Promoted as a dramatic balladeer

B. B. King, one of the founding fathers of Sixties rhythm'n'blues, uses his vibrato guitar technique to 'bend' a note

rather than a 'soul' singer, most of King's output was aimed at a pop audience, but with the right material he was as emotionally convincing as any soul star. 'Don't Play That Song', 'Tell Daddy', 'How Can I Forget', 'It's All Over', 'Seven Letters', 'So Much Love', and 'What Is Soul' were among his most exciting performances. He left Atlantic in 1969 for the Maxwell and Mandala labels and re-signed with Atlantic in 1974, hitting the US Top 10 in 1975 with 'Supernatural Thing – Part 1'. He was teamed with the **Average White Band** for a 1977 collaboration, *Benny and US* on Atco, and thereafter played the rock'n'roll revival circuit in both the US and the UK. 'Stand By Me' became a surprise UK chart-topper on reissue in early 1987. *See also the* **Drifters**

Singer-songwriter Carole King: her album Tapestry *was a massive hit*

KING, CAROLE One of the giants of pop songwriting and a major singing star of the early Seventies, Carole King was born Carole Klein in Brooklyn, New York, on 9 February 1942. During a brief college career she tried to write songs with **Paul Simon**, later leaving to become a full-time composer in **Don Kirshner**'s office at the Brill Building. Teaming up with Gerry Goffin, later to become her husband, she wrote dozens of hits between 1959 and 1967, when the partnership ceased. The grateful recipients of Goffin/King pieces included **Bobby Vee** ('Take Good Care of My Baby', 'Walking with My Angel', 'In My Baby's Eyes'); **Tony Orlando** ('Halfway to Paradise', 'I'll Never Find Another You' – both successfully covered in Britain by **Billy Fury**); the **Drifters** ('When My Little Girl Is Smiling', 'Up on the Roof'); **Shirelles** ('Will You Still Love Me Tomorrow'); **Little Eva** ('The Locomotion'); Cookies ('Chains', 'Don't Say Nothing Bad about My Baby'); and **Dusty Spring-**

field and the **Byrds** ('Goin' Back'). She had an international hit herself with 'It Might As Well Rain Until September' (Dimension, 1962). Previously she had recorded unsuccessfully for ABC-Paramount ('Babysittin''), RCA ('Short Mort') and Alpine ('Oh Neil!', her reply to **Neil Sedaka**'s 'Oh Carol!').

But by 1967, it seemed as though the new wave of predominantly West Coast music had swamped the craftsmanlike writers of the early Sixties. While Neil Sedaka and others disappeared from view, Goffin and King found themselves writing 'Pleasant Valley Sunday' for the **Monkees**, the creation of Don Kirshner.

An attempt to form an independent label, Tomorrow, foundered, but a new direction was signalled by 'A Natural Woman', the Carole King song recorded in 1967 by **Aretha Franklin**. In contrast to the earlier teenage love songs, it showed a new insight and maturity, already suggested by 'Goin' Back'. The opening lines seemed suffused with a very personal feeling – 'Looking out on the morning rain/ Sometimes I feel so uninspired' – an impression confirmed when King herself recorded it on *Tapestry* (1971).

Before that came the City, a group including Danny Kortchmar (guitar), Charlie Larkey (bass – her second husband) and Jim Gordon (drums). An unsuccessful album for **Lou Adler**'s Ode label was followed in 1970 by *Writer*, a Carole King album. It introduced the by now familiar instrumental sound, dominated by King's richly chorded piano, and was the prelude to *Tapestry* (1971), an international hit album which eventually sold over ten million copies. Containing 'You've Got a Friend', 'So Far Away', 'Smackwater Jack' and a low-key version of 'Will You Love Me Tomorrow', it placed Carole King at the forefront of the emerging 'singer-songwriters', alongside **James Taylor**, who took 'You've Got a Friend' to Number 1 in the US.

The initial critical welcome for *Tapestry* faded when *Music* (1971) and *Rhymes and Reasons* (1972) seemed little more than reiterations of the new formula. With *Fantasy* (1973), King tried with mixed success to deal with wider social issues as well as the themes of love and friendship. Despite the anti-climax of much of her later Seventies work, *Tapestry* remained a nodal album, marking the point at which rock lyrics proved themselves capable of handling adult as well as teenage themes. She has since recorded for Capitol (*Simple Things*, 1977), Avatar (*Welcome Home*, 1978), and Atlantic (*One to One*, 1982).

KING CRIMSON In the late Sixties, King Crimson were the prototype British 'progressive' band. Based on the lyrics of Pete Sinfield and the music and mellotron of **Robert Fripp** (born in 1946), Crimson first attracted attention at a **Rolling Stones** free concert in 1969. With Ian McDonald (flute, keyboards, born in 1946), Greg Lake (bass, vocals, born in 1948) and Mike Giles (drums, born in 1942), Fripp cut *In the Court of the Crimson King* (Island, 1969). Its baroque extravagances of word and sound set the tone for emerging progressive bands like **Yes** and, later, **ELP**, which included Lake.

From then on, a series of major personnel changes made Crimson's progress somewhat erratic. Only Fripp remained constant, with even the wordsmith Sinfield quitting in 1972 after *Islands*, the fourth album. The latter went on to produce the first **Roxy Music** album, make a solo record (*Still*, 1973) and publish a book of poems. The resulting line-up – Fripp, Mel Collins (saxes), Boz Burrell (bass) and Ian Wallace (drums) was more jazz-oriented and toured America in 1972, recording *Earthbound*, a live album.

The next year, Fripp reconstituted King Crimson with Bill Bruford, the former Yes drummer (born 17 May 1950), John Wetton (born in 1950), the bass player from **Family** who would later join **Uriah Heep**, David Cross (vocals, mellotron, born in 1948) and Jamie Muir, an *avant-garde* percussionist. They made *Larks' Tongues in Aspic* (1973) and the effective *Red* (1974) before Fripp announced the end of King Crimson in October 1974, declaring that he would now become 'small, intelligent and highly mobile'. He remained an enigmatic presence in British rock, producing a body of work which includes much that is eccentric and pretentious as well as genuinely experimental, including *No Pussyfootin'* (Island, 1974) and *Evening Star* (1975), two collaborations with Brian Eno. Bruford and Wetton played in a succession of other bands, the former eventually rejoining Fripp in Discipline in 1981. Fripp renamed the band King Crimson after the initial audience response was positive, and two albums resulted – *Discipline* (1981) and *Beat* (1982). *See also* **Robert Fripp**

KING CURTIS Born Curtis Ousley in Fort Worth, Texas, on 7 February 1934, King Curtis was the only rock-'n'roll saxophonist to become widely known outside the recording studios. At high school, he switched from alto to tenor and – prior to returning home to take up a musical scholarship – won an amateur talent contest at Harlem's Apollo Theatre. His studies abandoned, he formed a combo to play in Texas clubs.

By 1958, when he joined Atco, he had played with Lionel Hampton, formed a jazz trio with pianist Horace Silver and drummer Osie Johnson, and recorded under his own name for many independent labels, including Gem, Crown, Apollo and Groove. Apart from the odd Prestige jazz session, Curtis did not go in for improvisation. Nor (unlike Herb Hardesty with **Fats Domino**, any of **Little Richard**'s horn men or even Jimmy Wright with the Teenagers) is there any evidence that Curtis played on his back, shoulders heaving like pistons, blowing the reed from his instrument. Before becoming a full-time freelance studio player, his career had followed a mainstream path, absorbing the influence of Lester Young, Arnett Cobb and Gene Ammons. And, unlike the numerous apoplectic honkers of the period, Curtis brought a readily identifiable tone to whatever he played, whether blues (where he accompanied Roosevelt Sykes and Sunnyland Slim), R&B influenced pop (**Sam Cooke, Little Eva, Bobby Darin, Sammy Turner, Bobby Lewis** et al.) or jazz (Nat Adderley, Wynton Kelly) – the medium he preferred until the early Sixties when he discovered the warm ballad style which Southern soul men brought to Atlantic at that time.

Within each category he was not only prolific but versatile. The solos on Sammy Turner records are light years away from his tricky embellishments with the **Coasters**, but they are still natural, effortless and unmistakably King Curtis. He was particularly valuable to record companies who needed sessionmen to play exactly what was required of them. He was clean, note-perfect and solo breaks like those on the Coasters' records were unequalled in rock'n'roll. His tone – deep and fruity, with a characteristic burr – and his facility could combine in under twenty seconds to create a telling statement full of charm and utility. 'Charlie Brown', 'Along Came Jones', 'Shoppin' For Clothes' – all the classics have it.

In 1962, Curtis reached the Top 20 for the first time with 'Soul Twist' (Enjoy). Nothing else released under his own name was as successful, but later records – 'Beach Party', 'Soul Serenade' (for Capitol), 'Jump Back', 'Memphis Soul Stew' and 'Ode to Billy Joe' (all three on Atco) – also made the pop charts. By the late Sixties, his soul stylings had become indispensable to the records of **Aretha Franklin, Donny Hathaway** and other Atlantic stars. On the verge of increased recognition for his contribution to over a decade of rock history, Curtis was stabbed to death in Harlem on 13 August 1971.

KING, EARL Born in New Orleans on 7 February 1934, Solomon 'Earl King' Johnson was one of the major R&B artists to emerge from that city during the early Fifties. In 1954 he was featured vocalist with the legendary **Huey 'Piano' Smith** band, later cutting solo sides with Smith in accompaniment. By 1955 the singer/guitarist had signed with Johnny Vincent's newly-formed Ace label, scoring his biggest hit with 'Those Lonely, Lonely Nights'. King spent many years touring the Southern States, and his influence can be heard in the early work of **Little Richard** and **Lloyd Price**. His composition 'Let's Make a Better World' was included on **Dr John**'s album *Desitively Bonnaroo*.

KING, EVELYN 'CHAMPAGNE' Reputedly discovered while cleaning the bathroom at Philadelphia International, **Gamble and Huff**'s label, a task that she accompanied with a rousing rendition of **Sam Cooke**'s 'A Change Is Gonna Come', Evelyn King became the toast of the dance-floor in 1977 with her first single, 'Shame', off the album *Smooth Talk*, produced by T. Life. She was just 17 (she was born in 1960). A smallish woman with a big voice, King is also one whose form on record is more than usually dependent on the producer with whom she works. Thus, after another LP with Life, she worked with Morrie Brown, Willie Lester/Rodney Brown, Leon Sylvers, Andre Cymone, Bobby Watson, Hawk Wolinki, and Allen George/Fred McFarlane. Most successful was Morrie Brown whose assistants, Kashif and Paul Lawrence Jones, provided good material in the likes of 'Back to Love', 'Get Loose' and 'Love Come Down'.

KING, FREDDIE A pioneer of modern blues guitar, Freddie King was born on 30 September 1934, in Longview, Texas. While in his teens he moved to Chicago, and jammed with numerous bands including that led by **Muddy Waters**. He first recorded under his own name for El-Bee in 1956–7. In 1960, he signed with the Cincinnati-based Federal label, a subsidiary of Syd Nathan's King Records. The first session produced three hits: 'Have You Ever Loved a Woman', 'See See Baby' and his best-known number, 'Hide Away', a superb instrumental dedicated to a Chicago blues lounge of that name. Over a six-year period, Federal released 77 titles by King via singles and albums, and of these 30 were instrumentals. In 1968 he switched to Atlantic, cutting two **King Curtis**-produced albums. This eventually led to **Leon Russell** signing King to his newly formed Shelter Records. Three Shelter albums and numerous tours with Russell brought King superstar status. In 1974, however, **Mike Vernon** managed to lure him away to RSO Records, where in England he recorded 'Burglar', produced by Vernon and featuring **Eric Clapton** and Gonzalez.

King's influence on rock guitarists of the Sixties and Seventies was enormous. His many hits have been covered by Clapton/**Derek And The Dominos** ('Have You Ever Loved a Woman'), Clapton/**John Mayall** ('Hide Away'), Mick Taylor/John Mayall ('Driving Sideways'), **Peter Green**/John Mayall ('The Stumble', 'Someday After a While'), and Stan Webb/**Chicken Shack** ('San-Ho-Zay'). He died of hepatitis in Dallas, Texas, on 28 December 1976.

KING, JONATHAN Born in London on 6 December 1944, Jonathan King was a Cambridge University undergraduate when his nonsense protest song, 'Everyone's Gone to the Moon', became a surprise UK and US Top 20 hit. Rather than attempt a career as a singer and performer he turned to writing for and producing other groups, such as Hedgehoppers Anonymous, whose 'It's Good News Week' was a transatlantic hit in 1965. He briefly became a pop columnist, DJ and television personality before taking a part-time job as assistant to Sir Edward Lewis, the head of Decca Records, in the late Sixties. He signed **Genesis** to the label in 1968.

During this period, King released the occasional record, such as the bizarre 'Let It All Hang Out' (1969) and a version of **Dylan**'s 'Million Dollar Bash' (1970). In 1970 he started his own production company with a policy of looking for one-off pop hits, rather than artists, and leasing the masters to other record companies. He was immediately successful, scoring several British Top 20 hits in 1971, some of which were by him under different names: 'Sugar Sugar' (Sakharin, RCA), 'Johnny Reggae' (the Piglets, Bell), 'The Same Old Song' (the Weathermen, B&C), 'Keep on Dancing' (**Bay City Rollers**, Bell) and 'Leap Up and Down (and

Wave Your Knickers in the Air)' (St Cecilia, Polydor).

In 1972 King set up UK Records and was soon in the charts with Shag's 'Loop Di Loop'. However, such success was short-lived: he failed to break into the American market and his 1972 album, *Bubble Rock Is Here to Stay*, was excessively self-indulgent. For a while the mainstay of UK was **10cc**, whose only debt to King was their name – they wrote and produced their own records. Following the departure of 10cc and the failure for King of discoveries like **Marty Wilde**'s son Ricky, who was intended to capture the then vast teenybopper market, he reverted to a more traditional notion of a record company. In 1975 he signed one of the bright hopes of the pub circuit, the Kursaal Flyers, staying with them after the commercial failure of their first album, *Chocs Away* (1975). The year also saw him back in the British Top 20 with a cover of George Baker's 'Una Paloma Blanca' (UK). In 1976 the self-appointed Prince of Plasticity and scourge of 'progressive rock' released a collection of old and new tracks: *Jonathan King: Greatest Hits, Past, Present and Future*.

In the Eighties, King has remained a high-profile media figure, presenting programmes for Radio One, Capital Radio and BBC-2 (*Entertainment USA*) and regularly lambasting the latest teen idols and pop trends in the pages of *The Sun*.

KING RECORDS

The King Records group has included the Queen, De Luxe, Federal, Rockin', Glory, Bethlehem, Audio Lab and Starday-King labels. It was the most wide-ranging and successful independent recording operation during the Fifties.

Formed as a 'folk and country' label in Cincinnati during 1944 by Sydney Nathan, King acquired an impressive roster of artists such as the Delmore Brothers, Hawkshaw Hawkins, **Moon Mullican** and Cowboy Copas. Soon it launched a series of R&B/jazz/gospel issues (at first on Queen) and a 'popular' catalogue emerged in the Fifties and included Steve Lawrence and Ruby Wright. In 1947, **Henry Glover** began a twenty-five-year association with King as Artists and Repertoire manager and he was responsible for producing most of King's R&B artists and for mixing R&B with songs, styles and singers in an era when this was almost unknown. He began working with the bands of Lucky Millinder and Bullmoose Jackson, and singers **Roy Brown** and **Wynonie Harris**, and many

R&B hits were achieved. Through the Fifties, as rock'n'roll developed, King continued to be active in the full range of black music. 'Bloodshot Eyes' and 'Good Rockin' Tonight' gave way to **Jack Dupree**'s bluesy 'Walkin' the Blues', the group sounds of **Otis Williams** ('Hearts of Stone'), **Hank Ballard** ('Work with Me Annie'), and the instrumentals of **Bill Doggett** ('Honky Tonk'), Earl Bostic and Sonny Thompson.

Eventually, King found **Little Willie John** ('Fever' and 'All Around the World'), and **James Brown** ('Please, Please, Please'), who in their respective ways were important innovators of soul. In the Sixties, James Brown virtually carried the King group of labels. Something of the vital and pioneering spirit had, however, been lost, although various series of repackaged hits were successful. In 1970, the King company was bought by **Leiber and Stoller**, but the takeover was not a conspicuous success. *See also* **Henry Glover**

KING TUBBY

A Jamaican-born producer, sound-system operator and engineer *extraordinaire*, King Tubby was one of the most influential individuals in reggae of the Seventies. Pioneering the 'dub' sound in his studio, and featuring top deejays U Roy, and (later) I Roy, on his *No. 1* sound system, he, virtually single-handed, revolutionized the Jamaican music scene. Exploiting treble, in a bass-dominated music, Tubby produced a sound that perfectly complemented the direction in which reggae was moving – solid, heavy and immensely powerful. By 1975, virtually every dub recorded was engineered at Tubby's studios, many being dedicated to him: the most notable of which was Augustus Pablo's 'King Tubby Meets the Rockers Uptown'.

KINGSMEN

A vocal/instrumental quintet from Portland, Oregon, the Kingsmen comprised Lynn Easton (vocals), Gary Abbott, Don Gallucci, Mike Mitchell and Norman Sundholm. Formed in 1957 at high school, they developed a reputation while employing their driving, bluesy sound on TV commercials and one-nighter tours before signing with Wand in 1963. Their debut, a raw revival of **Richard Berry**'s 'Louie Louie' (produced by Jerry Dennon) delivered with virtually indecipherable diction, gained a gold disc in 1964. Numerous subsequent hits followed over three years, largely based on R&B songs.

KINGSTON TRIO

Formed at Stanford, California, in 1957, the Kingston Trio comprised Dave Guard, Bob Shane and Nick Reynolds who all played guitar and banjo and sang. As purveyors of folk songs to a larger pop audience, they marked a transitional and very successful phase between the more committed (Old Left) **Weavers** and (New Left) **Peter, Paul and Mary**. Their accessible harmonies (which owed as much to the cabaret tradition of the Four Freshmen and others as to folk) took them to Number 1 in the US in 1958 with 'Tom Dooley' on Capitol. A stream of successful albums and singles followed, including 'Worried Man' and 'Greenback Dollar'. In 1961, Guard was replaced by **John Stewart**. The Trio disbanded in 1966, outmoded by the newer folk-rock artists.

KINKS

At the centre of the mass of seeming contradictions that the Kinks represent is Ray Davies; his obsessions have charted the course the group have followed since the days when they were the Ravens, a smartly dressed – pink hunting jackets, frills and lace – if musically inept R&B group on London's deb circuit in 1962–3. The nucleus of the group was the Davies brothers, Raymond Douglas Davies (born in Muswell Hill, London, on 21 June 1944) and Dave (3 February 1947), who while at art school graduated from a passing interest in rock'n'roll and blues to fully fledged would-be R&Bers. They met up with ex-skiffler and drummer, Mick Avory (15 February 1944), and bassist Peter Quaife (23 December 1943), and got together originally to back singer Robert Wace who later became their manager.

Signed by Pye Records in the wake of the Merseybeat/R&B boom, the Kinks', as the group was renamed, first record – a very Beatles-influenced version of **Little Richard**'s 'Long Tall Sally' – failed, as did their second, 'You Do Something to Me'. However, their next single, 'You Really Got Me', was a British Number 1 and a US Top 10 record (on Reprise) in 1964. It marked the beginning of Ray Davies' songwriting career and the Kinks' prominence in the British (and world) charts for a couple of years. Produced by **Shel Talmy**, 'You Really Got Me' was both utterly primitive in conception and construction and completely devastating in performance. Over the next two years it was followed by seven British Top 10 hits, and sizeable American hits, all hewn from the same 'chunka chunka chunk' mould – as Ray Davies laconically put it later, 'Those three chords are part of my life, G, F, Bb.' These included 'All of the Day and All of the Night' (1964), 'Tired of Waiting for You' (a British Number 1), 'Set Me Free', 'See My Friends' and 'Till the End of the Day' (1965), which when taken together as a group of songs gave a foretaste of the aura of disenchantment and melancholy that was to pervade most of Ray Davies' songwriting. 1966 saw the first indication of the group's change in direction. At a time when the rest of the world was glorifying the idea of 'Swinging London' and Britain was smugly celebrating her lead in fashion and pop music, the Kinks chose to question the whole giddy scene in songs like 'Well Respected Man' and 'Dedicated Follower of Fashion' (1966). Amazing though they were at the time, these songs and others like 'House in the Country', 'Session Man' and 'Exclusive Residence for Sale', from *Face to Face*, their first thematically linked album, can in retrospect be seen as transitional. They showed that Ray Davies was quite sure of what he *didn't* like, but, as yet, this was only expressed in a superficial and wholly negative way. It wasn't until 'Sunny Afternoon' (a British chart-topper), 'Dead End Street' (1966), the glorious 'Waterloo Sunset' and 'Autumn Almanac' (1967) that Davies found the mellow melodic sound that was to characterize the Kinks' next phase and began to write compassionately rather than merely satirically.

For a while the change in direction seemed a smart move and the hits kept coming, though at a slower rate. But 'Days', a British Top 20 hit in 1968, marked the group's end as consistent hitmakers, especially in America where, after a disastrous tour in 1965, they weren't to perform again until 1969, due to their banning by the American Federation Of Musicians for 'unprofessional conduct'. In part the reason was that Ray Davies was involved in other projects. He wrote the music for the film *The Virgin Soldiers*, as well as songs for a variety of acts – e.g. 'I Go to Sleep', recorded both by the Applejacks (which included Ray's sister Megan on bass) and Peggy Lee, and 'Dandy', a Kinks album track that was an American Top 5 hit for **Herman's Hermits** in 1966 – and produced *Turtle Soup* for the **Turtles**.

Face to Face (1966), *Live at Kelvin Hall* and *Something Else* (1967) – Shel Talmy's last production for the group – found Davies still writing three-minute songs, but they were no longer aimed purely at specific audiences, the charts

or at the underground, as was demonstrated most noticeably on the live album. It consisted not of lengthy solos by members of the group but of one long 30-minute scream of applause by the audience, over which the Kinks could hardly be heard. And it wasn't an accident, as the credit 'musical direction: Ray Davies' made clear.

As the group was no longer performing very frequently, Dave Davies decided temporarily to branch out on his own as well. His first single, 'Death of a Clown' (1967), on which he was backed by the Kinks, was a British Top 5 hit. He planned a solo album, but when follow-up singles flopped, as did the Kinks' records of this period, it was scrapped. Despite the group's absence from the charts for a year, the Kinks had amassed a lot of material similar to that on *Something Else*. Initially only available in America – on *The Kink Kronikles* (Reprise, 1972) and *The Great Lost Kinks Album* (1973) – where the group had developed a fanatical cult following that saw them as the most English of all British groups, this material wasn't released in Britain at the time because Pye was only interested in hit singles and thought that if they couldn't sell singles, they certainly couldn't sell albums.

(The Kinks Are) The Village Green Preservation Society (1968), the group's first 'official' concept album, saw Ray Davies looking back at a make-believe Edwardian Britain when life seemed more ordered. Its follow-up, *Arthur (or the Decline and Fall of the British Empire)* (1969), which began life as a TV musical Ray Davies had written with Julian Mitchell, and saw John Dalton (born 21 May 1943) replacing Peter Quaife on bass, was again a look back. But this time the past was not seen as a haven but as a burden on the present, and flight – whether from the town to the country as in 'Drivin'', or from Britain to Australia in 'Australia' – was seen as the only solution. Having summed up the pressures of the past, the Kinks next moved on to a description of their own situation in *Lola Versus Powerman and the Moneygoround* (1970), produced while the group were preparing to leave both Pye and their old managers. More importantly, in career terms the album and its hit single, Ray Davies' salute to the ambiguous charms of 'Lola' – 'I'm glad I'm a man and so is Lola' – which reached both the British and American Top 10s in 1970, marked a new lease of life for the group.

In 1971, the group signed with RCA and recorded *Muswell Hillbillies*, by

Ray Davies leads the Kinks in typically flamboyant style

which time John Gosling had joined the group on piano and organ to fill out the group's sound. That and the next (double) album, *Everybody's in Showbiz – Everybody's a Star* (1972), which included another marvellous flop of a single, 'Celluloid Heroes', continued the themes of *Village Green* and *Lola* into the present day and, equally importantly, were relatively successful commercially. The tide seemed to be turning, and the group even began touring regularly again in America where they gained a new generation of fans with the increasingly theatrical approach to material which replaced the sloppy stage act of the Sixties. So successful were they with rock-theatre that all the following albums – *Preservation Act 1* (1973), which saw Alan Holmes (saxophone), Laurie Browne (trumpet) and John Beecham (trombone) joining as full-time Kinks, *Act 2* (1974), *Soap Opera* (1975) and *The Kinks Present Schoolboys in Disgrace* (1976) – would be accompanied by a stage presentation of sorts. While *Preservation* was too unwieldy to work either on stage or record, *Soap Opera* (which had its origins in a TV musical commissioned from Ray Davies by Granada and tells the story of a 'star' [Ray Davies] surveying suburbia for material for a new album and slowly succumbing to its 'attractions' until in the end he isn't sure if he's Norman

Normal or Ray Davies), was the group's most successful album of the Seventies and boded well for the future.

During their stay at RCA, the Kinks formed their own record label, Konk, which signed Claire Hammil among others, and Ray Davies returned to production with Café Society (whose line-up featured a young **Tom Robinson**). The Kinks' later albums, however, were commercial rather than critical successes. Their theatrical performances, featuring Ray Davies' camp swagger and the heavy-metal guitar of his brother, were now designed for American consumption; *Sleepwalker*, their first album for Arista in 1977, gave the group, now devoid of brass, an American hit album, even though it lacked a single hit to pave the way. But their concerts revealed a band that had lost inspiration, Ray Davies leading the audience through sing-along versions of the hits with little respect for the original sound. Records, too, lost virtually all their former distinctiveness; the concerns were similar but they were expressed with banal melodies, uninspired rock backings and tired clichés as present throughout *Low Budget*, the group's 1981 outing (and another American success). *Give the People What They Want* appeared in 1982. They returned to the UK chart in 1983 with 'Come Dancing' and in 1986 Ray Davies appeared in the film *Absolute Beginners*, singing 'Quiet Life'.

The Eighties found the Kinks back in vogue in their homeland as New Wave acts such as the **Jam**, Glen Matlock's Spectres (who recorded a version of 'This Strange Effect'), and the **Pretenders** (whose hits included versions of 'Stop Your Sobbing' and 'I Go to Sleep') paid tribute to the group's early sound.

KIRSHNER, DON

One of the most astute businessmen in American pop, Don Kirshner first made his mark on New York's fledgling rock industry in the mid-Fifties, as manager of **Bobby Darin** and **Connie Francis**. His early experience in songwriting, artist management and music publishing led him to form Aldon Music with Al Nevins, former member of the Three Suns vocal trio: with the aim of publishing and supplying songs specifically for the new teenage music market, they installed Aldon in offices within the Brill Building on New York's Broadway and recruited a stream of talented young songwriters from the city's high schools. These included **Neil Sedaka** and Howard Greenfield, Gerry Goffin and **Carole King**, **Barry Mann** and Cynthia Weil, and – a little later – **Neil Diamond**. All were hired on a nine-to-five basis and were expected to produce songs for a range of artists, from girl groups like the **Shirelles** to well-established teen idols of the **Bobby Vee** and **Tony Orlando** ilk.

In 1962, Kirshner set up Dimension Records as Aldon's recording arm and scored major hits with Carole King's 'It Might As Well Rain Until September' and **Little Eva**'s 'The Locomotion'. He became involved with Colpix, the new pop-oriented record subsidiary of Columbia Pictures, which used Aldon-published material almost exclusively and was run from Los Angeles by one of Kirshner's assistants, **Lou Adler**. In 1963, Kirshner sold his interest in Aldon to Screen Gems-Columbia and was appointed president of the film and television corporation's music division. As such, he devised the idea of a television series based on the life of a mythical pop group: called *The Monkees* and starring four unknown actor-musicians recruited through an advertisement in the showbusiness newspaper *Variety*, the series finally hit American screens in late 1966 and had the desired effect of turning 'the **Monkees**' into one of the biggest selling record acts in the world. All Monkee material was provided by Screen Gems-Columbia's publishing operation, whose contracted writers included not only such Aldon stalwarts as Goffin and King but relative newcomers like Michael Murphey and **Harry Nilsson**.

Following a dispute over percentages to be received by Kirshner for the Monkees, he left Screen Gems and wasted no time in starting a label of his own, Kirshner, and outdoing the Monkees with a new creation – the Archies. The concept was similar, with a weekly television show used to sell lightweight pop records to a very young audience, but this time the group in question were a bunch of cartoon characters, their voices and instrumental backing provided by a team of seasoned pop professionals. The scheme worked extremely well, with the debut Archies release 'Sugar Sugar' (1969) selling six million copies worldwide. A year later, Screen Gems-Columbia repeated the Monkee exercise – this time without Kirshner's help – by launching *The Partridge Family* on prime-time TV and promoting its star, **David Cassidy**, as a teen idol of the Seventies.

With the new decade, Kirshner began diversifying his various interests, re-launching the career of Neil Sedaka, discovering new writers, and plotting the rise of his eponymous record company. He became particularly involved in rock on television, creating a weekly late-night rock show called *In Concert* – which was later turned over to **Dick Clark** when its sponsors, ABC-TV, began insisting on artistic control – and establishing a syndicated live concert show, *Don Kirshner's Rock Concert*, as a television institution. His record label meanwhile continued to flourish, with his most successful discovery Kansas scoring a string of Top 40 hits between 1977 and 1982. *See also* **Bubblegum**; **Monkees**

KISS

Despite having sold over 50 million records worldwide, American hard glam-rockers Kiss will be remembered more for their make-up than their music. Formed by bassist Gene Simmons and guitarist Paul Stanley in New York in 1972, they recruited Peter Criss (drums) and second guitarist Ace Frehley. They immediately started gigging covered in greasepaint and retaining their facial anonymity, which became their main marketing gimmick.

Kiss developed their stage act to include horror special effects, mainly under the control of Simmons, and rode a critical onslaught to generate a strong young heavy metal following. Kiss released their first album in 1974, but it wasn't until 1976 and *Alive* that they broke into the US charts, the LP eventually going platinum. There followed a long string of successful releases, amassing 18 gold and 12 platinum albums. At one point Kiss became so popular (having broadened their audience with a more commercial sound) that Marvel created a comic around them.

Criss and Frehley left in 1979, to be replaced by Eric Carr and Bruce Kulick respectively and Kiss records continued to sell until the mid-Eighties. A change of make-up to a New Romantic image failed to impress and they eventually abandoned the camouflage altogether for fans to see their unadorned faces for the first time.

KNICKERBOCKERS

Formed in 1964 as the Castle Kings, the Knickerbockers – Buddy Randell from the Royal Teens (he co-wrote 'Short Shorts'), vocals and saxophone; Jimmy Walker, drums and vocals; John Charles, bass; and his brother Beau, guitar – took their name from Knickerbocker Avenue in their home town of Bergenfield, New Jersey. Discovered by Jerry Fuller, a moderately successful

Demon bassist Gene Simmons of Seventies hard rockers Kiss, the outrageously successful masters of make-up and comic horror effects

singer and very successful writer ('Travellin' Man', 'Young World', 'Over You' and 'Young Girl') and producer (Gary Puckett and the **Union Gap** and **Ricky Nelson**), they were signed to Challenge in 1965. They soon showed their skills as mimics when their **Beatles** pastiche, 'Lies' shot into the US Top 20 in the winter of 1965. Fuller's production of the Randell-B. Charles composition was perfect, sounding more like the Beatles than the Beatles. A follow-up, 'One Track Mind', reached the US Top 50 in 1966 but then failure set in and the group disbanded. Jimmy Walker briefly 'replaced' Bill Medley in the **Righteous Brothers** before attempting a solo career on Columbia and Buddy Randell tried the same on Uni and then Paramount.

KNIGHT, CURTIS Of mixed black/Indian parentage, R&B singer/guitarist Curtis Knight was born in Fort Scott, Kansas, in 1945. He moved to New York in 1961 where his own records on a number of labels (Gulf, Shell, R.S.V.P.) have since been overshadowed by an association with **Jimi Hendrix**. *Jimi*, Knight's 'intimate biography' of Hendrix, was published in 1974, but was not well received by critics or fans. Knight's best solo record was 'That's Why' on Gulf, which bubbled under the Hot 100 in 1961. Jimi Hendrix played and sang on tracks by Curtis Knight and the Squires made in 1965 for R.S.V.P.

KNIGHT, GLADYS Born in Atlanta, Georgia, on 28 May 1944, Gladys Knight was a child singer with the Morris Brown and Wings Over Jordan gospel choirs before joining her elder brother, Merald (2 September 1942) and cousins William (2 June 1941) and Elenor Guest to form the Pips

in 1952. It is reputed that she sang with the Magnificents on Vee Jay (1956–7) and some of their tracks have been reissued as by Gladys Knight, but she has since denied any part in them. Her 1958 debut release with the Pips – when another cousin, Edward Patten (2 August 1939), replaced Elenor – was 'Whistle My Love' on Brunswick. Three years later, their beautiful revival of 'Every Beat of My Heart', recorded for Atlanta-based Huntom (and leased to Vee Jay) and a re-recording for Bobby Robinson's Fury label, gave them simultaneous R&B hits with different versions of the same song. Further recordings for Robinson (on Fury, Enjoy and Everlast, 1961–3) included the fine 'Letter Full of Tears', a US Top 20 record in 1961. They next appeared on Maxx in 1964–5 with several excellent soul ballads (including 'Giving Up' and 'Either Way I Lose') written and arranged by **Van McCoy**, but remained unrecognized until a contract with Tamla-Motown in 1966 introduced them to a worldwide

In a recording career spanning three decades, Gladys Knight has received gold and platinum discs by the score, and still she sings on

audience. After minor success with 'Just Walk in My Shoes' they were placed with producer **Norman Whitfield**, who gave them nine exciting hits, including the first hit version of 'I Heard It Through the Grapevine' (1967), a wailing 'It Should Have Been Me' (1968), a revival of 'The Nitty Gritty' and the powerhouse 'Friendship Train' (1969). Later, several stunning ballad performances ('If I Were Your Woman' – 1970; 'Make Me the Woman That You Go Home To' – 1971; 'Help Me Make It Through the Night', 'Neither One of Us' – 1972) finally brought Gladys recognition as one of the great female soul singers of our time. In 1973 they transferred to Buddah and continued to win international acclaim with hits like 'Where Peaceful Waters Flow', 'Midnight Train to Georgia' (1973), 'The Best Thing That Ever Happened to Me' (1974), and 'The Way We Were' (1975). A legal dispute over the group's proposed switch to Columbia in 1977 – complicated by continuing legal difficulties with Motown over allegedly unpaid royalties – left them unable to record together for three years. Gladys and the Pips recorded separately, their reunion occurring in 1980 with *About Love*, produced by **Ashford and Simpson**.

KNIGHT, ROBERT Soul singer Robert Knight (born on 24 April 1945, in Franklin, Tennessee) first sang lead vocal with the Paramounts – Neal Hopper, Peter Hollins, Richard Simmons and Nashville super session man, Kenny Buttrey – on Dot in 1961. 'Young thrush sings lead on slow rockaballad' was how *Billboard* described their only disc. After solo sides for Dot – including 'Free Me' which **Johnny Preston** covered – Knight enrolled at Tennessee State University. In 1967, he was signed to Rising Sons by Mac Gayden and Buzz Cason who immediately wrote him a Top 20 smash hit, 'Everlasting Love', which was covered in Britain by the Love Affair. Knight's other light, frothy and magnificently danceable hits included 'Blessed Are the Lonely' (1968) and 'The Power of Love' (1972), whose flip, 'Love on a Mountain Top', reached the British charts in 1974. Knight who also recorded for Elf (e.g. 'Isn't It Lonely Together', 1968), continued an academic career in chemical research.

KNOX, BUDDY Born in Happy, Texas, on 14 April 1933, Buddy Knox was one of a wave of Southern country singers who broke into rock'n'roll in the Fifties. He formed the Rhythm Orchids locally, with Jimmy Bowen, and recorded at **Norman Petty**'s studio in Clovis, New Mexico. Petty placed 'Party Doll' and 'Hula Love' with Roulette in 1957, and both were big hits. Knox's style on these discs was basically country-rock but it was somehow lighter than other styles and was capable of adaptation into the teenballad genre of the later Fifties with hits like 'Somebody Touched Me' and 'Lovey Dovey'. In this, his career was paralleled by those of Texans Jimmy Bowen, **Roy Orbison** and **Buddy Holly**. Knox was a headliner on rock'n'roll extravaganza stage shows for five years with Roulette and Liberty Records, and he appeared in 'star-vehicle' movies like *Jamboree* (1957). During the Sixties, he turned towards country music and worked with minor success throughout Canada. He has recorded for Ruff, Reprise and United Artists.

KONGOS, JOHN A white South African – born in Johannesburg in 1946 – John Kongos emerged from the obscurity of the group Scrugg to enliven the UK music scene of 1971 with two tribal-like chants, 'He's Gonna Step on You Again' and 'Tokoloshe Man', both of which reached Number 4 in the chart. A writer/producer/performer of some promise, he became too identified too quickly with one, albeit highly original, rock sound and made no further impact, despite an interesting album for Elektra (*John Kongos*, 1971) that featured **Ralph McTell**, Ray Cooper, Lol Coxhill and others as guest musicians. His influence could be heard, however, in the Burundi-flavoured stomp of **Gary Glitter** and his later followers Adam and the Ants (see **Adam Ant**) and **Bow Wow Wow**, while 'Tusk' – a 1979 hit for **Fleetwood Mac** – was a straight re-creation of the briefly popular Kongos formula.

KOOL AND THE GANG A seven-piece black band led by bassist Robert 'Kool' Bell, Kool and the Gang disciplined their preference for free-form jazz to produce one of the hottest disco funk bands of the Seventies and early Eighties. Formed in Jersey City, New Jersey, in 1964 as the Jazziacs, they also doubled as the Soul Town Revue and the New Dimensions before adopting their present name in 1968 and signing to Gene Redd's De-Lite label the following year. After scoring minor hits with many ragged derivations of **Sly Stone** themes – 'Kool and the Gang' (1969), 'Let the Music Take Your Mind' (1970) and several loose albums, they tightened up to produce the million-selling 'Funky Stuff' (1973), the first of many equally exciting riffs ('Jungle Boogie', 'Hollywood Swinging', 'Higher Plane' – 1974; 'Spirit of the Boogie' – 1975) tailor-made for the growing disco boom.

They sang 'Open Sesame' on the soundtrack of *Saturday Night Fever* in 1977 and a year later were joined by singer James Taylor (not the white singer/guitarist of the same name), who debuted on the album *Ladies Night*. The title track reached Number 8 in the US and brought them their first UK chart entry, which was subsequently followed by such hits as 'Celebration' (1980), 'Jones vs. Jones' (1981), 'Get Down on It' (1982), 'Joanna' (1984) and 'Cherish' (1985). A new album, *Forever*, was issued in 1986.

KOOPER, AL Few musicians have had a more chequered or more fascinating career than Al Kooper, who was born in New York on 5 February 1944. At 13 he was a member of the Royal Teens who had a Top 10 hit with the novelty 'Short Shorts' on ABC in 1958. At 19, with a reputation as a session guitarist, he quit college to work as an apprentice engineer in a recording studio before teaming up with songwriters Bob Brass and Irvine Levine. Despite a Number 1 with 'This Diamond Ring' for **Gary Lewis and the Playboys** in 1965, Kooper didn't enjoy Tin Pan Alley life and spent his time between session work gigging round the folk clubs. Then Tom Wilson invited Kooper to a session by **Bob Dylan**. Kooper was determined to play on the session, but **Mike Bloomfield** was there to play guitar so Kooper muscled in to play organ. He didn't know the first thing about the instrument but felt his way through the take. Dylan was impressed by the amateurish squeezed organ sound and the take was used on the record, 'Like a Rolling Stone'. Kooper later joined Dylan at the famous 1965 Newport Folk Festival electric set before completing the *Highway 61* album. His association with both Dylan and Mike Bloomfield stood Kooper in good stead for the future.

In 1966, through Wilson, Kooper came to join the **Blues Project**. He played on three albums by the group, the two live ones and the studio *Projections*, until friction with guitarist Danny Kalb caused him to leave both the group and New York. In Los Angeles, he gigged around, and unveiled future **Blood, Sweat and Tears** songs at the Big Sur Folk Festival in 1967. Back in New York Kooper put together a temporary band to play a week at the Café A Go-Go in order to fund a trip to England. It was these musicians who became the nucleus for BS and T. However, after the remarkable *Child Is Father to the Man* album he found the band slipping away into an alien direction and left them to start work with Columbia as a producer. Filling in studio time, he started another trend by recording an album with Mike Bloomfield and **Steve Stills** (fresh from **Buffalo Springfield**) which became *Supersession* (1968). Its spectacular success led to a series of live concerts with Mike Bloomfield again captured on the, for the most part, excessive album, *The Live Adventures of Al Kooper and Mike Bloomfield* (1969).

In the early Seventies, Kooper released a series of usually weak solo albums of which only *Easy Does It* and *New York City You're a Woman* do him any real credit. A man never afraid to speak his mind and never the darling of the critics, Kooper's involvement with great projects and seminal schemes marks him out as someone special. He has been quiet since the mid-Seventies, devoting most of his time to production work – including albums for **Lynyrd Skynyrd**, the **Tubes** and **Nils Lofgren**. In the early Eighties, he played in a Blues Project reunion concert and on tour with Dylan.

KORNER, ALEXIS The godfather of the British R&B movement of the early to mid-Sixties, Alexis Korner (born in Paris on 19 April 1928) flirted with traditional jazz and skiffle before opening the London Blues and Barrelhouse Club with **Cyril Davies** in 1955. The pair first played together at the club's Thursday evening sessions, which attracted visiting American bluesmen as well as local enthusiasts. Inspired by **Muddy Waters**, **Chris Barber** introduced R&B into his jazz band's repertoire, and Korner (guitar) and Davies (harmonica) backed singer Ottilie Patterson. The popularity of the sets encouraged them to form their own R&B band, Blues Incorporated, in 1961 and, in March the following year, to open their own club in Ealing. The band's original personnel included Art Wood (vocals) and Charlie Watts (drums) and among those who passed through the constantly changing line-up during the next year were **Long John Baldry**, **Jack Bruce**, **Ginger Baker**, **Graham Bond**, Ronnie Jones and Phil Seamen. Despite his seminal influence on British R&B, the boom passed Korner by and he spent much of the

mid-Sixties working in television with his current rhythm section, Danny Thompson (bass) and Terry Cox (drums). In 1967, he formed a trio, Free At Last, with an initial line-up of Cliff Barton (bass) and Hugie Flint (drums), but which changed so much he decided to work on his own. While touring Scandinavia the following year he met Peter Thorup; their subsequent collaboration provided the nucleus of New Church in 1969, the studio band CCS and Snape, formed by chance on an American tour in 1972 with ex-members of **King Crimson**. Though Snape broke up within a year, Korner and Thorup continued to work together both as a duo and in CCS, whose hits included a cover of **Led Zeppelin**'s 'Whole Lotta Love' in 1970. He began a long-running association with BBC Radio 1 in the early Seventies, hosting a thoughtful and enterprising R&B show and narrating a number of documentary series. He died of cancer in 1984.

KRAFTWERK With **Can** and **Tangerine Dream**, Kraftwerk complete the Big Three of seminal German bands. They are also the most notable survivors from the German scene. Formed in 1971 out of Düsseldorf rock group the Organisation, the original duo of Ralf Hutter and Florian Schneider-Esleben took as their name the German word for 'power-station', and their inspiration came from the industrialized flatlands of the neighbouring Rhineland. With noted producer Connie Plank adding creative input, their first album – a double – *Kraftwerk* (1972) was inspired more by the German avant-garde than any rock sources, and it has yet to be improved on by any of the later, self-styled 'industrial' bands. The 1973 follow-up, *Ralf and Florian*, moved closer to their now-famous style of dense keyboard and rhythmic repetitions, quite probably influenced by recent exposure to the work of American minimal composer Philip Glass. Fame came with 1974's album *Autobahn*, notably the 20-minute long title track and the edited version released as a single. This established the Kraftwerk sound: seemingly innocuous melodies and rhythms straddling the avant-garde, the discotheque and traditional German song, often stretched to extraordinary length.

In 1975 they released *Radioactivity*, but it took 1977's *Trans-Europe Express* to establish them internationally. Notably predating the so-called 'New Europeans' tag that would be adopted by the likes of **Simple Minds** and **Ultravox**, it moved them

into position for the success of the following year's *Man Machine*.

Man Machine could not have arrived at a better time. It collided with punk's dalliance with avant-garde art (cover inspired by Russian Constructivist painter El Lissitsky; title taken from fashionable cybernetics; lyrics both German *and* alienated) and revealed that Kraftwerk had come clean about being a dance band. Critically acclaimed, it effectively re-wrote the history of German music overnight. With young bands such as the **Human League** and the Normal starting to release their own efforts under the Kraftwerk influence, it also firmly established the synthesizer as a punk instrument. You can thank, or blame, this album for the later electro-pop boom.

Publicity-shy perfectionists, Kraftwerk retreated into their Kling Klang Studios in Düsseldorf for three shrouded years before reappearing with 1981's *Computer-World* album and tour. It was initially mis-read as their most superficial, cynical record – six tracks of gleaming, faultless electropop – but soon revealed itself to be an album of irony, substance and political basis. The tour confirmed the rumours that the delay had largely been due to the extraordinary move of converting their studio equipment to enable them to take it on the road. Though further rumour had it that a cycling accident suffered by Hutter – their shared obsession for the sport resulted in 1985's signature-theme single for the Tour de France race – had delayed production of their eighth album, *Electric café* eventually surfaced in 1986.

Kraftwerk – humans or dummies?

KRAMER, BILLY J., AND THE DAKOTAS

Originally the lead singer with a Merseyside group, the Coasters, the handsome but bland-voiced Billy J. (born William Ashton, 19 August 1943) was teamed by **Brian Epstein** with a Manchester group, the Dakotas, and signed to Parlophone. Between 1963 and 1965 he had six records in the British Top 20, four of them Lennon-McCartney compositions: 'Do You Want to Know a Secret?', 'Bad to Me', 'I'll Keep You Satisfied' and 'From a Window'. The others were composed by Mort Shuman ('Little Children') and **Burt Bacharach** ('Trains and Boats and Planes'). In America, only 'Little Children' and 'Bad to Me' reached the Top 20, and as his recording career began to fade, Kramer followed many of his contemporaries into the lucrative north of England cabaret circuit. The Dakotas (Mike Maxfield, lead guitar; Robin McDonald, rhythm; Ray Jones, bass; and Tony Mansfield, drums) had an instrumental hit in 1963 with the **Shadows**-styled 'The Cruel Sea'.

KRISTOFFERSON, KRIS

Better known in the Eighties as a film star than as one of country music's premier songwriters, Kris Kristofferson was nevertheless a prime mover in the 'crossover' success that country enjoyed from the early Seventies onwards. IIe was born in Brownsville, Texas, on 22 June 1936 and was a country fan from an early age. He went as a Rhodes Scholar to Oxford University in 1958 where he had a couple of novels rejected by publishers and briefly became a 'genuine American' rock'n'roller, Kris Carson. Returning home, he joined the army for four and a half years, before eventually reaching Nashville in 1965, where his creative drive and love of country music could work for each other. The next four years were spent hustling songs he was writing, with increasing success. He got a publishing contract, provided hits for **Ray Stevens** and **Roger Miller** and finally started to cut his own demos. Around the turn of the decade he made several successful albums, the first and best of which, *The Silver Tongued Devil and I* (Monument, 1971), featured the fine musicianship of Nashville friends, Kris' less notable voice, and songs written with a fine turn of phrase. His most famous songs, like 'Me and Bobby McGee' and 'Help Me Make It Through the Night', have swiftly become contemporary standards. Between 1973 and 1977 he produced little of note, but he worked (*Kris And Rita*, 1973) and lived with

Rita Coolidge, whom he married in 1973. (They divorced six years later.) The late Seventies brought further albums – *Easter Island* (1978), *Shake Hands With the Devil* (1979) – but he seemed more intent on following a film career that had already blossomed impressively with roles in *Cisco Pike*, *Pat Garrett and Billy The Kid*, *Alice Doesn't Live Here Anymore*, *A Star Is Born*, *Convoy* and *Semi-Tough*. His Eighties films have to date included *Heaven's Gate* and *Rollover*.

KUTI, FELA ANIKULAPO

Nigerian singer/songwriter/bandleader Fela Kuti (born in 1938) faced vicious harassment from a succession of Nigerian regimes, an aspect of his life which has to be considered as important as the creation of his Afrobeat style of music. While popular music, both within Africa and outside it, has thrown up many politically oriented protest artists since the mid-Sixties, only a tiny proportion of these have ever had their commitments tested in the face of determined state repression. Indeed, the music and the persecution are inextricably linked, for Kuti's anti-establishment and anti-colonial-heritage politics – and their consequences for him – have contributed to the lyrics of many of his most powerful and lasting songs and record releases.

Though he later identified himself

Fela Kuti eventually took his politics more seriously than his music

wholly with the poorest, most under-privileged sections of Nigerian society, Kuti was actually born into a relatively well-off, middle-class environment – his parents paid for him to travel to London in 1958 to study at Trinity College of Music. Back in Nigeria in 1962 he joined Nigerian Broadcasting as a trainee radio producer before forming his first band, Koola Lobitos.

Initially basing his music on that of jazz musicians like John Coltrane and soul singers like **James Brown**, Kuti steadily increased the African content of his style – naming it Afrobeat in 1968 and renaming his band Africa 70 in 1969. He enjoyed his first Nigerian hit in 1971, and the same year founded the Shrine Club in Lagos, which became the focus of Afrobeat music for the next decade.

Kuti's most productive period was the mid-Seventies, when he released albums like *Gentleman*, *Alagbon Close* and *Expensive Shit*. Following the army sacking of his home in 1977, the balance between politics and music in Kuti's activities tipped so far in the direction of the former as to make his Afrobeat so unremittingly propagandist that it became ultimately unsatisfying music.

KWESKIN, JIM, JUG BAND

Formed at the suggestion of Al Grossman in 1963, from a nucleus of folk musicians who performed regularly at Club 47 in Boston, Massachusetts, the Jim Kweskin Jug Band comprised Jim Kweskin, vocals, guitar; Maria D'Amato (Muldaur) vocals, kazoo, tambourine; Geoff Muldaur, guitar, vocals, clarinet, washboard; Bill Keith, banjo, steel, guitar and Fritz Richmond, jug, washtub bass. They literally sparked off the whole jug band revival through their spectacular live appearances. Rarely captured on album, *Best of Jim Kweskin and his Jug Band* (1969) is the closest approximation of their craziness. They spanned six years and various personnel fluctuations. Fiddler Richard Greene joined towards the end and earlier Mel Lyman (then a harmonica player) had helped start the collapse. It was inevitable anyway, as jug band music became a pleasant anachronism. Kweskin became part of Lyman's authoritarian religious sect, 'The Family'. Geoff and Maria recorded together in Woodstock, then separated, Maria to some solo success, and Geoff tastefully in Better Days and then solo. Richmond and Keith are still in demand as musicians, Richmond also as an engineer. *See also* **Maria Muldaur**

LABELLE, PATTI From high heels, bouffant hairstyles and Broadway show tunes to sci-fi fashion, revolutionary image and aggressive 'black rock', LaBelle's metamorphosis was one of the most extraordinary phenomena of the Seventies. Patricia Holt (alias Patti LaBelle, born 4 October 1944) and Cindy Birdsong (15 December 1939) grew up together in Philadelphia. They joined the Ordettes, while their friends Sarah Dash (24 May 1942) and Nona Hendryx (18 August 1945) joined the Del Capris. The four girls amalgamated as the Blue Belles and Newtown Records hit the Top 20 with their 'I Sold My Heart to the Junkman' in 1962. As Patti LaBelle and the Bluebells they became a part of the girl group scene of the Sixties, hitting with 'You'll Never Walk Alone' (Parkway, 1964) and 'All or Nothing' (Atlantic, 1965). But their stream of discs became less and less successful. Cindy Birdsong took up an offer to replace Florence Ballard in the **Supremes** and the team re-grouped as a trio.

With new manager Vicki Wickham (late of Britain's *Ready Steady Go* TV programme) and a new, streamlined name – Labelle – the girls moved first to Warner Bros in 1972 and then to RCA where their image sharpened up with the use of strong material, like **Gil Scott-Heron**'s 'The Revolution Will Not Be Televised'. A contract with Columbia/Epic brought forth the *Nightbirds* album produced by New Orleans mastermind **Allen Toussaint**. With the million-selling 'Lady Marmalade' (1975) their rebirth was complete, though the line-up lasted only until 1977. Patti then enjoyed solo success with Columbia and, in 1982, joined **Al Green** in the Broadway show *Your Arms Too Short to Box With God*. 1986 found her back in the US and UK charts with 'On My Own', on which she duetted with Michael McDonald.

LAINE, DENNY A founder member of the **Moody Blues** and a long-time associate of **Paul McCartney** in Wings, Denny Laine was born Brian Arthur Hayes in Birmingham, UK, on 29 October 1944. He led his first group, Denny and the Diplomats, from 1962 through to 1964, and after being sacked formed the Moody Blues with Mike

Pinder, Clint Warwick, Graeme Edge and Ray Thomas. He sang the plaintive lead vocal on the group's first major international hit, the UK chart-topping 'Go Now', but left in 1966, frustrated by the failure of their follow-up releases. In 1967 he fronted the short-lived Electric String Band and wrote and recorded 'Say You Don't Mind'. Laine's own version was an unaccountable chart failure, but a 1972 recording of the song by **Colin Blunstone** reached Number 15 in the UK. With Trevor Burton of the **Move**, Laine formed Balls in 1969 (a putative supergroup financed by Tony Secunda) but was again unable to engender much public interest. The group, which also included at various times Steve Gibbons, Dave Morgan, Keith Smart, Richard Tandy and Alan White, made one single, 'Fight for My Country', and played ten dates before breaking up in 1971. After a brief spell with **Ginger Baker**'s Airforce, Laine joined Wings as rhythm guitarist. He remained a key member of the McCartney camp for a decade, pausing to record the solo albums *Aah Laine* (1973), *Holly Days* (a McCartney-produced tribute to **Buddy Holly**, 1976) and *Japanese Tears* (1981). He left McCartney in 1981 and later sold the inside story of Wings to a Sunday newspaper.

LAINE, FRANKIE A big-voiced balladeer who formed part of Mitch Miller's strategy – as head of A&R at American Columbia – to import a hint of country and western into pop during the Fifties, Frankie Laine was born Frank LoVecchio on 30 March 1913, in Chicago. His earliest claim to fame was the setting of the all-time marathon dance record of 145 days in 1932. Laine's professional singing career began when he replaced Perry Como in Freddie Carlone's band in 1937. He moved on to Los Angeles, where Hoagy Carmichael is supposed to have discovered him singing in a night-club. He signed to Mercury Records, and the first big hit came in 1947 with 'That's My Desire'. He had thirteen million sellers in the next decade. Most were for Columbia, to whom he was signed by Miller in 1951. Hits like 'Jezebel' and 'High Noon' were in the muscular-ballad mould favoured by Miller for his artists (Guy Mitchell was another). He appeared in films and continued having hits throughout the Fifties, but moved into cabaret work during the Sixties. His best-known recording since has been 'Blazing Saddles', the theme song from Mel Brooks' 1975 film of the same name.

LANCE, MAJOR A figurehead of the Chicago soul scene of the Sixties, Major Lance was born in the city on 4 April 1941 and recorded unsuccessfully for Mercury before finding success on the Okeh label. There, the combination of Carl Davis' production, Johnny Pate's brassy arrangements and **Curtis Mayfield**'s songs gave him a stream of hits on both the pop and R&B charts between 1963 and 1967. 'The Monkey Time', 'Hey Little Girl', 'Um Um Um Um Um Um' and 'The Matador' were all Top 20 records, while 'It Ain't No Use', 'Rhythm' and 'Come See' were lesser hits. In 1968, he went with Carl Davis to Dakar Records and had a small R&B hit with 'Follow the Leader'. Later records on Curtis Mayfield's Curtom label included 'Stay Away from Me' and 'Must Be Love Coming Down'. In 1972, Lance recorded for Volt, toured Britain where he had become a cult figure on the Northern soul scene and recorded for Contempo and Warner Brothers. *See also* **Curtis Mayfield**

LANE, RONNIE After leaving the **Faces** in mid-1973, Ronnie Lane (born 1 April 1948) formed his own group, Slim Chance, and had a UK hit with his first single release, 'How Come' (GM, 1973). He then undertook an overambitious tour, the Passing Show, using a circus big top, which financial pressures forced him to abandon uncompleted, and his band (which included Benny Gallagher and Graham Lyle – see **Gallagher and Lyle**) broke up after recording *Anymore for Anymore* (GM, 1974). Later that year he re-formed Slim Chance with Ruan O'Lochlainn (keyboards, saxophone, guitar), Charlie Hart (keyboards, violin, accordion), Steve Simpson (guitar, mandolin, violin), Brian Belshaw (bass), and Colin Davey (drums) – with himself handling vocals and guitar – for *Ronnie Lane's Slim Chance* (Island, 1975). However, he was best seen on stage where his eccentric and eclectic range of material was imbued with the jollity of a knees-up in an East End of London boozer. In 1976, the same line-up, minus O'Lochlainn, released *One for the Road*, and by 1977 Lane was solo again, though his next record – *Rough Mix* – was with Pete Townshend.

Little was then heard from Lane apart from one solo album, *See Me* (Gem, 1979), until it emerged that he was suffering from the debilitating disease, multiple sclerosis. Helped by numerous ex-colleagues, he organized and performed in a number of MS benefit concerts in the early Eighties.

LASALLE, DENISE During the early Seventies chunky and funky Denise Lasalle vied with **Ann Peebles** as the raunchiest writer/songstress out of Memphis. Born Denise Craig in Greenwood, Mississippi, she eventually settled in Chicago where she cut her first, unsuccessful, records for the Chess (1967) and Parka (1970) labels. After forming Crajon Productions with husband Bill Jones, sessions with **Willie Mitchell** and Gene Miller in Memphis yielded the first of several compulsive hits on Westbound, including 'Trapped by a Thing Called Love' (1971), 'Now Run and Tell That' and 'A Man Size Job' (1972). Recording in Muscle Shoals in the mid-Seventies, she continued to release the occasional hit but concentrated on songwriting and production for other artists. She made a welcome but unexpected return to the pop headlines during 1985, when her '(Don't Mess with) My Toot-Toot' (Epic) became a Top 10 UK hit.

LAUPER, CYNDI Born and raised in an Italian neighbourhood of Queens, New York, Cyndi Lauper paid her dues in the mid-Seventies as a vocalist with a number of New York bands. In 1977 she met saxophonist and keyboard player John Turi and together they formed Blue Angel, before signing with Polydor Records in 1979 and releasing the album *Blue Angel* the following year. The group gained favourable notices within the New York music scene but little followed on and in 1983 Cyndi quit the band to sign a new deal with Portrait Records as a solo singer. Portrait introduced her to producer Rick Chertoff, a happy collaboration which resulted in the 1984 album *She's So Unusual*. This provided her with a succession of hits, the lightweight, boppy 'Girls Just Want to Have Fun' and the chart-topping 'Time After Time', a superb production which, incidentally, caught the attention of **Miles Davis**, who went on to cover the song on his *You're Under Arrest* album.

LEADBELLY A legendary figure in black folk music, Leadbelly was born Huddie Ledbetter in Mooringsport, Louisiana, in 1885, into a family that included musicians from whom he learned the elements of playing guitar and accordion for dances and street entertainment. Discovery of his musical talent by the outside world did not come in those circumstances, however; he was serving a sentence for assault in the penitentiary at Angola, Louisiana, when, in the early Thirties, John A. Lomax, collecting prison songs for the

Library of Congress Archive of Folk Song, uncovered Leadbelly's vast store of traditional music. Throughout the Thirties and Forties, first for the Archive and (after his reprieve) for folk record companies in the East, he recorded many hundreds of blues, blues-ballads, dance songs and other specimens of black folk music, to his individual and thrusting 12-string guitar accompaniment. Though lionized by both the folk music establishment and society audiences, he died in comparative poverty in 1949.

Leadbelly's repertoire, easily the most extensive and valuable ever documented from a black folk musician, included many archaic pieces of the pre-blues era, and these – for example 'Midnight Special', 'Ella Speed', 'Pick A Bale O'Cotton', 'Rock Island Line' – became the standards of the folk revival of the Fifties, and, in Britain, of skiffle. Frequently, however, it was other artists who enjoyed success with his material; for instance the **Weavers** with 'Goodnight Irene'. With the coming, after his death, of a blues vogue, Leadbelly was underrated, though he was no negligible blues-singer, and his angry compositions 'Mr Tom Hughes' Town' and 'Bourgeois Blues' are among his best recordings. Gradually his uniqueness is becoming valued, and much of his repertoire has been made available on albums, notably *The Library of Congress Recordings* (Elektra, 1966) and *Last Sessions* (Folkways, 1962). These contain many of the songs which rock musicians in the Sixties and Seventies continually borrowed.

LEAVES Part of the first wave of Los Angeles folk-rock groups that followed in the wake of the **Byrds**' success in 1965, the Leaves were led by Jim Pons and Bill Rinehart. The group also included John Beck, Robert Reiner and Tom Ray; when Rinehart left a few months later he was replaced by Bobby Arlin. Signed to the local Mira label, they recorded a number of fine protest songs, the requisite number of **Dylan** tunes, and two versions of a song that later became a folk-rock standard (recorded by the Byrds, **Love**, **Tim Rose**, **Jimi Hendrix** and countless others) – 'Hey Joe'. The second version gave them their only national hit (when it reached Number 31) in May 1966. Its powerful beat, fuzz guitar and screaming vocals made it an all-time classic; the Leaves were later signed by Capitol who issued a second album. Pons joined the **Turtles** in 1967, and Arlin left to form the Hook, a trio who recorded two albums for Uni.

LED ZEPPELIN Giants of Seventies hard rock and one of that decade's greatest commercial success stories, Led Zeppelin had a history dating back to October 1968, when **Jimmy Page** (guitar, born on 9 April 1944) formed the band with Robert Plant (vocals, 20 August 1948), John Paul Jones (bass, keyboards, 3 January 1946), and John Bonham (drums, 31 May 1948). Page had had the idea for the band throughout the last months of the **Yardbirds**; he knew John Paul Jones from session work and a friend recommended Birmingham-based Robert Plant, in whose Band Of Joy John Bonham drummed. They recorded their first album in thirty hours and then toured Scandinavia fulfilling old Yardbirds obligations.

On their first American tour in early 1969 they supported **Vanilla Fudge** and played club dates. Their second, headlining tour came shortly after and the next shortly after that; by March 1970, they were performing their fifth tour. *Led Zeppelin* was released in February 1969 by Atlantic Records; within two months it was Number 8, and remained in the Top 20 for six months. *Led Zeppelin II*, released in October 1969, became Atlantic's fastest selling album, moving at 100,000 copies per week. This record was subsequently broken by the group's 1975 album, *Physical Graffiti*, which at one point was selling 500 an hour. All the group's albums are platinum.

The first group to establish a world reputation by heavily touring America while playing only sporadically elsewhere – a situation created partly by an initial lack of interest in them in Britain – much of their success lies with manager Peter Grant who guided the group's career with almost mechanical efficiency and timing. His policy that they should work only every other year kept the group in demand, a situation not hindered by the endless quest for perfection that held up the release of an album for several months due to cover problems, the year and a half of recording *Physical Graffiti*, or the endless delays of their feature film, *The Song Remains the Same*.

By 1975 they were the most successful group in the world, filling football stadiums across America and five days at London's 20,000-seat Earl's Court with an awesome display of lights, smoke, dry ice and laser beams. The group's focus was Plant and Page. Onstage they were opposites and complements: Plant a golden-ringleted Adonis marvellously parodying the sexual superstar while singing in a voice of limitless power, Page a dark, fragile guitarist of immense versatility and command clothed in black velvet and rippling dragons.

Presence (1976) and *In Through the Out Door* (1979) proved to be the last Zeppelin albums proper. Bonham was found dead at Page's home on 25 September 1980, and the band issued a statement to the effect that they could continue no longer. The suitably entitled *Coda*, comprising unreleased recordings and out-takes, was issued in 1982, the year that Plant made his solo debut with the album *Pictures at Eleven*.

LEE, ALBERT As **Chris Farlowe**'s guitarist in the Thunderbirds, Albert Lee (born 21 December 1943) earned a legendary reputation in London in the mid-Sixties among other musicians, though Farlowe's lack of recording success – apart from 'Out of Time' (Immediate, 1966), without the Thunderbirds – denied him wider acclaim. When Farlowe finally broke up his backing group in 1968, Lee spent eighteen months with Country Fever, during which time he also recorded as Poet and the One Man Band with Tony Colton (percussion) and Ray Smith (guitar). He later worked briefly with Fotheringay and recorded with Steve Gibbons before rejoining Smith and Colton as Heads Hands And Feet (together with Mike O'Neill (keyboards) and Pete Gavin (drums) for three albums, *Heads Hands and Feet* (Island, 1971), *Tracks* (1972) and *Old Soldiers Never Die* (Atlantic, 1973). He subsequently worked with the **Crickets** and in 1975 rejoined Farlowe for the latter's comeback tour, before becoming a member of **Emmylou Harris**' Hot Band. His solo album, *Hiding* (A&M, 1979), was completed after a two-year stint with the band. That same year, he toured with **Eric Clapton**'s band; a second album, *Albert Lee*, followed in 1982.

Led Zeppelin's John Bonham, loud and aggressive, drives the band forward

LEE, BRENDA Arguably the finest white female singer in pop during the pre-Beatle years, Brenda Lee was born in Atlanta, Georgia, on 11 December 1944. She was discovered and managed by Dub Albritten, country music star Red Foley's manager, and made her singing debut at the Ozark Mountain Jubilee in 1956. She then seemed set for an orthodox career as a country singer, especially when she had a minor country hit with her first record for American Decca, the standard 'Jambalaya'. However, in 1959, with **Connie Francis** established as the female singer of the period, Brenda Lee cut 'Sweet Nothins'. She still had the manner and appearance of a country-singing Georgia Peach, but the song was strong – and her singing even stronger – and it became a huge pop hit in both Europe and America.

Before retiring from the music business in 1967, she had well over twenty chart hits, including Number 1s with 'I'm Sorry' and 'I Want to be Wanted', and a string of Top 10s, 'Emotions', 'Dum, Dum', 'That's All You Gotta Do', 'Fool Number One', etc. Most of these were performed in a rock-ballad style, with integrated pizzicato strings and an electric rhythm section behind the voice. But if the backings were formula-ridden and the songs of a variable quality, what remained constant was Brenda Lee's voice; it suggested a mixture of despair, dissipation and sexual torment more often than not.

In 1971, married with two children, she returned to music and immediately gained country chart success with **Kris Kristofferson**'s 'Nobody Wins'. Her first return album, *Brenda*, was her biggest seller to date. She is now well established as a country singer in the Nashville mainstream.

LEE, CURTIS Born on 28 October 1941, in Yuma, Arizona, Curtis Lee was poised to follow in the footsteps of **Fabian** with whom he has been unfavourably compared. Blue-eyed and blond, his looks were his greatest asset, but his early sides on Warrior in 1960 also revealed a sweet voice with a countryish burr. The following year he was signed to Dunes by **Ray Peterson**. 'Pretty Little Angel Eyes', which capitalized on the Fifties trick of an over-employed bassman – Arthur Crier, who along with the rest of the Halos who provided the back-up singing on the disc – and 'Under the Moon of Love', a pounding party disc redolent of **Gary 'U.S.' Bonds**, were produced by **Phil Spector** and reached the Top 10 and Top 50 respectively.

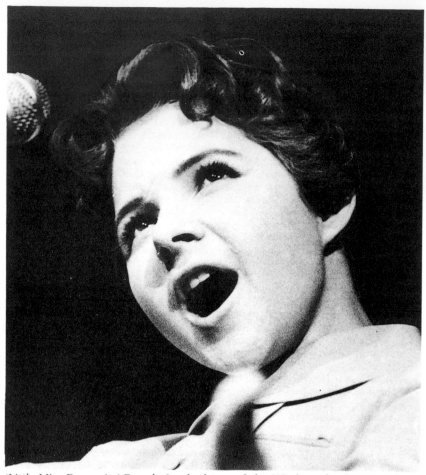

'Little Miss Dynamite' Brenda Lee had topped the US charts by the time she was 16; the power of her voice was astounding for her age

LEE, LAURA One of the first soul singers to champion liberated women, Laura Lee's early records (Chess, 1967–8) chastised ('Dirty Man'), and advertised ('Wanted: Lover, No Experience Necessary', 'Up Tight Good Man', 'A Man with Some Backbone'). She was equally convincing on romantic songs like **Jerry Butler/Curtis Mayfield**'s 'Need to Belong' and 'He Will Break Your Heart'. After a year with Cotillion she enjoyed greater success on Hot Wax with even more forthright material, including 'Wedlock is a Padlock' (1970), 'Woman's Love Rights' (1971), 'Rip Off', and 'Crumbs off the Table' (1972), but later releases on Invictus ('If I'm Good Enough to Love – I'm Good Enough to Marry') seemed to indicate a change of heart.

LEFT BANKE A **Beatles**-inspired five-man group from New York City, the Left Banke was formed by 18-year old piano and harpsichord student Michael Brown in 1966. His fellow members were Steve Martin (vocals),

Tom Finn (bass), Rick Brand (guitar) and George Cameron (drums). Their first hit single was 'Walk Away Renee', written by Brown some three years earlier and graced by an appealingly offbeat arrangement featuring ethereal vocals, heavy strings and harpsichord. A Number 5 hit in the US, it was followed by the similar 'Pretty Ballerina' (1967). None of the Left Banke's subsequent releases (including the brilliant 'Desiree') sold well and Brown left in 1969 to form the more experimentally-oriented Montage. From there, Brown moved on to **Stories** in 1972 and later worked as an A&R manager with Mercury Records in New York. The original members of the Left Banke, minus Brown, re-formed the group for one reunion single, 'Queen of Paradise', in 1980.

LEIBER AND STOLLER The first independent producers in the history of rock, Jerry Leiber and Mike Stoller were responsible for ushering out an era when records were made by pulling groups off the street into a studio to mouth 'doowop, doowah' into a mike for three minutes. Leiber and Stoller were also the first to introduce satire and social comment into a music previously concerned with songs about a boy who just had to have a girl. They may even have been the first blue-eyed soul brothers, writing and producing records for a host of bluesmen from 1949 onwards.

It was in that year that Leiber (born in Baltimore on 25 April 1933) met Stoller (born in New York on 13 March 1933) in Los Angeles. They pooled their skills and wrote blues, usually with the first line of each verse repeated – the classic twelve-bar form. The seeds of R&B were developing in the soil of country blues and the big bands. Small independent labels relied on local talent to perform the new, hybrid music. Leiber and Stoller had no difficulty in placing their songs.

The Robins, **Amos Milburn**, **Floyd Dixon**, Peppermint Harris, Preston Love, the Flairs, Bullmoose Jackson, **Jimmy Witherspoon** . . . as many as twenty blues singers mopped up their compositions as fast as they were written. In 1951, **Charles Brown** gave them their first 'race' hit, 'Hard Times'. Shortly after, Little Willie Littlefield cut 'K.C. Lovin'' (a million seller for **Wilbert Harrison** as 'Kansas City' in 1959) and **Willie Mae Thornton** recorded 'Hound Dog' (revived by Presley in 1956).

In 1954, Leiber and Stoller founded their own label, Spark. Among the artists they signed, none were more important than the Robins, whose records – 'Framed', 'Riot In Cell Block No. 9' – were of historic importance in the development of R&B production. On the strength of this, Atlantic Records signed the pair to an independent production deal in 1955. They headed for New York, but without three of the Robins who preferred to stay in LA. Quickly augmented on the East Coast, the group was renamed the **Coasters**. Leiber and Stoller produced and wrote for many of Atlantic/Atco's greatest performers (**Joe Turner**, **LaVern Baker**, the **Isley Brothers**, **Clyde McPhatter**, **Ruth Brown**), but had they never recorded anyone else, they would be secure in rock history for their work with the Coasters, for whom they created an astonishing figure of 18 ingenious hits.

They were also put in charge of Atlantic's other important black group, the **Drifters**. The liaison soon produced 'There Goes My Baby', arguably the greatest record with which Leiber and

Stoller were ever involved. It combined **Ben E. King**'s gospel-rooted voice with a Latin rhythm section and neo-classical strings. It sounded like two records playing at once and it sold a million in 1959. The combination of such eclectic ingredients unleashed a trend as significant as the invention of the electric guitar. By imposing themselves on a second black group, Leiber and Stoller had given the popular music industry entirely new ideas. After 'There Goes My Baby', black groups rarely recorded without strings, while Latin rhythms permeated the whole of pop from **Burt Bacharach** (who sat in on the Drifters' sessions) onwards. In keeping with the general softening of rock'n'roll, succeeding Drifters records were less intense and often decidedly lush. But they were extremely popular and it is probable that they inspired **Phil Spector**, who was 'apprenticed' to Leiber and Stoller at this time.

By maintaining their independence from Atlantic, Leiber and Stoller were able to work for many other companies during the Fifties and early Sixties. A brief list would have to include: Capitol (the Cheers), Checker (**Dale Hawkins**), Vee Jay (Christine Kittrell), Fabor (Larry Evans), Okeh (**Screamin' Jay Hawkins**), Modern (Young Jessie), MGM (**Roy Hamilton**), Jubilee (Betty Harris, Garnell Cooper), Big Top (**Sammy Turner**), United Artists (the **Clovers**, **Jay and the Americans**, Steve Lawrence, Mike Clifford, the **Exciters**) and RCA (June Valli, Perry Como, Julius LaRosa, David Hill). Here they also worked with **Presley**, who was already past his rock'n'roll peak. The urban blues satire at which they excelled would not have suited Elvis, and the atmosphere at RCA was not conducive to works of incisive wit. They were further handicapped by the need to operate within the limits of his unbearably stodgy film-scripts. But despite these restraints, they managed to write and produce some of Presley's better post-Sun records. 'Jailhouse Rock', 'Trouble' and 'Santa Claus is Back in Town' contain magnificently earthy lines.

Few of the innumerable discs made by Leiber and Stoller with lesser artists than Presley, the Coasters and the Drifters, were of significance. Sammy Turner's 'Lavender Blue' was exceptional, as were Ben E. King's passionate, Latin-flecked soul hits, notably 'Stand by Me'. And apart from records by the Exciters and Peggy Lee, their early Sixties' productions sold only moderately. Inventive perfectionists when fired by artists of exceptional ability, they

could do next to nothing with the plethora of MOR talent with which they worked outside Atlantic.

After fresh but abortive attempts to start labels of their own, they met up with **George Goldner** in 1964. This led to the formation of the Red Bird and Blue Cat labels, to which they signed a host of young songwriters and producers, including **Jeff Barry** and **Ellie Greenwich**, 'Shadow' Morton and Artie Ripp. With Goldner in charge of promotion, the labels had 25 hits in two years, among which the **Shangri-Las**, the **Dixie Cups**, the Jellybeans and the Adlibs are best remembered. Leiber and Stoller took little part in the creative end of the business: to them it was bubblegum pop, for which they had no liking. Weary of administration, they sold out to Goldner.

Next, after some brilliant but poor-selling Coasters records for Columbia, Leiber and Stoller retired from studio work and invested their capital in large and durable music publishing firms. In 1970, they bought the famous Starday/King company, which would have allowed them to record, market and promote whatever they wished. But they were writers and producers first and businessmen second, and the King takeover was not a success. In 1973 they produced 'Stuck in the Middle with You', a Top 10 UK hit and the album *Ferguslie Park* (both by Stealers Wheel). Other artists to benefit from their production touch during the Seventies were **Procol Harum** and **Elkie Brooks**, but in interviews they distanced themselves from the contemporary rock scene and professed to be more interested in writing for the film and theatre –a full-scale musical, *The International Wrestling Match*, for which Peggy Lee's hit 'Is That All There Is?' (1970) was originally written, remains unstaged to date.

LENNON, JOHN Until he opted out of recording and performing in 1975 to look after his son Sean, John Lennon (born 9 October 1940) was the most prolific and most controversial of the four former Beatles. His murder five years later ensured him a kind of immortality, bordering at times on deification, that complicates any kind of assessment of his musical worth. While **Paul McCartney** and **George Harrison** adopted conventional rock star personae (one a show business personality, the other a recluse), Lennon, often with **Yoko Ono**, tried a variety of strategies, often linked with the artistic or political avant-garde. Although the Beatles' split was not officially confirmed until 1970, Lennon had already distanced himself from the others in the previous year when he embarked on a series of 'Bed-Ins' and albums with Yoko (following their marriage in Gibraltar), which were rooted in the 'Happenings' philosophy, then went to New York to become part of the artistic community there. Three albums were released jointly by John and Yoko, consisting primarily of electronic and 'found' sounds (press conference tapes, for instance): *Two Virgins* (Apple, 1968) – with the celebrated nude photographs of the couple on the sleeve – *Unfinished Music No. 2: Life with the Lions* (1969) and *Wedding Album* (1969). However, by 1969 the Plastic Ono Band had emerged as the definitive vehicle for his more conventional musical activity. A shifting group of musicians centred on John and Yoko, its performance at the Toronto Rock Revival show, with **Eric Clapton**, Klaus Voorman (bass) and Alan White (drums), was released as *Live Peace In Toronto*. Included on this album were rock'n'roll oldies, two of Yoko's wailing compositions and 'Give Peace a Chance', the prototype of the other side of Lennon's new music – a simple, populist song, intended to be sung on the streets.

A further stage in Lennon's self-renewal was reached with *John Lennon/Plastic Ono Band* (1970). Described later as Primal Scream music (after Lennon revealed his treatment by psychotherapist Arthur Janov), the songs dug back into his formative childhood relationships ('Mother', 'My Mummy's Dead') and the Beatle experience ('Working Class Hero' and the riveting 'God', which coined the phrase, 'the dream is over'). By comparison, *Imagine* (1971), produced by **Phil Spector**, was calmer and more contained. The title song was to become the most widely known of Lennon's compositions, while 'How Do You Sleep' was interpreted by many as an attack on Paul McCartney's solo work. The re-election of Nixon as president in 1972 and pressures to have Lennon deported from America were perhaps contributory factors to the political commitment which was the driving-force behind *Some Time in New York City* (1972). Lyrics about the oppression of women, the Attica prison riots and Northern Ireland were attacked as simplistic and extremist, but the album's powerful musical impact was enhanced by spirited rock-'n'roll backings from the New York group Elephant's Memory. It was packaged with a second record containing

material from two live sessions, with the Mothers of Invention and a 1969 band, at London's Lyceum Theatre, including **Eric Clapton**, Keith Moon and **Delaney and Bonnie**.

With *Mind Games* (1973) and *Walls and Bridges* (1974), John Lennon returned to more conventional themes of love and personal interaction on meticulously crafted albums using top New York session musicians. 'Mind Games', with a powerful wall of sound behind Lennon's penetrating voice, was a Top 10 hit in America, while the starker 'Whatever Gets You Through the Night' reached Number 1 in America in 1974. In 1975, Lennon made his contribution to rock's re-examination of its own past when, on *Rock'n'Roll*, he reaffirmed his commitment to the archetypal strengths of Fifties music, which had always been

prominent in his own work. John and Yoko separated for eighteen months in 1973–5 and the birth of their son Sean in October 1975 marked the beginning of a long period of seclusion for Lennon. While Yoko took charge of the couple's business affairs, Lennon remained at home 'baking bread' and giving Sean the attention that he (Lennon) had never had as a child from his father. In 1980, however, he signed with Geffen Records and made *Double Fantasy*. Seemingly on the brink of a third important stage in his rock career, he was shot dead outside the Dakota Flats building (where he had his home) in New York on 8 December 1980 by Mark David Chapman. His single '(Just Like) Starting Over', became a transatlantic Number 1, beginning a predictable spate of posthumous best-selling releases.

A rock star who cared about much more than the size of his income or his position in the charts

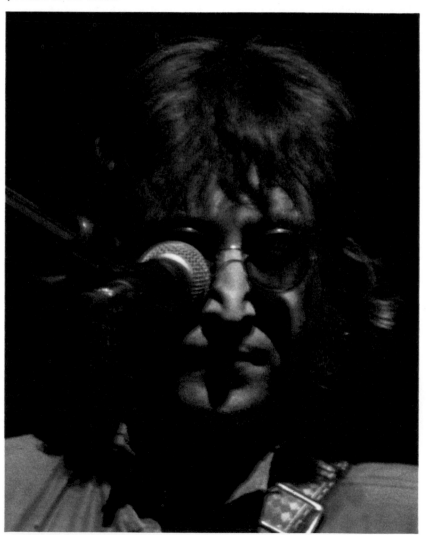

LENNON, JULIAN The son of **John** and Cynthia **Lennon**, Julian was born in Liverpool on 8 April 1963. When, at the age of five, his parents divorced, he stayed with his mother. At school he shared an interest in early rock'n'roll with his future musical partner, Justin Clayton, and they formed a schoolboy band.

His father was murdered in New York when he was seventeen, and Julian travelled there to share his grief with **Yoko Ono** and his half-brother, Sean. Eventually, back in London, after jamming with various musicians, he was offered a deal by Charisma, and sent to Nevers, France, to write material for an album. Phil Ramone (whose credits included **Billy Joel**, **Bob Dylan** and **Paul Simon**) was brought in to produce the mainstream pop/rock LP, *Valotte* (1984), which made the UK Top 20 and yielded the hit single 'Too Late for Goodbyes'.

Early in 1986 he released his second LP, *The Secret Value of Daydreaming*.

LESTER, KETTY Born in Hope, Arkansas, Ketty Lester was a refined 'torch' singer who worked with Cab Calloway's Orchestra and the Ziegfeld Follies in New York before signing with Ezra on the West Coast. She enjoyed her major success on this label in 1962 with the million-selling 'Love Letters'. Especially memorable were the marvellous piano embellishments and austere but smooth arrangement. This arrangement was copied for the first **Presley** version of 1966, although vocally he brought even more finesse to the song. Her attempts to follow 'Love Letters' quickly in 1962 depended too much on repeating its keyboard ploys but were none the less appealing, especially 'Moscow Nights' which added words to a reworking of 'Midnight in Moscow', a traditional jazz hit for Britain's Kenny Ball the year before. Leaning towards jazz, Ketty Lester's work is the living proof that 'soul' need not be raucous.

LEVEL 42 British band Level 42 were formed on the Isle of Wight in the late Seventies and through sheer persistence, hard work and a reluctance to copy American styles, became probably the UK's leading soul/funk outfit.

Led by virtuoso bassist and vocalist Mark King, Level 42 was completed by Mike Lindup (keyboards/vocals), Phil Gould (drums) and Boon Gould (guitar). King immediately gained recognition as a highly technically proficient musician (he was voted best bassist several times in UK music paper polls and was eagerly sought as a session player), and by the time they had released their fourth album *Standing in the Light* (1983), their particular British feel was beginning to make an impression in the US.

Although they never burnt up the charts, they plugged away, encouraged by their early minor single successes, releasing a string of competent dance records and slowly building a following. By the mid-Eighties they appeared regularly in the upper reaches of the UK charts and were selling records across the world. The fans were rewarded by a live LP *A Physical Presence* at the end of 1985, which was followed in 1986 by *World Machine*.

LEWIE, JONA One of Stiff Records' earliest signings, singer/songwriter Jona Lewie had wide experience with various groups on the rock/R&B circuit before scoring a couple of solo UK hits.

Through the late Sixties Lewie, a blues pianist, supported himself by playing sessions with a variety of people including veteran American bluesman **Arthur Crudup** (writer of Presley's 'That's All Right'). He then joined Brett Marvin and the Thunderbolts who had a UK Number 2 in 1972 (as Terry Dactyl and the Dinosaurs) with 'Seaside Shuffle'. After six months with another band, the Jive Bombers, Lewie released two abortive solo singles before signing to Stiff in 1977.

His first Stiff single, 'The Baby She's on the Street', sold badly but nonetheless, he joined his stablemates on the Be Stiff Tour, which led to a brief residency in the UK charts twice in the same year with two charming, offbeat singles, 'You'll Always Find Me in the Kitchen at Parties' and 'Stop the Cavalry', the latter a Number 3, in 1980.

LEWIS, BARBARA Born in a Detroit suburb on 9 February 1944, R&B singer Barbara Lewis began her career after submitting her own songs to Ollie McLaughlin in 1961. A contract with Atlantic led to regional hits, including 'My Heart Went Do Dat Da' and finally to the hauntingly sensual 'Hello Stranger', which reached the Top 3 in 1963. With various producers – McLaughlin, **Bert Berns**, Jerry Wexler – and good songs from Goffin and King and **Van McCoy**, Lewis was consistently successful in the soul field throughout the mid-Sixties. Her hits included 'Straighten up Your Heart', 'Puppy Love', 'Baby I'm Yours' and 'Make Me Your Baby' (both of which reached Number 11 in the US in 1965) and 'Make Me Belong to You'. Her distinctive voice, suggesting both coyness and sophistication, coped equally well with strong blues material and soft, romantic ballads.

LEWIS, BOBBY Born on 17 February 1933, in Indianapolis, Indiana, Bobby Lewis sang with the Leo Hines band and recorded for Chess, Spotlight, Mercury and Roulette in the years 1952–9. In 1961, 'Tossin' and Turnin'', his first record for Beltone, hit the Number 1 spot and stayed on the charts for 23 weeks. A throwback to the baritone jump blues singers of the early Fifties, Lewis commercialized the style by adding a chanting girl chorus (the Swanettes) who stayed with him for other hits, including 'One Track Mind' (Top 10) and 'What a Walk'. None were as good as 'Tossin'', written by producer Joe Rene and Ritchie Adams of the Fireflies. Lewis also recorded for ABC and, although further hits were not forthcoming, a dynamic stage act kept him in steady club work.

LEWIS, GARY, AND THE PLAYBOYS To get started in the Californian pop business during the mid-Sixties, it did no harm at all to have a famous father. Mickey Rooney Jr, Nancy Sinatra, and the Dean Martin/ Desi Arnez offspring Dino, Desi and Billy found no trouble securing recording contracts – and the same applied to Gary Lewis, the son of comedian Jerry Lewis. Gary (born Gary Levitch in Los Angeles on 31 July 1946) learned the drums at fourteen and formed his band, the Playboys, in 1964. The group comprised: Al Ramsey, guitar (born on 27 July 1943); John West, guitar (31 July 1939); David Walkes, keyboards (12 May 1943); and David Costell, bass (15 March 1944). They were signed to Liberty after a residency at the Disneyland complex and placed with up-and-coming producer **Leon Russell**, who supervised and also co-wrote many of their subsequent releases, among them the Top 10 US hits 'This Diamond Ring' (a Number 1 in 1965), 'Count Me In', 'Save Your Heart for Me', 'Everybody Loves a Clown' and 'Green Grass' (1966). They played solid teenage pop with the emphasis on heart-throb Gary's bright if unspectacular voice, but the band lost ground following Lewis' drafting into the US Army during 1966 and scored only two further chart hits after his discharge. In the early Seventies, Lewis was promoted as a 'sensitive' singer-songwriter, but his lack of progress prompted him to reform the Playboys in 1973 and try his luck on the cabaret circuit.

LEWIS, HUEY, AND THE NEWS

US mainstream rock band Huey Lewis and the News joined the multi-platinum set when the album *Sports* (1983) sold over six million copies. A session and country rock veteran, singer Huey Lewis had been a member of West Coast country rockers Clover who had backed **Elvis Costello** in London on his debut album *My Aim Is True*. Returning to America, Lewis met up with Sean Hopper (keyboards), Chris Hayes (guitar), Johnny Colla (guitar/sax), Mario Cipollina (bass) and Bill Gibson (drums), who joined him as the News; they were immediately snapped up by Chrysalis in 1981.

'Do You Believe in Love' was an instant US Top 10 single hit – the first of many – and two albums, *Huey Lewis and the News* (1982) and *Picture This* (1983) sold well before *Sports* put them on the map. In the UK, although receiving plenty of airplay, they had to wait until 1984 and 'If This Is It' for a Top 10 single, and in 1985 the success of 'Power of Love', the theme tune to the film *Back to the Future*, established them properly on both sides of the Atlantic.

LEWIS, JERRY LEE

One of the great originals of rock, Jerry Lee Lewis came to the fore in 1957 with Sun Records of Memphis, but was not lost in the famous 'Sun Sound' that had by then already spawned **Elvis Presley** and **Johnny Cash**. Rather, he added his own uniquely attacking style of vocalizing and piano playing, and made the sound even better.

He hit the American national headlines in 1957 with his second and third recordings, 'Whole Lotta Shakin' Going On' and 'Great Balls of Fire', classics of rock which have been copied by successive generations of musicians but never bettered. The Lewis style is one of the most immediately identifiable in rock. It is straightforward, powerful, even primitive, but also perfect. 'Whole Lotta Shakin'' was recorded with no trial runs. The drummer makes one mistake, but otherwise a sympathetic guitar and drum backing combines with Lewis's pumping piano in a relentless rhythm that emphasizes the soaring vocals and allows full appreciation of the top-note keyboard solo gymnastics. As always, Lewis displays a swaggering self-confidence in his own ability and a full command of his material, allowing the tempo to lull before storming back for a dynamic ending.

As a showman, too, Lewis was an original. He broke pianos, he threw chairs, he swore at the band and the audience, but his arrogance was compensated by his supreme talent. His uniqueness, his originality, is in no way countered by the fact that his material is rarely his own. He has an inherent ability to mould the songs of others to his own style to such effect that the question of sameness and rigidity hardly arises.

Lewis was born in Ferriday, Louisiana, on 29 September 1935, and learned his music from the country music radio shows and the local black juke-joints of his teens. He claims to have no influences, and certainly his first recordings, 'Crazy Arms' and 'End of the Road', made for Sun in 1956, show a fully developed style that he has never basically altered. However, his piano playing can be partly attributed to Texan honky-tonk pianist **Moon Mullican** and it is interesting that in 1954 Lewis recorded a demonstration record, in Shreveport, Louisiana, of two C&W songs that he sang and played very much in a straight country style. Between then and 1956, he acquired a driving ambition to become a success through music and he also saw the way to achieve this. Rock'n'roll had arrived, and there was room for a wildman pianist.

Following his successes of 1957 with 'Whole Lotta Shakin'' and 'Great Balls of Fire', Lewis hit with 'Down the Line' and 'High School Confidential' and appeared in movies – *Jamboree* (1957), *High School Confidential* (1958), and later, in 1960, *Young and Deadly*. His career was booming in 1958 when his marriage to a fourteen-year-old cousin led to scandal and the string of million sellers ceased for three years. His career was shattered, but he remained with Sun Records, experimenting with pop, country and R&B songs.

In 1961, he began recording R&B songs in Nashville and 'What'd I Say' restarted him on the trail of hits. Two years later he moved to Smash Records, later Mercury, and began to find a niche in the country charts. Hits such as 'Another Place, Another Time', 'She Even Woke Me up to Say Goodbye' and 'Think About It Darlin'' were identifiably country, but also unmistakably Jerry Lee Lewis and he has been able to develop his catch-phrases and clichés almost to the point of self-parody. He successfully brought off an unbelievably fast rendition of **Kris Kristofferson**'s 'Me and Bobbie McGee' as only he could. He has recorded with soul, rock, C&W and New Orleans jazz backings, and remained in command.

Currently, he operates in the C&W field, highly successfully, and his many interpretations of country songs are as

Meteoric Jerry Lee Lewis was cast as the dark star of rock'n'roll

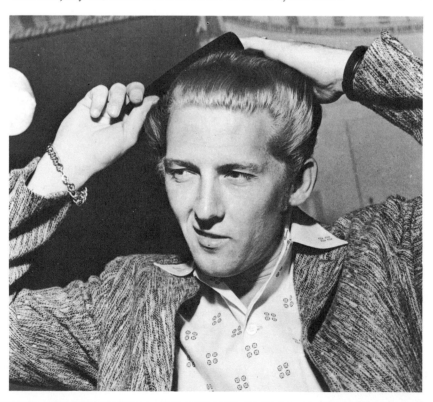

triumphant as his rock'n'roll songs. They are transformed, becoming Jerry Lee Lewis recordings rather than just another version of a particular song.

LEWIS, RAMSEY Although his background was in jazz, Ramsey Lewis had some success during the Sixties with instrumentals aimed at the pop chart. He was born on 27 May 1935, and studied piano at the Chicago College of Music and De Paul University. He formed his own jazz trio in 1956, working local night clubs and appearing on records by Sonny Stitt, Clark Terry and Max Roach, with albums of his own on American Argo. These, plus occasional gigs in New York City, earned the Ramsey Lewis Trio – bassist Eldee Young, drummer Isaac Holt and Lewis – a modest following until their 1965 recording of 'The In Crowd' (Argo) reached Number 5 on the US Hot 100. Other big hits included 'Hang on Sloopy' (1965) and 'Wade in the Water' (1966) before the Trio broke up. Since then Lewis has made a huge commercial success of transforming a variety of material with his strong keyboard touch, thick gospel chording and a rocking blues beat; he has toured extensively, including several dates in Britain. His *Sun Goddess* (Columbia, 1975) was produced by Maurice White of **Earth, Wind and Fire**, a former Lewis accompanist.

LEWIS, SMILEY An important figure in New Orleans R&B during the late Forties and Fifties, Smiley Lewis was born Overton Amos Lemons on 5 July 1920. His parents moved to New Orleans in 1931 and, soaked in the long musical heritage of the Crescent City, Smiley rose to become a major local R&B artist. A competent guitarist, he first recorded for De Luxe in 1947 as 'Smiling' Lewis but it was the consistent high quality of his Imperial recordings between 1950 and 1960 that established his reputation. He had two R&B hits in this time, 'The Bells Are Ringing'(1952) and 'I Hear You Knocking' (1955) but he never got the national recognition he deserved. His songs have, however, given hits to Gale Storm ('I Hear You Knocking'), **Elvis Presley** ('One Night') and in Britain, **Dave Edmunds** ('I Hear You Knocking'). After further isolated records for Okeh, Dot and Loma, he died of stomach cancer in 1966. *See also* **New Orleans**

LEWIS, STAN One of the American South's leading record entrepreneurs, Stan Lewis was born of Italian heritage in Shreveport,

Louisiana, and invested his savings in five jukeboxes in black locations at the age of 19. Finding it difficult to re-stock these jukeboxes, he became interested in the record business itself and with his wife, Pauline, took over a struggling record shop in a black location in Shreveport. After meeting Leonard Chess, then peddling Chess's R&B discs around the South by car, Lewis increased his involvement in the lucrative shop and mail-order house, supplying virtually anything for anyone wanting records. In 1951 Lewis decided to buy airtime on Shreveport's local radio station KWKH (home of the famed Louisiana Hayride) and soon found himself handling orders across 35 States. Eventually, labels like Specialty and Chess asked him to act as their local talent scout and in 1953, Lewis began recording local acts after hours at KWKH for $15 an hour and placed Slim Whitman and several lesser-known 'Louisiana Hayriders' with record companies. In 1957, Lewis recorded two national hits, **Dale Hawkins**' 'Susie-Q' and TV Slim's 'Flat-Foot Sam', both sold to the Chess combine with whom he maintained close connections. In 1963, he formed his own Jewel label, followed in 1965 by the Paula and Ronn labels. In 1967, Paula achieved a million-seller with **John Fred**'s 'Judy in Disguise'. Unlike some of his contemporaries, Lewis never forgot his roots and became America's most important producer of authentic blues and gospel music.

LEYTON, JOHN Born in Frinton, Essex, on 17 February 1939, John Dudley Leyton was another actor who turned to singing by chance. He played Ginger in the ATV *Biggles* series and then Johnny St Cyr in another TV series, *Harper's West One* which is where he got his first chance to sing 'Johnny Remember Me' and which led to the record's success in 1961. It was expertly produced by **Joe Meek** and featured an echo effect that masked the inadequacies of Leyton's voice. His other records were all remarkably similar and the public quickly tired of him. Written by Geoff Goddard, they were 'Wild Wind', 'Son This Is She' and 'Lonely City' in 1962. He later returned to acting and appeared in *The Great Escape* (1963), *Von Ryan's Express* (1965) and *Krakatoa* (1968). Possibly his only lasting claim to fame was that he was one of the first artists to be handled by Robert Stigwood, later to find his fortune as the producer of *Jesus Christ Superstar, Saturday Night Fever* and owner of RSO records.

LIBERTY RECORDS Liberty was formed in late 1955, in Hollywood by Si(mon) Waronker – whose son Lenny became a producer with Warner-Reprise – Alvin Bennett and Theodore Keep. Liberty immediately entered the rock'n'roll market with powerful acts like **Eddie Cochran**, **Johnny Burnette** and Troy Shondell. Al Bennett, originally brought in to promote the company's records, soon turned to A&R, becoming a West Coast version of **George Goldner**. But the company really prospered under **'Snuff' Garrett**, a Texas deejay who joined the A&R department in 1958 and transformed Johnny Burnette into a successful balladeer with 'Dreamin''. He was even more successful with **Bobby Vee** and, in 1961, was promoted to head of Liberty's growing A&R department. The early Sixties were equally profitable, thanks to the successes of **Jan and Dean**, the **Ventures** and **Gary Lewis and the Playboys**. In 1967, Trans-America, who had already purchased United Artists (UA), bought Liberty (and later Imperial); later that year Liberty set up its own British organization and in the early Seventies Trans-America merged its record interests under the United Artists logo.

LIGHT OF THE WORLD One of the earliest British jazz-funk acts to accomplish the difficult task of impressing American audiences, Light of the World were formed in the mid-Seventies but had to wait until 1979 before gaining any recognition.

Breeze McKrieth (vocals/guitar), Paul 'Tubbs' Williams (bass/vocals), Everton McCalla (drums), Gee Bello (percussion), Peter Hinds (brass), Canue 'Kenny' Wellington (brass) and Nathaniel Augustine (brass) spent a couple of years on the British gig circuit, building a small but loyal following. In 1979 they signed to Ensign and released 'Swingin'', proving that British acts were capable of matching their trans-Atlantic rivals in producing quality jazz-funk. They released a string of impressive singles without storming the UK charts, the best-selling being 'I'm So Happy', a Number 35 in 1981. They also released the albums *Light of the World* (1980) and *Round Trip* (1981), the latter causing a minor stir in the US, but Light of the World split shortly afterwards. The brass trio continued as Beggar and Co, scoring a couple of minor hits in 1981 – *Somebody Help Me Out* and *Mule (Chant No 2)* – and playing with the likes of *Spandau Ballet*. They guested on the latter's 1981 hit, *Chant No 1*.

LIGHTFOOT, GORDON One of the most prolific and consistent Canadian singer-songwriters since the mid-Sixties, Gordon Lightfoot was born in Orillia, Ontario, on 17 November 1938, and studied orchestration at Westlake College, Los Angeles. He became a professional jingle writer in Toronto and started playing in the folk clubs there around 1960, encouraged by the folk duo Ian and Sylvia, who recorded two of his early songs, 'Early Morning Rain' and 'For Lovin' Me'. He was given a recording contract by United Artists in 1966, his first albums reflecting his background in the York-town folk scene, Toronto's equivalent to New York's Greenwich Village. 'Canadian Railroad Trilogy' was an epic tribute to the building of the transcontinental lines, while 'Early Morning Rain' became a folk standard, recorded by **Peter, Paul and Mary**, **Bob Dylan** and many others.

In 1970, Lightfoot moved over to the Reprise label to start a fruitful professional relationship with producer **Lenny Waronker**. His first album for the company, *Sit Down Young Stranger* (1970), included the original recording of **Kris Kristofferson**'s 'Me and Bobby McGee' and **Randy Newman** and **Ry Cooder** were among the musicians involved.

His popularity increased throughout the Seventies as he developed a fluid style in which voice, melody and lyrics were merged in a resonant but seldom bland way. The title track of *Sundown* (1974) provided him with his first US Number 1 single, and 'The Wreck of the Edmund Fitzgerald' reached Number 2 during 1976. His albums have sold consistently well ever since and include *Summertime Dream* (1976), *Endless Wire* (1978), *Dream Street Wise* (1980) and *Shadows* (1982).

LIND, BOB Born in Baltimore in 1946, Bob Lind had a transatlantic Top 10 hit in 1966 with 'Elusive Butterfly' (World Pacific, Fontana in Britain). The subsequent album, *Don't Be Concerned* (produced by **Jack Nitzsche**), was a typical post-**Dylan** singer/songwriter production, with self-consciously poetic lyrics set to soft music. The follow-up, 'Remember the Rain'/'Truly Julie's Blues' reached the lower end of the American charts, but Lind's later albums on Verve and Capitol (*Since There Were Circles*, 1971) made no impact. Lind's songs 'Cheryl's Goin' Home' and 'Mr Zero' – both featured on his debut album – were minor UK hits during 1966 for **Adam Faith** and Keith Relf respectively.

Bob Lind was a short-lived success in the Sixties 'folk-poet' genre

LINDISFARNE An all-Newcastle band comprising Alan Hull, guitar/ vocals (born 20 February 1945), Rod Clements, bass/violin (17 November 1947), Ray Jackson, mandolin (12 December 1948), Simon Cowe, guitar (1 April 1948) and Ray Laidlaw, drums (28 May 1948), Lindisfarne was signed to Charisma Records in 1968 after a series of successful appearances at various festivals. Their first album, *Nicely out of Tune* (1969) full of rich Geordie humour and raucous harmonies, preceded their great moment of popularity but remains their best album. The band reached their peak in the early Seventies. With Nashville producer **Bob Johnston**, they recorded *Fog on the Tyne*, which eventually became the best-selling album in Britain, and had Top 5 hits with 'Meet Me on the Corner' and a re-release of 'Lady Eleanor' in 1972. They remained with Bob Johnston but Alan Hull lost the flair for writing and their final album *Dingly Dell* (1972) was salvaged only by resurrecting some of the old, never before recorded material. An arduous Pacific tour eventually took its toll and in 1973 the band split into two, Alan Hull and Ray Jackson retaining the name Lindisfarne, while Clements, Laidlaw and Cowe formed Jack The Lad. The new Lindisfarne, despite its greater musical strength, lacked the necessary temperament and dedication and split up in 1975. Three years later, all the original members of the band reunited to record *Back and Fourth* for Atco. Their comeback UK hit, 'Run for Home' (a Number 10 in 1978), also brought the band their first, albeit moderate American success, reaching Number 33.

LINX David Grant and Peter 'Sketch' Martin were, as Linx, the best band to emerge from the second wave of home-grown black artists (**Eddy Grant** and **Hot Chocolate** were the most lasting of the first wave). As writers of pop-funk they were rivalled in Britain only by Heatwave's Rod Temperton, and their string of hit singles ('You're Lying', 'Intuition', 'Throw Away the Key', 'So This Is Romance') in the late Seventies and early Eighties were the most lasting contributions to that era's Brit-funk movement. Their co-compositions had catchy melodies, good hooks, were well-produced and crisply performed. They were a 'sellable' couple, too. Grant, eloquent, intelligent, enthusiastic; Martin a somewhat quieter, more lugubrious presence. After their excellent debut album, *Intuition*, and the slightly less appealing *Go Ahead*, both out in 1981, the duo split up. Martin has been virtually silent ever since but Grant lost little time in establishing himself as a solo artist, recording two LPs – the eponymous debut (1983) and *Hopes and Dreams* (1985) – and has had several hit singles for Chrysalis, the label that had also nurtured Linx.

LITTLE ANTHONY AND THE IMPERIALS The career of Little Anthony – full name Anthony Gourdine (born on 8 January 1941) – began in Brooklyn in 1955, when he sang with the Duponts. However, they soon disbanded and Anthony then formed the Chesters, with Clarence Collins, Tracy Lord, Ernest Wright and Nat Rogers, who signed with End in 1958, debuting with the distinctive million seller 'Tears on My Pillow'. End renamed them Imperials, while DJ **Alan Freed** added the 'Little Anthony' prefix. Several hits followed, but personal problems caused them to split in 1960. Anthony, Collins, Wright and Sammy Strain re-formed the group in 1964, achieving a string of hits on DCP with plushly arranged, dramatic ballads like 'Going out of My Head', subsequently recording for Veep, UA, Janus and, in 1974, Avco. Gourdine signed a solo deal with MCA in 1980, while Strain joined the **O'Jays**.

LITTLE EVA Born Eva Narcissus Boyd on 29 June 1945, in Bellhaven, North Carolina, Little Eva moved to New York while in her teens. Here, legend insists, she was baby-sitting for **Carole King** and Gerry Goffin when they asked her to record a new song they had written. The result was 'The Locomotion'. With the Cookies, of

'Chains' fame, as back-up singers, it went to Number 1 in the US in 1962. A string of computerized dance hits followed, including 'Keep Your Hands off my Baby', 'Let's Turkey Trot' and 'Old Smokey Locomotion', all on **Don Kirshner**'s Dimension label, on which Eva's sister, Idalia Boyd, recorded 'Hula Hooping'. Despite several far more soulful records (on Amy, Spring and others), Eva had no further big hits.

LITTLE FEAT

Much admired by musicians and critics for the surreal imagery of their songs and the elaborate but fluid interplay between their guitars and rhythm section, Little Feat's career spanned the whole of the Seventies. The band was formed in 1970 by Lowell George (guitars, vocals), Bill Payne (keyboards, vocals), Roy Estrada (bass) and Ritchie Hayward (drums). Estrada and George had played with the Mothers of Invention, Hayward with the Fraternity of Man, while Payne had played with various Texas groups.

With **Ry Cooder**, 'Sneeky' Pete Kleinow and producer Russ Titelman, they cut *Little Feat* for Warner Brothers in 1970. The majority of the tracks, including the much-covered 'Willin'', were written or co-written by Lowell George. After a second album, *Sailin' Shoes* (1972), Estrada left to join **Captain Beefheart**. Little Feat was augmented by three new members: Ken Gradney (bass), Sam Clayton (congas) and Paul Barrère (guitars).

This line-up made *Dixie Chicken* (1973), but the lack of commercial success caused a lull in the band's activity soon afterwards, with George returning to session work. In 1974, they returned to the studio for their most commercially successful album at that time, *Feats Don't Fail Me Now*, followed by *The Last Record Album* (1975). *Time Loves a Hero* came in 1977, but their biggest seller was the live set, *Waiting for Columbus*, in 1978.

George became increasingly involved in his own projects – producing *Shakedown Street* for the **Grateful Dead** in 1978 and working on the solo set, *Thanks I'll Eat It Here*, which finally appeared in 1979 – and he took a unilateral decision to break up the band during the same year. Going on tour with a new band, he was found dead on 29 June 1979, at Arlington, Virginia. The remaining members of Little Feat disbanded after completing *Down on the Farm* (1979). Many of their best tracks were assembled for a final album, *Hoy Hoy* (1981), a fitting tribute to their subtle, funky music.

LITTLE MILTON

One of the leading blues singer/guitarists of the Sixties and Seventies, Little Milton was the performing persona of Milton Campbell, who was born in Inverness, Mississippi, on 17 September 1934. As a child he sang in his local church choir and became interested in the guitar at the age of 10. His first public performance was at 14 and his inspirations included **T-Bone Walker**, **B.B. King** and **Roy Brown**. In 1950, a trio Milton was leading became popular around Memphis and he came to the attention of Sun records where he was recorded with **Ike Turner**'s band. From Sun he switched to Meteor and, in 1958, to the St Louis-based Bobbin label where he cut several successful singles with bandleader/arranger, Oliver Sain. In 1961, Chess/Checker took over his contract, and Milton was turning out such hits as 'Who's Cheating Who', 'Grits Ain't Groceries' and 'We're Gonna Make It', a US Number 1 R&B hit in 1965. All featured Milton's throaty, gospel-inflected vocals, tastefully underscored by a full band – often with arrangements by **Donny Hathaway** and production by **Gene Barge**. This consistency led to his 1971 signing with Stax, where he re-established himself on the black music scene. An appearance in the film *Wattstax*, plus more commercially oriented single hits like 'Behind Closed Doors', turned Milton into an international pop/soul name who still retained his blues roots. He left Stax in 1976 and turned to record production.

LITTLE RICHARD

Of all the progenitors of rock'n'roll, Little Richard is still unclassifiable. However shattering an effect **Elvis Presley**, **Jerry Lee Lewis** and **Chuck Berry** had on the calm of Eisenhower's America, they were ultimately assimilable. A major reason for this was colour: the first two were white and though Berry was black, his material, almost from the beginning, was oriented towards white teenagers. In contrast to these, Little Richard – for better or worse – made no concessions.

If rock'n'roll was delicious drivel, he was its epitome – 'A-Wop-Bop-A-Loo-Bop-A-Lop-Bam-Boom'; and if rock-'n'roll was a threat, it was 'the Prince of Clowns' who represented its insane vigour. Richard alone represented the crude fantasy of absolute rebellion that lay at the heart of rock'n'roll. Accordingly, it isn't surprising that his endless fascination and power over us rests on the results of scattered moments in his career.

Little Richard, it seemed, didn't

develop but sprang at us fully grown. None the less, the twists and turns of his seemingly directionless career, in their own bizarre fashion, reflect the enigma that is Little Richard. Born in Macon, Georgia, on 5 December 1932, Richard Penniman was raised as a Seventh Day Adventist and spent his formative years singing in church choirs. He first performed professionally with a variety of itinerant medicine shows and then gained a club residency in Fitzgerald, Georgia, where his repertoire consisted primarily of **Louis Jordan** songs. During 1951–2, he cut his first records for RCA, mostly blues performed very much in the shadow of **Roy Brown**. His first release, in 1952, was 'Every Hour' coupled with 'Taxi Blues'. The follow-up, 'Get Rich Quick' was an exuberant shouter in the tradition of **Wynonie Harris**. The flip was the slow, reflective 'Thinkin' About My Mother', on which Richard's stark delivery was underpinned by a loquacious saxophone. On 'Why Did You Leave Me', he aped the unearthly banshee wails of a Roy Brown or a **Bobby Bland** in front of an arrangement one might expect from Memphis or Houston studios, Stygian and spare, leaving the voice in splendid isolation. His final sides for RCA were 'Please Have Mercy on Me' and 'I Brought It All on Myself'.

In 1952, he joined Don Robey's Houston-based Peacock label where he was backed for the most part (instrumentally and vocally) by the Tempo Toppers – Jimmy Swan, Billy Brooks, Barry Gillmore and organist Raymond Taylor. His first session, on 25 February 1953, resulted in 'Fool at the Wheel' and 'Ain't That Good News' (which bears no relation to the later **Sam Cooke** hit of the same title). In 1954, with the Tempo Toppers, he recorded Raymond Taylor's novelty composition 'Rice, Red Beans and Turnip Greens' and Robey's 'Always'. Richard used the **Johnny Otis** band next, and 'Little Richard's Boogie' – released in 1956 after he had joined Specialty – featured Otis on vibes. On the reverse was the first of several versions of 'Directly from My Heart', a plodding blues ballad bound for better days. Richard's last record for Peacock, in May 1957, coupled 'I Love My Baby' with 'Maybe I'm Right', with Otis on piano on the latter. His stay at Peacock had produced some agreeable music, but nothing that was out of the ordinary or made much improvement on the RCA sides which already saw him as an assured, if limited, singer.

A demonstration tape finally took

Little Richard from Peacock to success with Art Rupe's Specialty label in 1955. None the less, it was seven months before he went to New Orleans to make his first recordings for the company. That session, produced by **'Bumps' Blackwell** and engineered by Cosimo Matassa, took place at the J&M studios on 14 September 1955. From this came 'Tutti Frutti', his debut Specialty release in October and the first of seven accredited million-sellers. The song was cleaned up by local writer Dorathy La Bostrie from a scurrilous ditty, while Richard's maniac swaggering was accompanied by **Huey Smith** on piano. Its very banality ensured its success and in some measure the disc, although far from Richard's best, is the quintessence of anarchic rock'n'roll.

In 1956, 'Long Tall Sally' was released with 'Slippin' and Slidin''. The top side, with its traditional phallic metaphor, derives from the blues, and started life as 'The Thing', when first recorded by Little Richard in New Orleans. Later the title was switched to the more likely 'Bald Headed Sally' but still was unreleased until it was finally re-cut successfully in Los Angeles. It was immediately covered by **Pat Boone** – who had previously covered 'Tutti Frutti' – and by Presley and **Eddie Cochran** after a discreet interval. Connoisseurs, however, may prefer 'Slippin' and Slidin''. A typical New Orleans number, it begn life as 'I Got the Blues for You', by Al Collins on Ace, with the telling lyric 'Baby with the big box, tell me where your next stop is, I got the blues for you'. Prudently revised, but still alive with good humour, the song was next presented as 'I'm Wise' by Eddie Bocage on Apollo. Bocage's, possibly the definitive version of the song, serves as a reminder that there were plenty of piano-playing vocalists in New Orleans who could eclipse or equal Richard on record – but never in person.

Richard's other noteworthy records for Specialty include, 'Rip It Up', 'The Girl Can't Help It' (1956), 'Lucille' (1957) and 'Good Golly Miss Molly' (1957). The sidemen on these were usually a combination of Earl Palmer, drums; Red Tyler and **Lee Allen**, saxes; Frank Fields, bass; Ernest McLean and Justin Adams, guitars; with Huey Smith, Edward Frank, Little Booker and Salvador Doucette as supplementary pianists. On the New Orleans recordings brass, reeds and, of course, piano dominate the sound; only 'Whole Lotta Shakin' Goin' On' (released after Richard had left the

The usually frenzied Little Richard captured in a milder mood

company) deviated from this pattern to feature wild guitar breaks.

Little Richard's Specialty career ended in 1959 when he decided that religion mattered more than rock-'n'roll, but releases continued up to 1964 when he reappeared to cut 'Bama Lama Bama Loo' in Los Angeles and secure his first Hot 100 entry since 1959. From 1957 to 1964, apart from occasional secular forays, most of Richard's studio work was gospel, frequently inspired gospel at that. With the exeption of a little rock'n'roll on Little Star, his followers had to wait until the mid-Sixties and a succession of sides on Vee Jay, Okeh, Modern and Brunswick. 'Whole Lot of Shakin' Goin' On' (Vee Jay), 'Lawdy Miss Clawdy', both in 1964, and 'Without Love' in 1965 were excellent. His work for Modern saw Richard moving into a more contemporary soul field in 1966 with 'I'm Back' while his version of Sam Cooke's 'Bring It on Home to Me' featured excellent guitar work and his 1967 duet with an unnamed lady on the

Jimmy Reed blues 'Baby What You Want Me To Do' was compulsive. However, his Brunswick output was dire, apart from 'Soul Train'.

Richard's renaissance as a performer coincided with the boom in rock festivals during the late Sixties and continued into the Seventies under the general guardianship of the rock'n'roll revival movement. However, by the mid-Seventies – as demonstrated at the 1974 Wembley Rock'n'Roll Festival in London – the increasingly self-laudatory nature of his act, in which the theatrics came at the expense of both the music and the nostalgic expectations of much of his audience, had all but closed those arenas to Little Richard. None the less, the initial success of his return to favour with the white concert and festival audience brought with it a renewed interest by record companies. He joined Reprise and 'Freedom Blues', recorded in Muscle Shoals and a Top 50 record in 1970, gave him his first chart entry since 1965. The long instrumental jams such as 'The Rill Thing', from the album of the same name, saw him for the first time seriously adapt himself to current tastes fairly successfully. *Second Coming*, on which he was once more re-united with musicians like Earl Palmer and Lee Allen under the guidance of 'Bumps' Blackwell, whilst exhibiting many of the hallmarks of New Orleans R&B, also saw him recording, albeit a little tentatively, in the fashionable rock/soul mode of **Sly Stone** and the **Isley Brothers**. In the mid-Eighties he made another comeback of sorts, this time with WEA Records and with Stuart Coleman as producer. *Lifetime Friend* appeared in 1986.

Yet increasingly, as Little Richard has managed to come to terms with the present, his anarchic virtues are hidden – much more so than in 'live' performance. Perhaps the best thing would be to record the 'King of Rock-'n'Roll' without consideration for time, in the hope that even the seen-it-all-before consciousness of the Eighties could be dented by his wailings.

LITTLE RIVER BAND The international success of the Little River Band during the second half of the Seventies was a vital factor in the rise of antipodean rock music in general. The band was formed in 1975 from veterans of Australian bands the Twilights, the Zoot, Axiom and Mississippi – all of which had undertaken disastrous trips to the Northern Hemisphere since the Sixties. Their line-up was Glenn Shorrock (vocals), Graham Goble (guitar),

Beeb Birtles (guitar), Rick Formosa (guitar), Roger McLachlan (bass) and Derek Pellicci (drums). Established with the specific aim of developing a mass-appeal sound based on 'mature' musicianship and lush harmonies, the Little River Band effectively took coals to Newcastle when they toured the US in 1976; many fans were unaware that they were Australian.

After breaking into the US Top 30 in November 1976 with 'It's a Long Way There', the group commenced a regular chart profile that saw them honoured by *Billboard* magazine in 1982 as the only act in the world to have scored a US Top 10 hit every year for the previous five years. The biggest was 'Reminiscing', a gentle, almost traditional ballad, which reached Number 3 in 1978. The unbending musical attitude of Graham Goble resulted in a regular turnover of personnel and in 1982 Glenn Shorrock was replaced by British-born Australian pop star John Farnham. Though a fine singer, Farnham was unable to equal Shorrock's writing skills, which had produced songs such as 'Cool Change' and 'Home on a Monday'. Nevertheless, the group remained a top-ranking act in America.

LITTLE WALTER Born Marion Walter Jacobs on 1 May 1930 in Alexandria, Louisiana, Little Walter revolutionized blues harmonica technique with a style steeped in jazz phrasing which remains, to this day, unsurpassed. Influenced by **Sonny Boy Williamson** (No. 1) and jump saxophonist **Louis Jordan**, he arrived in Chicago in 1947, singing and playing for a living in the Maxwell Street market. But Walter's obvious talents resulted in his recording for several small Chicago labels, like Ora Nelle and Regal. From 1951, he was often hired by Chess Records as accompanist on the **Muddy Waters** sessions, his powerful, heavily amplified harp embellishing such hits as 'Standing around Crying', 'Hoochie Coochie Man' and 'I'm Ready'. He also backed singer-guitarist Jimmy Rogers on most of his big-selling singles like 'That's All Right' and 'The World Is in a Tangle'. In 1952, Chess signed Walter to their subsidiary, Checker, and his first session produced 'Juke', his best-known instrumental and a huge R&B hit. Then came 'Mean Old World', 'Off the Wall', 'Blues with a Feeling' and 'Last Night', all self-penned R&B chart hits featuring accompaniment by top Chess sessionmen Louis and David Myers, guitars, and Fred Below, drums. 1954 and 1955 were Walter's most successful years.

He stayed in the national R&B Top 10 throughout that period. More hits followed, including 'My Babe' and 'Confessin' the Blues' before Walter switched sidemen, cutting 'Everything's Gonna Be Alright' and several other sides with Freddy Robinson on lead guitar, who was later to succeed Mick Taylor in **John Mayall**'s Bluesbreakers. Walter died on 15 February 1968, from a thrombosis brought on by injuries received in a fight.

LIVE AID See **Band Aid**

LIVERPOOL (1960s) Virtually every major British city in the early Sixties had its nucleus of rock musicians dedicated to playing rougher and more rewarding music than the current Top 20. What made Liverpool different was the size of its beat group population and the richness and variety of their American musical influences.

As a port, Liverpool had strong connections with America, and local seamen would return from New York with ciggies, comic books and the latest R&B and pop records. Thus local groups were able to graft onto their rock'n'roll repertoire the music of early Motown, the **Shirelles**, the **Isley Brothers** and **Richard** (Ritchie) **Barrett** (whose **Ray Charles**-styled 'Some Other Guy' became a Merseybeat standard). By 1960 local entrepreneurs like Alan Williams were booking Liverpool groups led by Kingsize Taylor and the Dominos into the clubs along Hamburg's notorious Reeperbahn and, on Merseyside, folk and trad jazz clubs were switching to beat music. By 1962 the Cavern, opened four years earlier as a jazz cellar, was given over to the pounding rhythms of the **Big Three**, the **Beatles**, Rory Storm and the Hurricanes, Faron's Flamingos and many more of the 350 groups that Liverpool's own music paper, *Mersey Beat*, estimated were operating in the area. The same thing happened at the Iron Door, the Jacaranda, the Beachcomber, the David Lewis and Litherland Town Hall.

All this activity made little impact outside Merseyside and Hamburg until local record-shop owner **Brian Epstein** got the Beatles their EMI recording contract. The success of 'She Loves You' in early 1963 sent recording managers scurrying from London to find their Liverpool group. Pye signed the **Searchers**, the Undertakers, black vocal group the Chants and Johnny Sandon and the Remo Four. Decca had the Big Three, the Clayton Squares, Lee Curtis and the All-Stars, Freddie Starr

and the Midnighters and the Dennisons. Philips/Fontana grabbed the **Merseybeats**, Earl Preston and the TTs, Ian and the Zodiacs. EMI (Parlophone and Columbia) released the records of the Epstein stable, including those by **Gerry and the Pacemakers**.

Over 200 singles by Liverpool groups were released in Britain over the next few years. Most were sloppily produced and undistinguished and no groups outside the charmed circle of the Epstein stable and the Searchers and **Swinging Blue Jeans** established themselves on a national or international scale. If the first or second single failed, most Liverpool groups were dropped by the record companies as quickly as they had been snapped up.

Merseybeat was, in any case, essentially created in live performance. It was captured best on live recordings, notably those of the small Oriole label, which recorded a dozen or so groups in a short recording session at the Cavern under live conditions (some of the tracks are now available on a British United Artists album, *This Is Mersey Beat*). At its best it represented an exciting collision between the enormous enthusiasm of the musicians and their fairly rudimentary technique. Its essence was in the chugging rhythm section, with metallic guitar chords cutting across thumping bass lines and solid four-square drumming. Few of the groups could reproduce the atmosphere and energy of a night at the Cavern in a London recording studio with an unsympathetic producer, and hardly any wrote their own songs.

By 1965, the Liverpool music scene was almost dead. Drained of its best musicians by the record companies, yesterday's trend, its only consolation was that the graduates of Merseybeat had changed the face of pop music internationally. *See also* **the Beatles**

The Merseybeats on the Mersey

LOBO A US chart regular during the mid-Seventies, singer-songwriter Lobo (real name Kent Lavoie) was born in Tallahassee, Florida, in 1943. He began playing guitar in high school with a band called the Rumors, moved on to the Sugar Beats whose 'What Am I Doing Here with You' was a local hit around St Petersburg, then after a stint in the Army joined Me And The Other Guys, one of the more popular groups in the area. Three years later, he teamed up with Phil Gernhard (who had successfully produced the Royal Guardsmen, another Florida group, as well as **Dion** and many other Laurie artists) and signed with the new Big Tree label.

His first single for the label, 'Me and You and a Dog Named Boo', was a million-seller in early 1971, followed by several large hits over the next two years including 'She Didn't Do Magic', 'I'd Love You to Want Me', 'Don't Expect Me to Be Your Friend' and 'Standing at the End of the Line'. These records established Lobo as one of AM radio's most consistent stylists, identifiable by his smooth, rhythmic approach, acoustic guitar, warm vocals, and uncomplicated songs. He was in many ways a one-man Bread. Although he maintained a low profile, seldom toured, and shunned the teen magazines, Lobo remained a steady hit-maker until the late Seventies, made several well-received albums, and also co-produced hits for Jim Stafford.

LOFGREN, NILS Born in Chicago in 1952, guitarist/singer Nils Lofgren grew up in Maryland, just outside Washington DC, and became involved in rock at the age of 15, playing in a local band. In 1969 he formed Grin with Bob Berberich (born in Maryland in 1949) on drums from the Reekers, and Bob Gordon (born in Oklahoma in 1951) on bass, and recorded *Grin* (Spindizzy, 1971). Although it was recorded before **Neil Young**'s *After the Goldrush*, on which Lofgren was a featured guitarist, Lofgren's album was released after Young's. After recording with Crazy Horse, Lofgren returned to Grin to record *1+1* (Columbia, 1972) with David Briggs again producing. Divided into a 'dreamy' and 'rockin'' side, the album showcased Lofgren's eloquently eclectic guitar playing and songwriting at their most inventive. For *All Out* (Epic, 1973) the group was enlarged by the addition of Lofgren's elder brother Tom on guitar. A move to A&M produced the disappointing *Gone Crazy* after which Grin folded, and after performing and recording with various members of **Crosby, Stills,** Nash and Young (notably on Young's *'Tonight's the Night'*), Lofgren went solo. His first solo effort, *Nils Lofgren* (A&M, 1975) was a fine example of pop-rock. *Cry Tough* (1976) was produced by **Al Kooper** and Briggs. *I Came to Dance* (1977) featured some ponderous funk, while the live double *Night After Night* failed dismally to capture the excitement and fire of Lofgren on stage. However, *Nils* (1979) and *Night Fades Away* (1982) showed a return to form.

LOGGINS AND MESSINA

When Jim Messina (born 5 December 1947) left **Poco** to pursue more studio work and involve himself less in touring, Epic Records introduced him to Kenny Loggins (7 January 1948), a young songwriter at the publishing company ABC Wingate, whose songs had been recorded by the **Nitty Gritty Dirt Band** amongst others. Messina produced Loggins' first album using ex-Sunshine Company rhythm men Larry Simms and Merel Bregante, horn men Al Garth and Jon Clarke and keyboard player Mike Omartian. So successful was *Sittin' In* (Columbia, 1971), that the session team, with the exception of Omartian, formed a band to tour.

Between 1971 and 1976, Loggins and Messina were one of Columbia's most successful acts, selling albums by the truckload but generally failing to repeat the drive and urgency of their first two releases, *Sittin' In* and *Loggins and Messina*. Soon after their 1976 break-up, Loggins released a solo album, *Celebrate Me Home*, and followed that with the platinum-selling *Nightwatch* (1978). Since then, Loggins has consolidated his success as an AOR superstar with a succession of big-selling albums and the hit theme songs from two films, 'I'm Alright' from *Caddy Shack* (1980) and 'Footloose' (1983), from the film of the same name. Messina had less success, and by the early Eighties he had returned almost exclusively to production work.

LOMAX, ALAN

Ethnomusicologist Alan Lomax was an important figure in the folk revivals of both Britain and America. With his father, John A. Lomax, he went on field recording trips in the Thirties, collecting songs for the Library of Congress archive for which he also recorded **Woody Guthrie**. On one of these they met **Leadbelly** who was brought by the Lomaxes to perform in front of white, urban audiences. A 1941 trip included the first recordings of a young singer, McKinley Morganfield, better known as **Muddy Waters**. In the post-World War II period, Lomax travelled to Britain to collaborate with Ewan MacColl in such ventures as the *Ballads and Blues* radio series. He returned to America in the Fifties to undertake the last major field recording journey in the South, the results of which were issued on Atlantic's *Southern Folk Heritage* series.

LOMAX, JACKIE Singer-songwriter Jackie Lomax was born in Wallasey, near Liverpool, on 10 May 1944. During the Merseybeat era, he fronted first Dee And The Dynamites, then the Undertakers, who recorded **Rosco Gordon**'s 'Just a Little Bit' in 1963. He next formed Lomax Alliance, an unsuccessful group, before signing with Apple Records in 1968.

Supervised by **George Harrison**, Lomax's work for the label – three singles and an album, *Is This What You Want* (1969) – showed him to be a skilful writer and singer. With the demise of Apple, he moved to Warner Brothers for the critically acclaimed *Home Is in My Head* (1970) and *Three* (1971), produced by John Simon. With Badger he recorded *White Lady* (Epic, 1974), produced by **Allen Toussaint**, but left them a year later and emigrated to California where he recorded the solo album *Livin' for Lovin'* in 1975. Both it and the follow-up, *Did You Ever Have That Feeling?*, sold poorly and his label, Capitol, dropped him.

LOPEZ, TRINI Born in Dallas, Texas, on 15 May 1937, Trini Lopez was discovered by Don Costa of Reprise. In 1963, Trini Lopez emulated **Peter, Paul and Mary** and took 'If I Had a Hammer' into the US Top 10, with a totally different treatment. Costa produced and arranged 'If I Had a Hammer' – which reached Number 3 – and his subsequent recordings, giving them a party atmosphere of handclapping and enthusiastic yelping – from Hollywood's PJ's club – around rhythm guitar and Lopez's clear vocal. The formula was used over the years on a string of hits – 'Kansas City', 'America' (like 'Hammer', taken from the gold album *Trini Lopez at PJ's*), 'La Bamba' and 'Lemon Tree'. Throughout the mid-Sixties he had a large following in South America and Europe, especially in France. He later turned up singing and acting in the film *The Dirty Dozen*.

LORDAN, JERRY A songwriter and performer of the pre-Beatle era, Jerry Lordan was born in Paddington, London, in 1933 and began his career in Royal Air Force camp shows. On his demobilization in 1955, he tried his luck as a comedian but failed and turned instead to songwriting and recording as one half of Lee and Jerry Elvin. Although the duo made no progress, one of London's early songs, 'A House, a Car and a Wedding Ring' was a minor hit for Mike Preston in America in 1958 and Lordan turned to songwriting full-time. **Anthony Newley**'s 'I've Waited So Long' came next in 1959 and on the strength of that he secured a recording contract with Parlophone. His first single, 'I'll Stay Single', reached Number 26 in the UK and 'Who Could Be Bluer', the follow-up, peaked at Number 17 early in 1960. Ironically it was the instrumental 'Apache' that really established him when it topped the British charts (by the **Shadows**) and reached Number 2 in the USA (in a version by Jorgen Ingmann) later that year. Since then he has written songs for **Cliff Richard**, Matt Monro and the Shadows.

LOS ANGELES
While Philadelphia and New York teemed with managers and agents looking for brooding, pudgy-faced youths to transform into teenage idols, a rather different rock'n'roll culture was developing on the West Coast during the late Fifties. There were no big talent agencies or Svengalic managers in Los Angeles. Instead, scattered inconspicuously across LA's huge sprawl were numerous small record labels, distributors and recording studios.

This fledgling record industry began after World War II when independent labels like Aladdin and Specialty sprang up to satisfy a huge demand for urban blues, created by the migration of blacks to the North and West. This R&B boom lasted until the late Fifties when white rock'n'roll caused many of the original blues labels to founder while others like Imperial, with **Ricky Nelson**, quickly moved into the lucrative pop market before it was too late. From then on, the West Coast bred literally dozens of small, short-lived and often domestically-run record labels. Unlike their predecessors, few of these newer companies catered for any one market but recorded virtually anyone and anything sounding vaguely commercial (local sales alone provided adequate profit for such firms), and many companies simply made one-shot 'product' oriented records using session-singers and musicians.

Back in the late Fifties, LA's rock community comprised several interrelated cliques which encompassed white Southerners who had come to Hollywood to try their luck (**Eddie Cochran**, **Johnny Burnette**, **Leon Russell**, **P.J. Proby**, etc.); a variety of black artists ranging from pop singers like **Bobby Day** and **Sam Cooke** to dozens of vocal groups which changed personnel at every session; and, finally, white middle-class high school kids like **Jan and Dean**, **Phil Spector**, **Herb Alpert**, **Terry Melcher** and the **Beach Boys**.

With the advent of rock'n'roll, many West Coast labels began recording high school kids who were glad to be given a chance at what was basically a pastime, encouraged by the rock'n'roll craze and California's sunny, recreational environment. It also became possible for an enthusiastic and latently talented college kid to squeeze into a peripheral position at one of these firms in order to learn about the record business. From this tutorial musical environment of the late Fifties and early Sixties came a new breed of youthful entrepreneurs who wrote songs, made records and even managed artists while maintaining a semi-professional status. Later-to-be-successful record producers like Herb Alpert, **Frank Zappa**, **Shel Talmy** and Terry Melcher cut their teeth on the occasional hit and many obscure failures during this period.

Until 1965, LA's record business was still searching for an identity. Unable to compete with the thriving New York scene, dozens of local labels struggled for local sales and occasionally surfaced with a national hit like the **Teddy Bears**' 'To Know Him is to Love Him' and Jan and Arnie's 'Jenny Lee', two records which are acknowledged as having instigated the entire West Coast rock movement. LA's rock'n'roll future would lie in this state of frivolous apprenticeship until the mid-Sixties when the **Byrds**, **Sonny and Cher** and TV shows like *Shindig* turned the Coast into rock's new focal point.

Other 'classic' West Coast-recorded hits from this period include 'Chicano' rockers such as **Ritchie Valens**' 'La Bamba' and **Chris Montez**'s 'Let's Dance'; archetypal teen-ballads such as 'A Thousand Stars' by Kathy Young and the Innocents and 'Image of a Girl' by the Safaris and novelty discs like 'Monster Mash' and 'Alley-Oop'.

In 1965, the new thing was **Dylan** and protest. The familiar Los Angeles session crew played behind **Roger McGuinn** on the Byrds' 'Mr Tambourine Man', an immaculate and influential record. The key figure of this era in Los Angeles, however, was **Lou Adler**, who brought together **P. F. Sloan**'s punk lyrics and **Barry McGuire**'s hairy 'protest' image to make 'Eve of Destruction', a million-seller on his own Dunhill label. Other Los Angeles protest successes came with Sonny and Cher (their records owing much to the skill of arranger **Harold Battiste**), **Glen Campbell** and the **Turtles**. The Turtles soon became part of the Los Angeles vocal group trend into which 'protest' evolved. Adler contributed the **Mamas and the Papas**, who blended rich harmonies with hip or witty lyrics, while in 1966 two San Francisco-based groups – the **Beau Brummels** and **Harpers Bizarre** – began to record with producer **Lenny Waronker** when Warner Brothers bought out their label, Autumn.

The local club scene blossomed in the mid-Sixties, through venues like Ciro's, the Moulin Rouge (later the Kaleidoscope), the Crescendo and the Cheetah and Shrine Explosion ballrooms. From them came a series of groups, including the **Doors**. Los Angeles also had a youth culture centred on Sunset Strip, the scene of anti-curfew riots which became the subject of **Buffalo Springfield**'s single, 'For What It's Worth', in 1967, and also inspired a run of teen-exploitation movies and soundtracks which often featured local groups like the **Standells** and the Chocolate Watch Band.

From 1967 onwards, former members of the Byrds and the Springfields regrouped in a bewilderingly kaleidoscopic series of changes, the most obvious example being **Crosby, Stills, Nash and Young**, who more than any other group managed to bring together the traditional Los Angeles attention to pure craftsmanship and the San Franciscan devotion to live enthusiasm. CSN&Y were the real superstars, living in the Los Angeles canyons, but other ex-Byrds and ex-Springfields, together with an influx of country-influenced musicians like 'Sneeky' Pete Kleinow, Bernie Leadon and Al Perkins, were gathering in clubs like the Troubadour.

Country music was the most important new influence. The Byrds, who had electrified Dylan's folk songs, now electrified the country music into which he retreated, creating the 'country rock' which would form the core of the city's music during the first half of the Seventies. **The Flying Burrito Brothers**, Manassas, the **Eagles**, **Loggins and Messina** all followed, creating a rhythmic sound that featured country-associated instrumentation like the pedal steel guitar and the mandolin. In between group sessions, these same musicians would make the odd solo album and join together to back a steady stream of female vocalists which included **Linda Ronstadt**, Wendy Waldman, **Maria Muldaur** and **Bonnie Raitt**.

Of the pre-folk-rock groups only the Beach Boys remained still touring and making records, still in part under the direction of the genius recluse Brian Wilson. Newer names, however, emerged from within the recording and publishing companies that had mushroomed in Los Angeles since the mid-Sixties: the early Seventies, in particular, saw a rash of new singer-songwriters sign to LA labels like the fast-expanding Warner-Reprise organization – many of whom, like **Randy Newman** and **Van Dyke Parks**, once worked on a nine-to-five basis for the city's Metric Music publishing house. David Gates was another ex-Metric writer: he formed **Bread** in 1969 with two session musicians, Jimmy Griffin and Robb Royer, and masterminded their masterly mix of lush instrumentation and rich vocal harmonies. From out of the folk clubs came **Jackson Browne** and **Joni Mitchell**, who formed, with **Neil Young** of CSN&Y, a triumvirate of writer/performers who continued the Los Angeles tradition of 'topical' music, exploring in song the state of America mirrored in their relationships with loved ones and their audiences. All three were principally concerned, early in their career at least, with the alternatives available in the aftermath of the Sixties' failure to realize its dreams.

From Randy Newman's black irony to the Beach Boys' ecological concerns, from Joni Mitchell's self-doubts to the Eagles' reflections on the Californian superstar lifestyle, Los Angeles music in the Seventies had variety and depth, although it came to be identified – as the decade went on – with blandness, predictability and a general air of safety. From the late Seventies through the first half of the Eighties, West Coast rock as a whole retained this image while throwing up a number of oddball talents – numerous punk-influenced bands, a handful of highly-regarded Sixties-influenced groups (Dream Syndicate, Green on Red, the Long Ryders) who were nevertheless ignored by mainstream audiences, and quirky singer-songwriters like Stan Ridgway. However, more successful were the Bangles, an all-female band whose music was essentially a clever and often affecting distillation of approximately twenty years of LA rock – sweet harmonies, jingle-jangle guitar, romantic teen songs shot through with a streak of realism, and clinically perfect production.

LOS LOBOS With a potent blend of R&B, soul and Tex-Mex, Los Angeles' Los Lobos almost instantly gained critical acclaim after the release of their mini-LP . . . *and a time to dance* (1983), which won them a Grammy award, and they were soon after voted band of the year in a *Rolling Stone* poll.

David Hidalgo (vocals/guitar/harmonica), Steve Berlin (sax), Conrad Lozano (bass/vocals), Cesar Rosas (guitar/vocals/banjo) and Louis Perez (drums/guitar) converted their local live reputation to rave record reviews with that first release. Taking to the road to promote the mini-album, they found a wider audience, riding on the wave of popularity for 'honest American music', that is basic, no frills, homegrown rock music. The debut LP, *How Will the Wolf Survive* (1984) was similarly well-received.

LOUDERMILK, JOHN D. Born in Durham, North Carolina, on 31 March 1934, John D. Loudermilk has enjoyed a moderately successful recording career since the early Sixties but is best known as a songwriter. His first hit came when **George Hamilton IV** took 'A Rose and a Baby Ruth' to Number 6 in the American pop charts in November 1956. Subsequent hits included Stonewall Jackson's 'Waterloo' (1959) and Johnny Ferguson's 'Angela Jones' (1960), covered in Britain by Michael Cox. As 'Tommy Dee' he recorded 'Three Stars', a maudlin tribute to **Buddy Holly**, **Ritchie Valens** and the **Big Bopper**, in 1959. Loudermilk's biggest period was 1961–2: Sue Thompson had successive hits with 'Sad Movies' and 'Norman', and the writer himself scored with 'The Language of Love', 'Thou Shalt Not Steal', 'Callin' Doctor Casey' and 'Road Hog'. Writing successes in the mid-Sixties included 'Abilene' and 'Tobacco Road'.

Loudermilk has never sounded particularly convincing as a recording artist; even his own hits sound more like the demo records that they probably started out as, due to his light voice and simple backings. As a songwriter, though, his work has passed beyond the Country and Western field into the pop and 'novelty pop' categories. He continues to prosper as a live entertainer, armed with guitar, harmonica, and plenty of patter.

LOVE Along with the **Doors**, Love were arguably the most outstanding product of the Los Angeles rock scene of the mid-Sixties. The group was the brainchild of Arthur Lee, guitarist, singer and songwriter, and began in 1965, playing the city's club scene with a music that synthesized black R&B and the new 'folk-rock' of the **Byrds**. The original line-up comprised Lee (born in Memphis, Tennessee, in 1944), guitarist John Echols, guitarist/vocalist Bryan Maclean, bassist Ken Forssi, drummer Alban 'Snoopy' Pfister, and percussionist Michael Stuart. Their first two albums, *Love* (Elektra, 1966) and *Da Capo* (1967), featured Lee's eerie voice intoning surreal lyrics over a smooth blues sound dominated by acoustic guitars. However, their third album – *Forever Changes* (1968) – was the one with which they came to be most associated. With horn player Tjay Cantrelli (who had joined after the first album) now departed along with Pfister, Lee's music schizophrenia had full rein. The album contained the same elements as earlier, but rather than coexisting peacefully they now glared at each other, R&B being as absent from the music as traditional folk-rock themes were from the lyrics.

LA groups had a reputation for performing badly outside the city. Love solved this by simply staying there, rarely leaving their horror-film mansion in Hollywood. The triumph of *Forever Changes* was followed by an album, apparently too awful to release, and the old Love was no more. From 1968, the name belonged to Arthur Lee and whatever musicians he chose to work with. Among these was **Jimi Hendrix**, an indication of Lee's progression into straighter, blacker R&B. Hendrix performed on one track of *False Start* (1970) and made a whole album with Lee which has never been released. Lee released a solo album, *Arthur Lee and Band Aid*, on A&M in 1972, and in 1974, signed to RSO with a completely reconstituted Love. The band made one album, *Reel to Real*, before folding. Lee has recorded sporadically since.

LOVE, DARLENE Best known for her recording work with **Phil Spector**, Darlene Love was born Darlene Wright in 1938. She joined the Blossoms, a Los Angeles high-school girl group which recorded unsuccessfully for Capitol in 1958–60: between 1960 and 1962, they recorded for Challenge and Okeh but mostly did session work in Los Angeles for **James Darren**, **Bobby Darin**, **Nino Tempo and April Stevens** and many others. As a session singer, Darlene sang lead on several Phil Spector-produced singles on Philles, including 'He's a Rebel' and 'He's Sure the Boy I Love'(which was credited to the **Crystals**) and 'Zip-A-Dee-Doo-Dah' by the dubiously named Bob B. Soxx and the Bluejeans. She also recorded six singles for Philles in her own right, notably 'Christmas (Baby Come Home)', 'Today I Met the Boy I'm Gonna Marry' and 'A Fine Fine Boy', and scored in 1963 with 'Wait Till My Bobby Gets Home' which reached Number 26 in America. Throughout the Sixties, the Blossoms continued to work sessions (they were regulars on the *Shindig* TV show) and went on the road with **Elvis Presley** during an early Seventies tour.

LOVERS ROCK A British reggae phenomenon of the mid-Seventies, lovers rock was – depending on your point of view – either a dispiritingly anodyne and tackily produced balladic style, or just the thing for cuddling up to your loved one on the living-room sofa. The genre took its name from London producer Dennis Harris' label Lovers Rock. At its best, singers like Janet Kay and Jean Adebambo transcended the limitations of lovers rock, while Jamaican-based artists who periodically recorded lovers rock material – **Gregory Isaacs**, **Dennis Brown**, Sugar Minott – gave added muscle and credence. At its worst, the artists are not only best forgotten, but actually *are* forgotten.

LOVICH, LENE Born Marlene Premilovich in Detroit, Lene Lovich came to prominence in Britain in 1978 when her kooky good looks, wild saxophone playing and distinctive vocal style made her the star of the Be Stiff tour. She capitalized on this by scoring three UK hit singles (on Stiff) the next year, including the repetitive, mesmeric 'Say When' and the quirky 'Lucky Number'.

Collaborating with boyfriend/co-writer Les Chappell, Lovich released two confusing, absorbing albums (*Stateless* [1979] and *Flex* [1980]) before disappearing from the music scene for two years.

She re-emerged in 1982 with a new album, *No Man's Land*, betraying her European folk ancestry and achieved a minor hit with 'It's You, Only You'. Her successful starring role in a musical based on the life of Mata Hari proved her artistic ability, but her need for commercial success was probably slightly less than all-consuming.

LOVIN' SPOONFUL Specialists in what came to be known as 'good-time music' – a streamlined jug-band sound set to rock accompaniment – the Lovin' Spoonful came together in

Lovin' Spoonful on British TV: Zally Yanovsky (left) and John Sebastian

Greenwich Village during 1964. **John Sebastian** (born 17 March 1944) was a local boy, the son of a classical harmonica player. He had played mouth-harp himself on sessions for **Tim Hardin**, the Even Dozen Jug Band and others before producer Eric Jacobsen encouraged Sebastian to put a group together to record his own songs. Zally Yanovsky (born 19 December 1944, in Toronto) had been with Sebastian in the Mugwumps, which also contained **Cass Elliott** and Denny Doherty, later of the **Mamas and the Papas**. Joe Butler (born 19 January 1943, Glen Cove, Long Island) was one of the few drummers in the Village and Steve Boone (23 September 1943, North Carolina) was a rhythm guitarist in search of a band. All were extroverts with a wild sense of humour who combined traditional folk and blues elements with updated rock'n'roll to produce a streamlined jug-band sound that came to be known as good-time music.

The Spoonful signed to Kama Sutra and followed up the success of their first record, 'Do You Believe in Magic',

with six successive Top 10 singles in 1965–6. At a time when everyone else in America seemed to be imitating the **Beatles**, the Spoonful were among the few to create an American equivalent to the Merseybeat synthesis. They had a similar zany, casual image which, however, seemed to extend to their musical activity as well. They did not progress in the way the Beatles or **Dylan** did: each album was just a collection of songs, nearly always Sebastian originals or reworkings of traditional songs, from which hit single after hit single was taken – lazy, old-fashioned celebrations of love on a summer's day like 'Daydream'; eulogies to the power and appeal of pop music like 'Do You Believe in Magic' and 'Nashville Cats'; delicate description of adolescent love like 'You Didn't Have to Be so Nice' and 'Younger Girl'. Sebastian was a supreme pop craftsman and an unashamed romantic, yet he was best at capturing a mood – the sweaty tension of 'Summer in the City', their only American Number 1, or the resignation of 'Didn't Want to Do It'.

The Lovin' Spoonful had an effect on nearly everybody, including the Beatles, whose 'Good Day Sunshine' had exactly the same carefree attitude as Spoonful tracks like 'Daydream' (their biggest British hit, reaching Number 2 on Pye). But by 1967, they had begun to dissipate their energies and were producing work like Sebastian's uneven score for Francis Ford Coppola's first film, *You're a Big Boy Now*. The break-up of the group was, however, precipitated by a non-musical event. A drug bust in San Francisco in 1967 resulted in Zal Yanovsky incriminating others involved in the city's drug scene, under threat of deportation – he was still technically a Canadian citizen. The band were ostracized and Yanovsky left. He was replaced by Jerry Yester, former **Association** producer and folk singer, but they split up after a couple of worthy albums.

Sebastian made a comeback in 1970 when he took the stage at the Woodstock Festival during a storm, and for a couple of years his records sold well and his live appearances drew the crowds, though mostly on the strength of his association with the Spoonful. His new material was not as good, but rather more like his new adopted stage manner, too cloying and too sentimental. Four years later he re-formed the Spoonful, apparently without consulting Joe Butler, but the reunion was brief and Sebastian resumed his solo career. *See also* **John Sebastian**

LOWE, JIM Best known for his composition 'Green Door', Jim Lowe was born in Springfield, Missouri on 7 May 1927 and worked in Chicago and New York as a DJ after graduating from the University of Missouri. He retained a liking for country music, writing songs such as 'Gambler's Guitar' for Rusty Draper. He recorded country material for Mercury and joined Dot from 1955 until 1960. In 1956 'Green Door' became a national rock'n'roll hit for Lowe and was covered by **Bill Haley** and, in Britain, by Frankie Vaughan. Other recordings included 'Blue Suede Shoes' and 'Talkin' to the Blues', and two minor hits, 'Rock a Chicka' and 'He'll Have to Go'. A version of 'Green Door' by **Shakin' Stevens** was a UK Number 1 in 1981.

LOWE, NICK Once a member of infamous pub-rock band **Brinsley Schwarz**, Nick Lowe (born 25 March 1949) went on to have success both as a member of Rockpile with **Dave Edmunds** and as a solo artist and producer.

After the demise of Brinsley Schwarz in 1975, Lowe released a number of singles parodying various styles and under a variety of names, revealing a talent for sardonic lyrics and artful plagiarism. In 1976 he became the first artist to release a record on Stiff with the single 'So It Goes', and then became house producer for the label, operating the controls for **Elvis Costello** and the **Damned** among others.

In 1977 Lowe and Costello left Stiff to form Radar with Jake Riviera, and Lowe's most successful chart period began with 'I Love the Sound of Breaking Glass' (UK Top 10) and the album *The Jesus of Cool* (titled *Pure Pop for Now People* in the US), both in 1978. Lowe followed this in 1979 with *Labour of Lust* which gave him his sole US Top 40 single, 'Cruel to be Kind' (a Number 12 on both sides of the Atlantic).

Lowe continued as a producer, working with the **Pretenders** on their first single, as well as on several albums with Costello, a couple of albums by his wife Carlene Carter (daughter of **Johnny Cash**) and many others. Up to 1981 most of his time as a performer was spent working with Rockpile, but then the band split and Lowe was able to concentrate on his solo work, resuming with two albums, *Nick the Knife* (1981) and later *The Abominable Showman* (1983), but despite their snappy titles, Lowe never rediscovered the tempo and smart pop of his first two albums.

LULU Lulu and the Luvvers (originally the Gleneagles) were Scotland's most successful contribution to the British beat boom of 1963–5. Lulu – born Marie Laurie on 3 November 1948, in Glasgow – possessed a potentially great blues-shouting voice that was heard to good effect on their first hit, a 1964 version of an old **Isley Brothers** number called 'Shout'. Within a year, however, she had parted company with the Luvvers – Ross Nelson, Jim Dewar, Alec Bell, Jimmy Smith, Tony Tierney and David Miller – and was being groomed by her record label, Decca, as a rival to **Cilla Black**. A switch to EMI's Columbia label did much to revive her chart fortunes, as new producer **Mickie Most** provided her with material more appropriate to her original tomboy-ish image, such as the million-selling 'To Sir with Love' – the theme song from the film of the same name and a chart-topper in the US – and **Neil Diamond**'s 'The Boat that I Row' (both 1967). Despite breaking with Most in 1967, she was soon fronting her own television variety show and representing the UK in the 1968 Eurovision Song Contest – Britain's entry, 'Boom Bang-a-Bang', tied for first place. From then on, the world of cabaret seemed set to claim her for good, but she made a welcome return to the UK Top 10 in 1974 with an enigmatic version of **David Bowie**'s

Lulu personified the youth and vigour of the Swinging Sixties

'The Man Who Sold the World', which Bowie himself produced. Although she never really lived up to her initial potential, Lulu recorded some interesting sides under the direction of Jerry Wexler and **Arif Mardin** for Atlantic. Between 1969 and 1973, she was married to Maurice Gibb of the **Bee Gees**. In mid-1986 she scored a surprise UK hit with a re-recording of 'Shout'.

LYMON, FRANKIE Born in Washington Heights on 30 September 1942, Frankie Lymon fronted the accurately named Teenagers who, with **Little Anthony**'s Imperials, were prototypes for later soul groups like the **Jackson Five**. Apart from Lymon, the group comprised Sherman Garnes (8 June 1940), Joe Negroni (9 September 1940), Herman Santiago (18 February 1941), and Jimmy Merchant (10 February 1940). Hy Weiss, owner of New York's Old Town label passed Lymon on to rival **George Goldner** of Gee Records.

Young Frankie Lymon points to his poster outside the London Palladium

In 1955, the group sold two million copies of 'Why Do Fools Fall in Love?'. In 1956 came the mawkish 'I'm Not a Juvenile Delinquent', an apologia for rock'n'roll that was both ghastly and ironic, though the sound was undeniably attractive if you discounted Goldner's lyric. Finally there was Lymon's exultantly youthful voice, almost feminine, tackling the standard 'Goody Goody' to full orchestral accompaniment. The same year, 1957, the group disintegrated. Theirs had been the typical story of exploitation of blacks and teenagers in the first rock'n'roll boom – a handful of calculated and rather bland hits, some film appearances, then fade. Frankie Lymon went solo on Roulette in 1957 and soldiered into oblivion in the early Sixties. He died of drug abuse in February 1968.

LYNN, BARBARA

Born Barbara Lynn Ozen on 16 January 1942 in Beaumont, Texas, Barbara Lynn was discovered singing blues in Louisiana clubs by **Huey P. Meaux**, who went on to produce nearly all her records.

Early sides were cut in Cosimo's New Orleans studio but leased to the Philadelphia-based Jamie label. The first of these, 'You'll Lose a Good Thing', was written as a poem when Lynn was 16. It topped the R&B chart and reached the national Top 10 in 1962, later becoming an R&B standard. Other Jamie singles (12 in all) made the middle reaches of the Hot 100, including 'Second Fiddle Girl' (1963), 'Oh Baby We Got a Good Thing Goin'' (1964 – revived by the Rolling Stones) and 'You're Gonna Need Me' (1965).

After a less eventful period on Meaux's Tribe label, she returned to the charts on Atlantic with 'This Is the Thanks I Get' (1968), 'Until Then I'll Suffer' (1971) and 'Daddy Hotstuff' (1972). Barbara Lynn's recordings consistently displayed a bluesy experience-laden voice, low-key, frequently throwaway vocal style, her own simple but gutsy left-handed guitar work, and Meaux's tasteful horn arrangements. The lack of strings and lazy, down-home flavour was redolent of **Jimmy Reed**. See also **Huey P. Meaux**

LYNN, LORETTA

Born on 14 March 1940 in Butcher's Hollow, Van Leer, Kentucky, Loretta Lynn is, simply, the best female country singer of the past decade in the tradition of Molly O'Day and Kitty Wells. She began recording on Zero in 1960, transferred to Decca in 1962, and by 1966, with hits like 'Don't Come Home a' Drinkin'', 'With Lovin' On Your Mind',

'First City' and 'You're Not Woman Enough (to Take My Man Away from Me)' and a regular TV guest spot with the Wilburn Brothers, she had established the image of the simple country girl who could fight back. She recorded with established star Ernest Tubb. During the Seventies she developed as a vocalist and writer to produce classic country albums like *Coalminer's Daughter* (MCA) which was also the title of her best-selling autobiography, upon which the film *Coalminer's Daughter* (1983) was based. Fellow country singer **Crystal Gayle** is Loretta's sister.

LYNNE, JEFF

The creative force behind the **Electric Light Orchestra**, Jeff Lynne (born in Birmingham on 12 December 1947) was an active participant in the city group scene from about 1964. He started in school bands, picking up guitar, keyboards and bass, then replaced **Roy Wood** in Mike Sheridan's Nightriders, one of Birmingham's top groups of the mid-Sixties, along with the **Moody Blues**, the Uglys, Keith Powell and the Valets, and Carl Wayne and the Vikings. In late 1966, Sheridan went solo, leaving Lynne in charge of the Nightriders. He reorganized them as the Idle Race, who went on to become one of Britain's most impressive late-Sixties progressive-commercial groups. Although they never had a hit, their two United Artists albums, *Birthday Party* (1968) and *Idle Race* (1969), and several additional singles remain among the most prized collectors' items of their era, and hold up amazingly well.

After three years of going nowhere with the Idle Race, Lynne joined the **Move** in 1970. His influence became immediately apparent, as he co-produced the next two albums, with *Looking On* in particular reflecting Lynne's Idle Race sound. He wrote the B-sides to their 1970–1 hits, and the A-side of their biggest American hit, 'Do Ya'. His real interest, though, was the Electric Light Orchestra, an idea proposed by Carl Wayne (who ironically left the Move before Lynne's arrival). Wayne saw the ELO as a conceptual outgrowth of the Move, playing rock with a large classical orchestra. Wood and Lynne took the idea further, hoping to develop a fairly small group of rock musicians who could mix classical ideas and motifs into a rock format, using limited instrumentation but creating a sound with the fullness of a symphony orchestra.

A first album laid the groundwork for the ELO, with Lynne writing and sing-

ing at least half, including the British hit singles '10538 Overture' and 'Roll Over Beethoven' (1973). Soon after, Wood went off on his own, claiming that Lynne's approach to the ELO lacked the proper amount of rock'n'roll raunch and formed Wizzard to prove his point. In Lynne's hands, the ELO went on to develop the classical/rock synthesis, and became one of the most successful progressive groups of the early Seventies with albums like *Eldorado* (Warner Brothers, 1974) – their first big American hit – and singles like 'Evil Woman' (Jet, 1975). Lynne's only outside project in recent years has been to collaborate with **Del Shannon** (who, along with **Bobby Vee** and **Jerry Lee Lewis**, he credits as his greatest influence). See also **Electric Light Orchestra, Roy Wood**

LYNYRD SKYNYRD

Trailblazers of **Allman Brothers**-style Southern rock between 1972 and 1977, Lynyrd Skynyrd was founded by lead singer Ronnie Van Zant, from Jacksonville, Florida, in 1965. With fellow high-school students, guitarists Allen Collins and Gary Rossington, he named the group after an unpopular teacher. In 1972, with Ed King (guitar), Billy Powell (keyboards), Leon Wilkeson (bass) and Robert Burns (drums), they signed to **Al Kooper**'s newly formed Sounds Of The South label.

The band soon won a reputation as a fundamentalist Southern boogie unit, their name being linked with the Allman Brothers Band. Their music, however, made no concessions to sophistication, with Van Zant's songs concentrating on established themes, including the notable 'Sweet Home Alabama' (a Top 10 hit in 1975 on MCA), which effectively responded to **Neil Young**'s anti-redneck 'Southern Man'. Two tours of Britain endeared them to big beat boogie fans there and the massive sales of *Gimme Back My Bullets*, for which guitarist Steven Gaines joined the group, and *One More from the Road* (both 1976) placed them in the top league of American stadium bands. However, during the same week that saw the release of their sixth album, *Street Survivors*, the crash of the band's privately chartered plane claimed the lives (on 20 October 1977) of members Van Zant, Steven Gaines and his sister Cassie.

In 1980, three of the surviving members resurfaced in the Rossington-Collins Band, who recorded two albums – *Anytime, Anyplace, Anywhere* (1980) and *This is the Way* (1981) – for MCA before disbanding in 1982.

M

MABON, WILLIE Singer and pianist Willie Mabon was born in Memphis on 24 October 1925 and was a major presence in the R&B charts between 1952 and 1954. His hits for Chess included 'I Don't Know' (originally on Parrot), 'I'm Mad' and 'Poison Ivy'. The first two both reached the Top 10. He had previously recorded for Apollo as Big Willie. A suave and sophisticated performer, Mabon's singing was laconic and dry, leaning more towards the urban blues of the West Coast than the style of the Chicago musicians with whom he often worked. His 'Got To Have Some' was released on Sue in Britain and was included in the repertoire of white R&B performers, like **Georgie Fame**, in the early Sixties. Mabon's economical blues piano and occasional harmonica playing – also heard on subsequent records for Delta, Mad, Formal and USA – delighted audiences in France during the Seventies, where he recorded several albums. He died on 19 April 1985.

McCARTNEY, PAUL Following the break-up of the **Beatles** and the release of two low-key solo albums, *Paul McCartney* (Apple, 1970) and *Ram* (1971), McCartney formed Wings, which initially comprised Paul McCartney, bass, vocals (born 18 June 1942); Linda McCartney, keyboards, vocals (24 September 1942); **Denny Laine**, guitar, vocals (29 October 1944); Henry McCullough, guitar and Denny Seiwell, drums – in 1971. With the group he recorded a series of successful, but generally uninteresting singles – 'Give Ireland Back to the Irish', 'Mary Had a Little Lamb' (1972); the BBC-banned 'Hi Hi Hi' and its inoffensive flip 'C Moon'; 'My Love', 'Live and Let Die' (both American chart toppers); 'Helen Wheels' (1973) – and two albums – *Wild Life* (1971) and *Red Rose Speedway* (1973) – which were streaked with his by then familiar mawkishness and lack of consequence, before the release of the superior and highly successful *Band on the Run* at the end of 1973. By this time McCullough and Seiwell had left, and Wings continued as a three-piece group until the arrival of guitarist Jimmy McCulloch and drummer Joe English. This combination produced the weak but

Paul McCartney's post-Beatles career flourished, thanks to an easy gift for melody and sharp commercial sense

even more commercially successful *Venus and Mars* (1975).

McCartney is generally thought to have precipitated the demise of Apple through his dispute and lawsuit with the other Beatles and their business nominee, Allen Klein. He nevertheless enjoyed the largest and most varied following of any of the Beatles as a solo artist, and by the mid-Seventies was a major figure within, and influence on, mainstream pop.

Wings toured extensively during 1976 and a resulting live set, *Wings over America*, became the world's best-selling triple album. A year later, they achieved another record: 'Mull of Kintyre', released just in time for the Christmas market, became the UK's all-time biggest-selling single (a status it held until **Band Aid** sold even more with 'Do They Know It's Christmas?' in 1984–5). Meanwhile, McCartney used his money wisely, obtaining the rights to stage shows like *Annie* and *Grease* and the publishing rights to **Buddy Holly**'s back catalogue.

Two desultory albums followed in 1979 – *London Town* and *Back to the Egg*, which featured the Wings debut of drummer Steve Holly and guitarist Lawrence Juber, who had joined in

place of the departing McCulloch and English. In 1980, McCartney was busted for possession of marijuana in Tokyo, and his eventual deportation thwarted the planned Wings gigs. Laine then left Wings in disgust and McCartney plunged himself into solo work: *McCartney II* (1980) afforded two strong singles in 'Coming Up' and 'Waterfalls'.

Paul reunited with producer **George Martin** for *Tug of War* (1982), his finest album since *Band on the Run*. It included a tribute to **John Lennon**, 'Here Today', the UK single 'Take It Away', and the chart-topping 'Ebony and Ivory', a duet with **Stevie Wonder**. That same year, he duetted with **Michael Jackson** on an almost equally successful single, 'The Girl Is Mine', and paired with him again in 1983 for 'Say Say Say'. His film *Give My Regards to Broad Street* (1984) was a critical disaster but a respectable commercial success and included the single 'No More Lonely Nights'.

Although criticized in rock circles for the open commercialism of his work and the sometimes puerile sentimentality of songs like 'Pipes of Peace' (1983) and 'We All Stand Together' (1984), McCartney remains a master song craftsman and a man of amazingly consistent commercial judgment. Without progressing very significantly in any creative sense, he has proved himself a capable pop showman, a prolific composer and one of pop history's most enduring personalities. *See also* **Denny Laine**

MacCOLL, KIRSTY Daughter of traditional folk singer Ewan, Kirsty MacColl (born 10 October 1959) signed to Stiff in the late Seventies and immediately made her mark with 'They Don't Know', a self-penned song that received rave reviews but had to wait for **Tracey Ullman** to take it into the charts in 1983.

Signed to Polydor, MacColl scored her first hit in 1981 with the wacky, country-tinged 'There's a Guy Works Down the Chipshop Swears He's Elvis' reaching Number 14 in the UK. It was followed by her debut LP *Desperate Character*, which was greeted by predictions of future superstardom by the critics, but apart from one UK Top 10 hit with a cover of **Billy Bragg**'s 'A New England' in 1985, large-scale success has continued to elude her. Her time in the mid-Eighties has been spent raising a young family and providing backing vocals on records by the **Smiths**, Billy Bragg and the **Rolling Stones**.

McCOY, CHARLIE Recognized as the best harmonica player in country music, Charlie McCoy (born in Oak Hill, West Virginia, on 28 March 1941) was a one-time member of Stonewall Jackson's back-up band and became one of the top Nashville session players from the early Sixties onwards, playing on hundreds of country records as well as every **Bob Dylan** album from *Highway 61 Revisited* to *Nashville Skyline*.

As an instrumentalist, McCoy was heard to good effect on the two albums by Area Code 615, the Nashville session supergroup, during 1969–70. Following a minor 1961 hit ('Cherry Berry Wine', on Cadence), he signed to Monument as a solo artist in 1963, though his own records, such as *The Nashville Hit Man* (1974) tend to be less effective than his work with others.

McCOY, VAN One of the most successful songwriters and producers in Sixties soul and Seventies disco music, Van McCoy was born on 6 January 1944 in Washington DC. He sang with the Starlighters, a local group who recorded a few unsuccessful singles for End, before forming his own record label, Rockin' Records. A McCoy solo disc, 'Hey Mr DJ' (1959) was picked up for national distribution by Scepter Records, whom he joined as an A&R man, but left after a year to work freelance – he arranged the **Drifters'** small 1963 hit for **Leiber and Stoller**, 'Rat Race' – and recorded for Columbia and Epic ('Keep Lovin' Me', 'I Started a Joke') in a **Johnny Mathis** vein. At Maxx he produced a couple of sophisticated soul hits for **Gladys Knight and the Pips**, including the Top 40 'Giving Up' (1964), before returning to Columbia as a producer and writer. There he produced an unlikely hit for **Chad and Jeremy** ('Before and After', 1965) and a series of syrupy tunes for **Peaches and Herb** (1966–7), and also wrote 'Baby I'm Yours' for **Barbara Lewis**. In 1967 he formed Van McCoy Productions (VMP) and Vanda Records which had an immediate Top 40 hit with Christ Barley's smooth recording of 'The Sweetest Thing This Side of Heaven'. After Vanda folded he continued working as an independent producer, masterminding such hits as 'I Get the Sweetest Feeling' (**Jackie Wilson**, 1968), '5-10-15-20 (25-30 Years of Love)' (the Presidents, 1970) and 'Right on the Tip of My Tongue' (Brenda and the Tabulations, 1971) before settling down to work virtually full-time with the **Stylistics** as their arranger, following the departure of **Thom Bell**. Though his work with the group over-senti-

mentalized their sound, the records were phenomenally successful and **Hugo and Luigi**, the group's producers, invited him to record an album of symphonic versions of soul hits for Avco. That sold only moderately well, but he recorded a further instrumental album, *Disco Baby* (Avco, 1975), which included the transatlantic smash 'The Hustle'. He died on 6 July 1979.

McCOYS Best remembered for their 1965 US Number 1, 'Hang on Sloopy', the McCoys were formed in 1962 when Rick Zehringer (guitar), then 13, and his younger brother Randy (drums), 11, formed a high-school rock group with Randy Hobbs (bass) and Bobby Peterson (keyboards) in Union City, Indiana, and named it after a **Ventures** track, 'The McCoy'. They supported and backed leading acts in Dayton, Ohio, and three years later, after a few name-changes (Rick and the Raiders, Rick Z. Combo), reverted to the McCoys to record **Bert Berns'** 'Hang on Sloopy', a smash throughout America and Britain. Only one big hit followed – the Top 10 'Fever'/'Sorrow'. They lived down the teenage image with *Infinite McCoys*, and through regular appearances at Steve Paul's Scene in New York. Paul took over management in 1969, and later they became back-up for **Johnny Winter**, recording *Johnny Winter And . . .* with Rick producing. Rick, now Derringer, teamed up with Edgar Winter and debuted as a solo artist with *All American Boy* for Paul's Blue Sky label. See also **Rick Derringer**

McCRACKLIN, JIMMY Perhaps the most prolific if uneven R&B singer/pianist that the American West Coast produced, Jimmy McCracklin worked his way through just about every popular form of R&B in his thirty years of recording. Born in St Louis in 1931, he first recorded in the mid-Forties for the Los Angeles-based Globe label, eventually signing to Modern in 1949 and Swingtime in 1951. He cut his best sides over this period, usually hard-rocking blues highlighted by the nimble guitar work of Lafayette Thomas. As the Fifties progressed, McCracklin began to alter his style to suit the rock-'n'roll market. The trick worked, for while he was at Chess he cut his biggest-ever hit, 'The Walk', now regarded as a rock'n'roll classic. Apart from 'Just Got to Know', an R&B Number 2 in 1961 (Art-Tone), his record sales dropped off during the Sixties, culminating in an all-time low with Imperial where he cut dire material, like 'These Boots Are Made for Walking'. Fortunately,

Stax Records salvaged him in the Seventies, teaming him up with the Memphis Horns for an excellent album, *Yesterday Is Gone*, produced by Al Jackson and **Willie Mitchell**.

McCRAE, GEORGE Born in West Palm Beach, Florida, on 19 October 1944, George McCrae enjoyed overnight fame in 1974 on the strength of the transatlantic Number 1, 'Rock Your Baby', which helped launch that decade's disco craze. He played in a US Navy band called Astugi Express in the mid-Sixties and formed an unsuccessful partnership with his wife Gwen before retiring temporarily to study law. After a gap of two years, he returned to the recording studios by courtesy of Henry Stone's TK label, where he was placed with producer/writers Rick Finch and Harry Wayne Casey (K.C. of **K.C. and the Sunshine Band** repute). 'Rock Your Baby' was originally written by Finch and Casey for the Sunshine Band, but Casey's inability to sustain the high notes on the track prompted them to look elsewhere for a vocalist. McCrae's vocal resulted in a worldwide 15 million-seller, but his only chart success of note came in the UK, where 'I Can't Leave You Alone' (1974) and 'It's Been So Long' (1975) were both Top 10 hits. He later recorded for Gold Mountain, a US label distributed by A&M.

McDANIELS, GENE Born on 12 February 1935, in Kansas City, and a gospel singer from Omaha University and Conservatory of Music, Gene McDaniels joined Liberty in 1960. His stay there produced a string of melodic pop hits in the early Sixties including 'A Hundred Pounds of Clay' (a Number 3 in 1961, covered in Britain by Craig Douglas), 'A Tear', 'A Tower of Strength' (an American Top 5 record, covered in Britain by Frankie Vaughan), 'Chip Chip' (Top 10 in 1962), 'Point of No Return' and 'Spanish Lace', both Top 40 records in 1962. These songs, produced by **Snuff Garrett**, were provided by, among others, **Bacharach** and David, Goffin and King (see **Carole King**) and **Pomus and Shuman**. His moody version of 'Another Tear Falls' was the undoubted highspot of Dick Lester's *It's Trad, Dad*. With the dawn of the new black consciousness in the Seventies, McDaniels spurned the synthetic pop trappings of his past, and his records for Atlantic as Eugene McDaniels – including the album, *Outlaw* – dealt frankly and angrily with America's social problems.

McDONALD, JOE

McDONALD, JOE The founder of **Country Joe and the Fish**, Joe McDonald was born in El Monte, California, on 1 January 1942, and spent much of his youth listening to R&B on the radio and absorbing the political outlook of his parents, who were organizers for the local Communist Party. After enlisting in the Navy for a few years, McDonald's next major influence was the early work of **Bob Dylan**, and by 1965 he had formed his own group, Country Joe and the Fish, in Berkeley, successfully amalgamating electric music with the campus sensibility of dope, political protest, and personal explorations.

After the demise of the Fish, McDonald returned to his roots and recorded *Thinking of Woody Guthrie* (Vanguard, 1970), a superbly vital collection of the songs of America's seminal political folk singer, backed up by some of Nashville's finest session players, who also worked on his tribute to country music, *Tonight I'm Singing Just for You* (1971). *War War War* (1971), his next album, set Robert Service's World War I poems to music, providing a pertinent comment on both the Vietnam war and McDonald's own experience of the mystique and monotony of military life. It was folowed by *Incredible Live*, perhaps his most straightforwardly political record, made when he was working in the FTA (Free the Army) anti-war show with Donald Sutherland and Jane Fonda. In 1973 he released *Paris Sessions*, a collection of songs dealing primarily with the oppression of women and the manipulative powers of the media (including the rock-music industry). It was a powerful, and frequently painful, contrast with the zany exuberance of the songs that the Fish recorded, and confirmed McDonald's position as one of the few musicians who not merely survived the Sixties, but actually analysed and placed the failures of the Acid Test culture in a wider American context. *Paradise and Ocean View* (Fantasy, 1975) was a less impressive album. Subsequent solo albums included *Love is a Fire* (Fantasy, 1976), *Goodbye Blues* (1977) and *Rock'n'Roll from Planet Earth* (1978), while during 1977 he engineered a Fish reunion that resulted in the album *Reunion*, also on Fantasy.

McGARRIGLE, KATE AND ANNA

McGARRIGLE, KATE AND ANNA Canadian sisters Kate and Anna McGarrigle's marriage of folk and pop provided them with a recording career of their own, although in the US at least their songs became better known when covered by other artists such as **Linda Ronstadt**.

The sisters grew up bilingual in Montreal (Kate was born on 6 February 1946 and Anna on 4 December 1944) and in the late Sixties were part of the Mountain City Four, a group commissioned by the National Film Board of Canada to write the score for the film *Helicopter Canada*. Both sisters continued to write songs, Kate writing for **Maria Muldaur** while Anna wrote, for Linda Ronstadt, 'Heart Like a Wheel', the title track of a multi-platinum album. In 1973, Kate married fellow singer/songwriter **Loudon Wainwright III**.

Their songwriting talents led to Warner Brothers flying the sisters to California to record their warm, romantic debut album *Kate and Anna McGarrigle* (1976), which was an instant critical success but failed to win over radio programmers, a situation that continues to exist. Successive albums on Warners and then *Love Over and Over* (1983) on Polydor, supported by occasional tours, failed to break them into the US mainstream, although *French Record* (1981), a compilation of material in French, had been a bestseller in Canada.

The sisters' striking and very attractive harmonies are complemented by their playing on keyboards, banjo, guitar and accordion; Kate also plays violin. In the mid-Eighties their sister Jane (born 26 April 1941) joined them for live performances, singing and playing keyboards. She has recorded with her sisters, but her principal role is to act as their business manager.

McGHEE, BROWNIE

McGHEE, BROWNIE See **Terry, Sonny, and McGhee, Brownie**

McGUINN, ROGER

McGUINN, ROGER After the demise of the **Byrds** in 1972, Roger McGuinn – born James Joseph McGuinn on 13 July 1942, in Chicago (he changed his name to Roger in 1968) – embarked on a solo career. His first solo album, *Roger McGuinn* (Columbia), was released in 1973, hot on the heels of the unspectacular *Byrds* reunion album (which featured the five original members of the group). *Peace on You* appeared in 1974 and after a British tour that same year he formed a band consisting of ex-members of Shiloh and the Stone Canyon Band – Steve Love, Richard Bowden, Greg Attaway and David Lovelace – and recorded *Roger McGuinn and Band* (1975) with them. He toured with Dylan's Rolling Thunder revue in 1976 and cut *Cardiff Rose* with **Mick Ronson**

producing. *Thunderbyrd* followed in 1977 – its tracks including McGuinn covers of **Peter Frampton**'s 'All Night Long', **George Jones**' 'Why Baby Why' and **Tom Petty**'s 'American Girl' – and in 1978 he joined forces once again with **Gene Clark** and **Chris Hillman** for a European tour and the albums *McGuinn, Clark and Hillman* (1979) and *City* (1980). A collaboration with Hillman, *McGuinn Hillman*, was released in 1981. McGuinn toured the US as a solo act in 1983–4 and guested on the **Beach Boys**' 25th anniversary album in 1986, adding his immaculate 12-string guitar work to a version of 'California Dreamin''.

McGUINNESS FLINT

McGUINNESS FLINT McGuinness Flint was a band formed in 1969 by ex-**Manfred Mann** bassist Tom McGuinness (born 2 December 1941) and former **John Mayall** drummer Hughie Flint (15 March 1942). With singer Dennis Coulson and multi-instrumentalists and songwriters Benny **Gallagher** and Graham **Lyle**, they had considerable success with their thoughtful blend of good-time, country and folk music. 'When I'm Dead and Gone' (Capitol, 1970) and 'Malt and Barley Blues' (1971) both entered the Top 5 in Britain. Soon after, Gallagher and Lyle left and were replaced by bass player Dixie Dean. *Lo and Behold* (DJM, 1972) was a selection of obscure **Dylan** material, continuing the Manfred Mann tradition of recording little-known Dylan songs. In 1973, Coulson left to try a solo career and the group added Lou Stonebridge (keyboards, vocals) and Jim Evans (pedal steel, fiddle). The group's final album, *C'est La Vie* (Bronze, 1974) was an interesting collection of original songs, produced by veteran session guitarist Big Jim Sullivan. Gallagher and Lyle subsequently enjoyed some success as a performing and songwriting duo. See also **Gallagher and Lyle**

McGUIRE, BARRY

McGUIRE, BARRY The kingpin of the brief protest pop phase of the mid-Sixties, Barry McGuire was born in Oklahoma City on 15 October 1937. He was the gruff lead voice on the New Christy Minstrels' US hits 'Green Green' and 'Saturday Night' (Columbia, 1963), but left them in 1964 and headed out to California. At the **Byrds'** club debut at Ciro's in Los Angeles, he met producer/entrepreneur **Lou Adler** and songwriter **P.F. Sloan**; in autumn 1965 he recorded Sloan's 'Eve of Destruction' – the archetypal protest song – for Adler's Dunhill label. A rushed album of mainly **Dylan** and

Sloan's imitatory Dylan material proceded *This Precious Time*, for which Adler brought the future **Mamas and the Papas** to the sessions. The Mamas and the Papas' 'California Dreamin' is the same as McGuire's hit with Denny Doherty's voice substituted for McGuire's. His finest album was *Barry McGuire and the Doctor* (1969), after which he discovered salvation in Christianity – and the musical inspiration for albums like *Seeds* and *Lighten Up* for the religious Myrrh label.

MACK, LONNIE

Born in Harrisburg, Indiana, in 1941, Lonnie Mack had just one big hit, and that was a fluke. In the summer of 1963, at the end of someone else's session, he cut an instrumental version of Chuck Berry's 'Memphis'. His tense, rhythmic guitar style propelled it straight into the US Top 10 on the Fraternity label and some lesser selling releases, a fine album and a few months of fame all followed. In 1969, he tried again, recording three albums for Elektra (his 1963 album was also re-released). His voice still carried the fullness and conviction of the gospel singer and his guitar work was still roadhouse tough – his music was a unique and fully realized blend of black music (gospel, blues and soul) with a country tinge, best exemplified by such tracks as 'Why', 'What Kind of World is This' and 'Where There's a Will There's a Way'. A shy, retiring man with none of the flash (or drive) essential for stardom, he dropped out of the music business, apparently for religious reasons. Though he returned to Indiana to drive a truck for a while, he also recorded singles for various labels in the Seventies, including the Troy Seals-produced 'Highway 56' (Roulette, 1975).

McKENZIE, SCOTT

Scott McKenzie will eternally be remembered for the flower-power anthem of 1967, 'San Francisco (Be Sure to Wear Some Flowers in Your Hair)'. He was born on 1 October 1944, in Arlington, Virginia, and served his musical apprenticeship in the folk clubs of the East Coast. He joined the Journeymen in 1963, alongside John Phillips; when Phillips moved west to California to start the **Mamas and the Papas**, McKenzie stayed in New York and recorded a few ballads for Capitol. By early 1967, folk-rock had become a booming industry in Los Angeles and Phillips persuaded McKenzie to come out and join in. The Phillips-produced 'No, No, No, No, No', (Epic, 1967) established McKenzie's ability within

the genre and soon thereafter he appeared on **Lou Adler**'s newly formed Ode Records with Phillips' 'San Francisco (Be Sure to Wear Some Flowers in Your Hair)'. Perhaps the ultimate hippie eulogy, it was a heart-tugging production with a genuine innocence and sense of wonder that inspired thousands of kids to make pilgrimages to San Francisco when it became an international hit. According to interviews, McKenzie was apparently very sincere in his flower philosophy, which may also explain why he stopped recording when the hippie era ended save for a lack-lustre country-rock album *Stained Glass Morning* (Ode, 1970) three years later.

McLAREN, MALCOLM

Coming from an art school background, Malcolm McLaren joined the ranks of the great rock entrepreneurs when he became the instrumental force in the formation of the **Sex Pistols**. Since then he has been involved in countless other band projects as well as a lucrative solo recording career and, in the process, gained a reputation as something of a sharp operator and a shrewd arbiter of tastes and trends.

Born in London in 1947, he had his first serious brushes with music in the Fifties and early Sixties, becoming an aficionado of rock'n'roll. From that point on, McLaren has been a great believer in the potency of rock'n'roll, especially as a means of stepping outside the boundaries of normal society. He built up a political consciousness while at various art schools and allied himself with Situationism, a surrealist/libertarian art movement that engineered 'situations' to expose social repression. An equally bizarre involvement was with a West London anarchist group called King Mob who once invaded Selfridges, a large department store in London, dressed as Father Christmases and gave away free gifts to the customers. This background later enabled him to engineer the stunts that gave the Sex Pistols so much publicity.

In 1971 McLaren opened a clothes shop on the Kings Road with his girlfriend, designer Vivienne Westwood, but his interest in music was rekindled by the visit to London in 1973 of US band the **New York Dolls**. He followed them to New York and managed them there for six months in 1974, dressing them in shiny red leather, draping communist flags over the stage and providing a backdrop of Chairman Mao. By 1975 he was back at the shop, now named Sex and selling a selection of bondage clothing and rubberware. It

was an important return, because it was there that he met the boys that would become the Pistols, and became aware that something like punk was on its way.

After McLaren's fantastic achievements with the Sex Pistols, his courting of controversy, his orchestration of their destructive image and his ability to manipulate record companies, he became a notorious character, treated with suspicion but also with a great deal of respect. His innate ability to sense underlying changes of taste helped Adam and the Ants (*see* **Adam Ant**) find success when he created their new, swashbuckling image – for a fee. He later also created **Bow Wow Wow**, discovering teenage vocalist Annabella Lwin in a local launderette, and then pitched the group for the adolescent market, which he correctly predicted would become the most important for pop music.

In the early Eighties McLaren began to work with the scratchers, breakers and rappers of New York (again before their widespread popularity), then moved on to American traditional country and gospel forms, musical wanderings that culminated in his first solo album *Duck Rock* (1983), and two big UK single hits, 'Buffalo Gals' and 'Double Dutch'. In 1985 he fused rock with opera in the 'Madame Butterfly' single, an experiment that was indicative of his continuing quest for the new and unconventional.

Malcolm McLaren, cultivating rock entrepreneurship as a creative art

McLAUGHLIN, JOHN Jazz-rock guitarist John McLaughlin was born on 4 January 1942 in Yorkshire, and began playing the guitar at the age of 11. During the Sixties he played with various London jazz and rock combos, including the **Graham Bond** Organisation (which included **Jack Bruce** and **Ginger Baker**) and released his first solo album, *Extrapolation* (Polydor) in 1969. McLaughlin's guitar style utilized elements from blues, jazz, and Eastern musical modes. He combined a dazzlingly fast technique with an ability to use space and unexpected chord configurations in his solos. In 1969 McLaughlin moved to New York; the day after his arrival he played on **Miles Davis**' *In a Silent Way* sessions. McLaughlin's 'open-ended' guitar sound was well matched to the musical areas Davis was beginning to explore: more metrically free, using a dense variety of sound textures emphasized by electronic manipulation. On Davis' *Bitches' Brew* (1970) albums, McLaughlin developed a more integrated style fusing blues/rock riffs with spiralling solos. On Carla Bley's jazz opera *Escalator Over the Hill* (1971), McLaughlin's abrasive guitar work (again accompanied by Jack Bruce) was played off against the sparse, Eastern texture of Don Cherry's trumpet work.

In 1972, McLaughlin formed his own group, the **Mahavishnu Orchestra**, which was extremely successful both critically and commercially. Its identity was dominated by McLaughlin's adherence to the philosophy of Sri Chinmoy, a Bengali mystic. In 1974, he recorded an intermittently powerful album with Carlos **Santana**, *Love Devotion Surrender* (Columbia), dedicated to Sri Chinmoy and strongly influenced by the work of the late John Coltrane. He later formed a Mahavishnu Mark II and recorded *Apocalypse* (1974), *Visions of the Emerald Beyond* (1975) and *Inner Worlds* (1976). In the late Seventies, he formed Shakti with Indian musicians and the One Truth Band, after which he returned to his pre-Mahavishnu state, appearing with other superstars of jazz-rock and issuing occasional (and mostly acoustic) albums under his own name. *See also* **Mahavishnu Orchestra**

McLEAN, DON Born in New Rochelle, New York on 2 October 1945, Don McLean became an overnight success in late 1971 with the release of his epic lament for the state of rock, 'American Pie', which reached Number 1 in the US and Number 2 in the UK.

He had been a folk singer since 1963 and in 1969 accompanied **Pete Seeger**, Louis Killen, Gordon Bok and a crew of musicians on the Hudson River sloop, *Clearwater*, in a campaign to clean up the Hudson River. His first album for the United Artists subsidiary Mediarts, *Tapestry*, paved the way for *American Pie* (1972). McLean followed up his sudden fame by touring all over the world. He was called awkward, over-emotional, unco-operative, but it was basically a refusal to change his music that characterized McLean. His interest was in folk music, and when the record company wanted a follow-up to his second international hit single, 'Vincent' (1972), McLean instead put out the vitriolic *Don McLean* and an album of standards, *Playin' Favourites* (both 1973). *Homeless Brother* (1974) saw McLean returning to a more traditional notion of folk in his songs (the celebration/examination of the hobo) and instrumentation (banjo and acoustic guitar). After one more album, *Solo* (1976), McLean left UA for Arista, for whom he recorded one album, *Prime Time* (1977). By 1981, he was recording for Millennium and enjoying a chart revival – a version of **Roy Orbison**'s 'Crying' gave him a UK Number 1 and a Number 5 in the US, where 'Since I Don't Have You' and 'Castles in the Air' were also Top 40 hits.

McNEELY, BIG JAY His fame as a rock'n'roll contortionist – Big Jay was one of the first to play tenor sax lying on his back – went hand in hand with his brash, swinging, coarse-toned style. Born Cecil McNeely on 29 April 1928, he recorded for Exclusive in 1946 and for Savoy in 1949, when 'Deacon's Hop' made the R&B charts. His best-known composition was 'There Is Something on Your Mind', a Number 5 R&B hit in 1959, which also reached the national pop charts. This often-revived soul ballad was an even bigger hit for New Orleans singer Bobby Marchan in 1960. The original version featured Little Sonny Warner, the McNeely band's vocalist, and was released on Hunter Hancock's Swingin' label. McNeely also recorded for Aladdin, Federal and Warner Brothers.

McPHATTER, CLYDE The son of a Baptist minister, Clyde McPhatter was born on 15 November 1933, in Durham, North Carolina, and formed a gospel group (the Mount Lebanon Singers) at the age of 14. He entered the secular field in 1950, joining Billy Ward's **Dominoes** as lead tenor, record-

ing successfully for Federal. Leaving in 1953, he formed the **Drifters** and his distinctive high-tenor lead is evident on such hits as 'Money Honey' and 'White Christmas'. Drafted into the USAF in 1954, Clyde embarked on a solo career with Atlantic on discharge in 1956, enjoying a string of R&B best-sellers including 'Treasure of Love' (also a British hit), 'Without Love', and the million-selling 'A Lover's Question'.

He signed with MGM in 1959, but one year and four minor hits later moved to Mercury, soon finding himself in the upper reaches of the charts with 'Ta Ta'. In 1962 the jumping, percussive 'Lover Please' was an American Top 10 hit. Two more smaller hits followed – Mercury also released seven McPhatter albums over three years – before he switched to Amy in 1966, recording five pleasant but unsuccessful singles. The following year Clyde moved to London, England, but two 1968 Decca sessions failed to find a winning formula: 'Denver', a solitary 1969 disc on B&C, was well-received but flopped, and he was obliged to return to America in 1970 when his work-permit expired. Clyde Otis persuaded American Decca to record him, and a fine but unsuccessful album resulted. He died in June 1972. Jerry Wexler's was the best epitaph: 'The great, unique soul singer of all time.'

McTELL, RALPH Although the success of his song 'The Streets of London' has tended to overshadow the rest of his work, Ralph McTell was one of the best songwriters to emerge from the British folk revival of the early Sixties. Born Ralph May on 3 December 1944 in Farnborough, Kent, he took his new surname from country-blues singer/guitarist Blind Willie McTell, and played blues and ragtime guitar in the London clubs before cutting his first album, *Eight Frames a Second*, for Transatlantic in 1968. *Spiral Staircase* followed a year later and featured his original recording of 'The Streets of London'. By the time McTell moved to Paramount/Famous in 1971, he had completed the transition from folk-singer to a singer/songwriter of intelligence and commitment. *You Well-Meaning Brought Me Here* was, in some ways, his best album. Produced by Gus Dudgeon, it contained songs dealing with militarism and political commitment, as well as the whimsy of 'Old Brown Dog'.

Moving to Reprise, McTell made *Not Till Tomorrow* (1972), which included the perceptive 'Zimmerman Blues'. By

1975, after two more albums, a successful national tour and a surprise Number 2 UK hit with a strings-laden re-recording of 'The Streets of London', McTell was given a major American launch by Warner Brothers, the relative failure of which left him disillusioned and interested only in returning to England. Back in the UK by 1977, he once again played the folk clubs and small-scale concerts. He also became a familiar figure on children's television, appearing in and writing songs for *Alphabet Zoo* and *Tickle on the Tum*. In 1985, he made a minor impression on the UK album chart with *At the End of the Perfect Day* (Telstar), a made-for-TV album that featured versions of songs by **Lennon** and **McCartney**, Roger Whittaker, **Paul Simon** and others, and yet another re-recording of 'The Streets of London'.

MADNESS A product of the ska revival prompted by the emergence of 2-Tone, Madness became one of the most successful British chart acts of the early Eighties. Their 'nutty sound', a highly individualistic brand of bluebeat-based dance pop, allied with their infectious sense of humour and ability to make consistently cheap and hilarious videos, helped them score a long run of hit singles (nineteen consecutive Top 20 hits between '79 and '84) and albums.

Together in one form or another since 1976, the original group, consisting of Lee Thompson (sax), Mike Barson (keyboards), Chris Foreman (guitar) and Carl 'Chas Smash' Smyth (vocals) performed first as Morris and the Minors and later as the Invaders. With the arrival of Suggs (Graham McPherson) on lead vocals, they changed their name to Madness (after a **Prince Buster** song) in 1978 and added Daniel 'Woody' Woodgate (drums) and Mark 'Bedders' Bedford to the line-up.

After gigging around North London for a while, they met Jerry Dammers, and when the **Specials** started the 2-Tone label in 1979, they released Madness' first single, a manic ska knees-up called 'The Prince'. It peaked at Number 16 and inspired Dave Robinson of Stiff (after having them play at his wedding reception) to sign them up in the face of strong competition from the majors. Madness' first Stiff single and album were called 'One Step Beyond', and both sold well, especially after the band had teamed up with the Specials and impressed young audiences with their energetic live shows on the 2-Tone tour. This was the beginning of Madness' runaway commercial success.

The manic energy of Madness' live performances and videos won them a large following, but more sophisticated music kept them at the top

In 1981 they made *Take It or Leave It* (scripted and directed by Dave Robinson), a documentary-style profile of Madness' early days in which the members of the band all played themselves. That year they also went on the 'Absolutely Madness One Step Beyond Far East Tour' which proved a tremendous success and confirmed their popularity down under.

The year 1982 saw the release of *Complete Madness*, their greatest hits compilation, which went gold on advance orders and spawned the enormously popular single, 'House of Fun'. It was Madness' twelfth consecutive hit but only their first Number 1; the album and single occupied the top UK chart spot simultaneously. In 1983 their success story continued and they finally cracked the US market, achieving a Number 7 hit with 'Our House'. The same year, Mike Barson announced his departure from the band to settle into

quiet domesticity in Amsterdam with his Dutch wife Sandra.

Keep Moving, Madness' sixth album, was released in February 1984 and was the last to feature Barson, ex-**Squeeze** and Ace keyboards man Paul Carrack being recruited for their US dates in March. Shortly afterwards, in May, came the end of Madness' five year collaboration with Stiff, a partnership that had spawned eighteen UK Top 20 singles, most notably 'Baggy Trousers', 'Embarrassment' and 'House of Fun', and six Top 10 albums, including the outstanding *Absolutely*.

The same year Madness founded their own Zarjazz label and signed a marketing and distribution deal with Virgin. The first release was 'Listen to Your Father' by **Feargal Sharkey**, in October, and they started off 1985 with the Fink Brothers' 'Mutants in Mega City One' (a Suggs and Carl Smyth pseudonym). In February they released a single, 'Starvation', Zarjazz's own contribution to the Ethiopian famine relief cause, featuring various names from the ska, reggae and jazz fields, and later in the year Madness released their seventh album *Mad Not Mad*. The LP made the charts but did not have the major success of its predecessors, although it produced the hit singles 'Yesterday's Men', 'Uncle Sam' and their cover of **Scritti Politti**'s 'The Sweetest Girl', which entered the UK charts early in 1986 as their twenty-second consecutive hit. These failed to burn a trail into the uppermost reaches of the charts, however, suggesting that Madness had reached a crucial point in their career. For the first time they were finding it difficult to sustain the outstanding level of their success, and later that year, after a string of failed hit singles, and continued dissatisfaction with the development of an album in progress, the band split up.

MADONNA Born on 16 August 1959 in Rochester, Michigan, Madonna Louise Ciccone was the most successful female pop singer of the mid-Eighties, and the undoubted pop phenomenon of 1985. Sheer hard work and her versatility as a dancer, singer and actress won Madonna legions of admirers and imitators and enabled her to sell enormous quantities of records all over the world.

In high school, Madonna had shown a talent for ballet which won her a dance scholarship to the University of Michigan. But her hunger for success was such that she left after a year for New York and continued her dance training while working as a waitress to support herself. Anxious to make a career, she made a film, posed for nude pictures and played in a series of rock bands (in one of which she was the drummer).

Eventually in 1982 she recorded some songs that borrowed heavily from the New York club sound, an aggressive brand of pop with a strong dance beat. Mark Kamins, a New York club DJ and Madonna's lover of the time, took the tape round the record companies, and she signed a deal with Sire/ Warners. The first two singles, 'Everybody' and 'Physical Attraction', made no impression on the US charts but sold well among dance audiences. Her debut album, *Madonna*, was released in June 1983, and soon after the single, 'Holiday'.

With 'Holiday', Madonna finally conquered the US Top 40, reaching Number 16 in December '83, but it wasn't until the fourth single, the mildly pornographic 'Burnin' Up', that a Madonna video appeared on MTV and exposed her lacy, tacky sex-kitten image to a large audience. After that her success seemed to be assured, sales of her first album passing the million mark and spawning six singles. 'Holiday' was also a hit in the UK, and 1984 proved to be a good year for Madonna on both sides of the Atlantic.

It was in 1985, however, that Madonna really came to the fore. Her second album, *Like a Virgin* and the single of the same name made it into the US charts in January and broke her into the superstar bracket in Europe. Both topped the charts all over the world paving the way for a long string of hit singles (most notably the irrepressible party record 'Into the Groove'), five of which came from the album. In the UK Madonna had five singles in the Top 40 and three in the Top 10, all at the same time, and in the US she repeated the feat with six in the Top 40. A memorable appearance on Live Aid (*see* **Band Aid**) came just at the time when Madonna-fever had reached a high, with teenage lookalikes packed in the audience, and the shops swamped with lace, lingerie and trashy jewellery.

The same year Madonna married Hollywood brat-pack actor Sean Penn, making front-page news everywhere, providing the celebrity story of the year and confirming her status as a superstar. She never made any secret of her quest for fame, irrespective of the field, and it seemed that her ambitions as an actress, especially after the success of the film *Desperately Seeking Susan*, would be likely to push her singing career into the background. Her next film, however, *Shanghai Surprise*, which she made with her husband, was a critical failure. This set-back had no effect on her singing career; her third album, *True Blue*, was released in 1986 and continued her chart success.

Desperately seeking success: Madonna projected a streetwise sexuality that had virtually never been exploited by earlier female singers

MAGAZINE After a stint as vocalist with the **Buzzcocks, Howard Devoto** formed five-piece band Magazine in his hometown of Manchester in 1977, in the thick of the punk explosion. He was joined by John McGeogh (guitar), John Doyle (drums), Barry Adamson (bass) and Dave Formula (keyboards). Their debut single, 'Shot By Both Sides', is one of the finest songs to have come out of that era and was described in *Rolling Stone* as 'the best rock'n'roll record of 1978, punk or otherwise'.

Universal critical acclaim came again with the release soon afterwards of the LP *Real Life*, and although both album and single were only minor commercial successes, they established Magazine, at least as far as the critics were concerned, as one of the most important bands of the time. With such a weight on their shoulders, it was no surprise that the second album, *Secondhand Daylight* (1979), received terrible treatment at the hands of the reviewers, despite its considerable polish and its efforts to experiment within the confines of popular music.

During this time, the articulate Devoto became one of the premiere figures of the post-punk fraternity, and his opinions on a number of issues were widely sought by the UK music press. His marked reluctance to assume the role of spokesman, however, generated a great deal of hostility and bad press from a headline-hungry music media.

Magazine released their third album, *The Correct Use of Soap*, in 1980, and it marked their return to critical favour with a host of good reviews. That year they successfully toured the UK, the US, Europe, New Zealand and Australia, and while on the latter leg of the tour, they recorded the excellent live set *Play* which was rush-released in December.

Earlier, McGeogh had left the band (later to join **Siouxsie and the Banshees**) and was temporarily replaced by ex-**Ultravox** man Robin Simon for the recording of the live album. Ben Mandelsen, an old friend of Devoto's, finally became the full-time guitarist. In 1981, this line-up produced *Magic, Murder and the Weather*, an album that sustained Magazine's position as one of the most influential bands to have come out of the punk period. Just before its release, however, Devoto announced that he was leaving the group to pursue his own solo interests; this was a move that effectively meant the demise of the band, since the remaining members decided not to continue operating under the name Magazine.

MAHAL, TAJ One of the new breed of late Sixties/early Seventies intellectual/cosmic bluesmen, Taj Mahal was born Henry St Clair Fredericks of Caribbean descent in New York City on 17 May 1942. He grew up under the influence of Marcus Garvey and of Haile Selassie rather than **Muddy Waters** and **Howlin' Wolf**, eventually taking a degree in animal husbandry at the University of Massachusetts and moving to California. His debut album for Columbia in 1967, *Taj Mahal*, none the less highlighted a driving, electric blues-band that included such notables as **Ry Cooder** and Jesse Ed Davis who had been with him in the Rising Sons. His two best singles came from the same period: 'Statesboro' Blues' and 'Give Your Woman What She Wants'. He subsequently cut nine albums for Columbia, each one more ethnic in approach and many featuring acoustic African instruments. He moved to Warner Brothers in 1976 and later recorded for Crystal Clear and Margaret. He wrote the scores for the Seventies films *Sounder* and *Brothers*.

MAHAVISHNU ORCHESTRA Formed in 1972 by guitarist **John McLaughlin** (Mahavishnu being the name that McLaughlin was given by his religious adviser Sri Chinmoy), the Orchestra swiftly became the most successful fusion, commercially and critically, of jazz and rock. Their ability to integrate virtuoso solo work within a tightly disciplined instrumental framework made their second album, *Birds of Fire* (Columbia), one of the few masterpieces of this rather nebulous genre. The Orchestra featured the violin of Jerry Goodman (ex-Flock), the pyrotechnically dazzling drumming of Billy Cobham, and **Jan Hammer**'s keyboard and synthesizer work, but was dominated by McLaughlin whose aura of burning spiritual zeal was conveyed by superfast tempos and an *ethereal* heavy metal sound. The original group disbanded in 1974, and was replaced by a larger line-up, including violin maestro Jean-Luc Ponty. The last album under the Mahavishnu name was *Inner Worlds* (1976). *See also* **Jazz-rock**; **John McLaughlin**

MAMAS AND THE PAPAS The Mamas and the Papas produced music that, for some, was the epitome of high-class folk-rock, a perfect merging of California beat and Greenwich Village melody. But despite their beginnings in the New York club scene of the early Sixties and their close association with the **Lovin' Spoonful**, their musical style owed little to the American folk and blues tradition and was more a contrived product of shrewd pop thinking on the part of leader John Phillips (born in Parris Island, South Carolina, on 30 August 1935) and their producer/manager **Lou Adler**. Their policy was to match the sweet harmonies of Phillips, his wife Michelle (née Gilliam, born in Long Beach, California on 6 April 1944), **Cass Elliott** (born in Alexandria, Virginia, on 19 September 1943) and Denny Doherty (born in Halifax, Nova Scotia, on 29 November 1941) with a rock backing and to market them in terms of their hippie image – which, though fairly common among solo performers, was almost unheard of in groups.

Most of the Mamas and the Papas' material was written by John and Michelle Phillips, including their breakthrough hit 'California Dreamin'' (released on Adler's Dunhill label in 1966), which rivalled another of John's compositions – 'San Francisco' for **Scott McKenzie** – as a popularizer of the Californian flower-power philosophy. A dozen more hits followed in the next two years, including 'Monday Monday', 'I Saw Her Again Last Night', a revival of the **Shirelles**' 'Dedicated to the One I Love' and 'Creeque Alley', the lyrics of which told the story of the group from Cass and Denny's days alongside Zal Yanovsky and **John Sebastian** (both later of the Lovin' Spoonful) in folk group the Mugwumps. After a while, however, their records began to sound pedestrian, too much like the Ray Conniff cover versions of their songs, and in 1968 they finally disbanded. Cass Elliott and Denny Doherty went solo, with varying degrees of success; John made an intriguing solo album, *The Wolfking of LA* (1970), and joined the rock jet set with his wife Michelle, who became a film actress. The group re-formed briefly in 1971 and again ten years later – Cass having died and the Phillipses having divorced in the meantime – John re-launched the group with Spanky Macfarlane from **Spanky and Our Gang** taking Cass' place. *See also* **Cass Elliott**

MAN South Wales' leading progressive rock outfit of the early and mid-Seventies, Man grew out of a Swansea group called the Bystanders who first came together in 1965 with a line-up of Jeff Jones (drums), Clive John (keyboards), Mickey Jones (guitar) and Ray Williams (bass). The Bystanders recorded for Piccadilly, a subsidiary of

Pye, between 1966 and 1968, and had one small success in 1967 with '98.6', which reached Number 45 in the UK. In 1968, with guitarist Deke Leonard (formerly with Dream) joining, they rechristened themselves Man and made their recording debut under that name with *Revelation* (Pye). Williams and Jeff Jones left in 1970 and were replaced by Martin Ace and Terry Williams, though Ace in turn left in 1970; Phil Ryan (keyboards) and Will Youatt (bass) joined in 1972. The band recorded prolifically during the Seventies, for Pye, Dawn, United Artists and (from 1975 onwards) for MCA, and Leonard cut the solo album *Iceberg* for United Artists in 1972. Although never a major concert attraction in the UK, Man were popular with European audiences and won a sizeable following in the US with the release of *Slow Motion* in 1974. They toured the UK in 1975 with John Cippolina of **Quicksilver Messenger Service** in support, and the live album *Maximum Darkness* resulted. The band broke up in early 1977. Terry Williams joined **Dave Edmunds'** Rockpile.

MANASSAS *See* **Stephen Stills**

MANDEL, HARVEY Blues guitarist Harvey Mandel was born in Detroit on 11 March 1945, but spent his formative years in Chicago, where he learnt guitar in similar clubs to those nurturing the then nascent **Paul Butterfield/Mike Bloomfield** school of white blues. Since 1968, he has made solo albums for Philips, Ovation, Dawn and Vanguard, as well as playing at various times during the late Sixties and early Seventies with **Canned Heat** and the ever-changing **John Mayall**'s Bluesbreakers. As a session guitarist, he has played on records by such diverse talents as the **Ventures** and **Love**, as well as more obvious contemporaries like Charlie Musselwhite and **Barry Goldberg**. *Cristo Redentor* (Philips, 1968) remains his finest solo work.

MANFRED MANN One of the most commercially successful groups to emerge from London's blossoming R&B club scene in the mid-Sixties, Manfred Mann took their name from their South African-born leader and founder. He formed the Mann-Hugg Blues Brothers in 1962 with Mike Hugg: they had played in the same jazz quartet, on piano and vibes respectively, at a Butlin's holiday camp that summer. Mann (born Michael Lubowitz on 21 October 1940) took up organ, Hugg (11 March 1940) swapped to drums, and with **Paul Jones** (vocals, harmonica, born on 24 February 1942), Mike Vickers (alto, clarinet, born on 18 April 1941), and Dave Richmond (bass), dropped jazz for R&B. An immediate success on the rapidly expanding R&B club circuit, they made their first single, 'Why Should We Not?' (HMV), in July 1963. Their third release, '5-4-3-2-1', in January 1964, coincided with Richmond's replacement by Tom McGuinness (2 December 1941 in London); its gimmicky pop qualities made it the theme tune of British television's *Ready Steady Go!* and a big hit. Thereafter Manfred Mann's A-sides – e.g. 'Do Wah Diddy', 'Pretty Flamingo' (both British Number Ones) – stuck to a strong pop formula with a consistent success unaffected by the departure of Vickers – McGuinness switched to lead and was replaced by **Jack Bruce** on bass – at the end of 1965, the brief addition of a brass section (Lyn Dobson and Henry Lowther), and the substitution of **Mike d'Abo** from A Band Of Angels for Paul Jones and Klaus Voorman for Bruce, who left after six months for **Cream**. No material was exempt from the Manfred touch and the group's string of 15 British hits included two **Dylan** numbers, 'Just Like a Woman' and 'The Mighty Quinn' (a Number 1). After the group split in 1969, Mann and Hugg stayed together for a while in Manfred Mann Chapter III, then Mann formed his eponymous Earth Band in 1971. *See also* **Paul Jones**; **McGuinness Flint**; **Manfred Mann's Earth Band**

Paul Jones, seen here in the recording studio, contributed vocals and harmonica to the early Manfred Mann sound

MANFRED MANN'S EARTH BAND After the demise of the group Manfred Mann Chapter III (see **Manfred Mann**) in 1971, Mann switched to a heavier rock format to put together a new outfit, the Earth Band.

Mann was joined by Mick Rogers (vocals/guitar), Colin Pattenden (bass) and Chris Slade (drums) and they set about touring extensively, concentrating on the US. Apart from one UK hit single, 'Joybringer' in 1973, the Earth Band had a lean time in the charts until 1976 when they scored a US Number 1 with a version of **Bruce Springsteen**'s 'Blinded by the Light', prompting a boost in sales for the album *The Roaring Silence*. The single also reached Number 6 in the UK as did 'Davy's on the Road Again' in 1978, their last hit of any magnitude. Despite further LP releases leading up to *Somewhere in Afrika* (1983) and the live set *Budapest* (1984), they were unable to re-enter the charts. *See also* **Manfred Mann**

MANHATTAN TRANSFER

Vocal harmony fourpiece Manhattan Transfer graduated from the New York cabaret scene to the international stage with a unique, eclectic repertoire that spanned swing, doo-wop, jazz and Sixties pop styles.

Formed in 1972 by Tim Hauser and Alan Paul, they were joined by Janis Siegel and Laurel Masse and quickly became a favourite New York cabaret act. In 1975, they released an album, *Manhattan Transfer*, which contained their first US hit single, 'Operator' and were immediately offered a TV series. Surprisingly, they failed to capitalize on this exposure and turned their attention to Europe. 'Tuxedo Junction' was a UK Top 30 hit in 1976 and 'Chanson d'Amour', the song that made their international reputation, was a Number 1 the next year.

Masse left in 1979 to be replaced by Cheryl Bentyne, and her arrival saw an updating of the group's image, introducing a jazz-rock feel as heard on the single 'Twilight Zone/Twilight Tone', which returned Manhattan Transfer to the US charts in 1980. They scored their biggest US hit single in 1981 with a cover of 'The Boy from New York City' (Number 7), yet despite continuing popularity as a live act and several Grammy awards over the years, they have never managed to sustain a long-term, regular presence in the charts.

In 1985, Manhattan Transfer released their ninth album, *Vocalese*, which featured a host of jazz musicians and indicated a new, heavily jazz-oriented direction for the band.

MANHATTANS Formed in Jersey City in 1964, the Manhattans were George 'Smitty' Smith, Winfred 'Blue' Lovett (born in 1940), Sonny Bivins (1941), Kenny Kelly (1948), and Richard Taylor (1939). Spotted at an Apollo Theater talent contest, the group were signed to Carnival Records and launched into a successful singles career, interspersing doo-wop ballads with Motown dance beat discs. R&B hits included 'I Wanna Be (Your Everything)' (1965) and 'Can I' (1966). Moving to King's Deluxe label, more soul hits occurred like the lovely 'If My Heart Could Speak' (1970) before tragedy struck – Smith, whose poignant lead shaped the group's sound, died of spinal meningitis in 1970. But Gerald Alston (born in 1951) proved a fine replacement, singing on the beautiful, Philadelphia-recorded 'There's No Me Without You' (1974) and 'Hurt' (1975) – both American hits on Columbia. The Manhattans are unquestionably sweetly superior soul music, as shown by their last two major US hits, 'Kiss and Say Goodbye' (1976, a Number 1) and 'Shining Star' (1980, a Number 5).

MANN, BARRY Leading Sixties pop songwriter Barry Mann was born on 9 February 1939, in Brooklyn, New York. A would-be architect, he became a songwriter when Paul Case, the general manager of the Aberbach family-owned Hill and Range Music, put one of Mann's first songs on the flip of Bobby Pedrick's 'White Bucks and Saddle Shoes' on Big Top – which was affiliated to Hill and Range – in 1958.

In 1961, Mann married Cynthia Weil, with whom he was to write most of his hits, and turned briefly to recording when his own 'Who Put the Bomp' – with the bomp supplied by New York session singer, Ronald Bright – became a US Top 10 hit on ABC in the summer of that year. Further records failed, as did his return to recording when, in the wake of the success of **Carole King**, he attempted a comeback with solo albums in 1971 and 1975.

However, if Mann's recording career was unspectacular, he and Cynthia Weil were one of the most successful non-performing American songwriting teams of the Sixties. In the years 1959–70 – on his own, with Cynthia Weil, and with others – Mann wrote nearly fifty Hot 100 records – only failing to score in 1967. They included: 'Bless You' (for **Tony Orlando**, 1961), 'Uptown' (the **Crystals**, 1962), 'On Broadway' (the **Drifters**, 1963), 'I'm Gonna Be Strong' (**Gene Pitney**, 1964), 'We Gotta Get Out of This Place' (the

Animals, 1965), 'You're My Soul and Inspiration' (the **Righteous Brothers**, 1966), 'I Love How You Love Me' (**Bobby Vinton**, 1968, but originally recorded by the Paris Sisters in 1961), 'Walking In the Rain' (**Jay and the Americans**, 1969), 'I Just Can't Help Believing' (B. J. Thomas, 1970). He continued writing hit songs well into the Seventies, his later hits for others including 'Sometimes When We Touch' for Dan Hill and 'Here You Come Again' for **Dolly Parton** (both 1977).

MARCELS A racially mixed group from Pittsburgh, the Marcels – Cornelius Harp (lead), Ronald Mundy (first tenor), Gene Bricker (second tenor), Dick Knauss (baritone) and Fred Johnson (bass) – hit the Number 1 spot in both Britain and American in 1961 with 'Blue Moon'. The goofy 'bom, ba ba bom' introduction was effective in restoring the much-neglected bassman to respectability, and the Marcels were much copied. They applied the same novelty treatment to other standards, including 'Summertime', 'Heartaches' – a Number 7 hit by the then all-black group, Allen Johnson and Walt Maddox replacing Knauss and Bricker – and 'My Melancholy Baby', all Colpix records arranged by Stu Phillips and Bert Keyes.

MARDIN, ARIF Born in Istanbul, Turkey, on 15 March 1932, Arif Mardin became a leading record producer with Atlantic during the Sixties and subsequently reached the position of vice-president and musical director of the company. He was awarded a jazz scholarship to the Berklee School of Music in 1958 and later worked there as a teacher. Joining Atlantic in 1963, he co-produced and/or arranged albums and singles for many of the label's biggest names, including **Aretha Franklin**, the **Rascals**, Herbie Mann, **Wilson Pickett**, **Stephen Stills**, **John Prine**, **King Curtis**, the **Average White Band**, **Roberta Flack**, and **Laura Nyro**. He also cut two solo instrumental albums for Atlantic, *Glass Onion* and *Journey*. He produced the **Bee Gees**' 1975 album *Main Course* – the first Bee Gees album in a quasi-soul mode, and an important precursor of their *Saturday Night Fever* soundtrack work – and in the Eighties was as much in demand as ever, working with **Chaka Khan** (her 'I Feel for You' in 1985 was a Mardin production), **Culture Club**, Peabo Bryson, **Scritti Politti**, **David Bowie** and many others. Mardin is particularly noted for the clarity of his productions.

MARESCA, ERNIE Born on 21 April 1939, Ernie Maresca reached the Top 10 on Seville in 1962 with 'Shout Shout (Knock Yourself Out)', which has claims to being one of the first punk rock records. The chaotic cacophony of the disc contained echoes of **Dion**, for whom Maresca had written 'Runaround Sue', 'The Wanderer' and others. A minor league figure in the doo-wop revival of the early Sixties, he also provided songs for the Belmonts ('No One Knows', 'Come On Little Angel'), the Regents ('Runaround'), Nino and the Ebbtides, the Five Discs, the Del-Satins and other New York groups. The Del-Satins backed him on 'Shout Shout' and worked with Dion on his solo records for Laurie. In the Seventies, Maresca moved to an executive post with Laurie.

MARILLION Generally regarded as the forerunner of a new breed of progressive rock outfits, Marillion operated at the sophisticated, and at times gentle, end of hard rock.

The quintet, based at Aylesbury, Buckinghamshire, first stepped out under the name Silmarillion in 1979, but by 1982 and a series of line-up changes they had dropped the first syllable and signed a deal with EMI. Led by enigmatic Scottish vocalist Fish (who had an early penchant for face paint), Steve Rothery (guitar), Mark Kelly (keyboards), Peter Trewavas (bass) and Mick Pointer (drums), they released their first single, 'Market Square Heroes'. This was well received and their second, 'He Knows You Know', made the UK Top 40 in 1983.

Marillion later released the albums *Script for a Jester's Tear* (1983), *Fugazi*, and the live set *Real to Reel* (both 1984), all well received and selling reasonably well, but it was not until 1985 and *Misplaced Childhood* that they locked on to the large-scale success that had been predicted for them. The LP (now with Ian Mosley on drums), which included their UK Number 2 single 'Kayleigh', remained in the upper reaches of the UK charts for most of the year, and their popularity greatly increased around Europe.

MAR-KEYS Originally known as the Royal Spades, the Mar-Keys had a Top 10 US hit with their first disc, 'Last Night' (Satellite, 1961), written and arranged by Chips Moman. Other, smaller hits included 'Morning After', 'Popeye Stroll', and (in 1966) 'Philly Dog', all on Stax. The first of many Mar-Keys line-ups contained Packy Axton (tenor sax), **Don Nix** (baritone sax),

Wayne Jackson (trumpet), Jerry Lee Smith (organ), **Steve Cropper** (guitar), Don 'Duck' Dunn (bass) and Terry Johnson (drums). All were white, two of whom – Cropper and Dunn – also played in the MGs with black musicians **Booker T.** and Al Jackson, who in turn went on to play in both groups. As staff musicians at the Stax-Volt studios, the Mar-Keys were at the centre of the Memphis soul boom of the mid-Sixties, providing accompaniment to hits by **Otis Redding**, **Sam and Dave**, **Wilson Pickett** *et al.* Axton subsequently formed the Packers, whose 'Hole in the Wall' was a hit on the Pure Soul label in 1965. Wayne Jackson, Andrew Love (tenor sax) and Floyd Newman (baritone sax) played in both the Mar-Keys and the famed sextet, the Memphis Horns. *See also* **Don Nix**; **Booker T. and the MGs**; **Steve Cropper**

MARLEY, BOB, AND THE WAILERS

A reggae band from Kingston's Trench Town district in Jamaica, Bob Marley and the Wailers won critical acclaim with their first Island album *Catch a Fire* (1973). Two years – and two albums – on, they had achieved international recognition and Marley was being hailed as 'the black **Bob Dylan**'. The Island contract meant a number of departures for the group, to the increasing dissatisfaction of founding members Peter 'Tosh' Mackintosh (vocals, guitar) and Bunny Livingston (vocals, percussion) – later repalced by Al Anderson (guitar), Tyrone Downie (organ) and the I Threes female back-up trio – but Marley's music retained much of its earthiness.

The Wailers came together in 1963 – the other members at this time were Junior Braithwaite (vocal), and backing singers Beverley Kelso and Cherry Smith – to cut 'Simmer Down' for producer Coxsone Dodd, Robert Nesta Marley (vocals/guitar, born in St Ann, Jamaica, on 6 February 1945) having previously recorded 'Judge Not' and 'One Cup of Coffee' for Leslie Kong. The group remained with Dodd until 1967, establishing itself with songs of love and rebellion, rudie style, like 'It Hurts to be Alone', 'Rule Them Rudie', 'Put It On' and 'Bend Down Low'. Braithwaite having split, Marley became an ethnic hero in Jamaica. Following a series of false starts, they joined producer **Lee Perry** in 1970, adding two Upsetters, brothers Carlton and Aston 'Family Man' Barrett (drums and bass) to record 'Small Axe', 'Duppy Conqueror' and 'Trench Town Rock'.

Success did not blunt Marley's songwriting skill, as *Natty Dread* (1975)

Bob Marley delivers one of the classic songs that are his legacy

amply illustrated. He continued to preach love, sex, Rastafarianism and anti-establishment politics with consummate passion, and cuts like 'No Woman No Cry' and 'So Jah Seh' became confirmed classics. His 'I Shot the Sheriff' was an American chart topper for **Eric Clapton** in 1974. A live version of 'No Woman No Cry', first featured on *Bob Marley and the Wailers Live* (1975), gave the group its first UK hit, a Number 22, and paved the way for their biggest success – *Rastaman Vibration* (1976), which included the outstanding 'War', in which the words of a speech by the late Emperor Haile Selassie of Ethiopia were set to music.

The next Marley album, *Exodus*, was recorded in London and Miami in 1977, and tracks for the follow-up, *Kaya*, were cut at the same sessions. He returned to Kingston in March 1978 for a concert that attempted to bring together the politicians and gunmen who were turning the city into a battleground, and he set up his own Tuff Gong label there. *Survival* (1979) was a more militant record than anything he had recorded previously and was partly inspired by his visit to Ethiopia, the spiritual home of Rastafarianism, during the preceding year. The influence of African music could be distinctly heard on the track 'Africa Unite', while 'Zimbabwe' was adopted by that country's Patriotic Front party as its anthem. *Uprising* (1980) had a similar mood and there was a strange, prescient irony in the fact that 'Redemption Song', the final track of the album, concluded the body of work

released during Marley's lifetime.

In September 1980, Marley and the Wailers arrived in New York for a series of concerts that would, it was hoped, finally launch the band in the one territory that had so far remained lukewarm towards their music. Three days later, Marley had a stroke while jogging in Central Park; he completed the dates, then flew to the Bavarian Alps clinic of Dr Joseph Issels for cancer treatment. His condition was diagnosed as hopeless and he returned to Miami, where he died on 11 May 1981.

MARMALADE A British singles group of the late Sixties, Marmalade originally comprised Dean Ford, lead vocals (born on 5 September 1946); Junior Campbell, lead guitar (31 May 1947); Pat Fairlie, rhythm guitar (14 April 1946); Graham Knight, bass (8 December 1946); and Raymond Duffy, drums. They initially called themselves Dean Ford and the Gaylords, and became a leading Scottish group – they came from Glasgow – on a par with the Poets and the Beatstalkers. They made entertaining and inventive singles such as 'The Name Game' and 'Little Egypt' but national impact eluded them until a change of name and a contract with CBS brought them a debut hit with 'Lovin' Things' in 1968. During the same year they reached Number 1 in the UK with a cover version of the **Beatles**' 'Ob La Di Ob La Da'. More hits followed – 'Baby Make It Soon', 'Reflections of My Life' (both 1969, the latter their first hit for Decca), 'Rainbow' (1970), 'Cousin Norman' (1971) – but a series of personnel changes, beginning with the departure of Ray Duffy and the arrival of Alan Whitehead, undermined the group's stability. Most serious was the departure of Junior Campbell, co-writer with Dean Ford of 'Reflections of My Life', their finest hit. He made a string of highly successful Tamlaesque singles under his own name for Deram, while Hughie Nicholson, his successor in Marmalade, formed the much-praised Blue with fellow ex-Poets. Reduced to a four-piece, Marmalade – now comprising Ford, Knight and Duggie Henderson (drums) and Mike Japp (lead guitar) – continued to make polished singles though with less good fortune. Knight left in 1973 and Ford embarked on a solo career before emigrating to the US. Knight briefly re-formed the group in 1976 to promote the Top 10 single, 'Falling Apart at the Seams', and thereafter retained the Marmalade name.

MARTHA AND THE VANDEL-LAS
One of Motown's great triumvirate of girl groups – the others were the **Supremes** and **Gladys Knight and the Pips** – Martha and the Vandellas originally came together as the Del-Phis in high school in their native Detroit. Martha was Martha Reeves (born 18 July 1941), who was joined in the group by Rosalind Ashford (2 September 1943) and Annette Sterling. Martha was employed as a secretary by Motown Records where one of her jobs was to sing lyrics on to tape for artists to learn. When an artist fell ill, Martha was asked to sing on a session and the studio, impressed with the results, hired her and her friends as backing vocalists. Their first disc as a session group was backing **Marvin Gaye**'s 'Stubborn Kind of Fellow' hit. The girls were then given a contract with Gordy Records – 'Vandellas' was derived from 'vandal', as they were jokingly accused of stealing the limelight from Gaye.

Martha Reeves fronts the Vandellas, a Motown hit trio of the Sixties

The group's second record, 'Come and Get These Memories', a husky beat ballad, was a Top 30 US hit in 1963 and the follow-up 'Heatwave', which saw a change of style to a rocking, brassy dance sound, set the US charts alight, rising to Number 4. At this point Annette quit the group to marry and was replaced by Betty Kelly (16 September 1944), another Detroiter. The follow-up, 'Quicksand', was also successful and in 1964 'Dancing in the Street' (co-written with Gaye), another storming dance record with crashing percussion, hit the Number 2 spot. Numerous other hits followed and in 1967 the billing changed to Martha Reeves and the Vandellas. The following year Martha's sister Lois replaced Betty, but in 1969 Martha's illness interrupted activities. When they resumed in 1970, ex-Velvelette Sandra Tilley had replaced Rosalind, but success now dwindled, and the group split in 1972. Martha Reeves became established as a solo singer on MCA in 1974, signing with Arista in 1975.

MARTIN, GEORGE
The producer of the majority of the **Beatles**' EMI recordings, George Martin was born in London on 3 January 1926. He trained at the Guildhall School of Music and joined EMI Records in 1950, later graduating to head of the company's Parlophone label – a haven during the Fifties for comedy acts and ballad singers. He was responsible for hits by the **Temperance Seven**, the **Goons**, Peter Sellers, Matt Munro, Shirley Bassey, Bernard Cribbins, Charlie Drake and others. Signing the Beatles in 1962, he acted as their factotum, his role as arranger becoming more crucial as the group's music grew in complexity. In addition to his string arrangements ('Eleanor Rigby') or harpsichord playing ('In My Life'), Martin's knowledge of studio techniques enabled **Lennon** and **McCartney** to translate their musical intuitions into sound collages on innovative tracks like 'Strawberry Fields Forever'. He also produced records by many other acts in **Brian Epstein**'s management stable, including **Cilla Black**, **Billy J. Kramer** and **Gerry and the Pacemakers**.

In 1965, Martin left EMI to set up his own independent record production company, AIR London, and after the Beatles' dissolution, turned to other projects, including production work for the West Coast group Sea Train, the British band Stackridge, and **America**. He also produced albums by **John McLaughlin**, **Cheap Trick**, Ella Fitzgerald and **Neil Sedaka**, and in 1982 was reunited with Paul McCartney for *Tug of War*.

MARTYN, JOHN
Folk-based singer/songwriter John Martyn was born in Glasgow in 1948 and was signed by Island Records in 1968. His first albums – *London Conversation* and *The Tumbler* – were typical examples of the British folk genre of the time, but *Stormbringer* (1970) and *The Road to Ruin* (1970), featuring his wife Beverley, presented a more individual talent. The first was produced by Joe Boyd in Woodstock and included Garth Hudson of **The Band** among the musicians, while on *The Road to Ruin*, Martyn introduced a jazz influence which would play a great part in the development of his style.

On *Bless the Weather* (1971) and particularly *Solid Air* (1972), Martyn's amplified guitar with electronic accoutrements accompanied his unique, scat-style singing. He also began to tour extensively, accompanied by ex-**Pentangle** bassist Danny Thompson. *Inside Out* (1973) and *Sunday's Child* (1975) found Martyn's approach fully formed, with its roots in various folk and jazz modes. A live album – *Live At Leeds* – was released by Island in 1975, and distributed by mail order. A period in Jamaica working with reggae kings **Lee Perry** and Jack Ruby directly influenced the content of *One World* (1977), while *Grace and Danger* (1980) was co-produced by **Phil Collins**, who also assisted with percussion and vocal backing. *Glorious Fool* was released in 1982.

MARVELETTES
Motown vocal quintet the Marvelettes – Gladys Horton (lead singer), Katherine Anderson, Wanda Young, Georgeanna Tillman and Juanita Cowart (all born in 1944) – came together at Inkster High School in Detroit. The girls won the school talent contest and a teacher introduced them to Berry Gordy, who signed the group to Tamla Records. Their debut disc 'Please Mr Postman', an intense, gospel-inspired beat ballad featuring Gladys Horton's rasping lead vocal, was a Number 1 hit and million-seller in the US in 1961. The next four years brought a succession of Top 50 hits with such songs as 'Playboy', 'Beechwood 4–5789' and 'Too Many Fish in the Sea', but it was the Motown sound with a difference since the Marvelettes' vocal delivery had a bluesy edge not found in most of the Corporation's teen dance output. 1966 brought a return to the Top 10 with the mellower, gospel blues-flavoured 'Don't Mess with Bill', notable for its searing tenor sax solo. The group was reduced to a trio when Georgeanna and Juanita quit, but continued to make hit records. When lead singer Gladys left in 1968 – replaced by Anne Bogan – the distinctive sound went, too; 'That's How Heartaches Are Made', which crept into the Hot 100 at 97 for one week in 1969, reflected an altogether softer pop sound. The group disbanded soon afterwards.

South African exile trumpeter Hugh Masekela consciously sought innovation, but never lost his roots in black African urban sounds

MASEKELA, HUGH Born near Johannesburg, South Africa, in 1939, trumpeter Hugh Masekela went into voluntary exile in the early 1960s, and has subsequently lived in Britain, the USA, Ghana, Nigeria, Guinea and (most recently) Botswana. Though firmly rooted in the black South African urban dance music known as *mbaqanga*, his music has absorbed much from Afro-American funk and soul and even more from jazz. Like Cameroonian hornman **Manu Dibango**, Masekela is an aggressive believer in African music's right to experiment and move forward, and his zest for innovation has led him to make some injudicious music over the years, including a number of very bland and best forgotten 'crossover' albums. At his best, however, he remains the most exciting trumpeter South Africa has produced. Among his best albums are *Home Is Where the Music Is* (made with fellow expatriate saxophonist Dudu Pukwana in London in 1972) and the mid-Seventies series made with Ghanaian band Hedzoleh Soundz, notably *I Am Not Afraid*. More recent releases, like 1985's *Technobush* set, combine fiery *mbaqanga* pieces with examples of blandly anonymous crossover.

MASON, DAVE Born on 10 May 1947 in Worcester, singer/guitarist Dave Mason went through several Worcester and Birmingham bands (the Jaguars, the Hellions, Deep Feeling, Julian Covey and the Machine) and jobs (including being a roadie for **Spencer Davis**) before he, **Stevie Winwood**, **Jim Capaldi**, and Chris Wood retired to Berkshire to form **Traffic**. 'Hole in My Shoe', the first song he ever wrote, was the group's biggest single hit, reaching Number 2 in Britain in 1967. He left after the release of the first album in December 1967 to go to Greece but returned to produce the first **Family** album. He rejoined Traffic in May 1968 to cut the *Traffic* album but left again to pursue a solo career and cut a single, 'Little Woman', only to team up again with Capaldi and Wood in the short-lived Mason, Capaldi, Wood And Frog. He moved to the States and played with **Delaney and Bonnie** and eventually used many of their associates to record the classic *Alone Together* (Blue Thumb, 1970). Over the next few years he played with Mama **Cass Elliott** and **Derek and the Dominoes** before rejoining Traffic for the six live dates that resulted in *Welcome to the Canteen*. He returned to the States and formed a band only to discover that his record label, Blue Thumb, had decided to release some unfinished tapes (*Headkeeper*) totally against his wishes. Contractual problems of that sort plagued him until he signed to Columbia in late 1972. Three competent albums followed – *Dave Mason* (1974), *It's Like You Never Left* (1974, with **Stevie Wonder** and **Graham Nash** accompanying) and *Split Coconut* (1975) – without reaching the heights of *Alone Together*. 1977 saw considerable success in the US, with *Let it Flow* selling well and a single, 'We Just Disagree', reaching Number 12. *See also* **Traffic**

MATCHBOX Operating in an essentially revivalist field, rockabilly specialists Matchbox nevertheless succeeded in bringing their sound sufficiently up to date to score several hit singles in the early Eighties.

Originally formed in London in 1977, the steady line-up of Graham Fenton (vocals), Steve Blomfield (guitar), Dick Callan (guitar), Gordon Scott (guitar), Fred Poke (bass) and Jim Redhead (drums) did not achieve success until 1979 and the UK Top 20 single, 'Rockabilly Rebel'.

Over the years they continued to play Fifties rock'n'roll with a country swing, although, ironically, their biggest hit has been the **Presley**-style ballad, 'When You Ask About Love', which reached Number 4 in 1980.

MATHIS, JOHNNY Born on 30 September 1935, Johnny Mathis is said to have been the first black American to become a millionaire. Ironically, his success came through his adoption of a white pop ballad approach. He was signed to Columbia in 1956, and at first recorded in a jazz style, before Mitch Miller decided that Mathis should switch to ballad singing. His run of hits between 1956 and 1959 included 'A Certain Smile' and 'Misty'. Ever since, his ethereal but schmaltzy voice has haunted the album charts (and, less frequently, the singles charts) on both sides of the Atlantic. Principally choosing conventional ballads ('The Shadow of Your Smile', 'The Twelfth of Never'), in 1974 he had a big hit with a re-make of the **Stylistics**' Philly-soul song 'I'm Stone in Love with You' and subsequently scored major UK hits with 'When a Child is Born' (a Number 1, 1976) and 'Too Much, Too Little, Too Late' (a duet with **Deniece Williams**, 1978). In a sense, Mathis was and remains the natural successor to **Nat 'King' Cole**, though he lacks the depth of Cole's best work.

MATTHEWS, IAN Since leaving **Matthews Southern Comfort** in 1970, the career of Ian Matthews (born Ian MacDonald in Lincolnshire in 1946), potentially one of Britain's best singer/songwriters and interpreters in the country/folk idiom, has been erratic. None of his albums has achieved the commercial success of his earlier work with **Fairport Convention** or Matthews Southern Comfort.

A solo contract with Vertigo produced two low-key albums during 1971, *If You Could See Thro' My Eyes* and *Tigers Will Survive*. Relationships between artist and label were soon strained, however, and the third record made under this agreement, *Journeys from Gospel Oak*, did not appear until 1974 when producer Sandy Robertson released it through Mooncrest.

Matthews' next venture was Plainsong, a group involving Andy Roberts (guitar), Dave Richards (bass) and Bob Ronga (guitar). After one Elektra album (*In Search of Amelia Earhart*, 1972), the restless Matthews left for America. In Los Angeles he linked up with **Mike Nesmith** who produced his next solo venture (*Valley Hi*, Elektra, 1973). After a further Elektra record, the fine *Some Days You Eat the Bear* (1974), Matthews quit the label to join Columbia, making his debut with *Go for Broke* (1976). *Hit and Run* (1977) and *Stealin' Home* (1978) followed, together with the traditional folk-oriented *Siamese Friends* (1979). Moving to Seattle in the late Seventies, he formed Hi Fi with David Surkamp.

MATTHEWS SOUTHERN COMFORT *Matthews Southern Comfort* was originally the title of the first solo album by former **Fairport Convention** singer **Ian Matthews**, released by Uni in 1970. The album was produced and written by **Ken Howard** and **Alan Blaikley**, hitherto best known for their work with **Dave Dee, Dozy, Beaky, Mick and Tich** and the **Herd**, and was an exciting amalgam of folk and country music. Among the tracks was 'I've Lost You', later a hit for **Elvis Presley**. Characterized by Matthews' high, clear voice and Gordon Huntley's pedal steel guitar, the album won critical acclaim and led to the formation of a band with the same name. The line-up of Matthews, Huntley, Mark Griffiths (harmony vocals), Andy Leigh (bass, vocals), Carl Barnwell (guitar, vocals) and Ray Duffy (drums) soon had a UK Number 1 hit with a version of **Joni Mitchell**'s 'Woodstock' (Harvest, 1971), which launched their career as Britain's first West Coast-style country rock band. Within a year, however, it was all over. After three MCA albums, the temperamental Matthews quit the band to go solo. Barnwell, an American, kept the remainder together as Southern Comfort through three further Harvest albums, none of which had the authority of the Matthews-led recordings. The group disbanded in 1972. *See also* **Ian Matthews**

MATUMBI In the mid- to late Seventies, Matumbi were the outstanding British reggae band – a position only lost when the departure of key musician and songwriter **Dennis Bovell** led to the disintegration of the group. Before the arrival of Matumbi – the group formed in London in 1972 and had a frequently changing line-up – British reggae had been in a generally sorry state, the musicians feeling massively inferior to their Jamaican counterparts and consequently attempting to do little else than ape Jamaican initiatives. Bovell and Matumbi, however, had sufficient nerve and originality to break that mould – and, importantly, to convince the British reggae audience that the mould now deserved to be broken. Originally recording for pioneering British reggae label Trojan, Matumbi's first big success came in 1976 with 'After Tonight', their first release on the Safari label. The 1977 album *Scientific Higher Ranking Dub*, recorded under the pseudonym 4th Street Orchestra, was another first for homegrown reggae. 'Point of View' reached Number 35 in the UK chart in 1979. Ultimately, however, Matumbi proved too limiting a framework for Bovell, whose decision to go solo at the end of the Seventies led to the band's eventual disappearance.

MAYALL, JOHN A protégé of **Alexis Korner**, John Mayall developed a multi-instrumental technique from the Fifties onwards, playing harmonica, piano, organ and guitar. Born in Manchester on 29 November 1933, he established his group, the Bluesbreakers, on the R&B club circuit with a line-up of Roger Dean (guitar), John McVie (bass) and Hughie Flint (drums), which remained unchanged until **Eric Clapton** replaced Dean in April 1965. When Clapton left to form **Cream** just over a year later after making his own reputation, and Mayall's, with his unparalleled virtuosity – both live and later on record with *Blues Breakers* (Decca, 1966) – his replacement, **Peter Green**, introduced a new and equally creative phase in the band's career. Mayall was the Midas of British rock: Green and McVie went on to form **Fleetwood Mac**; Green's successor, Mick Taylor, joined the **Rolling Stones**; his drummers included Aynsley Dunbar, Keef Hartley and Jon Hiseman; and both **Jack Bruce** and Andy Fraser played bass for a while. As each musician came and went, so Mayall's reputation grew. He has experimented frequently with the Bluesbreakers' line-up, adding horns, a violin, excluding drums, and attempting a fusion of jazz and blues with *Jazz-Blues Fusion* (Polydor, 1971) and *Moving On* (1972), recorded in America where he now lives. In 1974 he signed with ABC, for whom he recorded *New Band, New Company* (1975) with singer Dee McKinnie. **Allen Toussaint** produced *Notice to Appear* (1976), but neither this nor his two subsequent ABC albums (*A Banquet in Blues*, 1976; *The Hard Core Package*, 1977) were well received. He cut *Bottom Line* for DJM in 1979 and in 1982 was involved in a short Bluesbreakers reunion tour of the US and Australia with Mick Taylor and John McVie.

MAYFIELD, CURTIS After twelve years as the mainstay of the **Impressions**, Curtis Mayfield launched himself on a solo career in 1970 with the highly acclaimed *Curtis* album on Buddah, followed the next year by a live recording (*Curtis – Live*) and *Roots*, which established him as a leading figure in the new wave of soul stars. Combining his old skill for lilting melodies and simple, effective lyrics with a keener view of society's confusion, Mayfield (born in Chicago on 3 June 1942) reflected life's ups ('The Makings of You', 'Move on Up', 'Beautiful Brothers of Mine') and downs ('If There's a Hell Below', 'Stone Junkie', 'Underground') with a compelling grace that reached its peak in 1972 with his soundtrack for *Superfly* (including the million-seller 'Freddie's Dead'). Although he scored other successful soundtracks, *Claudine*, for **Gladys Knight** (Buddah, 1974) and *Let's Do It Again* for the **Staple Singers** (Curtom, 1975), his own releases lost direction and by the end of 1974 he was jumping on every available bandwagon with songs like 'Kung Fu' and 'Sweet Exorcist'.

In 1977, Mayfield provided the soundtrack score for the film *Short Eyes*, but then began a disastrous flirtation with disco music that resulted in *Do It All Night* (1978) and *Heartbeat* (1979). 1982 found him back to something like his old form on *Honesty*.

MAYFIELD, PERCY A blues-based vocalist and pianist from Minden, Louisiana, Percy Mayfield (born in 1921) recorded for the Supreme label in Los Angeles before joining Specialty Records, the company on which he hit Number 1 on the R&B charts in 1950 with his own composition, 'Please Send Me Someone to Love'. Other Mayfield records to figure in the R&B chart included 'Lost Love', 'What a Fool I Was', 'Cry Baby' and 'The Big Question'. His gentle Creole phrasing and urbane style returned to the same charts in 1963 with 'River's Return' (Tangerine), and in 1970 with 'To Live in the Past' (RCA). He wrote a number of hit songs for **Ray Charles**, including 'Hit the Road, Jack' (a national Number 1 in 1961), 'Hide Nor Hair' and 'Danger Zone'. He died on 11 August 1984, in Los Angeles.

MC5 Detroit-based band the MC5 – Rob Tyner, vocals, harmonica; Fred 'Sonic' Smith, guitar; Mike Davis, bass; Dennis Thompson, drums; Wayne Kramer, lead guitar – were thrust to national prominence in 1969 by manager John Sinclair. They were originally part of the Trans Love commune that housed Sinclair's White Panther Party, but the raw revolutionary energy and 'punk' stance of the live *Kick Out the Jams* (Elektra, 1969) was rejected, along with Sinclair, as their attitudes and political ideas diverged. They replaced Sinclair's philosophy with rock'n'roll, and guided by rock critic Jon Landau, they recorded *Back in the USA* (Atlantic, 1970), one of the most interesting rock albums of the Sixties. Sandwiched between these two rock-'n'roll classics was a new expression of teenage consciousness Seventies-style, but in concise, three-minute epics ('Teenage Lust', 'American Ruse', 'Call Me Animal'). *High Time* had the same drive and energy and instrumental precision. They toured Europe in 1972, but were badly received. Davis stayed behind, and the others moved back to Detroit and called it a day. Fred Smith married **Patti Smith** in Detroit in March 1980.

MEAT LOAF Born Marvin Lee Aday on 27 September 1947 in Dallas, Texas, 20-stone mainstream rock singer Meat Loaf sold a phenomenally surprising five-million copies of his first solo LP, *Bat Out of Hell*, in 1978.

Having already acquired the nickname Meat Loaf at high school, he moved to California in 1966 where he performed in various bands, but his big break came in New York when, in 1973,

Meat Loaf's sweaty overweight image was instantly unforgettable, and with a tough vocal style earnt him a brief glory in the Seventies

he met songwriter/playwright Jim Steinmann, the man who was later to mastermind his success. In 1975 Meat Loaf played Eddie in the cult film *The Rocky Horror Picture Show*, and later sang backing vocals on heavy metal merchant **Ted Nugent**'s platinum LP, *Free for All*. Meat Loaf and Steinmann then toured together with the National Lampoon Show, and Steinmann wrote a musical, *Never Land*, from which much of the material for *Bat* was taken.

When the pair came to make the LP, they recruited **Todd Rundgren** to produce it; at first the critics failed to respond, as did the public, but then Meat Loaf went on the road and as a result the album was platinum by the end of the year. The extremely rotund Meat Loaf became an unlikely superstar, his tough vocal style and the dream imagery of the songs charming the crowds; the live shows continued, punctuated in 1980 by an appearance with Deborah Harry in the film *Roadie*, but finally the strain of being on the road took its toll and he was forced to rest his voice.

An LP, *Dead Ringer*, the title track a lively duet with **Cher**, finally arrived in 1981 but, inevitably, was doomed to suffer by comparison to its predecessor and failed miserably to emulate its success. Meat Loaf parted company with Steinmann for *Midnight at the Lost and Found* (1983), and with its successor *Bad Attitude* (1985), it seemed that he had got stuck in an unremarkable, and unsuccessful, rock rut from which he was unlikely to emerge.

MEAUX, HUEY P. At various times a disc jockey, barber and independent record producer, Huey P. Meaux was born in Kaplan, Louisiana, on 10 March 1929. Of Cajun origin, he founded a number of local record labels which were devoted to this ethnic music, including Crazy Cajun, on which Meaux himself recorded. His first pop production, Jivin' Gene's 'Breaking up Is Hard to Do', became a hit in 1959. Meaux's influence throughout Texas and Louisiana spread as his ability to pick hit records increased. 'My plan,' he told *Billboard*, 'is to pick up masters and place them with various companies. I want to set aside certain hours every day when I do nothing but listen to masters.' The degree of responsibility was somewhat blurred, and he was often credited with producing records which he may simply have arranged for a major company to purchase or distribute. Meaux's name has cropped up in connection with **Dale and Grace**'s 'I'm Leaving It All up to You' (from Sam Montel) and Archie Bell's 'Tighten Up' (from Skipper Lee Frazier). But Meaux certainly produced many records himself, including Joe Barry's 'I'm a Fool to Care', 'She's About a Mover' by the **Sir Douglas Quintet** (released on his own Tribe label), **Barbara Lynn**'s major hit 'You'll Lose a Good Thing', the profits from which he ploughed into his own studios, including Pasadena Sounds in Houston and Grits and Gravy Studios in Jackson, Mississippi.

Other records he 'placed' include the Hombres' 'Let It Out' (1967), **Roy Head**'s 'Treat Her Right' (Backbeat in 1965), and B. J. Thomas's 'I'm So Lonesome I Could Cry' (Scepter in 166). He also worked with T. K. Hulin, Jimmy Donley, Joey Long (three key but little-known figures in Texas rock), **Chuck Jackson**, Johnny Copeland, **T-Bone Walker** and **Jerry Lee Lewis**, whose fine *Southern Roots* album was a Meaux production. Freddy Fender's huge success in 1975 with three hit singles and two albums was in great part due to Meaux's 'old fashioned' approach to production: 'always highlight the song'.

MEEK, JOE Britain's first independent record producer of note, Joe Meek (born Robert George Meek in 1929) came from Newent, Gloucestershire, and spent his National Service in the RAF as a radio technician in the early Fifties. On his release in 1953, he went to work as an engineer at the IBC studio, at that time one of only two independently-owned studios in London. There he engineered records by Frankie Vaughan ('Green Door'), Denis Lotis, Lita Roza, Shirley Bassey, Anne Shelton, Harry Secombe and Petula Clark. In 1956, he began working for Denis Preston at Lansdowne Studios, where he was engineer on several of **Lonnie Donegan**'s early hits, including 'Cumberland Gap' and 'Don't You Rock Me Daddy-O', as well as trad jazz recordings by Humphrey Lyttelton and **Chris Barber**. He also began dabbling in songwriting and in 1958 wrote 'Put a Ring on Her Finger' for **Tommy Steele**.

Leaving Lansdowne in 1960, Meek built his own studio in a flat above a shop in Holloway, North London, equipping it with £3,000 worth of second-hand gear. He called the studio RGM Sound and simultaneously started his own label, Triumph – this at a time when British pop was dominated by the three major labels, EMI, Pye and Decca. A cover version of a US hit, Michael Cox's 'Angela Jones', reached the UK Top 10 in June 1960, but none of Triumph's other releases was successful and Meek discontinued the label in favour of tape-lease deals with the majors. He scored the following year with **John Leyton**'s eerie, futuristic 'Johnny Remember Me' and 'Wild Wind', Mike Berry's poignant 'Tribute to Buddy Holly' and several smaller hits by Berry's group the Outlaws (whose line-up included Ritchie Blackmore), who backed many of Meek's artists on record.

In 1962, a combination of Meek's session musicians recorded his instrumental composition 'Telstar': released under the name of the **Tornados**, it became his biggest-selling production, reaching Number 1 in both the US and the UK. The Tornados followed it up with several less successful discs including 'Robot', 'Globetrotter' and 'Ice Cream Man' before being swamped in the ensuing Merseybeat craze. Nevertheless, the Meek-produced 'Don't You Think It's Time' was a hit for Mike Berry in 1963 and another of his productions, the Honeycombs' 'Have I the Right', was a Top 10 hit in 1964. He had no hits in 1966 and, anxious over personal problems, he shot himself on 3 February 1967.

MEL AND TIM Cousins and lifelong buddies, Mel and Tim were Mel Hardin and Tim McPherson. Brought up in Holly Springs, Mississippi, they moved to St Louis where they mixed with all the big names on the southern soul scene. Working with veteran artist/producer **Gene Chandler** they had a Top 10 hit with the Stax-influenced 'Backfield in Motion' (1969), written by Tim and released on the small Scepter-distributed Bamboo label owned by Chandler. Another big hit, 'Good Guys Only Win in the Movies', followed in 1970. After contractual fights the duo began recording in the Muscle Shoals studio where they cut the beautiful, lilting ballad, 'Starting All Over Again'. Written by Phillip Mitchell, and leased to Stax Records in Memphis, it was a major soul hit in 1972 but subsequent releases have had less success.

MELANIE Singer Melanie was born Melanie Safka in New York on 3 February 1947. Emerging in 1969, she carried the obligatory acoustic guitar of the singer/songwriter, though her unusual vocal style owed most to jazz and to the French *chanteuse* approach of Edith Piaf.

Her first big hit was a hoarse, dramatic rendition of the **Rolling Stones**' 'Ruby Tuesday', which reached the Top 10 in Britain in 1970. Other hits on Buddah followed, including 'Look What They've Done to My Song Ma' and 'Brand New Key', an American chart topper in 1971. Her songwriting sometimes tended towards the coy and some found her on-stage warmth embarrassing.

In 1972, Melanie formed Neighbourhood Records with her husband and producer Peter Schekeryk. She moved away from the girlish persona of some of the early work on albums like *Madrugada* (1974) and *As I See It Now* (1974). *Sunset and Other Beginnings* (1975) contained a mixture of Safka originals and contemporary standards, while Neighbourhood continued to foster a number of other folk-based acts including Mike Heron's Reputation. The label folded in 1976 and Melanie moved to Atlantic for *Photograph* (1976) and *Phonogenic* (1978). She still performs regularly, particularly at European peace festivals and benefits for radical causes.

MELCHER, TERRY Born on 8 February 1942, in New York City, Terry Melcher was a leading West Coast record producer of the Sixties and early Seventies. He made his singing debut in 1962, cutting several solo sides for Columbia under the name of Terry Day. They failed miserably, so he shifted into production work, turning out a string of moderate hits in the surf-sun genre by people like **Pat Boone**, Wayne Newton, the Rip Chords and his mother, Doris Day. In between sessions, he cut a few singles with future Beach Boy Bruce Johnston as Bruce and Terry. But it was as a producer that Melcher really excelled, and when his work with groups such as **Paul Revere and the Raiders** and the **Byrds** established him as a consistent hit-maker, his singing career faltered. During the years 1963–71 Melcher was responsible for the numerous hit albums by the Byrds: *Mr Tambourine Man*; *Turn, Turn, Turn*; *Easy Rider*; *Untitled* and *Byrdmaniax* as well as eight best-selling albums by Paul Revere and the Raiders, two by the Rip Chords, and one by Doris Day.

In 1973, Melcher signed to Reprise as a solo artist and cut the introverted *Terry Melcher*, which featured names like Clarence White, **Roger McGuinn**, **Chris Hillman** and **Ry Cooder**. However, it didn't sell, and Melcher redirected his energies into his own company, Equinox Records. Distributed by RCA, Equinox includes California Music (Bruce Johnston's group) and, of course, Melcher. As a production subsidiary, it released albums by such diverse artists as **Barry Mann** and **David Cassidy**.

MELVIN, HAROLD, AND THE BLUE NOTES

Featuring the exhortative soulful wail of **Teddy Pendergrass**, Harold Melvin and the Blue Notes were perhaps the group most closely identified with the black 'Philly Sound' of the early Seventies. Originally a street-corner group, their early work included 'If You Love Me' (Josie, 1956) and 'My Hero' (Value, 1960). Club work on the chittlin' circuit led to a slicker tie'n'tails approach (at Martha Reeves' suggestion) and the white supper-club circuit. 'Get Out' was an R&B hit in 1965 on Landa. When offered a chance to work with **Gamble and Huff**, at the same time as lead John Atkins left to make way for Teddy, the group – Bernard Wilson, Lloyd Parkes, Lawrence Brown, Melvin and Pendergrass – began to produce the brand of sweepingly symphonic yet utterly soulful music that became their hallmark. Starting with a soul hit, 'I Miss You', they progressed to smoulderingly poignant international hits, 'If You Don't Know Me By Now' (1972), 'The Love I Lost' (1973) and 'Where Are All My Friends' (1974).

The group lasted as long as the 'Philly Sound' retained public favour: by 1976, Pendergrass had departed for an immensely successful solo career and the remaining members had moved on to ABC, where they enjoyed a few hits on the soul chart but none in the pop listings. In 1979, the group joined Source Records for *The Blue Album*; a year later, they were contracted to MCA and recording *All Things Happen in Time*. *See also* **Teddy Pendergrass**

MEMPHIS

For anyone from the rural Mississippi Delta on their way to find work in the industrial North, Memphis is traditionally the first stop. White and black musicians from Louisiana and Arkansas, Mississippi and Tennessee, heard each other's music in person and on the radio, and the results were sounds which inspired musicians far beyond the city limits. Thus the recording history of Memphis reveals an amazing range of styles and a series of complex developments.

It was first known as a blues town, with a number of field recording sessions held there in the Twenties and Thirties. But there was no Memphis recording studio as such until after World War II, and much of the jazz, hillbilly, gospel and blues tradition of the town went unrecorded. Sam Phillips was the post-war pioneer. In 1950, he set up the Memphis Recording Service and in 1952, Sun Records. Soon, other labels like Flair (with **Elmore James**), Meteor, Blues Boy, Buster, Wasco and OJ began to record R&B and country music. Meanwhile, Sun launched the careers of **Rufus Thomas**, **Junior Parker**, **Elvis Presley**, **Carl Perkins**, **Johnny Cash**, **Jerry Lee Lewis**, **Charlie Rich**, **Roy Orbison** and **Billy Lee Riley**.

Following Sun's success with blues and especially rockabilly, a new clutch of labels emerged. Hi, founded by record distributor Bill Cuoghi, had consistent success with the **Bill Black** Combo ('Smokie', 'White Silver Sands') and occasional hits from Gene Simmons ('Haunted House') and Ace Cannon ('Tuff'). Fernwood scored with Thomas Wayne's 'Tragedy' and Rita Records had Harold Dorman's 'Mountain of Love'.

Even smaller labels had to lease successful records to larger companies, as Renay did with the Matt Lucas rocker 'I'm Movin' On' (to Smash), and Penn with **Sam the Sham**'s 'Woolly Bully' (to MGM). The enterprise of Sam Phillips and the success of rockabilly had established Memphis as a major recording centre by the early Sixties, and the city retained its importance throughout the decade. Foremost among the Memphis labels after Sun's eclipse remained Hi Records, to which former Sun session man Bill Black had moved in 1958. He had a series of hits during the early Sixties with his sax-led combo. Paralleling this success with a similar sound was altoist Ace Cannon; **Willie Mitchell** followed on from Black in the mid- and late Sixties.

Cuoghi died in 1968 and Mitchell largely took control of Hi's output, being responsible for the success of **Ann Peebles** and **Al Green**. In each case, Mitchell's band provided support with mellow, precise horn/rhythm arrangements, and his hornmen, Wayne Jackson and Andrew Love, forged a link with rival Memphis giant, Stax, which was formed in 1959 as Satellite (by Jim Stewart and Estelle Axton) but changed its name to avoid confusion with a like-named West Coast label. The Stax sound, developed throughout the mid-Sixties with artists like Rufus and **Carla Thomas**, **Sam and Dave**, **Johnnie Taylor** and the **Mar-Keys**, was characterized by more punchy horn arrangements played by the Mar-Keys, whose line-up (including Jackson and Love) backed most Stax artists on sessions. House arrangers included **Isaac Hayes** and David Porter, also prolific songwriters, who were both later to become successful solo artists.

Short-lived competition emerged in 1964 with Quinton Claunch and Doc Russell's Goldwax label, who had some success with the Ovations and **James Carr** with an intense, deep-soul style. In 1967, Chips Moman and Tommy Cogbill quit Fame Studios to set up their own American Group Productions in Memphis, and recorded the **Box Tops**, B. J. Thomas, **Dionne Warwick**, Elvis Presley, **Dusty Springfield** and others. *See also* **Sun Records**

MEMPHIS SLIM

The barrel-houses of Beale Street in Memphis, Tennessee, where he was born Peter Chatman in 1916, probably gave Memphis Slim his declamatory vocal and pianistic style, which was introduced to the blues market in 1940 with the hit 'Beer Drinking Woman'. He continued to record for this audience through the Forties and Fifties, but by the Sixties had discovered a second role as blues and boogie interpreter for whites, a part he developed in cafés, concerts and a series of Folkways albums. From the mid-Sixties onwards he lived in France, dividing his recording activity between somewhat sentimental commemorations of the past and somewhat undirected sessions with European (or, occasionally, visiting American) blues, jazz and rock musicians. Though rarely recapturing the unassuming vitality of his small-group recordings in the Fifties he had a significant influence as an *émigré* bluesman.

MEN AT WORK

The Australian rock success story of the early Eighties, Men At Work became international stars in 1983 when 'Down Under' developed into a massive worldwide hit. Formed at the end of the Seventies, Men At Work secured a residency at the Cricketer's Arms Hotel in Melbourne. The band – Colin Hay (vocals), Greg Ham (sax), John Rees (bass), Ron Strykert (guitar) and Jerry Speiser (drums) – were passed over by virtually every A&R manager in the country before Peter Karpin, a young CBS employee, returned from a New York posting and placed his job on the line to get them signed and into the studio with American producer Peter McIlan.

The group's debut album, *Business as Usual*, shot to the top of the LP chart in Australia and produced three hit singles. Accepted for American release by CBS (more out of obligation than enthusiasm), *Business as Usual* broke the **Monkees**' record for the longest-running debut album at Number 1, with 15 weeks at the top. 'Who Can It Be Now?' gave Men At Work their first American Number 1 single and 'Down Under' their first global chart-topper.

The band returned to the top in the US with a second album, *Cargo* (1983). Initially accused of sounding like the **Police** – through reggae-influenced rhythms and Hay's high-pitched singing style – they eventually found their own musical style, a bland, lightweight rock sound, designed to appeal to an international market.

MERCURY RECORDS Formed

in 1947 in Chicago by Irving B. Green, Berle Adams and Art Talmadge as an independent, Mercury quickly became a label of major standing, setting up its own pressing facilities and national distribution network in its first year. The company had immediate hits by **Frankie Laine** (which helped it buy up Majestic Records in 1948), Vic Damone and Patti Page, under the supervision of Mitch Miller (who later joined Columbia) and Talmadge (who later left to set up Musicor Records).

Mercury's R&B division was headed by Clyde Otis – the first black A&R man in a major company – and Nat Tarnapol and included Eddie Vinson, **Dinah Washington**, **Brook Benton**, Damita Jo and Roy Byrd. However, it was in the mid-Fifties when the company entered the rock'n'roll field that it really prospered, first with white covers of R&B songs – 'Sh-Boom' (the Crewcuts), 'Tweedle Dee' and 'Dance With Me Henry' (Georgia Gibbs) and 'Little Darlin'' and 'Silhouettes' (the **Diamonds**), all of which were gold records – and then with originals by the **Platters**, the **Big Bopper** and others. The Platters provided Mercury with their biggest hits of the rock'n'roll years and came to the company almost by accident – Mercury signed the Buck Ram-managed **Penguins** whose 'Earth Angel' had been covered by the Crewcuts, and as part of the contract got Ram's other group, the Platters.

With this success behind them Mercury continued to search out rock-

'n'roll talent, signing up **Freddie Bell and the Bell Boys** and employing **Shelby Singleton** as a free, floating Southern A&R man. Singleton's signings were the most interesting – **Johnny Preston**, **Bruce Channel**, the Big Bopper and, possibly even more important, **Jerry Kennedy** who was later to produce a string of hits for Mercury with **Tom T. Hall**, **Charlie Rich**, **Jerry Lee Lewis** and others.

Smash, originally a pop subsidiary, was set up in 1959 and in 1962 the company was bought up by North American Philips bringing Mercury into the worldwide Phonogram set-up and creating another pair of labels, Philips and Fontana. Through its British organization Fontana became an important source of new talent – the **Troggs** and the **Mindbenders** – while Philips had success with acts as varied as Paul and Paula, the Singing Nun and the **Four Seasons**.

By the Seventies, Mercury's roster included **Rod Stewart**, **Bachman-Turner Overdrive**, **Don Covay**, **Spirit** and **10cc**, together with country artists **Roger Miller**, Johnny Rodriguez, Faron Young and the Statler Brothers. In the Eighties, Mercury acts included **Tears for Fears**, the Scorpions, and **Dexys Midnight Runners**.

MERSEYBEATS The Merseybeats

– Tony Crane (lead guitar), Aaron Williams (rhythm guitar), Billy Kinsley (bass) and John Banks (drums) – were one of the few Liverpool groups to achieve a recorded sound worthy of their impact in live performance. Produced by Jack Baverstock on Fontana, they made a series of slow, atmospheric rock ballads (the **Shirelles**' 'It's Love That Really Counts', **Jackie DeShannon**'s 'Wishin' and Hopin'), though none was as successful as the jaunty Peter Lee Stirling number, 'I Think of You', which reached Number 5 in 1964. Various personnel changes led, in 1966, to the dissolution of the group, but Kinsley and Crane re-emerged as the Merseys to score a massive hit with 'Sorrow', later to be enshrined as a Sixties classic by **David Bowie** on his *Pin-Ups* album. Kinsley became a session musician in the early Seventies and played for a while in the **Jackie Lomax** Band before forming Liverpool Express, who had Top 10 hits in the UK with 'You Are My Love' and 'Every Man Must Have a Dream', in 1976. Tony Crane, meanwhile, toured the cabaret centres of Britain with the New Merseybeats, although he was the only member who had any connection with the group in its earlier incarnation.

The Merseybeats at the Cavern, Liverpool, in April 1963, when A&R men were just becoming aware of the potential of Mersey talent

METAL-BASHING A media term for music made literally by hammering junk metal, metal-bashing was a short-lived but high-profile phenomenon of the early and mid-Eighties. The inspiration came largely from the European classical avant-garde, and the style grew on both sides of the English Channel, notably in Berlin and London.

Berlin's contribution began with Einsturzende Neubauten ('Collapsing New Buildings', after a Berlin government building which did just that prior to its official opening). Part of Berlin's nihilist punk scene, Neubauten originally claimed to be providing the soundtrack to the Collapse of Western Civilization. Live performances were exciting, and sometimes dangerous, spectacles; conventional instruments mixed with road drills, jackhammers, buzzsaws and industrial grinders. Three albums, *Kollaps* (1982), *Zeitnungen der Patienten O.T.* (1984) and, most successfully, *Halber-Mensch* (1985) proved their terminal pop could translate to vinyl.

London rejoined with Test Dept, a young, politically-committed group who risked, and once suffered, arrest for staging unofficial events in industrial buildings in the city. Dressed for the foundry, backed by propaganda films and accompanied by harrowing electronics, Test Dept beat out hypnotic rhythms on huge structures rescued from scrapyards. Their debut album, *Beating the Retreat* (1985), did not make the stage-to-vinyl transition so successfully, although in 1986 their *Unacceptable Face of Freedom* EP saw them moving on to the experimental scratch dance-floor.

More political commentary than entertainment, the style was fully defined by the two groups so did not spread far. However, underground groups such as Last Few Days and Yugoslavia's Laibach are among those working in a similar area of mixing industrial sounds and social comment. Amusingly, metal-bashing as a sound-effect soon became incorporated in the production of chart singles. **Genesis**'s 'Mama' was among the first, and **Depeche Mode** have also taken the effect into the charts. It is now a staple part of funk, scratch and hip-hop, albeit reproduced on computerized keyboards.

METERS A clinically precise rhythm section from New Orleans, the Meters were formed in 1967 and comprised veteran keyboard player **Art Neville**, with Leo Nocentelli (guitar), George Porter (bass), and Joseph Modeliste (drums). Their distinctive, choppy back-beat drove countless

Allen Toussaint productions (including hits by **Lee Dorsey**, Betty Harris and **Dr John**) and gave them several minor hits in their own right, on Josie: 'Sophisticated Sissy' (1968), 'Cissy Strut', 'Look-ka Py Py' (1969), 'Chicken Strut' (1970), 'Good Old Funky Music' (1971), and Reprise: 'Cabbage Alley' (1972), 'Chug Chug Chug-a-Lug' (1973), 'Hey Pocky-a-Way' (1974). However, their rhythms were too tricky and their sound too thin to compete with the most popular disco bands, though after their signing to Reprise, their albums – *Cabbage Alley* (1972), *Rejuvenation* (1974) and *Fire on the Bayou* (1975) – did attract interest among the (white) rock audience. Cyril Neville joined in 1976, after guesting as vocalist on *The Wild Tchoupitoulas*. A year later, they broke up with Toussaint and took on Dave Rubinson as producer for *New Directions*. When Toussaint and his partner Marshall Schorn lay claim to the Meters' name, the band broke up. *See also* **Art Neville**

MGM RECORDS An outlet for MGM's movie scores, MGM Records was formed in Hollywood in 1946. A C&W series was launched with **Hank Williams**, whose recordings had a deep influence on most country-oriented rock'n'rollers. Although the label recorded jazz-blues artists like Billy Eckstine and **Ivory Joe Hunter**, occasionally in an R&B vein, it was not successful in the rock field until 1958.

Producers like Jim Vienneau began experimenting with country singers and writers and **Marvin Rainwater** and **Conway Twitty** brought considerable success to the label with 'Whole Lotta Woman' and 'It's Only Make Believe' respectively. MGM followed up with **Connie Francis** whose 'Who's Sorry Now' (1958) began a lengthy series of hits. An MGM subsidiary, Cub, recorded R&B acts the **Impalas** and **Jimmy Jones**. In the mid-Sixties, MGM's success in the pop field was limited to that of British groups the **Animals** and **Herman's Hermits**, and **Sam the Sham and the Pharaohs**, but MGM did attempt to gain some credibility in the folk and rock markets through its development of another subsidiary, Verve, as a rival to Elektra Records. Originally established as a jazz label in the Fifties, Verve's roster included **Tim Hardin**, **Laura Nyro**, **Janis Ian**, **Richie Havens** and the **Velvet Underground**, all signed to the label by the former Columbia producer Tom Wilson. In the late Sixties, the fortunes of both MGM and Verve were put in the hands of **Mike Curb**.

MIAMI Despite its many small companies and obscure record labels, Miami's musical output stems almost entirely from two sources during the Sixties and Seventies – Criteria (a modern studio associated with Atlantic but used for outside productions), and Tones/TK (a converted attic in Henry Stone's distribution/production company). Stone arrived in Miami in the early Fifties, started the Rockin' label, and shared interests in Federal and DeLuxe with King Records. By 1960 he'd relinquished these to concentrate on distribution, continuing to run smaller labels (Glades, Marlin, Dade) for local consumption. Throughout the Sixties, he used producers Brad Shapiro and Steve Alaimo but failed to secure any notable hits, although it was Alaimo who discovered **Sam and Dave**, later to find fame with Stax Records of Memphis.

Meanwhile, two black writer/producers, Willie Clarke and Johnny Pearsall, started the Deep City and Lloyd labels, featuring local acts including Frank Williams, Little Beaver, Paul Kelly, Helene Smith, and later, **Betty Wright**. Clarke teamed with singer/songwriter Clarence Reid and together they joined Henry Stone in 1968. After scoring national success with Betty Wright ('Girls Can't Do What the Guys Do', 1968), Reid, Clarke, and Alaimo gradually fostered more hits, until by the early Seventies various Stone labels (Alston, Glades, TK, Cat, Dig) represented two aspects of a popular 'Miami Sound': deep soul and the new wave of disco music. Artists included J. P. Robinson, Jimmy 'Bo' Horne, Timmy Thomas, Benny Latimore, Little Beaver, **K.C. and the Sunshine Band** and, most successfully, **George** and Gwen **McCrae**.

Simultaneously, Criteria emerged as one of the most popular studios in the south (along with Muscle Shoals, Alabama). Shapiro left Stone in the late Sixties to work there with arranger Dave Crawford, producing many sessions for Atlantic, while other top names (from **Aretha Franklin** to **Steve Stills**, **James Brown** to **Dr John**) regularly placed the studios in the credits of best-selling albums.

During the disco boom of the mid- to late Seventies, Miami labels were responsible for a steady flow of hits, including Anita Ward's transatlantic Number 1, 'Ring My Bell' (TK, 1979) and a stream of K.C. and the Sunshine Band tracks. However, TK's increasing specialization in a de-energized disco music proved its undoing, and it filed for bankruptcy in 1981.

MICKEY AND SYLVIA Blues guitarist McHouston 'Mickey' Baker, born 15 October 1925 in Lexington, Kentucky, and singer Sylvia Robinson (née Vanderpool), born 6 March 1936 in New York, met in 1955 when Mickey gave Sylvia guitar lessons. Both had previously recorded solo, and their partnership was some two years old when their fifth disc 'Love Is Strange', became a 1956 million-seller on Groove. They separated in 1961 after playing on **Ike and Tina Turner**'s 'It's Gonna Work Out Fine' (Sue) and had a last hit on their own Willow label the same year, 'Baby You're So Fine'. They reunited briefly in 1965, after which Mickey began a solo career as a blues artist and a writer of guitar instruction books.

Sylvia recorded solo for Sue and Jubilee, but in 1968 she emerged on the other side of the fence as co-owner of the All Platinum label with husband Joe Robinson. After a slow start the company became one of the most successful independents in north-east America, hitting with heavy soul (Linda Jones), smooth vocal groups (the Moments, the Whatnauts), and disco-stompers (Shirley and Co, the Rimshots, Retta Young). She also had a major hit of her own in 1973, with 'Pillow Talk' on Vibration, another self-owned label. In 1978, she relaunched All Platinum as Sugar Hill and turned it into New York's premier rap label, signing such acts as the Sugar Hill Gang and **Grandmaster Flash** and the Furious Five. *See also* **Rap**

MIDLER, BETTE The self-styled 'Divine Miss M', singer-actress Bette Midler (named after Bette Davis) was born in Paterson, New Jersey, on 1 December 1945, and brought up in Hawaii. She was variously a folk singer, go-go dancer and bit player in Broadway musicals before performing solo at a New York gay club, the Continental Baths; with Barry Manilow as her accompanist and musical director, she developed a camp stage act incorporating rock, jazz and Hollywood songs, dazzling costumes and an outrageous line in stage patter. She debuted for Atlantic with *The Divine Miss M* album in 1972 and won a Grammy award for that year's Best New Artist. In 1973, she scored three US Top 40 hits with 'Do You Want to Dance', 'Boogie Woogie Bugle Boy' and 'Friends'. Her recording career went into decline as the decade went on, but in 1979 she made a triumphant appearance in the film *The Rose*, playing a washed-out rock singer; she won

an Oscar nomination and the title song gave her a Number 3 US hit in 1980. Later films included *Jinxed* in 1982, and *Down and Out in Beverly Hills* in 1986. Although it is as a rock age cabaret entertainer that Midler has established her reputation, she remains an actress of considerable depth and a singer of no mean range.

MILBURN, AMOS Born in Houston, Texas, on 1 April 1927, Amos Milburn played an important role in the development of West Coast R&B. His husky blues voice and sophisticated jazz-tinged piano identified the club-style blues of Los Angeles and San Francisco. In 1946 he signed with newly-formed Aladdin Records, whose roster was later to boast **Charles Brown**, **Shirley and Lee** and the Five Keys. A year later, Milburn cut his most famous hit, the million-selling 'Chicken Shack Boogie'. Other huge sellers included 'One Scotch, One Bourbon, One Beer' and 'Bad, Bad Whiskey'. As the Fifties progressed, Milburn's records veered more and more towards rock'n'roll, but he had only the minimum of chart success. In later years he cut one album for Motown, *Return of the Blues Boss*. He was partially paralysed after a stroke in the late Sixties and performed only occasionally thereafter, mostly in and around Cincinnati. He died in Houston on 3 January 1980.

MILES, BUDDY A rock drummer best known for his associations with **Jimi Hendrix** and the **Electric Flag**, Buddy Miles was born on 5 September 1946, in Omaha, Nebraska. He was a backing musician for the **Ink Spots** at the age of 15 and played on numerous recording sessions during the early Sixties. While playing with **Wilson Pickett**'s band he was approached by **Mike Bloomfield** to join the Electric Flag. Miles' soul combined with Bloomfield's blues background, their personalities outweighing the other players, to create in the Flag both adventuresome ideas and consolidatory rock/soul music, as on *A Long Time Coming*. Following Bloomfield's departure, the Flag fell apart. Miles, in the driving seat for their second indifferent album *An American Music Band*, formed Buddy Miles Express out of its ruins. More brass-oriented, the Express folded when Miles joined Jimi Hendrix (guitar) and Billy Cox (bass) in the Band Of Gypsies' tour through the winter of 1969–70. After Hendrix's death, Miles and Cox picked up the pieces in the Buddy

Miles Band, and had a hit with 'Them Changes', a song continually recycled by Miles' bands ever since. He relinquished his **James-Brown**-meets-**Blood, Sweat and Tears** sets to tour with Carlos **Santana**, releasing a live album in 1972 on which their styles rarely met convincingly. Another band in between led to the re-formation of Electric Flag in spring 1974 and a typically uneven album, *The Band Kept Playing* (Atlantic). The band stayed together for a year before splitting up. In 1978, Miles was convicted of grand theft and committed to the California Institution for Men, where he formed a prison band.

MILLER, FRANKIE Born in Glasgow in 1950, Frankie Miller began his singing career in the Stoics, a late Sixties blues band, and from there joined **Robin Trower** and Jim Dewar in Jude. As a solo artist, Miller recorded *Once in a Blue Moon* (Chrysalis, 1972) with **Brinsley Schwarz** as his backing group. That album showed his blues-influenced singing style, but it wasn't until *High Life* (1973), produced by **Allen Toussaint** in New Orleans, that he fully revealed his feisty, gravelly voice and his songwriting abilities. A critical success, the album included songs that became hit singles for **Three Dog Night** and **Betty Wright**, but sold poorly. In 1975, Miller, an erratic and infrequent performer, formed the Frankie Miller Band with Henry McCullogh and Mick Weaver from the Grease Band on guitars, Christ Stewart from **Spooky Tooth** on bass, and Stu Perry on drums, and released *The Rock*, again to critical success and poor sales.

The Miller Band evolved into Full House, which recorded one eponymous album before disbanding in 1978. The solo release *Perfect Fit* included 'Darlin'', which reached Number 6 in the UK in late 1978. Later albums – *Easy Money* (1980), *Standing on the Edge* (1982, recorded in Muscle Shoals) sold only moderately.

MILLER, ROGER One of country music's great songwriting talents, Roger Miller was born on 2 January 1936, in Fort Worth, Texas. He worked in Nashville for a decade (as a songwriter, backing musician and RCA recording artist) before signing to Smash and scoring his first hit with 'Dang Me' in 1964. Both that and his other 1964 million-seller, 'Chug-a-Lug', represented his best qualities: humorous lyrics, sung tongue-in-cheek and set to infectious melodies. The following year he scored again with the blander 'King of the Road', which reached Number 1 in the UK. 'Engine Engine No. 9', 'England Swings' (an invitation to all Americans to sample the delights of 'swinging' London) and 'Little Green Apples' brought him further hits before the decade was over, but he was comparatively quiet as a chart artist during the Seventies and his songs were rarely heard outside country music radio stations. He sang the title part in the late Seventies Walt Disney cartoon film, *Robin Hood*.

MILLER, STEVE/STEVE MILLER BAND

One of the most durable American rock bands of the Sixties and after, the Steve Miller Band was the brainchild and vehicle of guitarist/ singer Miller, who was born in Milwaukee, Wisconsin, on 5 October 1943. He was raised in Texas, where, as a child, he learned about the blues – bluesman **T-Bone Walker** would play at parties for his doctor father. His first band was the Marksmen Combo, the line-up of which included **Boz Scaggs**, who later joined him in the Ardells while both attended the University of Wisconsin. Moving to Chicago, he began associating with young white blues musicians like **Mike Bloomfield** and **Paul Butterfield** and formed a band with **Barry Goldberg**.

Miller headed west to San Francisco in 1966 and formed the Steve Miller Blues Band, a tighter, more professional outfit than most in the city. With Scaggs and Miller as joint lead guitarists, drummer Tim Davis, bassist Lonnie Turner and keyboards player Jim Peterman, the band picked up a large ballroom following in no time and, during 1967, signed for Capitol for an unprecedented advance of $75,000. Now called simply the Steve Miller Band, they made their debut with *Children of the Future* (1968, recorded in England with Glyn Johns as producer): stepping well past the blues, the first side of the album featured an extended suite that meshed electronic effects and meticulous harmonies with the basic band tracks. *Sailor* (1968) was in the same vein. Scaggs and Peterman left the band in 1969, after which Miller usually stuck to a trio or quartet formation and took a higher profile than he had hitherto. There was a constant turnover of sidemen and the sound became more diffuse, but Miller managed to keep a stable, good-sized audience without actually scoring hit singles.

Top 40 success finally came in 1973 with 'The Joker', a US chart-topper,

from the platinum album of the same name. *Fly Like an Eagle* (1976) repeated this success and brought further Top 10 US hits in the shape of the title track (a Number 2) and another Number 1, 'Rock'n'Me', which also brought the Miller Band its first UK hit. Another track, 'Take the Money and Run', reached Number 11 in the US. The album heralded their best period, commercially if not musically, though a long time elapsed between the release of the follow-up album, *Book of Dreams* (1977), and their next effort – *Circle of Love* in 1981, which Miller described as an album of 'mood pieces'. It was a relative failure, the single from it ('Heart Like a Wheel') reaching only Number 24 in the US, but Miller returned to commercial form with *Abracadabra* (1982), the title song of which was another Number 1. Featured strongly on the album were new members Kenny Lewis (guitar) and John Massaro (guitar), and drummer Gary Mallaber, who co-produced all the tracks and contributed several songs. An immaculate live album, simply called *Live*, was released during 1983.

MILLIE Born Millie Small in Jamaica where she recorded a few unmemorable sides for Coxsone Dodd and one classic, 'Oh Shirley' with Roy Panton, Millie was brought to England at the peak of the bluebeat craze by the astute Chris Blackwell, who produced her international hit, 'My Boy Lollipop' (1964). Her follow-up, 'Sweet William', in similar vein, failed to register and from then on it was the long road down – a high-pitched screech based on Shirley of **Shirley and Lee** being the sum of her musical vocabulary.

MIMMS, GARNET, AND THE ENCHANTERS

After unsuccessful recordings with the Gainors on Cameo, Mercury and Big Top, Mimms (born 26 November 1937 in Ashland, West Virginia) struck lucky with the Enchanters (Sam Bell, Charles Boyer, Zola Pearnell) under the guidance of fellow-Philadelphian, **Jerry Ragavoy**. The group recorded twelve beautiful sides for United Artists, including million-selling 'Cry Baby', 'Baby Won't You Weep', and a revival of 'For Your Precious Love' (1963) before splitting into two acts for the price of one. Enchanters releases on Warners and Loma were ignored, but Mimms succeeded with further recordings for United Artists ('Tell Me Baby', 'One Woman Man' – 1964; 'It Was Easier to Hurt Her' – 1965; 'I'll Take Good Care of You' – 1966) and its subsidiary Veep

('It's Been Such a Long Way Home' – 1966; 'My Baby' – 1967). By then, however, Ragavoy was getting more reaction with another ex-Gainor, **Howard Tate**, and his sporadic productions with Mimms on Verve (1968–70) were a poor second-best. Two more releases on GSF (1972) were no improvement.

MINDBENDERS Formed in Manchester in 1963 as the backing group of singer **Wayne Fontana**, the Mindbenders comprised Eric Stewart (guitar, born 20 January 1945), Bob Land (bass) and Ric Rothwell (drums).

They released their first solo single, 'A Groovy Kind of Love', in December 1965 for Fontana. An attractive beat ballad, it reached Number 2 in January 1966, and a month later the group officially split from Wayne. They recorded five more singles, but only one, 'Ashes to Ashes', reached the charts. Two albums were released – one in 1966 and one in 1967 – containing mostly cover versions of R&B hits like 'Just a Little Bit' and 'Cool Jerk'. The group made its final bow in the 1967 film *To Sir with Love*. In later years, Eric Stewart formed Hotlegs – of 'Neanderthal Man' fame – which was eventually to become **10cc**.

MINK DEVILLE Largely a vehicle for the talents of singer/guitarist Willy DeVille (born on 27 August 1953 in New York City), Mink DeVille emerged as one of the leading bands of the New York punk and new wave explosion.

Mink DeVille were formed in San Francisco in 1974 where DeVille met Ruben Siguenza (bass) and Tom Allen (drums). Inspired by the **Ramones** and the burgeoning New York scene, they formed the band and moved to the East Coast. *Cabretta* (1977) was their well-received debut LP, but like so many new US bands of the time, they went to Britain to find their first success. 'Spanish Stroll', a strongly dance-oriented rock single with a Hispanic feel, was a UK Top 20 hit, but they failed to repeat this achievement.

DeVille came to Europe to record his third album, *Le Chat Bleu*, in 1980, by which time he had fired most of the band, and the lack of commitment shown by his label, Capitol, to his new, Cajun-influenced sound caused a change of label to Atlantic. *Coup de Grace* (1981) and *Where Angels Fear to Tread* (1983) followed but failed to fulfill DeVille's early promise.

MIRACLES *See* **Robinson, Smokey and the Miracles**

MITCHELL, GUY Born Al Cernik on 27 February 1927, of Yugoslavian parents, Guy Mitchell was a child actor in the Thirties, then joined the Navy and set about becoming a singer when he was demobbed in 1946. In 1949, he won an Arthur Godfrey Talent show and was signed to Columbia by Mitch Miller the following year. He scored with a series of million-sellers – 'My Heart Cries for You' (1950), 'The Roving Kind' (a cover of the **Weavers**' original version) and 'My Truly Truly Fair', another diluted adaptation of a folk song by Bob Merrill – who wrote most of Mitchell's hits – both in 1951. But it was 1956 that produced his best-remembered record, 'Singing the Blues' – covered in Britain, as was its follow-up, 'Knee Deep in the Blues', by **Tommy Steele**. Despite the overly cheerful backing provided by Mitch Miller, Mitchell somehow suggested he really was singing the blues. That song, however, was the exception; and when he recorded 'Heartaches by the Number', another Number 1 in 1959, Mitchell was in complete accord with Miller's backing.

MITCHELL, JONI Arguably the most outstanding female singer-songwriter of the post-Woodstock years, Joni Mitchell was born Roberta Jean Anderson on 7 November 1943, at Fort McLeod, Alberta, Canada. She turned to folk singing while at art college and performed in the folk clubs of Toronto's Yorktown area. From there she became a regular on the East Coast folk circuit in 1967, with her folksinger husband Chuck Mitchell. Some early songs were recorded by **Judy Collins** and **Tom Rush**, and minus her husband, she moved west to Los Angeles, to make her first album, *Joni Mitchell* (Reprise, 1968) under the guiding and skilful hand of ex-Byrd **David Crosby**.

Her main assets at this stage were a quirky self-taught acoustic guitar style, a voice with an exceptionally wide range, and her poetic talent. In the meantime, her first album and the two that followed – *Clouds* (1969) and *Ladies of the Canyon* (1970) – were most notable for the delicate mirror they held to the Californian peace and love ethos, a theme that culminated in her anthemic song of the festival, 'Woodstock'. Most of the time, though, the rather fey approach to reality was more than compensated for by her melodic originality, a gift for words, and her singing.

In 1970, Joni took a year off, went to Europe, went sailing with **Graham**

Joni Mitchell at Wembley in 1979: the Sixties folksinger moving into jazz

Nash and Crosby on the latter's boat. She returned to make *Blue* (1971), an album which marked a change in emphasis, shared by *For the Roses* (1972) and *Court and Spark* (1974).

A major impetus for her work at this time was the struggle to make sense of a personal failure to find lasting satisfaction in any of her well-publicized relationships. The central dilemma she experienced in these relationships – caught between security and freedom, between her consciousness and her emotional needs – was first expressed on her first album. Staring warily at each other over the accumulated paraphernalia of the hippie dream were the two Jonis – in 'I Had a King' the one who finds romance restrictive, in 'Cactus Tree' the jet-setting lady who finds freedom insufficient. These two personae fight each other with increasing sophistication, awareness, and musical skill through all her albums.

Progress in her lyrics was matched by the music. *Ladies of the Canyon* saw piano share predominance with acoustic guitar for the first time, and since then her musical range has steadily expanded. *Blue* had more of a rock rhythm; *For the Roses* (Asylum) and *Court and Spark* overlaid this with Tom Scott's immaculate woodwind and brass playing. Through this progress, Joni's melodies grew ever more imaginative, and her singing reached

new heights of expression on the luxuriant *Hissing of Summer Lawns* (1975). The power of her live performances accompanied by Scott's LA Express is captured on *Miles of Aisles* (1974).

Her subsidiary theme reflected her subsidiary relationship – that with her audience. Like **Neil Young** she produced a string of songs exploring the paradox of selling her personal life-history. 'For Free' and 'For the Roses' explore, as the titles suggest, the two sides of the coin: playing for oneself, to one's own standards, and being part of the corporate machine churning out product. 'Carey' and 'Free Man in Paris' both lament the conflict between a lost freedom and the rewards it brings.

Her privileged position in one way added to the power of her music. Being a woman free of the usual costs of living in a male-dominated society, like financial dependence and lack of opportunity for self-expression, her songs of relationships probed a deeper conflict, that between romantic love and the liberation of women. *Court and Spark* explored this area, of a woman 'raised on robbery', but looking for love, and showing how the singer herself connives against her own aspirations, caught in a double bind of a heart seeking romance and security that offends her mind, and a mind seeking freedom to find only the painful transience of love affairs.

Court and Spark was one of *the* albums of the Seventies and a difficult act to follow; *The Hissing of Summer Lawns* was, by comparison, poorly received, but it marked an ambitious change of direction in the dearth of confessional material it contained. Musically, it confirmed her new interest in jazz styling, as did *Hejira* (1976), which included some of the most beautifully impressionistic songs she had yet recorded – 'Amelia', a tribute to the aviator Amelia Earhardt, and 'Furry Sings the Blues' among them. Only *Don Juan's Reckless Daughter* (1977) seemed to suggest that Joni might be losing her creative momentum, her devotion of one side of the album to the autobiographical 'Paprika Plains' seeming something of a misjudgement. The album was notable, however, for the support work of Wayne Shorter and Jaco Pastorius from **Weather Report**, a collaboration that inspired her to take her jazz leanings one step further by recording an album with one of the giants of post-war jazz, Charlie Mingus. Called *Mingus*, this 1979 release won critical plaudits but was a commercial failure.

1982 found Joni Mitchell returning with *Wild Things Run Free*, a far less adventurous album than its predecessors, and this was followed in 1985 by *Dog Eat Dog*, a collection of songs on political issues of particular application to her adopted home state of California.

MITCHELL, WILLIE A writer/producer/arranger turned company executive, Willie Mitchell led **Al Green** and Hi Records along the same trail from Memphis to international success that **Otis Redding** and Stax had blazed a few years earlier. Born in Ashland, Mississippi, in 1928, Mitchell was raised in Memphis where he learned trumpet at high school before playing professionally with the Tuff Green and Al Jackson dance bands. In 1954, he formed his own R&B combo whose popularity throughout the South led to a recording with vocalist Billy Taylor (Skipper, 1960) and a contract as house band with Home Of The Blues records.

His work behind R&B stars like **Roy Brown** and the Five Royales and his own instrumental releases (including 'One Mint Julep', 1961) brought him to the attention of Hi's owner Joe Cuoghi. Within a year of his signing in 1963, Mitchell's hits were competing with the company's only other regular sellers, **Bill Black**'s combo and Ace Cannon. For a while he aped the winning formulas of Stax's bands ('20–75',

'Percolatin'' in 1964, 'Buster Browne' in 1965) or Tamla's **Junior Walker** ('Everything Is Gonna Be Alright', 'That Driving Beat', both 1966), but by 1968 hits like 'Soul Serenade' and 'Prayer Meeting', and his outside productions for O. V. Wright (Back Beat), Syl Johnson (Twinight), and Otis Clay (Cotillion), were beginning to display the steady, rolling rhythms and simple brass figures that typified all his later triumphs.

After becoming Hi's vice-president in 1969, Mitchell and arranger Gene 'Bowlegs' Miller groomed two new signings, **Ann Peebles** and Al Green, to project their 'Memphis Sound'. The following year, 'Part Time Love' (Peebles) and 'I Can't Get Next to You' (Green) were the first successes of the new formula. Green then scored a dozen smash hits to become one of the top five black stars in America while Ann Peebles followed in his wake. Hi has continued to expand its roster of talent, while many outside artists (including **Denise Lasalle** and the Detroit Emeralds) successfully used Mitchell's band and studio. See *also* **Al Green**

MOBY GRAPE A San Francisco group who tend to be remembered for all the wrong reasons, Moby Grape was formed in 1967 by Matthew Katz, the one-time manager of **Jefferson Airplane**. Built around Skip Spence (born 18 April 1946), the Airplane's original drummer, as rhythm guitarist and singer, Moby Grape boasted two other lead guitarists – Jerry Miller (10 July 1943) and Peter Lewis (15 July 1945) – plus Bob Mosley (4 December 1942) on bass and Don Stevenson (15 October 1942) on drums. All sang and their vocal diversity and harmonies set against the fluency of three guitars established their melodic style. After playing the city's Fillmore venue late in 1966, only weeks after formation, they were inundated with record offers. David Rubinson, of Columbia, won out and then was responsible for a wave of promotional overkill in launching their album, *Moby Grape*, in May 1967, culminating in the simultaneous release of five singles drawn from it. The group's credibility was destroyed.

Ironically, *Moby Grape* was a rare attempt by an early 'Frisco group to actually create a structured album rather than simply capture a live sound. Each member contributed songs and the magic of interweaving guitars and rapturous singing ('8.05', for example, clearly foreshadowed **Crosby, Stills and Nash**) resulted in an album

that has matured well with time. Dogged by more hype techniques and, later, an ever-fluctuating line-up, the group floundered. *Wow* was a fascinating exercise in excess with only occasional glimmers of their potential. Skip Spence left soon after to make the extraordinary *Oar* and the four-piece cut *Moby Grape '69*, complete with a disclaimer about the earlier hype. However, it was a poor album and when Mosley quit before its release, the Grape folded. Clutching at straws, the remaining trio went to Nashville to record the unimpressive *Truly Fine Citizen*, with local bassman Bob Moore depping for Mosley. They fell apart again only to return *in toto* in 1971 for the largely forgettable *20 Granite Creek*.

There's little doubt that the Grape were something special, but a never-ending saga since 1974 of re-forming and splitting did little to redeem their tarnished past reputation. Despite it all, *Moby Grape* alone reveals what a tragedy it was that they were never able to develop freely.

MODERN RECORDS Standing as one of the great R&B blues labels of the postwar era, Modern Records was formed in April 1945 in Los Angeles by white American businessman Jules Bihari and his three brothers Saul, Joe and Lester. In a few years the brothers had achieved one of the most streamlined distribution networks in the country, with a regional office in New York and contacts throughout the South.

In 1948, a deal was arranged to distribute the Texas-based Gold Star label, thus bringing the talents of country blues singer **Lightnin' Hopkins** to a mass public. That same year, Modern discovered and signed **John Lee Hooker**, one of the best and most prolific postwar bluesmen. His debut single, 'Boogie Chillen' became a nationwide R&B hit. It was **B.B. King**'s records that established the RPM label which got under way in September 1950 and became the longest surviving Modern subsidiary. King recorded literally hundreds of sides for the Biharis including his first big seller, 'Three O'Clock Blues'.

At about this time, band leader **Ike Turner** joined Modern as a talent scout. Josea, Taub and Ling, credited with writing much of Modern's output were in fact Joe, Saul and Florette Bihari. During this period the company issued product by **Howlin' Wolf, Bobby Bland, Junior Parker, Etta James, Rosco Gordon, Jimmy Witherspoon,**

Smokey Hogg, Saunders King, **Floyd Dixon**, the Cadets, Johnny Moore's Three Blazers and dozens more. In 1954, Modern signed Mississippi bluesman, **Elmore James**, to another of its subsidiaries, Flair. In 1956, the brothers decided to slacken off production of singles and concentrate on the growing market in albums via a low-budget line on Crown. Artists like Hooker and James were dropped, only B.B. King being retained. In 1957 production of all labels ceased bar Crown and Modern's latter-day successor, Kent.

MONEY, ZOOT A stalwart of the London R&B scene of the early to mid-Sixties, George Bruno 'Zoot' Money (born on 17 July 1942 in Bournemouth – then in Dorset but now in Hampshire) had a spell with Blues Incorporated in 1963 before forming Zoot Money's Big Roll Band. Backing his keyboards and vocals were Paul Williams (bass, vocals), Andy Summers (guitar), Nick Newell (tenor), Clive Burrows (baritone), and Colin Allen (drums). Although the band had no success on record, either with Decca or Columbia, Zoot rapidly became a favourite of the Flamingo audience for both his music and his clowning and took over **Georgie Fame**'s residency. A victim of psychedelia and flower power – he appeared in robes and short-lived euphoria as Dantalion's Chariot – he re-emerged in 1971 with Steve Ellis of Love Affair in the group Ellis. After recording two albums for Epic, the group broke up. Money subsequenty performed in the rock revue, Grimms, and backed Kevin Coyne. His one-time guitarist Andy Summers went on to spectacular success in the late Seventies as one third of the **Police**. In the mid-Eighties he concentrated more on developing a career as an actor and writer of film music but he played occasionally with the Big Roll Band.

MONKEES The Monkees were formed in the spring of 1966 to star in a new television comedy series about the life of a mythical pop group. The chosen four from among the hosts of unknowns auditioned for the parts were former British child star Davy Jones, vocals (born in Manchester on 30 December 1945); former American child star Mickey (Circus Boy) Dolenz, drums, vocals (8 March 1946 in Los Angeles); Peter Tork, bass, vocals (13 February 1945 in Washington, DC); and Michael Nesmith, guitar, vocals (30 December 1942 in Houston, Texas). They had talent but, initially at least, were given no chance to develop it:

they were told what to sing and how to sing it and were not allowed to play their respective instruments on recording sessions. For two years virtually every single made under the Monkees' name (on Colgems, and RCA in Britain) reached the Top 10 in both America and Britain, and for a short time it really did appear, in terms of the hysteria they created and actual record sales, that here were the new Beatles.

The musical supervision of the series was by **Don Kirshner** the head of Screen-Gems Music, who used material from the people he had worked with earlier in New York: **Carole King** and **Gerry Goffin** ('Pleasant Valley Sunday'), **Neil Diamond** ('I'm a Believer', 'A Little Bit Me, A Little Bit You'), **Neil Sedaka** and **Barry Mann**. A few of the hits were from newer writers, who would later make their mark elsewhere. **Harry Nilsson** wrote 'Daddy's Song' and 'The Puppy's Song' for them while 'Daydream Believer' was by **John Stewart**. Kirshner's approach, like that of the show's producers and publicity men, was unashamedly commercial. It secured ten gold records within eighteen months, but it also ensured that the group would rebel against the

machine that had created them. When, led by Nesmith, they won greater control over their records – at the time of *Headquarters*, the third album – Kirshner was content to manufacture another television pop group who existed only in cartoon form, the Archies.

The Monkees themselves never quite made the leap from teen idols to 'serious' rock group, 1967 style, though *Head* (the soundtrack of their one feature film) was an above-average album. The beginning of the end came, however, on 30 December 1968 when Peter Tork left, breaking his contract. Each member of the group subsequently went his own way, although the impact of the Monkees operation itself was major. A new, sub-teenage audience had been identified – an age-group which previously had shown no interest at all in pop – and it was proved that the centralization of control over an artist's material, production and the means of exposing them to the public could hardly fail. The creators of the Partridge Family (see **David Cassidy**) and the **Osmonds** were not far behind.

In 1975, the Monkees re-formed with Dolenz and Jones joined by Tommy Boyce and Bobby Hart, who had written

The Monkees, from left to right, 'cute' Davy Jones, 'dumb' Peter Tork, 'crazy' Mickey Dolenz, and 'thinker' Mike Nesmith, hand-picked for the market

many of the group's early songs ('Last Train to Clarksville', 'I'm Not Your Steppin' Stone'), as well as having hits of their own ('I Wonder What She's Doing Tonite', 1967, and 'Alice Long', 1968). They toured successfully and recorded for Capitol. Nesmith became a noted singer/songwriter, performing mainly in a country-rock vein, while Tork disappeared from view for some years before re-emerging with a band, the New Monks, in 1981. Since the late Seventies, Dolenz has been resident in the UK, where he works as an independent television producer. Davy Jones appeared in the London stage version of Nilsson's *The Point* (in which Dolenz also appeared). He also performed in pantomimes, and for a time was an on-board entertainer on the liner QE2. The group – minus Nesmith – re-formed for a very sucessful US concert tour in 1986. *See also* **Michael Nesmith**

MONOTONES
'Book of Love' by the Monotones – on Argo – soared into the Top 5 of both the R&B and pop charts early in 1958. Founded in Newark, New Jersey in 1954, the group comprised Charles Patrick (lead vocal, born 11 September 1938), Warren Davis (1 March 1939), George Malone (5 January 1940), Warren Ryanes (14 December 1937), John Smith (13 May 1938) and John Ryanes (16 November 1940). Based on a Pepsodent commercial, the arrangement – featuring a snappy drumbeat – occurred to the group when kids outside threw a ball against the window of the room in which they were practising: 'That ball hit the window, "boom", so we kept it in as the drum part.' Other discs for Argo (leased from Hull) were unsuccessful and the group disbanded when several members were conscripted.

MONTEZ, CHRIS
Singer Chris Montez was born in Los Angeles on 17 January 1943, and attended the same school in Hawthorne, California, as the **Beach Boys**. He made his first record, 'She's My Rocking Baby' at 17, in 1960. After graduating in 1961, he met Jim Lee, a young writer-producer working at Indigo Records in Hollywood. Leaving Indigo, Lee formed Monogram Records around Montez, whose first record for the label, 'All You Had To Do Was Tell Me' (a duet with Kathy Young) became a local hit. The sequel, 'Let's Dance', sold a million late in 1962, as did the follow-up 'Some Kinda Fun' (although it only reached Number 43 in the US), and Montez toured Britain with **Tommy Roe** early in 1963,

The Moodies show off their hefty collection of high-selling discs

headlining over newcomers the **Beatles**. Montez's subsequent releases flopped in 1964, Jim Lee abandoned the label to pursue a singing career. Montez came back on A&M in 1966 with 'Call Me' and 'The More I See You', the latter being a major hit in both the US and the UK.

MONTGOMERY, BOB
Songwriter/performer/producer Bob Montgomery was born in Lampass, Texas, in 1936 and moved to Lubbock where he met **Buddy Holly** in 1949. Buddy and Bob, 'Singers of Western and Bop', recorded a number of unimpressive bluegrass and country sides (later released by American Decca as the *Holly in the Hills* album) before Holly formed the **Crickets**.

Montgomery helped with the engineering in **Norman Petty**'s Clovis studios and wrote a number of songs with and for Holly, including 'Heartbeat' and 'Love Made a Fool of You'. In 1959, he moved to Nashville and his songs were soon recorded by Bob Luman, Sue Thompson ('Two of a Kind') and Mel Tillis. After several successful compositions including 'Misty Blue' (recorded by Wilma Burgess) and 'Wind Me Up' (recorded by **Cliff Richard**), he joined United Artists as a staff producer in 1966. His work there with Johnny Darrell, **Buddy Knox**, Earl Richards and Del Reeves resulted in a stream of country hits, and his silky and imaginative productions for **Bobby Goldsboro** helped to bring 'country-pop' into being. During the Seventies and Eighties he produced albums for a variety of artists, among them **Randy Crawford**, the **Crickets**, **Lobo**, B. J. Thomas, Slim Whitman and Janie Fricke.

MOODY BLUES
Heavyweights in the field of ponderous, pseudo-mystical, vaguely arty rock music, the Moody Blues first came together in Birmingham, England, in 1964. The original line-up comprised Mike Pinder (keyboards, vocals, born in Birmingham on 19 December 1942), Graeme Edge (drums, born in Rochester, Staffordshire, on 30 March 1942), Ray Thomas (vocals, harmonica, flute, born in Stourport, Hereford and Worcester on 29 December 1942), **Denny Laine** (guitar, born in Jersey, Channel Islands, on 29 October 1944) and Clint Warwick (bass, born in Birmingham on 25 June 1949).

Originally an R&B group, they had a British Number 1 hit the next year with the Bessie Banks song, 'Go Now', on Decca. Subsequent singles were unsuccessful and in 1967 Laine and Warwick left to be replaced by guitarist Justin Hayward (born in Swindon, Wiltshire, on 14 October 1946) and bass-guitarist John Lodge (born in Birmingham on 20 July 1943). The group changed direction with *Days of Future Passed*, a concept album making full use of electronic and orchestral effects, which was hailed as a successful fusion of rock and classical music. Hayward's 'Nights in White Satin' was issued as a single, reaching the British Top 20 in 1968. On re-release in 1975, it was an even bigger hit.

There followed a series of six gold albums, developing the *Days of Future Passed* formula which included Peter Knight's lush strings, quasi-philosophical lyrics of greatly varying quality and the high, vulnerable vocal tones, mainly of Hayward and Thomas. The whole was held together by the immaculate production techniques of

Tony Clarke, 'the sixth Moody'. The occasional single was released, with 'Question' (1970), 'Isn't Life Strange?' (1972) and 'Singer in a Rock and Roll Band' (1974), the most successful.

The Moody Blues' following is vast and intensely loyal, although after *Seventh Sojourn* in 1972 and its attendant world tour, the group members concentrated on separate projects, with Hayward and Lodge working together as the Blue Jays and the others as solo artists. The resulting albums appeared in 1975 on the group's Threshold label. 'Blue Guitar', by the Blue Jays, was a major hit single.

The Moodies reconvened for *Octave* in 1978, after which Pinder left to be replaced by Patrick Moraz of **Yes**. *Long Distance Voyager* followed in 1981 and *The Present* in 1983.

MOONGLOWS Bobby Lester (born on 13 January 1930), **Harvey Fuqua** (27 July 1929), Alexander Graves (17 April 1930) and Prentis Barnes (born in 1921) first came together as the Moonglows, with Billy Johnson (born in 1924) on guitar, in 1952. They recorded briefly for the Champagne label before disc jockey **Alan Freed** introduced them to Chance Records, with whom they stayed until the label folded in 1955. They then joined Chess Records, debuting with the Fuqua-Freed ballad 'Sincerely', an R&B hit covered for the pop market by the McGuire Sisters. The group led a schizoid career for a while, recording occasionally as Bobby Lester and the Moonlighters on Checker and as the Moonglows on Chess. As the latter, they scored a national Top 30 hit in 1955 with a jump tune, 'See Saw', which was featured in the film *Rock, Rock, Rock*. Their peak came in 1958 when 'Ten Commandments of Love' reached Number 22 in the Hot 100. The original line-up split up shortly after this, and though Moonglows discs appeared on Chess in 1960, the personnel had completely changed – those making up the 'new' Moonglows went on to form the core of Motown group the **(Detroit) Spinners**. Fuqua reformed the Moonglows in 1970 for revival concerts, and the group – featuring Fuqua and unspecified other members – recorded for RCA in 1972. *See also* **Harvey Fuqua**

MOORE, MERRILL Born in 1923 in Algona, Iowa, Merrill Moore was part of a small school of country-boogie pianists whose style predated rock-'n'roll. His pounding right-hand improvisations, chopped rhythms and steady drum backings on titles such as 'House of Blue Lights', 'Rock Rockola' and 'Down the Road Apiece' were an important link between the boogie-woogie and Western Swing of the Forties and the early rock styles. Moore moved to San Diego in the late Forties and has worked the club scene steadily, recording for Capitol 1952–8 and B&C in 1969. He was employed, too, as a session pianist, backing Tommy Sands' and **Wanda Jackson**'s Capitol hits.

MOORE, SCOTTY Born in December 1931, in Gadsden, Tennessee, Winfield Scott (Scotty) Moore served a musical apprenticeship in conventional country music on radio station WBRO Washington and in Nashville session work. Moving to Memphis in 1954, he formed **Elvis Presley**'s first group and was his first manager. Moore's guitar style developed out of R&B and country and western and his contribution to Presley's Sun and RCA rockabilly recordings was crucial to their sound. He toured with Presley, and appeared in movies such as *Loving You* before buying into Fernwood Records in Memphis and producing Thomas Wayne's hit 'Tragedy'. He inspired a wide range of guitarists from **James Burton** through **Lonnie Mack** to Amos Garrett.

MORODER, GIORGIO Italian producer/composer Giorgio Moroder was one of the first to realize the potential of the synthesizer; he virtually invented Eurodisco; he launched the career of **Donna Summer** and he won an Oscar for the film soundtrack to *Midnight Express* (1978).

Born in Northern Italy and educated at the local Academy of Fine Arts, he went on the road with various bands as a bassist. Playing mainly dance-oriented music he eventually wrote, produced and performed on several hit records in Germany, where soul was popular due to the US Military presence and American forces radio.

He teamed up with producer/lyricist Pete Bellotte and in 1972 had some success with 'Son of My Father', a song taken to Number 1 in the UK by Chicory Tip. Even at this early stage, the synthesizer played an important part in Moroder's compositions. The duo set up as a production team in Munich where they became major architects of the 'Munich Sound', and there they met up with Donna Summer in 1974. Two years later, 'Love To Love You Baby' was a huge international hit for Summer. Moroder went on to produce seven of her LPs.

Moroder also made synthesizer-dominated albums of his own, recording the first digitally recorded and mastered LP with $E = MC^2$ (1979) and scored a UK Top 20 solo single in 1977 with 'From Here to Eternity'. After *Midnight Express*, Moroder moved to Los Angeles and worked on the soundtrack for *American Gigolo*, which included **Blondie**'s big 1980 hit 'Call Me'. His film-score writing continued with *Cat People* in 1982, and he later collaborated with Phil Oakey of the **Human League** for the UK Top 5 single 'Together in Electric Dreams' from the film *Electric Dreams* in 1984. He continued to work as a composer and producer, scoring the dubious credit of being at the desk for **Sigue Sigue Sputnik's** debut LP.

MORRIS, DOUG A producer, songwriter and record executive, Doug Morris was one of the more significant behind-the-scenes record men of the Sixties and early Seventies. Born in 1938 in New York, Morris entered the business around 1962, writing songs for some of the artists on Laurie Records and soon becoming involved in production, working with Elliott Greenberg, one of the label's owners. One of his first productions was 'Send Her to Me' by **Gary 'U.S.' Bonds**, followed by records with many of the other Laurie/Rust/Legrand artists. His biggest hits were in 1966, with the **Chiffons**' 'Sweet Talkin' Guy' and the Barbarians' 'Are You a Boy Or Are You a Girl?' both of which he wrote and produced.

In 1970, Morris started his own label, Big Tree, whose first hit was **Lobo**'s 'Me and You and a Dog Named Boo' in April 1971. Distributed by Ampex, the label had other hits with Dave and Ansel Collins' 'Double Barrel' (one of the first reggae hits in America) and 'White Lies, Blue Eyes' by Bullet, but their biggest hitmaker was Lobo. In 1972, Big Tree switched distribution to Bell, and in two years issued over fifty singles which included, besides Lobo's hits, records by April Wine, **Duane Eddy**, Thundermug, the Happenings, and their biggest hit, 'Smokin' in the Boys' Room' by Brownsville Station (1974). Distributed after 1974 by Atlantic, Big Tree continued releasing many singles, having hits with Fancy's 'Wild Thing' and **Hot Chocolate**'s 'Emma', while Lobo and Brownsville Station were consistent sellers. In an era dominated by albums and record business bureaucracy, Big Tree was one of the last important independent singles labels in the US.

MORRISON, VAN

One of the most outstanding singing and song-writing talents to emerge out of Sixties UK rock, Van Morrison was born George Ivan Morrison in Belfast, Northern Ireland, on 31 August 1945. Through his parents – his mother Violet had been a jazz singer – he developed an early interest in blues and jazz, and left school at 15 to play music. He formed **Them** in 1963, but after two hit singles and an American tour, Morrison became disillusioned with the music business, and returned to Ireland. Later, producer **Bert Berns** invited him back to America to record for his new Bang label. Morrison agreed, and his first single, 'Brown Eyed Girl', reached the American Top 10 in 1967. Two solo albums were released on Bang, including the classic *Blowin' Your Mind* (1968).

Until then, Morrison's music had been heavily rooted in R&B. Them used it to express a distinctively punk *angst*, and although the Bang recordings showed Morrison maturing both as a singer and a songwriter, his talent still appeared derivative rather than original. *Astral Weeks* (1968), his first album for Warner Brothers, changed all this. It remains unique amongst his work: fresh, subtle and infinitely delicate. The lyrics are stream-of-consciousness romanticism, magically evoking a wealth of moods, feelings, locations, all superbly enhanced by the music. Swelling and tumbling gently, guitar, flute, sax, drums (Connie Kay) and flowing acoustic bass (Richard Davis) create a finely textured backdrop for Morrison's vocals, which in turn make brilliant use of scat and repetition.

Moondance (1970) saw him bring together the emotional vigour of his earlier, R&B-influenced work and the lighter, jazzy sound of *Astral Weeks*. All his later albums of the Seventies including *His Band and Street Choir* (1971), *Tupelo Honey* (1971), *St Dominic's Preview* (1972) and *Veedon Fleece* (1974) built on the musical synthesis of *Moondance*, central to which was the work of guitarist John Platania. Morrison's music continued to show a love of blues, country, jazz and soul; while his lyrics further explored the many moods of a singular romanticism. In 1973, he embarked on his first full-scale tour of Europe and North America, backed by a ten-piece band, the Caledonia Soul Orchestra, which included a string quartet.

Veedon Fleece was Morrison's most introspective work since *Astral Weeks* and it marked his temporary retirement from the rock limelight; he finally re-emerged out of seclusion in Ireland in 1977 to record the generally disappointing *A Period of Transition*. *Wavelength* followed in 1978 and *Into the Music* in 1979, both albums openly devotional in tone, and the spiritual theme was pursued on *Common One* (1980), a romantic celebration of the countryside that was larded with references to Wordsworth and Coleridge. These and his subsequent Eighties albums – *Beautiful Vision* (1982), *Inarticulate Speech of the Heart* (1983), *Live at the Grand Opera House, Belfast* (1984), and *A Sense of Wonder* (1985) – amply demonstrated Morrison's commitment to explore music that acts as 'a healing force ... a medicine'.

At his best, Morrison is a compelling performer. Nervous, intense, he stands motionless midstage, eyes closed, while his voice seems first to take him over, then enrapture the entire theatre. Luckily, some of his vintage live performances are available on the double album, *It's Too Late To Stop Now* (1974).

Above everything, Van Morrison is a great singer. He can take a few phrases and repeat them over and over, weaving his voice around the music, gradually working his way deeper into the listener's consciousness. When this comes off, on tracks like 'Madame George', 'Stoned Me' or 'Listen to the Lion', his music is truly spellbinding.

Van the Man from Belfast, still singing on in the Eighties

MORTON, GEORGE 'SHADOW'

Something of a cult-figure, George 'Shadow' Morton's reputation as a record producer outweighs his actual achievements which amount to a few hits in the middle-to-late Sixties by the **Shangri-Las**, **Janis Ian** and **Vanilla Fudge**. Born in 1942 in Richmond, Virginia, he nicknamed himself 'Shadow' – possibly because of his tendency to excuse himself from business meetings, ostensibly to visit the toilet and not be seen again for several days. Raised in Brooklyn, he sang with a local group, the Gems, during the late Fifties, then had numerous jobs including bouncer, ice-cream vendor and hairdresser before launching his record career in 1964 with a hit song he wrote in twelve minutes – the exotic 'Remember (Walkin' in the Sand)' by the Shangri-Las. Although Morton wrote the song, he did not produce the session, as commonly supposed. However, he did produce the group's subsequent output on the Red Bird label and established a reputation for his theatrical approach exemplified on Top 10 American hits such as 'Leader of the Pack' (a Number 1 in 1964) and 'I Can Never Go Home Anymore' (1965) and such minor hits as 'Past, Present and Future' (1966), 'Out in the Streets' and 'Give Us Your Blessing' (1965).

In 1968 Morton entered the heavy-rock field with his 'pop-art' production of 'You Keep Me Hanging On', by Vanilla Fudge and also scored with 'Society's Child' by singer-songwriter prodigy Janis Ian. He also supervised **Richie Havens**' debut album for Verve

but achieved very little commercial success in subsequent years, although he was hired to produce the **New York Dolls**' second album in 1974. An autocrat in the studio, Morton did his own arranging and most of his engineering.

MOST, MICKIE

One of the most astute independent record producers in British pop history, Mickie Most was born Michael Hayes in 1938 in Aldershot, Hampshire, but was brought up in Harrow, North London. He befriended would-be rock'n'roll star Terry Dene during the skiffle craze and both appeared as extras in a crowd scene in the film *Joan of Arc*, made at Pinewood in 1956. The following year, Dene shot to stardom as an early British teen idol while Most worked the espresso machine at the famed 2 I's coffee bar in Soho. In 1958, Most and friend Alex Murray formed the Most Brothers, recorded unsuccessfully for Decca and toured with the young **Cliff Richard**. Following his marriage in 1959 to a South African girl, Most spent the next three years in that country where he formed Mickie Most and the Playboys and covered American hits for the South African market, achieving eleven consecutive local Number 1s. Returning to England in 1962, Most attempted to break into the burgeoning R&B/beat scene but turned instead to record production. 'Baby Let Me Take You Home' by the **Animals** reached the Top 20 but the follow-up, 'House of the Rising Sun', topped charts internationally. From then on, Most achieved an impressive success ratio with a stream of international pop hits by the **Nashville Teens** ('Tobacco Road'), **Brenda Lee** ('Is It True'), **Herman's Hermits**, the Animals, **Donovan** and **Lulu**. The last two were both 'cold', chartwise, when Most took over their recording careers and furnished them both with comeback hits – respectively, 'Sunshine Superman' and 'The Boat That I Row'. He also recorded the original **Jeff Beck** Group and put Beck in the Top 10 with 'Hi-Ho Silver Lining' but was criticized for treating the guitarist like any other pop singer whose career depended on chart success. In 1969, Most formed his own label, RAK, which achieved an all-time high ratio of hits in 1973 with 14 from 18 releases; his artists included **Suzi Quatro**, **Mud** and New World. Later in the Seventies, he produced the ITV show *Revolver*, then one of the few showcases for punk rock on television, and early in the Eighties masterminded the rise to fame of his old pal **Marty Wilde**'s daughter, **Kim Wilde**.

MOTHER EARTH

Starting out in that melting-pot of music, Texas, in 1967, Mother Earth were: Tracy Nelson (born on 27 December 1944 in Madison, Wisconsin), piano, vocals, once a folk singer with a debut album on Prestige behind her; R. Powell St John, singer, once part of a bluegrass band (with **Janis Joplin**) which was resident at the legendary Threadgill's Bar in Austin; Mark Naftalin, keyboard player, then fresh out of the **Paul Butterfield** Blues Band; Bob Arthur, bass; John 'Toad' Andrews, guitar; George Rains, drums – once three-quarters of a Texas University R&B band, the Wigs, completed by **Boz Scaggs**. Rains, like the final member of the group, Martin Fiero, an accomplished sax player, had been with the **Sir Douglas Quintet**.

Their first recorded work was on *Revolution*, a soundtrack album from the film about San Francisco, their adopted home. Along with Doug Sahm, Mother Earth were the most successful in drawing from the wide Texas musical experience – blues, Cajun, soul, rock and country – and in creating a strong group identity highlighted by Tracy Nelson's full-throated singing and R. Powell's distinctive guttural tones, and by playing which was rough without being ragged, warm and mellow without being too laid-back.

Their first album, *Living with the Animals* (Mercury, 1968), is deeply rooted in both soul and blues in a highly personalized manner. If anything, their second album *Make a Joyful Noise* (1969) was even more impressive with a city side and a country side, the latter a fascinating blend of dobros, fiddle and bottlenecking offsetting Tracy Nelson's singing and an early exposition of country rock. John Andrews' funkier guitar-playing fitted surprisingly neatly into the country mould. Augmented by Nashville players they cut *Tracy Nelson Country* the same year, 1969, the group having moved to Nashville from San Francisco. They went through numerous personnel changes, with only Tracy Nelson and Andrews remaining constant, and produced a series of weaker albums, the best being *Bring Me Home* (Reprise, 1972) featuring Boz Scaggs, then arousing interest with the same rich-textured sounds Mother Earth music always conveyed. Nelson's solo albums were relatively undistinguished, though *Tracy Nelson* (Atlantic, 1974), did include a duet with **Willie Nelson**, 'After the Fire is Gone', which was nominated for a Grammy award. She later recorded for MCA, Flying Fish and Adelphi.

MOTHERS OF INVENTION
See **Zappa, Frank**

MOTÖRHEAD

Always at the forefront of the British heavy metal revival, Motörhead came to prominence at the height of punk in the late Seventies. Fronted by the awesomely ugly bassist and singer Lemmy (real name Ian Kilminster, born 24 December 1945 in Stoke-on-Trent, Staffordshire) they endeared themselves to rock and punk audiences alike with their primal combination of speed and volume, and went on to become one of the most consistently popular bands as the 'new wave' of hard rock got into full swing.

After Lemmy left his previous band, **Hawkwind**, in 1975 he formed Motörhead (a US term for a speed freak) with ex-Pink Fairies guitarist Larry Wallis and drummer Lucas Fox and played, among other gigs, support to the **Blue Öyster Cult**. The papers hated them, and they were dubbed 'the worst band in the world'. Motörhead recorded an album for United Artists, during which time Fox was replaced by unknown Phil 'Philthy Animal' Taylor (born 21 September 1954 in Chesterfield, Derbyshire) on drums, and shortly after which guitarist 'Fast' Eddie Clarke replaced Wallis.

UA refused to release the record and as the band's relations with the label stagnated, Jake Riviera suggested they record a one-off single with his new Stiff label. 'White Line Fever' was the result, but UA blocked the release and the song only surfaced later in compilation and boxed-set forms. Eventually, UA dropped the band and they recorded an album, *Motörhead* (1977) on independent label Chiswick. After an unproductive period with a new American manager, Tony Secunda, they returned to their old manager, Doug Smith, who got them a deal with Bronze Records. The first release was a tough version of an old live standard, the **Kingsmen** hit 'Louie Louie', with which they appeared on BBC TV's *Top of the Pops* – the song became a very minor hit in September 1978.

With the release of the next album, *Overkill*, in March 1979, Motörhead built up a routine of recording and touring that continued uninterrupted for three years, culminating in the live LP *No Sleep Till Hammersmith*, which reached Number 1 in the UK on 27 June 1981 and confirmed them as a top-flight band. Aspiring to international status, Motörhead supported **Ozzy Osbourne** on a forty-date US tour, returning to headline the Heavy Metal Holocaust bill at Port Vale Football Club.

Iron Fist appeared in 1982 and while the band were on tour to promote the album, Fast Eddie suddenly quit. Disagreements over projects outside Motörhead (like his teaming up of the band with **Girlschool** for the *St Valentine's Day Massacre* EP) had come to a head with Lemmy's recording of 'Stand By Your Man' with Wendy O'Williams of trash punks the Plasmatics. Ex-**Thin Lizzy** guitarist Brian Robertson (born 2 February 1956 in Clarkston, Scotland) replaced Clarke for a while, only to leave at the end of 1983. The next LP, *Another Perfect Day* came out the same year, and the fans bought it in their droves, confirming the staying power of Motörhead despite the upheavals.

The next album, *No Remorse*, did not appear for another two years and featured a whole new line-up apart from Lemmy. Taylor had gone, and the band consisted of Pete Gill (drums, born 9 June 1951 in Sheffield, South Yorkshire) and the two guitarists, Wurzel (real name Michael Burston, born 27 October 1949 in Cheltenham, Gloucestershire) and Phil Campbell (7 May 1961 in Pontypridd, Wales), but none of the venom had gone as Motörhead proved to their fans that they were as powerful a live act as ever. In 1986 they signed with GWR and put out a single, 'Death Forever' and an album, *Orgasmatron*.

MOTOWN In the beginning, there was Berry Gordy Jr. He spent the mid-Fifties working part-time on Ford Motor Company's production lines in Detroit, but the rest of his time was spent rather more creatively – writing songs and producing record sessions. By early 1960 he had written or collaborated on eighteen Hot 100 entries, six of which made the Top 20 and four selling over a million. There had also been innumerable misses and album fillers. Moreover, Gordy produced virtually all of those hits, and often ensured that the songs were published by his own firm, Jobete. His collaborators included his sister Gwen, Tyran Carlo, Janie Bradford, and **Smokey Robinson**, and artists to record his songs included **Jackie Wilson**, **Marv Johnson** and **Etta James**. Berry's production work included the Miracles (*see* **Smokey Robinson**), and he leased their masters first to End, then to Chess where 'Bad Girl' made the Hot 100 late in 1959. At this time, his sister Gwen had her own Detroit label, Anna (named after another sister), distributed by Chess, on which Paul Gayten made the Hot 100 in November 1959, and the following February **Barrett Strong** began a climb to the Top 30 with 'Money'.

These successes prompted Berry into action, and in June 1960, the Motown label (derived from Detroit's 'Motortown' tag) was launched with 'My Beloved'/'Sugar Daddy' by the Satintones, followed a month later by Tamla – he wanted to call it Tammy, after Debbie Reynolds' 1957 hit, but was prevented for copyright reasons – whose first release was a pickup of Barrett Strong's 'Money' hit from Anna. The eighth release on Tamla was 'Shop Around' by the Miracles, which by early 1961 had risen to Number 2 in the charts, selling a million copies on the way. At the same time, Motown's fourth release, **Mary Wells'** 'Bye Bye Baby', reached the Top 50, and by the end of that year the **Marvelettes'** 'Please Mr Postman' had provided Tamla's second gold disc and first chart-topper, while Eddie Holland's 'Jamie' was soon to put Motown in the Top 50 again. Success followed success, and another string was added to the Motown Recording Corporation's bow with the debut of the Gordy label early in 1962. By autumn, the **Contours'** 'Do You Love Me' had given the new label a Number 3 hit and a gold disc. Meanwhile several small Detroit independent labels with Gordy family connections were experiencing financial difficulties, having scored hits but not received payment from distributors. By the end of 1962 such labels as Harvey, Tri-Phi, Miracle, Melody and Anna had been absorbed into the Motown Corporation, and with them came the contracts of Lamont Anthony (Dozier), **Jimmy** and **David Ruffin**, **Johnny Bristol**, **Junior Walker**, the **Temptations** and **(Detroit) Spinners**. Dozier forsook his performing career to employ his writing talents in partnership with Eddie and Brian Holland (*see* **Holland, Dozier and Holland**) – a trio that was to provide Motown with a constant stream of hit records over half a decade – and Bristol also turned his attention to writing and producing, while the others were placed with the Corporation's now established labels.

The Temptations went to Gordy, where after a shaky start they reached the Top 20 in 1964 with 'The Way You Do The Things You Do', and the next year went to Number 1 with 'My Girl', written by Miracles' leader and Motown vice-president, Bill 'Smokey' Robinson, arguably the most poetic popular songwriter of his time. The Temptations have proved to be the label's most consistent hitmakers over the years, despite numerous changes of personnel and style. Their closest rivals on Gordy were **Martha and the Vandellas**, whose 1963–4 hits 'Heat-

Motörhead's macho image centred around the band's liking for studded black leather, strong beer and loud, loud music

wave' and 'Dancing in the Street' were followed by consistent chart entries up to 1970. Other artists to enjoy chart success on Gordy include the Contours, Bobby Taylor and the Vancouvers and **Edwin Starr**, who joined the label following Motown's acquisition of the Ric Tic/Golden World combine in 1967. Tamla's success continued with the Miracles and Marvelettes, while in 1963 **Marvin Gaye** – married to Anna Gordy – began a string of Top 30 hits with 'Hitch Hike', later augmenting his success in duets with Mary Wells, **Kim Weston** and **Tammi Terrell**, and the million-selling chart-topper 'Fingertips' set blind, harmonica-playing keyboard virtuoso **Stevie Wonder** on the road to fame and fortune; 1966–7 saw a brief spell of chart entries for the **Isley Brothers**.

Motown's initial momentum was maintained by Mary Wells with a succession of hits up to her departure in 1964, when the **Supremes** inherited the mantle of prime hitmakers, followed by the **Four Tops** – the Supremes recorded no less than twelve chart-toppers between 1964 and 1969 and the Tops were rarely out of the Top 50. In 1970, when these groups were waning somewhat, the **Jackson Five**, a male sub-teen group signed from the small independent Steeltown label, revitalized Motown's potency with four consecutive Number 1s, spending a total of ten weeks at the top of the charts that year. 1964 had also seen the opening of two further outlets, VIP and then Soul. VIP seems to have been intended for experimental product, with novelty items by Ray Oddis ('Happy Ghoul Time') and the Vows, material licensed from overseas (Richard Anthony), a tentative dabble with local white acts (R. Dean Taylor, the Lewis Sisters, Chris Clark) and 'mainstream' soul. It is perhaps significant that only soul brought chart success: the Velvelettes' 'Needle in a Haystack' reached the US Top 50 late in 1964, and there were subsequent hits by the Monitors, **Elgins** and (Detroit) Spinners. Meanwhile, soul soon became established when the seventh release, Junior Walker's 'Shotgun', reached the Top 5 early in 1965 – the first in a succession of hits for his combo. Shorty Long (killed in a boating accident in 1969), Jimmy Ruffin, the Originals and **Gladys Knight** and the Pips subsequently kept the label well represented in the charts.

In 1970, the Motown Corporation took a step into the rock market with the Rare Earth label, which achieved

Label boss Berry Gordy who put Motown on the move in June 1960

four Top 10 hits in its first year – three by **Rare Earth**, a group of white Detroiters restyling Sixties hits in 'heavy' fashion, and one by R. Dean Taylor. The following year, the Corporation moved its administrative quarters to Hollywood as Berry Gordy became involved in movies, grooming **Diana Ross** for stardom in the title role for a biographical film on Billie Holiday, *Lady Sings the Blues*. The move also brought a new label, aptly named Mowest, with a roster including Gloria Jones, Sisters Love, G. C. Cameron and Tom Clay, a disc jockey who took the second release into the Top 10, 'What the World Needs Now Is Love – Abraham, Martin and John', a bizarre but striking collage of radio station tape clips pertaining to various political assassinations, with tasteful musical background. In 1973, Gordy took the chairmanship of his conglomerate, relinquishing the presidency to **Ewart Abner**, whose pedigree included presidency of Vee Jay during the Sixties and Motown staff production duties.

Meanwhile, Motown stalwarts Marvin Gaye and Stevie Wonder set off on less formula-ridden, more personal musical directions with *What's Going On?* and *Where I'm Coming From* respectively; Wonder renegotiated his financial and personal terms for staying with Motown and re-signed in 1975 for $13 million, at that time the biggest advance in US record industry history. Meanwhile, other popular Motown acts like Gladys Knight, Martha Reeves, the Four Tops and the Spinners all left the label, and the Holland, Dozier, Holland team set up their own rival company, Invictus, though the Jackson

Five, the Miracles (without Smokey Robinson, who quickly established himself as a solo artist), **Eddie Kendricks** were among the Corporation's most notable Seventies acts. The Jackson Five left Motown in 1976 to sign with Epic and rename themselves the Jacksons, while Diana Ross stayed until 1980 and Marvin Gaye until 1982, by which time the label's principal artists were the **Commodores** and their long-time singer/songwriter **Lionel Richie**, **Rick James**, Debarge and – as ever – Stevie Wonder.

MOTT THE HOOPLE Named after a book by Willard Manus, Mott the Hoople originally called themselves Silence and comprised Mick Ralphs (guitar, born 31 May 1944), Dale 'Buffin' Griffin (drums, 24 October 1948) and Pete 'Overend' Watts (bass, 13 May 1947), all of whom had been playing together in the Hereford area since the mid-Sixties. Completing the line-up by 1969 was Verden 'Phally' Allen (organ, 26 May 1944). Ralphs shopped demo tapes around the London record companies and struck gold with Island Records A&R man Guy Stevens, who was responsible for their change of name. Their vocalist, Stan Tippens, left the group to become their road manager and Ian Hunter (3 June 1946), an avid **Dylan** fan who knew only two songs on the piano, joined in his place. From the first album his constant wearing of sunglasses (due to weak eyes), long curly hair and his blatant Dylan stylings provided the group with a focal point.

In 1972 – after four albums, notably *Brain Capers* (1971) – they broke up due to bad luck and debts, but were encouraged by **David Bowie** to re-form and signed with Columbia Records. Bowie penned 'All the Young Dudes', their first hit in 1972. Hit singles continued in Britain – notably 'All the Way from Memphis' (1973), 'Roll Away the Stone' (1974) – while albums took off in America – *Mott* (1973) and *Mott The Hoople* (1974). In early 1973 Verden Allen left; later that year Mick Ralphs left to join **Bad Company**. He was replaced by Ariel Bender (Luther Grosvenor, ex-**Spooky Tooth**). Later, Blue Weaver (organ) and Morgan Fisher (piano) were added. In mid-1974 Weaver and Bender left; Fisher took over the keyboards while Bender was replaced by **Mick Ronson**. In December the pressures became too much for Hunter and without warning he and Ronson left to pursue a career together. After several months of auditions they were replaced by Ray Majors (guitar) and Nigel Benjamin (vocals), the group's name being shortened to Mott. Two albums followed before the group broke up for good. The Hunter-Ronson Band folded after one disastrous tour and Hunter began a solo career. Verden Allen formed Cheeks, whose personnel included James Honeyman-Scott and Martin Chambers, both future members of the **Pretenders**.

MOUNTAIN The original line-up of Mountain was Leslie West (guitar, born Leslie Weinstein in New York on 22 October 1945), **Felix Pappalardi** (bass, born in New York in 1939), Steve Knight (keyboards), and Corky Laing (drums, born in Montreal, Canada, on 28 January 1948). A heavy guitar-led outfit, they were based on the **Cream** model, Pappalardi having produced several of the British band's albums. West had previously been a member of Long Island's favourites the Vagrants.

Formed in 1969, they had a Top 30 hit the next year with 'Mississippi Queen' (Windfall), and in their three-year existence produced five albums, all acceptable to Cream fans starved of their heroes. In 1972, Pappalardi left to be replaced by **Jack Bruce**. As West, Bruce and Laing, the new trio cut two further albums during 1972-3. To complete the circle, the original Mountain re-formed in 1974 to cut *Avalanche* (Windfall), before splitting up again in 1975. West produced two solo albums, *The Great Fatsby* and *The Leslie West Band* (both 1975); Laing's solo offering, *Makin' It on the Street*, appeared in 1977. Pappalardi moved to Japan, where he produced and played with heavy metal band Creation. On 17 April 1983, he was shot dead by his wife and songwriting partner Gail Collins. *See also* **Felix Pappalardi**.

MOVE Formed in late 1965 from the cream of the Birmingham, England, beat groups, the Move comprised guitarist and songwriter **Roy Wood** (born on 8 November 1946), drummer Bev Bevan (25 November 1945), bassist Ace 'The Singing Skull' Kefford (10 December 1946), guitarist Trevor Burton (9 March 1949), and vocalist Carl Wayne (18 August 1944). Manager Tony Secunda booked them into London's Marquee Club in late 1966 where their violent and dramatic approach to performing caused a sensation and won them a following among London's burgeoning underground. Their first record, 'Night of Fear' (Deram), a pastiche of Tchaikovsky's '1812 Overture', which reached Number 2 in Britain in January 1967, was a Roy Wood composition, supposedly

inspired by Secunda's prompting. Subsequent Top 20 hits of note included: 'I Can Hear the Grass Grow', 'Flowers in the Rain', 'Fire Brigade', 'Blackberry Way', 'Curly', 'Brontosaurus', 'Tonight' and 'California Man' – all by Wood, who developed into a sucessful and consistent formula pop-writer of little originality but with a flair for mimicking and reworking styles.

The Move veered uneasily between psychedelia and a career as a hit singles band with only one minor hit album, their first *The Move* (1968), at a time when singles and album charts were developing in different directions. A late flirtation with heavy metal on *Looking On*, which yielded 'Brontosaurus', was largely unsuccessful. Secunda's flamboyance backfired when Prime Minister Harold Wilson sued successfully over a postcard caricature designed to publicize the 1967 single, 'Flowers in the Rain' (Regal Zonophone). Internal dissent led to the departure of Ace Kefford, then Trevor Burton, and finally, after a disastrous excursion into cabaret, Carl Wayne. Birmingham musicians Rick Price, bass (born 10 June 1944) and **Jeff Lynne**, guitar and vocals (12 December 1947) replaced them; the latter avowedly to launch a new project with Wood – the **Electric Light Orchestra** (ELO). The final line-up made one brief trip to America in 1971 before coming off the road for good. The last hit, 'California Man' (the B-side of which, 'Do Ya', was their only American chart entry), appeared in May 1972, just three months before ELO's first hit '10538 Overture' signalled the end of the Move.

See also **Roy Wood**; **Electric Light Orchestra**.

MOYET, ALISON Born in Billericay, Essex, on 18 June 1961, Genevieve Alison 'Alf' Moyet first came to prominence when she was recruited by Vince Clarke to sing in the electro-pop outfit, **Yazoo**. Previously she had been doing the rounds on the Essex R&B pub circuit, singing in a succession of bands like the Vicars and the Screaming Abdabs. After her brief, hugely sucessful partnership with Clarke came to an end in 1983, Moyet signed a lucrative solo deal with CBS Records.

Even though her vocal delivery had been critically acclaimed when she sang with Yazoo, it wasn't until she embarked on a solo career, and was freed of the limitations of the electronic format, that her resonant, versatile voice was allowed full rein. After a long delay during which she gave a couple

of live jazz and blues performances, her first solo release was the single 'Love Resurrection', a booming dance number that reached the UK Top 10 in June 1984; the second single, 'All Cried Out' was similarly well received (reaching Number 8). Her debut solo LP *Alf* sold over a million copies in the UK and established Moyet in that growing band of solo performers who achieved star status by appealing to a crossover audience consisting of chart-obsessed teenagers as well as the more serious adult listeners.

In 1985 she braved the wrath of the critics by covering a legend when she released a version of Billie Holiday's 'That Ole Devil Called Love'. (Holiday's voice had been a favourite yardstick for critics when seeking to draw comparisons to Moyet's.) It was favourably received by even the most diehard Holiday fans and became a huge hit. Later that year, she took part in the summer's Live Aid (see **Band Aid**) extravaganza, and her duet with **Paul Young** was one of the highlights of the occasion. Early in 1987, 'Weak in the Presence of Beauty', produced by Jimmy Iovine, got to Number 6 in the UK Top 10.

Alison Moyet, one of the most distinctive voices of the Eighties

MTV American cable music channel MTV (Music TeleVision) opened on 1 August 1981, and by mid-1983 had become second in importance only to radio as a promotional vehicle for music industry products. Launched by Warner Communications Inc., MTV offered a 24-hour menu of rock videos, music news, interviews and chit-chat, presided over by a team of 'VJs' (video jockeys) and aimed unequivocally at the teenage television market. Because the promotional use of video was comparatively undeveloped in the US at this time, MTV relied heavily in its early days on videos imported from the UK, and its extensive exposure of UK products helped immeasurably to pave the way for the so-called 'British Invasion' of rock acts from 1982 onwards. Although initially positive in its influence on a rather stagnant US rock scene, in time MTV appeared staid and reactionary in its programming policy – its apparent exclusion of black musicians and singers on the grounds that soul and disco music were not 'rock' was particularly criticized. Also, as US record companies moved into video in a major way, so MTV became less reliant on British imports and became more of a vehicle for mainstream American rock and pop. In 1985, Viacom International bought out Warner Communications' holding in MTV in a reported £550 million deal, and a year later the channel suffered its first serious ratings drop. By 1987, a European version of MTV, to be beamed across the Continent by satellite, was in the planning stage, jointly financed by Viacom, British Telecom and Robert Maxwell's Mirror Group Newspapers.

MUD A group adopted by songwriters Nicky Chinn and Mike Chapman (Chinnichap) in the early Seventies after their success writing and producing for the **Sweet**, Mud were altogether homelier than their flash stablemates. Their line-up was Les Gray (vocals), Rob Davis (guitar), Roy Stiles (bass) and Dave Mount (drums). The collaboration with Chinn and Chapman produced a series of hit singles between 1973 and 1975, starting with 'Crazy' (RAK, 1973) and culminating in the clever **Presley** parodies, the chart-topping 'Lonely This Christmas' (1974) and 'The Secrets That You Keep' (1975). Dissatisfied with the slim financial return from enormous record sales, the group split with Chinnichap and RAK early in 1975. Their departure was followed by the release of two hit singles from their old partnership, 'Oh Boy' (a Number 1) and 'Moonshine Sally'. None the less, their first self-produced singles on Private Stock, 'L-L-Lucy' and 'Show Me You're a Woman', easily made the Top 20. Their last hit was 'Lean on Me' in 1976, though a now-solo Gray did reach the chart during the following year with a Presley-like rendition of the **Mindbenders'** hit, 'A Groovy Kind of Love'.

MULDAUR, MARIA For a time in the mid-Seventies, Greenwich Village-born Maria Muldaur appeared to have blended jazz, blues, gospel, bluegrass and country music into a successful hit formula. Influenced by the records of blues singer **Bessie Smith** and the early bluegrass musicians, she started singing in local folk clubs, and at sixteen formed a girl group, the Cashmeres. They signed with Gone records and did some back-up work for other artists. Maria (née Maria Grazia Rosa Domenica d'Amato on 12 September 1943 in Greenwich VIllage, New York) later became interested in Appalachian music as performed by Doc Watson and others. She learned to play fiddle from the great Gaither Carlton, Watson's father-in-law. At 21 she joined the Even Dozen Jug Band which included **John Sebastian**, **Stefan Grossman** and Joshua Rifkin. They cut an album, played two shows at Carnegie Hall, did some TV work and then disbanded.

Maria moved to Cambridge, Massachusetts, and married Geoff Muldaur, a member of **Jim Kweskin's Jug Band**. She soon became a full-time group member, staying with them for six years and recording several albums. When the band broke up, Maria and Geoff moved to Woodstock and cut two albums for Reprise – *Pottery Pie* and *Sweet Potatoes*. When her marriage faltered, Maria struck out on her own. Her first album, *Maria Muldaur*, released in June 1974, was well received and included the hit single 'Midnight at the Oasis', a Top 20 success on both sides of the Atlantic. Produced by **Lenny Waronker** and Joe Boyd, the album featured an assortment of musicians including **Dr John**, **Ry Cooder**, Clarence White and Amos Garrett, who played the exceptional guitar solo break on 'Midnight'. Her second album, *Waitress in a Donut Shop*, released in December 1974, included three songs arranged and conducted by the eminent jazz saxophonist Benny Carter, who was joined by some of the best jazz musicians in the world. Maria then became well known in jazz as well as rock circles, her wispy, fragile voice and Bohemian looks winning her a top-of-the-bill spot at the 1975 Newport and Montreux Jazz Festivals. After this promising start, however, her career suffered a setback when her third album for Reprise, *Sweet Harmony*, sold poorly. For *Southern Winds* (1978), she switched to Warner Brothers but this failed to re-establish her momentum. In 1980, she moved to the Takoma label and began recording in a straight gospel vein.

MULLICAN, MOON A popular country-and-western pianist of the Forties and Fifties whose pumping left hand and 'two-finger' right hand style influenced **Jerry Lee Lewis**, Moon Mullican was born in Corrigan, Texas, in 1909 and gained experience as a pianist in the clubs of Houston, Beaumont and Nashville before recording for Decca in the Thirties and appearing in several Western movies. He earned the title 'King of the Hillbilly Piano Players' with C&W hits for King such as 'Jole Blon' in 1947 and 'I'll Sail My Ship Alone' in 1951. Between 1956 and 1958, Mullican recorded several rock songs including 'Seven Nights to Rock' with Boyd Bennett's band, whose 'Seventeen' had been a rock hit in 1955.

MUNGO JERRY Featuring a line-up of skiffle revivalists, Mungo Jerry was dominated by the personality of lead singer Ray Dorset (born 1946 in Ashford, Kent). Originally known as Good Earth, the Mungoes – Dorset, Paul King, Mike Cole and Colin Earl – were the hit of the Hollywood (Newcastle) Festival in 1970 and simultaneously released their million-seller and UK Number 1 'In the Summertime' (Dawn). The majority of their subsequent singles were successful, including 'Baby Jump' (1971, another Number 1) and 'Alright Alright, Alright' (1973). When critics attacked the group's music for being very monotonous, Dorset brought out a solo album (*Cold Blue Excursion*, 1972) in which he experimented unsuccessfully with a variety of styles. Long after the group's break-up, Dorset turned to record production – among his hits was Kelly Marie's 1980 UK Number 1, 'Feels Like I'm in Love'.

MUNICH The Eurodisco phenomenon of the mid- to late Seventies was the work of a handful of producers, based almost exclusively in the West German city of Munich, who crafted a sound that sold millions of records all over the world, and took America by storm. Most of the artists that these producers made famous were actually British or American, although they had in many cases spent years working in Europe. The producers, who closely controlled their artists' material and sometimes the artists themselves, had a background of working in European pop.

Very popular for most of the Sixties, interest in disco had waned by the end of the decade and it wasn't resurrected until **Barry White** and **Gloria Gaynor** scored enormous hits in 1974 with the soul dance numbers 'Can't Get Enough of Your Love, Babe' and 'Never Can Say Goodbye' respectively. At the same time in Europe, especially in the holiday resorts, the occasional good-time disposable dance number became a big hit like the George Baker Selection's 'Paloma Blanca' in 1975, but it was only when Munich-based Italian producer **Giorgio Moroder** teamed up with **Donna Summer** and recorded the 17-minute dance epic, 'Love to Love You Baby' (an international chart success early in 1976), that Eurodisco proper was born. Moroder, along with his English partner Pete Bellotte, was the most successful of the Continental producers and did more than anyone to define the mesmeric metronome beat that characterized Eurodisco.

While Moroder and Bellotte were creating Donna Summer's sound, other producers continued to plug away, like Michael Kunze with his Silver Convention project who had a US Number 1 with 'Fly Robin Fly' in 1975, but one spectacularly successful exponent was German producer Frank Farian. Successful as a solo singer before taking up production, Farian was the man behind **Boney M**'s string of huge international hits which started in 1976 with 'Daddy Cool' and included 'Rivers of Babylon' and 'Mary's Boy Child', although the band failed to make significant inroads into the American market.

Although Moroder has said that they might have all been successful earlier had they been based in London or Los Angeles, the fact is that they were based in Munich which was where, in the mid-Seventies, everything came together at the right time. It was German record companies – Oasis, Jupiter and Hansa – who put faith, time and money behind Eurodisco. With that support, and as a result of the work of all those producers mentioned above, Eurodisco became a significant strand of international popular music in the late Seventies.

MURRAY, ANNE Top easy-listening singer Anne Murray was born in Spring Hill, Nova Scotia, Canada, on 20 June 1946, and started singing professionally when she was signed by Brian Ahern – later her producer – for a season on Canadian TV's folksy *Sing-Along Jamboree*. She joined Arc Records and then Canadian Capitol with whom she had her first hit, 'Snowbird', in 1970. In America it inaugurated a series of country hits, including 'Talk it Over in the Morning', 'Cotton Jenny' (1972) and 'He Thinks I Still Care' (1974).

However, while her country hits and

singles like 'Danny's Song' (a Top 10 hit in 1973) and 'Love Song' (1974) showed the pleasant and gentle side of her singing, album tracks like her soulful version of Barbara George's 'I Know' and singles like the Top 10 'You Won't See Me' – originally the flip of 'He Thinks I Still Care' – also showed her to be a strong interpretative and expressive singer. Unlike many of the new breed of MOR/country singers, Murray (and producer Ahern) did not allow her early successes to set the pattern of her career. Thus she continues to live in Canada and record Canadian writers like Bruce Cockburn and **Gordon Lightfoot**. Among her late Seventies and early Eighties hits were 'You Needed Me' (a US Number 1 in 1978) and a revival of the **Monkees**' hit 'Daydream Believer' (1980).

MUSCLE SHOALS The reputation of Muscle Shoals as a recording centre is the result of the industry and perseverance of **Rick Hall** of Fame Studios. After years of touring locally with a small combo, doing session work for Hi Records in Memphis and writing songs with **Billy Sherrill**, Hall opened his studios in 1961 in Florence, Alabama, where he lived. He quickly collected around him a group of white musicians with their heads and hearts in southern R&B, among them **Spooner Oldham** and Barry Beckett, organ; Jimmy Johnson, guitar; David Hood, bass; and Roger Hawkins, drums. Unlike Memphis or New Orleans, Muscle Shoals offered no readily identifiable 'sound' as such, though arrangements on slow numbers tended to be church-like, with solemn, elegaic keyboard work and Hall tended to feature a repeated guitar riff on faster songs.

During the early Sixties, artists like **Tommy Roe** and the **Tams** (from Bill Lowery's Atlanta-based stable) recorded at Fame, and in 1964 Hall launched his own Fame label, scoring immediately with Jimmy Hughes' 'Steal Away'. **Joe Tex**'s 'Hold What You've Got' was another Muscle Shoals creation that year, and a year later Hall negotiated a distribution deal with Atlantic that prompted Jerry Wexler to venture south with such artists as **Aretha Franklin** and **Wilson Pickett**. **Arthur Conley**'s first hits were cut at Fame, while Chess used the studios to record **Etta James**, **Irma Thomas**, Maurice and Mac, and Bobby Moore's Rhythm Aces. In later years the diverse styles of **Otis Rush**, **Ronnie Hawkins** and others benefited from the Rick Hall touch, and during the Seventies the famous rhythm section – who in 1968

set up their own studio in neighbouring Sheffield, Alabama – played on sessions for the **Staple Singers**, **Paul Simon**, Bob Seger, **Millie Jackson** and many others. *See also* **Rick Hall**

MUSICAL YOUTH Leaping to a fairytale success that was helped initially by their novelty value, Birmingham (England) youngsters Musical Youth scored one of the biggest worldwide hits of 1982 with the highly commercial reggae track, 'Pass the Dutchie'. The boys, all aged between 11 and 15 at the time of their first hit, had been brought together by Frederick Waite, the father of Junior (drums) and Patrick (bass). Schoolfriends Dennis Seaton (vocals) and brothers Kelvin (guitar) and Michael Grant (keyboards/vocals) completed the line-up.

Freddie Waite had sung in the Sixties with Jamaican band, the Techniques, and after emigrating to England he pursued his musical interests, playing in bands and giving music lessons to local children at Saltley Music Workshop, a community arts centre in Birmingham. Musical Youth were assembled there in 1980 and, initially fronted by Freddie, they played pubs in the area, although these venues presented certain difficulties since at the time, Kelvin Grant was a mere eight years old. They recorded one single, 'Political'/'Generals', on Birmingham's 021 label, and sent demo tapes to DJ **John Peel**.

Eventually Seaton replaced Freddie Waite as full-time vocalist, and aided by the fervent support of Peel, plus an appearance at the Notting Hill Carnival, the group were signed by MCA Records in January 1982. Under the guidance of producer Peter Collins, they released a cleaned-up version of an old Jamaican ganja song 'Pass the Kutchie', which had been covered by the Mighty Diamonds. The irresistible 'Pass the Dutchie' (a dutchie being a communal cooking pot, as opposed to the dope bowl of the original) was released in September and became an instant hit, selling 115,000 copies in one day, reaching the UK Number 1 spot and clocking up worldwide sales of over 4 million.

The single came from the LP *Youth of Today*, on which they proved the extent of their talents by playing all the instruments and writing most of the material, including the excellent pop/reggae hit 'Never Gonna Give You Up'. A string of lesser hits and a poorly received second album, *Different Style!* in 1983 were followed by a long period of inactivity.

NAPIER-BELL, SIMON One of the most fabled, respected, ridiculed, outspoken, successful and deeply-tanned rock managers through three decades, Napier-Bell has steered the careers of both the influential and the trashy, seemingly with three guiding principles: that they earn money, make headlines and do a fair bit to cultivate his own image. From co-writing Dusty Springfield's 'You Don't Have to Say You Love Me' he graduated to managing the **Yardbirds**, Marc Bolan of **T. Rex** and John's Children and, after a lengthy retirement, **Japan**. A two-year management of **Wham!** with ex-partner Jazz Summers included an historical exploratory tour of China in 1985, but ended in controversy when his Nomis management complex engineered a £5m buy-out deal with a company strongly linked to the owners of South Africa's Sun City. As a result of this action, Wham!'s George Michael broke away. Napier-Bell, ever-keen to prolong his distinctly exotic lifestyle, branched out into journalism and television soaps in the mid-Eighties.

NASH, GRAHAM A leading member of the Manchester group, the **Hollies**, Graham Nash – born on 2 February 1942, in Blackpool – co-wrote and sang harmony on most of that group's successful singles in the mid-Sixties. Becoming disenchanted with their commercialism and the lack of recognition of his own work, he joined **Stephen Stills** and **David Crosby** in California in 1968 as one-third of **Crosby, Stills and Nash**, where more lasting music and stardom were to come. His songs for CSN and Crosby, Stills, Nash and Young and those on his two early Seventies solo albums – *Songs for Beginners* (1971) and *Wild Tales* (1973) – straddled the line between a powerful emotional simplicity and a naïve sentimentality. 'Lady of the Island' and 'Our House' were good examples of the two poles. Nash's problem has always been that his superb harmony voice is not really suited to extensive lead singing. The three CSN reunion albums – *CSN* (1977), *Daylight Again* (1982) and *Allies* (1983) – provided a better showcase for his vocal talents than his 1980 solo album, *Earth and Sky* (EMI), confirming that he has always tended to be at his best in a group context.

NASH, JOHNNY Born in Houston, Texas on 19 August 1940, Johnny Nash (real name John Lester Nash Jr) has been into more bags than a wrongly addressed envelope. As the (black) teenage star of KPRC's *Matinee*, he broke the Houston TV colour bar and attracted the attention of ABC-Paramount, for whom he scored with 'A Teenager Sings the Blues', 'A Very Special Love' (Top 50 in 1957), 'The Teen Commandments' (Top 30 in 1958) on which he shared the vocal chores with **Paul Anka** and **George Hamilton IV**, and 'As Time Goes By' (Top 50 in 1959).

While Nash went on to star in films like *Take a Giant Step*, *Key Witness* and the Swedish *Love Is Not a Game*, his recordings – which hovered unsuccessfully between soul and night-club easy listening – appeared on a variety of labels including Warner Brothers (1962–3), Groove, Argo (1964) and MGM (1970). His own labels, Joda and Jad, which operated intermittently between 1965 and 1970, brought him back to the charts with 'Let's Move and Groove Together' (1965) and the even more successful Byron Lee Jamaican studio recordings, 'Hold Me Tight' (a Number 5 in 1968), 'You Got Soul' and 'Cupid' (1969). Nash subsequently built his own studio on the island and established himself as the leading exponent of commercial reggae with internationally successful discs for Epic, including 'Stir It Up' (1971), 'I Can See Clearly Now' (an American Number 1), the eloquent 'There Are More Questions Than Answers' (1972), 'Tears on My Pillow' (a UK Number 1) and 'Let's Be Friends' (1975). His composition for **Joey Dee**, 'What Kind of Love Is This', hit the Top 20 in 1962 and he also produced Sam and Bill's Hot 100 entry, 'For Your Love', in 1965.

NASHVILLE The state capital of Tennessee, Nashville is often called 'Music City USA', and with good reason. It boasts a multi-million dollar recording industry which developed from country music. In 1925, radio WSM started a *Barn Dance* programme which became known as the *Grand Ole Opry*, a country music institution which continues to this day.

No record labels were based there until Bullet was formed in 1945 and recorded country music, R&B, gospel and popular music in the WSM studios. Nashville quickly became the country capital after radio engineers Aaron Shelton and Carl Jenkins had set up their Castle Recording Studio in the Tulane Hotel, providing facilities for major companies like Decca, while Acuff-Rose and Hill And Range Publishers were formed in 1942 and 1945 respectively, opening the way for a thriving recording and business network. The Tennessee and Republic labels were formed locally, and soon all the major companies followed Decca in establishing an office in the city. The music itself had not substantially altered at this time, however, being mainly traditional and played on acoustic instruments.

Ironically, the catalyst in the development of the 'Nashville Sound' was rock'n'roll. Country took a battering from the sales of rock records and many labels based in Nashville began to record the style. **Elvis Presley** was imported from nearby Memphis, the **Everly Brothers** recorded there, and the session musicians learned to adapt. By now, amplified guitars were the rule, while the piano also came to the fore as traditional country fiddle and banjo accompaniment went into disfavour. By the late Fifties, a group of musicians including **Chet Atkins**, **Floyd Cramer**, Grady Martin, Bob Moore, Buddy Harman and Boots Randolph had evolved a sound that became known as the most slick, professional studio back-up in popular music. The guitar was rock, but smooth, and vocal choruses added sophistication to the sound of singers like **Patsy Cline**, **Don Gibson**, **Jim Reeves** and Faron Young. Very soon the full range of orchestral and choral effects were being utilized in the Nashville studios.

In 1958, the Country Music Association (CMA) was formed and in 1960 the city grossed 35 million dollars through its music activities. Studios such as RCA and Bradleys became renowned, and producers and A&R men – recording popular singers like **Connie Francis** and Petula Clark as well as country artists – provided hit after hit. By 1963, half the recordings made in the US came out of Nashville, and men such as Shelby Singleton, Don Law, Ken Nelson, Steve Sholes and Jim Vienneau could fairly claim to have transformed the country music industry.

Nashville continued to cater for the needs of popular singers during the Sixties, but 1968 was largely a watershed year. The **Byrds** came to town to record with country session men and the classic *Sweetheart of the Rodeo* album resulted. Then **Bob Dylan** came to the city to record *Nashville Skyline*, including a duet with an established Nashville figure, **Johnny Cash**.

The story of Nashville since 1969 has

been that of the further development of these two trends: the country-pop confluence and the country-rock tributary. The popular music of the Seventies made increasing use of the steel guitar behind ballad singers and country artists like **Tammy Wynette**, Faron Young and **Charlie Rich** topped charts internationally – while **Olivia Newton-John** managed to do the same thing by copying the Nashville approach in London.

Apart from the forays of West Coast groups, including the important recordings of the **Nitty Gritty Dirt Band** in Nashville, the city also produced its own brand of 'modern' singer/songwriters like **Kris Kristofferson**, **Mickey Newbury**, **Tom T. Hall**, **Waylon Jennings** and **Billy Swan**. Instrumentally, a group of 'Nashville Sound' musicians formed Area Code 615 in the country-rock style, and bluegrass veteran **Earl Scruggs** recorded with folk and rock artists like **Joan Baez** and the Byrds.

However, the music business itself largely remains in the hands of the same major labels and publishers, though several new independent labels did emerge in the mainstream country field, like Mega, Stop, Chart and the temporarily successful Cinnamon.

NASHVILLE TEENS

NASHVILLE TEENS A British R&B band who found some chart success in the mid-Sixties, the Nashville Teens were formed in 1962 in Weybridge, Surrey, and comprised Arthur Sharp (vocals), Ray Phillips (vocals, bass), John Hawken (piano), John Allen and Pete Shannon (guitars), and Barry Jenkins (drums). They learned their craft in the clubs of Hamburg between 1963 and 1964: from this period, only a live album backing **Jerry Lee Lewis** (on which their contribution was mixed down) remains. In 1964, managed by Don Arden and with **Mickie Most** as producer, they cut a version of **John D. Loudermilk**'s 'Tobacco Road'. Featuring strident piano, a fierce beat and the two singers up front, it reached both the British and US Top 10s. However, their label (Decca) failed to grasp how original an R&B outfit they were – tracks like 'Parchman Farm' and 'I Need You Baby' from a 1964 EP bear witness to that originality – their pop singles were a travesty of their excellence. The band continued working into the Eighties, though with a much changed line-up still led by Ray Phillips. Sharp left in 1972, while Jenkins joined the **Animals** and Hawken joined Keith Relf in **Renaissance**. Nowadays, the Teens play mostly small clubs, pub venues and the occasional revival show.

NAZARETH When they moved to London from Fife, Scotland, Nazareth were able to prove one of the fundamental formulas of rock – that heavy rock projected with the aid of the right business expertise was a guaranteed success. The band turned professional in late 1971 and was launched at a fashionable Soho strip club but it was frequent touring throughout Britain and Europe that produced success. They had to wait eighteen months for their first Top 10 hit, 'Broken Down Angel' (1973). Then it all came at once for them – a headline British tour, follow-up hits 'Bad Bad Boy' and 'This Flight Tonight' (written by **Joni Mitchell**), and a hit album, *Razamanaz* (Mooncrest, 1973). They had the right stage image, projecting sex and mean rock through their singer

Dan McCafferty, drummer Darrell Sweet, bassist Pete Agnew and guitarist Manny Charlton.

They gradually moved into the heavy metal bracket and suffered from overkill in 1974, but 1975 saw them back in the charts with a version of 'My White Bicycle' (originally recorded by **Tomorrow**), while McCafferty released a solo album, *Dan McCafferty* (Mountain), and Nazareth's 'Love Hurts' reached Number 8 in the US. Guitarist Zal Cleminson joined the line-up in 1978 but stayed for just two albums, *No Mean City* (1978) and *Malice in Wonderland* (1980, produced by Jeff Baxter of the **Doobie Brothers**). In 1982, Nazareth's number swelled to six with the addition of guitarist Billy Rankin and John Locke, formerly keyboards player with **Spirit**.

Nashville Teens were the Home Counties contribution to the Liverpool-dominated beat explosion of 1964, scoring with 'Tobacco Road'

NEIL, FRED Singer-songwriter Fred Neil came to the fore in the Greenwich Village folk scene of the early Sixties. Although Neil made five albums between 1962 and 1970, his public performances were rare and other artists have been responsible for bringing his songs to large audiences. Born in St Petersburg, Florida, in 1937, he appeared on the *Grand Ole Opry* before moving to New York. His first Elektra album, *Bleeker And MacDougal* (1967) contained arguably the definitive versions of 'Candy Man' and 'Other Side of This Life', later recorded by **Roy Orbison** and the **Lovin' Spoonful** respectively. Neil later moved back to Florida, emerging only to cut occasional albums. Meanwhile, his songs were still being recorded by other artists, notably 'Everybody's Talkin' (by **Nilsson** on the soundtrack of the film *Midnight Cowboy*) and 'Dolphins' (by **Linda Ronstadt** and **Tim Buckley**). His last album was *Sessions*, released by Capitol in 1971: little has been heard from him since.

NELSON, RICK Late Fifties teen idol and Seventies country-rock singer Rick Nelson was born Eric Hilliard Nelson in Teaneck, New Jersey, on 8 May 1940, into a showbusiness family. His parents, Ozzie and Harriet, had a popular radio show and Ricky joined the cast in 1948, making his film debut the following year. In the Fifties, the show moved into television, and as a result of his nationwide popularity Ricky gained a recording contract with Verve in 1956. In May of the following year he scored a double-sided US hit with 'A Teenager's Romance' and the **Fats Domino** cover 'I'm Walkin' and followed this three months later with 'You're My One and Only Love'. He was then signed to Imperial, and stayed with the label through thirty-six Hot 100 titles (usually double-sided hits) until 1963 – among them were 'Stood Up' (Number 5 in 1957), 'Believe What You Say' (Number 8 in 1958), 'Poor Little Fool' (Number 1 the same year), 'Never Be Anyone Else But You'/'It's Late' (Number 6 and 9 respectively in 1959) and 'Travellin' Man'/'Hello Mary Lou' (Number 1 and 9 in 1961). In 1961 he changed his name to Rick, moved to Decca, and began a brief film career.

Nelson had his first hit at the age of sixteen and he was carefully packaged to appeal to a young audience; greased hair, lop-sided grin and slightly rebellious (but not dangerous) stance. His voice, though distinctive, was rather weak and limited in range and was bolstered up by double-tracking. The

Photogenic Rick Nelson oozed teen appeal on record and on film

songs he was given were carefully tailored to suit his image and above all he was provided with first-rate musicians. The most notable was guitarist **James Burton**, whose innovative guitar solos were central to the success of Nelson's records until well into the Sixties.

Although the late Sixties were a lean time as far as chart success was concerned, Nelson's growing interest in country music resulted in a maturing of his style and more satisfactory albums than many of his 'teen idol' years. He returned to the Hot 100 in 1969 with a version of Dylan's 'She Belongs to Me', and in 1972 reached the Top 10 with his classic autobiographical song 'Garden Party'. This described his reception at a Madison Square Garden 'rock'n'roll revival' show and his difficulty in getting over his new work in the face of his long list of teenage hits. During the previous year, Nelson had formed his Stone Canyon Band, the unit with whom he continued to work throughout the Seventies. It was the albums *Bright Lights and Country Music* (1966) and *Country Fever* (1967) which showed Nelson's determined attempt to find a new direction now that he had slipped past the age of twenty-five. His progress took him to an individual position in 'country rock' though the promise of his late Sixties and early Seventies material was never quite fulfilled. He recorded one album for RCA in 1974, *Windfall*, and was then dropped; it was 1981 before he was recording again, this time for Capitol (the album *Playing to Win*). He was killed when his private aircraft caught fire *en route* to a gig on 31 December 1985.

NELSON, SANDY Born Sander Nelson in Santa Monica, California, on 1 December 1938, Sandy Nelson attained considerable popularity in the early Sixties with a series of instrumentals which pitched his monotonous drumming against a solitary guitar playing menacing riffs. Originally a member of the same West Coast high school clique with **Jan and Dean**, **Phil Spector** and Nancy Sinatra, Nelson first played drums in an obscure local band called Kip Tyler and the Flips, which recorded for the Ebb and Challenge labels (**Beach Boy**-to-be Bruce Johnston played piano). In 1958, he played drums on the million-seller 'To Know Him Is to Love Him', by the **Teddy Bears**, with whom he also travelled during a follow-up tour. Turning to session work, he played on **Gene Vincent**'s *Crazy Times* album (1959), shortly before recording 'Teen-beat' for the small Original Sound label. The record sold a million worldwide and Nelson immediately moved to the larger Imperial label where he had to wait two years for his second hit 'Let There Be Drums'. Shortly before recording it, Nelson lost his left foot in a car crash but his drumming was unimpaired. During the Sixties, he recorded a series of near-Muzak instrumental albums covering a variety of contemporary themes.

NELSON, WILLIE In the early Seventies, Willie Nelson became the reluctant head of a country-rock 'movement' that grew around him and centred itself on Austin, Texas. He and his songs are in the country mainstream, but his importance was in rebelling against the Nashville business centre.

Born on 30 March 1933 in Abbott, Texas, Nelson worked as a band member with Ray Price and wrote hits like 'Nightlife', 'Family Bible' and 'Funny How Time Slips Away'. Having previously recorded for Betty, D, and Bellaire, he joined Liberty in 1962 and hit with 'Touch Me', and again on RCA in 1965 with 'The Party's Over' and 'Once More with Feeling'. Later, wishing to have room to experiment and develop his more than usually complex phrasing and melody lines within traditional country themes, he moved to Austin and to Monument and Atlantic Records. Two albums in particular, *Shotgun Willie* (Atlantic, 1973) and *Phases and Stages* (1974), were the classic statement of his style and paved the way for great commercial success with the 1975 singles 'Blue Eyes Crying in the Rain' and 'Red Headed Stranger'.

Both were released by Columbia, to whom Willie was signed after Atlantic phased out its country music catalogue. Other notable albums of the Seventies included *The Sound in Your Mind*, *The Troublemaker*, and (in 1978) *Stardust*, a collection of Nelson interpretations of popular music standards like 'Georgia on My Mind' and 'Blue Skies'. He started his own label, Lonestar, which later folded, and in 1980 made his film debut in *Honeysuckle Rose*: a song from the film, 'On the Road Again', reached Number 20 in the US national chart. Two years later, he scored his biggest hit of all, 'Always On My Mind', one of his own compositions that had been a UK hit some ten years earlier for **Elvis Presley**.

NESMITH, MICHAEL

The only former Monkee to establish himself as a solo artist, Michael Nesmith (born on 30 December 1942 in Houston, Texas) was always the most likely of the foursome to succeed – his compositions for the group ('Sweet Young Thing', 'Mary, Mary') showed a promising songwriting talent, and his one solo release while still a Monkee (the experimental jazz orchestral album, *The Wichita Train Whistle Songs*) in 1968 suggested a pleasingly idiosyncratic approach to music-making that was confirmed by his trilogy of California-style country music albums, *Magnetic South* (1970), *Loose Salute* (1970) and *Nevada Fighter* (1971), all for RCA.

In 1970, he formed his First National Band, featuring Orville 'Red' Rhodes (pedal-steel guitar, born in East Alston, Illinois, on 30 December 1930), John London (bass, born in Bryan, Texas, on 6 February 1942) and John Ware (drums, born in Tulsa, Oklahoma, on 2 May 1944). After *Nevada Fighter*, he put together a Second National Band, retaining Rhodes but bringing in drummer Jack Ranelli and bass-player Johnny Meeks, formerly with **Gene Vincent**'s Blue Caps and **Merle Haggard**'s Strangers. The idea was again to cut three albums, but only *Tantamount to Treason Vol. 1* (1972) appeared. The next Nesmith/Rhodes album, *And the Hits Just Keep on Comin'* (1972) is generally considered to be their best work to date. The title itself was a wry joke, since of the plethora of Nesmith recordings, only two singles – 'Joanne' and 'Silver Moon' – had reached the Top 50.

In 1972, Elektra offered Nesmith his own label, Countryside. Putting together a house band led by Red Rhodes, Nesmith produced four albums by Garland Frady, **Ian Matthews**, Rhodes himself and Nesmith's own final RCA album, *Pretty Much Your Standard Ranch Stash* (1973). When David Geffen replaced **Jac Holzman** at Elektra, Countryside was axed, leaving the talented but wayward Nesmith to plan his third attempt at a concept recording, released in 1975 as *The Prison* on his own Pacific Arts label.

In 1977, Nesmith became one of the first US artists to explore the possibilities of video technology: his promo for 'Rio' (a surprise UK hit that year) was a fascinating early example of a video/rock marriage. The albums *From a Radio Engine to a Photon Wing* (1977) and *Infinite Rider on the Big Dogma* (1979) followed, and in 1981 he was the recipient of the first-ever Grammy award for a video, for his 'video album', *Elephant Parts*. In 1986, he steadfastly refused all invitations to join the much-heralded Monkees reunion tour. *See also the* **Monkees**

NEVILLE, ART

Born Arthur Lanon Neville in New Orleans on 17 December 1937, Art Neville had a career spanning all the phases of New Orleans music-mambo, rock'n'roll, soul and modern funk. Heavily influenced by **Professor Longhair**, Neville joined the Hawketts – Carol Joseph (trombone), August Fleury and Israel Bell (trumpets), George Davis (alto), Maurice Bashman (tenor), Alfred August (guitar) and John Boudreaux (drums) – in 1955. Their record of 'Mardi Gras Mambo', with Neville on piano and vocals, is released annually by Chess to coincide with the local celebrations. Neville went solo on Specialty in 1958 with several rocking singles, all made with the assistance of studio owner Cosimo Matassa's finest sessionmen. **Jerry Byrne**'s 'Lights Out', also on Specialty, featured Neville's brain-bending piano solo. In 1961, Neville followed his brother Aaron to Minit, where he recorded under **Allen Toussaint**. He later formed the **Meters**, then formed a performing and recording partnership with Aaron.

NEW ORDER See Joy Division

NEW ORLEANS

The good-time, happy-go-lucky New Orleans R&B sound was a contributory factor to the rise of rock'n'roll music in the Fifties, and many rocking classics were cut at Cosimo Matassa's tiny studios in the French Quarter with the best sessionmen in support. It was a sound which Mac Rebennack (*see* **Dr John**) has described as 'strong drums, heavy bass, light piano, heavy guitar and light horn sound, and a strong lead vocal'.

With a long and colourful musical heritage to fall back on, the present scene really started in the immediate post-war years when David and Julian Braund of De Luxe Records, New Jersey, were the first record men to realize the vast potential that New Orleans and its artists offered. They recorded everybody in town between 1947–9, and got the big hit they were looking for with **Roy Brown** and 'Good Rockin' Tonight'. It was Lew Chudd and Imperial Records who struck real gold when they signed first **Dave Bartholomew** as A&R man, and then **Fats Domino** as artist in 1949. Fats' first record, 'The Fat Man', was an immediate success and it started an almost unbroken sequence of hits until 1963 when Chudd sold Imperial to Liberty: 'Ain't That a Shame', 'Blueberry Hill', 'Blue Monday', 'I'm Walkin'', 'Walking to New Orleans' – all familiar million-sellers which were largely responsible for putting New Orleans well and truly on the record map.

The success of Fats Domino inspired other labels to make the long trip down to Louisiana to seek out further talent. Aladdin scored with **Shirley and Lee**, Atlantic with **Ray Charles** and **Professor Longhair**, Specialty with **Lloyd Price**, **Guitar Slim** and **Little Richard**, Chess with Sugar Boy Crawford, the Hawketts, **Bobby Charles** and **Clarence Henry**, and of course Imperial with **Smiley Lewis**, Tommy Ridgley, the Spiders, Bobby Mitchell and Roy Brown. Most also made use of the talents of the famous Studio Band of New Orleans session musicians, including Earl Palmer (drums), later replaced by Charles 'Hungry' Williams, Frank Fields (bass), Red Tyler and Mel Lastie (horns), and **Harold Battiste** (with, later, **Allen Toussaint**) on piano. Regrettably, most companies were only on a get-rich-quick exercise, and the artists and indeed the city's overall music scene were the last to profit. So it was inevitable that when sales of R&B records dipped in the late Fifties, the independents dropped New Orleans like a hot potato, leaving the locals to their own devices.

Johnny Vincent's Ace label had been the first local company to operate in New Orleans in 1955 and with a star-studded roster of **Huey Smith** and the Clowns, **Earl King**, **Frankie Ford** and **Jimmy Clanton** they could hardly fail. Ace had several national successes which inspired other local operators to start their own labels – men like Joe

Ruffino (Ric and Ron), Joe Banashak and Larry McKinley (minit), and Irvine Smith (Instant). By 1960 the heavier rock'n'roll sounds of the Fifties were falling out of favour, and it was Minit, and producer Allen Toussaint in particular, who directed the new trend towards a softer, mellower yet funkier R&B approach. This policy paid handsome dividends when **Jessie Hill**, **Ernie K-Doe**, **Irma Thomas**, Benny Spellman and Aaron Neville all had hit records along with Instant's **Chris Kenner**. Several outside labels came back, and Chess scored again with Clarence Henry, Fire/Fury with **Lee Dorsey** and Bobby Marchan, while Imperial were still going strong with Earl King, Ford Eaglin and, of course, Fats Domino. In 1962 Harold Battiste, frustrated by so many bad record deals, set up AFO Records on a co-operative basis and although Barbara George had an immediate hit, the label soon crumbled in chaos and disillusionment.

By 1963, the New Orleans recording scene seemed quite derelict. Imperial/Minit Records had been sold by owner Lew Chudd to Liberty and the new management retreated to their West Coast home; AFO, likewise, had moved to California and Ace was having problems with its distributor, Vee Jay. Other major labels were not happy with the recording facilities available at Cosimo's tiny studio in Gov. Nicholls Street, nor were they pleased with the obstructing tactics of the local musicians' union. So, with the hits drying up and rock'n'roll and R&B in fast decline there seemed good reasons for long faces.

But there was light in the darkness and, as singer Earl King said, 'It seemed that New Orleans was at a standstill in production, but they had more recordings done during the Sixties, I imagine, than they did during the Fifties.' The departure of the outside independent labels had given the small local labels the chance to cash in on the homegrown talent. One of the first to come up with a local hit was Frisco, with Danny White, in late 1962 with 'Kiss Tomorrow Goodbye'; Rip did likewise with Deacon John, Reggie Hall and Eddie Bo and Watch had minor successes with Benny Spellman, **Johnny Adams** and Professor Longhair. The man responsible for these productions was Wardell Quezergue, who had learned his trade with Dave Bartholomew's band and now ran the most popular aggregation in the city, the Royal Dukes of Rhythm. Along with fellow-producer Allen Toussaint, Wardell more or less kept the New

Orleans scene alive in the Sixties. Like Toussaint, he was very much aware of the trend away from the old rocking R&B music towards the funkier, slicker soul sounds and this was reflected in his modern productions.

In late 1964, Wardell formed Nola Records with Clinton Scott and had early good-sellers with Smokey Johnson, Warren Lee and Willie Tee. Early problems with pressing, distributing and promoting facilities were solved when studio owner Cosimo Matassa formed his Dover Records Corporation to cover these vital aspects. Nola soon had a Number 7 US hit with Robert Parker's dance record, 'Barefootin'', in 1966 and another group label, Parlo, had a gold record with Aaron Neville's 'Tell It Like It Is' in early 1967. But Dover grew too big too quickly and collapsed in financial ruin in 1968 taking with it the 20 or so labels by then under its umbrella. Out of this debacle, only Instant and Sansu survived. Although Instant, who had early hits with Chris Kenner, was merely jogging along, Sansu – headed by Marshall Sehorn and Allen Toussaint – was enthusiastically clocking up international hits with Lee Dorsey on Amy. It was these two record-men who were willing and eventually able to inject new life into the long-standing New Orleans scene.

NEW RIDERS OF THE PURPLE SAGE
Formed out of the New Delhi River Band in 1969, the New Riders of the Purple Sage initially attracted attention through the presence in the line-up of part of the **Grateful Dead**. Dead members Jerry Garcia, Mickey Hart and Phil Lesh, plus lyricist Robert Hunter, all played for the band at some time, though only Garcia was featured on their initial, eponymous Columbia album in 1971. The nucleus of the band throughout its life was David Nelson (guitar, vocals) and John Dawson (guitar, vocals); Buddy Cage replaced Garcia on pedal-steel guitar in 1971, Spencer Dryden (ex-**Jefferson Airplane**) joined as drummer and Skip Battin (ex-**Byrds**) became bassist with the band. Their albums ranged from the country and rockabilly (*Powerglide*, 1972; *Gypsy Cowboy*, 1973) to good-time rock'n'roll (*Home Home on the Road*, 1974). Battin left in 1976 and was replaced by Steve Love, who had previously played with **Rick Nelson**'s Stone Canyon Band. The Riders switched to MCA in that same year and recorded two albums before the company dropped them in 1978.

NEW ROMANTICS
A term devoid of any precise musical meaning, 'new romantics' became a convenient label for a certain set of young white British pop bands who arrived at the start of the Eighties and who operated within a set of values that were markedly different from those of the punk period. A product of the ultra-fashionable and exclusive London nightclub scene of the time, the new romantics craved attention and sought to inspire envy with their extravagant attire and apparent material well-being.

Spandau Ballet had the highest profile, and remain the best example, of all the new romantic bands, gaining instant exposure when featured on a youth culture TV show, *20th Century Box*, in 1980. The band members embraced a set of attitudes – clothes, romantic escapism, shameless pleasure-seeking and the supremacy of the dance-floor – that spread quickly amongst London's young nightlife regulars, and soon places like Steve Strange's (see **Visage**) nightclub, the Palace, were jam-packed every night with *aficionados* dressed up as anything suitably 'romantic' – pirates, cowboys, dandies and other increasingly esoteric guises.

Many young bands emerging at the time were identified early on as new romantics, and although this categorization was often inappropriate, one factor which loosely linked obviously incompatible bands such as the **Human League** and **Duran Duran** was a common devotion to an electronic dance beat and the use of synthesizers. **Ultravox**, **Soft Cell**, **ABC**, **Depeche Mode** and many other acts came through in this way, and all proved to be quite different from each other.

More than anything else, the new romantics set in motion the trend which undid everything that the 'street' attitude of punk had managed to achieve. It re-established the mystique of the star and so ensured the domination of the British charts in the Eighties by a new generation of image-obsessed pop idols.

NEW SEEKERS
Formed in 1969 to cash in on the break-up that year of the hugely popular **Seekers**, the New Seekers had a run of eight UK Top 20 hits and several other minor successes between 1971 and 1974. Eve Graham (born in Perth, Scotland, on 13 April 1943), Lyn Paul (Melbourne, Australia, on 16 February 1949), Peter Doyle (Melbourne on 28 July 1949), Paul Layton (born in Beaconsfield, England,

on 4 August 1947), and Marty Kristian (born in Leipzig, Germany, on 27 May 1947) were brought together by the Seekers' original guitarist, Keith Potger and placed with Philips, for whom they debuted with a version of **Melanie**'s 'What Have They Done to My Song, Ma' in 1970. Released as 'Look What They've Done to My Song Ma' in the US, it reached Number 14. A cover version of **Delaney and Bonnie**'s 'Never Ending Song of Love' gave them a Number 2 hit in the UK a year later, but it was a recording of Roger Cook and Roger Greenaway's Coca Cola jingle, 'I'd Like to Teach the World to Sing' (Polydor), that established them as a global name, reaching Number 7 in the US, Number 1 in the UK and selling well over a million worldwide.

Other hits included Britain's 1972 Eurovision Song Contest entry, 'Beg Steal or Borrow', and MOR-type versions of **Harry Chapin**'s 'Circles' (1972), Pete Townshend's 'Pinball Wizard – See Me Feel Me' (1973) and **Lobo**'s 'Goodbye is Just Another Word' (1973). 'You Won't Find Another Fool Like Me' brought them another UK Number 1 at the close of 1973, but 'I Get a Little Sentimental Over You' (Number 5 in the UK in 1974) proved to be their last major hit. The group underwent several personnel upheavals during the following few years and in 1978 reached Number 21 in the UK with an outstanding a cappella record, 'Anthem (One Day in Every Week)'. *See also* the **Seekers**

NEW WAVE

A convenient and largely meaningless term coined to denote rock acts that emerged around or soon after the time of mid-Seventies punk but were not, strictly speaking, punk acts. 'New Wave' was often taken to mean 'superior to punk', in as much as the artists so identified were regarded as a new generation of talent who – while in many cases were charged with the energy and enthusiasm generated by punk – shared none of that form's musical amateurism and disregard for melody, and on the contrary marked a return to the traditional skills of songwriting and musicianship.

In Britain, names like **Elvis Costello**, **Joe Jackson**, **Police**, **Dire Straits** and many others began to get attention right at the height of punk, but clearly shared nothing of the punk ethic apart from a renewed zeal for making music. In several instances, the term was applied to acts like **Siouxsie and the Banshees** who began as a standard punk thrash outfit but went on to display greater

musical ambition and sophistication.

In the US, new wave took longer to get a grip and was generally perceived either to mean pop with punk influences – which covered a huge variety of bands from **Blondie** to the **Cars** – or to be an umbrella term for all rock bands that emerged after 1976 and could not be pigeon-holed as punk, mainly referring to bands that operated outside of the mainstream, like **Talking Heads** or **Père Ubu**.

NEW YORK – INDEPENDENT LABELS

The first New York independents (or 'indies') to start up were Apollo and Savoy – both in 1942 – although the latter was, strictly speaking, in New Jersey. Apollo was formed by Ike and Bess Berman and its artists included **Wynonie Harris**, the **Five Royales** and gospel singer **Mahalia Jackson**. Savoy, formed by Herman Lubinsky, had a wide range of R&B artists that included **Nappy Brown**, **Big Maybelle**, Paul Williams, and **Johnny Otis**, who in 1950 had eight Top 10 R&B hits. However, the company became less and less successful through the Fifties and became increasingly reliant on gospel singer James Cleveland. While both labels brought out some excellent songs that foreshadowed what was to come, neither had a rock-'n'roll hit and neither lost their artists (Johnny Otis, for example, had hits for Capitol in 1958) or succumbed, as others did, to cover versions.

Similarly, many labels, such as the various ones put out since 1953 by Bobby Robinson, were not hugely successful – despite a Number 1 on Fury with **Wilbert Harrison**'s 'Kansas City' in Robinson's case – due to copyright and distribution problems, always the bugbear of 'indies'.

National, the most successful independent up to 1950, was formed by **Al Green** in 1946, at a time when the New York record scene was becoming much more localized with the boom of the West Coast 'indies'. They had hits from Dusty Fletcher and the **Ravens**, plus million-selling records from Eileen Barton and crooner Billy Eckstine. But by the birth of rock'n'roll, they had folded – they had their own record plant but never made the transition from 78s to 45s.

Jubilee, with its subsidiary Josie, was founded in 1948 by Jerry Blaine, a distributor for lots of local labels who was therefore regularly in contact with managers. Jubilee was one of the first independents to achieve success with a black group, the **Orioles**, who had their first hit with the rhythm and blues song

'It's Too Soon to Know'. By 1953 they had moved towards a more sentimental style, with 'Crying in the Chapel', that other black groups like the Four Tunes (also on Jubilee) adopted. Other hits the label had were 'Speedoo' by the **Cadillacs** (1956) and Bobby Freeman's 'Do You Wanna Dance' (1958) but after they veered towards minority tastes that included 'party' records.

Archie Bleyer's Cadence Records (1950) differed from the rest of the 'indies' in that it catered for commercial rather than specialist tastes, with artists like the **Chordettes**, **Eddie Hodges** and the **Everly Brothers** (though they were not recorded in New York). Yet it was Herald/Ember, formed in 1952 by Al Silver, that had the most hits, specializing in group records with the **Nutmegs**, the Turbans, Charlie and Ray and the **Silhouettes**.

The disc-jockey's role in making more people aware of black music was considerable. Jocko Henderson, for example, on a so-called black station, oriented his programmes to the whites who began listening in, and **Alan Freed**'s role in particular on white stations was of paramount importance. Thus more 'indies' signed up black musicians in the hope of success; Rama, a subsidiary of Tico, founded by **George Goldner** in 1953, had many black groups that included the **Crows** ('Gee'), the **Cleftones**, the Valentines and the Harptones, as did Red Robin, also formed in 1953 by Bobby Robinson and Old Town (1955 by Hy Weiss) with Arthur Prysock.

With the continuing spread of audience taste, new 'indies' emerged. Roulette, the largest apart from Atlantic, was formed in 1956 by Phil Kahl and Maurice Levy, and George Goldner, who came in later, set up the subsidiaries Gone and End the following year.

The establishment of Scepter/Wand by Florence Greenburg in 1959 brought the first important rival to Atlantic. They had Luther Dixon to produce the compositions of Goffin and King (*see* **Carole King**), and **Bacharach** and David material for people like the **Shirelles**, **Chuck Jackson** and **Dionne Warwick** and in a sense it was Dixon's work that heralded **Phil Spector**'s era.

NEW YORK – LOCAL SCENES

Strange though it seems, major cities such as New York and Los Angeles have seldom developed the kind of strong local rock scene or identifiable regional sound that lesser American cities (Memphis, New Orleans, Cleveland, San Francisco,

Minneapolis, Atlanta, Austin, etc.) have always boasted. New York's street-corner vocal group scene in the Fifties was a notable exception, but following its demise there was little that the city could call uniquely its own.

The Greenwich Village club scene of 1965 produced many local groups, among them the Blues Magoos, Vagrants, Magicians, Fugitives, **Fugs**, **Blues Project**, and of course the **Lovin' Spoonful**. But although some of these rose to national fame, none defined a true local scene. This changed with the arrival of the Young Rascals (see **Rascals**), who seemed to reflect the attitudes and tastes of New York youth (especially the suburban Long Island contingent) as no group had before, and the **Velvet Underground**, who explored the extremities of the New York experience, from the self-destructive, burnt-out weariness of the street-corner junkie to the jaded brat from Scarsdale. In a real sense, these two bands *were* New York.

But the bands that followed in the late Sixties fell short of this standard, and what might have been a real New York scene, like the scene in San Francisco around that period, never actually materialized. Other New York bands, **Vanilla Fudge**, **Mountain**, the Insect Trust, the Group Image, the Illusion, the New York Rock And Roll Ensemble, NRBQ and Lothar and the Hand People, either ascended instantly into the ranks of international popdom or disappeared rapidly without ever making it beyond the clubs they started in.

It was only with the beginning of the Seventies that a new, vital scene began to emerge from the streets of New York. Concurrent with the rise of the glitter movement in England, New York's trendsetters were evolving a style and scene of their own, a nouveau-freakish bisexual camp, grotesque make-up and torn panty-hose, boys and girls alike posing as dropout sodomists in the Oscar Wilde room of the Mercer Arts Center, where trashy bands thrown together by kids off the street played for the hard-core faithful.

These bands, of whom the **New York Dolls** quickly became pre-eminent, played hard, basic rock'n'roll, with solid roots in the mid-Sixties British and punk styles. They dressed and acted like their audience, in varying degrees of drag, and they mixed choice oldies with original songs dedicated to the lifestyle of their small but dedicated following.

By 1973/4 the Dolls had spawned a large number of imitators, among them Wayne County, the Brats, Teenage Lust, the Miamis, the Harlots Of 42nd Street, New York Central, and Milk and Cookies. There were also other New York acts with a bold, mid-Sixties or glitter-pop approach, such as Elliott Murphy, **Kiss**, and **Blue Oyster Cult**.

This scene flourished for two years or so, with many small clubs opening to accommodate these bands, and much media attention was focused on it. But with the failure of the Dolls and Murphy to break through to a wider audience, and the inability of their imitators to establish an identity of their own, the scene as a whole began to taper off.

A third generation of Seventies bands began to appear in New York in early 1975, including such names as the Marbles, **Television**, the **Ramones**, the Dictators and Dolls offshoot the Heartbreakers (see **Tom Petty**). By 1976, a new 'underground' rock scene had established itself around such venues as CBGBs, Club 82 and Trax, but record company interest in it was limited to Arista's signing of **Patti Smith** and the efforts of Seymour Stein's Sire Records label, who signed the Ramones, **Richard Hell and the Voidoids**, the Dead Boys, **Talking Heads** and a number of other important acts. Warner Brothers agreed to a worldwide distribution deal with Sire during 1977, but the agreement bore little immediate commercial fruit – Sire's most important long-term signing turned out to be **Madonna**, who first had chart success in the US in late 1984.

New York's club scene of the latter Seventies made little direct commercial impact, but its influence on the developing London punk movement – followers of which first saw the Ramones, the Heartbreakers and Patti Smith in concert during 1976 – was incalculable. By the beginning of the Eighties, **Blondie** had gone from minor club fame to become a pop sensation in the UK, the Ramones were minor film stars and were playing in large halls to an army of dedicated fans, and Talking Heads were on the verge of success on a global scale, but most of the other old CBGBs bands had broken up. Although the number of venues for local talent swelled, the number of local bands to fill them dwindled. New bands did arrive but with a few exceptions – the Fleshtones, the Bush Tetras, the Raybeats, the Bongos, the Lenny Kaye Connection – they lacked spark, imagination and any compelling identity.

NEW YORK DOLLS With a repertoire derived from the **MC5**, **Velvet Underground**, **Shangri-Las** and early **Rolling Stones**, and a blasting double-lead guitar wall of sound, together with singer David Johansen's Jaggeresque voice, they had an impressive (if limited) style. But the group's flashy stage show and gutter transvestite costumes, and their songs of life and cheap love among the trashy New York glitter people, endeared them enormously to their audience.

The original group (late 1971) consisted of guitarists Johnny Thunders (born John Gonzales on 15 July 1954 in New York) and Rick Rivets, bassist Arthur Kane (3 February 1951, New York) and drummer Billy Murcia. Johansen (9 January 1954, New York) joined in early 1972. Murcia died on an early tour of England and was replaced by Jerry Nolan (7 May 1951, New York). Rivets was also replaced, by Sylvain Sylvain (real name Sil Mizrahi), before the first album.

Despite a Mercury Records contract (two albums, *New York Dolls* and *Too Much, Too Soon*), two singles ('Trash' and 'Stranded in the Jungle') and numerous tours, the Dolls never caught on nationally. In 1975 they broke up.

Guitarist Johnny Thunders camping it up with New York Dolls on stage

Johnny Thunders went on to form the Heartbreakers, whose appearances in Britain during 1976 helped lay the ground for the punk explosion to come. **Malcolm McLaren** managed the Dolls during their last days, an experience that helped him formulate his strategy for bringing together and launching the **Sex Pistols**.

NEWBEATS A three-man group, the Newbeats were based in Nashville and purveyed the sort of shrill, falsetto singing that was popular in the early Sixties (e.g. **Lou Christie**, **Four Seasons**, etc.). Originally a duo called Dean and Mark (who had a Top 50 hit with a cover of Travis and Bob's country number 'Tell Him No' on Bullseye, 1959) they became the Newbeats when joined by Larry Henley – born 30 June 1941, in Arp, Texas – in 1964. Their first release, 'Bread and Butter' (Hickory), was a Number 2 US hit in August of that year and was followed by two other Top 20 hits ('Everything's Alright', 'Run Baby Run') and several other chart entries over the next two years. A good, firm dance beat and strong material kept them going through 1965, after which they remained on Hickory. Larry Henley later recorded for Capricorn, while Dean and Mark Mathis – born on 17 March 1939 and 9 February 1942 respectively, in Hahira, Georgia – kept the Newbeats' name alive on Playboy Records.

NEWBURY, MICKEY Singer/ songwriter Mickey Newbury opened the Seventies with a Top 30 US hit, 'American Trilogy' (Elektra, 1971), a reworking of traditional songs, concerned, as the title suggests, with America. It was, however, untypical of his recordings which in the main deal with personal relations in the country-rock genre. Born in Houston, Texas, on 19 May 1940, Newbury left behind the small club bands to move to Nashville and starve there as a songwriter during the mid-Sixties. Eventually, he wrote hits for Ray Price ('Sweet Memories'), **Tom Jones** ('Funny Familiar Forgotten Feelings') and **Jerry Lee Lewis** ('She Even Woke Me Up To Say Goodbye'). Encouraged, he recorded himself for RCA, Mercury and Elektra. Though he has written fine songs like 'San Francisco Mabel Joy' and 'How I Love Them Old Songs', sustained success has continually eluded him.

NEWLEY, ANTHONY A child actor who became the darling of the Las Vegas night-club circuit, Anthony Newley flirted very briefly with rock-'n'roll during his transition period. Born in Hackney, London, in 1931, his most famous juvenile role was that of the Artful Dodger in *Oliver Twist* (1948). In 1959, having successfully bridged the gap to adult parts, he played a conscripted rock'n'roll singer in the film *Idle on Parade* and also sang and co-wrote the title song. An infec-

tious rock number despite the fact that it was primarily intended as parody (note the amount of voice echo) it entered the charts and launched Newley on a recording career. His follow-ups, however, were plaintive ballads ('Why?', 'Do You Mind?', 'D-Darling' etc.) and three more of these ('Gonna Build a Mountain', 'Once in a Lifetime' and 'What Kind of Fool Am I?') were the mainstays of *Stop the World, I Want to Get Off!*, the new-wave stage musical he wrote with Leslie Bricusse in 1961. The show not only broadened and revitalized the regimented structure of the musical, but also established the public image that Newley maintains today of the dynamic, but tortured, all-round entertainer.

From a rock point of view, his influence on the vocal style of **David Bowie** during the latter's 'Laughing Gnome' period is of particular interest.

NEWMAN, RANDY Once described as the Mark Twain of rock, Newman (born on 28 November 1943) is a humorist who has chosen the pop song as his medium. An adept song craftsman, he learnt his trade working in Los Angeles for Metric Music alongside **Glen Campbell**, **Leon Russell**, **Jackie DeShannon**, David Gates and others, and became a session arranger for Warner Brothers in 1967. A year later he recorded his first solo album, *Randy Newman* (Reprise), with the help of Van Dyke Parks and although it sold so badly that the company was forced into giving it away as an advertising gimmick, it set the tone of his later work. One of the chief reasons for public indifference was his voice, cracked and discordant, perfectly matching the spirit and tone of his songs, that were alternately cynical, ironic and serio-comic in effect.

Unlike most of his songwriting

Randy Newman's entertaining satires on the American Dream can be profoundly cynical or sweetly poignant, but never personal or introverted

contemporaries, Newman is one writer whose style is not strictly personal: he rarely writes about his own situation and prefers to create songs from inside the characters of others. He is equally at home writing in a jazz, country or ragtime vein as in rock, and in albums like *Twelve Songs* (1970), *Sail Away* (1972) and *Good Old Boys*(1974) he helped immeasurably to broaden the scope of the pop song in terms of subject-matter by exploring the other side of sex in his songs – inadequacy, impotence, even perversion. *Good Old Boys* was Newman's first attempt at a concept album – a sympathetic portrait of the South – and included one of his best-ever songs, 'Louisiana 1927', but it preceded a long lay-off during which he produced little. For *Little Criminals* (1977) he adopted the policy of working at songwriting on a nine-to-five basis in a Los Angeles office: the result was an uneven but very commercial album, more comic than satirical, which included the controversial Number 2 US hit 'Short People' and backing support from Glenn Frey and Don Henley of the **Eagles**.

Born Again (1979) found Newman railing against a number of targets – among them the Electric Light Orchestra (*see* **ELO**) and **Kiss**, two of Newman's pet hates – but it was an unfocused album, empty of any real character exploration and too self-consciously perverse in some of its subject matter. *Trouble in Paradise* (1983) was a vast improvement but lacked the observational qualities of his earlier albums. In between, he composed a marvellous score for the film *Ragtime* and won two Oscar nominations. His other film work has included *Performance* (1970), *Cold Turkey* (1971) and *The Natural* (1984).

NEWTON-JOHN, OLIVIA

A singer whose career has successfully touched on country music, disco, AOR-type easy-listening, a Eurovision Song Contest (in 1974) and starring roles in several musical films, Olivia Newton-John was born in Cambridge, England, on 26 September 1948. She emigrated with her family to Australia at the age of four and in her teens formed a vocal group, the Sol Four, with three high-school friends. At 16, she won a trip back to Britain in a talent contest sponsored by Johnny O'Keefe, Australia's answer to Elvis Presley. In the UK she starred in the little-shown film *Tomorrow*, produced by **Don Kirshner**, which was his attempt to create a cinematic follow-up to his earlier television creation, the **Monkees** – the 'Tomorrow' of

the title was a mythical futuristic pop group. When the venture failed, Olivia temporarily teamed up with another Australian, Pat Carroll, to work as a cabaret-oriented duo. Her association with the **Shadows** and **Cliff Richard** began at this time – she lived with Bruce Welch for a while – and she debuted on the UK chart in 1971 with a middle-of-the-road cover version of Dylan's 'If Not For You' (Pye), which also reached the US Top 30 on Uni. She followed this with UK Top 20 versions of 'Banks of the Ohio' (1971), **George Harrison**'s 'What is Life' (1972) and **John Denver**'s 'Take Me Home, Country Roads' (1973), at the same time consolidating her television and cabaret career.

One of the keys to her recording success was the production skill of John Farrar, a member of the Shadows offshoot Marvin, Welch and Farrar. 'Let Me Be There' (MCA), written by Shadow John Rostill, caused some astonishment in late 1973 by becoming first a hit in the US country chart, then a pop hit there, while barely denting the Top 40 in Britain. Having happily hit the precise meeting-point of country and easy-listening music in time and style, Newton-John continued plugging away, with Farrar's clean and sympathetic production behind her: 'If You Love Me, Let Me Know', 'I Honestly Love You' (1974), 'Have You Never Been Mellow' (1975) were all hits in the US – the latter two Number 1s – where she won three Grammy awards during 1974, two of which were for the Best Female *Country* vocalist and the other for Best Female *Pop* Performance. It was too much for some of the more traditional elements in Nashville, some of whom renounced their membership of the Country Music Association when it awarded her the Best Female Singer trophy in 1976.

Her appearance in the film *Grease* (1978), opposite John Travolta, helped her to dispel the girl-next-door image she had nurtured during her early career. Her two duets with Travolta, 'You're the One That I Want' and 'Summer Nights' were giant worldwide hits, both reaching Number 1 in the UK (the former was also a US chart-topper), and gave the basis on which to build a new musical personality for herself that crystallized on the albums *Totally Hot* (1978) and *Physical* (1980). Again produced by John Farrar, the albums found Olivia in a disco vein, and the latter in particular became a soundtrack to the growing health-and-fitness movement in the US. The title track was a US Number 1 in 1982. In 1980 she starred

with Gene Kelly in the film *Xanadu* which, while a box-office flop, featured a best-selling (and, in the UK, chart-topping) duet with the Electric Light Orchestra (*see* **ELO**) on the title track. She has also recorded with Cliff Richard ('Suddenly', a transatlantic Top 20 hit in 1980) and renewed her partnership with Travolta in the 1984 film, *Two of a Kind*.

NICE An important group in the development of progressive rock in the late Sixties, the Nice brought the name of Keith Emerson – later of Emerson, Lake and Palmer (*see* **ELP**) – to the fore for the first time. The band – comprising Emerson (born on 2 November 1944) on keyboards; Brian Davison (25 May 1942) drums; Lee Jackson (8 January 1943) bass, vocals; David O'List, guitar, vocals – had individually thorough groundings in the seminal British club scene of the mid-Sixties. They came together to back **P.P. Arnold**, often upstaging her with their impressive warm-up act. Managed by **Andrew Loog Oldham**, the original quartet made only one album, *Thoughts of Emerlist Davjack* (Immediate, 1968), featuring the climactic 'Rondo'. O'List left the group as he left **Roxy Music** later, on the verge of their breakthrough, removing one of the dynamic cornerstones of the band. Without O'List, Emerson's keyboard pyrotechnics dominated as he developed his penchant for rocked-up classics on *Ars Longa Vita Brevis* (1968) and his showmanship – exemplified by setting fire to the Stars and Stripes during 'America' – in live performances. Their three subsequent albums, including *Five Bridges* (Charisma, 1970), all reached the Top 10. Following the break-up in 1970, Emerson nurtured these aspects with ELP, while Davison and Jackson, after abortive attempts with their own groups, formed Refugee with another keyboard virtuoso, Patrick Moraz. In 1975, O'List formed Jet with Andy Ellison and Clive Townson (from John's Children) and Peter Oxendale and Martin Gordon (from **Sparks**), while Refugee folded when Moraz replaced **Rick Wakeman** in **Yes**. *See also* **ELP**

NICO An enigmatic singer of legendary cult status, Nico was born in Berlin in 1944 and came to New York early in the Sixties after a short spell as an actress in Italy – she appeared in Fellini's *La Dolce Vita* – and as a model in Paris. After appearing in Andy Warhol's *Chelsea Girls* and cutting one unsuccessful single for **Andrew Loog**

Oldham's Immediate label in 1965 ('The Last Mile', produced by **Jimmy Page**), she became the 'chanteuse' of the **Velvet Underground**. Her haunting, deadpan singing of 'I'll Be Your Mirror' and 'All Tomorrow's Parties' on *The Velvet Underground and Nico* (Verve, 1967) secured her a small but slavish following. Her subsequent albums – *The Marble Index* (Elektra, 1969), *Desertshore* (Reprise, 1971) and *The End* (Island, 1974) – were produced and arranged by former colleague **John Cale**. They extended her combination of Gothic, stylized singing, haunting harmonium accompaniments, and songs that suggest a glacial mental landscape of terminal psychosis.

In 1981, after sporadic appearances in the US and Europe, she re-emerged with *Drama of Exile*, which featured reworkings of songs by **Lou Reed**, **David Bowie** and others. A live album, *Do or Die*, appeared in 1983.

NILSSON, HARRY

Born in Brooklyn, New York, on 15 June 1941, Harry Nilsson became something of a cult figure during the late Sixties through his association with the **Beatles** and his gentle parody of their vocal and songwriting style. His early songs for West Coast pop and R&B artists (such as Bo Pete's 'Baa Baa Black Sheep Parts 1 and 2' on Crusader) are deservedly obscure and commercial success did not come his way until 1971 when his recording of 'Without You' (RCA), ironically not one of his own songs but written by Ham and Evans of **Badfinger**, reached the top of the charts in both Britain and America. Since then his albums have sold consistently well, although his Seventies recordings lacked the sheer finesse and offbeat originality of his first single and album releases, the best of which were *Pandemonium Shadow Show* (1967) and *Harry* (1969).

His trademark is the soft, melancholic ballad sung in a wistful, hurt voice and while he is arguably a far better singer than he is a songwriter many of his songs have been recorded by other artists, including 'Ten Little Indians' by the **Yardbirds** and 'Cuddly Toy' for the **Monkees**. An above-average pop talent, his main problem appears to be a lack of musical discipline: too often he records simply for the sake of recording. His albums include *A Little Touch of Schmilsson in the Night* (1973), a set of old-time standards orchestrated by Sinatra's long-time arranger Gordon Jenkins, and a rock'n'roll collaboration with **John Lennon**, *Pussy Cats* (1974). His film work includes the soundtrack scores for the cartoon *The Point* (1971, originally made for television from Nilsson's own draft story line), and *Son of Dracula* (1974, in which he appeared with **Ringo Starr**).

He has produced little of distinction since the mid-Seventies, both *Knilsson* (1977) and *Flash Harry* (1984) being rather tiresome collections of mannered ballads and hip novelty songs.

NIRVANA

Multi-instrumentalists Patrick Campbell-Lyons and Alex Spyropoulos came together as Nirvana in 1967 to produce two superb dreamlike singles, 'Tiny Goddess' and 'Pentecost Hotel'. They went on to produce *The Story of Simon Simopath* (Island, 1967) an impressive 'concept' album, although their second album, *All of Us* (1968), was in many ways more successful. However, the team began moving apart after the modest chart success of 'Rainbow Chaser' (1968) and Campbell-Lyons dominated the awkward-sounding *Dedicated to Markos III* (Pye, 1970). By the next album, Spyropoulos had vanished altogether and the three later Nirvana albums, solely under Campbell-Lyons' control, had only quiet flashes of their former excellence. Campbell-Lyons also worked as producer of a series of mostly unsuccessful albums by 'progressive' bands like Clear Blue Sky, Sunburst and Jade Warrior.

NITTY GRITTY DIRT BAND

A fascinatingly eclectic band, whose records contained a mixture of blues, jug-band music, bluegrass and original songs by writers like **Jackson Browne** and Kenny Loggins (*see* **Loggins and Messina**), the Nitty Gritty Dirt Band was formed in 1965 out of various high-school bands and originally comprised John McEuen (banjo, mandolin, guitar, vocals, born on 19 December 1945); Jeff Hanna (guitar, percussion, vocals, 11 August 1947); Jimmie Fadden (guitar, harp, drums, vocals, 9 March 1948); Les Thompson (bass, mandolin, vocals); and Jim Ibbotson (guitar, drums, accordion, vocals, 21 January 1947). Initially basing themselves in Los Angeles, the band signed with Liberty Records and made their debut with *Nitty Gritty Dirt Band* in 1967. They appeared in the film *Paint Your Wagon* in 1968 and disbanded for a short time, then re-formed to record *Uncle Charlie and His Dog Teddy* (1970), which included their surprise US Top 10 hit of that year, a version of Jerry Jeff Walker's 'Mr Bojangles'. That album and its follow-up, *All the Good Times* (1972), showed off the band's brand of country-rock to good effect – they moved their base in the early Seventies to the Denver and Aspen areas of Colorado – but the pinnacle of their success was the widely acclaimed triple album, *Will the Circle Be Unbroken* (1973), which was recorded in Nashville and included guest appearances by many country music veterans – among them **Roy Acuff**, **Earl Scruggs**, Maybelle Carter, Doc Watson, and Merle Travis. They recorded an album per year for the rest of the Seventies, amending their name to the Dirt Band in 1976 and becoming (in 1977) the first US rock band to tour the USSR. *Make a Little Magic* appeared in 1981 and *Jealousy* a year later, while *Let's Go* (1984) found the band assuming its original full name once more.

NITZCHE, JACK

Born in Michigan in 1937, Jack Nitzsche emerged as perhaps the most innovative pop arranger/composer/producer of the Sixties. At 21 he received a diploma in music and moved to Hollywood where he worked as an independent arranger and music copyist for Sonny Bono (*see* **Sonny and Cher**). In 1962, he was hired by **Phil Spector** to arrange 'He's a Rebel' by the **Crystals** and stayed on as his regular arranger, helping Spector create his famous 'wall of sound'. He arranged and orchestrated most of Spector's biggest hits, including the Crystals' 'Da Doo Ron Ron', the **Ronettes**' 'Be My Baby' and **Ike and Tina Turner**'s 'River Deep – Mountain High'. Although working primarily with Spector, Nitzsche signed a solo contract with Reprise in 1963, scoring several instrumental successes like 'The Lonely Surfer' (1963), which featured as sidemen such aspiring superstars as **Leon Russell** and David Gates.

Nitzsche later became friends with the **Rolling Stones**, playing piano and offering advice on many of their early records, including *Out of our Heads* and *Aftermath*. 1968 found him writing the score for the Mick Jagger movie *Performance*. That same year he arranged, produced and played piano on **Buffalo Springfield**'s 'Expecting to Fly', which led to a working relationship with **Neil Young**. Nitzsche wrote and arranged for Young's debut solo album, arranged and produced 'A Man Needs a Maid' and 'There's a World' on Young's *Harvest*, and played piano on *Time Fades Away*. He also recorded and toured with Crazy Horse, Young's regular back-up group, and worked on

Randy Newman's *Twelve Songs* album. 1972 saw a new departure for Nitzsche, who came to London to cut *St Giles Cripplegate* with the London Symphony Orchestra, an album containing a series of classically styled instrumental passages composed and arranged by Nitzsche with production by Elliot Mazer.

However, a year later he returned to a more familiar rock format and presented Reprise with a vocal/instrumental album which was subsequently rejected by the company. Nitzsche's growing dissatisfaction with the direction of rock music clearly showed through on the album, and resulted in his virtual retirement from the rock world. He continued composing and arranging for films, *The Exorcist* (1974) and *One Flew Over the Cuckoo's Nest* (1977), and producing a number of artists, including **Mink DeVille**.

NIX, DON Born in Memphis,Tennessee, on 27 September 1941, Don Nix was a saxophonist and singer of considerable repute in southern rock circles during the early Seventies. Of Cherokee Indian descent on his mother's side, he was part of a band at high school which became the **Mar-Keys**, the 'house' band for Stax Records during the mid-Sixties, backing **Otis Redding**, **Wilson Pickett** and **Sam and Dave**. In 1965, Nix moved to California, where he lived with **Leon Russell** and became involved with **Delaney and Bonnie** whose Stax album, *Home*, he produced. Subsequent production work with **Jeff Beck**, **Albert King**, **Freddie King** and **John Mayall**, together with three solo albums including the ragged *Living by the Days* (Elektra, 1971) and the masterminding of a tour by the Alabama State Troopers (which included Nix, **Lonnie Mack** and Jeanie Greene, although Mack dropped out at the beginning and was replaced by country-blues singer/guitarist Furry Lewis) made Don Nix a well-known if not hugely successful figure.

NOVELTY RECORDS Early in 1956, when rock'n'roll was itself a novelty, two young songwriters named Dick Goodman and Bill Buchanan conceived 'The Flying Saucer', a record that preserved in almost documentary form the impact of rock'n'roll on the media. It gave a phoney account of an invasion from outer space, integrating snatches of then popular rock records into the dizzy narrative. A record with such a structure was destined for heavy airplay, and by late August 1956 it was an American hit.

From then on, novelty items were seen as part and parcel of rock'n'roll. Indeed, reflecting the industry's ambiguous attitude to rock'n'roll, it often became the subject of novelty records. Examples of this are Stan Freberg's 'version' of 'Heartbreak Hotel' and, more obviously, his 'The Old Payola Roll Blues' in America and Peter Sellers' minor British hit, 'I'm So Ashamed', in which the singer is nine and worried that he may be too old since he hasn't had a Top 20 record for a whole three weeks.

But not all novelty records were inspired by rock'n'roll. One particular zany slice of humour in 1956 was 'Transfusion' by Nervous Norvus, actually Jimmy Drake, a 44-year-old truck driver living in San Francisco. Musically, it was a very quiet folksy record but the lyrics were about a speed-crazed driver who crashed repeatedly and required countless pints of blood. The grizzly narrative, sung nonchalantly in an adenoidal tenor, was punctuated at intervals by the screech of tyres, a deafening crash and choruses ending with lines like 'Hey Daddy-O, Make That Type O' and 'Pour the Crimson in Me, Jimson'.

In 1958, Ross Bagdasarian, an American actor turned songwriter, discovered that by speeding up tape, funny voices resulted and he made 'The Witchdoctor' ('Ooh-ee-ooh-aah-aah', etc.) a children's favourite in the late Fifties. Changing his name to David Seville, Bagdasarian then developed the sound into multiplicity and thus created the Chipmunks, a ghastly figment of the electronic imagination which helped establish Liberty as a major label.

The record industry apes itself with witless intensity and Sheb Wooley, another actor/songwriter, capitalized on 'The Witchdoctor' by recording 'The Purple People Eater' for MGM. It was the fastest-selling novelty record for five years, and manufacturers rushed on the market with Purple People Eater hats, T-shirts, buttons, 'The Cuban Purple People Eater' (in cha-cha rhythm) and 'The Purple Herring Fresser', a Yiddish version.

One of the better records to emerge from Philadelphia during the late Fifties was John Zacherle's 'Dinner with Drac', a rock'n'roll instrumental punctuated by horrific limericks which Zacherle clumsily related like a businessman telling a tasteless joke at a party, bursting into laughter at the offence he has caused. 'Drac' made America's Top 20 but was castigated when issued in Britain.

Dozens more obscure novelty discs were made by black vocal groups who often featured vocal gimmickry on the up-tempo sides of their records. 'Alley Oop' by the Hollywood Argyles (released in 1960) featured **Gary Paxton** – one half of **Skip and Flip** – croaking out contrived comic-book jargon backed by what sounded like a drunken Salvation Army choir playing a heavy walking beat. Two years later, Paxton snatched **Bobby 'Boris' Pickett** from a local bar band and had him perform his Boris Karloff imitation on 'Monster Mash' for Paxton's small Garpax label. Hoping for local sales, Paxton found he had an American Number 1 which has since become timeless in its appeal – re-released in 1973, it reached Number 10 in the US and Number 3 in the UK.

In 1963, Jeff Wayne, later **David Essex**'s producer, and two friends doctored up their voices electronically to produce the Dalek-like 'Martian Hop' which they released as by the Ran-Dells. Over the years we have had the insipid Napoleon XIV, the **Goons**, and the crown-prince of novelty, **Ray Stevens**, whose successes (which included 'Ahab the Arab', 'Gitarzan', 'Harry the Hairy Ape', 'Bridget the Midget' and 'The Streak') kept the novelty-record tradition alive beyond the era of rock'n'roll.

NUGENT, TED America's self-proclaimed king of ear-shattering, mind-numbing heavy metal, guitarist Ted Nugent was born in Detroit on 13 December 1948, and played in a number of bands – among them the Royal High Boys and the Lourdes – before forming the **Amboy Dukes** in Chicago in 1965. The band stayed together until the mid-Seventies, recording for Mainstream from 1972; in 1975, Nugent won a solo contract with Epic and formed a backing band with former Dukes bassist Rob Grange. His solo debut album was *Ted Nugent* (1975), but his best year was 1977, when both *Cat Scratch Fever* and *Double Live Gonzo* went platinum. A brilliant self-publicist with a penchant for challenging fellow guitar heroes to on-stage contests of guitar-playing dexterity, Nugent's career went into comparative decline by the beginning of the next decade, though a switch of labels to Atlantic in 1982 and the formation of a new band (including Carmine Appice, formerly of Beck, Bogert and Appice and **Vanilla Fudge**) helped. Nugent's Eighties albums included *Nugent* (1982) and *Penetrator* (1984). His style has barely changed over the years.

NUMAN, GARY A self-confessed plagiarist of **David Bowie**, as well as of William Burroughs and other SF writers, Numan (born in March 1958) shot to Number 1 in the UK singles chart in 1979 with 'Are Friends Electric?', an unsubtle but successful pointer to the electro-pop style that would pervade the charts in the following years. Previously, he had recorded two unsuccessful albums with his band Tubeway Army for the Beggar's Banquet label. He dropped the name Tubeway Army shortly after that success and launched out on a phenomenal, if relatively shortlived, solo career.

Seemingly always one breathless step behind his hero, Bowie, Numan constructed massive touring shows, one involving a hi-tech set complete with 'dancing' robots, and, like Bowie, went through a series of image changes: space cadet, futuristic soul boy, gangster, lounge lizard and brightly-coloured harlequin. Numan admitted his artistic shortcomings but got his own back on the critics by becoming hugely popular with the teenies, launching a massive and lucrative merchandising business. In the early 1980s he became rich enough to indulge a childhood fantasy, buying World War II airplanes, and dwindling success saw him continue to retreat into his hobbies like a junior Howard Hughes, leaving a series of unremarkable albums and singles (for example, 'We Take Mystery' and 'White Boys and Heroes', both 1982) to mark a career that did little for new wave music but wonders for his bank account. Since 1982, his chart appearances have been fleeting. However, despite this, he manages to retain a loyal following.

NUTMEGS In 1955, Leroy and James Griffin, William Emery, James Tyson and Thomas McNeil, from New Haven, Connecticut, formed a group and borrowed their State's 'nutmeg' emblem for themselves. Lead singer Leroy Griffin was a talented writer; thus the group were able to perform original material, arousing the interest of a local publisher who took them to Herald Records. Their first disc was 'Story Untold', a ballad of lost love featuring Leroy's mournful lead and wailing harmony – a massive R&B hit. The follow-up, 'Ship of Love', also sold well but further success eluded them. Leroy was killed in a smelting furnace accident in 1969 and replaced by nephew Harold Jaynes when the group re-formed in 1974 and recorded a fresh version of 'Story Untold'.

A series of synthesizer-based hits and spectacular hi-tech concerts earnt Gary Numan enough cash to indulge his private fantasy – piloting his own aircraft. Numan's popular success defied critical disapproval

NYRO, LAURA Although her songs have been recorded by a huge number of artists in the rock, pop and easy-listening fields, Laura Nyro (born in New York in 1947) has never made it beyond cult status as a performer. From an Italian-Jewish background, she attended Manhattan's High School of Music and Art and made her recording debut at the age of nineteen for the folk label Verve, with the album *More Than a New Discovery* (1966). A year later she made a disastrous appearance at the Monterey Pop Festival that left her in a state of almost permanent stage-fright, but Columbia boss Clive Davis signed her to his label in 1968 and placed her with a sympathetic producer, one-time **Four Season** Charlie Callello. The results, *Eli and the Thirteenth Confession* (1968) and *New York Tendaberry* (1969) were both very well received, and she also provided a steady stream of hit songs for other acts to record – among them the **Fifth Dimension** ('Stoned Soul Picnic', 'Wedding Bell Blues'), Barbra Streisand ('Stoney End', 'Time and Love'). Always inclined towards gospel and R&B, Nyro's next two releases – *Christmas and the Beads of Sweat* (1970) and *Gonna Take a Miracle* (1971) – were quintessential white soul, the latter featuring new versions of the Motown classics 'Dancing in the Street' and 'Jimmy Mack'.

In 1971, at just 24, she announced her retirement and stayed out of the rock limelight until 1975, when *Smile* was released. By then, however, the vogue for introspective singer/songwriters had passed, and she found it difficult to regain even the critical favour she had once enjoyed. This was unfortunate, because *Season of Light* (1977, produced by Felix Cavaliere of the **Rascals**) was an impressive album containing distinctive versions of what had become probably her best-known songs – 'And When I Die' and 'Sweet Blindness'. *Nested* appeared in 1978, but virtually nothing has been heard from her since.

OATES, JOHN See Hall and Oates

OCEAN, BILLY Born in Trinidad in 1952, but moving to the UK at an early age, singer Billy Ocean is one of the few British artists to top the US pop, black and dance charts.

Ocean left school in London, working as a tailor before financing his first single 'Scorched Earth' in 1974, and combining night shifts on a car assembly line with his daytime songwriting and recording activities. In 1975 he signed to GTO and released one minor single before 'Love Really Hurts Without You' made Number 2 in the UK in 1976 (US Number 12). In 1977, GTO was sold to CBS after Ocean had another UK Number 2 with 'Red Light Spells Danger', but under CBS his career floundered somewhat and he didn't manage to score a Top 40 record for seven years.

Signed to Jive, Ocean's career took off again in 1984 as he immediately scored a huge transatlantic hit with the easy dance rhythms of 'Caribbean Queen (No More Love on the Run)', a US Number 1 and a hit all over the world. His album sales blossomed as *Suddenly* (1984) sold over 2 million in the US and several hit singles followed. Early in 1986 'When the Going Gets Tough, the Tough Get Going', Ocean's theme song for the film *Jewel of the Nile*, topped the charts in eight countries (four weeks as UK Number 1) and established Ocean as an international star.

OCHS, PHIL A singer/songwriter primarily identified with Sixties topical protest, Phil Ochs was born on 19 December 1940 in El Paso, Texas. Ochs went as a disenchanted Ohio State University journalism student into the Greenwich Village radical folk scene as a logical progression. First influenced by Bob Gibson, he fell in with **Bob Dylan**, **Tom Paxton**, David Blue and the movement associated with *Broadside* magazine. He sang out against the Vietnam War as early as 1962, recorded for Elektra beginning in 1963, then switched to A&M, which released the controversial *Gunfight at Carnegie Hall* (1970) – a live record, complete with audience boos, of a concert he gave dressed in gold lame and with a rock backing band. His best known songs

include 'There But For Fortune' (a hit for **Joan Baez**), 'Power and Glory', 'Changes', 'I Ain't Marchin' Anymore', 'Draft-Dodger Rag', 'Flower Lady', 'Love Me, I'm a Liberal' and 'Small Circle of Friends'.

Especially fluent in the sardonic talking-blues style, Ochs eschewed the 'poetic' lyric fashion to stress logic and clarity, with a fine sense of melodic shaping. His career line became jagged as causes he espoused were either won, lost or abandoned. In the early Seventies he moved to London and contributed briefly to *Time Out*, but reappeared momentarily for a 1974 protest concert against the military coup in Chile; Dylan, with whom Ochs had long enjoyed a love-hate relationship, was also on the bill. An alcoholic and prone to bouts of severe depression – apparently traceable to a physical assault on him during a 1973 trip to Africa, which left his vocal cords badly damaged – he committed suicide on 9 April 1976, at his sister's home in New York.

O'CONNOR, HAZEL Best remembered for her part as the exploited singer in the film *Breaking Glass*, Hazel O'Connor (born 16 May 1955) never seemed happy being a mere pop star. Following stints as an exotic dancer in Beirut and an English teacher in Japan, she returned to London in 1979 and played several solo gigs, winning the attention of Albion Records. Their business contacts led to the making of the film for which O'Connor both played the starring role and wrote all the music: *Breaking Glass* was subsequently the surprise hit of the Cannes Film Festival, making O'Connor a star overnight.

A debut single, 'Writing on the Wall' entered the lower reaches of the UK chart but was soon eclipsed by 'Eighth Day', which reached Number 5 in September 1980. At the height of this success, she released a second album, *Sons and Lovers* (1980), was voted Variety Actress of the Year and had another hit single with 'D Days'.

She went on to form a touring band, provocatively called Megahype, and released a third album, *Cover Plus* (1981), but has since failed to score another hit single. She has also, surprisingly, refused to make another film, but she received excellent reviews for her portrayal of a disaffected single parent in the 1986 BBC-TV drama *Fighting Back*. She told her life story in the 1982 autobiography, *Uncovered Plus* (Proteus).

OHIO PLAYERS An eight-piece black band almost as well known for their striking album covers as for their music, the Ohio Players first hit the big time with a funky riff called 'Pain' on Westbound in 1971. Twelve years earlier the original members (from Dayton, Ohio) had got together as the Ohio Untouchables – the group that supplied the memorable backing to the **Falcons'** searing R&B hit 'I Found a Love' (Lupine, 1962). After innumerable personnel changes and a name switch they recorded several erratic sides for TRC (1967), Compass (1968) and Capitol (1969) before absorbing the ideas of **James Brown** and Sly Stone (see **Sly and the Family Stone**) to reach modern audiences. 'Pain' introduced a succession of throbbing variations ('Pleasure', 'Funky Worm', 'Ecstasy') climaxing in a new contract with Mercury and their chart-topping 'Fire' (from the album of the same name) in 1974. Subsequent releases – *Honey* (1975), *Contradiction* (1976), *Angel*, *Mr Mean* (1977) – enhanced their reputation as one of the tightest bands in the business. In 1978, the Players left Mercury for Arista; by 1981, they were recording for Boardwalk, though their days as major hit-makers were behind them.

O'JAYS Leading soul men the O'Jays – best known for their association with producers **Kenny Gamble and Leon Huff** – first came together in 1958. Eddie Levert, Walter Williams, William Powell, Bobby Massey and Bill Isles formed a doo-wop group while still at Canton McKinley High School, Eddie and Walter having previously sung as a gospel duo. As the Mascots, they recorded unsuccessfully for the Wayco label in 1961, before Cleveland disc jockey Eddie O'Jay gave them his name. After a record with producer Don Davis, **H. B. Barnum** took the group to Los Angeles where they cut a small hit with 'Lonely Drifter' (leased to Imperial in 1963). After a large number of Imperial recordings ('Lipstick Traces', 1965; 'Stand in for Love', 1966) the group moved on, to Minit and then Bell with producer George Kerr.

The group (by then a quartet following the departure of Isles) experienced a little success (including 'I'll Be Sweeter Tomorrow', 1967) before signing for Gamble/Huff's Neptune label. There, 'One Night Affair' (1969) and 'Looky Looky' (1970) hit but Neptune was dissolved in mid-1971. Bobby Massey left the group to work in production and the three-man O'Jays tried a little self-produced recording until

Gamble/Huff (now with a Columbia linkup) came bouncing back with their own Philadelphia International Records. The O'Jays signed in 1972 and had a string of big hits with 'Back Stabbers', 'Love Train', 'For the Love of Money', 'Sunshine' (cut live in London) and 'Give the People What They Want'. Eddie Levert's expressively soulful lead over the vibrant MFSB backings made O'Jays discs among the very finest examples of the famed 'Philly Sound'. Powell left in 1976 and died of cancer a year later. His replacement was Sammy Strain, a one-time member of **Little Anthony and the Imperials**. They remain one of the great soul acts of the post-Motown era.

OLDFIELD, MIKE After the success of *Tubular Bells* (1973), Mike Oldfield was acclaimed as the most significant composer of the decade. Born on 15 May 1953, in Reading, he first recorded acoustic songs with his sister Sally on *Sallyangie* (Transatlantic, 1968). He later joined **Kevin Ayers** and the Whole World on guitar and bass. There he met the classically trained *avant-garde* composer David Bedford, who was to orchestrate the later works for occasional live performances.

Signing to Virgin as a solo artist, he recorded *Tubular Bells*, a collage of melodic lines and varied instrumentation (guitar, bass, mandolin, organ, grand piano, voices), held together by the insistent bell motif. That theme was released as 'Mike Oldfield's Single', used in *The Exorcist*, and reached the American Top 10. Its unexpected and overwhelming international success was followed by *Hergest Ridge* (1974), a more unified but sadly less evocative work.

Both *Tubular Bells* and *Hergest Ridge* received live performances and Oldfield released a humorous single, 'Don Alfonso', with David Bedford, before his next major work, *Ommadawn* (1975). A more ambitious composition, it utilized African drummers, Celtic pipes and a choir of local children. Like Oldfield's previous works, it was a best-seller. Further success followed with the singles 'In Dulce Jubilo' (1975), 'Portsmouth' (1976) and 'Blue Peter' (1979), and the albums *Incantations* (1978), *Exposed* (1979, a live double) and *QE2* (1980). 'Moonlight Shadow' (1983), featuring Sally Oldfield on vocals, reached Number 4 in the UK.

In the Eighties, he had an audio-visual studio installed in his Buckinghamshire home at a cost of £2 million and began developing composi-

Mike Oldfield in his home studio: Tubular Bells may rank as the most unexpected megahit ever, making Virgin a fortune with its first release

tions in tandem with video treatments, his first such project being *Pictures in the Dark* (1986) made in collaboration with video director Pete Claridge. Unlike earlier attempts at classical/rock fusions, Oldfield's themes and harmonic progressions are firmly rooted in rock and folk modes. His achievement has been to become the first to extend such themes into coherent symphony-length works.

OLDHAM, ANDREW LOOG A failed teenage pop star and former publicist, Andrew Loog Oldham used his own persuasiveness – and Eric Easton's financial backing – to lure the **Rolling Stones** away from their verbal and unofficial understanding with **Georgio Gomelsky** one night in April 1963, at Gomelsky's Crawdaddy Club in Richmond. Though generally credited with moulding the group's unruly image – he sacked pianist Ian Stewart because he didn't look right – he initially tried to smarten up the Stones, forcing them into dog-check stage jackets for their

first British television appearance to promote 'Come On' on *Thank Your Lucky Stars*. He also controlled their early recordings, ignoring material from their popular club repertoire and, for a while, succeeded in diluting their style.

He modelled his own image – and some of his early productions – on **Phil Spector** and in 1966 formed his own record company, Immediate, whose artists included **Chris Farlowe**, the **Small Faces**, **P.P. Arnold** and the **Nice**. He split with the Stones in 1967 and retired altogether when Immediate folded in 1970, but returned to the business as a producer in 1973, working from an office in the Brill Building on New York's Broadway.

OLDHAM, SPOONER It was initially as keyboards player at **Rick Hall**'s Fame Studios that Spooner Oldham (real name Lyndon Oldham) came to prominence during the Sixties. He became part of the 'Muscle Shoals Sound' and later began a prolific songwriting partnership with **Dan Penn**, the duo being responsible for such hits as 'Out of Left Field' (**Percy Sledge**), 'She Ain't Gonna Do Right' (Clarence Carter), plus material for **James Carr**, **James and Bobby Purify** and many others. Oldham – full name Dewey Lyndon – was not, however, contracted to Rick Hall, and success spurred him to farm out his talents (with Penn) to other studios before setting up as an independent production team at the Lynn-Lou Studio. *See also* **Dan Penn**

ONO, YOKO Born in Japan on 18 February 1933, Yoko Ono moved to America with her parents when she was 14. She later entered the New York avant-garde scene as a poet, film-maker and conceptual artist before meeting **John Lennon** in London in 1968. They married the following year.

The media blamed Yoko for the **Beatles**' split; but her relationship with John was only one of several contributory factors, and there can be little doubt that she was vilified chiefly because she was a woman, an Oriental and an intellectual. John introduced Yoko to rock and she brought him her experience with electronic music and jazz. Their first albums together – *Two Virgins* (1968), *Wedding Album* (1969), *Life with the Lions* (1969) – were indulgently esoteric; but their development of the Plastic Ono Band created a new music that was spare, hard, often beautiful, always honest. Yoko's best work appeared on her *Approximately Infinite Universe* (1973) – cool, anguished, feminist rock that was among the most tough-minded and aware of Seventies music.

The murder of Lennon in December 1980 transformed media attitudes to Yoko, and her first solo release after the event – *Season of Glass* (Geffen, 1981) – was well received. *It's Alright* followed a year later. *See also* **John Lennon**

ORANGE JUICE Formed in Glasgow in 1977, Orange Juice were the brave young faces of Scottish new wave pop who promised a great deal but failed to live up to expectations.

Led by singer/guitarist Edwyn Collins, along with James Kirk (guitar), Steven Daly (drums, later replaced by Zeke Manyika) and David McClymont (bass), they joined forces with Alan Horne's newly formed Postcard label and released four singles during the late Seventies, 'Falling and Laughing', 'Love Sick'/'Blue Boy', 'Simply Thrilled Honey' and 'Poor Old Soul' – independent chart favourites and jangly pop records that remain minor classics of the period.

In 1981, Orange Juice signed to major label Polydor, seeking the breakthrough into the big league that never came. After a couple of albums, *You Can't Hide Your Love Forever* (1982) and *Rip It Up* (1982) and just one hit single, 'Rip It Up', a UK Number 8 in 1983, Orange Juice finally split in 1984. Collins and Manyika both continued to write and record as solo artists.

ORBISON, ROY Between 1960 and 1966, Roy Orbison had a string of nine American Top 10 hits and even more in Britain. In a period when most successful pop music was decidedly lightweight, his records were sensitive, sombre and overpoweringly emotional. Born in Vernon, Texas, on 23 April 1936, Roy Kelton Orbison began as a rockabilly singer with the Wink Westerners and then the Teen Kings, who included Johnny 'Peanuts' Wilson on rhythm guitar. His first records were cut at **Norman Petty**'s studio in Clovis, New Mexico, and released on Jewel. In 1956, Orbison recorded for Sun and 'Ooby Dooby' reached Number 59 in the national charts. Further Sun Singles – hard rockers, unsuited to Orbison's voice – were unsuccessful. In 1958, Orbison's song 'Claudette' was recorded by the **Everly Brothers** and he moved to Nashville to concentrate on songwriting. One single for RCA followed, then Orbison signed with **Fred Foster**'s Monument label. His second release on the label was 'Only the Lonely' which went to Number 2 in America and topped the British charts. It set the pattern for the string of big, mournful almost operatic ballads which followed – 'Blue Angel', 'Runnin' Scared', 'Dream Baby', 'Crying' and 'Blue Bayou' were among them. 'In Dreams' (Top 10 in 1963 on both sides of the Atlantic) was the Orbison song par excellence, with its spoken introduction, ringing tear-jerking theme, soaring falsettos and storming crescendo.

His romanticism was a legacy of his Southern upbringing. Many of his best songs reflect the emotional honesty of the best country music and tell of situations well loved by the Dixie audience: Orbison was the loner, the rejected lover, the born loser. He took his initial cue, no doubt, from country singer **Don Gibson** but there was something magical about the qualities of his songs which transcended even the best Gibson numbers. His voice, too, developed into something great – it contained within it something of Don Gibson's blue, lamenting quality, but it also exhibited much of the raw emotionalism of black music: it was the combination of these two qualities which created the mystique of the Big O's voice. It was tender, but the tenderness never seemed to slip into sentimentality – it was a tenderness permeated by toughness. The mystique of the Orbison voice was emphasized even more strongly at personal appearances, where his stunning lack of movement seemed oddly contradictory in the age of the Shadows and Freddy Cannon. Not only did he stand completely motionless but he also managed to sing his hard-hitting material (exact recreations of the records) without appearing to move his lips any more than the average ventriloquist.

In the middle Sixties Orbison's popularity and the quality of his material declined, although in Britain his appeal held fast in the face of beat group competition: both 'It's Over' and 'Oh Pretty Woman' topped the UK chart in 1964. 'Too Soon to Know' (on MGM, where he moved in 1965) also reached the British Top 10 in 1966. He was also dogged by domestic tragedy when his wife, Claudette, died in a motorcycle accident in 1966 and his house was destroyed by fire in 1968, killing his two children. He has continued performing and recording since, moving to Elektra for his 1979 album, *Laminar Flow*, and carving a career for himself in the country music field. He is still enormously popular with older audiences in Britain, and his songs have also provided hits for **Linda Ronstadt** ('Blue Bayou', 1977), **Don McLean** ('Crying', 1981) and **Van Halen** ('Oh Pretty Woman', 1982).

ORCHESTRAL MANOEUVRES IN THE DARK/OMD Liverpool synth-based outfit Orchestral Manoeuvres In The Dark were among the first to take electronic pop into the charts in the early Eighties and continued to be one of its most enduring successes.

Andy McCluskey (bass/vocals/keyboards) and Paul Humphreys (vocals/keyboards), with the aid of backing tapes, played their debut gig at Eric's club in Liverpool in 1978 and then sent a tape to Tony Wilson, TV presenter and head of the newly-formed Factory label, who put out the single 'Electricity'. This aroused a great deal of interest and by the beginning of 1980 they had recorded an album, *OMD*, and recruited Dave Hughes (keyboards) and Malcolm Holmes (drums) to replace the tapes that the duo had used up to then.

OMD founders Andy McCluskey (above) and Paul Humphreys drew their inspiration for electronic pop from Germany's Kraftwerk

The LP, a tuneful and fresh collection of songs, was enthusiastically greeted as was *Organisation* (1980) which yielded their biggest international hit, 'Enola Gay', a fixture on radio stations across Europe that summer. *Architecture and Morality* (1981) stayed largely in that lightweight vein before *Dazzle Ships* (1983) and *Junk Culture* (1984) became more experimental (including the use of electric typewriters as instruments), with varying degrees of success. Reviewers were less keen than formerly, however, and *Crush* (1985) saw a return to pop tunes, albeit with an increasing array of acoustic instruments that belied their 'electronic' tag.

ORIOLES Sonny Til (born Earlington Tilghman), George Nelson, Alexander Sharp and Johnny Reed were singing together in 1947 as the Vibra-Naires in local Baltimore clubs when they were spotted by Deborah Chessler, who booked them onto Arthur Godfrey's *Talent Scout* show. They lost to pianist George Shearing, but Godfrey was sufficiently impressed to invite them onto his daytime radio show.

In 1948, they met Jerry Blaine of Natural Records and cut 'It's Too Soon to Know', changing their name to Orioles after the Maryland State bird. Natural then became Jubilee, for whom the group recorded until 1956, scoring many R&B hits including chart-toppers 'Tell Me So' (1949) and 'Crying in the Chapel' (1953), characteristic senti-

mental love ballads with subtle instrumental accompaniment. Nelson quit in 1953, to be replaced by Gregory Carroll, but a year later the original group disbanded. Of the founder-members, Nelson died of asthma in 1959 and Sharp of a heart attack in 1970. Meanwhile Til 'adopted' the Regals (Albert Russell, Paul Griffin, Billy Adams and Jerry Rodriguez) as new Orioles, recording for Jubilee until early 1956 when, following problems with royalties and material, they moved to Vee Jay where they cut a further series of mellow love-songs before disbanding in 1957.

In 1962 Til put together a third 'Orioles' (Delton McCall, Billy Taylor and Gerald Gregory), cutting an album for Charlie Parker Records, and with personnel variations the group subsequently recorded for Lana, Sutton and, in 1971, RCA.

ORLANDO, TONY Born in New York, on 3 April 1944, Tony Orlando (real name Michael Cassavitis) first worked as a singer on demonstration discs for **Don Kirshner**'s famous Brill Building music publishing operation. Orlando cut the originals of 'Will You Still Love Me Tomorrow' and 'Some Kind of Wonderful' (hits for the **Shirelles** and the **Drifters**) before Kirshner realized his potential as a singer in his own right.

He specialized in the perfectly organized pop single and had three hits on Epic during 1961: 'Halfway to

Paradise' (a British hit for **Billy Fury**), 'Bless You' (Top 20) and 'Happy Times'. As a vocalist, he was one of the first 'blue-eyed soul' singers and the productions – by Kirshner and Al Nevins – were almost symphonic. But despite the rich strings, Spanish guitars, castanets and girl choruses, it was Orlando that you heard. Hours of practice in a cappella groups had helped to perfect a distinctive voice which often outshone the Goffin-King (*see* **Carole King**) songs he was given.

Although the Orlando voice disappeared later in the Sixties – he went into business, running April-Blackwood Music for its owners, CBS Records – he re-emerged early in the next decade as the leader of **Dawn**. After a long run of hits he became a born-again Christian in 1977. After working as a solo act in cabaret, he starred in the Broadway production of *Barnum* in the early Eighties.

ORLONS A four-girl, black vocal group of the early Sixties, the Orlons comprised Shirley Brickley, Rosetta Hightower, Stef Caldwell and Marlena Davis. They had a string of weak and watery dance hits on Cameo-Parkway Records between 1962 and 1964 and owed much of their success to frequent exposure on Philadelphia's *American Bandstand* TV show. 'The Wah Watusi' (Number 2), 'Don't Hang Up' (Number 4), 'South Street' (Number 3), 'Not Me' (Number 12), and 'Cross Fire' (Number 19) were their biggest hits, and the girls also sang on discs by Dee Dee Sharp and **Bobby Rydell**. The Orlons were not the best black singers around and, in 1964, Caldwell left and Audrey Birchley replaced Davis. After further discs for ABC and Calla as a trio, the group split up when Hightower left for a solo career in the UK, where the **Searchers** had earlier enjoyed a big hit with an Orlons original, 'Don't Throw Your Love Away'.

OSBORNE, JEFFREY Born on 9 March 1951 and raised in Providence, Rhode Island, Jeffrey Osborne had no formal musical training but taught himself to play drums when he was fifteen. In 1970 he accepted an offer to join LTD, a self-contained black band who recorded some excellent tracks. That was the start of a ten-year period with the band, initially as their drummer but later as lead singer. After leaving LTD in 1980, he negotiated a solo contract with A&M while writing songs, and in 1982 launched himself into the pop/R&B market with an eponymous album produced by **George Duke**. But it was his second set, *Stay With Me Tonight* (1983), that perfectly captured the richness of his voice, his interpretive powers and able handling of a good melody. A third Duke-produced album, *Don't Stop* (1984) and *Emotional* (1986) – with production credits including Osborne and Duke – established Osborne as one of the most interesting and capable male solo singers to emerge in the Eighties.

OSBOURNE, OZZY Having left British metal band **Black Sabbath** at the end of 1978, prime hard rock vocalist and frontman Ozzy Osbourne (born John Michael Osbourne on 3 December 1948 in Birmingham, England) continued to be a success across the world with his own group. His increasingly manic and cruel stage antics gave Osbourne a notoriety that he not only revelled in but played up to for the media.

After taking two years off, he re-launched his career in 1980, releasing an LP, *Blizzard of Ozz*, which sold surprisingly well worldwide, as did subsequent albums, especially *Bark at the Moon* (1983). His live shows were well attended, especially in America, where public outrage at his controversial stage act (he once bit the head off a live bat) generated masses of publicity. Osbourne continues to be one of rock's great frontmen. *See also* **Black Sabbath**

OSIBISA African rock music in Britain was pioneered by Osibisa. Founded in 1970, the group comprised Teddy Osei (tenor sax, flute) from Kumasi, Ghana, Loughty Amao (saxes) from Nigeria, Robert Bailey (keyboards) from Trinidad, Spartacus R (bass) from Grenada, Wendell Richardson (guitar, vocals) from Antigua, Mac Tontoh (trumpet) and Sol Amarfio (drums).

For MCA, Osibisa recorded *Osibisa* (1970) and *Woyaya* (1971), after which the group underwent major personnel changes, with only Osei and Amarfio remaining from the original line-up. A third MCA record (*Heads*, 1972) led to the band being featured on the soundtrack of *Superfly TNT*. In 1973, they moved to Warner Brothers, releasing *Happy Children* (1973) and *Osibirock* (1974). In 1976 they had their first British chart success with 'Sunshine Day' (Bronze) by which time lead singer Richardson had re-joined the group. Subsequent albums were *Welcome Home* (Antilles, 1976), *Ojah Awake*, *Black Magic Night* (1977) and – after a temporary disbandment – *Mystic Nights* (Calibre, 1980).

OSMONDS The musical progeny of George and Olive Osmond, the Osmonds are: Alan (guitar, born 22 June 1949), Wayne (guitar, sax, 28 August 1951), Merrill (bass, 30 April 1953), Jay (drums, 12 September 1955), Donny (keyboards, 12 September 1957), Marie (13 October 1959), and Jimmy (16 April 1963). The first five brothers showed musical inclinations at an early age and were encouraged to sing and play at family evenings. Their local church – they are Mormon and live in Utah – soon heard of the singing family and asked them to perform. Jay Williams, father of Andy, heard them and recommended his son to audition them for his TV show. They became regulars for the show's four-year history, switching to *The Jerry Lewis Show*, branching into other TV and variety shows, and touring with Williams, **Pat Boone** and Phyllis Diller, meanwhile recording for MCA.

Record success began in 1971 with the release of 'One Bad Apple', an American chart topper on the MGM label, then headed by **Mike Curb**, and continued with 'Down by the Lazy River' and 'Hold Her Tight' (1972). In 1972, at the height of their popularity in America, they turned their attention to Britain where astute promotion in the teeny-bopper market secured them an immediate hysterical following of riot-laden proportions. Donny Osmond was the first to score with a chart-topping solo record, 'Puppy Love' (1972) – the first of a stream of Fifties revivals, 'Too Young', 'Why', both Top 10 in 1972, 'Twelfth of Never' and 'Young Love', both Number 1s, and 'When I Fall in Love' (1973) – before he turned to duets with Marie Osmond with the chart-topping 'I'm Leaving It Up to You' (1974) and 'Morning Side of the Mountain' (1975).

Donny wasn't the only Osmond to tread the solo path: 'Little' Jimmy had a Number 1 hit in 1972 with his revival of a Beatles cash-in song of the early Sixties, 'Long Haired Lover from Liverpool' and a Top 10 hit with a revival of 'Tweedle Dee' in 1973, while in 1972 Marie Osmond had a huge hit with 'Paper Roses'.

The successes of these solo projects stemmed not so much from the chart successes of the Osmonds *en masse*, though that was considerable – 'Crazy Horses' (1972), 'Going Home' and 'Let Me In' (1973) were all Top 5 records – but from their in-person appearances, in which Donny and 'Little' Jimmy (and later Marie) provided easily identifiable foci for the group's audience. From November 1972, the date of their

first visit to Britain, to the end of 1974 they visited Britain frequently, culminating in an exclusive filmed performance, excerpts from which were shown daily on BBC TV for a week.

By 1975, the group's teenybopper popularity was on the wane in Britain too – significantly they had always sold more photographs of themselves than records. But the Osmonds began broadening their appeal with a convincing version of the **Johnny Bristol** soul ballad, 'Love Me for a Reason' (1974). Latterly, the group – minus Donny – have re-groomed themselves as a pseudo-country outfit; they headlined at the Wembley Country Music Festival in 1986.

O'SULLIVAN, GILBERT A lightweight singer/songwriter/pianist from Waterford, Ireland, where he was born on 1 December 1946, Gilbert O'Sullivan stands as a perfect example of how a minor but genuine talent can be spoiled by the star system. When he first appeared in England in 1970, singing 'Nothing Rhymed', he was dressed in short trousers and cloth cap, a parody of the working-class environment he was supposedly singing about in his songs and even his earliest recordings on MAM, the label owned by Gordon Mills, manager of **Tom Jones**, were marred by excessive easy-listening style orchestrations. A run of pleasantly idiosyncratic singles between 1970 and 1973, including 'We Will', 'Alone Again (Naturally)' and 'Clair' (all UK Top 10 hits), preceded his re-launch by MAM with a new image as an orthodox middle-of-the-road entertainer, partly with the US market in mind. After some further success, he dropped out of the public view around 1976 and became involved in litigation against MAM over bad career guidance – a case settled in O'Sullivan's favour in the mid-Eighties. Signed to CBS in 1980, he returned to the UK chart with 'What's in a Kiss'.

Gilbert O'Sullivan with flat cap

OTIS, JOHNNY One of the god-fathers of R&B, Johnny Otis was born in Vallejo, California, on 28 December 1921 to Greek immigrant parents, Alexander and Irene Veliotes. By 1940, the big band jazz of Count Basie and Duke Ellington had inspired him to start learning drums, later progressing to piano and vibes. In 1946 he switched from a small boogie/blues outfit to a 16-piece jazz/swing band, signed a contract with Excelsior Records and scored his first hit, 'Harlem Nocturne'. The band took off on a nationwide tour with **Louis Jordan**, **Nat 'King' Cole** and the **Inkspots**. They were later to record with such jazz greats as Lester Young, Illinois Jacquet and Jimmy Rushing.

In 1948, Otis opened the Barrelhouse Club in Los Angeles, thus launching the very first nightspot to feature R&B music exclusively. While at the Barrelhouse, he discovered 13-year-old Little **Esther** (**Phillips**). Throughout 1950, the pair cut numerous hits for Savoy records, usually billed as Little Esther with Johnny Otis and the Robins (who were another Otis find). Their first recording, 'Double Crossing Blues', was a Number 1 R&B seller. This was followed by 'Mistrustin' Blues', 'Wedding Boogie' and 'Deceivin' Blues'.

At about the same time, Otis saw the potential of a touring R&B review, and so 'The Johnny Otis R&B Caravan' took to the road – again the first of its kind. The package featured several Otis discoveries, including **Willie Mae** ('Big Mama') **Thornton**, who was later to cut the original version of **Leiber and Stoller**'s 'Hound Dog', with Otis in accompaniment. While in Detroit in 1951, he discovered **Jackie Wilson**, **Little Willie John** and **Hank Ballard**. A few years later the legendary **Johnny Ace** joined the Otis package, and quickly became the star of the show. Otis went on to arrange and produce most of Ace's recordings for the Texas-based Duke-Peacock label, including his smash hit of 1954, 'Pledging My Love'. **Little Richard**, **Etta James**, **Charles Brown**, **Johnny 'Guitar' Watson** and Sugarcane Harris are just a few of the other artists he has been associated with over the years.

As the Fifties progressed, Otis became more and more aware of the changing public taste in R&B, notably with the introduction of rock'n'roll styles into the music. By 1957 he had signed a contract with Capitol records in Los Angeles, and later that year cut 'Ma (He's Makin' Eyes at Me)', with Marie Adams and the Three Tons of Joy. Shortly after he recorded what was

to become his best remembered hit, 'Willie and the Hand Jive'. It was a novelty rock song aimed straight at the teenage market, and the Top 10 that exploited to the full the now famous '**Bo Diddley**' beat. Whether the arrangement was inspired by Diddley is open to debate, although Otis insists that he first played by this rhythm – known as 'shave-and-a-haircut, six-bits' – during the early Forties. The song was later covered in Britain by **Cliff Richard**.

Otis spent most of the Sixties working in a producer/arranger capacity until 1968 when he and his son, Shuggie, collaborated on a progressive album called *Cold Shot*. It was a surprise hit and led to a producer/recording contract with Columbia-Epic. By 1970, however, Otis had decided to re-form his original touring show of the Fifties, which has since played a string of successful concert dates throughout America and Europe.

OWENS, BUCK Country singer Buck Owens was born on 12 August 1939 in Sherman, Texas, as Alvin Owens. He moved to Bakersfield, California, in the early Fifties to play guitar in the bands of Bill Woods and then Tommy Collins. He also worked as an occasional sessionman for Capitol's Ken Nelson – he appears on some **Gene Vincent** recordings – before forming his own band, the Buckaroos, and signing with Capitol (after an abortive stay with the local Pep label) in 1957. Owens and his tight, spare 'Bakersfield Sound' have produced over 20 country chart-toppers since 1963 and, in the relatively small country market, have sold almost ten million records. His success meant the end of Nashville's dominance of the country charts and helped pave the way for Bakersfield's other country superstar, **Merle Haggard**, whose records are also firmly in the honky-tonk tradition. Although he is still active as a performer, the Seventies saw Owens, like **Roy Acuff** before him, increasingly turn his attention to business, building up his OMAC Artists Corporation into a base for a possible future in Republican politics as well as in music. His best-known composition is possibly 'Act Naturally', which the **Beatles** recorded on *Rubber Soul* in 1965.

OZARK MOUNTAIN DAREDEVILS Country-rock group the Ozark Mountain Daredevils originally comprised John Dillon (guitars, fiddle, etc.), Randle Chowning (lead guitars, harmonica), Steve Cash (harmonica), Buddy Brayfield (keyboards), Larry Lee

(drums) and Michael Granda (bass). All shared vocals, and each hailed from the vicinity of Springfield, Missouri, where they had played in various local bands before coming together in 1973.

Signed to A&M, their first, eponymous album was produced by David Anderle and Glyn Johns. It was a pleasant amalgam of country and rock, with graceful harmonies and strong compositions. 'Jackie Blue', written by Lee, from their second album *It'll Shine When It Shines*, was a major American hit (Number 3) in 1975. A third album, *The Car over the Lake Album*, recorded in Nashville, was released in 1975. Chowning went solo in 1976 and was replaced by Norwegian-born Rune Walle; Brayfield departed during the following year, his place being taken by Ruell Chapell. Jerry Mills (mandolin) and Steve Canday (guitar) also joined during 1977.

PAGE, JIMMY Born in Heston, Middlesex, on 9 January 1944, Jimmy Page became one of London's busiest session guitarists in the early Sixties. He turned down his first chance to join the **Yardbirds** when **Eric Clapton** left in March 1965, preferring to experiment with production – he produced **John Mayall**'s 'I'm Your Witchdoctor' (Immediate) later that year – continue his session work and make the occasional single, e.g. 'She Just Satisfies' (Fontana). He joined the Yardbirds as bass guitarist in place of Paul Samwell-Smith in June 1966, but soon swapped roles with Chris Dreja to share lead with **Jeff Beck**. He took over lead guitar work when Beck quit at the end of the year. When the Yardbirds split up in 1968, Page formed the New Yardbirds, later **Led Zeppelin**. *See also* **Led Zeppelin**, the **Yardbirds**

PALMER, ROBERT Born in Batley, West Yorkshire, on 19 January 1949, Robert Palmer served his musical apprenticeship with the Mandrakes and the Alan Bown Set before joining DaDa/Vinegar Joe in 1969. Palmer quit Vinegar Joe in 1974 to embark on a solo career, releasing his first album *Sneakin' Sally Through the Alley*, which featured a host of top US musicians including Lowell George and Bill Payne of **Little Feat**, Cornell Dupree and **Bernard Purdie**. The album became a radio hit in America and,

Jimmy Page; as enigmatic off-stage as he is flamboyant on-stage

Robert Palmer (right) working as a producer with Desmond Dekker in 1981

following a series of showcase gigs, Palmer decided to move to New York. His next two albums *Pressure Drop* (1975) – the title track a strong reworking of Toots Hibbert's classic – and *Some People Can Do What They Like* (1976), demonstrated his growing eclecticism; musicians included the Muscle Shoals Horns and the Motown rhythm section.

A major US success by the late Seventies – his single 'Every Kinda People' made Number 16 in the US chart in 1978 – he then began to find a new market in Europe. An American tour in the autumn of 1979 was followed by a sell-out series of European shows, including two nights at London's Hammersmith Odeon.

Palmer's greatest strength has been his blue-eyed soul vocals but his skills as a producer led to work on albums by **Desmond Dekker** and Peter Bauman among others. Studio work included collaborations with **John Martyn** and John and Andy Taylor of **Duran Duran**, with whom he formed the Power Station. **Chic**'s drummer Tony Thompson completed the line-up and in March 1985 'Some Like It Hot' was released, followed by a version of the **T. Rex** number 'Get It On', which made the US Top 10. In June 1985, Palmer quit the group to pursue his solo career and his album *Riptide* was released in October of that year.

PAPPALARDI, FELIX Bassist/producer/songwriter Felix Pappalardi was born in the Bronx, New York, in 1939, and studied music at Michigan University. Thrown out, he gravitated to Greenwich Village, playing guitar, singing and backing others like **Tom Rush** and **Fred Neil**. He did early sessions for Vanguard and Elektra, backing or arranging for an impressive roster – **Richard and Mimi Fariña**, **Tim Hardin**, **Richie Havens**, **Buffy Sainte-Marie** and **Joan Baez**, and producing New York's first folk-rock group, the Mugwumps. Later he worked with the **Lovin' Spoonful** and the **Youngbloods**, producing the latter's first two albums, before making his name with **Cream** as producer/arranger/writer on all their studio albums after *Fresh Cream*, and **Jack Bruce**'s *Songs for a Tailor*. In 1969, he produced and played bass on Leslie West's album, which led to the formation of **Mountain**. They made some of the most original heavy music on record on *Nantucket Sleighride* (1971). Pappalardi was shot dead on 17 April 1983, by his wife and songwriting partner Gail Collins. *See also* **Mountain**

PARKER, BOBBY

Singer/guitarist Parker's 'Watch Your Step', his own fierce, pounding, gospel-charged composition, reached Number 51 on V-Tone in 1961. The seminal guitar introduction influenced the Beatles ('I Feel Fine'), while the flip-side, 'Steal Your Heart Away', was revived by the **Moody Blues**. A club tour of Britain in 1968 revealed a dynamic modern blues performer.

PARKER, 'COLONEL' TOM

According to **Elvis Presley**'s celebrated and notorious manager, he was born on 29 June 1909, in West Virginia and went to work for his uncle's 'The Great Parker Pony Circus' as a child before setting up on his own on the Southern carnival circuit. However, evidence suggests that Parker was, in fact, born in Breda, Holland (on 26 June 1909) and christened Andreas Cornelius van Kuijk. Often in trouble with his parents, he fled to the USA at the age of eighteen where he worked with the travelling Royal American Carnival Show as a salesman and publicity agent. By the Forties he was promoting country acts on a tie-in basis with various Southern commodities, before signing Eddy Arnold to a management contract. In 1954 he took control of **Hank Snow**'s career, for one of whose tours he booked Elvis Presley, still managed then by Bob Neal. Parker, who knew Steve Sholes of RCA through his dealings with him on behalf of Arnold and Snow, organized the RCA contract for Presley, helped set up Elvis Presley Music with Hill and Range and became Presley's manager – all at once. He had taken complete control of the careers of Arnold and Snow – except for their music – and did the same with Presley. Once Presley's success was assured, Parker set about making him a superstar, creating a mystique about the singer and – coincidentally – making himself a legendary character. Though he never interfered with the musical decisions made for and on behalf of Presley, Parker's essentially hucksterish attitude to his charge must be partly responsible for the series of career decisions that led to Presley's awful Sixties film career and then to the way Presley's revival turned sour in the Seventies. *See also* **Elvis Presley**

PARKER, GRAHAM AND THE RUMOUR

British singer/songwriter Graham Parker (born in London on 18 November 1950) emerged from the Seventies pub-rock scene to a barrage of good reviews and flattering comparisons with the likes of **Bob Dylan** and **Elvis Costello**, but he failed to convert that acclaim into lasting commercial success.

In 1975 Parker, formerly a petrol-pump attendant, impressed Dave Robinson of Stiff Records with a demo and introduced him to the Rumour – **Brinsley Schwarz** (guitar), Bob Andrews (keyboards), Andrew Bodnar (bass), Martin Belmont (guitar) and Steve Goulding (drums) – who were his backing band until 1981. Two LPs, *Howlin' Wind* and *Heat Treatment*, followed the next year and showed a strong soul sensibility. Five albums and a change of label (from Mercury to Arista) later, came *Squeezing Out Sparks* (1979), Parker's best-selling LP and also one of his finest artistically, blending accessibility with passion. Three more albums up to 1983 failed to improve on this, a situation which continued after another change of label (to Elektra) and *Steady Nerves* (1985). In 1986 he moved within the WEA group to Atlantic.

PARKER, JUNIOR

Born Herman 'Little Junior' Parker on 3 March 1927 in West Memphis, Arkansas, Junior Parker was a well-respected and influential bluesman of the Fifties and Sixties. Originally a member of the legendary Beale Streeters – along with **Bobby Bland**, **B.B. King**, **Johnny Ace** and **Rosco Gordon** – he first recorded in 1952 for the Modern label, switching to Sun in 1953 where he scored a massive R&B hit with 'Feelin' Good'. His second Sun release, 'Mystery Train', was covered by **Elvis Presley** in 1955. Parker then signed with Duke, where he achieved his greatest sucess. His straightforward **Sonny Boy Williamson**-influenced harmonica-playing did not appear on record until 1956, but thereafter he played harp on many sessions. His best sides included 'Next Time You See Me', 'Mother-in-Law Blues' and 'Barefoot Rock', all featuring superb accompaniment by the Bill Harvey/Joe Scott band. (These tracks can be heard on *Blues Consolidated*, Duke.) Apart from 'Drivin' Wheel', 'Country Girl' and a few other titles, Parker's later records were pretty dismal, his velvet-tinged vocals fighting a losing battle with gimmicky arrangements and a huge, brass-dominated band. During the late Sixties, he recorded a number of contemporary-sounding soul and blues sides for Mercury, Capitol, Blue Rock, Minit and UA. Parker died in a Chicago hospital on 18 November 1971, following surgery to correct an eye problem.

PARKS, VAN DYKE

Best known for his various songwriting collaborations with Brian Wilson of the **Beach Boys**, Van Dyke Parks was born in Mississippi on 3 January 1941, and moved with his family to Hollywood in his teens. He became a budding child movie star, appearing opposite Grace Kelly in the 1956 film *The Swan*, before studying classical piano and composition at college. He recorded briefly for MGM in the mid-Sixties, debuting with the single 'Number Nine', based on Beethoven's Ninth Symphony, and became a freelance session musician, arranging and playing on dates for **Harpers Bizarre**, **Judy Collins**, the **Beau Brummels**, the **Byrds** and others. He began working with Wilson in 1966, on recordings originally planned for the Beach Boys' aborted *Smile* album, some of which (notably 'Heroes and Villains') appeared on *Smiley Smile* a year later and on *Surf's Up* in 1971. Also in 1967, Parks began working on a solo album (*Song Cycle*, eventually released in 1968) for Warner Brothers – a kaleidoscopic suite of songs featuring mind-bendingly allusive lyrics and breathtaking musicianship from around eighty of Los Angeles' finest sessionmen.

He co-produced **Randy Newman**'s first album for Warners in 1968 and **Ry Cooder**'s debut for Reprise in 1970 but did not record again under his own name until 1972, when Warners released *Discover America*. Warners also retained his services as director of the company's audio-visual department between 1970 and early 1972. In 1975, he took his interest in calypso music (already apparent in *Discover America*) a stage further with *The Clang of the Yankee Reaper*, which again featured the Esso Trinidad Steel Band. He played a cameo role in the film *Popeye* in 1979 and contributed to the score, but his major project at that time was a complete musical treatment of the Brer Rabbit stories, which eventually appeared in album form as *Jump!* during 1984. Later, Parks was reported to be planning a stage version of the album.

PARNES, LARRY

Known as 'Mr Parnes, Shillings and Pence', Larry Parnes was *the* British rock'n'roll manager of the late Fifties. He first became involved in management through a partnership with publicist John Kennedy to promote Kennedy's discovery, **Tommy Steele**. They billed Steele as 'Britain's first rock and roller' and invented his name to match. Despite the fact that Steele's metallic qualities were hardly apparent, Parnes lost no faith in the power of naming. The year following the Steele breakthrough, 1957, saw Parnes grooming singer Reginald Smith for stardom. Parnes changed his name to **Marty Wilde**, booked him in to BBC-TV's *Six-Five Special* and got him a record contract with Philips.

Parnes put most of his performers on a rising yearly wage (Wilde and Fury were signed on a percentage basis) – employing them under the terms of a five-year contract rather than taking a percentage. Another of Parnes' innovations was to promote shows using up to ten performers from the 'stable' – in many ways his operation provided a model for future managers, agents and promoters.

Of all the Parnes stable only Wilde, Steele, **Billy Fury** and **Joe Brown** were to make any significant impact during their time with him. **Georgie Fame** and Duffy Power (sticking with their Parnes names) became established – the latter only in a small way – after leaving the stable. Among the names consigned to the margins of rock history are Dickie Pride, Johnny Gentle, Nelson Keene, Peter Wynne, Davy Jones, Johnny Goode and Vince Eager. In 1961, the Silver Beetles auditioned for him to back another Liverpudlian, Billy Fury. Parnes booked them to back Johnny Gentle (also from Liverpool). But when they became the **Beatles** he turned down a deal with **Brian Epstein**, and as his contracts expired he slowly moved out of the business leaving Epstein to shoulder his mantle.

PARSONS, GRAM

A seminal figure in the development of country-rock, singer/songwriter/guitarist Gram Parsons was born Cecil Connor on 5 November 1946, in Winterhaven, Florida. He formed the International Submarine Band during 1966 and recorded *Safe at Home* (LHI, 1967) with them before joining the **Byrds** at **Chris Hillman**'s invitation for their first predominantly country-influenced album, *Sweetheart of the Rodeo*. He left the group in 1968, refusing to tour South Africa, and formed the **Flying Burrito Brothers** who recorded the definitive Southern country rock album, *The Gilded Palace of Sin* (A&M, 1969), a unique mixture of black and white Southern music performed from a rock perspective. After one more album with the group, *Burrito Deluxe* (1970), he left to pursue a solo career. Without Parsons the Burrito Brothers veered more and more towards a Los Angeles version of

country-rock. Signed to Reprise, after a lengthy series of delays he released *GP* (1973), which featured the harmonizing of Emmylou Harris and united him with top session musicians including Byron Berline (fiddle) and **James Burton** (guitar) under the direction of ex-**Crickets** Glen D. Hardin. They formed the nucleus of his Hot Band. *GP* and the following album, *Grievous Angel* (released posthumously in 1974), featured an impressive array of mournful country standards and Parsons originals that translated the traditional concerns of country music into a contemporary context. Though both were critically well received, they sold poorly. Following his sudden death on 19 September 1973, Emmylou Harris recorded two plaintive albums, *Pieces of the Sky* and *Elite Hotel* (Reprise, 1975), and toured with the Hot Band, achieving greater commercial success than Parsons.

PARTON, DOLLY

Born on 19 January 1946, in Locust Ridge, Tennessee, Dolly Parton was recognized by the beginning of the Eighties as one of the best female singer/songwriters of the modern era. She spent the early part of her career in the mainstream country circuit (touring with Porter Wagoner) and appeared on Wagoner's syndicated TV show as 'Miss Dolly', projecting both the phenomenal figure and cascading blonde locks of the Southern bombshell, and the down-home innocence integral to straight country. This tended to disguise the fact that she wrote perceptive songs about her background and lifestyle and sang them

Miss Dolly, the not-so-dumb blonde from down in Tennessee

brilliantly. Recording first for Goldband, Mercury and Monument, she hit with 'Dumb Blonde' in 1967 and joined RCA in 1968. From 1970 onwards, songs like 'Joshua', 'Jolene', 'Coat of Many Colors' and 'In My Tennessee Mountain Home' – all country hits – carried her quivering Appalachian soprano to a wider, international audience, and her 1977 album *New Harvest* brought her a new and loyal following within the pop market. 1978 brought major (and global) chart success with 'Here You Come Again' and 'Two Doors Down', while 'Baby I'm Burning' (1979) became a surprise disco hit. Her US chart-topping 'Nine to Five' (1980), from the film in which she made her acting debut, consolidated her status as one of the most successful 'crossover' acts ever to emerge out of country music.

PARTRIDGE FAMILY See **David Cassidy**

PATTO

An innovative but commercially unsuccessful London band of the early Seventies, Patto was formed from the remnants of Timebox. The group comprise Mike Patto (lead vocals, born Mike McCarthy on 22 September 1942 in Glasgow), Ollie Halsall (guitars, keyboards, born in Southport, Lancashire, on 14 March 1949), Clive Griffiths (bass, 16 May 1945) and John Halsey (drums, 3 February 1945).

With Muff Winwood producing, Patto cut two albums for Vertigo (*Patto*, 1970, *Hold Your Fire*, 1971) and one for Island (*Roll 'Em, Smoke 'Em, Put Out a Line*, 1972). All featured Halsall's aggressive guitar work and Patto's vocals on hard-edged jazz-influenced songs.

The group split at the end of 1972, with Mike Patto joining **Spooky Tooth** and Halsall playing with Jon Hiseman's Tempest and later **Kevin Ayers** as well as establishing himself as a leading session musician. In late 1975, he was reunited with Mike Patto in Boxer, with Tony Newman (drums) and Keith Ellis (bass); their three albums were *Below the Belt* (Virgin, 1975), *Bloodletting* (1976) and *Absolutely* (1977). Mike Patto died of throat cancer in 1979.

PAUL, BILLY

Born in Philadelphia on 1 December 1934, Billy Paul became one of the stars of **Kenny Gamble and Leon Huff**'s Philadelphia International label in the early Seventies. He had an early grounding in jazz, through his mother's record collection, and attended Temple University, West

Philadelphia Music School and Granoff Music School, amassing an impressive set of qualifications before beginning his recording career as a slick jazz singer on Jubilee.

Paul met writer/producer Kenny Gamble at Philadelphia's Cadillac Club, where they got together to record an album. Following Gamble to his Neptune and Philadelphia International labels, Paul retained his jazz styling but aimed for the pop/soul market. Late 1972 brought him a chart-topping million-seller, 'Me and Mrs Jones', a smoochy but vibrant ballad with 'love-triangle' implications which also reached the British Top 20. He continued to record for Philadelphia International in his smooth, jazzy style throughout the Seventies, his hits including 'Thanks for Saving My Life' (1974), 'Let's Make a Baby' and a version of **Paul McCartney**'s 'Let 'Em In' (both 1976).

PAUL, LES, AND FORD, MARY

A major figure in the development and marketing of the electric guitar, Les Paul (born Lester Polfuss on 9 January 1916, in Waykesha, Wisconsin) began playing guitar in hillbilly bands and then moved on to jazz combos, first with the Les Paul Trio in the late Thirties, before becoming a guitarist with Fred Waring and his Pennsylvanians and, later, Bing Crosby. He had always been interested in electronics and in 1941, while in hospital after a car crash, he had the idea of making a solid body electric guitar – the 'log' – which he eventually sold to Gibson as the 'Les Paul Guitar'. It was finally issued by the company, complete with its famous sustaining pick-ups in 1952.

In the late Forties, he met Mary Ford – born on 7 July 1928 as Colleen Summer, in Pasadena, California – and they began performing and recording as a duo, unsuccessfully, for Decca and Columbia. After their marriage, they moved to Capitol and almost immediately had a series of million-sellers – 'Mockin' Bird Hill', 'How High the Moon' and 'The World Is Waiting for the Sunrise', records which are remembered more for their originality – Mary Ford's voice complementing Les Paul's 'talking guitar' – than anything else. Their hits ceased in 1961, but by then Les Paul, who had built the first eight-track recorder in 1954, was far more interested in experimenting with guitars than playing them. Since his divorce from Mary Ford in 1963, he has devoted himself to 're-inventing the guitar'. Mary Ford died in 1977.

PAXTON, GARY

In the early 1960s, Gary Paxton was part of a circle of young producer/songwriter/singers/ who formed the second generation of Los Angeles studio manipulators. Others included **Kim Fowley**, Skip Battin (of **Skip and Flip**), Bruce Johnston, **Lou Adler**, and **Terry Melcher**. Paxton's first success was with the Hollywood Argyles, singing the lead on 'Alley Oop', a Number 1 record in 1960. He and Fowley subsequently sent over a dozen 'Hollywood Argyle' groups out on the road, and recorded, produced and released hundreds of records by groups of kids they found on the street, on a wide array of one-shot labels. Paxton's Lute and Paxley labels were among the longer-lived of these, featuring many novelty releases along the lines of 'Alley Oop', notably **Bobby 'Boris' Pickett**'s 'Monster Mash'. Around 1965, Paxton became involved with the growing country scene in Bakersfield, California, and went on to write and produce many country hits there and in Nashville, though he never entirely left novelty records behind. 'The Clone Affair' (Private Stock, 1975) had much of the old spirit to satisfy any Hollywood Argyles fan. *See also* **Skip and Flip**

PAXTON, TOM

As his triumphant appearance at the 1971 Isle of Wight festival proved, Tom Paxton was the only topical folk singer of the early Sixties to retain his influence until the end of the decade with minimal changes in style. He was born in Chicago, Illinois, on 31 October 1937, and studied at the University of Oklahoma before travelling to New York, the centre of the folk revival. Many of the songs Paxton wrote in those early years – accompanying himself on guitar – became folk club standards, including love songs ('The Last Thing on My Mind', 'Leaving London'), highway songs ('Rambling Boy', 'Bound for the Mountains and the Sea'), children's songs ('Jennifer's Rabbit', 'The Marvellous Toy'), and above all the topical protest lyrics. These ranged from the early 'Daily News' and 'Lyndon Johnson Told the Nation', through 'Talking Vietnam Pot Luck Blues' (1968) to 'The Hostage' (1973) and 'Forest Lawn'. In 1971, Paxton signed with Reprise after cutting seven albums for Elektra, and became semi-resident in the UK, where he cut *New Songs for Old Friends* (1973) with **Ralph McTell** and formed a songwriting partnership with the British arranger/composer Ed Welch. He later recorded for MAM, Vanguard and Flying Fish.

PAYNE, FREDA

Detroit-born Freda Payne (on 19 September 1945) is best remembered for one of the biggest international dance hits of 1970, 'Band of Gold'. A former student at the Detroit Institute of Musical Arts, she spent many years performing big band jazz standards and slinky bossa novas on the night-club circuit, and recording in this vein for ABC and MGM. Then, in 1969, she joined ex-Tamla writing team **Holland, Dozier, and Holland** on the Invictus label and reached younger audiences with several bright Motown-style hits, including 'Deeper and Deeper' (1970), and 'Bring the Boys Home' (1971). Later releases were less popular, and she re-signed with ABC in 1974. She became a television presenter in the early Eighties, hosting the chat show *For You Black Woman*.

PEACHES AND HERB

The story of black vocal partnership Peaches and Herb began when Marlene 'Peaches' Mack (born in Virginia in 1945) left a session group, the Joytones, in 1966. Joining Herb Fame, an unsuccessful solo artist, at the suggestion of producer **Van McCoy**, she signed with Columbia's newly-formed Date label and began recording with Fame as a duo. Their debut release, 'Let's Fall in Love' (produced by McCoy), was recorded in the style of an updated **Brook Benton/ Dinah Washington** duet, Herb's easy tenor blending with Peaches' wistful voice, and the result was a Top 30 hit. The follow-up, 'Close Your Eyes' (1967), reached Number 8 in the US, and seven subsequent releases became Hot 100 hits over the next two years. When Marlene opted out of the partnership in the late Seventies, Francine Barker joined as her replacement. When Date was discontinued, the duo moved briefly to Columbia before moving to Mercury and then to BS Records. Herb dropped out of recording in the early Seventies to become a policeman but was persuaded back by McCoy in 1976, who suggested pairing him with yet another new Peaches – Linda Green, former singer with the Rondells. Freddie Perren produced the duo's 'comeback' album, *2 Hot* (Polydor, 1979), and from it was taken the singles 'Shake Your Groove Thing' and 'Reunited', the latter reaching Number 1 in the US and Number 4 in the UK.

PEARLS BEFORE SWINE

Late Sixties New York band Pearls Before Swine originally comprised Tom Rapp, guitar, vocals; Wayne Harley, autoharp, banjo, mandolin, oscillator; Lane Lederer, bass, guitar, various horns;

and Roger Crissinger, organ, harpsichord. After two ESP albums, however, the band became Tom Rapp plus whoever he gathered around him in the studio. Rapp's individual songs were always the heart of the group, shrouded in innovative, mysterious arrangements and presenting a philosophical aura (especially *Balaclava*, 1968) that suggest his influence on his New York peers the **Velvet Underground**, especially **Lou Reed**. After *Balaclava*, he abandoned the dominant abstract themes (shared by the earlier album *One Nation Underground*) for a series of more conventional-sounding albums, erratic, but containing brilliant humanistic ('The Jeweller'), allegorical ('Rocket Man') and romantic ('Island Lady') songs. After six albums under the aegis of Pearls Before Swine, he subsequently recorded under his own name. The first, *Familiar Songs* (Reprise, 1972), was a re-recorded collection of some of his best earlier songs.

PEEBLES, ANN Best known for her worldwide 1973 hit 'I Can't Stand the Rain', Ann Peebles has been one of the finest exponents of **Willie Mitchell**'s Memphis soul sound since joining Hi in 1969. Born in St Louis on 27 April 1947, she debuted on Hi (in the same month as **Al Green**) with 'Walk Away'. The first of many raunchy R&B hits, it was followed by oldies – 'Part Time Love', 'I Pity the Fool' (1970–1) – and new songs – 'Somebody's on Your Case', 'Gonna Tear Your Playhouse Down' (1972–3). Releases since 'Rain' have been equally impressive (particularly 'You Keep Me Hanging On') but their formula-bound similarity inhibited sales. She is married to singer Don Bryant, with whom she co-wrote 'Rain'.

PEEL, JOHN A champion of non-mainstream, alternative music for over two decades, disc-jockey John Peel helped launch the careers of numerous major and minor rock acts from the mid-Sixties onwards. He was born John Ravenscroft in Heswall, near Liverpool, on 30 August 1939, and had a public school education before moving to the US in 1961, ostensibly to study the American end of the cotton business in which his father operated. He began his radio career working for a station in Dallas, Texas, but found himself much in demand in 1964–5, when the British beat invasion and the American success of the **Beatles** in particular turned anyone with a Liverpool accent into a celebrity. He worked for station KOMA in Oklahoma and KMEN

in California, where he became exposed to the San Franciscan hippie lifestyle and the music of underground acts like **Captain Beefheart** and **Frank Zappa**. Back in the UK by early 1967, he joined the pirate station Radio London and started a late-night programme called *The Perfumed Garden*, on which he showcased the best of the new American rock and its British equivalent. When the pirates were closed down, he joined BBC Radio One and repeated the formula on the shows *Night Ride* and *Top Gear*, giving session time to a host of avant-garde acts and pioneering what was loosely called 'progressive rock'. He also ran his own record label, Dandelion, but on his own admittance was too generous and too naïve to survive as an entrepreneur.

Peel gave early exposure to the likes of **Pink Floyd**, **Soft Machine** and **T. Rex**, but by the mid-Seventies he was distancing himself from what progressive rock had become, complaining of being fed up 'with superstars, fraud, pretension and quasi-mystical hoggery'. Craving something new, he was increasingly drawn to what he called 'hooligan music' – that of **Eddie and the Hot Rods**, the **Ramones**, the **Damned** and others. His support for the punk movement in 1976–7 was invaluable:

at a time when record companies were reeling in shock and few A&R men were prepared even to visit a punk club, Peel and his producer John Walters booked such bands for sessions and spread the punk gospel well beyond London. Getting a Peel session became the recognized way for young musicians throughout Britain to find an audience, and literally hundreds of bands – from **Siouxsie and the Banshees** to **Altered Images**, from the **Undertones** to **Joy Division** – owed their early reputations to his endorsement.

By the mid-Eighties, Peel was the only member of the original Radio One disc-jockey team to be still broadcasting regularly for the station – a tribute to his extraordinary ability to keep discovering new sounds and new names, and to the enduring cult appeal of his low-key, diffident and unfussy style of presentation.

PENDERGRASS, TEDDY Few lives can match the rise, fall and subsequent rehabilitation of black American soul singer Theodore 'Teddy' Pendergrass. It seems cruelly apt that the stories of many of the best black American soul singers should scale the heights and plumb the very depths of

The macho sexual charisma of Teddy Pendergrass won him a 'ladykiller' reputation – female fans bombarded him with underwear during concerts

emotional, physical, and financial experience, for that is what most of their songs are about – triumph and disaster in love and life on a grand scale.

Born in 1950 and brought up in Philadelphia, Pendergrass's tough, powerful voice – mixing the styles of gospel and blues shouters whose intense delivery blended bravado and impassioned pleading in equal measure – became the cornerstone of the best music made by producers **Kenny Gamble and Leon Huff**, founders of the Philadelphia International label, originators of the Seventies' 'Philly Sound'. Pendergrass, who started out as a drummer for **Harold Melvin and the Blue Notes**, became that group's lead singer and his sound dominated it from then on. Whether it was on comparatively sweet ballads such as 'If You Don't Know Me By Now', or achingly believable ones like 'I Miss You', or on urgent stomping songs such as 'Bad Luck', 'Wake Up Everybody', 'The Love I Lost' or 'Don't Leave Me This Way', Pendergrass held the attention with his accomplished singing. He mixed an earthy, sexual insistence on the more aggressively paced pieces with mellow, moodier vocal work on ballads which he'd gradually infuse with wilder, improvised and often quite histrionic outbursts. To women, he became the most charismatic black sex-symbol/singer since **Al Green** and it was not unusual for the stage to be strewn with items of women's underwear after a Blue Notes performance.

As inevitable as his move from drum stool to centre stage was his move from group lead singer to solo artist. His debut album, 1977's *Teddy Pendergrass*, merely took the established Pendergrass style away from the close harmony backing of the Blue Notes and set it down in the excellent settings provided by Gamble and Huff's Sigma Sound Studio musicians. The material – the power of 'You Can't Hide From Yourself' and 'I Don't Love You Anymore', the pain of 'And If I Had' and 'The Whole Town's Laughing at Me' – was written to emphasize the styles that had brought Pendergrass a large following. The albums *Life Is a Song Worth Singing*, *Ready for Teddy* (a compilation), *Teddy* and *TP* broadly kept to this pattern, though by 1981 Pendergrass was insisting that he was less interested in inflaming the emotions of his women admirers.

In March 1982, still hugely popular despite a couple of disappointing, stale albums, Pendergrass was involved in a car crash which, at the age of 32, left him paralysed and permanently confined to a wheelchair. Inevitably, his singing voice was also badly affected – he could no longer sing from the diaphragm – and his first album of new recordings after the crash, *Love Language* (1984) on Asylum, confirmed all the worst fears about the vastly weakened state of his once majestic voice. A second album, *Working It Back* (1985), showed a marked improvement in both his singing and in his ability to find material to suit his reduced capabilities.

PENGUINS 'Earth Angel' by the Penguins was reputed to have sold two million copies on Dootone in 1954. The song was written by **Jesse Belvin** and recorded by Cleveland Duncan (lead vocal, born on 23 July 1935), Curtis Williams (1935), Dexter Tixby (1936) and Bruce Tate (1935). Gently rock-inflected, it distilled the feeling of adolescent uncertainty perfectly. It remains America's favourite oldie. Subsequently managed by **Buck Ram**, the Penguins had no comparable success, but recorded a series of fine discs for Mercury, Wing, Atlantic, Dooto, Sunstate and Original Sound, where **Frank Zappa** wrote and produced 'Memories of El Monte' for them in 1963. During this period, Teddy Harper and Randolph Jones replaced Williams and Tate.

PENN, DON Songwriter/producer Don Penn first came to the fore as the 14-year old writer of 'Is a Bluebird Blue?', a Top 40 hit for **Conway Twitty** in 1960. In the late Fifties, he formed a group, Dan Penn and the Pallbearers – adopting their name after buying a hearse as a bandwagon – with David Briggs (piano), Norbert Putnam (bass), Jerry Carrigan (drums). They made several unsuccessful records, playing local Alabama clubs and bars, before **Rick Hall** hired them as a session band for his new Fame studio, where Penn began a lengthy and fruitful partnership with another Fame sessioneer, **Spooner Oldham**. As a songwriting partnership, Penn and Oldham produced several hundred songs, some used by artists from Hall's own Fame label, some artists from other labels doing individual sessions at the studio, and some passed on to artists in other local studios since Penn and Oldham were not contracted to Fame as writers. Penn also wrote with other renowned sessioneers, most notably with Chips Moman, which team was responsible for 'Do Right Woman – Do Right Man', a million-seller for **Aretha Franklin** and the magnificent doomy, country-soul ballad 'Dark End of the Street', recorded by **James Carr**, **Roy Hamilton**, **Linda Ronstadt**, **Ry Cooder** and numerous others. As a producer Penn worked with the **Box Tops** amongst others. He continued his partnership with Spooner Oldham, however, and they went on to form their own independent production company, working from Lynn-Lou Studios. He has recorded in his own right for MGM, Earth, Fame, Atlantic and Happy Tiger.

PENTANGLE Founded in 1967 by **Bert Jansch** and John Renbourn, Pentangle was an amplified folk group who briefly dented the UK pop charts with 'Once I Had a Sweetheart' in 1969 and, most memorably, 'Light Flight' (the theme song of the BBC-TV series *Take Three Girls*) in 1970. Both Jansch and Renbourn were already established as virtuoso solo guitarists and had made an album together for Transatlantic (*Bert and John*). With folk singer Jacqui McShee and jazzmen Danny Thompson (bass) and Terry Cox (drums) they worked up a repertoire of traditional songs, jazz instrumentals, blues and occasional contemporary songs.

Signing with Transatlantic, Pentangle cut five albums between 1968 and 1971, two of which – *The Pentangle* (1968) and *Basket of Light* (1969) – were big-selling albums. For the most part, Jansch and Renbourn played acoustic guitars into microphones, though a muted electric guitar was introduced on *Cruel Sister* (1970). McShee's soprano voice dominated the singing, sometimes in combination with Jansch's less polished voice.

Frequent tours, at home and abroad, were organized by their manager, Jo Lustig, who signed them to Reprise (which had earlier distributed their Transatlantic releases in the US) for *Solomon's Seal* (1972). That proved to be their last record, with Jansch, Renbourn and McShee going into semi-retirement for two years. Thompson formed a successful touring partnership with avant-garde guitarist John Martyn. Pentangle's recorded work was uniformly immaculate but often without the fire of Jansch and Renbourn's solo albums, which they continued to record throughout the life of the group. Several anthologies of Pentangle material were issued by Transatlantic in the mid-Seventies. They re-formed in the early Eighties for a series of concerts, their reunion neatly coinciding with the return of *Take Three Girls* to the screen after an absence of twelve years.

PÈRE UBU Taking their name from the absurdist play by French writer Alfred Jarry, Père Ubu arrived in Europe as part of the mid-Seventies 'industrial' wave from the American towns of Akron and Cleveland. While the band's image and the titles of their songs initially suggested the period's confused notion of 'industrial music', they later proved to have a very different style. Their line-up was David Thomas, vocals; Tom Herman, guitar, bass; Scott Krauss, drums; Peter Laughner, guitar; Dave Taylor, keyboards; Tim Wright, bass; Alan Greenblatt, guitar; Allen Ravenstine, keyboards; and Tony Maimone, bass.

Formed in the early Seventies, they released their first single, '30 Seconds over Tokyo', in 1975 on the Cleveland label Hearthan. Like its successor, 'Final Solution' (1976), it had more in common with early **Velvet Underground** and **Can** than the noise espoused by the infant punk scene. But the mixture of raw punk riffing, crude electronics and the wildman vocals of Crocus Behemoth (aka David Thomas) gave their 1976 debut album, *The Modern Dance*, new wave credibility.

Signed to Chrysalis in Britain, the group were given support from the label which allowed their style to encompass improvisation, jazz moods and Thomas' increasing interest in eccentric popular song. They recorded four albums for Chrysalis – *Dub Housing*, *New Picnic Time*, *The Art of Walking* and *Song of the Bailing Man* – but split in 1982. Singer Thomas still pursues a variety of solo songwriting/performance projects under a variety of different names, occasionally reappearing as his alter-ego Behemoth.

PERKINS, CARL The original fusion of musical strands that produced the first rock'n'roll sounds was the product of a particular environment at a particular moment in time. If, from the white standpoint, **Elvis Presley** was the best interpreter of that moment, then it ought to be conceded that Carl Perkins, his stablemate at Sun Records, Memphis, was the best chronicler.

Like Elvis, **Johnny Cash** and **Jerry Lee Lewis**, Carl Perkins was born into poverty in the South – on 9 April 1932, in Lake City, Tennessee. Like them, his principal musical influences were black blues and white country: 'The man who taught me guitar was an old coloured man. See, I was raised on a plantation in Lake County, Tennessee, and we were the only white people on it. White music, I liked Bill Monroe, his black stuff; for coloured, I liked **John**

Carl Perkins shot to stardom in 1956 with 'Blue Suede Shoes' but his success was brief, although he went on performing into the Eighties

Lee Hooker, **Muddy Waters**, their electric stuff. Even then, I liked to do Hooker songs Bill Monroe-style, blues with a country beat.'

Perkins was a restless teenager, and it wasn't until Elvis Presley made his mammoth psychological breakthrough with 'That's All Right' that he decided to enter the music business seriously. With the release of 'That's All Right', the secret was out – the poor young whites in the South had absorbed the music of the local black communities of places like Beale Street in Memphis – there had been a crucial shift in attitudes since the heyday of **Hank Williams**, and Sam Phillips and Elvis Presley had spotlighted this changeover.

Perkins differed from Presley in that he was primarily a guitarist, and his lead playing on his early Sun tracks acted as an inspiration for a whole generation of guitarists – the sound of his records was closer to the feel of the new generation than that provided by **Bill Black** and **Scotty Moore** on Presley's contemporary recordings. Moreover, Perkins' material was usually self-composed, and again his material has, in retrospect, more lasting value than Presley's – it was written from a better vantage point, from within the communal change itself. Carl Perkins wrote and sang about things that mattered – about 'the cat bug' biting him (in 'Boppin' the Blues'), about brawls in bars ('Dixie Fried'), about the importance of his clothes and his style ('Blue Suede Shoes'). He sensed the release inherent

in the new music for the poor ('All Mama's Children') and he wrote about the wild young girls of the local area ('Put Your Cat Clothes On'). In short, he wrote about life for the young hepcats in Tennessee in the mid-Fifties – and, in doing so, he captured the sense of fun, and at the same time the sense of urgency of that moment in time.

Perkins was a brilliant chronicler, and his records with Sun will remain as works of sheer magic for all time – but he was never a real star. Maybe his preoccupation with the development of his musical form prevented him from seeing the possibilities open to a talent like his. Maybe, as others have suggested, he was simply too modest and too honest to want to make the steps that his friends at Sun made. It is difficult to imagine the rawness of Carl Perkins attaining the heights of the Ed Sullivan TV show, though he was invited and but for a car crash in Delaware, on 21 March 1956, he would at least have had his chance to try and become a teenage idol.

Since the mid-Fifties, Carl Perkins has continued playing – notably as a member of the Johnny Cash extravaganza – and recording. He has made little impact in those years since his heyday at Sun (although a rock'n'roll revival album, *Ol' Blue Suede's Back*, sold well in the UK in 1978) but the impact he made then was enormously important. He was, and always will be, the King of the style he created on his guitar – rockabilly. See *also* **Sun Records**

PERRY, LEE Also known as Scratch and Upsetter, Lee Perry was born in 1940 in Jamaica, and won international recognition in the late Sixties with a series of rhythmic reggae instrumentals: 'Clint Eastwood', 'Return of Django' (a British Top 5 hit in 1969) and 'Live Injection', all produced in conjunction with studio musicians, the Upsetters.

An apprenticeship in the Fifties with Coxsone Dodd's legendary Downbeat Sound System led Scratch to Studio One where he produced artists Delroy Wilson ('Joe Liges'), Shenley Dufus ('Rukumbine') and himself ('Trials and Crosses'). He left Dodd in 1968, following the inevitable disagreements. He worked alongside producers Joel Gibson and Clancy Eccles, briefly, until the Seventies when he was responsible for the classic Wailers' sides ('Small Axe', 'Duppy Conqueror'), Junior Byles ('Beat Down Babylon', 'Curley Locks'), I Roy, U Roy and many others, as well as recording tracks like 'Station Underground News' under his own name.

Perry moved to Holland in the late Seventies but recorded in the UK, his production credits including **Bob Marley**'s 1977 single for Island, 'Punky Reggae Party'. In 1979, Island issued a compilation album of Lee Perry's most noteworthy productions, *Scratch on the Wire*.

PERSUASIONS Masters of a cappella singing (harmony voices without instrumental backing) for over two decades, the Persuasions – Joseph Russell (born 25 September 1939 in Henderson, North Carolina), Jerry Lawson (23 January 1944 in Fort Lauderdale, Florida), Jayotis Washington (12 May 1941 in Detroit), Herbert Rhoad (1 October 1944 in Bamberg, South Carolina) and Jimmy Hayes (12 November 1943 in Hopewell, Virginia) – came together in New York in 1962. After an inauspicious (accompanied) recording debut on Minit, in 1966, the group adopted their a cappella singing style, and **Frank Zappa** issued their debut album on his Straight label. Further a cappella albums followed when they signed with Capitol, to be greeted with interest and curiosity but little commercial acceptance. They joined MCA in 1973 for one album, moving to A&M in 1974 with Willie C. Daniels replacing Washington but their new label put a band behind them in an attempt to gain commercial success. Daniels left in 1975 and was replaced by a returning Washington, the revised line-up recording *Chirpin'* for Elektra in 1977 and *Comin' at Ya* for Flying

Fish in 1979. They guested on recordings and live gigs by a number of black and white artists during the Seventies and sang the distinctive doo-wop backing on **Joni Mitchell**'s album *Shadows and Light* in 1980.

PETER AND GORDON Peter Asher and Gordon Waller (vocals/guitar) – always had a lot going for them. Peter (born 22 June 1944) was quiet and well educated, and looked like every mother's hoped-for son. Gordon (4 June 1945) had the sex appeal. Peter also had an actress sister, Jane, who was **Paul McCartney**'s girlfriend. McCartney and **Lennon** contributed unrecorded songs to give them their early hits ('World Without Love', 'Nobody I Know' on EMI's Columbia label) and Paul also wrote 'Woman' for them under a pseudonym, but the secret leaked out. Their other hits were timely revivals and vaudevillian songs such as 'Lady Godiva'. Like **Chad and Jeremy**, their real success was in America where their commerciality and 'Englishness' had great appeal and where they toured frequently. They split up in 1968; Gordon went solo, unsuccessfully, and Peter Asher became a staff producer for Apple before going on to even greater success as the manager and producer of **James Taylor** (one of his Apple discoveries) and **Linda Ronstadt**.

PETER, PAUL AND MARY The most successful pop-folk group of the Sixties, Peter, Paul and Mary were responsible for bringing countless pop fans into contact with the folk and protest movements. Peter Yarrow (born 31 May 1938 in New York), Paul (christened Noel Paul) Stookey (30 November 1937, Baltimore, Maryland) and Mary Allin Travers (7 November 1937, Louisville, Kentucky) were brought together in 1961 by manager Albert Grossman, to provide a contemporary equivalent to the **Kingston Trio** and the **Weavers**. In addition to their topical and protest songs – they were the first to introduce **Bob Dylan** compositions to mass audiences – their repertoire included comic and children's songs, notably 'Puff the Magic Dragon', which was claimed to have drug connotations by conservative critics of the folk revival. Under musical director Milt Okun, the trio had nearly twenty chart entries on Warner Brothers between 1962 and 1969, when **John Denver**'s 'Leaving on a Jet Plane' provided them with their first US Number 1. Peter, Paul and Mary were the most popular attraction on campuses,

but also sang at civil-rights, peace and liberal-Left meetings throughout the Sixties. Their light, ebullient harmonies and two-guitar backing were technically polished, appealing to audiences world-wide. They disbanded in 1971 to pursue solo careers but reunited in 1972, for a George McGovern presidential campaign benefit, and again in 1978 for an album (*Reunion*) and a US tour.

PETERSON, RAY Singer Ray Peterson (born in Denton, Texas, on 23 April 1939) was discovered in Los Angeles by Stan Shulman, who signed him to RCA-Victor in 1958. His early discs, which included 'Let's Try Romance' (his very first record), 'Tail Light', a cover of 'Fever' and the bright rocker 'Shirley Purley', all failed to make the charts. 'The Wonder of You', a Baker Knight song, gave Peterson his first US Top 20 hit in 1959. His emotional and petulant voice, with its range of four-and-a-half octaves, was ideally suited to such classic death discs as 'Tell Laura I Love Her' (a Number 7 in 1960) and 'Give Us Your Blessing' (a Hot 100 entry in 1963). Between the two, he scored with the **Phil Spector**-produced 'Corinna, Corinna' and one of the finest Gerry Goffin-**Barry Mann** ballads, 'I Could Have Loved You So Well', both on his own label, Dunes, to which he also signed **Curtis Lee**. After less successful records on MGM, Peterson tried to establish himself as a country singer.

PETTY, NORMAN Best remembered as **Buddy Holly**'s producer, Norman Petty (born in 1927) originally ran a cocktail-lounge trio with his wife which recorded fairly successfully for Columbia and ABC in the mid-Fifties. Growing tired of being bundled in and out of recording studios under record-company pressure, they decided to build their own studio in their home town of Clovis, New Mexico. Completed in 1955, Petty discovered that he had unwittingly built the only *bona fide* studio in the area and before long began hiring it out to local talent for demo recording.

First to record there was **Roy Orbison** who made his first disc, 'Ooby Dooby', for the local Jewel label under Petty's supervision before leaving for Memphis and re-recording it for Sun. Next came **Buddy Knox** and Jimmy Bowen (from Dumas, Texas) who recorded 'Party Doll' and 'I'm Stickin' with You' respectively for their own Triple D label in 1956. These tracks were sold to Blue Moon, before the giant Roulette combine in New York bought the rights and released each title separately. Both songs became hits – 'Party Doll' reached Number 1 in America. It was these early successes that prompted Buddy Holly, a hitherto unsuccessful but ambitious Decca artist from Lubbock, Texas, to visit Petty's studio and record some demos.

Sensing Holly's potential, Petty secured Holly's group, the **Crickets**, a new contract with Decca and released 'That'll Be the Day' which sold a million in 1957. Under Petty, Holly also began recording as a solo artist. More hits followed ('Oh Boy', 'Maybe Baby') and by 1958, Petty, who not only produced but often co-wrote the Crickets records, headed a thriving concern. A shrewd businessman, Petty did not lease out his studio at an hourly rate but instead simply charged a standard fee for each song recorded and offered to publish it.

When Holly moved to New York late in 1958, his relationship with Petty grew strained and Petty was about to sue when Holly was killed in a plane crash. Petty spent the next decade processing and patching together remnants of Holly's considerable recording legacy and several of these songs became English hits in the early Sixties.

Although Petty never again discovered a talent comparable to Holly, he produced several more million-sellers including 'Wheels' by the Stringalongs in 1961, and 'Sugar Shack' by Jimmy Gilmer and the **Fireballs** in 1963. In 1976, Petty sold the publishing rights to Buddy Holly's song catalogue to **Paul McCartney**. He died of leukaemia on 15 August 1984. *See also* **Buddy Holly**, the **Crickets**

PETTY, TOM, AND THE HEARTBREAKERS

Along with **Bruce Springsteen**, Tom Petty (born in 1952 in Gainsville, Florida) emerged during the Seventies as the leading light in American mainstream guitar rock.

Leaving high school at 17 to join leading Florida band Mudcrutch, Petty eventually wound up in Los Angeles seeking that elusive recording contract. He managed to set one up in the early Seventies with **Denny Cordell** and **Leon Russell**'s Shelter Records, but the band didn't survive the move to the West Coast. Petty was offered a solo contract but nothing happened until he heard Mike Campbell (guitar) and Benmont Tench (keyboards), both ex-members of Mudcrutch, recording with Ron Blair (bass) and Stan Lynch

Tom Petty, the leading light in American mainstream guitar rock during the Seventies

(drums). They became the Heartbreakers in 1975 and recorded their first album the next year. *Tom Petty and the Heartbreakers* was a stunning debut, a collection of Sixties-inspired songs with a Seventies rock edge, plus a couple of outstanding slower numbers. The LP sold poorly despite universal rave reviews, but a successful visit to the UK encouraged the re-release of the single 'Breakdown' which finally broke the US Top 40 a year after its initial release.

You're Gonna Get It! (1978) confirmed the promise of the first LP and pointed to imminent large-scale success, but a delay over the release of the third album due to record company wrangles (Shelter had been sold to MCA) threatened to undermine that position. As it turned out, *Damn the Torpedoes* (1979) was the breakthrough album, selling nearly 3 million copies and yielding two US Top 20 singles, 'Don't Do Me Like That' and 'Refugee'. *Hard Promises* (1981) also went platinum, firmly establishing Petty as a strong voice in rock, a status that continued through the albums *Long After Dark* (1982) and *Southern Accents* (1985).

PHILLIPS, ESTHER

A singer with a consummate command of R&B, soul, blues and jazz stylings, Esther Phillips was born on 23 December 1935, in Galveston, Texas, as Esther May Jones and modelled her style around **Dinah Washington**'s gritty jazz-blues. As Little Esther, she won a talent contest at **Johnny Otis'** Los Angeles

Barrelhouse Club in 1949 and recorded a number of ballad and jump-blues sides in indistinctive, almost nasal tones for Savoy, Modern and Federal Records, backed by Otis' usually mellow 'city blues' orchestra, sometimes duetting with Mel Walker from the Otis troupe. Her discs enjoyed fair success – 'Double Crossing Blues' was an R&B Number 1 in 1950.

She joined King Records of Cincinnati in 1951, where she stayed for two years, using the Johnny Otis Orchestra and recording in Cincinnati, New York and Los Angeles. She even duetted with **Clyde McPhatter** of the **Dominoes**, before her final fling with Decca in New York and her temporary retirement in 1954. In 1960 she emerged to work with Warwick in New York and was rediscovered by Lelan Rogers who signed her to Lenox Records, Nashville. Her hard-edged style, very much an acquired taste, finally broke through in 1962 with a Top 10 hit in 'Release Me', one of the few country songs she had recorded under Rogers' supervision. When Lenox folded, Esther Phillips (she took her surname from a gas-station hoarding) signed with Atlantic, and from 1963 through 1970 recorded an assortment of blues, pop, jazz and soul songs (excepting a further brief retirement in 1966 and a 1969 Roulette jazz-blues session), making little impression on the charts apart from a moderate 1965 hit, 'And I Love Him'.

In 1971, she signed with Kudu and produced a series of artistically excellent, critically acclaimed jazz-blues albums. 1975 brought a surprise disco success with a revival of the Forties song 'What a Difference a Day Makes', which reached both the UK and US charts. By 1978, she was recording for Mercury. She died on 7 August 1984.

PICKETT, BOBBY 'BORIS'

A briefly popular novelty singer from Somerville, Massachusetts, Bobby Pickett was born on 11 February 1940. After an unsuccessful attempt to become an actor and comedian, he joined a vocal group, the Cordials. In 1961, **Gary Paxton** (the lead singer with the Hollywood Argyles of 'Alley Oop' fame) produced Pickett's novelty narrative, 'Monster Mash'. It went to Number 1 and was another big hit when reissued in the UK in the early Seventies. 'Mash' and other gory slices from the same cadaver – 'Monster's Holiday' and 'Monster Motion' – depended for their success more on Pickett's ability to imitate Boris Karloff than on musical content.

PICKETT, WILSON One of the first of the new breed of singers to carry aggressive black emotion to a mass audience, Wilson Pickett eventually hammered spontaneous excitement into a stylized cliché, lost his sense of purpose, and then struggled to revive a lukewarm career. Born in Prattville, Alabama (on 18 March 1941) but raised in Detroit, he was first noticed on record as the shrieking lead vocalist on the **Falcons**' apoplectic R&B hit 'I Found a Love' (Lupine), in July 1962. Leaving the group (and after one dismal release on Correctone) he wrote and recorded two impressive wailers for **Lloyd Price**'s Double L label – 'If You Need Me' and 'It's Too Late' (1963) – before joining Atlantic the following year. After two unsuccessful releases, Atlantic took him to the Stax studios in Memphis for sessions with **Steve Cropper**, **Booker T.** and co., resulting in the hits 'In the Midnight Hour' and 'Don't Fight It' (1965), and to Muscle Shoals for '634–5789', 'Ninety-Nine-and-a-Half (Won't Do)' (1966). These launched Pickett as a major soul star.

For the next three years, at Fame studios, Muscle Shoals, he recorded constant variations on the dance themes, scoring his biggest hits with coarse, pounding tunes – 'Land of 1,000 Dances', 'Mustang Sally' (1966), 'Soul Dance No. 3', 'Funky Broadway' (1967), 'She's Looking Good', 'I'm a Midnight Mover' (1968) – although his best performances were slow, searing ballads – 'I'm in Love' and 'People Make the World' (1967) written and accompanied by **Bobby Womack**; the **Beatles**' 'Hey Jude' (1968); and 'Back in Your Arms' and 'Hey Joe' (1969). By the end of the Sixties, that particular brand of sock-it-to-'em soul was pushed aside by far more complex productions, and after one session in Miami and a hit with a tribute record dedicated to **Nat Cole**, **Sam Cooke** and **Otis Redding** ('Cole, Cooke, and Redding') he was teamed with the new black money-spinners, **Gamble and Huff**, at Sigma Sound in Philadelphia, who gave him 'Engine No. 9' (1970) and 'Don't Let the Green Grass Fool You' (1971), which was reputedly his first million-seller. Back in Miami, he recorded 'Don't Knock My Love', for Atlantic, before signing with RCA in 1972. Their endeavours to transform 'The Wicked Pickett' into a black Tom Jones largely misfired, but he did succeed with 'Soft Soul Boogie Woogie' in 1974 and slowly got to grips with the demands of a new era. Early in the Eighties he moved from RCA to EMI America.

PIGBAG See the **Pop Group**

PIL/PUBLIC IMAGE LTD Formed by John Lydon (previously Johnny Rotten) following the collapse of the **Sex Pistols**, Public Image Ltd – quickly abbreviated to PiL – brought Lydon's love of reggae and European electronic rock into the punk arena. Abetted by Jah Wobble (bass, real name John Wordle – later to launch his own solo career), Keith Levine (guitar), Jeanette Lee (audio-visuals) and Jim Walker (drums), their 1978 debut album, *Public Image Ltd*, featured only four tracks – including the successful title-track single – and essayed a for-then radical departure: mixing dub techniques with the bass-heavy rhythmic improvisations characteristic of Germany's **Can**. Most controversial was the 1979 follow-up, *Metal Box*, three lengthy EPs contained in a metal canister like those used for cine film. 1981's *Flowers of Romance* was the most startling experiment: a dark, stormy beat, Lydon's keening voice at its wildest, and the style switching between swirling Arabic folk, gypsy violins, warped heavy metal and Belfast protest song. *Paris au Printemps* (1983) was a lacklustre live effort, and PiL seemed to go into abeyance, with Lydon moving to Los Angeles.

Lydon once more proved the success of his wilful experiments in 1984 with 'This Is Not a Love Song', from the album *This Is What You Want, This Is What You Get*. In 1986, he relented and returned to the studio, solo but abetted by stars from jazz, funk, electronics and hard rock, to produce *Album*, another poke in the eye for rock trend-setters that saw PiL re-writing the history of heavy metal, with **Cream** drummer **Ginger Baker** in attendance.

The Wicked Pickett bares his soul in exciting hot funk style

PINK FLOYD Founded in 1966, Pink Floyd soon became London's premier psychedelic band. But unlike most celebrities from the summer of 1967, they have not only survived but have continued to evolve as performers and composers. The initial line-up was Syd Barrett, vocals and guitar (born in Cambridge, 6 January 1946); Roger Waters, bass (Great Bookham, Surrey, 6 September 1944); Richard Wright, keyboards (London, 28 July 1945); and Nick Mason, drums (Birmingham, 27 January 1945). Originally a straight R&B group, they moved towards psychedelia largely under the influence of Barrett and acquired a hippie management (Blackhill Enterprises), a recording contract with EMI's Columbia label, and a hit single – the bizarre 'Arnold Layne' – in April 1967, just as flower-power was being discovered by the national media.

The group played frequently at UFO, London's leading hippie club, and consolidated their underground preeminence with an excellent first album, *The Piper at the Gates of Dawn* (1967). The album was dominated by Barrett's songs, their childlike imagery and unexpected structural twists skilfully combining the sinister and the naïve. Also impressive were Wright's keyboard work and the band's instrumental evocations of space travel. 'Astronomy Dominé' and 'Interstellar Overdrive' established their image as a psychedelic space-rock band. However, during the next year, Barrett's behaviour became increasingly erratic and the other members of the band decided to part company with him. As a result, Dave Gilmour, born in Cambridge on 6 March 1944, was brought in to replace him as lead guitarist in 1968.

Without Barrett, the Floyd felt unable to develop as a singles band, and concentrated on their instrumental abilities. The title track of their second album, *A Saucerful of Secrets* (1968), was an extended instrumental which evolved skilfully through several shifts of mood to a beautiful, choral climax. 'Set the Controls for the Heart of the Sun' continued their space identity, again through musical, rather than verbal, skills. Barrett appeared once on one of his own compositions, 'Jugband Blues', singing his own epitaph: 'And I'm most obliged to you for making it clear/That I'm not really here'. The Floyd began using more sophisticated lighting effects in their live shows and introducing their innovatory 'Azimuth Co-ordinator', a PA system that moved the sound around the auditorium, emphasizing the spatial quality of their music. As testimony to their prowess as a live band, they released a double album, *Ummagumma* (Harvest, 1969). One record contained live recordings, showing that the band's energy and willingness to take chances enabled them to carry off their complex music live; the other contained a studio contribution from each member of the band, and was not so successful – the band appeared to possess more awareness of studio techniques than musical ideas on this record. After *Ummagumma*, the Floyd's career went through a somewhat quiet phase. They continued to develop the theatrical elements of their spectacular live shows, but their recordings were unadventurous in comparison. They created soundtracks for a few films: *More* (1969), *The Body* (1970), *Obscured by Clouds* (1972), but only Antonioni's *Zabriskie Point* (MGM, 1970) began to match the power of their music, particularly in the closing sequence when 'Careful With That Axe, Eugene' was played over an apocalyptic sequence of explosions.

Their next major album, *Atom Heart Mother* (1970), seemed to find the Floyd short of inspiration, utilizing choirs, orchestras, and diverse sounds (doubtless the influence of Ron Geesin who helped to record the album) to curiously little effect. Mere musical spectacle proved inadequate, and the Floyd responded well to this problem by tightening their sound and focusing their effects to create *Meddle* (1971), which was chiefly remarkable for 'Echoes', an extended piece occupying one side of the album. It wove together hard-rock improvisation, powerfully

On the road: Pink Floyd after Syd Barrett's departure, from the left Rick Wright, Nick Mason, Dave Gilmour and Roger Waters

melodic themes, and passages of abstract sound to create a richly integrated kaleidoscope of music. At the same time as developing a form of subtle, but emotionally charged, electronically flavoured mood music, the Floyd also began to create powerful songs. Probably the most successful piece on *Atom Heart Mother* was 'If' by Roger Waters, a movingly understated account of fear of an approaching mental crack-up, and this theme subsequently expanded to form the basis of a cycle of songs, *The Dark Side of the Moon* (1973), about the mental and emotional devastation wrought by the social pressures of fear of failure, growing old, poverty, loneliness, and, lurking behind them all, madness. The album was an extraordinary and quite unpredictable triumph for the Pink Floyd. The instrumental passages with which they fleshed out their songs were recognizable developments from their earlier musical experiments; but the theme of the lyrics (all written by Waters) and the overall mood of bleak pessimism were an explicit rejection of escapism, romanticism, rural retreats, and space travel – the major themes previously utilized by the Floyd – in favour of an acknowledgement of immediate, everyday pressures. *The Dark Side of the Moon* was a massive commercial, as well as artistic, triumph. It was conspicuously successful in the British and American charts, and had sold four million copies within two years of release. Despite lukewarm critical reaction, *Wish You Were Here* (1975) looked like repeating that success, one of its most notable tracks being a tribute to Syd Barrett, 'Shine on You Crazy Diamond'.

Animals, released in February 1977, won them renewed critical favour, and on tour they again resorted to elaborate audio-visual effects, using additional musicians to boost the sound and featuring an enormous, inflatable pig which was very much the album's symbol. In 1978, Gilmour and Wright each produced solo albums, and a year later *The Wall* appeared – credited to the group as a whole but very much Roger Waters' own creation. Its songs were linked by the presence of a central character called Pink, who becomes a powerful symbol of society's oppression of the individual. The single, 'Another Brick in the Wall', became the band's first Number 1 single, and the album formed the basis of the Alan Parker film of the same name in 1982. *The Final Cut* followed in 1983, an appropriately titled album in the light of Rick Wright's departure from the

band soon after its completion. Late in 1986, Waters began legal proceedings to dissolve the Pink Floyd partnership and to prevent Gilmour and Mason from using the name.

PITNEY, GENE One of the most popular American singers of the Sixties, Gene Pitney was born on 17 February 1941, in Hartford, Connecticut. He had no less than 23 chart-making singles, and at least that many albums. Although he occasionally wrote songs (his first hit, 'Love My Life Away', on Musicor, 1961), Pitney was best known as a pop singer who worked with other people's songs and arrangements. He had a strong, distinctive tenor that was at its best in big productions, which all of his hit records were. These included 'Town Without Pity' (1961), 'Liberty Valance', 'Only Love Can Break a Heart', 'Half Heaven – Half Heartache' (1962), 'Mecca' (1963), 'I'm Gonna Be Strong', 'It Hurts To Be in Love' (1964), 'She's a Heartbreaker' (1968) and '24 Hours from Tulsa', his best-remembered British hit (composed by **Burt Bacharach**) in 1963. From 1961 through 1966, Pitney averaged three hits per year. His hits continued through 1969, but dropped off after that. He has done little recording since, preferring to devote his time to the occasional cabaret or revival concert appearance, and to his many business interests.

PLATTERS A black vocal group of the Fifties who, thanks to careful management grooming, became hugely popular in the mainstream pop and cabaret fields, the Platters came together in 1953. Singers Tony Williams, David Lynch, Alex Hodge and Herb Reed met **Buck Ram** in Los Angeles and signed with Federal Records. Their discs were unsuccessful so Ram replaced Hodge with Paul Robi, added a female voice, Zola Taylor, and placed the group with Mercury in a package-deal including the **Penguins**, the hottest group at the time.

They recorded for Mercury from 1955 until 1964, managing to combine a prodigious output with a vast quantity of hits, ranging in style from the virtual a cappella of 'Only You' and the piano triplets of 'The Great Pretender' to the vast, orchestral arrangement of 'Smoke Gets in Your Eyes' as Ram steered them towards the lucrative cabaret circuits. Sonny Turner took over as lead tenor when Tony Williams quit in 1961, and more changes followed when the group moved to Musicor in 1966: Sandra Dawn replaced Taylor and soon after-

wards Nate Nelson supplanted Robi. The Platters regained chart status with such contemporary soul songs as 'I Love You 1,000 Times' (1966) and 'With This Ring' (1967), which became transatlantic discotheque favourites, and also re-recorded most of their Mercury hits.

Following dwindling singles sales and changing personnel, they moved to UA in 1973 where a dismal year yielded but one 45, and returned to Mercury in 1974 as the Buck Ram Platters, now featuring the neo-operatic lead tenor of Monroe Powell. The group is still performing in the Eighties, although the line-up has completely changed since their mid-Fifties heyday.

POCO Following the demise of **Buffalo Springfield**, Poco was formed (as Pogo, in summer 1968) when Richie Furay (guitar, vocals, born 9 May 1944) and Jim Messina (guitar, vocals, born 5 December 1947) joined up with Rusty Young (pedal steel, vocals, 23 February 1946), George Grantham (drums, 20 January 1947) and Randy Meisner (bass, 8 March 1946). The group's name became Poco in spring 1969. Messina left in 1970 and was replaced by Paul Cotton (9 May 1944) from the Illinois Speed Press, by which time the band had found a regular bass player in Timmy Schmit (30 October 1947), who replaced Randy Meisner when he left to join **Rick Nelson**'s Stone Canyon Band. This line-up reached a musical highpoint with the fifth Poco album, *A Good Feelin' to Know* (Epic, 1973), but leader Richie Furay left after *Crazy Eyes* (also 1973) to join forces with **Chris Hillman** and J. D. Souther in the Souther-Hillman-Furay Band.

Ironically, the departure of Furay precipitated Poco's best spell saleswise, with their next four albums all faring better than their previous releases. They signed with ABC in 1975 and released *Rose of Cimarron* during the following year. In 1977, Schmit joined the **Eagles** – replacing Randy Meisner – and Grantham also left; their replacements were Charlie Harrison and Steve Chapman. 1979 finally brought major commercial success in the form of *Legend*, for which the group received a gold disc: two singles taken from it, 'Crazy Love' and 'Heart of the Night', were US Top 20 hits that year. In 1980, Poco moved to MCA for three albums – *Under the Gun* (1980), *Blue and Gray* (1981) and *Cowboys and Englishmen* (1982) – before switching labels once more, this time to Atlantic in 1982.

POGUES Starting life as Pogue Mahone (Gaelic for 'kiss my arse'), the Pogues emerged in the mid-Eighties as the unique exponents of boozy, punk-powered Irish folk and rebel songs.

Shane MacGowan (vocals) found in 1982 that the Irish rebel songs he busked with were provoking a strong reaction and with Spider Stacey (tin whistle) – his partner from a previous band, the Nips – they recruited Jem Finer (banjo), James Fearnley (accordion), Cait O'Riordan (bass) and Andrew Ranken (drums) to form Pogue Mahone. Their raucous pub gigs soon became packed out, and in August 1984 they released 'Dark Streets of London', a big independent hit.

As the Pogues, the band signed to Stiff Records amid growing critical acclaim and acquired a big fan in **Elvis Costello** who went on to produce them. *Red Roses for Me* (1984) received rave reviews as did their second LP *Rum Sodomy & the Lash* in 1985, by which time Philip Chevron (guitar) and Terry Woods (mandola/concertina) had joined. Even though their live shows always sold out, substantial chart success still eluded them in 1986.

POINTER SISTERS Ruth, Anita, Bonnie and June Pointer, born in Oakland, California's black ghetto in 1946, 1948, 1950 and 1954 respectively, comprise the Pointer Sisters. They became a camp *succès d'estime* after years of failure (including back-up work and two Atlantic singles in 1972) when they replaced a cancelled act at the Troubadour Club, Los Angeles in 1973.

Guided by manager David Rubinson, their exuberant nostalgic mix of jazz, gospel and R&B harmonies catapulted them from rags to riches with TV work, tours, a hit single, two gold albums (produced by Rubinson on Blue Thumb) and finally in 1974 a Grammy Award for Best Country Single with their self-penned 'Fairy Tale'. With a broadening appeal they moved into the lucrative Las Vegas cabaret circuit.

Bonnie left for an initially successful solo career with Motown in 1978 (she later joined Epic), while her sisters joined Planet Records and recorded with label boss Richard Perry. Their version of **Bruce Springsteen**'s 'Fire' (1979) reached Number 2 in the US, an achievement matched by 'Slow Hand' (also a Top 10 hit in the UK and a global million seller) during 1981. Enormously popular in the Eighties, their best year was 1984, when the platinum album *Break Out* produced three major transatlantic hits in 'Automatic', 'Jump (For My Love)' and 'I'm So Excited'.

POLECATS Putting the emphasis on being flash, fun and footloose, the Polecats rode to fame on the early Eighties British rockabilly boom, appealing to young pop fans and older diehard rock'n'roll traditionalists.

Formed in North London in 1980, the group, consisting of Tim Worman (vocals), Martin Boorer (guitar), Philip Bloomberg (double bass) and Neil Rooney (drums), built up a strong following playing local hops and went on to secure a deal with Phonogram records.

Their brash exuberance and zany approach to re-creating the sheer fun of early rock'n'roll placed the band closer to **Madness** than **Matchbox** and they soon scored hit singles with a reckless version of **David Bowie's** 'John I'm Only Dancing' and their own spoof 'Rockabilly Guy' (both 1981). Teaming up with producer **Dave Edmunds**, they recorded their debut album, the frantic *Polecats Are Go* (1981), but as the rockabilly boom petered out, the band failed to sustain their early success.

POLICE The most commercially successful group to emerge out of the new wave, the Police were formed in 1977 by ex-Curved Air drummer Stewart Copeland (born 16 July 1952) who met bassist/singer Sting (real name Gordon Sumner, born 2 October 1951) playing in Newcastle jazz band No Exit. They performed briefly as a four-piece with guitarists Andy Summers (31 December 1942) – formerly with **Zoot Money**'s Big Roll Band – and Henry Padovani but the latter bowed out, leaving them as a trio.

The same year they made their first record, the raw, punk-influenced single 'Fall Out' on Illegal Records, which was owned by Stewart Copeland's brother, Miles, who was their manager. The Police signed to A&M at the beginning of 1978 and with the release of 'Roxanne' in April, premiered their innovative blend of reggae rhythms and sparse rock. It wasn't until a year later, however, after the single had made the US Top 40, that the Police really took off in the UK.

Sting's sexy looks helped project the Police's sharp rock-reggae blend to a massive worldwide audience, making them the major group of the early Eighties. Here, from the left, Copeland, Sting and Summers

In 1979, they had four UK hit singles, including two Number 1s and a Number 2, a Number 6 album, *Outlandos D'Amour* (which had been virtually ignored when originally released the year before) and a Number 1 album, *Regatta de Blanc*, which broke the band internationally. They achieved mammoth sales worldwide, appealing to a crossover audience – Sting's photogenic looks combined with the band's craftsmanship attracted the teen market as well as the more serious record buyers.

Allowing themselves a little time in between albums to indulge their solo ventures (especially Sting who accepted parts in the films *Quadrophenia* and *Radio On*), they released two more albums, *Zenyatta Mondatta* and *Ghost in the Machine* in 1980 and '81 respectively, both of which built on their international commercial success and spawned several hit singles, but represented no major developments in their songwriting – a failure that reviewers were at pains to point out.

In 1982, Andy Summers teamed up with **Robert Fripp** to record an experimental album, *I Advance Masked*, and the same year Sting was heavily committed elsewhere, appearing on the bill at Amnesty International's concert, *The Secret Policeman's Other Ball* as well as taking a part in the film *Brimstone and Treacle*, and this meant that the next Police album, *Synchronicity*, did not appear until mid-1983. Again it was poorly received by the music press, but it sold in huge numbers worldwide and contained two of the band's finest singles 'Every Breath You Take' and 'Wrapped Around Your Finger', both massive international hits.

Amid constant speculation (and constant denials) that the band were on the point of splitting up, the Police entered 1986 having recorded nothing as a three-piece since their fifth LP, but with each member having gone off on solo ventures. Copeland had made a film and recorded an album, both entitled *The Rhythmatist*, while Sting had appeared in more films and recorded an international hit album, the highly jazz-influenced *The Dream of the Blue Turtles*.

POLYDOR RECORDS/POLYGRAM

In 1961 Deutsche Grammophon Gesellschaft, the company formed by Joseph and Emil Berliner, who invented the flat disc in 1897, formed Polydor Records to complement its Deutsche Grammophon label.

In 1965 Polydor opened a manufacturing plant in Britain – all previous records, such as Tony Sheridan's (and the **Beatles**') 'My Bonnie', a minor hit in 1963, being imported from Germany. Soon after, the company signed production and distribution deals with Robert Stigwood (which resulted in the short-lived Creation and Reaction labels, a string of British hits from the **Bee Gees** and **Cream**, and finally RSO Records), Kit Lambert and Chris Stamp (Track Records) and hits for the **Who**, **Jimi Hendrix** and **Thunderclap Newman** and **Giorgio Gomelsky** (the short-lived Marmalade label) and licensed Atlantic and Stax in Britain.

Although Polydor soon established itself in Britain, it was not until much later that it formed its own A&R department and began signing groups such as **Slade** (1971) and the **New Seekers** (1971). An American label was formed in 1967 which also pursued a policy of licensing other labels and buying other record companies (MGM-Verve in 1971).

One of the few major record companies to have little or no image, despite its involvement in the early Seventies in British and American rock – it licensed or distributed Capricorn, **Jonathan King**'s UK Records, Phil Spector International and Kudu/CTI amongst others – its biggest success at this time was bandleader James Last, whose succession of MOR albums consistently sold in even vaster quantities than records by groups such as Slade and the **Osmonds**.

Later in the decade, the Polygram organization (as it was renamed in 1972) grew in global influence with the success of RSO and the Bee Gees – particularly their *Saturday Night Fever* soundtrack – and took over Decca Records in 1979. Important punk/new wave signings included the **Jam** and **Siouxsie and the Banshees**, while in the disco field Polydor offered **Gloria Gaynor**, **Peaches and Herb** and (on affiliated label Casablanca) **Donna Summer**.

Polydor found limited international success during the early Eighties with such acts as **Vangelis**, **Bucks Fizz** and **Level 42**, while other Polygram-owned labels – RSO, Casablanca, Mercury, Riva, London, Vertigo – proffered names such as Fine Young Cannibals, **Big Country**, **Tears for Fears**, **Bronski Beat** and **Carmel**. An anticipated merger between the Polygram organization and Warner Communications was abandoned in 1984. *See also* **Mercury Records**

POMUS, DOC, AND SHUMAN, MORT

A leading songwriting team of the early pop era, Jerome 'Doc' Pomus – who was confined to a wheelchair as a polio victim from early on in his youth (born on 27 June 1925 in New York City) – and Mort Shuman (12 November 1936, also in New York City) had their first hit when **Dion and the Belmonts** took their classic expression of teenage anguish, 'A Teenager in Love', to Number 5 in the US during 1959. Prior to working together, Pomus had unsuccessfully recorded blues in a **Mose Allison** vein for a number of record labels and had written songs both on his own and with Reginald Ashby (including 'Lonely Avenue' for **Ray Charles** and 'Boogie Woogie Country Girl' for **Joe Turner**); Shuman had written more pop-oriented songs for **Charlie Gracie** and others. They teamed up while contracted to the Aberbach music publishing company, Pomus having been signed there by Jerry **Leiber and** Mike **Stoller** after writing 'Young Blood' for the **Coasters**, a US Top 10 hit in 1957.

After 'A Teenager in Love' came 'Save the Last Dance for Me', which provided the **Drifters** with their first Number 1 in 1960. The success of these two songs established Pomus and Shuman – with Leiber and Stoller – as *the* rock'n'roll songwriters; while 'Save the Last Dance for Me', in particular, was the model and inspiration not only for the Drifters' and **Ben E. King**'s subsequent records, but also for the budding writers of the Brill Building – Goffin, King, Mann, Weil, Sedaka, Greenfield, etc. – who were to write many of those songs.

If Pomus and Shuman were successful in America, in Britain they were respected too: British managers and A&R men queued outside their door for their songs – British rock'n'roll at that time consisting almost entirely of (usually less successful) cover versions of American hits – and **Jack Good** devoted a whole programme of his *Oh Boy!* TV show to their songs.

It was quite easy to do this because, in the early Sixties, Pomus and Shuman's output was phenomenal and generally very successful. For **Elvis Presley** they wrote 'A Mess of Blues' (Number 32, as the flip of 'It's Now or Never' in 1960), 'Surrender' (Number 1 in 1961), 'She's Not You' (Number 5 in 1962) and 'Viva Las Vegas' (Number 29 in 1964) among others. For the Drifters, 'This Magic Moment' (Number 16 in 1960) and 'I Count the Tears' (Number 17 in 1961); as well as writing for **Ral Donner**, **Gene McDaniels** ('Spanish

Lace' in 1962) and **Gary 'U.S.' Bonds** ('Seven Day Weekend' in 1962). For Ben E. King, they wrote both together ('Here Comes the Night') and individually with **Phil Spector** – e.g. 'Ecstasy' (Pomus and Spector) and 'Young Boy Blues' (Shuman and Spector).

By 1965 their string of hits was coming to a close – in the new atmosphere generated by the **Beatles**, there was less demand for their songs and what demand there was was for middle-of-the-road material which they weren't very interested in producing. They more or less retired as an active partnership. In 1966, Shuman wrote a few songs with **Jerry Ragavoy** for **Howard Tate** – including 'Get it While You Can' and Tate's minor US hit of 1966, 'Look at Granny Run Run' – before emigrating to Paris. There he wrote, produced and starred in his own show, a tribute to the French songwriter Jacques Brel called *Jacques Brel is Alive and Well and Living in Paris*, which successfully transferred to the Broadway stage. He also spent some time in the UK during the mid- to late Sixties, writing occasionally with Clive Westlake and Kenny Lynch – the **Small Faces'** 1966 hit, 'Sha La La La Lee', was a Shuman/Lynch composition. In 1986 he moved to London to become involved in the staging of two musical productions for which he wrote most of the material.

POOLE, BRIAN
Vocalist Brian Poole (born on 3 November 1941) formed the **Tremeloes** in 1959 in Dagenham, Essex. A competent group, they turned professional after the first of many regular appearances on the leading British pop radio show, *Saturday Club*.

Their speciality was playing other people's hits – they even recorded an album, *Big Hits of '62*, for Ace of Clubs. However, their fortunes turned with the beat boom when, despite an anachronistic appearance and approach, they covered the popular **Beatles'** album track, 'Twist and Shout', in summer 1963. It was the first of six Top 20 hits, including 'Do You Love Me?', a UK Number 1. Poole's chart reign lasted only as long as the unqualified group fever, barely into 1965. In 1966, he left the Tremeloes (who continued successfully without him) for an abortive solo career. He subsequently returned to his original chosen occupation, butchery. He then found a group called Tramline and made a comeback of sorts during 1983. However, this was not too successful. *See also* the **Tremeloes**

POP GROUP
If any group symbolized the potential of punk it was the Pop Group. When legal wrangles caused the group to split in 1980, the fall-out produced three spin-off groups within a short time and several more later.

The band, formed in Bristol in 1978, comprised Mark Stewart (lyricist/singer), Gareth Sager (saxophonist/guitarist), John Waddington (guitar), Simon Underwood (bass) and Bruce Smith (drums). Initial performances produced such excitement that the media afforded them lavish coverage before they even released a record. Their debut single, 'She Is Beyond Good and Evil' (1979) is now considered a minor classic, mixing Stewart's Beat poet howl, raging saxophones, hot jungle drumming and jazz-influenced bass. Their debut album that year, *Y*, produced by reggae supremo **Dennis Bovell**, went further, combining punk thrash, contemporary jazz, funk rhythms, African percussion and some of the most inspired, if indulgent, free improvisation to come out of punk. Live performances reproduced this to heady effect, but their uncommercial nature finally lost the group their contract. Left owing an estimated £90,000, they began a series of Pop Group 'benefit' gigs. They released 'We Are All Prostitutes', in 1979 and split.

No sooner had the group split – with leader Stewart disappearing into seclusion – than Sager and Bruce Smith launched Rip, Rig + Panic. Named after the Rahsaan Roland Kirk jazz composition, and featuring singer Neneh Cherry (daughter of famed jazz trumpeter Don) it had a style that was influenced by outrageous jazz improvisations, tough rhythm and blues, hard funk and strong doses of African rhythms. The line-up was completed by young bass-player Sean Oliver, and classical prodigy Mark Springer.

Meanwhile, the remaining members of the Pop Group had themselves split into two other bands, Pigbag, who enjoyed success with 'Papa's Got a Brand New Pigbag', and Maximum Joy, a successful live unit whose sound adhered closer to soul-funk, as heard on their album, *Station M.X.J.Y.*

Of these groups, Rip, Rig + Panic enjoyed the most success, becoming regular figures on the live music scene and recording two albums for Virgin: *God* (1981) and *Attitude* (1983). This success was not enough to secure their future with Virgin, however, and in 1984 they split. While pianist Springer went solo, producing an album of that title, most went on to form Float Up CP, as yet unrecorded. In late 1985, Sager

left to launch his own band, Head.

At the same time, former Pop Group frontman Mark Stewart made a belated comeback with Mark Stewart and the Mafia. With his single, 'Hypnotised', and album, *As the Veneer of Democracy Starts to Fade*, the final part of the Pop Group puzzle was back in place. With leading dub producer Adrian Sherwood at the controls, Stewart offered up a swiping brew of heavy dub rhythms, scratch effects, violent electronics, improvisation and, as the title would suggest, plenty of political paranoia theory.

POP, IGGY/IGGY AND THE STOOGES
American singer Iggy Pop (born James Jewel Osterberg in Ann Arbor, Michigan, on 21 April 1947), first acquired semi-legendary status as the gravel-voiced, outrageous, manic and at times psychotic frontman of the Stooges in the late Sixties, but then showed himself to be a capable and mature solo artist with a series of albums and collaborations, most notably with **David Bowie**.

The Stooges, formed in 1967 and consisting of Iggy, Ron Asheton (guitar), Dave Alexander (bass), Scott Asheton (drums) (later additions to the band were James Williamson on guitar and Scott Thurston on keyboards), were initially categorized as a heavy metal band, but in reality favoured a very hard, very basic form of R&B which, coupled with the band's anti-social stage antics, gives substance to claims that they were the first punk band. The band released five albums between 1969 and 1978, the most noteworthy being *Fun House* (1970) and the Bowie-produced, *Raw Power* (1973).

Moving to Berlin in the mid-Seventies, Iggy's first solo album was *The Idiot* (1976), again produced by Bowie. His popularity grew with successive albums and tours (including the 1977 US tour with Bowie playing unbilled on keyboards), but he was never able to mount a concerted and co-ordinated attack on the world market due to several protracted bouts of drug abuse. Iggy's success continued nevertheless, and, through the assistance of Bowie's international hit with a cover of the Iggy song, 'China Girl', in 1983, his reputation was further enhanced.

In 1986, a healthy Iggy Pop emerged after a lengthy period of de-toxification and produced the album *Blah Blah Blah* (A&M) which suggested that he was at last ready to conquer the world. A first step was made in early 1987 with the David Bowie-produced UK hit single 'Real Wild Child'.

POSEY, SANDY

Country-pop singer Sandy Posey – real name Martha Sharp – was born in 1945 in Jasper, Alabama, and in her late teens moved to West Memphis, Arkansas. She did session-work as a back-up singer in Memphis and Nashville, and sang on innumerable records including **Percy Sledge**'s classic 'When a Man Loves a Woman'. She was also a songwriter, and in 1966 began to work with producer Chips Moman. Her first single, 'Born a Woman' (MGM), reached Number 12 in America; the follow-up, 'Single Girl', was equally successful and also reached Number 15 in Britain. Her most successful single came in the following year, 1967 ('I Take It Back'), preceded and followed by 'What a Woman in Love Won't Do' and 'Are You Never Coming Home' respectively. Sandy Posey has a distinctive country voice, but success in the pop charts has eluded her since the Sixties.

POWER POP

Initially coined in the mid-Seventies by US critic Greg Shaw to describe bands like **Big Star**, 'power pop' became a convenient, if short-lived and usually inappropriate, umbrella term for such acts as **Nick Lowe**, the Rich Kids, the **Pretenders** and the **Jam** among others – all late Seventies bands who had clear Sixties references in their music.

By the mid-Seventies, pop had become a synonym for middle-of-the-road, insubstantial pap with very few 'serious' musicians showing any interest in the form that was the heart of the Top 30. The vital three-minute pop song, such a strong feature of the Sixties, had died a death. It was not until the onslaught of punk that pop's fortunes began to look up again.

Punk put the three-minute song back in fashion – short, sharp and energetic – but it took old hands like Nick Lowe to fuse punk's vitality with Sixties melodic sensibilities, and produce something akin to 'power pop'. Bands like the Jam, the Pretenders and the **Boomtown Rats** had also found a tuneful balance between passion and pop hooks without sacrificing a contemporary feel. However, others, like the Pleasers, the Smirks, the Yachts and Tonight were slaves to the Sixties and it was to these groups, and those like them, that the term 'power pop' was most applicable.

Of all the bands that could be legitimately termed 'power pop', the Rich Kids and the Motors were the only two good enough to crack the UK charts, while the Records, perhaps the ultimate practitioners of the form, inex-plicably failed to take off. By 1980, power pop had all but gone, although during the Eighties it resurfaced in other guises through 'psychedelic' bands like Mood Six, and Beatle soundalikes Scarlet Party, whose lead singer Graham Dye bore an uncanny resemblance to John Lennon.

PRE-BEATLE POP (UK)

During 1955, British pop pretended to be aloof from the shame of rock'n'roll, and on the face of it she was. Dickie Valentine, Ruby Murray, Eddie Calvert and the Stargazers topped the polls, and only the entry of 'Rock Around the Clock' into the UK chart spoilt this façade.

In 1956, however, resistance cracked and Britain entered the rock race in the only way she knew how: by studying and copying the American model. Consequently, Britain's first rock'n'roll band were Tony Crombie (a jazz drummer) and The Rockets, *doppelgänger* of **Bill Haley** and the Comets, and by the end of the year, Britain's rock contingent consisted of Crombie, the Dallas Boys, **Lonnie Donegan** and a blond version of Elvis Presley named **Tommy Steele**. In 1957, reinforcements began to arrive and first on the scene were lisping balladeer Russ Hamilton, bluegrass singer **Johnny Duncan** (a genuine American), fast-singing Don Lang, *Six-Five Special* discovery Jim Dale, and former child wonders, the King Brothers. Failures included Terry Mayne, Tommy Steele's brother Colin Hicks, and the Lanza-inspired Toni Dalli, while the briefly popular Terry Dene was better known for his unhappy relationship with the Army. The discovery of 13-year-old Laurie London, who went on to become the first Briton to top the American hit parade, resulted in an invasion of singing children including Sandra Alfred and kilted Jackie Dennis, who had a big hit with 'La Dee Dah'. Gimmicks also assisted blue-rinsed Larry Page, Olympic swimmer Peter Elliott, Frankie Vaughan's sister-in-law Joyce Shock, and one of the better rock'n'rollers, Wee Willie Harris.

A little glory came to a well-behaved trio, the Mudlarks, and to the stars of TV's *Oh Boy!*, many of whom (Vince Eager, **Billy Fury**, Johnny Gentle, Duffy Power, Dickie Pride and **Marty Wilde**) had been re-christened by the first entrepreneur of British pop, **Larry Parnes**. Others making good on TV included Mike Preston, South African organist Cherry Wainer, former Los Angeles heavy Vince Taylor and, in 1959, a family of Italians, Little Tony and His Brothers. 1959 sounded the death knell for the golden age of rock'n'roll. The year's most popular arrival, **Joe Brown**, had some personality. Other newcomers – Craig Douglas, Rikki Price, Gerry Dorsey (who re-emerged in the Seventies as Engelbert Humperdinck), Michael Cox – hadn't. In 1960 flashes-in-the-pan included Emile Ford and growling Tommy Bruce. **Johnny Kidd** was a lone hard rocker, unrepresentative of popular taste: the top male singer was **Cliff Richard**, the top female, Shirley Bassey, the top group, the King Brothers.

Nice tunes prevailed in 1961 with trad jazz the dominant force and bland songsters like Eden Kane and 14-year-old **Helen Shapiro** making headway. Actors Jess Conrad, **John Leyton** and Hayley Mills looked chartwards – Leyton with great success. The Allisons and the Brook Brothers were more than vaguely reminiscent of the Everlys; Mark Wynter covered everything in sight; and among the one-hit wonders were Ricky Valance, Mike Berry and Shane Fenton. In 1962, during the calm before the storm, **Frank Ifield** and Jimmy Justice warbled and looked smart, while instrumentalits thrived and an influx of 'teenage' girls (Susan Maughan, Julie Grant, etc.) tried to grab a piece of Miss Shapiro's action. Their stock in trade was, as always, the cover version. But the end of this practice was nigh, with the **Beatles** ushering in a new era of musical self-reliance and self-confidence.

PRESLEY, ELVIS

The incomparable Elvis Presley was the biggest symbol of, and idol within, rock'n'roll during the late Fifties. In the Sixties, under the astute guidance of his manager, **'Colonel' Tom Parker**, he gave up live performances for a prolific but uninspired career as a film star. Records became little more than a spin-off from the movies. His popularity scarcely waned, though, and when, in 1968, he returned to live appearances in Las Vegas with his image modified to fit the changing times, his legendary status was reaffirmed. His immense popularity was borne out by a 1971 survey that reckoned his record sales to be 155 million singles, 25 million albums and 15 million EPs, figures bettered only by Bing Crosby and the **Beatles**.

Born Elvis Aaron Presley in Tupelo, Mississippi, on 8 January 1935, the son of a poor white farmworker, his earliest musical experiences were of the gospel singing at the First Assembly of God church, where the impassioned swaying of preacher and congregation formed the basis of the notorious pelvic gyrations that would horrify/delight nationwide television audiences.

In 1948, having already made his first public appearance at the age of ten when he sang the tear-jerking country song 'Old Shep' at the Mississippi-Alabama Fair, Presley moved with his parents Vernon and Gladys to the city of Memphis. Here, he came into contact with professional musicians for the first time, sitting in occasionally with the Blackwood Brothers gospel quartet, and at one point nearly joining them. However, his own career began almost accidentally after a visit to the Memphis Recording Service studio to cut a record as a present for his mother.

The studio was owned by Sam Phillips, who had only recently started his Sun record label. His assistant, Marion Keisker, thought Elvis had potential and noted down his address. Nearly a year later, in June 1954, Phillips called him in to record a song he had received from Nashville. He also brought in local musicians **Scotty Moore** (guitar) and **Bill Black** (bass). However, the session didn't go well until Elvis began singing **Arthur Crudup**'s R&B song, 'That's All Right'. The result was his first Sun single, which quickly became a local hit.

Other records followed, and soon Elvis was touring as 'The Hillbilly Cat' and 'The King of Western Bop', names which reflected the combination of country and R&B music in his style. His popularity grew rapidly and in November 1955 he was named the most promising country-and-western artist in a disc jockey's poll. The same week Col. Parker became Presley's manager, Phillips sold his contract to the RCA-Victor label for $35,000. RCA had the national promotion and distribution facilities which Sun lacked, and those facilities coupled with Parker's masterminding of selected television appearances soon made Presley a national star, with each successive record moving into the upper reaches of the charts.

Sam Phillips had foreseen that a young white singer who sounded black would be a sensation. Presley was that singer, and offered a highly personal and experimental fusion of white and black music, at once fluid and brash. His Sun recordings were characterized by light, yet restless, vocal phrasing over a country-based instrumentation that veered towards black rhythms and the distinctive 'Sun sound' which derived from that studio's primitive recording facilities and Phillips' constant use of echo.

The Sun singles (issued on HMV in Britain) featured a blues song on one

Elvis rhymed with pelvis and Presley was soon rock'n'roll's first outlaw

side and a country song on the other, each performed in a radically different manner. They were: 'That's All Right' and Bill Monroe's 'Blue Moon of Kentucky'; 'Good Rocking Tonight'/'I Don't Care If the Sun Don't Shine'; 'Milk Cow Blues Boogie'/'You're a Heartbreaker'; 'Baby Let's Play House'/'I'm Left, You're Right, She's Gone'; and 'Mystery Train'/'I Forgot to Remember to Forget'. Material recorded at Sun but purchased by RCA before it was released included two versions of 'I Love You Because' (one of which – recorded in July 1954 – wasn't issued until the 1974 album *Elvis – A Legendary Performer: Vol. 1*) plus 'Blue Moon', 'I'll Never Let You Go (Little Darlin')', 'Just Because' and the mag-

nificent 'Trying to Get to You'. Further unissued material from this period is contained on a bootleg album, *Good Rocking Tonight*.

The vast majority of white rock'n'roll singers who tackled R&B material diluted the power of the original – for example, **Pat Boone**, Presley's arch-rival for the allegiance of the teenage audience. In contrast to Boone, Elvis showed a deep understanding of many black artists' styles in his Sun recordings. Presley didn't make cover versions; with the aid of Bill Black, Scotty Moore and D. J. Fontana (on drums), he created the songs anew.

His first recording sessions for RCA were in Nashville, in January 1956 with **Chet Atkins** and the Jordanaires among the backing musicians. (Later sides were mainly cut in the company's main studios in New York.) The critical consensus has been that the move to RCA heralded an immediate deterioration in the quality of Presley's work, and that it continued downhill ever since. But though the records made up until his Army call-up in 1958 saw a considerable change in Elvis' style and type of material, they also produced a body of work which in retrospect can be seen as the cream of mainstream Fifties rock'n'roll.

Songs like 'Don't Be Cruel' and 'One-Sided Love Affair' saw Presley halfway between the light, frenetic Sun style and the smouldering, ominous, heavy recordings which came soon after. The latter, although more calculatedly commercial, were no less exciting or sexually charged. Moreover, these were the songs that, principally through his traumatic appearances on prime-time TV, introduced so many white teenagers to rock'n'roll: 'Heartbreak Hotel' and 'Hound Dog'. And the same qualities were present on the material recorded earlier but only issued while Elvis was serving as a GI in Germany: 'One Night', 'I Got Stung', 'A Fool Such As I' and 'Big Hunk O' Love'.

By the late Fifties, Elvis' career was worth millions and was being handled with exceptional acumen. In September 1956, RCA had taken the unprecedented step of releasing seven Presley singles simultaneously, and he was at Number 1 in the US every week between August and December. Meanwhile Colonel Parker was busily exploiting the Elvis image – through the first of many films (*Love Me Tender*) and by licensing the manufacturers of everything from key-rings to pillowslips to produce official Elvis souvenirs. Similarly Presley's recorded output was an astute mixture of ballads ('Old Shep', 'Loving You', 'Don't') and rock'n'roll songs, with the added bonus of the mixture of religious ballads, carols and popular seasonal standards that made up the original *Elvis' Christmas Album*, released in 1957. None the less it was as much a testament to the quality of the music as to Parker's marketing skills that two years in the Army away from recording studios made no difference to the level of Presley's popularity.

In March 1960 Elvis returned to civilian life and a much changed music scene. Classic rock'n'roll of the kind he had pioneered had all but disappeared to be replaced by the softer and more conventional sounds of the Philadelphia school of teen idols. His first

release, 'Stuck on You'/'Fame and Fortune', was firmly in the tough, don't-mess-with-me style he had perfected in 1958. But the album, *Elvis Is Back* hovered between what seemed to be a renewed commitment to R&B and country music, and an entirely new softness of vocal delivery. This softness, however, did not involve any new sensitivity. Rather, it indicated a loss of intensity and of focus. The drama of his earlier work had become mere melodrama and with spasmodic exceptions, this would be true of all Presley's subsequent work.

Between 'Stuck on You' and the rise of Beatlemania in America, Presley still functioned primarily as a singles artist, though only the occasional record – 'A Mess of Blues' and 'His Latest Flame'/'Little Sister', for example – echoed the fire of his Fifties work. Now at the peak of his success in terms of worldwide record sales, his image was far less forceful than it had been in the Fifties. The majority of his hits were smooth ballads like 'It's Now Or Never', 'Are You Lonesome Tonight' and 'Surrender', or singles taken from the movies: 'Wooden Heart' and 'Wild in the Country'. Also many albums were released, a considerable proportion of which were soundtracks from the seemingly endless series of Hollywood musicals he was beginning to make.

In the early Sixties he settled down to a career which relied on making three films a year, each revealing a more tired and timid Hollywood orthodoxy than the last, in which he sang whatever third-rate songs had been chosen to fill out their plotless vapidity. The records of this era began with 'Good Luck Charm' and continued through 'She's Not for You', 'Return to Sender' and 'One Broken Heart for Sale'.

The earliest Presley movies – *Love Me Tender* (1956), *Loving You* (1957), *Jailhouse Rock* (1958) and *King Creole* (1958) – had made use of songs and songwriters of the same standard as the singles of the period. But after attempts to provide Elvis with scripts in which he could act – *Flaming Star* (1960), *Wild in the Country* (1961) – there followed a series of over twenty films notable only for their stunning anonymity.

By 1968, Presley was widely regarded as the epitome of all that was cynical, flaccid and regressive within pop. Moreover, the films were by now making less and less money (for a long time they had contributed significantly to his income of about $4m. a year). They were also getting worse and worse, with even Elvis apparently as

Film performances virtually took over Presley's career in the Sixties

bored with them as everyone else.

Then he made his first TV appearance since 1960 (when he had appeared, dressed in a dinner-suit – arm in arm with Frank Sinatra). This time, he had his own *TV Special* and was dressed in black leather. He performed on a small stage surrounded by an audience. Presley was charismatic, lithe and ominous; it seemed as though he had been reborn.

The show's success presented Elvis with a difficult choice. He could either use it as a starting-point for a renewal of musical application and risk-taking, or else return to the production-line procedures that had seen him through previous years, with merely a new formula. At first, the issue seemed in the balance. The single taken from the TV show, 'If I Can Dream', was especially powerful, seeming to show the sheer effort it took him to shake off the plasticity of the Sixties. Then early in 1969 he returned to Memphis to cut *From Elvis in Memphis* at Chips Moman's American Recording Studio, and using the cream of the local session musicians, he produced his most exciting album for some time.

However, he next opened in Las Vegas, giving his first live performances since 1961. But despite the quality of his band (led by guitarist

James Burton) and the strength of his material, Elvis' live act failed to live up to the expectations aroused by the *TV Special*. Rapidly his career became as safe a showbiz routine as the films had been, a fact attested to by the various album releases of 'live shows' – from New York, Hawaii and Las Vegas. All involved half-hearted, vulgarly scored renditions of his earlier hit songs, none of which bear comparison with the original. Even so, when the Hawaii album reached the top of the American charts in 1973 it came as a reminder – along with his hit singles of the Seventies – that Presley's career as a top-selling recording artist was not over.

The irony is that the generally downward trend of his work since 1960 suggested that Presley's choice of material shows a continuing interest in less calculatedly commercial music than he hmself has produced. His early policy of recording black material has been maintained right into the Seventies. He cut **Ivory Joe Hunter** songs in 1958 *and* 1973, while the post-Army records have included songs drawn from **Chuck Jackson**, **Little Walter**, **O. C. Smith**, the **Coasters**, **Jerry Butler**, **Ketty Lester**, **Chuck Berry**, the **Clovers**, the **Drifters**, **Rufus Thomas**, **Willie Dixon** and many others. In addition, Elvis turned to the newer breed of Southern writers, such as **Jerry Reed** ('Guitar Man'), **Mac Davis** ('In the Ghetto'), **Tony Joe White** ('Polk Salad Annie') and Dennis Linde ('Burning Love').

This enterprise in choice of material makes the frequently poor standard of execution all the more inexplicable. The exceptions in Presley's work since 1960 were few. The religious album, *His Hand in Mine* (1960), had a particular delicacy and purity of vocal tone, and on the B-side of 'Kissin' Cousins', 'It Hurts Me' (1965) there are sudden flashes of a Fifties brand of Elvis excitement and risk, with even that drawled Southern pronunciation. Also notable are the *From Elvis in Memphis* and *Elvis Country* (1971) albums, and the evocative 'live' version of 'American Trilogy' on the album, *Elvis: Aloha from Hawaii via Satellite* (1973).

By the mid-Seventies though, Presley was firmly stuck in his latest rut. He appeared once more to have given up any attempt to win respect as an artist. His voice was often less focused than ever – rougher at the peaks of volume, more inaccurately wavering on the lower notes, and altogether without the subtlety, or vitality, of which he had once been a master. Worse, he was gradually killing himself on a diet of pills, junk food and general excess.

It was a measure of the impact of the Fifties Elvis that in at least one generation of listeners there remained, right up until his death on 16 August 1977, a widespread fantasy that the ageing and now portly Presley could be restored to his pristine glory if only he were removed from his Las Vegas/Hollywood lifestyle and shut in a room with a jukebox full of the early records, thus forcing him to recognize how great a singer he once was and goading him into a renewed effort to emulate his former self. The fact that it never happened in no way diminishes Presley's importance to rock'n'roll. The rare and innovative talent he displayed in the Fifties (and intermittently thereafter) remains unaffected by any subsequent activity (or inactivity). His work – more than any other single factor in the history of rock'n'roll – determined the form that it was to take. It was Presley who gave teenagers their own musical identity for the very first time. *See also* **Sun Records**

PRESTON, BILLY A child prodigy turned superstar's sideman, Billy Preston was already an experienced veteran by the time mass audiences bought 'That's the Way God Planned It' (Apple, 1969). Born in Houston, Texas, on 9 September 1946, he was raised in Los Angeles where he first played organ behind gospel queen **Mahalia Jackson** before making a cameo appearance in the film *St Louis Blues* at the age of ten. Through the early Sixties, he toured with **Little Richard** and **Sam Cooke** while recording organ instrumentals for Contract, Derby and Vee Jay. Later recordings, on Capitol, regular appearances on the American TV show *Shindig*, and tours with **Ray Charles** brought him to the attention of the **Beatles** whom he accompanied on 'Get Back' and 'Let It Be' while recording in his own right for their Apple label. Singles like 'I Wrote a Simple Song', the Top 10 hit 'Outta Space', 'Will It Go Round in Circles' (1972) and several versatile albums (including *Music Is My Life* and *Everybody Likes Some Kind of Music* on A&M) continued to display his diverse talent, but it was still as an accompanist that he received most attention, notably on recordings by **Sly and the Family Stone** and as special guest on the 1975 **Rolling Stones** tour of America. He wrote **Joe Cocker**'s 1975 hit, 'You Are So Beautiful', and duetted with Syreeta Wright on 'With You I'm Born Again', which reached Number 4 in the US in early 1979.

PRESTON, JOHNNY Born in Port Arthur, Texas, on 18 August 1930, Johnny Preston sang with the Shades before going solo in 1959. Then, with the aid of the **Big Bopper**, who produced the 'oom-pah-pah' sounds, Preston made 'Running Bear', a Number 1 hit on both sides of the Atlantic. Other hits for Mercury (produced by **Jack Clement** at Bill Hall's Beaumont studio), included the crassly commercial follow-up 'Cradle of Love' (written by Wayne Grey and Jack Fautheree of the country duo Johnny and Jack), 'Feel So Fine' (previously made by **Shirley and Lee** as 'Feel So Good') and a rocking version of **Little Willie John**'s 'Leave My Kitten Alone'. Preston's East Texas vocals transformed these otherwise undistinguished pop novelty records. He was, however, a poor live performer, and despite other discs for Southern labels, he was soon forced out of music to work as a garage-hand, an obscurity from which he has not re-emerged.

PRETENDERS The Pretenders emerged at the end of the Seventies to become the first successful new wave band of the Eighties. They were led by singer/songwriter and guitarist Chrissie Hynde, whose distinctive vocal power added a tough but feminine edge to their sophisticated guitar rock.

Hynde (born in Akron, Ohio, on 7 September 1951) arrived in London in 1973, broke and planning to form a band. Back in Akron she had been in Sat Sun Mat, a band that also featured Mark Mothersbaugh, later of **Devo**. For a time she wrote for the *New Musical Express* and after a short stint working in Sex, **Malcolm McLaren**'s clothes shop, she eventually wound up in France, singing with a band called the Frenchies. Hynde was back in London at the genesis of punk in 1975, and using the contacts she had made through working for McLaren, she became involved in various unsuccessful line-ups, working with people like Mick Jones (later of the **Clash**) and **Nick Lowe** who went on to greater fame and fortune. During that time she was also building up a repertoire of original songs.

In March 1978 she met Dave Hill who, having just formed his own label, Real, signed her up and financed her while she put together a band. First she found a bassist, Pete Farndon, who had been playing with Australian band the Bushwackers. Farndon then enlisted guitarist James Honeyman-Scott and drummer Martin Chambers, both of whom he remembered from his native city of Hereford. Together they recorded under the guidance of Nick Lowe, and the result was the first single, a cover of the **Kinks**' 'Stop Your Sobbing'. It didn't do quite as well as predicted – by this stage the press had latched on to the band – but it did at least make the charts, reaching Number 34 in February 1979.

The band's breakthrough came with 'Brass in Pocket', which, after a false start, eventually made the UK Number 1 slot in January 1980. At the same time their first album, *The Pretenders* was top of the UK LP chart, thus becoming the first Number 1 album of the Eighties. It was universally acclaimed, and remains one of the strongest debuts of any band. As Europe and America fell under their spell, the pressure took its toll and they retired from the public eye, to return in August 1981 with *Pretenders II*. It received terrible reviews but sold well and had a notable hit with a wonderfully tender version of yet another Ray Davies song, 'I Go To Sleep', which reached Number 7 in November. Hynde had long been an admirer of Davies, and by this time they had met and become lovers.

The Pretenders then suffered a series of setbacks that seriously impaired their activities. First of all, eight weeks into a US tour, Chambers injured his arm and hand after punching a glass lampshade. The tour had to be postponed, losing them money and momentum. The dates were completed in 1982, but then Farndon's erratic and unreliable behaviour caused him to be sacked in June. Then, two days later on 16 June, Honeyman-Scott died of a drug overdose. Chambers and Hynde battled on, recording, with ex-Rockpile guitarist Billy Bremner and Tony Butler (later of **Big Country**), 'Back on the Chain Gang', which reached Number 17 in October. They then found replacements in Robbie McIntosh (guitar) and Malcolm Foster (bass).

In January 1983, Hynde gave birth to a daughter by Ray Davies, and then went back into the studio to record a long-awaited third album. In April, Farndon too died of an overdose, and although he was no longer part of the group, the death of one who had done so much to crystallize Hynde's ideas did little for morale. An LP, *Learning to Crawl*, was released in 1984, but the critical response was less than encouraging and since then the Pretenders' activities have been at a virtual standstill. The group's problems were compounded by an upheaval in Hynde's private life that involved her leaving Ray Davies, marrying Jim Kerr of

Simple Minds in May 1984 and having his child. In 1985 she had a Number 1 hit duetting with Ali Campbell of **UB40** on a reggae version of 'I Got You Babe', and on their tour she often joined UB40 on stage to sing the song as an encore, but it wasn't until the following year that a new LP, *Get Close*, was released. It spawned a UK Top 10 single 'Don't Get Me Wrong', which marked a welcome return to form.

PRETTY THINGS Formed by the **Rolling Stones**' original bass guitarist, Dick Taylor, and Phil May (born on 11 September 1944) at Sidcup Art College in the autumn of 1963, the Pretty Things were doomed by their scruffy image and Bo Diddley-based rhythm and blues to the role of poor man's Stones. With Taylor switching to lead guitar, the rest of the line-up was May (vocals, harmonica), Brian Pendleton (rhythm guitar), John Stax (bass, harmonica), and Viv Prince (drums). They were signed up almost at once as the R&B boom hit the music industry, but after early hits, the double-sided 'Big Boss Man'/'Rosalyn' (May 1964), 'Don't Bring Me Down' (November 1964) and 'Honey I Need' (March 1965) on Fontana, they failed to make the Stones' shift to their own material until, in a reorganized line-up, May and Taylor composed *S.F. Sorrow* (Harvest, 1968), supposedly an encouragement for – if not an influence on – Pete Townshend's *Tommy* project.

Following the departure of Taylor and the failure of the highly regarded *Parachute* album in 1969, the band folded for a time, re-forming to record *Freeway Madness* (Warner Brothers, 1972). In 1974, with May, Peter Tolson (guitar), John Povey (keyboards), and Skip Alan (drums) still together from the *Parachute* personnel, plus Jack Green (vocals) and Gordon Edwards (bass) they signed with Led Zeppelin's Swan Song label for *Silk Torpedo*. The group disbanded again during 1976, although May did put together a reshaped Pretty Things in 1980 with Dick Taylor, Wally Allen, Skip Alan, John Povey and Peter Tolson. The new line-up lasted a year.

PRICE, ALAN One of the driving forces behind the **Animals** and subsequently a commercially successful and critically acclaimed solo performer, Alan Price was born in Fatfield, near Jarrow, Co. Durham, on 19 April 1942. He founded and led Newcastle's Alan Price Combo, which became the Animals *en route* for London and success early in 1964. Price employed a

driving organ technique to good effect as a foil to **Eric Burdon**'s vocals. He left the group in May 1965 and did not re-emerge until almost a year later with his own Alan Price Set, whose line-up included John Walters (trumpet, flugelhorn), Clive Burrows (baritone), Steve Gregory (tenor), Boots Slade (bass), and Roy Hills (drums). His first single, 'I Put a Spell on You' (Decca, 1966), led to a string of hits, introducing the British public to the songs of **Randy Newman**, notably 'Simon Smith and His Amazing Dancing Bear'.

Following a number of popular 'guest' appearances on television with **Georgie Fame**, the pair had their own series in 1970, later extending their partnership into cabaret and recording, though without ever taxing their abilities. In 1973 he wrote several songs for the soundtrack of Lindsay Anderson's *O Lucky Man* and his bit part as a musician in the same film earned him a starring role in *Alfie Darling* (1975).

His 1974 album *Between Yesterday and Today* (Warner Brothers) and the Top 10 single taken from it – 'Jarrow Song' – found him in fruitful contact with his Tyneside roots. The following album – *Metropolitan Man* (Polydor, 1975) – was disappointing by comparison, though he has continued to write and record songs of an essentially nostalgic, retrospective nature – as, for example, on the albums *Rainbow's End* (1977) and *England My England* (1978). His last UK hit was the Top 40-placed 'Just for You' in 1979, but he still performs and records regularly. *See also* the **Animals**

PRICE, LLOYD One of the stars of Fifties New Orleans R&B, Lloyd Price was born in the city on 9 March 1934. He landed a contract with Specialty Records in 1952 after failing several auditions with other companies. Armed with a little tune called 'Lawdy Miss Clawdy' and backed by **Dave Bartholomew**'s band – with **Fats Domino** on piano – Price's first record became the Number 1 R&B Record of the Year on the *Billboard* and *Cashbox* charts, earning a gold disc in the process. More important, it was one of the first 'race' records to break out into the white markets, and it was this cross-fertilization which soon led to the new sound of rock'n'roll.

Price's recording career was hindered by a spell in the Army between 1954–6 but on his return he had an immediate hit with the ballad 'Just Because' on ABC Paramount in 1957. After dabbling with his own label (KRC Records, co-owned with Harold

Logan and Bill Boskent) he re-signed with ABC Paramount and his brash version of the old New Orleans folk song, 'Stagger Lee', went to Number 1 in the US in early 1959, giving Price another gold disc. It seemed he could do no wrong in 1959 and he had further hits with 'Personality' and 'I'm Gonna Get Married'. With the New Orleans content of his material almost extinguished, his later records on Double and Turntable had little distinction. However, he invested his cash wisely and was one of the few New Orleans R&B men to profit from his music. *See also* **New Orleans**

PRINCE Two young black American singers dominated global pop music in the Eighties. During the early part of the decade, **Michael Jackson** set standards in pop production, marketing, sales levels and media interest. When he took a break from the limelight, Prince was just reaching his peak.

Born on 7 June 1958 in Minneapolis, Minnesota, and christened Prince Rogers Nelson, he inherited his father's musical talent and was later able to harness it rather better. He built up a clique of musically inclined friends, and by the age of thirteen he had formed his first band, Grand Central; music became the one strong constant in his itinerant youth (his parents had separated when he was seven). He spent most of his spare time learning various instruments, production techniques, and composing skills. His persuasive, adamant nature enabled him to get a Warner Brothers contract and a debut album, *For You*, appeared in 1978. The startling albums with which Prince opened the Eighties, *Dirty Mind* and *Controversy*, contained tracks ('Sexuality', 'Jack U Off', 'Head', 'Sister' and so forth) which lyrically left little to the imagination. Sung in a high, light, breathy voice full of gasps and squeals, they were as clear as could be in their sensuous content. But they did not sell particularly well, despite their promotion by a wild stage show which in the late Seventies had featured Prince garbed in a raincoat, jock-strap and not a lot else besides. Still, for all his soft speech there's obviously a very hard core to Prince (just as there is to Michael Jackson) and he not only was able to record a double album, *1999* (1982), but he also found backers for a film, *Purple Rain* (1984) – in which he starred – which was fiction loosely based on his own story. The success of the album *Purple Rain*, featuring music from the movie, put Prince firmly at the top as a writer/singer/producer/multi-

Prince Rogers Nelson startled more than just the US 'moral majority'

instrumentalist. His sudden explosion into being the megastar of the mid-Eighties was fuelled by the previously noted film, by the increased use of videos in marketing and by the enormous interest shown in his supposed exotic private life by a media deprived of the reclusive, resting Michael Jackson. A large bodyguard, often surreal taste in clothes and a generally enigmatic silence (after 1981, interviews were rare, on account of his reclusive nature) all added up to an image irresistible to Press, radio and TV.

Musically, after *1999* Prince took a deliberate decision to alter his style and thus broaden its appeal. After the first indications of this on *Purple Rain*, *Around the World in a Day* – released in 1985 on his own Paisley Park label and featuring a new band, the Revolution – showed a much more eclectic face, recalling psychedelic music of the late Sixties as well as refining Prince's own sexy funk. Significantly, the album's sleeve was vaguely reminiscent of the **Beatles**' *Sergeant Pepper's Lonely Hearts Club Band* cover. Although not an entirely successful experiment in artistic terms, *Around the World* sold well enough. In

1986, Prince further evolved his eclectic, pot-pourri style on *Parade*. Wider appeal, however, made his occasionally lusty lyrics the subject of attention by the USA 'moral majority' backlash.

What is equally remarkable about Prince's career since 1978 is that not only has he maintained a steady output of music under his own name but he has also acted as mentor or producer or writer or adviser to a large number of fellow Minneapolitan acts and others from diverse parts of the USA. André Cymone emerged from an early Prince band, Flyte Tyme became the Time and from this band Morris Day and Jesse Johnson emerged as solo acts while Jimmy Jam, Terry Lewis and Monte Moir all became much-praised writers and producers. Other Prince protégés included such exotically beautiful women singers as Vanity, Apollonia, and Sheila E and yet another new band, the Family. Moreover, after the success of the film *Purple Rain*, which made some $100m for Warners, Prince took off for the south of France to film *Under the Cherry Moon* (from which the music for *Parade* came). It was a romantic tale of two young men out to make their fortune on the Riviera.

PRINCE BUSTER A pioneer of Jamaican ska and rock-steady, Prince Buster was born Buster Campbell in Kingston, Jamaica, on 28 May 1939, and achieved local fame as a boxer and disc-jockey before achieving national prominence with 'Wash Wash' and 'I Feel the Spirit' in 1962. A front-runner in the bluebeat craze, he spread the ska gospel with '30 Pieces of Silver', 'The Lion Roars' and 'Sammy Dead' (which was adopted by Chelsea Football Club as their anthem in 1964). Always as popular with white British youth as with the Jamaican audience, he was first a hero of the mods in 1964 and later achieved similar status among their skinhead counterparts during the rock-steady period with rude-boy litanies like 'Judge Dread' and 'Ghost Dance'. Other Buster songs featured unabashed sexism ('The Ten Commandments of Love', 'Big Five') or were straightforward cowboy/gangster deifications like 'Al Capone' (a UK Top 40 chart entry in 1967) and 'Lawless Street'.

A prolific songwriter and recording artist, Buster invariably employed the best session musicians in his back-up group, variously known as the Blues Busters or the All Stars, including members of the **Georgie Fame** band on occasion. A long understanding with the Melodisc label ensured that the majority of his sides were made available in the UK on its Bluebeat, Fab and Prince Buster subsidiaries. By the Seventies, he was no longer recording in his own right but producing the likes of Dennis Alcapone and re-releasing his old hits, professing a distinct dislike of contemporary reggae. He also had a cameo role in the **Jimmy Cliff** film, *The Harder They Come*. When the 2-Tone movement began in the late Seventies, Buster made a comeback of sorts to capitalize on the new interest in Sixties ska. **Madness**' debut UK hit, 'The Prince' (1979), was dedicated to him.

PRINE, JOHN Born in Maywood, Illinois, in 1946, John Prine was misleadingly hailed as a 'new **Dylan**' when his first Atlantic album appeared in 1971. With his close friend **Steve Goodman** he was a graduate of the Chicago folk scene, and the enthusiasm of **Paul Anka** was instrumental in arranging his recording debut. Cut in Memphis, the first album (produced by **Arif Mardin**) caused a stir through songs like 'Sam Stone' – a post-Vietnam piece – and 'Illegal Smile'.

Prine's drawling delivery and tight-lipped lyrics led to the inevitable Dylan comparisons, but subsequent albums like *Diamonds in the Rough* (1972) and *Sweet Revenge* (1973), which revealed a significant debt to country music, had little commercial success. Other performers, however, began to record his songs, notably 'Paradise' (**Everly Brothers**) and 'Hello In There' (**Bette Midler** and **Joan Baez**).

In 1975, Prine changed musical direction with the hard-rock-edged *Common Sense*, though *Bruised Orange* (Asylum, 1978) marked a return to a more acoustic style. *Pink Cadillac* (1978) was his most unusual album yet – a rockabilly album produced by Sam and Knox Phillips at the (reopened) legendary Sun Studios (*see* **Sun Records**) in Memphis. At the end of 1986 he released *Aimless Love* (Demon).

PROBY, P. J. One of rock music's great exhibitionists, P. J. Proby was born James Marcus Smith in Houston, Texas, on 6 November 1938 and spent his early twenties in Hollywood, doing odd jobs, playing bit parts, cutting demos, and recording as Jet Powers. He was brought to England in 1964 by **Jack Good** – for a **Beatles** television special – who produced his first single as P. J. Proby, a raucous revival of a 1939 ballad, 'Hold Me'. Good sold the record to Decca and it became a big hit that summer. After a similar follow-up, he changed labels (to Liberty) and styles, with melodramatic versions of 'Maria' and 'Somewhere' from *West Side Story*. Established as a star, he toured Britain with **Cilla Black** in February, 1965, but provoked a furore (and

P. J. Proby in Catch My Soul

eventually his expulsion from the tour) by frequently splitting his velvet breeches on stage. His lifestyle was tailored less tightly than his clothes and by 1968, long after the hits had ceased, he was bankrupt. He returned to America, but was tempted back to London at the end of 1971 to play Iago in Jack Good's long-projected rock *Othello*, *Catch My Soul*, and later revived his old stage act for Northern nightclub matrons.

PROCOL HARUM Precursors of, and participants in, the art-rock vogue of the late Sixties, Procol Harum evolved out of an R&B group from Southend, Essex, called the Paramounts whose line-up originally comprised Gary Brooker (born 29 May 1945), keyboards, vocals; **Robin Trower** (9 March 1945), guitar; B. J. Wilson (18 March 1947), drums; and Chris Copping (29 August 1945), bass. The Paramounts made a string of singles, 'Little Bitty Pretty One' becoming a minor hit, before frustration led to their break-up in 1966. Gary Brooker teamed up with lyricist Keith Reid (10 October 1946) and to record their songs they formed a group. Procol Harum in their original line-up – Gary Brooker, piano, vocals; Matthew Fisher (7 March 1946), organ; Dave Knights (28 June 1945), bass; Ray Royer (8 October 1945), guitar and Bobby Harrison (28 June 1943), drums – made only one single: 'A Whiter Shade of Pale' (Deram). The drum part was played by session musician Bill Eyden. Released in summer 1967 to spectacular British and American success, its mysterious words and haunting organ, based on a Bach cantata, seemed to epitomize the spirit of the day.

They began an album, but Royer and Harrison had to be replaced (they formed the short-lived Freedom) and Trower and Wilson were added. In this form they completed *Procol Harum* (Regal Zonophone, 1967) and made two stunning and highly praised albums, *Shine on Brightly* and *A Salty Dog*. Despite a second hit single, 'Homburg' in 1967, gigs had always been scarce in a Britain in the throes of a blues boom which, ironically, would have better suited the old Paramounts. America, where audiences were more appreciative, provided their salvation. Long periods between tours allowed them time to produce albums of continually high standard. *Broken Barricades* (Chrysalis, 1971), for which Chris Copping replaced Knights on bass, also marked Robin Trower's rising musical aspirations since it was the first album without organist Matthew Fisher. Trower himself left in July 1971, finding Procol's panoramic sound too stifling for his Hendrix-inspired guitar trips. After forming the abortive Jude (with **Frankie Miller**) he subsequently formed the very successful Robin Trower Band. Copping, meanwhile, switched to organ and Alan Cartwright (10 October 1945) came in on bass. They recorded *Live in Concert with the Edmonton Symphony Orchestra*, which with a hit (reissued) single 'Conquistador', opened things up in Britain once more. They also achieved a settled line-up once Mick Grabham took over from Trower's replacement, Dave Ball (30 March 1950); in this form, they consolidated their packed-house tours of Britain and the US with neatly balanced albums like *Grand Hotel* (1973), though *Exotic Birds and Fruit* (1974) and *Procol Ninth* (1975) sold poorly. Cartwright left the group in 1977 and Pete Solley joined on organ, but that year's *Something Magic* – produced by **Leiber and Stoller** – was another commercial failure and precipitated the group's break-up. Brooker recorded as a solo artist – *No More Fear of Flying* (1980), *Lead Me to the Water* (1982) – and became a member of **Eric Clapton**'s band in 1980. *See also* **Robin Trower**

PROFESSOR LONGHAIR Next

to **Fats Domino**, Professor Longhair must rank as New Orleans' most influential musician. Born Henry Roeland Byrd in Bogalusa, Louisiana, on 18 December 1938, his family moved to New Orleans when he was still a child. He soon picked up the wonderfully diverse styles of the old pianists who used to play the clubs and clip joints, and moulded them into his unique way of playing, with Spanish and rhumba accents predominating. He made his first record in 1949 for Star Talent as Professor Longhair and the Shuffling Hungarians and in 1950 'Bald Head' on Mercury was his one and only record to dent the R&B charts. Records for Atlantic, Federal, Wasco, Ebb, Rip and Watch flopped badly although his 1959 Ron recording of 'Go to the Mardi Gras' still sells well at New Orleans' annual blow-out. He was out of work for much of the Sixties, but there was a revival of interest in his music during the Seventies which led to many live appearances and a visit to Europe. He died on 30 January 1980. Posthumous releases included *Mardi Gras in New Orleans* (Krazy Kat, 1982), a live recording from 1975, and *The London Concert* (JJP, 1984). *See also* **New Orleans**

PSYCHEDELIC FURS Formed in southern England in 1977, post-punk outfit Psychedelic Furs originally comprised Richard Butler (vocals), his brother Tim (bass), Roger 'Dog' Morris (guitar), Duncan Kilburn (sax) and a succession of short-lived drummers. In 1978, John Ashton (guitar) was recruited as the fifth permanent member and they eventually found a stable drummer in Vince Ely in early 1979.

The band first gained recognition later that year through a **John Peel** radio session; this prompted CBS Records to sign them, and in November their exceptional debut single 'We Love You' was released. With their then current line-up, they achieved a modicum of commercial success, the LPs *Psychedelic Furs* (1980) and *Talk Talk Talk* (1981) both charting, and they proved a big favourite on the UK club and college circuit. Morris and Kilburn departed in '82 and the remaining members recorded *Forever Now* with **Todd Rundgren**. Ely then left and was briefly replaced by Phil Calvert (ex-Birthday Party), but the band slimmed down to a three-piece on a permanent basis, recording the album *Mirror Moves* and scoring their biggest UK single hit 'Heaven', which reached Number 29 in March '84.

'Pretty in Pink', a classic Furs track first recorded in 1980, became the title song to a feature film, a major box-office success in the US in 1986. The band re-recorded the song for the film, and the success of the film spurred a return to the recording studio for a new album.

PUB ROCK It may have been convenient for describing a phenomenon of the early Seventies in Britain, but 'pub rock' was a dangerous term. It implied that all the bands tagged with it have something more in common than that they have all played in pubs, and ignored the fact that music has always been an integral part of pub life. Before 1972, pub music was usually a solo pianist, a desultory trio, or a jazz band (jazz of all kinds and standards). Then, the American country-rock band, Eggs Over Easy, managed to get a booking at the Tally-Ho, in London's Kentish Town, one of the foremost jazz pubs. This paved the way for Bees Make Honey (whose leader, Barry Richardson, was known to the pub for his trad-jazz past), and the seal of approval came when **Brinsley Schwarz** played there. The Brinsleys, while never gaining the recognition they deserved, were fostering a move away from introspective 'head' music back to simpler roots, influenced by rock'n'roll, country and

R&B. If 'pub rock' had a typical sound, it was this; music best designed for jigging about, pint of beer in hand.

With the decrease in the number of small clubs (ironically, often in pub back rooms) it was becoming impossible for up-and-coming bands to gain exposure. Gradually, as more bars moved from jazz to rock (notably The Kensington) and breweries, or their managers, realized that a rock band would boost sales, a loose circuit of small venues arose. After the pioneers, four generations of bands passed through the pub circuit. The first (1972–3) included Ducks Deluxe, Clancy, Ace, Kilburn And The High Roads, Phoenix and Chilli Willi And The Red Hot Peppers; the second (1973–4) Kokomo and **Dr Feelgood**; the third (1974–5) FBI and the Kursaal Flyers; the fourth (1975–6) Moon and Roogalator. On some nights, a dozen A&R men, record executives and agents would be sniffing out new talent in the same tiny bar. While pub rock undoubtedly helped to reinject 'good-time' values into a rock mainstream in danger of becoming overloaded with 'significance', it's sadly ironic to note that many of the bands mentioned above broke up without tasting chart success, though a few (notably Dr Feelgood, Kokomo and Kursaal Flyers) gained a wider audience. Most significantly, it was out of pub rock that many of the stars of the late Seventies new wave emerged, including **Ian Dury** (ex-Kilburns), **Nick Lowe** (ex-Brinsleys) and **Elvis Costello** (ex-Flip City), all of whom had an initial association with the most successful new independent label of the decade, Stiff Records. *See also* **Stiff Records, New Wave**

PUBLIC IMAGE LTD *See* PiL

PUNK ROCK (1960s) In the earliest usage of the term, 'punk rock' described a style that reflected America's grassroots response to the British beat group invasion of 1964–6. Not only did American punk set the stage for rock as it evolved in the late Sixties, it also accounted in its time for one of the most prolific outpourings of records and groups in the history of rock.

Punk rock was the music of thousands of bands, mostly of high-school age, who formed in the aftermath of the **Beatles** and the influx of UK groups. Sociologically, they were an outgrowth of the local bands who played surf and twist music in the early Sixties. Musically, most were derived to greater or lesser degree from either the **Rolling Stones** or the Beatles, with occasional exceptions who took their style from the **Pretty Things** or the **Small Faces**.

But where these groups had a modicum of style, innovation, and either an innate sense of cool or a genuine innocence, the punkers took a stance of spoiled suburban snottiness. Most classic punk records shared a number of common attributes, from fuzztone on their guitars to an arrogant snarl in the vocals, and lyrics usually concerned with uncooperative girls or bothersome parents and social restrictions. In every city in America there were a few punk bands, and the larger cities often boasted hundreds. And, it seems, nearly all of them issued records locally, leading to the development of active local scenes and recognizable regional sounds. Despite its pervasiveness, however, punk rock never caught on commercially. Most of the records were either too crude or too intense for mass radio standards, and on the whole there were less than twenty punk groups who had hit records, and few of those ever had more than one. Some exceptions were **Paul Revere and the Raiders**, the **Standells**, the **Seeds**, the Outsiders, and the **Knickerbockers**. The music's main exposure was through live performances at teen clubs, teen fairs, high-school dances and local TV dance shows.

The product of kids who had little exposure to the music business mainstream, the punk idiom (much like its antecedent in the Fifties, the short-lived rockabilly style that was unimportant commercially but proved crucial in defining the basic spirit of the decade in its purest form) gave birth to a great deal of experimentation, resulting in some of the most bizarre, extreme, and ingenuously eloquent recordings of all time – and also some of the most powerful. Punk rock had its musical equivalents in other countries such as England and Holland, but the spirit that motivated it was peculiarly a product of the American youth of the time. With the increased popularity of psychedelic drugs in 1966, it was a logical development from there to acid rock, although something indefinable was lost in the transition. Among the most noteworthy punk groups were the **Kingsmen** ('Louie, Louie'), the Seeds, the Standells, the Thirteenth Floor Elevators, the Music Machine ('Talk Talk'), the **Shadows of Knight**, the Knickerbockers, the Barbarians, Count Five, **Question Mark and the Mysterians**, the Trashmen ('Surfin' Bird'), the Chartbusters ('She's The One'), Mouse and the Traps, the Gants,

Blues Magoos, the **McCoys**, and the Clefs of Lavender Hill. Most punk groups released only ephemeral local singles, but the cream of the crop can be heard on the superbly compiled anthology, *Nuggets* (Elektra, 1973).

PUNK ROCK (1970s) The punk rock revolution that transformed the British music scene in 1976–7 owed its origins to a variety of sources. On one hand, the expanding New York underground (on which **Iggy Pop** was a profound influence as a performer) provided punk with many of its sartorial style models – ripped clothing and safety pins – plus a suitably iconoclastic imagery – **Richard Hell**'s single 'Blank Generation' for example – while the British pub-rock circuit was the training ground for young punk-rockers in the making – Johnny Rotten of the **Sex Pistols** had been a regular attender at Kilburn and the High Roads gigs and Joe Strummer of the **Clash** had served his apprenticeship in the hard-rocking R&B combo, The 101ers.

Much of the nation's youth had become tired of the chart-dominating establishment rock bands of the Seventies, and by the middle of the decade there was a growing, if unfocused, mood for change. The mood became focused by a few key entrepreneurial figures – most notably **Malcolm McLaren** who helped transform incipient protest into musical revolution.

By the end of 1976, McLaren was beginning to become known for his management of the Sex Pistols, the group spearheading the British punk revolution. Throughout the first half of 1976, the Sex Pistols played regularly in London and began to generate a great deal of interest, due not only to the raucous nature of their gigs but also to their genuinely exciting music, a passionate blend of fast, primitive rock'n'roll and snarling, satirical protest lyrics.

A similarly savage sense of humour, together with a determined effort to debunk the false and phoney, also dominated the lyrics of the Clash, who began playing in London in the spring of 1976. The punk scene mushroomed throughout the first half of the year, reaching an early climax that September, when a punk festival, featuring the Sex Pistols, the Clash and others, was held at the 100 Club in London's Oxford Street.

In November 1976, the Clash signed to CBS Records. At the end of that month, the Sex Pistols' first single, 'Anarchy in the UK', was released on

EMI Records, followed by a notorious TV interview with presenter Bill Grundy that ended in a torrent of expletives and made the Sex Pistols the most talked-about group in the country.

The year 1977 proved a watershed: suddenly there were new punk bands everywhere, many picking up instruments for the first time and getting their names on the bill at the Roxy, London's premier punk venue, in the first three months. Apart from the other well-known and wildly different names like the **Damned** with their extreme horror-film image and fast thrashy sound, Manchester's **Buzzcocks** and their high-energy pop-punk romance, the unashamedly mod-influenced **Jam** and **Siouxsie and the Banshees**, featuring wailing guitar hymns, there were countless others who enjoyed their 15 minutes – or more – of fame. **X-Ray Spex**, for example, were fronted by the engaging Poly Styrene, who made tooth-braces and chainstore kitsch fashionable. With their committed left-wing stance and the distinctive wail of Lora Logic's saxophone, they were responsible for some of punk's more famous anthems for frustrated youth – songs like 'Oh Bondage, Up Yours!', 'Identity' and 'Warrior in Woolworths'.

Jimmy Pursey's agit-rock group **Sham 69** were also notable for their political stance, and were indirectly responsible for the growth of the musical style known as Oil later in the Seventies, while **Generation X**, fronted by **Billy Idol**, hit back at the Who with their debut single, 'Your Generation'. The **Adverts** – 'One Chord Wonders' as one of their songs proclaimed – had a Top 20 hit with the topical and tasteless 'Looking Through Gary Gilmore's Eyes' in August of 1977, while other regulars on the scene included Chelsea, 999, Eater – famed for their 14-year-old drummer Dee Generate – the Lurkers, the Vibrators and Australian band the Saints, Slaughter and the Dogs and the quaintly-named Ed Banger and the Nosebleeds emerged from the Manchester scene, while Penetration, from County Durham, had a distinctive and talented lead singer in Pauline Murray.

The punk explosion had extended way beyond London, and even if by this time it was clear that the term 'punk' already covered a growing variety of musical styles, everybody involved broadly shared a basic 'contempt for any kind of establishment values, a delight in confrontation and excess, a cultivation of a kind of gutter individualism and a curiously noble belief in pure amateurism', as one observer of the scene put it.

The first major event of 1977 was the Clash's White Riot Tour to promote their first, eponymous, LP. Also on the bill were the Jam – who left halfway through the dates to promote *their* first album – the **Slits** and the Subway Sect. True to the punk ethic, both these bands consisted of unashamed beginners; the Slits, an all-girl band, had met at a Patti Smith gig and decided to form a group. Vocalist Arri Up would sport a pair of Jubilee knickers over wet-look trousers – conventional standards of 'femininity' appalled them. Subway Sect sang weird, avant-garde numbers about alienation but later singer Vic Godard's preoccupation with BBC Radio Two took them into the realm of cocktail jazz and the band eventually parted from Godard to form the JoBoxers.

There was a fierce rivalry between the various punk acts. Those like the Pistols and the Clash, who had emanated from the Malcolm McLaren stable, paraded their ideological principles and were disparaging about the lack of political awareness of other British punk bands, particularly the Damned. Nevertheless the Damned had been the first to have a record nationally distributed when 'New Rose' was released on the Stiff label. As a result, the Damned toured Britain at an exhausting pace with their anarchic music-hall act for most of 1977.

Although many punk acts had initially dismissed BBC-TV's *Top of the Pops* for its crass commercialism, many of them – the Clash excepted – willingly accepted invitations to appear when their records entered the charts. Partly as a result of this national exposure, the Adverts, X-Ray Spex, the **Stranglers** and the Jam enjoyed early success.

In the heart of mainstream Britain, however, punk rock appeared to be nothing more than a hiccup: the dominant event of 1977 for most of the nation was Queen Elizabeth II's Silver Jubilee. It was at this time that the Sex Pistols were again at the heart of a controversy, with their highly irreverent 'God Save the Queen', released during the Jubilee celebrations in June, reaching Number 2 on the singles chart. Virgin records maintained that it had outsold the Number 1 song, Rod Stewart's 'I Don't Want To Talk About It', yet been kept from the top slot to prevent embarrassment to Her Majesty.

The mood of paranoia surrounding the group was fuelled by McLaren's claims that no council in Britain would allow them to appear. Despite – or

The punk look; do-it yourself was the order of the day

perhaps because of – the Pistols' problems, punk made massive strides. Individual groups and independent labels were taking on the majors and winning, the well-known acts were asserting themselves and impressing with the strength of their talent.

But by the end of 1978 the punk revolution had run its course. In January of that year the Sex Pistols disbanded, and over the following twelve months the other originals either followed the Pistols' lead or began to develop in ways that pushed them beyond the narrow confines that defined the real nature of punk. A few diehard groups remained in the fold, but, no longer part of the musical mainstream, they were pushed to the periphery along with the diehard fans who sustained them. Certainly, punk refused to lie down and die but by the mid-Eighties it had become little more than a musical curiosity.

Even though in the long term punk had little effect on an industry that essentially remains moulded by business rather than creative hands, it gave that industry a timely and much-needed shot in the arm. Many acts around at the time, even if they were not directly identifiable with punk in its truest sense, benefited nevertheless from the boundless enthusiasm that was generated at its height.

If punk is to be remembered for anything at all, then it must be for shattering the God-like status bestowed on the established rock musicians of that era and for showing young people that

anybody could pick up an instrument, take to the stage and make a worthwhile sound. This last factor alone broke down a whole host of musical barriers and paved the way for the experimentation and eclecticism that characterized the music scene that followed on into the Eighties.

PURDIE, BERNARD 'PRETTY'

R&B Drummer Bernard Purdy was born on 1 June 1939, in Elkton, Maryland, and learned to play the drums as a child. He gained his first practical experiencing deputizing in a local club when the resident drummer became drunk and incapable. He played in a variety of bands in a variety of styles and, after graduating, went to New York in 1961 for a one-week gig and session with **Mickey and Sylvia**. In these early days he mixed gigs with Lonnie Youngblood and Les Cooper with a laundry job, but he gradually became established as a first-rate session drummer. By 1966 he was playing on up to twenty sessions a week in various styles – among them sessions for **James Brown**, **Tom Jones** and **Nina Simone** – but he later found he could afford to be more selective. 1967 saw his debut as a solo artist with 'Funky Donkey' (Date), a plodding percussive opus which reached the Hot 100. Purdie continued as a prolific sessioneer and embarked on several solo ventures before joining **Aretha Franklin**'s backing combo as musical director.

PURIFY, JAMES AND BOBBY

Soul duo James and Bobby Purify first teamed up professionally in 1965. James was born in Pensacola, Florida, on 12 May 1944; Bobby was his Tallahassee-born cousin (2 September 1939) Robert Lee Dickey. Bobby originally played guitar with the Dothan Sextet, accompanying Mighty Sam, and James was brought in as the latter's replacement on Sam's departure from the band. James and Bobby's duets became a highlight of the band's act; A&R man Don Schroeder heard them, signed them to Bell Records and took them to the Muscle Shoals studios where they cut 'I'm Your Puppet', a gospel-like beat ballad which became a Top 10 US hit during 1966. Subsequent discs also sold well, though by 1969 their appeal had cooled and Bobby had left, to be replaced by a 'new' Bobby – Ben Moore. He re-recorded 'I'm Your Puppet' with James and, retaining the old name, they signed with Casablanca in 1975. By the end of the decade, the duo had split and Moore was recording as a solo act for DJM.

Q

QUATRO, SUZI A likeable bass-playing female rock singer who first made her name in the UK during the glam-rock days of the early Seventies, Suzi Quatro was born on 3 June 1950 in Detroit. At eight years old she was playing bongos with her father's jazz band, the Art Quatro Band, and at fourteen she was TV go-go dancer Suzi Soul. At fifteen, she formed an all-girl group, Suzi Soul and the Pleasure Seekers, with her sisters Patti and Nancy; they played in mini skirts from Las Vegas to Vietnam. In late 1970, **Mickie Most** in Detroit recording **Jeff Beck** at Motown, heard her and brought her to Britain, where she toured, third on the bill, and released singles that got nowhere.

In early 1973, she was teamed with songwriters/producers Nicky Chinn and Mike Chapman who wrote and produced 'Can the Can' – a British chart topper on RAK. With a new image, encasing her five-foot figure in a leather jump suit, the idea of her playing bass guitar in a band of large bruisers – Len Tucky (guitar), whom she later married, Alistair Mackenzie (keyboards), Dave Neal (drums) – made her an instant success. '48 Crash' and 'Daytona Demon' (1973) and 'Devil Gate Drive' (1974) consolidated that success which went unchallenged until late 1974, when she had two flops in a row. She spent the first six months of 1975 in America, gaining wide recognition via an **Alice Cooper** tour: a year later she became a regular in the TV show *Happy Days*, playing the part of Fonz's sidekick, Leather Tuscadero.

A duet with Chris Norman of **Smokie**, 'Stumblin' in', gave Suzi her first and only major US hit, reaching Number 4 on RSO during 1979, and after a spell with Mike Chapman's Dreamland label she returned to Britain to concentrate on her UK career. In 1986, she made her theatrical debut as Annie Oakley in a British revival of *Annie Get Your Gun*.

Suzi Quatro, gutsy, bawdy, packed with energy and fun, definitely no class: 'Girls identify with me because I haven't got big tits'

QUEEN Mixing art-rock, heavy metal and a sound pop sensibility, Queen emerged in the mid-Seventies as one of the most dilettantish yet undeniably commercial bands of the decade. The band was formed by drummer Roger Taylor (born 26 July 1949) and guitarist Brian May (19 July 1947) in 1971 and was originally called Smile; when singer Tim Stafell left, graphic design student Freddie Mercury (né Bulsara, born 5 September 1946) was recruited from a west London band called Wreckage. Bassist John Deacon (19 August 1951) joined a little later. They signed with EMI as a quasi-glam-rock outfit in 1973 and scored their first hit with their second release, 'Seven Seas of Rhye' (Number 10), during the following year. Mercury's ingeniously allusive lyrics and Roy Baker's immaculate production ensured that the albums *Queen* (1973) and *Queen II* (1974) were well received by the critics, although their commercial potential was most fully realized by *Sheer Heart Attack* (1974), which featured the Number 2 UK single 'Killer Queen'. *A Night at the Opera* (1975) kept up the momentum and included a stunningly contrived but brilliantly executed mélange of rock and operatics in the single 'Bohemian Rhapsody', which was a million seller and a Number 1 in the UK for nine weeks. Much of its success was due to the video promo (one of the first of its kind) used to publicize the single.

Their next album, *A Day at the Races* (yet another title borrowed from a Marx Brothers film), appeared in 1976 and was their first self-produced release. A world tour followed in 1977 that set new standards for opulent, pseudo-theatrical stage presentation, and it was unsurprising that – with punk-rock in the ascendant – they should find themselves perhaps the most critically pilloried and least fashionable bands of the late Seventies.

Nevertheless, their commercial success was inarguable, and *News of the World* (1977), *Jazz* (1978), *Queen Live Killers* (1979) and *The Game* (1980) consolidated their popularity in the US and Europe. In 1981, they joined forces with **David Bowie** on a Number 1 UK single, 'Under Pressure', though their soundtrack album for the film *Flash Gordon* sold poorly by their standards. Later Eighties hits for Queen included the Roger Taylor composition, 'Radio Ga Ga' (Number 2, 1984), and a string of macho crowd-stirring chants – 'I Want to Break Free', 'It's a Hard Life' (both 1984), and 'One Vision' (1986) among them.

Freddie Mercury strutted and preened through Queen's live shows

QUESTION MARK AND THE MYSTERIANS

A Mexican-American group, Question Mark and the Mysterians made one of the most timelessly moronic records ever, and one of the biggest US hits of 1966, in '96 Tears' (Cameo). Moving from Texas to Flint, Michigan, they issued the record on their own label before it was picked up for national release by Cameo boss Neil Bogart. It was a good song, with properly arrogant vocals but its true appeal lay in the relentless two-note punk-style organ part that ran through the record. Later releases, particularly 'I Need Somebody', lacked that magic quality. Despite his seemingly unbeatable gimmick of remaining anonymous, Question Mark – Rudy Martinez, born in 1945, who also composed '96 Tears' – soon faded from the scene, as did the four-man Mysterians – Bobby Balderamma, lead guitar (born in 1950); Frank Lugo, bass (1947); Eddie Serrato, drums (1947) and Frank Rodriguez, organ (1951).

QUICKSILVER MESSENGER SERVICE

One of the last San Francisco bands of the flower-power/acid-rock era to get a recording contract – due to their own wariness of the fate of some of their colleagues – Quicksilver first came together in the Bay area in 1965. Their first consistent line-up was as a five-piece with Gary Duncan (guitar, born 4 September 1946), Greg Ellmore (drums, 4 September 1946), David Freiburg (bass, 24 August 1938), John Cippolina (guitar, 24 August 1943) and Jim Murray (harmonica) and it was with this format that they appeared in the film *Revolution* (1968). By the time that the soundtrack was recorded, Murray had left. They finally signed with Capitol in January 1968. Their uneasiness in the studio was evident on the first, eponymous, album and so they decided to record their second, *Happy Trails* (1969), in a more familiar 'live' environment and immediately found themselves with songs like the side-long 'Who Do You

Love? Suite' and 'Mona', which remain two of the finest guitar 'statements' ever recorded. At this stage the chemistry of the band was irrevocably altered; Dino Valenti (born 7 October 1943), an early member who had twice spent time in prison on drug charges, reappeared and persuaded Gary Duncan to join him in a band called the Outlaws. Nicky Hopkins (keyboards, born 24 February 1944) was called in and they cut *Shady Grove* (1970) which lacked the grandeur of its predecessor. Despite the return of Duncan and Valenti a year later, the band never recaptured their early spark. Hopkins left and was followed by Cippolina, who had been occupying more and more of a back seat, after *What About Me* (1971). The group continued with Valenti at the helm but had quite clearly lost its original musical identity. Eventually Freiburg quit and the various permutations of musicians that made up the name of the group – and which released two albums, *Quicksilver* and *Comin' Thru* (1972) – were less than pale imitations of the band that had once been. *Solid Silver* (1975) was an unsuccessful comeback album featuring Cippolina and Freiburg.

QUINTESSENCE

A true product of the British underground scene of the late Sixties, Quintessence was formed in 1968 through ads in the *Melody Maker* and auditions held in All Saints Hall, Notting Hill Gate, London. Raja Ram (born Ron Rothfield in 1940 in Melbourne), flute, vocals, and Sambhu, bass, were the moving spirit, adding Jake, drums; Alan, lead guitar, vocals; Shiva, vocals and Maha Dev on rhythm guitar. Their music was a blend of jazz/rock and Eastern music, built around heavy dependence on jazzy flute and rock guitar, that attempted to achieve spirituality through the chanting of mantras until 'the audience becomes the musicians'. Their cult following was won through club performances rather than usually unsuccessful albums – *In Blissful Company* (Island), the first in 1969 which was recorded within weeks of their formation. The partly live *Self* (RCA) in 1972 captured them best. Shiva and Maha Dev left in spring 1972 (Shiva forming a similar group in Kala) and their final album *Indweller* featured a band drifting apart. In spite of a tendency towards the pretentious, the group's concerts were often awesomely and powerfully constructed, achieving a high degree of contact with the audience.

QUIVER See Sutherland Brothers

RADIO (UK) Before 1964 there was little British pop radio. The only alternative to the evening broadcasts of the independent Radio Luxembourg, with its firm commitment to pop – and the heavy backing from the record companies which leased air time – was the BBC's Light Programme. An old-fashioned counterpart to the more 'serious' Third Programme (classical) and Home Service (non-musical), its content was epitomized by the perennial *Music While You Work*, which featured dance-band arrangements of popular evergreens. Pop was virtually confined to two weekend shows, Saturday morning's *Saturday Club* – originally *Saturday Skiffle Club* – and Sunday morning's *Easy Beat*, hosted with avuncular benevolence by Brian Matthew. Both featured more studio sessions than records and a musical policy that was as broad as it was bland.

This situation was altered on Easter Saturday, 1964, when Radio Caroline, the brainchild of Ronan O'Rahilly, commenced broadcasting from international waters five miles off Harwich. Within a week, the GPO had begun its campaign to ban offshore commercial radio, but on 12 May, Radio Atlanta came on the air, merging with Caroline in July to create Caroline South and North (operating off the Isle of Man). Other stations followed, broadcasting from ships or disused wartime defence forts, and in December the businesslike Radio London opened. By this time the 'pirates' had an audience of millions.

Their popularity was easy to understand. Unrestricted needle time, flamboyant DJs, and American-style format complete with call signs, jingles and commercials made a refreshing change. Listening figures grew through 1965, but although increasing pressure was placed on the Government to outlaw the stations because of their interference with official wavelengths, there was no attempt at legislation until the introduction of the Marine Broadcasting (Offences) Bill in July 1966, apparently hastened by the killing of Radio City owner, Reg Calvert, and the resultant exposure of genuine piracy behind the stations' breezy façades.

In December 1966, the Government announced plans for broadcasting, including the establishment of a pop wavelength and local BBC stations.

The Marine Broadcasting (Offences) Bill became law on 15 August 1967 and only Caroline was prepared to risk prosecution, surviving until March 1968 and reappearing on several occasions since. BBC Radio One, meanwhile, began on 30 September 1967 with the voice of Tony Blackburn and the **Move**'s 'Flowers in the Rain': with a programme format and jingles closely based on those of the pirates, the new station sounded like an instant carbon copy, though a Top 40 playlist was not introduced until the early Seventies (in anticipation of commercial competition) and its music policy was heavily weighted towards the assumed tastes of a captive audience of housewives. By giving over part of its coverage to bands in the 'progressive rock' vein – notably in programmes like **John Peel**'s *Top Gear* – Radio One did much to emphasize the growing gap in the late Sixties between commercial chart music and the album-oriented rock favoured by student audiences.

When the Conservatives won the 1970 General Election, they promptly halved the BBC's local radio allowance and introduced plans for the establishment of commercial radio on a local scale, under the auspices of the Independent Broadcasting Authority. Capital Radio in London was second on the air in October 1973, and every independent station that followed adopted a similar format of Top 40 hits, oldies, commercials, jingles, DJ chat, phone-ins, and features and interviews of local interest. To the consternation of rock fans, Capital and its successors initially took little advantage of the potentially fruitful areas left untended by the BBC and followed Radio One's pattern of bland daytime listening. Rock as such tended to be confined to the evenings and weekends. There were exceptions – Glasgow's Radio Clyde, in particular, developed a local identity by placing special emphasis on Scottish pop – but in image and sound the majority of stations remained resolutely MOR.

To face the threat from the new commercial stations, the BBC narrowed the gap between its two popular music networks, Radio One and Radio Two, with the result that some records were played heavily on both stations. Radio One's transmission time was extended and the 10pm to midnight slot became the haven of the progressive rock fan, though by 1976 John Peel for one was tiring of this kind of stereotyping and beginning to give extensive coverage to the burgeoning punk movement in London. His espousal of punk and the

explosion of regional talent that followed was critical to the development of British pop and rock in the late Seventies, and he and his producer John Walters were responsible for giving bands such as **Siouxsie and the Banshees**, the **Undertones**, **Joy Division** and **Altered Images** their career starts.

Punk itself was handled gingerly by Britain's radio stations. Many of the independent stations steadfastly ignored it and Radio One was typically selective in what it played, promoting the more 'acceptable' new wave groups – the **Police**, the **Jam**, the **Pretenders** – but refusing to play certain hard-core punk records. On the whole, Radio One's late Seventies playlists were dominated by disco releases or those by reliable pop names like **Elton John**, **Leo Sayer**, **Rod Stewart** and **Abba**.

That said, Radio One developed a more coherent identity for itself as its broadcasting hours were steadily extended and its programme-sharing arrangement with Radio Two was abandoned. By the Eighties, it was far more of a young people's network than it had been in 1967, and its DJs at least gave the impression of being more involved in the music. The decision to oust the playlist in 1979 in favour of allowing presenters and producers more freedom of choice was an adventurous move, although it paradoxically led to greater repetition of chart sounds and a degree of blandness in music choices; it was re-introduced in 1986 by the station's new controller, Johnny Beerling, who also took steps to counter the infamous verbosity of certain of its daytime presenters.

Other developments in British radio at this time included a complete about-turn on music policy by Capital, who switched from a MOR policy to a deliberately 'young' mix of soul, funk and rock during 1984 and began (in 1986) a special VHF-only service, CFM, on Sundays in conscious pursuit of an affluent, compact-disc-playing yuppie clientele. Continued problems in attracting advertising and consequent demands by some of the stations for sponsored programmes and a relaxing of the IBA's 'public service' regulations suggested that Britain's commercial radio system was due for an overhaul, while the reappearance and renewed popularity of pirate stations – both offshore, like Laser 557 and a revitalized Radio Caroline, and in urban areas – strengthened demands for the expansion of radio and the establishment of community radio stations specializing in programmes for minority audiences.

RADIO (US) In America, radio was the ideal medium for the dissemination of rock'n'roll. It was not accidental that a DJ, **Alan Freed**, was responsible for giving the new music its name, and his shows, plus those of other radio men, built up its youthful audience in the Fifties.

As early as the Thirties, though, DJs had begun to assume an essential role in the process by which new songs were brought to the attention of the public. They had superseded the 'boomers' or promotion men of the pre-wireless, sheet-music era, whose job was to pitch songs to singers or band-leaders to perform in live shows. As records replaced sheet music, juke boxes and radio stations became central to the pop process. By the end of the Thirties, programmes like Al Jarvis' *Make Believe Ballroom* and the American Tobacco co-sponsored *Lucky Strike Hit Parade* (which introduced the notion of a ranking of records) were the targets of record men who wanted to get their new discs across. DJs became privileged beings. In the late Forties, Capitol Records hit on the idea of giving them promotional copies of new singles, pressed on expensive vinyl. Other companies followed suit.

Radio stations had played a large part in the upsurge of the country and R&B music which predated the emergence of rock'n'roll. The older school of Tin Pan Alley songwriters and publishers distrusted the medium. In 1939, a dispute between their monopolistic organization ASCAP (the American Society of Composers, Authors and Publishers) and the radio men led to the formation of Broadcast Music Inc. (BMI). BMI primarily represented country music and R&B interests, which provided most of the material used by stations in the South and West of the country. And it was the DJs on those stations who championed the new sounds of the Fifties. Radio had also played a part in shaping rock'n'roll itself, for while it was not possible in the segregationist South for white kids to watch black musicians perform, they could tune in to R&B stations and absorb the music that way.

As the Fifties progressed, DJs became more and more crucial to the fate of a new record. This was quickly recognized by the record companies and the practice of payola became endemic. After a lengthy investigation into payola in 1960, Congress was outlawed and a maximum fine of $10,000 introduced.

It was, in any case, being made less significant by the growth of the Top 40 radio format. Under this system, first introduced in 1955 by Todd Storz on his chain of stations in the Midwest, a rigid playlist based on the *Billboard* Hot 100 chart was enforced. There was no room for individual DJs to exercise personal choice. Just as rock'n'roll itself had given way to formula pop, by the start of the Sixties the idiosyncrasies and personal influence of jockeys like Freed had all but disappeared.

However, some things did not change: as in the Fifties, DJs accepted composer credits or other 'honorariums' in return for helping to expose a new record or artist. Because of the competition to 'break' and claim credit for new hits, it was relatively easy for America's thousands of local groups to get their records aired, if only locally. Out of this grew an incredible proliferation of groups, records, labels, and musical trends. The years 1964–7 probably saw more records released than any other 3-year period in history.

Then in 1965, a new programming theory took hold in American radio. A programme director named Bill Drake (at KHJ, Los Angeles) discovered that he could get higher ratings playing 20 records in constant rotation (as opposed to the 40 or even 60 aired previously), and within a year AM radio was plunged into a cut-throat competition to see who could play the fewest records – at one point, WLS in Chicago (the nation's most powerful station) was playing less than 15. While great for the ratings, it effectively eliminated all avenues for new acts to gain radio exposure. However, this coincided with the birth of 'progressive' FM radio and the dance/concert phenomenon developing in the big cities. So there grew up, for the first time in rock, a duality: certain groups (mostly studio concoctions) holding forth on AM and selling singles, while the 'underground' rock groups confined themselves to concerts, FM rock and album sales. Progressive FM was begun in early 1967 by KMPX in San Francisco, WABX in Detroit, WBCN in Boston, and a few other pioneers. At first, these stations and those who followed tried to offer a clear alternative to the restrictions of AM, playing whatever the jocks wanted (be it classical, folk, avant-garde jazz, electronic music, or obscure album cuts), but as ratings increased and commercial pressures grew, FM in turn became competitive, with most stations establishing limited playlists of 'most popular album cuts' from popular current albums, with only a small percentage of airtime allowed for oldies or other programming. This in turn spawned 'progressive AM' in the Seventies, leading to a great confusion of definitions and formats.

By the late Seventies, the distinctions between FM and AM stations had become much less marked and the prevailing format was 'AOR', which was defined as both 'album oriented radio' and 'adult oriented rock'. The AOR stations mixed album cuts, oldies and hand-picked singles from the Hot 100 and aimed their output at an affluent post-teenage audience, but they tended to exclude from their playlists both home-grown and British punk/new wave and disco. Disco carved out a temporary niche on AM radio, but the more imaginative black music of the late Seventies and early Eighties was mostly heard on black stations and the more adventurous American and European rock on a growing network of voluntarily-run college stations. Indeed, US radio in the Seventies and Eighties was almost a two-tier system, populated by mainstream AOR stations serving mainstream audiences on the one hand and more specialized (musically and demographically) stations on the other, the latter serving *aficionados* of everything from orchestral easy-listening to jazz-rock. Narrowness in music programming was matched by increasing concentration of station ownership, while yet another indicator of the trend towards homogeneity and standardization of output (undercutting, of course, US radio's strengths as a *local* medium) was the widespread use of syndicated material originating from specialist companies like Westwood One, who by the mid-Eighties were looking increasingly to British stations like Radio 1 and Capital for concerts and rock-magazine programmes.

RAFFERTY, GERRY A former member of Scottish folk act **Stealers Wheel**, Gerry Rafferty (born on 16 April 1947 in Paisley, Scotland) spent seven years seeking success as a solo artist, and finally did it in style in 1978. Rafferty had released a solo album, *Can I Have My Money Back*, as early as 1971, but he had to wait five years after his hit stint with Stealers Wheel before the solo album *City to City* (1978) yielded the classic international hit, 'Baker Street' (UK Number 3, US Number 2).

Something of a recluse, Rafferty also did well with *Night Owl* (1979), but his low profile meant subsequent releases like *Snakes and Ladders* (1980) and *Sleepwalking* (1982) registered only briefly on the charts.

RAGAVOY, JERRY Among the backroom white soul brothers of the Sixties, writer/producer Jerry Ragavoy rates just below Jerry Wexler and **Bert Berns**. From Philadelphia, he began his career in 1954 with a composition called 'This Silver Ring' for George Grant and the Castelles; he also produced several more misty doo-wop classics for them including 'My Girl Awaits Me', released on Herb Slotkin's Grand label. In 1959, Ragavoy formed a partnership with entrepreneur Bill Fox and produced several hits for Fox's group, the Majors, in New York. 'A Wonderful Dream', 'Tra La La', 'A Little Bit Now' and 'She's a Troublemaker' were all teen-styled falsetto bouncers written by Ragavoy under the pseudonym Norman Meade. He next switched to deep soul, producing everything by **Garnet Mimms** on United Artists, Verve and Veep, starting with the climactic 'Cry Baby', which Ragavoy has said he co-wrote with Bert Berns, although the label credits one 'Sam Bell'.

In 1966, he produced many records on the Loma label, including those by the Enchanters, Roy Redmond and **Lorraine Ellison**'s classic 'Stay with Me'. In the same year, Ragavoy wrote and produced a series of minor hits for **Howard Tate** on Verve, following up with Miriam Makeba's 'Pata Pata' and 'Malayisha' in 1967–8. At this time he was also involved with more middle-of-the-road artists like **Gene Pitney** ('Mecca'), Kai Winding and Ritchie Adams. Ragavoy also wrote and co-wrote (often with Berns with whom he shared the Webb IV/Ragmar company) for Erma Franklin ('A Piece of My Heart'), Freddy Scott, Bobby Freeman, **Irma Thomas** ('Time Is on My Side'), Baby Washington, Jon Thomas and many others. Lou Courtney enjoyed moderate success on Ragavoy's own short-lived label, Rags, in 1973. His production work during the Seventies included albums for **Bonnie Raitt** and **Dionne Warwick**, who had once sung backing vocals on the Ragavoy-produced Garnet Mimms track, 'Cry Baby'.

RAINBOW One of the three major hard rock groups to be spun off from **Deep Purple**, Rainbow was formed by Ritchie Blackmore soon after his departure in 1975. Based largely around Blackmore's reputation as a virtuoso guitar player, Rainbow became a dominant force in heavy metal during the late Seventies and early Eighties.

Rainbow went through several changes of line-up, but the first stable one consisted of Ronnie James Dio (vocals), Cozy Powell (drums), Jimmy Bain (bass) and Tony Carey (keyboards). This personnel recorded *Rainbow Rising* (1976), the second and by far the best album and the one that made the band's reputation; featuring grandiose tracks of epic lengths, it is considered a heavy metal classic.

Altogether Rainbow recorded eight albums, but only *Long Live Rock'n'Roll* (1978) came close to *Rainbow Rising* in quality and sales. In terms of chart success, *Down to Earth* (1979), featuring a new vocalist Graham Bonnet, not only did well in the album charts but also spawned three consecutive UK Top 10 singles, most notably 'I Surrender', which reached Number 3 in January 1981. The one success that had eluded Rainbow up to that point was in the American market, and after a major shake-up of personnel (with yet another new vocalist, Joe Lynn Turner), they produced *Difficult to Cure* (1981), which suppressed the harder edges of their sound in order to sell in the US. Nonetheless, the sought-after success never really came, and after a couple of pedestrian rock workouts ending with *Bent Out of Shape* (1983), Blackmore and bassist Roger Glover (another ex-Purple man who had been in Rainbow since 1979) finally succumbed, in 1984, to the great temptation to re-form Deep Purple.

Volatile guitar virtuoso Ritchie Blackmore leads Rainbow, the band he formed as a vehicle for his talents after leaving Deep Purple in 1975

RAINWATER, MARVIN An American Indian born in Wichita, Kansas, on 2 July 1925, Marvin Rainwater is best known for the 1958 rock'n'roll hit, 'Whole Lotta Woman', although he has since recorded in straight country styles. A country songwriter and singer-guitarist of some originality, Rainwater has had major successes in that field with 'Gonna Find Me a Bluebird', 'Half Breed' and 'I Miss You Already'. He has recorded for MGM, United Artists, and Warner Brothers, and has also contributed several songs in more traditional country styles, such as 'Tennessee Hound Dog Yodel' and 'Tea Bag Romeo'.

RAITT, BONNIE Born in Los Angeles, California, on 8 November 1939, Bonnie Raitt matured into one of America's best white blues and soul singers during the Seventies. The daughter of John Raitt, star of several major Fifties musicals on Broadway, she attended Radcliffe College and began playing as a duo with her ever-present bassist, Freebo. She signed with Warner Brothers in 1970 and recorded her eponymous debut album a year later. Rougher than her later work, it mixed blues, soul, Dixieland and contemporary ballads, including her own compositions. The looser *Give It Up* was recorded in 1972 with Woodstock musicians including Eric Kaz, whose 'Love Has No Pride' is the highlight of the album, and typical of her heart-rending approach.

Established as a local Boston star with feminist leanings, she appeared at the Ann Arbor Jazz Festival in 1972 with blues singer Sippie Wallace, and played club and college dates alongside blues-men **Otis Rush**, Son House and Fred McDowell. With Lowell George of **Little Feat** she produced a classic album, *Takin' My Time*, in Hollywood in 1973, featuring songs by **Randy Newman**, Eric Kaz, **Mose Allison** and Fred McDowell. Adding keyboards, drums and another guitar she toured in 1974 and recorded the disappointing *Streetlights* with producer **Jerry Ragavoy**, but returned to form with *Home Plate* (1975) and *Sweet Forgiveness* (1977), the latter her biggest seller to date. *The Glow* followed in 1979 and *Green Light* in 1982, on which she was joined by the Bump Band, who featured former **Faces** keyboard player Ian McLagan.

RAM, BUCK Born in Chicago in 1908, Buck Ram first came to the fore as a writer and arranger for the bands of Duke Ellington, Count Basie and the Dorsey brothers in the Thirties. However, during the Fifties, he moved over to the business side of music, handling the **Platters** and composing many of their hits.

He founded Personality Promotions in 1954, and the agency grew quickly, attracting many of the young Los Angeles R&B stars, including the Flairs, Dolly Cooper, the Harris Sisters, the **Penguins** and Linda Hayes. A talented lawyer, Ram was able to place the Penguins and the Platters with a major record company, Mercury. When the Platters' 'Only You' took off, demand for Ram's services trebled: the Teen Queens, Joe Houston, the Empires and the Colts (who had the original of the **Drifters**' hit 'Adorable') flocked to his stable. Ram worked with them on his own labels – Antler, Discovery and Personality – or through other companies which employed him as an arranger: Mercury, Capitol, Modern, Felsted, Press. By 1967, when the Platters had their last big hit, Ram had taken a back seat. 'I'm out of it now,' he said, 'the companies are going with the kids themselves.' *See also* the **Platters**

RAMONES Undoubtedly America's greatest punk band, the Ramones mastered the three-chord wall of noise and combined a thrash of incredible ferocity and drive with bright touches of melody to take the form to new heights.

Formed in New York City in 1974, by Joey Ramone (born Jeffrey Hyman, vocals), Johnny Ramone (born John Cummings, guitar), Dee Dee Ramone (born Douglas Colvin, bass) and Tommy Ramone (born Tom Erdelyi in Budapest, drums), the Ramones met at Forest Hills High School. They shared a love for surf music, **Buddy Holly** and comic culture, all of which had a profound influence on their material. Their half-hour sets of quick-fire, under-three-minute songs won them a strong following on the New York scene and they became the first band at the New York end of the punk explosion to sign a recording contract.

Ramones was released on Sire in 1976 and constituted the definitive Ramones album style – thirteen crude pop songs played at breakneck speed. Virtually all subsequent releases were variations on that theme, although *Rocket to Russia* (1977) softened the approach a little and included two singles, 'Sheena is a Punk Rocker' and 'Rockaway Beach' that made the lower reaches of the US charts.

The Ramones spent a while out in the cold as they experimented with more complex arrangements, first of all with producer **Phil Spector** on *End of the Century* (1980) and then with Graham Gouldman of **10cc** on *Pleasant Dreams* (1981). *Subterranean Jungle* (1983) featured a new drummer Ritchie Beau, the first Ramone to retain his own name, Tommy Ramone having been replaced by Marky Ramone (Marc Bell) in 1978. A revival of their original, basic sound, this album returned them to the critics' good books. *Too Tough to Die* didn't appear until 1985, but saw the Ramones thrashing away as intensely as ever.

Although the band was deprived of the large-scale commercial success they deserved, the New York punk scene, and the successful bands that it threw up, owed a great deal to their pioneering example.

RANDAZZO, TEDDY Singer Teddy Randazzo (born on 20 May 1937) first made an impression as a member of the Three Chuckles, which he formed with Tom Romano and Russ Gilberto in Brooklyn in 1955. Small hits, like 'Times Two I Love You' (1955) and 'And the Angels Sing' (1956) on RCA's X and Vik subsidiaries led to appearances in rock'n'roll movies, notably *The Girl Can't Help It*. In 1958, Randazzo, a skilful singer parading a multitude of styles embracing black R&B, Presley slurs and Latin rhythms, went solo but the hits were infrequent: 'Little Serenade' (Vik, 1958), 'The Way of a Clown' (ABC, 1960) and 'Big Wide World' (Colpix, 1963). In 1962, he cut 'Dance to the Locomotion', a wild sequel to the **Little Eva** hit. Other sides included 'Broken Bell', featuring some Italianate crooning, and a relaxed version of the traditional 'Cotton Fields'. Randazzo later moved into writing and production, most notably with **Little Anthony and the Imperials**.

RANDOLPH, BOOTS The top saxophone player on the Nashville recording scene is – and always was – Boots Randolph. The Western Swing element in country and western had always admitted wind instruments, but the country-pop revolution of the 'Nashville Sound' in the late Fifties saw Boots rise to the top as a session musician and then wade into the pop charts in 1963 with the instrumental 'Yakety Sax'. He has produced a string of solo recordings for RCA and Monument and interjected sax statements behind almost everyone who ever recorded in Nashville, memorably on *Elvis Is Back* in 1968.

RAP In 1979, the Sugarhill Gang's 'Rapper's Delight' marked the emergence of rap to the record-buying public. A new black underground music, it consisted of a vibrant amalgam of fast-talking catch-phrases and rhymes spoken over a stripped-down rhythm track. The roots of rap went back to radio where DJs, who spread the powerful urban R&B sounds over the airwaves, were stars, introducing records in a high-speed rhyming slang that had developed all the way from African boasting and praise songs, through black American oral traditions to the hip patter of bebop singers and bandleaders like Cab Calloway.

The manic DJ jive was taken up by Jamaican musicians in the Sixties – notably producer Coxsone Dodd – and developed into the full-scale toasting style of the battling sound systems where the DJ would work his patter right across the record. Although reggae was slow to gain a following in the US, a growing Jamaican preserve in New York meant that, sooner or later, the Caribbean toasting style of DJ talkover would be recycled into soul.

DJ Kool Herc – a resident of the Bronx who had moved there from Kingston, Jamaica, in 1967 – was one of the first of a new generation to popularize the idea of rapping over records. Since the dub records in his own collection failed to cut ice with local dancers, he switched to Latin-tinged funk. Kool Herc's innovations – rapping out street vernacular through an echo chamber over repeated instrumental breaks – were followed by Grand Wizard Theodor's invention of 'scratching' (manually turning the record so that the stylus moves back and forth in the record groove) and DJ **Grandmaster Flash**'s use of a drum machine (known as a beat box) in combination with montaged fragments of records. A street subculture developed with an identity, a name (hip hop) and a lifestyle; its members (called Beat Boys) had a uniform; the sound systems wired their amps into the street lighting – a handy source of free electricity – and created music from other people's records and their own imaginative skills.

Thus far, hip hop style was confined to the Uptown streets and clubs, but when the Fatback Band heard a tape of DJ King Tim III rapping over a Roy Ayers instrumental, they were sufficiently impressed to record with him. The effect was convincing, probably because Fatback were among the best of the street-funk groups, and the floodgates were opened. The label Sugarhill followed up in 1979 with 'Rapper's Delight' by the Sugarhill Gang; for the rhythm track they stole the memorable bass riff from **Chic**'s international hit 'Good Times'. It reached Number 36 in the US and Number 3 in the UK.

The arrival of the 12-inch single in the mid-Seventies had sparked a terrific advance in disco club mixing and the practice of putting the A-side backing track as the B-side became popular. Endless variations could be rapped over popular tunes, leading to re-recordings, Jamaican-style, over distinctive rhythms, each one a new rap single.

Afrika Bambaataa accomplished one of rap's most daring coups in 1982, by converting **Kraftwerk**'s 'Trans Europe Express' into rap for 'Planet Rock'. In collaboration with producer Arthur Baker and rappers Soul Sonic Force, Bambaataa put together a record that combined a club atmosphere with hard electronic rhythms, European melodies and a new style of rapping called DJ popping. One of the best groups, the Furious Five, retaliated with 'The Message' the same year, an equally tough rhythm with a lyric that outlined ghetto realities in no uncertain terms.

Soon after the release of 'Rapper's Delight', the music industry had begun to predict that rap would soon be finished, yet in the Eighties, its popularity showed no signs of abating. Electro-raps like the Fearless Four's 'Rockin' It, on Bobby Robinson's Enjoy label, and Warp 9's 'Light Years Away' were opening up yet another direction for countless would-be stars to follow, and by 1986 rap acts like Beastie Boys, Fat Boys, Doug E. Fresh and most notably Run DMC (who that year scored rap's first million-selling album with *Raisin' Hell*) had large followings on both sides of the Atlantic. *See also* **hip hop**, **toasting**

RARE EARTH A vocal and instrumental unit from Detroit, Rare Earth comprised Gil Bridges (sax, flute and vocals), Pete Rivera (drums, vocals), John Parrish (bass, trombone, vocals), Rod Richards (guitar, vocals) and Kenny James (keyboards). Signed to launch the Motown Corporation's Rare Earth label in 1969 they marked the company's entry into the 'heavy rock' field. Though their musical style was a departure from the Motown norm, their initial material wasn't; and it was a revival of the **Temptations**' 'Get Ready' and '(I Know) I'm Losing You' that brought them Top 10 hits in 1970. More original material was used sub-sequently, such as 'I Just Want to Celebrate', as the group developed an identity under **Norman Whitfield**'s close supervision. In 1970, Ray Monette replaced Richards, and in 1971 Rivera, Parrish and James were replaced by Pete Hoorelbeke, Mike Urso and Ed Cuzman. They remained with Motown until 1977, when they switched labels to Prodigal and released *Rare Earth*.

RASCALS For many the finest white soul band of the Sixties, the Rascals did far more than just play soul – they understood its inner tensions. Felix Cavaliere, organ, vocals (born 29 November 1944); Eddie Brigati, vocals (22 October 1946); Gene Cornish, guitar (14 May 1945) left **Joey Dee and the Starlighters** to join Dino Danelli, drums (23 July 1945) as the Young Rascals in February 1965. Debuting at the Choo Choo Club in Garfield, New Jersey, they quickly became renowned for their plus-fours and knickerbockers – and for their brand of rock'n'roll and R&B. They dropped the 'Young' two years later.

The group's first single 'I Ain't Gonna Eat Out My Heart Anymore' made the US Top 50 but it was 'Good Lovin', a Number 1 in 1966, that really set them on their way. They were particularly influential on the East Coast, spawning a virtual 'New York Sound' among groups like the Pigeons (later **Vanilla Fudge**) and the Vagrants. Significantly, they appealed to black and white audiences alike – and were also the first white rock group on Atlantic. In Europe, they were a musicians' group until the dramatic (and phenomenally successful) change of style on 'Groovin' exploded them worldwide. The classic 1967 song established a pattern which became the basis of the group's finest album, *Groovin'*, but in the long run saw them absorbed in good-vibe jazzy rock with more than an air of pretension on albums like *Freedom Suite* (1969) and *Island of Real* (Columbia, 1972). At the same time the group were actually doing something positive, announcing a new appearance policy of no more shows that didn't include at least one black act, thereby cutting their own financial throats by effectively banning themselves throughout the South. They also played the Soul Together show for Martin Luther King and the UNICEF benefit in London where they upstaged **John Lennon**'s Ono Band. Right up to their 1971 break-up they were a live band of the first order; only towards the end did they fail to communicate this on record.

RASPBERRIES The focal point of the Ohio music scene in the early Seventies, the Raspberries incorporated a mid-Sixties style and approach into a distillation of Seventies pop consciousness; they were the embodiment of the basic process of musical rejuvenation that was the most significant formative trend of their era.

Formed in 1971, the Raspberries were Eric Carmen (vocals, piano, bass, born 11 August 1949), Wally Bryson (guitar, 18 July 1949), Jim Bonfanti (drums, 17 December 1948) and Dave Smalley (guitar, 10 July 1949). They came from a series of groups including Cyrus Erie, the Choir, the Quick, and the Mods that collectively represented the cream of Cleveland's pop scene, which has always stood out from the rest of America as being strongly influenced by the best in British rock. From 1965 on, the various Raspberries had been local idols, adapting little-known records of the **Who**, **Small Faces**, **Kinks**, **Move** and their other heroes, the **Beatles**, **Lesley Gore** and the **Beach Boys**. 'It's Cold Outside' by the Choir was a regional hit in 1967, and remains the best American treatment of the British mid-Sixties sound.

In the Raspberries, these influences all came together in a fresh, dynamic new synthesis. Produced by Jimmy Ienner, their first album came out on Capitol and their second single, 'Go All the Way', entered the Top 10 in September 1972, becoming one of the year's biggest sellers. On top of influences ranging from the Beatles to **Free**, Carmen contributed a style of his own, a lush pop romanticism, singing in pure, rich harmony of idealized adolescent love, a theme he re-worked through many subsequent songs. The hard rock backing offset the material's latent schmaltz, and created an appealing, truly ingenuous sound.

The Raspberries' peak years were 1973–5, during which they released three brilliant albums (*Fresh*, *Side 3* and *Starting Over*) and had several more hits ('I Wanna Be with You', 'Let's Pretend', 'Tonight', 'I'm a Rocker' and 'Overnight Sensation'). With each new release they became more adept at blending their influences into an overall sound as original and enduring as those they strove to emulate.

As they improved, however, they became less popular. Not until their final album, *Starting Over* (1975), did critics begin raving. Within months the group broke up. Carmen's solo album for Arista maintained the Raspberries' sound and included a 1976 US and UK Top 20 hit, 'All By Myself'.

RAVENS An important R&B vocal group of the early Fifties, the Ravens first came together in 1945 when Warren Suttles and Jimmy Ricks, waiters in a Harlem club, contacted Leonard Puzey and Ollie Jones through a booking agency. After recording for Hub, Jones was replaced by Maithe Marshall and the group appeared at the Apollo Theatre with Stan Kenton and **Nat Cole** in 1947, gaining an incredible reaction to their bass lead voice, Ricks. They signed with National and immediately hit the R&B chart with a distinctive revival of 'Old Man River' – bass lead, gentle harmony support and sparse rhythm accompaniment. The Ravens recorded prolifically, with various personnel changes, for Columbia, Okeh, Mercury, Jubilee and Argo until 1956.

Perhaps the best of the post-Ink Spots doo-wop groups, the Ravens

RAY, JAMES A black New Yorker (born in 1941) with a gospel music background, James Ray recorded for Galliant in 1959, and moved to Caprice, where he made the charts with the Rudy Clark songs 'If You Gotta Make a Fool of Somebody' (Number 22) and 'Itty Bitty Pieces' (Number 41), in 1961–2. Both records owed as much to Hutch Davies' scintillating band arrangements as to Ray's vocals, but the songs themselves – singalong R&B at its very best – abounded with catchy hooks. While Ray went on to make obscure discs for Congress Barr and Dynamic Sound, **Freddie and the Dreamers**' insipid version of 'If You Gotta Make a Fool of Somebody' reached Britain's Top 10 in 1963.

RAY, JOHNNIE One of the most popular white singers of the immediate pre-rock'n'roll era, Johnnie Ray was born on 10 January 1927, in Dallas, Oregon, of part Blackfoot tribe ancestry. Although partially deaf since the age of nine as the result of an accident, the need to use a hearing aid didn't inhibit his musical progress. For his first professional engagement, aged 15, he shared the billing with Jane Powell on a child talent radio show in Portland, Oregon. He headed for the West Coast two years later, finding work in Hollywood and Los Angeles, where he became a resident night-club pianist. Moving to Detroit in 1951, he was spotted singing at the Flame Club by DJ Robin Seymour, who persuaded Columbia to sign him. Placed on the newly re-activated R&B/pop Okeh label, his second release, 'Cry'/'The Little White Cloud That Cried' became a double-sided million seller, topping the American charts for 11 weeks in 1952. 'Cry', with simple rhythm accompaniment to Ray's dynamic, emotional vocal and subtle harmony support from the Four Lads topped the R&B chart. Not surprisingly, he was subsequently switched to Columbia and his follow-up, 'Here I Am Brokenhearted', also went gold, as did 'Just Walking in the Rain' in 1956, while he enjoyed numerous other hits to the end of the decade.

Johnnie's popularity increased through reaction to his emotionally histrionic stage act – he put so much feeling into the sad songs that he literally cried the words, being variously nicknamed the 'Nabob of Sob', 'Cry Guy', 'Prince of Wails', etc. Ray still records sporadically and tours regularly.

RCA RECORDS The Radio Corporation of America was formed in Camden, New Jersey, in 1901, and operated record labels under the Victor (Talking Machine Co) and Bluebird logos. Bluebird issued mainly 'race' and 'folk' music while RCA Victor issued popular material. By the Fifties, Perry Como headed the RCA roster but there was a strong interest in R&B and country music, fostered by **Chet Atkins** in Nashville and Steve Sholes, the Southern area representative. Sholes was promoted to head RCA's A&R department – after his signing of **Presley** proved a success – in place of Joe Carlton, who left in 1957 to join ABC. There he discovered **Jack Scott**, before setting up his own Carlton label with Scott and Anita Bryant as his major artists.

The country representation was headed by Eddy Arnold, Hank Snow and, later, **Jim Reeves**, while **Arthur Crudup** was most successful in the black market. The subsidiary label, Groove, formed in 1953, also carried strong R&B singers such as Varetta Dillard and Piano Red. Through 1951–2, RCA recorded **Little Richard** but the style he used then was big band R&B; and RCA's first *bona fide* rock singer did not appear until 1955. This, of course, was Elvis Presley, acquired from Sun in October for a then record fee of $35,000 – and a Cadillac for Presley himself – which turned out to be the best investment ever made in rock music. Earlier, Perry Como had covered R&B hits like 'Ko Ko Mo' for RCA, but Presley came through 1956 with monumental hits such as 'Heartbreak Hotel' and 'Hound Dog' and as a result RCA's interest in R&B and in remoulding crooners was ended – **Sam Cooke** and **Della Reese** being left in the hands of independent producers **Hugo and Luigi**. The company issued records by several other rock'n'rollers, such as Jean Chapel (also from Sun), Janis Martin, the Rhythm Rockers and Joe Clay (on the short-lived subsidiary, Vik). As rock'n'roll merged into 'pop' they developed a strong country-pop roster under Atkins, with Jim Reeves and **Don Gibson** among others, and achieved the occasional hit by lesser-known artists like **Mickey and Sylvia** with 'Love Is Strange'. Other successes came from **Harry Belafonte** and various soundtrack albums.

During the Sixties, RCA achieved greater sales than ever with Elvis Presley and continued to thrive in the rock, pop and country fields. As mainstream pop sounds softened in the early Sixties, RCA scored heavily with **Neil Sedaka**, and Chet Atkins added a stream of smooth Nashville country-pop product by Don Gibson ('Sea of Heartbreak'), **Skeeter Davis** ('End of the World'), Eddy Arnold ('Make the World Go Away') and Jim Reeves, around whose death RCA built a multi-million dollar legend. In the year of Reeves' death, 1964, country artist **Bobby Bare** had a pop hit with 'Detroit City', for by now RCA had developed a promotional organization that could maintain a country-music hit factory while also enabling a really successful country record to be crossed over into the pop market.

RCA was able to repeat this in the soul field with Sam Cooke and **Nina Simone**. In pop, they were supplied with a massive series of hits by **Don Kirshner**, who supervised records by

the **Monkees** and the Archies for RCA-distributed labels, plus hits by **Duane Eddy** and Little Peggy March. The company also entered uncertainly into the progressive rock market in the late Sixties, signing the **Jefferson Airplane** and the **Youngbloods**, although their grandiose 'Groupquake' marketing campaign to promote acts like Autosalvage was less successful. In Britain, their 'progressive' subsidiary, Neon, made little impact.

In the Seventies, the picture was similar: the company fired efficiently on all fronts, continuing to score well with Presley (and enjoying a big rise in sales when he died in 1977) and signing a handful of major acts (Daryl **Hall and** John **Oates**, **John Denver** and country singer Ronnie Milsap). It scored a notable coup in the early Eighties with the acquisition of **Diana Ross**, but perhaps the most notable feature of RCA output in the first half of the decade was the success of its subsidiaries, particularly Salsoul, Pablo and Planet.

RED BIRD RECORDS

Jerry **Leiber and** Mike **Stoller** formed Red Bird and its subsidiary Blue Cat in 1964, in an attempt to rectify the failure of their previous attempts at running their own label, Daisy and Tiger. They jointly owned the companies with veteran New York record man, **George Goldner**, who took care of the promotion side. Apart from blues singer Alvin Robinson, Leiber and Stoller took little interest in the creative end of Red Bird, leaving the songwriting and production to a younger generation of pop operators: **Jeff Barry** and **Ellie Greenwich**, Gerry Goffin and **Carole King**, **Barry Mann** and Cynthia Weil, Steve Venet, **George 'Shadow' Morton**, Artie Ripp and Joe Jones.

Red Bird was a tremendous success, with twenty-five Hot 100 hits in its two-year existence, beginning with 'Chapel of Love' by the **Dixie Cups** and 'Remember (Walking in the Sand)' by the **Shangri-Las**. Both groups had further hits, as did two more all-girl teams, the Butterflies (in fact Ellie Greenwich double-tracking) and the Jelly Beans. In the summer of 1965, there were two dance hits, 'The Boy from New York City' by the soulful Adlibs (Mary Ann Thomas, Hughie Harris, Danny Austin and David Watt) and 'New York's a Lonely Town' by the Tradewinds, a harmony surfing record by **Anders and Poncia**. By 1966, Leiber and Stoller were increasingly unhappy with their involvement with music they felt no sympathy for – Greenwich and Barry

had brought **Neil Diamond** to them, but they saw no potential in him – and withdrew from the company. Goldner was not capable of holding it together and, soon after, Red Bird ceased operations. See *also* **Leiber and Stoller**

REDBONE

An American Indian band from a Cheyenne reservation in Washington State, Redbone comprised Lolly Vegas (lead guitar, vocals), Tony Bellamy (rhythm guitar, vocals), Pat Vegas (bass guitar), and Peter DePoe (drums). They came together in Los Angeles in 1967, naming themselves after an anglicized Cajun epithet for half-breed, 'rehbone', and spent their early years travelling between migrant camps, picking crops and backing people like Odetta and **John Lee Hooker** on recording dates. They also wrote songs: the Vegas brothers composed 'Niki Hoeky', which **P. J. Proby** took to Number 23 in the US during 1967. The group was signed by Epic in 1969 and released their debut album, *Redbone*, a year later; probably their best remembered hit, 'Witch Queen of New Orleans' (Number 21 in the US and Number 2 in the UK) followed in 1971, after which they expanded their hybrid form of swamp-rock into a smooth Las Vegas-oriented sound over a succession of albums. Their biggest US hit was the million-selling 'Come and Get Your Love', a Number 5 in 1974. The group disbanded in 1979, after eight albums.

REDDING, OTIS

Born in Dawson, Georgia, on 9 September 1941, Otis Redding – the son of a Baptist minister – imbibed gospel influences in his earliest years, but grew up in the late Forties and early Fifties to the sound of R&B and jump-blues shouters. As a high-school student in Macon, Georgia, he was so impressed by the adulation showered upon local luminary **Little Richard**, whose style was also modelled around intense blues-shouters like **Roy Brown**, that he decided to become a full-time performer, having already established a reputation in local clubs as a talented musician.

The road to fame began when high-school friend Phil Walden, later to become his manager, booked the band with whom Redding was vocalist, for a college party. Through Walden he met another local band, Johnny Jenkins and the Pinetoppers, whom he joined as general assistant and sometime singer. This outfit gave Otis his recording debut when, as Otis and the Shooters, they recorded 'She's Alright', a mid-tempo Little Richard imitation featur-

Otis Redding's emotional live performances in front of a blasting horn section overwhelmed his soul-loving fans in the mid-Sixties

straining emotion but tending to verge on the histrionic.

His appearance at the Monterey Pop Festival in 1967 brought Redding massive acceptance by American rock fans, just as his European tour later that year enlarged his audience there – so much so that he was voted World No. 1 Male Singer by *Melody Maker* readers. His cult-like following was deeply shocked when, on 10 December 1967, his aircraft plunged to the bottom of the frozen Lake Monona, Wisconsin, killing Redding and several members of his Bar-Kays band. 'Dock of the Bay', a wistful, shuffling ballad, was a posthumous American chart-topper and million-seller a month later (his only Top 10 hit), reaching Number 3 in Britain. Later in 1968, Stax/Volt was sold to Gulf & Western, but the previous distributors, Atlantic, retained Redding's material and managed to gain chart hits with six further posthumous releases, but on songs like 'Hard to Handle', 'Day Tripper' and 'Love Man', his exaggerated delivery had become a self-parody, worlds away from the soulful simplicity of his first Volt hit. *See also* **Stax Records**

REDDY, HELEN Born in Melbourne, Australia, on 25 October 1942, Helen Reddy topped the American charts in 1972 with her own composition 'I Am Woman' which quickly became associated with the American women's liberation movement. She arrived in America in 1966 as a little-known Australian performer, but her career didn't pick up until her manager (and husband) Jerry Wald signed her to Capitol Records in the early Seventies. 'I Don't Know How to Love Him' from *Jesus Christ Superstar* gave her a US Top 20 hit in 1971 and then came 'I Am Woman' which inaugurated a series of Top 10 hits: 'Delta Dawn' (1973), 'Keep On Singing', 'You and Me Against the World' and another US Number 1, 'Angie Baby' (1974), also a British hit in 1975, 'Emotion' and 'Ain't No Way to Treat a Lady' (1975). Even more impressive than the number of her hits though, were their careful production, the range of material – which went from the chilling 'Angie Baby' to the cheerful 'Keep On Singing' – and her powerful evocative voice.

The host of US TV's *Midnight Special* for much of the Seventies, she starred in the Disney film *Pete's Dragon* in 1978. She moved to MCA in 1982, the same year in which Reddy and Wald were divorced. Her MCA albums *Imagination* (1983) and *Play Me Out* (1984) show a mature vocal talent.

ing reedy organ, in 1959, for the local Finer Arts label. The following year they tried again, this time billed as Otis Redding, with an even more frantic Richard soundalike, 'Shout Bamalama', on Confederate, which made a little more noise and was picked up for national release by the King subsidiary, Bethlehem. Meanwhile Johnny Jenkins was signed to Atlantic, and during 1962 was booked for a session at the Stax studios in Memphis. Otis drove the band to the studio that day, and with a little time left at the end of the session Jim Stewart was persuaded to record Otis singing one of his own songs. The song was 'These Arms of Mine', a tender blues ballad, which Stewart released on his new Volt label, and its sheer simplicity carried it into the lower reaches of the Hot 100 in 1963. His third release, 'Pain in My Heart', another poignant ballad, was a Hot 100 hit, and the following four years brought a succession of chart hits on Volt, all recorded in Memphis, including ballads like 'That's How

Strong My Love Is', 'I've Been Loving You Too Long', 'My Lover's Prayer' and 'Try a Little Tenderness'; and brassy, raunchy, up-tempo items like 'Mr Pitiful', 'Respect', 'Satisfaction' and 'Fa Fa Fa Fa Fa'. The biggest hit of this period was 'I've Been Loving You Too Long', an intense deep-soul ballad written by **Jerry Butler**, which reached Number 21 in 1965, but it was generally the up-tempo items which were more successful, though none rose higher than Number 29 ('Fa Fa Fa' in early 1967).

It is significant that Redding's somewhat gruff baritone voice seems to have been more acceptable on up-tempo material, carried by raunchy horn arrangements, than on ballads where the emotional intensity of his delivery was striking, yet his voice lacked depth. This is evident in his version of the **Temptations**' 'My Girl', which took him into the British Top 20 in 1966 – the poignant pitch of the original version is lost as he stretches for falsetto notes that aren't his to reach; instead he produces a sound of

REED, JERRY Country singer, song-writer and guitarist Jerry Reed was born Jerry Hubbard on 20 March 1937, in Atlanta, Georgia. He made his recording debut for Capitol in 1955, as a rockabilly guitarist, and wrote 'Crazy Legs' for his label-mate **Gene Vincent** in 1956. After Army service, he moved to Nashville and scored two minor country hits – 'Hully Gully Guitars' and 'Goodnight Irene' – before becoming a sought-after session musician under the guidance of **Chet Atkins**.

But it was as a songwriter that Reed's impact spread beyond country music. Two of Reed's songs were hits for **Elvis Presley** in 1968 – 'Guitar Man' and 'US Male'. Other much-recorded Reed songs include 'A Thing Called Love' and the boasting 'Tupelo Mississippi Flash'. That song and the tall tale of 'Amos Moses' represent the 'swamp-rock' side of Reed's somewhat erratic writing talent. His own albums for RCA have tended to include more than their fair share of dross as well as good songs, though *Me and Jerry* (1974) was an outstanding album of guitar duets with Atkins.

REED, JIMMY One of the greats in the field of R&B, Jimmy Reed was born Mathis James Reed in Dunleith, near Leland, Mississippi, on 6 September 1925. He learnt guitar from bluesman Eddie Taylor, who was to contribute much to Reed's infectious boogie-blues sound of later years. By the late Forties, Reed had settled in Chicago, where he became well known singing and playing electric guitar with a harmonica strapped to a harness. In 1953, he signed with Chicago-based Vee Jay Records, scoring his first R&B chart hit two years later with 'You Don't Have to Go'. Reed's biggest successes came during the rock'n'roll era, and included 'Ain't That Loving You Baby' and 'Honest I Do', which reached Number 32 on *Billboard*'s Hot 100.

Easily the most popular bluesman recording in Chicago, topping even **Muddy Waters**, Reed's earthy, down-home sound was immediately identifiable by his lazy, dragged-out vocals and fierce, high-register harp playing set against a heavy, almost absurdly uncomplicated back-beat. His accompanying musicians usually included Taylor on second guitar and drummer Earl Phillips. The hits kept coming, and in 1960 Reed was back in the Top 40 with 'Baby What You Want Me to Do'. A year later came 'Big Boss Man' and 'Bright Lights, Big City', while, in 1964, he even dented the British pop charts with 'Shame,

Shame, Shame'. Over a twelve-year period, Reed notched up twenty-two chart entries, mostly for Vee Jay. His style influenced many blues artists in the Sixties, including **Slim Harpo**, **Tommy Tucker** and various British rock bands of the Sixties, especially the **Rolling Stones**, who featured his 'Honest I Do' on their first album. Other artists to cover Reed songs include **Elvis Presley** ('Big Boss Man'), **Pretty Things** ('Big Boss Man') and the **Animals** and **Them** ('Bright Lights, Big City'). He died in California on 29 August 1976.

Lou Reed, tense, mean and moody

REED, LOU One of the forces behind perhaps the most persistently influential American band of the late Sixties, the **Velvet Underground**, Lou Reed was born on Long Island, New York, on 2 March 1943. He led his first punk-rock bands (Pasha and the Prophets, LA and the Eldorados) at high school and attended Syracuse University, but dropped out and dabbled in courses in journalism and acting. Reed finally integrated these talents into the Velvet Underground.

After writing all the group's material, Reed quit in the summer of 1970. His first solo album, *Lou Reed* (RCA, 1972), contained some strong songs but was weakened by the inept production work of Reed and Richard Robinson. His next album, *Transformer* (1973), lived up to its title: produced by **David Bowie** and **Mick Ronson** just when Bowie was most in the media spotlight,

the association gave Reed the publicity he needed, while Ronson's string arrangement made 'Walk on the Wild Side' (an account of Warhol's Factory clan of freaks) into a classic single and a surprise hit: after eight years in the music business, it became Lou Reed's first hit single (Number 16 in the US, Number 10 in the UK) in 1973.

Berlin (1973), though not as commercially successful as *Transformer*, contained Reed's most compelling and disturbing work since the Velvet Underground: a cycle of songs about a sado-masochistic relationship which culminates in the woman committing suicide and the man wondering where his feelings went. Supported by an all-star cast of musicians, and Bob Ezrin's subtle production, Reed contributed some of the best vocals of his career and songs which were both understated and paralysingly bleak. His live album, *Rock'n'Roll Animal* (1974), combined Velvet Underground with ornate **Allman Brothers**-style guitar work, an unexpected but pleasant achievement. By contrast, his double album of electronic music, *Metal Machine Music* (1975), was widely regarded as the worst album ever made by a major recording artist.

His last four albums of the Seventies – *Rock'n'Roll Heart* (1976), *Street Hassle*, *Live – Take No Prisoners* (both 1978), and the embarrassing *The Bells* (1979) – all exhibited a distinct loss of power, while Reed's once-incisive voice became increasingly quavering until he seemed to be singing permanently through a tremelo unit. Reed seemed doomed to live out his own legend until, quite unexpectedly, he fell in love. Marrying for the second time in 1980, he responded with the album *Growing Up in Public*, on which he seemed to confront the demons that had been festering in his head for so long. All the music on the set was written and arranged by Reed's long-time keyboards player Michael Fonfara, leaving him free to concentrate on his lyric-writing and singing.

His next release, *The Blue Mask* (1981), was different again, marking a return to more sinister preoccupations. Phantoms that crowd into the head of a child lying awake at night, muggers, rapists, the spectre of alcoholism and a fear for the world's future all came flooding out into the new songs. *Legendary Hearts* followed in 1983, and songs like the harrowing 'The Last Shot' and the scathing 'Bottoming Out' showed him once again in good writing form. *Mistrial* was released in 1986. *See also* the **Velvet Underground**

REESE, DELLA Among the few black woman singers to make an impact on the pop charts in the Fifties, Della Reese was born Dellareese Taliafano on 6 July 1932. She began as a gospel singer, at first with **Mahalia Jackson**'s troupe and later with the Clara Ward Singers. On signing with Jubilee in 1957, she moved into the pop field. Her biggest US hit came in 1959, with 'Don't You Know', which climbed to Number 2 on RCA. Later records were on ABC and Avco.

REEVES, JIM The death of country singer Jim Reeves in a plane crash in Tennessee on 31 July 1964 resulted in the growth of a dedicated 'cult' following. His influence in spreading pop-country music internationally has been considerable. Reeves, nevertheless, came from a pure C&W background. Born on 20 August 1923, in Galloway, Texas, he became a pro baseball player and then a radio station manager before succeeding as a country singer. He recorded locally for Macy's Records, in 1949, and Abbott, in 1952, achieving success with 'Mexican Joe'. On joining RCA, his already smoother-than-usual vocal style was moulded into the 'Nashville Sound', blending with lyrical pop instrumentation and vocal choruses. His C&W roots were maintained only marginally in such giant hits as 'Four Walls', 'He'll Have to Go' and 'Distant Drums'. The year he died, he starred in the Embassy movie *Kimberley Jim*.

REGGAE A musical form that developed in the Sixties, reggae grew out of rocksteady; which grew out of ska; which, in turn, had roots in secular African/Caribbean musical traditions (*calypso*, *mento*), sacred revivalism and American – particularly New Orleans – R&B. At the same time the emergence of black pride was intrinsic to the music's subsequent development. Ska had been easily absorbed, even touted as a tourist attraction by the Jamaican establishment; rocksteady, however, could not be easily assimilated and remained the property of the aristocratic rudie; reggae declared its autonomy and became the music of struggle. One reason for this was the hitherto dormant Rastafarianism – a general term describing divergent, back-to-Africa cults, peculiar to Jamaica, of a millennarian nature. The Rastafarians saw Ethiopia as Zion and Haile Selassie (Ras Tafari) as the 'Living God'. But even whilst espousing Rasta (Rastafarianism) in songs like the Ethiopians' 'The Selah', the Charmers' 'Rasta Never Fails' and

Prince Jazzbo's 'Step Forward Youth', reggae retained its own particular dynamism.

By the Seventies, reggae had diversified considerably, encompassing rebel music from Junior Byles ('Beat Down Babylon'), Max Romeo, the Wailers; fervid, melodic piety from the Melodians ('Rivers of Babylon') and **Toots and the Maytals**; pop-reggae from the Pioneers and Greyhound; sentimental vocalists John Holt, Pat Kelly, the late Slim Smith; *sufferers* like Errol Dunkley, Delroy Wilson, **Dennis Brown**, etc.

Steel Pulse, Birmingham black sound

Producers were essential to the Jamaican music industry. Men like Duke Reid and Coxsone Dodd pioneered ska and the producers who monopolized Seventies reggae – Niney, **Lee Perry**, Bunnie Lee, Lloyd Clarke, Rupie Edwards (who had a British hit 'Ire Feelings' in 1975) and Clement Bushay, were as relevant as the artists they engineered. Dramatic vocals and instrumentation embellished clean, hard rhythms, emphasizing reggae's

inherent *dread* quality.

In this spirit, the talk-over, originated by sound-system DJs, was effected. Talk-over was eulogy – brotherhood, love, or merely self-advertisement – to a *skank* rhythm. Popularized by U Roy around 1970 ('Rule the Nation', 'Scandal'), the trend peaked during 1972–3 with, among others, Dennis Alcapone, I Roy and Scotty consistently scoring. **Big Youth** (Augustus Buchanan) usurped U Roy with singles ('Ace 90', 'Foreman v Frazier') and albums (*Chi Chi Run*, *Dread Locks Dread*). Prince Jazzbo, Jah Woosh, Topper Zukie, Jah Lloyd and Jah Ali were later exponents of the genre.

The talk-over engendered 'dub': backing tracks reduced to bass and drums, punctuated with the occasional, arbitrary vocal or guitar riff to make things interesting. Feedback extravaganzas, dubs were ideal DJ fodder and in vogue in 1975 with albums from **Keith Hudson** and Aston Barrett (*Pick a Dub*) and Rupie Edwards' *Dub Basket* amongst others. Augustus Pablo, who laid wistful melodic passages over throbbing dub ('Tales of Pablo') was particularly popular. 1974–5 also brought a new breed of rasta 'prophet': Johnnie Clarke ('Move out a Babylon'), Cornell Campbell ('Gorgon'), Sang Hugh ('No Potion a Gal') and, most auspiciously, **Burning Spear** (Winston Rodney) who led a trio of the same name and sang, with acute conviction, songs endemic to the Jamaican experience: 'Zion Higher', 'Marcus Garvey' and 'Slavery Days'.

In Britain, the sound systems of Duke Reid, Sir Coxsone, Count Shelley in London, and Duke Neville in Birmingham, provided the West Indians with their only escape, the church apart, from a hostile white society. Its popularity in the black clubs often ensured the music's subsequent British release. The metamorphosis of rocksteady into reggae had alienated the music's small white audience – the skinheads. As reggae preoccupations moved from the speedy and aggressive to the stoned and peaceful, they drifted away. The skinheads' brief patronage had been responsible for reggae's early appearances in the British charts, including Dave and Ansell Collins' 'Double Barrel' – Number 1 in 1970 – and 'Monkey Spanner'; Horace Faith's 'Black Pearl'; Harry J's 'Liquidator' and the Pioneers' 'Let Your Yeah Be Yeah'.

Following the demise of ska labels like Bluebeat, Rio and R&B, and with Island wooing the rock market, Trojan Records led the way in the late Sixties.

The label's commercial middle-of-the-road music appealed to pop tastes and the company established itself as the largest reggae outlet in Britain. Rivals included Pama, who hit with Max Romeo's 'Wet Dream' in 1969 (despite a BBC ban) and Creole. By 1975, dozens had surfaced, each situated in concentrated immigrant areas. Count Shelley, Lord Koos – both owned by British resident Sound System operators – Atra, Magnet, Ethnic and Dip were among those that established themselves. Attempts by the major companies to corner this market, EMI's subsidiary Rhino, for instance, made little impact on the reggae scene despite their occasional hits.

During the second half of the Seventies, however, the picture began to change. Island's success with **Bob Marley and the Wailers** brought new credibility to reggae in rock circles, and **Eric Clapton**'s covers of Marley material like 'I Shot the Sheriff' (1974) rendered the appropriation of reggae rhythms and the use of Jamaican musicians and producers newly fashionable. Reggae nevertheless continued to be identified as a rebel music, and in this respect it had a natural affinity with punk rock: the hippest punks declared that reggae was the only music to which they listened, and one of London's Roxy club's key attractions was Rastafarian disc jockey Don Letts, who played imported reggae discs between sets. Perhaps more significant was the emergence, in the late Seventies, of a number of home-grown British reggae bands – **Aswad**, Misty in Roots, **Black Slate**, Steel Pulse – who performed alongside punk bands in the many Rock Against Racism (RAR) benefit concerts – concerts from which bands like the **Specials** in Coventry and the **Beat** in Birmingham drew particular inspiration. With multi-racial line-ups and a musical philosophy born of punk and Jamaican ska and reggae, such bands personified the RAR ideal and became the major focus in British rock – especially after the launch of the 2-Tone label – between 1979 and 1982.

The other side of the UK reggae coin was lovers' rock. Sound systems still provided the main sources of musical entertainment in the black community, and lovers' rock was strictly studio music made for the party of the dance hall. Key roles in the development in this softer side of the music were played by **Matumbi** and particularly their guitarist, **Dennis Bovell**. Although artists like Jean Adebambo and Carrol Tompson remained cult names, one-off pop successes like Janet Kay's 'Silly Games' (a Number 2 pop hit in 1979) or Sugar Minott's 'Good Thing Going' (a Number 4 in 1981) proved the size of lovers' rock's potential audience.

By the Eighties, Britain had a flourishing reggae scene serviced by innumerable independent labels based in urban areas, though the impact of the music on the national charts was still patchy. The reggae influence had nevertheless become prevalent within white rock – as the success of **Culture Club**, **Scritti Politti**, the **Police** and numerous other acts showed – and it was clear that in some quarters UK-made reggae was taking on a distinctly political edge (not necessarily linked to Rastafarianism) in response to the wave of street disturbances and deteriorating relationships between black communities and the police that were a fact of early Eighties life. Alongside the development of rapping and 'toasting' techniques (the latter exemplified by disc jockeys/masters of ceremonies Tippa Irie and Smiley Culture) and the increased profile for reggae music due to the proliferation of black-oriented pirate radio stations, this trend was perhaps the most notable feature of mid-Eighties British reggae. *See also* **Lovers rock**

R.E.M. Among the leaders of a new generation of American guitar bands that mushroomed in the Eighties, R.E.M. took the **Byrds**' jangly guitar sound and gave it a tough, contemporary feel. Formed in Athens, Georgia, by Michael Stipe (vocals), Peter Buck (guitar), Mike Mills (bass) and Bill Berry (drums) in 1980, R.E.M. came to the attention of Miles Copeland, manager of the **Police** and owner of the label IRS, via his brother Ian, a tour promoter in the US. The group quickly became a favourite band with the critics and the albums *Chronic Town* (1982), and *Murmur* (1983), did the groundwork for *Reckoning* (1984) to reside in the US LP chart for over a year. *Fables of the Reconstruction* (1985) followed it into the charts.

RENAISSANCE Originally formed by ex-**Yardbirds** Keith Relf and Jim McCarty as a progressive folk-rock band, Renaissance became a force on Britain's campus circuit during the Seventies without ever quite making it into the major league of UK bands. Joining Relf and McCarty in the first line-up were Jane Relf, Keith's sister, on vocals and former **Nashville Teens** keyboard player John Hawken, and they made their debut in 1969 with the album *Renaissance* (Island). By 1972, the group's personnel had completely changed, with Rob Hendry (guitar), Jon Camp (bass), John Tout (keyboards) and Terry Sullivan (percussion) now playing behind the distinctive lead vocal of Annie Haslam. Hendry left after *Prologue* (1972) and was replaced by Michael Dunford, who had hitherto composed most of the band's music to lyrics by Betty Thatcher. They built up a cult following in the US and recorded steadily through the Seventies, even reaching the UK chart on one occasion – with 'Northern Lights' (Warner Brothers) in 1978. In the mid-Eighties, Renaissance was still a working entity. Representative albums include *Ashes Are Burning* (1973), *Turn of the Cards* (Sire, 1974), *Scheherazade and Other Stories* (1975), *Novella* (1977) and *Camera Camera* (1981).

REO SPEEDWAGON Yet another US FM rock band who muster enormous domestic sales but find difficulty sustaining a high profile in the charts elsewhere, REO Speedwagon were formed in Champaign, Illinois, in 1968. Made up of Kevin Cronin (vocals), Gary Richrath (guitar), Neil Doughty (keyboards), Alan Gratzer (drums) and Bruce Hall (bass), the group gigged constantly and slowly built up a strong following in the Midwest, but it wasn't until 1977, after six albums, that the band began to find success on a national level.

At this time, Cronin and Richrath decided to take on the producer's role, and their first self-produced album, the live set *You Get What You Play For*, became their first gold record, quickly followed by platinum in 1978 with *You Can Tune a Piano But You Can't Tuna Fish* and their first US Top 40 single, 'Roll with the Changes'.

The group graduated to large stadium status, filling huge venues coast to coast, and selling an enormous number of records, their popularity growing steadily until 1981 and the release of *Hi Infidelity*. The album stayed at Number 1 for nearly five months and yielded two huge hit singles, a Number 1 with 'Keep On Loving You' (also their biggest UK hit) and a Number 5 with 'Take It on the Run'. That year they sold 18 million records worldwide. Subsequent releases failed to make such an impression in world terms but the band managed to maintain their domestic popularity.

REPARATA AND THE DELRONS One of the many groups who produced one classic record during the 1962–5 'girl group era',

Reparata and the Delrons had their moment of glory with 'Whenever a Teenager Cries' (World Artists, 1965). Despite a number of fine follow-ups, particularly 'I'm Nobody's Baby Now' (RCA, 1966), the group had no more hits in America, though 'Captain of Your Ship' (Bell) was a British Top 20 hit in 1968. Reparata has, none the less, continued recording through the years. The Delrons were Mary Aiese, Lorraine Mazzola (who sang lead on 'Captain of Your Ship') and Nanette Licars.

REPRISE RECORDS After his contract with Capitol Records expired, Frank Sinatra formed Reprise Records in 1960. Sinatra headed the company and appointed Mo Ostin, a former Verve Records accountant, as Executive Vice-President, to run it. The first Reprise single was 'Second Time Around' by Sinatra, released February 1961; the first album was Sinatra's *Ring-a-Ding-Ding!* Into the Reprise fold, attracted by Sinatra, came many showbiz world friends: Sammy Davis was the first to join, followed by Dean Martin and Bing Crosby.

In June 1963, negotiations between Sinatra and Warner Brothers' film division began – Sinatra was hot property in film terms, and Jack Warner wanted to sign him up for four films. Sinatra's terms were that Warners should buy Reprise. Capitol, Sinatra's former label, had reissued his albums at cut-price, affecting his Reprise product, and there was a lawsuit between Sinatra and Capitol, later settled out of court. It was a large headache. Reprise was $2 million in debt and Sinatra wanted out. He retained a one-third interest in Warner-Reprise: Warner Brothers bought two-thirds for $2 million and a four picture deal. A month later, Reprise scored its first hit single – Lou Monte singing 'Pepino the Italian Mouse'. Then **Trini Lopez**'s 'If I Had a Hammer' was a hit, and Reprise moved into Warners' Burbank office in February 1964. Albums by comedian Allan Sherman and singer **Freddy Cannon** were subsequently released. In late 1964, Reprise aquired Petula Clark, **Sandie Shaw** and the **Kinks** from Pye records in Britain. Clark's 'Downtown' gave the label its first gold disc in March 1965.

Even bigger hits followed in 1966 – Nancy Sinatra's 'These Boots Are Made for Walking' became the company's best-selling single ever, Sinatra's own 'Strangers in the Night' went to Number 1 on both sides of the Atlantic, and Petula Clark's run of hits continued. In 1967, Reprise signed **Jimi Hendrix**, whose every release was to achieve

gold disc status. That same year, the label signed **Randy Newman**, **Arlo Guthrie** and **Joni Mitchell**, and other acts secured by the end of the decade included **Neil Young**, **Ry Cooder**, **Gordon Lightfoot** and the **Beach Boys**. When Warner Brothers was itself taken over by the Kinney Corporation, Reprise became one part of Warner Communications Incorporated and continued to find and nurture new talent – especially in the singer/songwriter field – throughout the Seventies.

RESIDENTS Simply the weirdest pop group in recorded history, the Residents were allegedly formed in Carolina in 1966. They adopted the name the Residents in 1970, inspired by the address-label on a demo tape sent to Warner Brothers and returned to its anonymous originators.

They began their career and continue to operate under a cloak of 'total obscurity', having developed a detailed mythology of aliases, front organizations and mystery personalities. Records were first advertised alongside 3-D glasses and Grow-Your-Own-Pet-Monkeys in cartoon comics. In their rare live performances, the band members were bandaged like mummies, dressed as large vegetables and, most famously, decked out in top hats and tails, wearing giant eyeball masks.

Persistent investigators have gone to great lengths to expose them, gatecrashing their San Francisco studios and publishing photographs of alleged 'members', but the band's campaign of secrecy is quite harmless except that it actually obscures considerable musical talent. Responsible for some twenty albums – *Third Reich-'n'Roll* (1975), a mischievous assault on numerous chart classics, being the most famous – they mix playful avant-garde exploration with mutant pop, all manner of ethnic musical styles and eccentric obsessions (such as classical composer Charles Ives, jazz bandleader Stan Kenton) in what has become a 'spot the reference' game between band and fans. Despite two world tours in the early 1980s, the group continue to work apparently undetected, in a San Francisco suburb.

REVERE, PAUL, AND THE RAIDERS Originally known as the Downbeats, Paul Revere and the Raiders hailed from Portland, Oregon, and built up a strong high school and college following on the North-west circuit on the strength of 'Like Long Hair', their progressively titled first hit. Disc jockey Roger Hart gave them their

next break, financing a tape that won them a Columbia Records contract. The result was a raunchy version of 'Louie Louie', but another local group, the Kingsmen, got in first with the hit. In 1965 'Steppin' Out' gave them their first national Top 50 hit; then **Dick Clark** signed the group for the weekly rock show *Where the Action Is*. It turned them, overnight, into the most heavily exposed group in the country and their well-rehearsed, slick stage act, eighteenth-century costume of jackets and tights, and comedy routines won over a vast audience. It also killed their underground appeal as they consistently put out Top 10 hits over the next two years – 'Kicks', 'Good Thing', 'Just Like Me', etc., many of which, usually recorded by Bruce Johnston or **Terry Melcher** in single studio visits and in only one or two takes, still hold up as instant pop classics. The original group were Mark Lindsay, lead vocals (born 9 March 1942); Paul Revere, piano, organ (born 1942); Drake Levin, guitar; Michael Smith, drums and Philip Volk, bass. Soon, however, they grew unhappy with the fantasy world of *Where the Action Is*. The resulting personnel shake-ups left Lindsay and Revere with the group's name, after the others formed the spin-off band, Brotherhood. Jim Valley, guitar (later replaced by Freddy Weller, born 9 September 1947); Joe Correro Jr., drums (19 November 1946) and Charlie Coe, bass (19 November 1944) were brought into the group who, by 1968, were just the Raiders. Their later material had a more pop amorphous sound which gave them their only Number 1, **John D. Loudermilk**'s 'Indian Reservation', in 1971. They were far less at home than in the punk metier of *Just Like Us* or *Greatest Hits*, which included their single, 'The Great Airplane Strike', from their best album, *Spirit Of '67*. In 1969, Lindsay launched himself on a parallel solo career with a string of hits beginning with the Top 10 'Arizona' in 1971 on Columbia. He also produced the later records by the group.

RICH, CHARLIE Although his style was not markedly different from that of previous decades, Charlie Rich was *the* country-pop superstar of the early Seventies.

Born 14 December 1932 in Colt, Arkansas, Rich grew up with an equal access to classical, blues and country music influences. By the time he was drafted into the Air Force he was playing jazz saxophone and piano and had married a jazz singer. By 1957 he was a staff composer, demo singer and arranger for the rock'n'roll and country stars of the Sun label in Memphis. His early songs 'Breakup' and 'It Hurts Me So' were recorded by **Jerry Lee Lewis**, and 'The Ways of a Woman in Love' and 'Thanks a Lot' by **Johnny Cash**.

In 1960, **Elvis Presley** recorded Rich's 'I'm Comin' Home' and Rich reached the Top 30 with 'Lonely Weekends'. By now a singer/pianist, he began to alternate between soul-blues and country music. Leaving Sun and Phillips International, he moved to Groove/RCA to work with producers **Bill Justis** and **Chet Atkins** and to move towards country. In the mid-Sixties he moved to Smash and recorded R&B for **Shelby Singleton**, coming up with a Top 20 hit 'Mohair Sam' in 1965. After a year with Hi Records in 1967, Rich settled for **Billy Sherrill**'s Epic label country sound and he expanded his country – and cult – following with a huge hit in 1973 with 'Behind Closed Doors'. Other hits – 'The Most Beautiful Girl in the World', 'There Won't Be Anymore' and 'A Very Special Love Song' – followed throughout the world.

The Sherrill sound was saccharine enough to move Rich into the international MOR market, and perhaps to widen the appeal of music based heavily in country and blues, elements which Rich retained strongly in his own voice and piano style.

RICHARD, CLIFF

The most enduringly successful performer in British pop, Cliff Richard was born Harry Rodger Webb in Lucknow, India, on 14 October 1940, and came to Britain with his family at the age of eight. After settling in Cheshunt, Hertfordshire, the young Webb went to Cheshunt Secondary Modern School where he sang with a vocal group called the Quintones – two boys and three girls. In 1957, Webb saw **Bill Haley** when he played at Edmonton, London, and after leaving school he joined a skiffle group run by Dick Teague.

Webb's ambition to form his own rock'n'roll group led him to leave the Dick Teague Skiffle Group, taking with him his neighbour and the group's drummer, Terry Smart. While with Dick Teague, Webb had picked up a little guitar playing and with Smart on drums and another local boy, Ken Pavey, on guitar, he started the Drifters. The group became quite popular around their home town and occasionally played at the legendary 2 I's coffee bar in Soho, London. While playing there one night they met up with guitarist Ian 'Sammy' Samwell, who joined the group. As bookings became more

Cliff fronts the Shadows, with his debt to Presley much in evidence

regular and Webb concentrated on singing, a change of name for the group seemed desirable. John Foster, who acted as a booking agent for London gigs suggested that Harry Webb become Cliff Richard and the group was billed from then on as Cliff Richard and the Drifters. A performance at a Carroll Levis audition led to the group's being taken up by agent George Ganjou.

Ganjou booked them into Butlin's Holiday Camp and arranged for a demo disc ('Breathless' b/w 'Lawdy Miss Clawdy') to be sent to Norrie Paramor, label manager at EMI's Columbia label. Paramor recorded the group doing a cover of Bobby Helms' 'Schoolboy Crush'. The B-side was an up-tempo number written by Ian Samwell, called 'Move It'. The publisher of 'Schoolboy

Crush' took the record to **Jack Good** who was preparing his *Oh Boy!* TV show and Good decided to use the group, but insisted that Richard abandon his sub-**Presley** image – shaving his sideburns and getting rid of the guitar he carried but rarely played. On 15 September 1958, Cliff Richard and the Drifters made their first appearance on *Oh Boy!* and two weeks later 'Move It', now the A-side, entered the British charts, and eventually made Number 2.

By 1959, the line-up of the Shadows – the Drifters changed their name to avoid conflict with the American vocal group – had altered to become Bruce Welch (rhythm guitar), Jet Harris (bass), Tony Meehan (drums) and Hank B. Marvin (lead guitar), Samwell having left to concentrate on writing and (later) production.

From the start, Richard was compared to Presley, and while the comparisons were invidious, Richard's early records were genuinely exciting: 'Move It', 'High Class Baby' and his first album, *Cliff* (recorded in a studio in front of an audience) showed that unlike, say, **Tommy Steele**, Richard understood rock'n'roll. In 1959, he was given a supporting role in the film *Serious Charge*, singing three numbers. One of the songs from the film, 'Living Doll' (written by Lionel Bart), was released as a single. A medium tempo number in an almost country vein, it became a million-seller, reaching Number 1 in Britain and Number 30 in America.

In 1960, he toured America with little impact and appeared in the film *Expresso Bongo*, in a major role, and subsequently in his own star vehicles, *The Young Ones* (1961) and *Summer Holiday* (1961). Richard topped polls as the best British male singer from 1959 to 1965, and withstood the onslaught of Beatlemania very effectively, though his announcement of his conversion to Christianity in 1967 and subsequent association with the Festival of Light made him a deeply unfashionable figure in rock circles. He represented Britain in the Eurovision Song Contests of 1968 and 1973, coming second on both occasions, made a number of Royal Variety appearances, had his own long-running television series and continued to have hits – although his career hit a low point in 1975, the first year in which he failed to register a single UK chart placing.

In 1976, however, he began a remarkable chart renaissance with 'Devil Woman', the closest he had come to recording a true rock number for years. His new production mentor – in the absence of Norrie Paramor, who retired as his producer in 1973 – was Bruce Welch, who also took the credit for the *I'm Nearly Famous* album (1976); critical opinion was favourable towards his new direction and **Elton John** was so taken with 'the new Cliff' that he organized the release of Richard's singles in the US through his own company, Rocket. 'Devil Woman' reached Number 6 in the US and finally established him there as a name artist. Final confirmation of the wisdom of Cliff's change of direction – which he attributed to becoming much more involved in the recording process, whereas previously he had tended just to record material over pre-recorded backing tracks – came with the Number 1 UK success of 'We Don't Talk Anymore', in 1979.

Cliff began the Eighties with a run of UK chart hits – 'Carrie', 'Dreamin'' (1980), 'A Little in Love', 'Wired for Sound' and 'Daddy's Home' (all 1981) among them – and in 1986 was back at Number 1 in the UK once more, with a remake (in aid of Comic Relief) of 'Living Doll', on which he was joined by the Young Ones comedy team.

RICHIE, LIONEL See the Commodores

RICHMAN, JONATHAN, AND THE MODERN LOVERS One of rock's great eccentrics, Jonathan Richman (born May 1951 in Boston) built up a cult following with simple, joyful rock'n'roll songs instilling the often bizarre material (from wacky, teen romance songs to 'I'm a Little Aeroplane') with a disarming boyish charm.

The early Modern Lovers (Richman's band) were inspired by the **Velvet Underground** and performed on the East Coast in the early Seventies, gaining most recognition for the chugalong road song 'Roadrunner'. By the release of the first album, *Jonathan Richman and the Modern Lovers* (1977), Richman's songs had lightened appreciably in tone. 'Egyptian Reggae', a camp instrumental that was an unlikely hit across Europe (UK Number 5 in 1977) gave Richman a sizeable following but also provided him with a credibility problem and a barrier to large-scale success since it had given him the reputation of a novelty act, something he never fully lived down. Over a series of broadly similar albums up to *It's Time for Jonathan Richman and the Modern Lovers* (1985) Richman did well in Europe and consistently reaped favourable reviews, but in his native America he remained virtually undiscovered.

RIGHTEOUS BROTHERS
Vocalists Bill Medley (born 19 September 1940, in Los Angeles), and Bobby Hatfield (10 August 1940 at Beaver Dam, Wisconsin) – the Righteous Brothers – were not related, but got their name from the patrons of the Black Derby, a small club in Santa Ana, California, where they played a six-month engagement in 1962 and whose patronage was about 25 per cent black. In 1963, they began recording for the small Moonglow label in Hollywood and had a small hit that year with 'Little Latin Lupe Lu' penned by Medley who had earlier recorded with a group called the Paramours.

Although they grew steadily popular in southern California, they did not break nationally until **Jack Good** heard them at Hollywood's Purple Onion Club and signed them to appear on *Shindig*, one of several dance-oriented TV rock shows which dominated American pop between 1964 and 1966. Through *Shindig*, the duo quickly reached a national audience of white teenagers, at the same time retaining a significant following amongst their black fans.

At this point **Phil Spector** stepped in and offered to record them, providing that Moonglow would permit him to release their records on his label in certain territories, notably America and Britain. Spector produced 'You've Lost That Lovin' Feelin'', which topped charts internationally in 1965 and is considered by some to be his greatest production. There followed a samey sequel, 'Just Once in My Life' (Number 9 in America) and big-selling revivals of 'Ebb Tide' and 'Unchained Melody'. By late 1965, however, Medley and Hatfield had grown restless with Spector. In 1966, they broke their contract to record the Spectoresque '(You're My) Soul and Inspiration' for Verve which topped the American charts, but they could not sustain their impetus for more than two records.

In 1968, they parted company; Medley recorded solo while Hatfield recorded solo and with new partner, Jimmy Walker. However neither achieved any notable success. In 1974, Medley and Hatfield reunited and scored American Top 10 hits on Haven with the death-disc 'Rock'n'Roll Heaven' and its follow-up, 'Give It to the People'. In 1982, Medley released the solo effort *Right Here and Now* (Planet). The 'brothers' still get together to perform occasionally, though it would seem that their partnership is unlikely to be permanent. See *also* **Phil Spector**

RILEY, BILLY LEE Launched by Sun Records in 1957 as a successor to Elvis Presley, Billy (later Billy Lee) Riley was a talented multi-instrumentalist who recorded vocal and instrumental discs in virtually every rock style related to country and blues. A prolific sessionman in Nashville, Memphis and Hollywood, he was born on 5 October 1933, in Pocohontas, Arkansas, and left Sun in 1960 to form a label, Rita, which had several hits. He recorded country for Sun, Mojo, Pen, Hip, Entrance; backwoods blues for Rita; R&B for Dodge, Checker and Hip; rock for Brunswick and Home of the Blues; and soul for Smash, Fire, Fury, Mojo and Myrl. His most successful rock recordings were 'Red Hot' and 'Flying Saucers Rock'n'Roll' for Sun (both had **Jerry Lee Lewis** on piano), and the latter title inspired Riley to form for a short while a backing band called the Little Green Men: this group was basically the Sun house band which comprised Riley (guitar, bass), Roland Janes (guitar, bass) and James Van Eaton (drums). Although he is now largely inactive on the music scene in the US, he still tours occasionally in the UK and Europe.

RILEY, JEANNIE C. A native of Anson, Texas, who moved to Nashville as a secretary-cum-hopeful singer, Jeannie C. Riley (born 19 October 1945) had the rare distinction for a country singer of becoming a worldwide pop star at the same time as she first topped the country charts in 1968 with 'Harper Valley PTA'. It launched Jeannie C., the song's writer **Tom T. Hall**, and also **Shelby Singleton**'s Plantation label. The campaigning, liberated young mother in the song was an image the media propagated to such an extent that it could not be erased by other, different, hits for Plantation, Capitol and MGM. Despite fine country recordings like 'The Girl Most Likely', 'Back Side of Dallas' and 'Houston Blues', her record sales declined in the Seventies.

RIP, RIG + PANIC See the **Pop Group**

RIPERTON, MINNIE Born in Chicago on 8 November 1947, Minnie Riperton had, reputedly, the largest vocal range in rock – her voice spanned five octaves. Her first records were with the Gems, a Chess Records session vocal group. In 1966 she cut some unsuccessful solo records as Andrea Davis before joining Rotary Connection, a racially mixed progressive group created by Chess.

From 1968, Riperton sang on six Rotary Connection albums. When the group dissolved, she cut a solo record (*Come into My Garden*) produced by her husband Richard Rudolph. Next she moved to Epic where 'El Toro Negro' (alias Stevie Wonder) produced a well-received album, *Perfect Angel* (1974), which included the trans-atlantic hit 'Lovin' You'. *Adventures In Paradise* (1975) was less interesting, but only two more albums followed – *Stay in Love* (Epic, 1977) and *Minnie* (Capitol, 1979) – before her death from cancer on 12 July 1979.

RIVERS, JOHNNY American pop singer Johnny Rivers had US Top 40 hits in a three-year spell in the mid-Sixties. He was born John Ramistella on 7 November 1942, in New York City. The name change came after he began playing in a high-school band and was at the suggestion of **Alan Freed**, who also secured him his first recording contract with Gone.

His big break came when he discovered a successful format of live performance at the Whisky A Go-Go in Los Angeles. Since 1963, Rivers has sold over twenty million records, and has had more than twenty chart entries, notably 'Memphis', 'Mountain of Love' (1964), 'Seventh Son' (1965), 'Secret Agent Man' and the chart-topping 'Poor Side of Town' (1966), 'Baby I Need Your Lovin'' and 'Tracks of My Tears' (1967), all of which were Top 10 records on Imperial.

At the end of the Sixties, Rivers formed his own label, Soul City, and the first signings to the label were the **Fifth Dimension**, who immediately won several gold records. The combination of the production of Johnny Rivers and Bones Howe, the harmonies of the Fifth Dimension, and the songs of the then little-known **Jimmy Webb**, became an almost unassailable force during the first few years of Soul City's existence, but when the group left the label, Rivers returned to serious record-making on his own account on UA. The hand-clapping disco format was abandoned and was replaced by the backing of a studio band comprising the best Hollywood session men, and several successful albums and singles resulted. In the mid-Seventies he succeeded in persuading Brian Wilson to return to the studios, if only to add distinctive back-up vocals to Rivers' own version of the **Beach Boys**' 'Help Me Rhonda' (Epic). A change of label (to Big Tree) in 1977 brought him his first Top 10 hit for five years, with 'Swayin' to the Music (Slow Dancin')'.

RIVINGTONS With 'Papa-Oom-Mow-Mow', the craziest of all novelty vocal group records, the Rivingtons reached the US Top 50 on Liberty in 1962. Al Frazier, Carl White, Rocky Wilson and Sonny Harris had already worked together as the Sharps for various labels including the Jamie, where they sang behind **Duane Eddy**'s twangy guitar. Individual members of the Rivingtons had also sung with the Lamplighters and the Tenderfoots on Federal.

Their other Liberty discs – 'Mama-Oom-Mow-Mow' and 'The Bird's the Word' (Top 50 in 1963) were as wild as their hilarious predecessor. The group also recorded unsuccessfully for Reprise, Vee Jay, Columbia, RCA and Wand, while the Trashmen of 'Surfin' Bird' fame based their brief career entirely on the Rivingtons' sound.

ROBBINS, MARTY The career of country singer/songwriter Marty Robbins effectively illustrates the development of country music in relation to rock. Born in Glendale, Arizona, on 26 September 1925, Robbins began his country career in Phoenix at Radio KTYL in 1948. In 1952, he joined Columbia, recording singly and duetting with manager Lee Emerson. Through 1954–6 he recorded several rockabilly songs, easily outselling Presley's version of 'That's All Right'. Through 1956–8, Robbins' country-based rock stylings on 'Singin' the Blues', 'A White Sports Coat' and 'Story of My Life' provided national hits, the vocal choruses and pop arrangements of these songs being later accentuated in a string of ballad recordings when Robbins was known as 'Mr Teardrop'.

Robbins also became known for gunfighter ballads following his recording of 'El Paso' and the inclusion of 'The Hanging Tree' in the movie of the same name. He appeared in several Westerns, like *Buffalo Guns* in 1958, and had a Top 5 hit in the UK during 1962 with his composition, 'Devil Woman' (CBS). He operated mainly in the country field during the Sixties and Seventies, recording for Columbia and MCA, but was plagued by heart trouble that cut down his appearances during the latter decade. He died on 8 December 1982.

ROBERTS, ANDY An underrated guitarist and songwriter, Andy Roberts' own work has been overshadowed by his association with the various manifestations of poetry, comedy and rock in Britain. From Harrow, London, he joined the Liverpool Scene on its formation in 1967, accompanying the poetry of Adrian Henri and 'playing Spider John Koerner numbers'.

His solo career began with *Home Grown* (B&C, 1970), which included the fine 'Moths and Lizards in Detroit'. In 1972 he formed Plainsong with **Ian Matthews**. The band made one country-inflected album for Elektra before Matthews' departure caused it to fold. Roberts continued to record for Elektra (*The Great Stampede*, 1973) while playing in the Grimms live show, another mixture of music and humour for which he wrote the theme song, 'Clowns on the Road'. His subsequent recording work included sessions for **Kevin Ayers**, **Roy Harper**, Maddy Prior and Yellow Dog.

ROBINSON, ALVIN Born in New Orleans on 22 December 1937, Alvin Robinson was originally a guitarist with the **Joe Jones** band. As a solo artist he recorded for Imperial in 1961 and Post the following year before the **Chris Kenner** song 'Something You Got' provided him with his first hit on Tiger in 1964. Arranged by Jones, it was a fine performance, slow and heavy, with a vocal reminiscent of Robinson's idol, **Ray Charles**. The B-side, a revival of the **Coasters**' 'Searchin'', was stark, deep and fiercely black. Other Robinson sides – notably 'I'm Gonna Put Some Hurt on You' – captured the essence of New Orleans R&B, and though his chart success was slight, the quality and influence of his work was undeniable. The **Leiber and Stoller** composition 'Down Home Girl' (on Red Bird) was later recorded by the Coasters and the **Rolling Stones**, while on 'Let the Good Times Roll' (Bluecat), Robinson's thick, cracked and guttural voice was in fine form. He also recorded for Joe Jones (his arranger/manager's label) and Atco, before moving to the West Coast to work with **Harold Battiste** and Mac Rebennack (*see* **Dr John**) and record for Pulsar.

ROBINSON, SMOKEY, AND THE MIRACLES 'America's greatest living poet' was what **Bob Dylan** called him some years ago, and America's most influential living poet wasn't joking. Smokey Robinson has, without question, written some of the finest words and melodies in pop's entire canon; he is also one of the most expressive of its singers, and a producer of brilliant resource.

Born in Detroit on 19 February 1940, as William Robinson, he was just fifteen when – with a group of school friends – he made his first private tape

The Miracles and Smokey Robinson (second from right)

recording, a version of a song called 'Adios, My Desert Love' which had been popularized by Nolan Strong and the Diabolos. The tape betrays Smokey's debt to Strong – even at that early age he'd developed a very personal falsetto voice, half-choked and pleading. Smokey and his friends quickly coalesced into a group called the Miracles, and in 1957 they were heard at an audition by a young composer called Berry Gordy Jr, who'd just written 'Reet Petite' for **Jackie Wilson**. Gordy saw the potential of the six – Smokey, lead; Claudette Rogers, first tenor (born 1942); Bobby Rogers, second tenor (1940); Ronnie White, baritone (1939); Warren 'Pete' Moore, bass (1939) and Marvin Tarplin on guitar – and helped them acquire a record deal for one of Smokey's own songs, 'Got a Job' (an 'answer' record to the **Silhouettes**' smash hit 'Get a Job'). The record came out on End in 1958. The group's next record, 'Bad Girl', was released by Chess in 1959. An aching ballad, 'Bad Girl' provided an early definition of one aspect of Smokey's unique writing; the subsequent release, 'Way Over There' (Tamla, 1960), provided another. A straight dance record, it featured Smokey at his most frothy and bubbling. Where 'Bad Girl' previewed a whole series of heart-wrenching tragedies, 'Way Over There' was the forerunner of many matchless dance classics.

The group's first major hit was 'Shop Around', an up-tempo song which revealed Smokey's increasingly clever way with words which made Number 2 on the pop charts in 1960. On 'You've Really Got a Hold on Me' (Top 10 in 1962), 'I Gotta Dance (to Keep from

Crying)', 'I Like It Like That', 'That's What Love Is Made Of', and 'Mickey's Monkey' (Top 10 in 1963), all part of the group's first golden age, Smokey's use of the 'Hitsville USA' session musicians quite paralleled that made by Motown's other top producers, **Holland, Dozier and Holland** and William Stevenson. In his writing for other Motown artists, Smokey was showing even greater talent: 'The Way You Do the Things You Do' for the **Temptations**, for instance, displayed a wholly idiosyncratic deployment of homespun similes, piling one atop another with an almost dizzying effect. Similarly, 'What's Easy for Two', 'The One Who Really Loves You', and 'My Guy' brought out all the romantic quality latent in **Mary Wells**' voice, and her version of Smokey's 'Two Lovers' is simply one of the finest R&B ballads of all time.

By 1964, Motown Records was established as one of the strongest single forces in popular music: it appeared to have less trouble than any of its competition in getting its records to 'cross over' from the R&B charts to the national pop lists. It was at this time that Smokey's period of highest achievement began. Exactly when is difficult to say, but it may have been with the Temptations' 'My Girl'. This initiated a sequence of luscious slow love songs which form a quite distinct body of work, including, amongst others, 'Since I Lost My Baby', 'Fading Away', 'It's Growing', and 'Don't Look Back' for the Temptations, and 'My Girl Has Gone', 'Swept for You Baby', 'You Must Be Love', and 'The Tracks of My Tears' for the Miracles. This last song, generally – and rightly – considered his greatest single piece, is a beautiful combination of thoughtfully contrived words, darkly introspective singing, and Marvin Tarplin's slowly unfolding melodies. Tarplin's contribution has been consistently underrated: besides his memorable guitar intros and mellow rhythm playing, he also wrote the music for some of their best songs. Smokey's up-tempo songs were at their best in this era, too: the Miracles scored with the Top 20 'Going to A Go-Go' (1965), a discotheque anthem, while **Marvin Gaye** received a new impetus to his career from 'Ain't That Peculiar', 'One More Heartache', and 'Take This Heart of Mine', all of which hummed along on the motorway of Smokey's crisp, driving production. Robinson's singing had by now achieved full maturity: on a neglected item like 'A Fork in the Road' he was producing some of the most audacious phrasing ever attempted by an R&B singer – the kind of inventiveness that his imitators, like the **Stylistics**' Russell Thompkins Jr in the early Seventies, could never begin to equal.

By 1967 his writing had lost some of its youthful freshness and had gained a new depth. With the loss of innocence came lyrics like those of 'I Second That Emotion' and 'The Love I Saw In You Was Just a Mirage': 'Just like the desert shows a thirsty man a deep oasis where there's only sand, you lured me into something I should've dodged . . . the love I saw in you was just a mirage'. There was, too, 'If You Can Wait', with the economy of this marvellous couplet: 'Just like "push" can turn to "shove", "like" can turn to "love"'. Musically, though, some of the magic was disappearing, and the hits were now less frequent. Perhaps it was the rigours of touring, perhaps creative exhaustion, perhaps the demands on Smokey's time made by his other role as vice-president of the Motown Record Corporation. Whatever the reason, the most interesting songs were now usually buried in albums which consisted mostly of adequate versions of other people's songs. Understandably, the general audience never dug deep enough to find 'You Must Be Love' on *Make It Happen*, 'You Neglect Me' and 'I'll Take You Any Way That You Come' on *Time Out*, or 'A Legend in Its Own Time' on *Four in Blue*.

However, Smokey and the group never fell completely into the doldrums and in 1970 the British success of a 1967 track 'The Tears of a Clown', prompted American Motown to issue the record, finally giving the group their first Number 1 on the pop charts. Close listening to this magnificent record reveals the lines, 'Just like Pagliacci did, I try to keep my sadness hid', and the key to most of Smokey's lyrics. Preoccupied with the heartbreak behind the smile, with the 'lipstick traces from kisses you only pretended to feel', his most moving songs all concentrate on hidden pain.

In 1972, after a long series of farewell concerts, he left the Miracles, who continued with a new lead singer, and embarked on a solo career. *Smokey*, the first album, was uneven but promising; *Pure Smokey*, the second, was much more coherent and considered, showing him coming to terms with the preoccupations of men of his age. Instead of parties and discos, he sang about his wife and children, and the complexities of family relationships. 'It's Her Turn to Live', 'She's Only a Baby Herself', and 'The Love Between Me and My Kids' showed concern and understanding, as well as an awareness of changing fashions in music (he employed a tough, funky rhythm section well able to cope with the current clichés). *Quiet Storm*, the third solo album, appeared in 1975 and found him singing in a slightly lower register. Musically, it was sometimes more far-ranging than anything he'd done before: the title track, for instance, included rhythmic figures which would not have been out of place on a Miles Davis Quintet album in 1965. Another track, the more straightforward 'Baby That's Backatcha', put him back at the top of the US R&B singles charts.

There followed a quiet period in Smokey's career, with *Deep in my Soul* (1977), *Love Breeze* and *Smokin'* (1978) selling well but not spectacularly. 1979, however, brought one of his biggest successes for years – 'Cruisin'', a Number 4 hit in the US. Smokey's chart renaissance continued with 'Being with You', a US Number 2 and a UK chart-topper in 1981.

The Miracles, too, enjoyed a measure of continued success, albeit on a far less notable scale. Billy Griffin joined as Robinson's replacement, and sang on several transatlantic hits, notably the US chart-topper (and a Number 3 in the UK) 'Love Machine' in 1976. *See also* **Motown**

ROBINSON, TOM One of the very few openly gay rock musicians, singer/songwriter Tom Robinson (born on 1 June 1950 in Cambridge, England) premiered his rousing, radical brand of rock'n'roll in 1977 during the early days of punk. Although he was extremely important as the first gay to frame his sexual preference successfully in a musical context, as in his song 'Glad to be Gay', his continually thoughtful approach to rock embraced a much wider field.

Robinson's musical career began in 1973 with Café Society, a band signed to Ray Davies' Konk label, but their lack of success caused him to quit in 1976. Inspired by the energy rather than the sound of punk, he teamed up with guitarist Danny Kustow, a friend from his days at a school for maladjusted boys. In a unit consisting of Robinson on bass and vocals, Kustow, Dolphin Taylor (drums) and Mark Ambler (keyboards), the Tom Robinson Band gigged around London and impressed sufficiently to be signed by EMI in 1977.

In October '2-4-6-8 Motorway', an agreeable, life-on-the-road slice of

Tom Robinson in action, rousingly radical and candidly gay

boogie at odds with TRB's usual socio-political stance, reached Number 5 in the UK. But after having toed the commercial line for their debut, they released in February '78 the *Rising Free* EP, a collection of four songs making strong political statements – especially on gay rights. *Power in the Darkness*, TRB's first album, appeared in May and the band became the darlings of the British music press. But then the band's success – the album reached Number 4 – caused internal friction and a change of line-up. The second album *TRB 2*, produced by **Todd Rundgren**, was released in 1979, but after a poor set of reviews and an uneventful US tour, Robinson broke up the band.

The demise of TRB caused Robinson to have a nervous breakdown and he joined his next band, Sector 27, on the basis that he would not be the leader. They released various singles and an album *Sector 27* in 1980, but it became clear that the band would never take off and Robinson left.

In January 1982, Robinson moved to Hamburg, where he recorded a solo album on his own Panic label, *North by Northwest*, a mature work that garnered much critical acclaim. Robinson's renaissance became complete when he scored an unexpected Top 10 hit with the single 'War Baby' in 1983. He spent the summer touring the UK, including a set at the Edinburgh Festival, released another single and then took a long rest until releasing a cover of **Steely Dan**'s 'Rikki Don't Lose That Number' in September 1984.

ROBYN, ABE Recording engineer Abe 'Bunny' Robyn pioneered today's multi-microphone techniques in Los Angeles during the Fifties. Working as an engineer at Universal Studios, Hollywood, in the late Forties, Robyn, a former classical violinist, became popular with the area's newly-formed independent R&B labels because he produced quality records despite the era's primitive lacquer recording techniques. In 1952, with the guaranteed patronage of labels like Imperial and Specialty, Robyn built his own independent studio in Hollywood – Master Recorders – which he specially designed to record the era's boisterous R&B combos. Utilizing as many as twelve microphones and acoustically separating each instrument, Robyn engineered some of the era's outstanding records; 'Searchin'', 'Long Tall Sally' and 'Willie and the Hand Jive'. In 1959, he demolished Master Recorders and built LA's then largest studio, United, before retiring in 1962.

ROCK AGAINST RACISM

Prompted into existence as a response to the increased activity in Britain by fascist groups, Rock Against Racism existed briefly during the late Seventies, an organization dedicated to combating racism among young rock audiences.

Although music has been a medium for some form of political expression or other for centuries, rock, from the Fifties onwards, was little more than a symbol of rebellion. Apart from a brief abortive fling during the hippie era, it wasn't until the arrival of punk that rock and politics combined effectively. The youthful zeal and anarchic appeal of punk brought together large numbers of young people, and with establishment rock stars like **David Bowie** and **Eric Clapton** expressing racist and fascist views in public in 1976, allied to a fear of the rising neo-fascist movements, the Rock Against Racism organization grew quickly in punk and related circles and staged many benefit gigs to raise money for anti-racist organizations.

Rock Against Racism also produced a lively fanzine, *Temporary Hoarding*, which successfully adapted punk graphics to convey a political message. It also had close links with another anti-racist organization, the Anti-Nazi League. Together they arranged a massive, successful rally in East London in 1978, at which a huge gathering saw the **Clash**, the **Tom Robinson** Band and **X-Ray Spex** perform and align themselves to an overtly political message.

In spite of allegations that they were merely front organizations for extreme left-wing political groups, Rock Against Racism and the Anti-Nazi League undoubtedly succeeded in combining rock music, striking graphics and a flair for organizing demonstrations and carnivals to make rock audiences aware of anti-fascist and left-wing ideas. In so doing they inspired similar campaigns of the time from Rock Against Sexism to Rock Against Thatcher, and undoubtedly provided a role model for later mobilizations of rock musicians behind a cause, most notably **Band Aid** and Red Wedge.

ROCK FILMS

Rock'n'roll's emergence in the mid-Fifties could not have come at a more opportune moment for a cinema fighting TV for survival and using films such as *Rebel Without a Cause* and *Blackboard Jungle* in an effort to cling to the youth market. To Hollywood executives, therefore, rock music was just another means of getting arses on seats, and

since the fans never complained, rock films were thrown together on low budgets, and invariably revolved around the same plot – a teenager is prevented from rocking by an older figure of authority, who is eventually won round. Musical content was variable, many acts being cheap and talentless, while others were plainly inhibited by having to mime playback. Exceptions to these rules were few.

One was the first rock film, *Rock Around the Clock*, a piece of pure corn that magically captured the high-octane emotion that surrounded **Bill Haley** in 1956. The film started the seat-slashing craze, was banned in many cities and still incites a desire to misbehave today. Also unique was *The Girl Can't Help It* (1956), the only film of the period in colour and the only one to sandwich its obligatory seventeen musical numbers in between a witty satire of the contemporary rock scene (Tom Ewell is given the task of turning Jayne Mansfield, who can't sing, into a rock star). Otherwise the many films of 1956–9 served only to record the acts of pioneer rock stars, many of whom (the **Platters**, **Chuck Berry**, **Fats Domino**, **Jerry Lee Lewis**, **Little Richard** and disc jockey **Alan Freed** in particular) made regular appearances.

Some rock idols were also called upon to act. The first and most successful was **Elvis Presley**, a natural. His early films (from *Love Me Tender*, 1956) creaked with sentimentality, but had guts – more than could be said for the soulless glossies to which he progressed. In 1960, Hollywood bowed out of rock movies and moved into Beat Generation dramas. When the Twist attacked in 1961, it was briefly exploited (*Rock Around the Clock* was re-made as *Twist Around the Clock*), but there was no further activity until a wave of beach musicals began in 1963.

In Britain, meanwhile, some American trends were reflected, while others were not. During 1956, British producers felt that the kids would be content with *It's a Wonderful World* featuring Dennis Lotis and Ted Heath and his Orchestra. The first British rock film, a tatty variety bill called *Rock You Sinners*, arrived in 1957, the same year that producers realized the potential of **Tommy Steele**. It was through his films that Steele gradually extended himself into the all-round entertainer he had always aspired to be. There was only one equivalent (*Six-Five Special*, 1958) of the American rock movie and only one British rocker who was regularly expected to act: **Cliff Richard**. Tried out in *Expresso Bongo*, Richard was given his head in *The Young Ones* (1961) and the string of all-singing, all-dancing musicals that ensued were acclaimed (in the absence of American counterparts) as major achievements.

Unfortunately, the later additions to the series did not move with the times. There were no other musical developments in the British cinema until 1962 when *It's Trad, Dad*, a mixture of pop music and the Goonish humour of director Dick Lester, showed the shape of things to come. The two **Beatles** films – *A Hard Day's Night* (1964) and *Help!* (1965) led the way in changing the manner of rock's presentation on celluloid. Although the first stuck to a showbiz theme, Dick Lester's direction and Alun Owen's script showed the influence both of zany British comedy (the **Goons**) and of the gritty realism that dominated British fiction and film-making at that time. *Help!* took the surreal comedy further, and in both the four Beatles were given parts which seemed to extend their natural wit. Other films featuring British beat groups were less enterprising (*Ferry Cross the Mersey* with **Gerry and the Pacemakers**, *Catch Us If You Can* with the **Dave Clark Five**) although *What a Crazy World* had **Joe Brown** as a cockney layabout in a film version of an excellent Joan Littlewood play.

In America, beach-party movies like **Fabian**'s *Ride the Wild Surf* (1965) continued unabated and screen exploitation of the new rock was at first limited to television, though a series of low-budget movies began to appear about the 'youth question', including *Riot on Sunset Strip*, *Wild in the Streets* and *Revolution*. The soundtrack music for these was generally provided by punk bands such as the **Standells** and the Chocolate Watch Band, though *Revolution* included the **Steve Miller Band, Quicksilver Messenger Service** and **Mother Earth**. These films were the forerunners of more sustained examinations of rock and youth culture. In Britain, Peter Watkins' *Privilege* had ex-Manfred Mann singer **Paul Jones** as a pop star manipulated by the authorities to channel the energies of the kids in a conformist direction. And Peter Fonda's *Easy Rider*, the odyssey of two hippie bikers with a soundtrack featuring the **Byrds** and other luminaries, rivalled Mike Nicholls' *The Graduate* (featuring music by **Simon and Garfunkel**) as the definitive late Sixties statement on American youth.

By this point, it was almost *de rigeur* for smart film-makers to use rock music almost as an earlier generation of film-makers felt it obligatory to set a scene in a sultry night-spot. Francis Ford Coppola used a **John Sebastian**-composed soundtrack score for his first feature film, *You're a Big Boy Now* (1966), while Antonioni's relentlessly swinging *Blow Up* (1967) had a sequence in which the Yardbirds' **Jimmy Page** was shown smashing a guitar, Pete Town-shend-style. All these developments were carried over into the Seventies, by which time the success of *The Graduate* and *Easy Rider* with rock soundtracks had alerted film producers to the fact that a rock score could not only enliven a film but maybe help to sell it too. No movie of the late Sixties or early Seventies seemed complete without a trendy chart name on the composing credits. **Nilsson** appeared on those for *Skidoo* (1969), Ray Davies (*see the* **Kinks**) worked on *Percy* (1971), **Elton John** on *Friends* (1971), and the fashion still continues today.

However, a more enduring and more profitable marriage between rock music and the cinema came about with the advent of the concert documentary. *Festival* (1967), a film about Newport, was the progenitor of this but *Monterey Pop* (1970) was the first to succeed, and for the next three years it seemed that no self-respecting garden fête was without its squad of cameramen. The most famous of the cycle and the most accomplished technically was *Woodstock* (1970), decked out with every conceivable gimmick to make one act look different from the next. None the less *Monterey Pop* and *Gimme Shelter* (1971) were of much greater significance and indeed, in their respective ways, offered truer accounts of rock festivals. By 1973 the market for concert films had been saturated and it was just as well that *Let the Good Times Roll*, an account of a revival concert that featured Haley and **Chubby Checker**, was one of the last entries in the field. *Let It Be* (1970), a documentary about the Beatles at work and play, had to be thrown together for contractual purposes, and it looked it. **Frank Zappa**'s uncontrollable flight of fancy, *200 Motels* (1972), was an utter mess. And the film version of *Jesus Christ Superstar* (1973) consisted of a crowd of hippies jumping up and down in the desert *ad nauseam*. During the first half of the Seventies rock stars also seemed particularly reluctant to try their hands at dramatic art. After one or two films apiece Jagger and **Dylan** showed no interest in continuing; most didn't bother to start. Only one recruit made good, the lugubrious **Kris Kristofferson**, still in demand for macho lover roles (*Alice Doesn't Live Here Anymore, A Star is Born*). During 1974–5 there was every indication of a revival of interest in the rock musical. Certainly, for better or worse, *That'll Be the Day* (1973), *Stardust* (1974) and *Flame* (1974) were among the most commercially successful films on the pop music business that Britain had produced. These were films that were as much about rock as they were films that used rock. However, in the mid-Seventies it was the latter category that produced the most interesting films, for example the first Jamaican feature film, *The Harder They Come*, the bizarre *Tommy* (1975), a commercial if not an aesthetic success, *American Graffiti* (1974) which was both, the assured *The Lords of Flatbush* (1974) and *Nashville* (1975).

The late Seventies was the era of the disco movie and especially *Saturday Night Fever*, based on a magazine article by Nik Cohn and starring dancer John Travolta. The success of the soundtrack album, and individual songs taken from it – including 'How Deep is Your Love', 'Stayin' Alive', and 'Night Fever', all US Number 1s – marked the phenomenal re-emergence of the **Bee Gees** as a chart force and set a new marketing precedent: after *Fever*, films and soundtrack albums were effectively used to promote each other. The wisdom of this strategy was proved again in 1978, when **Olivia Newton-John** and Travolta were paired – again by the Robert Stigwood Organisation (RSO), which had backed *Fever* – in a comparatively small budget production, *Grease*, based on a Broadway musical. The soundtrack album was one of that year's biggest sellers, and hits from the film dominated the UK charts in particular. However, the strategy failed abysmally once the product itself was seen as below-par – RSO's *Sgt Pepper's Lonely Hearts Club Band*, a lavish musical fantasy based on the Beatles' album and starring the Bee Gees and other RSO artists, was a critical and commercial flop.

Martin Scorsese's film of **The Band**'s last concert, *The Last Waltz*, was premièred in 1978 to almost universal acclaim, the same year that Derek Jarman's *Jubilee* – a punk fantasy featuring then-unknown names like **Adam Ant** and **Toyah** – was released. *Thank God It's Friday* attempted to repeat the success of *Fever*, while Motown invested heavily in *The Wiz* – an update of *The Wizard of Oz* starring **Diana Ross** and **Michael Jackson**. There was also a spate of teen movies in the *American Graffiti* mould (including a sequel, *More American Graffiti*), and at least two films that used rock music in innovative fashion – Chris Petit's *Radio On* (1979) and a film representation of the **Who**'s album *Quadrophenia*, both of which featured Sting of the **Police** in cameo roles. Meanwhile, *The Buddy Holly Story* was a sincere (if partially inaccurate) cinematic account of Holly's life.

The Eighties brought forth a multitude of films with some degree of rock content – some with rock stardom as its subject matter (*The Rose* starring **Bette Midler**, *Breaking Glass* starring **Hazel O'Connor**, some little more than excuses for appearances by a succession of rock acts (*Roadie, Dance Craze*), and one caricaturing the whole pop process – *The Great Rock'n'Roll Swindle*, which told the story of the **Sex Pistols**' short, turbulent career. None of these films were exactly box-office blockbusters, however, and even *Absolute Beginners* – the much anticipated, much-hyped film version of Colin MacInnes' novel – was only a qualified commercial success on its release in 1986.

ROCKABILLY

The musical style rockabilly was, simply, the white Southerner's rock'n'roll. It derived from honky-tonk and juke-joint music of the early Fifties' South. From the Western-Swing, country-boogie and Hank Williams-influenced hillbilly music of the whites came the basic instrumentation of acoustic guitar and bass with their chopped rhythms, while black R&B and boogie provided the drum styles and – most importantly – the electric lead guitar styles. Sometimes the piano, steel guitar, fiddle or saxophone would be added, but basically rockabilly was a raw acoustic rhythm with a heavy backbeat and cutting electric guitar solos. Throughout the South, this music developed with young bands using the traditional C&W booking circuits. It was dance music, it was wild, it was fun, but it was not quite rock'n'roll.

The catalyst that transformed rockabilly was the emergence of Sun Records in Memphis, and in particular **Elvis Presley**'s first record, 'That's All Right'. The enthusiastic high-pitched vocals, the slapping bass rhythm of **Bill Black** and the violent guitar runs of **Scotty Moore** caused a stir among DJs, but Presley's attitude, sex-appeal and downright outrageousness drew attention to the music even more. When Presley was transferred to RCA Victor, he became a national phenomenon, and for two years, at least, rockabilly

was the music of most white kids.

Sun took off with **Carl Perkins** and others whose music typified and exemplified the style. Perkins' 'Blue Suede Shoes' topped all charts and the music of 1956 became the basis for the careers of **Rick Nelson**, the **Everly Brothers**, **Roy Orbison**, **Conway Twitty**, **Buddy Holly**, **Buddy Knox**, **Johnny Burnette** and a host of others. Most of them forsook rockabilly with the demise of rock'n'roll in the late Fifties, but the style has remained embedded in the rock tradition. Its influence has been of prime importance, on the early **Beatles**, on West-Coast country-rock and on **Creedence Clearwater Revival**.

During the heyday of rockabilly – between 1954 and 1958 – small and major companies alike recorded the style profusely. In Nashville, the larger labels recorded **Gene Vincent**, Eddie Bond, Johnny Carroll, the Everly Brothers, **Charlie Feathers** and Mac Curtis, and **Sanford Clark**. These labels (Capitol, Mercury, Decca, Cadence, King, Dot, and Columbia) were joined in a dozen other recording centres by independent companies who recorded almost anyone who would attempt the style. Fine regional variations were sometimes achieved. In Beaumont, Starday were one of the first and the songs of Sonny Fisher and guitar style of Hal Harris were as near perfect as Perkins and Presley. The output from the studios at Houston-Fort Worth, the Lowery studios of Atlanta, the Louisiana sounds of Goldband, Feature, Zynn and others, the Shreveport sound of **Dale Hawkins**, the Clovis studio of **Norman Petty**, the **Al Casey** sound from Phoenix, Westport in Kansas City, Imperial in New Orleans and Hollywood and a dozen other labels and studios – all provide evidence of the grass-roots appeal of rockabilly and its influence on later developments in rock. *See also* **Sun Records**

ROCKIN' BERRIES

A Birmingham-based group, the Rockin' Berries finally scored in 1964 after a number of misses with a cover version of the **Tokens**' American hit, 'He's in Town' (Pye). Their close harmonies and dominant falsetto lead (Geoff Turton) also sounded like the Tokens, and sustained the resemblance for their next two hits. In 1965, they made their debut in pantomime and subsequently began embellishing their act with comedy routines and impersonations by singer Clive Lea. In 1967, Lea quit to become a solo impersonator. Today, as the Berries, they remain a popular family cabaret act. Personnel changes

have been frequent, but the original line-up was Roy Austin (born 1943), Terry Bond (1943), Chuck Botfield (1943), Lea (1942) and Turton (1944).

RODGERS, JIMMIE

Although not the first white country singer to draw on the blues, nor the first to employ the yodel, 'America's Blue Yodeler' – born in Meridian, Mississippi, on 8 September 1897 – was unquestionably the initiator of an important and enduring idiom. Jimmie Rodgers' blue yodels, blues songs couched in rural black phrasing and imagery with yodelled refrains, were inspirations for countless singers after him. His influence, however, resides in his whole output, which included railroad songs, parlour balladry, novelty songs and rearranged fragments of traditional Southern themes. He performed these in a warm, relaxed vocal style, to a highly characteristic guitar accompaniment (sometimes augmented), on a series of recordings between 1927 and 1933, the year of his death from tuberculosis (in New York City on 26 May).

The massive popularity of his records, which sold in tens of thousands, established Rodgers as the first rural artist to attain the commercial status of the Northern popular singers. The image of personal success he generated was tempered by his retention of Southern homeliness, humour and unaffectedness, and despite his easy command of the market, he made few changes in the presentation of his music; his last recordings were little more sophisticated than his first.

Among his most typical pieces were the first of the blue yodels, also known as 'T for Texas'; the railroad songs 'Waitin' for a Train' and 'Hobo Bill's Last Ride' – another of his nicknames was the 'Singing Brakesman'; and many evocations of Southern locales, such as 'Peach Picking Time in Georgia' and 'Mississippi River Blues'. These and their companion pieces have been both specifically and generally recalled in the work of such later singers as Ernest Tubb, Webb Pierce, Lefty Frizzell, **Merle Haggard** and **Hank Snow**. (Tubb, Frizzell, Haggard and Snow have all recorded album-length tributes to Rodgers.) Western Swing and bluegrass repertoires also reflect very sharply the impact of Rodgers' work. It has become commonplace to refer to Rodgers as the father of country music, and, unlike some such tributes, he has maintained this role through the continued currency of his songs.

RODGERS, JIMMY The son of veteran country singer **Hank Snow**, Jimmy Rodgers was named after the great 'Singing Brakesman' (**Jimmie Rodgers**) and was born on 18 September 1933, in Camus, Washington. Rodgers was the most successful folk-pop (not folk-rock) performer of the late Fifties and early Sixties. Although his material was folksy, he sounded more like the contemporary, soft-voiced teenage singers than the **Kingston Trio**. His Roulette recording career began with two US hits in 1957: 'Honeycomb' (Number 1) and 'Kisses Sweeter Than Wine' (Number 3) and two in 1958: 'Oh, Oh, I'm Falling in Love Again' (Number 7) and 'Secretly/Make Me a Miracle' (Number 3). After that, he began to fade, though an album-track, 'English Country Garden' was a British hit in 1962. He later recorded for Dot and A&M, but a severe accident in 1967 curtailed his career.

ROE, TOMMY A rising star of early Sixties US pop who survived the coming of the **Beatles** and the British invasion far better than most of his contemporaries, Tommy Roe was born Thomas David Roe in Atlanta, Georgia, on 9 May 1942. He formed his own group, the Satins, at Brown High School at the age of 16; they played local dances and high-school hops and began recording in 1960 for the local Judd label. As Tommy Roe and the Satins, he first recorded 'Sheila' for Judd during that year, but without success. He switched to ABC Paramount in 1962, where, under the supervision of Felton Jarvis (later **Elvis Presley**'s producer), he cut 'Save Your Kisses'. Unexpectedly, however, it was the flip-side, a re-recording of 'Sheila', which registered internationally, topping the US chart and reaching Number 2 in the UK late in 1962.

Roe proved durable: his follow-up, a revival of Robin Luke's 'Susie Darlin'', flopped but his third ABC release, 'The Folk Singer', was a Number 4 in the UK despite failing to chart in the US. Roe made a solid comeback when his fourth disc, the futuristic 'Everybody', reached Number 3 in the US and Number 8 in Britain. Three relatively barren years followed until Roe began his career anew with a series of 'bubble-gum' hits beginning with 'Sweet Pea' (a million-seller) and 'Hooray for Hazel' in 1966, and 'Dizzy' (a transatlantic Number 1) and 'Jam Up Jelly Tight' in 1969. He returned to his native Georgia in the mid-Seventies before signing a recording deal with Warner/Curb Records.

ROGERS, KENNY A hugely successful country crossover artist in the late Seventies and beyond, Kenny Rogers (born in Houston, Texas, on 21 August 1941) began his performing career as one of the New Christy Minstrels, though he had sung with various local bands in the early Sixties. He formed a rock outfit, the First Edition, in late 1966 with a line-up consisting entirely of fellow ex-Minstrels: Terry Williams (born on 6 June 1947), guitar; Mike Settle (20 March 1941), rhythm guitar; and Thelma Camacho. They accurately gauged the anti-Vietnam war mood of the time with their massive 1969 hit, 'Ruby, Don't Take Your Love to Town' (Reprise), a version of a Mel Tillis song originally written with the plight of Korean war veterans in mind. Lesser hits followed in the shape of 'Reuben James', 'Something's Burning' (written by **Mac Davis**), and 'Tell it All Brother', before the band broke up in 1972. Rogers then spent a period in the rock wilderness, unsure of which direction to take, until a move to United Artists in late 1976 precipitated his metamorphosis from would-be hippie to smooth country music entertainer. The hits began with 'Lucille' in 1977 – a UK Number 1 – and continued with 'The Gambler', 'She Believes in Me', 'Coward of the County' and others before the end of the decade. Both 'The Gambler' and 'Coward of the County' inspired TV-movie dramatizations in which Rogers took the leading roles.

In 1980, Rogers topped the US chart with the **Lionel Richie**-composed 'Lady' and began to consolidate his mainstream middle-of-the-road appeal by recording best-selling duets with **Kim Carnes** ('Don't Fall in Love with a Dreamer', 1980), Dottie West ('What Are We Doin' in Love', 1981), **Sheena Easton** ('We've Got Tonight', 1983) and **Dolly Parton** ('Islands in the Stream', 1983, a US Number 1). His solo Top 20 hits of the Eighties included 'I Don't Need You' (1981), 'Share Your Love with Me' (1981), 'Through the Years' (1982) and 'Love Will Turn You Around' (1982). He moved to RCA in a $20 million deal in 1983, debuting for the label with the gold album *Eyes That See in the Dark*.

ROLLING STONES On 21 July 1962, the Rolling Stones played their first gig – deputizing for Blues Incorporated at the Marquee Club in London – because **Alexis Korner**'s group was appearing on BBC radio's *Jazz Club*. Mick Jagger was quoted in *Jazz News* as saying, 'I hope they don't think we're a rock'n'roll outfit.' The magazine also announced the line-up: Mick Jagger (vocals), born 26 July 1943 in Dartford, Kent; Keith Richard, born 18 December 1943 in Dartford and Elmo Lewis (guitars); Ian Stewart (piano), Dick Taylor (bass), Mick Avory (drums). Whether the future **Kinks** drummer played that night is not clear, though he did rehearse with the group, as did one Tony Chapman, before Charlie Watts (2 June 1941) – who had previously worked with Korner – joined. Elmo Lewis turned out to be Brian Jones' (26 February 1944) notion of an appropriate name for a bluesman; Dick Taylor quit to stay in art school, whereupon Bill Wyman (24 October 1936) took his place; and Ian Stewart was kicked out soon after by manager **Andrew Loog Oldham** because his face didn't fit. The 'sixth Stone' became the group's roadie and occasional session pianist. (He died in 1986.)

Following their debut at the Marquee, the Stones played a few support gigs there and then were dropped because, as **Chris Barber** put it, 'they weren't authentic enough'. However, if their repertoire of **Chuck Berry**, **Bo Diddley** and **Jimmy Reed** numbers and their energetic, unsophisticated style were too close to rock'n'roll for the smug purists of the self-styled London Jazz Centre, they impressed **Giorgio Gomelsky** sufficiently for him to offer the group a residency at his Crawdaddy Club in Richmond. There the Stones' reputation spread so rapidly by word of mouth that within a matter of weeks Gomelsky was faced with long queues and the need to move to larger premises. Then, in the first week of May 1963, his unwritten contract with the group ended when Andrew Oldham, with immense self-confidence and Eric Easton's financial support, signed a management deal with them.

Easton purchased the demo tapes the group had made at IBC studios, and under Oldham's supervision they recorded 'Come On' and 'I Wanna Be Loved', which were released as the group's first single in June on Decca. The choice of the A-side, a Chuck Berry song not featured in the Stones' club repertoire, and its vocal harmonies and double-tracking were early indications of Oldham's attempt to mould the group into a form that would be more readily acceptable to the pop public; another was their appearance on television's *Thank Your Lucky Stars*, to promote the record, in matching check stage jackets, and photographic sessions in collar and tie. The success of this manipulation was limited, for the

The Stones' live performances earnt their status as 'the greatest rock'n'roll band in the world' despite less than earth-shattering albums

record failed to reach the Top 20. Nevertheless, 'Come On' did well enough to land the group a spot on a national package tour headed by the **Everly Brothers**, **Little Richard**, Bo Diddley and **Gene Vincent**, and their second single, 'I Wanna Be Your Man', **Lennon** and **McCartney**'s concept of the Stones' sound and a further step away from the group's original style, eventually made Number 10 at the beginning of January 1964.

Their third single, released in February, was a reworking of the **Crickets**' 'Not Fade Away' and the group's first significant interpretation, for their Diddleyesque adaptation made Buddy Holly's song their own; along with their treatment of the **Valentinos**' 'It's All Over Now', their fourth single and first British Number 1, it anticipated the

approach of Jagger and Richard's songwriting partnership. Not unnaturally, however, their first efforts – 'Little by Little' and 'Tell Me', for example – were heavily derivative of the R&B they had been playing. It wasn't until they had moved beyond R&B to the more openly emotive and declamatory style of soul that the writing of Jagger and Richard flourished. To do this, they had first to confront Oldham who, though he had quickly learnt how to manipulate the group's improvised image and was especially good at capitalizing on the group's frequent brushes with the authorities, was less astute in his proposals for their musical direction. Obsessed with **Phil Spector**, whose Philles label he hoped to emulate with his own Immediate Records, Oldham – as can be clearly seen on the out-takes

of that period finally released in 1975 on *Metamorphosis* (London) – made inept attempts at his own 'wall of sound'. Fortunately, however, the Stones found their own way, as 'Satisfaction', their first American Number 1 in the summer of 1965, demonstrated. That record was the perfect synthesis of the musical styles that had influenced the group – particularly **Solomon Burke**, Chuck Berry and **Muddy Waters** – and, for the first time, generalized feelings entered the Stones' lyrics as Jagger screamed out his anger at the attempt at complete manipulation he saw around him. Aggression also marked the songs Jagger and Richard fashioned out of their election to the exclusive, but supposedly egalitarian, club of 'Swinging London' – 'Play with Fire', 'Out of Time' and 'Stupid Girl' – songs in which class hatred, and sexual aggression and frustration are to be found in equal parts.

However, 'Satisfaction' marked not only the Stones' discovery of a musical way forward, it also confirmed the social stance the group had evolved in the two years since 'Come On'. For the Stones had not merely won pop polls, topped the charts and toured the world, they had also caused riots in Blackpool, Belfast and Paris, at London Airport and on *Ready Steady Go!*; been barred from hotels and restaurants; walked out on press receptions; been banned by the BBC, and convicted for driving offences and using insulting behaviour; and they'd angered hairdressers, schoolteachers, television viewers and magistrates. Seen from this perspective, the phenomenal popularity of 'Satisfaction' said as much for the accuracy with which it reflected the feelings of a generation in the mid-Sixties as it did for the song's construction and the group's performance. None the less, because of a stylistic restlessness that verged on whimsy, only a few of the half-dozen hits of the next two years came near to 'Satisfaction', though success was assured for every single and album – 'Get Off of My Cloud' (1965), 'Paint It Black' (1966) and 'Ruby Tuesday' all made Number 1 in America.

The albums of that period, *Out of Our Heads* (1965), *Aftermath* (1966) – the first to consist entirely of Jagger-Richard originals – and *Between the Buttons* (1967), were equally eclectic, but the most significant development in the group's career between 1965 and 1967 was the inordinate growth of their image and the increasing seriousness with which it was treated by the establishment, culminating in the *News of the World* witch-hunt, the drugs busts in February (Jagger and Richard) and May 1967 (Jones), and the subsequent disproportionate jail sentences which prompted the famous *Times* editorial 'Who Breaks a Butterfly on a Wheel?' and were quashed on appeal. Out of all this came a wilting flower-power single, 'We Love You' (August 1967), featuring back-up vocals by Lennon and McCartney, who also introduced them to the Maharishi Mahesh Yogi; a break with Andrew Oldham; virtual withdrawal from public performances; and the unsuccessful post-*Sergeant Pepper* psychedelic album, *Their Satanic Majesties Request* (December 1967). Then in May 1968, the group emerged from the months of retirement with 'Jumping Jack Flash', their finest single since 'Satisfaction', and played their first British concert in two years. And finally, after a five-month delay due to Decca's opposition to the sleeve artwork, *Beggar's Banquet* was released in December. Though its superficially radical themes drew the Stones greater attention than they perhaps deserved, it was their most complete album to date, seeing the cutting edge of their music restored (in part by Jimmy Miller's production) as Jagger-Richard returned to their theme on frustration in songs like 'Street Fighting Man'.

In June 1969, Brian Jones left the group, explaining his decision in the unquestionable understatement, 'I no longer see eye-to-eye with the others over the discs we are cutting', and within a week Mick Taylor – born 17 January 1948 – had left **John Mayall** to join as lead guitarist. Jones announced his intention to form his own band, but on 3 July was found dead in his swimming pool. Mick Jagger transformed the group's free concert in Hyde Park that weekend into a memorial service by quoting Shelley and releasing several thousand butterflies. Following the sensation of Jones' death, the group continued to provide newspaper copy: Jagger with his girlfriend, **Marianne Faithfull**, and the shooting of *Ned Kelly* in Australia, but more disturbingly at the year's end when, during their set at the notorious Altamont Festival, a black youth was stabbed to death by Hell's Angels in front of the stage as they played. The killing made prophetic sense of 'Gimme Shelter', the opening cut on their excellent *Let It Bleed* album (December 1969): 'Rape, murder – it's just a shot away'. In turning the Woodstock dream into a nightmare, it emphasized the group's total

remoteness from their audience.

After an initial burst of energy which brought about the foundation of their own record company – Rolling Stones Records, launched with *Sticky Fingers* in April 1971, their last Decca recording being *Get Yer Ya Yas Out* (September 1970), a live set to foil concert bootleggers – the Seventies saw complacency setting in. The group moved to France after a farewell gig at London's Roundhouse in March 1971, and thereafter public attention drifted away from their music to focus on Jagger's much-publicized courtship of Bianca Pérez Morena de Macías and their trendy San Tropez wedding in May. The couple at once joined the international jet set, attending society parties and winning fashion polls. The rest of the group declined to follow suit. They worked less, and not surprisingly the music suffered. Jagger's songs, especially, lost the force provided by his earlier stance outside conventional society. *Exile on Main Street* (1972) was a sprawling double album with no core; *Goat's Head Soup* (1973), old-fashioned: and although *It's Only Rock'n'Roll* (1974) revived confidence in their universally unquestioned status as 'the greatest rock'n'roll band in the world', it is as a live act that their reputation has been best preserved.

Keith Richard's collaboration with Ron Wood of the **Faces** in 1974 – the former's first work outside the group – gave rise to speculation about the future of both groups; when Mick Taylor quit at the end of the year it was indeed Wood who took his place on the Stones' 1975 US tour. Since then, the line-up has remained stable and the group has shown no sign of even contemplating disbandment. Their albums – *Black and Blue* (1976), *Some Girls* (1978), *Tattoo You* (1981) – have been hardly earth-shaking affairs, but the Stones have shown a willingness to update their sound (exploring disco rhythms on the latter two albums, for example) while never wholly departing from their R&B roots. Mick may have become the darling of the gossip columns, but it is Keith who still makes the front pages with every misdemeanour. Charlie Watts launched his own big band jazz project in 1986, while Bill Wyman (besides recording solo – his 'Si Si, Je Suis Un Rock Star' was a UK Top 20 hit in 1982) has put much energy into maintaining a complete computerized record of the band's history. The Rolling Stones' other albums of the Eighties comprise *Undercover* (1983), *12 × 5* (1984) and *Dirty Work* (1986).

ROMERO, CHAN Born in Billings, Montana, on 27 July 1941, Chan Romero was a 'chicano' rock'n'roller best remembered for his original rendition of 'Hippy Hippy Shake'. He was first discovered in 1957 by Specialty A&R man **'Bumps' Blackwell** but Specialty's boss, Art Rupe, automatically shunned white artists and Romero had to wait until 1959, when Los Angeles deejay Don Redfield took him to Bob Keene's Del-Fi label who were urgently seeking a Latin-styled singer to fill a spot vacated by the recently killed **Ritchie Valens**. Using the same studio and musicians as Valens, Romero recorded his own frantic 'Hippy Hippy Shake' on which he demonstrated a lusty, hiccoughing vigour untypical of the late, more restrained Valens. Although popular on the West Coast, 'Shake' failed to register nationally, nor did his follow-up, the even more pulsating 'My Little Ruby'. Before recording gospel music for his own Warrior label he cut discs on Challenge and Philips. In 1963 the **Swinging Blue Jeans** took an exact facsimile of 'Hippy Hippy Shake' to Number 2 in Britain.

All in the family – the three Ronettes, two sisters and a cousin

RONETTES Although best remembered for their recording work with **Phil Spector**, the Ronettes – sisters Veronica (born 10 August 1943) and Estelle Bennett (22 July 1944) and their cousin Nedra Talley (27 January 1946) – began as a pubescent dance-act the Dolly Sisters before branching out into singing, after taking harmony tuition at New York's Camilucci Studios. In 1961, at the height of the twist craze, they worked as resident dancers at the Peppermint Lounge and in 1961 they went out as a utility dance-act, touring with the Clay Cole Twist Package and appearing with Cole (a deejay) in the exploitation film, *Twist Around the*

Clock. Signing with Colpix in 1961, they recorded five singles without success until 1963 when the Phil Spector-produced singles, 'Be My Baby' and 'Baby, I Love You', sold a million copies each on Spector's Philles label. Several smaller hits followed including 'Walkin' in the Rain' and 'The Best Part of Breakin' Up', but the trio faded with the demise of Philles in 1966. They re-emerged, briefly, in 1969 on A&M and with a revised line-up, on Buddah, in 1973. Veronica (Ronnie) Bennett married Spector in 1965; they separated in 1973.

RONSON, MICK Guitarist Mick Ronson's musical training began with violin at school (where he also learned to read music) and private piano lessons. Bored with the slowness of the other pupils he began playing his violin like a guitar, soon graduating to the real thing. In the mid-Sixties he formed a local band, the Rats, who recorded singles but didn't gain popular attention.

He left to record with Michael Chapman, meeting **David Bowie** soon after. He provided the major musical impetus for Bowie's albums *The Man Who Sold the World* (1970) and *Hunky Dory* (1971) and was instrumental in forming the Spiders From Mars. Ronson's stinging guitar and spare arrangements attracted much acclaim and were viewed by many as the backbone to Bowie's success. After the demise of the Spiders and the recording of *Pin Ups* in 1973, he turned to a brief solo career. But without other forces and personalities to bounce off, his two solo albums were patchy and disappointing; his solo tours likewise. In mid-1974 he joined **Mott the Hoople**, leaving in December with Ian Hunter to perform and record as Hunter-Ronson, before touring with **Bob Dylan**'s Rolling Thunder revue. He subsequently co-produced **Roger McGuinn**'s *Cardiff Rose* album and releases by Ellen Foley and David Johansen.

RONSTADT, LINDA Singer Linda Ronstadt was acclaimed but unsuccessful in the country-rock field until her potential was realized in 1974 with the Peter Asher-produced album, *Heart Like a Wheel* (Capitol – Asylum in Britain). Born in Tucson, Arizona, on 15 July 1946, she started out as a folk singer in the **Joan Baez** vein, before joining the Stone Poneys in 1965.

A surprise Top 20 hit came in 1967 with **Mike Nesmith**'s 'Different Drum' (Capitol), but Ronstadt went solo soon after. A series of albums containing reworked versions of country and rock songs followed, foreshadowing the similar approach of other women singers by several years. They included *Hand Sown, Home Grown* (1969) and *Silk Purse* (1970).

Her career was hampered by problems in maintaining a stable line-up in her backing group and by unimaginative record production. In 1973 she signed to Asylum and the new confidence on *Don't Cry Now* produced by John Boylan and Peter Asher (*see* **Peter and Gordon**) heralded her later success with the chart-topping singles 'You're No Good' and 'When Will I Be Loved' from the *Wheel* album, her last for Capitol under the existing contract. (Peter Asher became her manager and produced all her subsequent albums.) Her success continued with a Top 10 album (*Prisoner in Disguise*) and single 'Heat Wave' on the Asylum label. The albums *Hasten Down the Wind* (1976), *Simple Dreams* (1977), and *Living in the USA* (1978) consolidated her status as a new, hip easy-listening superstar, though she never quite repeated her American success in the UK.

To her credit, later albums like *Mad Love* (1980) and *Get Closer* (1982) found her exploring new musical territory beyond the country-rock bias of her earlier releases – in the former case, with versions of three **Elvis Costello** songs. She took a lead role in the rock version of Gilbert and Sullivan's *The Pirates of Penzance*, which was premiered in New York during 1980, and received wide critical acclaim for a trio of albums recorded with bandleader Nelson Riddle, *What's New* (1985), *Lush Life* (1985) and *For Sentimental Reasons* (1986). All three albums featured repertoire from the pre-rock era, including versions of songs by Gershwin, Rodgers and Hart and Irving Berlin.

ROSE ROYCE Initially the tool of former Motown producer Norman Whitfield, Rose Royce grew into one of the better, more lasting self-contained funk'n'ballads bands to emerge in the mid-Seventies. The style which they were to pursue throughout their career was established by Whitfield's writing and production of the *Car Wash* movie soundtrack, a substantial part of which Rose Royce performed. Poignant, gossamer-textured ballads like 'I Wanna Get Next to You' and hard-driving funk pieces such as the title track and 'Put Your Money Where Your Mouth Is' set the pattern for later hits from gorgeous ballads like 'Wishing on a Star', 'Love Don't Live Here Anymore', 'And You Wish For Yesterday' and 'Golden Touch' to the insistent power of 'Is It Love You're After', 'It Makes You Feel Like Dancin'' and 'Do Your Dance'. Although the solid backing of eight male musicians kept the band's music moving, it was the work of the female lead singer which caught and held the attention, particularly on the band's ballad work. At first Gwen Dickey (who changed her name to Rose Norwalt) held centre-stage with her caressingly wistful readings of the slower tunes. When she left to take up a solo career, Ricci Benson took her place and showed equal aptitude for light, tuneful compositions. After 1980's *Golden Touch* LP, the band and Whitfield produced some fairly mediocre works but in 1984, after they'd parted company with their former mentor, Royce returned to form with *Music Magic*, co-produced by various members of the band, the songwriters and Bobby Eli.

ROSE, TIM A powerful singer and songwriter with roots in the early Sixties American folk scene, Tim Rose – born in Washington DC in September 1940 – was a member of folk-rock trio the Big Three (alongside Mama **Cass Elliott**) before signing with Columbia and gaining attention with an eponymous 1967 debut album. It contained a song he had written with Canadian folk singer Bonnie Dobson, 'Morning Dew', which became something of a folk club standard, and a slow arrangement of 'Hey Joe', a hit that year for **Jimi Hendrix**. A second album, *Through Rose Coloured Glasses*, followed in 1969, after which he left Columbia to sign (in 1971) with Playboy Records. He recorded little during the Seventies and settled in the UK, at one time partnering **Tim Hardin** on club dates. He signed with Atlantic in the mid-Seventies and recorded *The Musician* (1976).

ROSS, DIANA The jewel in Motown's crown during the late Sixties and early Seventies, Diana Ross was born on 26 March 1944 and grew up in Detroit's ghetto area Brewster Housing Project. She began singing at an early age with neighbourhood friends, Florence Ballard and Barbara Martin. With Mary Wilson replacing Martin, the group evolved into the **Supremes**, who became Diana Ross and the Supremes in 1968. Despite the phenomenal success of the group, Diana (by now married to Motown boss Berry Gordy Jr) left to pursue a solo singing and acting career: during spring 1970, her solo debut 'Reach Out and Touch' was a Top 20 US hit. By the autumn, 'Ain't No Mountain High Enough' was topping the US chart and earning Diana a second gold disc; in 1973, she won an Oscar nomination for her portrayal of the late Billie Holiday in *Lady Sings the Blues*, the Motown Corporation's first step into film production. In 1975, she starred in the even glossier *Mahogany*, directed by Gordy, and the following year its theme song, 'Do You Know Where You're Going To', took her back to Number 1.

Her chart career then hit a comparative slump until 1980, when she began working with producers Nile Rodgers and Bernard Edwards of **Chic**: the result of their collaboration, the *Diana* album, became her biggest selling solo effort, though the single taken from the

album, 'Upside Down', was remixed by Russ Terrana and Ross herself prior to release. More hits followed – 'My Old Piano', 'I'm Coming Out' (1980), 'It's My Turn', 'One More Chance' (1981) – but in 1981 Diana severed her connections with Motown and signed with RCA for the US market and EMI-Capitol for overseas release. 'Why Do Fools Fall in Love' and 'Muscles' maintained her success rate in 1981–2, but ironically it was a Motown-released track, 'Endless Love', a duet with **Lionel Richie**, which achieved the highest sales of all her post-Supremes singles. By 1985, she was recording with Barry Gibb of the **Bee Gees**, who produced and co-wrote (with brothers Robin and Maurice) her 1986 UK Number 1, 'Chain Reaction'. *See also* the **Supremes**

Diana Ross won an Oscar nomination for her performance as the legendary Billie Holiday in Lady Sings the Blues, *Motown's first film*

ROTHCHILD, PAUL A staff producer for Elektra Records in the mid-Sixties, Paul Rothchild produced records by the label's main rock bands, including the **Doors**, the **Paul Butterfield** Blues Band and **Love**. He was involved in six records by the Doors, and once tried to record the group on LSD. Before joining Elektra, Rothchild had worked with **Tom Rush** for the Prestige label, and though he did not continue to produce Rush at Elektra, he was a prolific producer throughout the Sixties. Clear Light, Goodthunder and the heavy rock 'supergroup' Rhinoceros (which he had been instrumental in forming) were among his later, mainly unsuccessful, projects. Leaving Elektra he produced **John Sebastian**'s first solo album and, in 1973, made an abortive attempt to set up his own label, Buffalo Records.

ROUGH TRADE Successful independent record label and distributor Rough Trade was originally begun by Geoff Travis in 1976 as an independent record shop in West London. They began distributing records by mail order, and by the end of 1977 had established a wholesale business. Since they were constantly receiving tapes from exciting groups who could not get a record deal, it seemed logical to start their own label; their first single was 'Paris Maquis' by the French punk band Métal Urbain. The label really took off, however, after the release of the label's first LP, *Inflammable Material*, by the Northern Irish punk outfit **Stiff Little Fingers** in February 1979; by July the album had gone gold.

This success enabled Rough Trade – an employee-managed co-operative – to build up a range of services for its artists: a publishing company, Rough Trade Music, an independent press and promotional service and a booking and tour management agency. Their roster grew to include **Robert Wyatt**, Red Crayola, **Père Ubu**, the Fall, the Raincoats, **Scritti Politti** and the **Smiths**, but they continued to act as distributors for other less established names.

In 1982, Rough Trade streamlined the independent distribution by setting up the Cartel, a group of regional companies – Backs in Norwich, Fast Product in Edinburgh, Probe in Liverpool, Red Rhino in York and Revolver in Bristol – all of which had started as small record shops. These outlets serviced the 'indie' (independent) shops in their region, while Rough Trade acted as a central clearing house.

As the Eighties progressed, and the major labels brought their massive resources into play to recapture their dominance of the market, the independents had a hard time, but Rough Trade managed to keep its head above water, largely through the continuing success of the Smiths but also by making an all-out effort to put the unlikely all-girl punky outfit We've Got a Fuzzbox and We're Gonna Use It into the charts early in 1986.

ROULETTE RECORDS Morris Levy and Phil Khals formed Roulette Records in 1956 as an adjunct to their music publishing operations. Their partner was **George Goldner**, into whose Rama and Tico organization the company was slotted. The company was more or less taken over by **Hugo and Luigi** in 1957, leaving Goldner free to concentrate on his new enterprises, Gone and End, which were distributed through Roulette. Roulette itself had limited success with a variety of acts ranging from **Buddy Knox**, through **Jimmy Rodgers** (of 'English Country Garden' fame) to **Ronnie Hawkins** whose 'Forty Days' in 1959 with the Rock-a-Teens' 'Woo Hoo', was the label's only hard piece of Fifties rock-'n'roll. By 1962, however, the company was concentrating on repackaging its own oldies, as well as signing new talent. Its principal successes in the Sixties were **Joey Dee and the Starliters**, the Royal Teens and **Tommy James and the Shondells**.

ROXY MUSIC In its conception, Roxy Music was not so much a band as a musical workshop presided over by Bryan Ferry. While an art student in Newcastle, Ferry (who was born in Washington, County Durham, on 26 September 1945) worked as a disc jockey and singer with soul band Gas Works. After leaving college he became a teacher and an occasional artist, then realized that the quickest and most effective way to put over his ideas was within a rock band. He began to put together Roxy Music – the name picked from a list of old cinema names – after teaching himself to play piano in ten days and developed his concept of the band as one of elegance and glamour, with a hint of nostalgia rubbing against futuristic rock. The 1971–2 line-up was Ferry on vocals and keyboards, David O'List (ex-**Nice**) on guitar, Paul Thompson (born on 13 May 1951) on drums, Graham Simpson on bass, Andy Mackay (23 July 1946) on saxophone and oboe, and Brian Eno (15 May 1948) who had initially been taken

Bryan Ferry in the Eighties, an image of sleazy sophistication

on as sound man, through Mackay, but he soon graduated to the stage, where he played synthesizer and co-ordinated tapes of special effects.

Signed by Island Records, their first album *Roxy Music* was released in mid-1972 in a blaze of attention, though by this time Simpson had been replaced by Rik Kenton (31 October 1945) who himself left a few months later to be replaced by a series of guest bassists that included ex-**Big Three** member John Gustafson. In September, 'Virginia Plain' reached Number 4 in the UK, and 'Pyjamarama' and 'Street Life' provided further Top 10 hits during 1973. In time, however, the androgynous-looking Eno began to attract attention in his own right, an event not foreseen in the Ferry plan. On *For Your Pleasure* (1973), guitarist Phil Manzanera (31 January 1951) replaced O'List and subsequently Eddie Jobson (violin, keyboards, born on 28 April 1955) replaced Eno, who pursued a studiedly eclectic solo career thereafter. *Stranded* (1974) featured compositions by both Manzanera and Mackay, and *Country Life* gave them their first, if modest, American success with a Number 37 album chart placing. 'Love is the Drug', taken from *Siren* (1975) went to Number 30 in the US that year, after which Ferry broke up the group and continued with a solo career that had begun in 1973 with *These Foolish Things* and yet had been intended only as complementary to Roxy Music's activities. Mackay provided the music for the ITV series, *Rock*

Follies, in 1976–7, while Manzanera played on sessions and with a short-lived band (featuring Eno) called 801.

In 1978, Ferry re-formed the band – minus Jobson – for the album *Manifesto*, but by 1980 and the release of *Flesh and Blood*, Roxy Music was a threesome: Ferry, Mackay and Manzanera. It set the pattern for the band's career in the Eighties, offering Ferry originals in a stylish, clinically clean, soul-inflected musical setting. The band seemed more of a Bryan Ferry vehicle than ever, his languid-loner songs dominating their albums and the personnel changing with each tour. *Avalon* was released in 1982 and an extended-play single, *The High Road*, during the following year.

RUBY AND THE ROMANTICS Originally known as the Supremes, Edward Roberts (first tenor), Ronald Mosley (baritone), Leroy Fann (bass, from Ohio) and Alabama-born George Lee (second tenor) changed their name to the Romantics when Ruby Walsh (also from Ohio) joined them as lead singer in 1962. Their recording of Bob Hilliard's Latin-flavoured song, 'Our Day Will Come' on Kapp, topped both pop and R&B charts the following year. They were managed by orchestra leader Leroy Kirkland and their other Top 50 hits, all on Kapp, included 'My Summer Love', 'Hey There Lonely Boy' (later revived by **Eddie Holman** with a change of gender), 'Young Wings Can Fly' and 'When You're Young and in Love'. The group also recorded for ABC-Paramount.

RUFFIN, DAVID The son of a Baptist preacher, David Ruffin began his career singing gospel with the Dixie Nightingales. Born in Meridian, Mississippi, on 18 January 1941, Ruffin had a brief spell as a racehorse jockey in Arkansas, where he met Billy Davis and signed with Anna Records, which Davis was forming with the Gordy family. In Detroit he soon joined the **Temptations**, and it was his distinctive, gritty baritone voice that carried such hits as 'Ain't Too Proud to Beg'. He left the Temptations in 1968 to go solo, scoring a Top 10 hit with 'My Whole World Ended', and after a short period of duetting with his brother **Jimmy**, he reverted to his successful solo career with Motown. 'Walk Away from Love' (produced by **Van McCoy**) brought him a Number 9 US hit in 1975. He rejoined the Temptations with another ex-member, **Eddie Kendricks**, in 1982. See *also* the **Temptations**

RUFFIN, JIMMY

RUFFIN, JIMMY Best remembered for the plaintive beat ballad, 'What Becomes of the Broken Hearted', Jimmy Ruffin was born in Collinsville, Mississippi, on 7 May 1939, and moved to Detroit in 1960. One of the members of Motown's **Contours** group introduced him to Berry Gordy, who signed him to the Miracle label, though much of his early time at Motown was spent providing vocal backings for groups like the **Supremes**. Neither of his first two singles, 'Don't Feel Sorry for Me' (1961) and 'Since I've Lost You' (1964), were big hits, and Ruffin supplemented his Motown earnings by working on the Ford assembly lines. Ruffin declined to join the **Temptations** when the opportunity was offered, a decision that was vindicated by the success of 'What Becomes of the Broken Hearted' in 1966, when it became a transatlantic Top 10 hit. Subsequent discs were smaller hits – 'I've Passed This Way Before' (1966), 'Gonna Give Her All the Love I've Got' (1967) – but he remained particularly popular in the UK until the early Seventies, scoring three Top 10 hits in 1970 alone ('Farewell is a Lonely Sound', 'I'll Say Forever My Love', 'It's Wonderful'). He recorded an album with his brother **David Ruffin**, *I Am My Brother's Keeper* (1971), before departing from Motown in 1972 for a spell with Atlantic and then Polydor. He made a comeback to the transatlantic charts in 1980 with 'Hold On to My Love' (RSO).

RUFUS Originally a West Coast splinter-group from Chicago-based popsters American Breed, Rufus started out as Ask Rufus before personnel changes resulted in a bi-racial soul band featuring the versatile lead vocal of **Chaka Khan**. Signed by ABC in 1973 they recorded a moderately successful debut album, *Rufus*, from which three singles were drawn, but the breakthrough came with their compelling treatment of a Stevie Wonder song, 'Tell Me Something Good', from their second album, *Rags to Rufus*, the following year.

Further personnel changes left Chaka fronting Tony Maiden (guitar), Bobby Watson (bass), Kevin Murphy and Nate Morgan (keyboards), and André Fischer (drums). This line-up went on to join the major league, bridging pop and soul markets with *Rufusized* (1974) and the single hits 'Once You Get Started' and 'Please Pardon Me' (1975). From 1975 until Chaka's break with the band in 1978, the line-up was billed as Rufus featuring Chaka Khan. *See also* **Chaka Khan**

RUNDGREN, TODD Master engineer/producer and multi-faceted recording artist Todd Rundgren was born in Upper Darby, Pennsylvania, on 22 June 1948. He was lead guitarist with various local groups, including Money and Woody's Truck Stop, before making his first albums with the Nazz. Three albums appeared on SGC between 1968 and 1970, showcasing a band clearly influenced by the British groups of the Sixties. The group had a small hit with 'Hello It's Me' in 1969, which Rundgren re-recorded in 1973 with even greater success.

In 1970, Rundgren changed direction to work as house engineer and producer for the Bearsville label. He was associated with albums by **Paul Butterfield**, Ian and Sylvia, Jesse Winchester, **Badfinger** and **The Band**. He also put together his own recording trio, Runt, with Tony Sales (bass) and Hunt Sales (drums). The result was *Runt* (Bearsville, 1970) and *The Ballad of Todd Rundgren* (1971). The former included Top 20 US single 'We Gotta Get You a Woman'.

Dropping the Runt tag and working as a solo artist, Rundgren went on to make *Something/Anything*, a double album released in 1972 on the Bearsville label. The title was accurate: the record included neat pop songs like the hit single, 'I Saw the Light', but also self-indulgent pieces of electronic trickery and artless jams. Then came *A Wizard, a True Star* (1973), which he modestly described as 'the first stream-of-consciousness album'. As well as a medley of old soul songs, it included critical lyrics about politicians, rock

Producer, songwriter and performer Todd Rundgren, live in Paris, 1977

revolutionaries and Top 40 androgyny.

Todd (1974) was a suitably ego-centric title for what many consider to be Rundgren's best album. It again contained socially conscious songs ('Sons of 1984', 'Number One Lowest Common Denominator') as well as a dazzling tour of various then-current rock styles. He continued to produce such artists as **Grand Funk Railroad**, **Hall and Oates** and Felix Cavaliere of the **Rascals**, as well as recording further albums, among them *Todd Rundgren's Utopia* (Bearsville, 1974) and *Initiation* (1975).

In 1977, Rundgren returned to outside production with **Meat Loaf**'s *Bat out of Hell* and released two further Utopia albums, *RA* and *Oops, Wrong Planet*; a double live set, *Back to the Bars*, followed, together with a solo effort, *Hermit of Mink Hollow*. In 1979, he produced recordings by the **Tom Robinson** Band, the **Tubes** and **Patti Smith**. The Eighties saw him continuing to record prolifically, both on his own and with Utopia, while accepting the occasional production job like the **Psychedelic Furs**' *Forever Now* in 1982.

RUSH Progressive Canadian rock trio Rush started life in the North American hard guitar rock mould but developed into a subtle, ambitious and complex unit. High-pitched vocals, epic guitar work and lengthy musical structures place Rush in similar musical territory to that of **Yes** and early **Genesis**.

Formed in a high school 200 miles from Toronto in 1969, Geddy Lee (bass/keyboards/vocals), Alex Lifeson (guitar) and John Rutsey (drums) played school dances and private parties before graduating to the Toronto club circuit. By 1974 they had gained a reputation as a hard rocking outfit, and, faced with record company indifference, they self-financed the debut album *Rush*. This sold well on the strength of their local following, and they were finally signed by Mercury. At this point Rutsey was replaced by Neil Peart, who also became responsible for Rush's later apocalyptic science fantasy lyrics.

In 1976, three albums and several tours later, they released both a concept album, *2112*, and a double live album, *All the World's a Stage*; these established Rush as a major draw on both sides of the Atlantic, a status they consolidated by touring Europe for the first time in 1977. Subsequent recordings enhanced Rush's reputation for powerful rock with progressive/art rock tinges, proving they were not just another heavy metal band.

RUSH, OTIS Blues singer Otis Rush was born in Philadelphia, Mississippi, on 29 April 1934, and first recorded for Cobra in Chicago. In 1956, he cut sixteen tracks of exceptionally high quality, one of which – 'I Can't Quit You Baby' – reached the R&B Top 10. An important, but often unremarked, influence on the more 'purist' of the British R&B musicians, he is a left-handed guitarist with an unparalleled sustained note technique. The superb 'So Many Roads' heralded Rush's move to Chess in 1960 and he has recorded for Duke, Vanguard and, in 1969, Cotillion, with **Mike Bloomfield** and Nick Gravenites producing. He remains one of the few younger bluesmen whose work is comparable with that of the older generation.

RUSH, TOM A singer/songwriter from Portsmouth, New Hampshire, Tom Rush (born on 8 February 1941) started his folk career while attending Harvard University. He soon gravitated towards the Boston/Cambridge coterie of the Club 47. Influenced by Eric Von Schmidt, he developed his twelve-string and bottleneck style to a highly individual level on his first Elektra album, *Tom Rush*, and the acoustic side of the 1966 *Take a Little Walk with Me*. These, and two earlier Prestige albums, reveal a stronger traditional and country blues emphasis than his Dylanesque contemporaries. He shunned the protest era and though he fell in with the electric trend on the 1966 album, it was by playing rock'n'roll classics by **Chuck Berry**, **Bo Diddley** and **Buddy Holly**, with **Al Kooper** on lead guitar. In 1968 he abandoned folk music with *The Circle Game*, a lavishly arranged album of heavily poetic material, including the restrained 'No Regrets', his finest song, and others by the then unknown writers **Joni Mitchell** (the title song), **Jackson Browne**, and **James Taylor**. Three patchier albums followed with more good interpretations but weaker self-written songs and less thoughtful arrangements. *Ladies Love Outlaws* (Columbia, 1975) glimpsed at a return to former glory. In 1985 a new album, *Late Night Radio*, appeared on the independent Nightlight label.

RUSHENT, MARTIN Working in recording studios since 1969, Martin Rushent made his name in the early Eighties as the producer for the **Human League** and became an important influence on the development of electronics in pop.

Born on 11 July 1948, Rushent began as a tape operator in London's Advision Studios, then worked as engineer with **Yes**, **ELP**, **T. Rex** and others during the early Seventies before an abortive attempt to build his own studios led him into A&R at United Artists (though he did manage to produce one hit, Stretch's 'Why Did You Do It?' in 1975). He signed the **Buzzcocks** and the **Stranglers** and went on to produce them both, scoring the first hit new wave album with the Stranglers' *Rattus Norvegicus* (1977). During this time he also produced **Generation X**.

After these successes, he concentrated on his ambition to build his own lavishly-equipped recording studio, Genetic. Since it had been, at first, just a simple, informal set-up (which nevertheless produced the million-selling *Visage* LP in 1980), the more ambitious construction involved threw up financial problems and it was only his work with French band Téléphone that pulled Rushent through.

The first album produced in the newly-completed Genetic studios was the Human League's phenomenally successful *Dare* (1981) which took advantage of Rushent's skill with synthesizers, and this led him to win the British Phonographic Institute's Producer of the Year award in 1981. The next year, 1982, was also a good one for Rushent as only one week out of 52 had no Genetic product in the UK charts.

Rushent also worked with **Altered Images** and the **Go Gos**, but after 1982 his influence tailed off as other producers started to gain prominence, although his studios continued to be fully booked as Genetic became established as one of the UK's leading recording studios.

RUSSELL, LEON A leading California-based arranger, producer and songwriter during the Sixties, Leon Russell emerged from the relative anonymity of session work towards the end of the decade to mastermind **Joe Cocker**'s American success and establish his own label, Shelter Records. He was born in Lawton, Oklahoma, on 2 April 1941 and was part of a small circle of musicians – David Gates, Carl Radle and **J. J. Cale** among them – who developed their own kind of rockabilly on the Kansas/Oklahoma borders and went on to become internationally famous musicians in other styles. Russell played piano with **Ronnie Hawkins**' Hawks and in 1959 began recording as Russell Bridges.

After playing briefly with **Jerry Lee Lewis**' touring band, he moved to Los Angeles and became a full-time session pianist, working on tracks by the **Crystals**, the **Ronettes**, the **Righteous Brothers**, the **Byrds** and many others. He graduated to arranging, working mainly with **Gary Lewis and the Playboys** and, in 1967, **Harpers Bizarre**, but his attempt to embark on a solo career – with a country version of Erroll Garner's 'Misty' in 1967 – was not a success. In 1968, he began a fruitful association with **Delaney and Bonnie** Bramlett, arranging all the tracks on their debut album *Accept No Substitute* and touring with them; through them he met Marc Benno, a folk-rock performer with whom he cut his first album, a *tour de force* of gospel-rock called *Asylum Choir* (Smash).

Leon Russell plays it standing up

During 1969, Russell and producer friend **Denny Cordell** bought a share in the Shelter label, a subsidiary of Blue Thumb Records, and began scouting for talent. Their signings included **Freddie King** and J. J. Cale, but the most significant of Shelter's early releases proved to be Russell's eponymous solo album, which included Delaney and Bonnie, **Rita Coolidge**, **Steve Winwood**, **Eric Clapton**, **George Harrison**, **Ringo Starr**, Charlie Watts, Bill Wyman and **Joe Cocker** as guest artists. A tour consolidated Russell's growing critical reputation, but it was his involvement in Joe Cocker's US tour of 1970 that finally made his name widely known. Russell put together a huge

touring band, including himself, and suggested that the event be filmed: the result, *Mad Dogs and Englishmen*, was a box-office success and threw the spotlight firmly on Russell himself, picturing him continually coaching, rehearsing, arranging, playing and cheerleading. Following that, he recorded a post-tour album for Shelter in four different studios, co-wrote and recorded an album with Eric Clapton, wrote and recorded 'Watching the River Flow' with **Bob Dylan**, and produced George Harrison's single 'Bangla Desh', appearing with the latter in the 1971 Concert for Bangla Desh.

Legal difficulties hit Shelter during 1971 in a dispute with National Comics over the label's logo and a year later Russell suffered a nervous breakdown on a British visit. Within months he was back, with the album *Carney*, but his followers noted a lack of fire in his new work and his star began to fade somewhat. *Leon Live* (1973) sold well but he began to distance himself from mainstream rock with excursions into country music (*Hank Wilson is Back*, 1973), jazz (*Stop All That Jazz*, 1974) and soul (*Make Love to the Music*, 1977, recorded with his wife Mary McCreery). Subsequent albums included *Americana* (1978) and *Willie and Leon* (Columbia, 1979), made with **Willie Nelson**, while the early Eighties found him leading a bluegrass outfit called the New Grass Revival. Their *Live Album* (1981) featured bluegrass versions of songs by **Hank Williams**, Jagger and Richards, **Lennon** and **McCartney** and Russell himself.

RUTS Best known for their storming punk anthem 'Babylon's Burning', the Ruts had a promising career cut short by the death of singer Malcolm Owen in 1980. Owen, Dave Ruffy (drums), Segs (bass) and Paul Fox (guitar) were a unit of extraordinary power and ferocity, and seemed likely to carry on the spirit of punk long after its premature demise in 1978.

'Babylon's Burning' reached Number 7 in 1979, and was quickly followed into the charts by the superb singles 'Something That I Said' and 'Staring at the Rude Boys'. These, plus the powerful debut album *The Crack* (1980), pointed to the Ruts becoming a major band, but Owen's death from a heroin overdose had broken the group's spirit. Although the remaining trio plus Gary Barnacle (sax/keyboards) made the albums *Animal Now* (1981) and *Rhythm Collision* (1983), as the Ruts DC, they never recaptured that original vitality.

RYDELL, BOBBY Born Robert Ridarelli in Philadelphia on 26 April 1942, Bobby Rydell became a regular on Paul Whiteman's local Teen Club TV show in Philadelphia at the age of nine, singing and doing impersonations. In 1957, he joined a local rock- 'n'roll group, Rocco and his Saints, but went solo under the close guidance of manager Frankie Day. Rydell recorded two flops for Day's Veko label – formed after Capitol, Decca and RCA had turned Rydell down – then joined Cameo, recording three more flops before registering with 'Kissin' Time' in 1959. Clean-cut Rydell went on to become an American teen idol of gigantic proportions and during 1959–63 he notched up a further sixteen American hits, including 'Volare', 'Sway', 'Swingin' School', 'Wild One' and 'Forget Him', until Beatlemania caused his fortunes to wane rapidly in 1964. He appeared with Ann-Margret in the film version of *Bye Bye Birdie* (1964).

RYDER, MITCH, AND THE DETROIT WHEELS Although they came along with the wrong sound at the wrong time, Mitch Ryder and the Detroit Wheels made it work anyhow. 'Jenny Take a Ride' (on New Voice), a frenetic Little Richard remake that broke at the end of 1965, was much earthier than just about anything else on the charts at a time when rock was becoming increasingly sophisticated. Born in 1945, Mitch (real name Billy LaVere) had spent his teenage years roaming the black clubs of Detroit, sometimes getting onstage to test his pipes against those of his Motown idols. He was a screamer with style, perhaps the best of the white rhythm and blues singers, with a stage act modelled after **James Brown**'s.

By 1968, the group – John Badanjek, Jimmy McCarty, Earl Elliot and Joe Cubert – had rocked up ten more chart items, the biggest of which were 'Devil with a Blue Dress On'/'Good Golly Miss Molly' (1966) and 'Sock It to Me Baby' (1967). But manager-producer **Bob Crewe** felt Ryder was the sole attraction, and neglected the rest of the band. He tried to mould a Las Vegas-type show with full orchestra and elaborate choreography. Ryder went along with it only for a few months before returning to Detroit, bitter and deep in debt. In 1971, at the height of the Motor City's heavy-metal mania, he resurfaced as leader of the Wheels under their new name of Detroit. Their one album for Paramount was a metallic blues-rock classic featuring Mitch's rendering of the **Falcons**' 'I Found a

One of rock's most talented misfits, Mitch Ryder, in all-action sock-it-to-me mood as the Detroit Wheels go roaring up the charts

Love', a song he had by then been singing for eleven years. But this band was short-lived, a victim of little promotion and much in-fighting. Mitch temporarily retired not to the car wash, but to the car factories of his home-town, where, as Billy LaVere once more, he worked as a foreman and nursed a throat infection that threatened to finish his singing career for good. Late in the Seventies, however, he made a

solo recording comeback with *How I Spent My Vacation* (Seeds and Stems), while one-time Wheels Rusty Day and Jim McCarty joined Carmine Appica and Tim Bogert in Cactus. Ryder's songs are best known these days as fixtures in **Bruce Springsteen**'s on-stage repertoire. 1983 saw Ryder back in the studio for *Never Kick a Sleeping Dog*, produced by John Cougar Mellencamp.

S

SAD CAFÉ Formed in Manchester in 1976, British mainstream rock band Sad Café seemed destined for international superstardom but never quite made it. Soon after their formation, Paul Young (vocals) (not the mid-Eighties solo singer), Ian Wilson (guitar/vocals), Victor Emerson (keyboards), John Stimson (bass), Ashley Mulford (guitar), Lenni (sax) and Tony Cresswell (drums) were snapped up by RCA. At odds with the punk movement dominant at that time, Sad Café decided to concentrate on breaking the US, and over several tours and two albums, *Fanx Tara* (1976) and *Misplaced Ideals* (1977), built up a steady following.

Their album, *Façades* (1979), proved to be a major success, spawning three hit singles, the biggest being 'Everyday Hurts', a UK Number 3, but that success was never followed up as they only made one more album, *Sad Café IV* (1981), on RCA and then had a brief abortive fling with Polydor before management problems eventually caused the band to split up in 1983.

In 1985, Wilson and Young reformed as Sad Café, releasing the LP *Politics of Existing*, but the comeback was briefly interrupted as Young sang with Mike Rutherford of **Genesis** on his Mike and the Mechanics project.

SADE Ex-model and clothes designer Folasade Adu (born in Nigeria on 16 January 1960), known as Sade, cultivated a cool, sophisticated image and married it with an effortlessly smooth brand of jazz-tinged pop/soul.

Sade's career was launched in a mountain of hype in 1983 as her label Epic capitalized on her stunning good looks. With such media support, it was only a matter of time before her records started to sell, and the single 'Your Love Is King' became a UK Number 6 in February 1984. *Diamond Life* was released later that year, and though it was a seamless collection of commercial tunes, its massive success came as something of a surprise as it sold over 4 million copies very quickly, and was still in the UK charts two years after its release.

Promise (1985) could never follow such an act and suffered by comparison, not marking any progression in her work, but nevertheless followed its predecessor into a lengthy chart run.

SAHM, DOUG

Born in Texas on 6 November 1941, Doug Sahm started out playing country music. At the age of five he was a regular on a local radio show. He recorded for the Sarg label and, billed as Little Doug, toured with the big names in early-Fifties country music. He also recorded for Warrior (with The Pharaohs), Harlem (with the Markays), Personality (Doug Sahm and the Spirits) and Renner (as Doug Sahm). The variety of styles he has subsequently mastered is explained by the area in which he was brought up, San Antonio. He heard as much Texas blues as country music (his first band, the Knights, which he formed when he was 14, played blues music) and a Mexican influence is also found in the so-called 'Tex-Mex' music of the **Sir Douglas Quintet**. The Quintet lasted on and off until the early Seventies, and since then Sahm has occasionally returned to the studios as a solo artist. His *Doug Sahm and Band* (Atlantic, 1973) album features such guests as **Bob Dylan**, **Dr John** and David Newman; it is a relaxed and inspired studio jam covering Western Swing, country, blues, R&B and rock. In 1974 he formed his Tex-Mex Trip band with Doug Clifford and Stu Cook (both late of **Creedence Clearwater Revival**), Link Davis Jr. and Frank Rodarte. The music still ranged wide, but with more emphasis on Sahm's own brand of country-rock, and was well represented on *Groovers' Paradise* (Warner Brothers, 1974).

He was associated with the Austin, Texas, country scene during the late Seventies and in 1980 recorded a third solo album, *Hell of a Spell*, for Takoma. A year later, he re-formed the Sir Douglas Quintet with former members Johnny Perez and Augie Meyer: a reunion album, *Border Wave*, was released, again on the Takoma label. *See also* **Sir Douglas Quintet**

SAINTE-MARIE, BUFFY

Compositions like 'Universal Soldier' (a hit for **Donovan** and **Glen Campbell**) and her strong, idiosyncratic voice made Buffy Sainte-Marie – born in Maine on 20 February 1941, of Cree Indian descent – an important figure within the New York folk scene during the early Sixties. A number of her songs dealt with the past and present situation of the American Indian, notably 'Now that the Buffalo's Gone' and 'My Country 'Tis of Thy People You're Dying', though she is probably best-known to mainstream audiences for her songs 'Until It's Time for You to Go' – a US Top 40 hit for **Elvis Presley** in 1972 and since recorded by numerous artists – and 'Soldier Blue', a Top 10 UK hit for her during 1971. She began recording in 1964, for Vanguard, and started to develop beyond folk music in the late Sixties, cutting her *I'm Gonna Be a Country Girl Again* album in Nashville in 1968 and subsequently experimenting with indigenous Indian styles, rock accompaniments and orchestral settings on albums such as *Illuminations* (1970), *She Used to Wanna Be a Ballerina* (1971) and *Moon Shot* (1972). She moved to ABC Records in 1974, making her debut with *Sweet America* two years later. She co-wrote the Academy Award-winning 'Up Where We Belong', from the film *An Officer and a Gentleman* (1983), with **Jack Nitzsche** and Will Jennings.

SAM AND DAVE

Soul duo Sam Moore (born in Miami, Florida, on 12 October 1935) and Dave Prater (Ocilly, Georgia, on 9 May 1937) were discovered by Morris Levy, of Roulette, in 1960. Sam's musical grounding was singing gospel with the Melonaires, but he soon realized that only secular music would yield sufficient financial reward to support his family and began doing solo gigs around the Miami area. He was playing the King of Hearts Club in Miami, in 1958, when Dave Prater joined him onstage, and the audience response persuaded them to form a partnership. The duo signed with Roulette in 1960 and spent four years making fine gospel-soul discs under the wing of **Henry Glover**, but without any commercial impact. They left Roulette, in 1965, to sign with Atlantic. There, Jerry Wexler arranged for them to record at Stax, whose owner, Jim Stewart, required that their records were released on his label. They were teamed with writers/producers **Isaac Hayes** and David Porter to record a series of gospel-tinged hits supported by the renowned Memphis Horns, both up-tempo and ballads, commencing with 'You Don't Know Like I Know' and 'Hold On I'm Coming' (1966) and culminating with 'Born Again' (1969), peaking with million-selling Number 2 hit 'Soul Man' (1967).

When Stax was sold to Gulf & Western in 1968, the duo reverted to the Atlantic label, but later discs, recorded in Miami, were unsuccessful and they split in 1970, intent on furthering solo careers, Sam with Atlantic and Dave with Alston. But a year later they teamed up again, signing with United Artists after a short spell back with Atlantic. In 1980, memories were jogged by the film *The Blues Brothers*, in which the stars John Belushi and Dan Ackroyd modelled themselves closely on Sam and Dave. They were backed by the appropriate musicians and even succeeded in making 'Soul Man' a hit again for Sam and Dave. In early 1987, Sam Moore formed a brief temporary partnership with **Lou Reed** to record 'Soul Man' yet again.

SAM THE SHAM AND THE PHARAOHS

Christened Domingo Samudio, Sam the Sham was a Texan-Mexican who, with his Pharaohs (David Martin, Roy Stinnet, Jerry Patterson and Butch Gibson, also of Tex-Mex origin and musical inspiration), launched a rocking good-time sound at the public in the mid-Sixties. The group recorded unsuccessfully in Memphis in the early Sixties, but a cover version of Gene Simmons' novelty rock hit, 'Haunted House', was followed by 'Woolly Bully', 'Ju Ju Hand' and other top hits. 'Woolly Bully' was a monster hit for MGM in 1965, to whom it had been leased from Stan Kesler's Pen Records in Memphis. The group transferred permanently to MGM thereafter and followed up with 'Red Hot', an old rockabilly tune, and 'Lil Red Riding Hood'. In 1970, Sam attempted a comeback with an uneven album (*Sam, Hard and Heavy*) under the name of Sam Samudio on Atlantic. In 1981, he contributed two songs to the soundtrack of the film *The Border*.

SAN FRANCISCO

For many years, San Francisco had provided a hospitable environment for both artistic and political radicalism even before the growth of the 'hippie' culture in the mid-Sixties, whose main expression was the music of dozens of locally-based rock bands. In the space of a few months during 1967, this localized phenomenon had an international impact as San Francisco groups, led by the Charlatans, the **Jefferson Airplane** and **Country Joe and the Fish**, were signed to major record labels. **Scott McKenzie** sold vast numbers of his ersatz hippie anthem 'San Francisco (Be Sure to Wear Some Flowers in Your Hair)', and the city's counter-culture was the subject of countless magazine and television features. In addition, the so-called 'psychedelic music' of San Francisco groups inspired other musicians to experiment within a rock format throughout America and Western Europe.

Before 1965, there had been a small but flourishing rock scene in the city itself and a lively folk music scene in the university centre of Berkeley across the Bay. The local labels were Fantasy (Lenny Bruce, Vince Guaraldi, the Golliwogs, later **Creedence Clearwater Revival**) and **Tom Donahue**'s Autumn Records. Donahue was a well-known local DJ and pioneer of 'underground radio', who employed Sylvester Stewart (later Sly Stone) as producer on hits by the **Beau Brummels**, the Mojo Men and others. By 1965, the city was feeling the first ripples from the British Invasion and the new American rock of the **Byrds** and **Lovin' Spoonful**. Dances were organized at the Longshoreman's Hall by a community organization called the Family Dog, at which the Charlatans, the Great Society (featuring Grace Slick), the Jefferson Airplane, the Warlocks (later the **Grateful Dead**) and the pre-Janis Joplin **Big Brother and the Holding Company** played. Meanwhile, in Berkeley, the Instant Action Jug Band was becoming Country Joe and the Fish as acid became as important as protest in their lifestyle. LSD was not yet illegal in California and soon the influence of its apostles, notably Ken Kesey, was felt. The Grateful Dead developed their long, meandering numbers as a kind of musical equivalent of an acid trip, while the Airplane reached the American Top 10 with a thinly disguised drug song, 'White Rabbit'. Closely associated with the groups and dances was the development of poster art and of light shows.

In 1967, the first major free outdoor concert, the Human Be-In, inspired the Monterey Festival at which the leading San Francisco groups appeared outside their home town for the first time. The Airplane had just been signed to RCA, and, sensing a trend, other big companies moved in. The Grateful Dead joined Warner Brothers, **Moby Grape** and **Janis Joplin** went to Columbia, the Fish to Vanguard, the Sons of Champlin and Mystery Trend to Verve. As those groups began to have hit albums, other musicians were among the thousands flocking to San Francisco's Haight-Ashbury district to join the 'love generation': **Sir Douglas Quintet**, **Mother Earth**, **Electric Flag**, Linn County and Mad River were among them. But the hippie community was crumbling, music had become big business (**Bill Graham**, former Mime Troupe member, was now a big-time promoter) and the successful local bands were setting their sights on wider horizons. By 1969, there was no longer a specifically San Francisco sound. It was underground music and of international significance.

SANTANA Emerging at the end of the Sixties from San Francisco's Haight-Ashbury area, Santana were the first band to find success with a merger of electric rock and the percussive rhythms of Africa and Central America. Initially known as the Santana Bluesband, the band came together in 1966 with a line-up comprising guitarist Carlos Santana (born in Autlán, Jalisco, Mexico on 20 July 1947), percussionist Mike Carabello, organist Gregg Rolie and guitarist Tom Frazier; among their first gigs were bottom-of-the-bill performances at Bill Graham's Fillmore West in San Francisco, supporting acts like the **Who** and **Paul Butterfield**. In the summer of 1967, Frazier left and David Brown joined on bass and Marcus Malone on percussion, and the band's name was shortened to Santana. Drummer Michael Shrieve joined during the following year. Largely due to Malone's influence, the music started to move away from its blues roots towards a more Afro-Cuban sound; when Malone was convicted on a manslaughter charge two years later, his mantle was inherited by mid-1969 recruit José 'Chepito' Areas.

Santana's appearance at the Woodstock festival in August 1969 launched them into rock's premier division and their debut album for Columbia, *Santana*, became one of the year's biggest sellers. The *Woodstock* film (1970) helped introduce the band to a wider audience: a second album, *Abraxas*, sold well and their version of Fleet-

wood Mac's 'Black Magic Woman' reached Number 4 in the US. Another track from *Abraxas*, 'Samba Pa Ti', became a UK Top 30 hit when issued as a single in 1974. Throughout 1971, various additional recruits joined the line-up and by the time the band came to record *Santana III*, guitarist Neal Schon had joined along with another percussionist, Coke Escovedo. Following a drugs bust in 1971, bassist David Brown left to be replaced by Tom Rutley, and the band stood in danger of breaking up in considerable acrimony. Schon and Rolie went on to form Journey, while Carlos Santana recorded the jazz-influenced *Caravanserai* (1972) with selected personnel. During that year, he came to embrace the religious teachings of the guru Sri Chinmoy, later adopting the name Devadip Carlos Santana as a mark of his conversion, and that September he unveiled a new line-up for his band, retaining only the services of Areas and Shrieve. Newcomers included jazz vocalist Leon Thomas, keyboardist Tom Coster and percussionist Armando Peraza.

Carlos also collaborated at this time with the Mahavishnu Orchestra's **John McLaughlin** to produce *Love Devotion Surrender* (1973), a compendium of rock guitar bombast. *Welcome* continued the progression towards a more jazz-dominated fusion and was the last to feature Santana's longest surviving collaborator, Mike Shrieve, who was replaced after falling ill on the eve of a

Santana in the late Sixties; the man himself is second from the left. No one else could quite match the sweet sound of Carlos' singing guitar

1974 US tour and went on to form the band Automatic Man. Santana's 1974 release, *Borboletta*, was again in the jazz-rock idiom, but its follow-up, *Amigos*, was a clear and commercially successful attempt to return to the band's Latin roots. *Festival* (1976) and the double *Moonflower* (1977) continued in this vein, the latter album yielding their biggest UK hit single, a remake of the Zombies' 'She's Not There', a Number 11 in the UK in 1977. Between then and the end of the decade, Carlos toured and recorded with the band, produced a solo album *Oneness/Silver Dreams Golden Reality* (1979), and contributed to albums by Narada Michael Walden and Herbie Hancock. The Santana albums *Inner Secrets* (1978) and *Marathon* (1979) flirted with disco rhythms, but the band returned to a more traditional formula on *Zebop!* (1981) and *Shango* (1982). In 1983, Carlos recorded the solo album *Havana Moon*, with Jerry Wexler producing and Booker T. Jones (see **Booker T.**) and **Willie Nelson** making guest appearances, and during the following year, *Live*, was released of his on-stage collaboration with **Buddy Miles**. *Welcome* appeared in 1984 under the Santana banner and was well received.

Santana's main impact was to alert many rock and soul bands to the possibilities of using percussion to embellish their music, and their influence can be easily heard in the music of acts as diverse as Sly Stone, **Talking Heads**, **Steely Dan** and Pigbag (*see* **Pop Group**). Despite continued activity and international success into the Eighties, it is their earlier work that remains their most significant contribution to the history of rock.

SARSTEDT, PETER

In 1969, Peter Sarstedt emerged from the shadow of his brother, **Eden Kane** (one of the minor figures of pre-**Beatles** British pop) with his own composition, 'Where Do You Go to My Lovely' which was a Number 1 UK hit on United Artists. It was a perfect distillation of middle-class *angst* that temporarily fitted the mood of the times. None of Sarstedt's other projects – which included the forming of a group with his brothers – came to anything, nor did his albums for Warner Brothers (e.g. *Trees*, 1975) meet with any success. His brother Robin had a Number 3 UK hit in 1976 with a version of the Hoagy Carmichael song, 'My Resistance is Low'. With Robin (now recording as Clive Sarstedt), Peter made an instrumental album of New Age music, *Asia Minor* (Kenwest), in 1986.

SAXON

Emerging with their self-titled debut album in 1979, Saxon, from Barnsley in Yorkshire, came onto the scene just in time to join the ranks of the new breed of British heavy metal bands. Peter 'Biff' Byford (vocals), Graham Oliver (guitar), Paul Quinn (guitar), Steve Dawson (bass) and Pete Gill (drums) aroused further interest with well-received support slots to **Motörhead** and **Nazareth**, and then released another LP, *Wheels of Steel* (1980), to underline their ability to play fast, accomplished heavy metal.

Strong Arm of the Law (1980) was a disappointment but *Denim and Leather* (1981) re-established Saxon and broke them in the US, confirming the band's status among the cream of British heavy metal. Pausing only to replace drummer Gill with Nigel Glockler, Saxon continued to produce powerful albums with *Power and the Glory* (1983) and *Crusader* (1984). The group signed with EMI in 1985 and issued the successful *Rock the Nation* later that year. While not achieving the huge international success of a band like **Def Leppard**, Saxon nevertheless had strong followings around the world and retained great critical approval.

SAYER, LEO

Like **David Essex**, Leo Sayer – born Gerard Hugh Sayer on 21 May 1948 in Brighton, Sussex – was one of a new breed of pop showmen in the mid-Seventies who combined flamboyant stage acts with 'meaningful' songs, yet avoided the camp connotations of **Gary Glitter** *et al.* Born in Shoreham, Sussex, Sayer led a band named Patches before teaming up as a songwriter with Dave Courtney; their work first appeared on **Roger Daltrey**'s debut solo album, from which 'Giving It All Away' was a hit in 1973. Managed by **Adam Faith**, Sayer was signed to Chrysalis, reaching the Top 10 with his first single, 'The Show Must Go On'. He developed a striking stage act using mime and a harlequin outfit. Both *Silverbird* (1973) and *Just a Boy* (1974) entered the British album charts, while the latter also provided him with a transatlantic Top 10 single, 'Long Tall Glasses'. In 1975 Dave Courtney released a solo album, *First Day*, and Sayer, now writing with Frank Farrell, released the more assured *Another Year*, which included the Top 3 single 'Moonlighting'.

With the American market in mind, Sayer soon dropped the theatrical trappings and began writing and recording in a more poppified, mainstream style, typified by the two biggest hits of his career, 'You Make Me Feel Like Dancing' (1976) and 'When I Need You' (1977). Both were US Number 1s, the latter a chart-topper in the UK as well. He continued to record in a disco-cum-AOR vein for the rest of the Seventies – 'How Much Love' and 'Thunder in My Heart' (both 1977) were entirely representative – and in the early Eighties gained a BBC television series on which he developed his skills as a would-be-all-round entertainer, learning the arts of comic timing and Young Generation-style choreography. By 1985, the hits had become far less frequent but, like David Essex, he seemed to have found his niche as a middle-of-the-road pop star and was resolutely sticking to it.

Leo Sayer, pop showman and professional nice guy, on the hop

SCAFFOLD

A trio of Liverpudlian humorists with an appeal similar to that of London's Alberts, Scaffold first attracted national attention with their recordings of such schoolboyish ditties as 'Thank U Very Much' and 'Lily the Pink', a million-seller in 1968. None the less, Scaffold were primarily stage and club performers, who also maintain disparate individual careers. Mike McGear (Michael McCartney, stepbrother of Paul, born 7 January 1944) released a solo album in 1975; Roger McGough (9 November 1937) was a poet particularly renowned for his P.C. Plod cycle; John Gorman (4 January

1937) was a comedy actor. In the early Seventies, all three men became associated with the larger unit, Grimms. In the Eighties, McGear wrote a book of reminiscences – *Thank U Very Much* – about his and Paul's early life, while Gorman became a resident performer on ITV's notorious late-night show, *OTT*.

SCAGGS, BOZ

Born on 8 June 1944, in Ohio, Boz (William Royce) Scaggs made a major impact in the mid-Seventies with an innovative brand of white soul music. His performing and writing style developed in Dallas, Texas, and Madison, Wisconsin, where he was one of the singer/guitarists with the Ardells, whose members included **Steve Miller** and Ben Sidran. After a trip to Europe which produced a hastily made and obscure album, *Boz* (Polydor, 1966), Scaggs joined the Steve Miller Band in its San Francisco heyday, and many regard his time with Miller as having produced the band's most memorable work, *Children of the Future* (1968) and *Sailor* (1968). After leaving Miller in 1968, Boz made an album at Muscle Shoals, Alabama, *Boz Scaggs* (Atlantic, 1968), produced by Jann Wenner, the editor of *Rolling Stone*, which contained some impressive guitar playing by the then little-known Duane Allman (see **Allman Brothers Band**). From that date on, Scaggs produced a new album every fifteen months, for a small but loyal following, until he began to explore the soul idiom on the albums *My Time* (1972) and, particularly, *Slow Dancer* (1974), which was produced by ex-Motown staffman **Johnny Bristol**. *Silk Degrees* (1976) crystallized the new direction in Scaggs' work and sold over five million copies worldwide and included the hits 'Lowdown' Number 3 in the US) and 'What Can I Say' (a Top 10 hit in the UK in early 1977).

Scaggs found difficulty reaching these commercial heights again, though *Down Two, Then Left* (1977) and *Middle Man* (1980) were worthy successors to *Silk Degrees*.

SCEPTER-WAND RECORDS

The Scepter-Wand story began in 1958, when Florence Greenberg launched the Scepter label in New York. Her only act at the time was a female vocal quartet – the **Shirelles** – which she had discovered at a school talent-show and subsequently managed. Early Scepter product was channelled through Decca's distribution, but when the third release, the Shirelles' 'Dedicated to the One I Love', sold a million in 1959 the label went into its own full-scale production, promotion and distribution. Two further Shirelles discs went gold over the next year, giving Scepter a firm financial footing, and, in 1961, the Wand subsidiary was started. The first five releases remain obscure but the sixth, **Chuck Jackson**'s powerful ballad 'I Don't Want to Cry', reached the Top 10, and the same year saw Lenny Miles and Tommy Hunt with solo debut hits. The Shirelles' 'Will You Love Me Tomorrow' was Scepter's first chart-topper, and the girls had some twenty further chart entries before moving to Bell in 1967, while Chuck Jackson also enjoyed a stream of hits before he, too, left in 1967 for Motown. Further major hits came with the **Isley Brothers** ('Twist and Shout', 1962), novelties by the Rocky Fellers (1963), the **Kingsmen** ('Louie Louie', 1964) and B. J. Thomas's chart-topping original of 'Raindrops Keep Falling on My Head' (1969), but the company's biggest success was with **Dionne Warwick**, who between 1962 and 1971 achieved some thirty-eight Hot 100 entries, eight of them American Top 10 hits, largely with material written by **Burt Bacharach** and Hal David including 'Walk On By', 'I Say a Little Prayer', and 'This Girl's in Love with You'. Both Scepter and Wand remain active, mainly in the R&B field.

SCHENKER, MICHAEL

German heavy metal guitarist Michael Schenker (born in Saustedt, West Germany, on 10 January 1955) first made his reputation as a virtuoso rock player at the start of the Seventies with German outfit the **Scorpions**, but gained wider recognition on joining the British group **UFO** in 1974.

After five successful years with UFO, Schenker left in 1979, briefly rejoined the Scorpions, with whom he played on an album and half a European tour, and then promptly disappeared. He reappeared soon after on Chrysalis Records with his band, the Michael Schenker Group, in the autumn of 1980, and scored almost instant success throughout Europe, America and Japan with the eponymous debut album, a no-frills, straightforward collection of riff-ridden hard rock.

Three further albums followed, plus several changes of line-up, which at one time included ex-**Rainbow** men Cozy Powell and Graham Bonnet, confirming Schenker's band as a solid but unexceptional hard rock outfit. But with *Built to Destroy* in 1983, Schenker's fortunes started to go into decline after the album received a critical panning, and its release was followed by a long period of inactivity. Schenker spent the early part of 1986 in the US trying to put together a new band.

SCORPIONS

West Germany's Scorpions evolved from a vaguely jazz-tinged rock band in the early Seventies to an out-and-out screaming heavy metal band in the Eighties. The original – short-lived – line-up of guitarists Michael and Rudolf Schenker, Klaus Meine (vocals), Lothar Heimberg (bass) and Wolfgang Ziony (drums) recorded the first album *Action* in 1972. Through the next four albums (to *Tokyo Tapes* in 1977) and several changes of personnel, Meine and Rudolf Schenker were the nucleus of the band as its popularity grew in Japan and Germany.

Michael Schenker had left in 1973 to become a renowned guitarist with **UFO** and later to form his own band, but when he briefly returned to contribute to the Scorpions' sixth album *Lovedrive* in 1979, he added a tough metallic edge to the record, which broke them worldwide. Subsequent albums *Animal Magnetism* (1980), *Blackout* (1982) and *Love at First Sting* (1985), as well as a series of sell-out concerts across the world, further served to establish the Scorpions' status among the leading heavy metal bands of the time.

SCOTT, JACK

In 1957, Jack Scott appeared on the rock'n'roll scene and, while he recorded several powerful rockers in a Southern style, he found that a career as a rock balladeer was more acceptable to the late Fifties public. Born Jack Scafone on 24 January 1938, in Windsor, Ontario, he was living in Detroit when he joined ABC Paramount in 1957, having first gained a writing contract with Southern Music. Rockers like 'Two Timin' Woman' and 'Baby She's Gone' had some play by disc jockeys, but in 1958 producer Joe Carlton left ABC to form Carlton Records and took Scott with him. A rockabilly tune about a buddy named 'Leroy' who had been sent to jail was a hit, but the ballad flip 'My True Love' was bigger. It was followed into the charts by 'With Your Love', 'Goodbye Baby' and a latter-day rockabilly song that fought off the vocal choruses, 'The Way I Walk'. Scott joined Rank and then Capitol in 1960–1, scoring with the ballads 'What in the World's Come Over You' and 'Burning Bridges'. He recorded unsuccessfully for Jubilee in the mid-Sixties and later re-emerged as a country singer on Dot.

SCOTT, PEGGY, AND BENSON, JO JO
A briefly popular soul pairing of the late Sixties, Peggy Scott and Jo Jo Benson had US Top 40 hits with 'Lover's Holiday', 'Pickin' Wild Mountain Berries' (1968) and 'Soul Shake' (1969). Peggy Scott – born in Pensacola, Florida, in 1948 – sang in various gospel groups before adopting a secular style in 1966. She toured with **Ben E. King**, but, after hospitalization following a car crash, became resident with the Swinging Sextet in Pensacola, where she met Jo Jo Benson in 1968. Jo Jo – born in Columbus, Ohio, in 1940 – sang with the Bluenotes before joining the **Chuck Willis** Show, with which he toured until Chuck's death, later singing with the Upsetters and Enchanters. Both recorded as solo artists, but with little success.

SCOTT-HERON, GIL
One of the first performers to have integrated the political impetus behind the black struggles of the late Sixties and early Seventies into the mainstream of black music, Gil Scott-Heron was born in Chicago in 1949 and grew up in Jackson, Tennessee. He moved to New York and studied at Lincoln University where he met his later collaborator Brian Jackson (born in 1954). He published two novels, *The Vulture* (1969) and *The Nigger Factory*, and a collection of 'rap' verses, *Small Talk at 125th and Lennox*, before turning to music with Jackson. He recorded three albums for Bob Thiele's Flying Dutchman label, amongst which were *Pieces of Man* – which included 'The Revolution Will Not Be Televised', recorded by **Labelle** and *Free Will* (1973), before moving to the co-operative Stata/East label. There, with Jackson, he cut *Winter in America* (1974), which included the incisive 'H-20 Gate Blurs' and 'The Bottle', a disco discourse on the problems of alcoholism in the black ghetto. They signed with Arista in 1975 as the label's first act and recorded *The First Minute of a New Day* and *From South Africa to South Carolina* (which included the disco hit, 'Johannesburg'). Both albums sold well.

Scott-Heron's partnership with Jackson ended during the late Seventies, but albums such as *Secrets* (1978), *The Mind of Gil Scott-Heron* (1979), *1980* (1980) and *Reflections* (1981) consolidated his reputation as one of the most original and influential American jazz-funk artists: 'B Movie' on *Reflections* was a brilliant put-down on Reaganite policies, while 'We Almost Lost Detroit' became something of an antinuclear anthem.

SCREEN STARS
It was the actor Tab Hunter – born on 11 July 1931 – who first proved that an image could sell records as well as, if not better than, a sound, with his watered-down version of Sonny James' 'Young Love'. He had a 21-week run in the US chart with that disc in 1957, by which time the one thing that was clear about rock'n'roll to the record industry was that it had defined a totally new market – the teenager – that would buy almost anything specifically aimed at it.

Eddie 'Kookie' Byrnes – born on 30 July 1938 – the mandatory teenager of TV's *77 Sunset Strip*, had possibly the most bizarre Top 10 hit ever with 'Kookie Kookie Lend Me Your Comb' (Warner Brothers) in 1959, on which he did little but listen to Connie Stevens plead with him. Meanwhile, the recording career of Ms Stevens herself – the resident teenager of *Hawaiian Eye*, born on 18 April 1938, as Concetta Ann Ingolia – continued beyond 'Kookie Kookie' with a Number 3 hit, 'Sixteen Reasons' (also Warner Brothers) in 1960.

Rick Nelson had featured regularly in his parents' television show, *The Adventures of Ozzie and Harriet*, and these appearances made his name familiar before he became a major recording star. The first chart success of Academy Award winner Walter Brennan – born 25 July 1894, died 1974 – came in 1960 with the monologue, 'Dutchman's Gold', on Dot. Two years later, he reached the Top 5 with the tear-jerking 'Old Rivers' on Liberty – the flip of which was the equally bizarre 'The Epic Ride of John H. Glenn'. But perhaps the strangest case of misrepresentation was that of Lorne Greene – born in 1914 and known to the world as 'Pa Cartwright' of the Western series *Bonanza* – and his 1964 US Number 1, 'Ringo' (RCA). Supposedly a narrative based on the life of the notorious gunfighter Johnny Ringo, the record's success can be attributed partly to its release at the height of American Beatlemania. After the Beatles, a few film and television stars still scored in the charts – Richard Harris ('Macarthur Park', 1968), Lee Marvin ('Wanderin' Star', 1970), Telly Savalas ('If', 1975) and David Soul ('Don't Give Up On Us', 1976 and 'Silver Lady', 1977). John Travolta had spectacular success (with his co-star, **Olivia Newton-John**) with two songs from the film *Grease*: 'You're the One That I Want' and 'Summer Nights', both 1978). It was more common, however, for rock stars to become screen stars than vice versa.

SCRITTI POLITTI
Formed in the late Seventies, Scritti Politti (whose name was a corruption of a generic Italian term for political magazines, *scritti politici*) were initially a dreadlocked shambolic group whose style was a mixture of dub, punk and improvisation. Responsible notably for the Rough Trade single 'Skank Bloc Bologna', the group eventually foundered and control was taken by charismatic leader 'Green' Gartside (vocals, guitar).

The streamlined Scritti Politti re-emerged in 1981 with the more sophisticated album *Songs to Remember*, a lighter mix of pop, reggae, soul, jazz, and Gartside's preoccupation with French philosophers, notably those of the structuralist and semiotic schools (one track was in fact called 'I'm in Love with Jacques Derrida'); it produced one successful single, 'The Sweetest Girl'. By Gartside's admission *Songs to Remember* almost bankrupted Rough Trade, and by mutual agreement he took his solo ambitions to the larger Virgin Records, who allowed him some three years and an alleged half-million pounds to work on 1985's LP *Cupid & Psyche*. One of the biggest critical successes of the year, the LP was seamless, hi-tech dance music, criticized by admirers of the earlier, ramshackle Politti. It remains a critical favourite, and Gartside continues to work largely in seclusion.

SCRUGGS, EARL
An outstanding country instrumentalist of the Fifties and Sixties, Earl Scruggs was born in Flint Hill, North Carolina, in 1924 into a musical environment where an unusual, three-finger five-string banjo style was prevalent. Scruggs perfected this style and brought it to Bill Monroe's band in 1945, contributing much to the formative recorded statements of 'bluegrass' music. Later, with Lester Flatt, he contributed songs like 'Foggy Mountain Breakdown' to the legacy of bluegrass, and soundtracks to the *Beverly Hillbillies* and the movie *Bonnie and Clyde*. In the Seventies, he formed a widely different band, the Earl Scruggs Revue, electric and eclectic, playing folk, college and rock venues with artists like **Arlo Guthrie**, **Bob Dylan**, the **Byrds**, **Linda Ronstadt** and **Joan Baez**. His many notable albums include a collaboration with singer-songwriter **Tom T. Hall**, *The Storyteller and the Banjo Man* (1982), and *Top of the World* (1983), which featured guest artists Ricky Scaggs, the **Flying Burrito Brothers** and Lucy J. Dalton.

SEALS AND CROFTS

Jimmy Seals (born in Sidney, Texas, in 1940) and Dash Crofts (born in Cisco, Texas, in 1940) were former members of the **Champs** – an instrumental group from the late Fifties who had a major hit with 'Tequila' in 1958 – who re-emerged in the Seventies as a successful singer/songwriter duo.

Seals and Crofts signed first to the TA label and then to Warner Brothers and began recording a series of albums whose sound owed much to the recently disbanded **Simon and Garfunkel**, with lyrics often expressing the duo's newly found Baha'i faith. Critics found them unenterprising and sanctimonious, but Top 10 hits like 'Summer Breeze' (1972) and 'Diamond Girl' (1973) demonstrated their immense appeal, especially to college audiences. They released an album per year between 1972 and 1978, the last being *Takin' It Easy*; *The Longest Road* appeared in 1980.

SEARCHERS

Named after the John Ford movie, the Searchers were second only to the **Beatles** on Merseyside in terms of musicianship and local popularity. On their signing to Pye in 1963, the line-up was Mike Pender, lead guitar (born Mike Prendergast, 3 March 1942), John McNally, rhythm (30 August 1941), Tony Jackson, bass (16 July 1940), and Chris Curtis, drums (16 August 1941). Their first single, the **Drifters**' 'Sweets For My Sweet' went to Number 1 and featured the high-pitched, light harmonies that became the group's trademark. Other covers of American hits followed and were equally successful: **Jackie DeShannon**'s 'Needles and Pins' (written by **Jack Nitzsche** and Sonny Bono – of **Sonny and Cher**), the **Orlons**' 'Don't Throw Your Love Away' and 'When You Walk in the Room', another DeShannon hit. The Searchers were also regular visitors to the American Top 20 on the Kapp label, and their combination of tight harmonies with jangling guitars anticipated the sound of the **Byrds**. By 1965, however, their lack of original songs for singles was becoming a liability. Two folk/protest numbers (Malvina Reynolds' 'What Have They Done to the Rain' and **P. F. Sloan**'s 'Take Me for What I'm Worth') barely scraped into the UK Top 20 and Jackson left to be replaced by Frank Allen from **Cliff Bennett**'s band. In 1969, the Searchers lost Curtis who tried a solo career briefly and then went into production. The group continued to tour during the Seventies and became stalwarts of the north of England cabaret scene before making a recording comeback with *The Searchers* (Sire, 1979) and *Love's Melodies* (1981). Pender left in 1986, leaving McNally as the only original member.

The Searchers line-up in 1965 after Tony Jackson quit: left to right, John McNally, drummer Chris Curtis, Mike Pender and new-boy Frank Allen

SEBASTIAN, JOHN

Born on 17 March 1944, in Greenwich Village, New York, John Sebastian wrote some of the finest hit records of the day for his group the **Lovin' Spoonful** between 1965 and 1968 – among them 'Daydream', 'You Didn't Have to Be So Nice', 'Younger Girl', and 'Do You Believe in Magic'. Following the group's break-up, he went into a brief retirement before re-emerging at the Woodstock festival in August 1969, stealing the show with an impromptu acoustic performance when the rain came. He appeared at the Isle of Wight festival a year later, following the release of his first solo album, *John B. Sebastian* (Reprise). That album suffered a long gestation period because of contractual problems and was followed by a live album, *Cheapo Cheapo Presents* (1970): both included songs celebrating Woodstock-type togetherness, and the subsequent *The Four of Us* (1971) was a set of songs about life on the road with his family. He then settled down in a Los Angeles suburb to work with a small backing combo, recording occasionally (for example, the album *Friends Again* in 1973), until he resurfaced in 1976 with a single, 'Welcome Back', written as the theme song of the television series *Welcome Back, Kotter* starring John Travolta. Co-produced by **Steve Barri**, it reached Number 1 in the US chart during May 1976. That led to further television and film work, notably a number of songs for the children's series *Strawberry Shortcake* and *The Care Bears* in the Eighties – a path also followed, interestingly, by another major Sixties songwriter, **Carole King**. *See also* the **Lovin' Spoonful**

SEDAKA, NEIL

Although trained as a classical pianist, Brooklyn-born Sedaka (13 March 1939) initially won fame as a composer of 'Stupid Cupid' (1958) one of **Connie Francis**' biggest hits. In 1960 he joined **Don Kirshner**'s stable of young writer/performers based at the Brill Building on New York's Broadway and teamed up with lyricist **Howie Greenfield** to write over 500 songs, many of which Sedaka himself recorded for RCA. Their intention was to groom him as yet another teen idol in the style of **Frankie Avalon** and **Rick Nelson**. Far too tubby to be taken seriously in that role, he none the less had a string of Top 40 hits in America – a total of thirteen – before 1964, some of which, in retrospect, encapsulate the flavour of the early Sixties almost better than any other records: 'Oh Carol' (written in honour of girlfriend **Carole**

Chubby and cheerful, Neil Sedaka was an unlikely rock success of the early Sixties. His comeback in the Seventies brought a string of hits, appealing to older listeners who remembered him from first time round

SEEDS One of the more unusual groups spawned in Los Angeles during the folk-rock era, the Seeds were formed by the charismatic Sky Saxon (real name Richard Marsh) in early 1965, the group including Jan Savage, Daryl Hooper and Rick Andridge. Their music was raw, simplistic, and featured one-note guitar runs, but it was Saxon's weird, idiosyncratic growls and free-association ramblings that made them special. After being out nearly a year, 'Pushin' Too Hard' (their second single) was picked up by a local radio station and spread to become a national Top 40 hit at the end of 1966. Although they had only three subsequent chart singles – 'Mr Farmer', 'Can't Seem to Make You Mine' and 'Thousand Shadows' – the Seeds remained immensely popular with discotheque audiences in Los Angeles, and with fans around the country who saw them on tours and bought their albums, which were full of overt (if innocent) drug references and blatant sexual overtones. Everything they did was grossly overdone, notably their 'psychedelic' album, *Future*, and a ridiculous blues album with liner notes by **Muddy Waters**. But through it all Saxon's appeal remained. They dissolved around 1969, with no further recordings by any of the members – although Saxon was still making the rounds of record companies during the Seventies with tapes he describes as 'better than the **Beatles**'.

SEEGER, PETE Generally acknowledged as 'the father of the American folk revival' through thirty years of performing, collecting, songwriting and proselytizing, Pete Seeger has always linked music and radical humanism. Born on 3 May 1919 in New York, he is the son of ethnomusicologist Charles, and half-brother of singers Peggy and Mike. After 'conversion' at a 1935 visit to a North Carolina folk festival, he dropped out of Harvard and established contact with the Lomaxes, **Leadbelly** and **Woody Guthrie**. During World War II, he performed with the Almanac Singers before Army service. He helped found the **Weavers** in 1949 and made several hit records with them. Seeger went solo in the Fifties, and became a perennial on the college, camp and union benefit concert circuit. He helped reactivate the Newport Folk Festival in 1960, and has long been a leading columnist on *Sing Out!* and a patron of *Broadside*. Seeger's many recordings on Folkways, Vanguard and Columbia have shown an enormous range of style and material, with his

King who replied with 'Oh Neil'), 'Calendar Girl', 'Happy Birthday Sweet Sixteen' (all Top 10 records) and his 1962 chart topper, 'Breaking Up Is Hard To Do'.

With the coming of the **Beatles** and the new cult of self-sufficiency, demand for songs of such engaging cuteness declined and, though he continued writing material for the **Monkees**, **Tom Jones**, and others, Sedaka stopped recording. The success of Carole King's *Tapestry* encouraged him to try again but it was in Britain that his revival started. First caught up

in the rock'n'roll revival with songs like 'Standing on the Inside' and 'Laughter in the Rain', which also became his first American Top 10 record for over ten years, he managed to distance himself from the revival by carving a niche for himself as an easy-listening entertainer, writing songs for older record buyers who remembered his success first time around. His albums – including *The Tra La Days Are Over* (1973, recorded with **10cc**), *The Hungry Years* (1975) and *Now* (1981) – have sold consistently well since.

light tenor voice and commanding instrumental work. He is a great believer in audience singalongs, and has been the greatest popularizer of the five-string banjo, though he also plays six- and 12-string guitar, chalil, and steel drums. His nicknames – 'the Johnny Appleseed of folk song' and 'America's tuning-fork' – indicate the missionary appeal. Among his most famous songs are 'If I Had a Hammer', 'Where Have All the Flowers Gone', 'Waist Deep in the Big Muddy', and 'Guantanamera'.

SEEKERS Australia's most successful musical export of the Sixties, the Seekers specialized in an easy-going brand of folk-pop of the type made popular by the **Springfields** at the beginning of the decade. Most of their hits were in fact written and produced by Tom Springfield (Dusty's brother), including their debut million seller for Columbia, 'I'll Never Find Another You' (Number 1 in the UK in 1965). The group first came together in Melbourne, Australia, in 1964, with a line-up comprising singer Judith Durham (born on 3 July 1943), guitarists Bruce Woodley (25 July 1942, also in Melbourne) and Keith Potger (2 March 1941, in Colombo, Sri Lanka), and double-bassist Athol Guy (5 January 1940 in Victoria, Australia). Based in the UK from late 1964 onwards, they had a run of eight UK Top 20 hits and three US chart placings, the highest of which was the Oscar-nominated title song from the film *Georgy Girl*, a Number 2 in early 1967. Most of their material was safely middle-of-the-road, in keeping with their homely image, but they had the distinction of being the first act to have a hit with a **Paul Simon** song – 'Someday One Day', a Number 11 in the UK in 1966. The Seekers broke up in 1969, bidding farewell with an emotional televised concert, but Keith Potger subsequently put together the **New Seekers** in a successful bid to capitalize on his old group's following. Judith Durham recorded as a solo artist, initially in a straight easy-listening vein but subsequently as a jazz singer. *See also* the **New Seekers**

SEGER, BOB Born in Ann Arbor, Michigan, on 6 May 1945, Bob Seger is a high-energy white rocker, singer, composer and guitarist in the **Springsteen** vein. He formed his first band, the Last Heard, in Detroit in 1964 and recorded for his manager Eddie 'Punch' Andrews' record label, but success came only with a solo single, 'Ramblin' Gamblin' Man', which reached Num-

The passion and energy of Bob Seger's performances were legendary. Here he fronts the Silver Bullet Band in Paris in 1980

ber 17 in the US during 1969 when released by Capitol. For the latter label he also cut *Brand New Morning* in 1971, a singer-songwriter set in the then-fashionable **James Taylor** mode, before switching to Reprise for two albums, *Back In '72* and *Seven*. He formed his Silver Bullet Band, consisting mainly of unknown musicians from his home-town area – Drew Abbott (guitar), Chris Campbell (bass), Charlie Allen Martin (drums) and Rick Manasa (keyboards). Manasa was replaced by Robyn Robbins in 1973, and Alto Reed (saxophones) joined in 1975. Seger and his band rejoined Capitol during the same year.

The hard-edged playing of the Silver Bullet Band became the perfect foil for Seger's gritty vocals, although *Beautiful Loser* (1975) was a reflective album containing some untypical ballad material. The albums which really launched him as a national name were *Live Bullet* and *Night Moves* (both 1976), though his success was blunted by tragedy when Martin was paralysed as a result of a car accident; his place was taken by David Teegarden, with whom Seger had recorded and toured during the early Seventies.

Stranger in Town (1978) and *Against the Wind* (1980) sold a total of seven million copies, and by 1983 he was one of the USA's most respected and sought-after acts. *Nine Tonight*, another love set, appeared in 1981 and *The Distance* in 1983.

SELECTER Lining up alongside the **Specials**, **Madness** and the **Beat** as the first bands to record on the 2-Tone label, during their short existence the Selecter were at the forefront of the Midlands' ska explosion. The name of the band started life merely as the title of the flipside (penned by guitarist Neol Davis) of the Specials' debut single 'Gangsters', but the success of the record encouraged Davis to assemble a group around him to perform as the Selecter. Through the intercession of the Specials' Lynval Golding, Davis met up with singer Pauline Black in mid-1979 and recruited the rest of the band: Desmond Brown (keyboards), Compton Amanour (guitar), 'Gaps' Hendrickson (vocals), Charley 'H' (drums) and Charley Anderson (bass).

The high chart placing of 'Gangsters' plus rigorous touring pushed their first single, 'On My Radio', into the UK Top 10 in late '79. An album, *Too Much Pressure*, made the UK Top 5 in February 1980 and another single, 'Three Minute Hero', also made the Top 10 the same year.

Following a successful UK and US tour, the band became disillusioned with 2-Tone towards the end of 1980 and left the label. Just one more album followed, *Celebrate the Bullet* (1981), and its lack of success – added to abortive attempts to re-jig the line-up of the band – caused the Selecter to split in 1981. Pauline Black later found moderate success as a TV presenter.

SELF, RONNIE Born in Springfield, Missouri, in 1939, Ronnie Self is best known in country music circles as a prolific songwriter and recording artist, but his career began in the late Fifties as a rockabilly singer. In 1957, he recorded twice for ABC Paramount, 'Pretty Bad Blues' being a good harsh-voiced rocker. In 1958, he moved to Columbia, adapting Bill Monroe's bluegrass tune 'Rocky Road Blues', and making the popular charts with a violent screaming rocker 'Bop a Lena'. He also recorded unsuccessfully for Decca, Knapp and Amy while writing hits for **Brenda Lee** and **Jerry Lee Lewis**.

SENSATIONAL ALEX HARVEY BAND

During the Seventies, Alex Harvey's was one of the most unusual success stories in British rock. An R&B and beat group leader in the previous decade, he re-emerged with his Sensational Alex Harvey Band and a mixture of rabble-rousing stage antics and studiedly outrageous songs.

Born in Glasgow on 5 February 1935, he led the Alex Harvey Soul Band on guitar and vocals from 1958 to 1966, playing much of the time in Hamburg and recording occasionally, notably *Big Soul Band* (Polydor, 1964). Dissolving the group, he joined the pit band for the London production of *Hair*, where he stayed for five years. In 1972 he teamed up with the Scottish group Tear Gas to form his 'Sensational' band which included Zal Cleminson (guitar, born on 4 May 1949), Chris Glen (bass, 6 November 1950), Hugh McKenna (piano, 28 November 1949) and Ted McKenna (drums, 10 March 1950).

Signing to Vertico, the band gradually built up an enthusiastic following through Harvey's oddball songs and his dramatic delivery, and they made their chart debut in 1975 with a sardonic version of the old **Tom Jones** hit, 'Delilah'. A year later they switched to Mountain Records and recorded *SAHB Stories*, scoring again with the single 'Boston Tea Party'. Without Harvey, the SAHB cut *Fourplay* (1976). One further album followed – *Rock Drill* (1977) – before the band broke up, Cleminson joining **Nazareth** and Ted McKenna joining **Rory Gallagher**'s regular band. Alex continued performing in his own right and with other musicians until his death in Belgium in February 1982. A compilation album, *The Best of the Sensational Alex Harvey Band*, was released by RCA in 1982. In 1983, Pinnacle released *The Soldier on the Wall*.

SEX PISTOLS Coming to national fame in a glorious blaze of obscenity-induced publicity, the Sex Pistols were the personification of the British punk revolution. Their total disregard for the establishment, their shredded clothes, their calculated anti-social behaviour and their anarchic lifestyle influenced a generation and they served as perfect role models for hoardes of would-be punks.

Although it was manager **Malcolm McLaren** who finally brought the Sex Pistols together, the nucleus of the band had already formed as early as 1973 with Paul Cook, Steve Jones and an older friend called Wally. By 1975, Wally had gone and Glen Matlock, an assistant in *Sex*, McLaren's Kings Road clothes shop, had joined on bass. With Cook on the drums and Jones having shifted from his original role as singer to lead guitar, the trio rehearsed regularly, lacking only a singer. The solution came in the shape of one of Sex's customers, a repulsive, green-haired, perpetually sneering youth called John Lydon (born 30 January 1956), but re-named Johnny Rotten after the condition of his teeth.

The Sex Pistols (the name was coined by McLaren) played their first gig at St Martin's School of Art in London on a November night in 1975. It turned into a battleground, and amid a hail of bottles the promoters pulled out the plugs on the band's amplifiers. This set the pattern for future appearances. They continued to make sporadic appearances at college gigs, and it was clear that Rotten was a gem of a frontman, insulting their audiences and provoking violent scenes. As the Pistols terrorized the London circuit, many similar bands sprang up in their shadow and punk was born.

The Sex Pistols signed to EMI for £40,000 in October 1976 and released their first single, 'Anarchy in the UK', one of their live favourites and a potent, speeded-up hybrid of R&B and heavy rock. A tour had to be cancelled as local authorities banned them, and finally, in December, they made front-page news after uttering expletives in a live TV interview with presenter Bill Grundy. The publicity was phenomenal as the papers had a field day expressing their outrage. The single began to sell, and then staff at EMI's pressing plant refused to make any more copies. By the New Year, the Pistols were no longer with EMI.

The band spent the winter being refused permission to play anywhere – a factor that constantly generated publicity – and early in March they signed

Vicious-looking John Beverley making a political statement

to A&M. Matlock had departed, sacked for being too proficient a musician, and was replaced by the blatantly musically incompetent Sid Vicious (born John Beverley, 10 May 1957) who had a penchant for violent abuse. The signing was staged outside Buckingham Palace to an abusive press reception and a handful of violent squabbles, mostly involving Vicious, that ended with the group being sacked once more.

Despite, or perhaps more accurately, because of, all of this notoriety, record companies were still eager to sign the band, and their recording career proper started when they signed to Virgin in the spring of '77. In June a single, 'God Save the Queen', whose release had been timed to cause maximum embarrassment during the Queen's jubilee celebrations, reached Number 2, despite attacks in the press and a virtual TV and radio blackout; it proved to be their biggest chart success. By July and the third single, 'Pretty Vacant', the group actually managed to appear (on video) on TV's *Top of the Pops*, and again they made the Top 10. 'Holidays in the Sun' followed in October, as did their only legitimate LP *Never Mind the Bollocks Here's the Sex Pistols*.

Inside the Sex Pistols' camp things were not at all well – Rotten was resistant to McLaren's idea of making a film with Russ Meyer, tentatively called 'Who Killed Bambi?' – and after a European tour where they nearly met their deaths at the hands of a Stockholm street-gang, and a few bloodsplattered dates (mostly over Vicious) in Texas, Rotten quit. McLaren had planned to send the whole group to South America to record with Great Train Robber Ronald Bigs, but in the event only Cook and Jones were on hand to record the resulting single, 'No One Is Innocent', a truly awful record. The other song on the double A-sided single was Vicious' hilarious, mangled version of 'My Way', which carried it into the charts. This song also featured on the soundtrack of McLaren's pet movie project, *The Great Rock'n'Roll Swindle* (1978), which was eventually directed by Julien Temple.

The final nail in the coffin came with the death of Vicious on 2 February 1979 in New York. Put on bail after being charged with the murder of his girlfriend Nancy Spungen, he took a fatal heroin overdose. Cook and Jones carried on under the name the Professionals but did little of any note, although Cook later resurfaced in 1985 with the Chiefs of Relief while Rotten reverted to his real surname and formed **Public Image Limited**.

Together, McLaren and the Sex Pistols were a powerful force in the music, the image and the philosophy of punk. In some ways, however, they were perhaps punk's greatest failure, since having contrived an image of excess and outrage, they took it too far and destroyed themselves. The tragic part is that in Sid Vicious' case, the destruction was final – he wasted his life for the sake of an image.

SHA NA NA Sha Na Na – Scott Powell (vocals), Johnny Contardo (vocals), Frederick Dennis Greene (vocals), Don York (vocals), Rich Joffe (vocals), Elliot Cahn (vocals, guitar), Henry Gross (vocals, guitar), Chris Donald (guitar), Bruce Clarke (bass), Screamin' Scott Simon (piano), John

Baumann (piano), Lennie Baker (sax), Jocko Marcellino (drums), and Vinnie Taylor (guitar) – had been performing in New York coffee bars for two years before a brief appearance in *Woodstock* (1970) brought them international recognition. Since then their act has changed little: they present astute, hilarious parodies not only of the music of the Fifties but also of the teenage aggression associated with the era. Publicizing themselves as hoodlums, the band (once nicknamed 'the Dirty Dozen' but now reduced to a fluctuating membership of between eight to ten players) is a troupe of talented actors and musicians. However, they have generally not succeeded in capturing, on their albums and singles for Kama Sutra, the fun of their stage act. Guitarist Vinnie Taylor died in 1974 and Elliott Randall joined as replacement, since when their personnel has undergone numerous changes. Guitarist Henry Gross, who left in 1970, reached Number 6 in the US with 'Shannon' during 1976.

SHADOWS The most successful and influential British group of the pre-**Beatle** years, the Shadows originally came together under the name of the Drifters to provide backing for **Cliff Richard**. Their line-up in 1958 when they backed Richard on his first hit, 'Move It', was guitarists Hank Marvin (born on 28 October 1941), Bruce Welch (2 November 1941), Ian Samwell (composer of the record) and drummer Terry Smart. Marvin and Welch were regulars at the 2 I's coffee bar in Soho, having travelled to London from their native Newcastle in search of work during 1957, after spells in various local skiffle groups. In 1959, Samwell and Smart were replaced by Jet Harris (bass, born 6 July 1939) and Tony Meehan (drums, 2 March 1942) and the Drifters began recording in their own right. After three non-chart singles (only one an instrumental) they changed their name to avoid confusion with the American **Drifters**, began to concentrate on instrumental A-sides and reached the British Number 1 spot with the **Jerry Lordan** composition 'Apache' on Columbia in 1960.

From then on they pursued parallel careers as the country's leading instrumental group, and as the backing unit for Richard. Hits followed in unbroken succession, including four more chart-toppers – 'Kon Tiki', 'Wonderful Land', 'Dance On' and 'Foot Tapper'. The Shadows survived various personnel changes and the Merseybeat onslaught, and even

though the hits ceased by 1967, they were by then part of the rock establishment. After all, the new generation of British guitar heroes had all started by copying Hank Marvin's clean, melodic instrumental style and his heavy spectacles.

They had no impact at all in America, where the Dane, Jorgen Ingmann, had the hit with 'Apache'. Brian Bennett (born 9 February 1940) replaced Meehan late in 1961 and the following March Jet Harris left and was replaced by Brian Locking. Locking lasted a year and his successor, John Rostill (born 16 June 1942), was the band's bassist until they formally disbanded in 1969, while Brian Bennett became Cliff's on-tour musical director. In 1975, the group re-formed to present the UK entry in that year's Eurovision Song Contest. Marvin and Welch then formed a group with Australian guitarist John Farrar. They were also associated with the launching of **Olivia Newton-John**'s career, with Farrar producing and writing several of her early hits. The Shadows' instrumental sound was cleanly-recorded, simple and dramatic, with clear separation between the lead and rhythm guitars.

In the late Seventies, Marvin, Welch and Bennett re-formed the group on a semi-permanent basis and enjoyed a major return to chart form (sounding exactly as they did over fifteen years earlier) with instrumental hit versions of 'Don't Cry for Me Argentina' and the theme from 'The Deer Hunter'.

SHADOWS OF KNIGHT Mid-Sixties punk-rock, Chicago-style, was centred around the Dunwich label and Bill Traut's Dunwich Productions, and no group better typified this scene than the Shadows of Knight. Formed in 1965, the group (Jim Sohns, Warren Rogers, Jerry McGeorge, Tom Schiffour, Joe Kelley) paid the usual dues until their first single, 'Gloria', rose to the Top 10 nationally, nearly a year after **Them**'s original version had flopped. Soon every garage band in the country was doing the song, although the Shadows of Knight were unable to follow this classic with anything of equal impact. 'Oh Yeah' and 'Bad Little Woman' (1966) presented the band's crude, **Bo Diddley**-inspired sound at its best, and though the Kasenetz-Katz-produced 'Shake' (Team) was big regionally in 1968, like nearly every punk group, one hit was all they got. A reformed Shadows of Knight, without Sohns, began playing the local circuit from 1974 onwards.

SHAKATAK

SHAKATAK Mainstream British jazz-funk outfit Shakatak became a great favourite with club audiences, and converted this dance-floor popularity into chart success. Formed in 1980 by Bill Sharpe (keyboards and leader/songwriter), Roger Odell (drums) and Keith Winter (guitar) who met while playing with London band Tracks, they completed the line-up with Nigel Wright (keyboards) and Steve Underwood (bass, later replaced by George Anderson). They later added the vocalists Norma Lewis and Jill Saward.

'Easier Said Than Done', their fifth single, finally cracked the UK charts in 1981, reaching Number 12, and, spurred by this success, their second album *Nightbirds* emerged in 1982 and went gold. Subsequent releases have sold consistently well, most notably the UK Top 10 singles 'Night Birds' and 'Down on the Street'.

SHAKIN' STEVENS Born Michael Barrett on 4 March 1948 in Cardiff, Wales, Shakin' Stevens was something of a late starter: after his debut in the mid-Sixties he spent the next fifteen or so years touring the UK with little commercial success, his most noteworthy achievement being a lead role in the stage show *Elvis* in the mid-Seventies. But when his break came in 1980 (with the UK Top 30 hit 'Hot Dog') he never looked back, going on to score eighteen Top 20 UK hits, including four Number 1s, over a period of five years. Operating within the field of the up-tempo ballad – his roots are in rock'n'roll revivalism – Shaky's chart success in the UK and Europe remains one of the pop phenomena of the Eighties.

SHALAMAR Formed in 1977, soul/dance group Shalamar comprised Jody Watley (vocals) and Jeffrey Daniel (vocals/guitar), two dancers well known to regular viewers of the American TV show *Soul Train*, and Gerald Brown (vocals). Signed to Dick Griffey's Solar label, they cut two disco-biased LPs – *Uptown Festival* and *Disco Gardens*, the latter including the 1978 hit 'Take That to the Bank' – before Brown was replaced as lead singer by Howard Hewett (vocals/bass), a fine singer with a high, clear, distinctive tone. The addition of Hewett in 1979 and the fast-improving production of Leon Sylvers enabled Shalamar to outlast the Seventies disco boom, although their pop hits never lost their danceable pace. 'Right in the Socket', 'The Second Time Around', 'I Owe You One', 'Some Things Never Change' and

'Attention to My Baby' far outnumber the band's best ballads such as 'Somewhere There's a Love' and 'This Is For the Lover in You'. Successful albums such as *Big Fun* (1979) and *Three For Love* (1980) were promoted by bright and cheery stage shows. But 1982's *Friends* suggested that the trio was becoming stale, a feeling confirmed by *The Look* the following year. It was also clear that the group's direction, towards a rock audience, was not particularly suited to them. Inevitably, the band went through a major upheaval with Watley and Daniel leaving. Hewett continued in charge of the group – the new members were Delisa Davis and Micki Freez – and was still being pushed in a rock direction with less and less commercial or artistic success.

SHAM 69 The creation of singer Jimmy Pursey (from Hersham, in Surrey near London), Sham 69 had a short and violent career as the self-appointed punk spokesmen for working-class youth. Pursey encouraged his audience to acquire a greater political awareness and claimed idealistically 'if the kids are united they will never be defeated'. And yet the more frequently Pursey made his appeals for unity, justice and tolerance, the more the kids turned Sham 69 gigs into battlefields.

After an abortive start, Sham 69 came into being in 1977 comprising Pursey (vocals), Dave Parsons (guitar), Albie Maskall (bass) and Mark 'Doidie' Cain (drums). When the band signed to Polydor, Maskall left, to be replaced by Dave 'Kermit' Treganna. Their first single, the classic punk anthem 'Borstal

Intense and hyperactive, Jimmy Pursey wanted Sham 69 to be a focus to unite 'the kids', but 'the kids' were too violent for Pursey's idealism

Breakout' was followed in February 1978 by the album *Tell Us the Truth*, which reached Number 25 in the UK chart and exposed the group to a national audience. Two Top 10 singles – 'If the Kids Are United' and 'Hurry Up Harry' – capitalized on this success, and Sham 69 became a hot property for Polydor.

Their next album, *That's Life*, went silver, a success capped by the release in 1979 of *The Adventures of the Hersham Boys*, which reached Number 8 in the UK LP chart. Things were not going well with the band, however: Pursey was becoming increasingly frustrated by the workings of the music business and his failure to influence his audience towards greater solidarity. In addition, the aura of violence that was surrounding Sham 69 was preventing them from playing live; few venues would take the risk of rioting punks and skinheads.

At the end of 1979, Pursey wound up the group, and went on to make two solo LPs, *Imagination Camouflage* (1980) and *Alien Orphan* (1981). Sham 69 had promised much, but in the end had been destroyed by its notorious reputation.

SHANGRI-LAS The members of the Shangri-Las were Mary Weiss, her sister Betty, and Mary Ann and Margie Ganser (who were twins) who began singing semi-professionally while still attending Andrew Jackson High School in Queens, New York. Between 1964 and 1966, they cut a series of remarkable records best described as theatrical in their intensity, masterminded by producer **George 'Shadow' Morton**. The girls were brought to him by disc-jockey Babalu (Bob Lewis). Their first record was the defiantly morbid 'Remember (Walkin' in the Sand)', released on **Leiber and Stoller**'s Red Bird label. It reached Number 5, but the follow-up, 'Leader of the Pack', topped the US charts. Morton dubbed on motorcycle noises (after the seagulls of the earlier disc) and faced opposition from the more conservative members of the company over the record's adulation of black leather boys.

Minor hits of a more conventional nature followed until 'I Can Never Go Home Anymore', featuring lead singing from Mary Weiss expressing almost unbearable desolation, became the Shangri-Las' third Top 10 record in 1965. The even more ambitious 'Past, Present and Future' (a recitation set to Beethoven's 'Moonlight Sonata') followed, but in 1966 both Red Bird and the group folded.

SHANKAR, RAVI Born in Benares, India, in 1920, Ravi Shankar was raised in an orthodox Hindu Brahmin family and he began his musical career as a member of his elder brother Uday's travelling music and dance company. In 1939 he returned to India to study his native classical music and the sitar under Guru Baba Khan, eventually to become one of the greatest virtuosi in music – Eastern or Western. By the mid-Sixties, the Eastern influence found its way into the creatively expanding field of pop. **George Harrison**'s use of the sitar on 'Norwegian Wood', for example, had unleashed a torrent of interest in – and misuse of – the instrument. Few followed Harrison's example in studying the sitar seriously. He journeyed to Bombay to study under Shankar and later used his tuition well to produce the brilliant 'Within You Without You' on *Sergeant Pepper*. Others used the sitar like a fashionable gimmick; its ubiquity on albums was virtually the Carbon 90 test for 1967. In May 1967, Shankar inaugurated his Kinnera School of Music in Los Angeles and performed at the Monterey Pop Festival later the same year. He also played at Woodstock in 1969 and at the 1971 Madison Square Gardens Concert for Bangla Desh.

SHANNON, DEL An individualistic hit-maker and songwriter of the early Sixties, Del Shannon was born Charles Westover at Grand Rapids, Michigan, on 30 December 1939. He began playing guitar and singing at the age of 14 and entered the US Army in 1957, making his first public appearance a year later in Germany in the Army show *Get Up And Go*. On his discharge in 1959 he returned home to Battle Creek, Michigan, and took up a day job while playing nights in a local dive with a pianist friend, Max Crook. In 1960 he came to the notice of a local black entrepreneur and disc jockey, Ollie McLaughlin, who took Shannon to Detroit in order to sign a management contract with Harry Balk of Talent Artists Management, who also managed **Johnny and the Hurricanes**. Shannon's first session in New York followed soon after, but nothing was released after this and he returned to Battle Creek where he composed 'Runaway' with Crook one afternoon while jamming in a small club. Recorded late in 1960 and leased to Big Top in New York, 'Runaway' went on to become one of 1961's biggest hits.

Shannon followed up with another million-seller, 'Hats Off to Larry', and a

Michigan's Del Shannon was a runaway success in the Sixties

series of international hits including 'So Long Baby', 'Hey Little Girl', 'Swiss Maid' and 'Little Town Flirt', all of which reached Britain's Top 10, although they were less popular in Shannon's home country. Leaving Big Top in 1963, he formed his own Berlee label and recorded 'Sue's Gotta Be Mine', which flopped. In 1964 he signed with Amy records and made a comeback with 'Handy Man' and the excellent 'Keep Searchin'', which sold a million. In an era when pop music was dominated by malleable teenage idols who were told exactly what to sing in the studio, Shannon was a genuine self-contained talent who not only wrote his own material, but took an active interest in the production of his records. They remain classic pop productions, combining barnstorming arrangements (usually featuring pipe-organ) with Shannon's aggressive falsetto.

During the late Sixties, after joining Liberty, Shannon went into decline as an artist but took up production and supervised **Brian Hyland**'s 'Gypsy Woman', a Top 3 American hit in 1970. He continued to record in his own right, **Jeff Lynne** producing 'Cry Baby Cry' (1973) and **Dave Edmunds** producing 'And the Music Plays On' (1974), though neither were hits. Another unsuccessful release was a version of the **Zombies**' 'Tell Her No' in 1975, on Island. In 1981, he returned to the recording studio with Tom Petty as producer to cut *Drop Down and Get Me* (Network). A track from the album, 'Sea of Love', gave Shannon a Number 33 hit in the US during the following year.

SHAPIRO, HELEN A protégée of voice coach Maurice Burman and EMI's Norrie Paramor, Helen Shapiro was born in Bethnal Green, London, on 28 September 1946. She emerged in 1961 as a 14-year-old schoolgirl with a rich booming voice and an artfully aimed John Schroeder song, 'Please Don't Treat Me Like a Child'. Later that year, 'You Don't Know' and 'Walking Back to Happiness' both went to Number 1. Two more hits followed in 1962, as well as an appearance in the film, *It's Trad Dad*, but Shapiro was elbowed aside by Merseybeat, having decided to concentrate on 'quality' material. After a long spell in the cabaret doldrums, she recorded for DJM in the Seventies and appeared on the London stage as Nancy in a revival of *Oliver!* In the Eighties, she began performing in a jazz vein, made a marvellous album (*Straighten Up and Fly Right* for Oval) and appeared regularly with Humphrey Lyttleton and his Band.

SHARKEY, FEARGAL After the split of the **Undertones** in 1983, singer Feargal Sharkey (born 13 August 1958) immediately embarked on a solo career, scoring an instant UK Top 5 hit in November that year with the single 'Never Never' under the name of the Assembly, a project with ex-**Depeche Mode** and **Yazoo** member Vince Clark.

After that early success, Sharkey signed to Virgin, but a major follow-up hit eluded him for a surprisingly long time. He scored only a couple of minor UK chart entrants until 1985, when he had a surprise Number 1 with 'A Good Heart'. His debut album, *Feargal Sharkey*, produced by Dave Stewart of the **Eurythmics**, was released in December 1985 and instantly went gold in the UK.

SHAW, SANDIE Born Sandra Goodrich in Dagenham, Essex, on 26 February 1947, Sandie Shaw was transformed into a perpetually barefooted pop singer after demonstrating her vocal talents in **Adam Faith**'s dressing room, for the benefit of his manager Eve Taylor. In 1964, her second record '(There's) Always Something There to Remind Me' on Pye – a cover version of **Dionne Warwick**'s US hit – went to Number 1 in the UK and began a run of fifteen Top 40 placings, most of them produced (and some written) by **Chris Andrews**. Her career appeared to go into decline in 1966, when only 'Tomorrow' reached the Top 10, but a year later she was topping the UK chart once more with the Eurovision Song Contest winner, 'Puppet on a String'.

Sandie Shaw walked barefoot to the top of the charts in 1964 with her classic version of 'Always Something There to Remind Me'

After marrying fashion designer Jeff Banks in 1968, her public appearances became sporadic. She had no chart entries at all during the Seventies, when she spent much of her time helping to run Banks' business.

It was not until the early Eighties that she resumed her career, with a collaboration with the **Heaven 17** offshoot, the British Electric Foundation – ironically, with a version of 'Anyone Who Had a Heart', a song most associated with her Sixties chart rival **Cilla Black**. In 1984, aided by the **Smiths**, she made a chart comeback with the Rough Trade single, 'Hand in Glove'. By 1986, she was touring once more and earning much respect for her astute mixing of old and new material. A single released that year, 'Frederick' (the **Patti Smith** song), attracted general critical favour.

SHERRILL, BILLY As head of recording policy for Epic/Columbia in Nashville, Billy Sherrill is one of the most powerful figures in the recording industry of that city. He joined Epic in 1964 as a producer and was responsible for many country hits until, in the Seventies, he manufactured hits for three superstar country artists – **Tammy Wynette**, **Charlie Rich** and **Tanya Tucker**.

Born in Winston, Alabama, Sherrill came into music as a saxophonist and pianist with a local white R&B band in the mid-Fifties. Moving to Nashville in 1958, he played some sessions and recorded rockabilly for Mercury ('Like Makin' Love', covered in Britain by **Marty Wilde**) and other smaller labels, before joining Sam Phillips' Sun label as producer in charge of the new Nashville studio. This lasted from 1960 to 1964, when Phillips sold the studio, but Sherrill had the chance to work with top names like **Jerry Lee Lewis** and Charlie Rich. On joining Epic, Sherrill moved more into mainstream country and by 1968 had worked out a classic, sparse yet dramatic country sound to suit the tear-jerking songs of Tammy Wynette. With his Spectorish production of songs like 'Stand By Your Man' (Wynette) and 'Delta Dawn' (Tanya Tucker) he became country music's biggest hit maker.

In 1968 too, Sherrill acquired Charlie Rich for Epic. They had worked briefly at Sun, but now Sherrill directed Rich at the middle-of-the-road country pop market and scored massive hits with 'Nice'n'Easy', 'Behind Closed Doors' and 'The Most Beautiful Girl'. However, if Sherrill's production enhanced Tammy Wynette's singing, only too often it did the reverse for Charlie Rich, drowning him in a sea of melodrama and saccharin. Among the other artists Sherrill has worked with are **Ray Charles** and **Elvis Costello**, whose encounter with the producer for the recording of *Almost Blue* in 1981 was the subject of an ITV documentary programme.

SHIRELLES Among the most influential and enduring of all early Sixties girl groups, the original Shirelles – from Passaic, New Jersey – were Addie Harris (born on 22 January 1940), Shirley Alston (10 June 1941), Beverly Lee (3 August 1941) and Doris Kenner (2 August 1942). After recording briefly for Tiara, the group gained their first success with the buoyant 'Met Him on a Sunday', one of four releases on Decca. In 1960, their manager Florence Greenberg founded Scepter Records and the girls had their first million seller on the label with a haunting ballad, 'Tonight's the Night'. The same year saw 'Will You Love Me Tomorrow' (written by **Carole King** and Gerry Goffin) and 'Dedicated to the One I Love' (written by Lowman Pauling and previously recorded by his group, the Five Royales); 'Soldier Boy' followed in 1962. All were gold disc records. From New York, they utilized excellent material from Goffin and King, **Burt Bacharach** and Hal David, Luther Dixon and others, and sang mostly adolescent R&B ballads with fragile and naïve conviction and that slightly nasal suggestion of flatness common to black groups of the period. They were an important influence on the early **Beatles** – who recorded the Shirelles' 'Baby It's You' and 'Boys' on their first album – and stayed together until the late Sixties, re-forming in the following decade for revival shows.

SHIRLEY AND LEE Born Shirley Goodman (1937) and Leonard Lee (1935) in New Orleans, Shirley and Lee cut their first record 'I'm Gone' (1952) for Atlantic, soon a Number 2 R&B hit. They were just neighbourhood kids of 14 and 15 but as 'The Sweethearts of the Blues' they influenced many male/female rock'n'roll duos. For a while they were stuck with a series of sentimental boy-meets-girl love songs, but they dropped these shackles when the rollicking classic 'Let the Good Times Roll', written by Lee, became a million-selling hit in 1956. Backed by the best New Orleans sessionmen, and with Shirley's shrill, theatrical vocals and Lee's lovely blues voice, their records were certainly distinctive and deceptively good. After Aladdin folded, the couple recorded for Warwick and Imperial in the early Sixties before going their separate ways, occasionally reuniting for rock'n'roll revival shows. In 1974, Shirley had a major hit with 'Shame Shame Shame' on Vibration. The duo have been very influential on Jamaican girl singers such as **Millie** Small.

Looks – rather than musical talent – was the criterion when it came to deciding Sigue Sigue Sputnik's line-up

SHOWADDYWADDY British Fifties revivalists Showaddywaddy had phenomenal success with their easy-listening pop covers of rock'n'roll classics during the Seventies, notching up ten UK Top 10 singles, including a Number 1, and five Top 10 albums, again including a Number 1.

Discovered in the early Seventies on a television talent show, Showaddywaddy, who decked themselves out in drapes and crepe-soled shoes, built up a following among the diehard teddy boys and rockabilly fans, but their huge sales showed a much wider appeal. Dave Bartram (vocals), Billy Gask (vocals), Romeo Challenger (drums), Malcolm 'The Duke' Allured (drums), Rod Teas (bass), Al James (bass), Russ Fields (guitar) and Trevor Oakes (guitar) had their first hit, a Number 2 with 'Hey Rock'n'Roll' in 1974, and followed that with twenty-two other Top 40 singles up to 1982, including the Number 1 'Under the Moon of Love' in 1976. They scored two platinum albums with greatest hits compilations, the second of which reached Number 1 in 1978.

Although they still managed to break the lower reaches of the charts, sales diminished into the Eighties with 'Who Put the Bomp (in the Bomp-a-Bomp-a-Bomp)' their last Top 40 single in 1982, after which Showaddywaddy disappeared from the public eye.

SHUMAN, MORT See **Pomus, Doc, and Shuman, Mort**

SIGUE SIGUE SPUTNIK The apotheosis of the triumph of gimmick over talent, designer punks Sigue Sigue Sputnik arrived on the British rock scene in 1985 in an avalanche of publicity. They were led by Tony James (ex-**Generation X**), a veteran of the English punk scene, whose philosophy in recruiting the band had been simple – find people who look the part and musical proficiency will come in time.

The line-up consisted of James (bass), Martin Degville (vocals), Neil Whitmore (guitar), Chris Kavanagh (drums), Ray Mayhew (drums) and Jane Farrimond (sound mixing). The group's extreme haircuts and make-up, and the professed 'designer violence' theme of their attire, together with James' pedigree, made an irresistible package for the music media, so that only a handful of high-profile gigs in fashionable London venues brought them an overwhelming amount of press coverage. The band were eventually signed to EMI for a reputedly astronomical sum (the hype said £4m), and early in 1986 their noisy debut single 'Love Missile F-111' was released and made the UK Top 3, purely on its novelty value. The follow-up, '21st Century Boy', was virtually ignored, however, as was their dismal album *Flaunt It*, which was the first to feature commercials between tracks.

SILHOUETTES Four Philadelphians, Earl Beal, Raymond Edwards, Billy Horton and Richard Lewis – formed the Gospel Tornados in 1955, but it was not until 1958, as the Silhouettes, that they turned the charts upside-down when the startling sound of 'Get a Job' sold a million copies within three weeks of release – its bass chant, 'Sha-na-na-na', is now infamous in the annals of rock'n'roll. Released initially on DJ Kae Williams' Junior label and leased to Ember, the Silhouettes' song was strong social comment for its time, but was obscured by the lead singer's barely intelligible diction. The group recorded for Ember and Ace until 1961 without further success.

SIMON AND GARFUNKEL Paul Simon and Art Garfunkel made one of the biggest selling albums ever in *Bridge over Troubled Water* (1970), but it was by no means their only significant recording achievement. Previously, Simon and Garfunkel had provided songs for Mike Nichol's award-winning movie, *The Graduate*, a

Simon and Garfunkel formed the most popular and enduringly commercial act to emerge out of the folk-rock phase of the mid-Sixties

skilful comedy about the 'generation gap', which interpreted the 'youth revolt' of the Sixties for anxious parents. The unparalleled sales of the *Bridge* album suggested a similar impact. It bridged the division between the rock generation and those outside it through Simon's enigmatic songs and Garfunkel's soft, soaring tenor.

Paul Simon (born 13 October 1942) and Art Garfunkel (5 November 1942) grew up together in Queens, New York. At 15, they were Tom and Jerry, an **Everly Brothers**-type harmony team, with a small hit on Big called 'Hey Schoolgirl'. They made a few public appearances and appeared on *American Bandstand* before returning to their studies. Simon continued recording under various names, including Jerry Landis and Tico and The Triumphs (whose 'Motorcycle' made 99 in the Hot 100 on Amy in 1962). He met **Carole King** and tried unsuccessfully to write songs with her, and then took his acoustic guitar down to Greenwich Village to become a folksinger. His earliest songs were recorded with Garfunkel for Columbia but remained unnoticed until **Bob Dylan** unveiled his electric sound in 1965 and suddenly folk-rock was the thing. Paul Simon was in England playing the folk clubs, producing Jackson C. Frank and cutting his acoustic *Songbook* album and Garfunkel was in college when producer Tom Wilson added a rock backing to their recording of 'Sounds of Silence'. By early 1966 it was a Number 1 hit. Simon rushed back to the US, got together with Garfunkel and began touring. The pattern of their work together for the next five years was set.

From the start it was clear that Simon had his finger on the pulse of a college generation whose high-school adolescent angst was deepened as the Student Movement began. These songs were sometimes portentous ('Patterns', 'Sounds of Silence', 'I Am a Rock') but they were balanced by Simon's unequalled melodic sense and by a few love songs of enduring power, notably 'Kathy's Song' and 'Wednesday Morning 3 a.m.'. The singing, too, was exceptional: the restless generation had its own Everly Brothers.

On record, it took some time for Simon and Garfunkel to achieve an instrumental mode to match their songs and singing. Both Wilson's overdubbing and the 1966 studio album produced by **Bob Johnston** (then Dylan's producer) were shotgun marriages of folk songs and rock sounds. Later that year another album, *Parsley,*

Sage, Rosemary and Thyme, included more revamped versions of Simon's earlier acoustic songs. Meanwhile they had scored two more Top 10 hits, 'Homeward Bound' and 'I Am a Rock', and two further singles went Top 30. Simon and Garfunkel now took greater control of their career, resisting the pressure for more and more product. Throughout 1967 they concentrated on *The Graduate* and on the first self-produced album, with its sympathetic accompaniments to Simon's first 'State of the Nation' song, 'America', and the mysterious 'Fakin' It'. Like *Bridge over Troubled Water* and their later solo albums, it involved the collaboration of master engineer Roy Halee.

The stage was set for their greatest triumph and in 1970 both the single and album of *Bridge* headed the charts. The overwhelming success seemed to induce musical inertia in the duo and when Art Garfunkel turned his attention to film acting (*Catch 22* and others), the split was inevitable. Simon's later solo work showed greater experimentation and intensity, while Garfunkel contented himself with relatively lightweight but exquisitely made records. They briefly re-united in 1975 for 'My Little Town', an American hit which also appeared on their 1975 solo albums, and again in 1978 for a revival (with **James Taylor**) of **Sam Cooke**'s 'Wonderful World'. In 1981, they appeared together in a Central Park concert, the live recording of which – *The Concert in Central Park* – won a gold disc. *See also* **Paul Simon**, **Art Garfunkel**

SIMON, CARLY A big-voiced singer-songwriter who outlasted the early Seventies vogue for solo performers to become a star of the AOR field, Carly Simon was born in New York City on 25 June 1945, and first performed and recorded with her sister Lucy. As the Simon Sisters, they had a small hit with 'Winkin' Blinkin' and Nod' on Kapp in 1964. They sang mainly folk-oriented material, playing only in the New York area where Carly was still at college. When Lucy married they stopped performing and it was several years before Carly was 'rediscovered' at a party and given an Elektra contract in 1970.

In the intervening years she had started to write music, and met Jacob Brackman, lyricist and screenplay writer, with whom she started a lengthy collaboration. Their most famous song, from her first album *Carly Simon* (1971) was the successful 'That's the Way I've Always Heard It Should Be'.

Its theme – the conflict between aspirations inherited in childhood and the adult reality – was consistently pursued by Carly throughout the albums that have followed, notably on the second, *Anticipation* (1971). Her greatest asset, then as now, was her strong and confident singing voice, and if the level of insight on her album declined over the years, the standard of musicianship, and in particular Richard Perry's productions, increased. Following her huge international hit with 'You're So Vain' in late 1972 her albums (*No Secrets*, 1972; *Hot Cakes*, 1974; *Playing Possum*, 1975) sold consistently well, and in 1974 she had transatlantic chart success with 'Mockingbird', a revival of the old **Inez and Charlie Foxx** song, on which she duetted with husband **James Taylor**. In 1977, she returned to the international charts with 'Nobody Does it Better', from the James Bond film *The Spy Who Loved Me*. The early Eighties found Carly winning some critical acclaim and major commercial success with the single 'Why' (1982) and the album *Torch*, on which she took the then-fashionable route of reviving pre-rock standards. Simon and Taylor divorced in 1982.

SIMON, JOE Soul singer Joe Simon enjoyed his biggest success between the late Sixties and mid-Seventies, when his country soul renditions of songs like 'Your Time to Cry' and 'Drowning in the Sea of Love' achieved high placings in the soul chart and crossed over to the pop listings. He was born on 2 September 1943, in Simmesport, Louisiana. After mediocre releases on Irral and Hush, where he sang with the Goldentones, and a minor hit on Vee Jay, he joined the Nashville-based Monument subsidiary Sound Stage 7 in 1966. With John Richbourg – noted for his work in the country-flavoured soul area – as his producer, Simon scored sixteen R&B hits in four years, including 'Teenager's Prayer' (1966), 'Nine Pound Steel' (1967), a version of the much-recorded 'You Keep Me Hanging On' (1968), and the million-selling 'The Choking Kind' (1969). Recording for Spring since 1970, he maintained his success with hits produced by **Gamble and Huff** – 'Drowning in the Sea of Love', 'Pool of Bad Luck', Brad Shapiro ('Step by Step', 'Carry Me') and further recordings with Richbourg. He scored his first US Top 10 hit with a disco record, 'Get Down, Get Down (Get on the Floor)', and thereafter recorded mainly in a disco mode.

SIMON, PAUL Born on 13 October 1942 and raised in New York City, singer/guitarist Paul Simon survived the dissolution of his enormously successful partnership with **Art Garfunkel** in 1970 with his reputation as a songwriter, if anything, enhanced. His output as a solo artist has been small – one live and three studio albums by 1975 – but marked by meticulous attention to detail unequalled in rock.

The first record (*Paul Simon*, Columbia, 1971) was hailed as a significant personal statement, shedding the whimsy of much of the **Simon and Garfunkel** music. More significantly, it showed Simon exploring a wide range of musical forms, including reggae ('Mother and Child Reunion') and even the middle-of-the-road ballad ('Everything Put Together Falls Apart' – a song whose lyrics contradicted the chosen musical style).

This process continued on *There Goes Rhymin' Simon* (1973), with the inclusion of the **Dixie Humingbirds** gospel group among the accompanists for 'Loves Me Like A Rock', while the Peruvian group Urubamba appeared in live performances recorded on the *Live Rhymin'* album (1974). At the insistence of Columbia, singles were released from the first album, with both 'Me and Julio down by the Schoolyard' and 'Mother and Child Reunion' reaching the Top 30. A bigger hit came with 'American Tune' from the second album, chosen by *Rolling Stone* as the song of the year, for its ability to capture the mood of Watergate-era America.

During the Seventies, Simon has had to withstand pressures for a resumption of the Simon and Garfunkel operation, conceding to the extent of recording one track with his ex-partner ('My Little Town') which appeared on both singers' 1975 albums. Simon's *Still Crazy After All These Years* also produced more hits with 'Gone at Last', a duet with **Phoebe Snow**, and the American Number 1, '50 Ways to Leave Your Lover'.

That album was his last for five years – a *Greatest Hits* package apart – and he spent the latter half of the Seventies involved in film work, taking a cameo role in Woody Allen's film *Annie Hall* and scripting and composing the soundtrack for his self-financed project, *One Trick Pony*. Critical opinion on the film, in which he also starred, was divided, but the soundtrack album yielded a major hit single in 'Late in the Evening' (Warner Brothers, 1980). The track reached Number 6 in the US. He was reunited with Garfunkel for a

memorable Central Park concert in 1981.

In 1983, Warners released *Hearts and Bones*, an accomplished solo set that included Simon's tribute to **John Lennon**, 'The Late Great Johnny Ace'. He also duetted with **Randy Newman** on a track on the latter's album *Trouble in Paradise* called 'The Blues', which was issued (unsuccessfully) as a single. 1985 found Simon working on *Graceland* and defying calls for a cultural boycott of South Africa by recording there with black musicians. *See also* **Simon and Garfunkel**

SIMONE, NINA An intense gospel-based singer from Tryon, North Carolina, Nina Simone was born Eunice Wayman on 21 February 1933. She played organ at her Method minister mother's church, having begun to learn piano at the age of four. She had formal training at New York's Juilliard School of Music, and worked around Philadelphia's clubs until signing with Bethlehem Records in 1959. Her debut album yielded a million-selling single – a tortuous, gospel-drenched version of George Gershwin's 'I Loves You Porgy'. She moved to Colpix in 1960 and recorded numerous LPs and two minor hit singles before joining Philips in 1965, when 'Don't Let Me Be Misunderstood' and 'I Put a Spell on You' were R&B hits. She signed with RCA in 1967 and soon returned to the charts

Nina Simone shunned the limelight after a handful of powerful hits

with 'Ain't Got No – I Got Life' from *Hair* and the black anthem 'Young Gifted and Black'. She retired from performing in 1974 but returned to recording four years later with *Baltimore* (CTI), the title song of which was written by **Randy Newman**.

SIMPLE MINDS

SIMPLE MINDS Glasgow's Simple Minds emerged in 1977 from what was left of local band Johnny and the Self Abusers; original members Jim Kerr (vocals), Charlie Burchill (guitar) and Brian McGee (drums) were joined by Derek Forbes (bass) and Mick MacNeil (keyboards). Originally signed to Zoom Records, a distribution deal led to a move to Arista. Their first three albums – *Life in a Day*, *Real to Real Cacophony* (both 1979) and *Empires and Dance* (1980) – were a strange mixture of influences, from **Roxy Music** to Sixties psychedelia, and ranged from the studiously serious to the eminently danceable. It was the third of these that consolidated their reputation and contained the best song of their early days, 'I Travel'.

Relations with Arista had not been good for some time and after a prestigious tour with **Peter Gabriel** in 1980, they signed to Virgin Records. *Sons and Fascination* and *Sister Feelings Call* (initially issued together as a double-pack but later reissued separately) were the first fruits of this new partnership and their strongest contribution to date, making Number 11 in the chart. Simple Minds made a series of excellent promotional videos which kept them in the public eye during the extensive tours.

In 1982, their next album *New Gold Dream* soared to Number 3 in the UK and did well in the US, a reflection of their growing international status. After the departure of Brian McGee they made do with a number of fill-in drummers until the arrival of Mel Gaynor in 1982, and during a series of live dates it was clear they had found the near-perfect drummer. Three singles, 'Promise You a Miracle', 'Glittering Prize' and 'Waterfront' made the Top 20.

Teaming up with star producer Steve Lillywhite, Simple Minds began work on their next album *Sparkle in the Rain*, a major success which featured powerful tracks, such as 'Up on the Catwalk' and 'Speed Your Love to Me'. The album shot to Number 1 in the UK charts. During 1985 the band took on exhausting touring schedules and worked with the **Pretenders** before going into the studio to record the next album *Once Upon a Time* which was released in the autumn of 1985 and, like its predecessor, shot straight to Number 1, confirming Simple Minds as one of the most successful bands of the Eighties. They made a memorable appearance in the Live Aid concert (performing at Philadelphia's JFK stadium) in July 1985.

SIMPLY RED One of the UK's most successful pop/soul bands, Simply Red came together in Manchester early in 1985. Led by singer Mick Hucknall, it was his soaring voice that gave the band an authentic soulful feel and which made them much more than just another proficient soul outfit.

Many of the band's members were active in the busy Manchester post-punk music scene, Hucknall once the frontman for garage band the Frantic Elevators, while Tony Bowers (bass), Chris Joyce (drums) and Tim Kellett (brass), had all been members of cult band the Durutti Column. They were joined by Fritz McIntyre (keyboards) and Sylvan Richardson (guitar) and after a handful of gigs they were signed to Elektra, finally making their mark with a triumphant support slot on **James Brown**'s 1985 UK tour, proving a very tough act to follow.

Simply Red scored a UK Top 20 hit in the summer with 'Money's Too Tight (To Mention)' and followed it up with the release of their well-received debut LP, *Picture Book* (which went gold in the UK). Their popularity grew right across Europe and they finally hit the jackpot with the single, 'Holding Back the Years', which was a huge hit in both the US and the UK. Their second LP, *Men and Women*, was released early in 1987.

SINGLETON, SHELBY Of all the white Southern record entrepreneurs who emerged during the Fifties and Sixties, Shelby Singleton's career was the most phenomenal. He was working in Shreveport, Louisiana, in the early Fifties as promotion manager for radio KWKH's country artists when he met his wife-to-be Margie, a singer whom he placed with Starday and eventually with Mercury. Singleton moved to Mercury in the late Fifties and climaxed a successful selling career by taking over as country product manager. Immediately, he began to find a string of top sellers like the **Big Bopper** and **Johnny Preston**.

When Mercury formed Smash Records in Nashville in 1962, Singleton was put in charge. He had by then successfully recorded **Clyde McPhatter** and **Brook Benton**, but his forte was making pop hits of country material, and in 1962 he produced **Bruce Channel** from Louisiana, whose 'Hey Baby' went to Number 1. In the same year he became a vice-president of Mercury, and he went on to sign **Jerry Lee Lewis** and **Charlie Rich**. In 1969, Singleton pulled off a financial coup by buying out Sun Records,

setting up the Sun International Corporation, forming his own Plantation, SSS and Silver Fox labels and coming up with hits in all fields. **Jeannie C. Riley**, **Peggy Scott** and Jo Jo Benson, **Johnny Adams** and Harlow Wilcox all made the national charts, while the original Sun product of **Johnny Cash** and Jerry Lee Lewis made a fortune all over again.

SIOUXSIE AND THE BANSHEES Among the pioneers of the British punk movement, Siouxsie and the Banshees made their legendary debut appearance at London's 100 Club in September 1976. The less than competent band, comprising vocalist Siouxsie Sioux (real name Susan Ballion), Steve Severin (bass), Marco Pirroni (guitar) and Sid Vicious (drums), played an impromptu twenty-minute version of the Lord's Prayer.

They re-surfaced in 1977 with a new line-up of Kenny Morris (replacing Vicious) on drums and John McKay on guitar (replacing the short-lived Peter Fenton who had ousted Pirroni). The band gigged throughout the rest of the year to little acclaim, record companies feeling that their screeching sound, coupled with Siouxsie's ghoulish make-up, was a little too hard to take. But they were slowly building up a live following and were featured on a **John Peel** radio session.

The year 1978 saw a change in their fortunes. The band had moved on from the cacophony of their early work to develop a characteristic, hard-edged sophistication that lifted them out of the punk rut. Polydor signed them, and their classic first single 'Hong Kong Garden', released in August, made the UK Number 7 slot. The LP *The Scream* followed in November and entered the UK Top 20 to massive critical acclaim in its first week of release.

Further hits 'The Staircase Mystery' and 'Playground Twist' followed in 1979 and the second LP *Join Hands* was released in September. Immediately after its release, Morris and McKay quit the band on the second date of the promotional tour to be replaced by Budgie from the **Slits** on drums. The **Cure**'s Robert Smith was recruited to fill in temporarily on guitar.

January 1980 brought the arrival of John McGeoch from **Magazine** to fill the guitarist's post permanently. *Kaleidoscope* was released soon after, and this album, which showed a clear move away from punk towards their own swirling blend of Eighties psychedelia, was well received, but it sold poorly. In 1981 came *JuJu*,

Siouxsie mellowing from bondage and swastikas into erotica and exotica

containing some of their finest work including the single 'Spellbound', and even if this number just failed to make the Top 20, the album consolidated the Banshees' musical strengths as well as their status as an innovative band for the discerning modern music enthusiast.

Siouxsie and Budgie also got together that year to form the Creatures, a part-time duo who released the EP *Wild Things* in October. In 1983, they scored a Number 14 hit with their sparse version of Mel Torme's 'Right Now', and an LP, *Feast* was released the same year.

The single 'Fireworks', featuring the string arrangements of Virginia Astley, was released by the Banshees in April 1982 and marked a new, warmer sound that was markedly different from their early bleakness. This progression was confirmed with the release of *A Kiss in the Dreamhouse*, an atmospheric collection of rich, exotic sounds that constituted a significant step for the band. Shortly after the album's release, McGeogh was mysteriously sacked, to be replaced again by Robert Smith, who decided he could run a career with the Cure and the Banshees at the same time.

By 1983 the Banshees had formed their own label, Wonderland, through Polydor, which allowed them various side projects (the Creatures, and the Smith/Severin project the Glove), and the next Banshees single, 'Dear Prudence', did not appear until September '83. An off-beat cover of a **Beatles** song, this was a surprise – and their biggest – hit, reaching Number 3 in the UK. They had two sell-out nights at the Royal Albert Hall which provided them with the live album *Nocturne*.

The next studio album was *Hyaena*, appearing in 1984, followed by two unsuccessful singles. There then followed a long rest, broken at the beginning of 1986 with 'The Candyman', a single that returned the group to the UK Top 30 and preceded the release of their ninth album, *Tinderbox*.

Siouxsie and the Banshees had moved on from the bleak industrial feel of their early work to a warmer, more rounded and melodic sound, and their influence can be heard in the songs of such diverse acts as **Joy Division**, the **Cure**, **Echo and the Bunnymen**, **Soft Cell** and **Toyah**. Their greatest achievement was to orchestrate a whole area of sound and mood that was instantly recognizable as theirs, yet rich and complex enough to allow others to explore it.

SIR DOUGLAS QUINTET

One of the most important bands to emerge in the US at the time of the so-called 'British Invasion' of 1964–6, the Sir Douglas Quintet comprised Doug Sahm (born 6 November 1941 in San Antonio, Texas), Francisco Morin (13 August 1946), Harvey Kagan (18 April 1946), Augie Meyer (31 May 1940) and John Perez (8 November 1942). Sahm was a country music child prodigy – he played the steel guitar at the age of six – who turned to rock'n'roll in the Fifties, recording both solo and with a group, the Knights, for several local Texas labels, before forming the Sir Douglas Quintet in San Antonio in 1964. **Huey P. Meaux**'s simple recording of 'She's About a Mover', featuring the insistent organ of Meyer, was a Top 20 hit in 1965 on Tribe. After one more hit, 'The Rains Came' (1966), Sahm decamped to San Francisco – a journey that was to provide the theme of much of *Mendocino* (Smash, 1969), Sahm's best album to date – where an enlarged group (including George Rains and Martin Fierro) recorded the charmingly uneven *Honky Blues* (Smash, 1968). Sadly, the infectious 'Mendocino', a surprise million-seller in 1969, came too late to rescue the band's commercial potential. Henceforth, despite satisfying and pioneering albums – *Together After Five* (1970) and *1+1+1=4* (1971) – which mixed country music, Mexican rhythms, the blues and rock with Meyer's organ and Sahm's idiosyncratic songwriting – the group's audience was a minority one. In 1971, Sahm folded the band to embark on an erratic solo career. *See also* **Doug Sahm**

SISTER SLEDGE

American soul group Sister Sledge were guided to chart success by **Chic** mainmen Nile Rodgers and Bernard Edwards, who crafted a pulsating sound for the sisters.

Joni, Debbie, Kim and Kathy Sledge began singing in church in Philadelphia at an early age before doing session work at the famed Sigma Sound Studios. In 1973, while they were still at high school, they were signed to Atlantic, where a string of early albums established their reputation. The breakthrough came in 1979 with the album *We Are Family*, which gave them three killer translantic hits with the title track, 'He's the Greatest Dancer' and 'Lost in Music'. There then followed a lull as they disappeared from the charts for a couple of years, but then re-releases of 'We Are Family' and 'Lost in Music' both returned to the charts in 1984 to pave the way for 'Frankie' to be a UK Number 1 in 1985.

SKAGGS, RICKY

One of the leading lights in Eighties country music, vocalist/guitarist Ricky Skaggs was born in Cordell, Kentucky, on 18 July 1954, the son of professional musicians. He appeared on Lester Flatt and **Earl Scruggs**' Nashville television show at seven years old and joined Ralph Stanley's support band at fifteen. Moving to Washington DC, he formed a band called Boone Creek and graduated to session work before becoming a permanent member of **Emmylou Harris**' Hot Band, where his command of the bluegrass idiom won him a strong critical following. Signed as a solo act by Columbia in 1981, he made his debut for the label with the album *Waitin' for the Sun to Shine* during that year and followed it with *Don't Cheat in Our Home Town* (1983) and *Country Boy* (1984). His single 'Crying My Heart Out Over You' (from his first album) reached Number 1 in the US country chart in 1981, beginning a run of commercial success, and by the middle of the decade Skaggs was a pivotal figure in the 'New Country' movement, offering a potent mixture of traditional country instrumentation and rock rhythms that had crossover appeal.

SKIDS

One of the first of the Scottish bands to make a breakthrough at the end of the Seventies, the Skids' first single, 'Reasons', was released on No Bad Records Of Dunfermline in 1978. This and regular appearances in the pages of the punk fanzines and patronage of DJ **John Peel**, led to a contract with Virgin Records.

Together with guitarist Stuart Adamson, Jobson formed a songwriting team that produced ten hit singles in just over two years. Their first LP, the raw and punky *Scared to Dance*, spent ten weeks in the album charts early in 1979, while the single from it, 'Into the Valley', reached Number 10. Their second LP, *Days in Europa* (1979) contained the hit singles 'Charade' and 'Working for the Yankee Dollar'.

However, Jobson's growing artistic pretensions – evident on their third album *The Absolute Game* (1980) – alienated Adamson, who quit soon after the LP's release. Jobson carried on with bassist Russell Webb, recording a final album, *Joy* (1981), which explored Celtic folksong. He then retired from the music scene to pursue his interests in acting and poetry. He returned to rock singing in 1983 with a new band, the Armoury Show, but was overshadowed by his former sidekick Stuart Adamson, who had refined the Skids' sound with his new band **Big Country**.

SKIFFLE

This term was originally applied to the Chicago jug bands of the Twenties, in which 'found' instruments replaced the rhythm section of the traditional jazz band and voices replaced front line instruments. However, the British skiffle boom of 1956–8 bore little relation to such music.

Skiffle had its origins in the first British trad boom of the early Fifties – **Lonnie Donegan**'s 'Rock Island Line', for example, was recorded by Donegan when he was part of the Skiffle unit in **Chris Barber**'s Jazz Band (Donegan on guitar and vocals, Barber on bass and Beryl Bryden on washboard) – when it was played as the interval music. But it soon burst beyond these confines to become Britain's first do-it-yourself music. Donegan opened the door to the skiffle boom, but it was the ease with which skiffle could be played more than anything that ensured the movement's success. In contrast to rock-'n'roll which demanded electric guitars, saxophones and an American accent, skiffle required only a basic guitarist (three chords and a capo), somebody with a good sense of rhythm (on washboard), a stand-up bass (or tea chest) player and a lot of energy – even the ever-present American accent wasn't a strict necessity. In the wake of Donegan's success, various skiffle aggregations had hits, including Chas McDevitt and Nancy Whiskey ('Freight Train') **Johnny Duncan** ('Last Train to San Fernando') and the Vipers ('Cumberland Gap'). But the real importance of the movement lay outside the charts: it was in the church cellars and coffee bars of Britain – the 2 I's, where all Britain's rock'n'rollers were supposed to have been discovered was originally the skiffle club – where thousands of young people formed skiffle groups, including **John Lennon**'s Quarrymen.

Skiffle had no lasting impact. By 1958, would-be skifflers were hunting out electric guitars and forming rock-'n'roll groups. Yet it was skiffle more than anything else that laid the foundations of British rock. *See also* **Lonnie Donegan**

SKIP AND FLIP

A fairly lightweight American pop duo who achieved moderate American success in 1959–60 with 'It Was I' and 'Cherry Pie', Skip and Flip were Clyde Battin and Gary Paxton respectively. The duo independently recorded 'It Was I' in Phoenix, Arizona, and leased the tape to the Brent label in Los Angeles. The record reached Number 11 in the US in July 1959, precipitating a national tour.

By 1960, Battin had been replaced as Skip by an ex-dishwasher from Phoenix, Dave Martinez, who was in turn replaced by Rod Marshall. The duo registered again with 'Cherry Pie' (Number 11 in May 1960) but disbanded that year when Paxton became lead singer of the Hollywood Argyles of 'Alley Oop' fame. He later became a producer ('Monster Mash') while Skip Battin joined the **Byrds** in 1969 and then the **New Riders of the Purple Sage** in 1973, with whom he remained until 1976 when he joined a re-formed **Flying Burrito Brothers**. *See also* **Gary Paxton**

SKYLINERS Perhaps the finest of white R&B vocal groups, the Skyliners were based in Pittsburgh and were renowned for the stunning lead singing of Jimmy Beaumont (born 21 October 1940) and for the much-revived Top 20 hit, 'Since I Don't Have You', recorded for Calico in 1959. Their manager, Joe Rock, produced other hits for Al Capozzi's label: 'This I Swear', 'It Happened Today' and 'Pennies from Heaven'.

When the group – Janet Vogel Rapp (10 June 1942), Joe Verscharen (1940), Wally Lester (5 October 1941) and Jackie Taylor (1941) – split up, Beaumont made solo records for May, Colpix, Scepter and Bang. Taylor formed his own Skyliners in 1965 and cut 'The Loser', a minor R&B hit on Jubilee. In 1969, the original members re-formed to appear at rock revival shows and cut an album for Buddah.

SLADE Converted by Chas Chandler from an undistinguished club band into one of the biggest pop phenomena of the early Seventies via an unbroken string of hits that included six Number 1 singles and two Number 1 albums, Slade comprised Noddy (real name, Neville) Holder (vocals, guitar, born 15 June 1946), Dave Hill (guitar, 4 April 1952), Jim Lea (bass, 14 June 1950) and Don Powell (drums, 10 September 1950). They started out in the Midlands in the Sixties as the In-Betweens before changing their name to Ambrose Slade and then to Slade.

As Slade, they initially received attention because of their skinhead image, but as success rapidly followed their first hit single, a revamping of Bobby Marchan's 'Get Down and Get With It' (Polydor, 1971), this was modified into a kind of aggressive glitter. The development of Holder and Lea as composers of all the group's subsequent hits encouraged comparisons with early **Lennon-McCartney**, which were reinforced by the closeness of Holder's voice to John Lennon's. But more importantly, the dynamism of early hits like 'Mama Weer All Crazee Now' (1972) and 'Cum On Feel The Noize' (1973) paralleled Pete Townshend's anthems. In an effort to enlarge their public beyond teenyboppers and boot boys, they spent the second half of 1974 working on a film, *Flame*.

A serious car accident in 1974 left Powell suffering from almost total amnesia and forced the group to reassess its direction and its plans for a major launch in the US. The hits continued into 1977 and the group faded out of the limelight, to re-emerge during 1980 with an EP, *Slade Alive at Reading '80*, that captured their blistering performance at that year's heavy metal festival. That disc began a major Slade revival, culminating in 1983 in a Number 2 hit with 'My Oh My' and a Top 20 re-entry of 'Merry Xmas Everybody', originally a chart-topper over Christmas 1973. Still one of the best live bands around, their energy shows no sign of flagging despite their many years of hit-making.

SLEDGE, PERCY Born in Leighton, Alabama, in 1941, Percy Sledge shot to international fame with his first release, 'When a Man Loves a Woman' (Atlantic), in 1966. An intensely performed love ballad, it was the archetype for many Southern soul productions of the period and set the pattern for most of his own subsequent releases. Although several were better than the original hit, audiences gradually rejected his simple but compelling style in favour of the complex sounds of the Seventies. Among his greatest performances were 'It Tears Me Up' (1966), 'Out of Left Field', two album tracks, 'Dark End of the Street' and 'I Had a Talk with My Woman' (1967), 'Take Time to Know Her', 'Sudden Stop' (1968), 'Any Day Now' (1969), and 'Stop the World Tonight' (1971). In 1974, he made a welcome, if surprising, return to grace with the Muscle Shoals-recorded 'I'll Be Your Everything' (Capricorn) which was in the style of his earlier records. 'When a Man Loves a Woman' made a return to the UK chart in early 1987 following its use in a Levis Jeans advertisement.

SLITS All-girl punk legends the Slits emerged at the height of the punk explosion in 1977, but it quickly became clear that they were a cut above the thrash merchants and later came to be respected as an innovative band.

Ari Up (vocals), Palmolive (drums), Kate Korus (guitar) and Suzi Gutsy (bass) was the original line-up, based in London, that gigged as much as legally possible (Ari Up was only fourteen at the time), but it soon changed as Budgie, Vivien Albertine and Tessa Pollitt joined to replace Palmolive, Korus and Gutsy. Signed to Island, the Slits recorded their stunning but unsuccessful debut album *Cut* in 1979 with **Dennis Bovell** producing, but they only recorded one more album, *Return of the Giant Slits* (1982) before disbanding soon after its release.

Slade in their shorthair phase: the band provided stomping rhythms and a lot of noise and jollity. Their raw, simplistic, warm-hearted music appealed to an audience that was sick of sophistication and subtlety

SLOAN, P. F. Singer/songwriter Philip (P. F.) Sloan had his moment in 1965, the year of the harmonica holder and **Dylan** caps, as folk singers crammed image-laden syllables into all their rhymes. In Britain this trend was epitomized by **Donovan**, in the US by the likes of **Bob Lind** and Sloan. Earlier, in partnership with **Steve Barri**, Sloan had been a writer of surfing songs in Los Angeles. There he had met **Lou Adler** who brought him together with **Barry McGuire**; Sloan wrote 'Eve of Destruction', a classic hate-ridden supply of lines for McGuire to angrily spit out. A performer himself, he recorded an album for Adler (*Songs of Our Times*) of original songs, some written in collaboration with Steve Barri (who also produced the album). An imitatory Dylan period piece, the album was a mixture of *Bringing It All Back Home* and *Another Side*. Sloan's 'This Morning' borrowed the melody of 'Love Minus Zero – No Limit' and 'What's Exactly The Matter With Me' was Sloan's variation on 'All I Really Wanna Do'. Somehow, though, Phil Sloan did it with great personal style. **Jimmy Webb** (for his album *Words and Music*) wrote a song, 'P. F. Sloan', in tribute to him. Later albums, like *Measure for Pleasure* (Atco), and *Raised on Records* (1972) failed to measure up to earlier expectations.

SLY AND ROBBIE This duo consists of Sly Dunbar (drums) and Robbie Shakespeare (bass), two Jamaicans who have established a reputation as one of the hardest rhythm sections in contemporary music. Since the mid-1970s they have worked with a staggering array of artists; **Grace Jones**, **Black Uhuru**, **Dennis Brown**, **Ian Dury**, **Bob Dylan**, the **Rolling Stones**, **Joe Cocker**, Bunny Wailer and **Burning Spear** are just some. Additionally, as producers, Sly and Robbie have built up an impressive list of credits and they also run their own label, Taxi Records.

Sly Dunbar was born in Kingston, Jamaica, on 10 May 1952 and made his recording debut working on Dave and Ansel Collins' 'Double Barrel' in 1969. Soon he was working with most of the major reggae stars, and was acknowledged as the most innovative drummer in Jamaica. By moving away from the standard reggae style to incorporate more complex and fluid rhythms, Sly has made a lasting contribution to the development of the music.

In 1974 he formed Taxi Records and began his partnership with Robbie Shakespeare (born 27 September 1953, in Kingston) who had also built up a reputation as a session ace in Jamaica. Like Sly, Robbie had been variously a member of the Professionals (for producer Joe Gibbs), the Upsetters (for Lee 'Scratch' Perry) and in 1984 they became permanent members of Black Uhuru, who they had produced and worked with since the start of the 1980s.

SLY AND THE FAMILY STONE One of the most influential bands in late Sixties black music, Sly and the Family Stone was the brainchild of one man – Sly Stone, born Sylvester Stewart in Dallas, Texas, on 15 March 1944. His enduring contribution to rock was to show the rhythmic potential of 'funk' when transferred from riffing horns to electronic keyboards and wah-wah guitars. Stone was a child prodigy, recording 'On My Battlefield for My Lord' at the age of four. At high school he was lead singer of the Viscanes, a doo-wop group, and though he moved to music college he soon left to split his time between deejaying on San Francisco radio and working as a record producer for the city's Autumn Records label.

The discs that Stone wrote and produced for Autumn ranged from the uptown soul of Bobby Freeman to the Beatles-like pop of the **Beau Brummels**, and they also included intriguing instrumentals of his own like 'Buttermilk'. But Sly was becoming exposed to an environment totally different from the insularity of mainstream ghetto life: firmly entrenched in the San Francisco psychedelic trip with his backing band (originally formed in 1966 as the Stoners), he became ambassador extraordinary of the new drug and youth revolution cultures by bringing elements of the West Coast white rock bands into his music. Now performing as Sly and the Family Stone, the band was spotted by Columbia/Epic's head of A&R, David Kapralik, in 1967 and launched on the rock scene with the album, *A Whole New Thing*. The band's line-up was: Sly (vocals, guitar, keyboards), Freddie Stone (vocals, guitar), Larry Graham (bass), Cynthia Robinson (trumpet), Greg Errico (drums), Rosie Stone (piano) and Jerry Martini (sax).

The release of a classic dance single, 'Dance to the Music', took Sly and his band to Number 8 in the US in 1968. More pulsating fusions of wah-wah guitar, undulating bass rhythms and chanted vocals followed in the single 'Everyday People' (a US Number 1 in

Sly Stone married black music to rock and gave a boost to them both

1969) and the album, *Stand*, which contained the apocalyptic 'I Want to Take You Higher' – the number Sly performed at the Woodstock festival to shattering effect. In 1970, rock's most extrovert personality released one single, the double gold-selling 'Thank You (Falettinme Be Mice Elf Agin)'. Sly's huge success was damaged by frequent non-appearances at gigs but as late as 1971 his 'new direction' album *There's a Riot Goin' On* killed the critics, the public and possibly Epic's finances (it being rumoured to have cost a million dollars to make despite featuring Sly himself on most instruments). An increasingly frenetic private and public life and the coolly received *Fresh* and *Small Talk* albums seemed to throw his career into reverse by 1975, and the rise of disco at this time left the group stranded. *Heard Ya Missed Me* (1977) was a thoroughly dreadful set of songs representing the nadir of his career. *Back on the Right Track* (1979), his first for Warner Brothers, was a more accomplished set that justified its title, but it was far less successful commercially than the compilation album of remixed Stone hits, *Ten Years Too Soon*, that CBS released during the same year with the disco market in mind. He was featured on Funkadelic's *Electric Spanking of War Babies* (1981) and played tour dates with George Clinton in the early Eighties, but his best days seemed behind him.

Sly and the Family Stone's legacy was, however, vitally important. Such artists as the **Isley Brothers**, **Prince** and the Parliament/Funkadelic combine built on the foundation laid by Sly's extravagant image and stage act. The musical riot that Sly Stone instigated is still going on in the Eighties.

SMALL FACES Unlike the **Who** (whose mod image was their manager's creation) the Small Faces *were* mods. Formed in 1965 by Steve Marriott, born 30 January 1947 (vocals, guitar); **Ronnie 'Plonk' Lane**, 1 April 1946 (bass); Jimmy Winston (organ) and Kenny Jones, 16 September 1948 (drums), the group grew out of their mutual liking for the mods' favourite music – R&B and soul – and their first single, 'Whatcha Gonna Do About It?' (Decca), a hit in September 1965, took the riff from **Solomon Burke**'s 'Everybody Needs Somebody to Love'. The Marriott–Lane follow-up, 'I've Got Mine', released when Ian McLagan – born 12 May 1945 – replaced Winston, flopped, but within six months they were chart regulars as 'Hey Girl', 'All Or Nothing' – their only Number 1 and probably

their best record – and 'My Mind's Eye' followed each other into the Top 10. The success of these singles – all Marriott–Lane compositions – linked the group for ever with the Top 10, and despite a label change and less obviously 'pop' material, they couldn't stop the hits or change their image. Songs like the jokey 'Itchycoo Park' (Immediate, 1967) – their only American Top 20 record – and 'Lazy Sunday' (Immediate, 1968), released as singles against the group's wishes, only heightened the problem.

After making the brilliant *Ogdens Nut Gone Flake* in 1968, Marriott quit and joined **Peter Frampton** in **Humble Pie**. Lane, McLagan and Jones stuck together, turned down offers to back solo performers and eventually teamed up with **Rod Stewart** and Ron Wood as the **Faces**. The band re-formed in 1977, without Lane but with Jimmy McCulloch from **Wings** and bassist Ricky Wills. *See also* the **Faces**, **Humble Pie**

SMILEY CULTURE South Londoner David Victor Emanuel became, under the name of Smiley Culture, the first man to take toasting into the UK singles chart. Smiley had already attracted a great deal of attention among knowledgeable circles with the hilarious single 'Cockney Translation' in 1983, and it was this style of rapid patois toasting punctuated with shots of broad white cockney that took the later single 'Police Officer' into the charts late in 1984. Attempting to follow up this success, he released several more singles, but he has yet to make any further impression on the charts.

SMITH, BESSIE If not the greatest woman ever to sing the blues, Bessie Smith will do until that person comes along. It is difficult to find secure ground for disagreeing with this assessment; no other singer has possessed her expressive range, her capability with material of extremely variable quality and style, and her subtlety of inflection and beauty of tone.

Born in Knoxville, Tennessee, in 1898, she developed her music in travelling shows, a life vividly described in the biography *Bessie* by Chris Albertson. Between 1923 and 1933 she recorded more than 100 blues, quasi-blues and popular songs with accompanists sometimes apt (Louis Armstrong, cornettist Joe Smith, pianist James P. Johnson), sometimes mundane. Her contemporaries were undoubtedly affected by her work, but it was the jazz musicians perhaps more than the blues singers who learned

from her phrasing and delivery. Nevertheless, all the important women singers since her time, from Billie Holiday to **Janis Joplin**, have acknowledged her achievements, and her most famous performances, such as 'St Louis Blues', 'Nobody Knows You When You're Down and Out' or the rumbustious 'Gimme a Pigfoot and a Bottle of Beer', are plainly immortal components of the jazz/blues canon.

Bessie Smith died after a motor accident in 1937; her recordings have rarely been out of catalogue since, and were reissued in their entirety on five double albums by Columbia in 1971–3.

SMITH, HUEY 'PIANO' Born in New Orleans on 26 January 1934, Huey Smith was one of the brightest and biggest New Orleans R&B stars of the Fifties. He started out playing piano with **Guitar Slim** and **Earl King**, and did session work for **Smiley Lewis**, **Little Richard** and **Lloyd Price** before recording on his own for Savoy. An impeccable pianist whose style was a refined development of **Professor Longhair**'s and an unusually talented songwriter, his voice was not strong and this led to the formation of his famous vocal group, the Clowns. It was with the Clowns, and Bobby Marchan in particular, that Huey Smith had his biggest hits for Ace – 'Rockin' Pneumonia and the Boogie Woogie Flu' (1957), 'Don't You Just Know It' (1958) and 'Pop-Eye' (1962). He was able to make the adjustment from R&B to soul with comparative ease, but his later records never sold well. He gave up music in favour of religion when in his thirties.

SMITH, O. C. Soul balladeer O. C. (Ocie Lee) Smith was born in Mansfield, Louisiana, on 21 June 1936, and moved to Los Angeles with his family when he was three years old. Upon graduation, he was conscripted into the USAF, and on discharge signed with Cadence Records in New York. Smith's debut disc, 'Lighthouse', was a slow rock'n'roll ballad with dubbed-on seagull cries. He subsequently recorded for Citation, and in 1961 became vocalist with Count Basie's Band after recording under **Leiber and Stoller** on Big Top and Broadway. Further fame came in 1968 when 'Son of Hickory Holler's Tramp', a country rockaballad on Columbia, was a transatlantic Top 40 hit. Ensuing years have brought several further US hits, largely sentimental ballads like 'Little Green Apples' and 'Daddy's Little Man', and in 1977 he reached the UK chart once more with 'Together' (Caribou).

SMITH, PATTI Described on more than one occasion as 'the high priestess of punk', Patti Smith was born on 31 December 1946, in Chicago and raised in Pitman, New Jersey. She moved to New York in 1967 and spent the next few years writing poetry, studying painting and travelling. In 1971, introduced by **Dylan** sidekick Bobby Neuwirth to the literary and musical life of Manhattan, she began reading her poetry at St Mark's in the Bowery, backed by rock critic/guitarist Lenny Kaye. Her poems were also published in *Creem* magazine and *Rolling Stone* and, in 1974, she began singing in the New York clubs, accompanied by Kaye and Richard Sohl (piano). She recorded a single, 'Piss Factory' (Mer Records, 1974) and in the early spring of 1975 was signed by Arista Records boss Clive Davis. Ivan Kral (guitar) and Jay Daugherty (drums) were added to the Patti Smith group for the recording of *Horses* (1975), which was produced by **John Cale** and included guest appearances by guitarists Tom Verlaine of **Television** and Allen Lanier of **Blue Oyster Cult**.

She returned to the studio in 1976 after a tour of Europe to record *Radio Ethiopia*, but critics complained that she had sacrificed her personal vision to the inferior egalitarianism of her band and blamed producer Jack Douglas for drowning her voice in the mix. In January 1977, she broke her neck in a fall off the stage during a performance in Florida and was inactive for over a year, although she wrote a volume of poetry, *Babel*, and worked on songs for *Easter*, which eventually appeared in 1978. Her most commercial work to date, it included a **Bruce Springsteen** song, 'Because the Night', with additional lyrics by Smith, which became a hit single around the world. *Wave* followed in 1979, produced by **Todd Rundgren**, but its cultivated amateurism and the juvenile tediousness of its lyrics were poorly received. Soon after its release, Smith broke up the band. On 1 March 1980, she married former **MC5** guitarist Fred 'Sonic' Smith and moved to Detroit.

SMITHS Guitarist Johnny Marr discovered (Steven) Morrissey in a Manchester bed-sit and persuaded him into a joint musical venture where Marr would write the music and Morrissey would provide the lyrics. Deliberately choosing the nondescript name of the Smiths, the group was completed in the summer of 1982 by Andy Rourke (bass) and Mike Joyce (drums). A number of live gigs brought them to the attention of **John Peel**'s radio show producer

John Walters and the independent label, Rough Trade. Walters got the group to record a series of radio sessions for the BBC after which Rough Trade signed them up, releasing the first single, 'Hand in Glove', in May 1983. The radio sessions proved very successful and helped ensure that the second release, 'This Charming Man', was a surprise UK Top 30 hit.

By early 1984 the Smiths had crossed over from cult band to the pop mainstream, a fact underlined by the rapid progress of 'What Difference Does It Make' to Number 12 in the UK chart. This was followed by their debut album, *The Smiths*, a superb piece of work by their producer John Porter that showcased the florid blend of Marr's fluid, intricate guitar work and Morrissey's plaintive vocal style, and reached Number 2 in the UK LP chart. By this time Morrissey had become a poppundit, his opinionated comments on the rock world eagerly sought by the music press. His inflated self-esteem was only redeemed by his subtle self-mockery and his undoubted abilities as singer and front man for the Smiths.

The Smiths' third album, *Meat is Murder* (it had been preceded by *Hatful of Hollow*, a package of a couple of unreleased tracks and the BBC radio sessions), was released in 1985 and went straight to the top of the UK LP chart, achieving gold status in the first week of sales. American interest in the band grew and a fifteen-date US tour in April presented the Smiths to a new audience. Back in the UK, the single, 'The Boy With the Thorn in his Side' returned them to the Top 30 and paved the way for the release of their fourth album, *The Queen Is Dead*, in mid-1986.

SNOW, HANK In the forefront of country music for nearly fifty years, Hank Snow's impact on rock was unusual, and unintentional. Born 9 May 1914, in Liverpool, Nova Scotia, he gained fame as the 'Singing Ranger' before moving to the States in the Forties. Recording for RCA since 1936, he is known for 'The Lonesome Blue Yodel', 'The Golden Rocket' and 'Nobody's Child'. His best-known song 'I'm Movin' On' was recorded in 1950 with his usual pure country-and-western sound, but became popular with rockabilly artists, whose emergence Snow disliked. In 1954 he refused to complete a tour with **Elvis Presley**. His son recorded under the name **Jimmy Rodgers** and had hits with 'Honeycomb' and 'Kisses Sweeter Than Wine' in 1958.

The Smiths, who had a surprise hit in 1983 with 'This Charming Man'

SNOW, PHOEBE Born in New York on 17 July 1952, Phoebe Snow (real name Phoebe Laub) was a graduate of the city's folk club scene who made her recording debut with an eponymous album for **Leon Russell**'s Shelter label in 1974. A single taken from it, 'Poetry Man', reached Number 5 in the US during 1975. She toured with **Paul Simon** in the mid-Seventies and moved to Columbia for her second album, *Second Childhood*, in 1976. After three further albums, she joined the Mirage label in 1981 and debuted with *Rock Away*. While she remained a critics' favourite, however, she largely failed to capitalize commercially on her remarkable jazz-inflected voice. Her only UK success was the 1979 single, 'Every Night' (written by **Paul McCartney**), which reached Number 37. She has performed and recorded infrequently in the Eighties, her only major release being the compilation set, *The Best of Phoebe Snow*, in 1986.

SOFT BOYS British new wave band the Soft Boys surfaced during the early days of the punk period but took their inspiration from the psychedelic era. Although they never had any real commercial success, they built up a cult following on the West Coast of America and were major influences on many of the bands who were to come out of the area.

Formed in Cambridge in 1976, the Soft Boys were Robyn Hitchcock (guitar/vocals), Kimberley Rew (guitar/vocals), Andy Metcalfe (bass) and Morris Windsor (drums). Their first release was the EP *Give It to the Soft Boys* in 1977 on Raw Records, and in 1978 they signed, albeit briefly, to Radar. Their first LP, *A Can of Bees* (1979), an album criticized for its strong psychedelic roots, was released by the band on their own Two Crabs label. *Underwater Moonlight* (1980), a more coherent collection of pop songs, preceded a lengthy stint touring the US, and even though they had a strong following there, they returned to the UK where in January 1981, discouraged by the lack of success or wide recognition, the Soft Boys broke up.

Hitchcock carried on working with his band the Egyptians, while Rew joined the successful Katrina and the Waves.

SOFT CELL Of all the 'odd couple' bands thrown up by the synth boom of the early eighties, Soft Cell proved to be the oddest, most extreme and, initially at least, the most successful.

Formed in Leeds in 1979, the group, which consisted of Marc Almond (vocals) and Dave Ball (electronics), played their first-ever show at a Christmas party at a local nightclub, where they indulged their passions for tacky glamour, Sixties soul, cabaret camp and Seventies disco. In mid-1980 they released their 'Mutant Moments' EP, which immediately sold all 2,000 copies and became a collectors' item.

After featuring on the Some Bizarre compilation LP, Soft Cell retained the eccentric Stevo as their manager and signed a licensing deal (through the Some Bizarre organization) with Phonogram. The 12″ dance funk of 'Memorabilia' confirmed the band's appeal on the nightclub scene, but the next single 'Tainted Love', an energetic reworking of a Northern Soul classic, became a huge surprise UK Number 1 in 1981 and stayed in the chart for four months.

In 1981, they released *Non-Stop Erotic Cabaret*, a mixture of sleazy ballads and breathless dance tracks, from which the hit singles 'Bedsitter' and 'Say Hello, Wave Goodbye' were culled. Several tracks were remixed by Mike Thorne for the mini-album, *Non-Stop Ecstatic Dancing* (1982).

Having explored the frantic side of their nature, Soft Cell attempted to concentrate on the seedier aspects of their music, but there was a minor scandal over their video for 'Sex Dwarf' and it was promptly banned. Meanwhile Marc Almond's lyrics probed further into the areas of moral disorientation and despair, as typified by the second album, *The Art of Falling Apart* (1983), which featured the hits 'Numbers' and 'Loving You, Hating Me'.

The constant pressure of international success was by now taking its toll: Almond, an unstable, mercurial character, was becoming increasingly frustrated by the restrictions of pop stardom and briefly found solace in two albums with his own group, Marc and the Mambas – *Untitled* (1982) and *Torments and Toreros* (1983). In the meantime, Dave Ball released his own solo album, *In Strict Tempo*.

While Ball thoroughly enjoyed studio experimentation, Almond needed the uncertain thrill of live performance and this irreconcilable difference was what eventually caused Soft Cell to split. However, this was not before they had released one more album *This Last Night* (1984) and one more hit single, 'Down in the Subway'.

Marc Almond then pursued a solo career, releasing the albums *Vermin in Ermine* (1984) and *Stories of Johnny* (1985), backed by the Willing Sinners.

SOFT MACHINE Evolving through various jazz-oriented personnel, Soft Machine took their name from William Burroughs' novel after Australian guitarist, Daevid Allen, brought the influence of Terry Riley and tape-loops to the basic line-up of **Kevin Ayers** (bass, vocals), Mike Ratledge (keyboards, born 1943) and **Robert Wyatt** (drums, vocals), who all hailed from Kent. They appeared regularly opposite **Pink Floyd** in London, participated in a couple of abortive recording sessions in 1967, and presented their music (free improvisation over a rock base, plus vocals) in France with great success. Allen was refused re-entry to Britain because of visa and passport difficulties, and it was as a trio that the band undertook a gruelling American tour with **Jimi Hendrix** in 1968; they broke up after cutting their first LP for Probe in New York.

When the album proved successful, they re-formed with Hugh Hopper (born 1945, a sympathetic sideman from the days when they called themselves the Wilde Flowers) replacing Ayers on bass. More albums (on CBS/Columbia) followed, featuring Wyatt's songs and Ratledge's angular experiments with time-signatures. Four jazz hornmen were added for a French tour, and saxophonist Elton Dean stayed with them; their now strongly jazz-influenced sound, with fewer Wyatt vocals, represented rock at the London classical music Proms in 1970, and Wyatt left to form Matching Mole in September 1971, shortly after an appearance at the Newport Jazz Festival. The jazz flavour remained, with Phil Howard then John Marshall on drums, Roy Babbington replacing Hopper, and Karl Jenkins (keyboards, oboe and baritone saxophone) replacing Dean; on the *Six* album, jazz riff structures and Rileyesque pieces rubbed shoulders.

Guitarist Alan Holdsworth joined for one album, *Seventh*, in 1975, and Ratledge left during the following year, to be replaced by John Ethridge (guitar) and Alan Wakeman (saxophone). That upheaval in personnel left the band without any of its original Machinists, though Soft Machine has continued its existence under the direction of various newcomers, including bassist **Jack Bruce**, sax player Dick Morissey and guitarist Alan Parker. *See also* **Robert Wyatt, Kevin Ayers**

SOLAR Born out of Soul Train Records, black independent label Solar (Sound of Los Angeles Records) was formed in 1978 when former concert promoter Dick Griffey took all the artists from the Soul Train label (**Shalamar**, the Whispers and Carrie Lucas) to start his own company. Over the next five years Griffey made Solar, with its related interests in concert promotion, artist management and music publishing, into an organization second only to Motown itself among black-owned entertainment companies in the US. Furthermore Solar became one of black music's most consistently interesting workshops, launching many hits (over fifty on *Billboard*'s R&B Top 40 during 1978–83) and a number of successful careers (Shalamar, the Whispers, Lakeside, Dynasty, Midnight Star) to create its own distinctive brand of black pop music.

Like the major companies, Solar had its own house band: Lem Sylvers (bass), Ernest 'Pepper' Reed (guitar) and Wardell Potts Jr (drums) formed the core of the band, joined on occasion by guitarist Stephen Shockley of Lakeside and keyboard player Kevin Spencer of Dynasty. Sylvers gradually became a central figure at Solar, and by the end of the Seventies he was house producer and the main creative force behind the label. He and the rest of Solar's creative crew hit their peak at the end of 1979, first with Shalamar's 'The Second Time Around' (a US Number 8), then with the Whispers' 'And the Beat Goes On' (Number 19 in the US and Number 2 in the UK). Combined sales for the two singles topped the three million mark.

Griffey showcased his leading acts on nationwide promotional tours that were modelled on the Motown revues of the Sixties, and in 1980 his 'Galaxy of Stars' tour (comprising Dynasty, Lakeside, Shalamar and comedian Vaughn West as compere) was seen by over a million people in the US. Since the performers shared backing musi-

cians, roadies and other services, running costs were kept to a minimum.

A highly influential figure within the black musical community, Griffey was also forthright on political issues, providing the best example since Motown that blacks could succeed in the business side of the music industry.

SONNY AND CHER Once described as the pop world's answer to Nelson Eddy and Jeanette Macdonald, Sonny and Cher graced the US and UK charts of 1965–6 with an engaging brand of folksy romanticism. Sonny was Salvatore Bono, who was born in Detroit, Michigan, on 16 February 1935, and worked with his father on the Douglas Aircraft assembly lines in Los Angeles. Mapping out a career for himself as a songwriter and would-be singer, he touted himself around local record companies in the late Fifties. In 1957, his 'High School Dance' was recorded as the flip of **Larry Williams**' million-seller, 'Short Fat Fannie' (Specialty). It sold well in its own right, reaching Number 46 in America. On the strength of this he became a staff producer at Specialty, also recording as Don Christy (after his first wife, Donna, and his daughter Christy) for that and other labels. After the demise of Specialty in 1959, Bono continued writing and formed his own Dak and Thrush labels, but without success. In 1963, the year he wrote 'Needles and Pins' – a huge hit for the **Searchers** later – with **Jack Nitzsche**, he began working for **Phil Spector**. In 1964, he married his girlfriend, Cher.

Born Cherilyn Sarkasian LaPier in El Centro, California, on 20 May 1946, of Armenian and Cherokee extraction, Cher took up session-singing to earn extra money to pay for acting lessons. At a **Ronettes** recording session for Phil Spector in 1963 – she can be heard on

'Be My Baby' – Cher and Bono met and under his direction the couple began recording, as Sonny and Cher for the small Vault label and as Caesar and Cleo for Reprise. In 1965, they signed with Atco and recorded the million-seller, 'I Got You Babe'. Written, arranged and produced by Bono, the song owed a lot to Spector and **Harold Battiste** – who conducted the orchestra on it and subsequent Atco recordings – both of whom Bono had worked under. However, it was Sonny and Cher's image – both sported long hair and 'outrageous' clothes – as much as their sound and the generalized protest content of their lyrics that sustained their careers through 'Baby Don't Go' (a Reprise recording), 'Just You'(1965) and 'The Beat Goes On' (1967) until, in 1967, it became apparent that they were more inclined towards Las Vegas than Haight-Ashbury. 1965 also saw the release of solo records – Sonny had a Top 10 with the ersatz protest song, 'Laugh at Me' (Atco), while Cher began what was to become a stream of hits with a cover of **Dylan**'s 'All I Really Want to Do' (Imperial). After four years of chart failure, the duo resurfaced on Kapp with'All I Ever Need Is You' (Number 7 in the US in 1971) and 'A Cowboy's Work Is Never Done' (Number 8, 1972), both of which were produced by **Tommy 'Snuff' Garrett**. They hosted a popular television series but by 1974 the marriage – and the singing partnership – were over. *See also* **Cher**

SOUL STIRRERS Featuring the amazing high tenor of Robert Harris, the Soul Stirrers pioneered the use of dual lead singers, and changed from a jubilee quartet into the gospel quintet of the post-1945 era. Their unique sound, promulgated by recordings for Aladdin and then Specialty, enabled **Sam Cooke** – who succeeded Harris in 1951 – to establish a reputation as a black teenage idol even before he secularized their style, when he turned to popular music. Despite adding instrumentation, including songwriting guitarist, Leroy Crume, the Texan group maintained their sound with first **Johnnie Taylor** and later Willie Rogers filling Cooke's role.

SOUND SYSTEMS Essentially mobile discotheques within the reggae culture, sound systems, at their simplest, consist of a DJ with a turntable, amplifier and speakers. At their most sophisticated, the equipment more closely resembles that employed in a recording studio – mixing consoles, reverb and echo chambers, equalizers,

The harmless face of the protest boom: Sonny and Cher, moody and droopy

tape delays and so on. Most sound systems feature a toaster in addition to a DJ – toasters being reggae's equivalent of a funk rapper, delivering more or less spontaneous poetry over the instrumental passages of records.

Sound systems developed first in Jamaica in the Fifties, when legendary DJs like Duke Reid, **Prince Buster** and Count Machuki toured the island putting on 'sound-system dances' in village squares and school halls. They are as important to reggae music as the live-gig circuit is to rock music, and provide the aspiring recording DJ with an established forum for learning his/her craft and making contact with record producers (many of whom are also sound-system operators).

SOUTH, JOE

One hit, 'Games People Play', made Joe South's reputation but his career drew together most of the important musical developments of the Sixties: he was a producer, songwriter, arranger, singer, session musician, guitar virtuoso, and disc jockey. He was born in Atlanta, Georgia, on 28 February 1940, and worked locally as a session guitarist and singer. This led to a minor hit in 1958 with 'The Purple People Eater Meets the Witch Doctor' (NRC), a none-too-subtle attempt to cash in on the then-current novelty song craze. Another small success came three years later with his version of the country classic 'You're the Reason' (Fairlane).

Throughout the Sixties, South worked on many sessions in Atlanta and elsewhere, including **Dylan**'s *Blonde on Blonde* and records by **Simon and Garfunkel**, **Aretha Franklin**, and **Tommy Roe**. As a songwriter, he had hits with 'Untie Me' (The **Tams**, 1962), 'Down in the Boondocks' (Billy Joe Royal's Top 10 US hit of 1965), 'Hush' (by Royal in 1967 and **Deep Purple** in 1968) and 'These Are Not My People' (**Johnny Rivers**, 1969).

Joe South made his mark as a performer with *Introspect* (Capitol, 1968). A classic set of blue-eyed soul songs often aimed at the intolerance and hypocrisy of Southern society (straight and hip), it included two Top 10 hits: 'Games People Play' for South himself and Lynn Anderson's 'Rose Garden'. The next album, *Don't It Make You Want to Go Home*, was in the same righteous vein, producing more hits with 'These Are Not My People' and South's 'Walk a Mile in My Shoes'. Later Capitol releases were less successful and in 1975 he signed to Island to record a subdued album *Midnight Rainbows*.

SOUTHSIDE JOHNNY AND THE ASBURY JUKES

A white R&B outfit from New Jersey, Southside Johnny and the Asbury Jukes emerged in the mid-Seventies in the wake of the success of fellow New Jerseyite **Bruce Springsteen**. Formed in 1974, the original line-up comprised Southside Johnny (real name John Lyon, born on 4 December 1948, vocals), Billy Rush (26 August 1952, guitar), Kevin Kavanaugh (27 August 1951, keyboards), Al Berger (8 November 1949, bass), Kenny Pentifallo (30 December 1940, drums), Carlo Novi (7 August 1949, sax), Tony Palligrosi (9 May, 1954, trumpet), Eddie Manion (28 February 1952, sax), Ricky Gazda (18 June 1952, trumpet), and Richie Rosenberg (trombone). The association with Springsteen went back to the mid-Sixties, when Lyon, Springsteen and Steve Van Zandt had played together in various local bands, and Van Zandt managed and produced the Jukes during the mid- to late Seventies. The band debuted with the album *I Don't Wanna Go Home* (Epic) in 1976 and recorded Springsteen material regularly until their eponymous fourth album in 1979 (their first for Mercury), which contained entirely self-written material. *Reach Out and Touch the Sky* (1981), a live set, found the band in top form.

SPANDAU BALLET

Very much a product of the trendy London scene of the late Seventies, new wave band Spandau Ballet's first live appearance took place in November 1979, in front of the group's fashionable friends in a private rehearsal room. Tony Hadley (vocals), Gary Kemp (guitar), Martin Kemp (bass), Steve Norman (sax/percussion) and John Keeble (drums) were all part of the Soho nightclub scene, specifically in the fashion-conscious clubs Blitz, Billy's, Hell and St Moritz, that threw up the likes of **Culture Club** and Steve Strange (*see* **Visage**).

Spandau Ballet at first performed exclusively to followers of this scene, but as media interest in what became known as the 'new romantics' grew, the band's reputation spread beyond the confines of the nightclubs. Acutely conscious of their image, they played a showcase set on HMS *Belfast*, moored on the Thames opposite the Tower of London, which gained them plenty of press attention and spurred Chrysalis into signing a licensing deal with the group's own label, Reformation.

The continuous media coverage ensured that their debut single 'To Cut a Long Story Short', a tough blend of guitars and synthesizers, was an

Spandau Ballet, from left Gary Kemp, Tony Hadley, Martin Kemp Steve Norman and John Keeble

immediate UK Top 10 hit in November 1980. Subsequent hit singles and a hit album *Journey to Glory* followed into 1981, and it was becoming clear that they were moving away from a rock-tinged sound to a more slick, if watered down, blend of pop, funk and soul. The single 'Chant No. 1' confirmed this, with its use of London-based session-eers Beggar and Co. It was a worldwide dance-floor hit and became the first white British record to be played on UK black dance radio.

The album *Diamond* was released in 1982 and the dance format continued, with a special limited edition of dance remixes of every track made available to bring the point home, but it wasn't until the release of the next LP, *True*, in 1983 that Spandau Ballet really hit paydirt. An accomplished set of eminently commercial dance pop tunes, the album generated hit after hit, namely 'Lifeline', 'Communication' and 'Gold', and especially the smoochy single 'True', which gave them their one and only UK Number 1 and made Number 4 in the US.

Parade was released in 1984 and provided no surprises, but only more of the same slick, well-crafted pop that had made them a teenage favourite worldwide. There then followed a lengthy quiet period aggravated by a disagreement with their label about the unauthorized release of a compilation album, *The Singles Collection*, at the end of 1985. In 1986, Spandau Ballet signed a major new deal with CBS and in the autumn released a single, 'Fight for Ourselves'.

SPANIELS

SPANIELS Black vocalizers the Spaniels – James 'Pookie' Hudson, Gerald Gregory, Opal Courtney, Ernest Warren and Willis Jackson – started their recording career with the Chance label in the early Fifties, though the company soon folded. Signing to Vee Jay Records, they began a period of seven years' prolific and often successful recording. The personnel changed in 1954 – Donald Porter, Carl Rainge and James Cochran joined Hudson and Gregory when the others departed – and the new team recorded a diverse selection of love ballads, standards and jumping rockers for Vee Jay until 1960, their forte being contrasting tenor/bass parts on material such as 'Stormy Weather', 'Red Sails in the Sunset' and their own 'Goodnight Sweetheart Goodnight'. The group made one disc for Neptune in 1961 before disbanding. Hudson re-formed the outfit in 1969 for a revival concert, and they enjoyed further success, recording for Calla ('Fairy Tales') and Buddah (an updated re-recording of 'Goodnight Sweetheart Goodnight').

SPANKY AND OUR GANG

Fronted by singer Elaine 'Spanky' McFarlane, Spanky and Our Gang featured Nigel Pickering (guitar, bass), Malcolm Hale (guitar, trombone, vocals), John Seiter (drums), Kenny Hodges (replaced by Geoffrey Myers, bass, vocals) and Lefty Baker (lead guitar, vocals).

A pop-folk group from Chicago in the style of the **Mamas and the Papas** and the British group, the Seekers, they reached the US Top 10 with 'Sunday Will Never Be the Same' on Mercury in 1967. It was the first of a string of American hits ('Lazy Day', 'Like to Get to Know You') that celebrated the summer pleasures of golden sands, beautiful sunshine, lazy days and walks in the park on Sunday mornings. When flower power withered away, they took up the Bonnie and Clyde craze and performed in Thirties gear, but they could not keep pace with the acid revolution and finally split in 1970. In 1975, the band was re-formed by Pickering and McFarlane with new members, but they had no further hits. In 1982, McFarlane joined a reunited Mamas and Papas as Cass Elliott's replacement.

SPANN, OTIS

SPANN, OTIS Remembered as an impressive and markedly individual solo pianist, and by far the most responsive and sensitive of accompanying musicians in the whole modern blues idiom, Otis Spann was born in Mississippi on 21 March 1930. He moved to Chicago at 17 and joined forces with his half-brother, **Muddy Waters**. The Spann–Waters partnership proved to be one of the most enduring and perhaps the most fruitful in the entire history of the blues, the two men working together for over twenty years. Spann's powerful rolling piano style graced most of Waters' hit records, as well as those by **Chuck Berry**, **Bo Diddley**, **Howlin' Wolf**, **Sonny Boy Williamson** and **Little Walter**. In 1964, he came to London and recorded with **Eric Clapton** and **Jimmy Page** for Decca. In later years he worked with **Fleetwood Mac**, gaining American chart action with the British recorded 'Hungry Country Girl'. Spann died on 25 April 1970.

SPARKS

SPARKS The group Sparks was the vehicle for the bizarre songs of Ron Mael (born in Culver City, Los Angeles, in 1948) as shrieked by his brother Russell (born in Santa Monica, Los Angeles, in 1953) which stirred Britain during 1974. The Maels, ex-child models, formed their first group, Halfnelson, while studying at UCLA but were dissatisfied with the American rock scene after two Bearsville albums (the first produced by **Todd Rundgren**) in 1971–2, and accepted an offer to come to Britain, where they put together the definitive Sparks; the other members were Trevor White (guitar), Ian Hampton (bass) and Dinky Diamond (drums). The new line-up's first single, 'This Town Ain't Big Enough for Both of Us' (Island, 1974), had a startlingly unnatural quality, and the Maels performed it (and four more UK hits) with a fine sense of theatre. Following a series of uneven albums (including *Propaganda* and *Indiscreet*, both 1975) coupled with diminishing chart success, the Maels returned to California.

In 1977, they moved base to Germany and signed with Virgin Records. This resulted in a re-emergence a year later with a reshaped disco sound by courtesy of producer **Giorgio Moroder**. Ron's synthesizers came to the fore in singles like 'The Number One Song in Heaven' and 'Beat the Clock', both of which were Top 20 hits in the UK. They returned to the old, familiar Sparks sound with *Whop That Sucker* (1981) and followed that the following year with *Angst in My Pants*, their first for CBS. The 1982–3 boom in electro-pop 'odd couples' – **Yazoo**, **Soft Cell**, and **Tears For Fears** and so on – saw a return to a format Sparks once seemed to have copyrighted.

SPECIALS

SPECIALS The inspiration behind the 2-Tone label, Coventry-based band the Specials were one of the best and most exciting of the British groups that came to the fore in the post-punk period. They harnessed the powerful energy of punk to the tuneful, good-natured music of West Indian calypso and ska – an infectious enthusiasm that was the perfect antidote to the gritted-teeth nihilism of punk rock. But the fun was far from mindless: from their earliest days, the Specials showed a genuine concern for the social problems of unemployment, poverty, racism and violence that particularly affected their home town in Britain's industrial midlands. The multi-racial line-up of the band was evidence of the Specials' ideas in action.

Formed in 1977, the band went through a number of name changes before settling in the first instance on the Special AKA. The line-up consisted of guiding inspiration Jerry Dammers (keyboards), John 'Brad' Bradbury (drums), Roddy 'Radiation' Byers (lead guitar), Lynval Golding (rhythm guitar), Horace (Sir Horace Gentleman) Panter (bass) and lead vocalists Neville Staples and Terry Hall. The sound of the band was a remarkable fusion of seemingly disparate elements: a solidly swinging rhythm section; Roddy Radiation's venomous guitar breaks; Dammers' mad fairground organ and Terry Hall's sardonic vocal delivery set against the rumbustious toasting of Neville Staples. The Specials' outrageously energetic stage act would gather such momentum that by the end of most gigs, a large proportion of the audience had joined the band on stage.

As the band's leader, Dammers was nothing if not uncompromising, and, determined to deal with the music industry on his terms, he developed the 2-Tone project, a record label 'run by musicians instead of businessmen'. Their first record was the self-financed single 'Gangsters'; this was released on the 2-Tone label and Rough Trade initially took up the distribution, to be followed by the major label Chrysalis. 'Gangsters' more than fulfilled everyone's expectations by reaching Number 6 in the UK chart in the summer of 1979. The first LP *Specials* (the group had dropped the 'AKA' tag), produced by **Elvis Costello**, was a strong set, mixing social comment with a good-time feel in their songs. It also provided a second Top 10 hit with the skanking 'A Message to You Rudy'.

Following a US tour early in 1980, the Specials released the The *Special AKA Live!* EP which paid homage to their early live work under their original name and contained a vigorous version of their early song 'Too Much Too Young'. To the amazement of the music business, the single raced up the charts to give the Specials their first chart-topper. The year 1980 continued to be successful for the band, with further Top 10 hits 'Rat Race', 'Stereotype' and 'Do Nothing'. The follow-up LP *More Specials* received mixed reviews but nevertheless reached Number 5 in the UK album chart.

In 1981, the Specials experienced their finest moment: while riots raged through Britain's cities that summer, the single 'Ghost Town', was perched at the top of the charts. Released just before the start of the rioting, it seemed to predict the unrest and presented a chilling view of the deeper problems behind the troubles. The topical theme caught the spirit of the time and it soared to Number 1.

At the height of their success, however, the Specials were beginning to fall apart – Dammers' authoritarian control of the band was cited as the main cause, along with the increasing incidence of skinhead violence at their concerts – and in October 1981, Hall, Golding and Staples left to form the **Fun Boy Three**, followed by Roddy Radiation's departure for the Tearjerkers and Horace Panter's for the religious sect Exegesis.

After a period of inactivity, Dammers and original member John Bradbury put the band back together again under the old name, Special AKA. The new line-up was completed by Gary Mac-Manus (bass), John Shipley (guitar) and the three vocalists Rhoda Dakar (from the Bodysnatchers), Stan Campbell and Egidio Newton. By now Dammers' political interests had developed considerably and the Special AKA confronted the social and political problems of the day head-on. The establishment was not interested, however, and the singles 'War Crimes' and 'The Boiler' (a harrowing monologue from a rape victim) received no radio airplay. Despite this, the group broke through in 1984 with 'Nelson Mandela' (a plea to release the black nationalist leader imprisoned in South Africa), which was a Top 10 hit. A long-awaited album, *In the Studio*, was well-received critically, even if sales were moderate, and yet the Special AKA was not to last. The group gradually broke up in 1985, Dammers carrying on with various projects including work with **Robert Wyatt**, which saw the release of the single 'Winds of Change' with the Swapo Singers.

SPECIALTY RECORDS Thanks to massive hits by **Lloyd Price**, **Guitar Slim**, **Little Richard** and **Larry Williams**, Specialty Records was a top-selling R&B independent label, but the company's influence went back even further. It was founded by Art Rupe in Los Angeles in 1946 out of the remnants of his original label, Juke Box. Specialty had an early R&B hit with Roy Milton's 'RM Blues', one of the most important city blues records of the Forties. The success inspired Rupe to record more big bands doing ballads, jump and boogie numbers, a policy which paid off with a string of hits by Jimmy Liggins, Joe Liggins and Roy Milton. **Percy Mayfield**'s smoky blues ballad, 'Please Send Me Someone to Love' opened the Fifties in fine style but Art Rupe felt his West Coast recordings were getting stale.

He therefore went down South on a field trip looking for new blues and R&B material. He came back with the master of Lloyd Price's 'Lawdy Miss Clawdy' made in New Orleans, and the result was the biggest R&B record of 1952, which sold over a million. It was also in New Orleans that he signed the extrovert showman, Guitar Slim, and Slim's first record for Specialty, the archetypal 'The Things That I Used to Do', was another million-seller and No. 2 R&B record of 1954. Rupe's raid on New Orleans was complete when the Crescent City gave Little Richard that distinctive sound to make 'Tutti Frutti' a national hit in 1955.

By then the R&B market was being encroached on by rock'n'roll and Art Rupe cashed in on the new craze with a constant stream of hits from Little Richard between 1956–8 and Larry Williams chipped in with 'Short Fat Fannie' and 'Bony Moronie' in 1957. **Don and Dewey**, **Jerry Byrne** and **Art Neville** had regional hits, and it was only when rock'n'roll stopped dead in its tracks in 1959 that Specialty came to a grinding halt. Art Rupe didn't seem too concerned. All along he had preferred gospel music to R&B (Specialty released many such records). He refused to get involved in payola (which he could ignore with immunity when Little Richard was selling) and in the end he was having problems with his producers, **'Bumps' Blackwell**, Sonny Bono (see **Sonny and Cher**) and **Harold Battiste** in New Orleans. He invested all his earnings from Specialty in other profitable business enterprises, but revived the label in the Sixties and, thanks to researcher Barrett Hansen, a large and intelligent reissue programme was initiated.

SPECTOR, PHIL Probably the most celebrated record producer in rock history, Phil Spector was born in the Bronx, New York, on 26 December 1940. His father died in 1949, and in 1953, his mother moved the family to California. The Spectors settled in Hollywood, and that year Phil enrolled at Fairfax Junior High School where he met Marshall Leib. In 1957, Spector – who was dabbling in songwriting – and Leib – who played piano – began working together on musical projects. Early in 1958 they roped in another Fairfax pupil, Annette Kleinbard, and formed a high school trio, the **Teddy Bears**. After graduation in June, they approached Dore Records, one of the many tiny labels scattered across Los Angeles' huge sprawl, and were signed to a recording contract. Soon after, Spector wrote a soft teen ballad titled 'To Know Him Is to Love Him' (the title came from the inscription on his father's grave) and recorded it with the Teddy Bears. The record unexpectedly topped both the British and American charts and the Teddy Bears found themselves catapulted into national prominence. Like so many of their contemporaries, however, they were unable to consolidate their initial success and they disbanded in 1959. Spector worked as a part-time stenographer while also studying at UCLA. Late that year, he decided to re-enter the record business.

Still only 18, Spector approached the independent producers, Lester Sill and **Lee Hazlewood**, who agreed to take him under their wing. They were the immensely successful producers of **Duane Eddy** whom they recorded in an obscure studio in Phoenix, Arizona, and it was here that Spector was taken to observe and master the mechanics of record production. In 1960, Spector persuaded Sill to send him to New York where he studied under **Leiber and Stoller** as a studio factotum. Spector was then introduced to Stan Shulman, manager of **Ray Peterson** who had recorded the classic death-disc, 'Tell Laura I Love Her'. Peterson and Shulman had just formed their own label, Dunes Records, and they hired Spector to produce Peterson's follow-up for the new label. The result was a very professionally made revival of the old folk song 'Corrina, Corrina', which made the American Top 10 in December 1960 – giving Spector his first hit as a producer.

On the West Coast, Sill allowed Spector an enormous amount of studio time to produce and during 1961, Spector spent close on $100,000 conducting what amounted to his own producer's course in the studio. But Sill's faith in his protégé was justified in December 1961, when 'I Love How You Love Me', Spector's second production with a trio called the Paris Sisters, made the US Top 5 on Sill's Gregmark label. He also had a Top 10 hit with **Gene Pitney**'s 'Every Breath I Take', though one of his most interesting early efforts, **Johnny Nash**'s 'Some of Your Loving', flopped. Late in 1961, Spector and Sill formed the Philles (Phil-Les) label with a distributor in Philadelphia. Spector began recording a girl group, the **Crystals** in New York and had two straight hits with 'There's No Other' and 'Uptown'. However, despite these successes Spector grew increasingly dissatisfied with the Philles set-up and, in 1962, he bought out his partners. At 21, Spector had become the youngest ever label chief and now had total control, with only the public to answer to.

He began recording on the West Coast, recruiting a team of session musicians and technicians. They included **Leon Russell**, Larry Knechtel, **Glen Campbell**, **Hal Blaine**, Earl Palmer, Barney Kessel, arranger **Jack Nitzsche** and engineer Larry Levine. Within two years, this set-up had produced fifteen consecutive hits for Spector and Philles, including the **Ronettes**' 'Be My Baby', the Crystals' 'Then He Kissed Me' and the **Righteous Brothers**' 'You've Lost That Lovin' Feeling'. This was the era of the famous 'wall of sound', whose most formally perfect expression was perhaps the unusual *Christmas Gift for You* album (1963) on which Philles artists (including **Darlene Love**) performed traditional seasonal songs. With the wall of sound, Spector brought the art of record production to a new level of sophistication. Where others would employ a conventional four- or five-piece rhythm section, Spector (through overdubbing) used instruments in multiples, skilfully interlocking them to create massive polyphonic sound structures. His was, as he said, 'a Wagnerian approach to rock and roll: little symphonies for the kids'.

As a personality, Spector tended to be sensitive and egocentric and he made enemies as a matter of course. In 1966, a mixture of circumstances led to the boycotting, in America, of a record he considered to be the high point of his career, 'River Deep – Mountain High' by **Ike and Tina Turner**. Its American failure (it was a smash hit in Britain) caused an embittered Spector to withdraw from production and go into seclusion for two years. In 1969, after a shaky resurrection at A&M

Phil Spector: 'My records are built like a Wagner opera'

records, Spector re-emerged as producer of the newly liberated **Beatles**, **John Lennon** and **George Harrison**. He knew better than to swamp them with the excesses of a bygone sound and million-selling albums like *Imagine* and *All Things Must Pass* proved that he could make records which allowed the artist an identity within the overall framework of Spector's idiosyncratic production methods.

Leaving Apple in 1973, he formed Warner-Spector records with Warner Brothers in Los Angeles, while continuing to work with Lennon. Little of note came of the new arrangement and during 1974 rumours were rife of Spector's eccentric behaviour. He suffered a mysterious accident at this time, but returned in 1975 with a new company, Spector International, whose first signing included **Dion** and **Cher**. He also worked with **Nilsson**, Darlene Love (again), **Leonard Cohen** and – in the early Eighties – the **Ramones**, but his most productive and inventive years were clearly behind him. Numerous collections honouring Spector's production career have been issued, notably the nine-album box set *Wall of Sound* (Phonogram, 1981), and a compilation of some of his earliest work, *Early Productions '58–'61* (Making Waves, 1984).

SPIRIT Formed in Los Angeles during the summer of 1967, rock eclecticists Spirit originally featured Ed Cassidy (drums, born in Chicago on 4 May 1931), John Locke (piano, born in Los Angeles on 25 September 1943), Randy California (guitar, born in Los Angeles on 20 February 1951), Mark Andes (bass, born in Philadelphia in 1947) and Jay Ferguson (vocals, born in Burbank, California, on 10 May 1947). All the members had been musically active for some time: Cassidy first as a jazz sideman and then with the Rising Sons; Andes first as a session man – he was on **Bobby Pickett**'s 'Monster Mash' – and then with Ferguson and California in the Red Roosters; and Locke with the New World Jazz Company. They signed with Ode in 1968 and released *Spirit* to poor sales, but critical acclaim for their ability to play together in a loose yet structured way. Their only chart success was the Top 30 single, 'I Got a Line on You' (1969). After *The Family That Plays Together* (1969) and *Clear Spirit* (1969) they moved to Epic for the uneven *The Twelve Dreams of Dr Sardonicus* (1970), following which Andes and Ferguson formed Jo Jo Gunne and California released *Kaptain Kopter and the Twirlybirds* (1973) before re-forming for *Spirit of '76* (1975) and five subsequent albums. Locke and Andes left the band in 1977, the latter to join Firefall and Heart. Spirit finally disbanded in 1981.

SPOOKY TOOTH Formed in 1967, Spooky Tooth comprised Gary Wright, an American living in Berlin (keyboards, born 26 April 1945), Mike Harrison (keyboards, born 3 September 1945), Luther Grosvenor (guitar, 23 December 1949), Greg Ridley (bass, 23 October 1941) and Mike Kellie (drums, 24 March 1947). A popular club band in the progressive rock era, it was less successful on record. Signed to Island, *It's All About* (1968) and the highly-regarded *Spooky Two* (1969) were released before Ridley left to join **Humble Pie**, being replaced by Andy Leigh.

From this point on, the band started to lose direction as Wright left to form Wonderwheel and three ex-**Joe Cocker** Grease Band musicians (Chris Stainton, Henry McCullough and Alan Spenner) joined for the fourth album. Spooky Tooth disbanded between 1970 and 1973 while Harrison and Wright pursued unsuccessful solo careers. Re-forming in 1974, they cut two further albums and were joined by vocalist Mike Patto for the final record, *The Mirror* (Goodear, 1974). Patto died of throat cancer in 1979.

SPRINGFIELD, DUSTY Born Mary O'Brien in Hampstead, London, on 16 April 1939, Dusty Springfield had early successes with the folksy **Springfields** before she went solo in1963. She appeared regularly in the British Top 20 over the next four years, reaching Number 1 with the spectacular 'You Don't Have to Say You Love Me', on Philips, in 1966. Despite a later concentration on cabaret work, she still released the occasional gem – notably 'Son of a Preacher Man' in 1968, now regarded as a soul classic, and 'Who Gets Your Love' (1972). Although her best singles were superbly assured performances of pop melodrama, Dusty's music has been heavily influenced by her love of soul. The brilliant *Dusty in Memphis* (1969, on Atlantic in America), produced by Jerry Wexler, showed her to be among the most funky and mellow of white soul singers, while the later *From Dusty with Love*, a **Gamble and Huff/Thom Bell** collaboration, was a lovely example of early Seventies soft soul.

She moved to the US West Coast in 1973 and recorded nothing for five years, apart from a few sessions for singer **Anne Murray**. 1978 brought two comeback albums on United Artists (*It Begins Again* and *Living Without Your Love*), but she drifted out of the rock scene after their relative failure and did not emerge again until 1980, when she played a few dates in New York. *White Heat*, on Casablanca, was well received during 1982.

SPRINGFIELD, RICK Australian-born (on 23 August 1949) rock singer and actor Rick Springfield spent many years on the verge of major success before finding national fame in the US television hospital drama *General Hospital*. This large-scale exposure helped him score a US Number 1 (and Grammy Award-winning) single with 'Jessie's Girl' in 1981.

Raised in both England and Australia, Springfield, as a member of Zoot, had an Australian Number 1 with the single 'Speak to the Sky'. He was offered a solo deal in America and recorded an album, *Beginnings*, in London in 1972. He was promoted as a teen idol but successive releases flopped and Springfield finally abandoned music for acting in 1976. After appearances in several high-rating US TV shows, interest in Springfield was such that he signed a new deal with RCA. The LP *Working Class Dog* was released in 1980, and 'Jessie's Girl' from it came out just as he became a regular on *General Hospital*. The

album went platinum, as did the two subsequent ones, *Success Hasn't Spoiled Me Yet* (1982) and *Living in Oz* (1983).

In the UK, Springfield's success was limited to one Top 30 single, 'Human Touch', in 1984, the same year in which he made his first feature film, *Hard to Hold*. In 1985 he released his seventh album,*Tao*.

SPRINGFIELDS The original members of the Springfields were Tom and Mary O'Brien (**Dusty Springfield**) and Tim Field, who left in 1962 and was replaced by Mike Pickworth (*aka* Mike Hurst), who went on to produce **Cat Stevens**). According to their publicist, they got their name from practising in a field on a Spring day. Their first chart entry in Britain was 'Bambino', an old Neapolitan carol that exemplified their commercial approach to folk music, as did their later hits 'Island of Dreams' and 'Say I Won't Be There' which was adapted from 'Au Clair de la Lune'. They were one of the first British

artists to record in Nashville and 'Silver Threads and Golden Needles', a failure in Britain, was a Top 20 hit in both the country and pop charts in America. In 1963, the group split up when Dusty went solo. *See also* **Dusty Springfield**

SPRINGSTEEN, BRUCE A live performer of the first rank and a gifted and imaginative songwriter, Bruce Springsteen is unquestionably the most charismatic figure to have emerged out of American rock since the early Seventies. He was born in Freehold, New Jersey, on 23 September 1949, and played guitar in a local band called the Castiles during his high-school days. At college he formed Steel Mill with drummer Vini Lopez and keyboard player Danny Federici; the band became popular on the Atlantic coast and played numerous dates in and around San Francisco in 1969, where **Bill Graham** heard them and offered a deal with his Fillmore label. They turned it down, headed back east

Springsteen and saxophonist Clarence Clemons: billed as the future of rock'n'roll, Bruce was perhaps more a throwback to its glorious past

and took on Steve Van Zandt on bass before disbanding in 1971.

Steel Mill nevertheless formed the nucleus of the Bruce Springsteen Band, which incorporated a brass section and later evolved into the E Street Band. Sensing that his future lay as a solo artist, Springsteen broke up the original band within months and, by 1972, had signed a long-term management deal with Mike Appel's Laurel Canyon Productions, through whom he gained an audition with legendary industry talent-spotter **John Hammond**. Hammond took him to Columbia, who signed Springsteen to a ten-album contract. The first under the deal was *Greetings from Asbury Park, New Jersey* (1973), a striking debut which almost got lost amid the plethora of recordings released by other promising singer/songwriters of the time such as **John Prine**, **Steve Goodman** and **Loudon Wainwright III**, all of whom – like Springsteen – had to endure the mixed blessing of being hailed as 'the new **Dylan**' by the music press. *The Wild, the Innocent and the E Street Shuffle* appeared later in 1973 and marked Springsteen's departure from the singer/songwriter stereotype, confirmed in *Born to Run* (1975) – an intense, densely produced (by rock critic Jon Landau) album packed with highway imagery and rebel romanticism that was promoted by posters bearing the legend, 'I have seen the future of rock'n'roll and its name is Bruce Springsteen'.

Legal wrangles with Mike Appel prevented Springsteen from making another album for three years, during which time he built his reputation as possibly America's greatest live act by touring almost constantly with his E Street Band, whose regular members now included Roy Bittan (piano), Clarence Clemons (saxophone), Danny Federici (organ) and Max Weinberg (drums). In 1978 he was back in the studio to record *Darkness on the Edge of Town*, a bleaker album than its predecessors, the earlier romanticism tempered by realism. This was a feature, too, of the eagerly-awaited double album *The River*, released in 1980: it showed Springsteen extending his range, consolidating his strengths and balancing the moodier, more serious songs such as the title track and 'Independence Day' with exuberant rockers like 'Ramrod' and 'Hungry Heart'. It confirmed Springsteen as one of America's few truly *international* superstars in latter-day rock, its success overseas precipitating his first European tour in 1981.

Springsteen's next move was unpredicted: *Nebraska* (1982) dispensed with the familiar honking sax breaks of Clarence Clemons and the driving rhythmic pulse of his band and found the singer alone, accompanying himself on guitar and harmonica, and performing songs steeped in the folk and country traditions of **Woody Guthrie** and **Hank Williams**. Recorded straight on to a four-track machine in his home, *Nebraska* gave Springsteen an opportunity to re-examine his musical roots and artistic concerns with mature detachment. By contrast, *Born in the USA* (1984) was a return to rock-'n'roll form, a set of characteristic Springsteen rockers with lyrics hinting half-critically at the current state of the Union yet celebrating the traditional rock concerns of Saturday-night hedonism and escape from adult routines. The ambivalence in his music was exemplified by the fact that both Ronald Reagan and Walter Mondale quoted him in their attempt to win the youth vote during the 1984 presidential campaign.

His gruelling world tour of 1985 left a powerful impression, though after ten years his original labelling as 'the future of rock'n'roll' was beginning to wear thin. He seemed not so much the future of rock as a symbol of its past, its heritage, recalling Fifties rock'n'roll and mid-Sixties garage-band beat in equal measure, and reasserting the old virtues of live performing and loud, unfussy guitar work at a time when rock was becoming over-infatuated with the technology of the video and the synthesizer. Springsteen released in 1986 a phenomenally successful boxed set of five discs – a record of his concerts since 1975.

SQUEEZE Emerging behind the great punk explosion of 1976–7, Squeeze have always been a difficult band to categorize, displaying a diversity of style that few groups can equal. The original line-up, Chris Difford (rhythm guitar/vocals), Glen Tilbrook (lead guitar/vocals), Harry Kakoulli (bass) and Jools Holland (keyboards)– all old school friends from the Deptford area of South-East London – was completed by the arrival of Gilson Lavis, an experienced session drummer.

Their debut recording on Miles Copeland's Deptford Fun City label was the three track EP, *Packet of Three* (produced by **John Cale**), a trio of raw songs revealing a clear pop sensibility, which led to their signing with A&M and their first UK Top 20 hit with 'Take Me I'm Yours' in April 1978. The first

album, *Squeeze*, was a moderate success and led to tours of the US, where the abilities of songwriters Difford and Tilbrook earned them unwanted comparisons with **Lennon** and **McCartney**.

The album *Cool for Cats* was released in 1979 and marked Squeeze's move to the domestic big time, and even though it wasn't particularly successful (it reached Number 45 in the UK), it spawned two big hit singles, 'Cool for Cats' and 'Up the Junction', both reaching the Number 2 slot. Original bass player Harry Kakoulli left to be replaced by John Bentley and the departure of the extrovert Jools Holland (to form his own group the Millionaires and later to achieve success as a TV personality), led to the recruitment of keyboardist Paul Carrack from Ace.

This new line-up went into the studio with **Elvis Costello** as producer to record *East Side Story* (1981). Costello encouraged them to take more risks, and with Tilbrook's increasingly sophisticated song structures and Difford's ability to make a few crucial details speak volumes, *East Side Story* proved to be the best example of their pop craftsmanship. 'In Quintessence' and 'Is That Love' were pop gems, while in 'Labelled with Love' Tilbrook demonstrated how to sing a country and western song with an English accent and gave the group a UK Number 4 hit single. Another single, 'Tempted', written and sung by Paul Carrack, provided Squeeze with their first American success. The release of *East Side Story* saw the band consolidate a US following and they embarked on a heavy schedule of promotional appearances and live concerts. Paul Carrack left at this time, to be replaced by Don Snow.

Sweets From a Stranger, Squeeze's fifth album, was released in mid-1982, and shortly after, they made a surprise announcement that they were splitting up. They felt they'd achieved all they could as a unit; worldwide success continued to elude them and the rigours of touring, in addition to management problems, had taken their toll. The two songwriters plus a group of session players formed a new band, Difford and Tilbrook, and they released one album, *Difford and Tilbrook*, before disbanding in 1984. Then, in January 1985, four of the original members of the group – Difford, Tilbrook, Holland and Lavis – got together to play a gig in Catford, South-East London, and they enjoyed themselves sufficiently to re-form the band on a permanent basis, leading to the release of *Cosi Fan Tutti Frutti* later the same year.

STAIRSTEPS From Frankie Lymon's Teenagers through to the Jackson Five, black music has always abounded in vocal teams featuring the quavering voices of pubescent youth. The Stairsteps were originally formed as the Five Stairsteps, a family group arranged by their father, Chicagoan Clarence Burke. Discovered by soulman **Curtis Mayfield** in 1966, the group – Clarence, James, Aloha, Kenny and Dennis Burke – were recorded on a series of densely orchestrated songs ranging from lilting dance songs to poignant love ballads that were released, all with soul chart success on Mayfield's Windy C label, as by the Five Stairsteps and Cubie. Transferring to Buddah in 1967 ('Something's Missing') and to Curtom in 1968 ('Baby Make Me Feel So Good') it was when the group finally split from Mayfield that they experienced their biggest hit, 'O-o-h Child', in 1970 (for Buddah). Family arguments saw the group disintegrate by 1973.

STANDELLS 'Dirty Water' (Tower, 1966) by the Standells was one of the first truly classic mid-Sixties punk-rock records. It contained all the essential elements – **Rolling Stones** riffs, taunting vocals, nasty lyrics, and burning fuzz-tone guitar. In their two follow-up hits, 'Why Pick On Me' and 'Sometimes Good Guys Don't Wear White', the Standells spoke for young men everywhere who felt like protesting, not in favour of any political cause, but merely against the way they were treated by parents, girls and society. That was the stance that the Standells took, and it carried them through four albums and an appearance in the film, *Riot on Sunset Strip*. The group had come together in 1963 and were popular as a discotheque group – recording for MGM, Liberty and Vee Jay – before joining the garage-band movement. Their line-up was Larry Tamblyn, Tony Valentino, Gary Lane, and a former Walt Disney Mouseketeer, Dick Dodd. Dodd and Tamblyn dropped out of the group at the end of the Sixties, but the others were still performing as the Standells on club dates during the Seventies.

STAPLE SINGERS A family gospel quartet, the Staple Singers are noted for the striking guitar phrases of Roebuck 'Pops' Staples (born in Winona, Mississippi, on 28 December 1915) and the emotive vocals of his daughter, Mavis. Completing the group are singers Cleotha and Yvonne, the latter of whom joined following the 1971 departure of Pervis Staples. After a short spell with the United label, they joined Vee Jay Records in 1955 and recorded both original ('Uncloudy Day', 'Help Me Jesus') and traditional ('Will the Circle Be Unbroken', 'Swing Low') gospel material before moving to the Riverside label in 1960. Riverside tried unsuccessfully to broaden their appeal, but Epic (which they joined in 1964) had greater success with the same policy through releasing Staples interpretations of songs like the **Buffalo Springfield**'s 'For What It's Worth' and some **Dylan** and **Woody Guthrie** material. **Larry Williams** was their producer at this time.

The Staples signed with Stax in July 1968 and worked initially with producer **Steve Cropper**. He produced their first ever US Top 40 hit, 'Heavy Makes You Happy' (1971), but it was with another Stax producer, Al Bell, that they began moulding the sound that reached its zenith on the album *Be Altitude: Respect Yourself* and the single 'Respect Yourself', a Number 12 US hit in late 1971. A million-seller, the song introduced the Staples to a mass public and was followed soon after by the chart-topping 'I'll Take You There' (1972). Subsequent Top 40 hits included 'This World', 'Oh La De Da', 'If You're Ready (Come Go with Me)' and 'Touch a Hand, Make a Friend', and appearances in the films *Wattstax* and *Soul to Soul* consolidated their popularity. Having found international success as a soul act without denying their roots or compromising their reputation within gospel circles, the Staples again topped the US chart in 1975 with 'Let's Do It Again', the **Curtis Mayfield**-composed title song from the Sidney Poitier film. In the decade since, the Staples have recorded for three different labels – Fantasy, Warner Brothers and 20th Century – and Mavis Staples has also recorded a number of solo albums while retaining her place within the group.

STARDUST, ALVIN The extraordinary success story of Alvin Stardust gives heart to every ageing rocker who ever dreamed of a comeback. Born Bernard Jewry in London in 1942, his first break was passing an

Feeling like Buddy Holly but looking like a rocker in this thirties – Alvin Stardust clad in leather, comeback man of 1973, and again of 1981

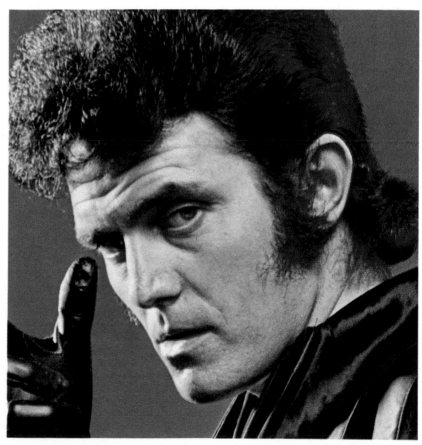

audition for BBC Radio's *Saturday Club*. He and his group (which included Bobby Elliott – later of the **Hollies** – on drums) became Shane Fenton and the Fentones, an energetic quintet in silver lamé, who had a hit with 'I'm a Moody Guy' on HMV (1962) and made a reasonable living until they were beaten back by the **Beatles**.

He returned with the rise of rock-'n'roll nostalgia and was working the Northern club circuit (still as Shane Fenton) when Peter Shelley of Magnet Records persuaded him to release 'My Coo-Ca-Choo' under the name Alvin Stardust. It was a Number 2 UK hit in 1973 and the five follow-ups, all Shelley compositions featuring more tape echo on the voice than had been heard since the heyday of **Gene Vincent**, fared almost as well. His image alternated between being a moody guy in black leather and a big brother to his youthful audience. When interviewed about his good fortune, he always seemed bemused by it.

In 1976, Roger Greenaway replaced Shelley as his producer but the hits dwindled, and little was heard from him until he signed with Stiff in 1981. Minus the black leathers this time, he made yet another chart comeback, reaching Number 4 with a revival of an old **Gerry and the Pacemakers** number, 'Pretend'. By 1984 he had switched to Chrysalis and was back in the chart with the elegaic 'I Feel Like Buddy Holly'. More hits followed ('I Won't Run Away', 'So Near to Christmas') and in 1986 he was chosen as the regular host of *The Rock Gospel Show* on BBC-TV. He is married to the actress Liza Goddard.

STARR, EDWIN A one-time Motown star who makes periodical appearances in the UK chart, Edwin Starr was born Charles Hatcher in Nashville, Tennessee, on 21 January 1942 and was educated in Cleveland. Upon graduation, he enlisted in the forces and was posted to Europe where he sang in clubs when off-duty. Discharged, he joined **Bill Doggett**'s combo before forming his own group and joining Detroit's Ric Tic Records, where his solo debut, 'Agent Double O Soul', a storming dance song with a fashionable spy lyric was a Top 30 hit in 1965. Further hits followed, including 'S.O.S.' and 'Headline News', before Ric Tic was swallowed by Motown. After some lean years, '25 Miles' and 'War' were Top 10 hits in 1969–70. With Motown's move to Hollywood, Starr began writing movie soundtracks. He left the Corporation soon after and

recorded for Granite and 20th Century during the Seventies – 'Contact', on the latter label, gave him a Number 6 UK hit in 1979. Later that year, he scored again with 'H.A.P.P.Y. Radio' on RCA. A long gap then ensued before Starr's name was seen in the charts again, this time with a revival of **Marvin Gaye**'s 'I Heard It Through the Grapevine' in 1986, which he originally recorded for a Levi Jeans commercial.

STARR, RINGO Despite predictions that he would suffer most from the break-up of the Beatles in 1970, Ringo Starr (born Richard Starkey on 7 July 1940) has successfully developed his cheerful, popular persona acquired in the group's seven years of stardom. *Sentimental Journey* (Apple, 1970) and *Beaucoups of Blues* (1970) were pleasant collections of childhood favourites and country standards respectively. Both reached the American album charts and *Sentimental Journey* entered the British Top 10.

Next, Ringo established himself as a major singles artist with a series of his own songs, including 'It Don't Come Easy' (1971 – his declaration of independence from the Beatle image), 'Back Off Boogaloo' (1972) and 'Photograph' (1973 – co-written with **George Harrison**). The *Ringo* album included the gold record 'You're Sixteen' and involved **Nilsson**, Marc Bolan (see **T. Rex**), Martha Reeves (see **Martha and the Vandellas**) and members of **The Band** as session musicians.

Ringo was produced by Richard Perry, as was *Goodnight Vienna* (1974), which provided further hit singles with 'Only You' and the title track. His film career developed from cameo roles in *Candy* (1967) and *The Magic Christian* (1970) to a much-acclaimed starring role in *That'll Be the Day* (1973) and a less satisfactory directorial debut in the Bolan documentary *Born to Boogie*.

None of his albums since *Goodnight Vienna* have sold particularly well, though he continues to record and perform for his own amusement or as a favour to friends – as, for example, on the 1977 'comeback' album by **Lonnie Donegan**, *Puttin' on the Style*. He married actress Barbara Bach in 1981. *See also* the **Beatles**

STATUS QUO One of the most consistent British chart bands of the Seventies and Eighties – by the mid-Eighties, they had in fact scored more hits on the UK chart (32) than any other group in pop history – Status Quo originally comprised Francis Rossi (guitar, vocals, born 29 May 1949), Rick Parfitt

(guitar, vocals, 12 October 1948), Alan Lancaster (bass, vocals, 7 February 1949) and John Coghlan (drums, 19 September 1946). As the Spectres, they had recorded some unsuccessful singles for Pye in the early Sixties with organist Roy Lynes (25 November 1943), later becoming Traffic Jam, and then Status Quo.

Rossi's 'Pictures of Matchstick Men' (Pye) provided them with a British Top 10 hit in 1968, and 'Ice in the Sun' was equally popular later in the year. Later singles flopped, Lynes left, and Status Quo's brief moment of glory seemed to have passed. But they transformed their uncertain, ornate pop style into basic four-square boogie and returned to the charts in 1970 with 'Down the Dustpipe'. Moving to Vertigo in 1972, they consolidated their position with further single hits (including 'Paper Plane' and 'Caroline' in 1973) and the albums *Piledriver* and *Hello*, which helped win them an enormous public, an army of faithful, denim-clad, long-haired consumers who cared not one jot for musical sophistication. Since then, the hit singles and albums have continued with regularity, among them some surprising reworkings of past hits like Hank Thompson's 'Wild Side of Life' (1976), John Fogarty's 'Rockin' All Over the World' (1977), **Tom Jones**' 'Something 'Bout You Baby I Like' (1981) and **Dion**'s 'The Wanderer' (1984). Coghlan left in early 1982 and was replaced by Pete Kirchner. Their appearance at the Milton Keynes Bowl in July 1984 was supposed to be their last, but Status Quo remain a recording and performing entity despite threatened personnel changes during early 1986.

Francis Rossi (left) and Rick Parfitt celebrate the Status Quo

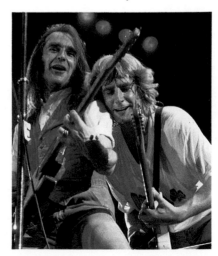

STAX RECORDS A pivotal label in the history of soul music, Stax Records had origins in the rock'n'roll heyday of 1957, when a Memphis bank-teller and country fiddler named Jim Stewart tried producing pop and country records in a garage after being turned down by Sam Phillips at Sun. Stewart's partner in this enterprise was local disc jockey Fred Bylar, but the crude results were unsuccessful, and Bylar soon pulled out. In 1958, Stewart formed another record company with his sister, Estelle Axton. Estelle mortgaged her house to finance Jim's purchase of an Ampex recording machine, which he installed in a garage with disastrous results – there was far too little space. Jim's barber offered him the use of a large store-room some 25 miles out of Memphis, and it was there that Satellite Records was launched in 1959.

The first release, Satellite 100, was 'Someday' by R&B vocal group, the Veltones. Success was not immediate, and country discs by Charles Heinz also failed to impress. In 1960, Jim found a vacant old theatre in McLemore Street, Memphis, and yet more property was mortgaged to finance the move back to the city. The theatre had a candy store out front, which Stewart turned into a record store, Estelle running it while Jim continued to work in the bank. Then **Rufus Thomas**, a disc jockey on local radio station WDIA, walked in with his daughter, **Carla**, to record ''Cause I Love You'. The disc was a regional hit, and was picked up by Atco for national release with a $1,000 advance, which was used to finance a solo disc by Carla, 'Gee Whiz'. This simple teen-ballad was a massive local hit, and again Atlantic took over national release and it became a Number 10 hit in the spring of 1961. The musicians on those sessions would work in the studios in their leisure time, and eventually they came up with an instrumental featuring a repetitive melody figure and horn riff, 'Last Night', which was issued in 1961 and hit the Number 3 spot that summer for the **Mar-Keys**. At this in time, a name-change was necessary to avoid confusion with another company, so Jim and Estelle decided to pool their surnames and came up with Stax.

Further Mar-Keys releases sold reasonably well in 1961, plus local hits by Barbara Stevens and **William Bell**. Then, in 1962, Stax had the idea of recording the Mar-Keys without their horn section, letting young black organist, Booker T. Jones, carry the melody. The result was the moody, bubbling 'Green Onions', which took **Booker T. and the MGs** to Number 3 in the charts in August 1962. Early 1963 saw the arrival of the Volt subsidiary, and the Stax combine committed to Atlantic for national distribution. Volt was soon in the charts with **Otis Redding**'s 'These Arms of Mine', and both Stax and Volt continued to enjoy a prolific number of chart entries with artists like Rufus Thomas, **Sam and Dave**, the Astors, **Johnnie Taylor**, **Eddie Floyd** and the **Staple Singers** (the last providing the label's first chart-topper, in 1972), the Mad Lads, Dramatics and Emotions (Volt). The late Sixties saw the inception of various smaller subsidiaries and distributed labels, including We Produce, KoKo, Respect, Hip, Weiss, Gospel Truth (now Truth) and Enterprise, which was introduced as a jazz outlet, but broke 'pop' when the elaborately arranged monologue/instrumentals of **Isaac Hayes**, who with David Porter had been a prolific writer/producer for the company, began to sell in vast quantities. His *Shaft* movie theme topped the charts in 1971.

The Atlantic distribution deal expired in 1968, and Stax opted to sell out for a production deal with the Gulf & Western conglomerate. The move was a financial and artistic disaster, and Stax bought themselves out of the contract, courtesy of a loan from Polydor, in return for international licensing rights. In 1972, they entered a distribution deal with Columbia, but despite a host of big-selling records on their various labels, they encountered financial problems which, in 1975, led to almost all their major artists joining other companies.

STEALERS WHEEL During 1973–4 Stealers Wheel came to international prominence with two Top 10 hits on A&M, 'Stuck in the Middle with You' and 'Star', produced by **Leiber and Stoller**. The group was formed in 1972 by two Scottish folk-club singers, Gerry Rafferty and Rab Noakes. The latter soon left to pursue an unsuccessful solo career with A&M and Warner Brothers. Rafferty, formerly with comedian Billy Connolly in the Humblebums, teamed up with another Scot, Joe Egan, to form a fruitful writing partnership.

Egan had previously sung harmonies on Rafferty's solo album for Transatlantic, *Can I Have My Money Back?* (1971). The pure strong harmonies were perfected on *Stealers Wheel* (1972) and *Ferguslie Park* (1973), named after a district of Paisley, their home town. A series of problems with backing musicians led to the duo forgoing live appearances, which may have contributed to the poor reception of their 1975 album, *Right Or Wrong*. Musically, it continued the Rafferty–Egan synthesis of Sixties rock in a Seventies framework, but the duo split up in acrimonious circumstances a year later.

Rafferty re-emerged in 1978 with the big-selling *City to City* album, produced (as was *Can I Have My Money Back?*) by Hugh Murphy. It contained the masterly evocation of big-city blues, 'Baker Street', which became a worldwide hit single and sold approaching $4\frac{1}{2}$ million copies. Further solo efforts included *Night Owl* (1979) and *Snakes and Ladders* (1980).

STEELE, TOMMY Born Thomas Hicks in Bermondsey, London, on 17 December 1936, Tommy Steele was Britain's first rock'n'roll star. Discovered singing **Hank Williams** material and calypsos, he became a teenage idol almost literally overnight. His first record 'Rock with the Caveman', was made just two days after his recording test in September 1956. Within a month it was a British Top 10 hit. Steele's first tour (of music halls rather than dance halls or concert venues) began in November 1956, and introduced the amplifier to the British stage.

With Lionel Bart and Mike Pratt, Steele wrote some of his British hits of the Fifties, including 'Rock with the Caveman' and 'A Handful of Songs' and he had further hits with cover versions of American records, 'Singing the Blues' (**Guy Mitchell**), 1957 and 'Tallahassee Lassie' (**Freddy Cannon**), 1959. The latter showed Steele in unfamiliar guise as a tough, heavy rocker. Heavy rocker he was not, however, and it was inevitable that Steele would leave rock-'n'roll. His personality was that of the archetypal cheery cockney, and clearly stemmed more from the vaudeville tradition than from an imported rock-'n'roll milieu. He was clearly far happier singing 'Little White Bull' than 'Knee Deep in the Blues'.

By the beginning of the Sixties, Steele had begun to succeed as an all-round entertainer, appearing in stage and film musicals like *Half a Sixpence*, *The Happiest Millionaire* and (in the Eighties) *Singin' in the Rain*. Steele's importance to British rock'n'roll simply derives from his having been there first, rather than from any subsequent creative contribution.

STEELEYE SPAN British folk-rock band Steeleye Span was formed in 1969 by Ashley Hutchings (bass), formerly with **Fairport Convention**, traditional folk singers Tim Hart (guitar) and Maddy Prior and Gay and Terry Woods (guitar, concertina), who had previously worked with Sweeney's Men, an early folk-rock experiment.

For the first two years, Steeleye Span remained a part-time band, as most of its members continued solo work in the folk clubs. As a group they set out in Hart's words to be 'not a rock band but traditional musicians working with electric instruments'. The first line-up didn't appear live and cut one album, *Hark! The Village Wait* (RCA, 1970), before the Woods left to form their own band.

They were replaced by the renowned folk guitarist and singer Martin Carthy and by violinist Peter Knight. During 1971, this line-up toured extensively and cut two albums for B&C, *Please to See the King* and *Ten Man Mop*. They also performed in Keith Dewhurst's play, *Corunna*, reaching new audiences beyond the folk scene.

At this point Hutchings left to pursue his more purist concern for English traditional music in the Albion Country Band and his partnership with Shirley Collins. Differences over whether the replacement should be another electric bassist or a multi-instrumentalist led to Carthy returning to solo work, which he continues. Two musicians with a rock orientation were brought in – Rick Kemp (bass) and Bob Johnson (electric guitar).

Manager Sandy Robertson was also supplanted by Joe Lustig, who signed them to Chrysalis and planned the strategy which made Steeleye Span a major international group in the mid-Seventies. On *Below the Salt* (1972) and *Parcel of Rogues* (1973), the dynamics of electric instruments were explored and arrangements were tight and dramatic. *Now We Are Six* (1974) saw the introduction of hard-rock drummer Nigel Pegrum.

The group's stage act, featuring five-part harmonies and focusing on Maddy Prior, was well-choreographed but almost predictable. In 1973, Steeleye Span added mummers' costumes to their act and the next year Hart presented a brief mummers' play on stage, to mixed reactions. 1975 saw another change of management (to Tony Secunda) and an unusual choice of producer for *All Around My Hat* – the Wombles' **Mike Batt**. Retaining their totally traditional repertoire, the group experimented with reggae backings and seemed to be increasing the heavy rock content of their sound at the expense of its folk roots. 'All Around My Hat' was a surprise Top 10 hit at the end of 1975.

In May 1977, Johnson and Knight left the band to complete work on their album, *The King of Elfland's Daughter*; Carthy and Kirkpatrick rejoined and John Kirkpatrick (accordion) became a group member for an album (*Tenth*) and a tour. The group's would-be final tour took place in March 1978, after which Maddy Prior and Tim Hart departed for solo careers and Nigel Pegrum devoted himself to his Plant Life record label. Prior and Kemp married in 1979.

However, pressures to re-form were enormous and a new album, *Sails of Silver*, duly appeared in 1980. Although their live performances were very much a re-creation of the Steeleye Span spectaculars of the mid-Sixties, their place in music history was assured. Between 1972 and 1976 they were the group that most extensively and logically explored the folk-rock formula: they put into practice the theory that the way to make traditional songs into contemporary ones was to detach them from their original settings and unite them with the sounds and rhythms of modern mainstream rock.

STEELY DAN One of the most enigmatic and least categorizable rock bands of the Seventies, Steely Dan was formed in 1972 after producer Gary Katz brought songwriters Walter Becker (born in Queens, New York, in 1951) and Donald Fagen (born in Passaic, New Jersey, in 1950) to the US West Coast as staff writers for ABC-Dunhill. Although they had previously composed the score for the film *You Gotta Walk It Like You Talk It* (1971), few artists were picking up on their material and Katz suggested that Becker and Fagen, who played bass and keyboards respectively, record an album themselves with the help of established session musicians. After the success of *Can't Buy a Thrill* and the two singles taken from it, 'Do It Again' and 'Reelin' in the Years' (both US Top 20 hits), drummer Jim Hodder and guitarists Denny Dias and Jeff 'Skunk' Baxter joined on a permanent basis, although the same policy of using outside people was followed through on all subsequent albums.

Steely Dan's sound, as it developed on *Countdown to Ecstasy* (1973), *Pretzel Logic* (1974) and *Katy Lied* (1975), was built on a marriage of styles, East Coast Latin-influenced R&B to Californian rock, shot through with a quirkiness – the group's name comes from that of a dildo in a William Burroughs novel – that stemmed from their jazz background. Frequently cynical, sometimes obscure but consistently interesting, Fagen and Becker's lyrics

The original Steeleye line-up, from left to right, Ashley Hutchings, Gay and Terry Woods, Maddy Prior and Tim Hart: 'Not a rock band but traditional musicians working with electric instruments'

were central to the group's success. Although they professed to enjoy jazz more than rock, they created in Steely Dan a rock band in which creativity and technical excellence played equal parts, and its stature was only marginally diminished by the departure of Hodder and Baxter – who joined the **Doobie Brothers** in frustration over Fagen and Becker's lack of interest in live performing – and, after *The Royal Scam* (1976) and *Aja* (1977), Denny Dias.

Fagen and Becker's jazz leanings became particularly apparent when bandleader Woody Herman recorded five of their compositions with his Thundering Herd Big Band, although *Gaucho* – the last Becker–Fagen album under the Steely Dan name – was their most musically straightforward yet, perfectly tailored to the needs of American FM radio. A single from *Gaucho*, 'Hey Nineteen', gave them their biggest US hit since 'Rikki Don't Lose That Number' in 1974, reaching Number Ten. Becker and Fagen dissolved their partnership in 1981, though rumours of an impending reunion have persisted ever since. Fagen made an outstanding solo debut with *The Nightfly* (Warner Brothers in 1982: a single taken from it, 'I.G.Y. (What a Beautiful World)', gave him a small US hit. Becker and Fagen played on Rosie Vela's *Zazu* (1986) and were reported to be re-forming Steely Dan.

STEPPENWOLF Formed in 1967 from the remnants of the Canadian blues group Sparrow, Steppenwolf comprised John Kay (born on 12 April 1944), vocals; Goldy McJohn (2 May 1945), keyboards; Jerry Edmonton (24 October 1946), drums; George Biondo (3 September 1945) bass and Kent Henry, guitar. They were a hard rock band with a fashionable name (after a Herman Hesse novel) and singles to match – 'Born to Be Wild', 'Magic Carpet Ride' (1968) and 'Rock Me' (1969) all of which made the American Top 10. Their first albums, *Steppenwolf* and *Steppenwolf the Second* (Dunhill) saw them straining to mix heavy rock and the blues, while later albums, like *Monster*, saw them content to live out a leather/bike-boy fantasy. Never successful in Britain and decreasingly so in America, the group disbanded in 1972. Kay made two solo albums before re-forming the band in 1974. They lasted a further two years before breaking up once more, although Kay did gather together a completely new line-up for a Steppenwolf re-launch in 1980.

STEVENS, CAT One of the most successful singer/songwriters of the Seventies, Cat Stevens (born Steven Georgiou on 21 July 1947 in London) became an international star before converting to the Muslim faith in 1979 and abandoning his musical career.

Stevens began writing his own songs while attending Hammersmith College in the mid-Sixties, and in 1966 scored his first UK single hit with 'I Love My Dog'. The next year 'Matthew and Son' hit Number Two and many of Stevens' songs were hits for other performers, including the **Tremeloes** and **P.P. Arnold**, who scored with Stevens' 'The First Cut Is the Deepest'.

In 1968, Stevens contracted tuberculosis, which interrupted his career, but he returned with the LP *Mona Bone Jakon* (1970), a more ambitious work that was well received and produced one hit single, 'Lady D'Arbanville'.

Another album, *Tea for the Tillerman* (1971) broke Stevens in America and started a run of seven consecutive US gold albums. With *Numbers* (1975) Stevens album sales started to drop off and he recorded only two more LPs, *Izitso* (1977) and *Back to Earth* (1978).

STEVENS, RAY One of pop music's great (and unsung) parodists, Ray Stevens was born in Clarksdale, Georgia, in 1939. Beginning as a session singer and writer for the Judd label in the late Fifties, he has since followed an unconventional musical path straddling country and pop. His first record, the comic 'Sergeant Preston of the Yukon' (1959) sold well before it had to be withdrawn following a lawsuit brought by the owners of the radio programme of that name. In 1961, Stevens signed to Mercury, recording several popular comedy tunes, 'Ahab the Arab' (a Top 5 US hit in 1962) being the most successful. Incidentally, Ahab's camel was named Clyde in honour of **Clyde McPhatter** who was present when the song was recorded. Moving to Monument, he wrote and recorded the powerful social comment of 'Mr Businessman' (1968) and the parody 'Gitarzan', a Top US pop hit in 1969. Further success followed with **Kris Kristofferson's** 'Sunday Morning Coming Down', 'Everything is Beautiful' (Stevens' first US Number One), and the country song 'Turn Your Radio On' on Barnaby, the label owned by Andy Williams. A brief return to comedy led to the topical international hit 'The Streak' (1974), recalling his 1971 success with 'Bridget the Midget'. Stevens switched back from comedy with the follow-up, a witty, countrified arrange-

ment of the pop standard, 'Misty' (Janus, 1975).

Since 1977 he has recorded for Warner Brothers but his only hit of note has been the totally bizarre 'In the Mood', the Glenn Miller standard as 'sung' by Stevens under the pseudonym of the Henhouse Five Plus Two. It consisted entirely of chicken noises.

STEWART, BILLY Born in Washington, DC on 24 March 1937, Billy Stewart gained his early musical experience in a family gospel group, the Stewart Gospel Singers, moving into the secular field at high school with the Rainbows, following which Billy joined **Bo Diddley**'s band as pianist. His solo debut came in 1956 with the instrumental, 'Billy's Blues' (Chess), followed by 'Billy's Heartaches' (Okeh) in 1957. He resurfaced in 1962 to hit with the vocal beat ballad 'Reap What You Sow' (Chess), introducing his trademark of 'word-doubling'. The following seven years brought a string of hits, largely with his own melodic beat ballads, such as 'I Do Love You' and 'Sitting in the Park', peaking in 1966 when his startling, original treatment of George Gershwin's 'Summertime', laden with word-doubling, yodelling, scat-singing and a dynamic, jazzy tenor sax solo, reached the Top 10. Subsequent sales dwindled but Billy toured constantly. He was killed on 17 January 1970 with three of his band when their car crashed off a bridge into the River Neuse, North Carolina, travelling between gigs.

STEWART, ROD With Elton John, Rod Stewart was the UK's most successful musical export of the Seventies and a performer of considerable staying power. Born in Highgate, London, on 10 January 1945, he resolved an early conflict between ambitions in soccer and music when he abandoned his apprenticeship at Brentford Football Club to busk around Europe. He sang and played harmonica with Jimmy Powell's Five Dimensions for a short time in 1963 before joining **Long John Baldry**'s Hoochie Coochie Men as second singer early in 1964. He made a solo single, 'Good Morning Little Schoolgirl' (Decca), released that October, and performed with the Soul Agents in the period between the disbandment of the Hoochie Coochie Men and the formation of Steampacket in mid–1965. He also played the harmonica on **Millie**'s single, 'My Boy Lollipop', in 1964.

Heavily influenced by **Sam Cooke**'s vocal style, he recorded 'Shake' (Columbia), backed by **Brian Auger**, in 1966, and after leaving Steampacket that summer he joined Shotgun Express, singing alongside Beryl Marsden, with **Peter Green** (guitar), Peter Bardens (keyboards), Dave Ambrose (bass), and Mick Fleetwood (drums).

As a founder member of the **Jeff Beck** Group early in 1967, he began a long-standing and fruitful association with Ron Wood. After a disastrous start in London, the group did well in America, and Stewart overcame his shyness on stage in vocal duels with Beck's guitar. By the time he and Wood left to join the **Faces** in 1969 he had developed a unique and spectacular stage act. He signed a solo recording contract before joining the Faces, and his first big success, *Every Picture Tells a Story* (Mercury, 1971), which was also his first solo production, was not as a member of the group. After the cult following of the previous *An Old Raincoat Will Never Let You Down* (Vertigo, 1969) and *Gasoline Alley* (Vertigo, 1970), both of which demonstrated his interpretative powers, *Every Picture*'s enormous popularity and that of the accompanying single, 'Maggie May' – for one week the single and the album were top of their respective charts in both Britain and America – immediately made him a star.

His concentration on a solo recording career became a factor in the patchiness and increasing rareness of the Faces' recordings, and by the time they disbanded in 1976 they existed almost solely as a performing band. Perhaps his strangest hit was in 1972 as Python Lee Jackson with 'In a Broken Dream' (Young Blood) which was a British Top 5 record and small American hit – Stewart had added a vocal to a backing track.

Never a Dull Moment (Mercury, 1972), the compilation *Sing It Again Rod* (1973) and the long-delayed *Smiler* (1974), using a nucleus of Ron Wood, his occasional co-writer, and Ian McLagan from the Faces, Martin Quittenton (mandolin and acoustic guitar) and Mickey Waller (drums), consolidated his position as one of the world's most successful artists. Perhaps disappointed by the poor public and critical response to *Smiler*, he changed the formula in 1975 to record the Tom Dowd-produced *Atlantic Crossing* (Warner Brothers, 1975) in America, where he moved the same year, using Muscle Shoals and Memphis session men and the **Meters**, from

New Orleans. It included the two hit singles, 'Sailing' and 'This Old Heart of Mine', and marked the beginning of Stewart's superstar period, when his relationships (notably that with film star Britt Ekland) and his increasingly flamboyant lifestyle made him a mainstay of gossip columns and tabloid scandal-seeking. Musically, his albums became slick and professional down to the last clinical detail, but the coming of punk and the new wave – which coincided with Stewart's excursions into disco with 'Hot Legs' (1978) and 'Do Ya Think I'm Sexy' (1979) – seemed to render him not only unfashionable but irrelevant.

Nevertheless, his sales continued to rocket, especially in the US, and by 1983 he was back topping the UK chart with 'Baby Jane', a composition that had some of the quality of his 'Maggie May'/'You Wear It Well' period. In 1986, Stewart began seriously to cultivate the UK market once more with a series of sell-out concerts and a single, 'Every Beat of My Heart', that was almost a rewrite of 'Sailing'. *See also* the **Faces**.

Ron Wood (left) and Rod Stewart had a long-standing and fruitful partnership

STIFF LITTLE FINGERS While most punk anger stemmed from nothing more than teenage frustration, the adrenalin-fired protest of Belfast band Stiff Little Fingers was fuelled by despair and disgust at the terrorism and brutality in Northern Ireland.

Their first single, 'Suspect Device', was like an aural Molotov cocktail – home-made, explosive and very effective. It sold 100,000 copies on their Rigid Digits label and earned them a place as support act on the **Tom Robinson** Band tour of late 1978. Original drummer Brian Faloon left when the band made the move to London to record the *Inflammable Material* (1979) LP for Rough Trade (which included the overtly political anthem 'Alternative Ulster') and the settled line-up of Jake Burns (vocals/guitar), Henry Cluney (guitar), Ali McMordie (bass) and Jim Reilly (drums) then signed a major deal with Chrysalis Records.

With Burns' furious, rasping vocal style and manager Gordon Ogilvie's biting lyrics, SLF built up a fervent following of hard-core fans and they scored several minor hit singles like 'Straw Dogs', 'At the Edge' and 'Nobody's Heroes', while the album of the same name also went Top 10 in 1980.

A live album, *Hanx* (1981), closed the band's first phase, but when SLF moved away from their guitar-thrash roots towards crafted pop with both a cutting edge and a social conscience (as in later singles 'Silver Lining' and 'Price of Admission'), they lost their early audience and failed to replace it.

Subsequent albums *Go For It* (1981) and *Now Then . . .* (1982), featuring new drummer Dolphin Taylor, ex-Tom Robinson band) showed plenty of musical progression and melodic structure but did not capture that blast of spontaneous imagination that had made early SLF so compelling.

Unsurprisingly, the band split in 1983, but Jake Burns thankfully returned two years later with a new group, the Big Wheel, and even had a minor hit with 'She Grew Up'.

STIFF RECORDS

The rise of Stiff records is without doubt the success story of the independent label boom of the mid- and late Seventies; of a total of just under 200 singles released by the early Eighties, Stiff had achieved chart entries with almost 50, a remarkably high figure considering that most majors count on six hits for every hundred releases. In addition, Stiff, along with Rough Trade and Cherry Red, proved one of the few labels to prosper once the euphoria of punk died down.

This remarkable independent was formed in mid-1976 by Dave Robinson and Jake Riviera (real name Andrew Jakeman). Robinson, the elder of the two, had a long track record in the music business and a reputation as a hustler without peer. Following a period as **Ian Dury**'s manager, Robinson set up and operated a recording studio at London's Hope and Anchor pub, the centre of the pub-rock scene. Riviera had a similar background, managing a succession of bands, and it was during an American tour with **Dr Feelgood** that he made two decisions: to start Stiff (the industry term for a flop record), and to make **Nick Lowe**, who happened to be with the Feelgoods' touring party, the first artist on the label. Lowe's single 'So It Goes' was recorded for £45 (the entire Stiff capital at the time was £400, a loan from Lee Brilleaux of the Feelgoods). From the outset, Stiff's witty marketing devices, the label design and the sheer cheek of their operation helped create a vital image that was perfectly in step with the sense of revolution of the time and set them apart from the majors whose products looked dull by comparison.

After Lowe, the label's subsequent artists were mostly old friends of Robinson and Riviera, such as Sean Tyla, the Pink Fairies and Lew Lewis. Towards the end of 1976, however, punk exploded on the scene. Stiff's biggest coup was to sign the **Damned**, who released the first nationally distributed punk record, 'New Rose'. Major companies began to sense that something was happening and Island records swiftly signed a distribution deal with Stiff. The label's next significant signing was **Elvis Costello**, who gave them their first Top 20 record in late 77, 'Watching the Detectives'.

Then in September, Riviera decided to leave and took Costello, Lowe and the Yachts with him to form Radar Records (the forerunner of Costello and Lowe's Eighties outlet, F-Beat). Riviera had been largely responsible for Stiff's public image, and the label's future became uncertain, few believing that Robinson could sustain it alone. But two factors helped him – the rise to stardom of Ian Dury and the success of the first Stiff tour earlier that year.

This tour, a package of their more prominent acts namely Dury, Costello, Lowe, Larry Wallis and Wreckless Eric, had been arranged to promote the label. The hits of the tour were Costello and Dury, who stayed to provide Stiff with their first Number One hit, 'Hit Me With Your Rhythm Stick', and its first platinum album, *New Boots and Panties* (1978). The label thus acquired a sound financial footing to nurture lesser-known acts such as **Lene Lovich**, Rachel Sweet and Wreckless Eric.

These three performers, plus **Jona Lewie** and Mickey Jupp, then embarked on Stiff's most ambitious project to date – the Be Stiff Tour, for which Robinson hired a special train to shunt the touring party around the UK. Fans queued to meet the train on arrival at every station, and the tour established Lovich, Sweet and Wreckless Eric as popular acts. The latter part of '78 and much of 1979 were spent promoting Lovich and Dury, who followed up his early successes with 'Reasons To Be Cheerful Part 3' and a smash album, *Do It Yourself* (1979). Lovich eventually scored two UK hits with 'Lucky Number' and 'Say When'.

The only blemish at the time was Stiff's failure in the US. Lovich had modest singles success there, but otherwise the Americans wanted nothing to do with British new wave groups and artists. Stiff's New York office eventually closed, but ironically it was only later, after its closure, that Stiff acts such as **Madness**, the **Belle Stars** and Yello, did well in the States through transatlantic licensing deals.

In October 1979, the label made its most important signing – Madness – and their huge commercial success enabled Stiff to develop such new talent as Any Trouble, Theatre of Hate, **Tenpole Tudor** and the Belle Stars. Madness took Stiff into the Eighties as the stars of a highly successful operation, a success that continued with the Belle Stars and **Tracey Ullman**.

At the beginning of 1984, Stiff merged with Island Records, Robinson becoming the managing director of both labels. Under Robinson, Island prospered greatly with **Bob Marley**, **U2** and **Frankie Goes to Hollywood** performing spectacularly well. But Stiff lost Madness shortly after the merger when the band left to start their own label, Zarjazz, and with the demise of Tracey Ullman and the Belle Stars in the charts, Stiff's fortunes went into decline. Of their signings, only Irish folk punks the **Pogues** and R&B troupe the Untouchables (from Los Angeles) made any impact.

Robinson, deciding that the Stiff label had been neglected long enough, resigned from Island in July 1985, but Stiff was not technically independent again until six months later, when it was installed in new North London premises. Robinson assigned himself to the task of rebuilding the label into a strong musical force once more, but it seemed that the damage had been done and the label found itself in severe financial difficulties, suffering a cash-flow crisis and finally going into receivership in the summer of 1986. But just as it seemed inevitable that Stiff records was going under for good, Jill Sinclair, a director of ZTT, bought out the label for a reputed £300,000. However, just how secure this development made Stiff's future remained a matter for speculation.

STILLS, STEPHEN

Born in Dallas, Texas on 3 January 1945, Stephen Stills not only played a crucial part in the success of two seminal West Coast groups – **Buffalo Springfield** and **Crosby, Stills, Nash and Young** – but carved an uneven but consistently interesting career for himself as a solo artist. His professional career began on the New York folk circuit, but in 1966 he moved west to found Buffalo Springfield, for whom he wrote 'For What's It's Worth', still a painfully accurate account of the contradictions of social confrontation. This theme – the need to fight with new weapons rather than the old – was to run through his subsequent music alongside a determined approach to relationships.

Stills, unlike Neil Young, earned a reputation as a musician rather than a songwriter, and appeared with **Al Kooper** and **Mike Bloomfield** on the 1968 *Supersession* album, one of the earliest teamings of individual talents from separate groups. In the same year, he formed Crosby, Stills and Nash and played most of the music on their eponymous debut album – electric and acoustic guitars, bass, and keyboards. With the addition of Young, Stills could better fulfil his role as a guitar virtuoso, shown to fine effect on the live *Four-Way Street*. On his two solo albums (Atlantic, 1970, 1971), and the two with Manassas, *Manassas* (1972), *Down the Road* (1973), Stills' wide musical vocabulary came more to the fore, expanding the basic West Coast sound to accommodate country music, Latin rhythms, and harder rock'n'roll. His lyrics were uneven, occasionally climbing to peaks in anthemic songs like 'Carry On', 'So Begins the Task', and 'Sugar Babe' which had simplicity allied to a reverberating depth. His major talent, though, remained in his guitar-playing. He learned much from the likes of **Hendrix** and **Clapton**, and became an important exponent of the wah-wah pedal, just one part of his formidable stylistic range as a guitarist. In 1975, Stills signed to Columbia, cut his fifth post-CSN&Y album (*Stills*) and formed a new touring band of whom only percussionist Joe Lala remained from the Manassas line-up.

In 1976, he resumed his partnership with Young for *Long May You Run*, but Young departed during a subsequent tour. From 1977 onwards, Stills became heavily involved in the CSN reunion, and he contributed most of the material on their *Daylight Again* album in 1982. *See also* **Buffalo Springfield, Crosby, Stills, Nash and Young.**

STONE, JESSE The arranger who brought a coherent rock'n'roll backbeat to the R&B of the Fifties, Jesse Stone had worked with big bands and recorded for RCA and MGM before moving to Atlantic. There, he accompanied the label's executives on early field trips, introduced **King Curtis** to session work, and wrote, rehearsed and arranged many classics, often under his real name, Charles Calhoun. They included 'Cole Slaw' (Frank Culley), 'Money Honey' (the **Drifters**), 'Shake, Rattle and Roll' (**Joe Turner**) and 'Your Cash Ain't Nothin' But Trash' (the **Clovers**). His success led to work for other companies, notably Aladdin, Capitol and Epic, where he wrote **Roy Hamilton**'s 'Don't Let Go'.

STONE THE CROWS See **Maggie Bell**

STRANGLERS Although the Stranglers' origins clearly predated punk, their first successes were undoubtedly related to it, as was their subversive stance, their arrogance and their tendency towards violence. As one of the core bands of the punk explosion, they cultivated a sneering, cynical image, but as punk subsided, their true identity as accomplished, subtle rock musicians emerged.

The Stranglers were originally formed in 1974 as the Guildford Stranglers when Hugh Cornwell (guitar/vocals), ex-teacher and a veteran of many small-time bands (most notably Johnny Sox in Sweden) teamed up with Jet Black (drums) and Jean-Jacques Burnel (bass). They played as a trio until Dave Greenfield was recruited on keyboards in the summer of 1975, then performed over 200 gigs in the next eighteen months. They appeared regularly at London rock venues, and after a support slot on **Patti Smith**'s '75 UK tour, the band were already on the verge of success when punk arrived.

They signed to United Artists for £40,000 in December 1976 amid much media attention – unlike most punk bands they could play their instruments, something the music papers valued highly before they fully embraced punk – and Burnel's abuse of journalists ensured its continuity. In February 1977, the Stranglers' first single '(Get A) Grip (On Yourself)' made Number 44 in the UK charts, Greenfield's swirling organ sounds and Burnel's distinctive bass playing giving them a tough sophistication that few, if any, punk bands could emulate and proving they were not really a punk band.

Rattus Norvegicus was released in April, reaching Number 4 in the UK LP

Colourfully dressed Stranglers give a smile for the camera: from left, Dave Greenfield, Jean-Jacques Burnel, Jet Black and Hugh Cornwell

chart. A moody, intense collection of songs that amply displayed their talents, it also revealed an extraordinary, and apparently deep-rooted, misogyny. Several tracks violently abused women, 'Peaches', 'Princess of the Street' and 'London Lady' being particularly offensive. Whether this was authentic sexism, or just empty macho posturing on behalf of their adolescent male audience, remains open to debate.

Regardless, the Stranglers enjoyed a successful period, releasing a string of successful singles and albums, culminating in their fourth studio LP, *The Raven*, in October 1979, by which time they had moved away from crude machismo to more apocalyptic themes. This LP marked a new level of sophistication, in which the last vestiges of punk power chords disappeared and Greenfield wove intricate tonal patterns with his synthesizers. Yet 1980 was to be a terrible year for them. After a riot at a concert in France, they were threatened with 20-year jail sentences for incitement (the charges were later dropped). Shortly after this, Cornwell spent three weeks in an English prison for a drugs offence, and, finally all their gear was stolen during an American tour. Heavily in debt they were on the verge of a break-up.

They weathered those storms, however, and released the disappointing LP *The Gospel According to the Meninblack* at the start of '81, but the November release of *La Folie* represented a return to form. It included their biggest hit single, the haunting 'Golden Brown' (which reached Number 2 in January '82) and provided them with the success they had been missing. In 1983, after a change of label to Epic, they released *Feline* which provided another Top 10 hit, 'European Female' in January. Since then the Stranglers have maintained a low profile and released singles only sporadically; a gap of nearly two years elapsed before their next Top 20 single, 'Skin Deep' (Number 15 in October '84). They released an album, *Aural Sculpture*, in 1984, which was widely derided by the music press and failed to re-establish the band as a hit act.

Again after a lengthy gap, the Stranglers produced their tenth album, *Dreamtime*, in 1986, a wholly more worthwhile effort and the band found themselves back in the UK singles chart with 'Big in America'.

STRAWBS A leading British folk-rock band of the early Seventies which enjoyed some chart success, the Strawbs were formed in 1967 as the Strawberry Hill Boys by vocalist/guitarist Dave Cousins (born 7 January 1945), then a student at Leicester University. The early line-up of Cousins, acoustic guitarist Tony Hooper and mandolin player Arthur Philips lasted until 1968, when bassist Ron Chesterman replaced Philips and vocalist **Sandy Denny** briefly joined. They signed with A&M in 1969 and debuted with *The Strawbs*, which was produced by Gus Dudgeon; *Dragonfly*, produced by Tony Visconti, followed a year later but its comparatively low-key reception prompted Cousins and Hooper to reshape the band with new members John Ford (bass), Richard Hudson (drums) and **Rick Wakeman** (keyboards). Wakeman's classical training and aspirations to a classical-rock synthesis, together with Cousins' increasing interest in the electric guitar, brought a new dimension to the band's previously heavily folk-accented work, though Wakeman left to join **Yes** after contributing to *Just a Collection of Antiques and Curios* (1970) and *From the Witchwood* (1971). His replacement was the former **Amen Corner** keyboard player, Blue Weaver.

Tony Hooper departed in 1972, soon after the release of *Grave New World*, to be replaced by Dave Lambert (electric guitar). Cousins recorded a solo album, *Two Weeks Last Summer*, while the group reached Number Twelve in the UK with a Cousins composition, 'Lay Down', late in 1972. Their biggest hit, however, was a satire on trade-union politics released early in 1973, 'Part of the Union', which was composed by Hudson and Ford and featured a lead vocal by Ford. Hudson and Ford's emergence from Cousins' shadow led to differences and they left to pursue a career as a duo after the release of *Bursting at the Seams* (1973). Weaver also left and Cousins reshaped the band once more with Lambert and new recruits John Hawken (keyboards), Chas Cronk (bass) and Rod Coombes (drums, ex-**Stealers Wheel**). The first album with the new line-up, *Hero and Heroine* (1974), was poorly received in the UK, though the band began to build a sizeable American following, where both *Ghosts* (1975) and *Nomadness* (1976) sold better than in the UK. Hawken left in 1976 and Coombes in 1978, by which time the band had released *Deep Cuts* and *Burning for You* for the Oyster label. After one album for Arista, *Deadlines* (1978), tracks were recorded for a follow-up, *Heartbreak Hill*, but it was never released so the Strawbs broke up. Cousins then made an album with Brian Willoughby (guitar) entitled *Old School Songs* on his own label, Old School Records.

Dave Cousins then went into commercial radio on the presentation and then management side, graduating to Programme Controller and Managing Director of the Exeter station, Devonair Radio. He put together a new band as the Strawbs during 1986 and played a number of pub and club dates in the UK, the US and Canada, but he insisted he had no plans to return to performing or recording full-time. In early 1987 a new album was being recorded with the following line-up: Cousins (vocals, guitar), Tony Hooper (vocals, acoustic guitar), Brian Willoughby (electric lead guitar), Chris Parren (keyboards), Richard Hudson (drums) and Rod Demick (bass). *See also* **Hudson Ford.**

STRAY CATS Strutting American rockabilly revivalists the Stray Cats first found success in the UK before returning to the US to become the surprise hits of 1982.

Formed in New York in 1979, the Stray Cats, comprising Brian Setzer (guitar/vocals), Slim Jim Phantom (Jim McDonell, drums) and Lee Rocker (Lee Drucker, bass), played the Long Island club circuit before coming to London in 1980. They soon became live favourites and signed to Arista, their brilliantly manic first single 'Runaway Boys' reaching Number 9 in November. 'Rock This Town' and 'Stray Cat Strut' followed it quickly into the charts.

Stray Cats (1981) made the UK Top 10 LPs but by the time the disappointing *Gonna Ball* (1982) was released, British interest in the band had waned and they concentrated on America. A compilation of the first two British albums, *Built For Speed* (1982) was released in America just as interest in the Stray Cats was building. The album sold over two million copies and 'Rock This Town' and 'Stray Cat Strut' made the US Top 10.

Their popularity was not destined to last long, however, and only one more album (which proved unsuccessful) *Rant 'n' Rave with the Stray Cats* (1984) was released before the demise of the band. Brian Setzer returned as a solo artist in 1986 with an album and single, *The Knife Feels Like Justice.*

STRONG, BARRETT Born in Mississippi on 5 February 1941, Barrett Strong moved with his family to Detroit where his cousin, Nolan, was singing with the Diablos. In 1960, Barrett was signed to Gwen Gordy's Anna label. Soon afterwards, he reached the Top 30 with the original version of the Janie

Bradford-Berry Gordy classic 'Money'. The gospel-charged riff and unadorned message ('Money – that's what I want') were perhaps the basic ingredients on which Gordy (the producer of the record) founded the Tamla-Motown empire later the same year. The song was equally influential during the British group boom, when it was recorded by the **Beatles** on their second album and a version by Bern Elliott and the Fenmen made the Top 20 in 1963.

After less exciting records on Tamla, Atlantic and Tollie, Strong returned to Tamla-Motown-Gordy, where he worked as a producer and writer alongside **Norman Whitfield**, turning out hits for the **Temptations** and Undisputed Truth in the Seventies.

STYLE COUNCIL

In 1982, soon after the demise of the **Jam**, Paul Weller (guitar) formed a new band, the soul-influenced Style Council, with keyboards player Mick Talbot, who had a pedigree that included **Dexys Midnight Runners**. Weller continued his association with the Jam's label, Polydor, and the first Style Council single, 'Speak Like a Child', was released in March. An instant UK hit (peaking at Number 4), it re-established Weller as one of the premier British songwriters, and in this new partnership with Talbot he blended a smoother soul feel with the vitality that characterized the Jam's output. The new venture also seemed to spur Weller to voice his political views more openly, and the band played their first gigs in the spring of 1983 as benefits for the Campaign for Nuclear Disarmament.

Further singles followed that year as Weller and Talbot based themselves in Paris; particularly noteworthy was the languorous 45 'Long Hot Summer' (a Number 3), that won the Style Council a new, older audience. The following year saw more singles and the LP *Café Bleu*, which received mixed reviews, the critics holding some reservations about the band's obscure rhetoric and apparent obsession with style. Fans, however, bought the record regardless and Style Council went on an extended tour of Europe and Japan.

Weller's left-wing politics acquired a high profile when he formed the Council Collective at the tail end of 1984. With the support of other artists including **Junior Giscombe** and Dee C. Lee, the Collective raised money for striking miners' families and for the widow of a taxi driver murdered while driving a working miner to the pit. All proceeds from the sale of the single 'Soul Deep' were donated to the cause.

Weller was named President of International Youth Year for Britain in 1985, and the Style Council's political stance became even more overt as shown clearly on the powerful, vaguely revolutionary single 'Walls Come Tumbling Down' (it reached Number 6) and their second album, *Our Favourite Shop*. The lyrics heavy with political comment, this LP received heavy treatment at the hands of the critics but it was in fact an accomplished, exotic set of jazz/soul-influenced songs.

Recognition of Weller's stature as a songwriter come with his commission, along with the likes of **David Bowie**, to compose a song for the British musical film *Absolute Beginners*.

STYLISTICS

A soul group from Philadelphia renowned for the distinctive lead falsetto of Russell Thompkins, the Stylistics came together in 1970: Thompkins, Airrion Love and James Smith were members of the Monarchs, while James Dunn and Herbie Murrell had sung with another local group, the Percussions. Their first R&B hit, originally released on the small Sebring label but picked up for national distribution by Avco Records, was 'You're a Big Girl Now', which was co-written by their road manager Marty Bryant and Robert Douglas. Avco then teamed the Stylistics with writer/producer/arranger **Thom Bell**, who – working with Linda Creed – gave them nine straight Top 40 hits, among them 'You Are Everything' (1971), 'Betcha By Golly Wow' (1972), 'Rockin' Roll Baby' (1973) and 'You Make Me Feel Brand New' (1974). All nine were Bell/Creed compositions, with the exception of 'You'll Never Get to Heaven' in 1973, a **Burt Bacharach**/Hal David song: apart from the untypical dance record 'Rockin' Roll Baby', all were romantic sweet-soul ballads.

In 1974, **Van McCoy** took over as the group's arranger and **Hugo and Luigi** as their producers. Although the subsequent cuts were generally less memorable than their collaborations with Bell and their US chart career went into decline, their European hits continued unabated. Their *Greatest Hits* anthology (1975) had unprecedented sales in Britain for a black vocal group. Dunn left in the late Seventies, and in 1980 the group were reunited with Bell when they left Avco for his Philadelphia International label.

Sweet soul harmonies from the ice-cool Stylistics: from the left, Airrion Love, James Smith, James Dunn, Herbie Murrell and Russell Thompkins Jr

STYX Along with **Foreigner** and **Journey**, Styx dominated the US easy-listening rock sphere during the late Seventies and early Eighties with a meticulous blend of pop and theatrical pomp (often called 'pomp rock'), and released a succession of multi-platinum albums.

The origins of Styx can be traced back to Chicago in 1963, when twins Chuck and John Panozzo (bass and drums respectively) started jamming with Dennis De Young (keyboards/vocals). The trio's efforts were restricted to rehearsals until the recruitment of guitarists James Young and John Curulewski in 1968, after which they began gigging, first under the name Tradewinds and later as TW4.

In 1970, they changed their name to Styx, signed a deal with the local Wooden Nickel label and released an LP, *Styx I*. Although it was a promising release, it lacked depth – as did a succession of albums up to 1975, when they moved to A&M. In that time they made a name for themselves by touring incessantly, and managed to score a US hit single, 'Lady' (Number 6 in 1975). Curulewski then left and was replaced by Tommy Shaw, whose vocal abilities allowed them to extend the intense haronizing that was coming increasingly into their work. Their first A&M album, *Equinox*, was released the same year.

They had to wait until 1977, however, before they hit on just the right mixture of syrupy vocal harmonies, pompous lyrics and ersatz rock'n'roll with *The Grand Illusion*, the album that finally broke the band nationally and assured their success. They packed out large venues across the country and sold vast quantities of records as each release followed its predecessor to platinum status. Even concept albums such as *Paradise Theatre* (1980) and *Kilroy Was Here* (1983) made the upper reaches of the US chart.

Their domestic success was never quite echoed elsewhere in the world; they scored a Top 10 single in the UK with their worldwide hit 'Babe' (1979), but it was a success they never followed up. Although they retained their status as a consistently top-selling mega-band in the US, they disbanded in the mid-Eighties.

SUMMER, DONNA One of a family of five sisters and one brother, soul/disco singer Donna Summer was born Donna Gaines on 31 December 1948 in Boston, Massachusetts, and raised in that city. She sang in church

and then secularly, in 1967, with a group named Crow. She left the USA later that year and at the age of 18 was in Munich singing in the cast of *Hair*, married Helmut Sommer and changed her name to Donna Summer. Singing in the evenings in musicals and light opera, she did sessions at Munich Musicland studios where eventually she met **Giorgio Moroder** and Pete Bellotte, who suggested that she sing on their productions. After a couple of minor hits on the Continent, the trio's sixteen-minutes-plus version of 'Love to Love You Baby', chiming in with the disco explosion and pushed by Casablanca Records, became a smash. Insistent, throbbing pace behind Summer's hot, breathy singing, it was an omnipresent sound in 1975, and the title of her first album. *A Love Trilogy* and *Four Seasons of Love* (both 1976) followed in quick order, refining the extended disco vamp style, but 1977's *I Remember Yesterday* revealed a desire for greater variety though the single 'I Feel Love', a big hit, was firmly in that original, successful vein. *Love's Unkind* took a slightly rockier stance while the title track sounded like Dr Buzzard's Original Savannah Band,

Donna Summer – a Seventies disco dream got up in fur and feathers

forerunner of **Kid Creole** and Stony Browder Jr. But Summer was, at this time, very prolific, recording on the soundtrack of the film *The Deep* and releasing a double LP, *Once Upon a Time*, a quite successful concept album telling a love story/fairy tale.

After a quiet 1978, a live album (*Live and More*) and a hit collection her only records, she released a second double album, *Bad Girls*. Further hit collections aside, it was her last good album for some while as she attempted to move from disco into the rock market with *The Wanderer* (1980, her first set for Geffen to which she moved from Casablanca in a welter of litigation), *Donna Summer* (1982, produced by Quincy Jones), *She Works Hard for the Money* (1983), and *Cats Without Claws* (1984). She also became a devout Christian and found a new husband, Bruce Sudano of the Brooklyn Dreams vocal group.

SUN RECORDS The label that more than any other has become identified with the emergence of white rock 'n'roll is that of Sun Records, of Memphis, Tennessee. The label was formed late in 1952 by Sam Phillips, a former radio announcer who in 1950 had set up the first permanent studio in Memphis, at 706 Union Avenue, to record the myriad local blues, R&B and C&W performers.

For two years he leased successful recordings to labels like Chess and his recordings of **Howlin' Wolf**, **B.B.King** and Jackie Brenston formed the basis of the Sun R&B sound of **Rufus Thomas** and **Junior Parker**, which in turn provided the inspiration for the rhythm of **Elvis Presley** and **Carl Perkins**.

The Sun label had scored several R&B hits by July 1954, when Presley's 'That's All Right' was issued. Less than two years later, Carl Perkins' record of 'Blue Suede Shoes' became a monumental hit and those two records defined a new area in the repertoire of Southern music, and eventually in the whole development of rock. The music was called 'rockabilly' and it drew together the many styles of Southern music. It became the local form of rock-'n'roll and the success of Presley, whose contract was sold to RCA in October 1955, and Carl Perkins was added to by a string of artists who have now emerged as top-selling stars – **Roy Orbison**, **Johnny Cash**, **Jerry Lee Lewis** and **Charlie Rich** were among them. The Sun catalogue was filled with the new music for around four years, during which time Sam Phillips became a millionaire.

Among the rockabilly artists were Warren Smith and **Billy Lee Riley** – two performers whose records were unjustly neglected in their heyday – Sonny Burgess, **Conway Twitty**, Dickey Lee and Ray Smith. Their music came from country roots, and in this style Sun recorded fine artists like **Charlie Feathers**, Mack Self and Malcolm Yelvington. Bluesmen **Rosco Gordon**, **Little Milton**, Walter Horton and Frank Frost started here, too, and during the Sixties several fine country and soul singers recorded at Sun. In 1960, Sun moved to 639 Madison Avenue, Memphis, and the company continued to be so successful that, in February 1961, Phillips moved yet again to a newly-built studio in Nashville and set up a new label, Phillips International.

In the early Sixties, however, the musical climate changed and Sun ceased to be a leader on the charts. It was financially stable, but musically it had already made its biggest contribution to rock. As the Sixties progressed, Sun mainly reflected local trends and provided a school of experimentation for musicians like **Steve Cropper**, **Booker T.**, and the new 'Memphis Sound'. Sun continued until 1 July 1969 when Sam Phillips sold the entire catalogue to producer **Shelby Singleton** – except for the Presley recordings which had already been bought by RCA in 1955. Singleton set up the Sun International Corporation and initiated a massive reissue programme in which the vaults were raided and a lot of Sun material has now appeared for the first time ever on the Charly label in the UK.

The very existence of Sun in the Fifties and its subsequent success enabled a tremendous number of talented performers to find their entry into recording. Sun was the foundation of the new huge music industry in Memphis.

SUPERTRAMP Brought into being in 1969 through the indulgence of a millionaire rock fan, Supertramp produced an accessible brand of soft rock that had sold over 25 million records by the mid-Eighties.

The band's founder, Richard Davies (vocals/keyboards) had been a member of an earlier group, the Joint, and when they split up, Dutch millionaire Stanley August Miesegaes, a keen fan, offered to finance Davies' career. Davies recruited Roger Hodgson (vocals/keyboards/bass, later guitar) and the duo, by then called Supertramp, became the nucleus of a band that went through several changes of line-up. After two dis-

astrous albums, *Supertramp* (1970) and *Indelibly Stamped* (1971), and an abortive tour of Norway, morale was low, but then their label, A&M, decided to get behind the band. As a result, their next LP, *Crime of the Century*, an immaculately crafted work, was accompanied by a massive promotional campaign on its release in 1974. It went to Number 1 in the UK.

The next two albums, *Crisis? What Crisis?* (1975) and *Even in the Quietest Moments* (1977) trod similar ground to *Crime*, achieved plenty of FM radio airplay in the US, and paved the way for the phenomenal worldwide success of *Breakfast in America* (1979). This LP, a Number 1 all over the world, broke the band in the US and scored three hit singles, the best-known (apart from the title track) being 'The Logical Song', a US Number 6 in 1979.

Supertramp found *Breakfast* a difficult album to follow and subsequent releases have not done as well, *Famous Last Words* (1982) being a particularly tired rerun of a bland formula. In 1985, slimmed down to a four-piece core of Davies, John Helliwell (sax), Dougie Thompson (bass) and Bob Siebenberg (drums) (Hodgson left in 1984), Supertramp released their tenth album, *Brother Where You Bound*.

SUPREMES The group who most typified the verve, glamour and style of Motown music in the Sixties, the Supremes originally comprised **Diana Ross** (born 26 March 1944, in Detroit), Florence Ballard (30 June 1944, in Detroit), Barbara Martin (born 1944, in Detroit), and Mary Wilson (6 March 1944, in Mississippi). They grew up together in Detroit's Brewster Housing Project and as the Primettes, played local clubs as sister group to the Primes (later the **Temptations**) and recorded for Lupine. In their last year at school, they won a talent contest which brought them to the attention of Berry Gordy at Motown, who insisted they complete their education before signing a contract, which they did in 1960. Their first release, 'Your Heart Belongs To Me', entered the Hot 100 in August 1962, soon after which Barbara left the group. Four other discs, including the *risqué* 'Buttered Popcorn', were small hits over the next two years, until the summer of 1964 when their seventh release, the husky, swinging 'Where Did Our Love Go', shot to the top of the charts, as did their next four releases, each selling a million on the way including 'Baby Love' and 'Stop!'. Then came failure – 'Nothing But Heartaches' only reached Number 11!

The classic Supremes line-up: Mary Wilson, Florence Ballard and Diana Ross

They were soon back on top with 'I Hear a Symphony' and 1966 and 1967 brought a further four consecutive US chart-toppers, ending with 'The Happening'. 'You Can't Hurry Love' and 'You Keep Me Hanging On' (1966), both **Holland, Dozier and Holland** compositions, were probably their finest recordings.

At this point Florence quit, replaced by Cindy Birdsong – born 15 December 1939 – and the next Number 1, 'Love Child', in late 1968 saw the group listed as Diana Ross and the Supremes. A year later, in December 1969, Diana Ross finally departed for a solo and movie career, and with her went the Supremes' last Number 1 – 'Someday We'll Be Together'. Jean Terrell replaced her as lead singer, but the magic touch was gone – 'Stoned Love' and 'Nathan Jones' were Top 20 hits, but later discs were comparative flops. In June 1972, Cindy Birdsong left to concentrate on married life, and was replaced by Lynda Laurence; later Jean Terrell left and was replaced by Shari Payne – born 14 November 1944 – leaving Mary Wilson as the only original Supreme. Florence Ballard, in the eyes of many the most vocally talented of all the women to grace the Supremes' line-up, died on 22 February 1976. *See also* **Diana Ross**

SURF MUSIC A broad trend that dominated grassroots teenage music in America during the years 1962–5, surf music actually breaks down into four distinct phases. It started as early as 1961, with such transitional records as 'Mr Moto' by the Belairs (Felsted),

'Stick Shift' by the Duals (Sue), 'Moondawg' by the Gamblers (World-Pacific), and 'Church Key' by the Revels (Impact), which had what later would be called a surf sound, but no overt connection with surfing. This was instrumental music, a direct outgrowth of the hard rock, sax-and-guitar instrumentals that were 1959's biggest trend (**Duane Eddy**, **Johnny and the Hurricanes**, Viscounts, **Ventures**, Rockateens, Royaltones, etc.), a style taken over by local dance bands everywhere. The catalyst that turned these thousands of instrumental bands into surf bands was Dick Dale, whose Eastern-influenced, staccato guitar sound was designed to simulate the feel of being on a surfboard. Dale's popularity at southern California dances became immense in 1961 and 1962, and he was soon imitated by a whole wave of surf bands including the Chantays, Rumblers, Tornadoes, Pyramids, Marketts, Surfaris, and Dave Myers and the Surftones.

This music established the audience for surf-related music, in California at least, but it took Brian Wilson and the **Beach Boys** to give it a commercial cast to which the rest of the world could relate. They pioneered surf lyrics in songs that were about going to the beach, surfing, partying, etc. In short, they had built surfing into a universal metaphor for being young and having fun. Their inspiration, however, had come from **Jan and Dean**, whose truly pioneering 1959 records such as 'Baby Talk' (Dore) had introduced the California style of falsetto and doo-wop-derived nonsense phrases used heavily in the early Beach Boys records. The vocal surf bands who followed made up the golden age of surf music – though, in reality, there were few real surf music bands besides the Beach Boys and the Surfaris who did vocal music. Most of the 'groups', including the Rip Chords, the Superstocks, the Four Speeds, the Rogues, the Fantastic Baggys, and many others, were the studio-created product of a small circle of writers/producers that included **Bruce Johnston**, **Terry Melcher**, Gary Usher, Roger Christian, **P. F. Sloan**, **Steve Barri**, and Brian Wilson and Jan Berry. These people, in various permutations, were so prolific they accounted for literally hundreds of surf (and later hot rod) recordings, including most of the acknowledged classics. Other notable acts of the period included the Astronauts and the Trashmen (the leading Midwest surfing bands), the Sunrays ('I Live for the Sun', Tower), and Nashville's Ronny and the

Daytonas; plus, of course, Jan and Dean, whose records always reinforced the basic non-seriousness of it all, and in fact were usually parodies of the broadest sort – which didn't hinder their being huge hits.

Late in 1963, the record industry decided that surfing was out, and hot rod music would be in. Cars and beaches were really part of the same culture and the same metaphor, so there was no problem adapting, since the Beach Boys, Jan and Dean, Dick Dale, the Surfaris, the Hondells, and others all contributed fine car tunes in the same basic instrumental and vocal style. This trend lasted a year or so, by which time the Beach Boys had evolved the music a stage further. Now it wasn't surf music or car music, but simply California music, or summer music. 'Summer Means Fun' by Bruce and Terry (Columbia, 1964) said it all. Summer means fun, California means summer, summer means beaches, beaches mean girls, girls mean cars, cars mean fun, etc., etc. Now 'fun' was the key word, and the world was given an image of California as a promised land where fun and summer were a year-round lifestyle. The Beach Boys' records of 1965–6, such as 'Dance, Dance, Dance', 'Help Me, Rhonda', 'California Girls' and 'Wouldn't It Be Nice' represented California music at its most sublime. The next step took it a little too far, however, as many Californian musicians began getting mystical and experimenting with drugs. From then on, nothing as literal as surf music, or anything reminiscent of it could be tolerated, although the effects of **Scott McKenzie**'s 'San Francisco (Wear Some Flowers in Your Hair)' showed the extent to which the rest of America still believed in California as the promised land.

Though surf music as a commercial trend died in 1966, 1974 saw a brief revival as a reissue of *Surfin' USA* by the Beach Boys became a large hit and several other surfing records made the charts. Surf concerts and surf revival bands have been popular in southern California since the early Seventies, and surf music seems destined to survive indefinitely as a classic form, at least in its home territory.

SUTCH, SCREAMIN' LORD A
somewhat legendary figure of the British rock netherworld, Screamin' Lord Sutch was born David Sutch in Harrow, Middlesex, in 1942, and formed his group, the Savages, in 1958. His 'wild man' act owed as much to Fifties horror movies as it did to

Screamin' Jay Hawkins, and Sutch caused much offence by running amok as Jack the Ripper or being carried onstage in a coffin. Rarely on television and never in the charts (although not for the want of trying) Sutch garnered much of his later publicity by standing for the British Parliament in the 1966 election, and opening a pirate radio station (Radio Sutch). Neither venture was financially rewarding, and he returned to the provincial club circuit whence he came. His 1970 album, *Lord Sutch And Heavy Friends* (Atlantic) brought together ex-Savages like Nicky Hopkins, with superstars like John Bonham, **Jeff Beck** and **Jimmy Page**, but to no avail. In the Eighties, he divides his time between playing rock-'n'roll revival shows and standing at parliamentary by-elections on behalf of his self-styled Monster Raving Loony party.

SUTHERLAND BROTHERS AND QUIVER
Gavin (guitar, bass, vocals) and Ian (guitar, vocals) Sutherland had recorded two albums, *The Sutherland Brothers Band* and *Lifeboat* (Island, 1972) and worked with a band, as a duo and with session men, before teaming up in 1973 with Quiver – Tim Renwick (guitar), Bruce Thomas (bass), Willie Wilson (drums), and from the time of the coalition, Pete Wood (keyboards). Quiver had themselves made two albums for UA, had played the opening night of the Rainbow Theatre in London, and had lost co-founder and songwriter Cal Batchelor. The Sutherland Brothers and Quiver's first session together produced '(I Don't Want to Love You But) You Got Me Anyway', which became an American Hot 100 hit as they toured the US supporting **Elton John** in September 1973. They failed to match its success, though the pop-rock harmonies of *Dream Kid* (1973) were critically well received. When Bruce Thomas left in mid-1974 and Pete Wood early in 1975, neither was replaced, as Gavin Sutherland switched to bass and the line-up was trimmed down to a four-piece. After *Beat of the Street* (1975), SB&Q left Island for Columbia and released *Reach Out for the Sky* (1975). Gavin Sutherland's composition 'Sailing' was a 1975 hit for **Rod Stewart** and the group's first UK hit, 'Arms of Mary', followed a year later. *Slipstream* failed to consolidate on this success and Renwick left during the recording of *Down to Earth* (1977). Quiver and the Sutherlands parted company in 1978 and the latter's *When the Night Comes Down* appeared during 1979.

SWAMP-POP Known locally as South Louisiana Rock'n'Roll, swamp-pop came out of the bayou lands of south-western Louisiana and was a rich hybrid of New Orleans R&B, cajun and hillbilly music. It hit its peak at the end of the Fifties with a series of national hits – Rod Bernard's 'This Should Go On Forever' (Argo), **Cookie and his Cupcakes**' 'Mathilda' (Judd), Jivin' Gene's 'Breakin' Up Is Hard to Do' (Mercury) and **Phil Phillips**' 'Sea of Love' (Mercury) and came back strongly in 1961 with Joe Barry's 'I'm a Fool to Care' (Mercury) and Cookie and his Cupcakes' 'Got You on My Mind' (Chess) in 1962.

The overall influence was **Fats Domino**; both black and white artists easily absorbed his lazy Creole vocals. There was a two-way flow of acts in and out of New Orleans and the Louisiana country towns which increased this musical cross-fertilization. The sound was nurtured by local Southern record men like George Khoury (Khoury's), Lee Lavergne (Lanor), **Huey Meaux** (Tribe), Jay Miller (Zynn), Sam Montel (Montel), Eddie Shuler (Goldband) and Floyd Soileau (Jin). Since the Seventies, only Soileau, Meaux and Shuler have been recording and promoting the infectious swamp-pop sound.

SWAN, BILLY A producer/performer with roots in country music and Fifties rockabilly, Billy Swan was born on 12 May 1944 in Cape Girardeau, Mississippi. In the mid-Fifties, he joined Mirt Mirley and the Rhythm Steppers and travelled to Memphis where **Bill Black**'s Combo recorded his composition, 'Lover Please', which two years later in 1962 was a Top 10 hit for **Clyde McPhatter**. By that time Swan had moved to Nashville where he worked at the city's various studios, occasionally being a roadie for country stars like Mel Tillis. In 1969 he joined Monument as a producer, being responsible for **Tony Joe White**'s US Top 10 hit, 'Polk Salad Annie'. As a recording artist, he released the lilting rockabilly-style 'I Can Help' in 1974, a US Number 1 and also a major UK hit. Subsequent singles, such as 'I'm Her Fool' (1975), were not so successful, but his albums, *I Can Help* (1974) and *Rock'n'Roll Moon* (1975) were a pleasantly archaic mixture of rock-'n'roll and relaxed country music. He moved to APM for his 1978 album, *You're OK, I'm OK*, and continued production and session work in Nashville. In 1986 he joined forces with Randy Meisner, former bassist with the **Eagles**, to form Black Tie.

SWAN SILVERTONES A smooth jubilee quartet in the Thirties, the Swan Silvertones evolved a gospel style around the silky falsetto of Claude Jeter and a succession of harsh, shouting lead singers including Rev. Percell Perkins, for King, and Rev. Robert Crenshaw, for Specialty. Their greatest success was for Vee Jay in the early Sixties when the rhythmic harmonies organized by Paul Owens provided the ideal foil for Jeter and gravel-voiced shouter, Louis Johnson. Jeter's influence spread into the secular field with hit versions of 'Oh Mary, Don't You Weep' and 'The Lord's Prayer'.

SWEET One of Britain's most popular teen-appeal chart groups of 1971–5, Sweet was formed in 1968 by Brian Connolly (vocals), Frank Torpy (guitar), Steve Priest (bass) and Mick Tucker (drums). After unsuccessful singles for Fontana and Parlophone, the group were taken under the wing of Nicky Chinn and Mike Chapman (Chinnichap) in 1970. By this time, Torpy had been replaced first by Mick Stewart and then by Andy Scott, who had once backed **Scaffold**.

The group was transformed into infallible hit-makers via a string of Chinnichap songs between 1971 and 1974, beginning with 'Funny Funny' (RCA, which reached Number 13), and typified by such alliterative titles as 'Co-Co' (1971), 'Wig Wam Bam' (1972) and the heavier 'Blockbuster' (1973, their only Number 1). The production, owing much to classic American bubblegum records, was by Phil Wainman.

The group's stage image underwent several transformations, including banning from some venues for too suggestive performances and their cheerily androgynous style adopted in the wake of **David Bowie**. Their new songs included the powerful 'Ballroom Blitz' and 'Hellraiser', and Chinnichap's philosophizing about the youth revolution, 'The Six Teens'. By 1974, they had become restive at the total control of their career exercised by Chapman and Chinn, and elected to leave them. Sweet's first original composition, 'Fox on the Run' (1975), reached Number 2 in the UK and showed how much they had learned from their former masters.

In 1978, 'Love is Like Oxygen' brought them major transatlantic sales, peaking at Number 8 in the US and Number 9 in the UK, but subsequent releases failed to make anything like the same impact. Considered not heavy enough by US fans and too teenybopper in orientation – despite their aspirations towards 'progressive' credibility – by UK record buyers, the band's fortunes flagged until the final break-up in 1981. The title of their last album – *Identity Crisis*, recorded without Connolly – seemed entirely apt.

SWINGING BLUE JEANS The Swinging Blue Jeans followed the classic Merseybeat route to success, from Liverpool skiffle groups to the Cavern and Hamburg and, finally, an HMV record contract in 1963. Previously known as the Bluegenes, they comprised Ray Ennis (lead guitar, born 26 May 1942), Ralph Ellis (rhythm, 8 March 1942), Les Braid (bass, 15 Sep-

Sweet tried to throw off an early teenybopper image and go for harder rock

tember 1941) and Norman Kuhlke (drums, 17 June 1942). Like many of their compatriots, the Blue Jeans were seldom able to reproduce the excitement of their live act on record, and they also suffered from a lack of strong original material. Their only three Top 20 records were all covers of American songs – **Chan Romero**'s 'Hippy Hippy Shake', **Little Richard**'s 'Good Golly Miss Molly' and **Betty Everett**'s 'You're No Good'. The first two in particular conveyed a certain enthusiasm and excitement which took them into the American charts on Imperial. Ellis left the group in 1965 and was replaced by Terry Sylvester, who in turn departed (to join the **Hollies**) in 1969. Ennis and Braid were still running the Blue Jeans in the early Eighties, with new members John Ryan (drums) and Colin Manley (lead guitar).

TALKING HEADS Drawing on a variety of musical influences, from funk and African rock to classic minimalism, Talking Heads have been one of the most innovative and influential bands to emerge, certainly out of the American new wave, producing a tight, individualistic and danceable sound, aptly described as 'urban funk'.

Guitarist and leader David Byrne met drummer Chris Frantz at art school where they played in a band called the Artistics. They shared an apartment in New York with Frantz's girlfriend (later his wife) Tina Weymouth, who was talked into taking up bass and together they formed Talking Heads in 1975. Their first live dates were at the New York club CBGB's in June, just as the local punk scene was beginning to take shape. In those early days ex-**Roxy Music** man Brian Eno worked with them but the tapes from these first collaborations have never been released. The line-up was completed when Jerry Harrison (guitar/keyboards), formerly with **Jonathan Richman and the Modern Lovers**, joined early in 1977.

Britons first saw Talking Heads in 1977 when they supported the **Ramones** on their European tour, which was followed by the release of the LP *Talking Heads '77*, a thumping, slightly eccentric debut featuring their early classic, 'Psycho Killer', a song that Byrne and Frantz had first performed with the Artistics. The album was only on the UK chart for one

By 1980 Talking Heads had begun to expand, giving a bigger sound with more funk and African influences to back Byrne's intense, distinctive vocals

week at Number 60. The year 1978 brought *More Songs About Buildings and Food* and under the guidance of Brian Eno at the mixing desk, Byrne and Co. began to indulge some of their less conventional musical ideas and experiment with dance rhythms, a process that expanded with successive albums. Allegedly recorded in five days, the album did capture a 'live' feel and scored the band their first domestic Top 30 single with their intense cover of **Al Green**'s 'Take Me to the River'. The partnership with Eno continued with *Fear of Music* (1979) and *Remain in Light* (1980), reaching a climax and taking the band's obsession with African polyrhythms and tough, driving funk to extremes. In early '81, the latter album provided Talking Head's first UK hit 45, 'Once in a Lifetime', a brilliant study of urban paranoia set to a minimalist funk beat that reached Number 14. During this period Byrne also made an experimental album with Eno, *My Life in the Bush of Ghosts*, which was not released until 1981.

Creative disagreements caused a rift between the band and Eno and, in 1981, the whole of the band took a long break from each other. Byrne took part in various avant-garde projects and produced records for the **Fun Boy Three** and the **B-52's**; Harrison released the solo album *The Red and the Black* (1981); but Frantz and Weymouth enjoyed the most success with their *Tom Tom Club* LP. A relaxed dance record, it stayed in the US charts for 30 weeks and spawned the UK Number 7 single, 'Wordy Rappinghood'.

A live album, *The Name of This Band Is Talking Heads* appeared in 1982, but it was not until 1983 and *Speaking in Tongues* that they made their next studio LP. It harked back to the stripped-down sound of the early Talking Heads and was in many ways a more accessible work than its Eno-influenced predecessors. The tour that followed its release was captured on the film *Stop Making Sense*, directed by Jonathan Demme, the soundtrack of which became the group's first LP release after switching labels, from Sire to EMI, in October 1984.

Talking Heads' eighth album *Little Creatures* was released in 1985, moving yet further away from the hard urban funk to more easily approached conventional song structures. The album received highly favourable reviews applauding their return to the kind of dismembered pop/punk of the first two albums, and a single from the album, 'And Then She Was', returned the group to the UK Top 30 in early '86. The same year also saw the release of Byrne's pet project, the feature film *True Stories* and an LP of the same name.

TALMY, SHEL A one-time classmate of **Phil Spector**, Shel Talmy arrived in Britain from California in 1963 with a letter of recommendation from another noted West Coast producer, Nik Venet. Impressed, Decca Records gave Talmy the chance to prove himself by assigning him as producer to the Bachelors, whom he transformed from a harmonica trio into a very successful pop harmony group with revivals of old standards like 'Charmaine' (1963) and 'Diane' (1964, a UK Number 1). By 1964, Talmy had set up an independent production deal with Pye which led to his involvement with the **Kinks** – whose records he produced prior to their *Something Else* album in 1967 – and then the **Who**, whom he first recorded as Kinks soundalikes. In 1965, he set up Planet Records as a wholly independent label, but it failed to secure any hits – the closest being Creation's 'Making Time' in 1966 – and ceased operation in 1967. Other notable Talmy productions included the **Easybeats**' 'Friday on My Mind' and *Good Friday* album (1966 and 1967 respectively) for United Artists, **Roy Harper**'s 1967 album *Come Out Fighting Genghis Smith* (CBS), and albums by **Pentangle**, String Driven Thing, the Sorrows, **Amen Corner** and ex-**Zombies** bassist Chris White. In the Seventies he moved into film production and book publishing with his company, Talmy-Franklin.

TAMS Black vocal group the Tams originally comprised Charles Pope (born 7 August 1936), Joseph Pope (6 November 1933), Robert Lee Smith (18 March 1936), Floyd Ashton (15 August 1933), and Horace Kay (13 April 1934). They spent three years singing around the clubs in their home town of Atlanta, Georgia, before their first hit, 'Untie Me', in 1962. It was recorded at **Rick Hall**'s Fame Studios in Muscle Shoals for Harry Finfer's Arlen label. Under Bill Lowery's management and with Albert Cottle (born in 1941 in Washington, DC) replacing Ashton, the Tams became one of the most popular soul acts in the South. Their long run of single hits on ABC-Paramount included 'What Kind of Fool' (Top 10 in 1963), 'You Lied to Your Daddy', 'It's All Right', 'Hey Girl Don't Bother Me' (which topped the British charts in 1971), 'Silly Little Girl' and 'Be Young, Be Foolish, Be Happy'. The deliciously hoarse lead vocals, the rough gospel harmonies and a series of good songs by white soul brother Ray Whitley made the Tams an admirable foil to the slicker Motown soul of the North. In 1968 the group also recorded for Lowery's 1-2-3 label and Capitol before rejoining ABC-Paramount in 1971.

TANGERINE DREAM A seminal synthesizer band from Germany, Tangerine Dream was formed by West Berlin music student Edgar Froese (born on 6 June 1944) in 1967. The group originally comprised Froese,

Klaus Schulze and Conny Schnitzler; later members included Chris Franke, Peter Baumann, Steve Schroyder, Udo Dennebourg and Roland Paulyck. They began playing music that was heavily influenced by West Coast acid rock (especially the **Doors**), and **Pink Floyd**. However, in the following years as the line-up settled down, they gradually dispensed with conventional instrumentation in favour of synthesizers, mellotrons, pre-set tapes and other electronic aids and the music became a texture of electronic drones and waves of shifting tones and volume. Their early albums, *Electronic Meditation* (Ohr-Musik, 1970), *Alpha Centauri* (1971, released in Britain by Polydor) and *Zeit* (1972) were 'conventional' experiments in electronic music, but by the time of *Phaedra* (Virgin, 1974), *Rubycon* (1975) and Froese's solo albums, *Aqua* (Virgin, 1974) and *Epsilon in Malaysian Pale* (1975), the group was creating sounds that veered from the romantic to the ethereal without any referent whatsoever. Their cult success grew in the UK and they were a considerable influence on the new wave of synthesizer bands who emerged in the late Seventies and early Eighties.

TATE, HOWARD Born in Macon, Georgia, in 1943, R&B singer Howard Tate moved to Philadelphia in the Sixties and spent two years singing with **Bill Doggett**'s band. Between 1966 and 1968 he had a number of successes in both pop and R&B charts with gospeltinged, climactic soul songs including 'Ain't Nobody Home', 'Look at Granny Run Run' and 'Stop'. All were written and produced for Verve by **Jerry Ragavoy**. Smaller R&B hits – 'These Are the Things That Make Me Know You're Gone' and 'My Soul's Got a Hole in It' – followed on **Lloyd Price**'s Turntable label in 1969 to 1970. The Ragavoy-produced *Burglar* was a classic of deep soul.

TAUPIN, BERNIE Born in Lincoln on 22 May 1950, lyricist Bernie Taupin began his partnership with **Elton John** when they met after the latter took part in a Liberty Records talent competition in 1967. His earliest lyrics were saturated with poetic aspirations but on the albums *Elton John* and *Tumbleweed* he emerged as a superb craftsman of romantic ballads with a fascination for old Americana and leanings towards a bed-sit or sophomore mentality much in evidence on his solo album *Taupin* (DJM, 1971). His superficial profundity

reached full flower on *Madman across the Water* but he switched to a more direct, jaunty style with *Honky Chateau* and turned from cowboys to film stars on *Goodbye Yellow Brick Road*. An obsessive fan, he produced **David Ackles**' classic *American Gothic* in 1972, and drew on his early experiences with John for the bitter autobiographical *Captain Fantastic and the Brown Dirt Cowboy* (1975).

He published a collection of poetry under the title *The One Who Writes the Words for Elton John* in 1976, but they ceased writing together after John's announcement of his 'retirement' in late 1977. After a spell collaborating with Gary Osborne, John resumed his partnership with Taupin in 1980, for the albums *21 at 33* and *The Fox*, since when they have collaborated regularly but not exclusively. A second Taupin album, *He Who Rides the Tiger*, was released in 1980.

TAYLOR, JAMES The archetypal introverted, melancholic singer/songwriter of the early Seventies, James Taylor was born on 12 March 1948 into a musical Boston family, and started to play guitar at an early age. In 1965 he met Danny Kortchmar, with whom he formed the Flying Machine in New York, some two years later. The group didn't do too well, and James, with a heroin addiction to cope with, went to England in 1968 where old friend Peter Asher (see **Peter and Gordon**) got him an album contract with the newly formed Apple. When *James Taylor* was released in 1969, a heroin-free James returned to the States for a second sojourn in a mental institution.

His second album, *Sweet Baby James* (Warner Brothers, 1970) and the single from it, 'Fire and Rain', catapulted him

Sweet baby James Taylor sings a sad and mournful song

to a stardom from which he has never really recovered. The simple world-weariness of the music seemed entirely apposite for the post-Kent State feelings of American youth. The music was basically acoustic folk-blues guitar; the lyrics were open to the point of vagueness. The tone of voice was the dominant factor: resignation and the sadness of a hopeless quest. James Taylor had fused together the simple pessimism of country music and the portentousness of much Sixties folk, so reflecting the 'failed hopes' ethos of the early Seventies.

Mud Slide Slim and *One Man Dog* followed in 1971 and 1972, featuring songs mostly dedicated to the salvations of love and the highway. Particularly noteworthy were the dignified 'Highway Song' and the huge hit 'You've Got a Friend' (actually written by **Carole King**) from the former, and the suite of songs that closed the latter. In late 1972, James married fellow-singer **Carly Simon** with whom he had a Top 10 hit with 'Mockingbird' in 1974. (They divorced in 1982.)

Walking Man (1974) and *Gorilla* (1975) followed, the latter featuring harmony singing from **Dave Crosby** and **Graham Nash**, while his US Top 10 success with a revival of **Junior Walker**'s 'How Sweet It Is' in 1975 indicated a new lightness in his musical approach. Switching to Columbia in 1977, Taylor scored heavily with another revival – 'Handy Man', originally recorded by **Jimmy Jones** and **Del Shannon**. His first Columbia album, *J.T.*, found him reunited with Peter Asher for the first time since *One Man Dog*. In 1978, he joined **Simon and Garfunkel** on a US Top 20 revival of **Sam Cooke**'s 'Wonderful World', and a year later he was back in the US chart with yet another reworking, this time of the **Drifters**' 'Up on the Roof'. *Flag* (1979) and *Dad Loves His Work* (1981) contained more original material which, while showing Taylor to be an essentially lightweight talent, more than consolidated his reputation as an AOR superstar. *That's Why I'm Here* (1985) carried on the same pattern.

TAYLOR, JOHNNIE Born in Crawfordsville, Arkansas, on 5 May 1938, Johnnie Taylor was the son of a church minister and sang in the choir at the age of six, and later enjoyed listening to **Sonny Boy Williamson** and **Junior Parker** on the radio. Leaving home at 15, he worked in a Cleveland chemical plant, singing with a gospel group in his spare time, then moved to Chicago and sang with the Five Echoes

on Vee Jay. He joined the **Soul Stirrers** on **Sam Cooke**'s recommendation (replacing him) and in 1961 reverted to secular music with Cooke's Sar label – 'Baby We've Got Love' was a 1963 hit on the Derby subsidiary, sounding very similar to Sam. In 1965, Taylor signed with Stax and soon found himself in the R&B charts with 'I Had a Dream', an intense blues ballad. Success grew and 1968 brought a million-seller with 'Who's Making Love', a brash, funky warning of infidelity, which became a Top 10 hit. Since then he continued to take his rasping, blues-tinged presentations of Memphis soul into the charts for Stax with songs like 'Jody's Got Your Girl and Gone' (an R&B chart-topper in 1971) and 'Hijackin' Love'. He maintained his consistency with his 1975 album, *Taylored in Silk*, and scored his biggest hit ever with the US chart-topper 'Disco Lady' in 1976.

TAYLOR, LITTLE JOHNNY Christened Johnny Young and born in Memphis in 1940, Little Johnny Taylor adopted the 'Taylor' tag in the early Sixties, manufacturing a fraternal identity with soul singer Ted Taylor. He began singing gospel with the Mighty Clouds of Joy with whom he recorded for RCA, but later moved to Los Angeles to perform solo blues where he was spotted by producer Cliff Goldsmith and signed to Galaxy Records. Having scored an R&B hit with his debut disc, the follow-up 'Part Time Love', an intense, emotional blues ballad, was a 1963 Top 20 smash. He recorded steadily for Galaxy throughout the Sixties in a soul-blues idiom before joining Ronn Records, where 'Everybody Knows About My Good Thing', in similar style, was a pop and R&B hit in 1971. He remained active on that label for much of the Seventies.

TEARDROP EXPLODES Formed in Liverpool in 1978 by Julian Cope after his involvement with Ian McCullough (**Echo and the Bunnymen**) and Pete Wylie (**Wah!**) in the Crucial Three, Teardrop Explodes were the quintessential psychedelic post-punk pop band, blending, with unique finesse, Sixties flower-power influences and a Seventies tough edge.

Going through a series of line-up changes for their early gigs and two independent singles, the nucleus of Teardrop Explodes eventually settled at Cope (vocals, guitar), David Balfe (keyboards), Alan Gill (guitar) and Gary Dwyer (drums). The first album, *Kilimanjaro* (1980), a fine collection of

acid-pop tunes, was largely dismissed as promising but undistinguished. The classic single 'Reward' changed all that as its irrepressible, brass-laden power stormed into the UK Top 10 and resuscitated interest in the LP, and a new version of the album (now to include 'Reward') stayed in UK album charts for 35 weeks.

'Treason' and 'Passionate Friend', equally vital singles, followed through 1981 and a second album, the inexplicably underrated *Wilder*, came out at the end of the year. The almost complete indifference with which the LP was received and the poor response the group encountered in their live shows through 1982 discouraged Cope to the extent that after just one more release, yet another joyous, swinging pop single 'When You Disappear From View', Teardrop Explodes disbanded in 1983.

Cope continued as a solo artist, releasing *World Shut Your Mouth* (1984) and *Fried* (1985) on Mercury before signing to Island in 1986, with whom he released the LP *Saint Julian*.

TEARS FOR FEARS Initially finding moderate success as an accomplished but lightweight pop outfit, Tears for Fears later built their sound into a tough blend of the most sophisticated rock arrangements with a refined pop sensibility, and as a result established themselves as a major act.

Formed in Bath in southern England out of the childhood friendship of Curt Smith (vocals, bass) and Roland Orzabal (vocals, guitar), they were signed to Polygram in 1981 on the strength of a two-song demo. Released as singles, neither of the songs made the charts and they had to wait until October 1982 and their third single, the plaintive 'Mad World', before scoring a UK hit. It reached Number 3, and there followed two further Top 5 singles and the album, *The Hurting* (1983), which sold close to a million copies worldwide. Despite Smith and Orzabal receiving most of the credit, Tears for Fears had at this point settled into a four-piece unit with Ian Stanley (keyboards) and Manny Elias (drums).

Apart from a minor hit single, Tears for Fears then disappeared to write and record *Songs from the Big Chair* (1985), an album that showed a marked progression from its pretty but insubstantial predecessor and elevated them to the big time. It spawned three huge international hit singles, 'Mothers Talk', 'Shout', and, most notably, the worldwide Number 1, 'Everybody Wants To Rule the World', and achieved multiple platinum sales.

TEDDY BEARS A white vocal group from Los Angeles, the Teddy Bears were the launching pad for the career of master-producer **Phil Spector**. He formed the group while still a student at the Fairfax Junior High School, LA, with Annette Kleinbard (born 1940) and Marshall Lieb (26 January 1939).

Spector had already written a song, 'To Know Him Is to Love Him', apparently inspired by an inscription on his father's grave. He booked a local studio and cut the record, with Annette Kleinbard's high-pitched, 'little girl' voice taking the lead vocal. The disc was leased to Dore and by the end of 1958 it was Number 1 on the Hot 100.

A follow-up on Dore made no impact, and the trio moved to Imperial, where 'Oh Why' crept in at the bottom of the charts for two weeks. Other Imperial singles were less successful and soon after Kleinbard changed her name to Carol Connors, the group split up. Later, the **Fleetwoods** had a massive hit with 'Come Softly to Me', which utilized the 'Teddy Bears' formula of girlish lead vocal backed by cooing male harmonies. See also **Phil Spector**

TELEVISION Leading lights of the New York new wave explosion of the late Seventies, punk band Television had as their guide and mentor, principal guitarist, composer and singer Tom Verlaine. Born Tom Miller in New Jersey in 1950, Miller moved to Greenwich Village, New York in 1968, adopted his new surname from the 19th-century French poet and later, in the early Seventies, formed the Neon Boys with two old school friends, drummer Billy Ficca and bassist **Richard Hell** (whose original surname had been the more prosaic Myers). Although the Neon Boys never played in public they recorded a couple of Verlaine/Hell compositions – 'That's All I Know (Right Now)' and 'Love Comes in Spurts' – which revealed Verlaine's distinctive and imaginative guitar style.

In 1974 the trio was augmented by second guitarist Richard Lloyd and with the new name 'Television' they played their first gig on March 2. Shortage of suitable venues was a major problem until Verlaine and Lloyd talked the owner of the Boney Street bar, CBGB's, into letting them play there. The group quickly gained a devoted following and CBGB's became the focus of the new wave in New York.

A&R men began to show an interest in Television and Island Records sent Brian Eno to engineer some demo tapes, but Island were not impressed with the result and the exercise came to nothing. Shortly afterwards, in April 1975, Richard Hell was ousted from the band, his primitive bass-playing no longer fitting Television's increasingly complex music, and he went off to form his own band, the Voidoids, **Blondie**'s Fred Smith was brought in as Hell's replacement and with this line-up, Television recorded 'Little Johnny Jewel' on their own Ork label. Verlaine's nasal tones and his free-ranging guitar solo combined with the group's sparse rhythms and spiky guitar noises to consolidate Television's style. An extraordinary record, 'Little Johnny Jewel' convinced Elektra of the group's potential, and they signed them to the label in 1976.

That winter, the group entered the studio with producer Andy Johns. Their first album, *Marquee Moon*, released in February 1977, was an astonishing debut; every song was compulsive listening, from the ravaging, driving 'See No Evil', through the sensuous 'Guiding Light' and the chilling 'Torn Curtain' to the title track, which featured a hypnotically sinister guitar riff that was nothing less than a masterpiece. The musical performances were outstanding in all departments, and if in print Verlaine's lyrics bordered on the pretentious, on record – with Verlaine's dry, engaging vocal delivery – they worked brilliantly.

In the US, reaction to *Marquee Moon* was lukewarm, and it failed to make the charts, but it drew justifiably ecstatic reviews in the UK and reached Number 28, while the singles 'Marquee Moon' and 'Prove It' made the Top 30. The follow-up album *Adventure* (1978) did even better in the UK, climbing to Number 7, and even if it did not measure up to the quality of its predecessor, it was, again, a marvellous record of shimmering guitars, exquisite arrangements and powerful Verlaine compositions. Critical response to *Adventure* was less than enthusiastic, a reflection of the music press' growing dislike of Television's aloof image and Tom Verlaine's undeniably arrogant public persona in particular.

In August 1978, Television suddenly split up: Smith and Ficca went into production and session work, while Verlaine and Lloyd pursued solo careers. Verlaine's first solo album, *Tom Verlaine* (1979) would have made an ideal third Television LP – much of *Marquee Moon*'s power and intensity was there – but subsequent efforts *Dreamtime* (1981) and *Words from the Front* (1982), were disappointing.

Lloyd, meanwhile, released a fine album of Sixties-sounding power pop in *Alchemy* (1979) yet he failed to follow it up. Whatever one thought of Television's image, their music was undeniably ahead of its time, and not only was their influence felt in groups well into the Eighties, but that era threw up few, if any, acts of similar invention and breadth of expression.

TELEVISION (UK) The first British television series to cater specifically for the 'under 21s' was *Teleclub*, a magazine programme with 'modern music', which was first broadcast on 9 October 1953. It faced stiff opposition from the BBC hierarchy, who were staunchly opposed to any form of youthful expression and suffered *Teleclub* only on the understanding that the noise be interspersed with features on sport and hobbies. On 24 March 1955, just as advance warnings of rock'n'roll were crossing the Atlantic, they took the show off the air and for the next two years both BBC and the commercial network steadfastly ignored the emergence of the new music. Finally, on New Year's Day 1957, the commercial channel (which had begun in 1955) timidly offered its 'intimate record programme' *Cool for Cats*, which featured a group of Beat Generation dancers interpreting the week's new releases. This may well have prompted the BBC to unveil – on Saturday 16 February 1957 – *Six-Five Special*, the first programme to fill the previously vacant six–seven p.m. slot.

Justly famous as the innovation of **Jack Good**, the programme is remembered today more for its style than its content, which was too often bogged down in sport, comedy and general-interest items. Before very long Good was tempted over to commercial ITV to set up his masterpiece, *Oh Boy!*, the first unadulterated rock show. He did away with the jiving teenagers of *Six-Five*, relegated his audience to the auditorium of a former music hall and focused attention on the stage, where he organized superb choreographed action between Lord Rockingham's XI, the Dallas Boys, the **John Barry** Seven, **Marty Wilde**, organist Cherry Wainer and the **Vernons Girls**. The show had an enormously successful run from 15 June 1958 to 30 May 1959, and bit so deeply into the BBC's viewing figures that on 27 December 1958, *Six-Five Special* was replaced by the *Oh Boy!*-inspired *Dig This!*. A pale imitation, the programme was succeeded after three months by *Drumbeat*, produced by Stewart Morris, (later to become associated with *Top of the Pops*). *Drumbeat* also failed to steal *Oh Boy!*'s thunder. Meanwhile, the BBC had introduced its pop panel show, *Juke Box Jury*, and for most of its eight-year run (1959–67) the stupidity of many of its guests made compulsive viewing.

Drumbeat was the BBC's last serious attempt to combat their rival's superiority in the pop field until it hit back with *Top of the Pops* in 1963. ITV followed *Oh Boy!* with *Boy Meets Girl* (1959), which was in turn replaced within a year by Jack Good's last British TV series, *Wham!* (1960). During the summer of 1960, the BBC's Josephine Douglas switched channels to produce *Tin Pan Alley Show*, a series that accurately reflected the blandness of pop music at the turn of the Sixties. It was aimed at 'teenagers and their mums and dads'. In 1961, the BBC cashed in with *The Trad Fad* for a few weeks, and on 9 September *Thank Your Lucky Stars* (ITV) started a new trend when it became the first programme to dispense with 'regulars' and present a completely different bill every week. *Lucky Stars* developed into an invaluable showcase for artists and, despite its conveyor-belt approach, enjoyed great popularity until it was axed during the death throes of the British pop boom in 1966.

In 1963, the **Beatles** made their television debut on a Granada TV magazine programme in Manchester and followed that with an appearance on the 23 February edition of *Lucky Stars*. A BBC appearance followed on 16 April, when they were four of the 'artists of the future' to be presented on Jimmy Young's *625 Show*. One of the countless side-effects of the Beatles' success was the creation by the end of that year of *Ready Steady Go!*, *Top of the Pops* and a dozen other programmes to accommodate the new-found enthusiasm for pop music. *Ready Steady Go!* swiftly developed into television's most invaluable pop barometer, faithfully recording the changing fashions in music, clothes and dance, while everyone who was anyone dropped into the jam-packed studio to perform. Atmospherically it carried a charge unapproached since the days of *Oh Boy!* (1958–9), but technically it was way ahead of its time: no British pop show since has bettered its direction and camerawork. *RSG!* made a star out of its ideally ingenuous *commère*, Cathy McGowan, who (with Keith Fordyce and Michael Aldred) was a co-presenter before taking total control after miming was ditched in favour of live performances in 1965.

Simultaneously, the programme was relocated in a larger studio, took some weeks to overcome the loss of intimacy, but triumphed. An arbiter of fashion to the last, it came off the air as British beat began to die.

Meanwhile, other programmes had sprouted. In 1963 both channels, acknowledging that 'the public for pops gets younger and younger', began supplying rock for children. The BBC offered Australian Rolf Harris in *A Swingin' Time*, while ITV revamped its two-year-old *Tuesday Rendezvous* as a junior version of *RSG!*, called *Five O'Clock Club*. New acts, trying to break into the charts, fought to appear even though it might mean sharing the bill with Sylvano's Sophisticated Chimps. On New Year's Day 1964, BBC-1 offered a challenge to *RSG!* in the undernourished shape of *Top of the Pops*, little more than an illustrated recital of the hit parade. At first clumsy and unimaginative, the programme has since become slick to the point of sterility. Also in 1964, BBC-2 presented its first pop show, *The Beat Room*, a sophisticated descendant of *Oh Boy!*

Most pop fans, however, remained tuned to ITV, whose coverage of contemporary music reached saturation point during that year. Apart from the programmes mentioned (plus the already established *Thank Your Lucky Stars*) the channel also staged the *RSG Mod Ball*, covered the *New Musical Express* Poll Winners' Concert and turned over peak-hour viewing to blues, gospel and folk as well as promoting *Ready, Steady – Win!*, a talent contest in which aspiring beat groups competed for £1,000 worth of musical equipment. The adverse criticism that such excesses aroused resulted in severe cutbacks the following year, and only the BBC premiered new shows. On BBC-2, *Gadzooks! It's All Happening* (*The Beat Room* in all but name) begat *Gadzooks! It's the In Crowd* (an experimental mixture of pop, folk and comedy), which in turn begat plain *Gadzooks!*, which was without issue. BBC-1 made a brave but unsuccessful attempt to catalogue the Glaswegian pop scene in *Stramash!* and, in 1966 – the year in which ITV axed practically all its pop shows – introduced *A Whole Scene Going*, the first programme to bring music into focus with the rest of pop culture (an idea expanded upon two years later when Tony Palmer presented his series *How It Is*). Between 1967 and 1968, TV relegated rock to the minority interests department, although two pop-based chat shows (**Jonathan King**'s *Good Evening* and

Simon Dee's legendary, awful *Dee Time*) won prime-time slots. Typical of the new attitude, however, was BBC-2's late-night *Colour Me Pop* (1968), not only the first pop show in colour but the first to highlight heavier rock. *Colour Me Pop* begat *Disco 2* (1969), which in turn begat the long-running *Old Grey Whistle Test*, hosted initially by journalist Richard Williams and one-time mid-Sixties teen idol **Ian Whitcomb**, and subsequently by Radio One's Bob Harris.

Old Grey Whistle Test remained a showcase for progressive rock and visiting American artists – especially the new wave of singer/songwriters – for much of the Seventies, and *In Concert* (produced by Stanley Dorfman) presented a succession of solo performers filmed through soft-focus lenses. Britain's new generation of teenyboppers, meanwhile, tuned in to shows like Mike Mansfield's *Supersonic* (1973–6), the sophisticated production effects of which influenced *Top of the Pops* to tidy up its presentation. Television's neat division between 'progressive' and teenybopper pop was, however, undermined by the onslaught of punk, the only outlet for which was the **Mickie Most**-produced *Revolver* (1977), which was presided over by a sneering Peter Cook in the guise of a shady club manager. To be fair, *Top of the Pops* accommodated far more punk and new wave acts than Radio One was prepared to give airtime to, and *Old Grey Whistle Test* gradually abandoned its by now outdated hard-rock and singer/writer orientation to feature many more new wave bands. A complete rethink in the early Eighties resulted in the programme being relaunched as simply *Whistle Test*, with three nicely sceptical presenters – David Hepworth, Mark Ellen and Andy Kershaw – and a new hour-long format.

The main innovation in pop television terms in the early Eighties, however, was the video promo – visual representations of records that freed performers from the necessity of appearing live on TV shows like *Top of the Pops*. Videos had become an essential element in pop shows by the middle of the decade – the *only* element, even, in the case of Channel 4's *The Chart Show*, which began in 1986 – and disquiet in the industry about their use as 'free programming' prompted pressure during that year for payments from the braodcasting companies for video usage. As for really effective television presentation of rock as *youth* music, the Eighties offered a brave near-miss in BBC-2's *Oxford Roadshow* and

Channel 4's innovative if over-rated *The Tube*, plus sundry other series like Paul Gambaccini's *The Other Side of the Tracks* (Channel 4), *Razzamatazz* (ITV) and the American import, *Soul Train*. Even though rock still tended to be treated as a minority taste on British television, it was noticeable that a pop element was becoming a standard feature of many a programme, from the competing breakfast-time shows to children's Saturday morning shows – all hosted by DJs who had made their name on radio. *See also* **Video**

TELEVISION (US)

TELEVISION (US) One of the great changes implicit in the rise of rock'n'roll was the end of the-song-not-the-singer adage, the central precept of Tin Pan Alley. By 1960, pop would have its own Tin Pan Alley (in the form of the Brill Building) but in the formative years of rock'n'roll it was the singer, not the song, that mattered – hence the demise of the cover-version syndrome once the originals were readily accessible.

For American TV, this meant that the format of *Lucky Strike Hit Parade*, which saw 'Snooky' Lanson and the other regulars weekly perform their interpretations of the hits of the day, would not survive the arrival of the raucous R&B and rock'n'roll songs of the Fifties. Essentially hostile to rock-'n'roll, yet fully aware of the increased viewing figures that a **Presley** could make to a TV programme, the networks were in a quandary, especially as putting Presley on TV was to make even more accessible a music they hated. TV's brief encounter with Presley in 1956 was, to say the least, an electrifying experience. His six appearances on Jimmy and Tommy Dorsey's *Stage Show* (starting on 6 January 1956) showing him from head to toe, gyrations and all, attracted a record mail for the programme, and ensured that 'Heartbreak Hotel' was a *national* hit. His chart success assured, Presley became a willing pawn in the ratings battle between Steve Allen and Ed Sullivan. They tried to deaden his impact – Allen, by dressing Presley in a tuxedo and then putting him in a comedy sketch, and Sullivan by showing Presley only from the waist up. The result was even more controversy. TV could control neither Presley's image nor his impact, and the next time he appeared on TV, it was by choice that he remained stationary and sang a duet with Frank Sinatra.

If Presley couldn't be contained, in **Dick Clark** television found someone who could tame rock'n'roll. *Bandstand* had been running since 1952 in Philadelphia, with Bob Horn as its presenter. In 1957, a year after local disc jockey Dick Clark took over its presentation, it went national as *American Bandstand* on Saturday afternoons. The show's success – it inspired innumerable local dance shows – depended on its concentration on records and teenagers dancing to them, with the odd guest now and then, in an atmosphere of good, clean fun to which parents couldn't object. Having weathered the payola hearings of 1960, Clark and *American Bandstand* continued, but the show, reflecting the mood of the times, was becoming less interesting. Fittingly, it was Ed Sullivan, the would-be castrator of Presley, who introduced the **Beatles** to America and – on the basis of the phenomenal ratings his British Invasion shows got – paved the way for TV's next battle with rock, **Jack Good**'s *Shindig* in 1964 and *Hullabaloo* in 1965. The former was a prime-time, weekly half-hour devoted to nothing but rock, presented in a go-go setting. The series was extremely successful, and within a year it had expanded to an hour, then twice a week, with competition from NBC with *Hullabaloo*. During this time, every major city developed local shows which presented a combination of nationally known stars and local groups, hosted by popular disc jockeys. Some of these were modelled on *Bandstand*, while others had a more theatrical cast, presenting live groups on stage. There were literally hundreds of these shows, many of them syndicated nationally.

They began dying off around 1967, however, after *Shindig* and *Hullabaloo* had been cancelled and the British Invasion had tapered off and, with it, the teen mania that had made the TV boom possible. The hardy *American Bandstand* survived, in addition to which Dick Clark launched other series, chiefly *Where the Action Is*, which lasted a few years and introduced a number of important groups, notably **Paul Revere and the Raiders**. Despite abortive attempts (such as ABC's *Music Scene*, in 1970) to present modern rock on TV, no successful format was evolved until 1973 when ABC's *In Concert*, NBC's *Midnight Special*, and **Don Kirshner**'s syndicated *Rock Concert* found their niche in late-night time slots. Otherwise, US television offered little for rock fans (beyond the folk, country and jazz concerts and documentaries broadcast by the Public Broadcasting System) until the launch in 1982 of cable channel MTV (Music TeleVision). Owned by Warner Communications, MTV was a 24-hour station that relied almost totally for its programming on a supply of promotional videos from record companies; owing to the paucity of videos at the begininng, MTV featured clips spotlighting British acts (video had, by 1982, become a very sophisticated business in the UK) and so paved the way for a huge influx of UK talent into the US chart. *See also* **Video**

TEMPERANCE SEVEN The nine-man Temperance Seven were a tongue-in-cheek attempt to re-create Twenties-style dance band music. Often lumped in with the trad scene, the Seven were purveyors of camp nostalgia rather than jazz, and were a formative influence on the **Bonzo Dog Doo Dah Band**. The Seven were formed in 1955 and settled down with a line-up of Captain Cephas Howard (trumpet, euphonium); Alan Swainston Cooper (soprano sax, clarinets, phonofiddle and Swanee whistle); Sheik Haroun Wadi el John R. T. Davies (trombone, alto sax, trumpet); Philip Harrison (baritone and alto sax); Dr John Gieves Watson (banjo, spoons); Martin Fry (sousaphone); Prof. Brian Innes (percussion); Clifford de Bevan (piano); and Whispering Paul McDowell (vocals). They had two British Top 10 hits in 1961 with 'You're Driving Me Crazy' – a Number 1 – and 'Pasadena', which came complete with a series of false endings. Personnel came and went – and returned – over the years, but the band continued performing well into the Eighties, mostly in cabaret. For some time in the Seventies Ted Wood, elder brother of the **Faces**' (and subsequently **Stones**') guitarist Ron Wood, was the vocalist.

TEMPO, NINO, AND STEVENS, APRIL A brother-and-sister duo from Niagara Falls, New York, Nino Tempo was born on 6 January 1937 and April Stevens 29 April 1936. After playing sax on Bobby Darin sessions on the West Coast, Tempo won a recording contract with Atco in 1962. The lines of hits which followed featured re-workings of pop standards through their unusual vocal harmonies. The most successful were 'Deep Purple' (a US Number 1 in 1963) and 'Whispering' (Number 11 in the same year). They re-emerged briefly on White Whale in 1968, and Tempo worked as an arranger in Los Angeles. He is credited on **Cher**'s 1974 record 'Dark Lady', which was produced by **'Snuff' Garrett**.

TEMPTATIONS A group subjected to a long and complex list of personnel changes and style variations, the Temptations initially consisted of **Eddie Kendricks** (tenor) – born on 7 December 1939 in Birmingham, Alabama; Otis Miles (baritone), subsequently known as Otis Williams – 30 October 1941 in Texarkana, Texas; Paul Williams – 2 July 1939 in Birmingham, Alabama; Melvin Franklin, christened David English, by which name he was later known (bass) – 12 October 1942 in Montgomery, Alabama; and Eldridge Bryant. During the late Fifties they congregated in Detroit and were singing with local groups; Kendricks and Paul Williams with the Primes, Franklin, Miles and Bryant with the Distants – along with Richard Street, destined to become a Temptation later on. Both groups had the same management, and when the Primes disbanded, Kendricks was drafted into the Distants as lead voice, Williams also joining. By 1959, the Distants had recorded for Northern and gained the interest of Berry Gordy, who signed them in 1960 and renamed them Temptations.

The group's first releases were on Gordy's Miracle label in 1961, basically straight doo-wop vocal style featuring baritone lead with burbling bass back-up. But with the introduction of the Gordy label in 1962 the Temptations were immediately switched to the new label, their first release, 'Dream Come True', becoming a substantial R&B hit that year. Follow-ups were less successful, however, and it was nearly two years later when their fifth Gordy release, 'The Way You Do the Things You Do', an imaginative **Smokey Robinson** beat ballad juxtaposing Kendricks' tender tenor lead with a tenor sax solo, went to Number 11 on the national chart. By this time, Eldridge Bryant had quit, to be replaced by baritone **David Ruffin** (born on 8 January 1941, in Meridian, Mississippi). Thus began the group's first 'golden age', lasting some four years with seventeen Top 30 US chart hits, six of them in the Top 10, including the 1965 Smokey Robinson-composed 'My Girl' (a Number 1) and 'Ain't Too Proud to Beg', a pounding anthem led by Ruffin's searing baritone.

Ruffin left in 1968 to go solo and was replaced by Dennis Edwards, a native of Birmingham, Alabama, who had previously sung with the **Contours**. The Temptations, now teamed with writer/producer **Norman Whitfield**, entered a musically 'heavier' phase, featuring rock-angled performances

Tough'n'tender Temptations of the mid-Sixties: from the left, Paul Williams, Melvin Franklin, David Ruffin, Otis Williams and Eddie Kendricks

with complex arrangements. 'Cloud Nine' was an immediate 1968 Top 10 hit in the US, and the next two years brought four more – among them a Number 1 in the US, 'I Can't Get Next to You', and a US Number 2, 'I'm Gonna Make You Love Me' (with **Diana Ross** and the **Supremes**) – both in 1969.

The year of great changes was 1971: 'Just My Imagination', a return to the tender ballad style, became their third Number 1 hit and then Kendricks left to go solo. His replacement, Ricky Owens from the **Vibrations**, proved unsatisfactory, and was himself replaced by Damon Harris after a mere six months. Meanwhile, Paul Williams had to quit on medical grounds (he was later found murdered in his car in Detroit) and Richard Street, a former member of the Monitors, joined. Further chart success followed – another Number 1, 'Papa Was a Rollin' Stone' (1972), 'Masterpiece' (1973), and a string of lower Top 40-ranked hits in 1973–5 – but by the middle of the Seventies the group had left Whitfield and were turning more to a mixture of ballads and thumping, discotheque-aimed funk. In 1975, Harris left and was replaced by Glenn Leonard; Edwards departed two

years later and was replaced by Louis Price. That same year, the group left Motown for a generally unsuccessful and unproductive spell with Atlantic, but by 1980 they were back with their former label and reunited with Edwards. In 1982, Ruffin and Kendricks rejoined for the album *Reunion*. *Back to Basics* followed, and a single, 'Treat Her Like a Lady', gave the Temptations their first Top 20 hit in the UK for over ten years in 1984. *See also* **Eddie Kendricks**; **David Ruffin**; **Motown**

TEN YEARS AFTER Hard-rock band Ten Years After was formed in late 1966 by Alvin Lee (guitar, vocals, born Graham Barnes in Nottingham on 19 December 1944), Chick Churchill (organ, 2 January 1946), Leo Lyons (bass, 30 November 1943), Ric Lee (drums, 20 October 1945). Brought up in Nottingham on his father's extensive blues collection, Alvin Lee established a successful local trio, the Jaybirds, with Leo Lyons, journeying to Hamburg directly after the **Beatles**, where they established the direction that ultimately surfaced as Ten Years After. Working in London in a West End production they met Ric Lee, a music scholar, and subsequently Chick Churchill, also well versed in musical styles. As Ten Years After they first gained attention at London's Marquee Club, soon signing a contract with Decca's Deram label, who released an eponymous debut album in 1967 without the benefit of the then obligatory establishing hit single. American promoter **Bill Graham** booked them into his Fillmore Auditoriums on the basis of this recording and they soon became a major concert attraction in the United States. In 1968 they gained major English and European attention, but it was their fast and furious rendition of 'Going Home' in the *Woodstock* film that established them as a top world attraction. Many of their subsequent audience, however, viewed this one song as their only style and were unprepared to accept anything else. The group disbanded in 1975.

In early 1974 Lee played a concert at London's Rainbow Theatre, subsequently performing a world tour as Alvin Lee and Co. before retiring once more to his country mansion-cum-studio, where he produced bands that interested him, such as FBI. From 1976 he fronted a number of bands with different names and different line-ups.

10cc Formed in Manchester, in 1972, 10cc's line-up originally comprised Eric Stewart (born 20 January 1945; vocals, guitar), Lol Creme (19 September 1947; vocals, guitar, keyboards), Kevin Godley (7 October 1945; vocals, drums), and **Graham Gouldman** (10 May 1946; vocals, bass). Stewart had been a member of the **Mindbenders** in the Sixties and in 1970 had played with Creme and Godley as Hotlegs, a group who had a surprise UK Top 5 hit with 'Neanderthal Man'. Gouldman had been a successful songwriter, his compositions including hits for the **Yardbirds**, the **Hollies** and **Herman's Hermits**. The group were based at Strawberry Studios, in Stockport, where they recorded a series of self-produced hits in the UK on **Jonathan King**'s label: 'Donna' (Number 2, 1972), 'Rubber Bullets' (Number 1), 'The Dean and I' (Number 10, 1973) and 'The Wall Street Shuffle' (Number 10, 1974), all of which showed total mastery of previous rock styles, performed with a wit and polish that marked a new self-consciousness in British rock.

In 1975, after two equally fine albums, *10cc* (1973) and *Sheet Music* (1974), they left UK for Mercury where they had a transatlantic hit with the ambitious *The Original Soundtrack* and the single from it, 'I'm Not In Love'

(UK Number 1; US Number 2), a fragile ballad that epitomized both their inventive use of the studio as a musical instrument and their craftsmanlike attitude to song construction. Their second Mercury album, *How Dare You* (1976) which was even more ambitious, saw them less sure of themselves. None the less, it and its single, 'Art For Art's Sake', were enormously successful. Godley and Creme left 10cc in 1976 to develop their 'Gizmo' guitar device (which enables orchestral sounds to be simulated electronically) and to launch their own video production company, which was used by the UK advertising industry before attracting record industry clients in the Eighties. They also recorded together, scoring a Number 3 hit in the UK with 'Under Your Thumb' and a Number 7 with 'Wedding Bells', both in 1981.

Stewart and Gouldman meanwhile carried on as 10cc, adding Stuart Tosh (drums) of Pilot to their line-up in 1977 – together with Rick Fenn (guitar) and Tony O'Malley (keyboards) – and recording *Deceptive Bends* (1977) and *Bloody Tourists* (1978) from which the UK chart-topping 'Dreadlock Holiday' was taken. Duncan Mackay (keyboards) joined in 1978. Subsequent albums have included *Look Hear?* (1980) and *Ten Out Of 10* (1982). *See also* **Graham Gouldman**

TENPOLE TUDOR Actor/singer Eddie Tudor-Pole first came to fame in the **Sex Pistols**' film, *The Great Rock-'n'Roll Swindle* in 1979, and also auditioned to join the Pistols as singer when Johnny Rotten departed the band. He formed his own band, Tenpole Tudor, with Bob Kingston (guitar), Munch Universe (guitar), Dick Crippen (bass) and Gary Long (drums) late in 1979, and they released their first single, 'Real Fun', on Korova Records.

The band then signed to Stiff, with whom they released a couple of albums and a string of singles including the two UK hits, the goodtime raucous punkabilly of 'Swords of a Thousand Men' and 'Wünderbar', both in the Top 20 in 1981. But Tenpole, who had been trained at the Royal Academy of Dramatic Art, soon tired of the music business and returned to acting full-time, landing a part in the 1986 film, *Absolute Beginners*.

TERRELL, TAMMI Christened Tammy Montgomery and the daughter of an actress, Tammi Terrell was born in Philadelphia in 1946, and attended the University of Pennsylvania to study medicine, majoring in psychology. She

appeared in many music talent shows and signed with Scepter Records in 1961, subsequently recording on Wand, Try Me and Checker before joining Motown in 1966. Briefly married to boxer Ernie Terrell, Tammi retained her married name and achieved two solo hits before being teamed with **Marvin Gaye** in 1967. Nine Top 50 hits followed over three years, including 'Ain't No Mountain High Enough' and the transatlantic smash 'The Onion Song', before she died on 16 March 1970, following a series of operations on a brain tumour.

TERRY, SONNY, AND McGHEE, BROWNIE The 45-year partnership of Sonny Terry (born on 24 October 1911 in North Carolina) and Brownie McGhee (born 30 November 1915 in Tennessee) had an incalculable influence on blues appreciation: its interplay of harmonica (Terry) and guitar (McGhee) left strong impressions on skiffle and every subsequent phase of blues revivalism.

After recording prolifically for black audiences in the Forties and Fifties, they discovered the white market and a new future which they were temperamentally suited to handle. McGhee's personable and articulate manner, coupled with Terry's virtuosity, clarified the blues for many non-American listeners at concerts and, during the Seventies, on film. Inevitably their repertoire became somewhat settled, but in performance they continued to retain a remarkable and communicative vivacity. Terry died on 12 March 1986.

TEX, JOE Born in Baytown, Texas, on 8 August 1933, Joe Tex became one of the top soul names of the Sixties after ten years of unsuccessful hustling. His early records on King (1955–7) and Ace (1958–60) were an erratic assortment of R&B, derivative rock, and pop novelties. But, influenced by **James Brown**, by the time he recorded for Anna (1960) he was attracting attention with an athletic stage routine. His first memorable records were two sermonizing responses to other people's hits, 'All I Could Do Was Cry' (**Etta James**) and 'I'll Never Break Your Heart' (**Jerry Butler**), and his own 'Baby You're Right' which Brown took into the charts. The following year he cut one single with Brown's band, 'Wicked Woman' (Jalynne), and was then signed by Nashville song publisher, Buddy Killen, who founded Dial records specifically to market Tex and his growing folio of material.

National success eluded them until Atlantic assumed distribution of the label four years later, when 'Hold What You Got' introduced a string of preaching hits ('A Woman Can Change a Man', 'I Want to Do Everything with You', 'A Sweet Woman Like You', 'The Love You Save'), each record a tongue-in-the-cheek slice of homespun philosophy. Acclaimed by Atlantic as the New Boss of the Blues, he began calling himself Soul Brother No. 1 until an onstage duel with James Brown put him firmly in his place. On record, he was alternatively a country singer, soul man, preacher, pop star, or a peculiar mixture of each, so that it was never clear whether Tex took himself or his songs seriously. However, his ingenious and prolific writing talent kept up the run of hits ('The Letter Song', 'Skinny Legs and All', 'Men Are Getting Scarce', 'Buying a Book', 'You're Right Ray Charles') and after a brief 'retirement' to the church at the end of the Sixties he bounced back with 'I Gotcha' (1972), still on Dial, now distributed by Mercury.

Another big hit, the self-deprecating 'Ain't Gonna Bump No More (With No Big Fat Woman)', followed in 1977, but between then and his death in August 1982 he devoted most of his time to the Muslim faith, in which he became a minister.

THEM In 1963, Them were formed as an Irish R&B group by **Van Morrison** (vocals), Jackie McAuley (keyboards), Billy Harrison (guitar), Alan Henderson (bass) and Ronnie Milling (drums). After a frenzied residency at Belfast's Maritime Hotel, Them crossed to London and enjoyed two British hits with Morrison's 'Gloria' and the soul-inflected 'Here Comes the Night' (Decca) produced by **Bert Berns**. The next year – 1966 – 'Gloria', 'Here Comes the Night' and 'Mystic Eyes' all entered the American charts on Parrot, and a tour followed. The group failed to consolidate their success, however, and Morrison returned to Northern Ireland before departing to the US to find major fame as a singer-songwriter in the late Sixties and early Seventies. A series of personnel changes ensued, with singer Ken McDowell and organist Peter Bardens among those passing through. 'Gloria' quickly became a punk-rock standard, while Them's own records remain of interest because of Morrison's adventurous vocals, combining the harshness of black R&B with a budding romanticism, which had its full flowering in his solo career. See also **Van Morrison**

Phil Lynott lines up with Scott Gorham (right) in one of Thin Lizzy's most explosive formations; the band suffered rapid changes of personnel

THIN LIZZY A hard guitar rock band led by the indefatigable bassist/vocalist Phil Lynott (born in Dublin on 20 August 1951), Thin Lizzy reached a peak during the late Seventies. Lynott's posturing cultivation of an image as a hip street urchin made a perfect focal point for the group; added to the prowess of the various guitarists that came and went, his personality made the group a major live attraction throughout the world.

Thin Lizzy was originally formed in Dublin in 1970, where Lynott was joined by Brian Downey (drums) and Eric Bell (guitar), and it was as Ireland's top band that they moved to London in 1971. They released a couple of albums but had to wait until 1973 before their first single, an up-tempo rock re-working of an Irish folk song, 'Whisky in the Jar', became a surprise hit. However, the song was so untypical of the band's other, more progressive, material that they failed to follow it up. Disillusioned, Bell left at the end of 1973.

Lynott and Downey continued with a succession of guitarists until 1974, when Scotsman Brian Robertson and Californian Scott Gorham were recruited, and the classic, hard-rocking Thin Lizzy line-up came into being. The duo developed a searing guitar harmony style as shown to best effect on the two outstanding albums, *Jailbreak* and *Johnny the Fox*, both released in 1976 and both major sellers. Apart from *Live and Dangerous* (1978), subsequent LPs failed to match up, though it was during the late Seventies that the band enjoyed its most consistent run of singles chart success. This was probably due to the instability of the line-up as Robertson left, rejoined and left again, and several guitarists (including Gary Moore, Snowy White and Midge Ure, later of **Ultravox**) passed through the ranks.

After a long period of only moderate success, the band split up in 1983, playing a triumphant farewell gig at the Reading Festival. Lynott continued as a solo artist, but became less and less active and died tragically on 4 January 1986 from a drug-related illness. Gary Moore has enjoyed considerable success as a solo artist since the group's break-up.

THOMAS, CARLA The daughter of disc jockey/singer/dance-craze originator **Rufus Thomas**, Carla Thomas was born in Memphis, Tennessee, in 1942. She gave the Stax studios their first hit with her own teen-dream ballad 'Gee Whiz (Look at His Eyes)', which was issued nationally on Atlantic in 1961. Noticeably more mature on her response to **Sam Cooke**, 'I'll Bring It On Home to You' (1962), and other successful releases on Atlantic, she reverted to Stax for duets with her father and solo hits, 'Let Me Be Good to You' and **Isaac Hayes'** composition 'B-A-B-Y' (1966). Dubbed the 'Memphis Queen', in 1967 she was teamed with 'King' **Otis Redding** for an album and hit singles 'Tramp' and 'Knock on Wood'. Later recordings with **Johnnie Taylor** and **William Bell** were not so popular, and her recording career effectively ended in 1975 with the demise of Stax. *See also* **Stax Records**

THOMAS, IRMA An outstanding singer, Irma Thomas – born in Panchatla, Louisiana, in 1941 – has a glowing reputation but little success to show for it. After local hits on New Orleans labels Bandy, Ron ('Don't Mess With My Man' – 1960), and Minit ('It's Raining' – 1962, 'Ruler of My Heart' – 1963, the model for **Otis Redding**'s 'Pain in My Heart'), she recorded her most famous performances for Imperial: 'Wish Someone Would Care', 'Anyone Who Knows What Love Is'/'Time Is on My Side' (1964), 'He's My Guy' (1965) and 'Take a Look' (1966). Although she had one more hit, 'Good to Me' (Chess) in 1968, equally fine records on Canyon, Roker, Cotillion, and Fungus were ignored.

THOMAS, RUFUS Best known for his series of dance-craze records in the Sixties and early Seventies, Rufus Thomas began his entertainment career as a comic with the Rabbit Foot Minstrels in 1935. Born in Carey, Mississippi, on 26 March 1917, he spent World War II in a Memphis textile factory by day and entertaining in the evenings, becoming a disc jockey on radio station WDIA. He began recording in 1949 with jump blues on Star Talent, appearing on Chess in 1951 and scoring an R&B hit on Sun in 1953 with 'Bear Cat'. Still with WDIA, he recorded a duet with daughter Carla, in 1959, for Satellite (soon to be Stax) and subsequently recorded a substantial number of solo hits on Stax with novelty dance songs like 'Walking the Dog' (1963), 'Funky Chicken' (1970), and 'Do the Funky Penguin' (1971).

THOMPSON, RICHARD AND LINDA The quiet genius in **Fairport Convention**, Richard Thompson (born 3 April 1949), an accomplished writer and influential guitarist, left the band after their fifth album *Full House* (1970). Following session work with **Sandy Denny**, **Ian Matthews** and other folk/rock musicians, he resurfaced with *Henry the Human Fly* (Island, 1972). That album was sadly neglected, and it was only when he teamed up with Linda Peters, whom he was later to marry, that Thompson's career took off. Through two albums – *I Want to See the Bright Lights Tonight* (1974) and *Hokey Pokey* (1975) – his genuine love for English traditional and American country music gave the term 'folk-rock' new meaning.

The recognition given to songs like 'The New St George', 'Calvary Cross', 'The End of the Rainbow' and 'When I Get to the Border' and their dramatic stage performances enabled the Thompsons to make the difficult transition from folk clubs to large concert halls. Having converted to Sufism in 1974, they started a Sufi community after the release of *Pour Down Like Silver* (1975) but made a recording comeback three years later with *First Light* (Chrysalis). *Sunnyvista* followed in 1979 and a solo album by Richard – *Strict Tempo!*, an instrumental set released on his own label, Elixir – in 1981. He and Linda toured on the strength of *Shoot Out the Lights* (Hannibal, 1982) but they separated soon after. Another solo set by Richard, *Hand of Kindness*, appeared in 1983, and was followed by *Small Town Romance* (Hannibal, 1984), *Across a Crowded Room* (Polydor, 1985) and *Daring Adventure* (Polydor, 1986). Linda Thompson made a solo album, *One Clear Moment*, for Warner Brothers in 1985.

THOMPSON TWINS Starting life as a ramshackle multi-rhythmic outfit in 1977, the Thompson Twins found international success after slimming down from a seven-piece to a three-piece in 1982 and developing a highly commercial pop formula. They also became a prime target for the detractors of 'chart-fodder'.

The original group (the name was taken from the brothers in the TinTin cartoon strip) became a great live favourite, building a reputation as a left-wing, politicized band who played some great punk/funk dance music. Record sales, however, did not reflect their live popularity and a string of singles and two albums were largely ignored until 'In the Name of Love' was released in January 1982. The single did little in the UK but it stormed to the top of the US dance charts. This success encouraged Tom Bailey (vocals, keyboards), Alannah Currie (vocals, sax, keyboards) and Joe Leeway to leave the rest of the band (amid accusations of a sell-out) and channel their efforts in the direction of dance pop.

'Love on Your Side' became their first of many UK hit singles and was quickly followed by the LP *Quick Step and Side Kick* (1983), which became a big seller worldwide. The next LP, *Into the Gap* (1984), established them as a top international act and it was followed late in 1985 by *Here's To Future Days*. Leeway left in 1986.

THORNTON, WILLIE MAE Born in Montgomery, Alabama, on 11 December 1926, Willie Mae ('Big Mama') Thornton recorded for Peacock between 1951 and 1957. Her version of the **Leiber and Stoller** composition 'Hound Dog' topped the R&B charts in 1953, selling the then phenomenal figure of 500,000 copies in the process. This classic song, featuring a guttural vocal and a tough guitar solo from Pete Lewis of the **Johnny Otis** band, was revived by **Elvis Presley** in 1956. Big Mama also recorded for Baytone and Sotoplay, and toured Europe with the 1965 Blues Festival, when she cut some of her finest sides for Arhoolie. She died in Los Angeles on 25 July 1984.

THOROGOOD, GEORGE One time semi-pro baseball player George Thorogood specialized in hard-driving slide-guitar blues in the Chicago style. Not seriously involved in music until 1970, singer/guitarist Thorogood recruited Ron Smith (guitar), Billy Blough (bass) and Jeff Simon (drums) to form his permanent band, the Destroyers, in Delaware in 1973.

They built up a strong reputation on the West Coast where they opened for a variety of big names and signed to the folk-based label Rounder, releasing the LP *George Thorogood and the Destroyers* in 1977. *Move It On Over* was released in 1978 and the title track gave Rounder a big US hit. In 1979 MCA released *Better Than the Rest*, an early demo tape that Thorogood had signed away. He publicly disowned it but the album still sold well.

Bad to the Bone (1982) marked a move to a new label, EMI America, followed by a long gap in releases, although regular live work continued in earnest, including an appearance on the US leg of Live Aid in 1985.

Originally a gritty soul group, the Three Degrees were groomed to be the queens of the international cabaret circuit, all glamour and gowns

THREE DEGREES Best known for their association with the Philadelphia International label during the early Seventies, the Three Degrees originally comprised Linda Turner, Shirley Potter and Fayette Pickney, all native Philadelphians. They teamed up with manager **Richard Barrett** for the first time in 1964; signed to Swan, their first hit was '(Gee Baby) I'm Sorry' in 1965. Barrett then took the girls to Boston, concentrated on their stage act, and the group graduated to posh niteries and supper-clubs. Fayette Pickney, Sheila Ferguson and Valerie Thompson recorded with Warner Brothers, Metromedia and Neptune before 'Maybe' was a Top 30 hit with Roulette in 1970. Signing with **Gamble and Huff**'s Philadelphia International in 1972, the trio finally broke through in a major way ('Dirty Old Man', 'Year of Decision', 1973; 'When Will I See You Again', 1974; 'Take Good Care of Yourself', 1975) though it was the European rather than the American audience who most warmed to their posturing, sequin-flashing cabaret-soul.

Leaving Philadelphia International in 1975 for Ariola, they continued their British success with 'Givin' Up, Givin' In' (1978), 'Woman in Love', 'The Runner' and 'My Simple Heart' (1979); none were US Top 40 entries.

THREE DOG NIGHT The beefy vocal harmonies and solid (if unimaginatively heavy) instrumentation of Three Dog Night were heard on a total of twelve gold albums and even more gold singles between 1969 and 1974. Although criticized for not writing their own songs, they displayed an unerring talent for finding great songs by little-known composers (among the authors of their hits have been **Randy Newman**, **Leo Sayer**, **Laura Nyro** and **Hoyt Axton**) and their instinct for raw material (a perfect example being B. W. Stevenson's plain, folkish 'Shambala' which they transformed into a fully produced pop smash) seldom failed.

The group was formed by veterans of the Los Angeles studio scene, primarily vocalists Danny Hutton (born 10 September 1946), who had auditioned for the **Monkees** and almost hit on his own with 'Roses and Rainbows', and Cory Wells (born 5 February 1944), whose band the Enemys were regulars at the Whiskey a Go-Go, with the addition of singer Chuck Negron from New York, and instrumentalists Joe Shermie (bass), Jim Greenspoon (keyboards), Mike Allsup (guitar) and Floyd Sneed (drums), from various local bands including Dyke and the Blazers and the East Side Kids. Their first big hit was 'One' (Dunhill), written by the then unknown **Harry Nilsson** in early 1969, followed by 'Easy to Be Hard', Nyro's 'Eli's Coming' (1969), 'Celebrate', Newman's 'Mama Told Me Not to Come' (1970), 'Out in the Country', Axton's 'Joy to the World', Russ Ballard's 'Liar', Paul Williams' 'An Old Fashioned Love Song', Axton's 'Never Been to Spain', Paul Williams' 'Family of Man', 'Black and White', 'Pieces of April', 'Shambala', Leo Sayer's 'The Show

Must Go On' and **Allen Toussaint**'s 'Brickyard Blues'.

Hutton left the band in 1976 for a career in rock management and his place was taken by Jay Gruska; new members Al Ciner, Ron Stocker and Denny Belfield also joined from **Rufus**, but the band enjoyed no further hits.

THROBBING GRISTLE While the **Sex Pistols** may have reaped all the national newspaper headlines at the time of the punk explosion, it was Throbbing Gristle who caused the most controversy inside the rock industry. They formed in 1975, arising out of the shock-tactic performance-art group COUM Transmissions, which featured artist/writer Genesis P. Orridge (vocals, bass) and one-time strip artist Cosey Fanny Tutti (electronics). Joined by artist/designer Peter 'Sleazy' Christopherson (electronics (of the album design company Hypgnosis) and musician Chris Carter (electronics), they caused immediate outrage with their loud, violent free electronic noise and 'ironic' games with the themes of sexual violence and totalitarianism. 'Music from the Death Factory' was an early slogan, 'Industrial Records' the influential name of their own label. Among their claimed mentors were American murderer Charles Manson and novelist William Burroughs, and at least one performance, accompanied by underground films, ended in a riot.

Their first album, *Throbbing Gristle* (1977), was an unlistenable stew of formless noise. The follow-up, *DOA* (1978), displayed a considerable progression but also gave hints of a stylistic split that was to widen: Orridge and Christopherson concentrating on more darker noise and imagery, Tutti and Carter essaying more melodic and disco-oriented material. While a number of live and out-take albums continue to appear on independent labels, the soundtrack *Heathen Earth* and the lighter *Twenty Disco Greats* complete their 'official' studio work. Throbbing Gristle split in 1982, Orridge and Christopherson forming Psychic TV (the latter then leaving to form the duo, Coil), Carter and Tutti marrying each other and recording electronic pop and dance albums as Chris and Cosey.

THUNDERCLAP NEWMAN Multi-instrumentalist Andy Newman (born in 1943), guitarist Jimmy McCulloch (born in 1953) and composer/drummer Speedy Keen (born on March 29, 1945, in Ealing, London) had an international hit in the summer of 1969 under the name of Thunderclap Newman, with the Pete Townshend-produced 'Something in the Air' (Track). The band's connections with the **Who** began when Newman and Townshend met at art school, and Keen later wrote 'Armenia City in the Sky' for the Who's album *The Who Sell Out*. The group's *Hollywood Dream* album (1969) very effectively combined the surreal psychedelia of Keen's lyrics and the precision of McCulloch's guitar work with Newman's distinctive piano solos. However, re-creating the sound in a live situation was a problem and not even the addition of Jim Pitman-Avory (bass) and Jack McCulloch (drums) could solve it. A couple of singles followed, notably the fine 'Accidents' (1970), but both were unsuccessful and the band split up. Newman and Keen both released solo albums – *Rainbow* and *Previous Convictions* respectively – while Jimmy McCulloch moved on to Stone the Crows (see **Maggie Bell**) and, later, **Paul McCartney**'s Wings.

TILLOTSON, JOHNNY Teen

star Johnny Tillotson was born in Jacksonville, Florida, on 20 April 1939. Originally a country singer, the baby-faced singer was discovered at the Nashville Pet Milk talent show and signed to Cadence Records. Between 1958 and 1966, he was rarely out of the pop charts and had over twenty-five records in the Hot 100. 'Poetry in Motion' (Number 2), 'Without You' (Number 7) and 'It Keeps Right On A-Hurtin'' (Number 3) were the most successful. Some of his hits had a stupendous beat, but he was clear-voiced with no rough edges, and parents liked him. He left Cadence for MGM in 1963, and again reached the Top 10 with 'Talk Back Trembling Lips'. Similarly melancholic country songs still keep him busy.

TOASTING The art of part-talking,

part-singing over the (essentially) bass and drum dub sides of reggae records – usually instrumental B-sides subjected to extensive treatment with esoteric recording studio techniques – toasting has its origins both in the jive-talking radio DJs on black American radio stations picked up by Jamaican listeners in the late 1940s and the travelling Jamaican sound systems of the 1950s. From simple exhortations to 'get up, dance and enjoy yourselves', toasting developed first into full blown verbal flights over the dub sides of records played at sound-system dances, then became a recording form where the toast was an integral part of the session.

Reggae folklore has it that the first sound-system DJ to toast over records was Count Machouki, a top Fifties DJ on the Coxsone Dodd Downbeat system. What is more certain is that the first full blown recording toasters were U Roy and **Big Youth**, both of whom started as travelling sound-system DJs before going on to become recording artists. With contemporary toasters like **Eek A Mouse**, Yellowman and (the British-based) **Smiley Culture** and Tippa Irie, the distinction between reggae singing and reggae toasting has become increasingly blurred.

TOKENS Various musicians includ-

ing **Neil Sedaka**, **Carole King** and **Neil Diamond** played and recorded with Jay Siegel (born 20 October 1939) and Hank Medress (19 November 1938) before Phil (1 April 1942) and Mitch Margo (25 May 1947) joined to make up the Tokens proper. Their first record 'Tonight I Fell in Love', which they produced, made the US Top 20. After a dispute with their record company, Warwick, they moved on to RCA and had further hits with 'When I Go to Sleep', 'Sincerely' and their American Number 1 'The Lion Sleeps Tonight'. While their material made them the first folk-rock group, their early harmonies and arrangements were influenced by the style of the **Skyliners** and **Dion and the Belmonts**. After leaving RCA they recorded with little success on B. T. Puppy, Warner Brothers, Buddah and Atco. Hank Medress began working with Dave Appell, producing **Tony Orlando**; the other members of the Tokens recorded as Cross Country.

TOMORROW An early product of

Britain's underground scene of the late Sixties, Tomorrow comprised Twink (drums), Steve Howe (guitar), Keith West (vocals) and John Wood (bass). West and Wood had once been members of the In Crowd, who had a minor UK hit in 1965 with a version of 'That's How Strong My Love Is'. Tomorrow built their reputation in the underground clubs on their 1967 single 'My White Bicycle', a song about Dutch provos, which was produced by Pete Townshend. Halfway through their album, producer Mark Wirtz involved West in 'An Excerpt from a Teenage Opera'; originally to be a Keith Tomorrow release, it came out as by Keith West. Ironically, its success marked the beginning of the end for the group. A second single, 'Revolution', and the album followed, though plans to mount the 'opera' onstage never materialized. Tomorrow folded in

1968, Twink joining the **Pretty Things** and the Fairies and Steve Howe, whose guitar pyrotechnics shone in Tomorrow, eventually found fame with **Yes** in February 1970. Keith West re-emerged in 1975 with 'Moonrider'.

TOOTS AND THE MAYTALS

A vocal group from Kingston, Jamaica, Toots and the Maytals comprise Frederick 'Toots' Hibbert (born in 1946), Jerry Mathias and Nathaniel Gordon. They came together in 1963, but they were formerly known as the Vikings ('Six and Seven Books of Moses') and V. Maytals ('Little Slea'). They recorded copiously for various producers: **Prince Buster** ('He Is Real'), Coxsone Dodd ('Hello Honey'), Dynamic ('If You Act This Way'). With dissonantly harmonic, hymn-like songs they established themselves as ska favourites, winning the Jamaican Song Festival in 1966 with 'Bam Bam'.

The group's subsequent successes included 'Pressure Drop', 'Monkey Man' and '54–46 That's My Number'. By the early Seventies, with Toots as leader and a recording contract with the fashionable Dynamic Studios of Byron Lee, they had notched up two further Festival hits – 'Sweet and Dandy' (1969) and 'Pomps and Pride' (1972). Following an appearance in *The Harder They Come* film and the rock-style promotion of their over-produced set *Funky Kingston* (Island, 1974), they were widely acclaimed by Britain's rock media and elite, gigging at Hyde Park during their 1974 tour. The follow-up album, *In the Dark* (1975), was less enthusiastically received but a definite improvement, and it acted as a prelude for their US and European tours that year, while the title of their next album – *Reggae Got Soul* (1977) – suggested that they were becoming more international in outlook and were absorbing other black styles. The backing musicians included old Jamaican hands like Rico Rodriguez alongside the likes of Dudu Pukwana and **Steve Winwood**.

With the rise of 2-Tone in the UK in 1979–80, Toots' early ska and rock-steady hits achieved new recognition, and following two further studio albums – *Pass the Pipe* (1980) and *Just Like That* (1981) – Island released a live album with a difference, *Toots Live*, which was mastered, pressed and in the shops just 24 hours after being recorded at the Hammersmith Palais on 29 September 1980. In the mid-Eighties, Toots and the Maytals remain as popular as ever, his superb vocal range one of the delights of reggae.

TORNADOS Instrumental group the Tornados – George Bellamy (guitar, born 8 October 1941), Heinz Burt (guitar, 24 July 1942), Alan Caddy (guitar, 2 February 1940), Clem Cattini (drums, 28 August 1939) and Roger Laverne Jackson (keyboards, 11 November 1938) – came together in 1960 to do session work for producer **Joe Meek**. Dubbed the Tornados when they became **Billy Fury**'s backing group, they had an enormous hit in 1962 with a solo record, 'Telstar'. Others followed, virtually indistingushable from the first and, as the group's popularity waned, Heinz left and had an erratic career singing eulogies to **Eddie Cochran**. The others eventually drifted into other branches of the music business. Momentarily the Tornados' up-tempo, organ-dominated instrumentals succeeded in stealing some of the **Shadows'** thunder.

TOSH, PETER One of reggae's most successful figures, Jamaican singer Peter Tosh (born Winston Hubert McIntosh on 19 October 1944) was a member of the Wailers from its inception until, disenchanted with **Bob Marley**'s elevation to group leader, he left in 1974. Tosh subsequently sustained a high media profile despite a patchy and generally very ordinary creative output. His best post-Wailers releases are undoubtedly the mid-Seventies albums *Legalise It* and *Equal Rights* – tough, memorable reggae combining the roots tradition with a strong international appeal – but subsequent outings have been far less successful.

Signed to the Rolling Stones' label in 1978, Tosh produced three generally unconvincing albums – *Bush Doctor*, *Mystic Man*, *Wanted Dread or Alive* – which pretty well destroyed any lingering credibility he had with the reggae audience while simultaneously failing to cross him over into the rock one. The Jagger link-up, together with Tosh's much publicized espousal of cannabis (and consequent beatings by the Jamaican police), continue to keep his name more or less in the limelight. However, it is hard not to conclude that, in being a founder member of the Wailers, he was just an averagely talented musician who had the good fortune to be in the right place at the right time.

TOTO Yet another American band who found fame with a slick brand of easy-listening rock, Toto were originally put together in Los Angeles in 1978 as a session musicians' band, but decided to remain a unit after the phenomenal success of the debut album, *Toto* (1979).

Most of the group had met at Grant High School in southern California in 1972, and gone on to become prolific sessioneers. The stable line-up of Bobby Kimball (vocals), Steve Porcaro (keyboards), Steve Lukather (guitar), David Paich (keyboards), David Hungate (bass) and Jeff Porcaro (drums) recorded the debut album, which was an instant success and yielded a two-million selling single, 'Hold the Line'.

Following albums held to a similar soft-rock pattern but did not outperform the first one until *Toto IV* in 1982, a winner that went on to net seven Grammy Awards including best album and song of the year for 'Rosanna'.

TOURISTS See **Eurythmics**

TOUSSAINT, ALLEN Born in New Orleans on 14 January 1938, Allen Toussaint kept the Crescent City sound prominent on the American pop scene from the late Fifties right through to the late Seventies. The son of a railroad worker, he began his professional musical career as touring pianist with **Shirley and Lee**. In 1955 he was spotted by **Dave Bartholomew**, long-time partner and collaborator with **Fats Domino**, and hired as a studio session player, working with the likes of **Smiley Lewis** and **Lloyd Price**. In 1958, he was given his first recording contract by RCA and cut an instrumental album called *Wild Sounds of New Orleans* featuring Al Tousan, as he was then known. Unaware at that time of the importance of his publishing royalties, he signed away the rights to some of his best-known compositions – among them 'Java', which made New Orleans trumpeter Al Hirt a national star. Another trumpet-player who benefited from Toussaint's writing talents was **Herb Alpert**, who recorded his 'Whipped Cream'. Despite the elusiveness of public stardom, Toussaint was becoming known in professional music circles as a talented writer and session musician. Working behind the scenes, he established his reputation and learned the art of producing discs (for Minit Records) with artists like **Ernie K-Doe**, **Joe Jones**, the Showmen, **Jessie Hill**, Aaron Neville, and **Irma Thomas**. He was also busy producing sessions for **Lee Dorsey**, **Chris Kenner**, the **Meters**, Lou Johnson, **Wilbert Harrison**, **Clarence 'Frogman' Henry**, Betty Harris and Barbara George. It's the songs that Allen has written, though, that are apt to be the most familiar to the casual listener. He's responsible for more R&B classics than

anyone would imagine could flow from the same pen: 'Ride Your Pony', 'Working in the Coalmine', 'Get Out of My Life Woman', 'Holy Cow' (all for Lee Dorsey), 'Mother-In-Law' (Ernie K-Doe) and 'Ruler of My Heart' (Irma Thomas). He also wrote under the *nom de plume* of Naomi Neville – really his mother's name. He recorded for Seville as Al Tousan (1959–63) and for Alon in 1965 as Allen Toussaint.

In 1965, Toussaint teamed up with Marshall Sehorn, a white man from Carolina and a former general manager for Fire and Fury records. Together they launched Sansu Enterprises and later opened Sea-Saint Recording Studios, now the leading studios in New Orleans. Toussaint's second solo album, simply titled *Toussaint*, was cut in 1971 for Tiffany Records and distributed by the New York-based Scepter Records. In 1972, Toussaint signed with Reprise and cut *Life, Love and Faith*, a disappointing album featuring the Meters in support, which contained the popular disco single 'Soul Sister'. His second and best solo album for the company, *Southern Nights* (1975), again failed to sell well though the title track saw Toussaint in a new and more adventurous light, dabbling with contemporary chord structures and studio electronics. Out of the limelight, however, his talent continued to blossom. Seventies productions included 'Lady Marmalade' by **Labelle**, *High Life* by **Frankie Miller**, 'Right Place, Wrong Time' by **Dr John**, plus all the Meters' Reprise albums. Toussaint's songs have been covered by many artists outside New Orleans, and the lengthy list is headed by **Paul McCartney**, **Ringo Starr**, **The Band**, **Little Feat**, **Maria Muldaur**, Frankie Miller, Jess Roden, **Bonnie Raitt**, **Joe Cocker**, **Esther Phillips**, Hues Corporation, Van Dyke Parks, and **Glen Campbell**. In 1978, he recorded a third solo album, *Motion*, for Warner Brothers, and worked on the soundtrack of Louis Malle's film, *Pretty Baby*, which was set in New Orleans.

TOWER OF POWER Founded by Emilio 'Mimi' Castillo, Tower of Power were formerly known as the Motown Soul Band. All white musicians with the exception of lead singer Rick Stevens, the band – originally Greg Adams, Stephen Kupka, Mic Gillette, Willie Fulton, David Garibaldi, Francis Peestia and Brent Byar – specialized in raunchy super-tight dance riffs in a style somewhere between that of the old Stax houseband and **Blood, Sweat and Tears**. Picked up by impresario

Bill Graham, they recorded an album (*East Bay Grease*) for his San Francisco label. In 1971, they joined Warner Brothers, and released the Memphis-recorded *Bump City* (a track from which, 'You're Still a Young Man', was their first US hit). After various personnel changes, Lenny Williams, an experienced West Coast soul singer, joined as vocalist. *Tower of Power* came out next, including the massive ballad hit 'So Very Hard to Go'. *Back to Oakland* followed in 1974. Williams left soon after for a solo career, to be replaced by Hubert Tubbs. They signed with US Columbia in 1976 and continued recording – their *We Came to Play* (1977) was produced, like *Bump City*, by **Steve Cropper** and with a wide range of artists, including **Santana**, **Elton John** and **Elvin Bishop**.

TOYAH Singer/actress Toyah Willcox (born 18 May 1958 in Birmingham, England) shot to fame in 1977 after appearing in Derek Jarman's punk film, *Jubilee*. By the next year she had formed her own band and set off on a musical career that, although frequently interrupted by film and TV work, was nevertheless successful.

With a band that went through various changes of line-up, Toyah developed a grandiose, epic blend of punk and pop with gothic overtones, which at its best was powerfully hypnotic, but at its worst was ultra-disposable.

Signed to the independent label Safari, Toyah released her first single, 'Victims of the Riddle' in 1979 and the mini-album *Sheep Farming in Barnet*, later the same year. These were the first in a string of successful releases including the UK Top 10 singles 'Four from Toyah', 'I Want To Be Free' and 'Thunder in the Mountains'.

Toyah spent half of 1983 and most of 1984 acting, both on stage and screen, but 1985 saw her return to her recording career with her fourteenth single, 'Don't Fall in Love (I Said)'.

At the beginning of 1987, she took over the role of Sally Bowles in the West End revival of *Cabaret*.

TRAFFIC In their long and traumatic history, taking in the years 1967 to 1975, Traffic produced some of Britain's finest rock music and displayed an honesty and integrity that equalled that of their much vaunted West Coast contemporaries. The group was formed after vocalist **Steve Winwood** (born 12 May 1948 in Birmingham) left the **Spencer Davis Group**; joining him were **Dave Mason**, vocals and guitars (10 May 1945); **Jim Capaldi**, vocals and drums (8 February 1944) – all of whom had played together in the Birmingham-based group, Deep Feeling – and Chris Wood, flute and sax (24 June 1944) from Locomotive. To 'get things together', the group took off to the famous Berkshire cottage in Aston Tirrold and only emerged some months later for the release of the wistful 'Paper Sun', their first single, highlighted by Mason's sitar runs, which climbed into the Top 5 in the summer of 1967. 'Hole in My Shoe', based on a dream of Mason's, reached Number 2 in the UK charts later that year, but resulted in cracks appearing in the band's set-up; Mason's more commercial tunes lent themselves to releases as singles – something that seemed to upset the rest – and when the first album, *Mr Fantasy* (Island 1967) was released it was clear that the songs fell into two categories – Mason's and the others.

After 'Here We Go Round the Mulberry Bush' – their last Top 10 single, taken from the film of the same name – Mason split, but returned six months later. In his next brief stay, they got their second album together, *Traffic* (1968), which saw them expanding skilfully on their R&B roots. However, Mason's decision to leave again in October 1968 resulted in the whole band disintegrating six months later. *Last Exit* (1969), a part live, part studio album released the following summer, was quite clearly a rushed job and didn't reflect the band's true potential.

After a brief spell with **Blind Faith**, Winwood started work on a solo album in January 1970, tentatively titled *Mad Shadows*, but it wasn't long before Capaldi and Wood had rejoined him to

Fantasy-men Traffic: from the left, Steve Winwood, Chris Wood, Jim Capaldi and Dave Mason

bring Traffic back into existence once more. The album became *John Barleycorn Must Die* and proved the strength of the Winwood/Capaldi/Wood Triumvirate – fusing R&B, rock, jazz and traditional folk into a style that was uniquely theirs. Playing live as a trio was limiting for Winwood, and later that year ex-**Family**/Blind Faith bassist, Rich Grech, was called in, followed six months later by drummer Jim Gordon, conga-player Reebop Kwaku-Baah and the return of Dave Mason. They played only six gigs with this line-up but the live *Welcome to the Canteen* (1971) is a remarkable testimony of just how good they were. Their next studio album, *The Low Spark of High Heeled Boys*, released while they were touring America in December 1971, featured both Grech and Gordon – yet when they returned to England both had, somewhat mysteriously, left. With Winwood ill with peritonitis for the first part of 1972, the band rested. Capaldi went to Muscle Shoals to make a solo album, *Oh How We Danced*, and established connections with David Hood and Roger Hawkins who were to become the rhythm section of the new Traffic. They played on the critically received *Shoot Out at the Fantasy Factory* (recorded in Jamaica in 1972) and on the following year's tour Traffic was augmented by another Shoalsman, Barry Beckett, on keyboards. This was probably the most impressive version of Traffic onstage and the magnificent *On the Road*, recorded in Germany in 1973, restored everybody's faith in the band – though the Muscle Shoals section left after the tour and returned to the States.

The remaining four went into their annual period of hibernation for the rest of 1973 to emerge again the following year for an English tour. They had a new member in Rosko Gee from Gonzalez – a fluid bassist who featured prominently on *When the Eagle Flies* (1974), an album that saw Winwood almost abandon his guitar totally for piano, organ and synthesizer. With the departure of Reebop during the tour, the band returned to its original state as a four-piece. In 1975 the band finally dissolved as Capaldi's solo career was launched. *See also* **Jim Capaldi**; **Steve Winwood**; **Dave Mason**

TREMELOES As **Brian Poole**'s backing group, the Tremeloes shared in a series of hits between 1963 and 1965 that included the chart-topping 'Do You Love Me'. When Poole tried for a solo career, the three Tremeloes – Rick Westwood (lead guitar, born in 1943),

Alan Blakely (rhythm guitar, 1942) and Dave Munden (drums, 1943) – brought in young, handsome Len 'Chip' Hawkes (born in 1946) as bass guitarist and front man. As Poole's career spiralled from singing to butchery, the 'Trems' notched up seven Top 10 hits between 1967 and 1970, typified by the bright harmonies and optimism of 'Silence Is Golden' (a UK Number 1) and 'Even the Bad Times Are Good' on CBS in 1967. Their popularity waned in the Seventies and Westwood spent two years out of the group, rejoining when a car accident forced Hawkes to quit at the end of 1974. Blakely left in January 1975, leaving Aaron Woolley and Bob Benham alongside the two originals, but the post-Poole line-up has since re-formed for cabaret and revival gigs. See also **Brian Poole**

T. REX The story of T. Rex is essentially that of Marc Bolan, who was born on 30 July 1947, in London, as Mark Feld. A self-styled mod and occasional male model in the early Sixties, he changed his name to Bolan for his first record, 'The Wizard' (Decca, 1965), and briefly joined John's Children under the management of **Simon Napier-Bell**. He then formed Tyrannosaurus Rex with Steve Peregrine Took (percussion, born 28 July 1949, in London) in 1967, which rapidly became an underground cult band. With Took, he recorded three albums, *My People Were Fair and Had Sky in Their Hair But Now They're Content to Wear Stars on Their Brows* (Regal Zonophone, 1968), *Prophets, Seers and Sages, the Angels of the Ages* (1969) and *Unicorn* (1969), all a mixture of flower-power philosophy and

Marc Bolan, founder of glam-rock and precursor of punk

magic. It was during this period that Bolan also had a book of his poetry published.

In 1970, Took left and was replaced by Mickey Finn (congas, born 3 June 1947) with whom Bolan recorded *Beard of Stars* (1970). On that album Bolan began to make the transition to electric guitar, a process that was accelerated when later that year, having shortened the group's name to T. Rex, Bolan had a surprise Number 2 hit with 'Ride a White Swan' (Fly). He immediately added a drummer, Bill Legend (born 8 May 1944 in Essex), and bassist, Steve Currie (born 21 May 1947 in Grimsby), and aimed his next single, 'Hot Love', directly at the emerging teenybopper audience.

A UK Number 1, 'Hot Love' was followed by a string of nine successive Top 10 records, including 'Get It On' (1971) – this record, which featured back-up vocals from Mark Volman and Howard Kaylan (see Flo and Eddie), was Bolan's only substantial American hit when it appeared under the title of 'Bang a Gong' on Reprise in 1972 – 'Telegram Sam', 'Children of the Revolution' (T. Rex, 1972) and '20th Century Boy' (EMI-Marc, 1973) and a stream of albums. Each single consolidated Bolan's temporary pre-eminence in the British world of glam and glitter rock. However, unlike **Bowie**, then mining the same genre, Bolan brought neither perception nor mystery to his work and by the end of 1973, when his teenybopper audience began deserting him for more exciting images like **Slade**, his songs and his act became even more hysterical. He attempted a series of comebacks, including a spell as a TV pop show host, but he was an unfashionable figure by the time of his death in a car, driven by his girlfriend Gloria Jones, that crashed on 16 September 1977. The circumstances of his death ensured him a degree of pop immortality, and there were many bands of the punk and new wave eras who acknowledged T. Rex as formative musical influences. Steve Took died on 27 October 1980.

TROGGS 'They're so far behind, they're in front' was a remark credited to **Graham Nash** about the Troggs and their ingenuously basic brand of mid-Sixties pop. The group came from Andover in Hampshire and originally comprised Reg Presley, vocals (born on 12 June 1943); Chris Britton, guitar (21 June 1945); Pete Staples, bass (3 May 1944) and Ronnie Bond, drums (4 May 1943).

Signed by manager/label owner Larry Page in 1966, they had a worldwide hit with **Chip Taylor**'s 'Wild Thing'. Subsequent hits, which continued until 1968, were written by Presley, with the exception of Taylor's 'I Can't Let Go'. The Troggs' musical limitations were bolstered by good songwriting and production, and a streak of amusing suggestiveness ran through most of their material, including 'I Can't Control Myself', 'Give It to Me' and 'Love Is All Around'. Leaving Page's management and the hit parade behind, the group survived 'the progressive revolution' playing cabaret dates. In the early Seventies, they began to get college bookings and critical notice again; a 'Trogg revival' was rumoured. In 1974 the band (who were joined by present bass-player Tony Murray in 1969, but who have had several lead guitarists) were reunited with Larry Page, but they failed to reappear in the charts, even with their original version of 'Good Vibrations'.

TROWER, ROBIN A guitar hero of the Seventies whose popularity, especially in the US, was matched by a considerable degree of critical acclaim, Robin Trower was born in Catford, London, on 9 March 1945. An original member of the Paramounts, an R&B group from Southend, Essex, he joined **Procol Harum** – whose line-up included another ex-Paramount, organist/singer Gary Brooker – just as they were making their first album in 1967, and stayed with them until 1971. After *Broken Barricades* (1971), the first Procol album to be dominated by guitar rather than organ (most notable on Trower's tribute to **Jimi Hendrix**, 'Song for a Dreamer'), he left. He then formed the short-lived Jude with **Frankie Miller** (vocals), Clive Bunker from **Jethro Tull** (drums), and Jimmy Dewar from Stone the Crows (see **Maggie Bell**) (bass). Dewar joined Trower in the Robin Trower Group, which debuted in 1973 with *Twice Removed from Yesterday* (Chrysalis), along with ex-Quiver drummer Reg Isadore. Bill Lordan from **Sly and the Family Stone** replaced Isadore after *Bridge of Sighs* (1974) and *For Earth Below* (1975). Trower built upon his R&B roots with these and later albums – *Long Misty Days* (1976), *City Dreams* (1977), *Caravan to Midnight* (1978), *Victim of Fury* (1980) – to create an atmospheric modern guitar sound that owed much to Hendrix. In 1981, he collaborated with **Jack Bruce** on *B.L.T.* (Chrysalis); another co-effort, *Truce*, appeared a year later.

TROY, DORIS Born Doris Payne in New York in 1937, Doris Troy was the daughter of a Baptist preacher, sang in the choir and subsequently with gospel groups, but later turned to jazz with a trio, the Halos. An established songwriter – she wrote **Dee Clark**'s 'How About That' hit – Doris was spotted by **James Brown** while working as an usherette, and after recording in a Jay and Dee duo, signed with Atlantic in 1963 when the staccato, shuffling 'Just One Look' was a Top 10 US hit. Subsequent discs for Atlantic, Capitol and Calla were less successful, and in 1969 Doris settled in England, becoming a prolific session-singer and recording for Apple, People and Polydor.

TUBES Initially making their name through notorious stage shows that were a wacky blend of rock, theatre and high camp, the Tubes found that critical acclaim does not always equate with sales; they later achieved US chart success with consciously commercial, radio-oriented mainstream rock.

Bill Spooner (guitar), Rick Anderson (bass) and Vince Welnick (keyboards) had played together in their home town of Phoenix, Arizona, during the late Sixties, but it wasn't until moving to San Francisco in 1972 that the group was born. They found a perfect frontman with a penchant for theatricality in singer Fee Waybill (real name John Waldo), and with numerous other musicians put together intricate stage shows that were at first ridiculed, but after three years they had developed a following sufficient to justify the first album, *The Tubes* (1975).

Though their shows got wilder and wilder and better attended (although apart from a short peak period, their appeal wasn't especially strong in the UK), five albums on A&M were commercial failures. In 1981, on new label Capitol, they scored an AOR hit with the single 'Don't Want To Wait Anymore' which boosted the sales of the album *The Completion Backward Principle*, and the limited chart success continued as the single 'She's a Beauty' became a US Top 10 record in 1983.

TUCKER, TANYA Born 10 October 1958 in Texas, Tanya Tucker became a major country pop star at the age of fourteen. With a sure-fire combination of a pretty voice, a sexy pubescent image and some of Nashville's finest talents behind her, she had her first country hit in 1972 with 'Delta Dawn', which was also a hit for **Helen Reddy**.

Encouraged by her construction-worker father who took her to country

shows and nurtured her interest in the music, Tucker appeared in the film *Jeremiah Johnson* when she was thirteen and shortly after began recording with producer **Billy Sherrill**, scoring several hits, including the country Number 1s 'What's Your Mama's Name', 'Blood Red and Goin' Down' and 'Would You Lay with Me (in a Field of Stone)', the latter a chart-topper for her when she was sixteen.

After this she moved from Columbia to MCA, abandoning Sherrill and attempting unsuccessfully to break into the rock market (the album *TNT* in 1978 being the best example) before returning to country music. She had a brief spell singing duets with **Glen Campbell** but from 1981 onwards she worked the country circuit alone, and there followed a long gap between releases before the LP *Girls Like Me* appeared in 1986.

TUCKER, TOMMY Pianist/singer Tommy Tucker, born Robert Higgenbotham in Springfield, Ohio, on 5 March 1939, began his career in the jazz field and formed his own band the Dusters, who recorded for Arc and Hudson in 1956. This was short-lived and he later played piano with jazz multi-instrumentalist Roland Kirk. After meeting Titus Turner, Tommy entered the R&B field on Atco in 1961 as Tee Tucker, and in 1963 recorded 'Hi-Heel Sneakers' in simple, down-home style at Herb Abramson's A-1 Studio. It was leased to Checker and became a 1964 Top 20 hit. Several subsequent discs in similar style failed to click, and after reviving 'That's Life' on Festival in 1966, Tommy returned to being a club pianist, though he visited Europe in 1975 as part of a 'Blues Legends' tour. 'Hi-Heel Sneakers' is an R&B standard that has been covered by everyone from the **Rolling Stones** to **Tom Jones**.

TURNER, IKE AND TINA This husband-and-wife team evolved one of the most dramatically successful stage acts in rock in a career embracing most forms of blues and soul. Ike Turner was born in Clarksdale, Mississippi, deep in the Delta cotton belt, on 5 November 1931. A disc-jockeying job at station WROX led to the formation of the Kings of Rhythm, a band of local musicians led by Turner. Their first record was 'Rocket 88' (Chess, 1951), sung by Jackie Brenston, a disc that is often cited as the very first rock'n'roll recording.

Next, Ike became a talent scout in the southern states for Modern Records, fixing sessions by **Bobby Bland**, **B.B.**

King, **Howlin' Wolf** and others. With the arrival of rock'n'roll in 1956, Turner moved north to St Louis, recording and playing in clubs with the Kings of Rhythm. With them he evolved a revue format featuring various singers, while playing piano and guitar himself.

He found the focal point for the act in Anna Mae Bullock, who was born on 26 November 1939 in Brownsville, Tennessee, and moved to Knoxville, where she sang in the choir of her father's church. She was known at first as Little Ann, but her first record, 'A Fool in Love', was credited to Ike and Tina Turner. Released on Sue in 1960, it reached Number 2 in the R&B charts and Number 27 in the pop charts, and it eventually sold a million. That success led to the formation of the Ikettes (of which **P.P. Arnold**, Merry Clayton and Bonnie Bramlett were all members at one time) to back Tina.

Like many black artists, Ike Turner proved himself able to adapt to changing moods in both black and white audiences while still producing worthwhile music on many of the thirty-odd albums he and Tina recorded for Sue, Warner Brothers, Philles, Blue Thumb and United Artists amongst others. Perhaps surprisingly, they have had few major hits. 'It's Gonna Work Out Fine' (Sue, 1961), a fiery blues classic, was the most successful until their Top 10 version of 'Proud Mary' (Liberty, 1971), the funky, futuristic 'Nutbush City Limits' (United Artists, 1973) – a Number 4 hit in the UK – and 'Sweet Rhode Island Red' (1974). In 1966, Ike Turner relinquished production control to **Phil Spector** for the remarkable 'River Deep – Mountain High'. It reached only Number 88 in America but was a Top 3 record in Britain.

By the Seventies, Ike had his own studios, Bolic, and recorded a highly personal solo album, *Blues Roots* (United Artists, 1971), which suggested that the increasingly spectacular and regimented stage act, centred on Tina's flaunting sexuality, might be less than satisfying for him. *See also* **Tina Turner**.

TURNER, JOE The most experienced of all the singers on the R&B charts in the early Fifties, Joe Turner was born in Kansas City on 18 May 1911. He was also a prominent part of the Kansas City jazz scene of the Thirties, often teaming up with boogie pianist Pete Johnson. Coming to New York in 1938, he made his first record, the very popular 'Roll 'Em Pete' (with Johnson on piano) for Vocalion, and

became a major figure in the boogie-woogie revival of 1938–41 (sparked off by his appearance on **John Hammond**'s legendary Spirituals to Swing concert at Carnegie Hall, one of the first instances of authentic black blues and jazz musicians winning a large white audience). By 1951, Atlantic records had signed him to a recording contract and released 'Chains of Love', the first of a string of Turner hits that lasted well into the rock'n'roll era. Of these, probably his most influential was the 1954 recording of 'Shake, Rattle and Roll', a **Jesse Stone** composition – written under the pseudonym of Charles Calhoun – that was to form the basis of **Bill Haley**'s bowdlerized version. Whether Turner was strictly a rock-'n'roll singer is debatable; he never changed his style from the way it was in 1938. But then, he didn't have to. No other artist from the Swing era became anywhere near as vital a force in the R&B music of the Fifties as Joe Turner. He died on 24 November 1985.

TURNER, SAMMY Born Samuel Black in Paterson, New Jersey, on 2 June 1932, Sammy Turner's sinuous, smoky tenor was one of the most underrated voices in pop. All his records shared an inimitable, highly stylized approach, while the accompaniment – a blend of violins, cellos and King Curtis' stuttering sax – produced some diverting and unusual sounds. Masterminded by **Leiber and Stoller**, 'Lavender Blue' reached Number 3 in the US in 1959, and three other discs – 'Always', 'Symphony' and 'Paradise' (all on Big Top) – entered the charts during that year. The highly regarded 'Raincoat in the River' missed out, however. Turner also recorded, unsuccessfully, for Motown, 20th Century Fox, Verve, and Singers Studio International.

TURNER, TINA Long hailed for her dynamic stage performances, top rock vocalist Tina Turner has enjoyed a career with two distinct phases. Born Anna Mae Bullock in Brownsville, Tennessee, on 26 November 1939, Tina met Ike Turner in St Louis and married him in 1958. During the period 1960–75, they made their name through recording and touring, and by the late Sixties the Ike and Tina Turner Revue was an extremely professional, exciting and well choreographed show (*see* **Ike and Tina Turner**).

In 1975, Tina played the Acid Queen in the film version of *Tommy*, and also during that year she split from Ike; in 1976 the couple divorced. She then

toured virtually non-stop for eight years playing small clubs to pay off debts incurred during her marriage. In 1981, she appeared on dates as support act to **Rod Stewart** and the **Rolling Stones** and was invited to take part in a British Electric Foundation project masterminded by Martyn Ware and Greg Walsh of **Heaven 17**. She signed with Capitol in 1982 and had a Number 5 UK hit with a revival of **Al Green**'s 'Let's Stay Together', produced by Ware and Walsh.

That hit began the second phase of Tina's career, her subsequent hits including the chart-topper 'What's Love Got To Do With It?' (1984, written by Graham Lyle of **Gallagher and Lyle** with her producer, Terry Britten), 'Private Dancer' (from the album of the same name), and 'We Don't Need Another Hero' (1985), from the film *Mad Max Beyond the Thunderdome*, in which she also starred. She appeared in the US Live Aid concert (*see* **Band Aid**) and sang a memorable duet with Mick Jagger. Despite a very heavy touring schedule later that year in the US, Australia and Japan, she completed her autobiography, *I, Tina*. Her second album, *Break Every Rule* (1986), featured the work of several top producers – including Terry Britten, Bryan Adams and **Dire Straits'** Mark Knopfler – and was a US Number 3 and a UK Number 2. In 1987 she embarked on a sell-out world tour.

TURTLES Records by the Turtles consistently echoed the old California surf sound while taking in contemporary influences – big-band arrangements, vast well-organized productions in the post-**Spector** style – and in the US between 1966 and 1968 they had a string of Top 40 hits ('Happy Together' and 'She'd Rather Be With Me' among them). They were labelled folk-rock artists because of their 1965 pop treatment of the **Dylan** song, 'It Ain't Me Babe' (on White Whale), but what eventually came to distinguish the Turtles was their character as performers. Although the emphasis in their act was on comedy, they became heavily involved in the flower-power scene and never quite survived it. Leaving the group in 1969, arch-lunatics Howard Kaylan (born 22 June 1945) and Mark Volman (born 19 April 1944) joined **Frank Zappa**'s Mothers of Invention but soon left to form their own act, Phlorescent Leech (Flo) and Eddie. Lead guitarist Al Nichol (born 31 March 1945) and drummer John Barbata started doing session work. *See also* **Flo and Eddie**

TWITTY, CONWAY Born in backwoods Mississippi at Friars Point on 1 September 1933, Conway Twitty developed through country and rockabilly into an extremely successful rock ballad singer in the late Fifties. 'It's Only Make Believe' was one of the turning points in white rock'n'roll, highlighting the move of Southern artists away from rockabilly.

Twitty took his professional name in 1957 from towns in Arkansas and Texas that he passed through while touring under his real name, Harold Jenkins. His group, the Rockhousers, was first formed in Helena, Arkansas, in 1947 as the Phillips County Ramblers and was then strictly down-home country. In 1956, they worked in Memphis as the Rockhousers and demo tapes were made for Sun. In 1957, Mercury released rock'n'roll singles that had been based on Conway Twitty's **Elvis** ability to sound like **Presley**. 'I Need Your Lovin'' was a minor hit.

His first real contribution to rock-'n'roll came after he signed with MGM in 1958 and 'It's Only Make Believe' was rivalled for success by 'Mona Lisa' and several other ballad hits. An intense, deep, throbbing vocal style that was more or less his own was the keynote to sucess. Top media exposure and several 'college' and 'teen' movies followed. By 1963, after a brief association with ABC-Paramount, Twitty was in decline as a pop singer. He joined Decca and made a successful return to his roots – and to the music he had always wanted to sing – as a country singer. By the Seventies he had established himself as one of Nashville's foremost artists, singing (often with **Loretta Lynn**) hard-bitten songs of love and marriage in a pleading and mournful manner.

2-TONE The independent label that put the ska revival onto vinyl and established the **Specials**, **Madness** and the **Beat**, 2-Tone originated in Coventry as the brainchild of Jerry Dammers, leader of the Specials.

When the Specials' efforts to secure a recording contract failed, the band pooled their resources to record the song 'Gangsters', but their funds could only stretch to cover the cost of one side. To overcome this, Dammers brought in Neol Davies, a local Coventry musician, to contribute the B-side which was attributed to the **Selecter**, a group that didn't actually exist at the time. Dammers, determined to release 'Gangsters' on the Specials own 2-Tone label, managed to set up an independent distribution deal with Rough Trade in early 1979. His group started to generate more interest, especially on the London circuit, and as 'Gangsters' began to threaten the charts, major record companies clamoured round with offers, and in the end a deal, guaranteeing complete artistic and commercial freedom, was signed with Chrysalis.

'Gangsters' became a Top 10 hit, 2-Tone became commercially viable and it was decided to scout round for other bands to sign to the label. The first such band was Madness, who had sent them a rough demo tape, and their first single, 'The Prince', was released to become the second 2-Tone hit out of two. By this time 2-Tone was already a buzzword, synonymous with an irresistible dance beat, good-natured youthful vigour and, above all, multi-racial fun. The music press was enthusiastic in its approval.

Neol Davis had finally assembled a group to perform as the Selecter, and they released 'On My Radio' – another hit for 2-Tone. The three bands set off on a forty-date 2-Tone tour in the autumn, by which time the ska revival was in full flight. The bands went from strength to strength, and both Madness and the Specials released albums in October (although by this time Madness had signed to Stiff). The tour was a fantastic success and a triumph of energy and visual excitement.

Madness having departed, 2-Tone signed the Beat, who, with their version of 'Tears of a Clown', provided the label with a sixth consecutive Top 10 single early in 1980. Then the Specials' own live EP 'Too Much Too Young' gave them their first Number 1 while they were away on tour. Soon another 2-Tone package tour was ready to go on the road, this time with the Selecter, the Beat and the Bodysnatchers (their latest signing), while at the same time the Specials were exhausting themselves on tour in America. The hits kept on coming, but the enthusiasm and the urgency was beginning to flag as the size of their success began to take its toll.

The Beat struck up a deal with Arista to form their own Go-Feet label, and eventually the Selecter signed to Chrysalis in the conviction that 2-Tone was no longer able to fulfil its original objective, that of providing a label for musicians run by musicians. The Specials continued with the label regardless, scoring several more hit singles culminating in 'Ghost Town', their last record before splitting up. With the Specials no longer in existence, 2-Tone activities continued on a much reduced scale so that when the compilation LP *This Are 2-Tone* was released in November 1983, it was seen largely as an epitaph to the label. Even though 2-Tone carried on signing undiscovered talent, none of these signings had any conspicuous chart success. In fact, it wasn't until the new incarnation of the Special AKA that 2-Tone had another UK hit with 'Nelson Mandela' in the Top 10 in March 1984. After the Special AKA split in 1985, 2-Tone product continued to be absent from the charts. However Dammers could look back on what the label had achieved with justifiable pride – for a brief period it flourished, and there was no doubt that the music it promoted would not be easily forgotten.

TYGERS OF PAN TANG British hard rockers Tygers of Pan Tang were formed in Whitley Bay, Newcastle upon Tyne, at the end of 1978 and they soon ascended to the forefront of the new wave of heavy metal.

Jess Cox (vocals), Rob Weir (guitar), Rocky (bass) and Brian Dick (drums) put out the first single, 'Don't Touch Me There' which aroused much interest. MCA signed them to a major deal and the debut album *Wildcats* was released in 1980. The next one, *Spellbound*, (1981) gained them even more exposure and the band became a big live draw.

Tygers of Pan Tang scored a handful of minor hit singles and recorded two more albums, the last of which was their finest work *The Cage* (1982), and they were on the verge of breaking in the US before calling it a day. A 'Best Of' album appeared in 1984.

TYMES Black vocal group the Tymes came together in 1959, with a line-up comprising George Hilliard, Donald Banks (from Franklin, Virginia), George Williams, Albert Berry and Norman Burnett (from Philadelphia). 'So Much in Love', their US Number 1 hit on Parkway in 1963, heralded the sweet soul boom of the Seventies. They followed it with other hits in the same style, including 'Wonderful Wonderful', 'Somewhere' (both Top 20) and 'To Each His Own'. After less successful records for Winchester (a label they owned with Leon Huff) and MGM, the Tymes returned to the charts on Columbia with 'People' in 1968. Billy Jackson's productions of 'You Little Trustmaker' and 'Ms Grace' (a UK Number 1) kept the same personnel – now minus Hilliard – in the soul and pop charts until the late Seventies.

U

U2 Arguably a perfect stadium rock band, U2 almost single-handedly engineered the return of the guitar sound. Bono Vox's all-encompassing electric stage presence and the Edge's searing guitar breaks have helped U2 to become Ireland's most successful rock band ever, growing from a cult post-punk guitar band to one of the biggest live draws in the world.

First coming together while still at school in Dublin, Bono (real name Paul Hewson), the Edge (David Evans), Larry Mullen (drums) and Adam Clayton (bass), started rehearsing in Mullen's kitchen in 1977. By the following year they had become the darlings of the Dublin scene and in 1979 they recorded a one-off EP, *U23*, for CBS Eire. In December, it had reached the Top 10 and won five categories in a domestic music paper's readers' poll, after which U2 came to England for the first time, wielding their guitars amid a tide of electro-pop. Despite poor attendances at small club and pub gigs,

Island Records were sufficiently impressed to sign them up. Their first single, '11 O'Clock Tick Tock', was released in May 1980.

The LP *Boy* was recorded during the summer with producer Steve Lilly-white, who helped them construct the 'loud, glorious and aggressive' sound they were after. This album occupied the middle ground between contemporary pop and tough rock and was warmly praised by reviewers, serving to showcase U2's distinctive noise. Bono's voice had an inspiring depth and resonance, the Edge's guitar work was the most original for years and Clayton and Mullen held the whole thing stylishly together with military precision. Audiences started to mushroom as U2's reputation as an uplifting live band grew, but record sales remained only moderate.

They finally broke into the British charts in July 1981 with the single 'Fire' reaching Number 35, and, exposed to a wider audience, they went from strength to strength. The LP *October* was released three months later and made Number 11; in January '83 'New Years Day' became their first British Top 10 hit and in March *War* was released, entering the UK LP chart at Number 1. Ironically, the least accomp-

lished musically of their albums to date, it broke U2 in America and by the summer the band were a worldwide musical force.

This promotion to the first division of world bands was not without its problems, however, and critics had not been kind to the album, highlighting the unadventurousness of their sound. U2's Christian beliefs were treated with a great deal of cynicism by journalists, and at a time when their popularity with audiences was growing daily, the critical response was at its most negative. However, the success of *War* gave the band some breathing space, and after the vital live mini LP *Under a Blood Red Sky* kept the fans happy at the end of '83, *The Unforgettable Fire* restored their credibility with the critics in 1984 – and in 1985 *Rolling Stone* lauded U2 as the 'Band of the Eighties'.

That year the group took part in Live Aid (see **Band Aid**), Bono turning in a star performance for a global audience of millions, and, like many of the acts performing that day, they found their record sales leapt virtually overnight. U2 remain a tremendously important band, playing to huge audiences in stadiums all over the world and epitomizing the musical heights that guitar rock can achieve in the right hands. Early in 1987, they released the LP *The Joshua Tree*.

UB40 Of all the bands to have come out of the UK Midlands post-punk, 2-Tone era, UB40 are the only one to have stayed the course and remained true to their original aims. Immensely popular all over the world, they have gained an international stage for their politicized, lightweight reggae, all the while operating outside the constraints of the British record industry and running their own label.

UB40 came together for the first time in 1977 when three students at Moseley Art College in Birmingham, Brian Travers (sax), Jim Brown (drums) and Earl Falconer (bass) decided that being unable to play a musical instrument should not be a barrier to forming a band. They selected instruments, virtually at random, and were joined by friends Robin and Ali Campbell (who chose lead and rhythm guitar respectively), Jimmy Lynn (keyboards), Norman Hassan and 'Yomi' Babyemi (both percussion). They all taught themselves to play, their early efforts as an ensemble helped no end by the musical background of the Campbell brothers, sons of British folk singer Iain Campbell.

Once described as the 'last of the rock idealists', U2 performed with power, passion and subtlety: from the left, Adam Clayton, Bono Vox and the Edge

The name (taken from the form number of a British social security card) was chosen and they started playing cover versions of reggae classics on the Birmingham pub circuit. At this time 'Yomi' was repatriated to Nigeria and Lynn was replaced by Mickey Virtue, but the group acquired a strong following and a focal point in toaster/dancer/trumpeter Astro (Terence Wilson). UB40 held out on the major labels and signed to Graduate, a small label based in Dudley, a local town.

In 1979 they were asked to guest on the **Pretenders**' first UK tour, and helped by this exposure, in addition to the growing popularity of ska, UB40's first single, the gently skanking 'King'/'Food for Thought' climbed the charts to Number 4 in March 1980. They scored another two Top 10 singles that year, and their debut album *Signing Off* reached Number 2 in September and stayed on the chart for 71 weeks. In 1981 they formed their own label, DEP International, and continued to produce hits until the start of 1982 when the public began to tire of Anglicized reggae and ska. Three singles in a row barely made the Top 30 and an album, *UB44* couldn't repeat the sales of its predecessors.

With the LP *Labour of Love* in 1983, however, they made a pronounced comeback. Consisting entirely of covers of early Seventies reggae songs, it scored a huge UK Number 1 and international hit with the single 'Red Red Wine', and three other UK Top 20 hits. The LP sold well worldwide and established UB40 as the top reggae band in the world. *Geffrey Morgan* came out in 1984 and received mixed

Ali Campbell of reggae politicos UB40

reviews. An ambitious album, it showed UB40 essaying widescreen production in their own newly-constructed studio, but didn't quite hit the mark.

But in 1985 UB40 again found it in them to score another UK Number 1, this time renewing their partnership with Chrissie Hynde of the Pretenders. Ali Campbell duetted with her on a memorable reggae version of Sonny and Cher's 'I Got You Babe', and on their sell-out tour, Hynde regularly joined them on stage for an encore.

UFO British hard rock band UFO were formed in 1971 by singer Phil Mogg, the one member who has remained through the various line-ups. At first going completely unnoticed in the UK, they initially found success in France, Germany and Japan before making inroads into the American market.

After releasing two albums, *UFO* (1971) and *Flying* (1972), on Decca, the group was joined by German guitarist **Michael Schenker** and they changed label to Chrysalis. The following three albums, all produced by ex-**Ten Years After** bassist Leo Lyons, sold well in America despite a poor critical response. By 1979, UFO had a sizeable heavy metal following across the world and a growing one in the UK, the albums *Lights Out* (1977) and *Strangers in the Night* (1978, a live double) becoming particular favourites with heavy metal fans. But in 1979 Michael Schenker left to form his own band, and while UFO continued to tour and record, their fortunes went into decline to the point that in 1983 they took a lengthy rest.

With yet another new line-up featuring agile Japanese/American guitarist Atomik Tommy M and founder-member Mogg, UFO were re-launched in 1985 with the album *Misdemeanour*.

UK SUBS Formed in 1977 around the nucleus of vocalist Charlie Harper and guitarist Nicky Garrett, the UK Subs were one of the second generation of British punk bands who – alongside such stalwarts as the **Angelic Upstarts** and the Anti-Nowhere League – were characterized by a raw live sound full of speed, volume and nihilistic aggression. In the winter of 1978 their first single, 'CID', came out on City Records, to be followed by a deal with Gem Records and a Top 30 hit in the spring of 1979 with 'Stranglehold'. In September 1979 the UK Subs consolidated their fortunes with the release of their first album, *Another Kind of Blues*, featuring Harper's crazed ravings over

manic guitar and drums.

From the brooding atmospherics of *Brand New Age* (1980), through the more widely experimental *Diminished Responsibility* (1981) and *Endangered Species* (1982) to the even more ambitious *Flood of Lies* (1983), the UK Subs widened their abilities and effectiveness without losing the powerful emotional and political thrust that had always been at the heart of their music. Nor did they lose their sense of oneness with the fans, their claim being that 'anybody could be a UK Sub' – that they were all in this together.

The desire to perform in the small venues that made possible this close relationship with their fans was at odds with the band's large-venue potential, and this conflict was to lead to the end of the Harper–Garrett partnership: Harper insisted that the band continue to play the small clubs and pubs alongside the larger venues they could now fill, while Garrett was afraid that the UK Subs would become too mainstream and lose a section of their following. In the ensuing split Garrett departed, leaving Harper to strike out on his own and attempt to rebuild the group. Although the band name continued, through one form or another, playing the small venue circuit into the late Eighties, there was no evidence to suggest that they had anything worthwhile left to contribute.

ULLMAN, TRACEY Actress/singer Tracey Ullman (born 30 December 1959) made her name on the BBC-TV comedy series *A Kick Up the Eighties* and *Three of a Kind*, a factor that helped her score UK Top 10 hits with three throwaway pop singles in 1983. She had previously performed in *The Rocky Horror Show*, *Elvis* and *Grease* on the London Stage.

A chance encounter in a hairdressing salon with Rosemary Robinson, wife of Stiff supremo Dave, led to her being signed to that label and scoring an immediate hit with the single 'Breakaway', reaching Number 4. This was followed by a cover of **Kirsty MacColl**'s superb 'They Don't Know', which made Number 2, and then Doris Day's 'Move Over Darling' (Number 8). 1984 brought further, lesser hits with versions of **Madness**' 'My Girl' (recorded as 'My Guy') and John D. Loudermilk's 'Sunglasses'. The album *You Broke My Heart in Seventeen Places* was re-eased in 1984, but Ullman then put her singing career on hold as she got married, had a baby and set about conquering Hollywood as an actress.

ULTRAVOX Ultravox first made their mark as the forerunners of synth/electro towards the late Seventies, but with a major change of line-up in1980, they went on to become a prominent voice in British mainstream pop.

Ultravox! (the exclamation mark was dropped for the third album) came together in London in 1974 under the leadership of John Foxx (born Dennis Leigh, vocals), with Warren Cann (drums), Chris Cross (bass), Billy Currie (keyboards/violin) and Stevie Shears (guitar) completing the line-up. Their early shows were an amalgam of their art-rock influences – **David Bowie**, Warhol, **Roxy Music**, etc. – contrasting heavily with the punk thrash prevalent at the time. They signed a deal with Island in 1977 and went on to release three albums culminating in the superb *Systems of Romance* (1978), a highly sophisticated fusion of guitars and synthesizers. As well as its innovative use of electronics, it featured the flamboyant guitar work of Robin Simon (Shears had left at the beginning of 1978) and came to be regarded as a major influence on the electro sound that dominated pop in the early Eighties. The album sold poorly, Island dropped the band and Foxx and Simon left, Foxx to pursue a moderately successful solo career.

Midge Ure (real name James Ure, vocals, guitar, synthesizer), former teenybop star with Slik, was recruited to Ultravox in 1979. An unlikely replacement for Foxx, Ure had acquired a reputation as a journeyman after stints with the Rich Kids and **Thin Lizzy**, but the move turned out better than anyone could have imagined. Ure brought a commercial pop elegance to the streamlined electronic style of Currie, Cross and Cann, and the product of this marriage was the triumphant LP *Vienna* (1980), a sweeping wave of exotic synth-pop, that did not crack the charts until the release of the single of the same name – a magnificently moody electronic hymn – made Number 2 in January 1981 and stayed there for a month. Sales of the album then picked up, and it remained in the charts for 71 weeks.

Having found a winning formula, Ultravox were reluctant to abandon it and successive albums, like *Rage in Eden* (1981) and *Quartet* (1982), have been little more than shallow stylistic re-runs of *Vienna*. Nevertheless, they managed to come up with at least one decent pop single on each album, and built up a sizeable international following.

Ultravox in the Eighties, with Midge Ure (all in white) providing the vocals in place of John Foxx: Ure helped give the band pop appeal

Band members' activities outside Ultravox began in 1980 when Ure and Currie joined Steve Strange in **Visage**. Then, in 1982, Ure released a solo single, a cover of the **Walker Brothers**' 'No Regrets', which made the UK Top 10; his extra-mural work then went into neutral until 1984/5 when he teamed up with Bob Geldof on the **Band Aid** project. In 1985 he also recorded a solo album, *The Gift*, scoring a surprise UK Number 1 with the single 'If I Was'.

UNDERTONES Northern Ireland punk favourites the Undertones wowed audiences with their breathless barrage of pop tunes and enthusiastic energy. Through four excellent albums they developed from a tuneful, basic garage band to a highly sophisticated but unpretentious pop outfit.

Formed in 1975, **Feargal Sharkey** (vocals), John O'Neill (guitar), Damien O'Neill (guitar) and Billy Doherty (drums) rehearsed and played local gigs for over two years before recording the *Teenage Kicks* EP in 1978. BBC Radio DJ **John Peel** played the record continually, winning the band legions of admirers, and as a result, the major label Sire signed them up.

They released their second single, 'Get Over You', in 1979, and soon after produced their debut album, *The Undertones* – releases that established their distinctive style of driving pop guided by Sharkey's intense, quavering voice. Although they were loved by the critics and all their concerts were well attended, the Undertones never achieved more than moderate record sales, achieving only one UK Top 10 single ('My Perfect Cousin') and one UK Top 10 album, *Hypnotised* (1980). Due to internal dissent they unexpectedly split in 1983 soon after releasing yet another fine LP, *The Sin of Pride*. The O'Neill brothers went on to form That Petrol Emotion, while Sharkey became a successful solo singer, scoring a surprise Number 1 with 'A Good Heart' in 1985.

UNION GAP Comprising Gary Puckett, vocals (born 1942), Dwight Bement, tenor sax (1944), Kerry Chater, bass (1944), Paul Wheatbread, drums (1945) and Gary Withem, piano (1944), the Union Gap were originally the Outcasts, a popular San Diego group noted for their ability to duplicate other people's songs. 'Woman Woman' brought their first success in 1967, but 'Young Girl' reached Number 1 on both sides of the Atlantic in 1968 (making a return visit in 1974). They made six albums (plus a greatest hits volume) all produced by **Jerry Fuller** and built on their familiar formula with Puckett's voice as the core of their sound. They disbanded in 1971, Puckett working with brother David on an album and studying acting. None of Puckett's solo recordings . . . including a version of **Paul Simon**'s 'Keep the Customer Satisfied' (1971) . . . were hits.

UNITED STATES OF AMERICA

A collection of experimental musicians from California, the United States Of America comprised Joseph Byrd, electronic music, keyboards; Dorothy Moskovitz, vocals; Gordon Marron, electric violin, ring modulator; Rand Forbes, bass; and Craig Woodson, electric drums, percussion. They cut their only album, *United States Of America*, for Columbia in 1968, a pioneering effort rarely surpassed in harmonizing electronics and rock. It was also an intelligent satire on contemporary rock, with an air of decadence. 'The American Metaphysical Circus' parodied *Sergeant Pepper* and 'Garden of Earthly Delights', with Dorothy Moskovitz sounding like Grace Slick, suggested the **Jefferson Airplane**'s 'White Rabbit'. Byrd later indulged in self-parody with the Field Hippies, on a 1969 album *The American Metaphysical Circus* (Columbia).

URE, MIDGE *See* Ultravox

URIAH HEEP

Occupying the middle ground between heavy metal bands like **Deep Purple**, progressive groups like **Emerson, Lake and Palmer**, and pomp-rockers such as **Queen**, Uriah Heep inspired a large and loyal following in the Seventies without either critical acclaim or any chart successes of any significance. The band was formed in 1970 when guitarist Mick Box (born in London on 8 June 1947) and singer David Byron (born in Epping, Essex, on 29 January 1947) were matched with keyboard player Ken Hensley (24 August 1945) and bassist Paul Newton by producer Gerry Bron. The line-up performed as Spice before adopting the new name and adding drummer Alex Napier, who was replaced by Keith Baker after the release of their first album, *Very 'eavy, Very 'umble*, on Vertigo in 1970. That title indicated their musical aims, and it was significant that it was in Germany and then the US (as the latest in a succession of heavy rock bands) that they were first successful. *Demons and Wizards* (Bronze, 1972) and *Magician's Birthday* (1972) both went gold in America, by which time Iain Clarke had replaced Baker and New Zealander Gary Thain (ex-Keef Hartley) had replaced Newton. The latter album also marked the beginning of a gradual acceptance in Britain that grew further after *Wonderworld* (1974), but the following year saw the departure of Thain – he died of a drugs overdose shortly after – and his replacement by John

Guitarist Mick Box was a founder-member of Uriah Heep and proved the mainstay of the band in the Eighties when Heep made a notable comeback

Wetton, formerly of **Family**.

Byron, who had already cut two solo albums, was sacked in 1976 and Wetton quit soon after: their replacements were John Lawton and former **David Bowie** bassist Trevor Bolder, who stayed with the band until Mick Box took the drastic step of dissolving it in 1981 in favour of a completely new line-up. With John Sinclair – formerly of the Heavy Metal Kids – on keyboards, vocalist Pete Goalby from Trapeze, Bob Daisley from **Rainbow**, and Lee Kerslake from **Ozzy Osbourne**'s band, he cut the fifteenth Uriah Heep album, *Abominog* (1982). This found Heep playing in a more fashionable 'adult oriented rock' vein and enjoying some of their biggest sales for years. Daisley left in 1983 after the completion of *Head First*, to be replaced by a returning Trevor Bolder. David Byron died on 28 February 1985.

USHER, GARY

It was as a songwriter in partnership with disc jockey Roger Christian from Los Angeles Radio KFWB that Gary Usher first made his mark. They churned out a string of surfing and hot rod hits, such as 'Hot Rod High', 'You're Gonna Ride With Me' and most of the Hondells' hits on Mercury. **Mike Curb** produced them and Usher did the arrangements before

cutting his producing teeth with the Surfaris. Usher also wrote songs with Brian Wilson, such as 'In My Room' and others recorded by the Hondells and the Surfaris. Later he became a house producer with Columbia and his credits include **Chad and Jeremy**'s *Of Cabbages and Kings* and *The Ark*, **Gene Clark**'s eponymous album, the Millennium, the Peanut Butter Conspiracy and the **Byrds** on their classic albums *Younger Than Yesterday* and *The Notorious Byrd Brothers* in which his sympathetic role was crucial. He also produced the Byrds' *Sweetheart of the Rodeo*. With help in the arrangements and vocals from Curt Boetcher, and support from **Terry Melcher** and Bruce Johnston, he was the brains behind Sagittarius, a highly polished harmony and studio group, noted for their orchestrations. Columbia released *Present Tense* by Sagittarius, and from it took the 1967 hit 'My World Fell Down'. Their second album, *Blue Marble*, was released on Usher's own Together Records, which he established in March 1969, with Curt Boetcher and Keith Olsen, as an 'artist-oriented label'. Certainly it released an impressive array of material in its brief history, including the Byrds' *Preflyte*, *The Hillmen*, *Early L.A.* and other archive material.

V

VALENS, RITCHIE Born Richard
Valenzuela of Mexican-Indian lineage
in Los Angeles, on 13 May 1941,
Ritchie Valens took up the guitar as a
child and had written songs and
formed his own group, the Silhouettes,
while still at Pacoima High School. In
the spring of 1958, Valens signed a
recording contract with Bob Keene's
Del-Fi label in L.A., and after considerable coaching recorded the quasi-Latin
rocker, 'Come On Let's Go' which
reached Number 42 in America in
October 1958, and was covered in
Britain by **Tommy Steele**. Valens consolidated his success in December that
year when both sides of his follow-up,
'Donna'/'La Bamba', reached the US
Top 10. Valens subsequently appeared
on the Perry Como TV show, toured
Hawaii and featured on package shows.
He also filmed a cameo spot in *Go
Johnny Go*. After an appearance at the
Surf Ballroom in Clear Lake, Iowa,
Valens and co-stars **Buddy Holly** and
the **Big Bopper** were killed while
travelling to their next gig in a private
plane on 3 February 1959. Valens was
the prototype chicano rocker and forerunner in the style of **Chris Montez**,
Chan Romero, Eddie Quinteros, Sunny
and the Sunglows and Cannibal and
the Headhunters.

VALENTINOS Formerly a gospel
group called the Womack Brothers, the
Valentinos recorded for **Sam Cooke**'s
Sar Records. In 1962, they sold half a
million copies of 'Lookin' for a Love',
written by Cooke's manager, J. W. Alexander, together with Zelda Samuels.
Lead singer and session guitarist **Bobby
Womack** subsequently made a vastly
superior recording in Muscle Shoals,
Alabama, in 1974. Born in Cleveland,
Ohio, he often contrived to sound like
his mentor Cooke in vocal style and
texture, especially on limpidly austere
ballads like 'Somewhere There's a
Girl'. The Valentinos – the other members were Curtis, Cecil, Friendly and
Harris Womack – recorded Cooke's
composition 'Tired of Livin' in the
Country', a fall-apart blues ballad, but
are best remembered for 'It's All Over
Now', a raunchy up-tempo item they
wrote themselves. It was covered by the
Rolling Stones in 1964, who took the
song to Number 1 in the UK chart. *See
also* **Bobby Womack**

VAN DYKE, LEROY Country
singer Leroy Van Dyke (born on 24
October 1929, in Spring Forks, Mississippi) began singing and playing guitar
in the US Army. On his discharge he
became a livestock auctioneer, and in
1956 had the idea of writing a novelty
song around the auctioneers' cry. The
result, his recording of 'The Auctioneer', was leased to Dot later that year
and became his first national hit. It was
covered in Britain by Don Lang of *Six-
Five Special* fame. Surprisingly,
however, the track did not sell well in
the US country market. Further chart
success eluded Van Dyke until 'Walk
On By' became a Number 1 in the
country chart and a Top 5 hit nationally
on the Mercury label. Another song of
illicit love, 'If a Woman Answers', gave
him his last pop hit in 1962. Although
he switched labels at regular intervals –
to Warner Brothers in 1966, to Kapp in
1969, to Decca in 1970 – further
national success was not forthcoming.

VAN HALEN One of the most
sucessful of the heavy rock bands playing the US stadium circuit in the late
Seventies and early Eighties, Van
Halen provided a near perfect parody
of the heavy metal genre on stage with
singer Dave Lee Roth's wild stage
antics and the over-the-top guitar work
of Eddie Van Halen. The Van Halen
brothers, Eddie and Alex, took up the
guitar and drums respectively in their
home country of Holland before
emigrating to California in 1968 where,
in the mid-Seventies, they teamed up
with Lee Roth. Michael Anthony
joined them on bass and after exhaus-
tive gigging on the local circuit, they
were noticed in 1977 by record
supremo Ted Templeman, who signed
them to Warner Brothers and then went
on to produce their records.

In 1978, the band recorded their
debut album *Van Halen*, which
featured the extraordinarily dextrous
guitar work of Eddie Van Halen that
characterized their sound. A series of
further albums followed, achieving
only moderate success, while it was as
a live phenomenon that the group were
at their best. Regular world-wide tours
guaranteed a loyal following, but it was
not until 1984 that they broke into the
singles chart when they scored a surprise transatlantic Number 1 hit with
'Jump', followed by two further Top 20
hits later in the year – 'I'll Wait' and
'Panama'. Eddie's guitar pyrotechnics
were highly regarded by public and
musicians alike, sufficiently so for him
to guest on **Michael Jackson**'s monster
hit album, *Thriller*.

At the end of 1985 internal dissent
between Lee Roth and the rest of the
band became too much of a strain and
he left to pursue acting ambitions and
embark on a solo career. In 1986 a new
Van Halen, featuring the vocal talents
of long established US heavy metal
singer Sammy Hagar, released *5150*
which became their most successful
album to date and spawned the US hit
single, 'Why Can't This Be Love?'.

VANDROSS, LUTHER One of
the most versatile soul stars of the
Eighties, Luther Vandross made his
mark as a session-singer, songwriter,
producer and solo star. Born in New
York into a musical family (an elder
sister sang with doo-wop group the
Crests), Vandross received his first
break in 1972 when one of his compositions, 'Everybody Rejoice (a Brand New
Day)', was used in the Broadway show
The Wiz. Two years later guitarist Carlos Alomar – an old school friend –
introduced him to **David Bowie**, and
Vandross ended up arranging vocals
and singing background on Bowie's
Young Americans album, including
his own song 'Fascination'. Through
Bowie he met **Bette Midler** and her
producer **Arif Mardin**, who began to
call on him for frequent session work
with **Carly Simon**, **Chaka Khan** and the
Average White Band, among others.

On the strength of his sessioneer's
reputation, Vandross formed his own
group Luther, which did moderately
well in the R&B market but later fell
apart, the other members then going on
to form Kleer and **Chic**. Vandross carried on in the commercial sphere as a
jingles singer (7-UP and Kentucky
Fried Chicken both made use of his
services) until 1981 when Epic
released his first solo album *Never Too
Much*. A great success – it went on to
sell a million copies – the record
brought him to a wider audience and
proved him a solo star. His next album
Forever, For Always, For Love confirmed his position: appearing in
December 1982, it remained in the
charts for a year, gaining platinum
status.

At the same time Vandross was busy
in his role as producer and arranger,
producing hugely successful albums
for two of his long-time idols, **Dionne
Warwick** (*How Many Times Can We
Say Goodbye*) and **Aretha Franklin**
(*Jump To It, Get It Right*). He also sang
backing vocals and arranged three
numbers for **Diana Ross**'s *Silk*. Alongside this he found time to work on his
third album, *Busy Body*: released in
January 1984, it was an immense hit

like its predecessors, selling over a million copies. In that year he embarked on major tours of the USA and Europe, establishing his reputation as one of the most exciting names on the pop/soul circuit.

The Night I Fell in Love was released in March 1985 and marked a contrast to the lush orchestrations of his previous albums, featuring instead a tougher, sparser sound, setting off Vandross's brilliant vocal arrangements across an expert rhythm section. A singer of great technical ability, Vandross has made a speciality out of his highly-mannered vocal delivery which is distinguished by operatic-like trills and embellishments, to the extent that it has earned him the title of the 'Pavarotti of pop'.

VANGELIS Born in Greece some time in 1944 and given the unpronounceable name Vangelis O. Papathanoussiou, this versatile composer/keyboard player first emerged at the beginning of the Seventies with the band Aphrodite's Child, which also featured Demis Roussos. Having moved to France, Vangelis dropped his middle initial and surname and became a leading light of the electronic keyboard rock scene, producing some twenty albums in various styles from British pomp rock to cod contemporary-classical. In the mid-Seventies he was asked to join **Yes** but refused, instead striking up a working relationship with singer Jon Anderson that saw the two producing albums and singles in a more song-oriented form. Responsible for the theme to the film *Chariots of Fire*, Vangelis continues in the keyboard-rock mould but success has seen him moving closer to the musical mainstream. In a different vein, he achieved success during 1985 with his original score for the Royal Ballet's *Frankenstein*, choreographed by Wayne Eagling.

VANILLA FUDGE Contemporaries of the **Rascals** and Vagrants in Long Island and New Jersey in the mid-Sixties, Vanilla Fudge began life as the Pigeons, playing a brand of organ-based white funk. By 1967, they became Vanilla Fudge – Mark Stein, piano, organ (born 1947); Vince Martell, guitar (born 11 November 1945); Tim Bogert, bass (born 1944); Carmine Appice, drums (born December 1946). They added semi-gospel harmonies and a familiar pop/soul repertoire which they immediately disguised. 'You Keep Me Hanging On' was a minor hit in Britain in 1967 and a year later in America. They wallowed in

pretentiousness through tedious, over-ambitious albums before disbanding in 1970. Bogert and Appice formed Cactus, then teamed up with **Jeff Beck**, while Stein formed the little known and short-lived Boomerang.

VEE, BOBBY Singer Bobby Vee was both the luckiest and prettiest of a generation of American 'college boy' soloists who jockeyed for precedence in 1959 and then fell back against the opposition of the beat groups in 1963. He was born Robert Thomas Velline in Fargo, North Dakota, on 30 April 1943, and his first claim to fame was that he and his brother were members of the group (the Shadows) who deputized for air-crash victim **Buddy Holly** at a gig in Mason City, Iowa, in 1959. Producer **'Snuff' Garrett** heard their disc, 'Suzie Baby', and took the group to Liberty Records, where Vee was groomed for a solo career.

Supervised by Garrett, it flourished. After four American releases, 'Rubber Ball' took off on both sides of the Atlantic in 1960 and, for the next three years, Vee extolled the pain and pleasure of chaste romance in a series of slick, bouncy hits that included 'Take Good Care of My Baby', 'Run to Him', 'Sharing You', 'A Forever Kind of Love', 'The Night Has a Thousand Eyes' and 'Bobby Tomorrow'. His popularity in Britain was immense and he seemed to be forever either touring with the **Crickets** or making guest appearances in British films and TV shows.

After the bubble burst, he continued to record – scoring a million-seller in 1967 with 'Come Back When You Grow Up' – but was fighting a losing battle and bowed out in 1969, a wealthy family man. He returned in 1972 and, under his real name, recorded an LP, *Nothin' Like a Sunny Day*, that included a dull new arrangement of 'Take Good Care of My Baby'. Response was slight, and little further was heard from Vee until he signed to United Artists in 1978 for an unproductive spell.

VEE JAY RECORDS Vivian Carter, from Tunica, Mississippi, and Jimmy Bracken, from Kansas City, Missouri (actually man and wife), owned Vivian's Record Shop in Chicago when they launched a record company (named after their initials) in 1953. Their first two acts, **Jimmy Reed** and the Spaniards, literally walked in off the street and asked to record. The Brackens remodelled a garage into a studio where they rehearsed local artists before sessions at Chicago's

Universal Recording Studio. Initially distributed by Chance Records, who soon folded, Vee Jay found their feet when the Spaniels' 'Goodnight Sweetheart Goodnight' hit in spring 1954, providing finance to establish the label, and **Ewart Abner** and Vivian's brother Calvin joined the A&R staff.

In 1957, the Falcon subsidiary was formed, later re-named Abner, scoring hits with the **Impressions** and **Dee Clark**, while Vee Jay secured a stream of hits over the years with Jimmy Reed, El Dorados and the **Dells** among others. These were Chicago artists, but a fair proportion of the label's output comprised masters leased from small companies all over the country, while there was also a substantial catalogue of gospel material. Randy Wood (see Dot Records) became a director in 1960, joined by Bill Shepherd. Bill brought in **Gene Chandler**, whose 'Duke of Earl' was a 1962 million-seller and further success followed – the **Four Seasons'** 'Sherry', plus two follow-ups, each sold a million in 1962–3. Then the **Beatles** broke in 1964 with their first half-dozen hits on Vee Jay and its new Tollie subsidiary. But for every hit there were twenty flops, and the company hit financial trouble. They moved to Hollywood and back to Chicago before suspending operations in May 1966. Vivian Carter became a Chicago radio personality, but James Bracken died in 1974.

VELVET UNDERGROUND Although they had no great commercial success and little more than a cult following in the late Sixties, the Velvet Underground had a major influence on Seventies and Eighties rock, especially in the UK. The group consisted originally of **Lou Reed**, vocals (born 2 March 1944, New York); **John Cale**, viola, bass, keyboards (born 5 December 1940); Sterling Morrison, guitar, and Maureen Tucker, bass. Reed came from Long Island, had dropped out of college to write songs and hustle music deals. Cale came from Wales, studied contemporary music in London, and reached America on a Leonard Bernstein fellowship. Reed and Cale met in New York in 1964 and began playing in various clubs. They impressed Andy Warhol and his clan, who decided that this was the right group to feature in the Exploding Plastic Inevitable mixed media show which Warhol staged in New York in 1966, and which then toured the States and Canada. **Nico** (Christa Päffgen from Cologne, West Germany), another Warhol protégée who had appeared in

Velvet Underground, the house band of New York pop-artist Andy Warhol

several of his films, was introduced to the Velvets as a *chanteuse*.

Warhol's newsworthiness helped the group to a contract with MGM where their first album utilized a garish Warhol screenprint of a banana on the cover, and incorporated his name into the title: *The Velvet Underground and Nico Produced by Andy Warhol* (1967). However, Warhol did not exercise a record producer's usual control over their sound. This first album was dominated by Reed's fascination with elements of city life normally excluded from pop songs – an up-tempo account of the problems of heroin scoring ('I'm Waiting for the Man'), a haunting anthem of paranoia ('Sunday Morning') and a powerful amoral vignette of sado-masochistic obsessions ('Venus in Furs'). But Reed's interests were tempered by a true pop sensibility, and a sharp eye for authentic *demi-monde* detail. The sound of that first album drew additional power from Nico's deadpan, world-weary enunciation, and Cale's innovatory contributions on viola and bass, adding to rock the repetitive layers of sound that he had created with avant-garde composer LaMonte Young. The album was a powerful, original statement, and, of course, its subject-matter rendered it unplayable on almost every American radio station.

In 1967, Nico left the group to pursue her own career, and the Velvet Underground parted company with Warhol's Factory and its financial support. Cale and Reed no longer totally agreed about musical policy, and out of the tensions surrounding the group in late 1967, they created their second album, *White Light/White Heat*. It lacked the pop elements of their first, and its sound was aggressively harsh. This was not simply a result of Cale's avant-garde preoccupations swamping Reed's songs, for it was Reed who played the radical, screaming feedback guitar solos. Two tracks on the album stood out. 'The Gift' consisted of Cale's dry, Welsh voice reading aloud an elegantly macabre short story by Reed. And next to Cale's voice is set the murky, muddled instrumental sound of the band warming up. It remains a truly bizarre creation. 'Sister Ray' is a 17-minute rambling, deranged narrative about some sailors visiting a drag queen and being interrupted by the police, in which the words are frequently swamped by the maelstrom of music, and Cale plays some frighteningly unorthodox organ solos. Reed later commented he was trying to create the rock'n'roll equivalent of Ornette Coleman. In 1968, Cale quit to pursue his own career; he was replaced by Doug Yule on bass, guitar, and keyboards. Reed had written all the lyrics of the first two albums, and from this point the group became an undisputed vehicle for his vision.

Their third album, *The Velvet Underground* (1969), was again in contrast to its predecessor. Although there was a coherent plot with subtle implications, the sound remained delightfully light and tuneful: pure pop with heavy contents. The theme was a girl's search for significance through nihilism ('Candy Says'), religion ('Jesus'), adultery ('Pale Blue Eyes'), to some sort of moral liberation ('I'm Set Free'), followed by a relapse into schizoid inco-herence ('The Murder Mystery') and ending with a desperately cheerful song of loneliness ('Afterhours') beautifully sung by Mo Tucker, the group's drummer. The final song seemed to point straight back to the opener, making the album a song cycle. But though the album was pop in sound, it was too subtle to grab popular attention, and for Velvets fans who thought the group were committed to depravity, songs about Jesus and liberation sounded like a sell-out. It was only with their final album, *Loaded* (Atlantic, 1970), that the group approached making a popular impact. This was a work of melodic rock, celebrating city kids with warmth and affection, qualities for which the Velvet Underground had not previously been famous. Particularly striking were 'Rock & Roll', an anthem to AM radio, 'Sweet Nuthin'', an account of city kids able to live on nothing at all, which was both a survival guide and a set of existential values, and 'Sweet Jane', the archetypal, resilient city girl. But before *Loaded* was released, Reed abruptly quit in the summer of 1970, just when they appeared to be on the verge of achieving popular recognition. For a time, Doug Yule kept the group going and released another album, *Squeeze* (Polydor, 1970), but without Reed they had really ceased to exist. A live album – poorly recorded at Max's Kansas City in New York – in the Velvet Underground's heyday was released by Atlantic in 1972.

They were probably the most influential New York group of the late Sixties, spawning a series of performers bent on outrageous statement and appearance. Popular recognition of a kind only came to Lou Reed and John Cale in the mid-Seventies, as solo artists, but the debt of **David Bowie**, **Jonathan Richman**, **Patti Smith**, the **Cars**, **Joy Division** and countless others to the Velvets has been widely acknowledged. *See also* **John Cale**; **Lou Reed**; **Nico**.

VENTURES Formed in 1959, the Ventures were Bob Bogle (born 16 June 1937) and Don Wilson (10 February 1937) on guitars and Nokie Edwards (9 May 1939) on bass, with Howie Johnston as the first of many drummers. Their first single, 'Walk Don't Run' was issued in June of that year on Dolton. Its distinctive features were the cleanness of the instrumental sound and liberal doses of the tremolo arm – a technique the **Shadows** used in their 1960 hit, 'Apache'. 'Walk Don't Run' and its follow-up, 'Perfidia', made the Top 20 in both Britain and America, but as an instrumental group the Ventures had little fire or imagination, depending for their popularity on simple and melodious arrangements of other people's hits. With the advent of the Beatles, the Ventures turned their attention away from America and Britain towards Japan, where they were rewarded by a fistful of golden albums.

VERNON, MIKE A key figure of the mid- to late Sixties British blues scene, Mike Vernon was born in Harrow, Middlesex, on 20 November 1944. He began collecting rock'n'roll records at school, which led to an interest in R&B, blues and jazz. In February 1964, he teamed up with fellow R&B fanatic Neil Slaven to edit and publish the authoritative *R&B Monthly* and later became a production assistant at Decca, working on records by such artists as Kenneth McKellar, Mantovani and Benny Hill. At the same time he launched the privately distributed Purdah record label – later Blue Horizon – issuing the first recordings by **John Mayall** and **Eric Clapton**, and Savoy Brown. Vernon soon had the London R&B scene tied up, producing *John Mayall's Bluesbreakers with Eric Clapton* and *A Hard Road*, featuring **Peter Green**. He also worked on four **Chicken Shack** albums, plus singles and albums by **Ten Years After**, **David Bowie**, Duster Bennett, and **Champion Jack Dupree**. Then came **Fleetwood Mac**'s 'Albatross', a million-seller on Blue Horizon in 1968. Vernon left Decca, in 1969, to concentrate fully on his fledgeling label, now distributed by CBS. Two years later he switched

outlets to Polydor, for whom as an independent producer he scored heavily with two of **Focus**' albums *Moving Waves* and *Focus 3* (both gold), and the singles 'Hocus Pocus' and 'Sylvia' (UK Number 4). At the same time Blue Horizon fostered British talent including Jellybread (featuring Pete Wingfield) and co-ordinated a series of prestigious blues items by **B.B. King**, Lightnin' Slim, **Otis Rush** and others until the label folded in 1972. Vernon came back straightaway with the black soul outfit, **Bloodstone**, with whom he cut eight albums and a million-selling single, 'Natural High'. He then worked exclusively with black acts like **Freddie King**, **Jimmy Witherspoon**, and a new discovery, the Jades.

During the late Seventies and early Eighties he produced five albums by rock revivalists Rocky Sharpe and the Replays, and for five years was the group's bass vocalist. In 1980 he was invited by Polydor to produce **Level 42**'s early records, and both the eponymous first album and the follow-up, *In Pursuit of Accidents* (1982), went gold. He set up his own production outlet, Brand New Records, in 1982. More recently, he has worked with **Chris Farlowe** and the Thunderbirds, has had some success with songwriting, and has set up Vernon Brothers Records. He still runs his own recording studio at Chipping Norton, Oxfordshire.

VERNONS GIRLS A troupe of singers and dancers whose matchless raw enthusiasm perfectly suited the late Fifties, the Vernons Girls were formed in 1957 by the Liverpool-based Vernons Pools, who wanted to encourage an interest in choral singing among their employees. Sixteen of the original seventy turned professional and made their TV debut in *Six-Five Special*, but it was *Oh Boy!* (1958) that fully exploited their athletic and sexual potential. Subsequently no TV pop show was complete without them.

During the sweet music era of 1961, they disbanded and later re-emerged in smaller units. One girl (Lyn Cornell) went solo; three (Maureen Kennedy, Frances Lee and Jean Owen (later known as Samantha Jones) retained the name the Vernons Girls and had some minor hits ('You Know What I Mean', 'Lover Please' and 'Funny All Over') while the Twist raged. A further trio (Vicki Brown, Margo Quantrell and Jean Hawker) became the Breakaways, a much in-demand backing group. Much later, the most popular member

of the original line-up, bespectacled Margaret Stredder, joined Gloria George and Marion Davis as the Ladybirds, whose background harmonies were to British TV's *Top of the Pops* in the Sixties and early Seventies what the original 'Vernons Girls' short shorts were to *Oh Boy!*

VIBRATIONS R&B group the Vibrations came together in 1959 with a line-up featuring Don Bradley (born in St Louis on 7 August 1936), Dave Govan (Los Angeles, 2 August 1940), Carl Fisher (Quardon, Texas, 27 December 1939), Ricky Owens (St Louis, 24 April 1939) and James Johnson (Brooklyn, New York, 13 September 1939). In 1956, Johnson, Fisher, Govan and Carver Bunkum had hit the Top 30 as the Jayhawks with the original version of 'Stranded in the Jungle'. Owens, who replaced Bunkum, came from the Sixteens. In 1961, the group had two hits: 'The Watusi' on Checker under their own name and 'Peanut Butter' on Arvee as the Marathons. **H.B. Barnum** had persuaded them to cut the latter record, but the Chess brothers sued successfully and 'Peanut Butter' was also released on their Argo label. The Vibrations' later successes included the original version of 'My Girl Sloopy' on Atlantic (Top 30 in 1964) and several hits on Okeh between 1965 and 1968, including 'Misty' and 'Love in Them There Hills'. They also recorded for Bet, Epic, Amy, Neptune and A&M.

VIDEO Historically, rock music and television have never been comfortable bedfellows, and Sixties and Seventies shows like *Top of the Pops*, *Thank Your Lucky Stars* and even the fondly remembered *Ready Steady Go!* rarely gave acts the opportunity to present their music in a visually exciting way. The advent of the promotional video film in the late Seventies provided that opportunity, offering visual and musical entertainment in pre-packaged, three-minute segments of the particular band's (or, more commonly, their management's) own devising. Promotional films in themselves were not new, but video was a cheaper and more adaptable medium than celluloid, being easier to edit (electronically, by means of computer, rather than physically).

Queen's 'promo' for their album *Bohemian Rhapsody* in 1975 is generally regarded as the first true pop video. Certainly it was influential, both in terms of the visual effects used and as a catalyst for commercial and creative exploitation of the new medium, but it was in the post-punk atmosphere that video really came into its own, with young directors like Steve Barron virtually having the field to themselves between 1978 and 1980. Several of the new video directors, like Barron, came from television commercial-making – an activity in which British expertise was commonly agreed to be a world leader. Barron met the **Jam** while filming the Reading Festival in 1978 and directed promos for 'When You're Young' and 'Going Underground'; he launched a video company, Limelight, whose roster of directors included Julien Temple, maker of 1980's *The Great Rock'n'Roll Swindle*, and Don Letts, the one-time reggae DJ who chronicled the punk era on film.

Video promos freed bands from having to perform on television pop programmes in which they had no creative say, but as the use of video grew – and by 1981 it was *de rigueur* for any new band with major label backing to receive the video treatment – so new outlets opened up beyond the previously established TV shows. Most important of these was the American cable channel MTV (Music Tele-Vision), which began round-the-clock rock broadcasts in August 1981. Because of the requirement to fill the screen 24 hours a day, MTV relied heavily from the outset on video promos; as video was a relatively undeveloped promotional technique in the US at that time, the channel gave huge exposure to British-made promos and helped immeasurably to activate the so-called 'British Invasion' of the US charts in 1982–3.

Video-making attracted a number of important film directors in the Eighties, including Lindsay Anderson, Ken Russell and Bob Rafelson, but generally the creative standard was haphazard – occasional flashes of brilliance like the computer graphics on **Dire Straits**' *Money for Nothing* promo or the 'newsprint' effect of **a-ha**'s *Take On Me* simply underlined the paucity of ideas in the average promo. Despite the claims made for video as an art form, essentially the promo video was and remains a high-tech, artfully-conceived selling vehicle, precisely in keeping with the advertising associations of many of its makers.

On the other hand, whether the advent of the promo video had quite the detrimental effect on musical creativity that some of its debunkers claimed – the common argument was that clever visuals simply covered up for poor music – was debatable.

Certainly it ushered in an era when image-making became all-important (**Adam Ant** and **Duran Duran** were masters of the art of self-projection on video), but predictions that sales of rock video-cassettes would threaten those of singles and albums – on the strength of the enormous sales rung up by **Michael Jackson**'s 20-minute 'Thriller' (directed by John Landis) in 1982–3 – were looking wildly inaccurate by the middle of the decade. By 1986, record companies in Britain were beginning to cut back on their expenditure on video and to adopt a much more belligerent attitude towards television use of promos: sensing that promos had become of more use to television companies as programme or filler material than to the record labels as promotional items, the British Phonographic Industry (BPI) began demanding payment from the BBC, ITV and Channel 4, on a similar basis to the payments made by radio stations to the record companies for the privilege of playing records on the air. It was a sign that the record industry now wanted direct financial return from their investment in video and, possibly, that the heyday of video-making as a marketing aid had passed.

VILLAGE PEOPLE
Dressed as a cross-section of gay clichés (a biker, a construction worker, a policeman, an Indian Chief, a GI and a cowboy) over-the-top camp disco group Village People had huge success in the late Seventies, selling a reported 20 million singles and 18 million albums worldwide.

With New York disco producer Jacques Morali at the helm, a number of gay disco tunes were written for actor/singer Victor Willis, and as the songs became highly popular with both gay and straight audiences, David Hodo, Felipe Rose, Randy Jones, Glenn Hughes and Alex Briley were brought in to form the group. Songs like 'Macho Man', 'YMCA', 'In the Navy' and 'Go West' became huge international hits from 1978 to '79.

In 1979, Ray Simpson, brother of Valerie Simpson (of **Ashford and Simpson**) became Willis' replacement, but by 1980, after their involvement in the box-office disaster *Can't Stop the Music*, Village People's popularity was on the wane. In a desperate attempt to regain their status, they released the album *Renaissance* (1981) in a new romantic guise, but became such a laughing stock that they quickly returned to their original look. In 1985 they again attracted some attention with the single 'Sex on the Phone'.

VINCENT, GENE
Born Vincent Eugene Craddock of a poor family in Norfolk, Virginia, on 11 February 1935, Gene Vincent left school at sixteen and joined the Merchant Navy as a boiler-tender, fully intending to pursue a lifelong career on the seas. In 1955, while riding motorcycle despatch on the naval base in Norfolk, Vincent suffered severe injuries to his left leg in a crash and was permanently disabled. During several months of convalescence in the naval hospital, Vincent began devoting more time to his favourite recreation – singing. Late in 1955, he began sitting in with a country band affiliated to Norfolk's country music radio station, WCMS, and by 1956 was appearing regularly on the station's *Country Showtime* talent show. At WCMS, Vincent met 'Sheriff' Tex Davis, a local DJ who took Vincent under his wing and had him record some demos (including 'Be-Bop-A-Lula') with a hand-picked band of local musicians. These tapes were submitted to Capitol, in Hollywood, who were urgently seeking an answer to RCA's **Elvis Presley** and signed Vincent as their man.

Vincent and his band of ingenuous but adept country musicians – Cliff Gallup, lead guitar; Jack Neal, bass; Willie Williams, guitar and Dickie Harrell, drums – by now called the Blue Caps, were flown to Nashville to record

Sweet Gene Vincent displaying his famous all-leather stage gear

'Be-Bop-A-Lula' and 'Woman Love' on 4 May 1956. So closely were Capitol treading in RCA's footsteps, they had the single in the shops within two weeks. Promoted as a double A-side, it was 'Be-Bop-A-Lula' which took off and launched one of the most erratic and traumatic careers in the history of rock. The excitement generated on 'Be-Bop-A-Lula' came primarily from Gallup's startling, dipping and swirling guitar runs behind Vincent's distorted soft voice – he had to be recorded in another room to be heard at all, so loud were the Blue Caps playing.

However, through appalling mismanagement and a series of much weaker follow-ups chosen by his elderly Capitol A&R man, Ken Nelson, Vincent's career lost its original impetus. He came back, none the less, in 1957 with a new band – Harrell, Paul Peek, **Tommy 'Bubba' Facenda**, Bobby Lee Jones and Johnny Meeks on lead guitar – and a second million-seller, 'Lotta Lovin''. Despite the hit, Vincent's greasy working-class viciousness was unacceptable to American media geared to middle-class respectability. By 1958, he was a virtual outcast in an American rock scene now dominated by younger boy-next-door types like **Fabian** and **Rick Nelson**.

Vincent came to Britain and entered a new phase in his career as a European idol, renowned for his newly-adopted all-leather stage gear. In his heyday, he was the most extraordinary and unique spectacle on stage and although major hits eluded him he was by far the most popular live draw in the country. By 1964, Beatlemania, combined with his alcoholism, had taken their toll on both his health and his audiences and he returned to America a year later. When he re-emerged in 1969 to tour England, it was hard to equate his portly appearance with that of the erstwhile wild-rocker – and his **Kim Fowley**-produced re-recording of 'Be-Bop-A-Lula' didn't help matters.

Later that year, he appeared at the Toronto Rock Festival but found work hard to come by in America and returned to Britain in 1971 only to be involved in alimony proceedings with his English former wife. He fled to the US and died in Hollywood a fortnight later, on 12 October 1971, after a seizure attributed to a bleeding ulcer.

VINTON, BOBBY A leading teen idol and balladeer of the early Sixties, Bobby Vinton was born in Canonsburg, Pennsylvania, on 16 April 1935. He helped form his high-school big band, which built a substantial following

around Pittsburgh with Vinton playing clarinet and doubling on various instruments. Leaving the US Army in 1961, he went back on the road as a bandleader, releasing two albums for Epic – *Dancing at the Hop* and *Bobby Vinton Plays for His Li'l Darlin's*. His recordings in February 1962 were as a singer, among them 'Roses Are Red', which launched a new career. It was a Number 1 in the US and his only UK hit.

Vinton had further US chart-toppers in 'Blue Velvet', 'There I've Said It Again' (both 1963) and 'Mr Lonely' (1964). He was managed at this time by Allen Klein, later to take charge of the business affairs of the **Rolling Stones** and the **Beatles**. He remained a hit-maker until the mid-Seventies, scoring a total of thirty US Top 40 entries between 1962 and 1975; interestingly, they included revivals of 'Take Good Care of My Baby', 'Halfway to Paradise' and 'Sealed with a Kiss' – songs formerly associated with Vinton's great rivals in the teen-idol stakes, **Bobby Vee**, **Tony Orlando** and **Brian Hyland**.

VIRGIN A highly diversified, multinational recording, publishing, film, video and entertainments company owned by entrepreneurial whizz-kid Richard Branson, Virgin began as a small mail-order record service, and it is the record company that remains the backbone of Branson's organization.

The mail-order service was started in 1969 to help finance *Student*, the national magazine Branson had founded. The service (named 'Virgin' due to his inexperience in the field), the first retail outlet to discount records, flourished and enabled Branson and his partners to start Virgin Records in 1972. Their first signing was the then unknown multi-instrumentalist **Mike Oldfield**, who went on to sell several million copies of the album *Tubular Bells* (1973), a success that put the company on the map.

Sticking to a policy of signing artists at the more esoteric and original end of the rock spectrum, the Virgin label released, in the early years, records by the likes of **Gong**, **Robert Wyatt**, **Tangerine Dream** and many others. At the height of punk they were the only label prepared to stick with the **Sex Pistols**, who proved to be a shrewd investment.

Into the Eighties Virgin began to sign more obviously pop-oriented bands, **Culture Club** being their most conspicuous international success, but with bands like **XTC** and **Cabaret Voltaire**, they proved that the label was still prepared to take risks.

VISAGE A prominent style-setter about the London New Romantic scene, Steve Strange (born Steve Harrington in Wales on 28 May 1959) was the frontman for electro-pop band Visage, a part-time non-performing project that drew together musicians whose main commitments were elsewhere.

Midge Ure (guitar/keyboards) and Billy Currie (violin/keyboards) from **Ultravox**, Rusty Egan (drums), an old friend and colleague of Strange's, Dave Formula (keyboards) and Barry Adamson (bass), ex-**Magazine**, came together in 1979 to record two singles, 'Tar', which attracted notice but not sales, and 'Fade to Grey' which reached Number 8 in the UK in March 1980.

The first album, *Visage* (1981), sold over a million copies, mainly on the strength of the single and its excellent follow-up, 'Mind of a Toy', and Strange's prominence in the media. A second album, *The Anvil*, was released in 1982, but it was a tired re-run of the previous work, and even though sporadic releases from Visage kept appearing when commitments from the changing line-up permitted, the initial success was not repeated.

WAH! Essentially the brainchild of Pete Wylie, a prominent member of the Liverpool music community in the late Seventies, Wah! went through a series of name changes (starting off as 'Wah! Heat', then 'Shambeko Say Wah!' among others) before sticking to the simple, monosyllabic name. Despite a string of extraordinarily powerful pop singles from 1979 onwards, Wah! managed only one UK Top 10 hit.

In 1977 Wylie had been a member of the short-lived legendary Liverpool group the Crucial Three, along with Ian McCullough of **Echo and the Bunnymen** and Julian Cope of **Teardrop Explodes**. While the other two began to find fame in 1978, Wylie's group Wah! Heat didn't surface with a record until 1979 and the impressive 'Better Scream'/'Joe' on the independent Inevitable label. Eventually the 'Heat' was dropped, and on their own Eternal label, distributed by WEA, they put out some superb singles, most notably 'Seven Minutes to Midnight' and 'Some Say', neither of which made any mark on the charts. Wah! also released the album *Nah Poo – The Art of Bluff* (1981) but that too failed commercially.

Eventually, Wylie and Wah! scored in 1983 with the Spector-inspired 'The Story of the Blues', reaching Number 3 and staying in the charts for three months, but the follow-up single 'Hope (I Wish You'd Believe Me)' made only Number 37 and heralded the demise of Wah!.

In 1986, after a long absence from the music scene, Wylie emerged as a solo artist under his own name, signed to MDM Records, and hit the UK charts with his first solo single, 'Sinful', which pointed him in a new commercial direction.

WAILERS See Marley, Bob, and the Wailers

WAINWRIGHT III, LOUDON
One of the more strident and harder-edged performers to emerge during the singer/songwriter boom of the early Seventies, Loudon Wainwright III was born in Chapel Hill, North Carolina, on 5 September 1946, and first made his name on America's college and folk club circuit. He signed with Atlantic in 1969 who released his debut album, *Album I*, a year later. This and its successors, *Album II* (1971) and *Album III* (1972), were starkly humorous, while his later records for Columbia – *Attempted Mustache* (1973), *Unrequited* (1975) – were more mellow in their irony. He was never more serious than when he was at his funniest, as in the track 'Dead Skunk' (featured on *Album III* and a US hit single), in which the skunk 'stinking to high heaven' rapidly becomes a metaphor for many a more offensive happening. His songs of love here and in subsequent albums were marked by the same attitude, centring on such activities as crawling under the snoring wife's bed in search of a midnight cigarette. In the process he managed to say more about relationships than many a more serious-minded writer.

His music increased in complexity with his move to Columbia and the addition of a backing group, and his albums for Arista (which he joined in 1976) featured session musicians of the calibre of Elliott Randall (guitar), Richard Davis (bass) and Eric Weissberg (banjo). However, neither *T Shirt* (1976) nor *Final Exam* (1978) enjoyed great sales and Wainwright moved to England, recording for Jake Riviera's Radar label (*A Live One* in 1979, *Fame and Wealth* in 1983) and becoming a frequent headliner at folk clubs and festivals. His later work, typified by the songs in *Fame and Wealth*, shows that Wainwright has lost little of his satiri-

cal edge or mordant sense of comedy. In 1986 he released *More Love Songs* (Demon). Between 1973 and 1977, he was married to fellow singer/songwriter **Kate McGarrigle**, who recorded his 'Swimming Song' on her 1976 debut album with sister Anna.

WAITS, TOM
Variously described as 'part comedian, raconteur, torch singer and poet' and 'a one-man Beatnik revival', Californian singer/songwriter Tom Waits has captivated audiences with his gravelly growl ever since his emergence on the West Coast small club circuit in the early Seventies. Cultivating the stage persona of a booze-crazed down-and-out, a studied blend of bum and low-rent pimp, Waits is best known for his songs about life on the breadline.

Born on 7 December 1949 (he insists it was on the back seat of a taxi), he was only in his early twenties when he first came to public notice. His major influence was Beat author Jack Kerouac, and even though his adolescence came during the acid-rock era of the Sixties, he turned to the Beat generation for inspiration, uncovering role models in the work of writers Kerouac, Allen Ginsberg and William Burroughs, and finding solace in jazz, especially **Miles Davis** and Charlie Parker.

After a few sporadic appearances in the late Sixties, he decided to concentrate on a singing/songwriting career, building up a cult following as an opening act, and he was signed to Asylum Records in 1972. Waits' first LP was *Closing Time* (1973), an indetermi-

Tom Waits in his favourite role as beat-poet

nate blend of country and folk that sold poorly. Two songs from the album established Waits' name however – 'Martha' was covered by **Tim Buckley** on *Sefronia* and '01' 55' by the **Eagles** on their platinum-selling *On the Border*.

Since then he has consolidated a reputation as a writer of cool, stumbling jazz songs and bluesy romantic ballads, accompanied live by his piano and usually a sax-led jazz fourpiece. Through a series of albums he continued his examinations of city low-life. *Small Change* (1976) and *Foreign Affairs* (1977) remained in the jazz vein, but later albums *Blue Valentine* (1978) and *Heart Attack and Vine* (1980) saw a move to a more abrasive, electric R&B sound.

In 1980 Waits got married. His wife Kathleen was a script analyst for 20th Century-Fox and the marriage signalled a move by Waits into the film world. He then began work on the music for Francis Ford Coppola's *One from the Heart* (1982), on which he shared the microphone for a series of love songs with country singer **Crystal Gayle** to create his gentlest, most accessible recording. He subsequently took an acting role in Coppola's *Rumblefish*.

Waits changed labels to Island in 1983 to release the eccentric album *Swordfishtrombones*, a startling collage of sounds from a brass band to raving R&B, followed two years later by *Rain Dogs*, a further study of life on the periphery of society. Many find his voice on record impenetrable, and this, coupled with a lack of radio airplay, has prevented Waits from generating more than a cult following, but in performance he creates an exciting, intimate relationship with his audience that few can resist.

WAKEMAN, RICK
The architect of some of the Seventies' most commercially successful fusions of classical and rock music, Rick Wakeman was born in Perivale, Middlesex, on 18 May 1949 and started studying classical piano at the age of seven. He joined a local beat group, Atlantic Blues, in 1963 and enrolled at London's Royal College of Music after leaving school with a career as a concert pianist in mind. After devoting more time to jamming in pubs and clubs than to his classical studies, he was dismissed from the college and began regular session work, playing on hits by such varied artists as White Plains, Brotherhood of Man, Edison Lighthouse, **Black Sabbath** and comic actor Clive Dunn. He also contributed the distinctive

Mellotron sound to **David Bowie**'s 'Space Oddity' in 1969 and continued to guest on others' sessions after joining the **Strawbs** in 1970 and **Yes** a year later: the sensitive piano work on **Cat Stevens**' 1972 UK hit 'Morning Has Broken' and on Bowie's 'Life on Mars' (1973) was his.

Although the music of Yes in particular suited Wakeman perfectly, with its incessant demands on the players to come up with new sounds and ideas to fit increasingly ambitious arrangements, he had solo ambitions. While working on the Yes album *Close to the Edge* (1972), Wakeman completed a project of his own, *The Six Wives of Henry VIII*, which was eventually released in January 1973. It was the first in a series of solo works, his next album – *Journey to the Centre of the Earth* (1974) – involving keyboards, orchestra and narration by David Hemmings of extracts from Jules Verne's novel: performed and recorded at London's Royal Festival Hall on 18 January 1974, *Journey* achieved even bigger sales than its predecessor and topped the British album chart. Still more grandiose was *The Myths and Legends of King Arthur and the Knights of the Round Table* (1975), which was premiered on ice at the Empire Pool, Wembley, and caused Wakeman severe financial problems in its mounting.

Also in 1975, Wakeman wrote the soundtrack score for Ken Russell's film *Lisztomania*; a year later, he provided the score for the official film of the 1976 Winter Olympics, *White Rock*, and released a third solo album, *No Earthly Connection*, the release of which coincided with his rejoining Yes after a two-year break. He stayed with the band until 1980 but recorded two further solo albums for A&M, *Criminal Record* (1977) and *Rhapsodies* (1979). In 1981 he collaborated with lyricist Tim Rice on a musical treatment of George Orwell's *1984*, despite initial opposition from the Orwell estate, and in 1983 composed the musical score for *Golé*, the film of the previous year's soccer World Cup. He also became the weekly host of UK Channel 4's rock show 'Gastank'. The immense popularity of the amiable Wakeman has consistently confused critics who seem unable to accept him as a master of contemporary light orchestral music.

WALKER BROTHERS At their peak in the mid-Sixties, the Walker Brothers – Scott Engel, vocals and bass (born 9 January 1944, in Hamilton, Ohio), John Maus, vocals and guitar (12 November 1943, in New York), and Gary Leeds, drums (3 September 1944, in Glendale, California) – rivalled even the **Beatles** in Britain as the subjects of mass idolization. **Jack Good** suggested they try the British market after they had made little impact in America. Scott and John had recorded individually and together – John usually preferring the surname Stewart – before joining ex-Jet Powers (**P. J. Proby**) drummer Gary Leeds in 1964.

The following year they struck the formula that propelled them to success with 'Love Her', on which Scott and John pitted their voices in dramatic style against a Spectoresque arrangement. Only a minor hit, it set them up for further international hits in 1965–6 ('Make It Easy on Yourself', 'The Sun Ain't Gonna Shine Any More'). Their first album, *Take It Easy* (Philips), featured fine varied material, especially a version of 'Love Minus Zero'. They never totally cracked the American market, and after 'Sun' they found their emotional and sexual impact wearing thin. Scott Walker began to take his moody image too seriously, and Gary Leeds' frustration reared forth in a terrible version of 'You Don't Love Me'. They split after the third album, *Images*, Scott predictably doing well as a solo act.

In 1975, they re-formed and recorded a fine version of **Tom Rush**'s classic 'No Regrets', which reached Number 7 in the UK. Their producer then, as ten years earlier, was Johnny Franz. The reunion lasted until 1978 since when the three Walkers have been involved in various solo projects. Scott won a cult following around 1979–80 when Julian Cope of **Teardrop Explodes** began extolling him in press interviews.

WALKER, JUNIOR Best known for his long association with Motown, saxophonist and singer Junior Walker was born Autrey de Walt in Blythesville, Arkansas, in 1942, and picked up his stage name from his stepfather. Early influences were Illinois Jacquet and Earl Bostic, and his punchy, driving alto-sax style reflects the latter's approach. He formed a band around 1961, which was heard by **Johnny Bristol**, who recommended them to **Harvey Fuqua** in Detroit. He signed them to his Harvey label, soon to be incorporated in the Motown organization.

The shifting line-up of Junior Walker and the All-Stars included Willie Woods, guitar; Vic Thomas, organ; James Graves, guitar; and Junior on sax/ vocal duties. They had three discs on Harvey in 1962 and one on Soul in 1964, before 'Shotgun' – a pounding dance tune that was largely instrumental with shouted lyrics – became a Number 2 US hit in 1965. Some twenty subsequent discs climbed the American Hot 100, mainly rousing dance tunes, though mellower ballads like 'These Eyes' and 'Way Back Home', augmented with strings, pervaded the group's Seventies' repertoire.

WALKER, T-BONE Born Aaron Thibaud Walker in Linden, Texas, in 1910, T-Bone Walker entered music as a country bluesman and medicine-show artist in the Dallas area. Joining a territory band in the Thirties, he began to use electric guitar (which he first heard played by **Les Paul**) and moved to the West Coast, where he played with Les Hite's orchestra. During the Forties, he recorded for both Chicago and Los Angeles independents, having particular success with 'They Call It Stormy Monday' (Black & White); in the Fifties he recorded chiefly for Imperial, and then made a variety of albums for different companies.

Walker's experiments with electric guitar in a small blues-band format were profoundly influential, and the whole school of postwar guitar-playing that centres about **B.B. King** owes its existence (whether it knows it or not) to Walker's early demonstrations of the medium's potential. An unremarkable but pleasant blues-singer, temperamentally he never seemed inclined to reach out for the status to which his influence clearly entitled him. He died in March 1975.

WALSH, JOE One of American hard-rock's few genuine guitar heroes of the Seventies, Joe Walsh was born in Wichita, Kansas, on 20 November 1947. He formed his first band, the G-Clefts, at school before joining the Nomads as bassist, then spent a spell with the Measles before moving on to the **James Gang** in April 1969. He shot to fame with the Gang (aided by praise from Pete Townshend) and left in November 1971, when it became clear that his talents were exceeding the capabilities of the rest of the band. Six months later he formed Barnstorm with Joe Vitale and Kenny Passarelli: their album *Barnstorm* (Dunhill, 1972) confirmed Walsh's status as both an inventive guitarist and a talented writer. The single 'Rocky Mountain Way' brought gold status to the unit's next album, *The Smoker You Drink, the Player You Get* (ABC-Dunhill, 1973).

After extensive touring, Walsh felt that the band had reached its limits and for his next album, *So What* (1974), used Barnstorm on only a handful of tracks. The presence of the **Eagles** on its other cuts fuelled speculation that Walsh would join them and, after recording the live set *You Can't Argue With a Sick Mind* (ABC, 1975) and producing albums for Dan Fogelberg and Joe Vitale, he duly became Bernie Leadon's replacement on lead guitar. The first Eagles album to feature Walsh as a fully-fledged member was *Hotel California* (1975), but he continued to record as a solo artist and scored a major singles success in 1978 with 'Life Been's Good' (Asylum), a self-deprecating account of rock stardom taken from the album *But Seriously Folks*. Walsh remained with the Eagles until their official break-up in 1981 and made further solo albums – *There Goes the Neighbourhood* (Asylum, 1981), *You Bought It, You Name It* (Full Moon, 1983) and *The Confessor* (Warner Brothers, 1985).

WAR Instrumental group War – Harold Brown (drums, born 17 March 1946), Howard Scott (guitar, 15 March 1946), B.B. Dickerson (bass, 3 August 1949), Charles Miller (saxes, flute, 2 June 1939) and Lonnie Jordan (keyboards, 21 November 1948) – originally worked the West Coast club scene of the Sixties under various names including the Creators, the Romeos ('Precious Memories', Mark II Records, 1967) and Señor Soul ('It's Your Thing', Whiz Records, 1969). As the Night Shift they linked up with **Eric Burdon**, changed names again and toured as his backing band, having been joined by Papa Dee Allen (percussion, born 19 July 1931) and Lee Oskar (harmonica, 24 March 1948). *Eric Burdon Declares War* on MGM was followed by *Black Man's Burdon* on Liberty.

Leaving Burdon, War's solo albums, *All Day Music* and *The World Is a Ghetto* (United Artists, 1971), went gold and established them as a potent new voice in progressive soul music, their style embracing jazz/funk, Latin, rock, and R&B. Their sometimes mellow, sometimes percussive sound appealed equally to black and white audiences though they lost ground when disputes with their management in 1974 meant a year's lay-off and the release of a relatively mediocre live album. Their problems resolved, they went on to an album, *Why Can't We Be Friends*, from which came the 1975 hit single of the same name and 'Low Rider', a Number 7 US hit that year and

a Number 12 UK hit early in 1976.

The band moved to MCA in 1976 and recorded in a disco vein with some moderate success, though major personnel changes occurred when Dickerson left in 1978 to be replaced by Luther Rabb, and Tweed Smith (vocals), Pat Rizzo (horns) and Ron Hammond (drums) all joined. War recorded for RCA from 1982 onwards, their releases including the outstanding *Outlaw* and a single taken from it, 'You Got the Power'.

WARNER BROTHERS RECORDS/WARNER COMMUNICATIONS

Although founded in 1958, Warner Brothers Records represented the second venture into the record industry by the famous film empire – the first was in 1930, when the three Warner brothers bought Brunswick Records, a venture that ended in disaster a year later. The Warner Brothers label launched in 1958 was run by former vice-president of Capitol, Jim Conklin, and its first signings were middle-of-the-road performers like Henry Mancini and Buddy Cole. Its chart success began with a spin-off from a television series produced by the parent company – 'Kookie Kookie Lend Me Your Comb' by Ed Byrnes, star of *77 Sunset Strip* (see **Screen Stars**). By 1960, comedian Bob Newhart and the **Everly Brothers** (signed from the small Cadence label in a then record-breaking 'transfer' deal) gave the company its first major album and singles hits. Two years later Warners moved into the growing folk field by signing **Peter, Paul and Mary**.

Warners also began extending their empire to other labels. Frank Sinatra's Reprise label was brought under the Warners umbrella in 1964, and in the next two years two small West Coast labels, Valiant and Autumn, were acquired. The deal brought **Harpers Bizarre** and the **Beau Brummels** to Warners, together with their producer **Lenny Waronker**, who was eventually to become company president. In 1966, Warners signed the **Grateful Dead** and had novelty hits with singles by the Marketts and Napoleon XIV. Warner-Reprise was itself taken over during the following year by Seven Arts, which then acquired the Atlantic group of labels. The Warners roster grew with artists like **Van Dyke Parks**, **Van Morrison**, Mason Williams, **Alice Cooper**, **Randy Newman**, together with **Frank Zappa**'s Straight label. The takeover process continued until 1969, when the giant Kinney Corporation, with interests in virtually every area of

American industry, purchased the Warner Brothers-Seven Arts group, including the Warner Brothers film company and the Atlantic label. (Kinney was originally a company started in the late Forties by three businessmen – Caesar Kimmel, Sigmund Dornbusch and Emmanuel Rosenstein – that diversified into funeral parlours and building maintenance. During the early Fifties, Kinney took long-term parking lot leases and made a fortune during the building boom that followed. The company went public in 1962.)

By the mid-Seventies, Warner Communications – the name Kinney adopted in 1971, under the presidency of Steve Ross – controlled the Warner Brothers-Elektra-Atlantic-Asylum-Nonesuch group of companies, Warner Brothers films and television, DC Publications (distributors of *Batman* and *Superman* comics) and Cable TV Communications, the second largest cable system in the US. It also had a controlling interest in the Garden State National Bank of Hackensack, New Jersey, whose assets totalled $500 million, and owned the Jungle Habitat Wildlife Park in New York and the New York Cosmos soccer club. Its publishing arm, Warner Brothers Music, also expanded enormously and by the end of the decade had a number of important songwriters on its books (including Randy Newman and many European writers and performers, among them the **Sex Pistols**, **Madness** and **Vangelis**).

Although just one part (albeit a very significant one) of Warner Communications, Warner-Reprise Records itself built its success in the Seventies on long-term development of talent – **Randy Newman**, for example, was first signed in 1968 but only became a mainstream chart artist in 1977 – and on cultivating good relations with its acts through matching them with sympathetic producers (for example, **Lenny Waronker**, Ted Templeman, Joe Wissert, Russ Titelman, **Joe Boyd**) and allowing them a large degree of creative freedom in the studio. The company dominated the singer/songwriter movement of the early Seventies, its roster including **James Taylor**, **Joni Mitchell**, **Neil Young**, **Gordon Lightfoot** and many others, and groomed a string of major rock bands – the **Doobie Brothers**, **Van Halen**, **ZZ Top** and a reshaped **Fleetwood Mac** among them. By the Eighties, Warners' investment in **Prince**, **George Benson** and ex-Doobie Brother Michael McDonald was paying off spectacularly, while the company's UK division introduced a whole range of British acts to the American market –

Dire Straits, the Pretenders, Depeche Mode and Scritti Politti included. Warner Communications also co-owned (with American Express) cable channel MTV, establishing it as the record industry's most crucial exposure vehicle after radio, until Viacom International bought out its interest in September 1985. *See also* **MTV**; **Reprise Records**

WARONKER, LENNY A&R head and chief producer of Warner Brothers Records, Lenny Waronker is the son of Liberty Records founder Si Waronker. He worked for Liberty's music publishing subsidiary, Metric Music, in the mid-Sixties and turned to record production in 1967 with **Harpers Bizarre** (supervising their first album, *Feelin' Groovy*, and the single of the same name) and **Van Dyke Parks** (taking the production credit on Parks' mammoth concept album, *Song Cycle*, which featured approximately eighty of Los Angeles' finest session musicians). Waronker went on to produce a string of successful albums by the **Everly Brothers**, **Ry Cooder**, **Arlo Guthrie**, **Randy Newman** (a long-time friend whom Waronker introduced to Warners), the **Beau Brummels**, **Gordon Lightfoot**, the **Doobie Brothers** (co-producing with Ted Templeman), **Maria Muldaur** (co-producing with Joe Boyd, **James Taylor**), and others. He has been described as a 'sound sweetener' and uses strings, vocal harmonies and synthesizer accompaniments to give a fuller flavour to melodies. His work with Lightfoot has been typical of his general approach.

WARWICK, DIONNE Formerly a session-singer, in the mid-Sixties Dionne Warwick became the outstanding exponent of the ballads of **Burt Bacharach** and Hal David. Born in East Orange, New Jersey, on 12 December 1941, she studied at Hart College of Music in Hartford, Connecticut, before joining Cissie Houston as backing vocalists on records by **Garnet Mimms**, the **Drifters** and others. Her first solo disc was Bacharach's haunting 'Don't Make Me Over', which reached Number 21 in the US on Scepter in 1962. Warwick's perfect phrasing was well suited to the almost operatic quality of later Bacharach classics, including 'Anyone Who Had a Heart' (Number 8 in 1963) and 'Walk On By' (Number 6 in 1964). Her ability was emphasized by the far cruder reading given to the former in Britain by **Cilla Black**. Virtually every Dionne Warwick record of the Sixties entered the charts, though

Sophisticated Dionne Warwick

only a few were Top 10 hits. Like her mentors' songwriting, her work veered away from soul-tinged pop towards a less exciting cabaret style, on numbers like 'I Say a Little Prayer' (Number 4 in 1967). Nevertheless the breathy, faultless vocals were highly influential, particularly in Britain where **Dusty Springfield**'s outstanding style was indebted to Warwick's singing. Moving from Scepter to Warner Brothers in 1971, she re-emphasized the soulful component of her approach on *Just Being Myself* (1973), with compositions by Brian Holland and Lamont Dozier (*see* **Holland, Dozier, Holland**). Later tracks were produced by **Jerry Ragavoy** while *Track of the Cat* (1975) was produced by **Thom Bell**, but her only hit between 1971 and 1978 was a duet, 'Then Came You' with the (**Detroit**) **Spinners** in 1974. Her career underwent a dramatic renaissance in 1979 with the million-selling *Dionne*, produced by Barry Manilow: the singles taken from it – 'I'll Never Love This Way Again' and 'Deja Vu' reached Number 5 and Number 15 respectively in the US. In the Eighties she came

under the production wing of Barry Gibb of the **Bee Gees** and scored her first UK chart successes since 1968 with the Gibb-composed 'Heartbreaker' and 'All the Love in the World' (Arista, both 1982). In late 1985, her benefit record for AIDS research, 'That's What Friends Are For' (with **Elton John** and **Stevie Wonder**), did well on both sides of the Atlantic.

WAS (NOT WAS) Detroit multi-instrumentalists Dave Weiss and Don Fagenson, as Was (Not Was), achieved instant recognition as rock/funk dancefloor innovators with the release of their first album, *Was (Not Was)* in 1981. Don and Dave Was, the St Was brothers, as the duo came to be known, had been sessionmen and engineers around the various Detroit studios for fifteen years before teaming up. During that period they had worked with and made friends with various musicians like the **O'Jays** and **Funkadelic**, many of whom appeared on the first album. The LP was a raging critical, but not commercial, success and a second LP, *Born to Laugh at Tornadoes* did not appear until 1984. A single from this album, 'Out Come the Freaks' made Number 41 on the UK chart.

WASHINGTON, DINAH Born Ruth Jones on 29 August 1924, Dinah Washington was a pianist in a Baptist church as a child. A spell singing with Lionel Hampton followed, setting her on a career as a jazz singer. She recorded a wide range of material for Mercury from the late Forties onwards. There were blues ('Trouble in Mind'), pop songs and even a **Hank Williams** number ('Cold Cold Heart' in 1951). Her biggest hits were 'What a Difference a Day Makes' (Number 10 in 1959) and a duet with **Brook Benton**, 'Baby You Got What It Takes' which got to Number 5 in 1960. She moved to Roulette in 1962, but died of an overdose of sleeping pills on 14 December 1963.

WATERS, MUDDY The king of Chicago blues, Muddy Waters was born McKinley Morganfield on 4 April 1915, in Rolling Fork, Mississippi. He moved to Clarksdale at an early age where he grew up working on a plantation. In the summer of 1941, he was recorded for the American Library of Congress by folk-music researcher **Alan Lomax**, the two tracks being 'I Be's Troubled' and 'Country Blues'. Muddy moved to Chicago in 1943, where he met and played with **Big Bill Broonzy**, gaining invaluable experience.

In 1945, his uncle bought him an electric guitar, and a year later he was recorded, first for Aristocrat, and then Columbia. The Columbia sides were never issued, and he signed an exclusive Aristocrat contract, which was later taken over by the newly formed Chess label. In 1948, Muddy cut his first solo single, 'I Can't Be Satisfied', accompanied by Big Crawford on string bass. It was a minor hit. He followed-up with 'Screamin'and Cryin'', and then 'Rollin' and Tumblin'', released in March 1950. Muddy's debut release under the Chess banner was 'Rollin' Stone', and was his first National R&B success. Soon after, he formed his now legendary group, which featured **Little Walter** on harmonica, **Otis Spann** on piano and Jimmy Rogers on second guitar. This was the classic Muddy Waters band, the pioneer city blues group that was to influence countless other blues musicians not to mention the entire white R&B movement of the mid-Sixties. Each member went on to record solo, and eventually Walter outsold Muddy, becoming the biggest-selling Chicago blues artist of the Fifties. But as a unit they recorded dozens of sides, the most famous being 'I've Got My Mojo Working', 'Hoochie Coochie Man', 'I'm Ready', 'Long Distance Call', 'I'm a Man', 'Honey Bee', 'Tiger in Your Tank', 'You Shook Me' and 'She's 19 Years Old'.

The Waters band at its best was tough and uncompromising. Muddy shouted and played bottleneck guitar over a pounding rhythm and amplified harmonica. This expressive technique reflected the spirit of the period – and was put across with almost terrifying effect. Between 1950 and 1958, Muddy notched up 12 *Billboard* national R&B chart hits.

His last album for Chess was *Can't Get No Grindin'* in 1973, after which he brought a law suit against the company's publishing subsidiary for recovery of back royalties. He recorded four albums for Blue Sky – *Hard Again* (1977), *I'm Ready* (1978), *King Bee* (1981), and *Hoochie Coochie Man* (1983), all of which were produced by **Johnny Winter**. Waters died of a heart attack in Chicago on 30 April 1983.

WATSON, JOHNNY 'GUITAR'

A leading rock'n'roll accompanist, an impressive singer and a pioneer who experimented with the electronic characteristics of the guitar during the early Fifties – Johnny 'Guitar' Watson was all of these.

Born 3 February 1935, in Houston, Texas, Watson was inspired by blues guitarists **T-Bone Walker**, **Clarence 'Gatemouth' Brown** and **Lowell Fulsom**. He moved to Los Angeles

Great blues guitarist and vocalist Muddy Waters rocks on stage

while in his teens, and worked with the bands of Big Jay McNeely and Chuck Higgins. Watson signed with King Records in 1952 and cut the futuristic instrumental 'Space Guitar' and the rock'n'roll-styled 'Motor Head Baby'. In 1955, he scored a huge hit with 'Those Lonely, Lonely Nights', a blues cut for RPM records. Watson went on to tour with **Sam Cooke**, **Jackie Wilson**, the **Drifters**, **Ruth Brown** and **Louis Jordan**. During this time he developed his showmanship with the guitar, even playing it with his teeth while doing a handstand, pre-dating **Jimi Hendrix** by a decade. More hits followed, including the atmospheric 'Three Hours Past Midnight' and 'Cuttin' In'. In the early Sixties, Watson teamed up with veteran rocker **Larry Williams**. The duo came to England and cut a live album produced by Guy Stevens. Watson's blistering guitar work can also be heard on Little Richard's 'Whole Lotta Shakin' Goin' On', recut in 1964.

Watson subsequently signed to Fantasy and worked in a producer/arranger capacity with such names as **Betty Everett** and **Percy Mayfield**. His guitar style has been absorbed by several white rock musicians, including **James Burton** and **Roy Buchanan**. He won renewed critical acclaim in the mid-Seventies for a series of inventive albums, beginning with *I Don't Want to be Alone, Stranger* (1975), in the funk mode. His singles for DJM, 'I Need It' and 'A Real Mother for Ya' were small hits in the UK. In 1981, he signed with A&M and debuted for the label with *That's What Time It Is*.

WE FIVE Folk quintet the We Five had their beginnings in 1962 when Mike Stewart formed the Ridge Runners in the mould of the **Kingston Trio**, of which his brother John was a member. The Trio's manager, Frank Werber, suggested they drop straight folk in favour of folk-pop. Three years later, the result was the We Five – Mike Stewart, Beverly Bivens, Jerry Burgan, Bob Jones and Pete Fullerton – and an archetypal pop-folk record, 'You Were On My Mind' (A&M) which reached Number 3 in the US in 1965. The follow-up, 'Let's Get Together', made the Top 40, but subsequent records failed and the group disbanded.

WEATHER REPORT Formed in 1971 by Joe Zawinul (ex-**Miles Davis** and Cannonball Adderley pianist, born in Vienna on 7 July 1932) and Wayne Shorter (ex-Davis and Art Blakey saxophonist and composer, born in New Jersey on 25 August 1933), Weather

Report epitomizes the style of music associated with graduates of Miles' band. Their most characteristic approach is to build a performance from melodic fragments, weaving them into shifting patterns and textures, often of great subtlety and charm. Their records from *Weather Report* (Columbia, 1971) to *Tale Spinnin'* (1975) were carefully constructed artefacts which frequently achieved a rather cold and formal beauty, and commercial success proved elusive until Jaco Pastorius joined the group for *Black Market* (1976) and the half-million-selling *Heavy Weather* (1977). Although the line-up changed numerous times during the Seventies, Zawinul and Shorter were ever-present and in 1978 were joined by drummer Pete Erskine, who stayed for three albums – *Mr Gone* (1978), *8:30* (1979) and *Night Passages* (1980). Their other Eighties releases include *Procession* (1983), *Domino Theory* (1984) and *Sportin'Life* (1985). *See also* **Miles Davis**

WEAVERS Along with the earlier Carter Family, the Weavers stand as one of the most influential early commercial American folk-song groups. The Weavers formed in 1949, disbanded three years later because of anti-Leftist blacklisting, reactivated in late 1955, and finally dissolved after a Chicago concert on 29 December 1963. The original group was **Pete Seeger**, Lee Hays, Ronnie Gilbert and Fred Hellerman. Their hits of the early Fifties included **Leadbelly**'s 'Good Night, Irene', 'Kisses Sweeter Than Wine' and the traditional 'When the Saints Go Marching In'. When Seeger decided on a solo career, he was succeeded as tenor by Erik Darling in 1958, then Frank Hamilton, and finally, in 1963, by Bernie Krause. The Weavers' name was chosen to suggest both rhythm and work. They cited Leadbelly as their earliest strong influence. Their Fifties recordings with the Gordon Jenkins Orchestra were extremely pop-oriented, but their later work was considered to be both pop and authentically true to tradition. Imitators by the score emerged after 1958. The group's various Carnegie Hall reunions were sentimental gala occasions. *See also* **Pete Seeger**

WEBB, JIMMY One of the true greats of Sixties popular songwriting, acclaimed equally by pop, rock and easy-listening artists, Jimmy Webb was born in Elk City, Oklahoma, on 15 August 1946. Moving to California in 1964, he worked as a contract song-

writer for Motown's publishing arm, Jobete Music, and met **Johnny Rivers**, who was then in the process of setting up his Soul City label. Webb wrote a number of songs for him, including 'By the Time I Get to Phoenix', but it was **Glen Campbell** who took the song into the US chart during 1967 – the same year that the **Fifth Dimension**, signed to Soul City, scored a major US hit with Webb's 'Up Up and Away'. Both Campbell and the Dimension continued to record Webb material extensively – Campbell enjoyed Top 5 hits with 'Wichita Lineman' (1968) and 'Galveston' (1969) – and actor Richard Harris recorded two concept albums, *A Tramp Shining* and *The Yard Went On Forever* (both 1968), with Webb as musical director. Harris' million-selling 'Macarthur Park', one of Webb's most recorded compositions, was taken from the former album.

Dissatisfied with other people's performances of his material and intent on developing a more personal writing style, Webb signed with Reprise in 1970 and made his performing debut in Los Angeles. His first proper album – *Jim Webb Sings Jim Webb*, released by Epic in 1968, was an unauthorized collection of Webb demos – was *Words and Music* (1970), which included the plaintive 'P.F. Sloan', a tribute to one of his lesser-known professional songwriting colleagues from the mid-Sixties. Both this album and *And So: On* (1971) were uneven in quality yet showed Webb to be a more thoughtful writer than his earlier hits had suggested. *Land's End* (Asylum, 1974) saw him producing himself, again with mixed results. He also worked with the **Supremes** and **Art Garfunkel** during the early Seventies – Garfunkel's 'All I Know', composed by Webb, was a Number 9 US hit in late 1973 – and produced albums by **Cher**, his sister Susan and a reunited Fifth Dimension. Signing with Atlantic in 1977, he recorded *El Mirage* with **George Martin** as producer. His only album of the Eighties so far has been *Angel Heart* (Columbia, 1982), while his other composing projects have included a musical version of *Peter Pan* and a choral work for children.

WEEDON, BERT The British session-guitarist Bert Weedon was already a little too old to be a pop idol when his cover version of 'Guitar Boogie Shuffle' (an American Top 10 hit for the Virtues) put him in the limelight in 1959. He had another instrumental hit the following year with 'Sorry Robbie', and it is reputed that his version of

Jerry Lordan's 'Apache', which made Number 1 for the **Shadows**, was the first. Bert then returned to session work and regular appearances on children's television, occasionally making an album under his own name, and had a surprise success in 1970 with *Rockin' at the Roundhouse*, a budget-price album recorded at a rock'n'roll revival gig. He has since made a string of such albums, several of which were produced by BBC radio *Saturday Club* DJ Brian Matthew. Weedon's other main claim to fame, beside his hits, was his best-selling guitar instruction manual, *Play in a Day*, which was first published in the late Fifties.

WELLS, JUNIOR A contemporary of blues harmonica king **Little Walter**, Junior Wells was born Amos Wells Jr. in West Memphis, Arkansas, on 9 December 1932. Inspired by the playing of **Sonny Boy Williamson** (John Lee), his big break came during the early Fifties, replacing Walter in the **Muddy Waters** band. Wells's first solo sides were cut in 1953 for the Chicago-based United/States label. Included in those sessions was the magnificent 'Hoodoo Man', with the Waters band in support. His later hits included 'Messin' with the Kid' (now a showstopper for **Rory Gallagher**) on Chief. In 1972, Wells teamed up with blues guitarist **Buddy Guy**, cutting one album for Atlantic, part-produced by **Eric Clapton**. The duo still work live dates together and have toured America and Europe supporting the **Rolling Stones**. He also recorded for Shad, Profile, U.S.A., Delmark, Vanguard, Bright Star, Hit Sound and Blue Rock.

WELLS, MARY One of the Motown Corporation's brightest stars in the early Sixties, Mary Wells was born in Detroit, Michigan, on 13 May 1943, began singing at the age of ten, and in her teens played local clubs and talent shows. She was discovered during Motown's regular audition sessions, having walked in off the street in the hope of selling a song. The song, 'Bye Bye Baby', a gritty slow-rock ballad, became her debut disc and a Top 50 hit in 1961. Mary's popularity soared and a string of hits followed, including Top 10 'You Beat Me to the Punch' and 'Two Lovers', peaking in 1964 with the chart-topping million-seller 'My Guy', a husky loping minor-key ballad from the pen of **Smokey Robinson**. She then quit Motown for a lucrative 20th Century-Fox contract, but the move was the beginning of the end – a handful of 20th Century releases climbed the charts, but fell way short of the Motown hits, and further moves to Atco and Jubilee failed to remedy the situation, though recent material on Reprise proved an artistic, if not commercial, improvement. She married and divorced songwriter **Cecil Womack** and then married singer Curtis Womack.

WESTERN SWING At the beginning of the Thirties, the Texas fiddle-band tradition spawned a curious new music: Western Swing. It began as an elaboration of the fiddle band, uniting the fiddler and guitarist with pianist and other stringed-instrument players, and developed into a form of hillbilly jazz, played by five- to eight-piece bands in a fashion that owed much to contemporary jazz, swing and blues.

In most groups there was a core of fiddler(s), steel guitarist and, in time, brass and reed players, supported by a rhythm section of piano, rhythm guitar, tenor banjo and string bass that laid down a brisk 2/4 time. The repertoire embraced traditional fiddle breakdowns and waltzes, jazz standards, Thirties blues and a wide range of Tin Pan Alley songs, and numerous writers within the genre proved capable of imitating virtually all these idioms.

The leading band, and the first to expand into a substantial group with brass and reed sections, was Bob Wills' Texas Playboys. Wills, the son of an old-time fiddler, began in 1935 the creation of a very diverse record output, including such hits as 'San Antonio Rose' and 'Steel Guitar Rag'. A somewhat more local reputation was enjoyed by Milton Brown's Brownies, who included the highly creative steel guitarist, Bob Dunn. Other leading bands were Bill Boyd's Cowboy Ramblers, the Light Crust Doughboys (most jazz-influenced and versatile of the groups) and Cliff Bruner's Texas Wanderers. All Western Swing bands were primarily dance bands, and toured incessantly through the small towns of Texas and Oklahoma. A couple of thousand recordings, by around fifty bands, formed the body of documented Western Swing in the Thirties and early Forties.

After World War II, small bands were less common, and the style was maintained by the large orchestras of Wills, Spade Cooley and Ted Daffan. By the Fifties, there was little left of the original sound, but the lessons of Western Swing had been learned by country and western musicians all over; both in instrumentation and in repertoire the format of country music had been vastly expanded.

WESTON, KIM Sixties Motown star Kim Weston (born Agatha Natalie Weston in Detroit, Michigan, in 1943) originally planned to be a swimmer, and took to singing to improve her breathing control. Her minister father persuaded her to join a gospel group, whence she moved into R&B. After various auditions, Kim finally found Berry Gordy receptive to her talents, and her 1963 debut on Tamla, 'Love Me All the Way', reached the pop and R&B charts. A switch to the Gordy label in 1965 brought a Top 50 hit with the insistent, swinging 'Take Me in Your Arms' and 1967 saw a Top 20 hit duet with **Marvin Gaye**, 'It Takes Two'. Kim married Motown executive Mickey Stevenson in 1966 and moved with him to the MGM, People, Banyan Tree and Pride labels. Stevenson produced her 1969 album of duets with **Johnny Nash**. Kim latterly joined Enterprise and featured in the 1973 *Wattstax* show and film.

WHAM! Formed out of the schoolboy partnership of George Michael, of Greek-Cypriot origin (real name Georgious Panayatiou, born 25 June 1963), and Andrew Ridgely (born 26 January 1963), Wham! became almost certainly the most successful British pop group of the Eighties, winning massive audiences worldwide with their up-tempo, lightweight, soul-tinged pop.

In 1979, as youngsters on the outskirts of North London, they played in a band called the Executive (with Ridgely on guitar and Michael providing the vocals), an outfit that early on revealed the heavy soul influence on their work. By 1982 they had left school, formed a duo, which they called Wham!, and, armed with a demo tape, did the rounds of all the London record companies. They eventually signed an unadvantageous deal with the small independent label Innervision, and in June released 'Wham! Rap', an excellent debut single laden with social comment, but it received very little airplay and was quickly superseded by the good-time second single 'Young Guns (Go for It)', which made the UK Number 3 spot and introduced the Wham! philosophy (at least

Andrew Ridgely and George Michael, by 1984 undisputed world leaders of pop

as far as their public image was concerned) – youth, suntans, the pursuit of pleasure – to an eager TV generation.

At this point **Simon Napier-Bell** saw their potential. Napier-Bell described their friendship as 'Butch Cassidy and the Sundance Kid' and realized that this would provide an effective promotional tool. He took on their management responsibilities, and at the end of 1983 guided the duo through a series of court cases as they fought to release themselves from a complicated contractual wrangle with Innervision that resulted in their selling millions of records worldwide without making any money. Yet, despite all the hitches, 1983 proved to be a very successful year. Their first LP, *Fantastic*, reached Number 1 in the UK chart, and they had four hit singles, three of which made the UK Top 10. They toured for the first time in the autumn with backing singers Shirley Holliman and Pepsi Demacque (replacing Dee C. Lee who went on to sing with the **Style Council** and forge a successful solo career).

The dispute was finally settled in March 1984, when Wham! signed to Epic Records, and the duo were able to resume their assault on the world's charts. Through the crass, superficial, glamorous image of Wham! there shone a phenomenal songwriting talent with massive popular appeal, and it paid dividends. 'Wake Me Up Before You Go Go' became Wham!'s first UK Number 1 (and later topped the charts in the US), followed by Michael's brilliant solo single 'Careless Whisper', and the Wham! single 'Freedom'. Michael also sang on the **Band Aid** single, which ironically kept the Wham! single 'Last Christmas' from the top slot and prevented George Michael outdoing **Elvis Presley** by scoring five UK Number 1s in the same year. The LP *Make It Big* went platinum in both Britain and America; the papers and magazines were full of photos of the duo sporting suntans and toothy grins, and the scandal columns were eager for any choice gossip. By the end of 1984 Wham!, the two mates from the suburban town of Bushey, were the undisputed world leaders in pop.

The year 1985 couldn't possibly outdo 1984, and Wham! spent most of the year on a world tour that included a historic trip to China. George Michael performed at the Live Aid (*see* **Band Aid**) concert, and while his talent was becoming widely recognized (he picked up the Ivor Novello Songwriter of the Year Award), the ever-outrageous Ridgely continued to dominate the headlines by crashing racing cars

and getting drunk in public. Their huge following of teenage girls kept on growing and late in the year returned them to the top of the charts with one of their lesser offerings, 'I'm Your Man'.

In February 1986, the surprise announcement came that the duo would be splitting up after recording one more single in the spring ('Edge of Heaven') and performing a farewell summer concert. They felt they had achieved all they could with the group, and were quitting while still at the top. Ridgely was set to carry on racing and take up an acting career in Hollywood, and Michael to fulfil his own prophecy: 'I'll still be writing derivative, catchy, huge-selling records in ten years' time'. In their short career, Wham! became the biggest band since the **Beatles**, and even though they never received the critical acclaim they undoubtedly deserved, they captivated millions with their accessible pop and their exuberant image. Their final concert was given on 28 June at Wembley Stadium in London. Later that year, Michael released his first post-Wham! solo single, 'A Different Corner'. Needless to say, it topped the UK charts.

WHITCOMB, IAN

Born in Surrey in 1941, Ian Whitcomb was almost the only mid-Sixties British artist to have a major hit in America, but not in his home country, when the novelty falsetto record 'You Turn Me On' (Tower) reached Number 8 in 1965. He had visited America while on vacation from Trinity College, Dublin, where his R&B group, Bluesville, had included the nucleus of Bees Make Honey, an important London pub rock band of the Seventies. Seattle record man Jerry Dennon recorded Whitcomb's version of the traditional blues 'Sporting Life', which was a minor hit and then flew to Ireland to record Bluesville. Follow-ups to 'You Turn Me On' failed and Whitcomb returned to his first love, the popular music of the early twentieth century. He wrote books, produced a rock album by Mae West and recorded albums of music-hall songs and ragtime piano tunes. *Rock Odyssey*, published in 1985, was his blow-by-blow account of his brief flirtation with Sixties pop stardom.

WHITE, BARRY

During the first few years of the Seventies, Barry White was one of the most enigmatic and controversial figures in black music, his work raising the question: where does soul stop and easy-listening begin? White was born in Galveston, Texas, on 12 September 1944, and was

the organist in the local church before joining an R&B group, the Upfronts, in Los Angeles. At the age of 17 he undertook his first professional arranging, under the name of Lee Barry, for Rampart Records, learned production skills and spent some time as road manager for **Bob and Earl**. In 1966, White was made head of A&R at Mustang/Bronco Records, where he worked with such artists as Felice Taylor, whose 1967 UK hit, 'I Feel Love Coming On', was a White composition. He also recorded unsuccessfully under his own name.

When Mustang folded, White met up with three girl singers he dubbed Love Unlimited. Their first single, 'Walking in the Rain with the One I Love', was a worldwide hit on Uni. Signing in 1972 (together with his protégées) to 20th Century Records, White began to sing again himself and 'I'm Gonna Love You Just a Little Bit More Baby' like all his subsequent discs used an invigorating blend of **Isaac Hayes**-influenced lush 'sophistisoul' production and a driving rhythm track with extraordinary 'presence' in the guitar and drums. White enjoyed a run of million-selling singles ('Never, Never Gonna Give You Up' and 'You're My First My Last My Everything') and albums (*Stone Gon'*, *Can't Get Enough* and *Just Another Way to Say I Love You*). In 1974, he also led the Love Unlimited Orchestra to the top of the US chart with 'Love's Theme'.

It was with his heavy-breathing vocals and growled and vivid descriptions of his sexual appetites, however, that White gained most success – titles such as 'I'll Do Anything You Want Me To' (1975), 'Baby We Better Try and Get It Together' (1976) and 'I'm Qualified to Satisfy' (1977) were typical. His chart career went into decline as the Seventies went on, although he still sold well in the UK, and a version of the **Billy Joel** song 'Just the Way You Are' gave him his last major hit of any description, reaching Number 12 in the UK in early 1979. White left 20th Century later that year and set up his own company, Unlimited Gold, for distribution through Columbia. *Change*, his third album for the label, achieved healthy sales in 1982, while his business interests – among them Sa-Vette Music, Soul Unlimited and Barry White Inc – continued to flourish.

WHITE, TONY JOE

An important artist in the development of Southern music during the early Seventies, Tony Joe White – born in Oak Grove, Louisiana, on 23 July 1943 – came out of the swamplands in 1969 with an internationally successful funk-country soul hit song, 'Polk Salad Annie'. The disc reached Number 8 in the US and featured a sparse, muffled electric sound behind mumbled vocals in the **Presley** style. Recording for Monument, his first album *Black and White* (1968) was produced by **Billy Swan** and marked him as one of the first in a new breed of country singer/songwriters. Unlike the records of **Bobbie Gentry**, however, who had emerged in similar style in 1967, White's did not sell in the country market.

'Polk Salad Annie' became a contemporary standard and was covered by Presley, **Tom Jones** and others. Two more White compositions, 'Rainy Night in Georgia' (**Brook Benton**, **Randy Crawford**) and 'I've Got a Thing About You Baby' (Presley), also became hits in other versions. Switching from Monument to Warner Brothers in 1971, White continued to show distinction on albums such as *Tony Joe White* (1971) and *The Train I'm On* (1972), though his music began to diverge somewhat from the heavy swamp rhythm so prevalent on his earlier work. In 1974, he appeared in the **Jack Good** film, *Catch My Soul*. He made one further album for Warner Brothers (*Home Made Ice Cream*, 1973) before joining 20th Century in 1976, but he has made no impact on either singles or album charts since.

WHITESNAKE

Along with **Rainbow** and **Gillan**, Whitesnake featured ex-**Deep Purple** members in their line-up – in this case vocalist David Coverdale and keyboard player Jon Lord who led the band to the top of the British heavy metal pile.

On Purple's disbandment in 1976, Coverdale recorded a couple of low-key solo albums before deciding to recruit a new band to return to live work. The first Whitesnake album proper was *Trouble* in 1978 but it was the following year's *Love Hunter* (featuring Ian Paice, another ex-Purple man, on drums) that established the band as a tough, abrasive rock unit. The next year saw two more chart albums, *Ready an' Willing* and *Live in the Heart of the City*, and a UK Top 20 single 'Fool For Your Loving'.

Come an' Get It was released in 1981 but Whitesnake's activities came to a halt while Coverdale sorted out management and legal problems. With a new line-up of Coverdale, Lord, ex-Rainbow man Cozy Powell (drums), Mel Galley (guitar), Mick Moody (guitar) and Colin 'Bomber' Hodgkin-son (bass) the band returned to form with *Saints and Sinners* (1982) and then *Slide It In* (1983). They headlined the '83 Castle Donington Rock Festival, then went into another inactive period, Coverdale ostensibly planning a full-scale assault on the US market.

WHITFIELD, NORMAN

One of the most creative record producers in black music, Norman Whitfield was born in New York in 1943 and joined the Motown Corporation in Detroit soon after its inception to take up writing, arranging and production duties. Among his earliest Motown successes as a writer was **Marvin Gaye**'s 1963 Top 10 hit, 'Pride and Joy'. After following mainstream Motown styles with songs for **Kim Weston**, the **Marvelettes**, the Velvelettes, etc., and scoring a giant hit with 'I Heard It Through the Grapevine' – a million-seller in successive years (1967–8) for **Gladys Knight and the Pips** and Marvin Gaye – Norman, with his collaborator **Barrett Strong**, transformed the **Temptations** into Motown's answer to psychedelia. The result was a series of Top 10 hits including 'Cloud Nine', 'I Can't Get Next To You' and 'Psychedelic Shock' during 1968–70. The group then took his beautiful ballad 'Just My Imagination' to Number 1 in the US chart in 1971, and a year later he shattered pop musical conventions with 'Papa Was a Rolling Stone', a masterpiece of near-symphonic proportion. The tune began life as a twelve-minute Temptations album track, and an edited version soared to the top of the US chart, thanks to its disco pulse.

Whitfield also enjoyed limited success with a protégé male/female vocal group, the Undisputed Truth, whose 'Smiling Faces Sometimes' reached Number 3 in the US in 1971. The Truth was one of the ex-Motown acts Whitfield took with him when he broke with the Corporation in 1974 to form his own label, Whitfield Records – Willie Hutch and **Junior Walker** also joined him – but he found most success with **Rose Royce**, formed by Whitfield out of the musicians he had hired to back the Temptations on recording and touring dates. He wrote and produced the soundtrack score for the 1976 disco movie *Car Wash*, which Rose Royce performed: the title song topped the US chart towards the end of that year and began a run of hits for Rose Royce that included 'I Wanna Get Next to You' (1977, also from *Car Wash*) and the much-covered 'Love Don't Live Here Anymore' (1979).

WHO

A seminal British group from the mid-Sixties to the early Eighties, the Who – Roger Daltrey, vocals (born 3 January 1944), Pete Townshend, guitar (19 May 1945), and John Entwistle, bass (10 September 1944) – had been through instrumentals, the **Beatles** songbook and R&B (as the Detours), acquiring Keith Moon on drums (23 August 1946) on the way, when publicist Peter Meaden changed their name to the High Numbers, dressed them in mod clothes, and transformed Slim Harpo's 'Got Love If You Want It' into the hip 'I'm The Face' (Fontana, 1964). The mod cult was spreading rapidly at that time in London's areas and Meaden's plan to associate the group with the mods was shrewdly timed. However, despite the superficial appropriateness of the lyrics, the song was weak and the record flopped.

The group's following among the mod audiences of the London clubs continued to grow, and it was the crowd as much as the music that impressed Kit Lambert and Chris Stamp and prompted them to take over the Who's management. The new managers not only restored the group's previous gimmicky name – the Who (who?) – but encouraged the development of the mod image, spending a great deal of money and time to create the correct appearance, and moulding to this identity a musical violence that matched the physical aggression of the mods. The Who, nevertheless, failed to impress EMI, and it was only through the influence of **Shel Talmy**, who had produced the demo of Townshend's song 'I Can't Explain', that they were offered a contract with American Decca. Released in January 1965, on the Brunswick label, the record didn't take off until the group took their fanatical Marquee club audience with them to the mod-oriented TV show *Ready, Steady, Go!* In many ways closer to the **Kinks**' style than the Who's – Talmy produced both groups – it eventually made the Top 10 as did the more characteristic and innovatory follow-up, 'Anyway, Anyhow, Anywhere', which Lambert and Stamp energetically promoted as 'pop art'.

Despite the transitory, exploitative nature of the group's identification with the mods, the lifestyle held deep fascination for Townshend and provided the inspiration for his first compositions, culminating in the phenomenally successful 'My Generation', which conveyed the mods' inarticulate, pill-head rebelliousness as much by its style as its content. Townshend's subsequent songs introduced a

Music in the streets: Daltrey, Entwistle, a manic Keith Moon, and Pete Townshend

cast of characters whose frequently eccentric personalities allowed him to explore such conventional themes as enforced transvestism ('I'm a Boy', Reaction, 1966), marital infidelity ('A Quick One While He's Away' on *A Quick One*, Track, 1966) and sexual fantasy ('Pictures of Lily', Track, 1967). 'A Quick One While He's Away', a nine-minute song cycle which closed the group's second album – the first, *My Generation* (Brunswick, 1965), was a hurried, though powerful, collection of R&B readymades and early Townshend songs – was Townshend's first attempt at rock opera and, along with the incomplete 'Rael 1 and 2' on *The Who Sell Out* (Track, 1967), the precursor of *Tommy* (Track, 1968). The enormous critical attention and extravagant praise that *Tommy* attracted stemmed partly from its scale and ambitions, but it was an undoubted, if flawed, masterpiece. It brought wealth, international fame, and artistic respectability to the Who, and it was performed in opera houses throughout the world, later being given an orchestral treatment and all-star cast by Lou Reizner (Ode, 1972) and adapted into a typically excessive film by Ken Russell (1975), although in the group's live performances it was eventually condensed as a medley of old hits.

The release of 'Pinball Wizard' from *Tommy* virtually signalled the end of the Who as a singles group, and over the next five years only two singles – 'Won't Get Fooled Again' (1971) and 'Join Together' (1972) – made either the British or American Top 10. *Live at Leeds* (1970), a set that only lacked the visual excitement of their stage performance, followed *Tommy*, while *Who's Next* (1971) contained material from the abortive *Lifehouse* project. Then, after a compilation of hits, *Meaty, Beaty, Big and Bouncy* (1971), came *Quadrophenia* (1974), an elaborate homage to the mods whose image the group had originally exploited and whose lifestyle had inspired Townshend's first songs. Though quadrophonic sound was abandoned, the theme of a four-sided personality as a reflection of the four members of the group remained, and the work's lack of unity underlined their divergent paths through the Seventies, a period that saw more emphasis on individual projects. *The Who By Numbers* (1975) confirmed this by virtue of its bittiness.

That album was their last for three years, during which time all four pursued solo projects: Townshend collaborated with **Ronnie Lane** on an acoustic album, *Rough Mix*; Entwistle recorded with his band, Ox; Daltrey continued with a parallel solo career that had begun well with the hit single 'Giving It All Away' in 1973; and Moon recorded a comic album, *Two Sides of the Moon. Who Are You* (1978) was, as it turned out, the last album to feature the original line-up – Keith Moon died after a party on 7 September 1978, and was replaced after considerable deliberation as to whether the group should continue by Kenney Jones, former drummer with the **Small Faces**.

Face Dances (1981) was the first album with Jones, and *It's Hard* was released during the following year, but it was clear by this time that the Who's career as a regular recording and touring unit was drawing to an end. Their last concert appearance was in December 1982, and the group's break-up was officially confirmed almost exactly a year later. Daltrey returned to his solo recording projects – among them a version of Townshend's 'After the Fire', one of the songs from the latter's album-cum-video of 1986, *White City*. Townshend, meanwhile, having earlier started his own publishing company (Eel Pie), began working for Faber as a commissioning editor. The Who were reunited for Live Aid (see **Band Aid**) in July 1985.

WILDE, KIM Daughter of Fifties British rock'n'roller **Marty Wilde**, Kim (born Kim Smith on 18 November 1960 in Chiswick, London) made her singles chart debut in 1981 with the single 'Kids in America', which reached Number 2 in the UK. Signed to **Mickie Most**'s RAK label, she produced a series of bright pop tunes that, combined with her pouting good looks, brought her five Top 20 hits in a row during 1981–2. By the end of 1982, however, Kim's teeny-idol career had begun to flag. A move to MCA in 1984 was undertaken as a means to rejuvenate it, but her chart success remained only moderate.

WILDE, MARTY Born Reginald Smith in Blackheath, London, in 1939, Marty Wilde had only two years at the top but his voice, appearance and style made him a major British sex symbol. He was singing at London's Condor Club in 1957 when he was discovered by **Larry Parnes**. His height (6′3″) and Presleyish sullenness were novelties, but it was his fourth record, a cover version of Jodie Sands' 'Endless Sleep', that brought him stardom. He was a resident on the TV rock show, *Oh Boy!*, the host of *Boy Meets Girl*, had a girls' magazine named after him and, in 1959, had four big hits in a row: 'Donna', 'Teenager in Love', 'Sea of Love', and 'Bad Boy'. Only the last (which he wrote) was not a cover version.

In the years that followed he failed to adapt to the changing climate as well as his Larry Parnes stablemate, **Billy Fury**. He lost fans through touring America for too long and getting married and, by 1962, he was more an actor than a musician. The Seventies saw Wilde pursuing a variety of occupations within showbusiness, although he had less success in promoting his son, Ricky, as Britain's answer to Little Jimmy Osmond. In 1981, however, he had better luck when his daughter Kim expressed a wish to enter the pop field. She had a string of UK chart successes under her father's astute management. *See also* **Kim Wilde**

WILLIAMS, DENIECE

While she was a trainee nurse Williams sang for Wonderlove, **Stevie Wonder**'s backing singers, before retiring for several months to write the songs that were to make up the seven tracks on her debut album, 1976's *This Is Niecy*, produced by **Earth, Wind and Fire**'s Maurice White. The single 'Free' epitomized her style – a light, feathery voice with a good range and effective flights into a tinglingly high falsetto. After a second collaboration with White, Williams went on to work with David Foster and Ray Parker Jr, the outstanding Philadelphia producer **Thom Bell** (twice) and with the more contemporaneous studio ace **George Duke**. She continues to make highly appealing music and has developed into a proficient self-producer.

WILLIAMS, HANK

Singer Hank Williams was to country music in the Forties what **Jimmie Rodgers** was to it in the Twenties, and more; and it is appropriate that, in his rise, he followed much the same track as Rodgers, from a poor family through local popularity to a sudden elevation. Born in Mt Olive, Alabama, in 1923, he was close to neither the Southeastern harmony style of the Thirties nor its Southwestern contemporary, Western Swing; if he was influenced by what he heard, it was by such bands as **Roy Acuff**'s. From Acuff, too, he may have derived the elements of his grieved yet resolute singing, which implied a commitment previously uncommon in country music.

When he emerged on record in 1946, he did so as a singer and bandleader of the honky-tonk school, yet capable of an emotional range that swept up audiences far from the honky-tonk environment. First among country singers, he impinged upon a nationwide pop market with such recordings as 'Lovesick Blues', 'There'll Be No Teardrops Tonight', 'Your Cheatin' Heart' and 'You Win Again': love songs of despair phrased with a succinctness that few Tin Pan Alley songwriters could emulate.

Other songs belonged to a more recognizable tradition of good-time music – 'Honky Tonkin'', 'Rootie Tootie', 'Jambalaya' – and there were occasional novelties like 'Kawliga'. More in keeping with the melancholy of his best-known hits was a group of blues-derived songs, ingeniously distinct from the blues as such: '(I Heard That) Lonesome Whistle' is a supremely affecting example. Williams preserved, too (as Rodgers had never sought to do), his responses to old-time religion, which produced a number of powerful renderings of traditional and newly-composed gospel songs. Finally, in a series of recordings under the name 'Luke the Drifter', he delivered monologues on leading a righteous life and the many possible pitfalls, such as 'Too Many Parties and Too Many Pals'.

Williams died of a drug overdose in the back of a car on New Year's Day 1953, possessed of a remarkable past and an incalculable future. Few country singers since his day have been entirely unaffected by his music, and the standard country repertoire contains perhaps more of his songs than anyone else's.

WILLIAMS, LARRY

Although born in New Orleans in 1935, Larry Williams learned to play piano on the West Coast. He started out singing and playing in the bands of R&B greats like **Lloyd Price**, **Roy Brown** and **Percy Mayfield** and it was while accompanying Price on a recording session that he was discovered by Art Rupe of Specialty Records. His first record was an unsuccessful cover of Price's 'Just Because', but he made it next time out with the R&B classic, 'Short Fat Fannie', which climbed to Number 6 in the Hot 100 in 1957. 'Bony Moronie' and 'Dizzy Miss Lizzy' completed a rocking hat-trick for Williams, who for a time looked like rivalling Specialty's label star, **Little Richard**. After a succession of records for many labels and a good British tour in 1964, Williams turned to record production. He was found dead from gunshot wounds on 2 January 1980.

WILLIAMS, MAURICE, AND THE ZODIACS

Vocal group Maurice William and the Zodiacs – including Henry Gasten, Willie Bennet and Charles Thomas – hailed from Lancaster, South Carolina, where they won a talent contest in 1955 and travelled west to Nashville in the hope of recording. There they signed with Excello Records as the Gladiolas, and their first disc was the mambo-styled 'Little Darling', written by Williams, an American Top 50 hit in 1957, while the Diamonds' cover-version was a transatlantic million-seller. Subsequent discs failed to register and in 1959 the group moved to New York where they signed with Herald Records as the Zodiacs. They struck gold immediately when the distinctive falsetto wail of 'Stay' sold a million in 1960, topping the American charts and just missing the British Top 10. Similar-sounding follow-ups, 'I Remember' and 'Come Along', were minor American hits, but by 1963 the Zodiacs' fortunes had expired, though Williams – composer of most of the group's material – subsequently recorded solo for Atco, Scepter and Veep.

WILLIAMS, OTIS, AND THE CHARMS

Based in Cincinnati, Ohio, Otis Williams and the Charms – Roland Bradley, Joe Penn, Richard Parker and Donald Peak – signed with local King Records in 1954 and immediately shot to fame when 'Hearts of Stone' sold a million in 1955. Next year, 'Ivory Tower' repeated the feat, and the group issued a prodigious quantity of discs featuring Williams' fine lead vocals on De Luxe and King until splitting up in 1964. Williams then went solo on Okeh and later on Stop, where he began a fresh career recording country material as Otis Williams and the Midnight Cowboys.

WILLIAMSON, SONNY BOY

There were two Sonny Boy Williamsons, both influential and innovative forces in the world of blues.

John Lee Williamson (Sonny Boy No. 1) was born in Jackson, Tennessee, on 30 March 1914. While in his teens he played harmonica behind Sleepy John Estes and Homesick James, coming to Chicago in 1937 where he cut his first sides for RCA's Bluebird label. They included the now classic 'Good Morning, Little Schoolgirl' and 'Sugar Mama'. During the early Forties, Williamson began to record, using a small group occasionally featuring **Big Bill Broonzy** on guitar. He was one of the first Chicago-based bluesmen to use accompanying musicians on record, thus anticipating by a decade the heavy, back-beat rhythm that characterized Chicago blues records of the Fifties. His style of harmonica playing, too, paved the way for artists like **Little Walter** and **Junior Wells**. Sonny Boy Williamson No. 1 died in Chicago on 1 June 1948, the victim of a brutal attack and robbery.

Rice Miller (Sonny Boy No. 2) was the better known of the two bluesmen, especially in Europe where he toured, frequently during the early Sixties. Born in Glendora, Mississippi, in 1897, he first came to prominence in 1941, singing and playing harmonica on the highly successful daily radio show, *King Biscuit Time*, which was broadcast over KFFA in Helena, Arkansas. In order to gain even greater popularity, Miller claimed to be *the* Sonny Boy Williamson (who was safely based in Chicago, though scoring national hits) – a decision he must have certainly regretted in later years. He first recorded in 1951 for the Jackson-based Trumpet label, switching to Chess/Checker in 1955. Often accompanied by the **Muddy Waters** band, Sonny Boy's many hits included 'Don't Start Me Talking' and 'Fattening Frogs for Snakes'. He first came to Britain in 1963, where he caused a sensation dressed in a bizarre, two-tone suit and a bowler hat. During subsequent visits he appeared on the TV show *Ready, Steady, Go!* and cut live albums with the **Yardbirds** and the **Animals**. His records have been covered by such artists as **Van Morrison** ('Help Me') and the **Moody Blues** ('Bye Bye Bird'). **Led Zeppelin**'s 'Bring It On Home' on *Led Zeppelin II* was remarkably similar to Sonny Boy's original. He died in Helena, Arkansas, on 25 May 1965.

WILLIS, CHUCK Born in Atlanta,

Georgia, on 31 January 1928, Chuck Willis first sang with Red McAllister's band. In 1951, he was signed to Columbia's 'race' subsidiary, Okeh, where under the astute management of the famed Atlanta R&B disc-jockey Zena Sears, his success was immediate. 'My Story', 'Going to the River', 'Don't Deceive Me', 'You're Still My Baby' and 'I Feel So Bad' – all Top 10 R&B entries in 1952–4 – were among his many hits. In 1956, Willis was signed to Atlantic, whose superb production transformed the R&B veteran into a major rock'n'roll artist. 'It's Too Late', 'Whatcha Gonna Do When Your Baby Leaves You', 'CC Rider' (Number 12 in 1957), 'Betty and Dupree', 'Hang Up My Rock'n'Roll Shoes', and 'What Am I Living For' (Number 15 in 1958) were classics of their period. A fine songwriter, his compositions were recorded by **Elvis Presley**, the **Drifters** and **Buddy Holly**. After collapsing with a stomach ulcer, Willis died on 10 April 1958.

WILSON, JACKIE With an output

ranging from quasi-operatic ballads to gritty, belting dance favourites, Jackie Wilson was a supreme R&B vocal stylist who helped pave the way for the soul music explosion of the Sixties yet never quite became part of it. He was born in Detroit, Michigan, on 9 June 1936, and was discovered by **Johnny Otis** at a talent show in 1951. An admirer of **Clyde McPhatter**, he replaced him as lead singer with Billy Ward's **Dominoes** in 1953. His solo career took off in 1957 when he recorded 'Reet Petite', written in part by Berry Gordy Jr of Motown fame, for Brunswick. It's said that **Elvis Presley** derived some of his singing style and presentation from watching Wilson's dynamic stage act.

In October 1958, Wilson had his first million seller in 'Lonely Teardrops', an unexceptional side after the initial shock of his suitably jerking, sobbing style. Once again, Gordy had a hand in the composition. His second million-seller came in March 1960, with his double-sided hit 'Night' and 'Doggin' Around'. The first was an adaptation of Camille Saint-Saëns' 'My Heart at Thy Sweet Voice' from *Samson and Delilah*, a hugely swelling ballad ambitiously standing in a direct line from Richard Tauber, Mario Lanza, and other operatic popularizers of the immediate post-war years. But perhaps 'Doggin' Around' was more characteristic of the R&B artist, replete with sanctified organ strains and unbelievable, wailing vocal peaks.

Wilson's best sides were less successful commercially. 'Reet Petite' represents him at his finest with a truly joyous performance pulling every local stop possible as he rolls and stutters and screams over the band. Equally wild were 'Baby Work Out', released in March 1963, a tough dance exhortation in that familiar, crying blues style to heavy brass accompaniment and an earlier recording, the greasily sliding 'A Woman, a Lover, a Friend' from July 1960. This was copied later by **Otis Redding**. Impressive ballad performances include 'To Be Loved', a semi-operatic styling from February 1958, and 'Alone At Last', based on Tchaikovsky's Piano Concerto in B Flat Minor and sung with barely contained power.

Jackie Wilson was a masterly 'live' performer and an artist of astonishing range, technically and generically. Unfortunately, his unique blend of big voice, gospel fervour and rock'n'roll rhythm gave way to the first soul boom of the Sixties. The girls stopped screaming although he continued to haunt the Hot 100. He saw some action on 'Whispers' in September 1966. 'Higher and Higher' made Number 6 in the US in 1967 and later that year he had a modest disco success with 'Since You Showed Me How To Be Happy'. His last noteworthy outing was 'I Get the Sweetest Feeling', released in July 1968 and a hit in the UK on its re-release in 1975.

On 29 September 1975, Wilson suffered a heart attack at the Latin Casino, Camden, New Jersey; he hit his head as he fell, lapsed into a coma and suffered severe brain damage owing to oxygen starvation. **Barry White** contributed $10,000 to his care, and the (**Detroit**) **Spinners**, the Asbury Jukes and others raised some $70,000 through benefit concerts. He finally died on 21 January 1984.

In late 1986, 'Reet Petite' was re-issued in the UK and became a Number 1. Jackie Wilson was one of the greatest popular R&B exponents to emerge from the Fifties and he has suffered shameful critical neglect. Unique and without parallel, only a handful of singers can come near him.

WINGS See **McCartney, Paul**

WINTER, EDGAR The younger

brother of bluesman **Johnny Winter**, keyboard player and saxophonist Edgar Winter was born in Beaumont, Texas, on 28 December 1946, and played with him in a local band called the Black Plague in the mid-Sixties. He became a full-time member of Johnny's band towards the end of the decade and left to go solo in 1969, debuting a year later with the Epic album, *Entrance*. He then formed White Trash for the albums *White Trash* (1971) and *Road Work* (1972), before putting together the Edgar Winter Group with vocalist/bassist Dan Hartman, guitarist Ronnie Montrose and drummer Chuck Ruff; their 1973 single, 'Frankenstein', became a US Number 1 and a Number 16 in the UK. **Rick Derringer** joined later that year and cemented the Group as a major stadium attraction. Edgar took time out from the Group to record a 1975 solo album for Blue Sky, *Jasmine Nightdreams*, and in 1976 (after cutting an album, *With Johnny Winter: Together*, with his brother) he took a lengthy sabbatical, making occasional guest appearances on other artists' albums (Derringer and Hartman's solo releases, **Bette Midler**'s *Songs for the New Depression*) but recording no new material under his own name. In 1979 he re-formed the Group, but subsequent albums were solid rather than spectacular and lacked the edge that Derringer and Hartman, in particular, had previously brought out in his playing.

WINTER, JOHNNY One of America's most outstanding white blues guitarists of the Sixties and early Seventies, Johnny Winter (an albino) was born in Beaumont, Texas, on 23 February 1944, of a musical family. He started playing clarinet at five but changed to ukelele and then guitar at the age of eleven. After playing in various rock'n'roll bands in his teens, he made a short pilgrimage to Chicago in 1962 and played with such later blues luminaries as **Barry Goldberg** and **Mike Bloomfield**. On returning to Texas he joined brother Edgar's band for three years and then settled in Houston, determined to emulate the success of other white blues guitarists then emerging. With John 'Red' Turner (drums) and Tommy Shannon (bass) he started playing original blues-inspired rock in the local clubs, slowly gaining a devoted following.

In 1968 a rave *Rolling Stone* article attracted New York club owner Steve Paul. Masterminding a record-breaking contract from Columbia Records, Paul helped catapult Winter to stardom with albums like *Johnny Winter* (1969) and *Johnny Second Winter* (1970). In 1970 the band dissolved and the **McCoys** – Rick Derringer (guitar), Randy Hobbs (bass) and Randy Z (drums) – joined for *Johnny Winter And* (1970). The pressures of imminent superstardom and endless tours caused the band to turn to heroin and by 1972 Winter had hospitalized himself to recuperate. In 1973, he returned to performing with *Still Alive and Well*, utilizing his brother's touring crew to make short, civilized tours possible.

In 1976, he joined brother Edgar once more to record *Together* but found himself increasingly standing in the younger Winter's shadow. *Nothin' but the Blues* (1977) found Johnny recording with his musical mentor, **Muddy Waters**, and he also produced three late Seventies Waters albums, namely *Hard Again*, *I'm Ready* and *Live*, and toured as part of Waters' band. By this time, however, Winter appeared to be the victim of culture lag: cut off from the Sixties' spirit of musical adventure and operating in an area increasingly dominated by heavy metal bands, he lost his constituency. He visited the UK in May 1979 to promote *White Hot and Blue* and released *Raisin' Cain* in 1980, but his best days seemed over.

WINWOOD, STEVE Once described by **Al Kooper** as 'the finest white blues singer I have ever heard', Steve (originally, Stevie) Winwood found early fame as a vocalist and keyboard player with Birmingham's **Spencer Davis Group** before joining **Traffic** in 1967. Born in Great Barr, Birmingham, England, on 12 May 1948, he was organist with a Muff Woody Jazz Band at the age of 14 and developed a command of diverse musical idioms including blues, jazz, folk, ska, bluebeat and rock. His involvement during 1966 in the studio project Powerhouse, with **Eric Clapton**, **Jack Bruce**, Paul Jones, Pete York and Ben Palmer, was an indicator of things to come; not only as a member of Traffic but as a contributor to other much-vaunted 'progressive' ventures like **Blind Faith** and **Ginger Baker**'s Airforce, of which he was a member during 1970–1. Traffic, meanwhile, carried on until 1975, after which Winwood played on sessions for **Sandy Denny**, Stomu Yamashta, **George Harrison** and **Toots and the Maytals**, but it was not until 1976 that he recorded his first solo album, *Steve Winwood* (Island). It contained a number of compositions co-written with fellow Traffic member **Jim Capaldi** and ex-**Bonzo Dog Doo Dah Band** member Viv Stanshall, on whose albums *Men Opening Umbrellas* (1974) and *Sir Henry at Rawlinson's End* (1978) Winwood also collaborated. He guested on Stomu Yamashta's *Go Live from Paris* (1976) – his vocal on 'Crossing the Line' one of its highlights – and released a second album, *Arc of a Diver*, in 1980. Featuring Winwood songs with lyrics by Will Jennings, George Fleming and Viv Stanshall, the album demonstrated his mastery of synthesizer technology and presaged the subsequent *Talking Back to the Night* (1982), on which he made innovative use of Multimoog and polysynthesizer. By the mid-Eighties, Winwood was one of Britain's great 'elder statesmen' of rock, though still fashionable enough to score a major success (during 1986) with the album *Back in the High Life* and the transatlantic Top 20 single, 'Higher Love'. *See also* **Traffic**

WIRE It is only in recent years that Wire have been afforded their proper place in the punk pantheon. Their 1977 debut album, *Pink Flag*, boasting no less than twenty-one short and fast tracks, was misread as just another subscription to the three-minute-thrash ethic. It took 1978's *Chairs Missing*, moving at a more relaxed pace with only fifteen tracks, to show their true colours. While their art-school background was evident – and would reveal itself at greater length in later years – this LP was a collection of perverse punk cameos using the form but with a complexity that was the antithesis of the three-minute thrash. Pointing back to earlier experiments and on to the **Joy Division** 'school', it was a punk landmark comparable to **Television**'s *Marquee Moon*.

Unfortunately, this turned out to be the peak of their accomplishments; after a brief foray into performance art, Wire split in 1980. Drummer Robert Gotobed fled to deepest Wales, synthesizer/singer Colin Newman attempted a solo career with albums such as *Not To* (1982), and the duo of Graham Lewis (bass) and Bruce C. Gilbert (guitar) became known on the fringes of the noise/performance scene, notably with such albums as *MZUI* (1982), *Will You Speak This Word?* and their work under the name Dome. The group re-formed in late 1985, playing low-key dates under their own name.

WISHBONE ASH Among the most durable bands to emerge out of Britain's progressive rock scene of the late Sixties, Wishbone Ash was formed in early 1969 from a nucleus of Steve Upton (drums, born 24 May 1946) and Martin Turner (1 October 1947), who hired guitarists Andy Powell (8 February 1950) and Ted Turner (2 August 1950) through a *Melody Maker* advertisement. Their twin lead guitar line-up was unusual for the time, such a style of presentation having previously been attempted only by **Jimmy Page** and **Jeff Beck** in the last phases of the **Yardbirds**. Though not a media favourite, the band quickly established a large popular following through their first two albums *Wishbone Ash* (1970) and *Pilgrimage* (1971); their third release, *Argus* (1972) reached Number 3 in the UK album chart. Although they failed to capture the dynamic live qualities of their act on record, they continued to be a major concert attraction in Britain and the US, where they decided to settle permanently during 1975. By that time, Ted Turner had left the band, his replacement being Laurie Wisefield, formerly lead guitarist with Home.

There's the Rub (1974) was followed by *Locked In* (1976), a disappointing set despite the presence of **Tom Dowd** as producer, and a succession of well-received albums that pleased their following without attracting many new converts – *New England* (1977), *Front Page News* (1977), *No Smoke Without Fire* (1978) and *Just Testing* (1979). Martin Turner departed in 1980 and was replaced temporarily by former **King Crimson** and **Family** member John Wetton, and ex-**Uriah Heep** bassist Trevor Bolder and singer Claire Hamill also joined the band for a brief period. Although their sound had, by the Eighties, become indistinguishable from innumerable bands producing hard rock, Wishbone Ash deserved credit for developing the dual guitar sound adopted so successfully by **Thin Lizzy** and others in the Seventies.

WITHERS, BILL Best known for his US chart-topping 'Lean On Me' (1972), singer/songwriter Bill Withers came comparatively late to professional music-making. Born in Slab Fork, West Virginia, on 4 July 1938, he spent nine years in the US Navy before joining IBM as a computer operator and writing songs outside working hours. Using his own material, Withers made a demonstration tape and hustled his wares around numerous West Coast record companies before being signed to Sussex by Clarence Avant. His debut album, *Just As I Am*, was produced by **Booker T.** and featured **Stephen Stills** among the accompanying musicians. One of the album's strongest songs, the plaintive and sparsely funky 'Ain't No Sunshine', gave Withers a Number 3 US hit during 1971 and became a major UK hit in a version by **Michael Jackson** a year later. The subtle, gospel-like 'Lean On Me' established Withers internationally during 1972, reaching Number 18 in the UK, and further US hits followed in the shape of 'Use Me' – particularly notable for its embryonic street-funk – and 'Kissing My Love' (1973). Legal wrangles with Sussex led to Withers'departure for Columbia in 1975, for whom he recorded four albums and the 1978 hit single 'Lovely Day', a Number 30 in the US and a Number 7 in the UK. Further hits have since eluded him, though his voice could be heard on Grover Washington Jr's 1981 hit, 'Just the Two of Us' (a US Number 2).

WITHERSPOON, JIMMY Born in Gurdon, Arkansas, on 8 August 1923, Jimmy Witherspoon was one of the big names in hard-driving blues shouting which developed in the Thirties (and on which R&B grew) particularly in and around Kansas City. In 1945, he teamed up with boogie pianist, Jay McShann, who led an earthy jump band on America's West Coast. Rapidly gaining experience, he went solo in 1952 and soon became established as an international name on the jazz and blues circuit. His biggest hits include 'Big Fine Girl', 'Ain't Nobody's Business' and 'No Rollin' Blues'. Since the mid-Fifties,

Witherspoon has travelled widely, increasing his reputation all the time. His musical activities have been diverse, ranging from straight jazz to a rock album with **Eric Burdon**.

WOMACK, BOBBY Now an international star in his own right, Bobby Womack was for ten years recognized only as the originator of the **Rolling Stones**' first UK Number 1, 'It's All Over Now', and as a shadowy composer/session guitarist behind countless other stars, among them **Sam Cooke** and **Wilson Pickett**. Born in Cleveland, Ohio, on 4 March 1944, he first recorded for Cooke's Sar label with his brothers Harris, Cecil, Curtis and Friendly, singing gospel under their own name and then R&B as the **Valentinos**. Their R&B hits included 'Looking for a Love' (1962) and 'It's All Over Now' (1964). Womack's solo releases on Him, Checker, Atlantic and Keymen were largely ignored, but while contracted to Minit/Liberty between 1967 and 1970 he began attracting attention with an unusual mixture of original songs ('What is This', 'It's Gonna Rain', 'More Than I Can Stand') and rearrangements of middle-of-the-road hits such as 'Fly Me to the Moon' and 'I Left My Heart in San Francisco'.

Encouraged by Sly Stone, he reached wider audiences by adopting a looser and more personalized format, including raps and extended instrumental passages, that earned him the nickname of 'The Preacher'. Recording for United Artists, Columbia and Arista, his best performances included 'Communication', 'That's the Way I Feel About Cha' (1971), 'You're Welcome, Stop On By' (1974), 'Check It Out' (1975), and new interpretations of several of his early songs. Towards the end of the decade, Womack's career appeared to be in decline, but such fears were soon arrested by his guest appearance on the album *Inherit the Wind* and the single of the same name, released by Wilton Felder of the **Crusaders** in 1980. The success of both prompted new interest in Womack's career and he recorded one of *the* R&B albums of the year – *The Poet*, on Beverly Glenn – in 1981 and a sequel album, *The Poet II*, produced by ex-Stones manager **Andrew Loog Oldham**, a year later.

WOMACK AND WOMACK Cecil, brother of **Bobby Womack**, and Linda, daughter of **Sam Cooke**, had enough family pedigree to ensure that their efforts as songwriters would be blessed with success. He was a member

of the Womacks gospel group which went secular as the **Valentinos** and had a big hit in 1964 with 'It's All Over Now', later covered by the **Rolling Stones**. Linda, meanwhile, had begun writing songs at the age of 14: 'I'm In Love', a hit for **Wilson Pickett** was an early composition and she also co-wrote 'Woman's Gotta Have It' for Bobby Womack.

Cecil married and divorced from pioneer Motown singer **Mary Wells**. By then the Womacks had moved to Los Angeles and were living near the Cookes, who had long been friends. The couple first met when aged thirteen and eight respectively. They started writing together in the early Seventies for Phil Walden's Capricorn label but it wasn't until they started working for **Gamble and Huff**'s Philadelphia International set-up that their work was heard on a wider platform; they married in 1979. 'TKO' for **Teddy Pendergrass**, 'I Just Want to Satisfy You' for the **O'Jays**, 'I Just Called to Say', again for Pendergrass, were among several written either by Cecil or as a couple for Philly's top Seventies stars. They also wrote for **Patti Labelle**, the Dramatics, Mary Wells, **Millie Jackson** and **Randy Crawford**, among many others. But when in 1983 they signed a recording deal with Elektra, they gave their own songs uniquely warm, 'real' readings on *Love Wars*, an album whose title track became a hit. This album also included their version of 'TKO' in a series of songs which, like brother Bobby's then current 'Poet' records on which their songs appeared, heralded a return of traditional soul writing and performing. A second album, *Radio M.U.S.C. Man*, was drawn in darker shades, more sombrely atmospheric. Live performances suggested that the studio was their forte as they had trouble finding the correct balance between man and woman as focus of the act.

WONDER, STEVIE In terms of sales and volume of hits, Stevie Wonder ranks as the Motown Corporation's most successful artist ever. Achieving fame initially as a child prodigy, he continued to develop musically until his vast audience in the Eighties spanned black and white, pop and rock. He was born Steveland Judkins on 13 May 1950 in Saginaw, Michigan, and was blind from birth. Taking up harmonica from an early age, he was brought to the notice of Motown founder Berry Gordy by Ronnie White of the **Miracles** in 1960.

A year later Gordy set up his own

label and recorded 'Little Stevie Wonder' as a falsetto R&B screamer and harmonica player. His third single, 'Fingertips Part 2' (Tamla) reached Number 1 in 1963 and for two years he was promoted as the Boy Genius, proclaiming his admiration for 'Uncle Ray' (**Ray Charles**) and enjoying minor hits including 'Hey Harmonica Man' (1964) and 'High Heel Sneakers' (1965).

'Uptight', a Top 10 hit in 1965, marked a change in style towards a more orthodox Motown sound and, as his voice deepened, his singles veered towards the romantic balladry of 'I Was Made to Love Her' (1967) and 'For Once in My Life' (1968). Like most of his early hits, the former was part-written by Wonder and his producer Henry Cosby, while the latter typified the middle-of-the-road reputation Wonder was beginning to acquire: it had previously been recorded by Tony Bennett.

With the release of the *Where I'm Coming From* album (1971), he abruptly turned towards the progressive rock music of the time, making extensive use of the Moog synthesizer and writing philosophical lyrics. In the same year he married Syreeta Wright and renegotiated his relationship with Tamla, for the first time retaining full artistic control over his work.

Music of My Mind (1972) and *Syreeta* (which he masterminded in the same year) were consummate examples of his new style of 'black rock'. On *Music*, he played every instrument, perfecting the interplay between a variety of electronic keyboard sounds, production techniques and his light, clear vocals. *Talking Book* (1972) and *Innervisions* (1973) confirmed Wonder's major status, and he recovered from a near-fatal automobile crash to release *Fulfillingness First Finale* in 1974. If that album was thought by some critics to be somewhat repetitive, his best songs during the Seventies ranged from the raunchy rock of 'Superstition' through the serene lyricism of 'I Believe (When I Fall in Love with You It Will Be Forever)' to the compassionate social comment of 'Living in the City'. In 1975, he re-signed with Motown for the biggest ever advance, a massive 13 million dollars.

Late 1976 brought the hitherto much-postponed release of a double album, *Songs in the Key of Life*, the highlights of which included a joyous homage to Duke Ellington, 'Sir Duke', and a much-covered track dedicated to Stevie's newly-born daughter, 'Isn't She Lovely'. A stunning creative and commercial success, the album took

Stevie Wonder offers the microphone to Motown boss Berry Gordy

Wonder into the megastar bracket, though critical reaction to his next release – the soundtrack for an unreleased documentary film, *Journey Through the Secret Life of Plants* (1979) – was by no means as favourable. By the early Eighties, however, the pattern of *tour-de-force* albums and astutely-chosen singles was well established, each release tending to highlight not only his faultless hit-making sense but a genuine and ever-increasing commitment to black and human rights issues. 'Masterblaster (Jammin')' was his 1980 tribute to **Bob Marley**, 'Happy Birthday' (1981) a campaign song for his (eventually successful) crusade to have Martin Luther King's birthday adopted as a national holiday, and he used his acceptance speech at the Academy Awards ceremony in 1985 – when his 'I Just Called to Say I Love You' from *The Woman in Red* won an Oscar for Best Original Song – to call for the release of jailed black South African leader Nelson Mandela.

More than any other artist, Stevie Wonder has rendered divisions between white rock and black music almost meaningless, his records the epitome of 'crossover' appeal yet devoid of the musical compromise that the term sometimes implies. Versatile and extraordinarily prolific – besides his own solo work, he has appeared on record with and/or written for artists as various as **Chaka Khan**, **Cliff Richard** and **Paul McCartney** (their duet 'Ebony and Ivory' was a multi-million seller in 1982) – Stevie Wonder remains one of the rock era's great originals.

WOOD, ROY A master of pop pastiche, Roy Wood's career as a performer, songwriter and producer has spanned over twenty years. He was born Ulysses Adrian Wood on 8 November 1946, in Birmingham, England, and learned guitar in his early teens, when he started forming and joining bands – the Falcons, the Lawmen, Gerry Levine and the Avengers, Mike Sheridan and the Nightriders and finally, in 1966, the **Move**. Their debut hit single, 'Night of Fear' (Deram, 1967), was a Roy Wood composition that cleverly incorporated the main theme from Tchaikovsky's 1812 Overture. Six hit singles later, in 1970, former Idle Race guitarist-singer **Jeff Lynne** joined the band and began formulating, with Wood, the idea of an Electric Light Orchestra (*see* **ELO**). The idea did not reach fruition until 1972, by which time the relationship between Wood and Lynne was uneasy. Wood left and formed Wizzard that year.

After an initial hit, 'Ball Park Incident' (Harvest, 1973), Wood unleashed his re-creation of **Phil Spector** productions with 'See My Baby Jive', appearing in multicoloured fright wig and warpaint to promote it. The record reached Number 1 in the UK in 1973, as did the follow-up, 'Angel Fingers', and he continued to mine this successful formula with a Spector-style Christmas record, 'I Wish It Could Be Christmas Everyday'. Wizzard's success continued into 1974 with 'Rock-'n'Roll Winter' and 'Are You Ready to Rock', but by this time Wood was concentrating more on a parallel solo career that had begun with *Boulders* (Harvest, released in 1973 but recorded three years earlier). Apart from playing all the instruments on the album, he also produced and engineered it and designed and painted its cover. Of his four solo hit singles, 'Forever' (1973), a tribute to both **Neil Sedaka** and the **Beach Boys**, achieved the highest placing by reaching Number 8. By 1975, he had appeared on more than twenty-five UK hit singles, either solo or as a member of the Move, ELO or Wizzard.

Apart from two successful reissues (in 1981 and 1984) of 'I Wish it Could Be Christmas Everyday', Wood has remained a chart absentee since 1975. After disbanding Wizzard he formed Wizzo and subsequently the Helicopters, and he produced the 1978 debut album by Annie Haslam of **Renaissance**, *Annie in Wonderland* (Sire), on which he also guested. Much of Wood's best recording work is represented on *The Singles* (Speed), a retrospective compilation released in 1982.

WORKING WEEK

WORKING WEEK Based around the nucleus of Simon Booth (guitar), Larry Stabbins (saxophone) and Julie Roberts (vocals), Working Week's powerful blend of jazz and soul made them the standout band of the so-called jazz revival in the mid-Eighties.

Booth and Stabbins had worked together on two LPs up to 1983 in Weekend, a critically respected rock–jazz–dance band. Weekend's sound had been increasingly jazz-influenced, and when Booth later witnessed the burgeoning London Latin-jazz dance scene he saw its potential and wrote the Latin-influenced 'Venceremos', Working Week's first single in 1984.

Booth and Stabbins worked with a varied line-up of musicians and guest vocalists including **Robert Wyatt** and Tracey Thorn, and the band's live appearances across the UK became major events, with an impressive presence on stage of musicians and dancers. The duo eventually recruited Roberts, a talented and powerful singer who had scored a UK Top 10 single as the vocalist on Funk Masters' 'It's Over', as their full-time singer. Working Week released their debut LP, *Working Nights* in 1985 to rave reviews.

WRAY, LINK Born of Shawnee Indian stock in Fort Bragg, North Carolina in 1930, Link (short for Lincoln) Wray played in a country band with his brothers Doug and Vernon before recording 'Rumble' for Cadence in 1958. It reached Number 16 in the Hot 100 and eventually sold over a million copies, chiefly on the strength of the harsh, menacing chords and progressively intense reverberation on Wray's lead guitar work. 'Rawhide' (Epic) gave Wray another instrumental hit a year later, reaching Number 23, but of his subsequent singles only 'Jack the Ripper' (Swan, 1963) achieved a hit placing. For the best part of a decade, Wray recorded in his own three-track studio in Maryland, some of these tracks surfacing on his 1971 comeback album, *Link Wray*, on Polydor. The album renewed critical interest and brought to light privately supervised recordings for Vermilion and Record Factory. Further albums followed – *Be What You Want* (Polydor, 1973), *Beans and Fatback* (Virgin, 1973), *Stuck in Gear* (Virgin, 1976) – and in 1977 he began an association with rockabilly singer Robert Gordon, the fruits of which could be heard on *Robert Gordon with Link Wray* (Private Stock, 1977). Wray's later solo releases include *Bullshot* (Charisma, 1979) and *Live at El Paradiso* (Instant, 1980).

WRIGHT, BETTY Born in Miami on 21 December 1953, Betty Wright was signed by local writer/producers Willie Clarke and Clarence Reid at the age of eleven. She sang on sessions and made a number of solo recordings for the Deep City and Solid Soul labels before Clarke and Reid took her to Henry Stone's TK Organization in 1967. The following year, 'Girls Can't Do What the Guys Do' (Alston) gave her the first of several romantic hits ('Pure Love', 'I've Found That Guy' in 1970; 'I Love the Way You Love'in 1971) until the funky 'Clean Up Woman' (1971) introduced a new mature image. Now considered a classic of its type (and featuring Little Beaver's crisp guitar work), 'Clean Up Woman' was followed by hits on similar themes ('Is It You Girl', 'Babysitter' in 1972; 'Let Me Be Your Lovemaker' in 1973; 'Secretary' in 1974) and two Hot 100 hits in 'Shoorah and Shoorah' and 'Where is the Love' (both 1975). One of the best-known of TK's family of artists, her best and most representative albums to date are arguably *Danger: High Voltage* (Alston, 1973) and *Betty Wright Live* (Alston, 1978). She switched from Alston to Epic in 1981 and has kept to the forefront of black music without achieving major crossover success.

WYATT, ROBERT One of the most imaginative presences in British rock since the early Seventies, Robert Wyatt was formerly drummer with **Soft Machine** between 1967 and 1971. An able and sardonic lyricist, the tone and title of his first solo album – *End of an Ear* (CBS, 1970) – presaged what·was to follow. He formed Matching Mole (from the French for Soft Machine, *machine molle*) with David Sinclair and Dave McRae (keyboards), Bill Mac-Cormick (bass), and Phil Miller (guitar) in late 1971. Two exceptional but commercially unsuccessful albums followed, *Matching Mole* (1972) and *Little Red Record* (1973), the former of which included the lyrical 'O Caroline'. Wyatt became a central figure in the loose circle of British avant-garde and jazz-rock musicians, appearing on Keith Tippett's Centipede album *September Energy* (1971) and giving encouragement to **Henry Cow**, but had a surprise UK hit in 1974 with a deadpan, cockney-style version of the **Monkees**' 'I'm a Believer'. Released on Virgin, it reached Number 29. An accident that same year left him paralysed from the waist down and confined him to studio and occasional live work, though 1974 also saw the release of his second album, *Rock Bottom. Ruth is Stranger*

than Richard appeared a year later, and he also guested on albums by Daevid Allen, Phil Manzanera and Brian Eno.

In the Eighties, a series of singles on the Rough Trade label – notably his 1983 anti-Falklands War single *Shipbuilding*, written by **Elvis Costello**, which reached Number 35 in the UK despite minimal airplay – showed that his distinctive vocal style, his idiosyncratic musical sense and his political commitments reained unimpaired. His 1982 album *Nothing Can Stop Us* contained brilliantly conceived reworkings of 'The Red Flag' and Billie Holiday's 'Strange Fruit', and he has since worked extensively with Jerry Dammers (*see the* **Specials**).

WYNETTE, TAMMY Variously described as the Queen of Nashville and the First Lady of Country Music, Tammy Wynette was born Wynette Pugh on 5 May 1942 in Itawamba County, Mississippi. She worked in a beauty parlour before turning to professional singing and secured a residency on the *Country Boy Eddy Show* in 1965. She then sang briefly with Porter Wagoner, after his partner Norma Jean had left but before he began his association with **Dolly Parton**, and worked as a song-plugger prior to her signing with Epic Records in 1966.

Her first record, produced by **Billy Sherrill**, was 'Apartment No. 9'. It reached Number 44 in Billboard's country chart but was followed in 1967 by her first major success, 'Your Good Girl's Gonna Go Bad', which peaked at Number 3. Her next release, 'I Don't Wanna Play House', inaugurated a string of country chart-toppers, mostly written by Sherrill, Glenn Sutton (husband of fellow country singer Lynn Anderson) and Wynette herself. However, it was only when 'D-I-V-O-R-C-E' and 'Stand By Your Man' (a UK Number 1 when re-released in 1975) entered the US Hot 100 in 1968 that she became a major force in country music: both were paeans to the traditional virtues of Southern family life and were vividly extolled by Wynette's searing vocals and Sherrills' Spectorish productions.

Her 1968 marriage to top country singer **George Jones** (which ended in divorce in 1975) and the mass of country awards she won that year confirmed her status. Despite her success in the pop market, she has doggedly refused to alter either the content of her songs – 'Don't Liberate Me' and 'Joy to be a Woman' were representative of her Seventies titles – or her vocal styling, which remains uncompromising and countrified beneath the banks of strings with which she is supplied by Sherrill. She charted her extraordinarily eventful life – which has included five marriages, serious illnesses, and a 1978 kidnapping – in her autobiography *Stand By Your Man*, published in 1979, which was subsequently dramatized for a made-for-television film.

X-RAY SPEX

X-RAY SPEX Punk legends X-Ray Spex were among the first to conquer the UK charts, notching up three hit singles and a hit album in a brief but dazzling career. Fronted by two of the leading ladies of punk, singer Poly Styrene (real name Marion Ellis) and sax-player Lora Logic, X-Ray Spex burst on to the scene in 1977, quickly becoming a huge favourite and a regular in punk clubs across the country.

They released the raucous feminist anthem 'Oh Bondage, Up Yours!', an instant classic, before the less raw 'The Day the World Turned Day-Glow' sneaked into the Top 30 in April 1978. Two further hits and a UK Top 30 album *Germ-Free Adolescents* (1978) followed before the band split, with Poly Styrene leaving the music business after undergoing a religious conversion and Lora Logic continued with her own band, Essential Logic.

XTC

XTC One of a clutch of bands who emerged out of the 1977 punk-new wave explosion but transcended that era's stylistic limitations, XTC had a constantly challenging and innovative pop vision that found plenty of critical approval on both sides of the Atlantic, but never quite managed to generate more than a strong cult following.

First formed in Swindon, Wiltshire, in 1973 by Andy Partridge (guitar/vocals), Colin Moulding (bass/vocals) and Terry Chambers (drums), the band toured their locality under various names, but it wasn't until the recruitment of Barry Andrews (keyboards) and their signing to Virgin Records that they surfaced as XTC. In 1977, their first release, an album called *3D-EP*, premiered Partridge and Moulding's eccentric, jerky pop concoctions. As the band's career progressed, the pair's sensitivity for a strong hookline brought invidious comparisons with various prominent bands, most notably the **Beatles**.

Andrews left in 1979, eventually to form Shriekback with Dave Allen of **Gang of Four**, and was replaced by guitarist Dave Gregory. XTC's most successful period then followed with three excellent albums, *Drums and Wires* (1979), *Black Sea* (1980) and *English Settlement* (1982), spawning five UK Top 40 singles, including 'Senses Working Overtime', which reached Number 10 in January '82. After the release of the LP *English Settlement*, however, Partridge became seriously ill, a factor that strongly influenced XTC's decision to retire permanently from their hectic touring schedule. This allowed the band to step outside the workings of the main body of the music industry, and subsequent recordings – the LPs *Mummer* (1983), *The Big Express* (1984) and the exceptional *Skylarking* (1986, produced by **Todd Rundgren**) – have been characterized by a unique parochial English feel that delights critics but continues to leave the vast majority of the public unmoved.

YARDBIRDS

YARDBIRDS Arguably the most innovative of all the groups to emerge from within the London R&B circuit during the early to mid-Sixties, the Yardbirds grew out of a Kingston art school band called the Metropolitan Blues Quartet. Inspired by the **Rolling Stones**' performances at the Station Hotel, Richmond, early in 1963, the five Yardbirds – Keith Relf, vocals, harmonica (born 22 March 1943); Anthony 'Top' Topham, lead guitar; Chris Dreja, rhythm guitar (11 November 1946); Paul Samwell-Smith, bass (8 May 1943) and Jim McCarty, drums (25 July 1943) – made their debut at Eel Pie island and, with **Eric Clapton** replacing Topham, took over the Stones' Crawdaddy residency. However, despite a strong following on the R&B club circuit and *Five Live Yardbirds* (the quintessential British R&B album), the Yardbirds had no chart success until 1965 when they recorded three Graham Gouldman compositions – 'For Your Love', 'Heart Full of Soul' and 'Evil Hearted You' – all of which reached the Top 3 on EMI's Columbia label. The overt commerciality of these caused Clapton to quit. He was replaced by **Jeff Beck**, whose penchant for electronic effects earned the group an American reputation as psychedelic pioneers.

The Yardbirds during the brief link-up between Jeff Beck and Jimmy Page (back row left and right) in 1966

In June 1966, the endless touring forced Samwell-Smith to retire and **Jimmy Page**, who had turned down the chance to join when Clapton left, took his place. Dreja moved to bass and Page joined Beck on lead: their unison riffs and interchanged solos were exciting, if inconsistent, but within six months Beck split. Their appearance in Italian film director Michelangelo Antonioni's film of the 'Swinging London' of the Sixties, *Blow-Up*, had a lot to do with Page's later impact with **Led Zeppelin** in the US. Although they continued as a four-piece until July 1968, the last eighteen months produced little of merit and on stage they turned increasingly into self-confessed puppets. Following the break-up, Relf and McCarty worked as a duo, Together, before forming **Renaissance**; Dreja took up photography, and Page put together the New Yardbirds – Led Zeppelin, managed by former Yardbirds road-manager, Peter Grant. On 14 May 1976, Keith Relf accidentally electrocuted himself while playing guitar at home. *See also* **Led Zeppelin**; **Jeff Beck**; **Eric Clapton**; **Jimmy Page**

YAZOO

YAZOO Formed in late 1981, the vocal duo Yazoo blended the songwriting and keyboard talents of ex-**Depeche Mode** man Vince Clarke with the warm, blues-influenced vocal power of **Alison Moyet**. During 1982–3 they scored a hatful of hit singles and two hugely successful albums, and were Britain's leading electro-pop outfit.

Clarke left Depeche Mode after writing their first three hit singles and decided to concentrate on solo work at his home in Basildon, Essex. He already knew Moyet (they'd been in the same oboe class), and they got together purely to do a one-off demo. The session was such a success that they decided to release one of the songs from it, 'Only You', on the small Mute label, and Yazoo was born. The record was a huge hit, reaching Number 2 in the UK in April '82 and staying in the chart for three months. This success was followed up by the Number 3 hit, 'Don't Go'. Their debut LP *Upstairs at Eric's* topped the UK Independent charts and reached Number 2 on the main LP chart, confirming Yazoo's status as a top-selling group.

But the duo was soon to end. The two had different approaches to music and Moyet found the electronic form too limiting for her vocal range. They agreed to split in mid-1983, after scoring two more hit singles and recording a second album, *You and Me Both*. Moyet went on to a highly successful solo career, and Clarke got involved in various other projects including a UK hit single, 'Never Never' (Number 4 in November '83), under the name the Assembly, which featured **Feargal Sharkey** on vocals. In 1986 he re-emerged with vocalist Andrew Bell in a new band, Erasure. A single, 'Oh L'Amour', was released in April with an album, *Wonderland*, following shortly after. The duo finally made it into the UK charts early in 1987 with the single 'It Doesn't Have to Be'.

YELLOW MAGIC ORCHESTRA

The best-known and most successful rock band to have come out of Japan, synth- and computer-based Yellow Magic Orchestra united the exceptional talents of three of Japan's most influential musicians – Haruomi Hosono, Riuichi Sakamoto and Yukihiro Takahashi.

Hosono, who had had a strong solo career since the early Seventies, Takahashi, once drummer with the Sadistic Mika Band (one of the few Japanese bands to gain international recognition) and Sakamoto, a respected sessioneer, joined forces in 1978 after working on a Hosono solo album, *Paraiso*. Their first LP, *Yellow Magic Orchestra*, was more of a critical than commercial hit but their second, *Solid State Survivor* (1979), sold over 2 million copies and established YMO worldwide.

The trio's success with music technology encouraged many others and their influence was strongly felt in the British electro boom of the early Eighties. All three work regularly outside the band as session players and solo artists (Sakamoto being the most

conspicuous with a couple of international hit singles and the widely praised soundtrack for the film *Merry Christmas Mr Lawrence*), a factor that has limited the number of YMO releases, but they nevertheless had four albums in the Japanese Top 20 in 1980.

People with Smiles (1983) broke a long silence and featured the first European to appear on a YMO album, Bill Nelson (from **Be-Bop Deluxe**).

YES

The leading practitioners of symphonic rock in the Seventies, Yes was formed in the summer of 1968 by Jon Anderson (born in Accrington, Lancashire, on 25 October 1944), former singer with his brother Tony's group, the Warriors, and Chris Squire (North London, 4 March 1948), who had played bass in the Selfs and the Syn, the latter of which released two unsuccessful singles on Deram in 1967. With Squire's fellow Syn members Bill Bruford, drums (17 May 1950), guitarist Pete Banks (Barnet, 7 July 1947), and keyboard player Tony Kaye (Leicester, 11 January 1946) completing the band, they signed to Atlantic and recorded their first album (*Yes*, 1969), which showed the influence of Keith Emerson's playing and the **Fifth Dimension**'s harmony singing. *Time and a Word* (1970) continued this approach, notably in the group's arrangements of **Richie Havens**' 'No Opportunity Necessary, No Experience Needed' and **Stephen Stills**' 'Everydays'.

Soon afterwards, Banks left to form Flash, a more conventional rock band, with vocalist Colin Carter. Apart from a minor American hit with 'Small Beginnings', the band had little success. He was replaced in Yes by Steve Howe, the former **Tomorrow** guitarist (8 April 1947). *The Yes Album* (1971) marked the beginning of the later Yes sound, with Kaye introducing Moog synthesizer and all the songs written from within the band.

Kaye was then replaced by the former **Strawb**, **Rick Wakeman**, whose mastery of classical keyboard styles – the result of an education at the Royal College of Music – had a liberating effect on the group on *Fragile* (1971). Yes, astutely guided by manager Brian Lane, were now ready to attempt the lengthy song-cycles and symphonic pieces on *Close to the Edge* (1972) and *Tales from Topographic Oceans* (1974), both of which featured drummer Alan White (14 June 1949), formerly with the Plastic Ono Band, who had replaced Bill Bruford in 1972. Though Anderson's lyrics veered towards incoherence, both albums

were full of contrasting passages in time, volume and tone, thrust together in powerful collages of sound. *Yessongs*, a triple live album, was released in 1973 and *Relayer* in 1974, when Rick Wakeman left to pursue a successful solo career with extended works like *The Six Wives of Henry VIII* (A&M, 1973) and *Journey to the Centre of the Earth* (1974). He was replaced by the Swiss musician, Patrick Moraz, who had previously played with Brian Davison and Lee Jackson in Refuge. Kaye's group Badger had by this time fallen apart.

During 1975 and 1976 the individual group members became involved in solo projects. By the time their next album (*Going for the One*, 1977) was released, Moraz had left the band over apparently insurmountable musical differences and Wakeman had rejoined. The album, very much a return to rock dynamism after the expansiveness of their preceding works, featured 'Wondrous Stories', which reached Number 7 in the UK chart when issued as a single during that same year. The album was also notable for the absence of a Roger Dean-designed cover and of producer Eddie Offord, who had severed his relationship with the group a year earlier. 1978 saw the release of *Tormato*, for the promotion of which they played tour dates on a circular stage with the audience all around, bringing band and audience closer together.

This closeness did not extend to the Yes membership, however, and in 1979 both Anderson and Wakeman left the band. Their replacements were Trevor Horn and Geoff Downes of **Buggles**, but the album *Drama* (1980) served mainly to emphasize the contradictions inherent in the new combination of talents. By the end of 1980 Yes was no more, Howe and Downes having joined **Asia** and Horn having moved into full-time record production. A live set, *Yesshows*, was released towards the end of that year. *See also* **Rick Wakeman**

YOUNG, NEIL

Born on 12 November 1945 in Toronto, Canada, Neil Young made his initial impact as a Dylanesque folksinger in Toronto's Yorkville in the mid-Sixties. He also played in folk-rock electric groups such as Neil Young and the Squires, before heading west to help form **Buffalo Springfield** in Los Angeles, early in 1966. He played lead guitar, wrote, and occasionally sang lead for the group.

His songs, for the Springfield and on his first solo album, *Neil Young* (Reprise, 1969), were notable for their blending of adult melancholy and childlike wonder and paranoia, their melodic invention, and the fluency of his guitar-playing. However, it was in 1969–70 that he came to the fore as a singer, with the albums *Everybody Knows This Is Nowhere* (1969) and *After the Goldrush* (1970). His high straining voice perfectly caught the mood of the Woodstock generation fighting a losing battle against political realities in a series of desperate love songs.

In summer 1969 he had joined Crosby and Nash and rejoined Stills in **Crosby, Stills, Nash and Young**, a grouping that lasted little over a year in recording terms, but which has been sustained as an amorphous institution ever since. His time with CSN&Y saw some of Young's best songs – notably 'Helpless' and 'Ohio' – and a chance to re-create onstage the twin guitar battles with Stills which had marked the Springfield's live performances and which Young had emulated with Danny Whitten on *Everybody Knows*.

The two years that followed the splitting of CSN&Y saw Young making an unsuccessful film, the soundtrack of which was eventually released as *Journey Through the Past* (1973) and preparing *Harvest* (1972), amidst trying to come to terms with the pressures of stardom and the interrelated death of friend Danny Whitten, caused by a drugs overdose in 1972. These two themes – the contradictions of stardom and death by drugs as a consequence of them – would henceforth rank with love and politics among the themes of his music.

Harvest, his most uneven and his best-selling album, also marked a new musical direction, away from the angry sadness of his lead guitar and graceful voice-dominated music. The new input was Ben Keith's pedal-steel playing, which provided a fatalistic tinge to the music from then on, as well as a sense of light and space to counterpoint Young's peculiarly repressed-anger style of lead guitar playing. On *Harvest*, 'A Man Needs a Maid', a song that dealt in role-playing in relationships with a depth and insight unthought of in previous years, marked the end of love as a major theme in his music.

The next three albums – *Time Fades Away* (1973), *On the Beach* (1974), and *Tonight's the Night* (1975) – explored three different aspects of Young's world-view. *Time Fades Away*, a live album, presented the positive persona, the determined dreamer and self-righteous moralist, featuring both solo performances on piano and Young's own blending of hard rock and country instrumentation. *On the Beach* was a more sombre album, less overtly personal, a despairing tour through Nixon's America. The lyrics verge on the surreal, the music dark and heavily restrained. *Tonight's the Night*, the last to be released but recorded between the other two, was the most personal, a collage of songs centring on junkie death. The lyrics were alternately obscure and lucid, the music a starker and rougher version of the *Time Fades Away* style. Surprisingly, that album was a big American hit, as was *Zuma* (1975), which was only marginally lighter in tone.

Young's next two album releases, *Stars'n'Bars* (1977) and *Comes a Time* (1978), were altogether mellower affairs, the cheerful cover of the latter revealing that he had come up smiling after his past vicissitudes (which included the break-up of his marriage). *Rust Never Sleeps* (1979), by contrast, contained one side of reflective material and one of electric rock: among its tracks were 'Powderfinger' and 'Sedan Delivery', both written with hard rockers **Lynyrd Skynyrd** in mind, and a song dedicated to the **Sex Pistols** – 'Out of the Blue'. *Hawks and Doves* (1980) and *Re-ac-tor* (1981) were similarly schizophrenic, the first featuring country material on one side and acoustic songs on the other, the second a much harder, heavier set; *Trans* (1982) found Young employing synthesizers, drum machines and vocoders to interesting and amusing effect, while *Everybody's Rockin'* (1983) was yet another change of pace – a 'roots' album of Young originals and versions of **Presley**'s 'Mystery Train' and **Holly**'s 'Raining in My Heart', in rockabilly arrangements. *See also* **Crosby, Stills, Nash and Young**

YOUNG, PAUL Born on 17 January

1956 in Luton, Bedfordshire, Paul Young's rise to international superstardom came suddenly after a long apprenticeship on the British gig circuit. With a resonant soul-influenced voice, an ambitious selection and reworking of cover versions, and the support of a superb group of musicians, Young appealed to a wide audience, a fact reflected in his huge sales worldwide.

After several years playing with small local rock groups, Young first found success with Streetband in 1978 and the jokey UK Top 20 single, 'Toast'. His contribution went unnoticed, and his vocal talents were recognized for the first time only when he joined roving brassy soul big band Q-Tips in 1979. Though a revered live act, the band were unsuccessful on record and by 1983 Young found himself on a solo deal with CBS. His version of **Marvin Gaye**'s 'Wherever I Lay My Hat' hit gold and made Number 1 in the UK in June, and from then on he scored with a consistently good string of hit singles. An album of mainly cover versions, *No Parlez*, made the UK Number 1 spot and sold well across the world.

Young's position in the top bracket of British acts was recognized as he contributed vocals to the **Band Aid** single, and the success continued into 1985 with a memorable appearance at Live Aid, (*see* **Band Aid**) a world tour and a second album, *The Secret of Association*, which consolidated his best-selling international status.

Paul Young performed with Streetband and Q-Tips before winning solo fame

YOUNGBLOODS A folk-rock

group who took the familiar late Sixties route from the East Coast coffee houses to the laid-back recording environment of California, the Youngbloods began performing in New York in 1966 as the houseband at the Café A Go Go. Jesse Colin Young (born 11 November 1944) had been a well-known New York folk singer with two albums (*Soul of a City Boy* and *Young Blood*) behind him. He met up with Jerry Corbitt, a Cambridge folk singer, and as a duo they recorded 'Hey Babe' for Mercury who later released the earliest Youngbloods' sessions on *Two Trips with Jesse Colin Young*. The duo had added Banana Lowell Levinger, a onetime bluegrass musician (born 1946) and more recently member of Boston's Trolls, who played banjo, mandolin, guitar, bass and piano and ex-jazz drummer Joe Bauer (born 26 September 1941). Young wound up playing bass. Their style was essentially East Coast: good-time, jug band, jazz and **Beatles** influences – highlighted by Young's delightful singing. He shared lead vocals with Jerry Corbitt, who wrote and sang their 'Grizzly Bear' (RCA), a minor hit when pulled from their album *The Youngbloods* in 1966. Their recording of Dino Valenti's summer 1967 anthem, 'Get Together' – a Top 10 record when it was re-released in 1969 – launched them in their future home on the West Coast. After *Earth Music*, Corbitt departed (to record two disappointing solo albums), and the Youngbloods went on to complete *Elephant Mountain* as a trio. Their most acclaimed album saw Banana taking a more dominant role, his lilting piano and refreshing guitar underpinning a freer, jazzier album. *Elephant Mountain* and the comparable *Rock Festival* marked their peak, the self-indulgent *Ride the Wind* their zenith. They added Michael Kane, on bass in 1971, to record two rock'n'roll-oriented albums full of old rock classics (*Good 'N' Dusty* and *High on a Ridge Top*). After 1969 their albums, solo and spin-off projects (notably Jesse Colin Young's work with the remarkable Michael Hurley) were recorded for their own Racoon Records. By 1973, though, they had folded. Only Jesse Colin Young has remained active, reverting to the style of *Elephant Mountain* in a series of tasteful and satisfying solo albums for Warner Brothers.

YURO, TIMI Born Rosemarie Yuro, in Chicago on 4 August 1940, Timi Yuro enjoyed a brief vogue in the early Sixties, coming closer than any other white female singer to the deep, raw and soulful sounds of authentic R&B balladeering. Her only rival in this respect was **Brenda Lee**. In timbre, texture and mannerisms Timi Yuro sounded very like blues vocalist **Esther Phillips**. Her biggest success was a throbbing, sobbing ballad entitled 'Hurt' on Liberty in 1961. Her powerful, cracked tones were recorded effectively up front and the rapping, talking passage continued a tradition developed in the Forties by Orville Jones of the **Ink Spots**, enlarged by **Presley**, and brought into full fashion by latter-day soul singers.

Her best single was her arrangement of 'Down in the Valley', a song generally associated with **Solomon Burke** and, later, **Otis Redding**, but here taken at a slower, bluesier pace with plenty of piano and brass. Coupled with it was a superb rendition of the standard 'Gotta Travel On'. Much of her subsequent material veered towards the supper-club style.

Z

ZAPPA, FRANK Born Francis Vincent Zappa Jr. in Baltimore, Maryland, on 21 December 1940, Frank Zappa was one of the great innovators in rock's development in the Sixties, though it was not until the Seventies that his records began to sell in large quantities. At the age of 10, Zappa moved with his family to California where he later emerged as a West Coast musician. A self-taught multi-instrumentalist, he passed through his school band and various other local groups before becoming a serious student of many musics. As interested in arranging as in playing, Zappa's first recording, in 1960, was his own soundtrack for a film called *The World's Greatest Sinner*. Characteristically, Zappa's score involved 52 musicians. In 1963 another film soundtrack, for *Run Home Slow*, gave him enough money to buy a five-track recording studio in Cucamonga, California.

He involved himself in a number of locally issued singles under various names and, in late 1964, pruned down the band with which he was working into a deliberately 'freak'-oriented group first called The Muthers and then The Mothers. The original line-up was Zappa, Elliott Ingber (later of the Fraternity Of Man and then in **Captain Beefheart**'s band), Roy Estrada (subsequently with Beefheart and **Little Feat**), Jimmy Carl Black (later in Geronimo Black) and Ray Collins. This band was signed to Verve/MGM by producer Tom Wilson in 1966 and a double album, *Freak Out!*, was issued. The album and its promotion emphasized the 'freak' element in Zappa's work, gave the leader a great deal of vivid publicity and implanted the Mothers Of Invention (their name by now) on the rock public's consciousness as a synonym for outrageousness. However, that first album, and those immediately following, were also innovative in their resourceful combinations of different kinds of music, lethally accurate parodies of other rock/pop genres. It was also apparent from even the earliest Mothers Of Invention albums that Frank Zappa was ahead of any other rock artist of the time as a tape editor. The second and third albums – *Absolutely Free* (1966) and *We're Only In It for the Money* (1967) – were predominantly satirical in their impact. The latter was presented as a parody of the **Beatles**' *Sergeant Pepper*, although its targets included the American Way Of Life as well as its ineffectual opponents, the flower children. Later records moved towards a greater emphasis on instrumental work or, with *Ruben and the Jets* (1967), the re-creation of the sound of Fifties vocal groups. In 1969, the Frank Zappa solo album, *Hot Rats*, established his claim as a significant jazz-rock guitarist.

Working with a consistent set of overall themes and methods, Zappa has, over a decade of work, continued to build up more pieces and new dimensions within what appears as the vast interlocking jigsaw of his output. Zappa masters time in the additional sense that he manipulates the past through montages of nostalgia. This now seems unremarkable because the recording industry latched on to the commercial possibilities of the process. Zappa, however, kept it all under control and gave us, long before the 'Rock Revival', an inspired montage of the American Fifties, spliced into parallel evocations of Sixties hippie lifestyles and a personal musical vision.

This musical resourcefulness has been matched by the precision Zappa has always demanded of his many different line-ups. On stage, the various different Mothers bands usually radiated an image of freakish dishevelment, but their musical performances have always been outstandingly disciplined. Zappa has also been a considerable sponsor of other people's talent. His attempts to augment his original line-up in 1965 resulted in several names passing through his band – **Dr John**, Henry Vestine of **Canned Heat**, **Jim Guercio**, **Van Dyke Parks**, Jim Fielder, Alice Stuart and **Kim Fowley**. Subsequent Mothers have included Billy Mundi, Ed Marimba (Arthur Tripp III), Lowell George and Aynsley Dunbar. Zappa has also brought a number of jazz musicians before a wider audience, including Ian Underwood, **George Duke**, Jean-Luc Ponty, Don 'Sugarcane' Harris and Bruce Fowler.

In 1968, Zappa formed Bizarre Records with his manager, Herb Cohen, to ensure total artistic control over his work and to provide an outlet for his protégés, who included **Alice Cooper**, Wild Man Fischer and the GTOs (Girls Together Outrageously, the first groupie group). Artists on the sister label, DiscReet (founded in 1973) included **Tim Buckley**, also managed by Cohen, and he used it as an outlet for his own solo releases between *Over Nite Sensation* (1973) and *Bongo Fury* (1975), after which he spent an acrimonious period with Warner Brothers. Their low-key promotion of *Zoot Allures* (1976) – which included the ten-minute melange of screams, guitar solos and unpleasant lyrics that was 'The Torture Never Stops' and a song about a vibrator, 'Ms Pinky' – and their delaying tactics over the release of *Zappa in New York* (1978) prompted Zappa to hang a huge banner at his concerts reading 'Warner Brothers Sucks' and to extricate himself from his contract. Once free of Warners, he formed a new label, Zappa, for which he recorded *Sheik Yerbouti* (1979) and two albums, *Joe's Garage Act 1* and *Joe's Garage Acts 2 & 3* that collectively made up the score of a rock opera.

A prolific recording artist, Zappa kept up his record of at least one album a year in the Eighties and in 1982 recorded six orchestral compositions with the London Symphony Orchestra. His other projects included the reissue of remixed versions of the entire Mothers of Invention catalogue, a Broadway musical, and a full-length animated cartoon called *Baby Snakes*.

Despite his many failings – the disastrous film *200 Motels* in 1971, the dating of most of his Sixties social commentary, and in particular the tendency of some of his work towards a cheap vulgarity (the kind of vulgarity he once attacked in others) – Frank Zappa has none the less proved himself a major figure in rock. The jazz-inclined album *Jazz from Hell* (EMI) appeared in 1986.

ZE RECORDS

For a while in the late Seventies, Ze was *the* hip New York record label. It was the brainchild of Michael Zhilka, heir to the Mothercare millions and an unlikely contender for the title of hippest rocker in Manhattan; despite his wealth and status, Zhilka remained a charming, amiable and enthusiastic man. Ze's most famous signing was **Kid Creole and the Coconuts**, at that time little more than a local, cultish spin-off from Dr Buzzard's Original Savannah Band. The next biggest signing was Christina, then Zhilka's girlfriend, and the label seemed to lean toward light, fizzy nightclub dance music with other signings the Waitresses and Davitt Sigerson. The label had another side, however, giving support to bassist Bill Laswell's experimental jazz-funk band Material, Suicide, the solo Alan Vega and the reclusive **Was (Not Was)**. Zhilka sold out his involvement in 1983 but in 1986 was preparing to launch a new, as yet unnamed, label.

ZOMBIES

A product of the great British beat boom of 1963, the Zombies was a group of five Hertfordshire school kids who had a million-selling hit, 'She's Not There', the week they turned professional. Rod **Argent**, piano (born 14 June 1945); **Colin Blunstone**, vocals (24 June 1945); Paul Atkinson, guitar (19 March 1946); Hugh Grundy, drums (6 March 1945), and Paul Arnold, bass, replaced within weeks of formation by Chris White (7 March 1943) formed the group in St Albans in 1963. They won a beat group competition held by the *London Evening News* and were signed by Decca, who were impressed by their tapes of 'Summertime'. That was the group's choice for a single but Decca's was 'She's Not There', which surprisingly proved to be their only British hit. However, in America the follow-up 'Tell Her No' – a flop in Britain in 1965 – gave them their second Top 10 hit on Parrot. Instant success persuaded the group to leave school. Their image stressed their grammar-school status (with fifty 'O' levels between them) at a time when other groups disdained any educational achievements. More important, their sound was quite devastating for 1964, dominated by Argent's jazz-tinged electric piano and Blunstone's breathy vocals. They anticipated a number of facets of future styles in a series of underrated singles and on their mixed, though at times adventurous, album *Begin Here* (1965).

Far better appreciated in America, by 1967 they were at a low ebb, but before splitting up took three months to write and record an album. The result was *Odyssey and Oracle* (CBS, 1968), a breathtaking album by a virtually forgotten group in Britain. One of the singles taken from it, 'Time of the Season', became a huge hit in America on Date, but the group had gone its separate ways and several bogus groups sprang up there, until they took legal action against them. The separate directions included a solo career for Blunstone, a namesake group for Rod Argent (working closely with Chris White, who took a non-playing but writing and producing role and was also part of Nexus).
See also **Argent**; **Colin Blunstone**

ZTT

Taking its name from a proto-fascist war poem by Italian 'Futurist' F. T. Marinetti, the record label Zang Tuum Tumb (ZTT) was formed in 1983 by producer Trevor Horn and rock journalist Paul Morley, bankrolled by Island Records. Initially meant as a vehicle for its controversial signing **Frankie Goes to Hollywood**, it later added other artists to its roster, among them German electropopsters Propaganda, French chanteuse Anne Pigalle, and 'systems music' composer Andrew Poppy. A mixture of cheeky marketing, sometimes dazzlingly inventive artwork and often obscure art theory gained the label great, mischievous success with FGTH, but no others. Within two years, the success of its post-**McLaren** shock tactics was on the wane.

ZZ TOP

Formed in late 1970 from remnants of various Texas punk groups, ZZ Top (lead guitarist Billy Gibbons from the Moving Sidewalks, drummer Frank Beard and bass player Dusty Hill from the American Blues) joined the growing numbers of Southern guitar boogie bands, playing constantly and building a solid following. Their second album on Warner Brothers (*Rio Grande Mud*, 1972) produced a small hit, 'Francene', and was responsible for propelling them onto the gruelling national tour circuit. Two albums followed, *Tres Hombres* and *Fandango!* and the group's popularity grew steadily.

They soon gained a reputation as the support band nobody wanted to follow, and their sell-out live shows were translated into vinyl success, every album apart from their first gaining at least gold status. Through the late Seventies and early Eighties their success continued to grow, and by that stage they had moved on from being essentially a minority interest boogie band to one of the world's foremost rock bands.

In the UK they failed to match their huge US following until the *Eliminator* album in 1983, when the combination of experience, excellent videos and the most famous pair of beards in rock (sported by Gibbons and Hill) gave them a hit with the single 'Gimme All Your Lovin''. The band's appealing sense of humour and the fact that they never took themselves too seriously endeared them to a music press that was otherwise hostile to mainstream hard rock, and their success throughout the world continued unabated with the release of *Afterburner* at the end of 1985.

ACKNOWLEDGEMENTS

Photographs were supplied by Cyrus Andrews, Graham Barker, BBC, John Beecher, Peter Benjaminson, BMI Archives/House of Bryant, Rob Burt Collection, Blues & Soul, CBS, Country Music Foundation, Andre Csillag, Culver Pictures, Henry Diltz, Bob Erskine, Rob Finnis, Flair Photography, Jeremy Fletcher, Jill Furmanovsky, Armando Gallo, Charlie Gillett, Fraser Gray, Island Records, Jamie Records, Peter Kanze Collection, Kindlight Ltd, Kobal Collection, J. P. Leloir, London Features International, Melody Maker, Bill Miller, Music Books, Michael Ochs, Steve Petrysyzn, Pictorial Press, Barry Plummer, Popperfoto, Michael Putland, Nick Ralph, Rare Pics, RCA, David Redfern, Rex Features, Steve Richards, Rocket Records, David J. Smith, Star File, Stiff Records, Barry Summer, Syndication International, Thames Television, John Topham Picture Library, Paul Vernon, Val Wilmer.